McGRAW-HILL'S

SAT I

SECOND EDITION

CHRISTOPHER BLACK

MARK ANESTIS

and the TUTORS of
COLLEGE HILL COACHING™

McGraw-Hill

NEW YORK / CHICAGO / SAN FRANCISCO / LISBON / LONDON / MADRID / MEXICO CITY
MILAN / NEW DELHI / SAN JUAN / SEOUL / SINGAPORE / SYDNEY / TORONTO

McGraw-Hill books are available at special quantity discounts to use as pre-
miums and sales promotions, or for use in corporate training programs. For
more information, please write to the Director of Special Sales, Professional
Publishing, McGraw-Hill, Two Penn Plaza, New York, NY 10121-2298. Or
contact your local bookstore.

SAT is a registered trademark of the College Entrance Examination Board,
which does not endorse this book.

College Hill Coaching® is a registered trademark under the control of
Christopher F. Black.

Visit the College Hill Coaching Web site at www.collegehillcoaching.com.

ACKNOWLEDGMENTS

We would like to gratefully acknowledge the help of those who have contributed to
this enormous project and have been committed to its success. This project would
not have been the same without the help of so many of our close friends and relatives: Elizabeth Black, the world's greatest teacher of mathematics, for her many
years of patience, wisdom and gracious support; Sarah and Anna Black for their
constant inspiration and marvelous good humor; Stephanie Anestis for her invaluable efforts in reading and editing the text and for her incredible love and support;
and Robert, Janice, Michael and Matthew Anestis who also gave their insight on
the work in progress. We would also like to thank Brigid Barry, Aulden Kaye, Peter
Obourn, Kristoffer Shields and the brilliant tutors of College Hill Coaching for
their thoughtful and valuable assistance. We appreciate the hard work of those at
McGraw-Hill who made this project work and the thoughtful help of our agent,
Grace Freedson. Finally, we would like to thank all of the students of College Hill
Coaching who have contributed to the growth of these materials over the years;
their insight and experiences have thoroughly inspired and informed this book.

CONTENTS

CHAPTER 1

WHAT YOU NEED TO KNOW ABOUT THE NEW SAT I

Tough Questions about a Tough Test

1. Questions and Answers about the SAT I

2. How the SAT I Has Changed for 2005

I QUESTIONS AND ANSWERS ABOUT THE SAT I

Why do colleges need to see my SAT I scores? Aren't my grades and SAT II scores enough?

Colleges use your SAT I scores to assess your readiness to do the tough academic work of college. The SAT I does something that your high school transcript can't, namely, assess your general academic problem-solving skills.

Course grades are, unfortunately, far from objective measures of your academic ability. Teachers occasionally inflate or deflate grades for reasons unrelated to intellectual ability, and rarely use objective standards for grading. Even when objective standards are used, they vary widely from teacher to teacher and school to school. Achievement tests like the SAT IIs are more objective, but they are designed to assess subject knowledge rather than problem-solving skills. Of course, subject knowledge is critical to a good education, but it is only a part of the puzzle. Also, much subject matter can be memorized and forgotten. Knowledge is effective only when it is incorporated into a meaningful and robust way of solving problems. The SAT I, although not perfect, does a good job of measuring how well you reason under pressure, an important academic and life skill.

Doesn't the SAT I do a poor job of predicting first-year college grades?

In fact, SAT I scores do correlate very well with real academic success, that is, *professional* success in an academic field. In many ways, this is more important to colleges than predicting grades. Some students can get good grades without showing great intellectual ability, by "playing the game" of school. The SAT I is often able to distinguish these students from the good thinkers. Rather than predicting your grades, your SAT I scores indicate your ability to read critically, write well, solve math problems intelligently, and think under pressure. The SAT I is *not* designed to predict how well you'll play the college grading game.

Admissions officers understand that grades often don't reflect sheer intellect, so they don't want a test that simply predicts grades. They value SAT I scores because they assess some of the reasoning skills that make people successful in life, regardless of their grades. They also provide a way of comparing students from widely varying academic backgrounds. College admissions officers know that high SAT I scores don't guarantee college success, but they also know that the scores indicate to some degree how ready you are to do college work.

Doesn't the SAT I just measure "test-taking skills"?

Many in the test-prep industry would like you to believe that the SAT I tests nothing more than "how well you can take a test." They portray the SAT I as a scary and meaningless test concocted by a cabal of student-haters at the ETS. They claim the SAT I can be "cracked" by simply memorizing a bunch of test-taking gimmicks. Of course, it's tempting to believe that the SAT I is so easy to crack. These marketing schemes sell a lot of courses and books, but they don't help you to improve your SAT I scores dramatically or to prepare meaningfully for college work.

Success on the SAT I has very little to do with memorizing test-taking tricks. The SAT I is a tough test of reasoning. To ace it, you have to improve your reasoning skills. It takes work.

Contrary to what many test-prep companies say, the SAT I isn't written by sadists who love to "trick" students and make college admissions as difficult as possible. The Educational Testing Service writes the SAT I for the College Board, a nonprofit association of over 4,200 colleges, very likely including the schools you will apply to. The SAT I assesses several important skills that college professors think incoming freshmen should have, like critical reading, persuasive writing, and mathematical problem-solving skills. The ETS doesn't write the SAT I in isolation. In 2002, the University of California suggested that the SAT I incorporate an essay and do away with some of the more "artificial" questions so that it would better reflect actual college work. The College Board and the ETS agreed to change the SAT I accordingly.

Isn't it unfair that so much rides on just a single test?

It may seem unfair that a four-hour test is so important. Remember, though, that the SAT I is not a one-shot, all-or-nothing affair. You can take it many times, and colleges will consider only the top individual scores from all of your tests. In other words, if you take the SAT I twice, and get scores of 460 Critical Reading, 530 Math and 500 Writing on the first test, and 540 Critical Reading, and 490 Math and 400 Writing on the second test, then your score is, for all practical purposes, 540 Critical Reading, 530 Math and 500 Writing. Colleges won't average the scores, or penalize you for being a bit inconsistent. They do this for their own benefit as well as yours: they fare better in the college rankings if they report higher scores.

The SAT I is only "unfair" if you allow it to be by not taking it seriously. If, instead, you look at it as an opportunity to hone important academic reasoning skills, and prepare for it meaningfully, you'll find the process rewarding rather than nerve-racking.

Are SAT I scores declining?

Every once in a while, you may hear someone claim that "declining SAT scores" show the declining quality of our schools. Claims such as these are generally uninformed and demonstrate a lack of understanding about the SAT I. Trends in average SAT scores mean nothing unless comparable populations of students take the test each year, and unless the difficulty of each SAT I can be measured independently of the students who take it. Changes in the student populations who take the SAT I and the evolution of the test itself make it hard to infer anything about trends in scores.

The first SAT I was administered to a few thousand students, virtually all white males. Today, the SAT I is administered each year to more than one million students of both sexes representing all races and socioeconomic backgrounds in many countries. Furthermore, each year, the SAT I is administered to a broader and more varied student population. In 2002, over one-third of all students taking the SAT I were first-generation college applicants, and over one-third were minorities. These changes in demographics alone account for much of the year-to-year variations in test scores.

A fascinating study illustrates the dangers of drawing broad conclusions about trends in SAT I scores. In 1997, the College Board conducted a study and discovered that, although *overall* verbal SAT I scores had *declined* slightly over the previous decade, the verbal SAT I scores of every significant racial group had actually *improved* over that time period. The scores of African-Americans had improved, the scores of Asian-Americans had improved, the scores of European-Americans had improved, and the scores of Hispanics had improved. Why did the average score of every group improve, yet the overall score decline? Because the test-taking population was changing. A larger portion of students with historically lower scores took the SAT I, thereby bringing the overall average down, even though the scores of each group were improving! In other words, 100% of the decline in scores was attributable to demographics. From these data, a case can be made that schools are actually doing a *better* job teaching students, since virtually every subgroup is improving.

Isn't the SAT I unfair to minorities and biased toward rich white males?

The SAT I was originally intended as a means of opening Ivy League admissions to more racial and socioeconomic minorities. It was intended to find the "best and brightest" students for the Ivy League, regardless of their backgrounds. The elite colleges of New England had become the exclusive domain of wealthy white males from elite New England prep schools, many of whom had dubious academic skills. The president of Harvard, James Bryant Conant, wanted to change that system to make American higher education a true meritocracy. The SAT I was designed as a tool for achieving that goal. (You may question whether the SAT I has really had its desired effects, or whether everyone who used the SAT I used it in the same way, but these were the goals of its chief proponents.)

Critics of the SAT I have not provided much evidence that the content of the SAT I is culturally biased toward rich white males. In fact, the ETS carefully reviews each test to minimize references to the American cultural elite and to ensure that historically underrepresented populations are frequently mentioned.

Many political groups have complained that the SAT I is unfair simply because certain minority groups have scored, on average, lower than whites. These discrepancies in scores, however, may reveal less about bias in the test than about bias in educational opportunity and about the ill effects of certain environments on academic achievement.

Don't wealthy students who can afford expensive coaching have an unfair advantage?

Undoubtedly, the ability to afford the best coaching is an advantage. This should come as no surprise. Athletes and musicians certainly benefit from good personal coaching, and students are no different. This fact does not impugn the integrity of the SAT I. On the contrary.

The SAT I does not assess the innate limits of your ability. It is not just an "aptitude" test but rather a test of reasoning skills, which can be learned. The right kind of training will pay off. If you follow the College Hill approach and take your preparation seriously, your efforts will be rewarded.

Is the SAT I an intelligence test?

This isn't a simple question, so there's no simple answer. "Intelligence" can be used to refer to many different qualities, and certainly the SAT I does not assess all of them. The common definition of intelligence as "an innate, general, and stable cognitive ability that determines one's ability to reason across a wide range of tasks" is outmoded and unhelpful. Most psychologists agree that humans possess many different "intelligences" that can improve or atrophy with use or disuse. These include musical intelligence, interpersonal intelligence, mechanical intelligence, verbal intelligence, mathematical intelligence, and analytical intelligence. The SAT I measures only certain aspects of verbal, mathematical and analytical intelligence.

When people ask whether the SAT I is an "intelligence" test, usually they really mean: "Do my SAT I scores put limits on how successful I can be?" The answer is: only if you misinterpret them. Rather than a measure of your innate "limits" for success, the SAT I indicates your mastery of a few basic but essential academic skills. If you improve these skills, you will be more successful academically. Of course, academic success isn't the only kind of success. We can all find wonderful success stories about people who have become successful artists, politicians, and business leaders despite having low SAT I scores. The SAT I doesn't measure artistic, athletic, intrapersonal, or interpersonal skills, and these are often key elements to nonacademic success. You will find, however, that success in academic fields correlates quite highly (but not, of course, perfectly) with SAT I scores.

Doesn't the College Board claim that you can't study for the SAT I?

They used to suggest this, but no longer. They openly acknowledge the fact that the SAT I assesses very learnable skills. In fact, the College Board itself publishes materials to help students study for the SAT I. What their research does show, however, is that just learning test-taking tricks doesn't help much. Only solid preparation in fundamental reasoning skills produces dramatic score improvements.

Do I have to take the SAT I?

Consult the web sites or publications of the colleges you are interested in to see if they require the SAT I. Most competitive schools will require the SAT I or a test like it (such as the ACT), but some colleges do not. Even if your college does not require the SAT I, you might consider taking it anyway. If you do well, your scores can make your application more attractive by demonstrating your reasoning skills. If you don't do well, just don't send the scores.

Do the colleges see all of my SAT I Scores?

No college will see any of your SAT I scores until you give the College Board permission to send the scores to that specific school. You will be given the opportunity to release your scores to specific schools when you register for the test, but you should be cautious about doing this. Don't release your scores until either you're satisfied with your entire score report or you have no other choice (such as when a deadline is approaching).

When you release your score report to a college, the report will contain all of the scores of the SAT Is and SAT IIs that you have taken up to that point. But remember: if you have taken any test more than once, the college will consider only the top score among all of the results.

Do I have to take SAT II: Subject Tests?

The SAT IIs are one-hour subject area tests. They are offered in most academic subjects, like mathematics, physics, chemistry, biology, literature, history, languages, and so on. Some colleges do not require you to submit any SAT II scores, while others may require you to submit up to three SAT II scores. (But you may submit more than three if you wish.) If you are planning to apply to highly competitive colleges, you should plan to take three or more.

If you believe you have academic strengths that are not shown by your class grades, the SAT IIs are an excellent way of showing colleges those strengths.

When should I take the SAT I and SAT IIs?

Plan to take an SAT II in June for any course you've finished successfully. If you do well in freshman biology, for instance, take the SAT II in biology in June of your freshman year. Likewise, consider taking the Math Level IC after completing algebra II successfully, the Math Level IIC after precalculus, etc. You will want to take any SAT II in a subject when you feel you are "at your peak" in that subject. Learn which SAT IIs your colleges require, and try to complete them by June of your junior year. You can take up to three SAT IIs on any one test date.

After you take the PSAT in October of your junior year, you can take the SAT I in late January, late March (or early April), or early May of your junior year and in early November, early December, and late January of your senior year. To give yourself ample time to prepare, you may wish to take the SAT I in March and May of your junior year and again in October of your senior year if necessary. Remember, you can take the SAT I more than once, and colleges will use only your top scores.

Test Date	Regular Registration Deadline	Late Registration Deadline
October 8, 2005 (SAT I and SAT II)	September 7, 2005	September 14, 2005
November 5, 2005 (SAT I and SAT II)	September 30, 2005	October 12, 2005
December 3, 2005 (SAT I and SAT II)	October 28, 2005	November 9, 2005
January 28, 2006 (SAT I and SAT II)	December 22, 2005	January 4, 2006
April 1, 2006 (SAT I only)	February 24, 2006	March 8, 2006
May 6, 2006 (SAT I and SAT II)	April 3, 2006	April 12, 2006
June 3, 2006 (SAT I and SAT II)	April 28, 2006	May 10, 2006

How do I register for the SAT I or SAT IIs?

If you have a credit card and don't need special testing arrangements (such as extended time or Sunday testing), you can register online at *http://www.collegeboard.com/student/testing/sat/reg.html*. If you do need special arrangements, you must register by mail. A mail registration form can be found in the *SAT I: Reasoning Test Bulletin* or *SAT II: Subject Tests Bulletin*, which you can get from your guidance counselor. If you don't have a guidance counselor, request a bulletin by calling (609) 771-7600. Read the bulletin carefully so that you know your many options.

If you've already registered for a previous test, you can register by phone for a $10 fee at (800) 728-7267 or (609) 771-7600. The TTY number is (609) 882-4118.

Explore the College Board web site at *http://www.collegeboard.com*. It has lots of useful information and can answer most of the technical questions you may have about the SAT I and other tests.

Are my SAT I and SAT II scores the most important part of my college application?

In most cases, no, but these scores are becoming more important as college admissions become more selective. Without exception, high SAT I scores will provide you with an admission advantage regardless of what kind of school you are applying to. Most colleges are also very interested in your high school curriculum, your high school grades, your essay, your teacher recommendations, your special talents or experiences, and your extracurricular activities. Generally, the more selective a college is, the more important the personal factors are, such as extracurricular activities and special talents. Some large or specialized schools will weigh the SAT I or ACT scores more heavily than others, and even declare a cutoff score for applicants. If you have any questions about how heavily a certain college weighs your SAT I or ACT scores, call the admissions office and ask.

How is the SAT I scored? Should I guess if I don't know the answer to a question?

Each of your three SAT I scores (Critical Reading, Math and Writing) will be between 200 and 800. Each scaled score is based on a raw score for that section.

On any multiple-choice question, if you get the question right, your raw score increases by 1 point. If you get it wrong, your raw score decreases by $\frac{1}{4}$ point. If you skip it, your raw score remains the same. Therefore, on multiple-choice questions, blind guessing will likely harm your score in the short run. If you are guessing on no more than five questions, be conservative and guess only when you can eliminate two or more choices. If you are guessing on more than ten questions, though, be more aggressive and just try to eliminate at least *one* choice before guessing.

On any math question in which you must "grid in" a numerical answer, if you get the question right, your raw score increases by 1 point. If you get it wrong *or* skip it, your raw score remains the same. Therefore, on grid-in questions, blind guessing won't harm you any more than leaving the question blank. This means that if you have any kind of guess, you should fill it in.

Can I take the SAT I with extended time?

Some students with special needs can take the SAT I with extended time. These administrations are available only to students with a formal recommendation and are strictly proctored. If you have a learning disability that has been diagnosed by a psychologist and feel that an extended-time SAT I would benefit you, talk to your guidance counselor about how to qualify and register.

When will I receive my scores?

You can get your SAT I or SAT II scores by phone or on the web about two weeks after you take the test. About ten days later, a written report will be mailed to you free of charge. Any schools to which you release your scores will receive them by mail at about the same time you do. If a college needs your scores sooner, you can "rush" them for a $20 fee.

Can I get the actual test back when I receive my scores?

On some SAT I administrations (usually those in October, January, and May), the College Board provides the Question and Answer Service for a $12 fee. This service provides you with a copy of the test booklet, a record of your answers, the answer key, scoring instructions, and information about the types and difficulty of each question. You may order this service when you register or up to five months after the date of the test. You may also order a copy of your answer sheet *only* for a $10 fee.

Are some SAT Is easier than others?

SAT Is are "equated" so that one test should be, on average, just as difficult as any other. Many people think that, since the SAT I is "graded on a curve," it is best to take the test when the "smart" kids are not taking the test, so the curve will be in your favor. They are wrong. The grading curves are determined ahead of time for each test.

Don't let such misconceptions dictate when you take the test. Take it when you are best prepared for it.

2 | HOW THE SAT I HAS CHANGED FOR 2005

Since its inception in 1925, the SAT has undergone at least ten significant "overhauls" to keep up with research in standardized testing, trends in education, and the needs of College Board member schools. It will almost certainly change again in the future. The 2005 SAT I will differ from its predecessors in several important ways:

- The name of the Verbal section of the SAT I has been changed to the Critical Reading section.
- The Critical Reading section of the test has been expanded to include a wider range of passages, including shorter, single-paragraph passages.
- Analogy questions like *MENDICANT : BEG :: braggart : boast* have been eliminated.

- You will be required to write a short (25-minute) essay on a general topic, to be graded on substance, organization, clarity, and style.
- One 35-minute section has been added consisting of multiple-choice questions regarding standard English grammar and usage.
- The Math section of the SAT I now includes more advanced topics from Algebra II, such as absolute value, rational equations, radical equations, rational exponents, direct and inverse variation, function notation, domain and range, and quadratic functions.
- Quantitative comparison questions, asking you to determine which of two quantities ("Column A vs. Column B") is greater, have been eliminated.

CHAPTER 2

HOW TO USE THIS BOOK

1. Find Out Where You Are

2. Write Out a Plan and Commit to It

3. Working with College Hill Lessons

4. Two Sample Plans: The 10-Week Study Plan and the 2-Week Crash Plan

I FIND OUT WHERE YOU ARE

The first step in Smart Training is to assess yourself. Evaluate yourself with the following quiz:

DISAGREE STRONGLY		AGREE STRONGLY		
1	2	3	4	5

1. I feel confident in my test-taking abilities.

   1   2   3   4   5

   If you feel very confident about your test-taking skills, great. If you don't, then you'll need to take a lot of practice tests to build your familiarity with and confidence in the test. These are found in Chapter 19. Also, after each test, review any lessons in this book that focus on problem areas. This book provides the most focused and substantial skill-building system available for the SAT I. Just do the lessons you need, and your skills will improve dramatically.

2. My nerves sometimes get the better of me on tests.

   1   2   3   4   5

   If your nerves are a problem, then carefully read section 3 of Chapter 4: Learn the Mind-Body Connection. This section discusses concrete practices for managing your nerves. Remember, it's very natural to feel nervous before a big test. This is your body's way of preparing for a challenging task. If you learn good nerve management practices as you prepare for the test, you will be focused and relaxed on test day, ready to do your best.

3. I know a lot about how the SAT I is formatted, scored, and used by colleges.

   1   2   3   4   5

   If you don't know everything about how the SAT I is formatted, scored, and used by colleges, carefully read Chapter 1: What You Need to Know About the New SAT I.

4. I love to read.

   1   2   3   4   5

   If you love to read, and continually read challenging fiction as well as nonfiction, then you will have an advantage on the SAT I Critical Reading section. If you are a good reader, use your skills on the SAT I. In other words, don't change your reading approach dramatically to try to "crack" the SAT I. If you are a good reader, this approach will probably harm you. You should still do Lessons 1, 2, 3, and 5 in Chapter 7: Critical Reading Skills. If you don't feel that

you are a strong reader, then do all of the Lessons in Chapter 7, and review them continually after each practice test.

5. I love to do math and logic puzzles.

   1   2   3   4   5

   Those who love math and logic puzzles have an advantage on the SAT I Math section. This is because the SAT I is a reasoning test rather than an achievement test, so it tests your ability to think creatively even more than your ability to apply a memorized procedure. If you don't think solving math and logic puzzles is fun, then carefully do the lessons in Chapter 9: SAT I Math and MAPS-CATCH to work on your reasoning skills, then work carefully through the math lessons in Chapters 9–14 as needed.

6. I love to do word puzzles.

   1   2   3   4   5

   If you do a lot of word puzzles like crosswords, you will probably have an advantage on the vocabulary-intensive questions on the SAT I, particularly the Sentence Completion questions. If not, then carefully read the introduction to Chapter 6: How to Build an Impressive Vocabulary with MAPS-CATCH and work on your vocabulary skills daily using the strategies discussed there. Also, carefully complete Chapter 8: Sentence Completion Skills, to hone your verbal inference skills.

7. I know specifically which skills or problems types I want to work on for the SAT I.

   1   2   3   4   5

   If you know that you have specific "problem spots," like working with fractions, or 3-D geometry problems, or tough sentence completion questions, or "spacing out" on the reading passages, then this book provides the right tools: skill-specific lessons that focus on every problem type and skill that is tested on the SAT I. Simply scan the Table of Contents or the subheadings under each chapter title page to find the skill you want to focus on, and do the appropriate lessons.

8. My scores are already good, and I need to focus only on the most challenging SAT I questions.

   1   2   3   4   5

   Every Lesson in Chapters 7–18 contains problems to challenge even the best test-takers. If you feel that your scores are already good, and you want to focus on only the toughest questions, then do the last few questions on each SAT I Practice worksheet and review the corresponding lessons to review any concepts. Also, take plenty of practice tests in Chapter 19, focusing on the last few questions in each section. If your goals are more modest, and you'd like to practice on the easy to moderate questions also, work through all problems on the Concept Review worksheets and all of the SAT I Practice worksheets, and review the Lessons and Answer Key explanations when necessary

9. I have a plan for when I will take all of my college admissions tests, and I know my options.

    1   2   3   4   5

    If you're not sure when you will be taking all of your college admissions tests, read Chapter 1: What You Need to Know about the New SAT I. It will answer all your questions about what, why, how, where, and when. Also, find out which tests your prospective colleges require and which are optional.

10. How many hours per week will I commit to SAT I prep?

    1   2   3   4   5 or more

    Intelligent preparation requires time, and it should not be time that you merely "squeeze in" among your other tasks. Rather, you should plan your study time carefully, and commit to it as you would to other important tasks, like doctor's appointments, team practice, club meetings, and so on. If you want to see the 300- to 400-point improvements that are common among our private students, then you'll have to work. (That's right—it's not just a quick bag of tricks to memorize.) To see that kind of improvement, you will probably need to commit at least 5 hours per week for 10 weeks. Nevertheless, many students see over 200-point increases with just 3 good hours a week for six weeks. Of course, any time you put into this book will pay off, even if you do the one- or two-week "crash course."

11. How many weeks do I have to prepare?

    1 or less   2   4   6   8 or more

    If you have 8 or more weeks to prepare, you can probably complete a full preparation program for the SAT I and "max out" your potential, learning lots of vocabulary and doing lots of focused and mindful practice. The following pages lay out a 10-week plan for those students who have the time and commitment for it. We also give you a 2-week "crash" plan, if time is at a premium. But you don't have to use these; make a schedule to fit your needs.

2   WRITE OUT A PLAN AND COMMIT TO IT

Determine when you will take your SAT I and SAT IIs and put these important deadlines in your calendar. (See the test dates on page 4.) In a few pages you will see the College Hill 10-Week SAT I Study Plan and the College Hill 2-Week SAT I Crash Plan. You can use these, or modify them to meet your needs and your schedule. Write your plan down in your daily planner or your weekly calendar. Commit to this work schedule just as you would commit to a doctor's appointment or a date with a friend. Tell the people around you about your study plans, so they will respect them and help you to commit to them.

Dedicate a minimum of 30 minutes for each four-page lesson you plan to complete in Chapters 7–16. Also, you will need at least 3 hours and 10 minutes to complete any practice SAT I (or 3 hours and 25 minutes if you include the "experimental" section).

3   WORKING WITH COLLEGE HILL® LESSONS

College Hill Coaching® has spent fifteen years developing the most effective self-guided lessons in education. The College Hill Lessons found throughout this book are especially designed to promote mindful workflow, which optimizes your understanding of essential skills and practices. These lessons are effective, but only if you use them properly. Follow the instructions below carefully to make your work as productive as possible.

Each College Hill Lesson is designed to be completed in about 30–45 minutes. This should allow you enough time to check your work thoroughly and be sure that you understand the key concepts. College Hill Lessons generally have a four-page format.

The Lesson

This presents the important concepts and gives key examples and sample problems and explanations, Always read each Lesson and examples completely and carefully and take notes before moving on to the exercises that follow.

The Concept Review

Many of the Lessons will be followed immediately by a Concept Review worksheet. This will reinforce your understanding of the key concepts in the Lesson. Work through each Concept Review problem without peeking back at the Lesson. As you work, circle the difficult questions. Only after completing the entire Concept Review, go to the Answer Key and check your work. Mark wrong answers with an "x," but try to understand what mistakes you made and why so you can avoid them in the future.

The Practice

Most of the Concept Review worksheets are followed by Practice worksheets. These provide you with practice, usually in the form of SAT I questions, in applying the key concepts as they will actually be tested on the SAT I. As with the Concept Review worksheet answer all of the questions on the Practice worksheet before checking your work on the Answer Key. If you get a question wrong, read the Answer Key explanation carefully so that you can avoid the mistake in the future.

The Answer Key

This provides detailed explanations of the answers and often shows different ways to approach the questions. Read the Answer Key solution to every question, even for those questions you get right. Often it will provide options for solving questions even more efficiently than you did.

---

4 | TWO SAMPLE PLANS: THE 10-WEEK STUDY PLAN AND THE 2-WEEK CRASH PLAN

On the next few pages, you will find two sample study plans: a complete 10-week plan that will give you plenty of practice in every skill area tested on the SAT I, and a 2-week crash plan that will hit the most common problem areas for most students. A smart plan, however, must take your own individual needs, strengths, and weaknesses into account. Perhaps you can't devote an hour a day for 10 weeks to SAT I preparation. Perhaps you only have three or four days each week to devote to it. Also, perhaps you don't need to worry about certain aspects of the test, because your PSAT scores in those areas are satisfactory. Think carefully about each of these factors,

and draw up your own personal study plan. Use those on the following pages as guides.

When making your plan, remember to be reasonable. Don't plan on doing an entire chapter in a day, or even a couple of days. You should devote at least 30 minutes to each lesson, and for particularly difficult ones, perhaps as much as an hour.

Whatever you decide to do, write your plan down on a calendar or day planner. If you don't keep track of your work, it will probably get away from you. Also, use your planner to keep track of your progress on the practice tests. Seeing this progress can be a great motivator when the work gets tough.

The College Hill® 10-Week SAT I Study Plan

	Monday	Tuesday	Wednesday	Thursday	Friday	Saturday	Sunday
Week 1	• Read and annotate Chapters 1 and 3	• Read Chapter 6 and begin Vocabulary Lesson 1 • Read Chapter 4	• Complete 30–40 Vocabulary study cards from Unit 1 and Review	• 10 minutes Vocabulary Review • Chapter 15 Lessons 1 and 2	• 10 minutes Vocabulary Review • Chapter 15 Lessons 3 and 4	Take and score Diagnostic Test in Chapter 5 M:_____ CR:_____ W:_____	Catch-up or rest
Week 2	• Vocab Review • Chapter 9 Lessons 1 and 2	• Vocab Review • Chapter 17 Lessons 1 and 2	• 30–40 Unit 1–2 study cards • Chapter 9 Lessons 3 and 4	• Vocab Review • Chapter 17 Lessons 3 and 4	• Vocab Review • Chapter 9 Lessons 5 and 6	Practice Test 1 in Chapter 19 M:_____ CR:_____ W:_____	• Vocabulary Unit 1 • Review Exercises in Chapter 6
Week 3	• Vocab Review • Chapter 7 Lesson 1 • Chapter 10 Lesson 1	• Vocab Review • Chapter 7 Lesson 2 • Chapter 10 Lesson 2	• 30–40 Unit 2–3 study cards • Chapter 7 Lesson 3 • Chapter 10 Lesson 3	• Vocab Review • Chapter 7 Lesson 4 • Chapter 10 Lesson 4	• Vocab Review • Chapter 7 Lesson 5 • Chapter 10 Lesson 5	Practice Test 2 in Chapter 19 M:_____ CR:_____ W:_____	• Vocabulary Unit 2 • Review Exercises in Chapter 6
Week 4	• Vocab Review • Chapter 7 Lesson 6 • Chapter 10 Lesson 6	• Vocab Review • Chapter 7 Lesson 7 • Chapter 10 Lesson 7	• 30–40 Unit 3–4 study cards • Chapter 7 Lesson 8 • Lesson from Chapter 15 or 18	• Vocab Review • Chapter 7 Lesson 9 • Lesson from Chapter 15 or 18	• Vocab Review • Chapter 11 Lesson 1 • Lesson from Chapter 15 or 18	Practice Test 3 in Chapter 19 M:_____ CR:_____ W:_____	• Chapter 11 Lesson 2 • Vocabulary Unit 3 • Review Exercises in Chapter 6
Week 5	• Vocab Review • Chapter 11 Lesson 3 • Lesson from Chapter 15 or 18	• Vocab Review • Chapter 11 Lesson 4 • Lesson from Chapter 15 or 18	• 30–40 Unit 4–5 study cards • Chapter 11 Lesson 5 • Lesson from Chapter 15 or 18	• Vocab Review • Chapter 11 Lesson 6 • Lesson from Chapter 15 or 18	• Vocab Review • Chapter 11 Lesson 7 • Lesson from Chapter 15 or 18	Practice Test 4 in Chapter 19 M:_____ CR:_____ W:_____	• Chapter 12 Lesson 1 • Vocabulary Unit 4 • Review Exercises in Chapter 6
Week 6	• Vocab Review • Chapter 12 Lesson 2 • Lesson from Chapter 15 or 18	• Vocab Review • Chapter 12 Lesson 3 • Lesson from Chapter 15 or 18	• 30–40 Unit 5–6 study cards • Chapter 12 Lesson 4 • Lesson from Chapter 15 or 18	• Vocab Review • Chapter 12 Lesson 5 • Lesson from Chapter 15 or 18	• Vocab Review • Chapter 12 Lesson 6 • Lesson from Chapter 15 or 18	Practice Test 5 in Chapter 19 M:_____ CR:_____ W:_____	• Chapter 13 Lesson 1 • Vocabulary Unit 5 • Review Exercises in Chapter 6
Week 7	• Vocab Review • Chapter 13 Lesson 2 • Chapter 8 Lesson 1	• Vocab Review • Chapter 13 Lesson 3 • Chapter 8 Lesson 2	• 30–40 Unit 6–7 study cards • Chapter 13 Lesson 4 • Chapter 8 Lesson 3	• Vocab Review • Chapter 13 Lesson 5 • Chapter 8 Lesson 4	• Vocab Review • Chapter 13 Lesson 6 • Chapter 8 Lesson 5	Practice Test 6 in Chapter 19 M:_____ CR:_____ W:_____	• Chapter 8 Lesson 6 • Vocabulary Unit 6 • Review Exercises in Chapter 6
Week 8	• Vocab Review • Chapter 13 Lesson 7 • Chapter 8 Lesson 1	• Vocab Review • Chapter 14 Lesson 1 • Lesson from Chapter 16 or 18	• 30–40 study cards • Chapter 14 Lesson 2 • Lesson from Chapter 16 or 18	• Vocab Review • Chapter 14 Lesson 3 • Lesson from Chapter 16 or 18	• Vocab Review • Chapter 14 Lesson 4 • Lesson from Chapter 16 or 18	Practice Test 7 in Chapter 19 M:_____ CR:_____ W:_____	• Chapter 14 Lesson 5 • Vocabulary Unit 7 • Review Exercises in Chapter 6
Week 9	• Vocab Review • Chapter 14 Lesson 6	• Vocab Review • Chapter 14 Lesson 7	• Complete Vocab Review • Problem-area math review	• Complete Vocab Review • Problem-area math review	• Write down a "game plan" for your SAT I, one week away	Practice Test 8 in Chapter 19 M:_____ CR:_____ W:_____	• Catch-up or rest • Review vocabulary
Week 10	Correct mistakes in an old SAT I	Correct mistakes in an old SAT I	Correct mistakes in an old SAT I	• Drive to test site (if unfamiliar)	• Relax • Get materials ready for test	SAT I	Celebrate!

The College Hill® 2-Week SAT I Crash Plan

	Sunday	Monday	Tuesday	Wednesday	Thursday	Friday	Saturday
Week 1	• Read and annotate Chapters 1 and 3 • Take and score Diagnostic Test in Chapter 5 M:_____ CR:_____ W:_____	• Study Vocab Unit 1, Lessons 1–7 and complete Exercise Sets I, II, and III at the end of Unit 1 • Read Chapter 9 • Review answers to Diagnostic SAT I	• Study Vocab from Unit 1 • Chapter 7 Lesson 1 (4 pages) • Chapter 10 Lesson 1 (4 pages)	• Chapter 7 Lesson 2 • Chapter 10 Lessons 2–3	• Review Vocab • Chapter 17 Lessons 1–2 • Chapter 10 Lesson 4	• Chapter 8 Lessons 1–2 • Chapter 10 Lesson 5	• Take and score Practice Test 1 in Chapter 19 M:_____ CR:_____ W:_____ • Chapter 17 Lessons 3–4
Week 2	• Vocab Review • Chapter 12 Lessons 1–2 • Chapter 8 Lesson 3 • Review answers to Practice SAT I	• Chapter 12 Lesson 3 • Chapter 8 Lesson 4 • Chapter 7 Lesson 5	• Vocab review • Chapter 12 Lessons 4–5	• Vocab Review • Chapter 11 Lessons 1–2 • Chapter 8 Lesson 5	• Vocab Review • Chapter 7 Lessons 6–7 • Chapter 13 Lesson 1	• Complete and score two "problem sections" from Practice Test 2 in Chapter 19 • Get all materials ready for tomorrow's test • Get to bed at a reasonable time	SAT I

CHAPTER 3

THE COLLEGE HILL METHOD

Helping your mind work better

❚ THE COLLEGE HILL METHOD IN A NUTSHELL: HELPING YOUR MIND WORK BETTER

The College Hill Method is a system for helping your mind to work better so that you can solve problems— on tests, in school, and in your life—more effectively. It is the ideal approach to preparing for reasoning tests like the SAT I, but it's much more than that. It is based on sound principles of teaching and sound psychological research.

Your Ancient Brain

The human brain has evolved, as all human organs have, to enable humans to solve the problems of survival. Just as the heart, liver, and kidneys have been "designed" to process blood, the brain has been "designed" to process *information*. Systems have evolved in the brain for distributing attention, processing sensory information, forming and elaborating concepts, analyzing and synthesizing information, and executing behaviors.

Evolution is powerful but very, very slow. Significant biological changes develop only over thousands of generations. As a result, your brain has had time to evolve systems for solving only the kinds of problems that our hunter-gatherer ancestors encountered long ago. Therefore, when you have difficulty learning something or solving a problem, it may be because your brain is trying to process information that it was not "designed" to process efficiently. In a real sense, it's because your brain is an ancient one.

Fortunately, your brain is very flexible and profoundly sophisticated. It processes some information in a very complex manner without any difficulty at all: you learn to talk and understand language, to move your body nimbly around obstacles, to infer the emotions and intentions of others, to classify objects, to predict outcomes of physical events, and so on, without even realizing how complicated such tasks really are. (Computer scientists have perhaps the best appreciation for how complex these tasks are, because they've struggled mightily to get computers to do them, with very limited success.) These abilities have been "programmed" into your brain by the powerful forces of natural selection. Because these abilities helped our ancestors to survive, they were passed down to us.

But your life is almost certainly more complicated than your ancient ancestors' lives were. Your mind encounters problems that no caveman ever faced. In a sense, your brain is outmoded.

Fortunately, your brain has many flexible systems for learning, by which it can adapt to solve the problems posed by your particular modern environment. Some of these learning systems are themselves "automatic," that is, hard-wired by evolution and beyond your conscious control, but others are "executive," that is, controlled by your conscious attention and decision-making processes.

The College Hill Method teaches you to manage your "executive" mind effectively, so that you can solve the problems of *your* world, rather than getting trapped in the automatic modes of your ancient brain.

Old Thinking for New Problems

In order to thrive, our ancestors had to hunt and gather food, and form social groups for child-rearing, clan protection, and the distribution of work. Therefore, over the millennia, our brains have evolved the ability to solve many problems involved with hunting, foraging, communicating, and maintaining unspoken agreements. Even today, we can still see these old thinking systems hard at work: Since we no longer need them to survive, they take control of our recreational activities.

For instance, although we no longer need to hunt, many of us still engage in sports, which are simply activities that utilize our "hunter skills," like throwing accurately, running far and fast, tackling things, and so on. Even though we no longer need to forage for food, many of us still enjoy "foraging" for hidden words in puzzles or for patterns in clouds, and sorting things into categories. Even though we no longer need to live with extended clans, many of us still enjoy learning the intimate details of other people's lives in novels and on television and figuring out who is being honest and who is being deceitful. These ancient thinking systems assert themselves in our lives even though they no longer play such an essential role in our survival. Most of us don't realize why we do these things; we are just "compelled" to do them.

Because so many of the problems we encounter today are not the problems of our ancestors, our brains have not yet evolved the systems to solve them effortlessly. Our ancestors did not need to solve algebraic equations, write fifteen-page essays on Romanticism, negotiate mortgages, or take the SAT I. To solve these problems well, we must become more self-conscious. We must adapt our innate mind skills to modern problems. This requires our "executive" systems, which control attention and decision-making.

Beware of the "Quick and Easy"

Sometimes you'll see an advertisement for an educational product that claims to have found the "natural" and "easy" way to read, write, or learn higher mathematics. Usually, such claims are not only untrue, but also harmful. There is no "natural" way to learn these things, because our brains are not pre-programmed to learn them. We are born with the ability to learn to speak with little effort, but not to read or write, and we are born with the ability to deal with basic quantities easily, but not to do algebra. Such claims encourage the false belief that learning academic subjects shouldn't require much conscious effort, thereby implying that if you're trying hard, you must be stupid. We sometimes accept too readily the notion that effort is bad and to be avoided at all costs.

It's a simple fact: because of the nature of our ancient brains, certain complex and abstract problems, like reading, writing, and higher math, can't be solved effortlessly. This isn't a bad thing: The most enjoyable and rewarding things always require effort. Why should learning mathematics, reading, or writing be any different? The key to success isn't making work *easier*, it's making hard work *more rewarding*.

The Danger of Automatic Thinking

The more you perform routine tasks, like brushing your teeth or driving a car, the more automatic the tasks become. The "automating" function helps you to perform routine tasks with a minimum of attention. Sometimes the tasks become so automatic that you can't even remember having done them.

Of course, automatic processing is often enormously valuable. It conserves your mental energy, and lets you do more than one thing at a time. But there are also many important situations in which it impedes effective problem solving. To become an effective problem solver, you must train your executive mind to take over when it could be helpful.

A Life of Problems

As your information-processing organ, your brain constantly scans incoming information "looking" for problems. The more conscious control you gain over your problem-solving abilities, the better your life works. The first step is to become aware of what is automatic about your thinking, and to train your "executive" mind to take over when it could be helpful, and otherwise let things be.

Imagine that you accidentally touch a hot stove. You don't think: your hand automatically withdraws. A simple circuit of neurons detects the heat and activates the muscles to pull back your hand in a fraction of a second. Problem solved! This doesn't require your brain: All the necessary nerves are in your arm, shoulder, and spine. So does this mean that problem-solving is beyond your control? Do all of your problem-solving mechanisms have to be hard-wired like this one? Not at all. Even the simple pain-reaction circuit in your arm *could* be modified by input from your "higher" brain, which can modify its action. That is, you can train yourself to hold your hand on the stove even when it gets terribly painful. (Personally, we don't think that's smart, but some more rugged folks disagree.) Likewise, many other automatic systems can be at least partially controlled if you train your mind effectively. Of course, your executive mind must understand when it's good to take conscious control of a problem, and when it's best just to let your automatic mind do its job.

Don't Learn to Avoid Hard Work; Learn to Make Hard Work Rewarding

School poses a dilemma. On the one hand, it often rewards routine performance over creativity and mindful problem solving. For instance, math quizzes often reward quick responses to routine math facts, and history papers get points for including regurgitated facts. These kinds of tasks reward "automatic" thinking rather than creative or analytical thinking. If you are lucky, however, you will get a teacher who encourages creativity and mindful problem solving—the executive mind over the automatic mind. Which kinds of experiences are more rewarding? The answer, I hope, is obvious. Good education—that which improves your competence as a human being—must continually focus on developing the executive mind over the automatic mind.

Unfortunately, most learning methods focus only on the memorization of facts, procedures, and habits. Their goal is to make memorization "quick and easy," so that you don't have to think hard. This is absolutely the wrong approach to learning. Good education should not encourage you to avoid hard work by automating tasks, but rather to make hard work effective and self-affirming.

Focusing exclusively on memorizing facts, procedures, and habits may help you to learn to solve a narrow class of specific problems, but this emphasis will make you *less* capable as a problem solver. Facts, procedures, and habits will quickly become "mindless"—that is, either automatic and beyond conscious control or merely forgotten—unless they are learned as part of a system that makes you more aware of what your mind is doing from moment to moment, anticipating problems and correcting them. If, instead, you just memorize them the "quick and easy" way, they will become inflexible and untrustworthy obstacles to solving the various complex problems you will encounter. You have probably seen this in your own education: you memorize a fact or procedure, but become lost or frustrated when the problem situation changes slightly, and the thing you memorized no longer "works." It can be a very frustrating experience!

FACTS, PROCEDURES & HABITS VS. THEORIES, SKILLS & PRACTICES

The College Hill Method does not teach facts, procedures, and habits, but rather theories, skills, and practices. What's the difference? Theories, skills, and practices are under the conscious control of your executive mind, while facts, procedures, and habits are under the unconscious control of your automatic mind. Your automatic mind removes routine mental activities from consciousness so that your conscious mind can be freed to do other things. Of course, this is often quite helpful. For instance, if you had to think about it too much, you might not pull your hand away from the stove in time to prevent a severe burn! But sometimes "automating" systems hurt your problem-solving ability by removing the conscious executive mind from the process. Your executive mind must play a role if you are to solve complex and novel problems, because these problems require awareness and flexibility. By including awareness and flexibility in every step of learning and problem solving, you strengthen your ability to solve problems of increasing variety and complexity.

THE KEY TO SUCCESS AND HAPPINESS

The College Hill Method helps you become more aware of how your brain works, so that you can help it to do its job better. It helps you build a strong executive mind so that you can solve problems flexibly, creatively, and effectively. It helps you to analyze your own problem-solving skills so that you fix problems as they arise. It helps you to solve a wide range of problems, rather than only narrow categories of problems. It will reveal the joy and empowerment of problem solving as a life practice, so that you can learn to love learning for itself, and confront the problems you encounter every day, rather than avoid them. Research has shown that this is a real key to happiness: Those who feel confident enough in their problem-solving abilities to seek rather than avoid daily problems are the most well-adjusted, successful, and happy people.

2   WHAT IS MAPS-CATCH?

A system for problem solving

The College Hill Method gives you tools for examining how your mind perceives and solves problems. Of course, your brain is a profoundly complex organ, and even brilliant scientists who spend their lives studying it can come to understand only a small part of what the brain can do. Nevertheless, you can learn to make your mind work much more effectively by simply paying attention to some basic tasks that it performs continually to solve the problems you encounter. A simple mnemonic to help you understand some of these basic tasks is "MAPS-CATCH."

M =	**Mapping** the problem—representing the problem situation and goal in your "working memory."
A =	**Analyzing** the problem—breaking it apart into its relevant pieces.
P =	**Pattern-finding**—using "inductive reasoning" to make generalizations from specific examples.
S =	**Simplifying**—reducing the information you must process by applying simplification theorems.

C =	**Connecting to knowledge**—recalling relevant theorems, meanings, and other concepts that relate to the problem situation.
A =	**Alternative-finding**—considering different approaches to mapping, analyzing, pattern-finding, or applying procedures to the problem.
T =	**Thinking logically**—using deductive reasoning to draw specific conclusions from general theorems.
CH =	**Checking**—verifying the results of your thinking against the problem situation itself, and assuring yourself that the solution "works."

In the routine problems you encounter every day, your mind performs many of these tasks automatically, so that you are hardly aware of them. When working on more complex problems, like those on the SAT I, you must become more aware of these tasks and "troubleshoot" them, if need be.

M is for Mapping

"Mapping" a problem means simply representing **the basic problem situation** and **the goal in your**

working memory. Say you're watching television and a problem arises: you want a snack. Your mind quickly—almost imperceptibly—conjures a "map" which represents where you are (the couch) and where you want to go (the bag of potato chips). This "map" doesn't provide instructions itself, but provides some basic information for your mind to create a plan of action. There still may be many daunting obstacles to overcome in actually solving the problem: getting off of the couch, avoiding tripping on the cat or bumping into the walls, recalling which cabinet holds the potato chips, etc.

Solving the problem requires keeping the problem situation and goal in mind. If an interesting person intercepts you on your way to the kitchen, you may be thwarted from getting your snack! Perhaps your map of the "snack" problem will be replaced by a map for a "saying something witty" problem. But your nervous system occasionally reminds you of the situation and goal automatically: your stomach growls and sends hunger signals to your brain.

Unfortunately, your brain doesn't have a system for automatically mapping most SAT I problems. You've got to do it with your executive mind. If you don't keep a good "map" of the basic situation and goal in working memory, you can't begin to analyze and solve it.

> On the SAT I, don't "mis-map" a problem by looking for just one small piece of the problem as a "key" to "cracking" it with a trick you've memorized. Instead, regard every problem as if it's brand new. Map the entire problem so that you can create the best plan of action for that unique problem. Remember: all "averaging" problems are not the same; all "triangle" problems are not the same; all essays do not have the same structure; and so on. "Pigeonholing" problems like this might help you to get started on a few simplistic problems, but it won't get you very far on tough ones.

A is for Analyzing

Analyzing a problem means **examining its parts.** Once you've mapped the problem, you often must look more closely at the information "on the blackboard" and think about how the parts fit together. It's like trying to fix a car: you usually need to take things apart to fix the problem. But because you have to get it back together in working order, you also must have a good memory, or at least a good system, like a detailed diagram, for keeping track of parts and where

they came from. **Mental or written representations** are essential.

> To analyze abstract problems successfully, you must be able to represent and manipulate essential abstract "forms," like the number line, the equation-as-scale, the geometrical forms, the forms of prose, the sentence, and the word. In other words, you should understand the essential parts of these things, and understand the rules by which they can be transformed. For instance, you will better understand multiplication when you can "see" numbers being transformed into other numbers on the number line according to the rules of multiplication. You will better understand words when you understand the rules for transforming nouns into adjectives, adjectives into verbs, etc. You will better understand angle-side relationships in figures when you can mentally transform geometrical figures in your mind's eye. You will better understand algebra when you understand the rules of transforming equations as being like the rules for transforming a balanced scale.

When a problem overwhelms you, it is quite likely because the problem has too many parts to keep track of easily. When this happens, you must be able to represent the information on paper with equations, graphs, notes, diagrams, and so on. Consider scratch paper an extension of your working memory: it holds the information that your memory might not be able to hold.

P is for Pattern-finding

In addition to seeing relationships among common "forms," you may also need to find new relationships that are unique to the problem at hand. For instance, given the numbers 3, 6, 12, and 24, you should be able to determine the next number in the sequence by *discovering* (through intelligent guessing and checking) the rule that relates the parts. Likewise, in good writing, sentences are related within paragraphs and the paragraphs are related within passages, so that you should be able to make an educated guess about what may come next in a given passage, even if you have never seen the passage before. Similarly, the unique pattern of words in a sentence should help you to figure out the meaning of a missing or mysterious word in the sentence.

Your mind often seeks patterns, even unconsciously. It may find "faces" in clouds and in the bark of trees. When your friend hesitates to find a word to complete a thought, your mind (if it's paying attention) may "step in" and try to complete the thought on its own.

> You may struggle with a problem because you do not consciously focus on **pattern-finding,** or because you get "trapped" in the first pattern you see. To succeed on the SAT I, you have to see how different patterns can relate the same information. For instance, you must see how different rectangles can have an area of 24, how different fractions can represent ⅔, how different sequences of words can convey the same meaning, and how different sequences of ideas can convey a thesis in an essay.

A good example of where rethinking patterns can pay off is this quote from Groucho Marx:

Time flies like an arrow; fruit flies like a banana.

At first, this doesn't make a lot of sense, or, to the extent that it does, it seems kind of dumb. But at second thought, the second clause follows a very different pattern from the first. Read it again. Do you get it?

If you still don't get it, here are the two ways to read the second clause:

fruit/flies/like a banana subj/ v / adj	(Fruit can fly through the air as a banana does.)
fruitflies/like/a banana subj / v / adj	(Fruit flies enjoy bananas.)

We get "trapped" into reading the sentence the first, nonsensical way, because it follows the grammatical pattern of the first clause. Until we can reconsider the pattern, we can't make any real sense of the sentence. This ability to find and exploit patterns in sentences is important to solving the sentence completion questions on the SAT I.

Often, more than one pattern fits the data. We can see a man in the moon, but people in India see a rabbit in the moon. Ever try to see it? Here are some number patterns and word patterns, each of which can be interpreted in at least two different ways. Try completing the number pattern in two different ways, and then see if you can interpret each

headline in two different ways. In each case, ask: which interpretation is probably the "intended" interpretation?

2, 4, 8, _____, _____, _____ or 2, 4, 8, _____, _____, _____

> *Squad Helps Dog Bite Victim*
> *12 on Their Way to Cruise Among Dead in Plane Crash*
> *Chou Remains Cremated*
> *Reagan Wins on Budget, More Lies Ahead*
> *N.J. Judge to Rule on Nude Beach*
>
> *—Newspaper headlines compiled by the* Columbia Journalism Review.

S is for Simplifying

> Many complex problems would quickly overwhelm your working memory unless you had a way of simplifying them. Many careful studies have shown that our working memories can hold only between five and nine pieces of information at a time. When we can reduce the number of pieces of information in a problem, our minds have a better chance of solving the problem. Many problems contain information that can be simplified by simple transformation rules.

The SAT I is filled with expressions that can be simplified. Consider these examples:

Mathematical expression:	$\dfrac{3x^2 + 3}{x^2 + 1}$ can be simplified to 3 by dividing the numerator and denominator by $x^2 + 1$
Mathematical equation:	$3x^2 + 5x - 7 = 3x^2 + 2x + 5$ can be simplified to $3x = 12$ by adding $-3x^2 - 2x + 7$ to both sides of the equation.
Sentence:	*Unconcerned with the reactions of her friends, Sheila declared herself a candidate for the office of vice-president and accepted the duties and responsibilities of the office* can be simplified to

Unconcerned, Sheila declared herself a candidate and accepted the duties and responsibilities

by eliminating all of the prepositional phrases.

C is for Connecting to Knowledge

Sometimes seeing a pattern does not require sophisticated knowledge. But other times it does. Formulas like the Pythagorean Theorem, the average formula, and the rate formula help you to relate different quantities in special math problems. Knowing the different rhetorical devices helps you relate the different ideas and paragraphs in an essay or the scenes and motifs in a story.

Tough problems often require you to apply knowledge stored in your long-term memory. In other words, **some stuff you just gotta memorize—that means not only getting it into long-term memory, but getting it out easily, too.** For a math problem, you may need to know the Pythagorean Theorem, arithmetic facts (like *top-heavy positive fractions are greater than 1* or *negative × negative = positive*), and more. To write a great essay, you may need to remember relevant experiences or examples from your studies to illustrate your points, and you need to know the strategies of good writers. To do well on Critical Reading questions, you need to know the meanings of many words and roots, and understand the purpose and structure of different kinds of prose.

A is for Alternative-finding

There's more than one way to skin a cat. That's kind of a gross thought, but still very true. There are often many different ways to solve a given problem.

Don't get stuck on looking for the "one best way" to solve every kind of problem. That's not how great thinkers solve problems. They look at each problem individually, consider their options for solving each one, and choose the method that best suits their strengths and the problem itself.

In the SAT I math section, there are often several ways to solve any given problem. Smart students can consider two or more options before deciding on a strategy: *Should I solve the equation traditionally? Should I guess and check? Should I try out the answer choices? Should I look for a pattern? Should I simplify the expressions first?* On the SAT I essay, good students carefully consider their options before deciding what to write about: *What if I agree with the statement? What if I disagree with the statement? What examples can I use to illustrate this point? What strategies can I use to persuade my reader? What objections might a reader have to my points?*

T is for Thinking Logically

The SAT I doesn't just test what you know; it tests how well you think. Logic is one of the most powerful thinking tools that you have. Logic isn't merely "using your head" (as many people seem to think); it is drawing valid conclusions from previous statements according to a strict set of rules. These rules allow us to "transform" old statements into new statements. For instance, logical rules allow you to turn the statement $3x + 15 = 48$ into the statement $x = 11$, or convert the three statements *All giraffes are tall*, *All giraffes are animals*, and *David has a giraffe* into the statement *David has a tall animal*.

Using logic means obeying established logical rules for making valid conclusions. **Deductive** logic means drawing specific conclusions from general "facts." This includes knowing and obeying the rules of equations and applying the theorems of geometry and arithmetic. It also includes recognizing the implications of statements in a passage. In your writing, it means following a clear train of thought so that the reader can follow you to your conclusion.

To be masterfully logical, however, you must know more than deduction. Another form of logic that you should understand is **indirect logic**. This is the method of assuming the *opposite* of what you want to prove, and showing that this assumption leads to an absurdity. This proves that the assumption is false, and therefore that *its* opposite, the claim you are trying to prove, is in fact true.

CH is for Checking

Checking your work is key to smart problem solving. Basic checking is just repeating your steps with a bit more attention. But good checking strategy is much more than redoing your work to make sure you get the same answer.

Do two different kinds of "checks" as you solve a problem: check for **efficiency** as well as **accuracy.** To check efficiency, ask: *Am I getting closer to my goal? Might there be a quicker way to get to my goal? Will I have to find something else before I can get to my goal?* To check accuracy, ask: *Did I show my steps clearly? Are they correct? Does my solution make sense when I re-read the problem?*

When checking to see that your answer is correct, try your best to **look at the problem from a different angle** rather than merely repeating the steps you already took. On Math: if you did precise calculations to get an answer, check it with estimation, or if you used "guess and check," try to check by solving more directly. On Sentence Completions: re-read the sentence one more time with your answer "filled in," and check that it makes common sense. On the Critical Reading section, check that your responses make sense, given the overall purpose of the passage.

CHAPTER 4

SMART TRAINING FOR THE SAT I

Using Intelligence, Not Gimmicks

1 SMART TRAINING FOR THE SAT I: USING INTELLIGENCE, NOT GIMMICKS

The SAT I has raised its standards. It now includes a written essay, more reading passages, tougher math concepts than ever before, and questions about grammar and usage. It is, more than ever, an academic reasoning test, requiring creativity, insight, knowledge, logic, and genuine academic skills. Real success on the SAT I requires smart training, not test-taking tricks.

The "crack the test" approach to preparing for the SAT I is even less effective now. For real improvement on the SAT I, you must strengthen your problem-solving skills. Students who ace the SAT I don't do it by memorizing test-taking tricks. Ask them. They do it by becoming **good problem solvers.**

Smart Training for the SAT I is not about memorizing the "best way" to solve each "type" of SAT I question. There are no such "magic bullets," and trying to memorize each possible "type" is silly, not to mention virtually impossible. This would be like training a baseball player to simply "memorize" every possible scenario in a baseball game, and respond to each one in a pre-programmed way. Ridiculous. Of course, fundamental skills are important to a good player, but even more important are the systems he or she uses to respond—flexibly and creatively—to the infinite possibilities that may arise in any game. A good player is one who thinks well. Similarly, to do well on the SAT I, you must improve your *general* problem-solving skills, so that you are ready for any crazy problem that might come your way. This process requires being open to new information and discoveries as they come, continually looking for new relationships and patterns in that information, evaluating and reevaluating your progress as you work through problems, and so on.

This is mindful practice, not mindless habit or "quick and easy" tricks.

Here are some important questions to think about:

- As you read, are you in control of how your eyes move through the page? Do you always know what to look for in a passage? Is your mind actively seeking to answer questions as you read and to "construct" a representation of what you read in your mind? Do you consolidate information as you read? Do you notice the structure of the passage as you read? If not, you are not reading mindfully. The College Hill Method will show you how to read mindfully and ace the SAT I Critical Reading sections.

- As you write, do you stay mindful of the central purpose of your essay? Do you think about different ways of phrasing and arranging your thoughts? Do you address the objections a reader might have to your points? Are you continually checking that your writing is clear and forceful to your reader? If not, you are not writing mindfully. The College Hill Method will show you how to write mindfully and ace the SAT I Essay.

- When solving a math problem, do you always represent the problem information in a way you can use? Do you look for patterns or repetition in the problem so that you can simplify it? Do you consider the different approaches you could take to solving the problem? Do you have good strategies for checking your work? If not, you are not working mindfully. The College Hill Method will show you how to work mindfully and ace the SAT I Mathematics sections.

2 CREATING A MINDFUL WORKFLOW: GETTING "IN THE ZONE"

Do you ever feel "in the zone," when you feel confident that you can meet any challenge, and even seek out challenges to conquer? When you have a heightened, exhilarating awareness of your surroundings? This is what we call a state of **mindful workflow.** It's the state you want to be in when you take the SAT I, so you should practice getting into this state as you study.

Get the Oxygen Flowing

Your brain needs a good supply of oxygen to work well, so a good aerobic exercise regimen will help your SAT I preparation tremendously. Do at least 20 minutes of good aerobic exercise (as long as your doctor says it's okay) before sitting down to do your

work. This will get the oxygen flowing to your brain, relieve stress, and enhance your mental agility.

Focus and Calm Your Mind

Although you are probably not nervous when you study, you should still practice "focusing" exercises to get your mind ready to concentrate on mindful work. The next section will describe some good focusing exercises. Practice them and use them just as you sit down to study.

Prepare Your Study Area

Most students waste a tremendous amount of study time because they don't prepare their work space and therefore do not work efficiently. Put yourself in a place where you can maintain mindful focus for an extended time. **Do not study on your bed.** Your bed is a place for sleep, and you can't study well when half of your brain is sending sleep signals to the rest of your brain. **Instead, sit in a quiet area (soft, unintrusive music with no lyrics, if you must—no hiphop or rock) in an upright chair at a table or desk with good lighting.** Also, make sure that all the tools you will need are within easy reach: **a dictionary, note cards, a calculator, and pencils with erasers.**

Make Your Practice Tests Feel Real

If you are taking a practice SAT I, **try to replicate the experience of the actual test as much as possible.** Start the test around 8 or 9 am, since that's when you'll take the real thing. Use a stopwatch that will beep when your time is up on each section, and take the test in one sitting. **If you want to see good results, practice the way you will play. If you can, have someone proctor you; have your proctor hold the stopwatch and let you know when time is up on each section. You won't be in control of the time on test day, so it's best to practice with a proctor.**

It may help to build your test-taking stamina slowly. Just as marathoners don't start their training with a full marathon, you might want to plan to take just a couple of sections of a test the first week, building up gradually until, in the last few weeks before the SAT I, you are taking full tests each week as part of your training.

Work Intelligently

If you are doing your normal SAT I homework, always keep in mind that your goal is to learn to solve SAT I problems independently, as you would on the real test. Give every worksheet question your best effort, and check it if you can. Even if you can solve a problem, try to find a simpler way. Try to find different angles on each problem.

3 | THE MIND-BODY CONNECTION

As marathon runners, we realize more and more how much SAT I training is like marathon training. First, those who finish happy are those who take their training seriously. Unfortunately, many students "train" to take the SAT I merely by memorizing tricks and gimmicks for "cracking" the test. This is like training for a marathon merely by buying a pair of magic socks. The socks may give you a little bit of extra confidence, but they're not going to make a big difference. Second, the vast majority of marathon runners know that they don't have any chance of coming in first, but the good runners are happy just running "their own race" as best they can. They listen to their own bodies, rather than chasing the other runners around them. Similarly, good test takers don't pay attention to the students around them when they are taking a test. Instead, they know what they can do and what they can't do, and they don't stress out about not being able to answer every single question.

Train Your Body with Your Mind

There are two great reasons to combine a regimen of vigorous physical exercise with your preparation for the SAT I. First, physical health yields mental benefits. Those who are in good physical shape can focus longer and think faster than those who don't exercise. Second, the task of getting your body in shape teaches you a lot about getting your mind in shape. When you are training to run a race like a marathon, for instance, you learn quickly that consistency pays off. Getting out there every day and logging miles is critical. Similarly, consistency pays off in SAT I prep. If you set aside only one day a week to do your work, you won't see nearly as much benefit as if you had spread it out over the week. Also, physical training teaches you to listen to your body; you learn when it's okay to push yourself hard, and when you need to ease up. Similarly, good SAT I training teaches you to listen to your mind; you learn which problems you can tackle easily, which are challenging but manageable, and which ones to skip. This will help you enormously on test day.

Practice Focusing and Relaxation Exercises

Top athletes and performers almost always do focusing and relaxation exercises before they perform. These exercises help them to eliminate distractions and unnecessary tension so that they can do their best. You should practice these exercises, too. Here are some that work wonders for good students.

1. FOCUSED BREATHING

Focused breathing is perhaps the oldest and most powerful technique for calming nerves and focusing the mind. It is also amazingly simple. Sit in an upright chair with your hands on your knees, or sit upright on the floor with your legs crossed. Close your eyes and focus your attention on your breathing. Do not alter your breathing at first, just notice it. After a few breaths, you will notice that it will become slower and deeper on its own. This deep breathing is the key to relaxation. When we are tense and anxious, our breathing becomes short and shallow, and the oxygen flow through the body is diminished.

Next, focus on gently controlling your breathing so that you extend both the in breath and the out breath. Your in breath should feel like you are filling your lungs completely with air. The out breath should be slow and controlled, and should produce a light, hollow, raspy sound at the back of your throat. **Do not hold your breath at any point.** Your in breath should move smoothly into an out breath.

After a few breaths like this, you will notice that your mind will begin to wander. You will think about other things, perhaps about responsibilities that you have, and your body will tense up briefly. Focus on "releasing" those thoughts from your mind in the same way that you are releasing the air from your lungs, and return your focus to the breath. **This practice of noticing and releasing distractions is an essential part of focused breathing practice.** It teaches you that these thoughts are normal, that you shouldn't get too anxious about them, and that you have control over them. You can "release" them from your mind easily.

After a few minutes of focused breathing, your body is relaxed and your mind is alert, so you are prepared to do your homework or take your test.

2. Systematic Relaxation

Another amazingly simple practice for releasing tension is systematic relaxation. Sit in an upright chair, or lie on the floor. Close your eyes. Bring your attention to the muscles in your head and face. These are usually the first muscles to become tense when we are anxious. As your attention moves around your face to the different muscles, "see" these muscles in your mind's eye at the same time that you consciously relax them. When your face and head feel relaxed, move to your neck and shoulders. **Don't rush.** Often, the tension in your muscles goes so deep that you must focus on it for a minute or so before that tension will release. Then move systematically down to your arms, your torso and back, your hips, your legs, and your feet. With each stage of relaxation, you should feel the tension flowing out of you like sand from a bag. After several minutes of systematic relaxation, your body is relaxed, but your mind is focused, so your are ready to do your work.

3. Yoga or Other Mindful Exercises

The problem with most exercise is that it is not mindful. If exercise to you means grunting out reps with a barbell, or running with music blasting from your earphones, then your exercise strategy may be more of an assault on your body and mind than a healthful practice. Certain exercise disciplines have evolved over centuries to provide mindful, healthful practices. Yoga, for instance, is not just about bending and twisting your body into odd shapes. It is about pushing your body's strength, flexibility, and stamina to their limits in a mindful way, so that not only does your body become stronger and more flexible, but your mind develops a much deeper "body awareness" that is so essential to good health. T'ai Chi is also a great practice for developing body awareness, although it is generally not as physically demanding as yoga can be. Learning these disciplines requires the help of an instructor. You can probably find such classes available at your local gym, or find some instruction tapes in the library or store. Incorporating these practices into your life can make you calmer and more prepared to handle life's problems.

Listen to Your Body

1. Don't slouch when you work; sit upright.

Your brain is constantly receiving signals from your body. When you are studying or taking a test, you don't want those signals to interfere with your thinking. When you are slouched in your seat, or slumped over the table or desk, your body is telling your brain that it's not really time to pay attention. **If you want to think effectively, then sit upright and lean slightly forward over your work. You will find that this position helps you to process information much more efficiently than if you are in a more relaxed position.**

2. Look at your book head-on, not at an angle.

You will find it much easier to read when your book is facing you directly, rather than at an angle. Try to read both ways. You will still be able to read when the book is at an angle, but your brain has to work harder to process the words. Don't make things harder than they need to be!

3. Take short breaks whenever you feel fatigued.

Whenever you begin to feel fatigued from studying, take a five-minute break. But be strict—don't let your break get out of hand. Five minutes is enough time to get a snack or use the bathroom but not long enough to do much else. Don't take a break to watch your favorite show; you can do that after your homework is done. **But a good short break can provide a great energy boost in the midst of your studying.**

Eat Smart and Get Your Rest

Keeping your brain healthy is part of keeping your body healthy. Most high school students don't put nutrition and sleep near the top of their daily priorities. If you owned a $70,000 sports car, would you leave it out in hailstorms, neglect changing the oil or transmission fluid, and use only the cheapest gasoline? Obviously not. So don't fool yourself that your brain will work just fine even if you neglect its basic needs. Here are some simple tips to make sure that your mind and body are getting what they need.

1. DRINK AT LEAST FIVE LARGE GLASSES OF WATER PER DAY.

Even though water contains no calories or vitamins, it is the most important part of a nutritious diet. Water vitalizes your cells by helping transport essential nutrients to them. It also helps to flush out the toxic by-products that can build up in your system. Even though soda and juice are mostly water, they add lots of other unnecessary stuff that your cells don't need. All of your vital systems require an ample supply of *pure* water to function well.

2. TAKE A GOOD MULTIVITAMIN SUPPLEMENT DAILY.

Even if you eat three square meals a day, you still may not be getting some of the nutrients your body and brain need to work at their best. Just one multivitamin supplement can ensure that you won't miss any nutrients even if you miss a meal. But remember: many essential nutrients, like Vitamin C, are not produced by your body, and so should be consumed regularly throughout the day. **Vitamin supplements are helpful, but they can't substitute for good general eating habits.**

3. EAT PROTEIN WITH EVERY MEAL.

Protein, which is found in eggs, milk, fish, poultry, and meat, is essential to a good diet because it provides the "building blocks" for a healthy body. If you eat a lot of cereal and processed, packaged foods, you probably aren't getting enough protein. Egg whites, fish, chicken, lentils, tofu, and beans are the best sources of high-quality protein.

4. EAT WHOLE GRAINS AND LOTS OF GREEN VEGETABLES.

There is some evidence that food additives can be harmful to the functioning of your organs, and this includes your brain. Try to eliminate processed foods from your diet: packaged crackers, cookies and cakes, processed cheeses, soda, and so on, because the additives in these foods generally offset any nutritional value they have. America is fat largely because of processed foods. Instead, eat more salads and green vegetables, fruits, and whole grains. Instead of sugary processed cereal in the morning, try yogurt with fruit and oatmeal. Instead of a fast-food hamburger or pizza, try a grilled chicken sandwich with lettuce and tomato (keep the sauces to a minimum). Cutting out processed food is not too hard, and your energy will skyrocket and you'll feel (and think) much better.

5. TREAT SLEEP TIME LIKE AN APPOINTMENT.

When a student walks into my office, I can always tell right away if he or she is well-rested or not. I wish I had a dime for every time a student told me she was up until 2 a.m. the previous night because she needed to finish an assignment that she had to postpone because of a game, or because her friend had an emotional crisis. Don't get me wrong, I'm not saying you should quit sports or abandon your friends, but it's crucial that you understand something about sleep: **if you don't get enough sleep, any difficulties you are having now are likely to get worse.** The problems will snowball: you have to stay up late to finish an assignment, but then you're too tired to pay attention in class the next day, and you can't wait to get home to nap. Then you find that you hardly have time to do your homework because you've been sleeping, and so on. Think of it this way: if you plan your schedule so that you get eight hours of rest instead of six, you will probably find that you make up those two hours with better focus, energy, and productivity each day. So **treat your bedtime like it's an important appointment,** and you'll find you'll be much happier and get more done every day.

---

4 SMART TIPS

On Training

KEEP CHECKING YOURSELF!

When training to take the SAT I, continually assess your strengths and weaknesses with the Practice Tests in Chapter 19 and focus on your weakest areas first. But don't ignore your strengths—they can probably be made stronger!

Look carefully at any troublesome math questions on your PSAT, Diagnostic Test, or Practice Tests. Did your geometry teacher, Mr. Polygon, confuse triangles and squares, making the geometry questions particularly tough for you? If so, make sure you focus your attention on Chapter 13, "Essential Geometry Skills."

Was pre-algebra so long ago that you forget what sums, products, and remainders are? If so, Chapter 10, "Essential Pre-Algebra Skills," is a good place to start.

> Take Practice Tests in the library, where there are no distractions, and go over each of your Practice Tests for a second time soon after you take them to help you to understand where and why you are going wrong.
>
> *Joia Ramchandani (700CR 770M: +260 points)*

Look carefully at any troublesome Critical Reading questions on your tests. What part was toughest? If it was the vocabulary, focus on Chapter 6, "How to Build an Impressive Vocabulary with MAPS-CATCH." If you struggled to read the passages, or find their main points, focus on Chapter 7, "Critical Reading Skills." If you missed more Sentence Completion questions than you'd like, work on Chapter 8, "Sentence Completion Skills."

Look carefully at any troublesome writing questions on your tests. Did you find yourself struggling with the essay? If so, Chapters 15 and 16 will teach you how to approach the essay more effectively. If the rules of grammar sometimes seem overwhelming, work on Chapter 18, "Essential Grammar Skills," and Chapter 17, "Attacking the Grammar Questions."

> Whenever you have the choice, turn off the TV and read a good book instead!
>
> *Elisha Barron (Yale student, 800CR 800M)*

TAKE CONTROL OF THE TEST

When you take the SAT I, you must complete the sections in strict order. Once you have completed a section, you can't look back at it. However, within a section you can skip around as necessary. Remember, your objective is to accumulate as many "raw points" as you possibly can. Of course, within each section, the questions are ordered *roughly* from easiest to hardest, but that is a matter of opinion! You may find the 7th Sentence Completion question easier to do than the 3rd one. Know your strengths and take control of the test. Also, you may find that you feel better starting with the Critical Reading questions rather than the Sentence Completion questions on a given section. **Be careful, though: if you skip around, make sure you keep extra careful track of your answers on the answer sheet!**

> Write on the test when you need to. Mark up the diagrams on math problems, write in your own words in the Sentence Completion questions, and summarize each paragraph of the reading passages.
>
> *Alex Davidow (+170 points CR)*

SET CLEAR GOALS

Head into the exam with a well-formulated strategy for attacking the test. Have clear score goals in mind, and know what percentage of questions you will need to answer correctly to achieve those goals. The score conversion table below will tell you this.

Remember that answering every question is a bad strategy unless you have a very realistic shot at breaking 700 per section. As a rule of thumb, remember that you need to get only about 50% (or ½) of the questions right in order to break 500, about 67% (or ⅔) of the questions right in order to break 600, and about 87.5% (or ⅞) of the questions right in order to break 700. It's best to focus the majority of your time on just that percentage of questions you will need to break your score goal. This strategy gives you more time to check your work on each question, and minimizes the chance of making careless errors.

Use your PSAT scores or your Diagnostic Test scores as a starting point. Then decide what score will make you happy. You should know what the median SAT I scores are for the schools you'd like to apply to. Set aggressive goals as you train (our students always expect to improve their scores by 100 points or so on each section), but pick a realistic goal as you get closer to the test date, based on your performance on the practice tests. If you've been getting 400s on all sections of your practice tests, don't expect to get 600s on the real thing!

PRACTICE, PRACTICE, PRACTICE

Whatever your strategy is, *practice* it on real tests so that you don't spend energy thinking about it during the test. Don't get too focused on "point-counting" during the test. This will take your focus away from the real problems.

FAMILIARIZE YOURSELF WITH THE TEST INSTRUCTIONS AND FORMAT

One of the simplest ways to increase your chances of success on test day is to familiarize yourself with the format of the exam ahead of time. Know the format and instructions for each section of the SAT I. This will save you time on the actual test. Why waste time reading the directions when you could memorize them beforehand? The rules won't change. Likewise, don't waste time looking at the practice examples for each section. Get that out of the way well before the test date.

> Do some review almost every day rather than cramming it into just one or two days each week.
>
> *Joia Ramchandani (700CR 770M: +260 points)*

Score Conversion Table

Raw Score	Critical Reading Scaled Score	Math Scaled Score	Writing Scaled Score	Raw Score	Critical Reading Scaled Score	Math Scaled Score	Writing Scaled Score
67	800			32	520	550	610
66	800			31	510	550	600
65	790			30	510	540	580
64	780			29	500	530	570
63	760			28	490	530	560
62	750			27	490	520	550
61	730			26	480	510	540
60	720			25	480	500	530
59	700			24	470	490	520
58	700			23	460	480	510
57	690			22	460	480	500
56	680			21	450	470	490
55	670			20	440	460	480
54	660	800		19	440	450	470
53	650	790		18	430	450	460
52	650	760		17	420	440	450
51	640	740		16	420	430	440
50	630	720		15	410	420	440
49	620	710	800	14	400	410	430
48	620	700	800	13	400	410	420
47	610	680	800	12	390	400	410
46	600	670	790	11	380	390	400
45	600	660	780	10	370	380	390
44	590	650	760	9	360	370	380
43	590	640	740	8	350	360	380
42	580	630	730	7	340	350	370
41	570	630	710	6	330	340	360
40	570	620	700	5	320	330	350
39	560	610	690	4	310	320	340
38	550	600	670	3	300	310	320
37	550	590	660	2	280	290	310
36	540	580	650	1	270	280	300
35	540	580	640	0	250	260	280
34	530	570	630	−1	230	240	270
33	520	560	620	−2 or less	210	220	250

BE STRICT WITH TIME

When taking practice tests, time yourself strictly. You may be tempted to take a few extra minutes per section, but this will only hurt your practice. If you get used to taking 28 minutes for a 25-minute section, you will feel enormously rushed on test day, and this could really hurt your score. It is helpful to know whether you are budgeting your time well on your practice tests so that you can work on your efficiency and fix the problem. Having a parent proctor your practice tests can really help.

Taking Practice Tests under real test conditions helps a lot!

Alex Davidow (+170 points CR)

TO GUESS OR NOT TO GUESS?

The SAT I is different from exams you take in the classroom because you get *negative* points for wrong answers. On a 100-question classroom math exam, if you answer 80 questions correctly and get 20 questions wrong, your score would be an 80. On the SAT I, if you answer 80 questions correctly and get 20 questions wrong, your score would be a 75. Why? Because the ETS includes a "wrong-answer penalty" to discourage random guessing. For 5-question multiple-choice questions, a correct answer is worth 1 "raw" point, a wrong answer costs you ¼ point, and an unanswered question costs you nothing.

It's better to leave a question blank than it is to get it wrong. If you can eliminate two or more choices, however, you should probably make an educated guess. Work on your guessing strategy as you practice. When you take a Practice Test, write a "G" on the test booklet next to questions you guess on (*not* on the answer sheet). After the exam, check to see how many of those guesses you got right. If you consistently get more than 20% (or ⅕) of your guesses right, you are "beating the odds," and your guessing strategy is better than omitting those questions.

> Don't be afraid to speak up and ask your teacher or tutor about what you don't know! Don't be embarrassed if you forget some very basic stuff that you were supposed to learn years ago.
>
> *Alexandra Schwarzman (690V 760M: +400 points)*

Just Before the Test

DON'T LEAVE HOME WITHOUT IT!

The night before the test, lay out everything you will need for the test on your nightstand or kitchen table. Don't forget any of the following:

- Admission ticket
- Photo ID
- Several #2 pencils with erasers
- Calculator (with *fresh* batteries)
- Stopwatch
- A light snack, like a banana or granola bar
- Your brain
- Earplugs (if you need them to shut out distractions)
- Directions to the test site (if you haven't been there before)

> Bring a light snack for energy on SAT day to eat during one of the breaks.
>
> *Joia Ramchandani (700CR 770M: +260 points)*

Few things are as awful as having your calculator conk out ten minutes into your first math section, so put in fresh batteries the night before. Forgetting your ticket would be disastrous. And they rarely have a spare brain available if you happen to forget yours.

THE NIGHT BEFORE—RELAX!

The night before the SAT I, your studying should all be behind you; cramming at this point will probably do more harm than good. Relax, go see a movie, grab dinner with your friends, do whatever you need to do to reward your brain for its efforts over the previous months. As long as you get a good night's rest, you're allowed to have some fun the evening before the exam. For a truly peaceful slumber, lay out everything you need for test day the night before.

> Prepare in advance, but don't study the night before, just get a good night's sleep. And don't forget a good breakfast the next morning! (Even if you're nervous!)
>
> *Julie MacPherson (+130 points V)*

KNOW YOUR WAY

If you will be taking the SAT I at an unfamiliar test site, make sure to get directions to the site well ahead of time. Drive (or take the bus or subway) to the test site at some point in the days before the test, so you can familiarize yourself with it. Even better, have someone else drive you to the test, but make sure that he or she knows the way, too. Leave yourself plenty of time to get to the test site by 8 a.m. so that you don't stress out if you hit traffic or get a little lost.

B.Y.O.S.: BRING YOUR OWN STOPWATCH

Your testing room will almost certainly have a clock, but it can be a big advantage to have your own stopwatch. (But make sure it doesn't make noise, or the proctor will confiscate it!) The best stopwatch is one that counts backwards from the time that you set. Make sure you practice setting, starting, and stopping the watch before you get to the test site. This will help you to manage your time and avoid that annoying mental arithmetic you would have to do to tell how much time you have left. Practice using your stopwatch when taking your practice exams so that you feel comfortable using it.

> Know how to budget your time appropriately on the test.
>
> *Alex Davidow (+170 points CR)*

DRESS RIGHT

Wear clothes that will keep you comfortable in any temperature. If it is late spring, bring an extra layer in case the room is too cold; if it is winter, wear layers so that you can remove clothing if you are too hot. Sometimes it seems as if NASA is using SAT I testing rooms to test human endurance at extreme temperatures.

POWER BREAKFAST

Eat a good breakfast before the exam, with protein to give your brain the energy it will need. Oatmeal is a good option, or eggs and bacon. Try to stay away from sugary cereals and syrup. While eating, you may want to relax to some peaceful music, or you may want to "start your engine" by looking over an SAT I Reading Comprehension passage or an interesting math problem to get your brain in the right mode.

EYE OF THE TIGER

Finally, head into the SAT I with a positive attitude. If you go in with an "I don't want to be here" attitude, the SAT I will eat you alive. Your attitude is critical to success on the SAT I. Any negative energy will detract from your thinking power and cost you points. Positive energy serves as motivation and puts you into a sharper mindset, helping you to focus on the tough questions.

In the Testing Room

IT STARTS—FOCUS!

Good preparation will be wasted if you can't **focus** on test day. When you step into the classroom to take your SAT I, you shouldn't be thinking about the things that could go wrong. Fight the urge to think about the sweet party you will go to that night, the argument that you had with your best friend the night before, or what you are going to have for lunch. Before the test begins, focus on relaxing and carrying out your game plan.

DOWN THE STRETCH THEY COME!

The SAT I is like a marathon, so pace yourself well. If you lose focus for the last section, it may cost you dearly. When you get near the end, don't think, "I'm almost out of here!" Focus by thinking, "Finish strong!" Keep yourself mentally sharp from beginning to end; don't allow yourself to let up until that final answer is filled in.

SHOULD I CHANGE MY ANSWER?

When should you change an answer and when should you leave it alone? The answer is amazingly simple: **only change your answer when you've reviewed the entire problem and discovered a mistake.** Resist the temptation to change your answer after reviewing the problem superficially, or changing it simply because "it can't be that easy!"

On your practice exams, whenever you change your answer, write a "Ch" next to the question in your test booklet. After you finish the exam, see how many of those changes were for the better. This will give you a better sense on test day of whether your checking strategy is an effective one.

WASTE NOT!

Don't waste too much time on any one question. Some students lose 30–40 points on a section simply by being too stubborn to let a problem go. If a question is going to take too much time, circle the question number in the test booklet, skip it on your answer sheet, and come back to it later. If you return to the problem 10 or 15 minutes later, your refreshed brain may well see things more clearly and find a simple way to solve the problem!

DON'T GIVE THE RIGHT ANSWER TO THE WRONG QUESTION

Don't go so fast that you answer the wrong question when doing a math problem. Always re-read the question to make sure you are giving the answer to the question it asks! For example, in the following question:

$$3x + 6 = 12, \text{ what is the value of } 3x?$$

even bright and focused students often solve for x and give the answer of 2. However, the question asked for the value of $3x$, which is 6. This is an example of giving the right answer to the wrong question. If you occasionally make this kind of mistake, get yourself into the habit of underlining what the question wants you to find. This will help you to focus on answering the right question.

BLOWING BUBBLES

Many SAT I horror stories begin with a student filling in the wrong spaces on the answer sheet (or "bubble sheet"). Practice using the answer grids when taking your practice tests so that you get comfortable with them. You might experiment with different strategies for putting your answers onto the answer sheet. Some students like to slide the answer sheet from under the test booklet, revealing just one space at a time for each question. Some prefer to fill in the answer after every question, and some prefer to wait until they've answered all of the questions on a page (circling their answers on the test booklet before transferring them to the answer sheet). There is no one "best way" to do it; just find the approach that is most efficient for you. If you skip a problem to come back to later, be *extremely* careful to skip that question on the answer grid as well. A small erasable dash next to the question number on the answer sheet works well as a reminder.

IF TIME IS RUNNING OUT

If you budget your time wisely, you should have plenty of time to do everything you need to do on the SAT I, and that probably includes leaving some hard questions unanswered. But what should you do if suddenly time is running out and you have several questions left that you *need* to answer? First, make *sure* that you really *do* need to answer them; answering *too many* questions is a common mistake. If you really *do* need to rush a bit, at least rush wisely. First answer the questions that can be done quickly. For example, a "word-in-context" Reading Comprehension question can usually be answered much more quickly than a "main idea" question. If your time is running out, attack the most doable questions!

CHAPTER 5

DIAGNOSTIC SAT I

Answer Sheet

SECTION

1

Write your essay for Section 1 in the space below and on the next page.

Section 1

Time — 25 minutes

Directions for Writing the Essay

Plan and write an essay that answers the question below. Do NOT write on another topic. An essay on another topic will receive a score of 0.

Two readers will grade your essay based on how well you develop your point of view, organize and explain your ideas, use specific and relevant examples to support your thesis, and use clear and effective language. How well you write is much more important than how much you write, but to cover the topic adequately you should plan to write several paragraphs.

Your essay must be written only on the lines provided on your answer sheet. You will have enough space if you write on every line, avoid wide margins, and keep your handwriting to a reasonable size. Your essay will be read by people who are not familiar with your handwriting, so write legibly.

You may use this sheet for notes and outlining, but these will not be graded as part of your essay.

Consider carefully the issue discussed in the following passage, then write an essay that answers the question posed in the assignment.

> In a culture obsessed with superficial appearances, our leaders should be those who can see beyond the surface. Judging a book by its cover is the job of the consumer, but reading the book—pondering its contents and perhaps seeking to write new chapters—is the job of a leader.

Assignment: **How important is it to look beyond superficial appearances?** Write an essay in which you answer this question and discuss your point of view on this issue. Support your position logically with examples from literature, the arts, history, politics, science and technology, current events, or your experience or observation.

Write your essay on your answer sheet.

Section 2

Time — 25 minutes
20 questions

2

Directions for Multiple-Choice Questions

In this section, solve each problem, using any available space on the page for scratchwork. Then decide which is the best of the choices given and fill in the corresponding oval on the answer sheet.

- You may use a calculator on any problem. All numbers used are real numbers.
- Figures are drawn as accurately as possible EXCEPT when it is stated that the figure is not drawn to scale.
- All figures lie in a plane unless otherwise indicated.

Reference Information

$A = \pi r^2$ $A = \ell w$ $A = \frac{1}{2}bh$ $V = \ell w h$ $V = \pi r^2 h$ $c^2 = a^2 + b^2$ Special Right Triangles
$C = 2\pi r$

The arc of a circle measures 360°.
Every straight angle measures 180°.
The sum of the measures of the angles in a triangle is 180°.

---

1 If $2m + k = 12$ and $k = 10$, what is the value of m?

(A) 0
(B) ¾
(C) 1
(D) 2
(E) 4

---

2 The average (arithmetic mean) of three numbers is 50. If two of the numbers are 35 and 50, what is the third number?

(A) 45
(B) 50
(C) 55
(D) 60
(E) 65

3

$$\begin{array}{r} A5 \\ A3 \\ A5 \\ + \ 2A \\ \hline 157 \end{array}$$

In the correctly worked addition problem above, each A represents the same digit. What is the value of A?

(A) 1
(B) 2
(C) 3
(D) 4
(E) 6

---

4 What number is the same percent of 225 as 9 is of 25?

(A) 27
(B) 45
(C) 54
(D) 64
(E) 81

GO ON TO THE NEXT PAGE ▶▶▶

5 If $2^{x-1} = 32$, what is the value of x?

(A) 4
(B) 6
(C) 9
(D) 16
(E) 17

6

VOTING RESULTS FOR REFERENDUM

	Yes	No	Total
Men	26		
Women			76
Total	59		137

The table above, representing the results of a vote taken by the Zoning Commission on a recent referendum, is only partially completed. Based on the table, how many women on the Commission voted no?

(A) 43
(B) 48
(C) 57
(D) 61
(E) 78

7 Kenny and Mike each begin with the same number of baseball cards. After Mike gives Kenny 12 cards, Kenny has twice as many as Mike. How many cards do they have all together?

(A) 36
(B) 48
(C) 60
(D) 72
(E) 84

8 A bag of Texas Tillie's Trail Mix contains x ounces of walnuts, 15 ounces of peanuts, and 20 ounces of pecans. Which of the following expressions gives the fraction of the mix that is walnuts?

(A) $\dfrac{x}{35}$

B) $\dfrac{35}{x}$

(C) $\dfrac{x}{35+x}$

(D) $\dfrac{35+x}{x}$

(E) $\dfrac{35-x}{35+x}$

9

In the diagram above, if $\ell \parallel m$, which of the following is equivalent to $a + d + f + g$?

(A) $2c + 2f$
(B) $b + c + e + h$
(C) $2d + 2e$
(D) $a + d + e + h$
(E) $2b + 2g$

10 For which of the following ordered pairs (x, y) is $2x + 3y > 6$ and $x - y > 6$?

(A) $(7, -1)$
(B) $(7, 1)$
(C) $(4, -3)$
(D) $(3, 3)$
(E) $(-3, 4)$

11 When n is divided by 12, the remainder is 6. What is the remainder when n is divided by 6?

(A) 0
(B) 1
(C) 2
(D) 3
(E) 4

GO ON TO THE NEXT PAGE ▸▸▸

12

The figure above shows a polygon with five sides. What is the average (arithmetic mean) of the measures, in degrees, of the five angles shown?

(A)   85°
(B)   108°
(C)   120°
(D)   324°
(E)   540°

13   At a pet store, if d represents the number of dogs and c represents the number of cats, then which of the following is equivalent to the statement "There are 3 fewer than 4 times as many dogs as cats?"

(A) $4d + 3 = c$
(B) $4d - 3 = c$
(C) $d = 4c + 3$
(D) $d = 4c - 3$
(E) $4d - 3c = 0$

14

In the figure above, if $PR = RS$, what is the area of triangle PRS?

(A) $9\sqrt{2}$
(B) $9\sqrt{3}$
(C) $18\sqrt{2}$
(D) $18\sqrt{3}$
(E) $36\sqrt{3}$

15   A $50,000 prize is divided among four winners in a ratio of $4:3:2:1$. What is the greatest amount of money that any winner receives?

(A) $5,000
(B) $10,000
(C) $12,500
(D) $20,000
(E) $40,000

16   For all non-zero integers a and b, let

$$a\{b\} = \frac{a^2}{b^2}.$$

If $m\{n\} = 9$, which of the following must be true?

   I. $m > n$
   II. $m^2 - n^2 = 8n^2$
   III. $|n|$ is a factor of $|m|$.

(A)   II only
(B)   I and II only
(C)   II and III only
(D)   I and III only
(E)   I, II, and III

17   A jar contains only red, white, and blue marbles. It contains twice as many red marbles as white marbles, and three times as many white marbles as blue marbles. If a marble is drawn at random, what is the probability that it is white?

(A) $\dfrac{1}{10}$

(B) $\dfrac{1}{6}$

(C) $\dfrac{3}{10}$

(D) $\dfrac{1}{3}$

(E) $\dfrac{3}{5}$

18 A certain class has 6 girls and 5 boys. Four of these students are to line up in the front of the room, with two girls on either end and two boys in between. How many such arrangements are possible?

(A) 20
(B) 200
(C) 462
(D) 600
(E) 900

19

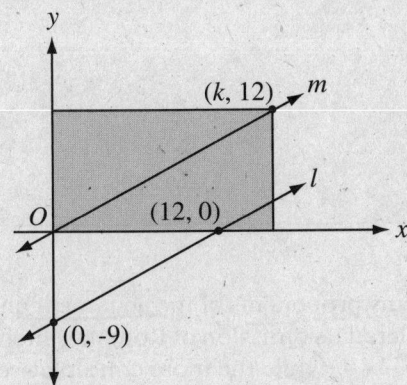

Note: Figure not drawn to scale

In the figure above, if $m \parallel l$, what is the area of the shaded rectangle?

(A) 96
(B) 108
(C) 144
(D) 192
(E) 204

20 A rectangular solid has a volume of p cubic centimeters, where p is an odd integer. The length, width, and height of the solid, in centimeters, are r, s, and t. If r, s, and t are all positive integers, which of the following must be true?

I. $p + s + t$ is odd.

II. $r = \dfrac{p}{st}$

III. The total surface area of the solid, in square centimeters, has an even value.

(A) I only
(B) I and II only
(C) I and III only
(D) II and III only
(E) I, II, and III

STOP

You may check your work, on this section only, until time is called.

Section 3

Time — 25 minutes
24 questions

Each of the sentences below is missing one or two portions. Read each sentence, then select the word or words that most logically completes the sentence, taking into account the meaning of the sentence as a whole.

Example:

Rather than accepting the theory unquestioningly, Deborah regarded it with -------.

  (A) mirth
  (B) sadness
  (C) responsibility
  (D) ignorance
  (E) skepticism

Correct response: (E)

1 They enjoyed each other's company enormously, but they rarely agreed on any issue; in fact, one could be sure that on any important topic their opinions would -------.

  (A) diverge
  (B) coincide
  (C) retreat
  (D) assemble
  (E) truncate

2 Once accepted as an incontrovertible truth, the theory that nine planets revolve around our sun is now regarded by astronomers as -------.

  (A) enacted
  (B) irrefutable
  (C) universal
  (D) dubious
  (E) conclusive

3 Having lost his wife and three children to untimely deaths, Rembrandt entered his dark period in 1642, when his immersion in painting often seemed his only ------- from abject -------.

  (A) salvation . . . prudence
  (B) remorse . . . adulation
  (C) solace . . . melancholy
  (D) elation . . . poverty
  (E) departure . . . cheerfulness

4 Many proponents of the new curriculum considered its omission of Romance literature to be -------, while the more conservative educators considered such a removal -------.

  (A) repugnant . . . premature
  (B) innocuous . . . deplorable
  (C) reprehensible . . . benevolent
  (D) malicious . . . disgraceful
  (E) auspicious . . . encouraging

5 As the expedition leader quickly realized, the recently accelerated program to acclimate the climbers to high altitudes was ------- as a result, several team members were soon ------- by the lack of oxygen.

  (A) illusory . . . initiated
  (B) excessive . . . mitigated
  (C) appropriate . . . confused
  (D) ineffective . . . enervated
  (E) venerable . . . absolved

6 Although the mainstream of most societies reviles the -------, nearly every culture reserves at least some small place for those who question its treasured norms and mores.

  (A) charlatan
  (B) surrogate
  (C) philanthropist
  (D) pragmatist
  (E) iconoclast

GO ON TO THE NEXT PAGE ▶▶▶

7 Steven Pinker is far from ------- about the heated controversy of whether the human mind is a *tabula rasa*; he stands ------- in the negative camp.

(A) ambivalent . . . unequivocally
(B) apathetic . . . furtively
(C) impartial . . . reluctantly
(D) adamant . . . vehemently
(E) subjective . . . stubbornly

8 Although Ivan Illich was dismissed as a ------- by many of his contemporaries, many modern thinkers now regard his revolutionary insights on the dehumanization of society as -------.

(A) pedant . . . derivative
(B) neophyte . . . vociferous
(C) radical . . . visionary
(D) partisan . . . conciliatory
(E) hermit . . . simplistic

Each passage below is followed by one or two questions based on its content. Answer each question based on what is stated or implied in the passage.

Questions 9–12 are based on the following passages.

PASSAGE 1

In many instances, the study of life on Earth ultimately involves the study of the molecules
Line of which living organisms are composed. How does photosynthesis convert the energy
5 of sunlight into the energy of sugar molecules? What is the structure of the cell membrane, and how does it function in controlling the movement of materials into and out of the cell? How do muscles contract? How
10 do the nerve cells in your brain communicate with one another? What causes cancer? To understand the answers to these questions, you must first learn about energy and matter, the properties of atoms, and how atoms interact with one another to form molecules.
15

PASSAGE 2

For centuries the idea that photosynthesis supports the earth's biosystem had been fundamental to our understanding of life on Earth. If the sun went out, we assumed, life
20 would soon follow. Yet in the 1970s, scientists discovered organisms thriving in deep-sea hydrothermal vents far from any light energy required for photosynthesis. These organisms relied on bacteria that harvest energy not
25 from light but from the chemical bonds in sulfides and other molecules that poured from the heat vents. This process is called chemosynthesis. Other organisms eat these bacteria or house the living bacteria in their
30 tissues. Such relationships mirror the myriad complex relationships we see in the photosynthetic food chain, in which bacteria are either consumed or co-opted by organisms to aid in breaking down or synthesizing chemicals that
35 the organisms' own tissues cannot.

9 Both passages focus primarily on

(A) how groups of cells form tissues
(B) the origin of life on Earth
(C) biochemical processes
(D) the importance of the sun to life on Earth
(E) unusual life forms

10 The questions listed in lines 4–11 of Passage 1 are presented as those that

(A) biologists have yet to explore in great depth
(B) inspire controversy within the scientific community
(C) necessarily concern those who are interested in a deep understanding of biology
(D) are difficult to investigate with current methods and technology
(E) researchers have not considered to be as important as those that concern ecology

GO ON TO THE NEXT PAGE ▶▶▶

11 Which of the five questions posed in Passage 1 is most relevant to the discussion in Passage 2?

(A) How does photosynthesis convert the energy of sunlight into the energy of sugar molecules?

(B) What is the structure of the cell membrane, and how does it function in controlling the movement of materials into and out of the cell?

(C) How do muscles contract?

(D) How do the nerve cells in your brain communicate with one another?

(E) What causes cancer?

12 Which of the following concepts is mentioned in Passage 2 but NOT in Passage 1?

(A) the structure of cells

(B) the conversion of light energy to food energy

(C) disease

(D) relationships among separate organisms

(E) bonds within molecules

The passages below are followed by questions based on their content. Answer the questions on the basis of what is stated or implied in the passage itself or the introductory material that precedes the passage.

Questions 13–18 are based on the following passage.

The following is an excerpt from a popular book on "innumeracy," the common inability of people to deal rationally with numbers.

Without some appreciation of common large numbers, it's impossible to react with the
Line proper skepticism to terrifying reports that
more than a million American kids are kid-
5 napped each year, or with the proper sobriety to a warhead carrying a megaton of explosive power—the equivalent of a million tons (or two billion pounds) of TNT.

And if you don't have some feeling for proba-
10 bilities, automobile accidents might seem a relatively minor problem of local travel, whereas being killed by terrorists might seem to be a major risk when going overseas. As often observed, however, the 45,000 people killed annu-
15 ally on American roads are approximately

equal in number to all American dead in the Vietnam War. On the other hand, the seventeen Americans killed by terrorists in 1985 were among the 28 million of us who traveled
20 abroad that year—that's one chance in 1.6 million of becoming a victim. Compare that with these annual rates in the United States: one chance in 68,000 of choking to death; one chance in 75,000 of dying in a bicycle crash;
25 one chance in 20,000 of drowning; and one chance in only 5,300 of dying in a car crash.

Confronted with these large numbers and with the correspondingly small probabilities associated with them, the innumerate will in-
30 evitably respond with the non sequitur,[1] "Yes, but what if you're that one," and then nod knowingly, as if they've demolished your argument with penetrating insight. This tendency to personalize is a characteristic of many who
35 suffer from innumeracy. Equally typical is a tendency to equate the risk from some obscure and exotic malady with the chances of suffering from heart and circulatory disease, from which about 12,000 Americans die each week.

40   There's a joke I like that's marginally relevant. An old married couple in their nineties contact a divorce lawyer, who pleads with them to stay together. "Why get divorced now after seventy years of marriage?" The little old
45 lady finally pipes up in a creaky voice: "We wanted to wait until the children were dead."

A feeling for what quantities or time spans are appropriate in various contexts is essential to getting the joke. Slipping between millions
50 and billions or between billions and trillions should in this sense be equally funny, but it isn't, because we too often lack an intuitive grasp for these numbers.

A recent study by Drs. Kronlund and
55 Phillips of the University of Washington showed that most doctors' assessments of the risks of various operations, procedures, and medications (even in their own specialties) were way off the mark, often by several orders
60 of magnitude. I once had a conversation with a doctor who, within approximately 20 minutes, stated that a certain procedure he was contemplating (a) had a one-chance-in-a-million risk associated with it; (b) was 99 per-
65 cent safe; and (c) usually went quite well. Given the fact that so many doctors seem to believe that there must be at least eleven

---

[1]A non sequitur is a statement that does not follow logically from previous statements.

GO ON TO THE NEXT PAGE ▶▶▶

people in the waiting room if they're to avoid being idle, I'm not surprised at this new
70 evidence of their innumeracy.

13 Which of the following can be inferred to be the author's view of the "reports that more than a million American kids are kidnapped each year" (lines 4–5)?

(A) They are typical examples of American journalism.
(B) They are evidence of a terrible problem that must be addressed.
(C) They are probably untrue.
(D) They properly use a number to convey a simple fact.
(E) They demonstrate an American obsession with statistics.

14 What fact is the list of probabilities cited in lines 21–26 intended to illustrate?

(A) that probability can be used in many different ways in everyday life
(B) that terrorism is far less a threat to Americans than many other common dangers
(C) that the world is filled with many dangers
(D) that a knowledge of probability can help Americans decide where to travel most safely abroad
(E) that bicycles are nearly as dangerous as cars

15 Which of the following is *not* an element of the discussion in this passage?

(A) a personal recollection
(B) a verifiable statistic
(C) a reference to an authoritative study
(D) a discussion of a common misconception
(E) a refutation of a scientific theory

16 What is the author's view of the "penetrating insight" mentioned in line 33?

(A) It is the result of careful analysis.
(B) It does not exist.
(C) It demolishes a statistical argument.
(D) It does not sufficiently personalize the situation being discussed.
(E) It is not found enough in everyday discussions.

17 In what way does the author suggest that the joke described in lines 41–46 is like "slipping between millions and billions" (lines 49–50)?

(A) They both involve a lack of appreciation for particular quantities.
(B) They both describe mistakes the elderly are likely to make.
(C) They both illustrate a common scenario.
(D) They both reveal the value of understanding probabilities.
(E) They both illustrate humor in mathematics.

18 The author mentions the time span of "approximately 20 minutes" (lines 61–62) in order to emphasize

(A) the doctor's inability to appreciate relevant time spans
(B) the comparison with the elderly couple in the preceding joke
(C) the frequency with which the doctor contradicted himself
(D) the common need to approximate rather than use precise numbers
(E) how quickly he was able to get an appointment

Excerpted from *Innumeracy* by John Allen Paulos, Hill and Wang, New York, 1988, pp. 7–8.

GO ON TO THE NEXT PAGE ▶▶▶

Questions 19–24 are based on the following passage:

The following is an excerpt from a memoir of Richard Feynman, a Nobel Prize–winning physicist, in which he describes the experience of having an artist friend named Jerry teach him to draw.

I promised to work, but still bet that he couldn't teach me to draw. I wanted very much to
Line learn to draw, for a reason that I kept to my-
self: I wanted to convey an emotion I have
5 about the beauty of the world. It's difficult to describe because it's an emotion. It's analo-gous to the feeling one has in religion that has to do with a god that controls everything in the universe: there's a generality aspect that
10 you feel when you think about how things that appear so different and behave so differ-ently are all run "behind the scenes" by the same organization, the same physical laws. It's an appreciation of the mathematical
15 beauty of nature, of how she works inside; a realization that the phenomena we see result from the complexity of the inner workings be-tween atoms; a feeling of how dramatic and wonderful it is. It's a feeling of awe—of scien-
20 tific awe—which I felt could be communi-cated through a drawing to someone who had also had this emotion. It could remind him, for a moment, of this feeling about the glories of the universe.
25   Jerry turned out to be a very good teacher. He told me first to go home and draw any-thing. So I tried to draw a shoe; then I tried to draw a flower in a pot. It was a mess!
      The next time we met I showed him my at-
30 tempts: "Oh, look!" he said. "You see, around in back here, the line of the flower pot doesn't touch the leaf." (I had meant the line to come up to the leaf.) "That's very good. It's a way of showing depth. That's very clever of you."
35   "And the fact that you don't make all the lines the same thickness (which I *didn't* mean

to do) is good. A drawing with all the lines the same thickness is dull." It continued like that: everything that I thought was a mistake, he
40 used to teach me something in a positive way. He never said it was wrong; he never put me down. So I kept on trying, and I gradually got a little bit better, but I was never satisfied.

19 In line 13, the word "organization" most nearly means

(A)   corporation
(B)   rules of physics
(C)   social group
(D)   arrangement of objects
(E)   system of emotional expression

20 Which of the following experiences is closest to what the author describes as "dramatic and wonderful" (lines 18–19)?

(A)   proving a physical law
(B)   creating a beautiful sculpture
(C)   appreciating the power of physical laws in nature
(D)   teaching another person how to play an instrument
(E)   seeing a masterful painting for the first time

21 What assumption does the author make about the appreciation of art?

(A)   It comes only through the experience of creating art.
(B)   It is enhanced by having experiences similar to those that inspired the artist.
(C)   It is not as important as the apprecia-tion of science.
(D)   It is difficult for a scientist.
(E)   It requires an understanding of the historical period in which the piece was created.

GO ON TO THE NEXT PAGE ▶▶▶

22 If Jerry is really a "very good teacher" (line 25) in the way that the author suggests, what would he most likely have done if the author had drawn the flower pot with lines of all the same thickness?

(A) Jerry would have shown the author how to vary the thickness of his lines.

(B) Jerry would have shown the author examples of how line thickness affects the quality of a drawing.

(C) Jerry would have mentioned that the drawing was dull, but could be made more lively with color.

(D) Jerry would have found something positive elsewhere in the drawing.

(E) Jerry would have made the author re-do the drawing.

23 The author suggests that the "way of showing depth" (lines 33–34) is actually

(A) unintentional

(B) unattractive

(C) difficult to accomplish

(D) not characteristic of true art

(E) a reflection of the author's theory of nature

24 In what way was the author "never satisfied" (line 43)?

(A) He was never able to fully appreciate great art.

(B) He was never able to draw a realistic flower pot.

(C) He was not able to replicate his teacher's talent for emphasizing the positive in his students.

(D) He never fully appreciated the talent of his teacher.

(E) He was never able to convey adequately his feelings about the beauty of the world.

3

STOP   *You may check your work, on this section only, until time is called.*

Section 4

Time — 25 minutes
35 questions

Directions for Improving Sentences Questions

Each of the sentences below contains one underlined portion. The portion may contain one or more errors in grammar, usage, construction, precision, diction (choice of words), or idiom. Some of the sentences are correct.

Consider the meaning of the original sentence, and choose the answer that best expresses that meaning. If the original sentence is best, choose (A), because it repeats the original phrasing. Choose the phrasing that creates the clearest, most precise, and most effective sentence.

EXAMPLE:
The children <u>couldn't hardly believe their eyes</u>.
(A) couldn't hardly believe their eyes
(B) would not hardly believe their eyes
(C) could hardly believe their eyes
(D) couldn't nearly believe their eyes
(E) could hardly believe his or her eyes

EXAMPLE ANSWER:
(C)

1 The anthology contains mostly the work of modern poets, but <u>which includes a few significant older works as well</u>.

(A) which includes a few significant older works as well
(B) it includes a few significant older works as well
(C) also it contains a few significant older works as well
(D) as well, it also includes a few significant older works
(E) which also include a few significant older works

2 The coach worked long and hard into the night <u>for preparing the team's strategy</u> for the next game.

(A) for preparing the team's strategy
(B) in preparing the team's strategy
(C) for the preparation of the team's strategy
(D) in order for proper preparation of the team's strategy
(E) to prepare the team's strategy

3 Although usually unflappable even in front of a crowd, <u>Carla's anxiety overwhelmed her</u> during the recital.

(A) Carla's anxiety overwhelmed her
(B) her anxiety overwhelmed Carla completely
(C) Carla being overwhelmed by anxiety
(D) Carla was overwhelmed by anxiety
(E) nevertheless Carla's anxiety was overwhelming

4 Those students who sit through her lectures <u>day after day, having been numbed into thinking</u> that history could never be even remotely interesting.

(A) day after day, having been numbed into thinking
(B) day after day being numbed into thinking
(C) day after day have been numbed into thinking
(D) day after day of being numbed into thinking
(E) day after day of having been numbed into thinking

5 Swimming in the deepest part of the lake, <u>the current pushed Justine farther from shore</u>.

(A) the current pushed Justine farther from shore
(B) Justine had been pushed farther from shore by the current
(C) Justine was pushed farther from shore by the current
(D) the current's push made sure that Justine moved farther from shore
(E) the push of the current moved Justine farther from shore

6 Writing a good twenty-page research paper is more difficult than <u>when you have to write</u> two good ten-page papers.

(A) when you have to write
(B) when one must write
(C) the writing of
(D) writing
(E) one's writing of

7 <u>If we had not stopped for gas</u>, we probably would have arrived in time for the movie.

(A) If we had not stopped for gas
(B) If we would not have stopped for gas
(C) If we didn't have stopped for gas
(D) Because we had stopped for gas
(E) If not for having been stopped for gas

8 The spectators watched <u>agape, they could not believe</u> what they were seeing on the playing field.

(A) agape, they could not believe
(B) agape having not believed
(C) agape, for the reason that they could not believe
(D) agape: they could not believe
(E) agape, therefore they could not believe

9 The evidence for clairvoyance has never been <u>persuasive, and many people continue to believe</u> that it is a widespread phenomenon.

(A) persuasive, and many people continue to believe
(B) persuasive; nevertheless, many people continue to believe
(C) persuasive, so many people continue to believe
(D) persuasive: and people continue to believe anyway
(E) persuasive, which is why people continue to believe

10 The strange theories that explain the atom <u>reveals how deeply the common and the bizarre are entwined</u> in the physical world.

(A) reveals how deeply the common and the bizarre are entwined
(B) reveal how common the entwining of the bizarre is
(C) reveals the deep bizarre common entwining
(D) reveal how the common and the bizarre are so entwined deeply
(E) reveal how deeply the common and the bizarre are entwined

11 The transportation board announced <u>their anonymous approval</u> of the new contract at the press conference that afternoon.

(A) their anonymous approval
(B) its anonymous approval
(C) their unanimous approval
(D) its unanimous approval
(E) about its unanimous approval

4

Directions for Identifying Sentence Error Questions

The following sentences may contain errors in grammar, usage, diction (choice of words), or idiom. Some of the sentences are correct. No sentence contains more than one error.

If the sentence contains an error, it is in one of the parts that are underlined and lettered. The parts that are not underlined are correct.

If there is an error, select the part that must be changed to correct the sentence.

If there is no error, choose (E).

4

EXAMPLE: SAMPLE ANSWER:

By the time <u>they reached</u> the halfway point
                   A   (D)

<u>in the race,</u> <u>most of the runners</u> <u>hadn't hardly</u>
       B   C   D

begun to hit their stride. <u>No error</u>
                                         E

---

12 The reporters failed to notice the <u>discrepancies</u>
                                                                  A

in the report that the Congressman presented,

because <u>his staff and him</u> had <u>successfully</u>
                B   C

diverted the media's attention <u>to other issues.</u>
                                                   D

<u>No error</u>
    E

13 The Warren family, whose ancestors

<u>founded</u> the town over <u>three hundred</u> years
     A   B

ago, <u>have ran</u> the general store <u>for</u> seven
            C   D

generations. <u>No error</u>
                          E

14 <u>Surprisingly</u> absent from the game <u>were</u> the
              A   B

crowd's <u>customary</u> <u>taunting of</u> the opposing
                   C   D

players. <u>No error</u>
                    E

15 <u>Much</u> of the class time <u>was dedicated</u> to
           A   B

discussing those theories that <u>seemed to be</u>
                                                     C

most commonly misconstrued

<u>by the students.</u> <u>No error</u>
          D   E

16 The refraction of light as it <u>passes from</u> air
                                                          A

into a denser <u>medium</u> like water or glass
                          B

often <u>produce</u> interesting kaleidoscopic
               C

<u>effects.</u>   <u>No error</u>
       D   E

17 Of the two films <u>that made</u> money
                                    A

<u>for the studio</u> this year, the <u>least</u> expensive
          B   C

garnered the more <u>favorable</u> reviews.
                                   D

<u>No error</u>
    E

18 Having invested so much effort in getting

her team <u>so far</u> <u>in the tournament,</u>
        A   B

Coach Moran could hardly be blamed for

reacting so <u>emotional</u> <u>to the foul</u> called on
          C   D

her player in the waning seconds of the

game.   <u>No error</u>
         E

19 To its most eminent proponents, anarchism

<u>implies</u> not a desire for lawlessness or
 A

chaos, but <u>rather it is</u> a respect <u>for the ability of</u>
         B   C

individuals <u>to manage</u> their own affairs
         D

justly without the intervention of a

government.   <u>No error</u>
          E

20 The senate adopted new rules to prevent

representatives <u>from serving</u> on a committee
         A

<u>while at the same time</u> maintaining an
      B

interest <u>in any company</u> that conducts
       C

business that is <u>affected</u> by that committee's
        D

decisions.   <u>No error</u>
        E

21 The labor coalition, <u>which consists</u> of
          A

representatives from all of the skilled labor

unions, <u>have expressed</u> concern <u>about</u> the
      B   C

new hiring policies <u>enacted by</u> the board.
            D

<u>No error</u>
 E

22 Most cognitive scientists <u>now believe</u> that
            A

the way the human brain <u>stores information</u>
            B

is <u>different</u> in many significant ways from
   C

<u>a computer hard drive.</u>   <u>No error</u>
     D   E

23 The museum, which <u>has sponsored</u> free
           A

programs in the arts for city children since

the late 1960s, was <u>cited</u> <u>by the mayor</u> for
          B   C

<u>their</u> many civic contributions.   <u>No error</u>
 D   E

24 <u>When given the choice,</u> Harlow's monkeys
      A

clearly preferred the warmer, cloth-covered

surrogate mother <u>more than</u> the wire
         B

surrogate, <u>even when</u> the latter was able
      C

<u>to provide</u> them with nourishment.
   D

<u>No error</u>
 E

25 Although both films <u>accurately depict</u> the
          A

horrors <u>of fighting</u> on the front lines, *Saving*
      B

Private Ryan is by <u>far</u> the <u>most</u> graphic.
        C   D

<u>No error</u>
 E

26 The debate team, <u>which</u> included
         A

Emma and I, <u>was</u> stuck on the bus for
     B   C

<u>more than two</u> hours.   <u>No error</u>
    D   E

GO ON TO THE NEXT PAGE ▸▸▸

27 By the time he <u>reached</u> the island, David
                   A
had already <u>swam</u> further than <u>anyone</u>
                   B   C
else ever <u>had</u>.   <u>No error</u>
              D   E

4 ➤ 28 <u>Far from</u> being a liberal fanatic, Davis
              A
actually <u>espouses</u> very conservative
                   B
<u>views on</u> social and <u>economic</u> issues.
       C   D
<u>No error</u>
       E

29 <u>For building</u> vocabulary skills, students
            A
should <u>try to</u> speak and write new words in
              B
<u>appropriate contexts</u>, rather <u>than</u> merely
            C   D
memorizing definitions.   <u>No error</u>
                                      E

Below is an early draft of an essay. It requires revision in many areas.

The questions that follow ask you to make improvements in sentence structure, diction, organization, and development. Answering the questions may require you to understand the context of the passage as well as the rules of standard written English.

Questions 30–35 are based on the following passage.

(1) *Maria Montessori, who was born in 1870, was a remarkable woman for her time. (2) She surprised her parents by telling them that she wanted to study engineering when she was young, a position that they thought was unladylike. (3) She later decided to switch to medicine and became the first female physician in Italy. (4) As a doctor, the treatment of children who they said were "deficient" bothered her. (5) She realized that isolating them and depriving them of stimulation was doing them a lot of harm.*

(6) *In 1907 Maria opened her* Casa dei Bambini, *or "Children's House," a daycare center where impoverished children could receive a stimulating learning environment. (7) She believed that there are specific time schedules where children's minds are ready to learn particular things at their own pace, and these periods are different for every child. (8) She decided it was important to help each child through his or her own curriculum rather than a standardized one for everybody. (9) What was most amazing, the children who used to be aggressive and unmanageable became very proud of their accomplishments and eager to learn more when they were taught skills that gave them control and independence. (10) There were fifty students in her first class.*

(11) *One of the things that Dr. Montessori did that might be the most important is not just treat children as small adults, but as people with their own special needs. (12) She designed special furniture, toys, and learning aids that were appropriate for their size and abilities.*

(13) *Her philosophy has had a profound effect on education throughout the world. (14) Today, even the most traditional and regimented schools acknowledge many contributions of Maria Montessori.*

30 Which of the following is the best revision of sentence 2 (reproduced below)?

She surprised her parents by telling them that she wanted to study engineering when she was young, a position that they thought was unladylike.

(A) When she was young, she surprised her parents by telling them that she wanted to study the unladylike position of engineering, they thought.

(B) When she was young, she surprised her parents by telling them that she wanted to study engineering, a subject they thought was unladylike.

(C) She surprised her parents by telling them that she wanted to study engineering, a subject that they thought was unladylike when she was young.

(D) She surprised her parents by telling them that she wanted to study the unladylike, so her parents thought, subject of engineering when she was young.

(E) She surprised her parents when she was young by telling them, who thought it was unladylike, that she wanted to study engineering.

31 Which of the following is the best way to revise the underlined portion of sentence 4 (reproduced below)?

As a doctor, the treatment of children who they said were "deficient" bothered her.

(A) she was bothered by the treatment of children who were said to be "deficient."

(B) the way children were treated who they said were "deficient" bothered her.

(C) the treatment bothered her of children who they said were "deficient."

(D) she was bothered by those children they said were "deficient" and the way they were treated.

(E) she was bothered by the children treated who were said to be "deficient."

32 The unity of the second paragraph can best be improved by deleting which of the following sentences?

(A) sentence 6
(B) sentence 7
(C) sentence 8
(D) sentence 9
(E) sentence 10

33 Where is the best place to insert the following sentence?

It was developed according to her theories about learning.

(A) after sentence 6
(B) after sentence 7
(C) after sentence 8
(D) after sentence 9
(E) after sentence 10

34 Which of the following is the best revision of sentence 7 (reproduced below)?

She believed that there are specific time schedules where children's minds are ready to learn particular things at their own pace, and these periods are different for every child.

(A) She believed that there are specific time schedules, and these schedules are different for every child, where children's minds are ready at their own pace to learn particular things.
(B) She believed that there are different time periods for every child where their minds are ready to learn particular things at their own pace.
(C) She believed different children at their own pace each have their own time schedules where they are ready to learn particular things.
(D) She believed that each child's mind has its own unique pace and schedule for learning.
(E) She believed that there are specific schedules that are different for every child's mind that make them able to learn at their own pace.

35 Which is the best sentence to insert between sentence 8 and sentence 9?

(A) Her need to blaze trails persisted well into her old age.
(B) It wasn't long until Dr. Montessori was recognized for her efforts.
(C) This focus on the individual child produced amazing results.
(D) She soon opened many of these schools throughout Italy.
(E) Even though she was a physician by training, she earned eminence as a teacher.

STOP

You may check your work, on this section only, until time is called.

Section 5

Time — 25 minutes
18 questions

Directions for Multiple-Choice Questions

In this section, solve each problem, using any available space on the page for scratchwork. Then decide which is the best of the choices given and fill in the corresponding oval on the answer sheet.

- You may use a calculator on any problem. All numbers used are real numbers.
- Figures are drawn as accurately as possible EXCEPT when it is stated that the figure is not drawn to scale.
- All figures lie in a plane unless otherwise indicated.

Reference Information

$A = \pi r^2$
$C = 2\pi r$

$A = \ell w$

$A = \frac{1}{2} bh$

$V = \ell wh$

$V = \pi r^2 h$

$c^2 = a^2 + b^2$

Special Right Triangles

The arc of a circle measures 360°.
Every straight angle measures 180°.
The sum of the measures of the angles in a triangle is 180°.

---

1   If $5y - 2 = 3y + 7$, what is the value of y?

(A)   3.0
(B)   4.5
(C)   6.0
(D)   7.5
(E)   9.0

2

In the figure above, three lines intersect in a single point. What is the value of $a + b$?

(A)   20
(B)   54
(C)   126
(D)   146
(E)   252

3 If $(2x)(3x) = \left(\dfrac{2}{8}\right)\left(\dfrac{3}{2}\right)$, and $x > 0$, what is the value of x?

(A) $\frac{1}{16}$
(B) $\frac{1}{8}$
(C) $\frac{1}{4}$
(D) $\frac{1}{3}$
(E) $\frac{1}{2}$

5

4 Two positive integers are "compatible" if their greatest common factor is a prime number. For instance, 15 and 25 are compatible because their greatest common factor is 5, which is prime. If m and 98 are compatible, and m is an odd number, then what is the greatest common factor of m and 98?

(A) 2
(B) 5
(C) 7
(D) 14
(E) 49

5 For how many integer values of k is $|k - 0.5| < 10$?

(A) 17
(B) 18
(C) 19
(D) 20
(E) 21

6 What is the greatest possible value of $f(x)$ over the interval $-1 \le x \le 2$ if $f(x)$ is defined by the equation $f(x) = \dfrac{10 - x^2}{2}$?

(A) 3.0
(B) 3.5
(C) 4.0
(D) 4.5
(E) 5.0

7 If m and n are integers and $1 < m^3 = n^2 < 100$, what is the value of $m + n$?

(A) 4
(B) 8
(C) 12
(D) 16
(E) 32

8 Amanda travels to work from home in 60 minutes. If, on her way home, she increases her average speed by 20% and she travels by the exact same route, how many minutes will it take her to get home?

(A) 48
(B) 50
(C) 54
(D) 60
(E) 64

Directions for Student-Produced Response Questions

Each of the questions in this section requires you to solve the problem and enter your answer in a grid, as shown below.

- If your answer is 2/3 or .666..., you must enter **the most accurate value the grid can accommodate,** but you may do this in one of four ways:

Start in first column

Grid result here

Start in second column

Grid as a truncated decimal

Grid as a rounded decimal

- In the example above, gridding a response of 0.67 or 0.66 is **incorrect** because it is less accurate than those shown above.
- The scoring machine cannot read what is written in the top row of boxes. You **MUST** fill in the numerical grid accurately to get credit for answering any question correctly. You should write your answer in the top row of boxes only to aid your gridding.
- Do **not** grid in a mixed fraction like 3½ as `3 1 / 2` because it will be interpreted as 31/2. Instead, convert it to an improper fraction like 7/2 or a decimal like 3.5 before gridding.
- None of the answers will be negative, because there is no negative sign in the grid.
- Some of the questions may have more than one correct answer. You must grid only one of the correct answers.
- You may use a calculator on any of these problems.
- All numbers in these problems are real numbers.
- Figures are drawn as accurately as possible EXCEPT when it is stated that the figure is not drawn to scale.
- All figures lie in a plane unless otherwise indicated.

---

9   What is 0.5 percent of 80?

10   If d is the middle number of three consecutive odd integers whose sum is s, what is the value of d divided by s?

11 If $\dfrac{4}{9}$ of c^2 is 24, what is $\dfrac{5}{9}$ of c^2?

15 If x and y are positive integers such that $x^2 + y^2 = 41$, then what is the value of $(x+y)^2$?

16 A jar contains fifteen marbles, five of which are white and the rest black. What is the *least* number of white marbles that must be added to the jar so that at least three-fifths of the marbles will be white?

5 →

12 The measures of the four angles in a quadrilateral have a ratio of $3:4:5:6$. What is the measure, in degrees, of the smallest of these angles?

17

In the figure above, $\overline{PT}$ is a straight line segment. What is the value of x?

13 If $5a + 6b = 13$ and $4a + 5b = 9$, then what is the value of $7a + 7b$?

14 If $m = \dfrac{1}{3}$, what is the value

of $\dfrac{\dfrac{1}{m+1} + \dfrac{1}{m-1}}{\dfrac{1}{m^2-1}}$?

18 In one basketball game, Tamara made 50% of her shots, and in the next game, she made 60% of her shots. In the two games, she made 52% of her shots altogether. If she took a shots in the first game and b shots in the second game, what is the value of $\dfrac{a}{b}$?

STOP   *You may check your work, on this section only, until time is called.*

Section 6

Time — 25 minutes
24 questions

Each of the sentences below is missing one or two portions. Read each sentence, then select the word or words that most logically complete the sentence, taking into account the meaning of the sentence as a whole.

Example:

Rather than accepting the theory unquestioningly, Deborah regarded it with -------.

  (A) mirth
  (B) sadness
  (C) responsibility
  (D) ignorance
  (E) skepticism

Correct response: (E)

1 Rather than giving Sandra thoughtful and useful advice, her father admonished her with hollow clichés and ------- platitudes.

  (A) irate
  (B) inane
  (C) homogeneous
  (D) flamboyant
  (E) altruistic

2 Maintaining a courageous ------- even while in prison, Nelson Mandela spent years trying to convince others that the fight against apartheid was not -------.

  (A) optimism . . . worthwhile
  (B) will . . . treacherous
  (C) hope . . . futile
  (D) fortitude . . . premeditated
  (E) instability . . . porous

3 The ------- of the construction near the building rendered the school far less ------- to learning; the teachers could hardly hear themselves talk.

  (A) din . . . conducive
  (B) efficiency . . . accustomed
  (C) noise . . . averse
  (D) precision . . . discernible
  (E) racket . . . irascible

4 Although no real problem in physics can be solved ------- an approximate solution by a simplified method is sufficient so long as the complicating factors are -------.

  (A) precisely . . . large
  (B) completely . . . difficult
  (C) exactly . . . negligible
  (D) plausibly . . . minimal
  (E) ethically . . . nonexistent

5 The ------- of a civil war depends on the factions' access to martial resources; the conflict may drag on for years or even decades so long as each side has sufficient ------- to continue fighting.

  (A) violence . . . mediation
  (B) popularity . . . opposition
  (C) length . . . reluctance
  (D) duration . . . means
  (E) value . . . skill

Each passage below is followed by questions based on its content. Answer each question based on what is stated or implied in the passage or the introductory material that precedes it.

Questions 6–7 are based on the following passage.

Jung was never dogmatic as to a single "cause" of schizophrenia,[1] although he inclined to the belief that a psychological, rather than a physical, origin was probable. He was also modest in his therapeutic claims, recognizing that only a limited number of cases responded to analysis, and that partial alleviation was more common than cure. Jung considered that there were many schizophrenics who never came near a mental hospital. If such people consulted him, he was cautious and sometimes dismissed them without attempting psychoanalysis. Jung was one of the first to recognize that a psychotic episode could be precipitated by psychoanalysis.

6 Based on the information in the passage, with which of the following statements would Jung most likely agree?

(A) Schizophrenia is much more common than most psychologists acknowledge.
(B) Schizophrenia has a single common cause.
(C) Psychoanalysis is not helpful to all mentally ill patients.
(D) Schizophrenia might be caused by physical trauma.
(E) Psychoanalysis, in the right measure, can cure all schizophrenic patients.

7 In context, "precipitated by" (line 14) most nearly means

(A) hastened by
(B) cured by
(C) responsive to
(D) made more efficient by
(E) composed of

[1] Schizophrenia is a type of mental illness characterized by a withdrawal from reality and, occasionally, delusions and mood disorders.

Questions 8–9 are based on the following passage.

The tragic (and the dramatic)—it is said—are *universal*. At a distance of centuries we still grieve at the tribulations of Oedipus and Orestes, and even without sharing the ideology of Homais we are distressed by the tragedy of Emma Bovary. The comic, on the other hand, seems bound to its time, society, cultural anthropology. We understand the drama of the protagonist of *Rashomon*, but we don't understand when and why the Japanese laugh. It is an effort to find Aristophanes comic, and it takes more culture to laugh at Rabelais than it does to weep at the death of the paladin Orlando.

8 Which of the following would the author consider most difficult for a modern American to find humorous?

(A) a farcical musical about animals who talk
(B) a comic film about gangsters set in Chicago
(C) a satirical poem written in 16th-century China
(D) a situation comedy based on the life of a plumber
(E) a funny movie with a tragic ending

9 The "effort" (line 11) to which the author refers is a task that requires which of the following?

(A) great planning
(B) the work of more than one person
(C) overcoming cultural obstacles
(D) a great many natural resources
(E) emotional fortitude

First paragraph: Anthony Storr, *The Essential Jung*. © 1983 by Princeton University Press. Reprinted by permission of Princeton University Press.

Second paragraph: *The Comic and the Rule* in *Travels in Hyperreality*, by Umberto Eco, Harcourt, Brace, Jovanovich, 1983, p. 269.

GO ON TO THE NEXT PAGE ▶▶▶

The questions below are based on the content of the preceding passage. The questions are to be answered on the basis of what is stated or implied in the passage itself or the introductory material that precedes the passage.

Questions 10–16 are based on the following passage:

The following is an excerpt from a book on the writing process in which the author describes an interview he gave by telephone to a radio show to promote a writer's conference.

The appointed evening arrived, and my phone rang, and the host came on and greeted me with
Line the strenuous joviality of his trade. He said he had three lovely ladies in the studio with him
5 and he was eager to find out what we all thought of the present state of literature and what advice we had for all his listeners who were members of the literati and had literary ambitions themselves. This hearty introduction dropped
10 like a stone in our midst, and none of the three lovely ladies said anything in response, which I thought was the proper response.
  The silence lengthened, and finally I said, "I think we should banish all further mention of
15 the words 'literature' and 'literary' and 'literati.' " I knew that the host had been briefed about what kind of writers we were and what we wanted to discuss. But he had no other frame of reference. "Tell me," he said, "what insights do you have
20 about the literary experience in America today?" Silence also greeted this question. Finally I said, "We're here to talk about the craft of writing."
  He didn't know what to make of that, and he began to involve the names of authors like Ernest
25 Hemingway and Saul Bellow and William Styron, whom we surely regarded as literary giants. We said those writers didn't happen to be our models, and we mentioned people like Lewis Thomas and Joan Didion and Garry
30 Wills. He had never heard of them. One of them mentioned Tom Wolfe's *The Right Stuff*, and he hadn't heard of that. We explained that these were writers we admired for their ability to harness the issues and concerns of the day.
35 "But don't you want to write anything literary?" our host said. The three women said they felt they were already doing satisfying work. That brought the program to another halt, and the host began to accept phone calls from his listeners, all of whom were interested in the craft
40 of writing and wanted to know how we went about it. "And yet, in the stillness of the night," the host said to several callers, "don't you ever

dream of writing the great American novel?"
45 They didn't. They had no such dreams—in the stillness of the night or any other time. It was one of the all-time lousy radio talk shows.
  The story sums up a situation that any particular practitioner of nonfiction will recognize.
50 Those of us who are trying to write well about the world we live in, or to teach students to write well about the world *they* live in, are caught in a time warp, where literature by definition still consists of forms that were certified as "literary"
55 in the 19th century: novels and short stories and poems. But in fact the great preponderance of what writers now write and sell, what book and magazine publishers publish and what readers demand is nonfiction.

10   In the first paragraph, the author suggests that he regards the host's introduction to be

(A)   insincere
(B)   inappropriate
(C)   erudite
(D)   flattering
(E)   incoherent

11   Throughout the passage, the author uses the term "literary" to mean

(A)   well-written
(B)   with regard to love stories
(C)   pertaining to the writing of fiction and poetry
(D)   concerning contemporary issues
(E)   persuasive

12   What is the main substance of the misunderstanding between the interviewer and the interviewees?

(A)   The interviewer believed that the writers had written books that they actually had not.
(B)   The interviewer lacked a frame of reference on writing beyond literary fiction.
(C)   The interviewees wanted to be more critical of classic authors, while the interviewer wanted to praise them.
(D)   The interviewer wanted to discuss current issues, while the writers wanted to discuss 19th-century literary forms.
(E)   The interviewer disagreed with the writers on the merits of *The Right Stuff*.

Excerpted from On Writing Well by William Zinsser, Harper Perennial, New York, 6th edition, 1998, pp. 95–97.

GO ON TO THE NEXT PAGE ▶▶▶

13 The authors in lines 29–30 are mentioned as examples of

(A) the most popular authors of the time
(B) authors who had set the trend for the "literary" style of that era
(C) authors who had influenced the work of the writers being interviewed
(D) authors whose works followed in the manner of Hemingway, Bellow, and Styron
(E) authors who wrote experimental fiction

14 In context, the word "harness" (line 34) most nearly means

(A) dominate
(B) make easier to understand
(C) influence the direction of
(D) witness
(E) reinforce

15 If the callers shared the sensibilities of the interviewees, then by saying that they had "no such dreams" (line 45), the callers were most likely suggesting that they

(A) did not wish to pursue literary fame in such a competitive environment
(B) had disdain for those who wrote fiction for profit
(C) knew that the public did not care for writers like Thomas, Didion, and Wills
(D) had been discouraged by their negative experiences with publishers in the literary world
(E) were happy doing what they were doing

16 In context, the word "preponderance" (line 56) most nearly means

(A) evidence
(B) domination
(C) majority
(D) heaviness
(E) quality

The questions below are based on the content of the preceding passage. The questions are to be answered on the basis of what is stated or implied in the passage itself or the introductory material that precedes the passage.

Questions 17–24 are based on the following passage.

The following is from a book on the history of Western philosophy by Bertrand Russell, in which he discusses ancient Greek philosophy.

To understand the views of Aristotle, as of most Greeks, on physics, it is necessary to apprehend
Line his imaginative background. Every philosopher, in addition to the formal system which he offers
5   to the world, has another much simpler system of which he may be quite unaware. If he is aware of it, he probably realizes that it won't quite do; he therefore conceals it, and sets forth something more sophisticated, which he believes be-
10   cause it is like his crude system, but which he asks others to accept because he thinks he has made it such as cannot be disproved. The sophistication comes in by way of refutation of refutations, but this alone will never give a posi-
15   tive result: it shows, at best, that a theory *may* be true, not that it *must* be. The positive result, however little the philosopher may realize it, is due to his imaginative preconceptions, or to what Santayana calls "animal faith."
20   In relation to physics, Aristotle's imaginative background was very different from that of a modern student. Nowadays, students begin with mechanics, which, by its very name, suggests machines. They are accustomed to auto-
25   mobiles and airplanes; they do not, even in the dimmest recesses of their subconscious imagination, think that an automobile contains some sort of horse inside, or that an airplane flies because its wings are those of a bird possessing
30   magical powers. Animals have lost their importance in our imaginative pictures of the world, in which humans stand comparatively alone as masters of a mainly lifeless and largely subservient material environment.
35   To the ancient Greek, attempting to give a scientific account of motion, the purely me-

Excerpted from *A History of Western Philosophy* by Bertrand Russell, Touchstone, Simon & Schuster, New York, 1945, 1972, pp. 203–204.

GO ON TO THE NEXT PAGE ▶▶▶

chanical view hardly suggested itself, except in the case of a few men of genius such as Dem- ocritus and Archimedes. Two sets of phenom-
40   ena seemed important: the movements of animals, and the movements of the heavenly bodies. To the modern man of science, the body of an animal is a very elaborate machine, with an enormously complex physico-chemical
45   structure; every new discovery consists in di- minishing the apparent gulf between animals and machines. To the Greek, it seemed more natural to assimilate apparently lifeless mo- tions to those of animals. A child still distin-
50   guishes live animals from other things by the fact that they can move them; to many Greeks, and especially to Aristotle, this peculiarity sug- gested itself as the basis of a general theory of physics.
55   But how about the heavenly bodies? They dif- fer from animals by the regularity of their move- ments, but this may be only due to their superior perfection. Every Greek philosopher, whatever he may have come to think in adult life, had
60   been taught in childhood to regard the sun and moon as gods; Anaxagoras was prosecuted for impiety because he thought that they were not alive. It was natural that a philosopher who could no longer regard the heavenly bodies
65   themselves as divine should think of them as moved by the will of a Divine Being who had a Hellenic love of order and geometric simplicity. Thus the ultimate source of all movement is Will: on earth the capricious Will of human be-
70   ings, but in heaven the unchanging Will of the Supreme Artificer.

17 Which of the following best summarizes the overall purpose of this passage?

(A) to compare Aristotle's philosophy with those of Democritus and Archimedes
(B) to describe the preconceptions behind Aristotle's physical theories
(C) to uncover the flaws in ancient Greek astronomy
(D) to show how Aristotle's theories facili- tated the development of modern tech- nology
(E) to contrast the modern conception of the animal with that of the ancient Greeks

18 According to the passage, in what way have animals "lost their importance" (lines 30–31)?

(A) Humans no longer treat animals as re- spectfully as they once did.
(B) Humans no longer need animals to do hard labor.
(C) Few religions today require animal sacrifices.
(D) Modern writers rarely write stories or fables with animals as main charac- ters.
(E) Animals no longer inspire modern physical theories.

19 Which of the following is most similar to the "imaginative preconceptions" (line 18) of Aristotle?

(A) the belief that animals are inferior to humans
(B) the belief that all scientific problems can be solved through rigorous philo- sophical analysis
(C) the belief that computers have minds and souls like humans or animals
(D) the belief that the body of an animal is a complicated machine
(E) the belief that the sun and moon are not alive

20 What does the author imply about the "men of genius" (line 38)?

(A) They believed that physics is essen- tially the study of the mechanics of motion rather than spirits or wills.
(B) They were able to precisely determine the orbits of the planets.
(C) They regarded the sun and moon as gods.
(D) They alone saw the similarity between the motion of animals and the motion of heavenly bodies.
(E) They regarded all movement as being produced by a Divine Being.

GO ON TO THE NEXT PAGE ▶▶▶

21 According to the passage, modern scientists diminish "the apparent gulf between animals and machines" (lines 46–47) by

(A) using machines to train animals
(B) studying the motivations of animals
(C) working to make machines function more like animals
(D) using technology to improve the lives of animals
(E) uncovering the mechanical laws behind biology

22 In line 48, the word "assimilate" most nearly means

(A) compare
(B) repeat
(C) attach
(D) refer
(E) elevate

23 In the final paragraph, which of the following does the author imply about Greek philosophers?

(A) Some of them were not rigorous in demonstrating their theories through experiment.
(B) They were more concerned with popularizing their theories than proving them.
(C) Some of them departed dramatically from their childhood teachings.
(D) They all regarded the planetary bodies as divine.
(E) Most of them disagreed strongly with Aristotle.

24 The "Hellenic love of order and geometric simplicity" (line 67) attributed to the "Divine Being" (line 66) can be inferred to involve which of the following?

I. a need to simplify mathematical equations
II. a desire to make astronomical objects move in elegant paths
III. a need to unify the laws of motion with a single theory

(A) I only
(B) II only
(C) I and II only
(D) II and III only
(E) I, II, and III

STOP

You may check your work, on this section only, until time is called.

Section 7

Time — 20 minutes
16 questions

Directions for Multiple-Choice Questions

In this section, solve each problem, using any available space on the page for scratchwork. Then decide which is the best of the choices given and fill in the corresponding oval on your answer sheet.

- You may use a calculator on any problem. All numbers used are real numbers.
- Figures are drawn as accurately as possible EXCEPT when it is stated that the figure is not drawn to scale.
- All figures lie in a plane unless otherwise indicated.

Reference Information

$A = \pi r^2$ $A = \ell w$ $A = 1/2\, bh$ $V = \ell wh$ $V = \pi r^2 h$ $c^2 = a^2 + b^2$ Special Right Triangles
$C = 2\pi r$

The number of degrees of arc in a circle is 360.
The measure in degrees of a straight angle is 180.
The sum of the measures in degrees of the angles of a triangle is 180.

---

1 The number that is $\dfrac{2}{3}$ of 60 is what fraction of 80?

(A) $\dfrac{1}{6}$

(B) $\dfrac{1}{3}$

(C) $\dfrac{1}{2}$

(D) $\dfrac{3}{4}$

(E) $\dfrac{8}{9}$

2 If $4x + 2y = 8$, then $x + \dfrac{1}{2}y =$

(A) 0.25
(B) 0.5
(C) 1
(D) 2
(E) 4

GO ON TO THE NEXT PAGE ▶▶▶

3

29 apples, 21 pears, and 64 oranges are to be distributed among three baskets, with each basket getting an equal number of apples, each basket getting an equal number of pears, and each basket getting an equal number of oranges. If as much of the fruit as possible is distributed in this way, what fruit will remain undistributed?

(A)   2 apples, 2 pears, and 1 orange
(B)   2 apples, 1 pear, and 1 orange
(C)   2 apples and 1 orange
(D)   1 pear and 1 orange
(E)   1 apple only

4

For all values of x and y, let "$x \& y$" be defined by the equation $x \& y = x(x-1) + y(y-1)$. What is the value of 1 & 2?

(A)   1
(B)   2
(C)   3
(D)   4
(E)   5

5

In $\triangle ABC$, $AB = 15$ and $BC = 9$. Which of the following could *not* be the length of AC?

(A)   5
(B)   7
(C)   9
(D)   16
(E)   22

6

What is the surface area of a cube that has a volume of 64 cubic centimeters?

(A)   64 square centimeters
(B)   96 square centimeters
(C)   256 square centimeters
(D)   288 square centimeters
(E)   384 square centimeters

7

The average (arithmetic mean) of x, 2, 6, and 10 is 8. What is the <u>median</u> of x, 2, 6, and 10?

(A)   4
(B)   6
(C)   7
(D)   8
(E)   9

8

Note: Figure not drawn to scale

In the figure above, $PS = SQ$ and $SQ = QT$. Which of the following expresses y in terms of x?

(A) $\dfrac{x}{2}$

(B) $90 - x$

(C) $90 - \dfrac{x}{2}$

(D) $180 - 2x$
(E) $180 - x$

9

The graph above represents the set of all possible solutions to which of the following statements?

(A) $|x - 1| > 1$
(B) $|x + 1| < 1$
(C) $|x - 1| < 1$
(D) $|x + 1| > 1$
(E) $|x + 1| > -1$

GO ON TO THE NEXT PAGE ▶▶▶

10

$$a > b$$
$$b < c$$
$$a = 2c$$

If a, b, and c represent different integers in the statements above, which of the following statements must be true?

I. $a > c$
II. $2c > b$
III. $ac > b^2$

(A) I only
(B) II only
(C) I and II only
(D) II and III only
(E) I, II, and III

11

How many different positive three-digit integers begin with an odd digit and end with an even digit?

(A) 125
(B) 180
(C) 200
(D) 225
(E) 250

12

A machine uses a laser beam to cut circles from a sheet of plastic, as shown in the figure above. The beam cuts at the rate of 3 cm per second. If circle A has an area of 64π square centimeters and circle B has an area of 16π square centimeters, how many more seconds will it take the machine to cut circle A than circle B?

(A) 2π seconds
(B) $\dfrac{8\pi}{3}$ seconds
(C) $\dfrac{16\pi}{3}$ seconds
(D) 8π seconds
(E) $\dfrac{48\pi}{3}$ seconds

7

GO ON TO THE NEXT PAGE ▶▶▶

13

Note: Figure not drawn to scale

In the figure above, the slope of *AC* is the opposite of the slope of *CB*. What is the value of *k*?

(A) 9
(B) 10
(C) 12
(D) 14
(E) 15

14

If *m* is the product of all of the integers from 1 to 10, inclusive, and 2^n is a factor of *m*, then what is the greatest possible value of *n*?

(A) 2
(B) 4
(C) 8
(D) 16
(E) 32

15

An equilateral triangle with area $36\sqrt{3}$ square centimeters is divided into two triangles by the bisector of one of its angles. What is the sum of the perimeters of these two triangles?

(A) $18 + 6\sqrt{3}$

(B) $18 + 9\sqrt{3}$

(C) $36 + 6\sqrt{3}$

(D) $36 + 12\sqrt{3}$

(E) $36 + 18\sqrt{3}$

16

A culture of bacteria doubles in population every 2 hours. A sample of 100 bacteria grows to 1,000 bacteria by 4:00 pm. At what time were there 250 bacteria in this sample?

(A)   11:30 am
(B)   12 noon
(C)   12:30 pm
(D)   1:00 pm
(E)   2:00 pm

STOP

You may check your work, on this section only, until time is called.

Section 8

Time — 20 minutes
19 questions

Each of the sentences below is missing one or two portions. Read each sentence, then select the word or words that most logically complete the sentence, taking into account the meaning of the sentence as a whole.

Example:

Rather than accepting the theory unquestioningly, Deborah regarded it with -------.

(A) mirth
(B) sadness
(C) responsibility
(D) ignorance
(E) skepticism

Correct response: (E)

1 To Clara's relief, the biopsy revealed that the tumor on her skin was -------.

(A) malignant
(B) irreverent
(C) serene
(D) benign
(E) mortal

2 The speaker's message was ------- by jargon that rendered it decipherable only to those few audience members familiar with her particular area of expertise.

(A) elated
(B) revealed
(C) obscured
(D) enlightened
(E) consoled

3 To those consumers who are more influenced by style than by performance, the ------- value of the sports car outweighs its functional flaws.

(A) utilitarian
(B) pragmatic
(C) approximate
(D) aesthetic
(E) inexplicable

4 A student becomes a thinker only when he or she realizes that most so-called facts are merely ------- claims, each serving its purpose only temporarily.

(A) provisional
(B) polemical
(C) authoritative
(D) dramatic
(E) pedantic

5 Traditionally, the role had been played demurely to provide a foil for the bolder personalities in the play, but Ms. Linney has decided to ------- convention and emphasize her character's -------.

(A) respect . . . bluster
(B) abandon . . . solitude
(C) forgo . . . coyness
(D) uphold . . . bombast
(E) eschew . . . impudence

6 Despite the attempts of popular analysts to depict the stock market as driven by predictable financial principles, an increasing number of investors believe that the price of any security is -------.

(A) invaluable
(B) complacent
(C) capricious
(D) responsive
(E) obscure

GO ON TO THE NEXT PAGE ▶▶▶

The questions below are based on the content of the two passages that precede them and the relationship between the passages. The questions are to be answered on the basis of what is stated or implied in the passage itself or the introductory material that precedes the passage.

Questions 7–19 are based on the following passages.

Since 1996, when scientists at the Roslin Institute in England cloned a sheep from the cells of another adult sheep, many inside and outside the scientific community have debated the ethics of cloning the cells of human beings. The following passages are excerpts of arguments on this issue.

Passage 1

With the specter of human cloning looming on the horizon, the dominant ethical question is: Line what is a human being? Until now, our respect for human life has rested fundamentally on the
5 deep understanding that human life is perhaps the ultimate gift of nature or God. This gift is made even more profound by the fact that we ourselves are not only its recipients but also its conduits: we receive life and we help create it.
10 But our participation in the creation of life must never be misconstrued as control. Rather, we must be humbled by the power of the life force at the moment of conception.

The idea of "outsourcing" the creation of
15 human life, of relegating it to a laboratory, of reducing the anticipation of childbirth to a trip to the mall or a selection from a catalog, leaves us with a profoundly hollow feeling. The mystery is replaced by design; the surrender to nature is re-
20 placed by arrogant control. Should we turn our noses up at one who would offer us the most precious gift in the universe, only to say: "Sorry, but I think I can do better?"

Cloning is the engineering of human life. We
25 have for the first time the ability to determine the exact genetic makeup of a human being, to thwart the essential random (or seemingly random) processes that form the basis of natural selection, to employ unnatural selection. A child
30 can be created that is no longer a unique creation but the end product of an assembly line, with carefully designed and tested features. Are the astonishing products of natural selection

that we find around us somehow deficient? Are
35 we so full of hubris[1] as to think we have a better way than nature or God?

If human cloning becomes acceptable, we will have created a new society in which the essence of human life is marginalized. Industries will
40 arise that turn human procreation into a profitable free-market enterprise. The executive boards of these companies, rather than nature or God, will decide the course of human evolution, with more concern for quarterly profit reports
45 than for the fate of humanity.

These are not idle concerns. Even as we ponder the ethical implications of human cloning, companies are forging ahead with the cloning of human stem cells for seemingly beneficial
50 purposes, marching steadily toward a Brave New World[2] in which humanity will be forever different from what it is today.

Passage 2

The irrational fears about human cloning that abound from all parts of the political spectrum
55 should not surprise anyone who knows a little bit about the history of technology. Hardly anything significant has been invented that no segment of the population has denounced as evil: factories, trains, automobiles, telephones,
60 televisions, computers. Not even medicine has been spared this vituperation, despite its obvious benefits to humanity. Before the merits of surgery became obvious, it was unimaginable that slicing the flesh of a human being could do
65 more harm than good.

At first glance, it might seem that cloning is a whole new ballgame. After all, cloning is "the engineering of human life," isn't it? It is the mass production of designer babies. It is the end
70 of evolution, or at least the beginning of its corporate management. It is certainly a slap in the face of God. Or is it?

One of scariest things to the opponents of cloning is the prospect of human beings having
75 identical genetic codes. As cloning foe Jeremy Rifkin has said: "It's a horrendous crime to make a Xerox of someone. You're putting a human into a genetic straitjacket." Logically, then, Mr. Rifkin must be repulsed by natural-
80 born identical multiples: there is no scientific way to distinguish the DNA of one's identical

[1] excessive pride or arrogance
[2] a futuristic novel by Aldous Huxley that describes the mass production of genetically identical human babies

GO ON TO THE NEXT PAGE ▶▶▶

twin from that of one's clone. Perhaps the whole system of natural human procreation is suspect, if it is capable of occasionally churning
85 out such monstrosities.

We need nothing more than the most rudimentary common sense to see how vacuous
such an argument is. We all know identical
twins who have their own unique thoughts,
90 talents, experiences, and beliefs. They are not
horrendous monsters. Human beings are more
than merely their DNA; they are the products of
the continual and inscrutably complex interactions of environment and biology. Human
95 clones would be no different.

The most common objection we hear from
the anti-cloning lobby is that those who would
clone human beings are "playing God," and
trespassing into territory that can only bring the
100 wrath of nature or its creator. Most of these arguments are basically theological, and rest on
the most effective tool of human control ever invented: fear of God. We can easily get people to
hate something by calling it "unnatural." But
105 this argument is even more easily demolished
than the previous one, because it falls so easily
in line with so many obviously silly claims. This
argument rests on the assumption that human
ingenuity has essentially no value, that improv-
110 ing on nature is the height of hubris. This is the
reasoning of the Dark Ages. Nature presents vegetables and meats only in raw form, so isn't the
cooking of food a human transgression against
nature? Nature gives us feet, not wheels, so
115 aren't bicycles evil? If we were to abandon all of
the "unnatural" practices and products from
our lives, we would be shivering in caves eating
uncooked leaves and bugs.

Maybe human procreation is a different arena,
120 however, more sacred than all of the others. But
then, why have the technologies of fertility
enhancement, in vitro fertilization, embryo
transfer, and birth control become so widely
accepted? They are telling examples: each of
125 these procreational technologies had legions of
vocal opponents—at first—but over time the
protests mellowed as people realized that the sky
wouldn't fall after all. Familiarity dissipates fear.

What most opponents of genetic technology
130 don't realize is that their supposedly "moral"
objections are impeding true moral progress.
With genetic engineering and stem cell research,
scientists finally have within their grasp technologies that can produce ample food for a
135 starving world and cure devastating illnesses.
Only ignorant superstition stands in their way.

tone

---

7 The "control" mentioned in line 11 is control over

(A) the effects of cloning
(B) the development of genetic technologies
(C) the process of conception
(D) the moral debate about cloning
(E) activities in a laboratory

8 Which of the following best describes the attitude of the author of Passage 1 toward "outsourcing" (line 14)?

(A) reluctant approval
(B) disdain
(C) strong support
(D) ironic detachment
(E) ambivalence

9 The statement "sorry, but I think I can do better" (lines 22–23) is intended to represent a comment from

(A) a religious person to a nonreligious person
(B) an opponent of cloning to a scientist
(C) a voter to a politician
(D) the author to the reader
(E) an advocate of cloning to nature or God

10 The parenthetical comment in lines 27–28 is intended to account for the possibility that

(A) life might be designed by a power beyond humanity
(B) cloning technologies might become uncontrollable
(C) two human beings might have the same genetic makeup by chance alone
(D) some scientific theories might not be reliable
(E) cloning technology might not succeed

GO ON TO THE NEXT PAGE ▶▶▶

11 Passage 1 mentions which of the following as elements of "unnatural selection" (line 29)?

  I.   mechanical procedures
  II. random processes
  III. selection of characteristics

(A) I only
(B) III only
(C) I and II only
(D) I and III only
(E) I, II, and III

12 In the first paragraph of Passage 2, the author suggests that the opponents of human cloning, as a group, are all of the following EXCEPT

(A) very religious
(B) unreasonable about the implications of cloning
(C) from widely varied political orientations
(D) ignorant of scientific history
(E) fearful of new ideas

13 Surgery is mentioned in lines 62–65 as an example of

(A) a practice that requires a great deal of education
(B) something that most people still fear
(C) a medical technology that was once denounced
(D) a viable alternative to genetic technologies
(E) a skill in need of more practitioners

14 The author of Passage 2 quotes Jeremy Rifkin (lines 76–78) in order to

(A) illustrate the dangers of cloning
(B) show a well-reasoned perspective
(C) indicate an illogical claim
(D) represent the views of medical professionals
(E) show how others support the author's thesis

15 The author of Passage 2 mentions that identical human twins "have their own unique thoughts" (lines 88–89) in order to suggest that those twins

(A) would likely oppose human cloning
(B) are not simply the product of their DNA
(C) are among the most vocal advocates of cloning
(D) are able to provide alternatives to pro-creational technologies
(E) are less likely to be swayed by illogical theories

16 Passage 2 suggests that those individuals who had previously denounced "procreational technologies" (line 125) have since come to accept them because those individuals

(A) became more familiar with the technologies
(B) realized that the technologies were indeed "natural"
(C) understood the theories behind the technologies
(D) realized that the technologies were inexpensive
(E) themselves needed to use those technologies

17 The tone of the last paragraph of Passage 2 is best described as

(A) indignant
(B) analytical
(C) resigned
(D) humorous
(E) whimsical

18 Which of the following best describes the relationship between the pair of questions presented in Passage 1 ("Are the astonishing products . . . nature or God?" [lines 33–36]) and the pair of questions presented in Passage 2 ("Nature presents . . . evil?" [lines 111–115])?

(A) The first two are not intended to be answered, while the second two are.

(B) The first two are scientific questions, while the second two are moral questions.

(C) Both pairs of questions indicate points of view criticized by their respective authors.

(D) The first two are intended as questions from cloning opponents, while the second two are intended as questions from cloning advocates.

(E) The first two are common questions, the second two are asked only by experts.

19 The last paragraphs of both passages indicate that both authors share what assumption?

(A) Cloning needs more scientific study.

(B) Genetic engineering will have profound global effects.

(C) Cloning will marginalize human life.

(D) Procreational technology can benefit the poor.

(E) Scientists are ill-suited to make moral decisions.

8

STOP

You may check your work, on this section only, until time is called.

Section 9

Time — 10 minutes
14 questions

Directions for Improving Sentences Questions

Each of the sentences below contains one underlined portion. The portion may contain one or more errors in grammar, usage, construction, precision, diction (choice of words), or idiom. Some of the sentences are correct.

Consider the meaning of the original sentence, and choose the answer that best expresses that meaning. If the original sentence is best, choose (A), because it repeats the original phrasing. Choose the phrasing that creates the clearest, most precise, and most effective sentence.

EXAMPLE:
The children couldn't hardly believe their eyes.
(A) couldn't hardly believe their eyes
(B) would not hardly believe their eyes
(C) could hardly believe their eyes
(D) couldn't nearly believe their eyes
(E) could hardly believe his or her eyes

EXAMPLE ANSWER:
(C)

9 ➤

1 One way to improve the effectiveness of the treatment is by moving the source of radiation more closely to the patient.

(A) by moving the source of radiation more closely
(B) to move the source of radiation more closely
(C) to move the source of radiation closer
(D) in moving the source of radiation closer
(E) to move more closely the source of radiation

2 Until becoming more affordable by standardizing its technology, cell phones were quite rare.

(A) Until becoming more affordable by standardizing its technology
(B) Having become more affordable through standardizing their technology
(C) Becoming more affordable through standardized technology
(D) Until they became more affordable in standardized technology
(E) Until standardized technology made them more affordable

3 The airline industry has adopted new pricing procedures; seeming to benefit both the consumers as well as the companies.

(A) procedures; seeming to benefit both the consumers as well as
(B) procedures; seemingly benefitting both the consumers and
(C) procedures seemingly in benefit of both the consumers as well as
(D) procedures that seem benefitting of both the consumers and
(E) procedures that seem to benefit both the consumers and

4 The thirty-foot-high stone wall, built over the course of eighty years, once protecting the city from invaders.

(A) wall, built over the course of eighty years, once protecting
(B) wall, built over the course of eighty years, once protected
(C) wall was built over the course of eighty years, which protected
(D) wall was built over the course of eighty years in protecting
(E) wall, built over the course of eighty years; it once protected

GO ON TO THE NEXT PAGE ▶▶▶

5 A concise and informative guide for writers, William Zinsser's *On Writing Well* has sold nearly one million copies.

(A) William Zinsser's *On Writing Well* has sold nearly one million copies

(B) nearly one million copies of William Zinsser's *On Writing Well* have been sold

(C) William Zinsser wrote *On Writing Well*, which has sold nearly one million copies

(D) William Zinsser's *On Writing Well* having sold nearly one million copies

(E) *On Writing Well* has sold nearly one million copies by William Zinsser

6 When you submit personal information to a website, one should make sure that it won't be used for unauthorized purposes.

(A) one should make sure

(B) and make sure

(C) then make sure

(D) be sure of

(E) make sure

7 Although passenger pigeons once filled the skies over Michigan, relentless hunting eliminated their entire population by 1901.

(A) relentless hunting eliminated their entire population by 1901

(B) it was relentless hunting eliminating their entire population by 1901

(C) its entire population was eliminated by relentless hunting by 1901

(D) by 1901 it was relentless hunting eliminating their entire population

(E) relentless hunting having eliminated their entire population by 1901

8 The failure of the relief effort was more a result of poor coordination than because of blatant corruption.

(A) poor coordination than because of blatant corruption

(B) coordination being poor than by blatant corruption

(C) poor coordination than by blatant corruption

(D) poor coordination than of blatant corruption

(E) coordination being poor than corruption being blatant

9 Until revealing that she had been working at a design firm, few of her friends realized that Amanda was interested in art.

(A) Until revealing that she had been working

(B) Having revealed that she had been working

(C) Until she revealed that she had been working

(D) Being that she revealed she had worked

(E) Until she revealed about her working

10 Inspired by reading about the great explorers, it was Gerald's decision to sail around the world.

(A) it was Gerald's decision to sail around the world

(B) Gerald decided to sail around the world

(C) the decision was made by Gerald to sail around the world

(D) sailing around the world was what Gerald decided to do

(E) Gerald having decided to sail around the world

11 The results of the election were so close that the club had it decided that they would have co-presidents.

(A) had it decided that they would have co-presidents

(B) decided to have co-presidents

(C) would have decided to have co-presidents

(D) decided they would have co-presidents

(E) had decided that they would have co-presidents

9

12 Writing skills are waning because the widespread use of e-mail and instant <u>messaging discourages students from developing their ideas and supporting</u> those ideas logically.

(A) messaging discourages students from developing their ideas and supporting

(B) messaging discourage students to develop their ideas and support

(C) messaging, which discourages students from developing their ideas and supporting

(D) messaging discouraging students from developing their ideas and supporting

(E) messaging discouraging students to develop their ideas and support

13 <u>To acknowledge</u> opposing viewpoints does not mean subverting your own thesis, and in fact usually creates a more cogent essay.

(A) To acknowledge
(B) In acknowledging
(C) Acknowledging
(D) While acknowledging
(E) For the acknowledgment of

14 To get the full benefit of any medication, avoid problems, and <u>for the reduction of possible side effects</u>, discuss your prescription with your doctor.

(A) for the reduction of possible side effects
(B) for reducing possible side effects
(C) reducing possible side effects
(D) also to reduce possible side effects
(E) reduce possible side effects

STOP

You may check your work, on this section only, until time is called.

ANSWER KEY

Section 2 Math	Section 5 Math	Section 7 Math	Section 3 Critical Reading	Section 6 Critical Reading	Section 8 Critical Reading	Section 4 Writing	Section 9 Writing
☐ 1. C	☐ 1. B	☐ 1. C	☐ 1. A	☐ 1. B	☐ 1. D	☐ 1. B	☐ 1. C
☐ 2. E	☐ 2. D	☐ 2. D	☐ 2. D	☐ 2. C	☐ 2. C	☐ 2. E	☐ 2. E
☐ 3. D	☐ 3. C	☐ 3. C	☐ 3. C	☐ 3. A	☐ 3. C	☐ 3. D	☐ 3. E
☐ 4. E	☐ 4. C	☐ 4. B	☐ 4. B	☐ 4. C	☐ 4. A	☐ 4. C	☐ 4. B
☐ 5. B	☐ 5. D	☐ 5. A	☐ 5. D	☐ 5. D	☐ 5. D	☐ 5. C	☐ 5. A
☐ 6. A	☐ 6. E	☐ 6. B	☐ 6. B	☐ 6. C	☐ 6. C	☐ 6. D	☐ 6. E
☐ 7. D	☐ 7. C	☐ 7. D	☐ 7. A	☐ 7. A	☐ 7. C	☐ 7. A	☐ 7. A
☐ 8. C	☐ 8. B	☐ 8. A	☐ 8. C	☐ 8. C	☐ 8. B	☐ 8. D	☐ 8. D
☐ 9. B	☐ 9. 0.4	☐ 9. D	☐ 9. C	☐ 9. C	☐ 9. E	☐ 9. B	☐ 9. C
☐ 10. A	☐ 10. .333 or 1/3	☐ 10. B	☐ 10. C	☐ 10. B	☐ 10. A	☐ 10. E	☐ 10. B
☐ 11. A	☐ 11. 30	☐ 11. E	☐ 11. A	☐ 11. C	☐ 11. D	☐ 11. D	☐ 11. B
☐ 12. B	☐ 12. 60	☐ 12. B	☐ 12. D	☐ 12. B	☐ 12. A	☐ 12. B	☐ 12. A
☐ 13. D	☐ 13. 28	☐ 13. E	☐ 13. C	☐ 13. C	☐ 13. C	☐ 13. C	☐ 13. C
☐ 14. B	☐ 14. .666 or .667	☐ 14. C	☐ 14. B	☐ 14. B	☐ 14. C	☐ 14. B	☐ 14. E
☐ 15. D	or 2/3	☐ 15. D	☐ 15. E	☐ 15. E	☐ 15. B	☐ 15. E	
☐ 16. C	☐ 15. 81	☐ 16. B	☐ 16. B	☐ 16. C	☐ 16. A	☐ 16. C	
☐ 17. C	☐ 16. 10		☐ 17. A	☐ 17. B	☐ 17. A	☐ 17. C	
☐ 18. D	☐ 17. 3		☐ 18. C	☐ 18. E	☐ 18. C	☐ 18. C	
☐ 19. D	☐ 18. 4		☐ 19. B	☐ 19. C	☐ 19. B	☐ 19. B	
☐ 20. E			☐ 20. C	☐ 20. A		☐ 20. B	
			☐ 21. B	☐ 21. E		☐ 21. B	
			☐ 22. D	☐ 22. A		☐ 22. D	
			☐ 23. A	☐ 23. C		☐ 23. D	
			☐ 24. E	☐ 24. B		☐ 24. B	
						☐ 25. D	
						☐ 26. B	
						☐ 27. B	
						☐ 28. E	
						☐ 29. A	
						☐ 30. B	
						☐ 31. A	
						☐ 32. E	
						☐ 33. A	
						☐ 34. D	
						☐ 35. C	

(Handwritten annotations across the page include: "I threw away first 7 but read last", "reading", "hot to what you know but whet he thinks makes a good teacher", "3 wrong missed last 2", "Did not do", "3 wrong lost 2", "no clay", "took too long", "didn't finish", "funny (ugh) 2 miss")

# Right (A):	Questions 1–8 # Right (A):	# Right (A):	# Right (A): ~~19~~	# Right (A):	# Right (A):	# Right (A):	# Right (A):
# Wrong (B):	—————— # Wrong (B):	# Wrong (B):	# Wrong (B): 3	# Wrong (B):	# Wrong (B):	# Wrong (B):	# Wrong (B):
# (A)–¼ (B): ————	—————— # (A)–¼ (B):	# (A)–¼ (B): ————	# (A)–¼ (B): 18.25	# (A)–¼ (B): 18.25	# (A)–¼ (B): 15.75	# (A)–¼ (B): ————	# (A)–¼ (B): ————
	Questions 9–18 # Right (A):						

(Handwritten circled number at bottom: 31)

SCORE CONVERSION TABLE

How to score your test

Use the answer key on the previous page to determine your raw score on each section. **Your raw score on each section except Section 5 is simply the number of correct answers minus ¼ of the number of wrong answers. On Section 5, your raw score is the sum of the number of correct answers for questions 1–8 minus ¼ of the number of wrong answers for questions 1–8 plus the total number of correct answers for questions 9–18.** Next, add the raw scores from Sections 3, 4, and 7 to get your Math raw score, and add the raw scores from Sections 6 and 9 to get your Writing raw score. Write the three raw scores here:

Raw Critical Reading score: _____ Raw Math score: _____ Raw Writing score: _____

Use the table below to convert these to scaled scores.

Scaled scores: Critical Reading: _____ Math: _____ Writing: _____

Raw Score	Critical Reading Scaled Score	Math Scaled Score	Writing Scaled Score	Raw Score	Critical Reading Scaled Score	Math Scaled Score	Writing Scaled Score
67	800			32	520	550	610
66	800			31	510	550	600
65	790			30	510	540	580
64	780			29	500	530	570
63	760			28	490	530	560
62	750			27	490	520	550
61	730			26	480	510	540
60	720			25	480	500	530
59	700			24	470	490	520
58	700			23	460	480	510
57	690			22	460	480	500
56	680			21	450	470	490
55	670			20	440	460	480
54	660	800		19	440	450	470
53	650	790		18	430	450	460
52	650	760		17	420	440	450
51	640	740		16	420	430	440
50	630	720		15	410	420	440
49	620	710	800	14	400	410	430
48	620	700	800	13	400	410	420
47	610	680	800	12	390	400	410
46	600	670	790	11	380	390	400
45	600	660	780	10	370	380	390
44	590	650	760	9	360	370	380
43	590	640	740	8	350	360	380
42	580	630	730	7	340	350	370
41	570	630	710	6	330	340	360
40	570	620	700	5	320	330	350
39	560	610	690	4	310	320	340
38	550	600	670	3	300	310	320
37	550	590	660	2	280	290	310
36	540	580	650	1	270	280	300
35	540	580	640	0	250	260	280
34	530	570	630	−1	230	240	270
33	520	560	620	−2 or less	210	220	250

SCORE CONVERSION TABLE FOR WRITING COMPOSITE
[ESSAY + MULTIPLE CHOICE]

Calculate your writing raw score as you did on the previous page and grade your essay from a 1 to a 6 according to the standards that follow in the detailed answer key.

Essay score: _____   Raw Writing score: _____

Use the table below to convert these to scaled scores.

Scaled score: Writing: _____

Raw Score	Essay Score 0	Essay Score 1	Essay Score 2	Essay Score 3	Essay Score 4	Essay Score 5	Essay Score 6
-2 or less	200	230	250	280	310	340	370
-1	210	240	260	290	320	360	380
0	230	260	280	300	340	370	400
1	240	270	290	320	350	380	410
2	250	280	300	330	360	390	420
3	260	290	310	340	370	400	430
4	270	300	320	350	380	410	440
5	280	310	330	360	390	420	450
6	290	320	340	360	400	430	460
7	290	330	340	370	410	440	470
8	300	330	350	380	410	450	470
9	310	340	360	390	420	450	480
10	320	350	370	390	430	460	490
11	320	360	370	400	440	470	500
12	330	360	380	410	440	470	500
13	340	370	390	420	450	480	510
14	350	380	390	420	460	490	520
15	350	380	400	430	460	500	530
16	360	390	410	440	470	500	530
17	370	400	420	440	480	510	540
18	380	410	420	450	490	520	550
19	380	410	430	460	490	530	560
20	390	420	440	470	500	530	560
21	400	430	450	480	510	540	570
22	410	440	460	480	520	550	580
23	420	450	470	490	530	560	590
24	420	460	470	500	540	570	600
25	430	460	480	510	540	580	610
26	440	470	490	520	550	590	610
27	450	480	500	530	560	590	620
28	460	490	510	540	570	600	630
29	470	500	520	550	580	610	640
30	480	510	530	560	590	620	650
31	490	520	540	560	600	630	660
32	500	530	550	570	610	640	670
33	510	540	550	580	620	650	680
34	510	550	560	590	630	660	690
35	520	560	570	600	640	670	700
36	530	560	580	610	650	680	710
37	540	570	590	620	660	690	720
38	550	580	600	630	670	700	730
39	560	600	610	640	680	710	740
40	580	610	620	650	690	720	750
41	590	620	640	660	700	730	760
42	600	630	650	680	710	740	770
43	610	640	660	690	720	750	780
44	620	660	670	700	740	770	800
45	640	670	690	720	750	780	800
46	650	690	700	730	770	800	800
47	670	700	720	750	780	800	800
48	680	720	730	760	800	800	800
49	680	720	730	760	800	800	800

Detailed Answer Key

Section 1

The following essay received 12 points out of a possible 12, meaning that it demonstrates *clear and consistent competence* in that it

- develops an insightful point of view on the topic
- demonstrates exemplary critical thinking
- uses effective examples, reasons, and other evidence to support its thesis
- is consistently focused, coherent, and well-organized
- demonstrates skillful and effective use of language and sentence structure
- is largely (but not necessarily completely) free of grammatical and usage errors

Consider carefully the issue discussed in the following passage, then write an essay that answers the question posed in the assignment.

> In a culture obsessed with superficial appearances, our leaders should be those who can see beyond the surface. Judging a book by its cover is the job of the plebeian or the consumer, but reading the book—pondering its contents and perhaps seeking to write new chapters—is the job of a leader.

Assignment: **How important is it to look beyond superficial appearances?** Write an essay in which you answer this question and discuss your point of view on this issue. Support your position logically with examples from literature, the arts, history, politics, science and technology, current events, or your experience or observation.

The creature that Victor Frankenstein created was horrible to all who saw it, including Victor himself. Huge, misshapen and awkward, the creature was not even considered human. Indeed, the creature began to fulfill the only role that humans allowed him to occupy: the role of a bloodthirsty monster. Yet what Mary Shelley's *Frankenstein* shows us is not so much how rare and horrible it is to alter the natural order, but how tragically simple it is to create a monster. Victor Frankenstein created a monster not by contravening nature, as many would believe, but by judging the creature by his outward appearance and treating him like an unworthy freak.

How simple it is to hate others, to consider them less than human, based on superficial analysis. Hatred is the desperate accomplice of fear. In recent years, too many of us Americans—denizens of the land of the free and home of the brave—have become imprisoned by our hatred and cowed by our fear of the unknown. Our leaders are too often complicit in rousing this fear and fueling this hate, and in mistaking a quick trigger finger for bravery in the face of threat. They become quick to imprison or kill people who scare us at first, rather than acknowledge that they are humans with rights. They see the populace cringing at foreigners because foreigners attacked us

in 2001. They can't see past their irrational fear to the enormous need to reach out to disenfranchised and subjugated cultures and listen to their concerns. If only Victor Frankenstein had tried to learn what his creature would need once it was given life.

Our leaders are often the blindest of all because, to survive, they must not edify but pander. They see the populace cringing in fear at the prospect of human cloning because they imagine Frankenstein's monster. They can't see past their irrational fear to the huge potential medical benefits of stem cell research. They refuse to see that clones are indistinguishable from twins, and that twins are not horrible monstrosities. We can't really expect politicians or the media—who pander to popularity polls and big corporate donations—to see the world for what it truly is. They judge the world book by its cover, as did the angry villagers of Ingolstadt.

Our current situation will get better only once a critical mass of the American population begins to see that we are creating monsters everywhere by our irrational fear of the new and the foreign. We value instant polls of superficial and uninformed opinions more than careful thought and deep analysis. Perhaps it's time to open the book and read it carefully rather than just glancing at the cover.

The following essay received 8 points out of a possible 12, meaning that it demonstrates *adequate competence* in that it

• develops a point of view on the topic
• demonstrates some critical thinking, but perhaps not consistently
• uses some examples, reasons, and other evidence to support its thesis, but perhaps not adequately
• shows a general organization and focus, but shows occasional lapses in this regard
• demonstrates adequate but occasionally inconsistent facility with language
• contains occasional errors in grammar, usage and mechanics

Whoever said you can't judge a book by its cover probably never had to drive on the highway behind a Hummer. Americans are obsessed with making a first impression, usually an impression of aggression and wealth. Certainly, first impressions about human beings are usually wrong, but American culture is, unfortunately, being increasingly defined by consumer items that give an aggressive first impression and last impression. These items, unlike human beings, are designed carefully, and their first impressions are intended to convey the entire product.

A good example of this is the Super Bowl. It has become a flashy, decadent display of consumption rather than what it should be, a display of athletic prowess. Our obsession with consumer goods that make us seem more attractive or stronger and more powerful have made it clear that we're not concerned with substance as much as appearances. Every commercial shouts at you that first appearances are everything. Our schools are filled with people who think that the most important things in their lives are what shoes they wear or what cell phone they use.

Popular psychologists like Dr. Phil appear on television and tell us how important it is for us to be ourselves and not let other people tell us who we are, and then a string of commercials comes on telling you how a beer or car or deodorant makes you look more attractive. Which message do we really hear?

The following essay received 4 points out of a possible 12, meaning that it demonstrates *some incompetence* in that it

• has a seriously limited point of view
• demonstrates weak critical thinking
• uses inappropriate or insufficient examples, reasons, and other evidence to support its thesis
• is poorly focused and organized, and has seriously problems with coherence
• demonstrates frequent problems with language and sentence structure
• contains errors in grammar and usage that obscure the author's meaning seriously

I think that definitely you can't judge a book by its cover. Like my friend Cal is a really good wrestler and he even got into the state finals for his weight class. Everybody thinks he's a total jock but not a lot of people know also that he works really hard every day after practice at his uncle's garage and a lot of people think he's as good as a lot of other mechanics. He's a lot smarter than people give him credit for and he get's really good grades in math.

As a matter of fact he's in the honors level of math and will probably take calculus next year, so he's not just a jock or even just a great mechanic. When you look at him, especially when he's got his game face on just before a match, you would hardly believe that he could be a good student.

The next time you see an athlete, don't assume that he is just a dumb jock. Professional athletes have sometimes become senators and business leaders, so sometimes they have minds as well as muscles.

Section 2

1. C Substitute $k = 10$ into $2m + k = 12$ to get
$$2m + 10 = 12$$
Subtract 10: $2m = 2$
Divide by 2: $m = 1$
(Chapter 11, Lesson 1: Solving Equations)

2. E If the average of three numbers is 50, then their sum must be $3(50) = 150$. If two of the numbers are 35 and 50, then the third is $150 - 35 - 50 = 65$
(Chapter 12, Lesson 2: Mean/Median/Mode Problems)

3. D Since the ones column has only one A, it is easy to figure out its value from there. The only value for A that yields a 7 in the ones column is 4.
(Chapter 12, Lesson 3: Numerical Reasoning Problems)

4. E The problem is best solved with a proportion:
$\dfrac{9}{25} = \dfrac{x}{225}$. Cross-multiply: $25x = 2025$
Divide by 25: $x = 81$
(Chapter 10, Lesson 4: Ratios and Proportions)

5. B Since $32 = 2^5$, we can substitute: $2^{x-1} = 32$
$$2^{x-1} = 2^5$$
$$x - 1 = 5$$
Add 1: $x = 6$
(Chapter 11, Lesson 3: Working with Exponents)

6. A Since there were 59 yes votes, 26 of which were from men, $59 - 26 = 33$ of them were from women. Since there were 76 women in total, 33 of whom voted yes, $76 - 33 = 43$ of them must have voted no.
(Chapter 14, Lesson 5: Data Analysis)

7. D They both start with x cards. After Mike gives Kenny 12 cards, Mike has $x - 12$ and Kenny has $x + 12$ cards. If Kenny has twice as many as Mike, then
$$x + 12 = 2(x - 12)$$
Distribute: $+ 12 = 2x - 24$
Add 24: $+ 36 = 2x$
Subtract x: $36 = x$
Since they each had 36 cards to start, they had a total of $36 + 36 = 72$.
(Chapter 11, Lesson 7: Word Problems)

8. C The fraction that is walnuts equals the amount of walnuts divided by the total amount: $\dfrac{x}{(x + 15 + 20)}$
Simplify: $\dfrac{x}{(x + 35)}$
(Chapter 10, Lesson 4: Ratios and Proportions)

9. B You might simplify this problem by plugging in possible values for the angle measures, remembering the parallel lines theorem. Your diagram might look like this:

This example shows that $a + d + f + g = 360°$, and the only other sum among the choices that equals 360° is (B).
(Chapter 13, Lesson 1: Lines and Angles)

10. A Either plug in the ordered pairs to check, or draw a graph, as long as you can do it quickly. Notice that the point $(7, -1)$ satisfies both inequalities:
$2(7) + 3(-1) > 6$ and $7 - (-1) > 6$
(Chapter 11, Lesson 6: Inequalities, Absolute Value, and Plugging In)

11. A If n has a remainder of 6 when it is divided by 12, it must be 6 more than a multiple of 12. Pick any one you like: 18, for example. When 18 is divided by 6, the remainder is 0.
(Chapter 10, Lesson 7: Divisibility)

12. B Any five-sided polygon can be divided into three triangles like so:

Since the sum of the angles in a triangle is 180°, the sum of the angles in this figure is $3(180) = 540°$. The average measure of the five angles, then, is $540/5 = 108°$.
(Chapter 13, Lesson 2: Triangles)

13. D It is perhaps simplest to rephrase the statement in terms of the number of dogs and the number of cats, so that it is easy to turn into an equation: "There are 3 fewer than 4 times as many dogs as cats" is the same as saying "The number of dogs is 3 fewer than 4 times the number of cats." This can be translated into $d = 4c - 3$.
(Chapter 11, Lesson 7: Word Problems)

14. B Mark up the diagram with the information given:

To find the area of the triangle, you need to use the formula *area = base × height*/2. Since the height divides the triangle into two 30° − 60° − 90° triangles, the other sides have lengths shown. The base of the triangle is $6(\sqrt{3})$ and the height is 3, so the area is $\frac{6(\sqrt{3})(3)}{2} 9\sqrt{3}$.
(Chapter 13, Lesson 3: The Pythagorean Theorem)

15. D The sum of the parts is $4 + 3 + 2 + 1 = 10$. Therefore, the parts are $\frac{4}{10}, \frac{3}{10}, \frac{2}{10}$ and $\frac{1}{10}$ of the whole. The largest share, then, is ($50,000)(4/10) = $20,000
(Chapter 10, Lesson 4: Ratios & Proportions)

16. C Use the definition to translate the equation:
$$m\{n\} = 9$$
Translate: $m^2/n^2 = 9$
Now think about what values of m and n will work. Notice that 3 and 1 will work, but so will −3 and −1. Now plug these into the statements, and see if any are false. Since −3 is not greater than −1, statement I can be eliminated, and so can answers (B), (D), and (E). Notice that this means you don't have to check statement II, because it's in both remaining answers. You can show that statement III is true by taking the square root of both sides of the equation: $\frac{|m|}{|n|} = 3$. This means that $|n|$ goes into $|m|$ 3 times, so it is a factor.
(Chapter 9, Lesson 7: Thinking Logically and Checking)
(Chapter 12, Lesson 1: New Symbol or Term Problems)

17. C Let's say there are x blue marbles in the jar. This means there are $3x$ white marbles, and $2(3x) = 6x$ red marbles, for a total of $10x$ marbles. Since $3x$ are white, the probability of picking a white is $3x/10x = 3/10$.
(Chapter 12, Lesson 6: Probability Problems)

18. D Think about how many options you have to fill each place, from left to right. Since the first person must be a girl, you have 6 options. Since the next must be a boy, you have 5 options. Since the next must be a boy, you have 4 options (one is already up there). Since the next must be a girl, you have 5 options left. This means that the total number of possible arrangements is $(6)(5)(4)(5) = 600$.
(Chapter 12, Lesson 5: Counting Problems)

19. D If the two lines are parallel, then they have the same slope. The slope of l is $\frac{9}{12} = \frac{3}{4}$, so the slope of m must be $\frac{3}{4}$ as well. Therefore $\frac{12}{k} = \frac{3}{4}$
Cross-multiply: $3k = 48$
Divide by 3: $k = 16$
Therefore, the rectangle has a width of 16 and a height of 12, so its area is $(16)(12) = 192$.
(Chapter 13, Lesson 4: Coordinate Geometry)

20. E If p is the volume of the solid, then $r \times s \times t = p$. Solving this for r gives $r = \frac{p}{(st)}$, so statement II is true.

This lets you eliminate choices (A) and (C). If r, s, and t are integers and p is odd, then r, s, and t must be odd, because if any of them were even, then p would be even. Therefore $p + s + t$ is odd, and statement I is true. This eliminates choice (D). To check statement III, you need to find an expression for the surface area of the solid, which is $2(rs) + 2(rt) + 2(st) = 2(rs + rt + st)$. Since this is a multiple of 2, it must be even, and statement III is true. So the answer is (E).
(Chapter 12, Lesson 3: Numerical Reasoning Problems)
(Chapter 13, Lesson 7: Volumes and 3-D Geometry)

Section 3

1. A The fact that they *rarely agreed* implies that their opinions would often *differ*. *diverge* = differ or move apart; *coincide* = fit together or occur simultaneously; *retreat* = move away; *assemble* = put together; *truncate* = cut short

2. D The sentence implies a contrast between what *once was* and what *is now*. If it is no longer an *incontrovertible* (irrefutable) *truth*, it must now be *in doubt*. *enacted* = put into effect officially; *irrefutable* = impossible to disprove; *universal* = true at all places and times; *dubious* = doubtful; *conclusive* = acting as final proof

3. **C**   One who has encountered such tragedy would be expected to look to his painting as a *departure* from such *abject* (wretched) *sorrow. prudence* = conservative wisdom; *remorse* = regret; *adulation* = admiration; *solace* = peaceful respite; *melancholy* = sadness; *elation* = extreme happiness

4. **B**   *Proponents of a new curriculum* are people who support the change, while *conservative educators* are those who want to keep things the same. *repugnant* = disgusting; *innocuous* = harmless; *deplorable* = regrettable; *reprehensible* = worthy of scorn; *benevolent* = kind; *malicious* = evil; *auspicious* = favorable

5. **D**   What effect should a *lack of oxygen* have on climbers? It should be expected to *weaken* them. But this implies that the expedition leader's plan to acclimate them (get them used to the environment) was a *failure. illusory* = like an illusion; *initiated* = started; *mitigated* = soothed or made better; *enervated* = weakened; *venerable* = worthy of honor; *absolved* = forgiven

6. **E**   One who *questions norms* (conventions) *and mores* (moral standards) is a *rebel* of sorts. *charlatan* = a fake; *surrogate* = one who stands in place of another; *philanthropist* = one who gives to charity; *pragmatist* = one concerned with practical matters; *iconoclast* = one who destroys sacred objects or traditions

7. **A**   If he *stands in the negative camp,* then he must have a firm opinion about the issue. *ambivalent* = having conflicting opinions on an issue; *unequivocally* = without doubt; *apathetic* = lacking concern; *furtively* = secretively; *impartial* = fair and unbiased; *adamant* = stubborn; *vehemently* = passionately; *subjective* = being a matter of opinion

8. **C**   If he was *dismissed* by his contemporaries, they must have thought negatively of him. The *although* implies a contrast, so modern thinkers must now think positively of him. *pedant* = a know-it-all; *derivative* = deriving from the work of others; *neophyte* = beginner; *vociferous* = loudly opinionated; *radical* = one with an extreme opinion; *visionary* = able to envision the future; *partisan* = marked by party loyalty; *conciliatory* = bringing people together; *hermit* = one who prefers to live alone

9. **C**   Passage 1 focuses on *the study of molecules of which living organisms are composed.* Passage 2 discusses the ways in which organisms harvest energy through chemical processes like photosynthesis and chemosynthesis, which are biochemical processes.

10. **C**   The main point of the paragraph is in the first sentence: the *study of life on Earth ultimately involves the study of molecules.* The questions that follow are therefore questions about molecules that concern those who study life on Earth, that is, biologists.

11. **A**   Passage 2 focuses on organisms that harvest energy in a way that is analogous to, but different from, photosynthesis. The process of converting energy into food for the organism, then, is a relevant topic for Passage 2.

12. **D**   Passage 2 discusses how *other organisms* utilize the bacteria that harvest energy from sulfides, either by consuming them or incorporating them into their tissues. This concept is not discussed in Passage 1. Both passages discuss the *conversion of light energy to food energy, and bonds within molecules.* Only Passage 1 discusses the *structure of cells and disease,* specifically cancer.

13. **C**   The author indicates that one should react with *proper skepticism* to those reports, thereby implying that they are *probably untrue.*

14. **B**   The author asks (in line 21) the reader to *compare* the probability of being a victim of terrorism to the list of probabilities that follow, which are much greater, thereby implying that terrorism is not much of a threat.

15. **E**   The personal recollection begins on line 60: *I once had a conversation. . . .* The verifiable statistics abound in paragraphs 1, 2, and 3. The authoritative study is mentioned in lines 54–60. Common misconceptions are mentioned multiple times, as in lines 12–13: *being killed by terrorists might seem to be a major risk.*

16. **B**   The author says that this *penetrating insight* is really a *non sequitur,* that is, something that doesn't follow logically. Therefore it is not a penetrating insight at all.

17. **A**   The author says that a *feeling for what quantities or time spans are appropriate in various contexts is essential to getting the joke* (lines 47–49), thereby implying that the couple, like those who slip *between millions and billions,* lack an appreciation for particular quantities.

18. **C**   In the span of *approximately 20 minutes* the doctor said three different things about the procedure, so he contradicted himself frequently.

19. **B**   The passage refines the usage of the word by saying *the same organization, the same physical laws,* thereby suggesting that the author meant *rules of physics* when he said *organization.*

20. C In lines 16–19, the author describes the *realization that the phenomena we see result from the complexity of the inner workings between atoms* as being *dramatic and wonderful.*

21. B In lines 20–22, the author says that his feeling of awe *could be communicated through a drawing to someone who had also had this emotion,* thereby suggesting that appreciating such art depends on having a similar experience as the artist.

22. D The author says that Jerry is a *very good teacher* in that *everything that I thought was a mistake, he used to teach me something in a positive way. He never said it was wrong; he never put me down.* We can infer, then, that Jerry would have done something positive and affirming.

23. A The parenthetical comment that precedes this sentence indicates that the fact that the line did not touch the flower pot was unintentional.

24. E The main point of the passage is that the author wanted to learn to draw to convey the awe he felt about the workings of nature and the physical world. So when he finishes by saying *I was never satisfied,* we know that he was *never able to convey adequately his feelings about the beauty of the world.*

Section 4

1. B The pronoun *which* is out of place because it is assumed to refer to the preceding noun *poets.* If the pronoun is eliminated, the meaning is clearer and the two clauses are **parallel.**
(Chapter 18 Lesson 5 and Lesson 15)

2. E This is an awkward usage of the gerund *preparing.* To convey purpose, the infinitive *to prepare* is much more effective.
(Chapter 18 Lesson 3)

3. D This contains a **dangling modifier.** The modifying phrase that begins the sentence describes *Carla* rather than *Carla's anxiety.*
(Chapter 18 Lesson 7 and Lesson 8)

4. C This is a sentence fragment without a verb. Choice (C) completes the thought and makes a complete sentence.

5. C The participle *swimming* **dangles** in this sentence. *Justine* should follow the **participial phrase** because she is the one swimming, not *the current.*
(Chapter 18 Lesson 7)

6. D The comparison is not **parallel.** The sentence should say that *writing* one thing is *more difficult than* **writing** something else.
(Chapter 18 Lesson 3)

7. A This sentence is correct.

8. D This is a **run-on sentence,** or a **comma splice.** Two sentences cannot be "spliced" together with only a comma; you must use a conjunction, a semicolon, or a colon. Since the second clause explains the idea in the first clause, a colon is most appropriate.
(Chapter 18 Lesson 15)

9. B The two clauses are not properly coordinated. Since the second clearly contradicts the first, a contrasting conjunction like *but* or a contrasting coordinating adverb like *nevertheless* should be used.
(Chapter 18 Lesson 15)

10. E The verb *reveals* does not agree with the subject *theories* and should be *reveal* instead.
(Chapter 18 Lesson 1 and Lesson 2)

11. D The pronoun *their* does not agree in number with its antecedent *board* and should be changed to *its.*
(Chapter 18 Lesson 5)

12. B The phrase *his staff and him* serves as the subject of the verb *had diverted,* and so it must be in the subjective case: *his staff and he.*
(Chapter 18, Lesson 6)

13. C This is incorrect **past participle** form; the **present perfect** form of *to run* is *have run.*
(Chapter 18, Lesson 9 and Lesson 13)

14. B The subject of the verb *were* is *taunting.* (This is an **inverted sentence** because the subject comes after the verb.) Since *taunting* is singular, the verb should be *was.*
(Chapter 18 Lesson 1)

15. E The sentence is correct.

16. C The verb *produce* does not agree with its subject *refraction.* It should be changed to *produces.*
(Chapter 18 Lesson 1)

17. C Since the sentence compares only **two** films, one of them is the *less* expensive.
(Chapter 18 Lesson 4)

18. C This word answers the question *how did she react?* Therefore it modifies a verb and should be in the form of an **adverb:** *emotionally.*
(Chapter 18 Lesson 12)

19. B This phrase is part of a **parallel construction:** *"not A but B."* The construction is parallel only if this phrase is eliminated.
(Chapter 18 Lesson 3)

20. B This phrase is **redundant.** The word *while* means *at the same time,* so the second phrase should be eliminated.
(Chapter 18 Lesson 12)

21. B The verb *have expressed* does not agree with its subject *coalition,* and should be changed to *has expressed.*
(Chapter 18 Lesson 1 and Lesson 2)

22. D This is an **illogical comparison.** A *way* cannot be compared to a *hard drive.* The phrase should be *the way a computer hard drive stores information.*
(Chapter 18 Lesson 4)

23. D The pronoun *their* does not agree with its **antecedent** *museum,* and should be changed to *its.*
(Chapter 18 Lesson 5)

24. B This is an **idiom error.** The correct form of this comparison is *"prefer A to B"* not *"prefer A more than B."*
(Chapter 18 Lesson 3 and Lesson 10)

25. D Since only two films are being compared, the comparative adjective *more* is required.
(Chapter 18 Lesson 4: Comparison Problems)

26. B The phrase *Emma and I* is the object of the verb *included,* and therefore should take the objective case *Emma and me.*
(Chapter 18 Lesson 6: Pronoun Case)

27. B The past perfect tense requires the past participle *swum.*
(Chapter 18 Lesson 9: Tricky Tenses)

28. E The sentence is correct as written.

29. A The participle *building* dangles in the original sentence. It should be changed to the infinitive *to build* so that it properly modifies the verb *try.*
(Chapter 18 Lesson 7: Dangling and Misplaced Participles)

30. B The modifying phrases are awkwardly placed. Modifiers should obey the **law of proximity** and be as close as possible to the words they modify.
(Chapter 18 Lesson 8)

31. A The modifying phrase at the beginning is **dangling.** Since *she* is *a doctor, she* should follow the opening phrase. (D) and (E) do not work because they improperly imply that she was bothered by the *children* rather than their *treatment.* You might notice that the correct choice contains verbs in the passive voice. Although you should minimize the use of the passive voice, it is not always incorrect.
(Chapter 15, Lesson 10: Write Forcefully)
(Chapter 18, Lesson 7 and Lesson 8)

32. E This paragraph discusses Montessori's methods and results in the *Casa dei Bambini,* and so the trivial and unrelated fact that *there were fifty students in her first class* is out of place.

33. A The pronoun *it* refers to Montessori's day care center, and so this sentence should follow the one that mentions the day care center, but precede the sentence that discusses her *theories* in detail.

34. D Revision (D) is the most concise and effective of the choices.

35. C Sentences 8 and 9 discuss Montessori's philosophy and its effectiveness. Sentence 8 indicates that Montessori *decided it was important to help each child through his or her own curriculum,* which is clearly a *focus on the individual child.*

Section 5

1. B $5y - 2 = 3y + 7$
Subtract 3y: $2y - 2 = 7$
Add 2: $2y = 9$
Divide by 2: $y = 4.5$
(Chapter 11, Lesson 1: Solving Equations)

2. D Since vertical angles are equal, $a = 20$. Since angles that form a straight line have a sum of 180°, $20 + b + 34 = 180$. Therefore $b = 126$. So $a + b = 20 + 126 = 146$.
(Chapter 13, Lesson 1: Lines and Angles)

3. C $(2x)(3x) = (2/8)(3/2)$
Simplify: $6x^2 = 6/16$
Divide by 6: $x^2 = 1/16$
Take the square root: $x = 1/4$
(Chapter 10, Lesson 3: Fractions)

4. C   Since the prime factorization of 98 is $2 \times 7 \times 7$, and since the greatest common factor of m and 98 is a prime number, that greatest common factor must be 2 or 7. Since it is not even, it must be 7.
(Chapter 10, Lesson 7: Divisibility)
(Chapter 11, Lesson 5: Factoring)
(Chapter 12, Lesson 1: New Symbol or Term Problems)

5. D

$$|k - 0.5| < 10$$

Translate: $-10 < k - 0.5 < 10$
Add 0.5: $-9.5 < k < 10.5$

The smallest possible integer value for k is -9 and the greatest is 10. The total number of integers between -9 and 10, inclusive, is $10 - (-9) + 1 = 20$.
(Chapter 9, Lesson 2: Analyzing Problems)
(Chapter 11, Lesson 6: Inequalities, Absolute Value, and Plugging In)

6. E   To maximize the value of $(10 - x^2)/2$, you must minimize the value of x^2. The smallest value that x^2 can have is 0, if $x = 0$. Since 0 is within the domain given, the maximum value of $f(x)$ is $(10 - 0)/2 = 5$.
(Chapter 14, Lesson 2: Functions)

7. C   It helps to know the perfect squares and the perfect cubes. The first seven perfect squares greater than 1 are 4, 9, 16, 25, 36, 49, and 64. The first three perfect cubes are 8, 27, and 64. Clearly, the only integer between 1 and 100 that is both a perfect cube and a perfect square is $64 = 4^3 = 8^2$. Therefore $m = 4$ and $n = 8$, so $m + n = 4 + 8 = 12$.
(Chapter 11, Lesson 4: Working with Roots)

8. B   This is a rate problem, so remember the basic rate formula: *distance = rate × time*. Start by picking a value for the distance from Amanda's home to work. No matter what distance you choose, the final answer will be the same, so choose a distance that's easy to calculate with, like 50 miles. If it takes her 60 minutes (1 hour) to get to work, she must be going 50 miles/hour. If she increases her speed by 20% for the trip home, then her speed coming home is (1.20) (50 miles/hour) = 60 miles/hour. To travel 50 miles at 60 miles/hour will take her (50 miles)/(60 mph) = 5/6 hour, which is 5/6(60 minutes) = 50 minutes.
(Chapter 12, Lesson 4: Rate Problems)

9. 0.4   Remember that "percent" means "divided by 100," so 0.5 percent of 80 means $0.5 \div 100 \times 80 = 0.4$
(Chapter 10, Lesson 5: Percents)

10. .333 or 1/3   Just pick three consecutive odd integers, like 1, 3, and 5. Since d is the middle of these, $d = 3$. Since s is the sum of these, $s = 1 + 3 + 5 = 9$. So d divided by s is 3/9 or 1/3.
(Chapter 12, Lesson 3: Numerical Reasoning Problems)

11. 30   4/9 of c^2 is 24
Translate: $(4/9)(c^2) = 24$
Multiply by 5/4: $(5/4)(4/9)(c^2) = (5/4)(24)$
Simplify: $(5/9)(c^2) = 30$
(Chapter 9, Lesson 4: Simplifying Problems)
(Chapter 11, Lesson 1: Solving Equations)

12. 60   The sum of the four angles in a quadrilateral is 360°. The sum of the parts in the ratio is $3 + 4 + 5 + 6 = 18$. Therefore the angles are 3/18, 4/18, 5/18 and 6/18 of the whole, which is 360°. So the smallest angle measures $(3/18)(360°) = 60°$.
(Chapter 13, Lesson 2: Triangles)
(Chapter 10, Lesson 4: Ratios and Proportions)

13. 28   Subtract the equations:

$$
\begin{array}{r}
5a + 6b = 13 \\
-(4a + 5b = 9) \\
\hline
a + b = 4
\end{array}
$$

Multiply by 7: $7a + 7b = 28$
(Chapter 9, Lesson 4: Simplifying Problems)
(Chapter 11, Lesson 2: Systems)

14. .666 or .667 or 2/3   A good way to simplify the messy fraction is to multiply the numerator and denominator by the least common multiple of all the denominators in the "smaller" fractions. Since $m^2 - 1 = (m + 1)(m - 1)$, $m^2 - 1$ is the least common multiple. Multiplying by $(m^2 - 1)/(m^2 - 1)$ simplifies the expression:

$$\frac{m^2 - 1}{m^2 - 1} \times \frac{\dfrac{1}{m+1} + \dfrac{1}{m-1}}{\dfrac{1}{m^2 - 1}} = \frac{(m-1) + (m+1)}{1} = 2m$$

Since $m = \dfrac{1}{3}$, $2m = \dfrac{2}{3}$.

(Chapter 10, Lesson 3: Fractions)
(Chapter 11, Lesson 5: Factoring)
(Chapter 9, Lesson 4: Simplifying Problems)

15. 81   By guessing and checking positive integers, you should be able to see that the only positive integers that satisfy the equation are 5 and 4. Therefore $(x + y)^2 = (5 + 4)^2 = 81$.
(Chapter 12, Lesson 3: Numerical Reasoning Problems)

16. 10   Five out of the 15 marbles are white. If x more white marbles are added, the probability of choosing a white marble is $\dfrac{(5 + x)}{(15 + x)}$. This fraction must be at least $\dfrac{3}{5}$, so

$$\frac{(5 + x)}{(15 + x)} \geq 3/5$$

Cross-multiply: $25 + 5x \geq 45 + 3x$
Subtract $3x$: $25 + 2x \geq 45$
Subtract 25: $2x \geq 20$
Divide by 2: $x \geq 10$.
(Chapter 12, Lesson 6: Probability Problems)

17. 3   By inspecting the angles of the two triangles, you can see that they must be similar, as the diagram shows.

This implies that the corresponding sides are proportional. Using the Pythagorean Theorem, you can find the hypotenuse of the larger triangle:

$$\sqrt{8}^2 + \sqrt{10}^2 = 8 + 10 = h^2, \text{ so } h = \sqrt{18}$$

Then you can set up a proportion of the corresponding sides: $\dfrac{\sqrt{8}}{\sqrt{4}} = \dfrac{\sqrt{18}}{x}$

Cross-multiply: $x\sqrt{8} = \sqrt{72}$
Divide by $\sqrt{8}$: $x\sqrt{9} = 3$

(Chapter 13, Lesson 6: Similar Figures)

18. 4   If she took a shots in her first game, and made 50% of them, then she made $.5a$ shots in the first game. Similarly, she made $.6b$ shots in the second game. If she made 52% of her shots altogether, then

$$\frac{.5a + .6b}{a + b} = .52$$

Cross-multiply: $.5a + .6b = .52a + .52b$
Subtract $.5a$ and $.52b$: $.08b = .02a$
Divide by $0.2b$: $4 = \dfrac{a}{b}$

(Chapter 10, Lesson 4: Ratios and Proportions)
(Chapter 10, Lesson 5: Percents)

Section 6

1. B   Sandra's father's words were not *thoughtful* or *useful*, but rather they were *hollow clichés*. They were *overused* and *thoughtless*. *irate* = angry; *inane* = pointless; *homogeneous* = the same throughout; *flamboyant* = lively; *altruistic* = selfless

2. C   If he was *courageous* in prison, he must not have given up his fight. *treacherous* = deceitful; *futile* = having no hope of success; *fortitude* = strength; *premeditated* = planned in advance; *porous* = full of holes

3. A   Since the teachers couldn't hear themselves talk, the construction must have been noisy, and therefore was not very *constructive* to learning (no

pun intended). *din* = noise; *conducive* = helpful, constructive; *averse* = opposed to; *discernible* = detectable; *irascible* = easily angered

4. C   The sentence implies that solutions to physics problems are *approximate*, so they cannot be *exact*. The approximate solution would be sufficient as long as the complicating factors are *small*. *negligible* = not significant; *plausibly* = with a good likelihood of success; *ethically* = with regard to moral standards

5. D   *Martial resources* are those resources that sustain an army's ability to fight; they are the *means* to continue fighting. If the factions both have *access* to these resources, the fight is likely to drag on. *mediation* = attempt to resolve a conflict

6. C   Since Jung was *modest in his therapeutic claims* (lines 4–5) and *cautious* (line 11) when consulted by schizophrenics, we can conclude that he did not yet believe that his therapy worked for all mentally ill patients.

7. A   The sentence indicates that psychoanalysis could *bring about* a psychotic episode.

8. C   The passage says that the *comic . . . seems bound to its time, society, cultural anthropology* (lines 7–8). This implies that it's harder to find something humorous if it is from another culture or time. Choice (C) is the most foreign to modern Americans.

9. C   Because the passage says that it is harder to understand the comedy of other societies and eras because of cultural obstacles, the *effort* is in overcoming these obstacles.

10. B   The author states that the host's introduction *dropped like a stone in our midst* (lines 9–10), and that no response at all to this introduction was *the proper response* (line 12). The rest of the essay makes clear that the author considers the host's comments, particularly with its focus on *literature*, to be inappropriate.

11. C   The author defines the term somewhat in lines 54–56 by listing the forms to which the term *literary* is applied: *novels and short stories and poems*. Throughout the passage, also the author distinguishes *literary* works from works of non-fiction, which can be very well-written.

12. B   The interviewer asked the writers about the "*literary experience*" (line 20) of the day, and then whether they "*write anything literary*" (lines 35–36), when in fact they did not write literature at all, but rather nonfiction.

13. **C**   Those writers are mentioned as *our models* by the author, suggesting that the author and the other writers have been influenced by them.

14. **B**   In saying that writers were admired for *their ability to harness the issues*, the author is saying that they make them easy to understand for their readers.

15. **E**   The writers being interviewed had said that *they felt they were already doing satisfactory work* (lines 36–37). The callers implied that they felt the same way.

16. **C**   The phrase *the great preponderance of what writers now write and sell* refers to the *majority* of what they write and sell.

17. **B**   The first sentence indicates the purpose of this passage: *To understand . . . Aristotle . . . it is necessary to apprehend his imaginative background* (lines 1–3), in other words, to understand the preconceptions behind his theories.

18. **E**   This paragraph discusses the ancient Greek idea that mechanical devices are somehow imbued with the spirit of animals with similar abilities, for instance, an airplane having the spirit of a bird. The comment that *animals have lost their importance in our imaginative pictures of the world* indicates that modern thinkers no longer suppose any link between the life-spirit of animals and the behavior of machines.

19. **C**   The *imaginative preconceptions* of Aristotle are explained in the second and third paragraphs, where it says that *to the Greek, it seemed more natural to assimilate apparently lifeless motions to those of animals* (lines 47–49).

20. **A**   The passage says that *the . . . mechanical view hardly suggested itself, except in the case of a few men of genius* (lines 36–38). So these men of genius had the *mechanical view*.

21. **E**   The passage says that *to the modern man of science, the body of an animal is a very elaborate machine* (lines 42–43). The difference between animals and machines is diminished with discoveries about the *physico-chemical structure* (lines 44–45) of animals, or the mechanical and chemical nature of biology.

22. **A**   In saying that, to the ancient Greek, *it seemed more natural to assimilate apparently lifeless motions to those of animals* (lines 47–49), the author is saying that Greeks were inclined to compare the motions of lifeless things to the motions of living things, and that these comparisons were *the basis of a general theory of physics* (lines 53–54).

23. **C**   The passage says that *Every Greek philosopher . . . had been taught in childhood to regard the sun and moon as gods* (lines 58–61), and then that *Anaxagoras was prosecuted for impiety because he thought that they were not alive* (lines 61–63). This implies that he *departed dramatically from his childhood teachings*.

24. **B**   The *Hellenic love of order and geometric simplicity* (line 67) is attributed to the Divine Being who moves the heavenly bodies. These heavenly bodies were said to move with *regularity* (line 56) and *superior perfection* (lines 57–58). Therefore, it can be inferred that this *love of order and geometric simplicity* pertains to the movement of the heavenly bodies.

Section 7

1. **C** $\frac{2}{3}$ of 60 is 40, and $\frac{40}{80} = 50\%$.
(Chapter 10, Lesson 3: Fractions)

2. **D** $$4x + 2y = 8$$

Divide by 4: $x + \left(\frac{1}{2}\right)y = 2$
(Chapter 9, Lesson 4: Simplifying Problems)

3. **C**   This question is asking what the remainder is when 29, 21, and 64 are each divided by 3. When 29 is divided by 3 the remainder is 2; when 21 is divided by 3 the remainder is 0; and when 64 is divided by 3 the remainder is 1.
(Chapter 10, Lesson 7: Divisibility)

4. **B**   1 & 2
Substitute using definition: $1(1 - 1) + 2(2 - 1)$
Simplify: $0 + 2 = 2$
(Chapter 12, Lesson 1: New Symbol or Term Problems)

5. **A**   In a triangle, any side must have a length that is less than the sum of the two other lengths but greater than the difference of the two other lengths. Therefore, the third side must have a length between $15 - 9 = 6$ and $15 + 9 = 24$, so a length of 5 is impossible.
(Chapter 13, Lesson 2: Triangles)

6. **B**   The volume of a cube is equal to s^3, where s is the length of one edge. If $s^3 = 64$, then $s = 4$, and so each square face has an area of $s^2 = 4^2 = 16$. Since a cube has six faces, the total surface area is $6(16) = 96$.
(Chapter 13, Lesson 7: Volumes and 3-D Geometry)

7. D $\dfrac{(x+2+6+10)}{4} = 8$, so $x+2+6+10 = 32$

Simplify: $x + 18 = 32$
Subtract 18: $x = 14$

So the numbers are 2, 6, 10, and 14. The median is the average of the two middle numbers: $\dfrac{(6+10)}{2} = 8$.

(Chapter 12, Lesson 2: Mean/Median/Mode Problems)

8. A Indicate the congruent sides with tick marks: in a triangle, the angles across from equal sides are equal; indicate this in the diagram. Your angles should be marked as shown. Since the angles in a triangle have a sum of 180°, $y + y + 180 - x = 180$

Subtract 180: $2y - x = 0$
Add x: $2y = x$
Divide by 2: $y = \dfrac{x}{2}$

(Chapter 13, Lesson 2: Triangles)

9. D Notice that the graph is of all the points that are more than 1 unit away from −1. The distance from a point to −1 is $|x - (-1)|$, or $|x + 1|$; if this distance is greater than one, then $|x + 1| > 1$.
(Chapter 11, Lesson 6: Inequalities, Absolute Value, and Plugging In)

10. B "Must be true" kinds of questions are often best answered by process of elimination with examples. Begin with a simple set of values, for instance $a = 0$, $b = -1$, and $c = 0$. Notice that these values satisfy all of the given information. This example clearly shows that statement I need not be true, because 0 is not greater than 0, and that statement III need not be true, because $(0)(0)$ is not greater than $(-1)^2$. This leaves only statement II as a possibility, so the answer must be (B).
(Chapter 9, Lesson 7: Thinking Logically and Checking)
(Chapter 12, Lesson 3: Numerical Reasoning Problems)

11. E You have five choices for the first digit: 1, 3, 5, 7, and 9; ten choices for the middle digit (any digit will do), and five choices for the last digit: 0, 2, 4, 6, and 8. So the total number of possibilities is $5 \times 10 \times 5 = 250$.
(Chapter 12, Lesson 5: Counting Problems)

12. B To find how many more seconds it will take the machine to cut circle A than circle B, you can find the length of time it takes to cut each circle and subtract them. The laser cuts the circumference of each circle, so you must find that first. Circle A has an area of 64π. Since the area of a circle is πr^2, the radius of the circle is 8. Since the area of circle B is 16π, its radius is 4. The circumference of a circle is $2\pi r$, so the circumference of A is $2\pi(8) = 16\pi$ and the circumference of B is $2\pi(4) = 8\pi$. The difference of their radii is $16\pi - 8\pi = 8\pi$. The time it takes to cut that length is given by the formula *time = distance/rate*.

$$\dfrac{(8\pi \text{ cm})}{(3 \text{ cm/second})} = \dfrac{8\pi}{3 \text{ sec}}$$

(Chapter 13, Lesson 8: Circles)
(Chapter 12, Lesson 4: Rate Problems)

13. E The slope of AC is *rise/run* = $\dfrac{(5-(-1))}{(8-1)} = 6/7$.

Therefore the slope of CB is −6/7. Using the slope formula: $\dfrac{(5-(-1))}{(8-k)} = -6/7$

Simplify: $\dfrac{6}{(8-k)} = -6/7$
Cross-multiply: $-6(8 - k) = 42$
Divide by 6: $-8 + k = 7$
Add 8: $k = 15$

(Chapter 13, Lesson 4: Coordinate Geometry)

14. C $m = 1 \times 2 \times 3 \times 4 \times 5 \times 6 \times 7 \times 8 \times 9 \times 10$. You can factor even further in terms of primes: $m = 1 \times 2 \times 3 \times (2 \times 2) \times 5 \times (2 \times 3) \times 7 \times (2 \times 2 \times 2) \times (3 \times 3) \times (2 \times 5)$. This shows that there are a maximum of eight factors of 2, so the greatest power of 2 that is a factor of m is 2^8.

15. D First draw a diagram to see how the area of an equilateral triangle is related to the lengths of the sides:

Notice that the height (which is also the bisector of the "top" angle) divides the triangle into two 30°-60°-90° triangles, with sides as shown. The area of a triangle is *base × height*/2, which in this case is

$$\dfrac{(2x)\left(x\sqrt{3}\right)}{2} = x^2\sqrt{3}.$$ Since the area is given as $36\sqrt{3}$, x must equal 6. Substituting this into the diagram, each smaller triangle has sides of length 6, $6\sqrt{3}$, and 12. Therefore the sum of the perimeters of the two triangles is $36 + 12\sqrt{3}$.
(Chapter 13, Lesson 2: Triangles)
(Chapter 13, Lesson 3: The Pythagorean Theorem)
(Chapter 13, Lesson 5: Areas and Perimeters)

16. B At 4:00 pm, there are 1,000 bacteria. Since the population doubles every two hours, there must have been half as many two hours ago. So at 2:00 pm there were 500 bacteria, and at 12:00 noon there were 250 bacteria. (Notice that the fact that there were 100 bacteria to start is irrelevant.)
(Chapter 12, Lesson 4: Rate Problems)

Section 8

1. D If she was relieved, the tumor must not have been dangerous. *malignant* = dangerous; *irreverent* = disrespectful; *serene* = calm; *benign* = harmless; *mortal* = capable of dying.

2. C If the jargon rendered the speech *decipherable only to* a few audience members, then it rendered the speech *undecipherable* to the rest of the audience. Therefore the message was *obscured*.

3. D If one prefers *style* to *performance*, then the *cosmetic* appeal of the car would be most important. *utilitarian* = concerned with practical uses; *pragmatic* = concerned with function; *aesthetic* = pertaining to beauty

4. A If something *serves its purpose only temporarily*, then it is by definition *provisional*. *provisional* = serving a temporary purpose; *polemical* = relating to a controversial intellectual position; *pedantic* = acting like a know-it-all

5. E A *foil* is a character that provides a dramatic contrast to the personality of another character. The *but* in the sentence indicates that Ms. Linney is *going against the tradition*, and does not portray her character *demurely* (modestly). *bluster* = brashness; *forgo* = abandon an inclination or plan; *coyness* = shyness; *bombast* = pompous speech; *eschew* = abandon; *impudence* = impertinence, rudeness

6. C *Despite* implies an ironic situation. If analysts have tried to depict the stock market as *driven by predictable principles*, it would be ironic if people believed that it was not predictable at all. *invaluable* = very valuable; *complacent* = self-satisfied; *capricious* = arbitrary, whimsical; *responsive* = tending to respond quickly; *obscure* = not widely known.

7. C The *control* is mentioned in the context of *the creation of life* (line 10). This is the *process of conception*.

8. B The author says that this *"outsourcing"* . . . *leaves us with a profoundly hollow feeling* (lines 14–18). This indicates a *disdain*.

9. E This statement is from those who *turn [their] noses up at one who would offer us the most precious gift in the universe*, that is, the advocates of cloning are turning up their noses at nature or God.

10. A The parenthetical comment suggests that the *essential random . . . processes that form the basis of natural selection* may be only *seemingly* random. This suggests that these processes may be planned rather than random.

11. D The *"unnatural selection"* is described as involving *an assembly line* (lines 29–31), which is a type of *mechanical procedure*, and *carefully designed and tested features* (line 32), which implies a *selection of characteristics*. The *random processes* (lines 27–28) are attributed to *natural* selection.

12. A The passage implies that those who know *a little bit about the history of technology* (lines 55–56) would not have such *irrational fears about human cloning* (line 53). Therefore you can eliminate choice (D). The fact that these *fears* are called *irrational* eliminates choices (B) and (E). Since these fears are said to *abound from all parts of the political spectrum* (line 54), you can eliminate choice (C). The passage never mentions that the opponents are *very religious*, so the answer is (A).

13. C Surgery is mentioned in line 63 as something *significant* (line 57) that was once *denounced* (line 58).

14. C After quoting Mr. Rifkin, the author then goes on to describe the illogic behind the quote.

15. B The passage mentions that human twins *"have their own unique thoughts"* in order to refute the claim that identical genes put *a human into a genetic straitjacket* (lines 77–78).

16. A The passage says that *familiarity* [with procreational technologies] *dissipates fear* (line 128), implying that these technologies become more acceptable as they become more familiar.

17. A This paragraph says that *ignorant superstition* (line 136) stands in the way of *technologies that can produce ample food for a starving world and cure devastating illnesses* (lines 133–135). This indicates anger at an unjust situation.

18. C In each case, the questions represent the perspective that the author argues against.

19. B The first passage says that cloning technologies will make the world *forever different from what it is today* (lines 51–52), and the second says that these technologies *can produce ample food for a starving world and cure devastating illnesses* (lines 134–135).

Section 9

1. C The infinitive *to move* more effectively conveys purpose than does the phrase *by moving*. Also, the modifier *more closely* has the incorrect form. It should be in adjectival form *closer*, because it modifies the noun *source*.
(Chapter 18, Lesson 12: Other Modifier Problems)

2. E The original sentence illogically suggests that cell phones standardized their own technology. The only choice that logically coordinates the ideas is choice E.
(Chapter 18, Lesson 15: Coordinating Ideas)

3. E The colon is misused in the original sentence, since it does not introduce a list of examples or an independent explanatory clause. Choice B has the same problem. Choices C and D use improper idioms. Only choice E conveys the idea clearly and idiomatically.
(Chapter 18, Lesson 15: Coordinating Ideas)

4. B The original phrasing is a sentence fragment; it contains no verb. Choices B, C, and D correct this mistake, but C and D do not clearly convey what protected the city. Only choice B conveys the idea logically.
(Chapter 15, Lesson 7: Write Logically)

5. A The original sentence is correct. The phrase preceding the comma is an appositive modifying *On Writing Well*. Therefore, B and C cause this modifier to be misplaced. Choice D is a fragment and E misplaces the modifier *by William Zinsser*.

6. E The original phrase shifts the pronoun from *you* to *one*. Choices B and C are illogical and D is unidiomatic. Choice E is concise and avoids these problems.

7. A The original sentence conveys the idea clearly and effectively. Choices B and C misuse the singular pronoun *it* to refer to the plural noun *pigeons*. Choice D is awkward and E produces a fragment.

8. D Choice D is the only choice that makes the comparison idiomatic, logical and parallel.
(Chapter 18, Lesson 3: Parallelism)

9. C In the original sentence, the participle *revealing* is misplaced, since it does not modify the closest noun *friends*. Choice B repeats this error, and choices D and E are unidiomatic. The only choice that fixes this problem and conveys the logical sequence of ideas is choice C.
(Chapter 18, Lesson 7: Dangling and Misplaced Modifiers)

10. B The participle *inspired* is left dangling in the original sentence. Its subject, *Gerald*, must follow the comma. Since choice E produces a sentence fragment, the best choice is B.
(Chapter 18, Lesson 7: Dangling and Misplaced Modifiers)

11. B The original phrasing does not clearly convey who *decided*. Also, the noun *club* is singular, so the plural pronoun *they* is inappropriate. Choice B concisely and clearly fixes these problems.
(Chapter 18, Lesson 5: Pronoun-Antecedent Disagreement)

12. A The original phrasing is clear, logical and effective.

13. C Since this sentence is giving general advice about a general practice, the gerund *acknowledging* is more effective than the infinitive *to acknowledge*. Further, the gerund is parallel with the gerund *subverting* with which it is compared.
(Chapter 18, Lesson 3: Parallelism)

14. E The sentence is not parallel. The first two items in the list establish the pattern: *get . . . avoid . . .* So the last item should be *reduce. . .*
(Chapter 18, Lesson 3: Parallelism)

CHAPTER 6

HOW TO BUILD AN IMPRESSIVE VOCABULARY

with MAPS-CATCH

1. Building an Impressive Vocabulary with MAPS-CATCH

2. Vocabulary Units 1–7

I BUILDING AN IMPRESSIVE VOCABULARY WITH MAPS-CATCH

Vocabulary building is one of the big challenges of preparing to take the SAT I. Building a vocabulary for college success requires discipline.

Map the problem: Build understanding, don't just memorize meanings

If you want to build a useful vocabulary, **your goal should not be just to memorize the meanings of words.** By only memorizing meanings, you are ensuring that your studies will be not only unsuccessful but very, very dull.

If you are a typical 16-year-old, then you have a 30,000- to 50,000-word vocabulary. How many of these words did you memorize with flashcards? How many did you look up in a dictionary? How many did you learn by using a memory trick? Only a tiny portion.

So how did you learn all those words so effortlessly? By using your mind's innate language-building system. This system is an "organ," very much as our hearts or kidneys are organs. In order to build a strong vocabulary, we have to keep that language-building system healthy with the right kinds of experiences and exercises.

> Your mind's language-building system does **not** respond well to mere repetition of words and their meanings. Don't try to build vocabulary simply by rote study of word meanings. Infants don't learn the meaning of words merely by having them repeated over and over. Rather, they learn words by trying to **understand and communicate with others.** If the words are separated from real everyday communication, our mind's language-building system doesn't work very well.

So what do our minds need to build a great vocabulary?

- **A vocabulary-rich environment.** When you were a baby, you were surrounded by people with much stronger vocabularies than yours. This is why your vocabulary grew so rapidly when you were very young. As you have gotten older, however, you have probably surrounded yourself with people whose vocabularies are more on a par with your own. So how do you improve your vocabulary? First, **read books with challenging vocabularies.** Watch college-level documentaries on television rather than mindless entertainment. Listen to National Public Radio. Read the *New York Times* Op-Ed page and magazine. Read articles and stories from *Harper's,*

The Atlantic Monthly, The New Yorker, The Nation, and *Scientific American.*

- **A willingness to use new vocabulary.** As we grow older, most of us become more and more self-conscious about our speech. We don't like to use words that our friends don't use, or to misuse words in front of our friends for fear of sounding stupid. This reluctance can hinder the growth of your vocabulary. **Find a friend or relative with whom you can practice your new vocabulary— perhaps someone who is also training for the SAT I.** Don't merely ask her or him to quiz you on meanings: talk about how to use and pronounce the words, about situations in which they are helpful, about related words, about their roots, and about creative ways to remember them.

- **A willingness to think about words as you read and speak.** Think about their roots, their origins, their synonyms, their antonyms, and their cognates (words that share a common root). Even when you are not *specifically* practicing your vocabulary, you can reinforce your new vocabulary by looking at everyday words in new ways.

Analyze: Break words apart

Analyzing means **breaking a problem into its parts.** Many words can be broken apart into **roots** and **affixes.** If you can recognize the parts of a new word, you can make good guesses about its meaning, part of speech, and usage. Consider the word *magnanimity.* This word has three parts: *magna-anima-ity,* which can help you to determine its meaning, part of speech, and usage. Its meaning derives from the roots *magna,* which means *great,* and *anima,* which means *spirit.* We can determine its part of speech from its suffix, *ity,* which is a *noun* suffix. We also can determine its usage, because *ity* indicates a *quality.* Thus, a good guess is that *magnanimity* is *the quality of having a great spirit.*

> **Learning word roots and affixes is an important part of building an impressive vocabulary.** But again, mere memorization is not enough: you must practice by analyzing the roots of the words you encounter every day. As you study the Vocabulary Lessons that follow, pay close attention to the roots and affixes that are indicated after many of the words, and think about the family of words that share each root or affix.

Find patterns: Learn how words relate in sentences, forms, and cognates

A pattern is a rule that relates the parts of a problem or sequence. There are many patterns that relate words to each other. One obvious pattern of words is a sentence or a phrase, in which the context gives you clues about the meanings of the individual words. Less obvious patterns of words are *form patterns* and *cognate patterns*. Let's use *magnanimity* as an example again. It can be part of a pattern of words in a **sentence** like

> *The college is filled with examples of the magnanimity of its early founders.*

Here, the sentence gives you important clues about the meaning of the word *magnanimity*: it is something that college founders can be considered to have, it is something whose effects can be seen in future generations, etc.

It can also be part of a **pattern of word-forms** that derive from the same basic word:

> *magnanimous* (generous), *ultramagnanimous* (super-generous), *pseudomagnanimity* (fake generosity)

It can also be part of a **cognate pattern** of words that derive from a common root:

> *pusillanimous* (cowardly), *equanimity* (even temper), *unanimous* (of one mind)

> The more we recognize how a word relates to others through **usage rules, word-form rules,** and **cognate rules,** the better we understand the word.

Simplify: Make word groups

Your brain doesn't store vocabulary words in the same way that a computer hard drive stores information, by making exact copies of "inputs." Your mind "processes" information rather than just recording it. To learn words efficiently, don't memorize merely individual words, but **related groups of words.** You can group words together as **cognates, related forms,** or **words with similar or opposite meanings.**

> The Vocabulary Lessons that follow allow you to group words in many ways: into **theme groups** (like "words that relate to talking"), into **synonym groups,** into **antonym pairs,** and into **cognate groups** (words with a common root). When you think of words in groups, learning them is easier.

Connect to knowledge: Connect new vocabulary to your own experiences

You don't really know a word until you are deeply familiar with the concept it represents. Don't treat word meanings as isolated facts to memorize. Rather, when you discover the meaning of a new word, think about how you could use that word right now. For instance, to learn the word *magnanimous*, you should ask: what people in my life are *magnanimous?* Who is the most *magnanimous* character I've read about in literature or seen in a movie? Do I want to be more *magnanimous*, and if so, what kinds of things would I do to become more *magnanimous?* The more you think about these questions, the more you build your understanding of *magnanimity*.

> You learn words by communicating about the concepts that the words represent. Since communication is a very personal activity, learning new vocabulary should be a personal thing, too. Think about how the concept behind a new word applies to your life and the people around you.

Find alternatives I: Use College Hill's ALIVE System for tough words

When you are trying to learn an obscure word, like *polemic*, College Hill's ALIVE visual mnemonic system is a great tool. Visualization is perhaps the most effective mnemonic strategy for learning difficult information quickly. Here's how it works:

1. Break down the sounds of the word, and turn them into a picture. For example, break down *polemic* into *pole* and *lemon*, and imagine a lemon on the end of a pole. (You might break it down differently. That's okay!)
2. Imagine a picture for the meaning of the word. *Polemic* means an unpopular or controversial intellectual position or argument, so you might imagine someone with a crazy philosophy—a hippie, perhaps—arguing with a senator at a debate. Try to picture someone you actually know, if possible. Get a vivid picture in your mind.
3. Put the two pictures together into one: see the hippie hitting the senator with a pole with a lemon on the end. The crazier the picture, the better!
4. Make your image come ALIVE. As you imagine your picture, check that it is

   Active: Make the picture **move**, like a wacky animated cartoon.

   Linking: Be sure that one picture links **both** images: the image for the sound and the image for the meaning.

Illogical: Don't try to make a "sensible" picture. Instead, make it **unique** and **bizarre.**

Vivid: See the picture in 3-D, in vivid color, and in **rich detail.** Work at painting a picture in your mind.

Exaggerated: The image that represents the meaning of the word should "pop out" of your picture. Make that part bigger than the rest, even if it makes the picture crazier.

Find alternatives II: Consider secondary meanings of words

Many words have more than one meaning. In *Webster's Collegiate,* for instance, the word *jack* has twenty-three meanings! Don't always assume you understand a particular usage of a word just because you happen to know *one* meaning of the word. Pay careful attention to how words are used, and realize that any word might mean something different than you assume!

The SAT I frequently tests your understanding of "secondary" meanings of words, particularly in "word-in-context" questions on the Critical Reading section, in which they ask things like, *In context, the word "apprehension" most nearly means.* . . . In these questions, the word has many possible meanings, and you must use the clues in the passage to determine which one is being used.

Think logically: Practice drawing inferences about meaning from sentences

Imagine hearing some new words in a sentence like

Heather said that Newton's Laws are pedestrian and obvious, but I find them inscrutable.

Perhaps you don't know what *pedestrian* and *inscrutable* mean, but the logical structure of the sentence allows you to make some educated guesses. For instance, since Heather said that Newton's Laws are *obvious,* she finds them easy to understand. Since she also finds them *pedestrian,* then *pedestrian* cannot mean *hard to understand.* Furthermore, the word *but* signals a contrast between statements, so it is likely that *inscrutable* does mean something like *hard to understand.* Also, *pedestrian* and *in-scrutable* must both be adjectives that can describe ideas.

This kind of logical work helps us to grasp the meanings of words when we hear or read them. To understand the function of a gear in a machine, we have to see and tinker with its connections to other parts of the machine, guided by the laws of physics. Likewise, to understand a word, we need to see and tinker with its connections to other parts of a sentence, guided by the laws of logic.

When you come across a new word in your reading, write it down in a notebook, and try to make a logical guess about its meaning. Then look it up to see if you're right.

Check: Test yourself continually as you speak and write

Education is what changes the way you think. Developing a good vocabulary means thinking carefully about your words as you use them. If you are truly to improve your verbal skills, *to educate yourself in language,* then you must practice by continually thinking about words in the ways we've discussed.

Check your understanding of the words you are learning by using them carefully as often as you can, and checking the way other people use the words. Make this practice more than just "test prep." Change the way you look at words. See them analytically, see their patterns, learn their histories, consider alternatives, and see how they are used. As you gain more control over your vocabulary this way, you will become a more articulate, persuasive, and confident speaker and writer.

The College Hill Word Study System

Building vocabulary requires good practice. The College Hill Word Study System allows you to build your vocabulary through mindful, creative practice.

Each week, carefully study three to seven of the Vocabulary Lessons in this chapter, and from those words, make 30–40 flashcards for those words you need to study in depth. Your flashcards should look something like this one:

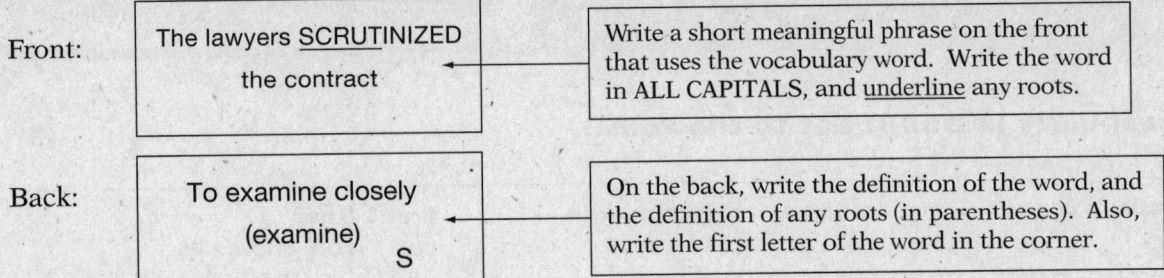

Front: The lawyers SCRUTINIZED the contract ← Write a short meaningful phrase on the front that uses the vocabulary word. Write the word in ALL CAPITALS, and underline any roots.

Back: To examine closely (examine) S ← On the back, write the definition of the word, and the definition of any roots (in parentheses). Also, write the first letter of the word in the corner.

After you've made a card for a word in the lesson, **check off that word from the list.**

You may also make cards of words you find on the lessons and worksheets in this book, or your practice SAT Is. When you do this, you should have a good collegiate dictionary, like *Webster's Collegiate*, to look up the words and their roots. In a dictionary, the roots of a word are often found in the etymology—the abbreviated history of the word—which is usually found in brackets just before the definition. In the vocabulary lessons that follow, the roots are given, when appropriate, in parentheses *after* the definition.

Study your cards **daily** for at least 10 minutes. Schedule this time with the rest of your homework. Review with a friend or relative whenever possible, using the following study techniques:

Study Technique 1: Have your friend read the word, and you create a **new and meaningful sentence** with it.

Study Technique 2: Have your friend read the word, and you give its **roots** and, for each root, **give as many other words as you can that share the root.**

Study Technique 3: Have your friend read the definition and the first letter, and you give the **word.**

Study Technique 4: **Discuss** appropriate uses of the word with your friend, and **teach** your friend how to apply the word in his or her own life.

Study Technique 5: **Teach** your friend any clever **mnemonics** you have created for your words using ALIVE.

Study Technique 6: Have your friend read the sentence, and you give the **definition.**

Study Technique 7: **Post** a bunch of flashcards around your room where you'll see them every day! Think of creatively appropriate places to post them, like *narcissist* on the mirror, *lethargic* on the bed, and so on.

After you finish a Vocabulary Unit (which consists of seven lessons), **complete the Exercise Sets** at the end of each Unit, and check your work with the answer key. These provide a great way to review and reinforce your word knowledge.

When you are reading, for school or for pleasure, **write down any new vocabulary words** in a small notebook, and keep your dictionary handy. Guess the meanings of new words from their context, then check your guesses with the dictionary. **If it is a good SAT word, make a flashcard for it.** Also, read at a desk rather than on a couch or bed; your brain works better when you are upright than when you are lying down.

Vocabulary Unit I

Vocabulary Lesson 1: Get to the Point!

Today's roots:	co-, con-	together, with	brev	brief
	cis	cut	cur	run, course

concise (adj)   brief and to the point (*con-* altogether + *cis* cut)

Ricky, try to be a bit more **concise** in this paper; the assignment was for a three-page paper; yours was 106.
Synonyms: *succinct, terse*   Antonyms: *prolix, discursive, protracted, circumlocutory, verbose*

laconic (adj)   disposed to using few words (from Latin term for Spartans, who spoke little)

I've known Lucy for ten years, but she's so **laconic** that I hardly know anything about her past.
Synonyms: *taciturn, reticent*   Antonyms: *garrulous, loquacious*

succinct (adj)   spoken or written in a clear and precise manner

Because commercial time during the Super Bowl runs over $3 million per minute, it's good to be **succinct**.
Synonyms: *terse, concise*   Antonyms: *prolix, discursive, protracted, circumlocutory, verbose*

brusque (adj)   rudely abrupt

My girlfriend tends to be **brusque** when she's mad; she just tells me to "talk to the hand."
Synonyms: *curt, abrupt, petulant*

abridge (v)   to shorten a written text

The dictionary was 1,400 pages long before it was **abridged** by the publishers to 850 pages.
Synonym: *abbreviate*   Antonyms: *augment, amplify, protract*

brevity (n)   quality of succinct expression (*brev-* brief + *-ity* quality of)

Speeches at the Academy Awards are not known for their **brevity**; they often go on long past their allotted time.
Synonyms: *conciseness, pithiness, succinctness, laconism*

conspire (v)   to plan together secretly to commit an illegal act (*con-* together + *-spire* breathe)
Synonyms: *collude, collaborate*

concur (v)   to agree (*con-* together + *-cur* run)   Synonyms: *accord, harmonize, cohere*

concord (n)   a state of harmony (*con-* together + *-cord* heart)   Synonyms: *unanimity, consensus*

congenital (adj)   existing at birth (*con-* together + *gen* born)   Synonyms: *innate, inborn*

schism (n)   a division into political or religious factions (*cis* cut)   Synonyms: *faction, rift, divergence*

incisive (adj)   having or indicating keen insight (*in-* in + *cis* cut)   Synonyms: *acute, keen, astute, canny, perspicacious, judicious, shrewd*

Vocabulary Lesson 2: Think Before You Judge

Today's roots:	jud	judge	leg	law
	jur	oath, law	scrut	to examine

judicious (adj)   showing sound judgment; prudent (*jud*- judge + *-ious* full of)

After much thought, I decided that the most **judicious** thing to do was to avoid the swamp full of alligators.
Synonyms: *prudent, sensible, circumspect, sagacious*   Antonyms: *improvident, rash*

adjudicate (v)   to hear and judge a case (*jud* judge + *-ate* to do)

Sometimes when my two children fight, I feel like I'm **adjudicating** a capital crime rather than settling a quarrel.

astute (adj)   shrewd; keen

The young Sherlock Holmes was quite the **astute** investigator; he always unraveled even the toughest mystery.
Synonyms: *sagacious, shrewd, incisive, canny, perspicacious*   Antonyms: *vacuous, vapid, obtuse*

scrutinize (v)   to examine carefully (*scruta* examine + *-ize* to do)

Before buying an apple, **scrutinize** it to be sure that it has no bruises.
Synonyms: *analyze, peruse*

perjure (v)   to lie under oath (*per*- through + *jur* oath)

The mobster told blatant lies while on the stand, **perjuring** himself to keep his partners out of jail.
Synonym: *prevaricate*

prudent (adj)   using good judgment (*prudentia* knowledge)

It would not be **prudent** to sneak out of your room again tonight; your parents will ground you if they catch you!
Synonyms: *judicious, sensible*   Antonyms: *improvident, rash*

jurisprudence (n)   the science or philosophy of law (*jur*- law + *prudentia* knowledge)

jurisdiction (n)   the sphere of authority or control (*jur*- law + *dictio* declaration)   Synonym: *domain*

adjure (v)   to command solemnly, as under oath (*ad*- to + *jur* oath)   Synonyms: *enjoin, entreat, beseech*

adjudge (v)   to determine based upon law (*ad*- to + *jud* judge)   Synonym: *adjudicate*

acumen (n)   keenness of judgment (*acus* sharp)   Synonyms: *discernment, perspicacity, shrewdness*

inscrutable (adj)   beyond comprehension or examination (*in*- not + *scruta* examine)
Synonyms: *enigmatic, recondite, abstruse*

allegation (n)   a formal accusation (*ad*- to + *legare* dispute)   Synonyms: *contention, assertion, charge*

Vocabulary Lesson 3: Let's Talk About It   Ap 5

Today's roots:	*locu, loqu* talk	*circum* around
	verb word	*e-, ex-* out

❑ *eloquent* (adj)   well spoken (*e-* out + *loqu* talk)

She is an **eloquent** spokeswoman for animal rights; she conveys her ideas with great ease and fluidity.
Synonyms: *articulate, fluent*   Antonym: *inarticulate*

❑ *loquacious* (adj)   very talkative (*loqu-* talk + *-ious* full of)

That guy never stops talking; now I understand why they call him "**Loquacious** Larry"!
Synonyms: *garrulous, voluble*   Antonyms: *laconic, taciturn, reticent*

❑ *circumlocution* (n)   evasive speech; talking around the subject (*circum-* around + *loqu* talk)

The politician had perfected the art of **circumlocution**; he knew exactly how to avoid answering direct questions.
Synonym: *evasion*

❑ *colloquial* (adj)   conversational; using everyday language (*co-* together + *loqu* talk)

I like Professor Thompson because she is so **colloquial**; yesterday she said my thesis idea was "really cool."

❑ *grandiloquent* (adj)   speaking in a pompous manner (*grand-* great + *loqu* talk + *-ent* adjective)

His speech was pompous and **grandiloquent**; it seemed he was just trying to use as many big words as possible.
Synonyms: *pontifical, portentous*

❑ *elocution* (n)   expressive delivery of public speech (*e-* out + *loqu* talk + *-tion* noun)

James is adept at **elocution**; his expressions and mannerisms add a new level of meaning to his words.

❑ *garrulous* (adj)   talkative <a **garrulous** gaggle of girls>   Synonyms: *loquacious, voluble*

❑ *pontificate* (v)   to speak pompously (*pontifex* high priest)   Synonyms: *declaim, sermonize, dogmatize*

❑ *verbose* (adj)   wordy (*verb-* word + *-ose* full of)   Synonyms: *prolix, discursive, digressive*

❑ *verbatim* (adv)   word for word (*verb-* word)   <I followed the recipe **verbatim**.>

❑ *soliloquy* (n)   a speech to one's self (*solo* alone + *loqu* talk)   <Hamlet's **soliloquy** begins "*To be or
                                                                    not to be. . . .*">

❑ *anecdote* (n)   a short and often humorous story
Don't confuse with *antidote* (n), a remedy.

❑ *discursive* (adj)   straying from the topic (*dis-* away + *curs* course)   Synonyms: *digressive, desultory*

Vocabulary Lesson 4: "Good, Thanks"

Ae 6

Today's roots:	ben, bene, bon good	eu good
	grat to please, thank	vole wish

❑ **benefactor** (n) one who supports or helps another (*bene-* good + *fact* to make)

Mr. King is the **benefactor** who generously donated the money for the new children's wing in the hospital.
Synonyms: *philanthropist, patron*   Antonyms: *malefactor, nemesis, antagonist, adversary*

❑ **benign** (adj) harmless (*bene* good)

She was relieved to find out that her tumor was **benign.**
Synonym: *innocuous*   Antonyms: *malignant, virulent*

❑ **benevolent** (adj) kind; considerate (*bene-* good + *vole* wish)

The **benevolent** Cub Scout did his good deed for the day when he helped a motorist change a tire.
Synonyms: *gracious, altruistic, magnanimous*   Antonyms: *malevolent, malicious, inimical, pernicious*

❑ **benediction** (n) an expression of good wishes (*bene-* good + *dictus* declaration)

At the reception, the father of the bride offered a **benediction,** wishing the couple never-ending love and happiness.
Synonyms: *blessing, sanction*   Antonyms: *curse, malediction, execration*

❑ **euphemism** (n) the substitution of an inoffensive term for an offensive one (*eu-* good + *pheme* speech)

A good journalist avoids the **euphemisms** of war, like "ordnance" for bombs and "collateral damage" for casualties.

❑ **eulogy** (n) a praising tribute (*eu-* good + *logia* discourse)

His touching **eulogy** for his fallen friend left all the mourners weeping.
Synonyms: *encomium, laudation, extolment, paean*   Antonyms: *denunciation, execration, censure*

❑ **ingratiate** (v) to put oneself in good favor with another (*in-* in + *grat* to please)

When starting at a new school, Mary sought to **ingratiate** herself with her classmates by being excessively nice.
Synonyms: *flatter, wheedle, toady, cajole*

❑ **beneficiary** (n) one who receives benefits (*bene-* good + *fic* to make)   Synonyms: *heir, recipient, legatee*

❑ **gratuity** (n) a small payment in gratitude (*grat-* thank)
Don't confuse with **gratuitous** (adj) unnecessary

❑ **gratis** (adj) free of charge (*grat-* thank)   <He let me borrow his car **gratis.**>

❑ **gratify** (v) to please (*grat-* please)   Synonyms: *appease, mollify, indulge*

❑ **euphoria** (n) a feeling of extreme happiness (*eu-* good)   Synonyms: *elation, rapture, jubilation, ecstasy*

❑ **euphonious** (n) sweet sounding (*eu-* good + *phon* sound)   Synonyms: *mellifluous, dulcet, lyrical*

Vocabulary Lesson 5: Changes

Ap 6

| Today's roots: | *rupt* break | *morph* form, shape |
| | *mut* change | *meta* change, beyond |

❑ **immutable** (adj)   unchangeable (*im-* not + *mut* change)

Emily is an immutable vegetarian. No matter how hard we try, we cannot get her to eat meat.
Synonyms: *permanent, inveterate*   Antonyms: *mutable, protean, vacillating, mercurial*

❑ **metamorphosis** (n)   a transformation (*meta-* change + *morph* form)

The old house underwent a **metamorphosis** from a rundown shack into a beautiful cottage.
Synonyms: *transformation, mutation, transmogrification*

❑ **rupture** (v)   to break open (*rupt-* break)

When the vat of smelly liquid **ruptured,** we picked up our feet to avoid getting the stuff on our shoes.
Synonyms: *burst, fissure, cleave*

❑ **transmute** (v)   to transform (*trans-* across + *mut* change)

Harry Potter was able to transmute a feather into a frog using a spell he learned in incantations class.
Synonyms: *metamorphose, alter, transmogrify*

❑ **amorphous** (adj)   lacking shape, changeable in form (*a-* without + *morph* shape)

Rather than marching in precise formation, the battalion broke down into an **amorphous** mass of charging soldiers.
Synonyms: *shapeless, nebulous, vague, nondescript*   Antonyms: *crystalline*

❑ **mercurial** (adj)   erratic, subject to wild changes in character (from the speedy god Mercury)

Molly is the most **mercurial** person in the office; we can never tell if she'll be the evil Molly or the sympathetic Molly.
Synonyms: *fickle, capricious, vacillating*   Antonyms: *immutable, stable*

❑ **protean** (adj)   capable of assuming different forms (from the form-changing sea god Proteus)

He has changed his position on issues so many times that he is considered the most **protean** member of Congress.
Synonyms: *polymorphous, labile*   Antonyms: *immutable, stable*

❑ **mutate** (v)   to change form (*mut-* change)   Synonyms: *transform, transmogrify*

❑ **fickle** (adj)   likely to change opinion unpredictably   Synonyms: *capricious, vacillating, mercurial*

❑ **fluctuate** (v)   to vary irregularly (*flux* flow)   Synonyms: *vacillate, waver*

❑ **vacillate** (v)   to change one's mind repeatedly   Synonyms: *fluctuate, waver*

❑ **revamp** (v)   to revise; to renovate (*re-* again)   Synonyms: *refurbish, renovate*

❑ **amend** (v)   to improve, to remove the faults of   Synonyms: *rectify, redress, ameliorate, mitigate*

Vocabulary Lesson 6: One Boring World

Ap 6

| Today's roots: | *vac* empty | *uni* one |
| | *mund* world | *anima* spirit, mind |

❑ **hackneyed** (adj)   overused, trite

This film was a **hackneyed** remake with a storyline that has been done a hundred times.
Synonyms: *trite, prosaic, banal*   Antonyms: *original, novel*

❑ **mundane** (adj)   ordinary, typical (*mund-* world)

Having worked for years behind a desk, she wanted to leave the **mundane** world behind for exotic adventures.
Synonyms: *routine, workaday, banal*   Antonyms: *singular, extraordinary, sublime*

❑ **vacuous** (adj)   lacking substance (*vac-* empty)

His latest book is widely criticized as **vacuous** and unintelligent.
Synonyms: *inane, asinine, fatuous*   Antonyms: *profound, thoughtful, deep*

❑ **prosaic** (adj)   unimaginative, ordinary

I don't understand why his oration was selected as the best; it was so **prosaic** that I nearly fell asleep.
Synonyms: *mundane, pedestrian*   Antonyms: *innovative, quixotic, whimsical*

❑ **insipid** (adj)   uninteresting, dull, without flavor (*in-* not + *sapere* taste)

Christine is the life of the party, but Tom is as **insipid** as they come; hardly anyone wants to talk with him.
Synonyms: *bland, nondescript, vapid*   Antonyms: *engaging, enchanting, piquant*

❑ **banal** (adj)   ordinary, trivial

That show used to be my favorite, but its story lines became so **banal** that I could no longer stand it.
Synonyms: *hackneyed, trite*   Antonyms: *extraordinary, singular, sublime*

❑ **pedestrian** (adj)   commonplace, ordinary   Synonyms: *prosaic, banal, vapid*

❑ **dormant** (adj)   inactive, sleeping (*dormire* sleep)   Synonyms: *inert, fallow*

❑ **unanimous** (adj)   in full agreement (*un-* one + *anima* mind)   Synonyms: *concordant, concerted*

❑ **uniform** (adj)   unvarying, always the same (*un-* one + *forma* form)   Synonyms: *homogeneous*

❑ **equanimity** (n)   the quality of being even-tempered (*equa-* same + *anima* mind)
Synonyms: *composure, imperturbability, aplomb*

❑ **magnanimous** (adj)   noble of heart, generous, forgiving (*magna-* great + *anima* mind)
Synonyms: *philanthropic, altruistic, merciful*

Vocabulary Lesson 7: The Humours

Today's roots:	*sanguis*	blood	*melan*	black
	choler	bile	*anima*	spirit, mind

In medieval Europe, it was widely believed that one's health and disposition were largely determined by the balance of four bodily liquids called "humours": blood (*sang*), phlegm, black bile (*melancholer*), and yellow bile (*choler*).

❏ **sanguine** (adj)   cheerfully optimistic (*sanguis* blood)

After acing his final, David was **sanguine** about his prospects for a good overall course grade.
Synonyms: *blithe, buoyant*   Antonyms: *morose, forlorn, melancholy, sullen*

❏ **phlegmatic** (adj)   sluggish

His prolonged illness turned Julio from a spry, happy bon vivant into a morose and **phlegmatic** bore.
Synonyms: *languorous, lethargic, somnolent, torpid*   Antonyms: *vigorous, vibrant, hale, spry*

❏ **melancholy** (adj)   sad, depressed (*melan-* black + *choler* bile)

She has been so **melancholy** ever since she broke up with her boyfriend; sometimes she stays in her room all day.
Synonyms: *morose, despondent, disconsolate, sullen*   Antonyms: *blithe, buoyant, sanguine*

❏ **choleric** (adj)   easily angered (*choler-* bile + *-ic* characterized by)

Gena's mom is really nice but her dad is **choleric;** he freaks out about the smallest things.
Synonyms: *irascible, fractious, bilious, splenetic*

❏ **recalcitrant** (adj)   stubbornly resistant to authority (*re-* back + *calcitrare* kick)

Christine is a talented volleyball player, but she's so **recalcitrant** that our coach often keeps her on the bench.
Synonyms: *refractory, intractable*   Antonyms: *compliant, docile, tractable, obsequious, obeisant*

❏ **lethargic** (adj)   sluggish; dully apathetic

After three weeks of factoring polynomials, my entire class became **lethargic;** we were bored to death!
Synonyms: *languorous, phlegmatic, torpid*   Antonyms: *vigorous, vibrant, hale, spry*

❏ **splenetic** (adj)   irritable, easily angered (*splen-* spleen)   Synonyms: *bilious, choleric*

❏ **querulous** (adj)   disposed to complaining   Synonyms: *peevish, captious, carping, caviling*

❏ **dolorous** (adj)   marked by or expressive of sorrow or pain (*dolor-* pain)   Synonyms: *lugubrious, doleful*

❏ **animosity** (adj)   hostility, ill-will (*animosus* bold)   Synonyms: *malevolence, antagonism, invidiousness*

❏ **pusillanimous** (adj)   cowardly (*pusillus* weak + *anima* spirit)   Synonyms: *timorous, craven, dastardly*

❏ **lassitude** (n)   feeling of weakness or listlessness   Synonyms: *lethargy, languor, torpor, stupor*

Vocabulary Unit I Exercise Set I

Ap 7

> Time—8 minutes
> For each questions, select the best answer among the choices given. Note any vocabulary words to review on the Hit List below.

1. Julia is amazingly ------ for a five-year-old: she adeptly persuaded her reluctant parents to let her stay up to watch another thirty minutes of television.
   (A) concise
   (B) astute
   (C) verbose
   (D) recalcitrant
   (E) capricious

2. He recited the President's speech back to me ------ ; it was almost as if he had written it himself.
   (A) loquaciously
   (B) insipidly
   (C) verbatim
   (D) curtly
   (E) diffidently

3. Those not used to Larry's ------ speaking style found him to be ------ and did not like him at first.
   (A) monosyllabic . . incisive
   (B) surly . . congenial
   (C) laconic . . brusque
   (D) circumlocutory . . direct
   (E) garrulous . . phlegmatic

4. During his first year at boarding school, Ricardo underwent ------ from a shy and reserved young boy to a garrulous and extroverted teenager.
   (A) a schism
   (B) an adjudication
   (C) a benediction
   (D) a soliloquy
   (E) a metamorphosis

5. Janice is so ------ that she ------ over even the simplest decision.
   (A) shrewd . . perjures
   (B) magnanimous . . denigrates
   (C) pusillanimous . . admonishes
   (D) surreptitious . . purges
   (E) fickle . . vacillates

6. Despite having always been ------ at heart, Paula found herself ------ about the near future at work.
   (A) pessimistic . . sanguine
   (B) lethargic . . placid
   (C) morose . . querulous
   (D) prudent . . verbose
   (E) succinct . . terse

7. Kemal was the ------ of his father's generosity while at the supermarket, because he got to eat an ice cream treat on the way home.
   (A) beneficiary
   (B) benefactor
   (C) benediction
   (D) patron
   (E) sanction

8. Because we are short on time, ------ would be appreciated; we need to leave in five minutes to catch the last bus of the night.
   (A) circumlocution
   (B) allegation
   (C) pontification
   (D) brevity
   (E) lassitude

9. The audience found the presentation to be ------ and vacuous; it was unimaginative and lacking substance.
   (A) dormant
   (B) unanimous
   (C) amorphous
   (D) dolorous
   (E) prosaic

10. The play was a blend of the mirthful and the ------; many scenes were ------, while others made me cry like a baby.
    (A) melancholy . . hilarious
    (B) reprehensible . . wistful
    (C) somber . . bitter
    (D) humorous . . jocular
    (E) despicable . . whimsical

HIT LIST

Ap 7

Vocabulary Unit I Exercise Set II

Write the meaning next to each root, then write as many words as you can that contain the root.

1. ANIMA _____

6. CIRCUM _____

11. JUD_____

2. VAC _____

7. EX-_____

12. CIS_____

3. BENE _____

8. LEG_____

13. CO-_____

4. EU _____

9. JUR_____

14. VOL_____

5. LOQU _____

10. VERB_____

15. GRAT_____

Vocabulary Unit I Exercise Set III

1. Should a talk show host be *laconic*?   Y N
2. Is wearing a seat belt *prudent*?   Y N
3. Should a politician be *perspicacious*?   Y N
4. Is something *innocuous* harmful?   Y N
5. Is a *beneficiary* one who gives?   Y N

Write the word with the given meaning

6. to change form   m_____
7. lacking substance   v_____
8. even-temperedness   e_____
9. commonplace   p_____
10. overused   h_____
11. sluggish   p_____
12. resistant to authority   r_____
13. disposed to complain   q_____
14. rudely abrupt   b_____
15. talkative   g_____
16. a political split   s_____
17. keenly perceptive   p_____
18. with sound judgment   j_____
19. to examine carefully   s_____
20. keenness of judgment   a_____
21. evasive speech   c_____
22. short humorous story   a_____
23. change one's mind often   v_____
24. able to change form   p_____
25. feeling of weakness   l_____

Write the correct form of the italicized word

26. the state of feeling *lethargic*

_____

27. the quality of being *pusillanimous*

_____

28. having the quality of a *euphemism*

_____

29. the act of *adjudicating*

_____

30. the act of *perjuring*

_____

Write the word with the given root

31. beyond comprehension (*scrut*)

_____

32. existing at birth (*con*)

_____

33. kind-hearted (*anim*)

_____

34. to command solemnly (*jur*)

_____

35. speaking in a pompous manner (*loqu*)

_____

36. a praising tribute (*eu*)

_____

37. harmless (*ben*)

_____

38. inoffensive term substituted for an offensive one (*eu*)

_____

39. to please (*grat*)

_____

40. expressive delivery of public speech (*loqu*)

_____

41. sphere of legal authority (*jur*)

_____

Unit I Exercise Set I Answer Key

1. (B) The colon (:) introduces an explanation. *Adeptly* means *with great skill*. A five-year-old would have to be pretty *sharp* to persuade reluctant parents.
   concise = brief and to the point
   astute = shrewd, keen
   verbose = wordy
   recalcitrant = stubborn
   capricious = whimsical

2. (C) The information after the semi-colon (;) describes the word in the blank. If he reads it as if he had written it himself, it implies that he knows it very well, and perhaps can read it word for word.
   loquaciously = in a talkative manner
   insipidly = in a painfully dull way
   verbatim = word for word
   curtly = in an abrupt manner, rudely
   diffidently = timidly, lacking confidence

3. (C) They did not like him at first, so the second blank is a negative word. The first blank should describe a speaking style that would cause someone to think that he is described by the second word.
   monosyllabic = one syllable; *incisive* = cogent
   surly = rude; *congenial* = friendly
   laconic = terse; *brusque* = rude, unfriendly
   circumlocutory = talkative
   garrulous = talkative; *phlegmatic* = sluggish

4. (E) Ricardo clearly changed from a shy person to a talkative extrovert. The word that fits the blank should mean *change*.
   schism = rift, large gap
   adjudication = judgment
   benediction = blessing
   soliloquy = speech to one's self
   metamorphosis = major change in form

5. (E) The second word is a verb that should complement the first word. Only E presents a pair that makes sense. Fickle people *do* tend to vacillate.
   shrewd = clever; *perjure* = to lie under oath
   magnanimous = generous; *denigrate* = to slander
   pusillanimous = cowardly; *admonish* = to scold
   surreptitious = sneaky; *purge* = to clear away
   fickle = erratic; *vacillate* = to go back and forth

6. (A) *Despite* indicates a contrast. So look for two words that are nearly opposite.
   pessimistic = negative; *sanguine* = optimistic
   lethargic = sluggish; *placid* = calm
   morose = sullen, gloomy; *querulous* = complaining
   prudent = wise, provident; *verbose* = wordy
   succinct = concise, to the point; *terse* = concise

7. (A) The recipient of generosity is a *beneficiary*.
   beneficiary = one who receives benefits
   benefactor = one who supports or helps another
   benediction = a blessing
   patron = a customer; someone who protects
   sanction = approval, permission

8. (D) A person short on time would likely appreciate something that is quick, which makes *brevity* a good choice.
   circumlocution = speaking in circles
   allegation = accusation
   pontification = speaking in a pompous manner
   brevity = briefness
   lassitude = fatigue, torpor

9. (E) The presentation was *vacuous*, which means lacking substance. This implies that the two clauses in the sentence are parallel, so the missing word must be similar to *unimaginative*.
   dormant = inactive
   unanimous = everyone agrees
   amorphous = lacking shape
   dolorous = causing pain or sorrow
   prosaic = dull, unimaginative

10. (A) Use the parallelism in the sentence. The two adjectives in the first clause are parallel to the two ideas in the second clause. The first word describes something that makes one cry, and the second word describes *mirthful* scenes. Two simple words to complete the sentence would be *depressing* and *funny*.
    melancholy = sadness; *hilarious* = funny
    reprehensible = blameworthy; *wistful* = sad
    somber = gloomy; *bitter* = unhappy
    humorous = funny; *jocular* = joking
    despicable = mean; *whimsical* = impulsive

Unit I Exercise Sets II and III Answer Key

Exercise Set II

1. ANIMA: spirit, life, mind
   unanimous, magnanimous, animosity, animation, animal, inanimate

2. VAC: empty
   vacate, evacuate, vacuum, vacuous, vacation, vacant

3. BENE: good
   benevolent, beneficiary, bonus, bona fide, benediction

4. EU: good
   euphemism, eulogy, euphony, euphoria, eugenics

5. LOQU: talk
   loquacious, eloquent, ventriloquist, elocution, circumlocution

6. CIRCUM: around
   circumference, circumnavigate, circumlocute, circuit, circuitous

7. EX-, E-: out
   emit, extract, exclaim, exit, egregious, enormous

8. LEG: law
   allege, legal, legitimate, legislate

9. JUR: oath, law
   jurisdiction, abjure, adjure, jury, jurisprudence

10. VERB: word
    verbatim, verbose, verbal, verbalize, proverb

11. JUD: judge
    adjudicate, judicious, adjudge, judiciary

12. CIS: cut
    incisive, scissors, concise, schism, decide, suicide

13. CO-: together, with
    cooperate, connect, correlate, committee, collect, conspire

14. VOL: wish
    voluntary, benevolent, malevolent, volition

15. GRAT: please, thank
    gratify, ingratiate, ingrate, congratulate, gratuity

Exercise Set III

1. N
2. Y
3. Y
4. N
5. N
6. mutate
7. vacuous
8. equanimity
9. pedestrian
10. hackneyed
11. phlegmatic
12. recalcitrant
13. querulous
14. brusque
15. garrulous
16. schism
17. perspicacious
18. judicious
19. scrutinize
20. acumen
21. circumlocution
22. anecdote
23. vacillate
24. protean
25. lassitude
26. lethargy
27. pusillanimity
28. euphemistic
29. adjudication
30. perjury
31. inscrutable
32. congenital
33. magnanimous
34. adjure
35. grandiloquent
36. eulogy
37. benign
38. euphemism
39. gratify
40. elocution
41. jurisdiction

AP 8

Vocabulary Unit 2

Vocabulary Lesson 8: Sneaky Sneaky

Today's roots:	*duplit* twofold	*pseudo* fake
	nym name	*rapere* to seize

❑ **spurious** (adj)   fake; counterfeit

The head of the FBI cursed the **spurious** lead that incorrectly led them to an abandoned warehouse.
Synonyms: *fictitious, dubious, fabricated*   Antonyms: *authentic, substantiated*

❑ **guile** (n)   trickery; deceit

The Big Bad Wolf deceived Little Red Riding Hood with **guile** and cunning.
Synonyms: *cleverness, cunning, duplicity*   Antonyms: *candor, straightforwardness*

❑ **beguile** (v)   to deceive with charm

The con artist **beguiled** me out of my money, convincing me to play his game over and over.
Synonyms: *charm, entrance, captivate*   Antonym: *disenchant*

❑ **strategem** (n)   a deceitful scheme (*strategos* army general)

The teenager devised an elaborate **strategem** to escape his parents' curfew.
Synonyms: *ploy, gimmick, ruse, subterfuge*

❑ **surreptitious** (adj)   deceptive; sneaky (*sub*- secretly + *rapere* seize)

The **surreptitious** movements of the lion lured the gazelle into a trap.
Synonyms: *covert, furtive, stealthy*   Antonyms: *honest, trustworthy, overt*

❑ **clandestine** (adj)   secret; hidden

The **clandestine** military facility in the capital city was unknown even to the President of the United States.
Synonyms: *stealthy, surreptitious, covert*   Antonyms: *forthright, straightforward, candid*

❑ **stealth** (n)   sneakiness; ability to avoid detection

The "**stealth** bomber" is so effective because it is undetectable by most radars.
Synonyms: *furtiveness, covertness*   Antonyms: *perceptible, observable*

❑ **duplicity** (n)   deceit; hypocritical deception (*duplit* twofold)   Synonyms: *chicanery, improbity*

❑ **specious** (adj)   false, but plausible (*specere* to look at)   Synonyms: *ostensible, sophistic*

❑ **furtive** (adj)   secretive; sneaky <a **furtive** plan to steal the diamond>   Synonyms: *stealthy, cloaked, guileful*

❑ **pseudonym** (n)   pen name (*pseudo*- fake + *onoma* name)   Synonyms: *alias, anonym*

❑ **fallacious** (adj)   deceptive; false (*fallacia* deceit + *-ious* full of)   Synonyms: *delusory, erroneous*

❑ **rapacious** (adj)   greedy; ravenous (*rapere* seize + *-ious* full of)   Synonyms: *ravenous, covetous*

Ap 8

Vocabulary Lesson 9: Time Is of the Essence

Today's roots:	*trans* across, through	*fluere* to flow
	chronos time	*tempus* time

❑ *transient* (adj) fleeting; short-lived (*transire* to go across)

We never understand the **transient** nature of childhood until we wake up one day and realize we're all grown up.
Synonyms: *ephemeral, evanescent, deciduous, transitory*   Antonyms: *permanent, interminable*

❑ *ephemeral* (adj) short-lived (*hemera* day)

Critics wrote off the band as a fad, their success as an **ephemeral** phenomenon.
Synonyms: *transient, evanescent, fleeting*   Antonyms: *permanent, everlasting, interminable*

❑ *sporadic* (adj) irregular or unpredictable; infrequent (*sporas* scattered)

He has experienced **sporadic** success as an actor, with occasional big roles amid many unmemorable parts.
Synonyms: *intermittent, episodic, mercurial*   Antonyms: *frequent, regular, permanent*

❑ *capricious* (adj) whimsical; impulsive

My English teacher runs her class **capriciously,** flitting from idea to idea with no reason or direction.
Synonyms: *fickle, volatile, mercurial, erratic*

❑ *evanescent* (adj) likely to vanish (*vanescere* to disappear)

The aurora borealis is beautiful but **evanescent,** a curtain of cascading light that can disappear in a heartbeat.
Synonyms: *transient, ephemeral, transitory*   Antonyms: *perpetual, enduring*

❑ *extemporaneous* (adj) done with little or no practice (*ex tempore* of time)

The speech was all the more remarkable because Dr. Sherman gave it **extemporaneously.**
Synonym: *impromptu*

❑ *anachronism* (n) something out of place in time (*ana-* backward + *chronos* time)

Her old-fashioned perspective on motherhood makes her an **anachronism** among her friends.
Synonyms: *archaism, incongruity, asynchronism*

❑ *transitory* (adj) lasting for a short time (*transitus* gone across)   Synonyms: *transient, fleeting*

❑ *expedite* (v) to speed up (*ex-* out + *pedis* foot)   Synonyms: *hasten, quicken, facilitate*

❑ *influx* (n) a flowing in (*in-* in + *fluere* to flow)   <an overwhelming **influx** of refugees>

❑ *superfluous* (adj) beyond what is necessary or sufficient (*super-* over + *fluere* to flow)

❑ *contemporaneous* (adj) existing or occurring at about the same time (*con-* together + *tempore* time)

❑ *interminable* (adj) never ending (*in-* not + *term* end)   Synonyms: *incessant, unremitting*

❑ *protracted* (adj) prolonged; extended in time (*pro-* forward + *tract* pull)   Synonym: *drawn out*

Ap 8

Vocabulary Lesson 10: If You Can't Say Anything Nice . . .

Today's roots:	*dia*	thoroughly, through	*de-*	down
	dictus	declared, word	*pugn*	to fight

❏ **censure** (n)   official condemnation; harsh criticism (*censor* Roman supervisor for morals)

Congress voted to declare **censure** on the representative who took money and gifts from a lobbyist.
Synonyms: *castigation, derision, rebuke*   Antonyms: *laudation, endorsement*

❏ **calumny** (n)   slander; false accusation

Too many tabloids know that **calumny** about celebrities is more profitable than the truth.
Synonyms: *libel, denigration, defamation*   Antonyms: *acclaim, extolment, approbation*

❏ **diatribe** (n)   malicious criticism or abuse (*dia-* through + *tribein* to rub)

A good debate must avoid vicious personal **diatribe,** and focus on a respectful discussion of issues.
Synonyms: *castigation, derision, harangue*   Antonyms: *laudation, extolment, honor*

❏ **caustic** (adj)   corrosive; sarcastic

James immediately regretted making such a **caustic** remark; he could tell his words truly hurt Vanessa.
Synonyms: *abrasive, acrimonious*   Antonyms: *mitigating, conciliatory, mollifying*

❏ **repudiate** (v)   to cast off publicly (*repudium* divorce)

The consumers **repudiated** the shoe company for using sweatshops, and began buying from its competitor.
Synonyms: *disavow, abjure, forswear*   Antonym: *condone*

❏ **derogatory** (adj)   disparaging; belittling (*de-* down, away)

Derogatory remarks are not allowed in class; discussions should criticize ideas, not people.
Synonyms: *pejorative, derisive, disparaging*

❏ **admonish** (v)   to reprimand mildly (*ad-* to + *monere* to warn)

The boy was **admonished** by his mom for spilling his soda on the brand-new rug.
Synonyms: *rebuke, reprove*   Antonyms: *laud, revere, endorse*

❏ **disparage** (v)   to belittle; to demean (*dis-* apart + *parage* rank, peer)   Synonyms: *deprecate, discredit*

❏ **impugn** (v)   to attack as untrue; to refute by argument (*in-* against + *pugn* to fight)

❏ **malediction** (n)   a curse (*mal-* bad + *dictus* declared)   Synonyms: *anathema, execration*

❏ **denigrate** (v)   to attack the character of; to disparage   Synonyms: *slander, decry*

❏ **harangue** (n)   a long, critical, and pompous speech   Synonyms: *diatribe, discourse*

❏ **pejorative** (adj)   tending to make worse (*pejor* worse)   <a **pejorative** comment>
Synonyms: *disparaging*

❏ **slander** (n)   comments that injure another's reputation (*scandalum* scandal)

Vocabulary Lesson 11: Holy Cow

Today's roots:	*sacer* sacred	*venus* respect, love
	sanctus holy	*vereri* respect

❑ **sanctimonious** (adj)   falsely pious or self-righteous (*sanctus* holy)

I prefer ministers who are real people, not **sanctimonious** know-it-all preachers.
Synonyms: *holier-than-thou, self-righteous, unctuous*   Antonyms: *sincere, unaffected, guileless*

❑ **sacrosanct** (adj)   profoundly sacred (*sacer* sacred + *sanctus* holy)

To Hindus, the cow is a **sacrosanct** creature to be treated with the utmost respect.
Synonyms: *inviolable, consecrated, divine, revered*   Antonym: *unholy*

❑ **sanctuary** (n)   a place of refuge; a sacred place (*sanctus* holy)

The Notre Dame cathedral is a **sanctuary** to all; anyone in need of a safe place to rest is welcome.
Synonyms: *shrine, asylum*

❑ **sacrilegious** (adj)   grossly irreverent; disrespectful of something sacred (*sacer* sacred)

To Hindus, to whom cows are sacred, the mass slaughter of cattle is considered **sacrilegious.**
Synonyms: *blasphemous, desecrating, impious*   Antonyms: *reverent, pious*

❑ **revere** (v)   to regard with honor and devotion (*re-* intensive + *vereri* respect)

Every genre of music has its stars, whom fans **revere** like gods.
Synonyms: *venerate, idolize, esteem*   Antonyms: *condemn, loathe*

❑ **pious** (adj)   showing religious reverence

Cotton Mather considered it his **pious** duty to hang anyone in Salem accused of witchcraft.
Synonyms: *devout, reverential*   Antonyms: *irreverent, blasphemous*

❑ **deference** (n)   respect for the wishes of others (*de-* away + *ferre* carry)

It is important to show **deference** to your elders and treat them with respect.
Synonyms: *courtesy, reverence*   Antonyms: *irreverence, impertinence*

❑ **sacrament** (n)   a formal religious act or oath (*sacer* sacred)   Synonyms: *rite, liturgy*

❑ **venerable** (adj)   worthy of respect (*venus* respect)   Synonyms: *revered, honorable*

❑ **venerate** (v)   to regard with reverence or respect (*venus* respect)   Synonyms: *revere, extol*

❑ **consecrate** (v)   to declare to be holy (*sacer* sacred) <**consecrate** a marriage>   Synonyms: *venerate, bless*

❑ **talisman** (n)   an object with magical powers (*telos* result)   Synonyms: *charm, amulet*

❑ **lionize** (v)   to treat as a celebrity   Synonyms: *glorify, exalt, panegyrize, apotheosize, deify*

Vocabulary Lesson 12: Power It Up!   *Ap 9*

Today's roots:	*potens*	strong	*in-, im-*	not
	domit	lord	*efficere*	to effect

❑ *formidable* (adj)   awesome; hard to overcome; dreadful (*formido* fear)

The Yankees are a **formidable** team; we'll be lucky to win a single game against them this year.
Synonyms: *indomitable, redoubtable*   Antonyms: *anemic, ineffectual*

❑ *potent* (adj)   strong and effective (*potens* strong)

Although the drug is clearly the most **potent** treatment for depression, it also has the strongest side effects.
Synonyms: *efficacious, forceful*   Antonyms: *impotent, enervated, feckless*

❑ *bulwark* (n)   a strong defense

The newly constructed dam is in place as a **bulwark** against future flooding.
Synonyms: *bastion, redoubt, rampart*

❑ *indomitable* (adj)   unable to be conquered (*in-* not + *domit* lord)

The **indomitable** castle has been under the control of the Spaniards for 6,000 years, despite repeated attacks.
Synonyms: *impregnable, invincible*

❑ *redoubtable* (adj)   arousing fear; formidable; awesome (*re-* intensive + *douter* to doubt)

The mob boss is a **redoubtable** figure who makes his enemies cower in fear.
Synonyms: *formidable, intimidating*

❑ *robust* (adj)   full of vigor

The **robust** young men were able to run miles at a time through the rugged terrain without breaking a sweat.
Synonyms: *brawny, athletic, potent*   Antonyms: *weak, delicate*

❑ *impervious* (adj)   incapable of being penetrated or affected (*im-* not + *per-* through + *via* road)

Bulletproof vests are almost always **impervious** to bullets.
Synonyms: *impenetrable, impregnable*   Antonyms: *permeable, penetrable*

❑ *efficacious* (adj)   capable of producing a desired effect (*efficere* to effect)   Synonym: *proficient*

❑ *stalwart* (n)   physically or morally strong person; strong supporter   Synonyms: *mainstay, partisan*

❑ *impotent* (adj)   lacking strength or power (*im-* not + *potens* strong)   Synonyms: *enervated, effete*

❑ *predominant* (adj)   most important (*pre-* before + *domit* lord)   Synonyms: *paramount, preeminent*

❑ *impregnable* (adj)   unable to be entered by force (*im-* not + *prehendere* grasp)
   <an **impregnable** fortress>   Synonyms: *impenetrable, invincible, indomitable*

❑ *brawn* (n)   muscular strength   <all **brawn** and no brains>   Synonyms: *robustness, vigor*

❑ *bastion* (n)   stronghold, fortress   <the college is a **bastion** of liberalism>   Synonym: *bulwark*

Vocabulary Lesson 13: Come Together   *Ap. 9*

Today's roots:	co-, com-, con- together	vocare to call
	syn- same, together	legere choose

❑ *coalesce* (v)   to blend or fuse together (*co-* together)

The Beatles' **coalesce** on microscopic particles in the atmosphere.
Raindrops are usually formed when water vapor **coalesces** on microscopic particles in the atmosphere.
Synonyms: *amalgamate, consolidate, fuse*   Antonyms: *disperse, diverge, dissipate*

❑ *anthology* (n)   a collection of works

The Beatles' **Anthology** is one of the best-selling greatest hits albums of all time.
Synonyms: *compilation, compendium, treasury*

❑ *convoke* (v)   to call together (*con-* together + *vocare* call)

The village elders **convoked** the citizens to discuss the sale of the ceremonial land.
Synonyms: *assemble, summon*   Antonyms: *dismiss, disperse*

❑ *synchronize* (v)   to arrange events to occur simultaneously (*syn-* same + *chron* time)

Nothing is harder for a dance teacher than trying to **synchronize** ten eight-year-old ballerinas.
Synonym: *coordinate*

❑ *synthesis* (n)   a fusion; a bringing together (*syn-* together + *tithenai* to put)

The **synthesis** of DNA occurs when many ribonucleic acids are joined together into one long double helix.
Synonyms: *amalgam, composite, fusion*   Antonyms: *division, disjuncture*

❑ *eclectic* (adj)   made up of parts from many different sources (*ec-* out + *legere* to choose)

Rob Mathes' **eclectic** compositions reveal a subtle yet effective blend of blues, gospel, classical, and jazz styles.
Synonyms: *multifaceted, multifarious, manifold, diverse, synthesized*

❑ *yoke* (v)   to join different things

Politicians often **yoke** unpopular legislation to popular bills so that they can sneak them through Congress.
Synonym: *couple*

❑ *amalgam* (n)   a combination of different substances into one mass   Synonyms: *composite, hybrid*

❑ *amass* (v)   to gather, to pile up   <We **amassed** a huge collection of CDs.>
Synonyms: *stockpile, accrue*

❑ *invoke* (v)   to call on for help or inspiration (*in-* in + *vocare* call)

<The judged **invoked** an old statute.>

❑ *compatible* (adj)   capable of living together harmoniously   <**compatible** roommates>
Synonym: *agreeable*

❑ *contemporary* (adj)   living or occurring during the same time period (*con-* together + *tempore* time)

❑ *predilection* (n)   disposition in favor of something (*pre-* before + *legere* to choose)
<a **predilection** for chocolate>   Synonyms: *inclination, bent, proclivity, propensity*

Vocabulary Lesson 14: Cruel and Unusual Ap 10

Today's roots:	*vilis* worthless	*de-* down
	super- above, beyond	*-less* without

❑ **ruthless** (adj)   cruel; merciless (*rue* regret + *-less* without)

Torquemada is widely regarded as the most **ruthless** interrogator of the Spanish Inquisition.
Synonyms: *brutal, callous*   Antonyms: *civilized, humane, merciful*

❑ **contempt** (n)   scorn; disrespect

Many eminent and successful scientists often show **contempt** for novel theories that question their own.
Synonyms: *disdain, scorn*   Antonyms: *respect, honor, reverence*

❑ **callous** (adj)   hardened; insensitive

Because they see so much suffering daily, emergency room doctors often struggle to avoid becoming **callous.**
Synonyms: *insensitive, dispassionate*   Antonyms: *compassionate, empathetic, sympathetic*

❑ **sadistic** (adj)   taking pleasure in the pain of others (from the *Marquis de Sade*)

The **sadistic** youngster smiled as he watched his classmate get hit in the head with a dodgeball.
Synonyms: *barbarous, savage, ruthless*   Antonyms: *civilized, humane*

❑ **supercilious** (adj)   full of haughty arrogance (*super-* above + *cilium* eyebrow)

Although he seems **supercilious** when you first meet him, Joe is actually a modest and down-to-earth guy.
Synonyms: *haughty, cavalier*   Antonyms: *diffident, unassuming, humble*

❑ **idiosyncrasy** (n)   a peculiar trait or habit (*idio* peculiar)

My history teacher has the **idiosyncrasy** of always squinting just before she asks a question of the class.
Synonyms: *quirk, affectation, eccentricity, singularity*

❑ **anomaly** (n)   unusual event (*an-* not + *homos* same)

The ninety-degree day in Siberia was an **anomaly**; the temperature had gone that high only once before.
Synonyms: *aberration, irregularity*   Antonym: *regularity*

❑ **incongruous** (adj)   inappropriate; not in keeping with a pattern (*in-* not + *congru* agree)

❑ **fetter** (v)   to tie up; to chain   Synonyms: *shackle, hamper*

❑ **notorious** (adj)   famous for bad things (*notus* known)   Synonyms: *infamous, disreputable*

❑ **decry** (v)   to speak out against (*de-* down + *crier* cry)   Synonyms: *vilify, condemn*

❑ **vilify** (v)   to slander; to defame (*vilis* worthless)   Synonyms: *denigrate, malign, libel, calumniate*

❑ **heinous** (adj)   cruel and unusual (*haine* hatred)   Synonyms: *atrocious, monstrous*

❑ **revile** (v)   to denounce abusively (*vilis* worthless)   <**reviled** as a coward>

Vocabulary Unit 2 Exercise Set I

Ap 10

> **Time—8 minutes**
> For each question, select the best answer among the choices given. Note any vocabulary words to review on the Hit List below.

1. The emotional outburst was quite unusual for Peter; he is typically one of the most ------ individuals you could ever meet.
   (A) stoic
   (B) demonstrative
   (C) extroverted
   (D) irascible
   (E) inimical

2. Ayn Rand, whose writing is considered by some awkward and contrived, is nevertheless ------ by many as ------ of individualism and objectivism, the cornerstones of her philosophy.
   (A) lionized . . . a stalwart
   (B) repudiated . . . a protagonist
   (C) censured . . . an advocate
   (D) praised . . . an antagonist
   (E) extolled . . . a skeptic

3. Fearing ------ from officials in their home country, the dissidents sought ------ in the American embassy.
   (A) veneration . . . solitude
   (B) oppression . . . sanctuary
   (C) impotence . . . asylum
   (D) calumny . . . disparagement
   (E) judiciousness . . . salvation

4. Because female authors were not treated as equals in the 19th century, many women used ------ in an effort to disguise themselves as males.
   (A) influxes
   (B) anachronisms
   (C) pseudonyms
   (D) diatribes
   (E) amalgams

5. The newly implemented tax cut was not as ------ as its supporters had hoped in ------ the economy by spurring investment and growth.
   (A) formidable . . . enervating
   (B) efficacious . . . invigorating
   (C) delicate . . . stimulating
   (D) ruthless . . . lauding
   (E) incongruous . . . encouraging

6. After many said that her last novel was too ------, she included a bizarre and shocking ending to her newest book in an effort to ------ her critics.
   (A) banal . . . support
   (B) elegant . . . pacify
   (C) spurious . . . silence
   (D) mundane . . . appease
   (E) contrived . . . endorse

7. When unhappy, Richard quickly becomes ------, picking fights with anyone around him.
   (A) sadistic
   (B) pious
   (C) capricious
   (D) belligerent
   (E) fallacious

8. Although sparrows appear to be weak and harmless, they can actually be quite ------ when their nest is threatened.
   (A) redoubtable
   (B) furtive
   (C) evanescent
   (D) fickle
   (E) laconic

9. Many societies detest ------, and as a result the ------ among them are often treated as outcasts.
   (A) compatibility . . . antagonistic
   (B) idiosyncrasy . . . callous
   (C) duplicity . . . perfidious
   (D) superficiality . . . profound
   (E) potency . . . sacrosanct

10. The ------ remarks made by the press hurt Kendra's feelings, but she vowed to ignore the ------ and continue toward her goal.
    (A) derogatory . . . consecrations
    (B) inimical . . . conciliations
    (C) sanctimonious . . . predilections
    (D) venerable . . . harangues
    (E) caustic . . . denigrations

HIT LIST

Vocabulary Unit 2 Exercise Set II

An 10

Write the meaning next to each root, then write as many words as you can that contain the root.

1. NYM_____

6. TRANS_____

11. TEMPUS_____

2. FLUERE_____

7. SACER_____

12. SANCTUS_____

3. CHRONOS_____

8. VERERI_____

13. POTENS_____

4. SYN_____

9. VOCARE_____

14. DOMIT_____

5. IN-, IM-_____

10. VILIS_____

15. DE-_____

Vocabulary Unit 2 Exercise Set III

1. Should a good boxer be *redoubtable?*   Y N

2. Is a *stalwart* weak?   Y N

3. Can a mountain be *evanescent?*   Y N

4. Do *compatible* things work together well?   Y N

5. Is a *diffident* person haughty?   Y N

Write the word with the given meaning

6. slander; false accusation c_____

7. reprimand mildly   a_____

8. irregular; infrequent   s_____

9. extended in time   p_____

10. trickery; deceit   g_____

11. sneaky   s_____

12. greedy; ravenous   r_____

13. to regard with honor   r_____

14. magical object   t_____

15. falsely pious   s_____

16. a strong defense   b_____

17. unconquerable   i_____

18. to slander; defame   v_____

19. scorn; disrespect   c_____

20. deceitful scheme   s_____

21. out of place in time   a_____

22. place of refuge   s_____

23. full of vigor   r_____

24. collection of works   a_____

25. call on for inspiration   i_____

Write the correct form of the italicized word

26. like an *anomaly*

_____

27. showing *contempt*

_____

28. having the quality of an *anachronism*

_____

29. to give *censure*

_____

30. having the tendency to *evanesce*

_____

Write the word with the given meaning and root

31. deceit (*duplit*)

_____

32. fake name (*nym*)

_____

33. disparaging (*de-*)

_____

34. to attack as untrue (*pugn*)

_____

35. falsely pious (*sanct*)

_____

36. regard with respect (*venus*)

_____

37. most important (*domit*)

_____

38. weak (*potens*)

_____

39. blend or fuse together (*co-*)

_____

40. full of haughty arrogance (*super-*)

_____

41. to denounce abusively (*vilis*)

_____

Unit 2 Exercise Set I Answer Key

1. **(A)** The sentence indicates that showing emotion is *unusual* for Peter. Look for a word that means *unemotional* to fill the blank.
   stoic = unaffected by pleasure or pain
   demonstrative = effusive, emotional
   extroverted = outgoing, gregarious
   irascible = easily angered
   inimical = unfriendly, harmful

2. **(A)** *Nevertheless* indicates that the blank should contrast *awkward and contrived*. A contrasting response would be *praise*. And if *individualism and objectivism* are the *cornerstones of her philosophy,* she must agree with them.
   lionized = worshipped; *stalwart* = unwavering person
   repudiated = cast off; *protagonist* = main character
   censured = condemned; *advocate* = supporter
   praised = commended; *antagonist* = opposed
   extolled = praised highly; *skeptic* = doubter

3. **(B)** The sentence indicates that they *fear* the first word and if they fear something, they should seek *comfort* of some sort.
   veneration = reverence; *solitude* = loneliness
   oppression = holding back; *sanctuary* = place of refuge
   impotence = lack of power; *asylum* = a safe place
   calumny = slander; *disparagement* = belittlement
   judiciousness = wisdom; *salvation* = being saved

4. **(C)** The word in the blank is something that they would use to disguise themselves as men. The only word that fits this description is *pseudonyms*.
   influxes = inward flows
   anachronisms = things out of place in time
   pseudonyms = false names
   diatribes = prolonged speeches
   amalgams = mixtures

5. **(B)** Supporters of the tax cut would obviously hope that it would do well and cause good things. So you want a positive word in the first blank. The supporters hoped it would "spur investment and growth" which shows they thought it would strengthen the economy.
   formidable = imposing; *enervating* = weakening
   efficacious = effective; *invigorating* = strengthening

   delicate = fragile; *stimulating* = causing activity
   ruthless = cruel; *lauding* = praising
   incongruous = not matching; *encouraging* = inspiring

6. **(D)** The second part of the sentence implies that the critics deemed her first novel to be lacking a *bizarre and shocking* ending. She would include a shocking ending to *silence* these critics. Two simple words to complete the sentence would be *predictable* and *quiet*.
   banal = trivial; *support* = to hold up
   elegant = refined; *pacify* = to soothe
   spurious = fake; *silence* = to quiet
   mundane = ordinary; *appease* = to quiet
   contrived = obvious; *endorse* = support

7. **(D)** As is often the case, the information after the semicolon tells us everything we need to know. When Richard is unhappy, he *picks fights*.
   sadistic = enjoying the pain of others
   pious = holy
   capricious = acting on impulse
   belligerent = warlike, prone to fighting
   fallacious = false

8. **(A)** *Although* shows a classic contrast. Sparrows appear to be *weak and harmless,* but when something important to them is threatened, they become the opposite of *weak and harmless*.
   redoubtable = formidable, intimidating
   furtive = sneaky
   evanescent = ephemeral, short-lived
   fickle = prone to change one's mind
   laconic = not inclined to speaking much

9. **(C)** If society *detests* it, the first word must indicate something negative. The *as a result* shows a cause and effect, so you'd expect the second word to describe a person who has the characteristic in the first blank.
   compatibility = ability to go together; *antagonistic* = hostile
   idiosyncrasy = odd behavior; *callous* = hardened
   duplicity = deceptiveness; *perfidious* = untrustworthy
   superficial = lacking substance; *profound* = deep
   potency = strength, power; *sacrosanct* = sacred

10. (E) The first word indicates something that would hurt one's feelings. The second word must be a noun to describe such remarks.
    derogatory = insulting; *consecrations* = blessings
    inimical = unfriendly; *conciliations* = actions or remarks that regain trust or friendship

sanctimonious = smug;
    predilections = inclinations
venerable = worthy of respect;
    harangues = tirades
caustic = harmful; *denigrations* = slander

Unit 2 Exercise Sets II and III Answer Key

Exercise Set II

1. NYM: name
   pseudonym, anonymous, synonym, antonym

2. FLUERE: flow
   fluent, superfluous, confluence, effluvium

3. CHRONOS: time
   synchronize, chronology, anachronism, chronicle

4. SYN: same
   synonym, sympathy, synchronize, synthesis

5. IN-, IM-: not
   intolerant, immoral, immodest, inconceivable

6. TRANS: across
   transparent, transmit, translate, transition

7. SACER: sacred
   sacrilegious, sacrament, sacrosanct, consecrate

8. VERERI: respect
   revere, reverent, irreverent, reverend

9. VOCARE: to call
   invoke, provoke, vocation, voice, revoke

10. VILIS: worthless
    vilify, revile, villain, evil

11. TEMPUS: time
    extemporaneous, temporary, contemporary

12. SANCTUS: holy
    sanctify, sanctuary, sacrosanct, sanctimonious

13. POTENS: strong
    potent, impotent, potential, despot

14. DOMIT: lord
    dominion, indomitable, domesticate, dominate

15. DE-: down
    descend, demoralize, demote, deride, decline

Exercise Set III

1. Y
2. N
3. N
4. Y
5. N
6. calumny
7. admonish
8. sporadic
9. protracted
10. guile
11. surreptitious
12. rapacious
13. revere
14. talisman
15. sanctimonious
16. bulwark
17. indomitable
18. vilify
19. contempt
20. stratagem
21. anachronistic
22. sanctuary
23. robust
24. anthology
25. invoke
26. anomalous
27. contemptuous
28. anachronistic
29. censure
30. evanescent
31. duplicity
32. pseudonym
33. derogatory
34. impugn
35. sanctimonious
36. venerate
37. predominant
38. impotent
39. coalesce
40. supercilious
41. revile

Vocabulary Unit 3

Ap 11

Vocabulary Lesson 15: Weak and Weaker

| Today's roots: | *batre* | to beat | *troph* | nourishment |
| | *sequi* | follow | *pli* | fold |

❑ ***atrophy*** (v)   to weaken from disuse (*a-* without + *troph* nourishment)

After surgery, extended bed rest often causes muscles to **atrophy** unless it is accompanied by physical therapy.
Synonyms: ***degenerate, deteriorate***   Antonyms: ***thrive, flourish***

❑ ***abate*** (v)   to subside; to decrease in intensity (*ad-* to + *batre* to beat)

The crews had to wait until the storm **abated** before they could begin to assess the damage to the coastal town.
Synonyms: ***wane, diminish***   Antonyms: ***expand, amplify***

❑ ***porous*** (adj)   filled with many holes (*porus* opening)

The teenager's story was a **porous** one that her parents could easily see through.
Synonyms: ***penetrable, pervious***   Antonyms: ***impervious, impenetrable, impregnable***

❑ ***wane*** (v)   to grow smaller or less intense

As the size of the moon **wanes** over the next few nights, it will get harder to see when it is dark.
Synonyms: ***abate, ebb*** Antonyms: ***wax, intensify***

❑ ***lassitude*** (n)   a feeling of weakness (*lassus* weary)

Although she tried valiantly to play through her illness, Danielle's **lassitude** overtook her in the second half.
Synonyms: ***listlessness, weariness***   Antonyms: ***vitality, vigor***

❑ ***undermine*** (v)   to weaken or diminish something

The continual setbacks to the project over many weeks **undermined** the morale of the workers.
Synonyms: ***undercut, attenuate***   Antonyms: ***fortify, strengthen***

❑ ***obsequious*** (adj)   overly submissive (*ob-* to + *sequi* follow)   Synonyms: ***fawning, compliant***

❑ ***attrition*** (n)   a wearing away of strength or morale   Synonyms: ***debilitation, weakening***

❑ ***enervate*** (v)   to weaken someone's vitality   Synonyms: ***debilitate***

❑ ***vulnerable*** (adj)   prone to attack or harm   Synonyms: ***assailable, susceptible***

❑ ***ebb*** (v)   to decrease or decline slowly   Synonyms: ***wane, abate***

❑ ***compliant*** (adj)   submissive (*pli* fold)   Synonyms: ***yielding, conciliatory***

❑ ***debilitate*** (v)   to sap the strength of (*de-* away + *bilis* strength)   Synonyms: ***cripple, enervate***

Vocabulary Lesson 16: Chillin'

Ap 11

> | Today's roots: | *status* | position, standing | *quies* | rest |
> | --- | --- | --- | --- | --- |
> | | *plac* | to please | *serenus* | calm |

❑ **placid** (adj)   calm (*plac* to please)

A relaxing day at the spa always makes me feel more **placid.**
Synonyms: *serene, tranquil*   Antonyms: *frenzied, frenetic*

❑ **inert** (adj)   sluggish; inactive (*in-* not + *ertem* active)

After his final exams, Ricky sat **inert** on his couch for two days watching soap operas and game shows.
Synonyms: *quiescent, torpid, phlegmatic*   Antonyms: *alert, lively*

❑ **listless** (adj)   sluggish; without energy (*-less* without)

I always feel **listless** on rainy days; sometimes I don't even want to get out of bed.
Synonyms: *enervated, inert, phlegmatic, lethargic*   Antonyms: *lively, robust*

❑ **quiescent** (adj)   resting; quiet (*quies* rest)

During the **quiescent** phase of cell division, the cell does not split or grow.
Synonym: *inactive*   Antonyms: *dynamic, active*

❑ **serene** (adj)   tranquil; calm; placid (*serenus* peaceful, calm)

There was not a single wave on the surface of the **serene** lake.
Synonyms: *quiescent, sedate*   Antonyms: *frenzied, turbulent*

❑ **static** (adj)   stationary (*status* standing)

The patient's vitals have been **static** for an hour. We hope this means he can be moved from intensive care.
Synonyms: *stagnant, inert*   Antonyms: *itinerant, peripatetic*

❑ **lethargic** (adj)   lazy; sluggish

The flu left me feeling **lethargic** even two days after my fever had broken.
Synonyms: *phlegmatic, dormant, enervated, listless*

❑ **moratorium** (n)   postponement   Synonyms: *deferral, delay*

❑ **stagnate** (v)   to become inactive; to become stale (*status* standing)   Synonym: *idle*

❑ **torpor** (n)   lethargy; apathy   Synonyms: *inertness, lassitude*

❑ **respite** (n)   rest; time of relief; pause (*respit* delay)   Synonyms: *hiatus, moratorium*

❑ **hiatus** (n)   a break in the continuity of something   Synonyms: *respite, discontinuity*

❑ **torpid** (adj)   hibernating; dormant (*torpere* be numb)   Synonyms: *inert, idle*

Vocabulary Lesson 17: Wanna Fight?

Ap 11

| Today's roots: | *bellum* war | *pro-* forward, forth |
| | *pugnare* fight | *ire* anger |

❑ **belligerent** (adj)   warlike; quarrelsome (*bellum* war)

My brother is a **belligerent** guy; he picks his fair share of bar fights.
Synonyms: *antagonistic, cantankerous, contentious*   Antonyms: *passive, peaceful*

❑ **irascible** (adj)   easily angered (*ire* anger)

Adam's **irascible** nature landed him in anger management therapy; he overreacts to the smallest things.
Synonyms: *choleric, splenetic, petulant*   Antonym: *even-tempered*

❑ **volatile** (adj)   explosive; tending to evaporate quickly (*vola* to fly)

The situation in the Middle East is a **volatile** one that must be handled with care.
Synonyms: *unsettled, temperamental*   Antonym: *stable*

❑ **rebuttal** (n)   refutation; opposing response to an argument (*re-* back)

After the opponent made his remarks, the debate team captain approached the podium to deliver her **rebuttal.**
Synonyms: *repartee, rejoinder*   Antonym: *agreement*

❑ **refute** (v)   to disprove; to rebut forcefully (*refutare* to drive back)

The judge found no evidence to **refute** your claim that the car is yours, so you get to keep it for now.
Synonyms: *contradict, rebut*   Antonyms: *support, endorse*

❑ **incite** (v)   to urge into action (*citare* to cause to move)

The rebels **incited** a revolt in the small city by convincing the citizens that their mayor was a crook.
Synonyms: *coax, cajole, instigate*   Antonym: *dissuade*

❑ **pugnacious** (adj)   quarrelsome; warlike (*pugnare* fight)

The **pugnacious** punk was happiest when his fists were pounding someone else's chin.
Synonyms: *truculent, belligerent*   Antonyms: *pacific, passive*

❑ **bellicose** (adj)   warlike in manner (*bellum* war)   Synonyms: *pugnacious, belligerent*

❑ **harass** (v)   to bother; to annoy   Synonyms: *irritate, torment*

❑ **assail** (v)   to attack or assault (*ad-* at + *salire* leap)   Synonym: *berate*

❑ **tumultuous** (adj)   violently agitated   Synonyms: *hectic, unruly*

❑ **instigate** (v)   to goad; to urge on   Synonyms: *incite, foment, coax, cajole*

❑ **provocative** (adj)   tending to aggravate or stimulate (*pro-* forth + *vocare* to call)
                                                                Synonyms: *goading, alluring*

Vocabulary Lesson 18: Bad and Ugly

Today's roots:	acri	bitter	caco	ugly
	noi	harm	phon	sound

❑ **acrimony** (n)   bitterness of feeling; harsh words (*acri* bitter + *monia* action or condition)

Her toast was inappropriately **acrimonious,** and we could all tell that she had not forgiven her friend.
Synonyms: *belligerence, rancor*   Antonym: *civility*

❑ **appalling** (adj)   shocking; causing dismay (*palir* to grow pale)

The way he yells at his wife is **appalling;** he treats her as if she were his servant.
Synonyms: *astounding, offensive*   Antonyms: *benevolent, virtuous*

❑ **cacophony** (n)   discord; harsh sounds (*cacos* ugly + *phon* sound)

How can this **cacophony** coming out of my son's room be today's popular music?
Synonyms: *disharmony, dissonance*   Antonym: *harmony*

❑ **abysmal** (adj)   extremely bad; wretched

The food at this hospital is **abysmal!** Is this bread or cardboard?
Synonyms: *deplorable, pathetic*   Antonyms: *commendable, laudable*

❑ **acrid** (adj)   harsh smelling or tasting (*acri* bitter)

Don't inhale too much of this chemical; it is known to be quite **acrid** and can make you pass out.
Synonyms: *astringent, pungent*   Antonyms: *savory, sweet*

❑ **blatant** (adj)   very conspicuous; annoyingly loud

The blaring of loud music despite my repeated requests for silence shows your **blatant** disregard for my needs.
Synonyms: *flagrant, impudent*   Antonym: *unobtrusive*

❑ **deplorable** (adj)   worthy of reproach or censure (*plorare* to cry out in sorrow)

Although they claimed to love animals, the conditions at their run-down shelter were **deplorable.**
Synonyms: *disgraceful, egregious*   Antonyms: *commendable, laudable*

❑ **egregious** (adj)   conspicuously bad; flagrant (*e-* out + *greg* herd)   Synonyms: *atrocious, deplorable*

❑ **lurid** (adj)   shocking; sensational   Synonyms: *graphic, vivid*

❑ **noisome** (adj)   offensive to the senses or the health (*noi* harm)   Synonyms: *loathsome, detestable*

❑ **flagrant** (adj)   offensively bad; reprehensible   Synonyms: *egregious, blatant*

❑ **heinous** (adj)   cruel; shockingly evil (*haine* hatred + *-ous* full of)   Synonyms: *atrocious, monstrous*

❑ **astringent** (adj)   caustic; pungent   Synonyms: *acrid, harsh*

Vocabulary Lesson 19: Moving Right Along

Ap 12

Today's roots:	*ambulare* walk	*flux* flow
	pel, pul force, drive	*peri-* around

❑ **ambulatory** (adj)   capable of moving around (*ambulare* walk)

He must stay in bed for a week, and once he is **ambulatory** he will need crutches.
Synonyms: *mobile, peripatetic*   Antonyms: *static, immobile*

❑ **deviate** (v)   to swerve or deflect (*de-* away + *via* path)

The tire sitting in the left lane of the highway caused the driver to **deviate** from her path.
Synonyms: *digress, veer*   Antonym: *conform*

❑ **influx** (n)   a flowing in (*in-* in + *flux* flow)

The school saw quite an **influx** of new applicants once it increased the number of scholarships.
Synonyms: *inundation, inpouring, immigration*   Antonyms: *efflux, emigration*

❑ **meander** (v)   to wander aimlessly (from *Maiandros,* a Greek river known for its winding path)

The confused lost child **meandered** through the streets with no apparent destination.
Synonyms: *roam, drift*

❑ **peripatetic** (adj)   traveling from place to place (*peri-* around + *patein* to walk)

The nomads were a **peripatetic** clan; they never stayed in the same place very long.
Synonyms: *itinerant, ambulant*   Antonyms: *stationary, static*

❑ **impel** (v)   to put into motion; to urge (*pel* force)

The zoo visitors were **impelled** into action by the announcement that a lion was loose.
Synonyms: *goad, spur*   Antonyms: *impede, dissuade*

❑ **expedite** (v)   to speed up the progress of (*ex-* out + *pes* foot: to free from entanglement)

The project was **expedited** once the CEO decided that its outcome reflected on him personally.
Synonyms: *facilitate, hasten, precipitate, advance*   Antonyms: *impede, hinder*

❑ **itinerant** (adj)   traveling from place to place   Synonyms: *peripatetic, ambulant*

❑ **nomadic** (adj)   wandering without a permanent home   Synonyms: *migratory, drifting*

❑ **peripheral** (adj)   located on the outer boundary (*peri-* around)   Synonym: *bordering*

❑ **compel** (v)   to urge into action by force (*com-* together + *pel* force)   Synonyms: *impel, coerce*

❑ **vagrant** (adj)   wandering from place to place (*vagus* wandering)   Synonyms: *nomadic, peripatetic*

❑ **perambulate** (v)   to move about (*per-* through + *ambulare* walk)   Synonyms: *wander, drift*

Vocabulary Lesson 20: Going, Going, Gone!

Ap 12

Today's roots:	purgare	cleanse	re-	back
	deplare	to empty	ab-	away

❑ **raze** (v)   to destroy completely

The massive level-five hurricane **razed** the entire port city, crushing everything in its path.
Synonyms: **obliterate, decimate**   Antonym: **preserve**

❑ **jettison** (v)   to throw overboard

The killer **jettisoned** the murder weapon into the lake as he sailed to his hideout in the cove.
Synonyms: **heave, dump**   Antonym: **retain**

❑ **abort** (v)   to terminate prematurely

The soldiers **aborted** their mission when they learned their cover was blown and it was no longer safe.
Synonyms: **scratch, cancel**   Antonyms: **execute, continue**

❑ **purge** (v)   to cleanse of something unwanted (*purgare* to cleanse)

It is satisfying to **purge** your email inbox of unwanted junk messages.
Synonyms: **remove, expunge**   Antonyms: **amass, collect**

❑ **forgo** (v)   to give something up (*for-* away + *go* go)

The woman decided to leave the hospital early and **forgo** further treatment on her injured hip.
Synonyms: **abandon, forsake**   Antonyms: **maintain, participate**

❑ **deplete** (v)   to decrease the supply of (*deplare* to empty)

The run on gasoline **depleted** the gas station of its fuel reserves, and it was forced to shut down.
Synonyms: **exhaust, diminish**   Antonyms: **replenish, restock**

❑ **dearth** (n)   lack; scarcity (*dear* greatly valued)

There has been a **dearth** of good will between the teams ever since the bench-clearing brawl.
Synonyms: **paucity, scarcity, want, deficiency**   Antonyms: **abundance, plenitude, bounty**

❑ **rescind** (v)   to take back; to cancel (*re-* back + *scindere* cut)   Synonyms: **annul, void**

❑ **efface** (v)   to erase by rubbing (*e-* out + *face* appearance)   Synonyms: **omit, cancel**

❑ **abdicate** (v)   to give up power (*ab-* away + *dicare* proclaim)   Synonyms: **relinquish, renounce**

❑ **renounce** (v)   to give up in a formal announcement   Synonyms: **abdicate, resign**

❑ **nullify** (v)   to make invalid (*nullus* none)   Synonyms: **cancel, void**

❑ **relinquish** (v)   to abandon or give up (*re-* back + *linquere* to leave)   Synonyms: **abdicate, vacate**

Vocabulary Lesson 21: Mr. Nice Guy

Ap 13

Today's roots:	*amicus* friend	*anthro* humankind
	munus gift, money, sharing	*phila* brotherly love

❑ *altruism* (n)   selflessness (*alter* other)

Tom's **altruism** pushes him to spend thirty hours per week working with the needy.
Synonyms: *humaneness, benevolence*   Antonyms: *egoism, malevolence*

❑ *amiable* (adj)   friendly; agreeable (*amicus* friend)

Mr. Richards is such an **amiable** guy, always smiling and laughing as he interacts with his customers.
Synonyms: *affable, amicable*   Antonyms: *surly, disdainful*

❑ *philanthropist* (n)   one who does good; lover of humankind (*phila* love + *anthro* humankind)

It is amazing that a penny-pincher like Paul is a **philanthropist** who has donated millions to charity.
Synonyms: *altruist, humanitarian*   Antonyms: *misanthrope, antagonist*

❑ *congenial* (adj)   friendly; pleasant (*con-* with + *genialis* pleasant)

After months of imagining her in-laws as monsters, Julia was surprised at how **congenial** they actually were.
Synonyms: *amicable, affable*   Antonyms: *hostile, surly*

❑ *munificent* (adj)   generous (*munus* sharing)

Donating that outfit to charity is quite a **munificent** gesture, considering that it is your favorite.
Synonyms: *beneficent, magnanimous*   Antonyms: *greedy, egoistic*

❑ *decorum* (n)   propriety; good manners (*decorus* proper)

While eating at the country club, you must behave with the utmost **decorum** and mind your manners.
Synonym: *etiquette*   Antonym: *impropriety*

❑ *amity* (n)   friendship (*amicus* friend)   Synonyms: *benevolence, amicableness*

❑ *decorous* (adj)   exhibiting decorum (*decorus* proper)   Synonyms: *civilized, dignified*

❑ *affable* (adj)   friendly; kind (*affabilis* easy to converse with)   Synonyms: *amiable, amicable*

❑ *gregarious* (adj)   sociable (*greg* flock)   Synonym: *friendly*

❑ *amicable* (adj)   polite and friendly (*amicus* friend)   Synonyms: *amiable, affable*

❑ *magnanimous* (adj)   generous; big-hearted (*magna* great + *animus* spirit)
      Synonyms: *altruistic, munificent*

❑ *geniality* (n)   cheerfulness (*genialis* pleasant)   Synonyms: *affability, amiability*

Vocabulary Unit 3 Exercise Set I

An 13

Time—8 minutes
For each question, select the best answer among the choices given. Note any vocabulary words to
review on the Hit List below.

1. Stephen's job as censor for the magazine was to
    ------ any material that might be objectionable to
    its readers.
    (A) abridge
    (B) amass
    (C) refute
    (D) expurgate
    (E) enervate

2. As more travelers have decided to ------ their
    garbage as they sail, the lake has become quite
    polluted.
    (A) pilfer
    (B) jettison
    (C) yoke
    (D) assail
    (E) impel

3. The movie critic refused to take back his ------ re-
    marks because he thoroughly intended to ------
    the director's abilities.
    (A) caustic . . compliment
    (B) derogatory . . revere
    (C) sanctimonious . . reveal
    (D) laconic . . lionize
    (E) scathing . . disparage

4. The ------ young salesman made his living wan-
    dering from town to town.
    (A) bellicose
    (B) inert
    (C) lethargic
    (D) acrid
    (E) peripatetic

5. Normally a ------ person, when stuck in horrible
    traffic on the highway Peter becomes even more
    ------, often provoking fisticuffs with other dri-
    vers.
    (A) congenial . . rapacious
    (B) contentious . . belligerent
    (C) listless . . dolorous
    (D) choleric . . serene
    (E) sanguine . . pugnacious

6. The normally ------ daytime television show had
    one surprisingly ------ episode and got yanked off
    the air.
    (A) decorous . . provocative
    (B) compliant . . obsequious
    (C) vulnerable . . porous
    (D) volatile . . tumultuous
    (E) deplorable . . altruistic

7. Coming off of the worst recession in the coun-
    try's 250-year history, the sudden ------ of money
    was a welcome sight to the rulers of the desti-
    tute nation.
    (A) depletion
    (B) influx
    (C) transgression
    (D) fluctuation
    (E) bulwark

8. The ------ from the construction work on the
    busy street below made it very difficult for me to
    concentrate with the window open.
    (A) torpor
    (B) cacophony
    (C) euphoria
    (D) anomaly
    (E) sacrament

9. As if he knew I was exhausted and in need of
    ------ from his interminable mischief, the puppy
    went to his bed and took a nap.
    (A) an elocution
    (B) a euphemism
    (C) a respite
    (D) a rebuttal
    (E) a testimony

10. Although it was nice to be ------ again after being
    bedridden for four weeks, the muscular ------
    that resulted from my immobilization was
    going to take a lot of work to fix.
    (A) itinerant . . deterioration
    (B) amiable . . bastion
    (C) ambulatory . . atrophy
    (D) amorphous . . attrition
    (E) pedestrian . . acrimony

_____
_____
_____
_____
_____

_____
_____
_____
_____
_____

Ap 13

Vocabulary Unit 3 Exercise Set II

Write the meaning next to each root, then write as many words as you can that contain the root.

1. A-_____

2. AN-_____

3. PERI-_____

4. AB-_____

5. ACRI-_____

6. BELLI-_____

7. AM-, AMICUS_____

8. ANTHRO_____

9. MUNUS_____

10. TROPH_____

11. PRO-_____

12. PHONO_____

13. PURG-_____

14. PEL-_____

15. SEQUI_____

Vocabulary Unit 3 Exercise Set III

1. Is a *heinous* act cruel?   Y N
2. Is a *gregarious* person friendly?   Y N
3. Is an *obsequious* person disobedient?   Y N
4. Is something *abysmal* good?   Y N
5. Is a *philanthropist* generous?   Y N

Write the word with the given meaning

6. traveling from place to place   i_____
7. hibernating, dormant   t_____
8. good manners   d_____
9. to destroy completely   r_____
10. to decrease the supply of   d_____
11. filled with many holes   p_____
12. capable of moving around   a_____
13. selflessness   a_____
14. to urge into action   i_____
15. to intentionally weaken   u_____
16. offensive to the senses   n_____
17. prone to attack   v_____
18. stationary   s_____
19. to terminate prematurely   a_____
20. to put in motion   i_____
21. politely friendly   a_____
22. warlike   p_____
23. to throw overboard   j_____
24. worthy of reproach   d_____
25. a break   h_____

Write the correct form of the italicized word.

26. characterized by *torpor*

_____

27. the act of *abdicating*

_____

28. the quality of being *volatile*

_____

29. how someone who displays *altruism* behaves

_____

30. the quality of being *pugnacious*

_____

Write the word with the given root

31. lazy, sluggish (*argos*)

_____

32. to erase (*fac*)

_____

33. to weaken from disuse (*a-*)

_____

34. postponement (*mora*)

_____

35. generous (*muni*)

_____

36. quarrelsome (*belli*)

_____

37. overly submissive (*sequi*)

_____

38. to swerve (*via*)

_____

39. easily angered (*irasci*)

_____

40. sociable (*greg*)

_____

41. harsh words (*acri*)

_____

Unit 3 Exercise Set I Answer Key

1. **(D)** A *censor* is one who removes objectionable material.
   abridge = to shorten
   amass = to accumulate or collect
   refute = to disprove
   expurgate = to remove inappropriate material
   enervate = to weaken

2. **(B)** The waters are becoming more polluted, which indicates that people are probably putting their garbage into the lake.
   pilfer = to steal
   jettison = to throw overboard
   yoke = to tie together
   assail = to attack
   impel = to provoke

3. **(E)** The critic *thoroughly intended* to say what he said. But if they were things he was expected to *take back*, they must have been pretty negative. The second word should be negative as well.
   caustic = harmful; *compliment* = to praise
   derogatory = offensive; *revere* = to respect
   sanctimonious = smug
   laconic = terse; *lionize* = to worship
   scathing = harsh; *disparage* = to put down

4. **(E)** This person makes his living *wandering from town to town*.
   bellicose = warlike
   inert = inactive
   lethargic = sluggish
   acrid = harsh
   peripatetic = traveling from place to place

5. **(B)** Peter sometimes picks fights (*fisticuffs*). The second word should be slightly stronger than the first.
   congenial = friendly; *rapacious* = ravenous
   contentious = inclined to argue; *belligerent* = warlike
   listless = lethargic; *dolorous* = painful
   choleric = easily angered; *serene* = peaceful
   sanguine = optimistic; *pugnacious* = combative

6. **(A)** It got yanked off the air, so the show must have done something bad. The word *surprisingly* indicates a contrast, so the first word is positive.

   decorous = proper; *provocative* = risqué
   compliant = obedient; *obsequious* = submissive
   vulnerable = susceptible; *porous* = full of holes
   volatile = explosive; *tumultuous* = turbulent
   deplorable = very bad; *altruistic* = selfless

7. **(B)** The nation is *destitute*, and therefore needs money to pour in.
   depletion = draining
   influx = inward flow
   transgression = violation
   fluctuation = shift back and forth
   bulwark = a defensive wall

8. **(B)** It is difficult to concentrate and the street is busy with construction; there must be lot of noise down there.
   torpor = sluggishness
   cacophony = harsh noise
   euphoria = elation, ecstasy
   anomaly = an abnormality
   sacrament = a formal religious act

9. **(C)** The owner of the puppy is exhausted and therefore in need of rest. *Interminable* means *never-ending*. The puppy's nap would provide the owner with a nice break from the mischief.
   an elocution = an expressive delivery of a speech
   a euphemism = an inoffensive expression substituted for an offensive one
   a respite = a rest
   a rebuttal = a retort
   a testimony = an account, evidence

10. **(C)** The first word describes one who is no longer bedridden. The second word describes a problem from being bedridden. *Atrophy* works because it is the result of disuse.
    itinerant = wandering; *deterioration* = degeneration
    amiable = friendly; *bastion* = a fortified area
    ambulatory = able to move; *atrophy* = withering
    amorphous = lacking shape; *attrition* = erosion
    pedestrian = common; *acrimony* = harsh words
    (*pedestrian* can also mean "on the move")

Unit 3 Exercise Sets II and III Answer Key

Exercise Set II

1. A-: without
   atheist, atrophy, apathy, asexual, amorphous, abyss

2. AN-: without
   anarchy, anecdote, anaerobic, analgesic, anemia, anesthesia, anonymous

3. PERI-: around
   peripatetic, perambulate, pericardium, period, perimeter, peripheral, peristalsis, periscope

4. AB-: away
   abdicate, abscond, abduct, aberration, absolve, abject, abscess, abomination

5. ACRI-: bitter
   acrimony, acrid, acrimonious

6. BELLI-: war
   belligerent, bellicose, rebel, rebellion

7. AM-, AMICUS: friend
   amiable, amicable, enemy, inimical, amity

8. ANTHRO: mankind
   anthropology, anthropocentric, philanthropist, misanthrope

9. MUNU: gift
   munificent, immunity, remuneration

10. TROPH: nourishment
    atrophy, phototroph, heterotroph, autotroph, dystrophy

11. PRO-: forward, forth
    procrastinate, prolific, prophesy, propagate, propensity, profound, provoke, provocative

12. PHONO: sound
    cacophony, phonetic, symphony, euphonious

13. PURG: to clean
    expurgate, purge, purgatory, spurge

14. PEL: to push
    compel, impel, expel, propulsion

15. SEQUI: to follow
    obsequious, prosecute, pursue, segue, subsequent

Exercise Set III

1. Y
2. Y
3. N
4. N
5. Y
6. itinerant
7. torpid
8. decorum
9. raze
10. deplete
11. porous
12. ambulatory
13. altruism
14. incite
15. undermine
16. noisome
17. vulnerable
18. static
19. abort
20. impel
21. amicable
22. pugnacious
23. jettison
24. deplorable
25. hiatus
26. torpid
27. abdication
28. volatility
29. altruistically
30. pugnacity
31. lethargic
32. efface
33. atrophy
34. moratorium
35. munificent
36. belligerent
37. obsequious
38. deviate
39. irascible
40. gregarious
41. acrimony

Ap 14

Vocabulary Unit 4

Vocabulary Lesson 22: Show Off!

Today's roots:	ped, paedere	instruct	grandis	great, big
	ostentare	to display	pomp	splendor

❑ **pedantic** (adj)   showy about knowledge (*paedere* to instruct)

Kim's **pedantic** teaching style bothers her students; she uses bizarre vocabulary words nobody understands.
Synonyms: *didactic, egotistic*

❑ **grandiose** (adj)   pretentious; ridiculously exaggerated (*grandis* great)

The castle's foyer was the most **grandiose** of its kind, adorned with crystal chandeliers and gilded banisters.
Synonyms: *ostentatious, flamboyant, lofty*   Antonym: *humble*

❑ **bombastic** (adj)   pompous; using inflated language

The **bombastic** language in the mayor's campaign speech made her seem arrogant and disconnected from the public.
Synonyms: *grandiose, overblown*   Antonyms: *understated, reserved*

❑ **braggart** (n)   one who boasts; a showoff (*braguer* to show off)

No one likes a **braggart,** son; it's best to be modest and humble about your successes.
Synonym: *egotist*

❑ **ostentatious** (adj)   showy; pretentious (*ostentare* to display + *-ious* full of)

That solid gold statue is the most **ostentatious** display of wealth I have ever seen.
Synonyms: *gaudy, grandiose, garish*   Antonyms: *understated, reserved*

❑ **pompous** (adj)   possessing excessive self-esteem; pretentious (*pomp* splendor + *-ous* full of)

His **pompous,** holier-than-thou attitude annoyed all of his classmates.
Synonyms: *conceited, self-centered, pontifical*   Antonyms: *modest, self-effacing, humble*

❑ **swagger** (v)   to walk or strut in an arrogant manner

Having beat their crosstown rivals handily, the players **swaggered** back to the locker room.
Synonyms: *brag, strut*

❑ **lofty** (adj)   haughty; overly proud   Synonyms: *cavalier, pretentious*

❑ **garish** (adj)   flashy; loud   Synonyms: *ornate, ostentatious, gaudy*

❑ **ornate** (adj)   overly decorated (*ornatus* to adorn)   Synonyms: *ostentatious, opulent, gaudy*

❑ **opulence** (adj)   luxuriousness (*opulentus* wealthy)   Synonyms: *grandeur, affluence*

❑ **pretentious** (adj)   ostentatious   Synonyms: *gaudy, grandiose, garish*

❑ **gaudy** (adj)   showy in a tasteless way   Synonyms: *ostentatious, garish*

Vocabulary Lesson 23: Like a Pit Bull

AN 14

Today's roots:	*tract* pull	*tenax* holding fast
	ob- against	*per-* very

❑ **dogged** (adj)   determined; unwilling to give up

Outmanned and overmatched, the **dogged** fighters nevertheless refused to surrender the Alamo.
Synonyms: *tenacious, inexorable*   Antonyms: *yielding, irresolute*

❑ **inexorable** (adj)   relentless (*in-* not + *exorabilis* able to be swayed)

Inexorable in his wooing, Jason vowed to send Kathy roses every day until she accepted his prom invitation.
Synonyms: *obstinate, dogged*   Antonyms: *yielding, irresolute*

❑ **obstinate** (adj)   stubborn (*obstinatus* to stand stubbornly)

No matter what she tried, she could not make her **obstinate** husband change his mind.
Synonyms: *adamant, relentless, obdurate*   Antonyms: *acquiescent, obsequious*

❑ **intransigent** (adj)   uncompromising (*in-* not + *transigente* compromising)

Pat's **intransigent** nature showed itself when he adamantly refused to shift his appointment from 5:00 to 5:05.
Synonyms: *obstinate, intractable*   Antonyms: *concordant, accommodating, complaisant*

❑ **contentious** (adj)   quarrelsome (*contendere* to strive after + *-ious* full of)

Julia sighed as her excessively **contentious** husband started another unnecessary argument with their waiter.
Synonyms: *pugnacious, belligerent*   Antonyms: *passive, conciliatory*

❑ **pertinacity** (n)   stubbornness (*per-* very + *tenax* holding fast)

Kyle showed incredible **pertinacity** after breaking his leg, making it back in time for the championship game.
Synonyms: *doggedness, steadfastness*

❑ **steadfast** (adj)   unchanging; unswerving (*stede* stand + *foest* firmly fixed)

Despite many hardships, the team was **steadfast** in its pursuit of the summit.
Synonyms: *obdurate, inexorable*   Antonyms: *fickle, vacillatory*

❑ **recalcitrant** (adj)   stubbornly rebellious   Synonyms: *defiant, stubborn, wayward*

❑ **tenacious** (adj)   holding firmly; persistent (*tenax* holding fast)   Synonyms: *persistent, steadfast, resolute*

❑ **disputatious** (adj)   inclined to arguing (*disputare* to argue)   Synonyms: *contentious, litigious, polemical*

❑ **obdurate** (adj)   intractable; not easily persuaded (*obdurare* to harden)   Synonyms: *inexorable, dogged*

❑ **intractable** (adj)   hard to manage; stubborn (*in-* not + *tract* pull)   Synonyms: *obstinate, headstrong*

❑ **adamant** (adj)   refusing to yield (*adamas* unbreakable)   Synonyms: *inexorable, obdurate*

❑ **litigious** (adj) prone to bringing lawsuits (*lis* lawsuit + *agere* to drive)   Synonym: *contentious*

Vocabulary Lesson 24: You're Good at That!   *Ap 14*

Today's roots:	*apt* fit	*summus* highest
	para- beyond	*dexter* skillful

❑ *adroit* (adj)   dexterous; skillful

An **adroit** con man, Clarence knew how to fool even the most skeptical eye.
Synonyms: *deft, proficient*   Antonyms: *clumsy, inept*

❑ *unerring* (adj)   committing no mistakes; perfect (*un-* not + *err* to make a mistake)

Her **unerring** sense of direction always puts her in the right place even if she has never been there before.
Synonym: *infallible*   Antonym: *inferior*

❑ *adept* (adj)   highly skilled

Roberto, an **adept** mathematician, completed the outrageously difficult calculus final in just 25 minutes.
Synonyms: *dexterous, adroit*   Antonyms: *incompetent, clumsy*

❑ *aptitude* (n)   a natural ability; intelligence (*apt* fit)

Kenneth showed a great **aptitude** for computers as a child, designing complex programs at the age of ten.
Synonyms: *competence, expertise*   Antonyms: *ineptitude, incompetence*

❑ *paragon* (n)   a model of excellence; perfection (*para-* beyond)

The head of several charities, Susan is the **paragon** of philanthropy.
Synonyms: *prototype; epitome*

❑ *deft* (adj)   adroit, skillful

The graceful ballerina kept from tripping on stage by **deftly** avoiding the poorly placed electrical wires.
Synonyms: *proficient, adroit*   Antonyms: *clumsy, inept, awkward*

❑ *preeminent* (adj)   outstanding

A **preeminent** psychologist, Dr. Carter is often asked to lend his expertise on difficult cases.
Synonyms: *unsurpassed, paramount*   Antonym: *inferior*

❑ *expertise* (n)   knowledge or skill in a particular area   Synonyms: *prowess, savvy, bailiwick*

❑ *discerning* (adj)   showing good judgment or keen insight (*dis-* off + *cernere* distinguish)
Synonyms: *astute, judicious, sage*

❑ *agility* (n)   nimbleness (*agilis* to move)   Synonyms: *spryness, litheness*

❑ *consummate* (adj)   perfect in every respect (*con-* with + *summus* highest)   Synonym: *impeccable*

❑ *dexterous* (adj)   skillful with the hands (*dexter* skillful + *-ous* full of)   Synonyms: *adroit, adept*

❑ *impeccable* (adj)   flawless (*im-* not + *peccare* to sin)   Synonyms: *immaculate, infallible, transcendent*

Ap 15

Vocabulary Lesson 25: Bad and Worse

Today's roots:	*mal*	bad, evil	*vol*	wish
	mis	bad, wretched, hatred	*anthro*	humankind

❑ **nefarious** (adj)   wicked; sinful (*ne-* not + *fas* lawful)

Cinderella's **nefarious** stepsisters took joy in making her do their daily chores.
Synonyms: *infamous, odious*

❑ **repugnant** (adj)   offensive; repulsive (*re-* back + *pugnare* to fight)

Christopher's mother found his superstition of not bathing after games **repugnant.**
Synonyms: *abhorrent, vile, abominable*   Antonyms: *alluring, admirable*

❑ **infamous** (adj)   famous for bad deeds; notorious (*in-* not + *famosus* celebrated)

The **infamous** "El Héctor" was remembered for the way he tortured the poor villagers of Santa Potula.
Synonyms: *contemptible, ignominious*   Antonym: *noble*

❑ **odious** (adj)   worthy of dislike; arousing feelings of dislike (*odiosus* hateful)

Jimmy was no longer afraid to go to school once the **odious** bully was suspended.
Synonyms: *abhorrent, loathsome, repugnant*   Antonyms: *delightful, laudable*

❑ **malevolent** (adj)   wishing harm to others; evil (*mal* evil + *vol* wish)

The **malevolent** dictator smiled as he ordered his soldiers to burn down the church.
Synonym: *sinister*   Antonym: *benevolent*

❑ **malefactor** (n)   an evildoer (*mal* evil + *facere* to perform)

Superman has found and stopped many a **malefactor** before the crime could actually be committed.
Synonyms: *scamp, delinquent*   Antonym: *benefactor*

❑ **abominable** (adj)   loathsome; unpleasant

His **abominable** behavior at the game included excessive drinking, loud swearing, and the removal of his clothes.
Synonyms: *contemptible, vile*   Antonyms: *delightful, laudable*

❑ **avarice** (n)   extreme greed   Synonyms: *miserliness, penuriousness*

❑ **bigotry** (n)   intolerance toward those who are different

❑ **hypocrite** (n)   one who says one thing but does another (*hypokrites* Gr pretender)

❑ **miserly** (adj)   lacking generosity (*mis* wretched)   Synonyms: *avaricious, penurious*

❑ **inimical** (adj)   unfriendly (*in-* not + *amicus* friend)   Synonyms: *antagonistic, hostile*

❑ **curmudgeon** (n)   a cranky person

❑ **misanthrope** (n)   one who hates humankind (*mis* hatred + *anthro* humankind)

Vocabulary Lesson 26: Ripped Off

Ap 15

Today's roots:	*sub-, subter-* under, secretly	*fugere* to flee
	larecin theft	*machina* device

❑ **charlatan** (n)   a fraud; a quack (*chiarlatino* It a quack)

June's family warned her that Chaz was a **charlatan** only pretending to be a successful lawyer.
Synonyms: *imposter, con man, swindler*

❑ **ruse** (n)   a crafty scheme

The clever criminal came up with a flawless **ruse** to steal the money from the bank.
Synonyms: *stratagem, machination*

❑ **subterfuge** (n)   a scheme; an attempt to deceive (*subter* secretly + *fugere* to flee)

It takes real **subterfuge** to sneak anything past Principal Guber; it's like he is able to see your every move.
Synonyms: *surreptitiousness, stratagem, ploy*   Antonyms: *forthrightness, candor*

❑ **dupe** (n)   one who is easily deceived

The con artist has a knack for picking the perfect **dupe,** someone who will easily fall for his scam.
Synonyms: *chump, pushover*

❑ **pilfer** (v)   to steal

The looters **pilfered** countless items from the electronics store during the riot.
Synonyms: *embezzle, filch*

❑ **swindle** (v)   to cheat

The street hustler **swindled** the unsuspecting man, tricking him into buying a fake designer watch.
Synonyms: *bamboozle, hoodwink*

❑ **gullible** (adj)   easily deceived

The **gullible** teenager was easily tricked by her friends into believing that one of them was a secret agent.
Synonym: *naive*   Antonym: *astute*

❑ **embezzle** (v)   to steal money from one's employer   Synonyms: *loot, pilfer*

❑ **machination** (n)   a crafty scheme (*machina* device)   Synonyms: *stratagem, ruse*

❑ **bilk** (v)   to cheat, to swindle   Synonyms: *hoodwink, defraud, cheat, fleece*

❑ **larceny** (n)   theft (*larcin* Fr theft)   Synonym: *thievery*

❑ **filch** (v)   to steal   Synonyms: *pilfer, embezzle*

❑ **fleece** (v)   to defraud of money, to swindle   Synonyms: *swindle, bilk, hoodwink, defraud*

Vocabulary Lesson 27: Good Guys and Bad Guys

Today's roots:	archos	leader, government	theos	god
	a-, an-	without	pacis	peace

❏ **hedonist** (n)   a pleasure seeker (*hedone* pleasure)

The '60s are often considered the age of the **hedonist,** a time when everyone felt they had the right to have fun.
Synonyms: *epicurean, epicure, sybarite, bon vivant*

❏ **ascetic** (n)   one who lives a holy life of self-denial (*asketes* monk)

Tim has spent years at a time as an **ascetic,** each time giving away all he owns and living on rice and prayer.
Synonym: *monk*

❏ **anarchist** (n)   one who opposes all political authority (*an-* without + *archos* leader)

Before the coup d'état, the dictator claimed to be an **anarchist;** that all changed once he was given power.
Synonyms: *insurgent, rebel*

❏ **pacifist** (n)   an individual who is opposed to violence (*pacis* peace + *facere* to make)

Forever a **pacifist,** Julie organized a rally protesting the war in the Middle East.
Synonym: *peace-seeker*   Antonyms: *warmonger, combatant*

❏ **atheist** (n)   one who does not believe that God exists (*a-* without + *theos* god)

Although she is an **atheist** and does not worship the Buddha, Cathy meditates with her Buddhist friends.

❏ **nihilist** (n)   one who rejects moral distinctions and knowable "truths"

Because she is a **nihilist,** Carrie likes to contend that the world may be a figment of her imagination.

❏ **despot** (n)   a tyrant; one who rules oppressively (*despotes* Gk absolute ruler)

The **despot** rules with reckless abandon, doing only what he wants, with no concern for the citizens.
Synonyms: *tyrant, oppressor*

❏ **narcissist** (n)   one in love with his/her own image (from Narcissus, who fell in love with himself)

❏ **zealot** (n)   one who engages passionately in a cause   Synonyms: *enthusiast, fanatic, devotee*

❏ **sybarite** (n)   an individual who seeks luxury   Synonym: *hedonist*

❏ **pessimist** (n)   an individual who focuses on the negative side of a situation (*pessimus* worst)
Synonyms: *alarmist, Cassandra, defeatist*

❏ **optimist** (n)   one who focuses on the positive side of a situation (*optimus* best)
Synonyms: *idealist, Polyanna, Pangloss, Candide*

❏ **fanatic** (n)   one who shows extreme enthusiasm for a cause (*fanaticus* enthusiastic)
Synonyms: *extremist, radical, zealot, enthusiast*

Vocabulary Lesson 28: That's Better

Ap.16

Today's roots:	*culpa* blame	*placare* to please
	ex-, e- out	*mollis* soft

❑ **vindicate** (v)   to clear from blame

The adroit defense lawyer was able to **vindicate** her client of all charges, and he was set free.
Synonyms: *exonerate, absolve*   Antonym: *convict*

❑ **assuage** (v)   to soothe anger or pain; to satisfy a hunger (*suavis* agreeable, sweet)

If your dog gets stung by a bee, place a wet washcloth on the area to **assuage** the pain.
Synonyms: *pacify, appease, quench, allay*   Antonyms: *provoke, vex, exacerbate*

❑ **mollify** (v)   to soothe the anger of (*mollis* soft)

The waiter attempted to **mollify** the angry customer by offering him a free dessert with his dinner.
Synonyms: *assuage, appease, placate, conciliate*   Antonyms: *rile, provoke*

❑ **exonerate** (v)   to clear from accusation (*ex-* out + *onus* burden)

When the principal found the spray paint in Rex's locker, Timmy was **exonerated** of all graffiti charges.
Synonyms: *acquit, exculpate, absolve*   Antonym: *incriminate*

❑ **placate** (v)   to soothe; to mollify (*placare* to please)

The mother attempted to **placate** her crying baby by handing him his favorite teddy bear.
Synonyms: *pacify, assuage, conciliate, appease*   Antonyms: *enrage, provoke*

❑ **exculpate** (v)   to free from blame (*ex-* out + *culpa* blame)

Although the DNA evidence did not identify the killer, it did **exculpate** the police's primary suspect.
Synonyms: *acquit, disculpate, exonerate*.   Antonyms: *impeach, convict*

❑ **anesthetic** (n)   something that reduces sensation (*an-* without + *aisthesis* Gk feeling)

Before closing the cut, the doctor administered an **anesthetic** to numb the area around the wound.
Synonym: *palliative*

❑ **pacify** (v)   to soothe the agitation or anger of (*pacis* peace)   Synonyms: *appease, conciliate*

❑ **invigorate** (v)   to energize (*in-* in + *vigor* liveliness + *-ate* to do)   Synonyms: *stimulate, rejuvenate*

❑ **alleviate** (v)   to relieve (think of "Aleve" to relieve body aches)   Synonyms: *assuage, allay*

❑ **emollient** (n)   a substance that softens (*mollis* soft)

❑ **absolve** (v)   to pardon (*ab-* from + *solvere* to loosen)   Synonyms: *exculpate, acquit*

❑ **placid** (adj)   peaceful; calm (*placare* to please)   Synonyms: *serene, tranquil*

Vocabulary Unit 4 Exercise Set I

AP!6

Time—8 minutes
For each question, select the best answer among the choices given. Note any vocabulary words to review on the Hit List below.

1. The ------ soldiers were commended for their refusal to surrender even when survival seemed to be an impossibility.
   (A) bombastic
   (B) dogged
   (C) disputatious
   (D) infamous
   (E) dexterous

2. Five months after the surgical procedure, the patient requested a stronger pain medication to help ------ the daily discomfort she felt in her shoulder.
   (A) exonerate
   (B) alleviate
   (C) invigorate
   (D) perambulate
   (E) scrutinize

3. The ------ golden statues added to the front of the house were excessively ------ even for the pretentious family that lived there.
   (A) ornate . . ostentatious
   (B) opulent . . nefarious
   (C) insipid . . pompous
   (D) splenetic . . grandiose
   (E) gaudy . . mercurial

4. In an effort to ------ his bitter opponents, the President passed a law they had been pushing unsuccessfully for years.
   (A) consummate
   (B) mollify
   (C) vindicate
   (D) purge
   (E) invoke

5. Sally's ------ made her a ------ for many a con artist.
   (A) loftiness . . chump
   (B) infallibility . . curmudgeon
   (C) pacifism . . charlatan
   (D) placidity . . ruse
   (E) gullibility . . dupe

6. Despite having ruled the nation for thirty years as ------ and ------ dictator, the prime minister was remembered for his munificence during the food shortage of 1987.
   (A) an abominable . . beneficent
   (B) a repugnant . . magnanimous
   (C) an obstinate . . lithe
   (D) a steadfast . . benevolent
   (E) an odious . . malevolent

7. The deft way in which the lawyer was able to deflect the negative testimony to his favor showed why he is the ------ of prosecution.
   (A) paragon
   (B) conviction
   (C) braggart
   (D) machination
   (E) misanthrope

8. The resort island is a fantasy vacation spot for a ------; one has rarely seen so much luxury and splendor in one place.
   (A) sybarite
   (B) zealot
   (C) nihilist
   (D) narcissist
   (E) ascetic

9. When a basketball player commits ------ foul in a flagrant attempt to hurt a player, the referee calls a "technical foul" and the team that is fouled receives two foul shots and retains possession of the ball.
   (A) a preeminent
   (B) a peripheral
   (C) a masochistic
   (D) an inexorable
   (E) an egregious

10. The young scamp has always shown ------ for larceny, having successfully ------ his first purse at the young age of six.
    (A) an equanimity . . filched
    (B) a bigotry . . bilked
    (C) an aptitude . . pilfered
    (D) a predilection . . exculpated
    (E) an agility . . razed

HIT LIST

_____   _____
_____   _____
_____   _____
_____   _____

Vocabulary Unit 4 Exercise Set II

Ap16

> Write the meaning next to each root, then write as many words as you can that contain the root.

1. GRAND_____

_____
_____
_____
_____

2. SUB-_____

_____
_____
_____
_____

3. SAUVIS_____

_____
_____
_____
_____

4. PACIS_____

_____
_____
_____
_____

5. SUMMUS_____

_____
_____
_____
_____

6. APT_____

_____
_____
_____
_____

7. PUGNARE_____

_____
_____
_____
_____

8. MIS_____

_____
_____
_____
_____

9. DEXTER_____

_____
_____
_____
_____

10. TRACT_____

_____
_____
_____
_____

11. CULP_____

_____
_____
_____
_____

12. MOLLIS_____

_____
_____
_____
_____

13. THEOS_____

_____
_____
_____
_____

14. PLAC_____

_____
_____
_____
_____

15. PED_____

_____
_____
_____
_____

Vocabulary Unit 4 Exercise Set III

1. Is an *ostentatious* person humble?   Y N

2. Is a *deft* person good at what she does?   Y N

3. Is a *recalcitrant* person *obsequious*?   Y N

4. Does an *anarchist* resist authority?   Y N

5. Is an *infamous* person known for   Y N
    kind things?

Write the word with the given meaning.

6. a fraud   c_____

7. showy about knowledge   p_____

8. a pleasure seeker   h_____

9. nimbleness   a_____

10. famous for bad deeds   i_____

11. to steal   p_____

12. luxuriousness   o_____

13. to clear from blame   v_____

14. worthy of dislike   o_____

15. to clear from blame   e_____

16. unswerving   s_____

17. a substance that softens   e_____

18. a crafty scheme   m_____

19. using inflated language   b_____

20. a resentful person   c_____

21. a tyrant   d_____

22. skillful   a_____

23. determined   d_____

24. relentless   i_____

25. one who seeks luxury   s_____

Write the correct form of the italicized word.

26. the quality of being *recalcitrant*

    _____

27. characterized by *agility*

    _____

28. characteristic of *hypocrites*

    _____

29. That which an *anarchist* seeks

    _____

30. To achieve *vindication*

    _____

Write the word with the given root.

31. wishing harm to others (*vol*)

    _____

32. stubbornness (*per*)

    _____

33. natural ability (*apt*)

    _____

34. a scheme (*subter*)

    _____

35. to soothe (*suavis*)

    _____

36. difficult to manipulate (*tract*)

    _____

37. to soothe (*mollis*)

    _____

38. wicked (*fas*)

    _____

39. to free from blame (*culp*)

    _____

40. model of excellence (*para*)

    _____

41. lacking generosity (*mis*)

    _____

Unit 4 Exercise Set I Answer Key

1. **(B)** If the soldiers are being *commended*, they must have done something good, which means that the missing word is positive. The phrase *refusal to surrender* tells us that *dogged* is the best choice.
   bombastic = pompous
   dogged = refusing to surrender
   disputatious = argumentative
   infamous = famous for evil acts
   dexterous = skillful with the hands

2. **(B)** The patient is having a lot of pain and discomfort and wants to get rid of it. *Alleviate* is a perfect fit.
   exonerate = to clear of blame
   alleviate = to lessen
   invigorate = to give strength to
   perambulate = to move around
   scrutinize = to examine closely

3. **(A)** The phrase *even for the pretentious family* leads us to believe that these statues must be quite pretentious. You want to pick words that relate to pretentiousness and luxury for both blanks.
   ornate = overly decorated; *ostentatious* = showy
   opulent = luxurious; *nefarious* = wicked
   insipid = dull; *pompous* = arrogant
   splenetic = irritable; *grandiose* = pretentious
   gaudy = showy; *mercurial* = changing

4. **(B)** The opponents are *bitter*, which means that they are quite unhappy about something. They have been trying to get a particular law passed, and finally this President helps them pass the law. You want a word that means to *soothe* or *please*.
   consummate = to make perfect
   mollify = to soothe the anger of
   vindicate = to clear from blame
   purge = to get rid of
   invoke = to call into being

5. **(E)** Con artists like to take advantage of people. Both words should describe a person who is easily taken advantage of. *Gullible* and *dupe* fit the best.
   loftiness = excessive pride; *chump* = a pushover
   infallibility = perfection; *curmudgeon* = resentful person
   pacifism = love of peace; *charlatan* = a fraud
   placidity = calm; *ruse* = a crafty scheme
   gullibility = easily fooled; *dupe* = a pushover

6. **(E)** *Despite* implies that the second half of the sentence should provide a contrast to the first. The leader is remembered for his munificence, or generosity, which is a positive quality. Therefore the two words should be negative.
   abominable = terrible; *beneficent* = doing good, kind
   repugnant = offensive; *magnanimous* = generous
   obstinate = stubborn; *lithe* = agile
   steadfast = determined; *benevolent* = kind
   odious = worthy of hate; *malevolent* = evil

7. **(A)** The lawyer *deftly* (skillfully) turns something that is negative into his advantage. This must mean that he is quite good at what he does. The word choice that best fits this is *paragon*.
   paragon = the model of perfection
   conviction = strongly held belief
   braggart = one who boasts
   machination = a crafty scheme
   misanthrope = a hater of humankind

8. **(A)** The sentence tells us that the resort island is filled with *luxury and splendor*. Who would love that? A *sybarite*.
   sybarite = an individual who seeks luxury
   zealot = one who engages passionately in a cause
   nihilist = one who does not believe anything can truly exist
   narcissist = a person in love with his or her own image
   ascetic = a person who lives a life of self-denial

9. **(E)** The technical foul is called when a player creates a foul that is obvious and *flagrant*. *Egregious* is a perfect choice.
   preeminent = outstanding
   peripheral = on the side
   masochistic = enjoying one's own pain
   inexorable = relentless
   egregious = flagrant, blatant

10. **(C)** A scamp is a mischievous person with a tendency toward crime. The word *having* indicates that the second word should support the first.
    equanimity = calmness; *filched* = stole
    bigotry = intolerance towards others; *bilked* = stole
    aptitude = talent; *pilfered* = stole
    predilection = preference; *exculpated* = freed from blame
    agility = swiftness; *razed* = completely destroyed

Unit 4 Exercise Sets II and III Answer Key

Exercise Set II

1. **GRAND**: great, big
   grandeur, grandparent, grandiose, grandiloquent

2. **SUB-**; under, secretly
   subtle, subcutaneous, subliminal, subterfuge, subservient, subconscious

3. **SAUVIS**: agreeable, sweet
   assuage, suave, sweet

4. **PACIS**: peace
   pacifist, peace, pacify, pacific

5. **SUMMUS**: highest
   summit, consummate, sum

6. **APT**: fit
   inept, aptitude, apt, adapt

7. **PUGNARE**: to fight
   pugnacity, impugn, pugnacious, repugnant

8. **MIS**: bad, wretched, hatred
   miserly, miserable, misanthrope, miser, misery, misogyny

9. **DEXTER**: skillful
   dexterity, dexterous, ambidextrous

10. **TRACT**: to pull
    subtract, abstract, attract, distract, contract, traction, intractable, tractor

11. **CULP**: blame
    exculpate, inculpate, disculpate, culprit, culpable

12. **MOLLIS**: soft
    emollient, mollify

13. **THEOS**: god
    atheist, theology, enthusiasm, pantheist, theocracy, monotheism

14. **PLAC**: to please
    placate, placid, placebo, complacent, complaisant, plea, please, displease

15. **PED**: instruct
    pedagogue, pedantic, pedant

Exercise Set III

1. N
2. Y
3. N
4. Y
5. N
6. charlatan
7. pedantic
8. hedonist
9. agility
10. infamous
11. pilfer
12. opulence
13. vindicate
14. odious
15. exonerate or exculpate
16. steadfast
17. emollient
18. machination
19. bombastic
20. curmudgeon
21. despot
22. adroit or adept
23. dogged
24. inexorable
25. sybarite
26. recalcitrance
27. agile
28. hypocritical
29. anarchy
30. vindicate
31. malevolent
32. pertinacity
33. aptitude
34. subterfuge
35. assuage
36. intractable
37. mollify
38. nefarious
39. exculpate
40. paragon
41. miserly

Vocabulary Unit 5

AP 17

Vocabulary Lesson 29: Make Me!

| Today's roots: | *ligare* to bind | *vocare* to call |
| | *ducere* to lead | *pro-* forth |

❏ *cajole* (v)   to persuade by using flattery

The clever eight-year-old girl successfully **cajoled** her parents into taking her to Disney World.
Synonyms: *coax, wheedle, deceive*

❏ *exhort* (v)   to urge strongly (*ex-* thoroughly + *hortari* to urge)

The doctor **exhorted** his patient to stop smoking by explaining how dangerous a habit it really was.
Synonyms: *provoke, instigate, rouse*   Antonyms: *inhibit, discourage*

❏ *coerce* (v)   to persuade through the use of force

The bully **coerced** the smaller boy into handing over his lunch money with threats of wedgies and deadarms.
Synonyms: *compel, intimidate*

❏ *induce* (v)   to cause (*in-* in + *ducere* to lead)

After thirty-six hours of labor, the doctors decided to **induce** the baby's birth with medication.
Synonyms: *sway, incite, impel*   Antonyms: *curb, stall*

❏ *coax* (v)   to persuade by using flattery

The charming man used well-placed compliments to **coax** the pretty waitress into meeting him for a drink.
Synonyms: *cajole, wheedle*

❏ *provoke* (v)   to stir up; to excite (*pro-* forth + *vocare* to call)

Eric **provoked** his older brother into fighting by whacking him on the head with his action figure.
Synonyms: *irritate, rile, incite*   Antonyms: *placate, assuage*

❏ *obligatory* (adj)   required (*ob-* to + *ligare* to bind)

The **obligatory** jumps in the skating competition must be performed or the competitor loses points.
Synonyms: *mandatory, compulsory*   Antonyms: *optional, elective*

❏ *wheedle* (v)   to influence by flattery   Synonyms: *coax, cajole*

❏ *goad* (v)   to urge into action   Synonyms: *spur, incite, catalyze*

❏ *begrudge* (v)   to give in to something reluctantly   Synonyms: *concede, acquiesce*

❏ *spur* (v)   to goad into action   Synonyms: *provoke, goad, incite*

❏ *prerequisite* (n)   a requirement   <don't confuse with *perquisite:* a perk>

Synonym: *obligation*

❏ *resigned* (adj)   accepting of one's fate   Synonyms: *begrudging, acquiescent*

Vocabulary Lesson 30: Come to Your Senses!

AP 17

Today's roots:	*audire*	to hear	*palpare*	to touch
	gustare	to taste	*cernere*	to separate

❏ **tactile** (adj)   able to be sensed by touch (*tactilis* to touch)

The petting zoo provides a fun **tactile** experience for children, allowing them to touch dozens of animals.
Synonym: *palpable*

❏ **olfactory** (adj)   relating to the sense of smell (*olere a* to smell of + *facere* to make)

For those with a strong **olfactory** sense the spray of a skunk is extremely pungent.

❏ **gustatory** (adj)   relating to the sense of taste (*gustare* to taste)

The meal was a **gustatory** extravaganza; her taste buds were exploding from all the savory spices.

❏ **auditory** (adj)   relating to the sense of hearing (*audire* to hear)

Kris's **auditory** deterioration prevented him from appreciating the subtle tonality of the music.
Synonym: *aural*

❏ **discern** (v)   to perceive as separate; to sense keenly (*dis-* away + *cernere* distinguish, separate)

The fog made it difficult for me to **discern** how many people stood at the far end of the parking lot.
Synonyms: *perceive, distinguish, ascertain*

❏ **pungent** (adj)   having a sharp or irritating odor (*pungere* to sting)

Many find garlic breath to be so **pungent** that they avoid cooking with the herb entirely.
Synonyms: *piquant, zesty*

❏ **palpable** (adj)   detectable by touch (*palpare* to touch)

As the tightrope walker attempted to regain his balance, the tension in the audience was nearly **palpable.**
Synonyms: *tangible, tactile*

❏ **ascertain** (v)   to learn for certain   Synonym: *discern*

❏ **savory** (adj)   pleasant tasting; appetizing   Synonym: *palatable*

❏ **putrid** (adj)   rotten; having a foul odor (*putris* rotten)   Synonyms: *rancid, decayed*

❏ **perceptive** (adj)   able to perceive; aware   Synonyms: *keen, insightful*

❏ **perceive** (v)   to become aware   Synonyms: *discern, ascertain*

❏ **aural** (adj)   relating to the sense of hearing (*auris* ear)   Synonym: *auditory*

❏ **tangible** (adj)   detectable by touch; substantial (*tangere* to touch)   Synonyms: *palpable, concrete*

Vocabulary Lesson 31: Stop It!

Ap 17

Today's roots:	*ab-, abs-* from	*terrere* to frighten
	tenere hold	*suadere* to urge

❑ ***thwart*** (v)   to stop something before it is able to succeed

Thanks to inside information, the police department was able to **thwart** the bank robbery before it even began.
Synonyms: ***circumvent, stymie, foil***   Antonym: ***abet***

❑ ***abstain*** (v)   to refrain from action (*abs-* from + *tenere* to hold)

An alcoholic for twenty years, Robert was unable to **abstain** from drinking when offered a beer.
Synonyms: ***forgo, eschew***   Antonym: ***indulge***

❑ ***deterrent*** (n)   something that acts to discourage (*de-* away + *terrere* to frighten)

The picture of the vicious lion baring his teeth was an effective **deterrent** against kids' reaching into the cage.
Synonyms: ***hindrance, impediment***   Antonym: ***incentive***

❑ ***impede*** (v)   to slow the progress of, to block

The orange cones did not do much to **impede** the progress of the cars; they just drove right over them.
Synonyms: ***hinder, obstruct***   Antonyms: ***assist, expedite***

❑ ***hinder*** (v)   to slow the progress of

The weed-killer sprayed on the garden successfully **hindered** the growth of the unwanted plants.
Synonyms: ***impede, obstruct, thwart***   Antonyms: ***promote, facilitate***

❑ ***curtail*** (v)   to make less (*curtus* short)

In an effort to lose weight, Mark tried to **curtail** his ice cream consumption.
Synonym: ***diminish***   Antonyms: ***extend, boost***

❑ ***impediment*** (n)   something that works to impede progress; a hindrance

Louise had a speech **impediment** that caused her to stutter, but that did not keep her from being a DJ.
Synonyms: ***impedance, encumbrance, hindrance***   Antonym: ***aid***

❑ ***stymie*** (v)   to present an obstacle to   Synonyms: ***hinder, impede***

❑ ***dissuade*** (v)   to persuade not to do something (*dis-* against + *suadere* to urge)

Synonyms: ***deter, divert***

❑ ***refrain*** (v)   to hold back from doing (*re-* back + *frenare* to restrain)   Synonyms: ***halt, inhibit***

❑ ***abstinence*** (n)   the voluntary avoidance of something (*abs-* from + *tenere* to hold)

❑ ***tentative*** (adj)   uncertain   <The **tentative** schedule was not set in stone.>
Synonyms: ***cautious, diffident***

❑ ***hamper*** (v)   to restrict the progress of   Synonyms: ***impede, hinder***

Vocabulary Lesson 32: Must Be the Money AP 18

Today's roots:	pecunia	money	parsi	to save
	pro-	ahead	indu	within

❏ **destitute** (adj)   completely penniless (*destitutus* abandoned)

The stock market collapse of 2000–2002 left many an adept investor **destitute.**
Synonyms: *impoverished, penniless*   Antonyms: *affluent, wealthy*

❏ **frugal** (adj)   economical; good with money (*frux* fruit, profit)

A **frugal** shopper does not make a purchase before checking many other places for a lower price.
Synonyms: *thrifty, parsimonious*   Antonyms: *squandering, prodigal*

❏ **remuneration** (n)   payment for services (*re-* back + *munerari* to give)

The job is tedious, but the **remuneration** is worthwhile—over fifty dollars per hour!
Synonyms: *income, earnings*

❏ **impecunious** (adj)   without money (*im-* not + *pecunia* money)

You would never guess that Marisa was so **impecunious** if you watched her spend money at the mall.
Synonyms: *destitute, penurious*   Antonyms: *affluent, wealthy*

❏ **improvident** (adj)   failing to provide for the future (*im-* not + *pro-* ahead + *videre* to see)

Despite once being a millionaire, Tom was now broke due to his **improvident** spending decisions.
Synonyms: *prodigal, negligent, spendthrifty*   Antonyms: *thrifty, frugal*

❏ **parsimony** (n)   excessive thriftiness (*parsi-* to spare, save + *monium* an action, a condition)

Al's **parsimoniousness** reached an extreme when he hand-delivered a bill rather than spending money on a stamp.
Synonyms: *miserliness, stinginess*   Antonyms: *magnanimity, munificence*

❏ **venal** (adj)   able to be bribed (*venalis* that is for sale)

The local outlaws knew that the **venal** sheriff could be paid to let them escape.
Synonym: *corruptible*

❏ **thrifty** (adj)   economical; good with money   Synonyms: *frugal, provident, parsimonious*

❏ **pauper** (n)   an extremely poor individual (*pau* little + *parere* to get)   Synonyms: *mendicant*

❏ **mercenary** (n)   one who gives his services to the highest bidder (*merces* pay, reward)

❏ **perquisite** (n)   payment or privilege received in addition to wages   <*perk* for short>

❏ **insolvent** (adj)   bankrupt (*in-* not + *solvent* able to pay what one owes)   Synonym: *broke*

❏ **indigent** (adj)   impoverished, poor (*indu-* within + *egere* to need, want)   Synonym: *destitute*

❏ **pecuniary** (adj)   pertaining to money (*pecunia* money)

Vocabulary Lesson 33: Saw That Coming

Ap 18

Today's roots:	*pro-, pre-, fore-* before	*scientia* knowledge
	monere to warn	*por-* forward

❑ **prophecy** (n)   a prediction of the future (*pro-* before + *phanai* to speak)

The **prophecy** told of a boy who would soon be born to save the human race from extinction.
Synonyms: *divination, prognostication*

❑ **harbinger** (n)   a precursor

Many consider the robin to be a **harbinger** of spring.
Synonyms: *omen, forerunner*

❑ **augur** (v)   to predict the future (an *augur* in ancient Rome was an official who foretold events)

The "psychic network" claims to **augur** what is to come for its callers, but most believe it to be a hoax.
Synonyms: *prophesy, divine*

❑ **premonition** (n)   a forewarning (*pre-* before + *monere* to warn)

The traveller had a **premonition** of the upcoming disaster and refused to board the plane.
Synonyms: *presentiment, hunch*

❑ **portend** (v)   to give advance warning (*por-* forward + *tendere* to extend)

The weather service looks for atmospheric signs that **portend** violent storms.
Synonyms: *foretell, foreshadow*

❑ **prescient** (adj)   having knowledge of future events (*pre-* before + *scientia* knowledge)

The seemingly **prescient** gambler made a fortune at the racetrack, always knowing which horse would win.
Synonym: *clairvoyant*

❑ **omen** (n)   a sign of something to come

The nervous bride took the death of the minister who was to marry them as an **omen** that her marriage was doomed.
Synonyms: *portent, prognostication*

❑ **foresight** (n)   the ability to see things coming (*fore-* before)   Synonyms: *anticipation, forethought*

❑ **clairvoyant** (n)   one with great foresight (*clair-* clear + *voyant* seeing)   Synonyms: *visionary, psychic*

❑ **portent** (n)   an omen of a future event (*por-* forward + *tendere* to extend)   Synonym: *omen*

❑ **preempt** (v)   to block by acting first (*pre-* before)   Synonym: *anticipate*

❑ **premeditate** (v)   to plan ahead of time (*pre-* before + *meditari* to consider)   Synonym: *plot*

❑ **prophetic** (adj)   able to tell the future (*pro-* before + *phanai* to speak)   Synonym: *prescient*

❑ **bode** (v)   to be an omen for something   <a red sky at dawn **bodes** ill for sailors>
        Synonym: *portend*

Vocabulary Lesson 34: Old and Worn Out   Ap 18

Today's roots:	*arch*	ancient	*per-*	through
	ante-	before	*ob-*	away, against

❑ **archaic** (adj)   ancient (*arch* ancient)

The boat's **archaic** navigation system confused the young sailor, who knew how to read only the newer consoles.
Synonyms: *primitive, antiquated*   Antonyms: *modern, novel*

❑ **relic** (n)   an object from an ancient time (*re-* back + *linquere* to leave)

The **relic** found at the ancient burial site once served as a water pitcher for an Aztec family.
Synonyms: *artifact, remnant*

❑ **decrepit** (adj)   worn out from old age or use (*de-* down + *crepare* to break, to crack)

The **decrepit** swing set in the schoolyard had been used by four generations of children.
Synonyms: *feeble, battered, threadbare*

❑ **antiquated** (adj)   obsolete; outdated (*antiquus* ancient)

The computer technology in rural Italy is quite **antiquated;** even Internet access is rare.
Synonyms: *archaic, primitive*   Antonyms: *modern, novel*

❑ **antediluvian** (adj)   very old (*ante-* before + *diluvim* a flood, in reference to the Biblical flood)

The piece of pottery they found was an **antediluvian** bowl that was made over 4,000 years ago.
Synonyms: *primeval, archaic*   Antonyms: *modern, novel*

❑ **defunct** (adj)   no longer in existence (*defunctus* dead, off-duty)

Telegrams as a means of communication are **defunct;** the existence of email and telephones made them obsolete.
Synonyms: *dead, extinct*   Antonym: *extant*

❑ **perpetuate** (v)   to keep from dying out (*per-* through + *petere* to seek, go to)

The myth that cigarettes don't harm you has been **perpetuated** by the cigarette companies.
Synonyms: *immortalize, commemorate*

❑ **outmoded** (v)   out of fashion; obsolete   Synonyms: *anachronistic, obsolete*

❑ **artifact** (n)   an object of historical interest (*arte* skill + *factum* thing made)   Synonyms: *relic, remnant*

❑ **obsolete** (adj)   outmoded (*ob-* away + *solere* to be used)   Synonyms: *anachronistic, antiquated*

❑ **dilapidated** (adj)   worn out   Synonyms: *decrepit, feeble*

❑ **threadbare** (adj)   shabby; worn down such that the threads show   Synonyms: *dilapidated, decrepit*

❑ **archive** (n)   a collection of historically interesting material (*arch* ancient)

Vocabulary Lesson 35: Feelings

Ap 19

Today's roots:	*pathos* emotion	*anti-* against
	con- with	*syn-, sym-* together

- ❑ **apathy** (n)   lack of feeling; lack of interest (*a-* without + *pathos* emotion)

  Mark was **apathetic** about Stephanie's desire to keep her laptop clean; he put his fingerprints all over the screen.
  Synonyms: *indifference, torpor*   Antonym: *intensity*

- ❑ **apprehensive** (adj)   anxious about what is to come

  It is normal to feel **apprehensive** on the morning of your driver's test; it is a nerve-wracking experience.
  Synonyms: *uneasy, concerned*   Antonyms: *fearless, intrepid, dauntless*

- ❑ **contrite** (adj)   repentant (*con-* with + *terere* to wear down)

  The **contrite** murder suspect scored points with the judge, who appreciated her remorseful attitude.
  Synonym: *remorseful*   Antonyms: *unrepentant, inveterate*

- ❑ **lament** (v)   to mourn, to show sorrow (*lamentum* a wailing)

  The fans **lamented** the passing of John Lennon; they cried as if they had lost a brother.
  Synonyms: *bemoan, grieve*   Antonym: *celebrate*

- ❑ **console** (v)   to comfort (*con-* with + *solari* to comfort)

  There were many family members on hand to **console** the grieving widow at her husband's funeral.
  Synonyms: *soothe, calm*   Antonyms: *enrage, provoke*

- ❑ **impassive** (adj)   lacking emotion (*im-* not + *passivus* capable of feeling)

  Joy's **impassiveness** about her grades upset her parents; they wanted her to care more about her work.
  Synonyms: *indifferent, apathetic*   Antonyms: *intense, demonstrative*

- ❑ **ignominy** (n)   humiliation; shame

  The **ignominy** of a jail sentence was too much for Jules to bear.
  Synonyms: *disgrace, dishonor*   Antonyms: *gratification, dignity*

- ❑ **pathos** (n)   pity; feeling of sorrow (*pathos* emotion)   Synonyms: *anguish, woe*

- ❑ **empathy** (n)   the ability to identify with another's feelings (*em-* in + *pathos* feeling)

- ❑ **penitent** (adj)   feeling remorse for one's actions   Synonyms: *repentant, contrite*

- ❑ **sympathy** (n)   the ability to share another's feelings (*syn-* together + *pathos* feeling)
  Synonym: *compassion*

- ❑ **poignant** (adj)   causing a sharp emotional response (*poindre* to prick)   Synonyms: *stirring, moving*

- ❑ **remorse** (n)   regret for past deeds (*re-* again + *mordere* to bite)   Synonyms: *anguish, contrition*

- ❑ **antipathy** (n)   strong feelings against something (*anti-* against + *pathos* feeling)

Vocabulary Unit 5 Exercise Set I

Ap 19

> Time—8 minutes
> For each question, select the best answer among the choices given. Note any vocabulary words to review on the Hit List below.

1. Elizabeth's assistant was ------ with his words and spoke only when it was absolutely necessary.
   (A) improvident
   (B) parsimonious
   (C) antiquated
   (D) clairvoyant
   (E) sympathetic

2. The salary Julia received for her job was unsatisfactory, but the ------ were phenomenal: a dental plan, five weeks of vacation, and a company car.
   (A) perquisites
   (B) harbingers
   (C) mercenaries
   (D) impediments
   (E) resolutions

3. In spite of his aggressive attempts to ------ us into doing something against the law, we were able to ------ from partaking in the illicit act.
   (A) goad . . refrain
   (B) cajole . . stagnate
   (C) coax . . rebound
   (D) impede . . abstain
   (E) dissuade . . recuperate

4. Because the team had been eliminated from the playoffs, they played with ------ in their final five games, losing by an average of forty points per game.
   (A) fortitude
   (B) apathy
   (C) dread
   (D) vigor
   (E) resolution

5. The wise old man who lived at the top of the mountain is visited often by villagers looking for him to use his ------ powers to ------ their future.
   (A) olfactory . . augur
   (B) tactile . . portend
   (C) prescient . . divine
   (D) prophetic . . console
   (E) clairvoyant . . perjure

6. A departure from the bland food and mundane atmosphere that characterized our recent dining experiences, Chez Henri provided ------ cuisine and ------ ambience.
   (A) pungent . . a hedonistic
   (B) savory . . a transcendent
   (C) piquant . . an artificial
   (D) obsolete . . a supreme
   (E) palatable . . an imperious

7. Management's decision to raise the salaries of the workers was more pragmatic than ------; the executives didn't want so much to be generous as to keep the assembly lines moving.
   (A) magnanimous
   (B) mellifluous
   (C) rigid
   (D) masochistic
   (E) frugal

8. After giving birth to her first child, the woman was finally able to ------ with her mother about the pain and discomfort that come with childbirth.
   (A) empathize
   (B) collaborate
   (C) perpetuate
   (D) premeditate
   (E) associate

9. The defendant's contrite behavior was not an act; he truly felt great ------ for the crime of which he was accused.
   (A) apprehension
   (B) indigence
   (C) foresight
   (D) bliss
   (E) remorse

10. Even though she was unable to walk without a limp, she did not allow this ------ to ------ her ability to run short sprints for the track team.
    (A) deterrent . . spur
    (B) barrier . . impel
    (C) abstinence . . thwart
    (D) impediment . . hamper
    (E) pathos . . hinder

HIT LIST

_____   _____
_____   _____
_____   _____
_____   _____
_____   _____

Ap 19

Vocabulary Unit 5 Exercise Set II

Write the meaning next to each root, then write as many words as you can that contain the root.

1. PATHOS_____

_____

_____

_____

_____

2. CITARE_____

_____

_____

_____

_____

3. TERRERE_____

_____

_____

_____

_____

4. ANTI-_____

_____

_____

_____

_____

5. AUD_____

_____

_____

_____

_____

6. FORE_____

_____

_____

_____

_____

7. SCIENTIA_____

_____

_____

_____

_____

8. VOCARE_____

_____

_____

_____

_____

9. POR-_____

_____

_____

_____

_____

10. SUADE_____

_____

_____

_____

_____

11. MONERE_____

_____

_____

_____

_____

12. TENERE_____

_____

_____

_____

_____

13. PALPARE_____

_____

_____

_____

_____

14. INDU_____

_____

_____

_____

_____

15. CERNERE_____

_____

_____

_____

_____

Ap 19

Vocabulary Unit 5 Exercise Set III

1. Can you be *parsimonious* with words?　　Y N
2. Is an *omen* necessarily bad?　　Y N
3. Does something *savory* taste good?　　Y N
4. Is something *obsolete* new?　　Y N
5. Does someone *thrifty* waste money?　　Y N

Write the word with the given meaning.

6. lacking emotion　　　　i_____
7. repentant　　　　　　　c_____
8. to foretell　　　　　　p_____
9. without money　　　　i_____
10. outmoded　　　　　　o_____
11. capable of being felt　p_____
12. to make less　　　　　c_____
13. to cause by persuasion　i_____
14. ancient　　　　　　　a_____
15. a forewarning　　　　p_____
16. relating to taste　　　g_____
17. to refrain from action　a_____
18. to persuade with flattery　c_____
19. deeply emotional　　　p_____
20. economical　　　　　　t_____
21. to urge strongly　　　e_____
22. humiliation　　　　　　i_____
23. payment　　　　　　　r_____
24. able to be bribed　　　v_____
25. to stop before it begins　t_____

Write the correct form of the italicized word.

26. showing *apathy*

_____

27. to act as a *deterrent*

_____

28. the act of *abstaining*

_____

29. the act of touching something that is *palpable*

_____

30. the act of *cajoling*

_____

Write the word with the given root

31. to urge into motion (*citare*)

_____

32. a prediction of the future (*pro*)

_____

33. lacking feeling (*a-*)

_____

34. relating to smell (*olere*)

_____

35. extremely poor individual (*pau*)

_____

36. to comfort (*solari*)

_____

37. economical (*frux*)

_____

38. to stir up (*vocare*)

_____

39. worn out (*crepare*)

_____

40. to make less (*curtus*)

_____

41. regret (*mordere*)

_____

Unit 5 Exercise Set I Answer Key

1. **(B)** If the assistant *only spoke when it was absolutely necessary*, then he was *frugal* or *sparing* with his words.
   improvident = not economical
   parsimonious = excessively thrifty
   antiquated = very old
   clairvoyant = having great foresight
   sympathetic = feeling pity

2. **(A)** The *but* indicates a contrast. Extra benefits like a dental plan, a vacation, and a car are called *perks* or *perquisites*.
   perquisite = a perk, a dividend
   harbinger = a sign of something to come
   mercenary = one who works for the highest bidder
   impediment = an obstruction
   resolution = firm determination

3. **(A)** The phrase *in spite* indicates a contrast in the second half of the sentence. If he was *aggressive* in getting us to do something *illicit* (illegal), the contrast suggests that we didn't give in. Words like *persuade* and *stay away* would work.
   goad = to urge; *refrain* = to hold back from doing
   cajole = to persuade; *stagnate* = to remain still
   coax = to persuade; *rebound* = to bounce back
   impede = to block; *abstain* = to avoid something
   dissuade = to deter; *recuperate* = to recover

4. **(B)** The sentence implies that the team has nothing left to play for. The fact that they also consistently lose by forty points indicates that they are playing with a *lack of heart*.
   fortitude = strength of mind; strength to endure
   apathy = lack of concern or effort
   dread = profound fear; anxious anticipation
   vigor = physical energy or strength
   resolution = firm determination

5. **(C)** The word *future* is the key context clue. What can one do to the future? A *wise* man in particular might be able to *predict* it.
   olfactory = related to smell; *augur* = to predict the future
   tactile = touchable; *portend* = to predict the future
   prescient = clairvoyant; *divine* = to predict the future
   prophetic = prescient; *console* = to comfort
   clairvoyant = able to predict future; *perjure* = to lie under oath

6. **(B)** The word *departure* indicates a contrast, and the parallelism between the clauses sets up the contrast. The two words must be the opposite of *bland* and *mundane*, respectively.
   pungent = strong; *hedonistic* = pleasure-seeking
   savory = delicious; *transcendent* = inspiring
   piquant = spicy; *artificial* = not genuine
   obsolete = outmoded; *supreme* = great
   palatable = edible; *imperious* = overbearing

7. **(A)** The second clause logically extends the idea of the first. The decision was done for *pragmatic* (practical) reasons rather than out of generosity to the employees. Look for a word that means *generous*.
   magnanimous = generous
   mellifluous = smooth-flowing
   rigid = inflexible
   masochistic = enjoying one's own pain
   frugal = thrifty; disinclined to waste money

8. **(A)** The woman now knows first hand about the pain and discomfort associated with childbirth. Because she has now experienced what her mother went through, she can now *empathize* with her about the sensations.
   empathize = to identify with another's feelings
   collaborate = work together
   perpetuate = cause to continue
   premeditate = plan in advance

9. **(E)** If the *contrite behavior was not an act,* then the defendant must truly feel regret for what was done.
   apprehension = nervousness
   indigence = neediness
   foresight = ability to see things coming
   bliss = extreme happiness
   remorse = regret

10. **(D)** *Even though* indicates an unexpected twist. The inability to walk without a limp is certainly a nuisance. It would make sense that the first word should mean *hindrance* and the second word should mean *prevent*.
    deterrent = something that discourages; *spur* = to goad into action
    barrier = a block; *impel* = to urge
    abstinence = avoidance; *thwart* = to stop
    impediment = barrier; *hamper* = to hinder
    pathos = sorrow; *hinder* = to obstruct

Unit 5 Exercise Sets II and III Answer Key

Exercise Set II

1. PATHOS: emotion
apathy, sympathy, empathy, osteopathy, pathogen, pathetic, psychopath

2. CITARE: to excite
incite, excite, recite, resuscitate, solicit, citation

3. TERRERE: to frighten
deter, deterrent, terrible, terrify, terror, terrific

4. ANTI-: against
antipathy, antibiotic, antonym, antiseptic, antagonist, antisocial

5. AUD: to hear
audition, auditorium, auditory, inaudible, audible

6. FORE-: before
foremost, foretell, forethought, forehand, forecast, forebear, foresight

7. SCIENTIA: knowledge
scientist, omniscient, prescient, conscientious

8. VOCARE: to call
vocabulary, convocation, provoke, revoke, convoke, vocation, invoke, advocate, equivocate

9. POR-: forward
portent, portend, portray

10. SUADE: to urge
sway, persuasion, persuade, dissuade

11. MONERE: to warn
premonition, summon, admonish, monitor

12. TENERE: to hold
sustain, abstain, contain, detain, entertain, tenable, tenacity, pertinacity, retain, obtain, pertain

13. PALPARE: to touch
palpate, palpable, palpatation

14. INDU: in, within
indigenous, industrial, indigent, industry

15. CERNERE: to separate
discern, certain, concern, excrement, secretary

Exercise Set III

1. Y
2. N
3. Y
4. N
5. N
6. impassive
7. contrite
8. portend
9. insolvent, impecunious
10. obsolete
11. palpable
12. curtail
13. impel, induce
14. archaic
15. premonition
16. gustatory
17. abstain
18. cajole
19. poignant
20. thrifty
21. exhort
22. ignominy
23. remuneration
24. venal
25. thwart
26. apathetic
27. deter
28. abstinence
29. palpation
30. cajolery
31. incite
32. prophecy
33. apathetic
34. olfactory
35. pauper
36. console
37. frugal
38. provoke
39. decrepit
40. curtail
41. remorse

Vocabulary Unit 6   Ap 20

Vocabulary Lesson 36: What the Heck?

Today's roots:	gradi	to step, to go	equi	equal
	crypto	secret	dis-	apart

❑ **ambiguous** (adj)   unclear in meaning (*ambigere* to wander)

The teacher's **ambiguous** instructions left us with no idea of what we were supposed to do.
Synonyms: *vague, obscure*   Antonyms: *apparent, lucid*

❑ **obscure** (adj)   not easily understood; indistinct (*obscurus* darkness)

The comedian's jokes contained **obscure** references that left the audience confused and silent.
Synonyms: *vague, enigmatic, cryptic*   Antonyms: *evident, lucid*

❑ **equivocal** (adj)   deliberately ambiguous or misleading (*equi* same + *vocare* to call)

The defendant's **equivocal** answers made it hard for the prosecutor to prove his case.
Synonyms: *evasive, indirect*   Antonyms: *straightforward, forthright, candid*

❑ **convoluted** (adj)   intricate and hard to follow (*con-* together + *volvere* to roll)

The instructions in this manual are so **convoluted** that I don't even know where to begin.
Synonyms: *cryptic, inscrutable, incomprehensible*   Antonyms: *coherent, intelligible*

❑ **cryptic** (adj)   enigmatic; mysterious (*crypto* concealed, secret)

The soldier's **cryptic** reply over the radio to his captain suggested that something was amiss.
Synonyms: *cryptic, obscure, incomprehensible*   Antonyms: *coherent, intelligible*

❑ **unfathomable** (adj)   impossible to comprehend (*un-* not + *fathom* to grasp)

The idea that time slows as our speed increases is **unfathomable** to most of us.
Synonyms: *baffling, impenetrable, inscrutable*   Antonyms: *coherent, intelligible*

❑ **nebulous** (adj)   vague; indefinite (*nebula* mist)

Bill's memory of the car accident was **nebulous;** he remembered only bits and pieces of the ordeal.
Synonyms: *hazy, unclear*   Antonyms: *lucid*

❑ **enigma** (n)   a mystery or riddle (*oenigma* riddle)   Synonyms: *conundrum, riddle*

❑ **esoteric** (adj)   difficult to understand (Gr *esoterikos* belonging to an inner circle)

❑ **ramble** (v)   to wander aimlessly, either verbally or physically   Synonyms: *stray, babble*

❑ **desultory** (adj)   aimless; prone to random digressions (*desultorious* skipping about)

❑ **digress** (v)   to go off topic (*dis-* away + *gradi* to step, to go)   Synonyms: *diverge, deviate, ramble*

❑ **profound** (adj)   deep; insightful (*pro-* forth + *fundus* bottom)   Synonyms: *philosophical, sagacious*

Vocabulary Lesson 37: True or False?

Ap 20

Today's roots:	*verax* true	*candere* to shine
	genuinus natural	*apo-* away

❏ *candor* (n)   honesty; straightforwardness (*candere* to shine)

I appreciated my doctor's **candor;** I prefer a straightforward approach when discussing my health.
Synonyms: *forthrightness, frankness*   Antonyms: *disingenuousness, fraudulence, equivocation*

❏ *affect* (v)   to put on airs; to behave unnaturally

Hoping to fit in while in London, Jules **affected** a British accent.
Synonyms: *feign, impersonate*

❏ *veracity* (n)   truthfulness (*verax* true)

Since we can't test the **veracity** of his statements, we will never know for sure if he was telling the truth.
Synonyms: *sincerity, candor*   Antonyms: *fallacy, falsehood*

❏ *debunk* (v)   to expose something as fraudulent

The DA knew that the cop was crooked and made it his mission to **debunk** the officer's claims.
Synonyms: *uncover, reveal*   Antonyms: *conceal, camouflage*

❏ *apocryphal* (adj)   of doubtful authenticity (*apo-* away + *kryptein* hide)

Before they found out it was a fake, the **apocryphal** Van Gogh painting sold for over a million dollars.
Synonyms: *counterfeit, forged*   Antonyms: *authentic*

❏ *forthright* (adj)   honest; straightforward

The student's **forthright** admission of guilt was appreciated by the principal, who reduced his suspension.
Synonyms: *candid, frank*   Antonyms: *deceitful, treacherous*

❏ *disingenuous* (adj)   insincere; crafty (*dis-* away from + *genuinus* natural)

Daphne's expression of remorse was clearly **disingenuous,** because she did not feel any regret for her actions.
Synonyms: *deceitful, treacherous*   Antonyms: *forthright, candid*

❏ *candid* (adj)   straightforward; honest (*candere* to shine)   Synonyms: *frank, forthright*

❏ *dubious* (adj)   doubtful (*dubium* doubt)   Synonyms: *suspect, questionable*

❏ *prevaricate* (v)   to lie (*pre-* before + *varicare* to straddle)   Synonyms: *equivocate, fabricate*

❏ *verisimilitude* (n)   the quality of appearing to be true (*verax* true + *similis* like)

❏ *outspoken* (adj)   candid and unsparing in speech   Synonyms: *forthright, frank*

❏ *fraudulent* (adj)   deceitful (*fraus* deceit)   Synonyms: *duplicitous; crooked*

❏ *facade* (n)   outward appearance; a false front (*faccia* face)   Synonym: *superficiality, frontispiece*

Vocabulary Lesson 38: Arts and Entertainment

Ap 20

| Today's roots: | *curare* to take care of | *levis* light in weight |
| | *jocus* joke | *para-* beside, beyond |

❏ **mirth** (n)   merriment; laughter

The little boy could not contain his **mirth** when playing with the bubbles.
Synonyms: *jollity, levity, gaiety*   Antonyms: *melancholy, dejection, despondency*

❏ **aesthetic** (adj)   relating to beauty or a theory of beauty (Gr *aisthetikos* perception)

The beautiful colors that emerged from the crystal when struck by the sunlight were **aesthetically** pleasing.

❏ **satire** (n)   a mocking literary or dramatic work (*satira* a poetic medley)

Animal Farm by George Orwell is a **satire** that mocks socialism.
Synonyms: *burlesque, parody, lampoon, travesty, spoof*

❏ **curator** (n)   the individual in charge of a museum (*curare* to take care of)

The **curator** in charge of the Louvre in Paris controls the Mona Lisa, perhaps the world's most famous painting.

❏ **witticism** (n)   a clever or funny remark

Will Rogers was famous for his **witticisms** about American life.
Synonyms: *epigram, bon mot, quip, badinage*

❏ **jocular** (adj)   done in a joking way (*jocus* joke)

Jeff's **jocular** tone relaxed the visitors trapped in the elevator; he even made a few people laugh.
Synonyms: *facetious, waggish, salty*   Antonyms: *despondent, somber, morose, plaintive, lugubrious*

❏ **malapropism** (n)   the outrageous misuse of a word

Saying "for all intensive purposes" instead of "for all intents and purposes" is a classic example of a **malapropism**.
Synonyms: *misusage, solecism, catachresis*

❏ **levity** (n)   a lack of seriousness (*levis* light in weight)   Synonyms: *frivolity, flippancy*

❏ **bard** (n)   a skilled poet   Synonyms: *sonneteer, versifier*

❏ **parody** (n)   a spoof (*para* beside + *ode* song)   Synonyms: *burlesque, lampoon, travesty, satire*

❏ **epic** (n)   a lengthy poem that celebrates the life of a hero (Gr *epos* word, story)

❏ **aesthete** (n)   a person interested in the pursuit of beauty (Gr *aisthetikos* sensitive)

❏ **dilettante** (n)   one who dabbles in an art (*dilettare* to delight)   Synonyms: *amateur*

❏ **lampoon** (v)   to make fun of   Synonyms: *satirize, mock, parody*

Vocabulary Lesson 39: You're in Trouble

Ap 21

Today's roots:	*culpa*	blame	*censura*	judgment
	dictare	to declare	*probus*	honest, worthy

❏ **chastise** (v)   to punish or criticize (*castus* pure)

The congressman was **chastised** in the media for his ties to big business.
Synonyms: *condemn, rebuke*   Antonyms: *applaud, hail*

❏ **reprove** (v)   to scold (*re-* not + *probus* worthy)

The teacher **reproved** her students strongly for talking during her lecture.
Synonyms: *rebuke, berate, reprimand*   Antonyms: *hail, compliment, acclaim*

❏ **reprehensible** (adj)   worthy of blame or censure

The woman could not believe that her son would do something so **reprehensible** as torturing small animals.
Synonyms: *culpable, disgraceful, censurable*   Antonyms: *laudable*

❏ **culpable** (adj)   deserving blame (*culpa* blame)

Although the DNA evidence clearly proved he was **culpable,** the defendant continued to claim innocence.
Synonyms: *guilty, blameworthy*   Antonyms: *innocent, blameless, sinless*

❏ **indict** (v)   to accuse of an offense (*dictare* to declare)

The mob boss was **indicted** on ten counts of money laundering.
Synonyms: *accuse, impeach*   Antonyms: *acquit, exonerate*

❏ **reproach** (v)   to blame; to express disapproval

After hitting the softball through the window, Ella was **reproached** by her mother for being so careless.
Synonyms: *censure, condemn, rebuke*   Antonyms: *compliment, commend*

❏ **rebuke** (v)   to scold (*re-* back + *buke* to strike)

Because Belinda was **rebuked** the last time she left her toys out, she cleaned up thoroughly to avoid another scolding.
Synonyms: *reprove, reproach, reprehend, reprimand, chide*

❏ **castigate** (v)   to punish severely   Synonyms: *reprimand, berate, chastise*

❏ **impeach** (v)   to accuse of wrongdoing (*im-* in + *pedica* shackle)   Synonyms: *indict, charge*

❏ **irreproachable** (adj)   beyond blame   Synonyms: *innocent, impeccable*

❏ **berate** (v)   to punish severely (*be-* thoroughly + *rate* to scold)   Synonyms: *reprimand, castigate, chastise*

❏ **culprit** (n)   one guilty of a crime (*culpa* blame)   Synonyms: *offender, criminal*

❏ **acquit** (v)   to clear of a charge (*a-* to + *quite* free)   Synonyms: *vindicate, exonerate*

❏ **reprimand** (v)   to scold (*reprimare* to reprove)   Synonyms: *reprove, castigate, censure*

AP 21

Vocabulary Lesson 40: Working Hard

| Today's roots: | *fatigare* tire | *sedere* to sit |
| | *metus* fear | *integer* whole |

❑ **diligence** (n)   hard work and dedication (*diligentia* attentiveness)

Ty's **diligence** paid off when his boss gave him a promotion and a raise.
Synonyms: *assiduousness, industry, perseverance*   Antonyms: *laziness, indolence*

❑ **scrupulous** (adj)   careful, ethical (*scruples* ethical standards)

Always a **scrupulous** student, Simone made sure she got her assignments in on time.
Synonyms: *conscientious, honorable, meticulous*   Antonyms: *immoral, wanton*

❑ **meticulous** (adj)   attentive to detail (*metus* fear)

The accountant was incredibly **meticulous;** no detail ever slipped by her.
Synonyms: *thorough, painstaking*   Antonyms: *lackadaisical, cavalier*

❑ **indefatigable** (adj)   untiring (*in-* not + *fatigare* to tire)

Despite working 100 hours per week, the lawyer was **indefatigable,** remaining energetic about his job.
Synonyms: *tireless, unremitting, dogged*   Antonyms: *listless, lethargic*

❑ **spartan** (adj)   full of self-discipline (from Sparta whose army was known for its discipline and valor)

Alissa's **spartan** regimen included learning fifty new vocabulary words each week.
Synonyms: *ascetic, rigorous*   Antonyms: *cavalier, lackadaisical*

❑ **painstaking** (adj)   meticulous; paying great attention to detail

After eleven **painstaking** hours in the operating room, the surgeon declared the brain surgery a complete success.
Synonyms: *thorough, meticulous*   Antonyms: *lackadaisical, cavalier*

❑ **assiduous** (adj)   hard working (*sedere* to sit)

My parents are always telling me that my grades would improve if I were more **assiduous** in my studies.
Synonyms: *diligent, industrious*   Antonyms: *indolent, slothful*

❑ **prolific** (adj)   extremely productive (*pro-* forth + *facere* to make)   Synonyms: *productive, abundant*

❑ **integrity** (n)   honesty and virtue (*integer* whole)   Synonyms: *purity*

❑ **enterprising** (adj)   full of initiative and imagination (*entreprendre* to undertake)

❑ **entrepreneur** (n)   a self-made businessman (*entreprendre* to undertake)
     Synonyms: *magnate, industrialist*

❑ **industrious** (adj)   hard-working; diligent   Synonyms: *assiduous*

❑ **resolute** (adj)   determined; willing to push on   Synonyms: *dogged, steadfast, tenacious*

Ap 21

Vocabulary Lesson 41: The Faithful and the Unfaithful

Today's roots:	orthos	straight, strict	sub-	under
	surgere	to rise	klan	to break

❑ **conform** (v)   to do what one is expected to do (*com-* together + *formare* to form)

His desire to avoid punishment at all costs causes him to **conform** to his parents' many rules.
Synonyms: *comply, obey*   Antonyms: *defy, rebel*

❑ **orthodoxy** (n)   strict adherence to tradition (*orthos* straight, strict + *doxa* opinion)

The Amish are well known for their **orthodoxy**; tradition is very important to their culture.
Synonyms: *conventionality, traditionalism*   Antonyms: *heresy, apostasy*

❑ **iconoclast** (n)   one who challenges tradition (Gr *eikon* image + *klan* to break)

Always an **iconoclast**, Michael did everything in his power to do the opposite of what was expected.
Synonyms: *heretic, apostate, rebel, nonconformist, infidel*   Antonyms: *conformist, traditionalist*

❑ **heresy** (n)   opinion or action that violates traditional belief

In many villages in colonial New England, to question religious doctrine was considered **heresy**.
Synonyms: *iconoclasm, apostasy*   Antonyms: *sycophancy, toadyism, compliance, submission, obsequy*

❑ **insurgent** (adj)   rebellious (*in-* against + *surgere* to rise)

The villagers became more **insurgent** each day that the army remained in their midst.
Synonyms: *insubordinate, mutinous*   Antonyms: *conformist, yes-man, toady, sycophant*

❑ **convention** (n)   a practice that comports with the norms of a society

Ms. Frazier's teaching style went against **convention** and thus angered the conservative school board.
Synonyms: *protocol, practice*   Antonyms: *irregularity*

❑ **insubordination** (n)   refusal to submit to authority (*in-* against + *sub-* under + *ordinare* arrange)

By punishing all **insubordination**, the commander showed his troops that no disobedience would be tolerated.
Synonyms: *agitation, subversion, rebellion*   Antonyms: *pacification*

❑ **renegade** (n)   an outlaw (*negare* to deny)   Synonyms: *defector, traitor*

❑ **insurrection** (n)   an uprising (*in-* against + *surgere* to rise)   Synonyms: *coup, mutiny, rebellion*

❑ **dissident** (n)   one who strongly opposes accepted opinion (*dis-* apart + *sedere* to sit)   Synonym: *rebel*

❑ **mutiny** (n)   a rebellion   Synonyms: *revolt, riot, uprising*

❑ **servile** (adj)   overly submissive (*servus* slave)   Synonyms: *obsequious*

❑ **heretic** (n)   one who dissents   Synonyms: *rebel, iconoclast*

❑ **apostasy** (n)   abandonment of a belief (*apo-* away from + *stanai* to stand)   Synonyms: *heresy*

Vocabulary Lesson 42: How Rude!

Ap 22

| Today's roots: | *pudere* | to cause shame | *trux* | fierce |
| | *solere* | accustomed | *haut* | high |

❑ **insolent** (adj)   rudely disrespectful (*in-* not + *solere* accustomed)

The despot punished the rebel's **insolence** with a lengthy prison sentence.
Synonyms: *impudent, impertinent*   Antonyms: *courteous, deferential, decorous*

❑ **affront** (n)   an insult (Fr *afronter* to confront)

When he found out that his dad had let him win, Frank took it as an **affront** to his tennis skills.
Synonyms: *slur, barb, aspersion, obloquy*   Antonyms: *tribute, exaltation, veneration*

❑ **haughty** (adj)   overly proud (*haut* high)

The **haughty** young goalie felt that he had no equal in the league.
Synonyms: *conceited, supercilious, cavalier, arrogant*   Antonyms: *modest, diffident*

❑ **crass** (adj)   unrefined

Luke's **crass** behavior at the dinner table horrified the princess, who had never seen such poor manners.
Synonyms: *boorish, oafish, philistine*   Antonyms: *decorous, civilized, refined*

❑ **impudent** (adj)   rudely bold (*im-* not + *pudere* to cause shame)

The young soldier's **impudence** would be punished; it is not wise to undermine the authority of a superior officer.
Synonyms: *insolent, impertinent, audacious*   Antonyms: *courteous, civilized*

❑ **boorish** (adj)   crude, barbaric (unrelated to *boar*, a wild pig, but *piggish* is a close synonym)

The **boorish** barbarians ripped at the meat with their bare hands and spit bones out onto the table.
Synonyms: *crass, oafish, barbaric, philistine*   Antonyms: *decorous, polite*

❑ **irreverence** (n)   disrespect (*ir-* not + *vereri* to respect)

The **irreverence** with which he mocked his teachers showed he had no respect for their authority.
Synonyms: *impertinence, flippancy*   Antonyms: *deference*

❑ **flippant** (adj)   disrespectfully jocular; using humor inappropriately   Synonyms: *irreverent, impertinent*

❑ **brazen** (adj)   bold and insolent   <a **brazen** midday robbery in the heart of downtown>
Synonym: *impudent*

❑ **truculent** (adj)   cruel and aggressive (*trux* fierce)   Synonyms: *obstreperous, bellicose*

❑ **effrontery** (n)   boldness, brashness   Synonyms: *insolence, impudence*

❑ **impertinent** (adj)   inappropriately bold (*im-* not + *pertinere* to concern)   Synonyms: *impudent, brazen*

❑ **glacial** (adj)   having a cold personality (like a *glacier*)   Synonym: *frigid*

❑ **rebuff** (v)   to refuse in an abrupt or rude manner   Synonyms: *reject, snub*

Vocabulary Unit 6 Exercise Set I

Ap 22

Time—8 minutes
For each question, select the best answer among the choices given. Note any vocabulary words to review on the Hit List below.

1. Those used to his frequent equivocation in describing his business dealings were shocked by his ------ description of his latest acquisition.
   (A) forthright
   (B) apocryphal
   (C) esoteric
   (D) boorish
   (E) indefatigable

2. Heidi's sudden indolence was ------ to her colleagues; until recently she had been an assiduous and exemplary employee.
   (A) an insurrection
   (B) a satire
   (C) an enigma
   (D) an indiscretion
   (E) an indictment

3. Decades after being appointed ------ of the renowned museum, Charles confessed to be only ------ who scarcely appreciated the significance of the great works he oversaw.
   (A) curator . . a dilettante
   (B) lampoon . . a dabbler
   (C) entrepreneur . . an amateur
   (D) fanatic . . a nihilist
   (E) philanthropist . . an ascetic

4. The film is a collection of lowbrow ------ that lampoon some of the more popular movies of recent years.
   (A) parodies
   (B) epics
   (C) anthologies
   (D) strategems
   (E) bards

5. The villager's ------ behavior was ------ to the queen, who was not used to being treated with such effrontery.
   (A) tenacious . . a malapropism
   (B) crass . . a witticism
   (C) jocular . . a moratorium
   (D) downtrodden . . an insult
   (E) insolent . . an affront

6. The press lambasted the congresswoman for her part in the scandal, but she knew that since she was not ------, the ------ was unfair.
   (A) seditious . . digression
   (B) guilty . . candor
   (C) veracious . . prevarication
   (D) jocular . . castigation
   (E) culpable . . censure

7. Helga was so ------ that she didn't even make eye contact with us as we greeted her at her door.
   (A) garrulous
   (B) glacial
   (C) loquacious
   (D) rapacious
   (E) industrious

8. The other medical residents were tired of Dr. Bob's ------; every other word out of his mouth was an obsequious compliment to a high-ranking doctor or hospital official.
   (A) belligerence
   (B) eloquence
   (C) munificence
   (D) xenophobia
   (E) sycophancy

9. Tom's ------ ideas contrasted sharply with the conventional views held by the strongly orthodox community.
   (A) truculent
   (B) diligent
   (C) iconoclastic
   (D) scrupulous
   (E) candid

10. They expected the funeral to be a sedate and somber affair, but were shocked by the grieving husband's ------.
    (A) orthodoxy
    (B) mirth
    (C) irrelevance
    (D) simplicity
    (E) decorum

HIT LIST

AP 22

Vocabulary Unit 6 Exercise Set II

Write the meaning next to each root, then write as many words as you can that contain the root.

1. CANDERE_____

_____
_____
_____
_____

2. LEV_____

_____
_____
_____
_____

3. JOC_____

_____
_____
_____
_____

4. VER_____

_____
_____
_____
_____

5. APO_____

_____
_____
_____
_____

6. EQUI_____

_____
_____
_____
_____

7. BUNK_____

_____
_____
_____
_____

8. DICTARE_____

_____
_____
_____
_____

9. FATIGA_____

_____
_____
_____
_____

10. PARA-_____

_____
_____
_____
_____

11. CRYPTO_____

_____
_____
_____
_____

12. ORTHOS_____

_____
_____
_____
_____

13. CURARE_____

_____
_____
_____
_____

14. SURGERE_____

_____
_____
_____
_____

15. DOXA_____

_____
_____
_____
_____

Ap 22

Vocabulary Unit 6 Exercise Set III

1. Is it honest to *equivocate*? Y N
2. Can a task be *painstaking*? Y N
3. Does a reprehensible person deserve *censure*? Y N
4. Is a *dilettante* very skilled and experienced? Y N
5. Does an *iconoclast* conform? Y N

Write the word with the given meaning.

6. merriment m_____
7. vague n_____
8. honest f_____
9. hard work d_____
10. strong disapproval c_____
11. unclear a_____
12. to do what is expected c_____
13. to reprimand r_____
14. candid o_____
15. rebellious i_____
16. incomprehensible u_____
17. skilled poet b_____
18. insubordination s_____
19. clever remark w_____
20. doubtful d_____
21. barbaric b_____
22. overly submissive s_____
23. lie p_____
24. rudely disrespectful i_____
25. insult a_____

Write the correct form of the italicized word.

26. a person who is *culpable*

_____

27. having the quality of *heresy*

_____

28. the quality of being *diligent*

_____

29. having the qualities of an *iconoclast*

_____

30. the act of *castigating*

_____

Write the word with the given root.

31. deserving blame (*culpa*)

_____

32. deliberately ambiguous (*vocare*)

_____

33. to punish (*rate*)

_____

34. deep, insightful (*pro*)

_____

35. done in a joking way (*jocus*)

_____

36. attentive to detail (*metus*)

_____

37. truthfulness (*verax*)

_____

38. untiring (*fatiga*)

_____

39. honesty (*candere*)

_____

40. overly proud (*haut*)

_____

41. of doubtful authenticity (*apo*)

_____

Unit 6 Exercise Set I Answer Key

1. **(A)** Those used to his *equivocation* (failure to be straightforward) would be shocked by *straight-forwardness*.
   forthright = honest, straightforward
   apocryphal = of doubtful authenticity
   esoteric = difficult to understand
   boorish = rude
   indefatigable = untiring

2. **(C)** Heidi had been *assiduous* (hard-working) and *exemplary* (worthy of imitation). Sudden *indolence* (laziness) would be surprising and puzzling, to say the least.
   insurrection = rebellion
   satire = mocking work of literature or drama
   enigma = puzzle
   ignominy = shame, embarrassment
   indictment = accusation

3. **(A)** One who lacks a sophisticated appreciation of art is a *dilettante*. One who oversees a museum is a *curator*.
   curator = person in charge of a museum;
   dilettante = dabbler in the arts
   lampoon = satirical work; *dabbler* = amateur
   entrepreneur = businessman; *amateur* = novice
   fanatic = passionate supporter; *nihilist* = one who denies moral absolutes
   philanthropist = benefactor; *ascetic* = monk

4. **(A)** Something that *lampoons* (makes fun of) something is a *satire, spoof,* or *parody*.
   parody = a spoof that makes fun of something
   epic = a heroic poem
   anthology = a collection of works
   strategem = a deceitful scheme
   bard = a poet

5. **(E)** The queen is not used to being treated with *effrontery* (rude boldness). This implies that the villager's behavior is probably *rude* and that such behavior would *bother* the queen.
   tenacious = intense; *malapropism* = incorrect use of a word
   crass = rude; *witticism* = funny remark
   jocular = joking; *moratorium* = rest, a break
   downtrodden = made submissive by constant harsh treatment; *insult* = rude remark
   insolent = rude; *affront* = insult

6. **(E)** The congresswoman is getting *lambasted* (harshly criticized) in the press. She feels that this *criticism* is unfair, so she must feel that she is not *guilty*.
   seditious = insubordinate; *digression* = aside
   guilty = blameworthy; *candor* = honesty
   veracious = truthful; *prevarication* = lies
   jocular = joking; *castigation* = punishment
   culpable = guilty; *censure* = criticism

7. **(B)** Helga did not make eye contact with her guests, a decidedly unfriendly thing to do.
   garrulous = friendly, talkative
   glacial = cold, unfriendly
   loquacious = talkative
   rapacious = ravenous
   industrious = hard-working

8. **(E)** The semicolon joins two clauses that support each other. *Obsequious* compliments are those that try to curry favor with others. He must be a *flatterer*.
   belligerence = inclination to picking fights
   eloquence = skill in speech
   munificence = generosity
   xenophobia = fear of foreigners
   sycophancy = excessive flattery

9. **(C)** Tom's ideas contrasted sharply with the *conventional* (typical) views held by the strongly *orthodox* (traditional) community. He must be a *nonconformist* who eschews tradition.
   truculent = cruel
   diligent = hard-working
   iconoclastic = resistant to tradition
   scrupulous = ethical, meticulous
   candid = honest

10. **(B)** The fact that they are *shocked* implies that the funeral was not so *sedate and somber*. It must have been *happier* than they expected.
    orthodoxy = strict adherence to dogma
    mirth = merriment
    irrelevance = lack of importance
    decorum = appropriateness of behavior

Unit 6 Exercise Sets II and III Answer Key

Exercise Set II

1. **CANDERE**: to shine
   candid, candor, incandescent, candle

2. **LEV**: light
   levity, relieve, elevate, elevator, levitate, alleviate, oblivion

3. **JOC**: joke
   jocular, jocund, joker, jocose, juggler, joke

4. **VER**: truth
   verisimilitude, veracity, verify, very

5. **APO-**: away from
   apocalypse, aphorism, apostate, apoplexy, apostle, apothecary, apocryphal, apology

6. **EQUI**: equal
   equinox, equivalent, equanimity, equipotential, equality, inequality, equitable, equator, equalize

7. **BUNK**: nonsense
   bunk, debunk

8. **DICTARE**: to declare
   dictate, indict, diction, dictum, dictionary

9. **FATIGA**: tired
   indefatigable, fatigued

10. **PARA-**: beyond, beside
    paraphrase, parasite, paramedic, paranoia, parallel, paramount, paradigm

11. **CRYPTO**: secret
    cryptic, crypt, cryptogram, cryptography

12. **ORTHOS**: right, strict
    orthography, orthodox, unorthodox, orthopedic, orthodontics, orthodoxy

13. **CURARE**: to take care of
    procure, curator, curate, pedicure, manicure

14. **SURGERE**: to rise
    resurrection, resurgent, insurgent, insurrection, surge

15. **DOXA**: opinion
    orthodox, paradox, heterodox

Exercise Set III

1. N
2. Y
3. Y
4. N
5. N
6. mirth
7. nebulous
8. forthright
9. diligence
10. censure
11. ambiguous
12. conform
13. rebuke or reprove
14. outspoken
15. insurgent
16. unfathomable
17. bard
18. sedition
19. witticism
20. dubious
21. boorish
22. servile
23. prevaricate
24. insolent
25. affront
26. culprit
27. heretical
28. diligence
29. iconoclastic
30. castigation
31. culpable
32. equivocal
33. berate
34. profound
35. jocular
36. meticulous
37. veracity
38. indefatigable
39. candor
40. haughty
41. apocryphal

Vocabulary Unit 7 ~~Ap 23~~

Vocabulary Lesson 43: Earth, Moon, and Sky

Today's roots:	astrum	star	luna	moon
	naus	ship	celum	sky

❑ **arid** (adj) extremely dry (*arere* to be dry)

Some regions of Africa have become so **arid** that entire lakes have evaporated.
Synonyms: *barren, parched*   Antonyms: *fecund, fertile*

❑ **astral** (adj) relating to the stars (*astrum* star)

The supernova is perhaps the most dramatic of **astral** events.
Synonyms: *celestial, cosmic*

❑ **nautical** (adj) pertaining to sailing (*naus* ship)

The southern tip of Africa poses many **nautical** challenges to even the most adept and experienced sailor.
Synonyms: *marine, maritime*

❑ **lunar** (adj) relating to the moon (*luna* moon)

The **lunar** vehicle can traverse some of the rockiest and most forbidding terrain on the moon.

❑ **fecund** (adj) fertile; fruitful (*fecundus* fruitful)

Over the summer, our **fecund** vegetable garden provided us with an endless supply of wonderful salads.
Synonyms: *prolific, abundant*   Antonyms: *barren, infertile, sterile*

❑ **fallow** (adj) unused; plowed but not cultivated

The **fallow** land would be replanted in two years, once all the nutrients had been restored.
Synonyms: *dormant, inactive, uncultivated*

❑ **cosmic** (adj) relating to the universe (Gr *kosmos* universe, order)

The enormous and unprecedented meteor shower was being hailed as the **cosmic** event of the century.
Synonyms: *astral, celestial, astronomical*

❑ **celestial** (adj) relating to the sky (*celum* sky, heaven)   Synonyms: *heavenly, astral*

❑ **arable** (adj) able to be cultivated (*arare* to plow)   Synonyms: *fertile, fruitful*

❑ **desiccated** (adj) completely dried out   Synonyms: *arid, parched*

❑ **quagmire** (n) swampy land; difficult situation (*quag* bog)   Synonyms: *marsh, swamp, bog*

❑ **aquatic** (adj) living in water (*aqua* water)   Synonym: *marine*

❑ **cultivate** (v) to nurture; to grow crops (*cultivus* tilled)   Synonyms: *farm, till, sow*

Vocabulary Lesson 44: More or Less

AP 23

Today's roots:	*facere*	to do	*plere*	to fill
	copia	abundance	*macer*	thin

❏ **paucity** (adj)   lack, scarcity (*paucus* few, little)

I love good food, so I'm frustrated by the **paucity** of good restaurants in town.
Synonyms: *dearth, scantiness*   Antonyms: *abundance, plenitude, copiousness*

❏ **surfeit** (n)   an excessive amount (*sur-* over + *facere* to do)

The **surfeit** of food on the table for Thanksgiving dinner left us all with bulging stomachs.
Synonyms: *glut, plethora, overabundance*   Antonyms: *deficiency, dearth, paucity*

❏ **copious** (adj)   abundant (*copia* abundance)

The **copious** mistakes in Robert's final paper showed his lack of effort.
Synonyms: *ample, bountiful*   Antonyms: *scanty, sparse, deficient*

❏ **barren** (adj)   infertile

The **barren** land was so devoid of life that it was difficult to find even a weed.
Synonyms: *sterile, desolate*   Antonyms: *fecund, fertile*

❏ **capacious** (adj)   having lots of room (*capax* able to hold a lot)

The **capacious** auditorium had enough seats for all 5,000 students with room to spare.
Synonyms: *spacious, voluminous*   Antonyms: *exiguous, scanty*

❏ **scanty** (adj)   meager; barely enough

The **scanty** portions the soldiers received left them hungry and weak.
Synonyms: *inadequate, meager, deficient*   Antonyms: *sufficient, adequate*

❏ **replete** (adj)   completely filled (*re-* again + *plere* to fill)

The old storage facility was **replete** with decrepit furniture that had far outlived its usefulness.
Synonyms: *crammed, stuffed*   Antonyms: *vacant, barren*

❏ **dearth** (n)   a lack, scarcity   Synonyms: *paucity, scantiness*

❏ **voluminous** (adj)   having great size (*volumen* roll of writing)

Synonyms: *cavernous, capacious, plentiful*

❏ **desolate** (adj)   deserted (*de-* completely + *solus* alone)   Synonyms: *uninhabited, barren*

❏ **diminutive** (adj)   tiny (*de-* completely + *minuere* to make small)   Synonyms: *undersized, miniature*

❏ **meager** (adj)   inadequate (*macer* thin)   Synonyms: *measly, paltry*

❏ **rarefy** (v)   to make less dense or less plentiful (*rarus* rare + *facere* to make)

❏ **rife** (adj)   plentiful   Synonyms: *abundant, rampant, widespread*

Vocabulary Lesson 45: Tough Times

Ap 23

Today's roots:	*logia*	speaking	*dolus*	grief
	epi-	over	*emia*	blood

❑ **eulogy** (n) an honorific speech at a funeral (*eu-* good + *logia* speaking)

Because Eric had been her best friend, he delivered an emotional **eulogy** at her funeral.
Synonyms: *panegyric, encomium, testimonial*   Antonyms: *denunciation, disparagement*

❑ **despondent** (adj) lacking hope (*de-* without + *sperare* hope)

With their team trailing by ten runs in the ninth inning, the fans became **despondent.**
Synonyms: *dejected, depressed, disheartened, desperate*   Antonyms: *ecstatic, elated, euphoric*

❑ **doleful** (adj) filled with grief (*dolus* grief + *-ful* full of)

The funeral for the child was a **doleful** affair; it is always so sad to see someone die at such a young age.
Synonyms: *crestfallen, depressed, woeful*   Antonyms: *ecstatic, elated, euphoric*

❑ **anemic** (adj) feeble; characterized by oxygen deficiency in the blood (*a-* without + *emia* blood)

Our offense was so **anemic** that we didn't hit the ball out of the infield the whole game.
Synonyms: *pallid, weak, feeble*   Antonyms: *robust, vigorous, hale*

❑ **malady** (n) a disease (*mal* bad)

The flu is a common **malady** that strikes millions of people each year.
Synonyms: *affliction, ailment, disorder*

❑ **anguish** (n) extreme suffering

The **anguish** Walter felt when his dog died was unbearable; he could hardly stop crying for a week.
Synonyms: *agony, grief, misery*   Antonyms: *ecstasy, elation, euphoria*

❑ **dirge** (n) a funeral song

You may think all **dirges** are depressing until you've been to a New Orleans jazz funeral.
Synonyms: *requiem, elegy*

❑ **blight** (n) a diseased condition   Synonyms: *curse, affliction*

❑ **affliction** (n) a disorder causing suffering (*ad-* to + *fligere* to strike)   Synonyms: *adversity, hardship*

❑ **elegy** (n) a poem or song relating to death (Gr *legos* poem of lament)   Synonyms: *dirge, requiem*

❑ **epitaph** (n) an inscription found on a gravestone (Gr *epi-* over + *taphos* tomb)

❑ **doldrums** (n) the blues; persistent unhappiness (*dolus* grief)   Synonyms: *depression, melancholy*

❑ **adversity** (n) hardship   <he fought back from **adversity** to win the title>   Synonym: *affliction*

Vocabulary Lesson 46: Good Learnin'

AP 24

Today's roots:	*arkhaios* ancient	*demos* people
	logos study, word, speech	*genea* descent

❑ **etymology** (n)   the study of the origin of words (Gr *etymon* true sense + *logos* word)

A good understanding of **etymology** can help you succeed on the SAT I.

❑ **archaeology** (n)   the study of past cultures (Gr *arkhaios* ancient + *logia* study)

There are many fascinating **archaeological** sites right in the center of Athens.

❑ **anthropology** (n)   the study of human cultures (*anthros* humankind + *logia* study)

Anthropologists are fascinated by the similarities between tribal rituals and modern social conventions.

❑ **ethics** (n)   the study of and philosophy of moral choice (*ethos* character)

The more deeply one studies **ethics,** the less one is able to think in terms of moral absolutes.

❑ **semantics** (n)   the study of the meanings of words and symbols (*sema* sign)

It's amazing that the noun *pedestrian* and the adjective *pedestrian* can be so different **semantically.**

❑ **theology** (n)   the study of religion (*theos* god + *logia* study)

While in Catholic school, we had many **theological** discussions about the role of God in daily life.

❑ **pathology** (n)   the study of disease (*pathos* suffering + *logia* study)

The tissue sample was sent to the **pathology** lab to determine if there was any disease in the liver.

❑ **sociology** (n)   the study of human social behavior and social institutions (*socius* fellow + *logia* study)

I was amazed to learn in **sociology** class that mandatory schooling until age sixteen is a fairly recent practice.

❑ **entomology** (n)   the study of insects (*entomon* insect + *logia* study)

Anna spends so much time burrowing in the yard that she may know more about bugs than most **entomologists.**

❑ **genealogy** (n)   the study of ancestry (*genea* descent + *logia* study)

Sarah was so fascinated by **genealogy** that she compiled a three-volume guide to her family ancestry.

❑ **demographics** (n)   the study of statistics relating to human populations (*demos* people + *graphein* to write)

The **demographics** reveal that Democratic candidates typically perform better in urban areas than in rural areas.

❑ **oncology** (n)   the study of tumors (*onco* tumor + *logia* study)

When my doctor discovered a tumor near my kidney, he referred me to the best **oncologist** on the staff.

❑ **paleontology** (n)   the study of fossils and ancient life (*palai* long ago + *logia* study)

I like to dig in my backyard and pretend I'm a **paleontologist** making an important fossil discovery.

❑ **neurology** (n)   the study of the human brain and nervous system (Gr *neuron* nerve)

I love studying the brain, but I don't want to cut it up; I think I prefer **neurology** to neurosurgery.

Ap 24

Vocabulary Lesson 47: All Alone

Today's roots:	*claudere* to close	*solus* alone
	insula island	*se-* apart

❑ **hermit** (n)   one who prefers to live alone (Gr *ermita* a person of solitude)

The **hermit** lived alone in a shack in the middle of the woods, more than ten miles from the nearest road.
Synonyms: *recluse, loner, eremite*   Antonyms: *socialite, extrovert*

❑ **ostracize** (v)   to exclude from a group

Her comments to the others were so self-centered and cruel that she was **ostracized** for months.
Synonyms: *exile, banish*   Antonyms: *welcome, accept*

❑ **exile** (n)   a banishment (*ex-* away)

After the dictator was overthrown, he lived a life of **exile** far away from his native country.
Synonyms: *banishment, ostracism, deportation, expulsion*   Antonyms: *inclusion, welcome*

❑ **expel** (v)   to force to leave (*ex-* away + *pellere* to push)

The student who slashed the bus tires was **expelled** and won't be seen back here again.
Synonyms: *discharge, evict*   Antonyms: *invite, admit*

❑ **recluse** (n)   one who likes to live alone (*re-* away + *claudere* to close)

In *To Kill a Mockingbird,* the **recluse** Boo Radley is endlessly fascinating to Scout.
Synonyms: *hermit, loner*

❑ **isolate** (v)   to place something apart from everything else (*insula* island)

The patient with tuberculosis was **isolated** from the other patients so he could not infect them.
Synonyms: *detach, segregate*   Antonyms: *include, embrace*

❑ **solitude** (n)   isolation; the quality of being alone (*solus* alone)

Before the two cosmonauts joined him, the lone astronaut on the space station had spent five months in **solitude.**
Synonyms: *seclusion, solitariness, detachment*   Antonyms: *camaraderie, companionship*

❑ **banish** (v)   to force to leave an area   Synonyms: *exile, ostracize, evict*

❑ **outcast** (n)   an individual who has been excluded from a group   Synonyms: *castaway, pariah*

❑ **seclusion** (n)   privacy (*se-* apart + *claudere* to close)   Synonyms: *isolation, solitude*

❑ **pariah** (n)   an individual who has been excluded from a group   Synonyms: *outcast, exile*

❑ **relegate** (v)   to banish, to demote in rank (*re-* back + *legare* to send)   Synonyms: *ostracize, exile*

❑ **quarantine** (n)   a period of isolation for someone infected with a contagion (*quaranta* forty [days])

Vocabulary Lesson 48: Go Forth

Ap. 24

Today's roots:	*supare* scatter	*satur* full
	vergere, vert to turn	*undare* to flow

❑ **disseminate** (v)   to spread information (*dis-* away + *seminare* to sow)

The members of the band **disseminated** flyers that advertised their debut concert this coming weekend.
Synonyms: *circulate, publicize, distribute*   Antonym: *suppress*

❑ **diverge** (v)   to go apart (*dis-* away + *vergere* to turn)

After traveling together for nearly 100 miles, the two cars finally **diverged.**
Synonyms: *divide, branch*   Antonyms: *converge, merge*

❑ **proliferate** (v)   to grow rapidly; to produce offspring at a rapid pace (*proles* offspring)

The bacteria **proliferated** at an alarming rate, multiplying tenfold in just 30 minutes.
Synonyms: *expand, multiply*   Antonyms: *wither, shrink*

❑ **amass** (v)   to accumulate; to gather together

Over the years, Rick has **amassed** quite a collection of CDs, accumulating over 1,000 of them.
Synonyms: *collect, gather, hoard*   Antonyms: *distribute, disperse*

❑ **distend** (v)   to swell; to increase in size (*dis-* apart + *tendere* to stretch)

Malnutrition can cause the abdominal cavity to **distend** and produce a bloated look.
Synonyms: *expand, dilate*   Antonym: *constrict*

❑ **propagate** (v)   to cause to multiply; to publicize; to travel through a medium (*pro-* forth)

Plants of all sizes and shapes **propagate** by forming seeds, which develop into new seedlings.
Synonyms: *procreate, breed*

❑ **inundate** (v)   to flood (*in-* into + *undare* to flow)

After days without work, the lawyer was astonished to suddenly find himself **inundated** with paperwork.
Synonyms: *engulf, overwhelm, swamp, deluge*

❑ **diffuse** (v)   to spread out, as a gas (*dis-* apart + *fundere* to pour)   Synonyms: *circulate, disseminate*

❑ **germinate** (v)   to sprout; to grow (*germen* sprout)   Synonyms: *bud, burgeon, develop*

❑ **disperse** (v)   to spread apart (*dis-* apart + *spargere* to scatter)   Synonyms: *diffuse, disseminate*

❑ **rampant** (adj)   growing out of control (*ramper* to climb)   Synonyms: *rife, predominant, prevalent*

❑ **dissipate** (v)   to scatter (*dis-* apart + *supare* to scatter)   Synonyms: *dispel, disperse*

❑ **saturate** (v)   to fill completely, as with a liquid or solute (*satur* full)   Synonyms: *soak, imbue*

Vocabulary Lesson 49: Even More

Ap 25

Today's roots:	*ad-* to	*scribere* to write
	post- after	*augere* to increase

❑ **annex** (v)   to attach; to acquire land to expand an existing country (*ad-* to + *nectare* to attach)

  When Hitler **annexed** Poland, the dictator's imperialist designs should have been clear.
  Synonyms: *acquire, appropriate, append*   Antonyms: *disengage, dissociate*

❑ **addendum** (n)   something added; a supplement to a book (*ad-* onto)

  After he completed the story, the author wrote an **addendum** explaining why he finished it the way he did.
  Synonyms: *appendix, supplement*

❑ **postscript** (n)   a message added after the completion of a letter (PS) (*post-* after + *scriber* to write)

  After my wife signed the postcard, she remembered something else she wanted to say and wrote a **postscript.**

❑ **epilogue** (n)   an extra chapter added onto the end of a novel (Gr *epi-* in addition + *logia* words)

  In the **epilogue,** the author described what the characters of the novel did 15 years after the main narrative.
  Synonyms: *afterword, postlude*   Antonyms: *prelude, forward, preface, prologue*

❑ **append** (v)   to affix something; to add on (*ad-* to + *pendere* to hang)

  The publishers **appended** an index to the end of the text to help the reader find things more easily.
  Synonym: *annex*

❑ **adjunct** (adj)   added in a subordinate capacity (*ad-* to + *jungere* to attach)

  Although principally a biologist, Dr. Carter was also an **adjunct** professor in the zoology department.
  Synonyms: *subordinate, subsidiary*

❑ **augment** (v)   to add onto; to make greater (*augere* to increase)

  One important way to **augment** your SAT I score is to study vocabulary.
  Synonyms: *enlarge, enhance, amplify, boost, strengthen*   Antonym: *diminish*

❑ **cession** (n)   the act of surrendering or yielding (*cessare* to yield)   Synonyms: *capitulation, relinquishment*

❑ **affix** (v)   to attach (*ad-* to + *figere* to fasten)   Synonyms: *annex, append*

❑ **appropriate** (v)   to take another's work or possessions as one's own (*ad-* to + *proprius* one's own)

❑ **encore** (n)   an extra performance at the end of a show (Fr *encore* again)   Synonym: *curtain call*

❑ **appendix** (n)   supplementary material at the end of a text (*ad-* to + *pendere* to hang)   Synonym: *addendum*

❑ **supplement** (v)   to add something to complete or strengthen a whole (*supplere* to complete)

Vocabulary Unit 7 Exercise Set I

Ap 25

Time—8 minutes
For each question, select the best answer among the choices given. Note any vocabulary words to
review on the Hit List below.

1. While most people would probably be ------ in her position, Stacey somehow managed to remain upbeat and was convinced that things would get better.
   (A) elated
   (B) diminutive
   (C) defamed
   (D) anemic
   (E) despondent

2. Seemingly without scruples, the professor ------ the work of his graduate students and published papers on topics he himself had not even researched.
   (A) isolated
   (B) relegated
   (C) appropriated
   (D) annexed
   (E) eulogized

3. It is shocking that someone who was once so ------ by the public can so quickly become ------ after just one social blunder.
   (A) belittled . . a malady
   (B) disparaged . . a pariah
   (C) saturated . . an exile
   (D) lionized . . an outcast
   (E) ostracized . . a recluse

4. The dearth of ------ land in this region of the country makes it very difficult to maintain plentiful harvests.
   (A) desiccated
   (B) arable
   (C) fallow
   (D) celestial
   (E) arid

5. The entrance of the cavern was so ------ that the indigenous tribes took advantage of its ------ shelter to keep entire clans dry during the heavy rain season.
   (A) voluminous . . capacious
   (B) enormous . . scanty
   (C) cavernous . . meager
   (D) fecund . . spacious
   (E) astral . . copious

6. Although many consider "Deadman's Run" to be the most ------ ski trail on the mountain, Tommy was able to maneuver through the course without ------ after having just learned to ski.
   (A) simple . . trouble
   (B) difficult . . speed
   (C) arduous . . exertion
   (D) pedestrian . . concern
   (E) pragmatic . . practical

7. Zach's knowledge of ------ helped him to identify and avoid the rare and poisonous African spitting beetle.
   (A) entomology
   (B) etymology
   (C) ethics
   (D) pathology
   (E) sociology

8. The spy was immediately ------ back to his country after he was caught attempting to pilfer information from the CIA database.
   (A) quarantined
   (B) secluded
   (C) disseminated
   (D) distended
   (E) deported

9. It is hard to imagine that this barren desert with little to no plant life was once ------ with farms and wildlife.
   (A) doleful
   (B) replete
   (C) germinated
   (D) rarefied
   (E) afflicted

10. After finishing a good novel, I'm always eager to see if an ------ follows to tell me what happened to the main characters after the conclusion of the narrative.
    (A) elegy
    (B) epitaph
    (C) epilogue
    (D) encore
    (E) eulogy

HIT LIST

Vocabulary Unit 7 Exercise Set II

Ap 25

Write the meaning next to each root, then write as many words as you can that contain the root.

1. EPI-_____
   _____
   _____
   _____
   _____

6. ASTRUM_____
   _____
   _____
   _____
   _____

11. ARCH_____
    _____
    _____
    _____
    _____

2. EU-_____
   _____
   _____
   _____
   _____

7. PLERE_____
   _____
   _____
   _____
   _____

12. DEMOS_____
    _____
    _____
    _____
    _____

3. SCRIBERE_____
   _____
   _____
   _____
   _____

8. SOLUS_____
   _____
   _____
   _____
   _____

13. PONERE_____
    _____
    _____
    _____
    _____

4. COPIA_____
   _____
   _____
   _____
   _____

9. GENEA_____
   _____
   _____
   _____
   _____

14. LOGOS_____
    _____
    _____
    _____
    _____

5. AQUA_____
   _____
   _____
   _____
   _____

10. POST-_____
    _____
    _____
    _____
    _____

15. CLAUDERE_____
    _____
    _____
    _____
    _____

Ap 25

Vocabulary Unit 7 Exercise Set III

1. Can a person be *capacious?* Y N
2. Is a *pariah* popular? Y N
3. Can a person be *fecund?* Y N
4. Is it fun to be *despondent?* Y N
5. Do people *germinate?* Y N

Write the word with the given meaning

6. a disease m_____
7. study of cultures a_____
8. to shun o_____
9. relating to the stars a_____
10. study of ancestry g_____
11. relating to the universe c_____
12. abundant c_____
13. one who lives alone r_____
14. lacking hope d_____
15. to accumulate a_____
16. able to be cultivated a_____
17. an extra chapter e_____
18. inadequate m_____
19. to flood i_____
20. unused, uncultivated f_____
21. to fill completely s_____
22. study of populations d_____
23. an extra performance e_____
24. excessive amount s_____
25. extreme suffering a_____

Write the correct form of the italicized word.

26. having *anemia*

_____

27. one who studies *sociology*

_____

28. the act of *ceding*

_____

29. in *solitude*

_____

30. the act of *proliferating*

_____

Write the word with the given root

31. relating to the sky (*celum*)

_____

32. to swell (*dis*)

_____

33. a poem (*legos*)

_____

34. an inscription (*taphos*)

_____

35. study of insects (*entomon*)

_____

36. a scarcity (*paucus*)

_____

37. tiny (*minuere*)

_____

38. banishment (*ex*)

_____

39. high praise (*eu*)

_____

40. to multiply (*pro*)

_____

41. to make greater (*aug*)

_____

Unit 7 Exercise Set I Answer Key

1. **E** *While* indicates a contrast. If she is *upbeat and optimistic*, it must be that most people would be the opposite: *depressed*.
   elated = extremely happy
   diminutive = tiny
   defamed = slandered
   anemic = weak
   despondent = lacking hope

2. **C** The professor lacks *scruples* (moral standards), so he must have done something bad to the work of his students. If he is publishing papers on topics that he has not researched, he is probably stealing the work.
   isolated = secluded
   relegated = banished
   appropriated = taken as his own
   annexed = added on to
   eulogized = praised

3. **D** The fact that it is *shocking* implies that the two words should contrast with each other.
   belittle = to put down; *malady* = illness
   disparage = to put down; *pariah* = outcast
   saturate = to fill completely; *exile* = outcast
   lionize = to worship; *outcast* = someone excluded
   ostracize = to exclude; *recluse* = loner

4. **B** If it is *difficult to maintain plentiful harvests*, it must be because there is too little *usable* land.
   desiccated = dry
   arable = fertile
   fallow = unused
   celestial = relating to the sky
   arid = dry

5. **A** An entrance that can accommodate *entire clans* must be pretty *large*.
   voluminous = large; *capacious* = having lots of room
   enormous = huge; *scanty* = inadequate
   cavernous = large; *meager* = inadequate
   fecund = fertile; *spacious* = full of room
   astral = pertaining to stars; *copious* = abundant

6. **C** *Although* indicates contrast. Although many think it's *hard*, Tommy must not have had difficulty with it.
   arduous = difficult, strenuous; *exertion* = effort, strain
   pedestrian = ordinary, mundane
   pragmatic = practical, concerned with results

7. **A** Zach had knowledge of insects that allowed him to identify the creature. *Entomology* is the study of insects.
   entomology = study of insects
   etymology = study of the origin of words
   ethics = study of moral choices
   pathology = study of disease
   sociology = study of social institutions

8. **E** If a country catches a spy *pilfering* (stealing) information, they will send the spy back to his country of origin.
   quarantined = isolated
   secluded = left alone
   disseminated = spread out
   distended = swollen
   deported = banished

9. **B** If the desert is now *barren* (infertile), it would be hard to imagine it *filled* with farms and wildlife.
   doleful = filled with grief
   replete = filled
   germinated = sprouted
   rarefied = thinned out
   afflicted = suffering

10. **C** The section of a novel that follows the main story is called an *epilogue*.
    elegy = song or poem about death
    epitaph = inscription found on a tombstone
    epilogue = extra chapter added at end of novel
    encore = an extra performance at the end of a show
    eulogy = high praise, speech given at funeral

Unit 7 Exercise Sets II and III Answer Key

Exercise Set II

1. EPI-: upon
   ephemeral, epitaph, epicenter, epidemic, epidermis, epilepsy, epitome

2. EU-: good
   eulogy, euphemism, eucalyptus, eucharist, eugenics, eukaryote, euphoria

3. SCRIBERE: to write
   inscribe, circumscribe, conscription, description, inscription, subscription

4. COPIA: abundance
   cornucopia, copious, copy

5. AQUA: water
   aquatic, aquarium, aqueduct, aqualung

6. ASTRUM: star
   astral, astronomy, astrology, disaster, astronaut

7. PLERE: to fill
   accomplish, complement, deplete, manipulate, replete, supplement

8. SOLUS: alone
   sole, soliloquy, solitaire, solitary, solitude, solo

9. GENEA: descent
   generation, genealogy, congenital

10. POST-: after
    posterior, posterity, posthumous, postpone, postscript

11. ARCH: ancient
    archaic, archaeology, archives

12. DEMOS: people
    demographics, democracy, epidemic, pandemic

13. PONERE: to place
    impose, appropriate, interpose, opponent, proponent, opposite

14. LOGOS: study of
    psychology, anthropology, oncology, geology

15. CLAUDERE: to close
    claustrophobia, conclude, exclude, recluse, seclude

Exercise Set III

1. N
2. N
3. Y
4. N
5. N
6. malady
7. anthropology
8. ostracize
9. astral
10. genealogy
11. cosmic
12. copious
13. recluse
14. despondent
15. amass
16. arable
17. epilogue
18. meager
19. inundate
20. fallow
21. saturate
22. demographics
23. encore
24. surfeit
25. anguish
26. anemic
27. sociologist
28. cession
29. solitary
30. proliferation
31. celestial
32. distend
33. elegy
34. epitaph
35. entomology
36. paucity
37. diminutive
38. exile
39. eulogy
40. propagate
41. augment

CHAPTER 7

CRITICAL READING SKILLS

Aprie 26

Aprie 27

Aprie 28

Lesson 1:
The Three Key Questions

Mapping the Problem of Academic Reading: The Three Key Questions

❑ Good academic reading skill is based on answering three Key Questions:

1. **What is the purpose of this passage?**
2. **What is the central idea of this passage?**
3. **What is the general structure of this passage?**

These are the three "higher-order" questions that form the basis of SAT I critical reading questions.

Questions First or Passage First?

Contrary to what some test-prep books may tell you, you can't ace the reading questions without reading the passage. You don't have to read super-carefully, but you have to read it to get the main ideas. The questions are constructed to distinguish good readers from those who just try to "crack" the questions without reading well.

❑ Some students think that it's best to read the questions before reading the passage. For the vast majority of students, however, this wastes time. It pulls them away from the Key Questions, and they lose sight of the all-important "big picture." This "piecemeal" reading makes understanding the passage much tougher. Most Critical Reading questions test whether you understand the substance of the passage, not whether you know test-taking tricks. Good readers make sure they get the passage first, then focus on the questions.

Don't Make the Passage Boring

A lot of students psych themselves out right off the bat by saying, "Oh, great, here's another one of those boring, pointless SAT I reading passages!" This is a perfect way to fail, because it sets up a self-fulfilling prophecy: if you *expect* that the reading will be boring and pointless, you won't look for the interesting points! And of course, finding those interesting points

is the key to "getting" the passage. If the passage seems boring, you probably haven't looked carefully enough for the interesting points. You haven't focused on the Key Questions.

❑ Good readers assume that there's something interesting to be gained from everything they read. This attitude profoundly changes the way they read: they become "active" readers rather than "passive" readers; that is, they read purposefully and with specific questions in mind, rather than merely hoping to be entertained or informed.

SAT I Questions vs. English Class Questions

The questions on the Critical Reading section aren't necessarily the kinds of questions your English teachers ask, because SAT I questions must be "objective," that is, have answers that every good English teacher will agree on, rather than "subjective," that is, based on an individual's point of view. Your English teachers often ask you to connect a reading to your personal life, or to explore symbolism, or to explore hidden meanings. Of course, the SAT I could never do that in a question, because the answer has to be cut-and-dried.

❑ Your job on the Critical Reading section is not to explore the "subjective" ideas that you explore in English class (those questions have their place, just not on the SAT I), but to understand just three things about each passage: the purpose, the central idea, and the general structure. The answers must be "objective," so
- They won't require you to draw on outside knowledge. Everything you need is in the passage.
- They won't ask you to make creative connections to the material in the passage.
- They won't ask you what "seems like it might be reasonable" about the passage, but rather what conclusions are clearly supported by the passage.

Concept Review 1:
The Three Key Questions

1. What are the three Key Questions that you should ask as you read prose?

• what is the purpose
general idea
structure

2. What are the disadvantages of reading the questions before the passage?

• you become passive
- you don't look for the
big pic. the main idea
- you look for answers

3. What are the differences between "active reading" and "passive reading"?

• active reading → get something out of it. (think
it will be informative), ask's ? ?'s
• passive → simply for entertainment
- not fishing for answers

4. What does it mean that the Critical Reading questions and answers must be "objective"?

- must have a def, non-subjective
answer

5. Each of the following is a question that your English teacher might ask you about something you have read. Cross out any question that is inappropriate to the SAT I. (Please note that the following questions *do not* refer to actual passages in this text. They are for review only, and aim to familiarize you with the types of questions found on the SAT I.)

   a. ~~What experiences in your life are similar to the experiences the author describes in the third paragraph?~~

   b. *What is one example of the "issues" the author describes in passage 1, line 4, that is discussed in passage 2?*

   c. *In line 20, "sustain" most nearly means*

   d. *The author uses the phrase "for better or for worse" in order to suggest that*

   e. ~~Drawing from your knowledge of the Civil War, what conflicts might the author be referring to in line 56?~~

   f. *In the third paragraph, Charles Wallace is characterized as*

   g. *What is the pendant described in lines 6–9 symbolic of?*

   h. *What is the best title for this passage?*

   i. ~~From what you have learned about Communism, is it likely that the author is a Communist?~~

   j. ~~Why might the author be so strident in her criticism of the anti-environmentalist movement?~~

SAT I Practice 1:
The Three Key Questions

The following is an essay regarding current knowledge of subatomic physics.

A tantalizing paradox peers out from every basic physics textbook, but rarely do students notice it or teachers exploit it. Despite the vast knowledge that scientists have accumulated about the subatomic realm, including aston-ishingly accurate equations for predicting the behavior of barely detectable particles, an ob-vious conundrum persists that they are only recently beginning to understand: protons stick together in atomic nuclei.

All first-year physics students learn that the atomic nucleus contains neutrons, which have no charge, and protons, which are positively charged. They also learn that while opposite charges attract, all like charges repel each other, just like the north poles of two magnets. So what keeps all of those positively-charged protons bound together in a nucleus? Physi-cists have long postulated that there must be another special force, called the nuclear force, that counteracts the electrical repulsion be-tween protons. But where does it come from?

One theory, proposed by Nobel laureate Hideki Yukawa in the 1930's, held that the nu-clear force is conveyed by a particle called a pion, which, he claimed, is exchanged among the neutrons and protons in the nucleus. Forty years later, physicists discovered that pions, not to mention the protons and neu-trons themselves, are actually composed of yet smaller particles called "quarks," which are held together by aptly-named "gluons." The force conveyed by gluons is called the "strong" force. Although experiments had clearly demonstrated that these gluons are responsi-ble for the force that binds quarks within pro-tons and neutrons, nothing suggested that gluons are exchanged between protons and neutrons. Nevertheless, by the early 1980's, most physicists became convinced that some combination of gluons and quarks perhaps the pion must be responsible for the nuclear force.

Professor Yukawa's theory, however, was dealt a blow by a series of experiments that were conducted at Los Alamos National Labo-ratory in the early 1990's. These experiments demonstrated that pions carry the nuclear

force only over distances greater than half a fermi—the radius of a proton—yet the distance between bound protons is far less than that. The pion seemed to be a giant plumber's wrench trying to do a tweezer's job.

In the years since, physicists have refined Yukawa's theory to suggest that closely bound protons or neutrons are held by a "residual" force left over from the strong forces binding quarks together into protons and neutrons, so that pions don't need to be exchanged. If the protons and neutrons are far enough apart within the nucleus, however, perhaps pions do the job.

---

1 Which of the following best summarizes the "paradox" mentioned in line 1?

(A) Teachers don't utilize educational materials effectively.
(B) A law of physics appears to be violated.
(C) Scientists continue to test hypotheses that they suspect are false.
(D) Hideki Yukawa's theory is incorrect.
(E) Scientists are increasingly reluctant to explore the difficult field of nuclear physics.

---

2 In lines 35–36, the phrase "responsible for" most nearly means

(A) guardians of
(B) guilty of
(C) representative of
(D) capable of conveying
(E) responsive to

3 According to the passage, the nuclear force cannot be completely explained in terms of the exchange of pions because pions

(A) are not composed of quarks
(B) have little or no effect in the distances between nuclear particles
(C) repel each other
(D) cannot coexist with the gluons that convey the "strong" force
(E) are positively charged

4 Which of the following best describes the purpose of the fifth paragraph in relation to the fourth paragraph?

(A) It resolves a problem indicated in the previous paragraph.
(B) It provides an example of a concept introduced in the previous paragraph.
(C) It presents a counterexample to a misconception described in the previous paragraph.
(D) It provides an example that is similar to the one presented in the previous paragraph.
(E) It logically analyzes a claim made in the previous paragraph.

5 Which of the following best describes the organization of this passage as a whole?

(A) presentation of a theory followed by refutation
(B) description of a problem followed by a history of attempts to solve it
(C) statement of fact followed by logical analysis
(D) description of a scientific discovery followed by a discussion of its implications
(E) analysis of a theory and suggestions on how it should be taught

Answer Key 1:
The Three Key Questions

Concept Review 1

1. What is the purpose of this passage? What is the central idea of this passage? What is the general structure of this passage?
2. It takes your focus away from where it should be: on answering the three Key Questions, rather than scanning for details or phrases in the passage.
3. Active reading is reading with specific questions in mind, and the expectation that you will find something interesting in everything you read. Passive reading is reading without specific questions in mind, in the hope of merely being entertained or informed.
4. "Objective" responses are those on which nearly all competent readers would agree, given the evidence from the passage. The answers must not be based on a reader's individual perspective or prior knowledge. The evidence for every answer must be clearly in the passage itself.

5.
a. Inappropriate: The SAT I would never ask you to make connections to your own life, although you may discuss such things in English class.
b. Appropriate: This question is a straightforward "interpretation" question, which asks you also to compare the content of two passages.
c. Appropriate: This is a "word in context" question.
d. Appropriate: This is a "purpose" question, in which you are asked to consider one part of the passage in terms of the overall purpose of the paragraph or passage.
e. Inappropriate: The SAT I would not ask questions requiring outside knowledge.
f. Appropriate: This is asking how a character is depicted by the author.
g. Inappropriate: The SAT I won't ask about symbolism.
h. Appropriate: This is a "main idea" question.
i. Inappropriate: This would require outside knowledge.
j. Inappropriate: This questions asks for speculation, but all SAT I questions should refer only to what is specifically mentioned in the passage.

SAT I Practice 1

1. **B** The paradox is that "protons stick together" even though a law of physics says they should repel each other.
2. **D** This is a **phrase in context** question. To answer it, you must consider how the phrase is used in that *particular* sentence: ". . . these gluons are *responsible for* the force that binds quarks within protons and neutrons. . . ." In other words, these particles, the gluons, bind the parts of protons and neutrons together. Since gluons are not people, they can't be (A) *guardians of* or (B) *guilty of* anything. This sentence is talking about what gluons *do*, not what they *represent*, so (C) *representative of* doesn't work. Choice (E) does not work because the sentence is discussing what *produces* the strong force, not what *reacts* to it, so (D) is the best choice.
3. **B** The phrase "according to the passage" means you should look for clear evidence in the passage. The answer to this question is found in the fifth paragraph (lines 47–49), where it says that "pions carry the nuclear force only over distances greater than half a fermi—the radius of a proton—yet the distance between bound protons is far less than that." This means that pions can't be what hold protons together, because they aren't effective between protons.
4. **A** The fifth paragraph explains how "physicists have refined Yukawa's theory" in order to resolve the problem described in paragraph four, namely, experimental evidence that showed that the pion is not effective in the narrow space between bound nuclear particles.
5. **B** This question is essentially Key Question #3: *what is the general structure of this passage?* The passage begins by describing a problem: physicists do not really know what holds a nucleus together. It then proceeds to discuss their attempts to find out. The passage ends, however, without the solution to the puzzle: scientists still don't know. Thus, the best description of the structure of the passage is (B) *description of a problem followed by a history of attempts to solve it.*

Lesson 2:
The Three Kinds of Prose

Analyzing the Three Kinds of Prose (Key Question 1)

SAT I Critical Reading passages will cover a wide range of topics, based on the kinds of reading you should expect to do at a good liberal arts college. They may cover subjects like philosophy, history, science, literature, literary criticism, psychology, and anthropology. Nevertheless, **these passages will have only three kinds of purposes: to tell a story, to persuade, or to analyze a concept.** A passage that tells a story is called a **narrative;** a passage that persuades or presents a point of view is called an **argument;** and a passage that examines a concept is called an **analysis.**

NARRATIVES are stories. They include biographies and memoirs. The purpose of a narrative is to **describe how a main character (the *protagonist*) deals with a problem (the *conflict*).**

ARGUMENTS are essays that persuade. They **present authors' points of view, and explain how it is better than one or more other points of view.** They are fundamentally **subjective;** that is, they focus on an **opinion** rather than on a set of facts.

ANALYSES are passages that **inform.** Every analysis is like the response to an essay question. They are fundamentally **objective;** that is, they stick to **facts** that no reasonable person would dispute, rather than opinions.

❏ The first Key Question, *What is the purpose of this passage?* is equivalent to asking: *is this passage a narrative, an argument, or an analysis?* In other words, *is its main function to tell as story, to persuade, or to inform?*

❏ The introduction to each passage often gives clues about the first Key Question. Read it carefully and notice clues like the following. When you see the clues, underline them, note the passage type, and think about the purpose.

Words that indicate narrative: *biography, story, autobiography, memoir, novel, fiction, account*
Words that indicate argument: *comment, argue, opinion, perspective, point of view, position*
Words that indicate analysis: *examine, analyze, scientific, historical, explore*

The Three Kinds of Central Ideas (Key Question 2)

❏ Every passage has a central idea. **This central idea is what "drives" the passage by focusing it, organizing it, and unifying it. It must be carried throughout the entire passage.** There are different kinds of central ideas.

NARRATIVES are focused on **CONFLICT.** The conflict is the **problem** that the main character must deal with. Conflict is the backbone of any narrative; it provides the overall structure of the story. Every narrative basically has three parts:

Part I. The conflict is introduced.
Part II. The conflict is developed.
Part III. The conflict is resolved.

ARGUMENTS are focused on **THESIS.** The thesis is simply what the writer is trying to persuade you to believe. A thesis must **take a side,** that is, state clearly whether a movie or philosophy or political movement or the like is **good** or **bad** or **right** or **wrong.** To understand a thesis, it is just as important to understand what an essay is arguing **against** as what it is arguing **for.**

ANALYSES are focused on an **OBJECTIVE RESPONSE TO A QUESTION** that would interest a college professor of history, literature, geology, philosophy, anthropology, literature or other discipline.

❏ Once you know what kind of passage you're reading, find the central idea. Find the **conflict** (if it's a narrative), the **thesis** (if it's an argument), or the **question** (if it's an analysis). You may want to jot it down in the margin.

❏ Check that every paragraph relates to the central idea. This is one of your most important tasks as a reader. No paragraph should stray from the point of the passage. **If a paragraph seems not to fit, re-read the paragraph or re-think the central idea.**

Concept Review 2:
The Three Kinds of Prose

1. Name the three kinds of prose, and describe the purpose of each.

2. For each type of prose, name four "key words" in the introduction that indicate that particular type of prose:

    a. Narrative

    b. Argument

    c. Analysis

3. What is the function of the "central idea" of a piece of prose?

4. The central idea of a narrative is the

5. The central idea of an argument is the

6. The central idea of an analysis is the

7. How do you know whether you've found the central idea of a passage?

8. After reading the passage on the next page, write what type of prose it is and its central idea.

9. Do the same for the previous passage (from SAT I Practice 1).

SAT I Practice 2:
The Three Kinds of Prose

The following passage was written in 1911 by Wassily Kandinsky, a renowned abstract painter. Here he discusses the relationship between Primitivism, an artistic movement that seeks to move away from technology and the divisions of modern society, and Materialism, which denies that there is a spiritual component of reality.

Every work of art is the child of its age and, in many cases, the mother of our emotions. It
Line follows that each period of culture produces an art of its own which can never be repeated.
5 Efforts to revive the art-principles of the past will at best produce an art that is still-born. It is impossible for us to live and feel as did the ancient Greeks. In the same way those who strive to follow the Greek methods in sculp-
10 ture achieve only a similarity of form, the work remaining soulless for all time. Such imitation is mere aping. Externally the monkey completely resembles the human being; he will sit holding a book in front of his nose,
15 and turn over the pages with a thoughtful aspect, but his actions have for him no real meaning.
There is, however, in art another kind of external similarity which is founded on a fun-
20 damental truth. When there is a similarity of inner tendency in the whole moral and spiritual atmosphere, a similarity of ideals, at first closely pursued but later lost to sight, a similarity in the inner feeling of any one period to
25 that of another, the logical result will be a revival of the external forms which served to express those inner feelings in an earlier age. An example of this today is our sympathy, our spiritual relationship, with the Primitives.
30 Like ourselves, these artists sought to express in their work only internal truths, renouncing in consequence all considerations of external form.
This all-important spark of inner life today
35 is at present only a spark. Our minds, which are even now only just awakening after years of materialism, are infected with the despair of unbelief, of lack of purpose and ideal. The nightmare of materialism, which has turned
40 the life of the universe into an evil, useless game, is not yet past; it holds the awakening soul still in its grip. Only a feeble light glim-

mers like a tiny star in a vast gulf of darkness. This feeble light is but a presentiment, and
45 the soul, when it sees it, trembles in doubt whether the light is not a dream, and the gulf of darkness reality. This doubt and the still-harsh tyranny of the materialistic philosophy divide our soul sharply from that of the Primi-
50 tives. Our soul rings cracked when we seem to play upon it, as does a costly vase, long buried in the earth, which is found to have a flaw when it is dug up once more. For this reason, the Primitive phase, through which we are
55 now passing, with its temporary similarity of form, can only be of short duration.

---

1 Which of the following is the best title for this passage?

(A) The Art of the Early 20th Century
(B) The Dangers of Materialism
(C) Why Primitive Art Cannot Be Rekindled
(D) The Similarities in Artistic Movements
(E) The Lack of Purpose in Art

---

2 In context, the word "aspect" (line 16) most nearly means

(A) meaningful perspective
(B) facial expression
(C) configuration
(D) contemplation
(E) minor part

3 Which of the following is an example of the "fundamental truth" mentioned in lines 19–20?

(A) the inability of great artists like Vincent Van Gogh to achieve fame in their lifetimes

(B) the tendency of artists from all cultures to eschew social conventions

(C) the failure to reproduce artwork that was created in the fourth century BC.

(D) the ability of apes to create paintings that resemble abstract works by humans

(E) the similarity between two paintings created a century apart, each in the midst of a great class war

4 In saying that the soul "trembles in doubt" (line 45) when it sees the "feeble light" (line 44), the author suggests that

(A) artists have doubts about whether the era of materialism is truly past

(B) the public is unsure that its hunger for art will be met

(C) artists do not know from where their next inspiration will come

(D) the Primitives found mysterious lights more frightening than modern people do

(E) artists usually do not work well under the harsh light of scrutiny

5 How would the author characterize the effect of materialism on the artist's soul?

(A) supportive
(B) confusing
(C) calming
(D) oppressive
(E) inspirational

Answer Key 2:
The Three Kinds of Prose

Concept Review 2

1. Narrative: to tell a story; Argument: to persuade; Analysis: to inform.

2. a. Narrative: *biography, story, autobiography, memoir, novel, fiction, account*
   b. Argument: *comment, argue, opinion, perspective, point of view, position*
   c. Analysis: *examine, analyze, scientific, historical, explore*

3. The central idea is the idea that *focuses, organizes,* and *unifies* the passage. Every paragraph must contribute to the central idea.

4. the conflict

5. the thesis

6. the question being analyzed

7. The central idea must "carry through" the entire passage, so to check that you've found the central idea, make sure that every paragraph contributes to that central idea. If not, then re-read the paragraph until it "fits" with the central idea, or reconsider what the central idea is.

8. This passage is an argument; the author is presenting a subjective theory about art and artistic movements. Its central idea, or thesis, is summarized in lines 3–4: *each period of culture produces an art of its own which can never be repeated.*

9. This passage is an analysis; the fact that it is about *"current knowledge of subatomic physics"* implies that it is likely objective and informative (although scientific articles are sometimes persuasive, too). The first paragraph indicates that the passage will discuss a scientific problem, not a point of view. The central idea, then, is the question that it is trying to answer, which is in lines 17–18: *what actually holds the nucleus of an atom together?*

SAT I Practice 2

1. **C** This is a "main idea" question, so it is based on Key Question 2. The title must capture the main idea of the passage, without being too broad or too narrow. This passage is an argument, and its thesis is that it's impossible to repeat the art of the past because art is "a child of its age" (line 1). It then goes on to explain how this pertains to the revival of ancient art forms called Primitivism. Therefore, choice (C) best summarizes the main idea in a title.

2. **B** The passage says that a monkey can look at a book with a "thoughtful aspect" but really have no understanding of the book. Since the monkey does not understand the book, choices (A) and (D) are illogical. The sentence is saying that the monkey only *looks* thoughtful, so choice (B) is the only sensible one.

3. **E** The "fundamental truth" described in the second paragraph is that a "revival of external forms" (line 26), that is, art forms that resemble those of the past, can occur only when there is "a similarity of inner tendency in the whole moral and spiritual atmosphere" (lines 20–22). The only example given that suggests that fact is (E).

4. **A** In these lines, the author is using a metaphor to describe how "our minds" and "the soul," by which he means the artistic, spiritual mind, are affected by the materialism of the age. Artistic inspiration is described as a "spark," and materialism as a "nightmare" and a "vast gulf of darkness." The soul "trembles" because it doubts that the light is "not a dream," meaning that the light might be a dream and the darkness reality. Therefore the author suggests that materialism might still hold the artistic soul in its grip.

5. **D** The metaphor in the final paragraph makes it clear that materialism "holds the awakening soul in its grip" (lines 41–42). This is not a nurturing grip, because the soul "trembles" (line 45) before the "nightmare of materialism" (line 39). Therefore, according to the author, materialism oppresses the artistic soul.

Lesson 3:
The Structure of Prose

Finding Patterns: What Is the Structure of the Passage? (Key Question 3)

SAT I passages are chosen for both their content and their structure. A good piece of writing is like a good **painting**; it must have effective structure. Looked at a different way, a good piece of writing is a unique **journey** through "narrative space," "argument space," or "analysis space." A good reader—particularly on the SAT I—recognizes how a good piece of writing moves through this space.

❏ Understanding an SAT I passage means understanding its parts. Those parts have a **sequence,** like the stops on a journey. This journey can be summarized with a line through "prose space," just as a real trip can be summarized with a red line through a geographical map. Of course, there are many ways of planning a journey, and there are many possible paths through a "prose space." Usually, though, a piece of prose travels from left to right from task to task in the "spaces" shown below. You might think of the boxes below as "cities" that must be visited in the journey, and the ovals as the optional sites you can visit within each city.

Narrative Space

This path describes the basic structure of a story in which a man's wife is murdered (crime), he pursues the criminal (adventure), discovers that his wife only staged her own death and ran off with another man (revealing experience) and becomes more aware of this vulnerability to deception (transformation).

Argument Space

This path describes the basic structure of an argument in which the author states that a particular philosopher's ideas are harmful (evaluation), explains why she believes this (explanation), gives an example of the potential harm of those ideas (example), and then discusses how this evaluation should affect how we think (implication).

Analysis Space

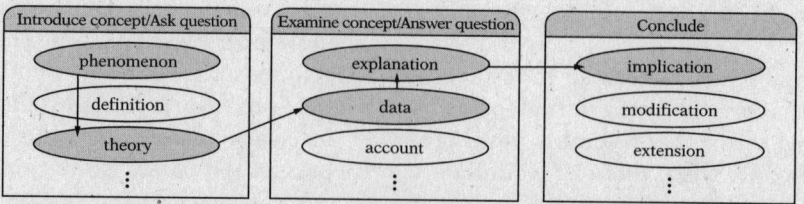

This path describes the basic structure of an analysis in which the author describes the discovery of a strange type of radiation from deep space (phenomenon), provides a theory to describe its origin (theory), gives data that supports the theory (data), explains why this data supports the theory (explanation), and discusses what this theory suggests about the composition of the universe (implication).

Concept Review 3:
The Structure of Prose

1. Name the three major "tasks" to be addressed in each of the three types of prose.

   a. Narrative: 1.   2.   3.

   b. Argument   1.   2.   3.

   c. Analysis   1.   2.   3.

2. Name three kinds of conflicts you might find in a narrative.

3. Name three kinds of theses you might find in an argument.

4. Name three kinds of questions you might find in an analysis.

5. Analyze the passage in SAT I Practice 3 as a journey through "analysis space." In the space below, indicate the structure of this passage by showing the tasks being performed in each of the four paragraphs.

   Paragraph 1   Paragraph 2   Paragraph 3   Paragraph 4

SAT I Practice 3:
The Structure of Prose

The following passage is excerpted from a text on the principles of zoology.

From ancient times, people commonly believed that life arose repeatedly by sponta-
Line neous generation from nonliving material in
addition to parental reproduction. For exam-
5 ple, frogs appeared to arise from damp earth,
mice from putrefied matter, insects from
dew, and maggots from decaying meat.
Warmth, moisture, sunlight, and even
starlight often were mentioned as factors that
10 encouraged spontaneous generation of living
organisms.

Among the accounts of early efforts to synthesize organisms in the laboratory is a recipe
for making mice, given by the Belgian plant
15 nutritionist Jean Baptiste van Helmont
(1648). "If you press a piece of underwear
soiled with sweat together with some wheat
in an open jar, after about 21 days the odor
changes and the ferment. . . . changes the
20 wheat into mice. But what is more remarkable
is that the mice which came out of the wheat
and underwear were not small mice, not even
miniature adults or aborted mice, but adult
mice emerge!"

25 In 1861, the great French scientist Louis
Pasteur convinced scientists that living organisms cannot arise spontaneously from
nonliving matter. In his famous experiments, Pasteur introduced fermentable ma-
30 terial into a flask with a long s-shaped neck
that was open to air. The flask and its contents were then boiled for a long time to kill
any microorganisms that might be present.
Afterward the flask was cooled and left
35 undisturbed. No fermentation occurred because all organisms that entered the open
end were deposited in the neck and did not
reach the fermentable material. When the
neck of the flask was removed, micro-
40 organisms in the air promptly entered the
fermentable material and proliferated.
Pasteur concluded that life could not
originate in the absence of previously
existing organisms and their reproductive
45 elements, such as eggs and spores. Announc-
ing his results to the French Academy,
Pasteur proclaimed, "Never will the doctrine

of spontaneous generation arise from this
mortal blow."
50 All living organisms share a common ancestor, most likely a population of colonial
microorganisms that lived almost 4 billion
years ago. This common ancestor was itself
the product of a long period of prebiotic
55 assembly of non-living matter, including
organic molecules and water, to form
self-replicating units. All living organisms
retain a fundamental chemical composition
inherited from their ancient common
60 ancestor.

1 Throughout the passage, the word "spontaneous" can best be taken to mean

(A) without reproductive elements
(B) in a medium
(C) unthinking
(D) free-spirited
(E) adult

2 In Pasteur's experiment, why was the neck of
the flask removed?

(A) to allow the air to escape
(B) to provide access to microorganisms
(C) to kill any microorganisms that may
     be present
(D) to permit the heating of the flask
(E) to introduce fermentable material

3 In line 49, the word "mortal" most nearly
means

(A) human
(B) impermanent
(C) fatal
(D) earthly
(E) malicious

Cleveland Hickman, Larry Roberts, and Allan Larson, *Integrated
Principles of Zoology*, ©2001 McGraw-Hill. Reprinted by permission of McGraw-Hill.

4 If both Pasteur's conclusion that "life could not originate in the absence of . . . eggs and spores" (lines 42–45) and the statement, "This common ancestor . . . units" (lines 53–57) are true, then which of the following statements must also be true about "prebiotic assembly" (lines 54–55)?

(A) It is not a "spontaneous" process.
(B) It does not depend on sunlight.
(C) It produces molecules unlike those in current life forms.
(D) It occurs in the absence of water.
(E) It occurs very quickly.

5 In what sense is the use of the word "water" (line 56) ironic?

(A) It is a substance in which many living organisms thrive.
(B) It has a relatively low boiling point.
(C) Pasteur did not mention it specifically in his description of his experiment.
(D) It was not one of the ingredients in Helmont's recipe.
(E) It was earlier mentioned as a factor in a debunked theory of how life was generated.

Answer Key 3:
The Structure of Prose

Concept Review 3

1. a. Narrative: 1. introduce the conflict, 2. develop the conflict, 3. resolve the conflict
   b. Argument: 1. state the thesis, 2. support the thesis, 3. conclude
   c. Analysis: 1. introduce the concept/ask the question, 2. examine the concept/answer the question, 3. conclude

2. types of conflicts include unrequited love, crime, and dissatisfaction

3. types of theses include the correction of a misconception, the evaluation of an artistic work, and the presentation of a controversial theory

4. types of questions include "what is the cause of this phenomenon?" "what are the implications of this theory?" and "what are the significant accomplishments of this historical figure?"

5. Paragraph 1: Describe misconception, Give example
   Paragraph 2: Give illustration
   Paragraph 3: Give account of a refutation
   Paragraph 4: Describe a generalization

SAT I Practice 3

1. **A** The theory of "spontaneous generation" is described as one in which life arises from substances that do not contain the reproductive elements of that life form.

2. **B** The important difference between the flask with the neck intact and the flask with the neck removed was the presence of microorganisms in the fermentable material. When the neck was removed, "microorganisms in the air promptly entered the fermentable material and proliferated."

3. **C** The experiment, Pasteur claimed, "killed" the theory of spontaneous generation, so it dealt a *fatal* blow.

4. **A** The "prebiotic assembly" is said to occur over a "long period." This must not be an example of "spontaneous generation," that is, generation of life over a short period of time from nonliving material, because the theory of spontaneous generation has been disproven.

5. **E** The first paragraph mentions that "warmth, *moisture,* sunlight, and even starlight often were mentioned as factors that encouraged spontaneous generation of living organisms," but the theory of spontaneous generation was then disproven. It is ironic, then, that water was found, in fact, to be a necessary precursor to life.

Lesson 4:
Paraphrasing and Visualizing

Simplifying by Consolidating and Paraphrasing

When you read, your brain doesn't simply record the information for playback the way a CD records music. Rather, your brain **consolidates** the information; that is, it **processes the information into a simpler form so that you can more easily recall and analyze it.** Paraphrasing is a way of expressing the consolidated information in a few tidy words.

❏ To ace Critical Reading questions, focus on **paraphrasing each paragraph quickly** as you read. This means **visualizing** and **simplifying** as you go. Don't make the mistake of thinking that this wastes time—the opposite is true: those who **don't** consolidate their understanding of a passage spend much **more** time answering Critical Reading questions, because they don't know how to "home in" on the right answers.

Visualizing

We first learn to read with picture books. As we move away from picture books, however, our minds still need pictures to consolidate information. So these pictures must become mental ones, and we must improve our skill of visualization. Often, however, we have trouble reading because we don't focus enough on "painting mental pictures" as we read.

Visualizing as you read enormously increases your interest level as well as your ability to retain and analyze what you read. Like any skill, you must consciously practice to get good at it. If you have trouble staying interested in or remembering what you read, focus on "creating a vivid movie" in your mind as you read.

❏ Visualization is essential to good comprehension of all prose: arguments and analyses as well as narratives.

- When reading a **narrative:** imagine it unfolding like a **movie** in front of your eyes. Try to visualize the characters in as much detail as possible as if you were painting a vivid picture in your mind. See the action clearly. In particular, "see" the conflict, like a "battle" between characters, or within a character, or between a character and a situation, etc. In particular, see its development and its resolution.

- When reading an argument: imagine it as a **battle,** with the author's thesis on one side and the "opposing thesis" on the other. The explanations and examples are like "weapons" against the enemy. See the battle in your mind's eye. **To understand an argument, you must see both sides of the battle.**

- When reading an analysis, imagine it like a **schematic diagram** unfolding before your eyes, with the central question in the middle of the diagram and the supporting points, explanations, or examples around it. This takes the most practice, because analytical prose is not as naturally "visual" as narrative prose is. You need to work harder to "see" an analysis in your mind's eye, but it will become easy with practice.

Reviewing After Each Paragraph

As you visualize, you may think of the start of each new paragraph as a "scene change" in your movie, and a jump to a new place in "prose space." Good readers use paragraphs to help them to check their understanding of the passage.

❏ **Every paragraph must contribute a new idea to the passage. To read well, you must find that new idea in each paragraph. Use the end of each paragraph as a "checkpoint" for answering these three questions:**

- What was the main idea of that paragraph?
- How is this idea related to the previous paragraph? (What's the transition?)
- How does this paragraph contribute to the main idea of the passage?

It may help to write a quick paragraph summary in the margins. Most students will have time to do this without rushing, but you should experiment under timed conditions to see if you can. This will help you to consolidate the information so that you can breeze through the questions!

Concept Review 4:
Paraphrasing and Visualizing

1. What kinds of things should you "see" when you are reading a narrative?

2. What kinds of things should you "see" when you are reading an argument?

3. What kinds of things should you "see" when you are reading an analysis?

4. What kinds of questions should you ask at the end of each paragraph?

Practice paraphrasing by writing a quick summary after each paragraph.

5. *When examined closely, "raising standards" does not often have the effect of improving education, despite all the rhetoric. When this game—and it is largely a game—is played right, the statistics improve, and its proponents claim victory. But we can do all sorts of horrible things to students in order to improve educational statistics: kick out slow learners, encourage cheating, employ superficial tests that are easily coached but reflect no real academic skill, and so on. We think that by saying we're "raising standards," we are challenging our children more intensely, and thereby producing smarter and more mature kids. For the most part, it's a con game, and we're all being taken in.*

   _____

   _____

   _____

6. *Art historians and aestheticians have long been confounded by Dadaism's complexities and seeming paradoxes. Few seem able to express its real meaning. Dadaism imbues art with the outrageous and the whimsical, but it is a mistake to think that it is mere child's play. It is a profound expression of art as life in the moment. Its works have sadly been lost on a public that expects erudition, archetypes, and allusions in its art, rather than the exuberance of life that art should be.*

   _____

   _____

   _____

SAT I Practice 4:
Paraphrasing and Visualizing

The following passage discusses the philosophical distinction between two methods of explaining scientific phenomena.

As our theories about the world around us have evolved and have become more useful, they
Line have become, almost without exception, less teleological and more mechanistic. A teleolog-
5 ical explanation of a phenomenon describes causes and effects in terms of desires or purposes: something happens simply because it serves a certain purpose, because it is "supposed" to happen, or because someone or
10 something "wants" it to happen. A ball falls to earth because, as it is in the air, it perceives that its more proper place is on the ground, and not because anything pushes it. Teleological explanations never survive as useful theories be-
15 cause they are backward: they place the cause after the effect.

A mechanistic explanation, on the other hand, requires that any discussion of causes and effects be restricted by the known laws of
20 how physical objects and substances interact as time moves *forward*. This is the language of the scientist. No right-minded chemist would say that trinitrotoluene explodes because it "wants to." It does so because the presence of
25 heat and oxygen releases the potential energy stored in its bonds.

Early scientific theories were almost exclusively teleological. If you could drive Socrates around in an SUV, he would be far more
30 likely to ask you about your vehicle's nature, or its desires, or its soul than about how the engine worked, how the odometer received its information, or how the different buttons on the CD player produced their effects. It would
35 seem to him that he was in the belly of a metallic animal, or at least a possessed machine.

Teleological explanations are convenient for explaining what people do, because most of us understand the concepts of "wants" and
40 "needs" far more deeply than we understand the mind's mechanisms for processing information. If you only have three minutes to explain to your friend why you are not going to a party, you don't very well have the knowledge,
45 not to mention the time or desire, to explain how your cerebral cortex processed the infor-

mation and concepts associated with the decision to stay home. You just give a reason why you don't want to, and your friend under-
50 stands.

This convenience persuades us that teleological explanations are the best for analyzing human behavior. Furthermore, we resist mechanistic explanations of behavior because
55 they seem to deny another preciously guarded concept: free will. If our decision to stay home from a party could be explained in the same way that the action of an internal combustion engine can be explained, then doesn't that
60 reduce us all to mindless machines?

No: the mind's understanding of the mind will always leave room for "free will," whatever that really means. Full understanding of a phenomenon depends on the mind's ability
65 to detach from and observe it, and the mind can never fully detach from itself. This complication may imply that a full understanding of the human mind is impossible, but it does not imply that we must be satisfied with mere
70 teleology. Perhaps this will require an entirely new conception of psychology, but if psychology is to remain relevant, we have no other choice.

---

1 Which of the following is the best title for this passage?

(A) Why Mechanism Should Replace Teleology
(B) The Science of the Ancient Greeks
(C) The Psychology of Wants and Needs
(D) The Causes of Scientific Ignorance
(E) Obstacles to a Full Understanding of the Mind

2 Which of the following is an example of a "teleological" explanation?

(A) water evaporates because it absorbs heat
(B) an engine works because it burns fuel
(C) a bird sings because it likes the sound
(D) a dog yelps because it perceives pain
(E) a ball falls because a gravitational field pulls it

3 The reference to Socrates in lines 28–36 emphasizes the fact that he was

(A) more influential than other Greek philosophers
(B) fearful of complicated machines
(C) concerned more with ethics than with physics
(D) aware of the mechanistic laws of physics
(E) inclined to explain phenomena in terms of purposes

4 In line 36, the word "possessed" most nearly means

(A) owned
(B) willful
(C) purchased
(D) determined
(E) spontaneous

5 The fourth paragraph suggests that teleological explanations persist chiefly because they

(A) are easier to use
(B) are more logically consistent
(C) agree with physical laws
(D) deny free will
(E) explain physical phenomena accurately

6 According to the author, which of the following describes the main difference between the "machine" in line 36 and the "machines" in line 60?

(A) The "machine" is modern, but the "machines" are ancient.
(B) The "machine" obeys mechanistic physical laws, but the "machines" do not.
(C) The "machine" cannot be explained teleologically, but the "machines" can.
(D) The "machine" is simple, but the "machines" are not.
(E) The "machine" is thought to have a soul, but the "machines" have had their souls attenuated.

Answer Key 4:
Paraphrasing and Visualizing

Concept Review 4

1. See the characters in vivid detail. See the setting and the action as if you were watching a movie. See the conflict as a "battle" between two characters, or within one character's mind, or between the character and a situation, etc.
2. See the argument as a battle between sides. Remember that to argue, one must argue *against* something. See the battle unfolding, with each point, example, or explanation as a weapon or a maneuver.
3. See a schematic diagram of the analysis, like a map of the journey through "analysis space."
4. At the end of each paragraph, ask: *What was the main idea of that paragraph? How does this new idea relate to the previous paragraph? and How does this paragraph contribute to the main idea of the passage?*

5. One possible paraphrase:
   "Raising standards," despite popular belief, can lead to bad things.
6. One possible paraphrase:
   Dadaism is hard to appreciate, but it is essentially art as life in the moment.

SAT I Practice 4

1. **A** The passage compares mechanistic explanations to teleological ones and explains why mechanistic ones are "more useful." Choices (B), (C), and (D) describe tasks that go far beyond what this passage accomplishes, and choice (E) describes an idea that is mentioned only in the last paragraph.
2. **C** "Teleological" explanations are those that "describe causes and effects in terms of desires or purposes." Saying that a bird sings because it "likes the sound" implies that the bird's action is caused by a desire.
3. **E** Socrates is said to "be far more likely to ask you about your vehicle's nature, or its desires, or its soul than about how the engine worked." This underscores the author's belief that Socrates explained things in terms of their "purposes."
4. **B** Socrates, the author tells us, would believe that the SUV possessed a soul, so the "possessed machine" is one with a living spirit and will.
5. **A** The fourth paragraph tells us that teleological explanations "are convenient," and goes on to explain why people continue to use them.
6. **E** The "possessed machine" in line 36 is the SUV that Socrates would believe has a soul. The "mindless machines" of line 60 represent the conception of human beings that many would have if human behavior were explained "mechanistically," thereby removing (they would think) our free will and soul.

Lesson 5: Understanding the Questions

Read Each Question Carefully and Know What It's Asking For

❑ Read each Critical Reading question very carefully—several times, if necessary—and look for the key words or phrases that tell you what to look for in the passage.

Also, make sure to re-read any lines that the question specifically refers to, then think of your own answer to the question before checking the choices.

Question Type	Asks you to . . .	So you should . . .
Purpose e.g., The overall **purpose** of the passage is to . . . The author mentions the "depth of division" **to suggest that.** . . .	explain why the author wrote the passage or used a particular term or phrase	reflect on the purpose of the whole passage (Key Question #1) as well as the purpose of the line mentioned
Central Idea e.g., Which of the following is the **best title** for this passage? What is the **main idea** of the passage?	describe the main idea, that is, the central thesis, question, or conflict of the passage	always be ready for a central idea question, because it's Key Question 2, which you should answer as you read the passage
Secondary Idea e.g., The "problems" mentioned in line 56 are those of. . . .	identify the points made in individual paragraphs or sentences	remember that secondary points generally support the central idea, so remind yourself of the answer to Key Question 2
Inference e.g., With which of the following statements **would** the author **most likely** agree? The author **suggests** that. . . .	draw conclusions based on the main or secondary points of the passage	understand not only the meaning of the reference, but also what it logically implies
Tone e.g., In the final paragraph, the author's cousin is characterized as. . . . The first sentence conveys a **tone** of. . . .	describe the author's attitude towards an idea, or the tone of a characterization	find the key words or ideas that convey a mood
Word or Phrase in Context e.g., In line 41, the word "final" most nearly means. . . .	give the meaning of a word or phrase as it is used in the passage	read the sentence with the given word or phrase, think about its meaning, and then replace it with your own word or phrase, and find the closest match
Structure or Device e.g., The **structure** of this passage is best described as. . . Which of the following **devices** is not used in the last paragraph?	describe the overall structure of the passage or identify certain devices, like similes, metaphors, anecdotes, etc.	always be ready for these questions, because they are based on Key Question 2, which you should answer as you read

❑ The SAT I often uses these words in "device" questions. Make sure you understand them.

Analysis—examination of parts
Anecdote—an illustrative story
Counterexample—an example that disproves a claim
Hyperbole—exaggeration for rhetorical effect

Irony—a reversal of expectations
Logic—systematic reasoning
Metaphor—saying one thing is another thing
Simile—comparison using like or as
Statistics—real-life quantities
Subjective—based on personal opinion
Objective—sticking to indisputable facts

Concept Review 5:
Understanding the Questions

State whether each of the following questions is a purpose question (P), a central idea question (CI), a secondary idea question (SI), an inference question (I), a tone question (T), a word (or phrase) in context question (WIC), or a structure or device question

(S/D) **Note: The passages that correspond to these questions are not given, so you can't actually answer the questions. This is only an exercise in identifying the question types, not answering them.**

1. *Which of the following best summarizes the "mystery" mentioned in line 1?*

2. *In line 29, the phrase "responsible for" most nearly means*

3. *According to the passage, pions are not likely the carriers of the nuclear force because*

4. *Which of the following best describes the organization of this passage as a whole?*

5. *Which of the following is the best title for this passage?*

6. *How would the author characterize the effect of materialism on the artist's soul?*

7. *The author describes the proposal as "solid" (line 16) in order to emphasize*

8. *The passage includes each of the following EXCEPT*

9. *The primary purpose of this passage is to*

10. *Which of the following is an example of the "trials" mentioned in line 23?*

11. *It can be inferred that one who supports Martin's proposal would likely do so because*

SAT I Practice 5:
Understanding the Questions

The following is an excerpt from a recent book by two science writers on the evolution of human intelligence.

Where can freedom be found? Perhaps in a flock of estuary birds? Flying together at high
Line speeds, thousands of birds maneuver with precise coordination. The flock flies this way
5 and then that. It turns as if a wave has passed through it. These "maneuver waves" start slowly in a few individuals but quickly spread. Unless the individual birds reacted together, the flock would disperse, exposing isolated
10 birds to predators. Sometimes it is "smart," in a survival sense, to give up your freedom and fit in with a group.

Once started, a wave travels through a flock at about 70 birds a second. Surprisingly, this
15 is much faster than a single bird's reaction time. Thus, individual birds cannot have seen their neighbors and said to themselves, "Hey, they've changed direction—I'd better copy them." Something else besides copying is
20 synchronizing the birds. Somehow they see themselves, if only for a short time, as part of a whole. They see the wave maneuver and time their own change of flight with it.

Individuals cease to be individuals in many
25 ways—not just when flying together. Humans can react physically as a group; a wave of legs passes down a chorus line at roughly 10 dancers every second. As with birds taking off, this is too fast for movements made in reac-
30 tion to neighbors. A similar thing, no doubt at a deeper level, organizes a jazz jam or a basketball team. This suggests that people are good—surprisingly good—at synthesizing their actions into a larger whole. Soldiers
35 marching in step with each other are not doing so as individuals.

We all have a sense of "we" that identifies with "our" group and favors "us" against outsiders. We have our fraternities, sororities,
40 and other old boy and girl networks. We seek out people who share the same club, school tie, or accent. Much of this activity is harmless, but our loyalties also have their darker side. When loyal group members are found to
45 be doing wrong—committing sexual or physical abuse, faking data, or taking bribes—other group members protect them. The bonds among group members may make them treat the whistle-blower, not the wrongdoer, as the
50 criminal. They do this especially if the whistle-blower is a member of their in-group—one does not squeal, tell tales, or inform on one's comrades.

Social psychologists find that we easily be-
55 come prejudiced. It takes the smallest hint that you belong to one group and other people to another for you to favor "your own" group. The reason you belong to one group rather than another may be no more than a prefer-
60 ence for abstract artists, Paul Klee rather than Wassily Kandinsky. You need not even meet and interact with the members of your own group, but prejudice will nonetheless rear its ugly head. It may be our football team, school,
65 town or nation, or the color of our skin. Once fully identified with that "we," people become sensitive to the needs of their group and callous toward other groups. Outsiders cease to matter. The stronger our identification with
70 the "we," the blinder we become to the humanity we share with "them." Out of this psychology comes the nasty side of history and the human race: the world of "ethnic cleansing," genocide, racial prejudice, and global
75 terrorism. Thus, we may be born alone, but we quickly learn to identify ourselves with a group, leading, in some cases, to barbaric consequences.

John R. Skoyles and Dorion Sagan, *Up from Dragons.* © 2002 McGraw-Hill. Reprinted by permission of McGraw-Hill.

1 The primary purpose of this passage is to

(A) examine a problem
(B) compare human behavior with bird behavior
(C) disprove a theory
(D) suggest an alternative
(E) analyze a phenomenon

2 The authors refer to the "freedom" (line 1) of "estuary birds" (line 2) in order to emphasize that

(A) birds are more physically free than humans
(B) something is not as it appears
(C) scientists do not yet understand how birds move in flocks
(D) the coordination of birds in flight is distinctly different from the coordination of human political movements
(E) birds do not appreciate the complexity of their actions

3 By saying that soldiers do not march "as individuals" (line 36), the authors suggest that the soldiers

(A) are compelled to march through coercion
(B) must obey the orders of their superiors
(C) react as a part of an organized whole
(D) lack leadership skills
(E) are reluctant

4 Klee and Kandinsky (lines 60–61) are mentioned as examples of

(A) artists whose works are closely related
(B) people who do not act as individuals
(C) men whose followers may form distinct groups
(D) those who belong to a privileged group
(E) individuals who express prejudice

5 On the whole, the authors' attitude toward group behavior is one of

(A) ambivalence
(B) disdain
(C) admiration
(D) skepticism
(E) fear

Answer Key 5:
Understanding the Questions

Concept Review 5

1. This is most likely a central idea (CI) question, because it is mentioned in line 1. It is possible, however, that in context it is a secondary idea (SI).

2. Word or phrase in contest (WIC)

3. Secondary idea (SI)

4. Structure or device (S/D)

5. Central idea (CI)

6. Tone (T)

7. Purpose (P)

8. Structure or device (S/D)

9. Purpose (P)

10. Secondary idea (SI)

11. Inference (I)

SAT I Practice 5

1. **E** This passage analyzes (examines closely) the phenomenon of group behavior, first in terms of birds flying together, then in terms of human beings acting as teams, and then in terms of human group identification. This passage is not focused on a "problem" because group behavior is often depicted as a positive thing, particularly in the first three paragraphs, so choice (A) is incorrect. Since the passage discusses birds only in the first couple of paragraphs, (B) must be incorrect. Also, since no alternative to a situation or refutation of a theory is presented, (C) and (D) cannot be right.

2. **B** The authors begin with a question: "Where can freedom be found?" and a rhetorical answer: "Perhaps in a flock of estuary birds?" This leads us to believe that the author might use the example of birds flying as an example of "freedom." However, the paragraph (and the passage as a whole) goes on to suggest that bird flight is not as "free" as it seems, and often typifies group behavior.

3. **C** The example of the marching soldiers follows the examples of the estuary birds, the chorus line, the jazz band, and the basketball team. All of these examples reinforce the common theme of group behavior being an organized whole.

4. **C** The sentence says that "The reason you belong to one group rather than another may be no more than a preference for abstract artists, Paul Klee rather than Wassily Kandinsky." This means that those who like the art of Klee might form a distinct group from those who like Kandinsky.

5. **A** The authors indicate the positive benefits of group behavior in the first three paragraphs, then its "darker side" in the last two paragraphs. This is an example of *ambivalence,* in which the authors are not saying that group behavior is always good or always bad.

Lesson 6:
Attacking the Questions

Rephrase the Questions to Make Them "Open-Ended" and Think of Your *Own* Answer First

❏ Have you ever thought that more than one choice "sounds right" on a Critical Reading question? This is usually a sign that you have not thought deeply enough about *your own* answer to the question before checking the choices. Remember, good test writers will always include choices that "sound right" but really *aren't right* if you think about the passage. You can get "talked into" these wrong answers if you don't formulate your own answer first. **Therefore, it's best to rephrase each Critical Reading question, if possible, so that it is an essay question or "open-ended" question rather than a multiple-choice question. Then, think of *your own* response before checking the choices. If you do it right, the right answer will "pop out" quickly and you won't waste time thinking hard about each choice.**

Practice "translating" Critical Reading questions to make them "open-ended" so you can think of your own answer:

Question: *The tone of the opening paragraph is best characterized as. . . .*
Translate: *What is the tone of the opening paragraph?*
Find an answer to this, re-reading if necessary, then look for a match among the choices.

Question: *The author implies that most people do not notice bias in the media because. . . .*
Translate: *Why (according to this author) don't people notice bias in the media?*
Find an answer to this, re-reading if necessary, then look for a match among the choices.

"Paired" Passages

Every SAT I will contain two "paired" passages that share a common theme, but are written by different authors. They will be followed by normal questions about the individual passages and then questions comparing or contrasting the two passages with each other. For the most part, it's best to approach these passages just as you would any other passage, but there are a couple of points to keep in mind.

❏ Remember that the two passages are written by different authors, and will likely have different perspectives on the same theme. As you read, then, ask yourself, "What is the common theme?" and "How do these two perspectives differ from each other?"

❏ **After reading the first passage, go directly to the questions.** The first few questions will deal with Passage 1 alone, so it makes sense to tackle these questions first. Once you've finished the questions that deal with Passage 1, read Passage 2 and then tackle the rest of the questions. This approach will help you to consolidate your understanding of the two passages separately, so that the separate perspectives don't "run together."

Single Paragraphs and "Paired" Paragraphs

Every Critical Reading section will contain several short passages that are single paragraphs about 100 words long, followed by one or two questions similar to the questions on the longer reading passages. There may also be two "paired" paragraphs, about 200 words long, with four questions based on the two passages and the relationship between the passages.

❏ The short, single-paragraph or "paired" paragraph passages should be approached in the same way as the longer passages. The questions will be of exactly the same type and basic difficulty as all the other Critical Reading questions.

Concept Review 6:
Attacking the Questions

Rewrite each of the following questions so that they are "open-ended," that is, phrased as "essay questions" rather than "multiple-choice questions" so that you can formulate your own response to check against the choices. Also, indicate what you should look for in the passage to verify your answer. **Note: The passages that correspond to these questions are not given, so you can't actually answer the questions. This is only an exercise in rephrasing the questions, not answering them.**

1. *The last paragraph suggests that Davis is motivated by*

2. *The author's attitude toward the "opposition" (line 42) is one of*

3. *The garden has become important to the narrator because*

4. *By saying that the mechanisms of proprioception "do not exist" (line 19) for most people, the author suggests that most people*

5. *The authors refer to the "freedom" (line 1) of "estuary birds" (line 2) in order to emphasize that*

6. *By saying that soldiers do not march "as individuals" (line 29) the authors suggest that the soldiers*

7. *The fourth paragraph suggests that teleological explanations persist chiefly because they*

SAT I Practice 6:
Attacking the Questions

PASSAGE 1

We have five senses in which we glory and which we recognize and celebrate, senses that
Line constitute the sensible world for us. But there are other senses—secret senses, sixth senses,
5   if you will—equally vital, but unrecognized, and unlauded. These senses, unconscious, au-tomatic, had to be discovered. Historically, in-deed, their discovery came late: what the Victorians vaguely called "muscle sense"—the
10 awareness of the relative position of trunk and limbs, derived from receptors in the joints and tendons—was only really defined (and named "proprioception") in the 1890s. And the com-plex mechanisms and controls by which our
15 bodies are properly aligned and balanced in space—these have only been defined in the 20th century, and still hold many mysteries. Perhaps it will only be in this space age, with the paradoxical license and hazards of gravity-
20 free life, that we will truly appreciate our inner ears, our vestibules, and all the other obscure receptors and reflexes that govern our body orientation. For normal man, in normal situations, they simply do not exist.

PASSAGE 2

Now the word "knowledge" we use in two dis-tinct senses; we speak of a person as "know-
Line ing" if he has knowledge but does not apply it, and also if he applies his knowledge. There
5   will be a difference then between doing wrong when one has knowledge, but does not reflect on it, and doing so when one not only has the knowledge but reflects on it. In the lat-ter case the wrongdoing seems strange but not
10 in the former. . . . For in a case where a per-son has knowledge but does not apply it, we see that "having" has a different meaning. In fact, in one sense he has knowledge and in an-other sense he does not have it, as, for exam-
15 ple, in sleep or madness or intoxication. Now this is the very condition of people under the influence of passion; for fits of anger and crav-ing for sensual pleasures and some such things do unmistakenly produce a change in
20 bodily condition, and in some instances actu-ally cause madness.

1 In line 1, the word "glory" most nearly means

(A)   acknowledge
(B)   praise
(C)   discover
(D)   become famous
(E)   take delight

2 By saying that the mechanisms of proprio-ception "do not exist" (line 24) for most peo-ple, the author suggests that most people

(A)   have not discovered how they work
(B)   do not appreciate their function
(C)   have difficulty maintaining balance
(D)   are seldom aware of the location of their limbs
(E)   are not scientists

3 According to the second passage, "wrong-doing seems strange" (line 9) when

(A)   the victim does not acknowledge the wrongdoing
(B)   the culprit does not think about his actions
(C)   the victim is capable of defending himself
(D)   the culprit reflects on his knowledge of right and wrong before committing the act
(E)   the culprit craves sensual pleasure

4 An individual with the "condition" described in line 16 can be inferred to

(A)   apply the knowledge he has
(B)   lack knowledge of right and wrong
(C)   value reflection over action
(D)   be incapable of passion
(E)   both have knowledge and lack it

PASSAGE 1

Researchers have been puzzling over modern human origins for decades. Numerous explanations have been put forward, but these have tended to lean toward one or the other of two competing theories.

One theory posits that modern humans arose as early as 200,000 years ago in Africa, then spread to the Near East, and then colonized the rest of the Old World. This "Out-of-Africa" theory claims that these early modern Africans replaced all indigenous populations of archaic humans, including the Neanderthals, by about 30,000 years ago and that all people living today are descended from these Africans. Support for this theory comes from the fact that fossils of modern humans from Africa and the Near East are much older than those found elsewhere. These fossils are 100,000 to 120,000 years old, and some may be even older. This is long before the period 30,000 to 40,000 years ago when modern humans began appearing in other regions. These early modern Africans and Near Easterners could therefore have served as source populations for subsequent migrations of modern humans.

Numerous genetic studies of DNA from living people also appear to support the "Out-of-Africa" theory. These studies indicate a relatively recent common ancestry for all the far-flung peoples inhabiting the globe today. They also consistently show present-day Africans to be the most genetically divergent, and therefore the most ancient, branch of humanity. These findings point toward a recent African origin for modern humans. These studies have recently been enhanced by analyses of ancient DNA from actual Neanderthal remains. The scientists studying this DNA have reported that the Neanderthal DNA differs significantly from our own, which they see as support for the Out-of-Africa theory.

The competing theory of modern human origins, the "multiregional evolution" theory, argues that present-day humans are descended not from a new type of humanity that appeared in Africa a mere 200,000 years ago, but from much earlier African emigrants.

This theory posits that our ancestry goes back to the hominids known as *Homo erectus* or *Homo ergaster*. These were the first hominids to spread out from Africa into Eurasia, beginning 1 to 2 million years ago, and they spawned the various archaic *Homo sapiens* populations of the Old World. The theory holds that these archaic *Homo sapiens* groups, including the Neanderthals, all evolved into modern humans within their own geographic regions. It sees this as the primary mechanism by which modern humans appeared, although it does not rule out the possibility of some migration between regions.

As support for their view of localized, regional evolution, multiregionalists claim that in each region of the Old World, certain distinctive traits can be identified in fossil bones from some of the earliest archaic humans to occupy the region. These traits then continue to show up in modified forms in subsequent human remains from the same region, down to the present day.

PASSAGE 2

We are a bright species. We have gone into space and walked on the moon. Yet you would never have guessed that if you traveled back to between 100,000 and 40,000 years ago. At that time our ancestors and Neanderthals coexisted. Neanderthals were like us but physically stronger, with large bones and teeth, protruding brows and face, and hardly a chin. Perhaps what we lacked in brawn we made up for in brains. But for most of our history, our species was not bright enough to act very differently from the Neanderthals, let alone be more successful than they were. Only around 40,000 to 32,000 years ago, in Western Asia and Europe, did Neanderthal people disappear, to be replaced by our species.

Why did we coexist with Neanderthals for 60,000 years—a far longer case of hominids living side by side than any other in human history? And why did we eventually win out? Brains alone cannot provide the answer, as Neanderthals may in fact have had the larger ones. Perhaps they lacked the long vocal chamber needed for speech. Equal certainty exists among those who study the base of their skulls that they did and that they did not. If they did lack one, then this could be the explanation, but maybe not, since even without a voice box, gestures can communicate, as can be seen among the deaf. Indeed, hunters find advantages in using sign language (speech sounds would warn off potential prey), and not just while hunting but in everyday life. Anthropologists find that hunter-gatherers use sophisticated sign languages to complement their speech. Sign language might even have other advantages—evidence even suggests

110 that it is easier to learn than speech: deaf children start to pick up signs earlier than hearing ones learn to speak. So "spoken speech" is not in all ways superior to "signed speech." It is not something that can explain our replace-
115 ment of the Neanderthals.

The reason we—anatomically modern humans—won out lies, we suspect, not in being brighter or better able to speak but in our very physical frailty and our resulting need to ex-
120 ploit our minds. Neanderthals, stronger than us, did not need to take this route. They could survive with their physical strength rather than tapping into the potential of their brains. An analogy is with countries: the richest ones,
125 such as Switzerland, Finland, Singapore, and Japan, are not blessed with, but rather lack natural resources. Without them, they have been forced to use their brains to innovate, providing products and services ranging from
130 mobile phones to diplomacy.

5 According to Passage 1, on which of the following issues do the "Out-of-Africa" theory and the "multiregional evolution" theory disagree?

 I. where modern humans first evolved
 II. whether modern humans descended from African ancestors
 III. whether Neanderthals evolved into modern humans
  (A) I only   (B) II only
  (C) I and II only   (D) I and III only
  (E) I, II, and III

6 According to Passage 1, proponents of the "Out-of-Africa" theory believe that present-day Africans must be the "most ancient" (line 34) branch of humanity because

 (A) their skeletal structure most resembles the most ancient relatives of humans
 (B) their DNA is more diverse than that of any other human group
 (C) they are the most successful hunters of all human groups
 (D) their ancestors were Neanderthals
 (E) they have settled in all regions of the world

7 According to Passage 1, which of the following pieces of evidence supports the "multi-regional evolution" theory over the "Out-of-Africa" theory?

 (A) distinctive human traits that have remained within regional populations since the earliest fossil records
 (B) genetic diversity among modern humans within a single region
 (C) genetic dissimilarities between modern humans and Neanderthals
 (D) the finding of modern human remains that date from 120,000 to 30,000 years ago
 (E) evidence of the migration of modern humans from Africa

8 The main purpose of the second paragraph of Passage 2 is

 (A) to make a suggestion
 (B) to examine some claims
 (C) to explain a situation
 (D) to present information objectively
 (E) to tell a story

9 In line 92, the phrase "win out" most nearly means

 (A) become justified
 (B) defeat our foes by force
 (C) come to dominate
 (D) become politically successful
 (E) become more popular

10 The evidence presented in the sentence "Anthropologists find . . . speech" (lines 105–108) is mentioned in order to

 (A) refute the misconception that hunter-gatherers were not good communicators
 (B) explain how modern humans replaced the Neanderthals
 (C) support the claim that hunter-gatherers have larger brains than Neanderthals
 (D) suggest that long vocal chambers may not provide an advantage to a particular species
 (E) show why some humans prefer gestures to spoken language

11 In Passage 2, "physical frailty" (line 119) is

(A) the reason our ancestors struggled to survive

(B) the result of a harsh physical environment

(C) an ironic advantage to modern humans

(D) something the Neanderthals exploited

(E) a trait that arose late in human history

12 In line 130, "mobile phones" and "diplomacy" are mentioned as examples of

(A) innovations that are used worldwide

(B) different ways of communicating

(C) luxuries that are denied to the physically frail

(D) inventions that Neanderthals could never use

(E) products or services that require intellectual rather than natural resources

13 With which of the following statements about the "multiregional evolution" theory would the authors of Passage 2 most likely agree?

(A) It is one of many possible ways of describing the dominance of modern humans over the Neanderthals.

(B) It is false because it posits that Neanderthals evolved into modern humans.

(C) It is true because it explains the variety of modes in human communication.

(D) It is unlikely to be true because it does not account for the violence of human societies.

(E) It is a helpful theory for explaining the similarities among countries like Switzerland, Finland, and Japan.

Answer Key 6:
Attacking the Questions

Concept Review 6

1. *What motivates Davis? (Check the last paragraph for the answer)*
2. *What is the author's attitude toward the "opposition"? (Check the sentences around line 42 for words or phrases that indicate tone.)*
3. *Why has the garden become important to the narrator? (This gives no line reference, so check the line references in the previous question and following questions to locate the portion of the passage to check.)*
4. *What does the author mean when he says that the mechanisms of proprioception "do not exist" (line 19) for most people? (Check the sentence containing line 19 as well as the sentence before and after.)*

5. *What are the authors trying to emphasize by mentioning the "freedom" (line 1) of "estuary birds" (line 2)? (Think about the overall purpose and central idea in this paragraph, then think about this reference in relation to that purpose.)*
6. *What are the authors saying about soldiers when they say that soldiers do not march "as individuals" (line 29)? (Check the sentence containing line 29, as well as perhaps the sentences immediately before and after.)*
7. *According to the fourth paragraph, why do teleological explanations persist? (Check the fourth paragraph.)*

SAT I Practice 6

1. **E** The sentence says that we "glory *in*" our five senses, but that others are "unlauded" (line 6). In this context, "glory in" means much the same as "take delight in."
2. **B** The previous sentence says that perhaps someday "we will truly appreciate our inner ears, our vestibules, and all the other obscure receptors and reflexes that govern our body orientation" (lines 20–23) but that for most people they "do not exist," thereby implying that most people do not appreciate them.
3. **D** The passage says that "wrongdoing seems strange" "in the latter case," which is the case in which "one not only has knowledge but reflects on it." In other words, it is strange when one does wrong while reflecting on his knowledge that it is wrong.
4. **E** A person with the "condition" "in one sense . . . has knowledge and in another sense . . . does not have it" (lines 13–14).
5. **D** The "Out-of-Africa" theory claims that "modern humans arose as early as 200,000 years ago in Africa" (lines 6–7), but the "multiregional evolution" theory says that modern humans evolved "within their own geographic regions" (lines 59–60) in Eurasia as well as Africa. They differ, also, on the question of Neanderthals: the "Out-of-Africa" theory claims that modern humans "replaced all indigenous populations of archaic humans, including the Neanderthals," (lines

12–13), while the "multiregional evolution" theory claims that "Neanderthals . . . evolved into modern humans" (lines 58–59). They agree, however, that the *ancestors* of modern humans came from Africa.
6. **B** The passage states that present-day Africans are "the most genetically divergent, and therefore the most ancient, branch of humanity" (lines 33–35). Therefore, because their DNA is more diverse than that of any other human group, they are the most ancient branch of modern humans.
7. **A** The "support" that multiregionalists cite for their claims is that "distinctive traits can be identified in fossil bones from . . . the region (lines 66–69)" that "continue to show up . . . in subsequent human remains from the same region" (lines 70–72).
8. **B** Words and phrases like "perhaps," "if," and "maybe not" indicate that Passage 2 is exploring possibilities.
9. **C** The passage is exploring the question of how modern humans "won out" over the Neanderthals, in other words, how they came to thrive while the Neanderthals died out; how we *came to dominate* them.
10. **D** The sentence "Anthropologists find . . . speech" is used to support the later claim that " 'spoken speech' is not in all ways superior to 'signed speech' " (lines 112–113), which would

cast doubt on the advantages of the "long vocal chamber needed for speech" (lines 95–96).

11. **C** The "physical frailty" of modern humans relative to Neanderthals created a need to exploit our creative brains, which led to our dominance over the Neanderthals.

12. **E** The "mobile phones" and "diplomacy" are examples of how countries that "lack natural resources" (lines 126–127) can still "use their brains to innovate."

13. **B** The authors of Passage 2 clearly believe that modern humans came to dominate Neanderthals, and are giving their explanation for this phenomenon. The "multiregional evolution" theory, however, claims that "Neanderthals . . . evolved into modern humans" rather than being supplanted by them.

Lesson 7: Thinking Logically

Think Logically: Use the Line References Intelligently

❑ Critical Reading questions, unlike the other questions on the SAT I, are not given in order of difficulty. Rather, they are arranged in roughly chronological order. In other words, the first question is about the beginning of the passage, and the last question is about the end of the passage. (See for yourself: look at the Critical Reading questions on an SAT I and notice that the "line references" in the questions get later and later.)

❑ If a question doesn't include line references, you may wonder where to look in the passage for the answer. When this happens, **refer to the questions just before and after,** and look for line references there. The answer to the question is probably found between those two line references. For instance, if question 25 does not refer to a line, but question 24 refers to line 46 and question 26 refers to line 55, you should look for the answer to question 25 between lines 46 and 55!

Find Your Evidence in the Passage

❑ Make sure that you have literal evidence from the passage for every answer you give. **You will *never* need to draw on background information or information that is not directly in the passage or the introduction.**

Use Logic on the Questions

❑ **Solid test-taking logic** can often help you decide among the answer choices on tough questions.

❑ **If two answers seem similar, the less extreme or less exclusive answer is more likely to be right.** Statements with "exclusive" words like "never" or "always" are less likely to be true than statements with "inclusive" words like "sometimes" or "often." Also, "extreme" statements are less likely to be true than banal, ordinary statements.

   e.g. What is the author's attitude toward the "transgressions" mentioned in line 12?

   (A) indifference   (B) vehement opposition
   (C) ambivalence   (D) disapproval
   (E) resignation

Of course, you must understand the passage to answer this question, but let's say you've thought about it, and you know it must be either (B) *vehement opposition* or (D) *disapproval*. Logically, since *vehement opposition* is a type of *disapproval* (but *disapproval* is not necessarily a type of *vehement opposition*), (B) cannot be the answer unless (D) is also correct, but of course two answers can't be right, so it must be (D).

❑ **Writers write about what they care about.** Some students forget about this obvious fact when answering questions. In the question above, for instance, choice (A) *indifference* is almost certainly not the right answer if the "transgressions" are a topic of discussion in the passage. Of course, it's remotely possible that the author is saying, "Here is something that some other people *think* is important, but it's really not; I'm not really interested in this idea." But even then, the author at least thinks it's important enough to discuss, right? So she's not really *indifferent* about it.

❑ **An author can do a lot in 400–800 words, but not too much.** It's easier, for instance, to "suggest a few political reforms" in 500 words than it is to "delineate the history of European political reform." So when answering Overall Purpose questions, use common sense about what can be done in 400–800 words and what can't.

   e.g. Which of the following best expresses the purpose of the passage as a whole?

   (A) to describe the relationship between literature and history
   (*too big a task for 500 words—eliminate*)

   (B) to belittle modern literary critics
   (*possible, but a very petty purpose—eliminate*)

   (C) to refute a misconception
   (*very possible and a worthwhile purpose—keep*)

   (D) to delineate a new mode of literary analysis
   (*too big a task for 500 words—eliminate*)

   (E) to suggest several remedies for a problem
   (*very possible and a worthwhile purpose—keep*)

❑ **Common sense alone won't get you many right answers, but a right answer will never *violate* common sense.** The authors of SAT I passages have widely different points of view, but none are clinically insane!

Concept Review 7:
Thinking Logically

1. How are the Critical Reading questions after a particular passage arranged?

2. When a Critical Reading question does not include line references, what can you do to determine where to look in the passage for the answer?

3. What is the difference between an "inclusive" answer and an "exclusive" answer?

4. Why does it help to consider the "inclusiveness" or "exclusiveness" of an answer when answering Critical Reading questions?

Use logic and common sense to eliminate choices in the questions below:

5. The first paragraph implies that art is primarily the product of
   (A) desire for wealth
   (B) anxiety
   (C) exact imitation
   (D) reason
   (E) intuition

6. With which of the following statements would the author most likely agree?
   (A) Voters always choose incapable political candidates.
   (B) Voters should be more educated about candidates.
   (C) Political candidates rarely campaign effectively.
   (D) Politicians do not represent their constituents well.
   (E) Voters are not interested in critical political issues.

7. Which of the following best expresses the purpose of this passage?
   (A) to dissuade students from studying political science
   (B) to describe the evolution of ethics in American history
   (C) to attack the credibility of politicians
   (D) to refute a misconception
   (E) to prescribe a solution to a problem

SAT I Practice 7:
Thinking Logically

The following is an excerpt from John Adams' A Dissertation on the Canon and Feudal Law, written in 1765. John Adams (1735–1826) was the first vice-president of the United States and the second president of the United States.

Liberty cannot be preserved without a general knowledge among the people, who have a
Line right, from the frame of their nature, to knowledge, as their great Creator, who does
5 nothing in vain, has given them understandings, and a desire to know; but besides this, they have a right, an indisputable, unalienable, indefeasible, divine right to that most dreaded and envied kind of knowledge; I
10 mean, of the characters and conduct of their rulers. Rulers are no more than attorneys, agents, and trustees, for the people; and if the cause, the interest and trust, is insidiously betrayed, or wantonly trifled away, the people
15 have a right to revoke the authority that they themselves have deputed, and to constitute abler and better agents, attorneys and trustees. And the preservation of the means of knowledge among the lowest ranks is of more im-
20 portance to the public than all the property of all the rich men in the country. It is even of more consequence to the rich themselves, and to their posterity. The only question is whether it is a public emolument;[1] and if it is,
25 the rich ought undoubtedly to contribute, in the same proportion as to all other public burdens—that is, in proportion to their wealth, which is secured by public expenses. But none of the means of information are more sacred, or
30 have been cherished with more tenderness and care by the settlers of America, than the press. Care has been taken that the art of printing should be encouraged, and that it should be easy and cheap and safe for any person to
35 communicate his thoughts to the public. . . .
    Let us dare to read, think, speak and write. Let every order and degree among the people rouse their attention and animate their resolution. Let them all become attentive to the
40 grounds and principles of government, ecclesiastical[2] and civil. Let us study the law of nature; search into the spirit of the British Constitution; read the histories of ancient ages; contemplate the great examples of

45 Greece and Rome; set before us the conduct of our own British ancestors, who have defended for us the inherent rights of mankind against foreign and domestic tyrants and usurpers, against arbitrary kings and cruel
50 priests; in short, against the gates of earth and hell. Let us read and recollect and impress upon our souls the views and ends of our own more immediate forefathers in exchanging their native country for a dreary, inhospitable
55 wilderness. Let us examine the nature of that power, and the cruelty of that oppression, which drove them from their homes. Recollect their amazing fortitude, their bitter sufferings—the hunger, the nakedness, the cold,
60 which they patiently endured—the severe labors of clearing their grounds, building their houses, raising their provisions, amidst dangers from wild beasts and savage men, before they had time or money or materials for com-
65 merce. Recollect the civil and religious principles and hopes and expectations which constantly supported and carried them through all hardships with patience and resignation. Let us recollect it was liberty, the hope
70 of liberty for themselves and us and ours, which conquered all the discouragements, dangers and trials. In such researches as these let us all in our several departments cheerfully engage—but especially the proper patrons and
75 supporters of law, learning and religion!

[1]Benefit.
[2]Related to church matters.

1 The "right" in line 7 is the right of the people to

(A) pursue happiness
(B) read what they wish
(C) know about their leaders
(D) set up printing presses
(E) run for public office

2 In context, the word "constitute" (line 16) most nearly means

(A) consist of
(B) produce
(C) remove
(D) install
(E) enjoy

3 It can be inferred from the passage that "our own more immediate forefathers" (lines 52–53) endured all of the following EXCEPT

(A) political oppression
(B) difficult terrain
(C) arduous labor
(D) hopelessness
(E) physical deprivation

4 As it is described in line 56, the "power" is

(A) a personal skill
(B) a national virtue
(C) a despotic agent
(D) a mysterious spirit
(E) a fearsome mirage

5 The tone of the second paragraph is best described as

(A) prescriptive
(B) critical
(C) objective
(D) melancholy
(E) joyous

6 Which of the following best describes the relationship between the first and second paragraphs?

(A) The first describes a current state of affairs, while the second describes a situation in the past.
(B) The first describes a right, while the second gives recommendations for exercising that right.
(C) The first describes a problem, while the second describes a way to remedy that problem.
(D) The first describes a theory, while the second describes the evidence for that theory.
(E) The first addresses the leaders of a country, while the second addresses its citizens.

Answer Key 7:
Thinking Logically

Concept Review 7

1. In general chronological order: the first questions are about the beginning of the passage, and the last questions are about the end.
2. Look at the line references in the questions before and after that question. The answer most likely can be found between those lines.
3. An "inclusive" answer uses words like "might," "can," "some," and "sometimes" that make a statement more likely to be true than if it had "exclusive" words like "must," "never," "all," and "always."
4. Because if two responses seem reasonable, the one with the more inclusive answer is more likely the correct one.
5. What would a reasonable person would say about where art *primarily* comes from? You don't need special outside knowledge here, just common sense.
   (A) desire for wealth (Are most artists money-grubbers? Probably not.)
   (B) anxiety (Are most artists anxious? Could be, but that's mean.)
   (C) exact imitation (Do most artists make exact copies? No.)
   (D) reason (Do most artists paint *logically*? Probably not.)
   (E) intuition (Do most artists rely on feelings and hunches? Seems reasonable.)

6. Since it asks which statement the author would *most likely* agree with, it's a good idea to focus on the exclusivity of the answers.
   (A) Voters always choose incapable political candidates. (*Always* is exclusive, and this is mean.)
   (B) Voters should be more educated about candidates. (This is reasonable and inclusive.)
   (C) Political candidates rarely campaign effectively. (Possible, but a bit exclusive and harsh.)
   (D) Politicians do not represent their constituents well. (Possible, but a bit exclusive and mean.)
   (E) Voters are not interested in critical political issues. (Since this answer would imply that (B) is also true, it must be wrong.)
7. Think about what can reasonably be accomplished in 400–800 words.
   (A) to dissuade students from studying political science (Reasonable but harsh.)
   (B) to describe the evolution of ethics in American history (Far too big a task.)
   (C) to attack the credibility of politicians (Reasonable but harsh.)
   (D) to refute a misconception (Reasonable.)
   (E) to prescribe a solution to a problem (Reasonable.)

SAT I Practice 7

1. **C** The "right" is described as the right to "knowledge . . . of the characters and conduct of their rulers."
2. **D** The sentence says that "the people have a right to revoke the authority that they themselves have deputed, and to *constitute* abler and better agents. . . ." This means that they can remove the leaders who don't lead well and replace them with those who do. So *constitute* means something like *replace them with,* or choice (D) *install.*
3. **D** The passage explains that "our own more immediate forefathers" experienced
   (A) political oppression: "that oppression . . . which drove them from their homes" (lines 56–57)
   (B) difficult terrain: "inhospitable wilderness" (lines 54–55)

   (C) arduous labor: "severe labors" (lines 60–61)
   (E) physical deprivation: "the hunger, the nakedness, the cold" (line 59)
   However, lines 69–71 say that it was "the hope of liberty . . . which conquered all the discouragements. . . ."
4. **C** The "power" is described as that "which drove them from their homes." So it is a despotic agent.
5. **A** Most sentences begin with "Let us . . . ," which indicates that he is strongly suggesting what his fellow citizens should do. He is *prescribing* action.
6. **B** The first paragraph describes the "right . . . to knowledge," while the second describes what kind of knowledge the citizens should acquire.

Lesson 8: Speed and Pacing

A Few Words About Speed

❑ **Good SAT I takers don't read too fast or too slowly; they read smart.** One of the most common mistakes on the Critical Reading section is reading too fast. Many students think that reading fast saves them time. The opposite is often true: **if you skim too quickly, you'll miss important points and get bogged down in the questions.**

As you take the Practice Tests in Chapter 19, time yourself carefully on the Critical Reading sections, and notice if you have much difficulty finishing each section. **Don't panic, though, if you don't finish in time for the first couple of tests;** you will probably improve your efficiency after a few tests, and the problem will go away. **If finishing in time is still a big problem after a few Practice Tests, however, you have four options:**

1. **Change the way you're attacking the questions (as discussed below).**
2. **Keep a stopwatch and budget your time: set aside 10 minutes for a short passage, 15 minutes for a long one.**
3. **Work on improving your reading speed (as discussed below).**
4. **Get tested to see if you qualify to take the SAT I with extended time.**

❑ **If you discover, after a few practice tests, that you would do considerably better on the Critical Reading section with more time, talk to your guidance counselor about how to qualify for extended time on the SAT I.** Be careful, though: extra time doesn't necessarily mean extra points. Some students actually score **lower** with extra time, because they don't use their time as effectively.

The "Attack the Questions as You Read" Approach

❑ Although many students prefer to read the whole passage before attacking the questions, you might want to experiment with an **"attack the questions as you read"** approach. First, **read the first paragraph or two, then answer the questions** that pertain to that section of the passage (skip any "central idea" or "overall purpose" questions for now). When you reach a question that refers to a portion of the passage that you haven't read, go back and read the next paragraph or two, and so on. **Always read whole paragraphs at a time: don't stop in the middle of a paragraph.**

Increase Your Speed Gradually

If you increase your reading speed the right way, your comprehension will increase as well. Imagine yourself driving a car when it suddenly accelerates beyond your control. What would you do? You'd pay very close attention to everything around you so you wouldn't crash! Similarly, when you speed up your reading, you break yourself of the habit of mindlessly moving your eyes over the page. You will pay better attention to the ideas. **The key, though, is to increase your speed gradually.**

❑ One barrier to fast reading is "subvocalization," or the tendency to "hear" in your head the words that you are reading. To break this barrier, **practice forcing your eyes to move over the words faster than you can speak them.**

Use Your Hand

❑ If you want to read faster or improve your focus, you must retrain your eyes to move smoothly and quickly through the page. Use your hand to help. Let your fingers sweep smoothly across the page to guide and focus your eyes on the words near your fingers. Work on "pushing" your eyes through the passage. Practice with different sweep techniques. Good hand-eye coordination will boost your comprehension as well as your speed.

Practice, Practice, Practice

❑ Daily "quick reading" exercises help you to hone your comprehension skills. Take out a stopwatch and try to get the key ideas of a newspaper or magazine article in 30 seconds. Try to get the key ideas of a book in only five minutes. "Quick reading" exercises will help you to locate important points in your reading and skim over unnecessary ones.

Concept Review 8:
Speed and Pacing

1. What four options should you explore if you consistently have difficulty finishing the Critical Reading questions?

2. Why does reading too fast often slow you down?

3. What is the "Attack the Questions as You Read" approach?

4. Experiment with the "Passage First" and the "Attack the Questions as You Read" approach, and write your comments about which method you prefer and why.

5. How can your hand help you to improve your reading speed and focus?

6. What are "quick reading" exercises, and why are they helpful to do every day?

SAT I Practice 8:
Speed and Pacing

The following is an excerpt from an essay written by David Pinching, a British writer, about the tyranny of maps.

Maps are one of the better inventions of humankind. Where we can see the problems that
Line develop from nuclear weapons (there goes a
city), labor-saving machines (there go our
5   jobs) and even books on the Internet (there go
our musty old libraries and old women telling
us to shut up and stop enjoying ourselves),
maps really get off extremely lightly. It is
probably fair to say that now, in the days
10 where one is unlikely to find the inscription,
"Here be dragons," maps in general are pleas-
ingly but boringly accurate. Things develop,
streets appear, one-way systems are created,
whole cities move three meters west (well,
15 sometimes) but nothing much changes. There
is no need to get lost with a map, even if we
do all too regularly as a result of our own ineptitude (always ending up on an industrial
estate—or is that just in England?). Instead,
20 the world is—as they tell us so inexplicably—
our oyster. Is that not a problem though? Is it
not an annoyance to rate at least alongside the
problem of where to put a sticky popsicle
wrapper when driving? I believe it is.
25   What, you may quite validly ask, brings me
to such a conclusion? I have, I will admit it,
no real wish to roam. Rambling will not be
the death of me. Anywhere I lay my hat is not
my home; it is where I ponder how I came
30 into possession of a hat at all. I did not, like so
many of my contemporaries, take a "gap" year
to roam foreign mountains armed only with a
rucksack, some cream crackers, a global positioning device and a Visa card. In fact, to find
35 me somewhere else but sitting on my couch
with a book and a cup of tea is akin to finding
a high street without an expensive but "stylish"
coffee chain on it. However, I have made a
discovery. It is perhaps more of a convenient
40 little excuse than a significant breakthrough
for mankind, but it matters to me nonetheless.
I have realized that it is maps themselves that
stop me going anywhere but back home. I
know exactly where the road that leads off left
45 from my road goes, not to mention right, and
I can make a pretty safe guess where I would

be if I jumped clean over the house opposite
us. Even if didn't, I could look on a map: convenient, useful, timesaving, but
50 horribly predictable. There is nothing new to
discover—anywhere. What is the point of
going anywhere when there is nothing to find
that someone hasn't seen and noted down before? I am no Francis Drake, Christopher
55 Columbus, or Marco Polo, but I am a descen-
dant of the great if disappointingly little-
known explorer Mungo Park (no, I really am)
and by God I should be exploring something!
And maps are getting in my way.
60   The Scottish adventurer Mungo Park left for
Africa in 1795 and, for reasons best known to
himself, travelled two hundred miles up the
Gambia, got caught by a native chief, escaped,
and then made it eighty miles down the Niger
65 to Ségou before running out of food and other
supplies (see his snappily-titled 1799 volume
Travels in the Interior Districts of Africa). Actually, he returned in 1805 and set off again, this
time from Ségou in a canoe before drowning
70 after being attacked at Bussa. The point is
that Park failed completely to live up to his
name. He did not park himself anywhere until
there was nothing he could do but go back,
and even then he was just waiting for the op-
75 portunity to start again in an even smaller
boat. With his blood in my veins, there had to
be hope for me. And still there are too many
maps and "Lonely Planet" guides. Everywhere is safely checked out for me in ad-
80 vance and rated for price, coziness and
cockroach quotient. Frankly, you can up and
take your life to anywhere on earth within
certain (usually icy or sandy) limits and live
it there in similar and often cheaper style.
85 With McBurgers. How disappointed would
old Mungo have been at Bussa if he had noticed that there was an outlet of his favourite
liquor bar stationed at his furthest point on
the Niger?

From "The Strange Tyranny of Maps," by David Pinching.
Reprinted by permission of the author.

1 The parenthetical remarks in the second sentence are intended to indicate

(A) what is lost with the advent of particular inventions

(B) what people like most about certain inventions

(C) the locations where certain inventions are most likely to be used

(D) what society gains from the use of maps

(E) the ways that different inventions are affected by maps

2 The "discovery" mentioned in line 39 is

(A) that maps are often wrong

(B) that there are many novel destinations to explore

(C) that he is related to an explorer

(D) that maps can discourage travel

(E) that maps are rarely used properly

3 The last sentence serves to emphasize

(A) the remoteness of a particular destination

(B) the dangers of a particular habit

(C) the difference between the author's world and that of his ancestor

(D) the beauty of a natural site

(E) the virtues of exploring uncharted territories

Answer Key 8:
Speed and Pacing

Concept Review 8

1. 1. Change the way you're attacking the questions.
   2. Keep a stopwatch and budget your time: set aside ten minutes for a short passage, fifteen minutes for a long one.
   3. Work on improving your reading speed.
   4. Get tested to see if you qualify to take the SAT I with extended time.

2. Because hasty reading often means missing the main points and tone of the passage, which means that answering the questions will require more re-thinking and rereading than necessary.

3. Stopping to answer any relevant questions after finishing each paragraph or so.

4. There is no right or wrong answer here. Just be sure that you consider both methods as options and practice with each one before deciding which to use.

5. By breaking your eyes of their "habit" of moving unevenly or mindlessly through the page. Your hand provides a point of focus and a means of pacing your eyes through the page.

6. "Quick reading" exercises are simply timed exercises in which you try to get the gist of a reading as short as an article or as long as an entire book. The goal is to perfect your "skimming" skills: your ability to focus on key ideas and skim over less important ideas.

SAT I Practice 8

1. **A** The parenthetical remarks indicate "the problems" that particular inventions cause, although the last one, "there go our musty old libraries and old women telling us to shut up and stop enjoying ourselves" is tongue-in-cheek. The fact they all begin with the phrase "there goes" or "there go" indicates that they are indicating something that is lost.

2. **D** The "discovery," the author explains, is "that it is maps themselves that stop me going anywhere but back home." In other words, maps can discourage travel.

3. **C** "Old Mungo" was, as the author explained at the end of the previous paragraph, an explorer who is also the author's ancestor. The author has explained that he has "no real wish to roam" and prefers "sitting on my couch with a book and a cup of tea." The last sentence implies that Mungo would be disappointed to find a convenience in a remote jungle locale, thereby emphasizing the different attitudes Mungo and the author have.

Lesson 9: Avoiding Common Mistakes

Deal with "Space-Outs"

Have you ever been reading for a while when suddenly you realize that you really **haven't** been reading? This is what we call a "space-out." Everyone does it from time to time. Your eyes are moving along on "automatic pilot," but your mind isn't really processing the words.

❑ When you space out when reading on the SAT I, **don't panic.** It happens to just about everyone, and it's nothing to worry about. **Just calmly go back to where you left off, and re-read normally.**

❑ The best way to minimize space-outs is to continually know what to look for. **When you have a conscious task, your mind stays focused and you're less likely to space out.** Constantly keep the three Key Questions in mind, and check your understanding at the end of each paragraph.

Sit Up Straight

❑ When taking the SAT I, and particularly when reading, **sit up straight.** Your body posture has a good deal to do with how well you focus on your reading. Ever try to read while lying in bed? It's hard to stay alert, isn't it? This is because your body is telling your brain that it's time for sleep, and so your brain **begins to shut down.** Hardly what you want to do when taking the SAT I! **Sit up straight and lean slightly forward as you read.** This keeps your brain in "alert" mode so that it's easier to focus.

Budget Your Time Well

Budget your time well. It should take you around 10 minutes to read and complete the questions for each short passage and 15 minutes for each long passage or set of "paired" passages. In other words, by the time you get to a long passage or set of paired passages, you should have about 15 minutes left on that section. If you don't have that much time, perhaps you spent too much time on the first part of the section, on the sentence completion and paragraph questions.

❑ If you consistently run out of time on the Critical Reading sections, consider keeping a stopwatch with you as you practice and budgeting time specifically for the reading. As a rule of thumb, you should budget 10 minutes or so for each short passage, and 15 minutes for every long passage or set of "paired" passages. As you learn more about your strengths and weaknesses, you can refine this plan as necessary.

Keep Your Eyes on the Prize

❑ **Unless you've got a good shot at an 800 Critical Reading score, you don't need to answer every question.** Don't get bogged down on tough questions. **If you can't decide between two answers, make your best guess and move on.** (But make a small mark next to the question number on your answer sheet so you know what to come back to if you have time.) **Keep in mind that to break 500, you need only to get about half of the questions right, and to break 600, you need to get only about two-thirds of the questions right.** To break 700, though, you'll need to get more than 86% of the questions right.

Be Selective

❑ Remember, reading questions are not arranged by difficulty, but rather "chronologically." **Be selective in choosing which ones to answer. Read each one before you decide. The first question is just as likely to be difficult as the last one.**

Concept Review 9:
Avoiding Common Mistakes

1. What is a "space-out?"

2. What should you do if you space out while reading on the SAT I?

3. What is the key to minimizing space-outs as you read?

4. Why is posture important in reading?

5. Approximately how much time should you budget to read and answer questions on a short passage?

a long passage?

two "paired" passages?

6. Approximately what percentage of the questions must you answer correctly to break 500?

600?

700?

SAT I Practice 9:
Avoiding Common Mistakes

The following is a college-level text on economics by Nobel Prize winner Paul Samuelson and professor William Nordhaus.

> *It is not from the benevolence of the butcher, the brewer, or the baker that we ex-*
Line *pect our dinner, but from their regard to their own interest.*

5   Adam Smith, *The Wealth of Nations* (1776)

Pause for a moment to consider the paradoxical words above, penned in 1776 by Adam Smith, the founder of modern economics. That same year was also marked by the
10 American Declaration of Independence. It is no coincidence that both ideas appeared at the same time. Just as the American revolutionaries were proclaiming freedom from tyranny, Adam Smith was preaching a revolutionary
15 doctrine emancipating trade and industry from the shackles of feudal aristocracy.

In the last two centuries, most of the world has experienced an era of unimagined prosperity. In the United States and other high-
20 income countries, most people today can afford to buy far more than the bare necessities of food, clothing, and shelter. Superfast personal computers, high-tech home entertainment centers, and fast air transportation to any part
25 of the globe are examples of an astonishing range of goods and services that have become part of everyday life. Developing countries have also seen their standards of living rise rapidly in recent years.
30   But widespread prosperity has not brought economic security. In an average year, 10 million Americans lose their jobs and almost 100,000 businesses go bankrupt. About 14 percent of households are designated as poor,
35 and the number is almost 50 percent among households headed by black females. Many families worry about the catastrophic financial consequence of illness because they have no health insurance. The affluent society is an
40 anxious society.

For most of human history, people who experience economic misfortunes lived on the mercy of their family or friends. Starting about a century ago, governments introduced
45 the "welfare state," which provided social in-surance and income support to needy people. Gradually, poor people in rich countries got access to minimal levels of income, food, and health care. But raising taxes and growing
50 government spending on health care and public pensions have produced a revolt of the middle class, which is the taxed class. In 1996, the United States removed its guarantee of income support for poor families. Everywhere,
55 countries are rethinking the boundaries between state and market, trying to balance the growing need for providing public services with the increasing clamor for cutting taxes and shrinking government.
60   This is the age of the global marketplace. Today, money, goods, and information cross national borders more readily than ever before. In earlier times, we did business with people down the street or in the next town,
65 and we bought mainly local goods. Today, we ride in the "world car." Look at this world car or at a fast computer. It incorporates materials, labor, capital, and innovations from around the world. The rise of the global mar-
70 ketplace raises new challenges. Who can best adapt to increased foreign competition? Who can quickly adapt to the information age? The stakes are high. To the winners go the profits, while the losers lag behind.

---

1 Which of the following best describes the overall purpose of the passage?

(A)   to describe a theory
(B)   to establish a context
(C)   to refute a misconception
(D)   to suggest a reform
(E)   to evaluate a work

---

2 In line 40, the word "anxious" most nearly means

(A)   eager
(B)   spirited
(C)   insecure
(D)   ill
(E)   angry

Paul Samuelson and William Nordhaus, *Economics*, 16th edition. © 1998 McGraw-Hill. Reprinted by permission of McGraw-Hill.

3 According to the passage, the "revolt of the middle class" (lines 51–52) is due to which of the following?

    I.   the growing costs of the welfare state
   II. lack of access to pension funds
 III. lower wages

    (A) I only
    (B) I and II only
    (C) I and III only
    (D) II and III only
    (E) I, II, and III

4 According to the passage, the "world car" (line 66) is a car that

    (A) is accessible to individuals of all nationalities
    (B) utilizes resources from many different places
    (C) is more efficient than others
    (D) is advertised worldwide
    (E) is adaptable to different purposes

Answer Key 9: Avoiding Common Mistakes

Concept Review 9

1. Your eyes make the motion of reading, but your mind doesn't process the words.

2. Don't panic: just calmly pick up where you left off and continue to read normally.

3. Focus on your tasks. Answer the three Key Questions, and check yourself at the end of every paragraph.

4. Because posture that isn't vertical tells your brain to begin to shut down for sleep, and focusing is much more difficult. So sit up straight and lean slightly forward when reading.

5. short passage: 10 minutes
long passage: 15 minutes
two "paired" passages: 15 minutes
(If you are taking the test under "extended time" conditions, budget 12 minutes, 22 minutes, and 22 minutes, respectively)

6. 500: about 50%
600: about 67%
700: more than 86%

SAT I Practice 9

1. **B** The passage describes the general economic situation "in the last two centuries" (line 17) without discussing any particular theories or misconceptions. The only mention of a potential "reform" is the "rethinking" of the "boundaries between state and market" mentioned in lines 55–56, but this is not a major theme of the passage. Although *The Wealth of Nations* is quoted at the beginning of the passage, it is not evaluated.

2. **C** The passage says that "widespread prosperity has not brought economic security" (lines 30–31) and "many families worry" (lines 36–37) about their lack of security. Therefore "anxious" is used to mean "insecure."

3. **A** The "revolt of the middle class" is due to "rising taxes and growing government spending on health care and public pensions" (lines 50–51). The passage does not mention wages or access to pension funds.

4. **B** The passage says that the "world car" "incorporates materials, labor, capital, and innovations from around the world" (lines 67–69).

The College Hill Coaching Reading List

Familiarize Yourself with Different "Voices"

If you really want to prepare for the Critical Reading portion of the SAT I, work on developing a well-rounded fluency in different kinds of prose. The SAT I will draw from readings in a wide variety of "voices," and it helps tremendously to be familiar with them. Good readers appreciate the work of a wide variety of writers. William Shakespeare, S. J. Perelman, Walter Lippmann, and Jane Austen are all masterful articulators of the English language, but their writing styles are vastly different.

Don't restrict yourself to reading just a narrow range of prose that you've enjoyed in the past. Expand your repertoire by delving into works of different genres, different eras, and different styles. The following list represents some of the most influential books in the liberal arts, and they represent a wide variety of voices. Push yourself to read the books on this list that go beyond your conventional reading.

Also, read to expose yourself to the vast world of ideas. The readings you will likely see on the SAT I will span the liberal arts and touch on many ideas that interest current scholars in those areas. The more familiar you are with these ideas, the easier it will be to understand passages that discuss them.

Narrative

One Hundred Years of Solitude,
    Gabriel García Márquez
Candide, Voltaire
The Wall, John Hersey
The Best American Short Stories of the Century,
    John Updike, editor
Frankenstein, Mary Wollstonecraft Shelley
The Grapes of Wrath, John Steinbeck
The Picture of Dorian Gray, Oscar Wilde
To the Lighthouse, Virginia Woolf
The Bell Jar, Sylvia Plath

Heart of Darkness, Joseph Conrad
The Three Musketeers, Alexandre Dumas
Things Fall Apart, Chinua Achebe
Madame Bovary, Gustave Flaubert
The Color Purple, Alice Walker
Metamorphosis (and other stories), Franz Kafka
The Autobiography of Frederick Douglass
The Painted Bird, Jerzy Kozinsky
Macbeth, William Shakespeare
Growing Up, Russell Baker
Baby, It's Cold Inside, S. J. Perelman
Pride and Prejudice, Jane Austen
Atlas Shrugged, Ayn Rand
The Life of Pi, Yann Martel
Crime and Punishment, Fyodor Dostoyevsky

Argument

The Op-Ed pages of *The New York Times*
Essays from *Harper's, The Atlantic Monthly*, and
    The New Yorker
Lanterns and Lances, James Thurber
Drift and Mastery, Walter Lippmann
The Best American Essays, Robert Atwan, editor
Walden, Henry David Thoreau
The Chomsky Reader, Noam Chomsky

Analysis

A Brief History of Time, Stephen Hawking
The Mismeasure of Man, Stephen J. Gould
The Republic, Plato
Civilization and Its Discontents, Sigmund Freud
A People's History of the United States, Howard Zinn
How the Mind Works, Steven Pinker
QED, Richard Feynman
The Lives of a Cell, Lewis Thomas
Democracy in America, Alexis de Tocqueville
The Language Instinct, Steven Pinker
The Man Who Mistook His Wife for a Hat,
    Oliver Sacks

CHAPTER 8

SENTENCE COMPLETION SKILLS

1. Verbal Inference

2. The Four Logical Relationships

3. Structural Keys

4. Simplifying the Sentence

5. Using Context Intelligently

6. The Toughest Sentences

Lesson 1: Verbal Inference

What Are Sentence Completion Questions?

❑ Every SAT I will contain about 20 Sentence Completion questions as part of the Critical Reading portion of the test. These questions test your **verbal inference skills.** Your verbal inference skills are the skills you use to figure out the meaning and usage of an unfamiliar word when you read or hear it in a sentence.

Consider the following sentence:

As part of our game, we ran twice around the cregiendo until we became so trepindant that we collapsed in a heap on the porch.

Is the word *cregiendo* a noun, a verb, or an adjective? How about *trepindant*? Since they are nonsense words, you could not have known the answer to those questions before reading the sentence above. After reading the sentence, though, it should be clear. *Cregiendo* must be a noun because it's the *thing* we ran around, and *trepindant* must be an adjective, because it describes us after we ran around the *cregiendo*. With your vast verbal inference skills, you've probably figured out more than just the part of speech of *cregiendo* and *trepindant*. Try these questions:

1. A *cregiendo* is about as big as (A) a spider (B) a pillow (C) a car (D) a house (E) a village.
2. Can a *cregiendo* be *trepindant*?

Even the world's smartest and most powerful computers find these kinds of questions very, very tough. It's easier to program a computer to become a chess grandmaster or to predict hurricanes than to answer such "common-sense" questions. Common sense seems simple, but this simplicity is deceptive. So revel in your brilliance!

Look at Question 1: A *cregiendo* is something that kids can run around, but running around it twice makes you so tired that you'd collapse. Your common sense tells you that such a thing would be roughly as big as a house. A village is way too big to run around in a game, and the other things are much too small to exhaust you.

Now look at Question 2: Since we became *trepindant* after running around the *cregiendo,* the word *trepindant* describes human beings, and perhaps other animals that can run, rather than, say, rocks. It also seems to describe a *temporary state* rather than a permanent trait, since we weren't *trepindant* before we started running around. What would make us collapse in a heap? Exhaustion, of course. So *trepindant* probably means *exhausted,* which big objects like *cregiendos* could never be.

Attacking the Questions

❑ Attack Sentence Completion questions systematically: (1) **Read the entire sentence,** saying "blank" in place of the missing words. (2) **Think about the logic** of the sentence. (3) **Complete the sentence with your own words.** (4) **Scan through the choices and look for a match.** (It probably won't be an exact match; pick the closest choice.)

e.g. Although these animals migrate, they are not -------; they remain loyal to their established ranges and seldom stray into new areas.

(A) predators   (B) burrowers
(C) grazers   (D) scavengers
(E) wanderers

Don't worry about the choices yet, just read the sentence. These animals *seldom stray,* so they must not be *wanderers.* It's possible that they are not *predators,* or *burrowers,* or *grazers,* or *scavengers* also, but the sentence doesn't provide any information about those traits. Your choice should be (E).

Check Your Work

❑ Always re-read the sentence with your selected response to check it. Too many students overlook this simple step. Re-reading helps you to avoid overlooking anything important. Check that the **logic** and the **tone** make sense.

Concept Review 1:
Verbal Inference

1. What is verbal inference?

2. What should you do before trying to complete a Sentence Completion question?

Read the following sentences, think about them, then answer the questions about the nonsense words.

Far from being an arnacular pastime, numismatics, or the study of currency, can purnade our appreciation of the history and economic development of a nation.

3. *Arnacular* is (A) a verb (B) a noun (C) an adjective (D) an adverb (E) a preposition (F) a pronoun.

4. Can a person be *arnacular*?

5. *Arnacular* most nearly means (A) invalid (B) obsessive (C) aimless (D) interesting (E) foreign (F) dangerous.

6. *Purnade* is (A) a verb (B) a noun (C) an adjective (D) an adverb (E) a preposition (F) a pronoun.

7. Is *purnading our appreciation* of something probably a good thing or a bad thing?

8. *Purnade* most nearly means (A) undermine (B) complicate (C) heighten (D) clarify (E) ignore (F) adore.

Car buyers, when given a choice of engines, will typically choose the most powerful and gas-guzzling option, refuting the popular belief that fellinance is the primary concern of consumers.

9. *Fellinance* is (A) a verb (B) a noun (C) an adjective (D) an adverb (E) a preposition (F) a pronoun.

10. Are all car engines *fellinant*?

11. Is *fellinance* more likely to be associated with a small sedan or a large pickup truck?

12. *Fellinance* most nearly means (A) longevity (B) continuity (C) propriety (D) efficiency (E) luxury.

SAT I Practice 1:
Verbal Inference

Each of the sentences below is missing one or two portions. Read each sentence, then select the word or words that most logically complete the sentence, taking into account the meaning of the sentence as a whole.

Example:
Rather than accepting the theory unquestioningly, Deborah regarded it with ------.
(A) mirth
(B) sadness
(C) responsibility
(D) ignorance
(E) skepticism

Correct response: (E)

1. Although he clearly was obsessed with the ------ of moral perfection, he was also aware of its potential ------: self-righteousness, arrogance, and condescension.
    (A) pursuit . . . pitfalls
    (B) likelihood . . . dangers
    (C) contemplation . . . insights
    (D) morality . . . tenets
    (E) sanctity . . . inequities

2. Whereas Gerald was always the frivolous one, Bernard felt compelled to compensate for his brother's indiscretions by exercising profound moral ------.
    (A) hysteria
    (B) embarrassment
    (C) prudence
    (D) acceptance
    (E) equivocation

3. In need of a ------ from persecution, many young refugees wandered far from their homeland seeking ------ communities in which to settle.
    (A) nightmare . . . just
    (B) haven . . . tolerant
    (C) plight . . . magnanimous
    (D) pledge . . . malevolent
    (E) sanctuary . . . invidious

4. The synthesized voices from today's computerized machines are a far cry from the ------ sounds of older machines; rather, they sound almost like real human speech.
    (A) melancholy
    (B) cordial
    (C) fervid
    (D) inflammatory
    (E) mechanical

5. Even in communities that value ------, investment in technologically advanced industries can be an important source of ------.
    (A) progress . . . prestige
    (B) liberty . . . concern
    (C) competition . . . decay
    (D) tradition . . . income
    (E) profits . . . dismay

6. Some contend that the quatrains of Nostradamus ------ events that would not take place for centuries, including ------ like wars, conflagrations, and earthquakes.
    (A) foreboded . . . cataclysms
    (B) mitigated . . . marvels
    (C) impersonated . . . myths
    (D) transcended . . . auguries
    (E) disrupted . . . coincidences

7. While the script for the movie consummately depicted the wit and charm of Oscar Wilde, the incompetent actor portraying him mutilated the most ------ lines.
    (A) tactless
    (B) sober
    (C) ingenious
    (D) unintelligible
    (E) unnecessary

8. Rather than ------ the attitude of the entire community from that of a few individuals, she was willing to concede that there were many conflicting opinions on the matter.
    (A) distinguishing
    (B) concealing
    (C) protecting
    (D) inferring
    (E) expelling

9. For all Nick's ------ at the office, his close friends knew that this trait ------ his true contemplative and introspective nature.
    (A) bluster . . . belied
    (B) pomposity . . . determined
    (C) sarcasm . . . revealed
    (D) presumptuousness . . . emphasized
    (E) shallowness . . . bolstered

Answer Key 1: Verbal Inference

Concept Review 1

1. The ability to determine the tone, meaning and usage of unknown words when they are read or heard in context.

2. Read the entire sentence, saying "blank" when you encounter a missing word; think about the overall meaning of the sentence; and try to complete it with your own words before checking the choices.

3. (C) an adjective

4. Probably. Words that describe pastimes, like *fun*, *popular*, or *dangerous*, can often be used to describe people.

5. (C) aimless

6. (A) a verb

7. Probably good, because *studying* usually *helps* you to appreciate things, rather than the opposite.

8. (C) heighten

9. (B) a noun

10. No. Since buyers can choose between engines with *fellinance* or without it, it must not be universal.

11. A small sedan. Since *fellinance* is not a quality of *powerful and gas-guzzling* engines, it is more likely a quality of smaller engines.

12. (D) efficiency

SAT I Practice 1

1. **A** The colon introduces examples. What are *self-righteousness, arrogance,* and *condescension* examples of? Certainly not something good! So *insights* and *tenets* (core beliefs) don't make sense. The *likelihood of perfection* doesn't have *dangers,* the *sanctity of perfection* doesn't have *inequities* (unequal treatments), but the *pursuit of perfection* can certainly have *pitfalls* (negative consequences) like those listed.
   contemplation = deep thought; *sanctity* = holiness

2. **C** *Whereas* indicates a contrast. *Frivolous* means lacking soberness or seriousness. The missing word has to indicate a quality that a serious person would have, like *prudence* (conservative wisdom).
   hysteria = irrational and excessive emotion; *equivocation* = failure to commit to a position

3. **B** *Refugees* are people in search of safety, usually from war. They wouldn't seek *malevolent* (ill-wishing) or *invidious* (causing resentment) communities. They are not in need of a *nightmare* or a *plight* (difficult situation). The only choice that makes sense indicates that they are seeking a *haven* (safe place) from persecution in a *tolerant* community.
   just = proper and righteous; *magnanimous* = generous; *pledge* = oath; *sanctuary* = safe place

4. **E** *Today's computerized machines* make sounds that are *almost like real human speech,* so they must be *a far cry* from artificial-sounding speech, or *mechanical* speech.
   melancholy = depressed; *cordial* = friendly; *fervid* = passionate; *inflammatory* = tending to incite anger

5. **D** *Even in* indicates irony (a reversal of expectations). If *technologically advanced industries* bring something *important,* that will certainly not be *concern, decay,* or *dismay.* Since technological advances are far from traditional, it would be ironic that a *traditional* community would value *technology.*
   prestige = public esteem; *liberty* = freedom

6. **A** If the events *would not take place for centuries,* he must have *predicted* them. *Wars, conflagrations, and earthquakes* are types of *cataclysms* (events that cause widespread destruction).
   foreboded = predicted; *mitigated* = improved a situation; *transcended* = rose above; *auguries* = predictions

7. **C** If the script *consummately* (with superior skill) depicted wit and charm, it must be very good. An *incompetent* (unskilled) actor would *mutilate* the *ingenious* (brilliant) lines.
   tactless = inconsiderate; *sober* = serious; *unintelligible* = hard to understand

8. **D** If you aren't *willing to concede that there were many conflicting opinions,* then you must believe that everyone shares the same opinion. Therefore, you would not have to ask everyone's opinion, but could *infer* (make a generalization about) everyone's attitude from those of just a few individuals.
   distinguishing = recognizing as distinct; *expelling* = throwing out

9. **A** Here the phrase *for all* is an idiom meaning *despite,* so it indicates irony. If Nick's true nature is *contemplative and introspective,* it would be ironic if he were outgoing and *blustery* in the office. This trait would *misrepresent* or *belie* his true nature.
   pomposity = haughtiness; *sarcasm* = bitter insulting attitude; *presumptuousness* = overconfidence; *bolstered* = supported

Lesson 2:
The Four Logical Relationships

Logic Is As Important As an Enormous Vocabulary

❑ **It's important to keep in mind that the Sentence Completion questions on the SAT I are logical questions.** That is, they are asking you to find the best word or phrase to complete each thought logically. They are not asking you to find the "most interesting" or the "most complicated" word or phrase. **Each question will include *only one* choice that will complete the sentence in a way that makes logical sense.** The other choices will be illogical or incomplete in one way or another.

   e.g. *What Mr. Harrison's writing lacked in clarity it made up for in -------, for it contained enough information for a clever craftsman to re-create his invention down to the most minute detail.*

   At first reading, it may seem as if there are many different ways of completing the sentence. That is, there are many ways that a piece of writing might make up for a lack of clarity: it might be clever, or funny, or useful, or thought-provoking. But when you look at the sentence **as a whole,** there is only one logical way to complete the sentence. The second part of the sentence is key: it says that his writing contains *enough information for a clever craftsman to re-create his invention down to the most minute detail.* In other words, it provides a lot of *detail.* This must be what makes up for its lack of clarity! So while there are many "good" ways to complete the sentence, only a word like *meticulousness, comprehensiveness, completeness, detail,* etc., will make the sentence **logically complete.**

The Logical Scheme of a Sentence

❑ **Every sentence in a Sentence Completion question has a logical scheme that shows the logical relationship among the ideas in the sentence.** That scheme will always include one or more of the four basic logical relationships:

A contrast between ideas

   e.g. ***Although*** *we waited over two hours for a table, it seemed like only a few minutes.*

The support of one idea with another

   e.g. *We loved staying at the cottage; the sounds of the ocean calmed us and the sea air invigorated us.*

A cause-and-effect relationship between ideas

   e.g. *We were irritated by the noise,* ***so*** *we moved to the next room.*

A definition or explanation of a word or idea

   e.g. *Joel was a nihilist,* ***someone who doesn't believe that any truth is absolute.***

❑ **Many sentences have an overall logical scheme that includes more than one logical relationship.** Think carefully about each sentence and make sure you see all of the logical relationships.

   e.g. *The motion of the region's glaciers is both ------ and ------: they seem not to be moving at all, yet they transform the landscape more profoundly than any other force of nature.*

   When you first read the phrase *both ------ and ------,* it may seems that the two missing words must be similar, because they are joined with *and* rather than *but* or *yet.* But you must get the **overall** logical scheme first. The colon indicates that the two statements **support** each other, and the use of *yet* in the second statement shows a **contrast** between the two ideas within the second statement. Therefore, the first missing word should mean *seemingly motionless,* and the second word should mean something like *having a profound effect. Imperceptible* and *dramatic* work nicely.

Concept Review 2:
The Four Logical Relationships

1. What are the four basic logical relationships a sentence may include?

After each sentence, describe its "logical scheme" by circling each logical relationship—contrast, support, cause and effect, or definition—that you can find within the sentence. (Remember that a sentence may show more than one relationship.)

2. Although he clearly was obsessed with the ----- of moral integrity, he was also aware of its potential -------: self-righteousness, arrogance, and condescension.

       support   contrast   cause and effect   definition

3. Few of us appreciated our group leader's ------; we were too intelligent and had too much self-esteem to be persuaded by her constant use of insult and humiliation.

       support   contrast   cause and effect   definition

4. In need of a ------ from persecution, many young refugees wandered far from their homeland seeking ------ communities in which to settle.

       support   contrast   cause and effect   definition

5. Because the population of bacteria soon ------ the food supply, their once rapid proliferation soon slows, and may even stop altogether.

       support   contrast   cause and effect   definition

6. Deer in the wild often seem ------ to the concept of death; they are utterly unaware of any danger even when they notice their friends nearby dropping one by one.

       support   contrast   cause and effect   definition

7. Some contend that the quatrains of Nostradamus ------ events that would not take place for centuries, including ------ like wars, conflagrations, and earthquakes.

       support   contrast   cause and effect   definition

8. While the script for the movie consummately depicted the wit and charm of Oscar Wilde, the incompetent actor portraying him mutilated the most ------ lines.

       support   contrast   cause and effect   definition

9. The herd of lemmings always acted ------, thus ensuring that either they all survived or they all perished.

       support   contrast   cause and effect   definition

10. By ------ his announcement of the new promotions, Carl felt that he could maintain his employees' eagerness with the element of anticipation.

       support   contrast   cause and effect   definition

SAT I Practice 2:
The Four Logical Relationships

Each of the sentences below is missing one or two portions. Read each sentence, then select the word or words that most logically complete the sentence, taking into account the meaning of the sentence as a whole.

Example:
Rather than accepting the theory unquestioningly, Deborah regarded it with ------.
(A) mirth
(B) sadness
(C) responsibility
(D) ignorance
(E) skepticism

Correct response: (E)

1. Possessing seemingly boundless energy, DeVare fights for the causes she supports with a ------ that would leave others ------ at the end of the workday.
(A) grace . . . scandalized
(B) commitment . . . uncertain
(C) loyalty . . . contrite
(D) vigor . . . exhausted
(E) sincerity . . . disillusioned

2. The members of the committee saw Vance's reign as chairman becoming more and more ------; his decisions seemed based more on personal whim than on the opinions of his fellow members.
(A) inclusive
(B) abstract
(C) irresistible
(D) illusory
(E) arbitrary

3. The boundary between Canada and the United States is more a political than a cultural ------; the people on both sides ------ a great deal in terms of artistic sensibilities.
(A) demarcation . . . share
(B) partition . . . estrange
(C) event . . . partake
(D) affiliation . . . admit
(E) division . . . conflict

4. Some criminal investigators believe that polygraphs reliably ------ deception by recording ------ reactions in a subject such as slight changes in breathing rate or perspiration elicited by a set of questions.

(A) judge . . . imaginative
(B) detect . . . physiological
(C) predict . . . imperceptible
(D) subvert . . . simulated
(E) induce . . . verifiable

5. The author intentionally combines the vernacular of the Bronx with pretentious academic jargon, creating a uniquely ------ style that makes her novel particularly difficult to translate into other languages.
(A) mundane
(B) taciturn
(C) alliterative
(D) idiosyncratic
(E) orthodox

6. The fact that polar bears are tremendously strong indicates the degree of ------ they must have in their aggressive play, for they never hurt each other.
(A) intensity
(B) stamina
(C) concentration
(D) instinct
(E) restraint

7. Long an advocate of deterrence, General Wallace had hoped that the ------ display of force would ------ further military action.
(A) formidable . . . obviate
(B) subtle . . . require
(C) impressive . . . generate
(D) unnecessary . . . prevent
(E) unbridled . . . sustain

8. Disillusioned and ------, the impoverished young writer was ready to ------ the artistic life for a real job.
(A) capable . . . abandon
(B) complacent . . . invoke
(C) dejected . . . forsake
(D) gracious . . . deny
(E) crushed . . . capture

9. The meal of raw eggs and vegetables, while ------, in fact ------ all requisite nutrition to the young athlete in training.
(A) meager . . . denied
(B) sumptuous . . . supplied
(C) spartan . . . provided
(D) doleful . . . restored
(E) appropriate . . . allowed

Answer Key 2:
The Four Logical Relationships

Concept Review 2

1. support, contrast, cause and effect, and definition
2. support (*colon* indicates examples), contrast (*although*)
3. support (*semicolon* indicates development), definition (missing word means *constant use of insult and humiliation*)
4. support (------ *communities* must provide ------ *from persecution*), cause and effect (the *need* caused their *search*)
5. cause and effect (*because*)
6. definition (missing word means *utterly unaware*)
7. support (*examples* are given)
8. support (the *script* was *consummate* so the *lines* must have been good, too), contrast (*while*)
9. cause and effect (*thus*)
10. cause and effect (*by . . .*)

SAT I Practice 2

1. **D** *Boundless energy* is the **definition** of *vigor*. This is the kind of thing that would **cause** someone to be *exhausted* at the end of the day.
   grace = elegance; *scandalized* = shamed publicly; *contrite* = filled with regret; *vigor* = great energy; *disillusioned* = with lowered esteem for another

2. **E** This sentence contains a **definition.** The missing word means *based more on personal whim than on the opinions of his fellow members.* This is what *arbitrary* means.
   inclusive = including; *abstract* = not concrete; *illusory* = based on or characteristic of illusion; *arbitrary* = based on whim or random power

3. **A** The semicolon indicates **support.** The phrase *more . . . than . . .* indicates a **contrast.** The word *boundary* is the **definition** of the first missing word.
   demarcation = boundary; *estrange* = cause to grow apart; *partake* = participate; *affiliation* = close association

4. **B** *Such as* indicates **support** through example. *Breathing rate* and *perspiration* are examples of *physiological* reactions. (They aren't *imperceptible* because they're being recorded!) The word *by* indicates a **cause and effect** relationship. The recording of such reactions would not *induce* (cause) deception, but might just *detect* it.
   imperceptible = incapable of being detected; *subvert* = undermine; *simulated* = artificial; *induce* = cause; *verifiable* = capable of being proven true

5. **D** The sentence shows a **cause and effect:** something about the novel *makes* it (causes it to be) *difficult to translate.* The description makes it sound *quirky*, which would indeed make it hard to translate.
   mundane = ordinary; *taciturn* = not talkative; *alliterative* = tending to use words that begin with the same sound; *idiosyncratic* = quirky; *orthodox* = adhering strictly to teachings

6. **E** This sentence shows a **cause and effect.** Some quality of the bears causes them not to hurt each other, even in *aggressive play.* Particularly since they are so **strong,** they would have to have a lot of *restraint.*
   stamina = endurance; *concentration* = focus; *instinct* = inborn ability; *restraint* = ability to hold back

7. **A** This sentence **supports** the main idea with a description of the General's beliefs. *Deterrence* is the belief that a strong offensive capability will *deter* (prevent) attack from one's enemies, that is, that a *formidable* (awesome) display of force would *obviate* (render unnecessary through foresight) further military action.
   subtle = hard to detect; *unbridled* = lacking restraint

8. **C** This sentence **supports** the main idea with a description of the writer's mood. If a writer is *disillusioned* and *impoverished,* she would probably not want to stay in that situation for much longer. She would want to *give up* the artistic life. The first word should be a negative adjective that describes the life she wants to give up.
   complacent = self-satisfied; *invoke* = call in; *dejected* = sad; *forsake* = abandon; *gracious* = full of grace

9. **C** The word *while* and the phrase *in fact* indicate a **contrast.** A meal of raw eggs and vegetables sounds pretty *minimal,* but it must *provide all requisite* (necessary) nutrition to the young athlete.
   meager = minimal; *sumptuous* = bountiful; *spartan* = minimal, stark; *doleful* = sad

Lesson 3: Structural Keys

The Structural Key Words

Structural key words are the words or phrases that show the logical relationship between the statements in the sentence. Certain logical relationships require key words: for instance, it's almost impossible to say that one thing **caused** another thing without using a word like *because, therefore, thus, in order to,* or *consequently.*

❑ As you read the sentences, try **underlining** or **circling** any structural key words you see, because completing the sentence logically may require you to think about these key words first.

Here is a partial list of some structural key words:

Contrast	*but*	*however*	*in contrast*	*nevertheless*
	whereas	*although*	*instead of*	*rather*
	despite	*unusual*	*unexpected*	*surprising*
	abnormal	*anomalous*	*curious*	*illogical*
Cause and Effect	*because*	*thus*	*consequently*	*therefore*
	so that	*in order to*	*if . . . then*	*since*
Support	*furthermore*	*likewise*	*moreover*	*also*
	besides	*additionally*	*similarly*	*like*
	for instance	*that is*	*for example*	

Semicolons and Colons

Some punctuation marks can also help you determine the logical relation between parts of a sentence. Semicolons and colons, for instance, indicate a "supporting" relationship between statements, but they mean slightly different things. **A semicolon (;) between two statements indicates that the second statement *extends* or *develops* the previous statement. A colon (:) between two statements indicates that the second statement *explains* the previous one.**

e.g. Newton inferred that the law of gravity was ------: even the gravitational pull of an ant on Earth will ------ a star millions of light-years away.

   (A) universal . . . influence   (B) inconsequential . . . accelerate   (C) intense . . . support
   (D) minute . . . affect   (E) complete . . . replace

The colon after the first statement indicates that the second statement **explains** the first, in this case by giving an example. To understand the sentence as a whole, it's probably best to try to understand the second statement first and then ask: "What general idea does that example explain?" The second part says that *the gravitational pull of an ant will* ------ *a star* far away. Well, a scientist like Isaac Newton wouldn't be so silly as to say that an ant's gravity could *support* or *replace* a star, so it must *influence, accelerate,* or *affect* it. If this is true, then even small gravitational effects must travel a long, long, long, long way. This is the important point of the example, so Newton's theory must have been that gravity is *universal.*

e.g. The string arrangements by Rob Mathes are unobtrusive yet ------; the violins rise ------, but soon they reach deeply into the piece and transform it into a lyrically rich and moving experience.

   (A) carefree . . . stiffly   (B) reserved . . . involuntarily   (C) profound . . . subtly
   (D) detached . . . carefully   (E) hesitant . . . methodically

The semicolon indicates that the second statement **develops** the first, repeating the same general idea but with more detail. The two clauses are **parallel,** that is, they have similar grammatical structures. The first says: *These are A yet B; they do C but then D.* The structure indicates that A and C go together, and B and D go together. If the arrangements are *unobtrusive* then they rise *subtly,* and if they *reach deeply into the piece and transform it,* they must be *profound.*

Concept Review 3: Structural Keys

1. Name as many structural key words or phrases as you can that indicate a contrast of ideas.

2. Name as many words or phrases as you can that indicate a cause-and-effect relationship.

3. What do colons and semicolons indicate about the statements they join, and what does a colon do that a semicolon does not do?

Circle each structural key word, phrase, or punctuation mark in each sentence, and indicate above the word, phrase, or mark whether it shows **support, contrast, cause and effect,** or **definition.**

4. Although the words coming from his mouth were refined and deferential, his eyes betrayed a subtle ------ for his subject.

5. In order to be newsworthy a story should be ------; that is, it should not merely warm over old facts the reader has heard many times before.

6. The building should be ------ not only for its long-recognized architectural merit but also for its ------ in the history of Black American theater.

7. Because the President was used to receiving the support of his advisers, he was ------ when he discovered that their views on the handling of the crisis were ------ with his own.

8. Some criminal investigators believe that polygraphs will reliably ------ deception by recording ------ reactions such as slight changes in breathing rate or perspiration rate elicited by a set of questions.

SAT I Practice 3:
Structural Keys

Each of the sentences below is missing one or two portions. Read each sentence, then select the word or words that most logically complete the sentence, taking into account the meaning of the sentence as a whole.

Example:
   Rather than accepting the theory unquestioningly, Deborah regarded it with ------.
   (A) mirth
   (B) sadness
   (C) responsibility
   (D) ignorance
   (E) skepticism

                              Correct response: (E)

1. The ------ of the neighborhood is revealed by subtle practices, like the fact that so many people in the community use the same hand gestures when speaking.
   (A) diversity
   (B) adaptability
   (C) modernization
   (D) cohesiveness
   (E) creativity

2. During the day crabs move slowly and ------, but at night they roam ------ across sandy sea bottoms, climbing reefs or foraging for kelp.
   (A) frantically . . . wildly
   (B) cautiously . . . freely
   (C) gradually . . . sluggishly
   (D) deliberately . . . carefully
   (E) rashly . . . rapidly

3. Because the President was used to receiving the support of his advisers, he was ------ when he discovered that their views on the handling of the crisis were ------ with his own.
   (A) stunned . . . irreconcilable
   (B) relieved . . . inconsistent
   (C) amused . . . consonant
   (D) oblivious . . . compatible
   (E) sorry . . . commensurate

4. The building should be ------ not only for its long-recognized architectural merit but also for its ------ in the history of Black American theater.
   (A) designed . . . role
   (B) commissioned . . . usefulness
   (C) preserved . . . importance
   (D) demolished . . . future
   (E) constructed . . . place

5. The lecture on number theory and its applications might have been particularly trying for the nonspecialists in the audience had the professor not ------ it with humorous asides.
   (A) exhorted
   (B) leavened
   (C) intercepted
   (D) countermanded
   (E) rebuffed

6. His ------ maintained that Mr. Frank was constantly at odds with the corporate officers; yet the truth was that his ideas were not at all ------ with the officers' reasonable goals.
   (A) detractors . . . in accord
   (B) supporters . . . at variance
   (C) advocates . . . harmonious
   (D) disparagers . . . incompatible
   (E) apologists . . . in conflict

7. In spite of the ------ of Larry's speech, most of the audience was ------ well before he had finished.
   (A) conciseness . . . cheering
   (B) humor . . . intrigued
   (C) appropriateness . . . enrapt
   (D) brevity . . . asleep
   (E) cleverness . . . reluctant

8. If a child is ------ by arbitrary parental restrictions and denied the opportunity to exercise personal responsibility, at adolescence the child is likely to engage in dangerous and self-destructive behavior.
   (A) nurtured
   (B) appeased
   (C) confined
   (D) fascinated
   (E) liberated

9. Although the government has frequently ------ some parental responsibilities, at heart it must still be parents, not agencies, who are ------ to care for children.
   (A) obscured . . . assumed
   (B) precluded . . . adjured
   (C) exulted . . . incompetent
   (D) disavowed . . . impelled
   (E) usurped . . . obligated

Answer Key 3: Structural Keys

Concept Review 3

1. *but, however, in contrast, nevertheless, whereas, although,* etc.

2. *because, therefore, thus, by,* etc.

3. Colons indicate that an explanation or a list of examples will follow; semicolons indicate that the statement that follows will extend or develop the previous one.

4. *Although* (contrast)

5. *In order to* (cause and effect); semicolon (support); *that is* (definition)

6. *not only . . . but also* (support)

7. *Because* (cause and effect); *discovered* (contrast)

8. *by* (cause and effect); *such as* (support)

SAT I Practice 3

1. **D** The word *like* indicates examples. What are common hand gestures examples of? The unity or sameness of the community.
   diversity = variety; *adaptability* = ability to fit in; *cohesiveness* = unity

2. **B** The *but* indicates contrast. The first missing word must fit well with *slowly*.
   frantically = wildly; *sluggishly* = slowly; *rashly* = hastily

3. **A** *Because* indicates cause and effect. The word *discover* indicates surprise. If the President *was used to receiving the support of his advisers*, then it would be surprising to discover that they didn't agree with him on something.
   irreconcilable = unable to be made to agree; *consonant* = in agreement with; *oblivious* = unaware; *compatible* = fitting well together; *commensurate* = in proportion to

4. **C** *Not only . . . but also . . .* indicates a supportive relationship between the ideas.
   commissioned = paid for an artistic work to be created; *demolished* = destroyed

5. **B** It *might have been trying* (difficult to tolerate) *had the professor not ------ it with humorous asides.* What do humorous asides do to make something easier to tolerate? They *lighten* it up.
   exhorted = urged strongly; *leavened* = lightened with humor; *intercepted* = caught in transit; *countermanded* = cancelled; *rebuffed* = refused abruptly

6. **D** It's not particularly good to be *constantly at odds with the corporate officers,* so this is something that *critics* would say of him. The word *yet* indicates a contrast. If the officers' goals were *reasonable*, then one would likely *not disagree* with them.
   detractors = critics; *accord* = agreement; *variance* = disagreement; *advocates* = supporters; *harmonious* = in pleasant agreement; *disparagers* = critics; *incompatible* = difficult to reconcile; *apologists* = those who make supportive arguments

7. **D** *In spite of* shows irony. It would certainly be ironic if the speech were short and yet still put people to sleep.
   conciseness = brevity; *enrapt* = enthralled; *brevity* = briefness

8. **C** *Parental restrictions* by definition are things that *confine; nurtured* = cared for; *appeased* = made less angry; *liberated* = freed

9. **E** *Although* indicates contrast. The sentence makes it clear that although government has *overtaken* some parental responsibilities, still, parents, not agencies, *should* care for children.
   obscured = made less clear; *precluded* = prevented; *adjured* = commanded solemnly; *exulted* = rejoiced; *disavowed* = renounced; *impelled* = urged to action; *usurped* = took over; *obligated* = morally compelled

Lesson 4:
Simplifying the Sentence

Simplify

Some sentences are hard. But don't give up immediately just because you can't think of a good way to complete the sentence right away. When that happens, try to simplify your task using one of these strategies.

Process of Elimination

❑ **If you understand any part of the sentence, see if that understanding can help you to rule out any choices.**

e.g. Statistics are often ------ information, but this is an ------ impression, because they must, by definition, obscure data by reducing many values to a single number.

    (A) equated with . . . erroneous
    (B) mistaken for . . . aesthetic
    (C) superior to . . . inaccurate
    (D) relegated to . . . insidious
    (E) substituted for . . . interesting

This sentence may be tough to understand at the first reading (or two). But you may know that statistics can't be *relegated to* (assigned to the lower status of) information, because data *is* information. If you just focus on the relationship between *statistics* and *information*, you can probably eliminate choices (C), (D), and (E). From there, you can try out the remaining choices and see that (A) works best.

❑ **If a sentence does contain two blanks, it is usually easier to complete the second blank first.** Why? Because by the time you get to the second blank, you will have read more context clues. Of course, the example we just used is an exception, but you will find that *usually* the second blank is easier to complete than the first.

Focus on Tone

❑ **If you can't find the right word or words to complete the sentence, try to at least determine the** *tone* **of the word, that is, whether it's** *positive,* *negative,* **or** *neutral.* **Then eliminate any choices that don't have the right tone.**

e.g. Without David's ------, the dispute between the parties might never have been resolved so tactfully.

    (A) conciliation   (B) antagonism
    (C) embarrassment   (D) indelicacy
    (E) ridicule

The right word might not come right to mind, but it *should* be pretty clear that whatever David used was a *good* thing, because it helped resolve the dispute *tactfully*. Therefore, if you notice any words that are **negative** or **neutral,** you can eliminate them! The beauty of this strategy is that you don't have to know all of the words: just go to the ones you **do** know, and eliminate them if they're not the right tone. (The answer, by the way, is (A).)

Paraphrase

❑ **You may also often find it helpful to paraphrase the sentence, that is, restate it in your own words.** This helps you to focus on the logic of the sentence as a whole, without getting stuck on **any particular** words or phrases. Just read the sentence completely, then try to restate the idea in the simplest terms possible. When you read the sentence again, you will probably find it easier to complete it, or at least to eliminate wrong choices.

Don't Be Afraid to Cut and Paste

❑ **Remember that you don't have to find the perfect word to fill the blank; you simply want to capture the right idea.** Often, you will find it easy to just **pick a word (or a form of a word) from elsewhere in the sentence.**

e.g. *Her account was so sterile that it made all of the other* ------ *seem* ------ *by contrast.*

To complete the sentence, just reuse the words: *accounts* and *unsterile* sound a bit redundant, but they do the job!

Concept Review 4: Simplifying the Sentence

1. Why is it important to pay attention to tone?

2. What does *paraphrase* mean?

Place a + (positive), – (negative), or = (neutral) next to each word based on its tone.

3. lurid

4. purchase

5. euphoria

6. innocuous

7. pretentious

8. overwhelm

9. rejuvenate

10. modify

11. insidious

Place a +, –, or = in each blank to indicate whether the word should be positive, negative, or neutral in tone, then use the tone to determine and check the answer.

12. A ------ politician, Congresswoman Andrews worked hard and made so few mistakes that her opponents seemed to be ------ by contrast.

    (A) shrewd . . . sages   (B) slothful . . . drones   (C) canny . . . blunderers
    (D) dynamic . . . firebrands   (E) conscientious . . . geniuses

13. His inability to relate to the latest trends in art led him to fear that his critical faculties had ------ during his long hiatus.

    (A) diversified   (B) atrophied   (C) converted   (D) enhanced   (E) multiplied

14. To her chagrin, Ellen soon learned that she could not hide her ------; her friends at the party could see the signs of weariness on her face.

    (A) amusement   (B) incoherence   (C) gratitude   (D) sorrow   (E) exhaustion

15. McLanham's ------ prose, particularly when compared to that of his more flamboyant ------, illustrates how artists of the same era can reflect startlingly different perspectives on the same reality.

    (A) stark . . . contemporaries   (B) spartan . . . enemies   (C) imprecise . . . role models
    (D) flowery . . . friends   (E) well-crafted . . . teachers

SAT I Practice 4:
Simplifying the Sentence

Each of the sentences below is missing one or two portions. Read each sentence, then select the word or words that most logically complete the sentence, taking into account the meaning of the sentence as a whole.

Example:
Rather than accepting the theory unquestioningly, Deborah regarded it with ------.
(A) mirth
(B) sadness
(C) responsibility
(D) ignorance
(E) skepticism

Correct response: (E)

1. In genetic research, ------ mice are often essential because their ------ allows scientists to pose questions answerable only if all the mice in a group have similar hereditary traits.
(A) sedated . . . temperament
(B) cloned . . . unpredictability
(C) adaptable . . . vigor
(D) inbred . . . uniformity
(E) adult . . . familiarity

2. Historians generally ------ the film, not only for its excessive sentimentality and unrealistic dialogue, but because it did not ------ a true understanding of the problems of the era.
(A) advocated . . . exhibit
(B) challenged . . . hinder
(C) panned . . . demonstrate
(D) exalted . . . ascertain
(E) censured . . . eliminate

3. The fact that even the most traditional European languages have ------ such words as "e-mail" seems to indicate that no language is impervious to foreign influences.
(A) originated
(B) prohibited
(C) invalidated
(D) recounted
(E) incorporated

4. Although many have ------ the theoretical undergirdings of her research, her experimental protocols have always been beyond reproach.
(A) lingered over
(B) disputed
(C) presumed

(D) interpreted
(E) publicized

5. Director T. C. Kehrwuld, whose mastery of stark objectivity in film has long been recognized by critics, has released another cinematic masterpiece which, while bound to satisfy those same critics, may be too ------ for public acceptance.
(A) flamboyant
(B) maudlin
(C) ecstatic
(D) austere
(E) humane

6. The humanists in the class emphasized the ------ of scientific discovery, asserting that although the world could have formulated calculus without Newton, it would never have produced the Hammerklavier Sonata without Beethoven.
(A) monotony
(B) triviality
(C) symmetry
(D) impersonality
(E) intricacy

7. Even Emily, who had to be ------ to participate at first, eventually confessed that she ------ a great deal from the workshop.
(A) cajoled . . . benefitted
(B) inclined . . . intuited
(C) restrained . . . resented
(D) persuaded . . . obscured
(E) discouraged . . . recalled

8. Although his manner was didactic and imperious, this fact was generally ------ and occasionally even ------ as qualities befitting a man of his stature.
(A) encouraged . . . dismissed
(B) overlooked . . . ignored
(C) discussed . . . denounced
(D) criticized . . . glorified
(E) tolerated . . . applauded

9. The novel's realistic depiction of social injustice in early-nineteenth-century America was an unmistakable ------ of the new republic's ------ to its democratic ideals.
(A) denunciation . . . infidelity
(B) disavowal . . . reversion
(C) trivialization . . . devotion
(D) revelation . . . gratitude
(E) commendation . . . allegiance

Answer Key 4:
Simplifying the Sentence

Concept Review 4

1. Because it is often easier to attend to tone than to meaning, and it can be used to eliminate inappropriate choices.
2. To restate in your own, simpler terms.
3. lurid (–)
4. purchase (=)
5. euphoria (+)
6. innocuous (+)
7. pretentious (–)
8. overwhelm (=)
9. rejuvenate (+)
10. modify (=)
11. insidious (–)
12. (C) A (+) politician, Congresswoman Andrews worked hard and made so few mistakes that her opponents seemed to be (–) by contrast.
shrewd = smart; *sages* = wise people; *slothful* = lazy; *drones* = mindless laborers; *canny* = smart; *blunderers* = people prone to mistakes; *dynamic* = energetic; *firebrands* = troublemakers; *conscientious* = attentive

13. (B) His inability to relate to the latest trends in art led him to fear that his critical faculties had (–) during his long hiatus.
diversified = made more various; *atrophied* = weakened from disuse; *converted* = changed; *enhanced* = made more valuable, effective, or beautiful
14. (E) To her chagrin, Ellen soon learned that she could not hide her (–); her friends at the party could see the signs of weariness on her face.
incoherence = confusion
15. (A) McLanham's (=) prose, particularly when compared to that of his more flamboyant (=), illustrates how artists of the same era can reflect startlingly different perspectives on the same reality.
stark = plain; *contemporaries* = peers; *spartan* = stark

SAT I Practice 4

1. **D** If mice all have similar traits, they are *uniform*, probably because they are very closely related. They must be *clones* or *close family members*.
sedated = put to sleep; *temperament* = disposition; *vigor* = energetic health; *inbred* = bred with family members; *uniformity* = lack of variation
2. **C** If the film has *excessive sentimentality and unrealistic dialogue*, historians must not like it. They would *criticize* the film. It must not have *shown a true understanding of the problems of the era*.
advocated = spoke in favor of; *exhibit* = display; *hinder* = impede; *panned* = criticized harshly; *exalted* = praised highly; *ascertain* ≠ determined the truth of; *censured* = criticized
3. **E** If this fact indicates *that no language is impervious to foreign influences*, it must reveal a strong influence from foreign sources. *Incorporating such words as "e-mail"* would show that influence.
originated = started; *invalidated* = made worthless; *recounted* = retold; *incorporated* = assumed into a whole
4. **B** *Although* indicates contrast. Although her *protocols have always been beyond reproach*, many must have *questioned* the undergirdings of her research.
lingered over = considered carefully; *disputed* = called into question; *presumed* = assumed to be true
5. **D** *Stark objectivity* in film means plain, unadorned perspective. *Stark* and *austere* are synonyms.
flamboyant = ornate; *maudlin* = depressed; *ecstatic* = very happy; *humane* = compassionate
6. **D** To say that *the world could have formulated calculus without Newton* is to suggest that scientific discovery does not depend on the creativity of particular individuals.
monotony = tedium; *triviality* = ordinariness; *impersonality* = detachment from personal qualities; *intricacy* = complicatedness
7. **A** If Emily only *eventually* confessed about the workshop, she must have *had to be forced to participate* at first, but then she must have gotten a lot out of it.
cajoled = coaxed persistently; *intuited* = determined by a hunch; *restrained* = held back; *obscured* = made unclear

8. **E** If being *didactic* (preachy) *and imperious* (overbearing) were thought *befitting* (appropriate), they must have been *accepted*.

9. **A** What is the relationship between a *depiction of social injustice* in a society and that society's *democratic ideals?* Such a depiction would certainly call those ideals into question, perhaps even *denounce* them.

denunciation = harsh criticism; *infidelity* = unfaithfulness; *disavowal* = swearing off; *reversion* = return to a previous state; *devotion* = strong commitment; *revelation* = revealing experience; *commendation* = praise; *allegiance* = faithfulness

Lesson 5:
Using Context Intelligently

Parallelism

❑ **Parallelism** is often an essential element of the logical scheme of a sentence. Noticing parallel structures often makes completing sentences much simpler. What is parallelism? Well, it's discussed in a bit more detail in Chapter 18, Lesson 3, entitled "Parallelism." In short, it is the similarity among phrases that are **listing** things or **comparing** things.

For instance, consider the sentence

Rather than being dull and arcane, her lecture on galaxy formation was ------ and ------.

This contains two ideas that are parallel: *dull and arcane,* and *------ and ------.* By the **law of parallelism,** the first missing word is an adjective that contrasts with *dull,* and the second is an adjective that contrasts with *arcane* (obscure and hard to understand). The missing words should contrast with the **tone and meaning** of the first two adjectives, preferably **in order.** So a nice, tidy, logical way to complete the sentence would be:

*Rather than being dull and arcane, her lecture on galaxy formation was **exciting** and **easy to understand.***

Modifiers

❑ The modifiers (that is, adjectives and adverbs) in Sentence Completion questions are not chosen casually. **Modifiers usually play key roles in the logical scheme of the sentence.** If you read a sentence a couple of times, and its main idea isn't perfectly clear, try reading it through once more, this time focusing primarily on the **adjectives** and **adverbs.**

e.g. The training center, clean and regimented, is ------ to those seeking the ------ once associated with boxing.

(A) surprising . . . austerity
(B) disappointing . . . seediness
(C) convincing . . . chaos
(D) refreshing . . . camaraderie
(E) inspiring . . . ambition

At first, you might focus on the modifiers *clean* and *regimented.* These could be pos-

itive descriptions, so such a training center might *impress* people who seek *cleanliness and order.* But no choice really fits this reading. The real key word is hard to miss: *once.* This word implies that people are seeking something that was *once* part of boxing but *is not any more.* Therefore, they would be disappointed by its absence, and so they must have been seeking something that is the *opposite* of *clean and regimented,* like *seedy and undisciplined.* (It may seem strange, but some people like that kind of stuff!)

Context and Common Sense

❑ Your common sense is one of your best tools on Sentence Completion questions. For instance, if a sentence refers to a *scientist,* it's not just for decoration. Think: what do scientists do or think that makes them different from nonscientists? Or how about *teachers,* or *politicians,* or *advocates,* or *critics,* etc.? Of course, the sentences won't always show people acting in typical ways, but they generally require you to understand how these folks *typically* act or think.

e.g. *An inveterate procrastinator, Pat could always be counted on to ------ any assignment he is given.*

The only real context clue we have here is the fact that Pat is a procrastinator. If you know what a procrastinator does, then you know how to complete the sentence. Procrastinators *postpone* things.

Practice Your Verbal Inference Skills

Just like every other reading skill, verbal inference skills can be improved best by reading. **Read books and articles with challenging vocabulary so that you can practice "figuring out" the meaning of unfamiliar words.** Some students think it's best to look up new vocabulary words as soon as they encounter them. Wrong! It's best to make an educated guess about the meaning before you look it up. Of course, once you do look it up, you should make a flashcard using the College Hill flashcard system described in Chapter 6, and practice it so that you never forget it.

Concept Review 5:
Using Context Intelligently

1. What is parallelism, and how can it help you to complete sentences?

2. What is a modifier?

3. What should you do when you encounter an unfamiliar word in your reading?

Each of the three following sentences contains some of the same information, but in very different *logical contexts*. Complete each sentence with your own word or phrase according to the logical context.

4. Britain can hardly be considered _____, despite the fact that it is separated from the European continent both physically and linguistically.

5. Even while it maintains a deep respect, even reverence, for its history, Britain can hardly be considered _____.

6. Britain can hardly be considered ----------------------------, having been reduced to a mere shadow of the vast dominion it once was.

Complete the following sentences with your own words or phrases, utilizing any parallelism in each sentence.

7. The speakers ran the gamut from the eloquent to the bumbling; some were ---------------------------- while others spoke with profound ----------------------------.

8. I did not want to sit through another lecture that was rambling and mind-numbing; rather, I was hoping for one that was ---------------------------- and ----------------------------.

SAT I Practice 5: Using Context Intelligently

Each of the sentences below is missing one or two portions. Read each sentence, then select the word or words that most logically complete the sentence, taking into account the meaning of the sentence as a whole.

Example:
Rather than accepting the theory unquestioningly, Deborah regarded it with ------.
(A) mirth
(B) sadness
(C) responsibility
(D) ignorance
(E) skepticism

Correct response: (E)

1. Most art critics regard her early style as pedestrian and conventional, utterly devoid of technical or artistic ------.
(A) lucidity
(B) analysis
(C) articulation
(D) mediocrity
(E) innovation

2. Historical buildings in many developing towns, rather than being razed, are now being ------.
(A) constructed
(B) renovated
(C) described
(D) condemned
(E) designed

3. Some linguists claim that French is characterized by brevity of expression and therefore may be the most ------ of all languages.
(A) beautiful
(B) vivid
(C) concise
(D) accessible
(E) concrete

4. The melée that punctuated the meeting between the rival factions was not entirely ------; the groups have long ------ each other on many important issues.
(A) surprising . . . supported
(B) unusual . . . copied
(C) explicit . . . evaluated
(D) unanticipated . . . opposed
(E) expected . . . encountered

5. Having been devastated by the earthquake, the freeway was virtually ------ to all but the most rugged of vehicles.
(A) destroyed
(B) impassable
(C) improper
(D) winding
(E) unnecessary

6. Those who assume that they can easily be ------ chefs in the classic tradition are almost as ------ as those who think they can write a novel if they simply sit down and type.
(A) amateur . . . candid
(B) renowned . . . skeptical
(C) superb . . . timid
(D) clumsy . . . pessimistic
(E) competent . . . naive

7. Many opponents of psychoanalysis contend that since its assumptions cannot be tested with scientific rigor, it is properly characterized as merely ------ system rather than a reliable therapeutic method.
(A) a concise
(B) a courageous
(C) a necessary
(D) an intuitive
(E) an ornamental

8. Paranoia, extreme competitiveness, and many other ------ of the modern rat race, despite what many cutthroat executives are saying, are hardly ------ to long-term success in the business world.
(A) by-products . . . conducive
(B) responsibilities . . . detrimental
(C) ornaments . . . helpful
(D) establishments . . . reliable
(E) inequities . . . charitable

9. Under certain conditions, the virus can mutate into ------ strain, transforming what was once simply ------ into a menacing poison.
(A) a new . . . an epidemic
(B) a deficient . . . a derivative
(C) an erratic . . . a rudiment
(D) a virulent . . . a nuisance
(E) an advanced . . . a disease

Answer Key 5:
Using Context Intelligently

Concept Review 5

1. Parallelism is the grammatical and logical consistency in phrases that list or compare things in a sentence.

2. A modifier is a word or phrase that describes another word. A word that modifies a noun is called an *adjective*, and a word that modifies a verb, an adjective, or another adverb is an *adverb*.

3. Try to infer its meaning from its usage in the sentence, then look it up in the dictionary to see if you are correct, then make a flashcard for the word using the College Hill system described in Chapter 6.

4. Britain can hardly be considered *an island*, despite the fact that it is separated from the European continent both physically and linguistically.

5. Even while it maintains a deep respect, even reverence, for its history, Britain can hardly be considered *archaic*.

6. Britain can hardly be considered *an empire*, having been reduced to a mere shadow of the vast dominion it once was.

7. The speakers ran the gamut from the eloquent to the bumbling; some were *articulate* while others spoke with profound *ineptitude*. (You may have used different words, but be sure that the first word is *positive* in tone and corresponds roughly to *articulate* and that the second word is negative and corresponds roughly to *ineptitude* in meaning.)

8. I did not want to sit through another lecture that was rambling and mind-numbing; rather, I was hoping for one that was *focused* and *engaging*. (You may have used different words, but be sure that both words are *positive* in tone and that the first corresponds roughly to *focused* and that the second word corresponds roughly to *engaging* in meaning.)

SAT I Practice 5

1. **E** Something *pedestrian and conventional* is ordinary and uses methods that have been used many times before. Therefore it is not *new*.
   lucidity = clarity; *analysis* = examination of parts; *articulation* = expression; *mediocrity* = averageness; *innovation* = novelty, creativity

2. **B** To *raze* something is to destroy it completely. If a historical building is not *razed*, it is preserved or, even better, made new again.
   renovated = made new again

3. **C** *Brevity of expression* is *conciseness*.
   vivid = full of lively forms or colors; *concise* = to the point; *accessible* = easily understood; *concrete* = perceived through the senses

4. **D** A *melée* is a fight. If the groups were fighting, they probably have *disagreed with* each other. Therefore the melée was not *unexpected*.

5. **B** A highway that has *been devastated by the earthquake* would be *hard to travel through*.
   impassable = unable to be travelled through

6. **E** Those who *think they can write a novel if they simply sit down and type* are probably unaware of how challenging such a task is. They are *naïve*.
   amateur = nonprofessional; *candid* = frank and honest; *renowned* = reputable, well-known; *skeptical* = inclined to doubting; *superb* = exceptional; *timid* = shy; *naïve* = lacking a sophisticated understanding

7. **D** If something cannot be *tested with scientific rigor* and is not a *reliable method*, it must be without a reasonable, scientific basis.
   intuitive = based on hunches rather than reason; *ornamental* = decorative

8. **A** *Despite* indicates contrast. *Paranoia* and *extreme competitiveness* are certainly bad things. Of course, *cutthroat executives* would claim that they help, but they can't really be *helpful* to *success in the business world*.
   by-products = results of a process; *conducive* = helpful; *detrimental* = harmful; *inequities* = unfair situations

9. **D** If something is *transformed* into a *menacing poison*, then it must not have been so bad before. Perhaps it was only a little bit *troublesome*.
   epidemic = a broad outbreak; *derivative* = repetitive of previous works; *rudiment* = basic element; *virulent* = dangerous; *nuisance* = annoyance

Lesson 6: The Toughest Sentences

Tough Sentences

❑ **Some sentences are tough not because they have tough vocabulary, but because they have a complicated or ambiguous logical structure.**

Negatives

❑ Negatives can easily complicate a sentence, and are easily overlooked. Watch carefully for negative words like *not, hardly, rarely, lacking*, etc., because they are as important as the key words! **When you encounter a sentence with negatives, it may help to paraphrase the sentence more "positively."**

> e.g. *Their approach was not unlike that of the Neo-Darwinians, whose lack of respect for quasi-scientific methods was far from unknown in the University community.*
>
> This sentence is easier to work with if it is first paraphrased without so many negatives:
>
> *Their approach was **like** that of the Neo-Darwinians, whose **support for the scientific method** was **well known** in the University community.*

Ambiguous Sentences

❑ **Some sentences are tough to work with because they are ambiguous; that is, they have more than one possible interpretation, usually one positive and one negative.** Since there are usually only two possibilities, just try them both.

> e.g. The recent trend of using ------ dialogue in films can be traced to directors who have ------ the natural half-sentences and interrupted thoughts that characterize genuine human speech.
>
> (A) halting . . . embraced
> (B) formal . . . assumed
> (C) imperfect . . . eschewed
> (D) stilted . . . adopted
> (E) passionate . . . endured

There are two ways to complete this sentence. Modern film directors might *like* or *dislike* the *natural half-sentences and interrupted thoughts that characterize genuine human speech.* If they like them, they would use them; choice (A) supports this reading. If they don't like them, they would prefer more *formal* dialogue. Choice (B) gives *formal* and (D) gives *stilted*, which convey that idea. But if the directors use *formal* language, they wouldn't *assume* imperfect dialogue, so (B) is out. Likewise, if they used *stilted* (formal) dialogue, they wouldn't *adopt* imperfect dialogue. So (A) is the correct response.

Abstract vs. Concrete

❑ Concrete nouns, which usually represent *people* and *objects*, are typically easier to understand than abstract nouns, which typically represent *quantities, qualities,* or *ideas*. When we focus on the concrete nouns in a sentence more than the abstract ones, we can misread the sentence. **Pay special attention to abstract nouns in sentences.**

> e.g. The dissent regarding the new restrictions on student parking was ------ those who wanted to be able to drive freely to school.
>
> (A) spearheaded by
> (B) surprising to
> (C) troublesome to
> (D) disputed by
> (E) disregarded by

This sentence is not about the *parking restrictions,* but rather about the *dissent.* It's easy to misread if you don't focus on the word *dissent.* (We overlook it because it's so **abstract.**) If you wanted to drive freely to school, how would you feel about the *dissent regarding parking restrictions*? You'd probably be one of the people dissenting! You may even *initiate* the dissent, which is why (A) is the best choice.

Concept Review 6:
The Toughest Sentences

1. What, other than tough vocabulary, can make a sentence hard to understand?

2. What are abstract nouns, and why should you pay close attention to them in sentences?

3. Circle the abstract nouns and draw boxes around the concrete nouns in the sentence below.

   The lack of interest among the voters ensured that the referendum about the new playground could sneak through, even though it contained some objectionable clauses.

Paraphrase the following sentences to minimize negatives.

4. *It is not uncommon to find people who refuse to deny that ghosts exist.*

5. *The council did not fail to block a single motion.*

Complete the following ambiguous sentences in two ways, with different tones.

6. Despite the _____ of the climb, the explorers were beginning to believe that the trek would soon become _____.

   Despite the _____ of the climb, the explorers were beginning to believe that the trek would soon become _____.

7. Far from being _____ on the issue of gun control, Will has _____ on the issue for many years.

   Far from being _____ on the issue of gun control, Will has _____ on the issue for many years.

SAT I Practice 6:
The Toughest Sentences

Each of the sentences below is missing one or two portions. Read each sentence, then select the word or words that most logically complete the sentence, taking into account the meaning of the sentence as a whole.

Example:
   Rather than accepting the theory unquestioningly, Deborah regarded it with ------.
   (A) mirth
   (B) sadness
   (C) responsibility
   (D) ignorance
   (E) skepticism

Correct response: (E)

1. The country's confidence, formerly sustained by an ------ sense of power, was replaced by an equally exaggerated sense of ------ following the hasty evacuation of its troops from three foreign capitals.
   (A) inflated . . . weakness
   (B) overwhelming . . . inviolability
   (C) erratic . . . hysteria
   (D) unquestioned . . . omnipotence
   (E) arbitrary . . . resolution

2. According to their detractors, the leaders of the Union for Progressive Politics do not truly ------ change, but simply rehash old and discredited theories of political philosophy.
   (A) admonish
   (B) censor
   (C) advocate
   (D) caricature
   (E) hinder

3. Dr. Cuthbert often ------ his former associates for not continuing to support him; apparently he harbored great animosity because of their ------ of him.
   (A) disparaged . . . endorsement
   (B) excoriated . . . abandonment
   (C) exonerated . . . denunciation
   (D) extolled . . . betrayal
   (E) venerated . . . dismissal

4. Despite her gregariousness, Andrea seems to have been a woman who cherished her ------ highly.

   (A) colleagues
   (B) friendships
   (C) privacy
   (D) integrity
   (E) humility

5. It is extremely rare to see a politician ------ any opinion that is widely unpopular; it seems that, for them, public censure is more ------ even than death.
   (A) conform to . . . desirable
   (B) tolerate . . . exciting
   (C) reject . . . feared
   (D) espouse . . . painful
   (E) manipulate . . . natural

6. The cogency and animation he showed in private belied his reputation for a notably ------ style of lecturing.
   (A) tepid
   (B) incisive
   (C) versatile
   (D) infrequent
   (E) fluent

7. The haiku, with its ------, its reduction of natural and everyday events to their mere essence, seems to economically depict the ------ of even the simplest human experience.
   (A) casualness . . . destructiveness
   (B) optimism . . . barrenness
   (C) capriciousness . . . rigidity
   (D) digressiveness . . . precariousness
   (E) conciseness . . . poignancy

8. Sadly, most people who say they want change in public schools will struggle to resist it, or at least ------ its effects on them.
   (A) initiate
   (B) distort
   (C) palliate
   (D) defend
   (E) enhance

9. Despite the ------ literature debunking the theory of ESP, a critical and rational awareness of the subject continues to ------ most of the public.
   (A) vivid . . . pervade
   (B) voluminous . . . elude
   (C) provocative . . . captivate
   (D) ambiguous . . . perplex
   (E) incomprehensible . . . escape

Answer Key 6:
The Toughest Sentences

Concept Review 6

1. Complicated or ambiguous logical structure.
2. Abstract nouns are nouns that represent ideas, quantities, or qualities; that is, they represent things that cannot be directly perceived.
3. *The lack (abstract noun) of interest (abstract noun) among the voters (concrete noun) ensured that the referendum (abstract noun) about the new playground (concrete noun) could sneak through, even though it contained some objectionable clauses (abstract noun).*
4. *It is common to find people who believe in ghosts.*
5. *The council blocked every motion.*

6. Despite the *ease* of the climb, the explorers were beginning to believe that the trek would soon become *treacherous.* (or some similar words)
   Despite the *arduousness* of the climb, the explorers were beginning to believe that the trek would soon become *easier.* (or some similar words)
7. Far from being *passive* on the issue of gun control, Will has *pontificated* on the issue for many years. (or some similar words)
   Far from being *consistent* on the issue of gun control, Will has *equivocated* on the issue for many years. (or some similar words)

SAT I Practice 6

1. **A** What would follow a *hasty evacuation* of a country's troops? A feeling of being overwhelmed and defeated, most likely. This feeling of *weakness*, we are told, is just as *exaggerated* as the sense of power just prior to the withdrawal.
   inviolability = invincibility; *erratic* = irregular; *hysteria* = irrational and exaggerated emotion; *omnipotence* = supreme power; *arbitrary* = based on whim and random power; *resolution* = determination
2. **C** If their *detractors* (critics) believe that they only *rehash old and discredited theories*, then they are suggesting that they do not really *speak out for* change.
   admonish = reprimand; *censor* = eliminate objectionable material; *advocate* = speak in favor of; *caricature* = exaggerate comically; *hinder* = get in the way of
3. **B** If his associates did not continue to support him, they must have *abandoned* him. If he harbored *animosity* for them, he must have *criticized* them.
   disparaged = criticized harshly; *endorsement* = show of support; *excoriated* = criticized harshly; *exonerated* = proved innocent; *denunciation* = condemnation; *extolled* = praised highly; *venerated* = honored
4. **C** *Despite* indicates contrast. *Gregariousness* is sociability. Its opposite is *solitude, reclusiveness,* or *privacy.*
5. **D** If *public censure* is like *death*, politicians must not like it. They must never *openly adopt* a widely unpopular opinion.

conform = do what is expected; *espouse* = adopt publicly; *manipulate* = take control of
6. **A** *Cogency* is *persuasiveness* and *animation* is *liveliness.* To *belie* is to *misrepresent,* so he must **not** have a reputation for being lively and persuasive, so people must think he's dull.
   tepid = dull, lukewarm; *incisive* = keen and thoughtful; *versatile* = well-rounded; *fluent* = smooth, flowing
7. **E** The first word must mean something like *reduction to its essence,* and the second word must mean something like *essence.*
   barrenness = starkness; *capriciousness* = whimsy, randomness; *digressiveness* = tendency to go off topic; *precariousness* = danger; *conciseness* = brevity; *poignancy* = sharpness of feeling
8. **C** If they *resist* it, then they want to prevent its effects on him, or at least *minimize* its effects on them.
   initiate = begin; *distort* = twist; *palliate* = make less severe; *enhance* = make better
9. **B** *Despite* indicates irony. If there is *literature debunking the theory of ESP*, it would be ironic if the public *failed to develop* a critical and rational awareness of the subject. What would make it even more ironic is if the literature were *plentiful.*
   vivid = full of vibrant imagery; *pervade* = fill completely; *voluminous* = plentiful; *elude* = escape capture or understanding; *provocative* = tending to elicit strong reactions; *captivate* = capture; *ambiguous* = unclear; *perplex* = confuse; *incomprehensible* = beyond understanding

CHAPTER 9

SAT I MATH AND MAPS-CATCH

1. Mapping Problems

2. Analyzing Problems

3. Finding Patterns

4. Simplifying Problems

5. Connecting to Knowledge

6. Finding Alternatives

7. Thinking Logically and Checking

Lesson 1: Mapping Problems

Mapping: Thinking about the Situation and the Goal

❑ If you want to solve a tough problem, your first job is to "map" it, that is, represent the basic problem situation and the goal. If you map a problem correctly, you will save yourself a lot of time and effort. If you map it incorrectly, you can't solve the problem.

Think about the Problem Situation

- Represent all the useful information in the problem with a *diagram, equation,* or *table.* **Write it down!**
- Know the *restrictions* on the unknown(s). Do they have to be *integers* or *positive* numbers or *multiples* of some number? Are they measures of angles or segments or areas in a figure?
- Know the *definitions* of all the terms.
- Know whether the unknowns in the problem are *variables* or *constants.* In other words, can the unknowns take values that I choose, or do they have only one particular value that I have to find?

Understand the Goal

- **Know what *exactly* the problem is asking for.** Does the problem ask you to solve an equation? Find the value of an expression? Find an area? Read carefully and make sure it's really asking for what you **think** it's asking for.
- **Notice whether the question is multiple choice;** if so, **what is the range of the answer choices?**

How are the choices expressed? As fractions, decimals, radicals, algebraic expressions?

- **Check whether you can estimate** to answer the question, or at least eliminate some of the choices.
- **Check whether the problem has choices that you can test** to see which one works.
- **On a multiple-choice question,** notice that the answer choices tell you in what form the answer should be, and may tell you what range of values to consider for the answer.

Use the Test for Scratchwork

❑ **Underline key words in the problem, and use the space on the test to do any scratchwork you need—diagrams, notes, tables, etc.** You don't get points for keeping the test clean! Don't get a question wrong simply because you "lost track" of important information!

Avoid the Common Confusions

❑ Even the brightest test takers sometimes get questions wrong because they misread the problem by overlooking or misinterpreting key terms. **Avoid this by paying special attention to these terms:**

- **Perimeter** (*distance around a figure*) is often confused with **area** (*number of unit squares that fit inside a figure*).
- The **circumference formula** for a circle ($2\pi r$) is often confused with the **area formula** of a circle (πr^2). To avoid confusing them, remember that *area* is always measured in square units, so its formula contains the "square."

- **Odd** (*integer **not** divisible by 2*) is often confused with **negative** (*less than 0*), because the two are "negative" in tone.
- **Even** (*integer divisible by 2*) is often confused with **positive** (*greater than 0*), because the two are "positive" in tone.
- **Integers** (*positive **and negative** whole numbers*) are often confused with **whole numbers** (*non-negative integers: 0, 1, 2 . . .*)
- **Product** (*the result of **multiplication***) is often confused with **sum** (*the result of **addition***).

Don't Rush—Avoid Quick Gimmicks

❑ **Always read the whole problem carefully before deciding how to solve it.** Using quick gimmicks is never a good test-taking strategy. **Careful mapping will save you time overall, not waste it.** Remember, SAT I problems are often not as hard as they seem at first glance.

Concept Review 1:
Mapping Problems

1. Describe what it means to "map" a problem.

2. Why is it important to consider the choices (in a multiple-choice question) as part of the problem?

Define the following terms, and indicate what terms they are sometimes confused with.

3. *Odd* means   and is sometimes confused with

4. *Even* means   and is sometimes confused with

5. *Perimeter* means   and is sometimes confused with

6. *Integers* are   and are sometimes confused with

Equations or inequalities are powerful "mapping" tools. Translate the following statements into equations or inequalities. Be sure to specify the meanings of any unknowns you may use.

7. The sum of two consecutive odd numbers is 28.

8. Ellen is twice as old as Maria.

9. Last year, Jennifer was twice as old as Brian is now.

SAT I Practice 1:
Mapping Problems

Map each of the following problems before solving it. Use the space for scratchwork, and underline any key words in the problem. Then solve each problem.

1 The product of five consecutive even integers is 0. What is the greatest possible value of any one of these integers?

Do Your Scratchwork Here

2 The perimeter of a rectangle is 28 inches, and its area is x square inches. If x is an even number, what is the greatest possible value of x?

3 Carlos begins with twice as much money as David. After Carlos gives $12 to David, Carlos still has $10 more than David. How much money did they have underline combined at the start?

(A) $32
(B) $66
(C) $68
(D) $92
(E) $102

4 Corinne travels from home to work at an average speed of 50 miles per hour, and returns home by the same route at 60 miles per hour. It takes her 10 more underline minutes to get to work than it takes her to get home. How many miles is it from Corinne's home to work?

(A) 25
(B) 35
(C) 50
(D) 75
(E) 90

Answer Key I: Mapping Problems

Concept Review I

1. To map means to represent the general problem situation and goal, either mentally or on paper.
2. Because the choices tell you the range of values to consider, as well as the form of the numbers (integers, fractions, etc.) and format (factored, decimal, etc.).
3. *Odd* means *an integer not divisible by 2*, and is sometimes confused with *negative*, because of the "negative" tone of both words.
4. *Even* means *an integer divisible by 2*, and is sometimes confused with *positive*, because of the "positive" tone of both words.
5. *Perimeter* means *distance around a figure*, and is sometimes confused with *area*, which is the *number of square units that fit inside a figure.*
6. *Integers* are *whole numbers and negative whole numbers* and are sometimes confused with *counting numbers, which are the **positive** positive integers: 1, 2, 3, 4 . . .*

7. Let n be the smaller of the two numbers. Then the next odd number is $n + 2$, so an equation that says that the sum of two consecutive odd numbers is 28 is $n + n + 2 = 28$.
8. Let e stand for Ellen's current age and m stand for Maria's current age. An equation that says that Ellen is twice as old as Maria is $e = 2m$.
9. Let j stand for Jennifer's age now and b stand for Brian's age now. Last year, Jennifer was $j - 1$ years old, so an equation that says that last year, Jennifer was twice as old as Brian is now is $j - 1 = 2b$.

SAT I Practice I

1. **8** If the product of a set of integers is 0, then one of the numbers must be 0. To maximize the value of any one of them, let 0 be the smallest of the integers. If they are **consecutive even** integers, they must be 0, 2, 4, 6, and 8. If your answer was 4, then you overlooked the fact that the numbers are **even.**

2. **48** Your first tool in mapping a geometry problem is a good diagram. This one has no diagram, so you must draw your own. Draw a rectangle, labeling its width w and its length l:

Since the perimeter of the rectangle is 28 inches, you can set up an equation: $2w + 2l = 28$. Divide both sides of the equation by 2 to get $w + l = 14$. Since the area is x, you can set up the equation $lw = x$. If x is even, then l and w can't both be odd. (Can you see how we know that?) You should be able to see that the possible values for w and l are 2 and 12, 4 and 10, and 6 and 8. (Check them and see.) This means that x can have values of $2 \times 12 = 24$, $4 \times 10 = 40$, or $6 \times 8 = 48$. The greatest of these, of course, is 48.

3. **E** Let c be the number of dollars Carlos had to start and d be the number of dollars David had to start. The question asks for the value of $c + d$. If Carlos begins with twice as much money as David, then $c = 2d$. After Carlos gives $12 to David, he has $c - 12$ dollars, and David has $d + 12$ dollars. If Carlos still has $10 more than David, then $c - 12 = (d + 12) + 10$

Simplify:	$c - 12 = d + 22$
Add 12:	$c = d + 34$
Substitute $c = 2d$:	$2d = d + 34$
Subtract d:	$d = 34$
Plug back in:	$c = 2(34) = 68$

So $c + d = 34 + 68 = 102$

4. **C** To "map" this problem, you must know that distance = speed × time. You must find the number of miles from Corinne's home to work, so call that d. If she travels from home to work at an average speed of 50 miles per hour, then it must take her $d/50$ hours, or $60 \times d/50 = 6d/5$ minutes. If she returns home at 60 miles per hour it must take her $d/60$ hours, or $60 \times d/60 = d$ minutes. If it takes her 10 more minutes to get to work than it takes her to get home, then:

$$\frac{6d}{5} - d = 10$$

Simplify:	$\dfrac{d}{5} = 10$
Multiply by 5:	$d = 50$

Lesson 2: Analyzing Problems

Break Complicated Problems Down into Simpler Ones

❏ **Analyzing** a problem means **breaking it down into smaller parts.** Analyzing a problem often helps you turn a big, difficult problem into smaller, simpler ones.

6 feet   6 feet

e.g.   For a certain fence, vertical posts must be placed 6 feet apart with supports in between, as shown above. How many vertical posts are needed for a fence 120 feet in length?

Answer: You may want to divide 120 by 6 and get 20, which seems like a reasonable answer. But how can you tell that this is correct without drawing a fence with 20 posts? Just change the question to a much simpler one: how many posts would you need for a 12-foot fence? The figure above provides the answer: it's 3! But 12 divided by 6 is 2. What gives? If you think about it, you will see that dividing only gives the number of spaces between the posts, but there is always one more post than spaces. So a 120-foot fence will require 20 + 1 = 21 vertical posts.

If You Can't Find What You Want Directly, Find What You Can!

❏ If you can't find what you want right away, just look at the parts of the problem one at a time and find what you can. Often, going step by step will eventually lead you to the answer you need.

Look for Simple Relationships

❏ Once you see the parts of a problem, look for simple relationships between them. Simple relationships usually lead to simple solutions.

e.g.   If $2x + 5y = 19$, then what is the value of $20x + 50y$?

Answer: There is no need to worry about "solving" for x and y. You need only see that $20x + 50y$ is 10 times $2x + 5y$. So, by substitution, $20x + 50y$ must equal 10 times 19, or 190.

e.g.   The figure above shows a square in which a smaller square is inscribed. The vertices of the smaller square are the midpoints of the sides of the larger square. If the area of the smaller square is 5, what is the area of the larger square?

Answer: When you are given the area of the square, the first relationship that probably comes to mind is the relationship between the area of a square and its side: $A = s^2$. You might try to find the length of the side of the small square, then try to find the length of a side of the larger square. But of course, there is a much simpler relationship between the "given" information and the information you need to find. Draw the two lines shown below, and it becomes clear that the smaller square is half the area of the larger square. So the big square has an area of $5 \times 2 = 10$.

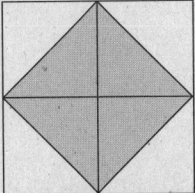

Concept Review 2:
Analyzing Problems

1. What does it mean to analyze a problem?

Given: $\ell_1 \parallel \ell_2 \parallel \ell_3$

2. Analyze the diagram above by indicating the measures of as many angles as possible.

3. If $20,000 is divided among three people in the ratio of 2:3:5, how much does each person get?

4. If $(x)(x-1)(x-2)$ is negative, and x is greater than 0, then what can be concluded about $x-1$ and $x-2$?

SAT I Practice 2: Analyzing Problems

1 How many odd numbers are there between 1 and 99, not including 1 and 99?

(A) 46
(B) 47
(C) 48
(D) 49
(E) 50

2

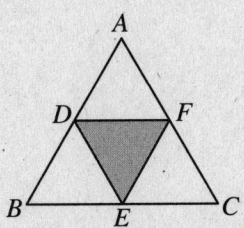

In the figure above, equilateral triangle *ABC* has an area of 20, and points *D*, *E*, and *F* are the midpoints of their respective sides. What is the area of the shaded region?

3 In the sophomore class at Hillside High School, the ratio of boys to girls is 2 to 3. The junior class contains as many boys as the sophomore class does, and the ratio of boys to girls in the junior class is 5 to 4. If there are 200 students in the sophomore class, how many students are there in the junior class?

4

Note: Figure not drawn to scale.

In the figure above, $\ell_1 \parallel \ell_2$, $AD = 8$, $EF = 4$, $GF = 3$, and $BG = 9$. What is the total area of the shaded regions?

(A) 32
(B) 36
(C) 40
(D) 42
(E) 44

Answer Key 2: Analyzing Problems

Concept Review 2

1. To analyze a problem means to look at its parts and find how they relate to each other.

2. Your diagram should look like this:

3. If the total is divided in the ratio of 2:3:5, then it is divided into 2 + 3 + 5 = 10 parts. The individual parts, then, are 2/10, 3/10, and 5/10 of the total. Multiplying these fractions by $20,000 gives parts of $4,000, $6,000, and $10,000.

4. If $(x)(x - 1)(x - 2)$ is negative, and x is greater than 0, then $(x - 1)(x - 2)$ must be negative, which means that one of the factors is positive and the other negative. Since $x - 2$ is less than $x - 1$, $x - 2$ must be negative and $x - 1$ must be positive.

SAT I Practice 2

1. **C** You might start by noticing that every other number is odd, so that if we have an even number of consecutive integers, half of them will always be odd. But this one is a little trickier. Start by solving a simpler problem: How many odd numbers are between 1 and 100, inclusive? Simple: there are 100 consecutive integers, so 50 of them must be odd. Now all we have to do is remove 1, 99, and 100. That removes 2 odd numbers, so there must be 48 left.

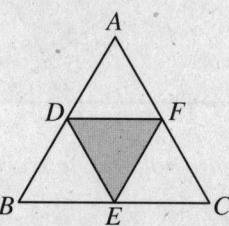

2. **5** Don't worry about finding the base and height of the triangle and using the formula *area* = (*base* × *height*)/2. This is needlessly complicated. Just notice that the four smaller triangles are all equal in size, so the shaded region is just 1/4 of the big triangle. Its area, then, is 20/4 = 5.

3. **144** If the ratio of boys to girls in the sophomore class is 2 to 3, then 2/5 are boys and 3/5 are girls. If the class has 200 students, then 80 are boys and 120 are girls. If the junior class has as many boys as the sophomore class, then it has 80 boys, too. If the ratio of boys to girls in the junior class is 5 to 4, then there must be $5n$ boys and $4n$ girls. Since $5n = 80$, n must

be 16. Therefore there are 80 boys and 4(16) = 64 girls, for a total of 144 students in the junior class.

4. **C** Write what you know into the diagram. Because the lines are parallel, $\angle GEF$ is congruent to $\angle GCB$, and the two triangles are similar. (To review similarity, see Lesson 6 in Chapter 13.) This means that the corresponding sides are proportional. Since GF and BG are corresponding sides, the ratio of corresponding sides is 3/9, or 1/3. Therefore EF is 1/3 of BC, so $BC = 12$. To find the areas of the triangles, you need the heights of the triangles. The sum of the two heights must be 8, and they must be in a ratio of 1:3. You can guess and check that they are 2 and 6, or you can find them algebraically: if the height of the smaller triangle is h, then the height of the larger is $8 - h$.

$$\frac{6}{8 - h} = \frac{1}{3}$$

Cross-multiply: $3h = 8 - h$
Add h: $4h = 8$
Divide by 4: $h = 2$

So the shaded area is (4)(2)/2 + (12)(6)/2 = 4 + 36 = 40.

Lesson 3: Finding Patterns

Look for Repetition

☐ Exploit any repetition in the problem to simplify it. Usually, repetition implies cancellation of some sort.

e.g.   If $5x^2 + 7x + 12 = 4x^2 + 7x + 12$, then what is the value of x?

Answer: This question is much simpler than it looks at first because of the repetition in the equation. If you subtract the repetitive terms from both sides of the equation, it reduces to $5x^2 = 4x^2$. Subtracting $4x^2$ from both sides then gives $x^2 = 0$, so $x = 0$.

Play Around to Find Relationships

☐ **Play around with the parts of a problem until you find simple patterns or relationships.**

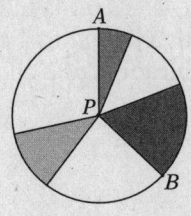

e.g.   If P is the center of the circle above, AP = 3, and $\angle APB$ has a measure of 120°, then what is the total area of the shaded regions?

Answer: This one is much easier than it looks. Remember from the last lesson: if you can't find what you want, at least find what you can. You can find the area of a circle: Since AP is the radius, the area of the circle is $\pi(3)^2 = 9\pi$. Now, play around with the pieces, as if they are part of a jigsaw puzzle. Do you notice how they all fit together inside $\angle APB$? Cool! Since $\angle APB$ is 120°, which is one-third of 360°, the shaded region is just 1/3 of the whole circle, or $9\pi/3 = 3\pi$.

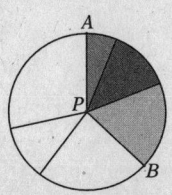

Sequence Questions

Some SAT I questions will specifically ask you to analyze a sequence. For instance:

$$1, 0, -1, 1, 0, -1, 1, 0, -1 \ldots$$

e.g.   If the sequence above continues according to the pattern shown, what will be the 200th term of the sequence?

Answer: Well, at least you know it's either 1, 0 or –1, right? Of course, you want better than a one-in-three guess, so you need to analyze the sequence more deeply. The sequence repeats every 3 terms. In 200 terms, then the pattern repeats itself 200/3 = 66 times with a remainder of 2. This means that the 200th term is the same as the 2nd term, which is 0.

☐ When given a sequence question, **write out the terms of the sequence until you notice the pattern. Then use your understanding of division with remainders to find what the question asks for.**

e.g.   What is the units digit of 27^{40}?

Answer: Remember that the units digit of an integer is the "ones" digit, or the last digit. You won't be able to find it with your calculator, though, because when 27^{40} is expressed as a decimal, it has fifty-eight digits, and your calculator can only show the first twelve or so. To find the units digit, you need to think of 27^{40} as a term in the sequence 27^1, 27^2, 27^3, 27^4. . . . If you look at these terms in decimal form, you will notice that the units digits follow a pattern: 7, 9, 3, 1, 7, 9, 3, 1. . . . The sequence has a repeating pattern of four terms. Every fourth term is 1, so the fortieth term is 1 also. Therefore, the units digit of 27^{40} is 1.

Concept Review 3:
Finding Patterns

Solve the following problems by taking advantage of repetition.

1. If 5 less than 28% of x^2 is 10, then what is 15 less than 28% of x^2?

2. If m is the sum of all multiples of 3 between 1 and 100 and n is the sum of all multiples of 3 between 5 and 95, what is $m - n$?

3. How much greater is the combined surface area of two cylinders each with a height of 4 cm and a radius of 2 cm than the surface area of a single cylinder with a height of 8 cm and a radius of 2 cm?

Solve each of the following problems by analyzing a sequence.

4. What is the units digit of 4^{134}?

5. The first two terms of a sequence are 1 and 2. If every term after the second term is the sum of the previous two, then how many of the first 100 terms are odd?

SAT I Practice 3:
Finding Patterns

1 If $\dfrac{3}{y} + \dfrac{x}{2} = 10$, then $\dfrac{6}{y} + x =$

(A) 5
(B) 15
(C) 20
(D) 40
(E) 60

2 Every term of a sequence, except the first, is 6 less than the square of the previous term. If the first term is 3, what is the fifth term of this sequence?

(A) 3
(B) 15
(C) 19
(D) 30
(E) 43

3 $-4, 0, 4, -4, 0, 4, -4, 0, 4 \ldots$

If the sequence above continues according to the pattern shown, what is the sum of the first 200 terms of the sequence?

(A) −800
(B) −268
(C) −4
(D) 0
(E) 268

4

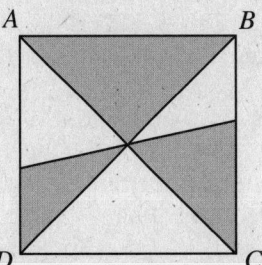

In the figure above, $ABCD$ is a square and $BC = 10$. What is the total area of the shaded regions?

5 What is the units digit of 3^{40}?

(A) 1
(B) 3
(C) 6
(D) 7
(E) 9

Answer Key 3: Finding Patterns

Concept Review 3

1. Don't worry about the percent or about finding x.
   Translate: 5 less than 28% of x^2 is 10 means
   $$.28(x^2) - 5 = 10$$
   Subtract 10: $.28(x^2) - 15 = 0$
   So 15 less than 28% of x^2 is 0.

2. $m = 3 + 6 + 9 + \ldots + 93 + 96 + 99$
   $n = 6 + 9 + \ldots + 93$
   When you subtract n from m, all the terms cancel
   except $3 + 96 + 99 = 198$.

3. Don't calculate the total surface area. Instead, just
   notice that the two small cylinders, stacked together, are the same size as the large cylinder. But
   remember that you are comparing **surface areas,**
   not **volumes.** The surface areas are almost the
   same, except that the smaller cylinders have two

extra bases. Each base has an area of $\pi(2)^2 = 4\pi$, so
the surface area of the smaller cylinders is $2(4\pi) = 8\pi$ greater than that of the larger cylinder.

4. Your calculator is no help on this one, because
   4^{134} is so huge. Instead, think of 4^{134} as a term in
   the sequence $4^1, 4^2, 4^3, 4^4. \ldots$ What is the units
   digit of 4^{134}? If you write out the first few terms,
   you will see a clear pattern to the units digits: 4,
   16, 64, 256 . . . Clearly, every odd term ends in a
   4 and every even term ends in a 6. So 4^{134} must
   end in a 6.

5. The first few terms are 1, 2, 3, 5, 8, 13, 21. . . . Since
   we are concerned only about the "evenness" and
   "oddness" of the numbers, think of the sequence as
   odd, even, odd, odd, even, odd, odd, even. . . . Notice that the sequence repeats every three terms:
   (odd, even, odd), (odd, even, odd), (odd, even,
   odd). . . . In the first 100 terms, this pattern repeats
   $100/3 = 33 \frac{1}{3}$ times. Since each pattern contains
   2 odd numbers, the first 33 repetitions contain
   66 odd numbers, and account for the first 99 terms.
   The last term must also be odd, because each
   pattern starts with an odd number. Therefore, the
   total number of odds is $66 + 1 = 67$.

SAT I Practice 3

1. **C** $\dfrac{6}{y} + x = 2\left(\dfrac{3}{y} + \dfrac{x}{2}\right) = 2(10) = 20$

2. **A** If every term is 6 less than the square of the pre-
   vious term, then the second term must be $(3)^2 - 6 = 9 - 6 = 3$. The third term, then, is also $(3)^2 - 6 = 3$, and so
   on. Every term, then, must be 3, including the fifth.

3. **C** The sequence repeats every three terms: (−4,
   0, 4), (−4, 0, 4), (−4, 0, 4). . . . Each one of the groups
   has a sum of 0. Since $200/3 = 67 \frac{2}{3}$, the first 200 terms
   contain sixty-seven repetitions of this pattern, plus two
   extra terms. The sixty-seven repetitions will have a sum
   of $67(0) = 0$, but the last two terms must be −4 and 0,
   giving a total sum of −4.

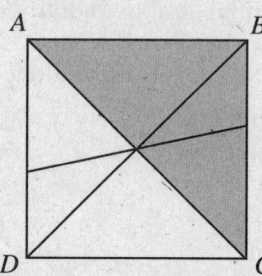

4. **50** Move the shaded regions around, as shown
   above, to see that they are really half of the square.
   Since the area of the square is $(10)(10) = 100$, the area
   of the shaded region must be half of that, or 50.

5. **A** The number 3^{40} is so big that your calculator is
   useless for telling you what the last digit is. Instead,
   think of 3^{40} as being an element in the sequence $3^1, 3^2$,
   $3^3, 3^4. \ldots$ If you write out the first six terms or so, you
   will see that there is a clear pattern to the units digits:
   3, 9, 27, 81, 243, 729. . . . So the pattern in the units digits is 3, 9, 7, 1, 3, 9, 7, 1. . . . The sequence repeats every
   four terms. Since 40 is a multiple of 4, the 40th term is
   the same as the 4th and the 8th and the 12th terms, so
   the 40th term is 1.

Lesson 4: Simplifying Problems

Reduce the Amount of Information You Have to Think About

❑ Once you've represented and analyzed a problem, it may still seem to have "too much information." When the problem has more information than you can handle, try to simplify the problem. **To simplify means to reduce the amount of information you have to think about.** There are several ways to simplify a problem: **beeline, substitute, combine,** and **cancel.**

Look for the Direct Route, the "Beeline"

❑ **Many problems can be simplified greatly by simply avoiding the knee-jerk response, mapping the problem well, and looking for the direct route—the "beeline"—from the given information to the information you want.**

e.g.   If $\dfrac{3a}{2b} = \dfrac{1}{4}$ and $\dfrac{b}{5c} = 3$, what is the value of $\dfrac{a}{10c}$?

Answer: This seems like a tough problem because there are so many unknowns. A knee-jerk response might be to try to solve for a, b, and c. But the question doesn't ask for the individual values of a, b, and c, and there is a much more direct route to the answer you need. Notice that just multiplying the two given expressions gets you almost there: $\dfrac{3a}{2b} \times \dfrac{b}{5c} = \dfrac{3a}{10c}$

Substitute: $\left(\dfrac{1}{4}\right)(3) = \dfrac{3a}{10c}$

Divide by 3: $\dfrac{1}{4} = \dfrac{a}{10c}$

Substitute to Simplify

❑ **One of the easiest ways to simplify a problem is to substitute a simple expression for a complicated one.**

e.g.   If $3x^2 + 5x + y = 8$ and $x \neq 0$, then what is the value of $\dfrac{16 - 2y}{3x^2 + 5x}$?

Answer: Both the equation and the fraction look complicated, but you can simplify by using the law of substitution, which says that if two things are equal, one can always be substituted for the other. Notice that $3x^2 + 5x$ appears in both the equation and the fraction. What does it equal? If you subtract y from both sides of the equation, you get $3x^2 + 5x = 8 - y$. If you substitute $8 - y$ for $3x^2 + 5x$ in the fraction, you get $\dfrac{16 - 2y}{8 - y} = \dfrac{2(8 - y)}{8 - y} = 2$

Combine to Simplify

❑ **Another easy way to simplify a problem is to combine parts that can be easily combined.** For instance, in Lesson 4 we saw how a tough geometry problem was made much simpler by combining the shaded regions. You can also simplify by combining algebraic terms.

e.g. $3m - (2m - 1)$ can be simplified by combining like terms: $3m - (2m - 1) = 3m - 2m + 1 = m + 1$

Cancel to Simplify

❑ To simplify fractions, cancel common factors in the numerator and denominator.

e.g. $\dfrac{4x^2 - 4}{x^2 + 3x + 2}$ can be simplified by factoring and cancelling: $\dfrac{4(x - 1)(x + 1)}{(x + 1)(x + 2)} = \dfrac{4(x - 1)}{(x + 2)}$

Concept Review 4:
Simplifying Problems

Simplify the following expressions.

1. $-2n - (6 - 5n) - n$

2. $\dfrac{2x^2 - 18}{x^2 + 2x - 3}$

3. $\dfrac{2}{x} + \dfrac{1}{2}$

4. $\dfrac{6x^3 + 4x^2 + 10x}{2x}$

5. $x\sqrt{x^6}$

Solve the following problems with substitution.

6. If $y = 1 - x$ and $2y + x = 5$, then what is the value of x?

7. If $3 + m + n = n^2 + m^2$, what is the value of $\dfrac{\left(n^2 - n\right) + \left(m^2 - m\right)}{6}$?

8. For all real numbers x, let $<x> = (1 - x)^2$. What is the value of $<<4>>$?

SAT I Practice 4:
Simplifying Problems

1 If $3y - 4z = 6$ and $2y + z = 10$, then $y - 5z =$

(A) 12
(B) 6
(C) 4
(D) 0
(E) –4

2 If $a + b = 3$, $a + c = 5$, and $b + c = -6$, then $a + b + c =$

(A) 4
(B) 2
(C) 1
(D) 0
(E) –1

3 If $\dfrac{a+b}{b} = 3$ and $\dfrac{a+c}{c} = 5$, what is the value of $\dfrac{b}{c}$?

(A) $\dfrac{1}{2}$

(B) $\dfrac{3}{5}$

(C) $\dfrac{5}{3}$

(D) 2
(E) 8

Questions 4 and 5 pertain to the following definition:

For all nonzero real numbers k, let $^\wedge k = 1 - \dfrac{1}{k}$.

4 Which of the following is equivalent to $^\wedge 3 - {^\wedge 2}$?

(A) $^\wedge \dfrac{1}{6}$

(B) $^\wedge \dfrac{5}{6}$

(C) $^\wedge 1$

(D) $^\wedge \dfrac{6}{5}$

(E) $^\wedge 2$

5 Other than 0, what is the only value of k for which $^\wedge{^\wedge}k$ is undefined?

Answer Key 4:
Simplifying Problems

Concept Review 4

1. $-2n - (6 - 5n) - n = -2n - 6 + 5n - n = 2n - 6$

2. $\dfrac{2x^2 - 18}{x^2 + 2x - 3} = \dfrac{2(x-3)(x+3)}{(x+3)(x-1)} = \dfrac{2(x-3)}{(x-1)}$

3. $\dfrac{2}{x} + \dfrac{1}{2} = \dfrac{4}{2x} + \dfrac{x}{2x} = \dfrac{4+x}{2x}$

4. $\dfrac{6x^3 + 4x^2 + 10x}{2x} = \dfrac{6x^3}{2x} + \dfrac{4x^2}{2x} + \dfrac{10x}{2x} = 3x^2 + 2x + 5$

5. $x\sqrt{x^6} = x \times x^3 = x^4$

6. Substitute $y = 1 - x$ into $2y + x = 5$ to get
$$2(1 - x) + x = 5$$
   Distribute: $\qquad\qquad 2 - 2x + x = 5$

Simplify: $\qquad\qquad\qquad\qquad 2 - x = 5$
Subtract 2: $\qquad\qquad\qquad\qquad -x = 3$
Multiply by -1: $\qquad\qquad\qquad x = -3$

7. $\qquad\qquad\qquad\qquad 3 + m + n = n^2 + m^2$
Subtract n and m: $\qquad 3 = (n^2 - n) + (m^2 - m)$

Substitute: $\dfrac{(n^2 - n) + (m^2 - m)}{6} = \dfrac{3}{6} = \dfrac{1}{2}$

8. $\qquad\qquad\qquad\qquad\qquad\qquad\quad$ <<4>>
Substitute for <4>: $\qquad\qquad = <(1 - 4)^2>$
Simplify: $\qquad\qquad\qquad\quad\; = <(-3)^2>$
Simplify: $\qquad\qquad\qquad\qquad = <9>$
Substitute for <9>: $\qquad\qquad = (1 - 9)^2$
Simplify: $\qquad\qquad\qquad\qquad = (-8)^2$
Simplify: $\qquad\qquad\qquad\qquad = 64$

SAT I Practice 4

1. **E** Subtract the equations: $\quad 3y - 4z = 6$
$$\underline{-(2y + z = 10)}$$
$$y - 5z = -4$$

2. **C** Add the equations:
$$(a + b) + (a + c) + (b + c) = 3 + 5 + -6$$
Simplify: $\qquad\qquad 2a + 2b + 2c = 2$
Divide by 2: $\qquad\qquad\; a + b + c = 1$

3. **D** Start by simplifying the expressions:
$$\frac{a + b}{b} = \frac{a}{b} + \frac{b}{b} = \frac{a}{b} + 1$$

$$\frac{a + c}{b} = \frac{a}{c} + \frac{c}{c} = \frac{a}{c} + 1$$

Substituting into the original equations gives

$$\frac{a}{b} + 1 = 3 \text{ and } \frac{a}{c} + 1 = 5$$

Subtract 1: $\qquad \dfrac{a}{b} = 2 \text{ and } \dfrac{a}{c} = 4$

Divide the fraction: $\quad \dfrac{\frac{a}{c}}{\frac{a}{b}} = \dfrac{4}{2}$

Simplify: $\qquad\qquad \dfrac{a}{c} \times \dfrac{b}{a} = 2$

Simplify: $\qquad\qquad\qquad \dfrac{b}{c} = 2$

4. **D** Begin by simplifying $^3 - {}^2$ by substitution:

$$^3 - {}^2 = (1 - 1/3) - (1 - 1/2) = 2/3 - 1/2 = 1/6$$

But be careful not to pick (A) $^1/6$ because

$$^1/6 = 1 - 6 = -5$$

Notice that the choices must be evaluated first before we can see which one equals 1/6. Notice that choice (D) is $^6/5 = 1 - 5/6 = 1/6$.

5. **I** Begin by simplifying $^{^}k$ by substitution:

$$^{^}k = {}^{^}\left(1 - \frac{1}{k}\right) = 1 - \frac{1}{1 - \frac{1}{k}}$$

Yikes! That doesn't look simple! But think about it: why is it that k can't be 0? Because division by 0 is undefined, and k is in a denominator. But notice that $1 - \dfrac{1}{k}$ is also in a denominator, so $1 - \dfrac{1}{k}$ can't be

0, either! Solving: $\quad 1 - \dfrac{1}{k} \neq 0$

Add $\dfrac{1}{k}$: $\qquad\qquad\qquad 1 - \dfrac{1}{k}$

Multiply by k: $\qquad k \neq 1$
Then check by noticing that $^{^}1$ is undefined:
$^{^}1 = {}^{^}(1 - 1/1) = {}^{^}0 = 1 - 1/0$, and $1/0$ is undefined.

Lesson 5:
Connecting to Knowledge

What You Need and What You Don't

❑ The SAT I math section is not a test of your calculation skills. If you're taking a lot of steps or doing a lot of calculations to solve an SAT I math problem, you're probably doing something wrong. **You should never need to do complicated calculations to solve an SAT I math problem.**

Reference Information

❑ Every SAT I math section begins by giving you this reference information. **Know what's included.**

$A = \pi r^2$ $A = \ell w$ $A = \frac{1}{2}bh$ $V = \ell w h$ $V = \pi r^2 h$ $c^2 = a^2 + b^2$ *Special Right Triangles*
$C = 2\pi r$

The arc of a circle measures 360°.
Every straight angle measures 180°.
The sum of the measures of the angles in a triangle is 180°.

Make the Connections

❑ To solve some SAT I math problems, you have to make quick connections to key math facts. **The faster you can make these connections and see if they are helpful, the faster you will solve the problems.**

Rate Problems

Problems involving speed or work are usually rate problems. **To solve rate problems, you need to know the rate formula: *distance (or work) = rate × time*.** Often, you simply need to **substitute the given information into the formula and solve for the missing part.** For more practice with rate problems, see Lesson 4 in Chapter 12.

If a problem says *at this rate . . .* it implies that two rates are equal, which usually lets you set up a proportion. For practice with these kinds of problems, see Lesson 4 in Chapter 10 and Lesson 4 in Chapter 12.

Mean/Median/Mode Problems

Some problems will ask you to deal with averages (arithmetic means), medians, or modes. Here, the important thing is knowing how to find each one (and not mixing them up). **The average (or arith-**metic mean) is the *sum of the numbers divided by how many there are.* The median is the *middle number or the average of the two middle numbers* when the numbers are listed in order. The mode is the *number that appears most frequently* in the set.** For more practice with these kinds of problems, see Lesson 2 in Chapter 12.

Right Triangle Problems

If a problem includes a right triangle, you should connect to two important things: the **Pythagorean Theorem** and the fact that **angles in a triangle add up to 180°.** If you know two sides of a right triangle, you can always find the third with the Pythagorean Theorem (see Lesson 3 in Chapter 13). If you know one of the acute angles in a right triangle, you can always subtract its measure from 90° to find the other angle.

Parallel Lines Problems

Whenever you see parallel lines in a diagram, **mark up the equal angles or supplementary angles.** If you have trouble finding them, see Lesson 1 in Chapter 13. You should be able to look at a diagram with parallel lines and tell quickly which angles are equal and which are supplementary.

Concept Review 5:
Connecting to Knowledge

Write out each formula, theorem, definition, or property.

1. The Pythagorean Theorem

2. The Zero Product Property

3. The Parallel Lines Theorem

4. The Rate Formula

5. The Average (Arithmetic Mean) Formula

6. The Definition of the Median

7. The Definition of the Mode

8. The Circumference Formula

9. The Circle Area Formula

10. The Triangle Area Formula

SAT I Practice 5:
Connecting to Knowledge

1 If x is the average (arithmetic mean) of k and 10, and y is the average (arithmetic mean) of k and 4, what is the average of x and y, in terms of k?

(A) $\dfrac{k+14}{4}$ (B) $\dfrac{k+14}{2}$ (C) $\dfrac{k+7}{2}$

(D) $7k$ (E) $14k$

Key formula(s):

2 If, on average, x cars pass a certain point on a highway in y hours, then, at this rate, how many cars should be expected to pass the same point in z hours?

(A) xyz (B) $\dfrac{xy}{z}$ (C) $\dfrac{z}{xy}$

(D) $\dfrac{xz}{y}$ (E) $\dfrac{x}{yz}$

Key formula(s):

3

h feet

8 feet

3 feet

4 feet

Note: Figure not drawn to scale.

A straight 8-foot board is resting on a rectangular box that is 3 feet high, as shown in the diagram above. Both the box and the board are resting on a horizontal surface, and one end of the board rests on the ground 4 feet from the edge of the box. If h represents the height, in feet, of other end of the board from the top of the box, what is h?

Key formula(s):

Answer Key 5: Connecting to Knowledge

Concept Review 5

1. The Pythagorean Theorem: In a right triangle, if c is the length of the hypotenuse and a and b are the lengths of the two legs, then $c^2 = a^2 + b^2$. (Lesson 3 in Chapter 13)

2. The Zero Product Property: If a set of numbers has a product of zero, then at least one of the numbers is zero. Conversely, if zero is multiplied by any number, the result is zero. (Lesson 5 in Chapter 11)

3. The Parallel Lines Theorem: If a line cuts through two parallel lines, then all acute angles formed are congruent, all obtuse angles formed are congruent, and any acute angle is supplementary to any obtuse angle. (Lesson 1 in Chapter 13)

4. The Rate Formula: *distance (or work) = rate × time* (Lesson 4 in Chapter 12)

5. The Average (Arithmetic Mean) Formula: *average = sum ÷ number of things* (Lesson 2 in Chapter 12)

6. The Definition of the Median: The "middle number" of a set of numbers when they are listed in order. If there are an odd number of numbers, the median is the "middle number," and if there are an even number of numbers, it is the average of the two middle numbers. (Lesson 2 in Chapter 12)

7. The Definition of the Mode: The number that appears the most frequently in a set. (Lesson 2 in Chapter 12)

8. The Circumference Formula: *circumference* = $2\pi r$ (Lesson 5 in Chapter 13)

9. The Circle Area Formula: *area* = πr^2 (Lesson 5 in Chapter 13)

10. The Triangle Area Formula: *area = base × height/2* (Lesson 5 in Chapter 13)

SAT I Practice 5

1. **C**   Key formula: *average = sum ÷ number of things*. So if x is the average of k and 10, then $x = \dfrac{k+10}{2}$.

And if y is the average of k and 4, then $y = \dfrac{k+4}{2}$.

The average of x and y, then, is

$$\dfrac{\dfrac{k+10}{2}+\dfrac{k+4}{2}}{2} = \dfrac{k+10}{4}+\dfrac{k+4}{4} = \dfrac{2k+14}{4} = \dfrac{k+7}{2}$$

2. **D**   Key formulas: *number of cars = rate × time*, and $rate = \dfrac{number\ of\ cars}{time}$. Since x is the number of cars and y is the time in hours, the rate is x/y cars per hour. Using the first formula, then, the number of cars that would pass in z hours is

$$(x/y \text{ cars per hour})(z \text{ hours}) = \dfrac{xz}{y}$$

You should notice, too, that simply plugging in values for x, y, and z can make the problem easier to think about. Say, for instance, that $x = 10$ cars pass every $y = 2$ hours. In $z = 4$ hours, then, it should be clear that 20 cars should pass by. Plugging these numbers into the choices, you will see that (D) is the only one that gives an answer of 20.

3. **1.8**   Key Formula: The Pythagorean Theorem: $c^2 = a^2 + b^2$. Key Theorem: In similar triangles, corresponding sides are proportional. Notice that the figure has two right triangles, and they are similar. The hypotenuse of the bottom triangle is 5 because $3^2 + 4^2 = 5^2$. Therefore, the hypotenuse of the top triangle is 8 − 5 = 3. Since the two triangles are similar, the corresponding sides are proportional:

$$\dfrac{3}{5} = \dfrac{h}{3}$$

Cross-multiply: $5h = 9$
Divide by 5: $h = 1.8$

Lesson 6: Finding Alternatives

Don't Just Memorize "One Best Way"—Consider Your Options

❏ **There is rarely "one best way" to solve an SAT I math problem.** What works best depends on your strengths, the particulars of the problem, and the situation. **Understanding different approaches to a problem also gives you a great way to check your work: if two different approaches give you the same answer, you are almost certainly right.**

Testing the Choices

e.g.   Which of the following represents all of the solutions of the equation $5x - 9 = x^2 - 9$?

    (A) $\{0, 1.8, 5\}$
    (B) $\{1.8, 3, 5\}$
    (C) $\{5\}$
    (D) $\{0, 5\}$
    (E) $\{-3, 3\}$

Answer: In this problem, you can simply "test" each choice by plugging its values back into the equation, and work by process of elimination. The easiest number to test in the choices is 0, so plug it in: $5(0) - 9 = (0)^2 - 9$ gives you $-9 = -9$, so 0 is a solution. This lets you eliminate choices (B), (C), and (E). Since both of the remaining choices, (A) and (D), also contain 5, you don't need to test 5 to know that it works. Just test 1.8 now: $5(1.8) - 9 = (1.8)^2 - 9$, which simplifies to $0 = -5.76$, which obviously isn't true, so 1.8 is not a solution. Therefore, by process of elimination, the answer is (D).

Another approach is to solve algebraically:
$$5x - 9 = x^2 - 9$$
Add 9: $5x = x^2$
Divide by x: $5 = x$

But this contains a subtle error: the last step involved dividing by x, and that's not allowed if x is 0! Checking that possibility by plugging $x = 0$ into the original equation shows that that is indeed a solution: $5(0) - 9 = (0)^2 - 9$. To avoid missing the extra solution, you should solve with a better method:
$$5x - 9 = x^2 - 9$$
Add 9 and subtract $5x$: $0 = x^2 - 5x$
Factor: $0 = x(x - 5)$
Use the zero product property: $x = 0$ or 5

❏ When solving a multiple-choice question by "testing" the choices, **if the choices are given in numerical order, start by testing choice (C).** If it doesn't work, you might still be able to tell whether it's too big or too small, and eliminate two more choices, leaving you with only two choices remaining. **If there is no pattern to the choices, start with the number that's easiest to test.**

Plugging In

❏ **If the choices in a multiple-choice question contain unknowns, you can usually "plug in" simple values for the unknowns to simplify the problem.** If you do this, **(1) check that the values satisfy any given equations or other restrictions, (2) write down the values you are plugging in for each unknown, (3) solve the problem *numerically* and write down this number,** and **(4) plug in the values to *every* choice and eliminate those that don't give the right answer.** If more than one choice gives the right answer, plug different numbers in.

e.g.   If $3m = mn + 1$, then what is the value of m in terms of n?

  (A) $n + 1$ (B) $n - 2$ (C) $\dfrac{1}{3 - n}$

  (D) $\dfrac{1}{3 + n}$ (E) $\dfrac{2}{3 + n}$

Answer: Since the answer choices contain unknowns, you can probably plug in to simplify. Plug in a simple number for m to start, like 1. Write down m = 1 on your paper. This gives $3(1) = 1n + 1$. The only way this will work is if $n = 2$. Write this down, too, and check that the equation works. Now the question asks "what is the value of m?" Obviously it's 1, so write that down and circle it. Now plug n = 2 into all of the choices and see what you get: (A) 3 (B) 0 (C) 1 (D) 1/4 (E) 2/5. Only (C) gives the right answer, so you're done! You could also have solved algebraically:
$$3m = mn + 1$$
Subtract mn: $3m - mn = 1$
Factor: $m(3 - n) = 1$

Divide by $(3 - n)$: $m = \dfrac{1}{3 - n}$

Concept Review 6:
Finding Alternatives

1. When can a multiple-choice problem be solved by just "testing the choices"?

2. When solving by testing the choices, why is it often best to start with choice (C)?

3. When testing the choices, when is it not necessarily best to start with choice (C)?

4. When can you simplify a multiple-choice question by plugging in values?

5. What are the four steps to solving by plugging in values?

6. Why is it best to understand more than one way to solve a problem?

SAT I Practice 6:
Finding Alternatives

Try to find at least two different ways of solving each of the following problems, and check that both methods give you the same answer.

1 If $m = 2x - 5$ and $n = x + 7$, which of the following expresses x in terms of m and n?

(A) $\dfrac{m = n + 2}{2}$

(B) $m - n + 2$

(C) $\dfrac{m - n + 12}{2}$

(D) $m - n + 12$

(E) $2(m - n + 12)$

2 Three squares have sides with lengths a, b, and c. If b is 20% greater than a, and c is 25% greater than b, then by what percent is the area of the largest square greater than the area of the smallest square?

(A) 20%
(B) 50%
(C) 75%
(D) 125%
(E) 225%

3 Jim and Ellen together weigh 290 pounds. Ellen and Ria together weigh 230 pounds. All three together weigh 400 pounds. What is Ellen's weight?

(A) 110 lbs
(B) 120 lbs
(C) 130 lbs
(D) 140 lbs
(E) 170 lbs

4 A painter used one-fourth of her paint on one room and one-third of her paint on a second room. If she had 10 gallons of paint left after painting the second room, how many gallons did she have when she began?

(A) 19
(B) 24
(C) 28
(D) 30
(E) 50

5 If $r = \dfrac{s}{5}$ and $4r = 7t$, what is the value of s in terms of t?

(A) $35t$

(B) $\dfrac{35t}{4}$

(C) $35t - 4$

(D) $31t$

(E) $70t$

Answer Key 6: Finding Alternatives

Concept Review 6

1. There are many situations in which this is possible, but perhaps the most common is where you're asked to find the solution of an equation, and the choices are ordinary numbers.

2. Because the answer choices are usually presented in numerical order. If choice (C) doesn't work, you may be able to tell whether it is too big or too small, and thereby eliminate two other answers as well. This way, you will only need to "test" one more choice to get the answer.

3. When it is not easy to tell whether the choice is "too big or too small," or when there is no pattern to the choices.

4. Usually, when the answer choices contain unknowns or represent ratios of unknowns; also when the problem contains more unknowns than equations.

5. (1) Check that the values satisfy any given equations or other restrictions, (2) write down the values you are plugging in for each unknown, (3) solve the problem *numerically* and write down this number, and (4) plug in the values to *every* choice and eliminate those that don't give the right answer. If more than one choice gives the right answer, plug in different numbers.

6. Because the two methods can provide a "check" against one another: if they both give the same answer, you are almost certainly right!

SAT I Practice 6

1. **Method 1:** The problem asks you to solve for x in terms of m and n. Notice that every choice contains the expression $m - m$.

   By substitution: $m - n = (2x - 5) - (x + 7)$
   Simplify: $m - n = x - 12$
   Add 12: $m - n + 12 = x$
   So the answer is **(D)**.

   Method 2: Just plug in simple values for the unknowns. If $x = 1$, then $m = (2)(1) - 5 = -3$ and $n = (1) + 7 = 8$. Since the problem asks for x, write down its value, 1, and circle it. Then plug in $m = -3$ and $n = 8$ to every choice, and simplify:

   (A) −4.5 (B) −9 (C) 0.5 (D) 1 (E) 2
   So the answer is **(D)**.

2. **Method 1:** Plug in numbers. Let a be 100. If b is 20% greater than a, then $b = 120$. If c is 25% greater than b, then $c = 150$. The area of the largest square, then, is $(150)^2 = 22,500$, and the area of the smallest square is $(100)^2 = 10,000$. The percent difference is $(22,500 - 10,000)/10,000 = 1.25 = 125\%$ (D).

   Method 2: Use algebra. $b = 1.2a$ and $c = (1.25)(1.2a) = 1.5a$. So the area of the smallest square is a^2 and the area of the largest square is $(1.5a)^2 = 2.25a^2$. Since $2.25a^2 - a^2 = 1.25a^2$, the area of the bigger square is 125% larger.

3. **Method 1:** Test the choices, starting with (C). If Ellen weighs 130 pounds, then Jim weighs $290 - 130 = 160$ pounds and Ria weighs $230 - 130 = 100$ pounds. All together, their weight would be $130 + 160 + 100 = 390$ pounds. Close, but too small. This means that our guess for Ellen's weight is too *big* (because increasing Ellen's weight decreases *both* Jim and Ria's weight by the same amount, for a net *decrease*.) This lets us eliminate choices (C), (D), and (E). Since our guess wasn't

   far off, it makes sense to test choice (B) next. If Ellen weighs 120 pounds, then Jim weighs $290 - 120 = 170$ pounds and Ria weighs $230 - 120 = 110$ pounds. In total, they weigh $120 + 170 + 110 = 400$ pounds. Bingo! The answer is **(B)**.

   Method 2: Use algebra. Let e = Ellen's weight, j = Jim's weight, and r = Ria's weight. Translate the problem into equations:

   $$e + j = 290$$
   $$e + r = 230$$
   $$e + j + r = 400$$
   Add first two equations: $2e + j + r = 520$
   Subtract third equation: $-(e + j + r = 400)$
   $$e = 120$$

4. **Method 1:** Use algebra. Let x be the number of gallons of paint that she starts with. Translate the problem into an equation: $x - (1/4)x - (1/3)x = 10$
   Simplify: $(5/12)x = 10$
   Multiply by 12/5: $x = 24$

   The answer is **(B)**.

   Method 2: Test the choices. Look at the problem carefully. She uses one-fourth of her paint, then one-third of her paint and is left with 10 gallons of paint, a *whole number*. This suggests that she started with a quantity that is divisible by 3 and 4. Since 24 is divisible by 3 and 4, it's a good choice to test. One-fourth of 24 is 6, and one-third of 24 is 8. This means she would be left with $24 - 6 - 8 = 10$. Bingo!

5. **Method 1:** Plug in. Let $s = 35$, so $r = 35/5 = 7$ and $t = 4$. (Check that they "fit.") Since the question asks for the value of s, write down 35 and circle it. Plugging these values into the choices gives

   (A) 140 (B) 35 (C) 136 (D) 124 (E) 280.

   Answer: **(B)**.

   Method 2: Use algebra. Solve the first equation for s: $s = 5r$. Then solve the second equation for r: $r = (7/4)t$. Then substitute: $s = 5(7/4)t = 35t/4$.

Lesson 7: Thinking Logically and Checking

Guessing and Checking

❑ A lot of students think they should never guess and check on the SAT I, because math is all about memorizing standardized procedures for solving particular problems. Hogwash! **Guessing and checking is the essence of good mathematical reasoning.** In fact, much of what professional mathematicians do is guessing and checking; it's just that their guesses are very educated and their checks are more sophisticated. **Don't hesitate to guess and check to solve problems, as long as you're logical with your guesses and careful with your checking!**

e.g.   A bin in a sporting goods store contains a total of 20 basketballs and soccer balls. If there are 8 more basketballs than soccer balls in the bin, how many soccer balls are in the bin?

Answer: There are no choices given here, but don't worry: you can make an educated guess. Your first thought might be that there are $20 - 8 = 12$ soccer balls. But a quick check shows that this doesn't make sense, because if there are 12 soccer balls, there must be only 8 basketballs (for a total of 20), but the problem says that there are 8 more basketballs than soccer balls. So your guess was too big. Your next guess might be to subtract 8 from your last guess: $12 - 8 = 4$. Does that work? No—too small, because if there are 4 soccer balls, there must be 16 basketballs to make a total of 20, and there would be 12 more basketballs than soccer balls, not 8. So increase your guess a bit, to 6. Does this work? Yup: if there are 6 soccer balls, then there must be $20 - 6 = 14$ basketballs, and 14 is 8 more than 6!

Algebra provides a cool and easy shortcut, if you prefer. Let x be the number of soccer balls. Then $x + 8$ represents the number of basketballs, and the total number of balls is $(x) + (x + 8) = 20$

Simplify:	$2x + 8 = 20$
Subtract 8:	$2x = 12$
Divide by 2:	$x = 6$

Use All of the Information (Usually)

❑ One important way to check your work on the SAT I math sections is to **check that you've used all of the information in the problem.** If you have to "leave out" a big piece of information, you've probably made a mistake. Every once in a while a problem will contain a piece of "unnecessary" information, but this is rare. **If you have to leave out a piece of information, make sure that you can explain why.**

Check the Little Things

❑ **As a last step, always re-read the problem to make sure you've satisfied all the restrictions of the problem, considered all of the important terms, and answered the question it asks.** I wish I had a dime for every time a student missed a question because he or she simply failed to re-read the question before choosing the answer. So often, a word is missed or an expression is misread or the student simply thinks that the question is asking something other than what it is asking.

Process of Elimination

❑ Perhaps the simplest logical strategy on a multiple-choice question is the **process of elimination.** Showing that four out of five choices are wrong is just as good as showing that one of the choices is right!

e.g.   If $(b)(b - 1)(b - 2)$ is negative, which of the following must also be negative?

(A) b (B) $b - 1$ (C) $b - 2$
(D) $b^2 - 1$ (E) $2 - b$

Answer: First find a value of b that works. $b = -1$ works, because $(-1)(-1 - 1)(-1 - 2) = (-1)(-2)(-3) = -6$, which is negative. But if b can equal -1, then we can eliminate choices (D) and (E) because (D) would equal 0 and (E) would equal 3, which aren't negative. Now you might notice that (C) has the lowest value of the remaining choices, so it's most likely to be negative. Notice that b could equal 1.5 because $(1.5)(1.5 - 1)(1.5 - 2) = (1.5)(.5)(-.5) = -375$, and this option shows that (A) and (B) don't have to be negative, so the answer is (C).

Concept Review 7: Thinking Logically and Checking

1. What should you do just before filling in your response to an SAT I math problem? Why should you do it?

2. Is it okay to guess and check on the SAT I? Why or why not?

3. What should you do if you don't use some of the given information to solve an SAT I math problem?

4. What does it mean to solve a multiple-choice SAT I math problem by the process of elimination?

5. Which problems are best to solve by the process of elimination?

SAT I Practice 7: Thinking Logically and Checking

1

Try to solve this problem by guessing and checking. If a, b, and c are positive integers greater than 1; ab = 15; and bc = 21, then what is the value of a + b + c?

2

Solve the following problem, then indicate why it is particularly important to re-read a problem like this one before filling in your response.

If $4x - 10 = 20$, what is the value of $2x - 10$?

3

Try to solve this problem by process of elimination.

If $a > b$ and $b(b - a) > 0$, which of the following must be true?

    I. $b < 0$
    II. $a - b < 0$
    III. $a < 0$

(A) I only
(B) II only
(C) I and II only
(D) I and III only
(E) I, II, and III

4

Solve the following SAT I problem and then indicate what is so unusual about it.

One-third of a liter of a liquid fertilizer concentrate must be mixed with four liters of water to form enough fertilizer to feed 800 square feet of grass. At this rate, how much of the concentrate is required to form enough of the mixture to feed 300 square feet of grass?

Answer Key 7: Thinking Logically and Checking

Concept Review 7

1. Re-read the question one more time, in order to make sure that you've answered the question it asks.

2. It is certainly okay to guess and check on the SAT I, and this may often be the best way to solve many problems. If it is never an efficient method for you, you probably need to work on strategies for educated guessing and efficient checking.

3. Check your work carefully, and make sure that the "extra" information is not necessary to solving the problem. Very very few SAT I questions will give unnecessary information. It happens occasionally, though, so just be sure that you can explain why any information in the problem is unnecessary.

4. It means eliminating the four wrong answers by finding counterexamples, and choosing the one remaining answer by default.

5. Three common problem types that are usually best solved by the process of elimination are problems in which you "plug in" arbitrary values for the unknown (see Lesson 6), "which of the following must be true?" problems, and problems with statements enumerated by Roman numerals (I, II, and III).

SAT I Practice 7

1. **15** If a and b must be positive integers greater than 1 and $ab = 15$, then they could only be 3 and 5. (15 and 1 don't work; they must both be *greater* than 1.) Let's guess that $a = 3$ and $b = 5$. Does this work? Check with the other equation: if $bc = 21$, then $5c = 21$ and $c = 4.2$. But that can't be, because the problem says that c must be an integer. So make a better guess: $a = 5$ and $b = 3$. If this is true, then $3c = 21$ and $c = 7$. This must be the solution, because all of the given information is satisfied: the equations both "work," and the numbers are integers greater than 1. Therefore, $a + b + c = 5 + 3 + 7 = 15$.

2. **5** It is particularly important to re-read this problem before filling in your response because it is easy to make two common mistakes: first, to solve for x and fill in the answer of 7.5, and second, to think that $2x - 10$ is half of $4x - 10$ and fill in an answer of 10. Both of these answers are wrong, because if

$$4x - 10 = 20$$

Add 10: $\qquad 4x = 30$

Divide by 2: $\qquad 2x = 15$

Therefore $\qquad 2x - 10 = 15 - 10 = 5$

3. **A** Start by picking simple values for a and b that satisfy the conditions. If $a > b$, then you might start with $a = 2$ and $b = 1$. This doesn't work, though, because $b(b - a) = 1(1 - 2) = -1$, which is not > 0. To

change the sign, we should pick a negative value for b. So try $a = 2$ and $b = -1$. This satisfies both inequalities. This example clearly rules out statement II, because $a - b = 2 - (-1) = 3$, which is not < 0. This means that we can also eliminate any choice that contains statement II in it, so (B), (C), and (E) are eliminated. This example also rules out statement III, because if a can be 2, it doesn't have to be less than 0. This lets us eliminate choice (D), so (A) must be the right answer by process of elimination.

4. **0.125 or 1/8 liters** The ratio of liters of concentrate to square feet of grass is 1/3:800. This simplifies to 1:2400. To find how much concentrate is required to feed 300 square feet of grass, we simply set up a proportion:

$$1/2400 = x/300$$

Cross-multiply: $\qquad 2400x = 300$

Divide by 240: $\qquad x = 0.125$ or $1/8$

This problem is very unusual because it contains a piece of "unnecessary" information, namely, that the first mixture requires four liters of water. Unnecessary information like that is very unusual in SAT I questions, and you should be able to explain why you don't need to use it. Because the question asked only for the number of liters of concentrate, and because we knew a direct link—the ratio—between the amount of concentrate and the area of grass covered, we did not need to use the information about the water.

CHAPTER 10

ESSENTIAL PRE-ALGEBRA SKILLS

1. Numbers and Operations

2. Laws of Arithmetic

3. Fractions

4. Ratios and Proportions

5. Percents

6. Negatives

7. Divisibility

Directions
1. [ ] READ each Lesson slowly and carefully. Underline important points and take notes in the margins. Think about each example and what concept it illustrates.
2. [ ] COMPLETE the Concept Review without referring back to the Lesson. Use the Concept Review to assess your understanding of the concepts.
3. [ ] REVIEW the Lesson and make any necessary corrections to your Concept Review answers.
4. [ ] CHECK your Concept Review answers with the Answer Key.
5. [ ] ANSWER all of the questions in the SAT I Practice. Answer every question to the best of your ability.
6. [ ] CHECK your SAT I Practice answers with the Answer Key.
7. [ ] REVIEW the questions you missed and try to find where your mistakes were.
8. [ ] NOTE any questions that you may want to review with your tutor or teacher.

Lesson 1:
Numbers and Operations

Number Sets

You need to know only two number sets for the SAT I. **An integer is a positive or negative whole number,** like . . . $-3, -2, -1, 0, 1, 2, 3.$ . . . **A real number is any number that you can imagine on the number line, including integers.** Real numbers include decimals, negatives, fractions, and roots.

Only two operations produce numbers that are not real: dividing by 0 and taking the square root of a negative.

❑ **Every number on the SAT I is a real number, but not necessarily an integer, unless you are specifically told that it is.**

e.g.   If you are told that $x > 3$, **don't** assume x is just 4 or 5 or 6. . . . It **might** be 3.125 or the like.

Operations

The SAT I deals only with the basic operations: *addition, subtraction, multiplication, division, powers,* and *roots.*

❑ A **sum** is the result of an **addition** and a **product** is the result of a **multiplication. Don't confuse the two!**

Inverse Operations

❑ **Every operation is paired with its inverse:** addition/subtraction, multiplication/division, powers/roots. **Inverse operations** are operations that "undo" each other. In other words, if you do an operation, then do its inverse, you're back where you started!

e.g.   *Dividing by* 6 is the inverse of *multiplying by* 6 because $x \times 6 \div 6 = x$.

❑ **Taking a square root is** *almost* **the inverse of squaring, but not quite!** Think: does $\sqrt{(-3)^2} = -3$?

❑ You **must** use inverse operations to "isolate" a variable when solving simple equations.

e.g. $3x - 7 = 38$ 1. Adding 7 is the inverse of subtracting 7 (do it to both sides): $3x = 45$
2. Dividing by 3 is the inverse of multiplying by 3 (do it to both sides): $x = 15$

Alternative Ways of Expressing Operations

❑ Any operation can be expressed in terms of its **inverse.** That is, any **subtraction** can be expressed as an **addition** (and vice versa), any **division** can be expressed as a **multiplication** (and vice versa), and every **root** can be expressed as a **power!** Be sure to consider your options when evaluating an operation.

e.g.   *Dividing by* 6 is always the same as *multiplying by* ⅙.   (Just change the number to its reciprocal.)

Subtracting −3 is always the same as *adding* 3.   (Just change the number to its opposite.)

Taking a square root is always the same as *raising to the* ½ *power.*

The *Real* Order of Operations

❑ The **real** order of operations has a "GERM" in it: **PG-ER-MD-AS.** These are the steps you should use when evaluating an expression:

1. **PG:** Evaluate what is in **parentheses** or within the two other **grouping symbols:** fraction bars and radicals.

2. **ER:** Evaluate any **exponentials** and **roots, from left to right!**

3. **MD:** Evaluate any **multiplication** and **division, from left to right!**

4. **AS:** Evaluate any **addition** and **subtraction, from left to right!**

Concept Review 1: Numbers and Operations

1. What is the greatest integer less than –9.5?

   1. _____

2. Express the answer to Question 1 as a fraction **in two different ways.**

   2. _____

3. When is taking the square root of a number **not** the inverse of squaring a number? Be specific.

   _____

   _____

4. Four consecutive even integers have a sum of 76. What is the greatest of these numbers?

   4. _____

5. If $-2 < x < 2$, how many possible values may x have?

   5. _____

6. The result of an addition is called a _____.

7. The result of a subtraction is called a _____.

8. The result of a multiplication is called a _____.

9. What is the difference between the product of 12 and 3 and their sum?

   9. _____

What is the **alternative** way to express each of the following operations?

10. $- (6)$ _____ 11. $\div (4)$ _____ 12. $\times -\dfrac{5}{3}$ _____ 13. $\div \dfrac{6}{7}$ _____

What is the **inverse** of each of the following operations?

14. $- (6)$ _____ 15. $\div (4)$ _____ 16. $\times -\dfrac{5}{3}$ _____ 17. $\div \dfrac{6}{7}$ _____

Simplify **without** a calculator:

18. $4 - 6 \div 2 \times 3 + 1 - (2 + 1)^2 =$ _____

19. $9 - \left(\sqrt{25} - \sqrt{16} \div 2\right)^2 =$ _____

20. $\dfrac{1}{2}\left(6^1 + 2^2\right)^2 =$ _____

21. $\left(1 - \left(2 - \left(1 - 2\right)^2\right) - 2\right) - 2 =$ _____

22. Circle the **real numbers** and underline the **integers:** 3.75 1.333... $\sqrt{25}$ $\sqrt{-7}$ $-\dfrac{2}{5}$ $\dfrac{56}{7}$ 0

23. The **real** order of operations is _____.

24. Which two symbols (besides parentheses) are "grouping" symbols? _____

25. If $\dfrac{x}{5}, \dfrac{x}{6}, \dfrac{x}{8}$, and $\dfrac{x}{12}$ are all positive integers, what is the least possible value of x?

    25. _____

26. List the three operations that must be performed on each side of this equation (in order!) to solve for x:

    $3x^2 + 7 = 34$ Step 1 _____   Step 2 _____   Step 3 _____ $x =$ _____

SAT I Practice 1:
Numbers and Operations

1 Which of the following is NOT equal to ⅓ of an integer?

(A) ⅓   (B) 1   (C) ⅔   (D) ½   (E) 10

2 Which of the following can be expressed as the product of two consecutive even integers?

(A) 22   (B) 36   (C) 48   (D) 60   (E) 72

3 $\left(1-\left(1-\left(1-3\right)\right)\right)-\left(1-\left(1-\left(1-2\right)\right)\right)=$

(A) −3   (B) −2   (C) −1   (D) 2   (E) 3

4 If $\sqrt{k}-3=8$, what is the value of k?

(A) 11   (B) 64   (C) 67   (D) 121   (E) 132

5 In the country of Etiquette, if 2 is a company and 3 is a crowd, then how many are 4 crowds and 2½ companies?

(A) 14   (B) 17   (C) 23   (D) 28½   (E) 29

6 For what integer value of x is $3x + 7 > 13$ and $x − 5 < − 1$?

7 For all real numbers x, let $\{x$ be defined as the least integer greater than x.

$\{−5.6 =$

(A) −6   (B) −5.7   (C) −5.5   (D) −5   (E) 1

8 Dividing any positive number by ¾ and then multiplying by −2 is equivalent to

(A)   multiplying by −⅔
(B)   dividing by ⅜
(C)   multiplying by −½
(D)   dividing by ⅜
(E)   multiplying by −⅜

9 When 14 is taken from 6 times a number, 40 is left. What is half the number?

10 If the smallest positive four-digit integer without repeated digits is subtracted from the greatest four-digit integer without repeated digits, the result is

(A) 8,642   (B) 1,111   (C) 8,853
(D) 2,468   (E) 8,888

11 If $x > 1$, the value of which of the following expressions increases as x increases?

I. $\dfrac{1}{x^2}$

II. $\sqrt{x}$

III. $10 - \dfrac{1}{x}$

(A)   II only   (B)   III only
(C)   I and II only   (D)   II and III only
(E)   I, II, and III

Answer Key 1: Numbers and Operations

Concept Review 1

1. −10 (Remember: "greatest" means farthest to the right on the number line.)

2. −10/1, −20/2, −30/3, etc. (Fractions can be integers.)

3. If the original number is negative, then taking a square root doesn't "undo" squaring the number. Imagine that original number is −3. The square of −3 is 9, but the square root of 9 is 3. This is the *absolute value* of the original number, but not the original number itself.

4. 22 (16 + 18 + 20 + 22 = 76. Just divide 76 by 4 to get the "middle" of the set = 19.)

5. Infinitely many (If you said 3, don't assume that unknowns are integers!)

6. sum

7. difference

8. product

9. 21 ((12 × 3) − (12 + 3) = 36 − 15 = 21)

10. + (−6)   11. × (1/4)   12. ÷ (−3/5)   13. × (7/6)

14. + (6)   15. × (4)   16. ÷ (−5/3)   17. × (6/7)

18. −13 (If you said −5, remember to do multiplication/division from left to right.)

19. 0

20. 50

21. −4

22. Circle all numbers except $\sqrt{-7}$ and underline only 0, $\sqrt{25}$ (= 5) and 56/7 (= 8)

23. PG-ER-MD-AS (Parentheses/grouping (left to right), exponents/roots (left to right), multiplication/division (left to right), addition/subtraction (left to right))

24. fraction bars (group the numerator and denominator), and radicals (group what's inside)

25. 120 (It is the least common multiple of 5, 6, 8, and 12.)

26. Step 1: subtract 7; Step 2: divide by 3; Step 3: take the square root; $x = 3$ or −3 (not just 3!)

SAT I Practice 1

1. **C**   ½ is not ⅓ of an integer because ½ × 3 = 1½ = 7.5, which is not an integer.

2. **C**   48 = 6 × 8

3. **C** $(1 − (1 − (1 − 3))) − (1 − (1 − (1 − 2)))$
   $= (1 − (1 − (−2))) − (1 − (1 − (−1)))$
   $= (1 − 3) − (1 − 2)$
   $= −2 − (−1)$
   $= −2 + 1$
   $= −1$

4. **D** $\sqrt{k} − 3 = 8$
   Add 3: $\sqrt{k} = 11$
   Square: $k = 121$

5. **B**   (4 × 3) + (2½ × 2) = 12 + 5 = 17

6. **3** $3x + 7 > 13$ and $x − 5 < −1$
   $3x > 6$ and $x < 4$
   $x > 2$ and $x < 4$

7. **D**   −5 is the least (farthest to the left on the number line) of all the integers that are greater than (to the right on the number line of) −5.6.

8. **A**   Dividing by ¾ is equivalent to multiplying by ⁴⁄₃:

   $x ÷ ¾ × −2$
   $=   x × ⁴⁄₃ × −2$
   $=   x × −⁸⁄₃$

9. **4.5** $6x − 14 = 40$
   Add 14: $6x = 54$
   Divide by 6: $x = 9$
   (Don't forget to find *half* the number!)

10. **C**   9,876 − 1,023 = 8,853
    Don't forget that 0 is a digit, but it can't be the first digit of a 4-digit integer.

11. **D**   You might "plug in" increasing values of x to see whether the expressions increase or decrease. 1 and 4 are convenient values to try. Also, if you can graph $y = 1/x^2$, $y = \sqrt{x}$ and $y = 10 − ¼$ quickly, you might notice that $y = \sqrt{x}$ and $y = 10 − 1/x$ "go up" as you move to the right of 1 on the x-axis.

Lesson 2: Laws of Arithmetic

The Laws of Arithmetic

When evaluating expressions, you don't always have to follow the order of operations strictly. Sometimes you can play around with the expression first. You can **commute** (with addition or multiplication), **associate** (with addition or multiplication) or **distribute** (multiplication or division over addition or subtraction). Know your options!

❑ When simplifying an expression, consider whether the laws of arithmetic help to make it easier.

e.g. $57(71) + 57(29)$ is much easier to simplify if, rather than using the order of operations, you use the "distributive law" and think of it as $57(71 + 29) = 57(100) = 5,700$.

The Commutative and Associative Laws

❑ **Whenever you add or multiply terms, the order of the terms doesn't matter, so pick a convenient arrangement.** To **commute** means to move around. (Just think about what commuters do!)

e.g. $1 + 2 + 3 + 4 + 5 + 6 + 7 + 8 + 9 = 1 + 9 + 2 + 8 + 3 + 7 + 4 + 6 + 5$

(Think about why the second arrangement is more convenient than the first!)

❑ **Whenever you add or multiply, the grouping of the terms doesn't matter, so pick a convenient grouping.** To **associate** means to group together. (Just think about what an association is!)

e.g. $(32 \times 4) \times (25 \times 10) \times (10 \times 2) = 32 \times (4 \times 25) \times (10 \times 10) \times 2$

(Why is the second grouping more convenient than the first?)

❑ Whenever you **subtract** or **divide,** the grouping of the terms **does** matter. Subtraction and division are neither commutative nor associative.

e.g. $15 - 7 - 2 \neq 7 - 15 - 2$ (So you can't "commute" the numbers in a difference until you convert it to addition: $15 + -7 + -2 = -7 + 15 + -2$.)

$24 \div 3 \div 2 \neq 3 \div 2 \div 24$ (So you can't "commute" the numbers in a quotient until you convert it to multiplication: $24 \times \dfrac{1}{3} \times \dfrac{1}{2} = \dfrac{1}{3} \times \dfrac{1}{2} \times 24$.)

The Distributive Law

❑ When a **grouped sum or difference** is **multiplied or divided** by something, you can do the multiplication or division **first** (instead of doing what's inside parentheses, as the order of operations says) as long as you "distribute." Test these equations by plugging in numbers to see how they work:

e.g. $a(b + c) = ab + ac$

$\dfrac{(b+c)}{a} = \dfrac{b}{a} + \dfrac{c}{a}$

❑ **Distribution is never something that you *have* to do.** Think of it as a tool, rather than a requirement. Use it when it simplifies your task. For instance, $13(832 + 168)$ is actually much easier to do if you **don't** distribute: $13(832 + 168) = 13(1,000) = 13,000$. Notice how annoying it would be if you distributed.

❑ **Use the distributive law "backwards" whenever you factor polynomials, add fractions, or combine "like" terms:**

e.g. $9x^2 - 12x = 3x(3x - 4)$

$\dfrac{3}{b} + \dfrac{a}{b} = \dfrac{3+a}{b}$ $5\sqrt{7} - 2\sqrt{7} = 3\sqrt{7}$

❑ **Follow the rules when you distribute!** Avoid these common mistakes:

e.g. $(3 + 4)^2$ is **not** $3^2 + 4^2$
(Tempting, isn't it? Check it and see!)
$3(4 \times 5)$ is **not** $3(4) \times 3(5)$

Concept Review 2:
Laws of Arithmetic

Simplify the following expressions, and indicate what law(s) of arithmetic you use to do it. Write **D** for distribution, **CA** for commutative law of addition, **CM** for commutative law of multiplication, **AA** for associative law of addition, and **AM** for associative law of multiplication.

1. $3 + x + 9$ _____

2. $-2x(x - 3)$ _____

3. $(5m^2n)(2mn^3)$ _____

4. $5 + (7 + 2y) + 5y$ _____

Look carefully at the following equations. If the equation is always **true,** write the law of arithmetic that justifies it (D, CA, CM, AA, or AM). If it is **false,** rewrite the right side of the equation to make it true.

5. $\dfrac{2x}{y} + \dfrac{3x}{2y} = \dfrac{5x}{3y}$ 5. _____

6. $15(67) + 15(33) = 15(100)$ 6. _____

7. $(a + b)^2 = a^2 + b^2$ 7. _____

8. $5c(c \times 3x) = 5c^2 \times 15cx$ 8. _____

9. $3(2^6 + 3^4) = 6^6 + 9^4$ 9. _____

10. $\dfrac{6 + y}{3y} = \dfrac{2}{y} + \dfrac{1}{3}$ 10. _____

Rewrite the expression $3x^2 + 12x^3$ according to the following laws:

11. distributive law: 12. commutative law of addition: 13. commutative law of multiplication:

_____   _____   _____

Do the following calculations **mentally** (no calculator!) by using the appropriate laws of arithmetic.

14. $25 + 48 + 75 + 60 + 52 + 40 =$ _____

15. $(4y)(6y)(25)(y^2)(5) =$ _____

16. $19(550) + 19(450) =$ _____

17. $(25 \times 5x)(4x \times 20) =$ _____

If a and b are not 0:

18. What's the relationship between $a \div b$ and $b \div a$?   18. _____

19. What's the relationship between $a \times b$ and $b \times a$?   19. _____

20. What's the relationship between $a - b$ and $b - a$?   20. _____

21. The distributive law says that only _____ or _____ can be distributed over grouped _____ or _____.

22. Which operations are **not** commutative?   22. _____

23. Are powers commutative? That is, is $(x^m)^n$ always equal to $(x^n)^m$?   23. _____

SAT I Practice 2:
Laws of Arithmetic

1 The difference of two integers is 4 and their sum is 14. What is their product?

(A) 18   (B) 24   (C) 36
(D) 45   (E) 56

2 For all real numbers x and y, $4x(x) - 3xy(2x) =$

(A) $12x^2y(x - 2x)$
(B) $2x^2(2 - 3y)$
(C) $xy(-x)$
(D) $2x^2(2 + 3y)$
(E) $4x^2(x - 3y)$

3 If $3x^2 + 2x = 40$, then $15x^2 + 10x =$

(A) 120   (B) 200   (C) 280
(D) 570   (E) 578

4 The expression $-2(x + 2) + x(x + 2)$ is equivalent to which of the following expressions?

  I. $x^2 - 4$
  II. $(x - 2)(x + 2)$
  III. $x^2 - 4x - 4$

(A) none   (B) II only
(C) I and II only (D) II and III only
(E) I, II, and III

5 If $(x + y) + 1 = 1 - (1 - x)$, what is the value of y?

(A) -2
(B) -1
(C) 0
(D) 1
(E) 3

6 For all real numbers x, $1 - (1 - (1 - x) - 1) =$

(A) x
(B) $x - 1$
(C) $x - 2$
(D) $1 - x$
(E) $2 - x$

7 If $a = 60(99)^{99} + 30(99)^{99}$, $b = 99^{100}$, and $c = 90(90)^{99}$, then which of the following expresses the correct ordering of a, b, and c?

(A) $c < a < b$
(B) $b < c < a$
(C) $a < b < c$
(D) $c < b < a$
(E) $b < a < c$

8 Which of the following is equivalent to $5x(2x \times 3) - 5x^2$ for all x?

(A) $5x^2 + 15x$
(B) $5x^2 \times 15x$
(C) $10x^2 \times 15x - 5x^2$
(D) $145x$
(E) $25x^2$

9 Which of the following statements must be true for all values of x, y, and z?

  I. $(x + y) + z = (z + y) + x$
  II. $(x - y) - z = (z - y) - x$
  III. $(x \times y) \times z = (z \times y) \times x$

(A) I only
(B) I and II only
(C) I and III only
(D) II and III only
(E) I, II, and III

10 The symbol $\lozenge$ represents one of the fundamental arithmetic operators: $+$, $-$, $\times$, or $\div$. If $(x \lozenge y) \times (y \lozenge x) = 1$ for all positive values of x and y, then $\lozenge$ can represent

(A) $+$ only
(B) $\times$ only
(C) $+$ or $\times$ only
(D) $-$ only
(E) $\div$ only

Answer Key 2: Laws of Arithmetic

Concept Review 2

1. $x + 12$ (commutative law of arithmetic)

2. $-2x^2 + 6x$ (distributive law)

3. $10m^3n^4$ (commutative law of multiplication and associative law of multiplication)

4. $7y + 12$ (associative law of arithmetic and commutative law of arithmetic)

5. false: $\dfrac{7x}{2y}$ (Find a common denominator, then add numerators.)

6. true: distributive law

7. false: $a^2 + 2ab + b^2$ (Don't ever distribute a power over addition. Expand and "FOIL" (First + Outside + Inside + Last))

8. false: $15c^2x$ (Don't ever distribute multiplication over multiplication. Use the associative and commutative laws of multiplication.)

9. false: $3(2)^6 + 3^5$ (You can distribute, but don't multiply before doing the powers!)

10. true: distributive law (Remember you can distribute division over addition!)

11. $3x^2(1 + 4x)$

12. $12x^3 + 3x^2$

13. $x^3 \times 12 + x^2 \times 3$

14. 300 (Reorder: $(25 + 75) + (48 + 52) + (60 + 40)$)

15. $3,000y^4$ (Reorder: $(4 \times 25)(6 \times 5)(y \times y \times y^2)$)

16. 19,000 (Use the distributive law.)

17. $10,000x^2$ (You can't "FOIL" here! Reorder: (4×25) $(5 \times 20)(x)(x) = (100)(100)(x^2)$)

18. They're reciprocals. (Their product is 1.)

19. They're the same.

20. They're opposites. (Their sum is 0.)

21. multiplication or division over addition or subtraction

22. subtraction and division

23. yes

SAT I Practice 2

1. **D**
$$\begin{array}{r} m - n = 4 \\ \underline{m + n = 14} \\ 2m \quad = 18 \\ m = 9 \qquad n = 5 \qquad 9 \times 5 = 45 \end{array}$$

2. **B** $4x(x) - 3xy(2x) =$
$4x^2 - 6x^2y = 2x^2(2 - 3y)$

3. **B** Don't solve for x. It's too hard, and it's unnecessary.
$$15x^2 + 10x = 5(3x^2 + 2x) = 5(40) = 200$$

4. **C** $-2(x + 2) + x(x + 2)$
$= (-2 + x)(x + 2)$ Distributive law
$= (x - 2)(x + 2)$ Commutative law of addition
$= x^2 - 4$ Distributive law ("FOILing")

5. **B** $(x + y) + 1 = 1 - (1 - x)$
associate: $\quad x + y + 1 = 1 - (1 - x)$
distribute: $\quad x + y + 1 = 1 - 1 + x$
simplify: $\quad\;\; x + y + 1 = x$
subtract x: $\;\; y + 1 = 0$
subtract 1: $\quad y = -1$

6. **E** $1 - (1 - (1 - x) - 1)$
distribute: $\;\; = 1 - (1 - 1 + x - 1)$
distribute: $\;\; = 1 - 1 + 1 - x + 1$
commute: $\quad = 1 - 1 + 1 + 1 - x$
simplify: $\quad = 2 - x$

7. **A** Each number has 100 factors, to make them simpler to compare:
$$\begin{array}{lll} a = 60(99)^{99} + 30(99)^{99} & = 90(99)^{99} \\ b = 99^{100} & = 99(99)^{99} \\ c = 90(90)^{99} & = 90(90)^{99} \end{array}$$

8. **E**
$$\begin{array}{ll} & 5x(2x \times 3) - 5x^2 \\ \text{parentheses:} & = 5x(6x) - 5x^2 \\ \text{multiplication:} & = 30x^2 - 5x^2 \\ \text{subtraction:} & = 25x^2 \end{array}$$

9. **C** Just remember that only addition and multiplication are commutative and associative. If you're not convinced, you might plug in 1, 2, and 3 for x, y, and z, and notice that equation II is not true.

10. **E**
$$(x \div y) \times (y \div x)$$
$$= \frac{x}{y} \times \frac{y}{x}$$
$$= \frac{xy}{xy}$$
$$= 1$$

Lesson 3: Fractions

Adding and Subtracting Fractions

Just as 2 apples + 3 apples = 5 apples, so 2 sevenths + 3 sevenths = 5 sevenths! So it's easy to add fractions if the denominators are the same. But if the denominators are different, just "convert" them so that they *are* the same.

❑ **When "converting" a fraction, always multiply (or divide) the numerator and denominator by the same number.**

e.g. $\dfrac{2}{5} = \dfrac{2 \times 5}{5 \times 5} = \dfrac{10}{25}$ $\dfrac{12}{18} = \dfrac{12 \div 6}{18 \div 6} = \dfrac{2}{3}$

❑ **If the denominator of one fraction is a multiple of the other denominator, "convert" only the fraction with the smaller denominator.**

e.g. $\dfrac{5}{18} + \dfrac{4}{9} = \dfrac{5}{18} + \dfrac{4 \times 2}{9 \times 2} = \dfrac{5}{18} + \dfrac{8}{18} = \dfrac{13}{18}$

❑ **One easy way to add fractions is with "zip-zap-zup": cross-multiply for the numerators, and multiply denominators for the new denominator.** You may have to simplify as the last step.

e.g. $\dfrac{x}{3} + \dfrac{2}{5} = \dfrac{x}{3} \diagdown \diagup \dfrac{2}{5} = \dfrac{5x}{15} + \dfrac{6}{15} = \dfrac{5x+6}{15}$

$\dfrac{5}{6} + \dfrac{7}{8} = \dfrac{5}{6} \diagdown \diagup \dfrac{7}{8} = \dfrac{40}{48} + \dfrac{42}{48} = \dfrac{82}{48} = \dfrac{41}{24}$

Multiplying and Dividing Fractions

❑ **To multiply fractions, don't worry about getting "common denominators." Just multiply straight across.**

e.g. $\dfrac{3}{4} \times \dfrac{7}{11} = \dfrac{3 \times 7}{4 \times 11} = \dfrac{21}{44}$

$\dfrac{y}{4} \times \dfrac{3}{x} = \dfrac{y \times 3}{4 \times x} = \dfrac{3y}{4x}$

❑ **To multiply a fraction and a non-fraction, multiply just the numerator by the non-fraction.**

e.g. $\dfrac{4}{7} \times 5 = \dfrac{4 \times 5}{7} = \dfrac{20}{7}$

$5y \times \dfrac{3x}{5} = \dfrac{5y \times 3x}{5} = \dfrac{15xy}{5} = 3xy$

❑ Don't confuse multiplying fractions with **cross-multiplying a proportion.** (That's in the **next** lesson!)

❑ To divide by a fraction, just **multiply by its reciprocal,** just as we did in Lesson 1.

e.g. $\dfrac{\frac{2}{5}}{\frac{7}{3}} = \dfrac{2}{5} \times \dfrac{3}{7} = \dfrac{6}{35}$

$\dfrac{\frac{3m}{7}}{\frac{5}{2m}} = \dfrac{3m}{7} \times \dfrac{2m}{5} = \dfrac{6m^2}{35}$

Simplifying Fractions

❑ If a fraction contains other fractions, or if the numerator and denominator have a common factor, it should be simplified. **Simplify fractions by dividing common factors or multiplying common denominators on top and bottom.**

e.g. $\dfrac{4x+2}{2} = \dfrac{2(2x+1)}{2} = 2x+1$

$\dfrac{\frac{2}{5} + \frac{2}{3}}{\frac{1}{4}} = \dfrac{60 \times \left(\frac{2}{5} + \frac{2}{3}\right)}{60 \times \left(\frac{1}{4}\right)} = \dfrac{24+40}{15} = \dfrac{64}{15}$

❑ **Don't cancel terms that are not common factors.** (Remember that a factor is part of a product.)

e.g.

Wrong: $\dfrac{x^2 - 1}{x - 1} = \dfrac{x^2}{x} = x$

Right: $\dfrac{x^2 - 1}{x - 1} = \dfrac{(x+1)(x-1)}{(x-1)} = x+1$

Concept Review 3: Fractions

Simplify the following expressions:

1. $\dfrac{1}{7} + \dfrac{2}{5} =$ _____

2. $\dfrac{5}{\dfrac{2}{3}} =$ _____
   $\dfrac{3}{8}$

   (rendered as) $\dfrac{\dfrac{5}{2}}{\dfrac{3}{8}} =$ _____

3. $\dfrac{56}{21} =$ _____

4. $\dfrac{2}{9} \div \dfrac{5}{4} =$ _____

5. $\dfrac{4}{7} + \dfrac{2}{3x} =$ _____

6. $\dfrac{\dfrac{3x}{2}}{\dfrac{9z}{8}} =$ _____

7. $\dfrac{12m+4}{8m+4} =$ _____

8. $-\dfrac{2}{9x^2} \div \dfrac{4}{3x} =$ _____

9. $\dfrac{1}{2} + \dfrac{1}{3} + \dfrac{1}{4} =$ _____

10. $\dfrac{3}{4} - \dfrac{x}{2} =$ _____

11. $\dfrac{x^2 - 25}{x - 5} =$ _____

12. $\dfrac{6n+9}{12n} =$ _____

Convert each expression to a fraction:

13. $25\% =$ _____

14. $0.20 =$ _____

15. $10\% =$ _____

16. $0.333\ldots =$ _____

17. How do you divide a number by a fraction?

_____

18. How do you add two fractions by "zip-zap-zup"?

_____

19. What can be cancelled to simplify a fraction?

_____

20. How do you convert a fraction to a decimal?

_____

21. If a class contains 12 boys and 15 girls, then what fraction of the class is boys?   21. _____

22. If 2/3 of a class is girls, and there are 9 boys in the class, what is the total number of students in the class?   22. _____

23. If m and n are positive, and $m < n$, then what is true about $\dfrac{m}{n}$?   23. _____

SAT I Practice 3: Fractions

1 If 4 quarts of apple juice are mixed with 5 quarts of cranberry juice and 3 quarts of grape juice, what part of the total mixture is apple juice?

(A) $\dfrac{1}{6}$ (B) $\dfrac{1}{4}$ (C) $\dfrac{1}{3}$

(D) $\dfrac{4}{9}$ (E) $\dfrac{2}{3}$

2 For what value of y does $\dfrac{1}{y} = -3$?

(A) -3 (B) $-\dfrac{1}{3}$ (C) $\dfrac{1}{3}$

(D) 3 (E) 6

3 Which of the following is greatest?

(A) $\dfrac{2}{3} \times 1$ (B) $1 - \dfrac{2}{3}$ (C) $1 \div \dfrac{2}{3}$

(D) $\dfrac{2}{3} \div \dfrac{2}{3}$ (E) $\dfrac{2}{3} \div 1$

4 If $\dfrac{\frac{1}{2}}{x} = 5$, then $x =$

(A) $\dfrac{1}{10}$ (B) $\dfrac{1}{5}$ (C) $\dfrac{2}{5}$

(D) $\dfrac{5}{2}$ (E) 10

5 If $\dfrac{1}{2} + \dfrac{1}{m} = \dfrac{5}{6}$, then $m =$

(A) $\dfrac{1}{3}$ (B) $\dfrac{2}{5}$ (C) $\dfrac{2}{3}$

(D) 3 (E) 5

6 If $x \neq y$ and $x + y = 0$, then $\dfrac{x}{y} =$

(A) -1 (B) 0 (C) $\frac{1}{2}$
(D) 1 (E) 2

7 If $\dfrac{m}{4} + \dfrac{n}{2} = \dfrac{7}{8}$, then $m + 2n =$

(A) $\dfrac{7}{4}$ (B) $\dfrac{7}{2}$ (C) 5 (D) 7 (E) 14

8 If $z \neq 0$, which of the following is equivalent to $\dfrac{1}{z + \frac{1}{z}}$?

(A) 1 (B) $\dfrac{1}{2z}$ (C) $\dfrac{2}{z}$

(D) $\dfrac{z}{z+1}$ (E) $\dfrac{z}{z^2+1}$

9 Five-eighths of Ms. Talbott's students are boys, and two-thirds of the girls do not have dark hair. What fraction of Ms. Talbott's students are girls with dark hair?

(A) $\dfrac{1}{24}$ (B) $\dfrac{1}{10}$ (C) $\dfrac{1}{8}$

(D) $\dfrac{1}{4}$ (E) $\dfrac{1}{3}$

10 If $\dfrac{2}{3} + \dfrac{6}{7} - \dfrac{1}{6} = \dfrac{2}{3} - \dfrac{1}{6} + \dfrac{1}{x}$, then $x =$

11 If $n > 1$, and $\dfrac{nx}{m+x} = 1$, then $x =$

(A) $\dfrac{m}{n-1}$ (B) $\dfrac{m}{n+1}$ (C) $\dfrac{m+1}{n}$

(D) $\dfrac{m+1}{n-1}$ (E) $\dfrac{m+1}{n+1}$

Answer Key 3: Fractions

Concept Review 3

1. 19/35 (Use zip-zap-zup: it's better than using your calculator!)

2. 20/3 (Change to $5/2 \times 8/3$.)

3. 8/3 (Divide numerator and denominator by their common factor: 7.)

4. 8/45 (Change to $2/9 \times 4/5$.)

5. $(12x + 14)/21x$ (Use zip-zap-zup.)

6. $4x/3z$ (Change to $3x/2 \times 8/9z$ and simplify.)

7. $(3m + 1)/(2m + 1)$ (Factor and cancel 4 from the numerator and denominator.)

8. $-1/(6x)$ (Change to $-2/(9x^2) \times 3x/4$ and simplify.)

9. 13/12 (Change to $6/12 + 4/12 + 3/12$.)

10. $(3 - 2x)/4$ (Use zip-zap-zup and simplify.)

11. $x + 5$ (As long as $x \neq 5$.) (Factor as $\dfrac{(x-5)(x+5)}{(x-5)}$ and cancel the common factor. For factoring review, see Chapter 11, Lesson 5.)

12. $(2n + 3)/4n$ (Divide numerator and denominator by the common factor: 3. Don't forget to "distribute" the division in the numerator!)

13. ¼ 14. ⅕ 15. ⅒ 16. ⅓
(Knowing how to "convert" numbers back and forth from percents to decimals to fractions can be very helpful in simplifying problems!)

17. Multiply by the reciprocal of the fraction.

18. "Cross-multiply" to get the new numerators, and multiply the denominators to get the new denominator, then just add (or subtract) the numerators.

19. Only common *factors*. (Factors = terms in *products*.)

20. Just divide the numbers by hand or on a calculator.

21. 4/9 (Not 4/5! Remember the fraction is a part of the *whole*, which is 27 students, $12/27 = 4/9$.)

22. 27 (If 2/3 are girls, 1/3 are boys: $t/3 = 9$, so $t = 27$.)

23. It must have a value between 0 and 1 ("bottom-heavy").

SAT I Practice 3

1. **C** $4/(4+5+3) = 4/12 = 1/3$

2. **B**
$$\frac{1}{y} = -3$$
multiply by y: $\quad 1 = -3y$

divide by -3: $\quad -\dfrac{1}{3} = y$

3. **C** $\dfrac{2}{3} \times 1 \qquad\qquad = 0.666\ldots$

$1 - \dfrac{2}{3} = \dfrac{3}{3} - \dfrac{2}{3} = \dfrac{1}{3} \quad = 0.333\ldots$

$1 \div \dfrac{2}{3} = 1 \times \dfrac{3}{2} \qquad = 1.5$

$\dfrac{2}{3} \div \dfrac{2}{3} = \dfrac{2}{3} \times \dfrac{3}{2} = \dfrac{6}{6} \quad = 1$

$\dfrac{2}{3} \div 1 = \dfrac{2}{3} \times 1 \qquad = 0.666\ldots$

4. **A** $\dfrac{\frac{1}{2}}{x} = 5$ multiply by x: $\dfrac{1}{2} = 5x$

multiply by ⅕: $\dfrac{1}{10} = x$

5. **D** $\dfrac{1}{2} + \dfrac{1}{m} = \dfrac{5}{6}$ multiply by $6m$: $3m + 6 = 5m$

subtract $3m$: $\qquad 6 = 2m$
divide by 2: $\qquad 3 = m$

6. **A** The quotient of opposites is always -1. (Try $x = 2$ and $y = -2$ or any other solution.)

7. **B** To turn $\dfrac{m}{4} + \dfrac{n}{2}$ into $m + 2n$, we only need to multiply by 4!

$$m + 2n = 4\left(\frac{m}{4} + \frac{n}{2}\right) = 4\left(\frac{7}{8}\right) = \frac{28}{8} = \frac{7}{2}$$

8. **E** You can solve this by "plugging in" a number for z or by simplifying algebraically. To plug in, pick $z = 2$ and notice that the expression equals ⅖ or .4. Substituting $z = 2$ into the choices shows that only (E) is .4.

Alternatively, you can simplify by just multiplying numerator and denominator by z:

$$\frac{1}{z + \dfrac{1}{z}} = \frac{z \times 1}{z\left(z + \dfrac{1}{z}\right)} = \frac{z}{z^2 + 1}$$

9. **C** ⅜ are boys, so ⅝ must be girls. Of the girls, ⅔ do not have dark hair, so ⅓ do. Therefore, ⅓ of ⅝ of the class are girls with dark hair. $⅓ \times ⅝ = ⅝$.

10. **7/6 or 1.16 or 1.17**

Begin by subtracting 2/3 from both sides and adding −1/6 to both sides, to simplify. This gives $\dfrac{6}{7} = \dfrac{1}{x}$. Just "reciprocate" both sides or cross-multiply.

11. **A** $\dfrac{nx}{m+x} = 1$ multiply by $m + x$: $nx = m + x$

subtract x: $nx - x = m$

factor: $x(n-1) = m$

divide by $(n-1)$: $x = \dfrac{m}{n-1}$

Lesson 4:
Ratios and Proportions

Ratios

- **Many simple ratios are just like fractions.** For instance, *the ratio of 5 to 7 is 5:7,* or $\dfrac{5}{7}$.

- In a **"ratio of parts,"** the sum of the parts represents the whole. **Think of each part as a fraction of the whole.**

  e.g.   If something is divided into parts in a ratio of 3:4:5, then the whole is $3 + 4 + 5 = 12$, so you think of the ratio as $\dfrac{3}{12}:\dfrac{4}{12}:\dfrac{5}{12} = \dfrac{1}{4}:\dfrac{1}{3}:\dfrac{5}{12}$, which shows each part as a fraction of the whole.

- Rates are ratios, too. In a rate, the word **per** means **divided by**.

  e.g.   *miles per gallon* means *number of miles: number of gallons.*

Proportions

- **A proportion** is a statement that **two fractions are equal,** like $\dfrac{3}{5} = \dfrac{9}{15}$.

- **The Law of Cross-Multiplication:** If two fractions are equal, then their **"cross-products" are always equal.**

  e.g.   If $\dfrac{3}{7} = \dfrac{9}{21}$, then $3 \times 21 = 7 \times 9$.

  If $\dfrac{x}{3} = \dfrac{y}{4}$, then $4x = 3y$.

- **If two fractions are equal, terms may be "cross-swapped" without changing the equality.**

  e.g.   If $\dfrac{3}{7} = \dfrac{9}{21}$, then $\dfrac{21}{7} = \dfrac{9}{3}$.

  If $\dfrac{x}{3} = \dfrac{y}{4}$, then $\dfrac{4}{3} = \dfrac{y}{x}$.

- The phrase **". . . at this rate . . ."** indicates that two rates are the same, so **you can usually set up a proportion.**

  e.g.   A bird can fly 420 miles in one day. *At this rate,* how many miles can the bird fly in 14 hours?

  The rate, in *miles per hour,* is the same in both situations,

  so $\dfrac{420 \text{ miles}}{24 \text{ hours}} = \dfrac{x \text{ miles}}{14 \text{ hours}}$

  Cross-multiply: $420 \times 14 = 24x$
  Divide by 24: $= 245$ miles

- **When setting up a proportion, you will find it helpful to make sure that the units "match up."** For instance, in the example above, the "miles" go in the numerators and the "hours" go in the denominators.

Similarity

- Two triangles are *similar* (have the same shape) if their corresponding angles all have the same measure. **If two triangles are similar, then their corresponding sides are proportional.**

  e.g.

  In the figure above,

  $$\dfrac{m}{k} = \dfrac{n}{l} \text{ or } \dfrac{m}{n} = \dfrac{k}{l}$$

- **When setting up proportions of sides in similar figures, double-check that the corresponding sides "match up" in the proportion.** For instance, notice how the terms "match up" in the proportions above.

Concept Review 4: Ratios and Proportions

1. A speed is a ratio of _____ to _____.   2. An average is a ratio of _____ to _____.

3. Define a proportion:

   _____

   _____

4. Write the Law of Cross-Multiplication as an "If . . . then . . ." statement:

   If _____

   then _____

5. Write three equations that are equivalent to $\dfrac{2}{x} = \dfrac{y}{3}$.   5. a)_____

                                                                                          b)_____

                                                                                          c)_____

6. Three people split a $24,000 prize in a ratio of 2:3:5. What is the value of each portion?   6. a)_____

                                                                                                          b)_____

                                                                                                          c)_____

7. A machine, working at a constant rate, manufactures 25 bottles every 6 minutes.   7. _____
   At this rate, how many *hours* will it take to produce 1,000 bottles?

8. If m meteorites enter the Earth's atmosphere every x days ($m > 0$), then, at this rate,   8. _____
   how many meteors will enter the Earth's atmosphere in mx days?

9. In the diagram above, $\ell_1 \parallel \ell_2$, $AC = 4$, $BC = 5$, and $CE = 6$. What is DE?   9. _____

10. There are 12 boys and g girls in Class A, and there are 27 girls and b boys in Class B.   10. _____
    In each class, the ratio of boys to girls is the same. If $b = g$, then how many
    students are in Class A?

SAT I Practice 4:
Ratios and Proportions

1 If x is the product of .03 and .2, then x is equivalent to the ratio of 6 to what number?

2 Jar A contains six red marbles and no green marbles. Jar B contains two red marbles and four green marbles. How many green marbles must be moved from Jar B to Jar A so that the ratio of green marbles to red marbles is the same for both jars?

(A) 0   (B) 1   (C) 2   (D) 3   (E) 4

3 90 students are at a meeting. The ratio of girls to boys at the meeting is 2 to 3. How many girls are at the meeting?

(A) 30   (B) 36   (C) 40
(D) 54   (E) 60

4 If $\dfrac{x}{y+1} = \dfrac{3}{5}$, then $5x + 1 =$

(A) $3y + 1$ (B) $3y + 2$ (C) $3y + 3$
(D) $3y + 4$ (E) $3y + 5$

5 On a map that is drawn to scale, two towns that are x miles apart are represented as being 4 inches apart. If two other towns are $x + 2$ miles apart, how many inches apart would they be on the same map?

(A) $4(x + 2)$ (B) 6   (C) $\dfrac{4x}{x+2}$

(D) $\dfrac{4(x+2)}{x}$ (E) $\dfrac{6}{x}$

6 If 3,600 baseball caps are distributed to 4 stores in the ratio of 1:2:3:4, what is the maximum number of caps that any one store receives?

(A) 360   (B) 720   (C) 1,080
(D) 1,440   (E) 14,400

7 David's motorcycle uses $\dfrac{2}{5}$ of a gallon of gasoline to travel 8 miles. At this rate, how many miles will it travel on 5 gallons of gasoline?

8 On a blueprint that is drawn to scale, the drawing of a rectangular patio has dimensions 5 cm by 7.5 cm. If the longer side of the actual patio measures 21 feet, what is the area, in square feet, of the actual patio?

(A) 157.5
(B) 294.0
(C) 356.5
(D) 441.0
(E) 640.5

9 To make a certain purple dye, red dye and blue dye are mixed in a ratio of 3:4. To make a certain orange dye, red dye and yellow dye are mixed in a ratio of 3:2. If equal amounts of the purple and orange dye are mixed, what fraction of the new mixture is red dye?

(A) $\dfrac{9}{20}$ (B) $\dfrac{1}{2}$ (C) $\dfrac{18}{35}$

(D) $\dfrac{27}{40}$ (E) $\dfrac{1}{1}$

Answer Key 4: Ratios and Proportions

Concept Review 4

1. distance to time

2. a sum to the number of terms in the sum

3. A proportion is a statement that two fractions or ratios are equal to each other.

4. If two fractions are equal, then the two "cross-products" must also be equal.

5. a) $6 = xy$ b) $\dfrac{3}{x} = \dfrac{y}{2}$ c) $\dfrac{2}{y} = \dfrac{x}{3}$

6. $4,800, $7,200, and $12,000. The sum of the parts is $2 + 3 + 5 = 10$, so the parts are 2/10, 3/10, and 5/10 of the whole.

7. 4.
$$\frac{25 \text{ bottles}}{6 \text{ minutes}} = \frac{1{,}000 \text{ bottles}}{x \text{ minutes}}$$

Cross-multiply: $25x = 6{,}000$
Divide by 25; $x = 240$ minutes

Convert to hours: $240 \text{ mins} \times \left(\dfrac{1 \text{ hour}}{60 \text{ mins}}\right) = 4 \text{ hrs}$

8. m^2. "At this rate . . ." implies a proportion:

$$\frac{m \text{ meteorites}}{x \text{ days}} = \frac{? \text{ meteorites}}{mx \text{ days}}$$

Cross-multiply: $m^2 x = ?x$
Divide by x: $m^2 = ?$

9. 12.5. Because $\ell_1 \parallel \ell_2$; $\triangle ABC$ is similar to $\triangle ADE$. Thus, $\dfrac{AC}{AE} = \dfrac{BC}{DE}$. Substituting x for DE gives

$$\frac{4}{4+6} = \frac{5}{x}.$$

Cross-multiply: $4x = 50$
Divide by 4: $x = 12.5$

10. 30. Since the ratios are the same, $\dfrac{12}{g} = \dfrac{b}{27}$.

Cross-multiply: $bg = 324$
Substitute b for g: $b^2 = 324$
Take the square root: $b = 18$
So the number of students in Class A $= 12 + 18 = 30$.

SAT I Practice 4

1. **1000.** $.03 \times .2 = 6/x$
   Simplify: $.006 = 6/x$
   Multiply by x: $.006x = 6$
   Divide by .006: $x = 1{,}000$

2. **D**   Moving 3 green marbles from Jar B to Jar A leaves three green marbles and six red marbles in Jar A and one green marble and two red marbles in Jar B. $3{:}6 = 1{:}2$.

3. **B** $2{:}3$ is a "part to part" ratio, with a sum of 5. Therefore 2/5 of the students are girls and 3/5 are boys. 2/5 of $90 = 36$.

4. **D**   Cross-multiply: $5(x) = 3(y + 1)$
   Simplify: $5x = 3y + 3$
   Add 1: $5x + 1 = 3y + 4$

5. **D**   Since the map is "to scale," the corresponding measures are proportional:
$$\frac{x}{4} = \frac{x+2}{?}$$

Cross-multiply: $?x = 4(x + 2)$

Divide by x: $? = \dfrac{4(x+2)}{x}$

6. **D**   The ratio is a "ratio of parts" with a sum of $1 + 2 + 3 + 4 = 10$. The largest part, then, is 4/10 of the whole. 4/10 of $3,600 = .4 \times 3{,}600 = 1{,}440$.

7. **100.**   "At this rate" implies a proportion:

$$\frac{\frac{2}{5} \text{ gallon}}{8 \text{ miles}} = \frac{5 \text{ gallons}}{x \text{ miles}}$$

Cross-multiply: $\dfrac{2}{5}x = 40$

Multiply by $\dfrac{5}{2}$: $x = \dfrac{5}{2} \times 40 = \dfrac{200}{2} = 100$ miles

8. **B**

Set up the proportion: $\dfrac{7.5}{5} = \dfrac{21}{x}$

Cross-multiply: $7.5x = 105$
Divide by 7.5: $x = 14$ feet
Find area: Area $= 21 \times 14 = 294$ ft^2

9. **C**   Each ratio is a "ratio of parts." In the purple dye, the red dye is $3/(3 + 4)$, or 3/7, of the total, and in the orange dye, the red dye is $3/(3 + 2)$, or 3/5, of the total. If the mixture is half purple and half orange, the fraction of red is

$$\frac{1}{2}\left(\frac{3}{7}\right) + \frac{1}{2}\left(\frac{3}{5}\right) = \frac{3}{14} + \frac{3}{10} = \frac{72}{140} = \frac{18}{35}$$

Lesson 5: Percents

Translating percent problems

❑ **Many percent problems practically solve themselves, as long as you know the translation key. Use the following key to turn basic percent problems into simple equations:**

percent	means	÷100
is	means	=
of	means	×
what	means	x, y, n, etc.

e.g.   What number is 5 percent of 36?

Translate the question: What number is 5 percent of 36

$$x = \frac{5}{100} \times 36, \quad \text{so } x = 1.8.$$

❑ If the problem is worded in a tricky way, you can use "*is* over *of* equals the *percent*" to set up the problem.

e.g.   *What percent is 24 of 18?* This can be translated as: *what percent of 18 is 24?* or can be set up correctly with "*is* over *of* equals the *percent*":

$$\frac{24}{18} = \frac{x}{100}$$

❑ **To convert a percent to a decimal, just move the decimal point two places to the left.** (This is equivalent to dividing by 100, which is what *percent* means!)

e.g.   5% is .05   125% is 1.25
                35.7% is .357   100% is 1

Finding "percent change"

❑ **To find a "percent increase" or "percent decrease," just use this simple formula:**

Percent change =

$$\frac{\text{final amount} - \text{starting amount}}{\text{starting amount}} \times 100\%$$

e.g.   What percent greater than 25 is 30? 25 is the "starting amount," because it's the amount we're comparing 30 to, using the formula:

Percent change =

$$\frac{30 - 25}{25} \times 100\% = \frac{5}{25} \times 100\% = .20 \times 100\% = 20\%$$

Changing Quantities by Percents

❑ **The simplest way to change a number by a given percent is to simply multiply it by the "final" percentage.** That is, to increase a number by $x\%$, simply multiply it by $(100 + x)\%$, and to decrease it by $x\%$, simply multiply it by $(100 - x)\%$.

For instance, if you want to **reduce** a number by 15%, your final percentage is 100% − 15% = **85%.** So just multiply by 0.85. If you want to **increase** a number by 20%, your final percentage is 100% + 20% = **120%,** so just multiply by 1.20!

e.g.   To calculate the final cost of a $22.60 dinner bill with a 15% tip added, just multiply by 1.15 (because the "final percentage" is 100% + 15% = 115% = 1.15). $22.60 × 1.15 = $25.99

❑ Here's a cool and (occasionally) useful fact about percents: ***a*% of *b* always equals *b*% of *a*!**

If you translate, it's easy to see why:

$$a\% \text{ of } b = \frac{a}{100} \times b = \frac{ab}{100} \quad b\% \text{ of } a = \frac{b}{100} \times a = \frac{ab}{100}$$

e.g.   36% of 25 = 25% of 36 = 1/4 of 36 = 9

Concept Review 5: Percents

1. Complete the translation key:

Word(s) in problem	Symbol in equation
what, what number, how much	
of	
	=
percent	

2. Write the formula for "percent change":   Percent change =

3. To increase a quantity by 30%, multiply it by _____   4. To decrease a quantity by 19%, multiply it by _____

5. To increase a quantity by 120%, multiply it by _____   6. To decrease a quantity by 120%, multiply it by _____

Translate the following word problems and solve them:

7. 5 is what percent of 26?   Translation: _____   Solution: _____

8. 35% of what number is 28?   Translation: _____   Solution: _____

9. 60 is 15% of what number?   Translation: _____   Solution: _____

10. What percent is 35 of 20?   Translation: _____   Solution: _____

11. What percent greater than 1,200 is 1,500?   11. _____

12. If the price of a sweater is marked down from $80 to $68, what is the percent markdown?   12. _____

13. The population of a city increases from 32,000 to 44,800. What is the percent increase?   13. _____

14. What number is 30% greater than 20?   14. _____

15. Increasing a number by 20%, then decreasing the new number by 20%, is the same as multiplying the original by _____.

16. Why don't the changes in problem 15 "cancel out"?

_____

17. If the sides of a square are decreased by 5%, by what percent is the area of the   17. _____
    square decreased?

18. 28% of 50 is the same as _____percent of _____, which equals _____.

19. 48% of 25 is the same as _____percent of _____, which equals _____.

SAT I Practice 5: Percents

1 David has a total of $3,500 in monthly expenses. He spends $2,200 per month on rent and utilities, $600 per month on clothing and food, and the rest on miscellaneous expenses. On a pie graph of his monthly expenses, what would be the degree measure of the central angle of the sector representing miscellaneous expenses?

(A) 45°   (B) 50°   (C) 70°
(D) 72°   (E) 75°

2 In one year, the price of one share of ABC stock increased by 20% in Quarter I, increased by 25% in Quarter II, decreased by 20% in Quarter III, and increased by 10% in Quarter IV. By what percent did the price of the stock increase for the whole year? (Ignore the % symbol when gridding.)

3 On a two-part test, Barbara answered 60% of the questions correctly on Part I and 90% correctly on Part II. If there were 40 questions on Part I and 80 questions on Part II, and if each question on both parts was worth 1 point, what was her score, as a percent of the total?

(A) 48%   (B) 75%   (C) 80%
(D) 82%   (E) 96%

4 If x is $\frac{2}{3}$% of 90, then $1 - x =$

(A) −59   (B) −5   (C) 0
(D) 0.4   (E) 0.94

5 The cost of a pack of batteries, after a 5% tax, is $8.40. What was the price before tax?

(A) $5.60
(B) $7.98
(C) $8.00
(D) $8.35
(E) $8.82

6 If the population of Town B is 50% greater than the population of Town A, and the population of Town C is 20% greater than the population of Town A, then what percent greater is the population of Town B than the population of Town C?

(A) 20%   (B) 25%   (C) 30%
(D) 35%   (E) 40%

7 If the length of a rectangle is increased by 20% and the width is increased by 30%, then by what percent is the area of the rectangle increased?

(A) 10%   (B) 50%
(C) 56%   (D) 65%
(E) It cannot be determined from the given information

8 If 12 ounces of a 30% salt solution are mixed with 24 ounces of a 60% salt solution, what is the percent concentration of salt in the mixture?

(A) 45%   (B) 48%   (C) 50%
(D) 52%   (E) 56%

9 The freshman class at Hillside High School has 45 more girls than boys. If the class has n boys, then what percent of the freshman class are girls?

(A) $\dfrac{n}{n+45}\%$ (B) $\dfrac{n+45}{2n+45}\%$

(C) $\dfrac{100n}{2n+45}\%$ (D) $\dfrac{100(n+45)}{2n+45}\%$

(E) $\dfrac{100(n+45)}{n+45}\%$

Answer Key 5: Percents

Concept Review 5

1. x, y, or any unknown; $\times$; *is*; $\div 100$

2. $\dfrac{\text{final amount} - \text{starting amount}}{\text{starting amount}} \times 100\%$

3. 1.30   4. 0.81   5. 2.20   6. −20

7. $5 = \dfrac{x}{100} \times 26$ $x = 19.23\%$

8. $.35x = 28$ $x = 80$

9. $60 = .15x$ $x = 400$

10. 175%. Rephrase: *What percent of 20 is 35?* (or remember *is over of* equals the *percent*)

    $\dfrac{x}{100} \times 20 = 35$ or $\dfrac{35}{20} = \dfrac{x}{100}$

    $3,500 = 20x$ $x = 175(\%)$

11. 25%. Use the "percent change" formula:

    $\dfrac{1,500 - 1,200}{1,200} \times 100\% = \dfrac{300}{1,200} \times 100\% = 25\%$

12. $-15\%.\ \dfrac{168-80}{80} \times 100\% = \dfrac{-12}{80} \times 100\% = -15\%$

13. 40%.

    $\dfrac{44,800 - 32,000}{32,000} \times 100\% = \dfrac{12,800}{32,000} \times 100\% = 40\%$

14. 26. To increase a number by 30%, multiply by 1.30: $20 \times 1.30 = 26$

15. 0.96. $x(1.20)(.80) = 0.96x$

16. Because the two percentages are "of" different numbers.

17. 9.75%. Assume the original square has sides of length x and area x^2. The new square, then, has sides of $.95x$ and area of $.9025x^2$.

    $\dfrac{9025x^2 - x^2}{x^2} \times 100\% = \dfrac{-.0975x^2}{x^2} \times 100\% = -9.75\%$

18. 50% of 28, which equals 14

19. 25% of 48, which equals 12

SAT I Practice 5

1. **D** Miscellaneous expenses = $3,500 − $2,200 − $600 = $700. As a percent of the total, 700/3500 = 20%. The total number of degrees in a pie graph is 360°, so the sector angle = 20% of 360° = .20 × 360 = 72°

2. **32%** Assume the starting price is x. The final price is $x(1.20)(1.25)(.80)(1.10) = 1.32x$, which represents a 32% increase. Notice that you can't just "add up" the percent changes, as we saw in Question 16 of the Concept Review.

3. **C** The total number of points is 40 + 80 = 120. The number of points she earned is .60(40) + .90(80) = 24 + 72 = 96.   96/120 = .80 = 80%

4. **D** If you chose (A), remember: 2/3% is NOT the same thing as 2/3! Don't forget that % means ÷ 100.
   $x = 2/3\%$ of 90 = (2/3) ÷ 100 × 90 = 0.6
   $1 - 0.6 = 0.4$

5. **C** If you chose (B), remember that the tax is 5% of the starting amount, not the final amount. The final price must be 5% higher than the starting price. If the starting price is x, then $8.40 = 1.05x$.
   Dividing by 1.05, $x = \$8.00$.

6. **B** Let a = population of Town A, b = population of Town B, and c = population of Town C. Since b is 50% greater than a, $b = 1.50a$. Since c is 20% greater than a, $c = 1.20a$.

   $\dfrac{1.5a - 1.2a}{1.2a} \times 100\% = \dfrac{.3a}{1.2a} \times 100\% = 25\%$

   You can also set $a = 100$, so $b = 150$ and $c = 120$.

7. **C** If the rectangle has length a and width b, then its area is ab. The "new" rectangle, then, has length $1.2a$ and width $1.3b$ and so has an area of $1.56ab$, which represents an increase of 56%.

8. **C** The total amount of salt is .30(12) + .60(24) = 3.6 + 14.4 = 18 ounces. The total amount of solution is 36 ounces, and 18/36 = 50%. Or you might notice that 24 is twice as much as 12, so the concentration of the mixture is the average of "two 60s and one 30."
   $(60\% + 60\% + 30\%)/3 = 50\%$

9. **D** The number of girls is $n + 45$, so the total number of students is $2n + 45$. So the percentage

   of girls is $\dfrac{100(n+45)}{2n+45}\%$.

Lesson 6: Negatives

Visualize the Number Line

❏ **Visualize the number line when comparing, adding, or subtracting numbers.** *Greater than* always means *to the right on the number line* and *less than* means *to the left on the number line.* **A negative number is *greater* than another if it is *closer to 0.***

e.g.   Which is greater, –2/5 or –7/5? Answer: Visualize the number line. Although 2/5 is less than 7/5, on the negative side this relationship is "flipped." –2/5 is closer to 0 than –7/5 is, so –2/5 is greater.

Adding and Subtracting with Negatives

❏ **To add, visualize the number line. To add a positive, jump to the right. To add a negative, jump to the left.**

e.g.   To add –5 + –12, start at –5 and move 12 spaces to the *left* (negative), to land on –17.

(Or you could start at –12 and jump 5 spaces to the left!)

❏ **To subtract, you can change the subtraction to addition by changing the sign of the second number.**

e.g.   To subtract –5 – (–12), change it to addition by changing the sign: –5 + 12 = 12 – 5 = 7.

❏ **To subtract, you can also "swap" the numbers and change the sign of the result,** because $a - b$ is the opposite of $b - a$.

e.g. $4 - 18 = -(18 - 4) = -14$

❏ Remember these helpful facts about subtracting:

• $a - b$ is *positive* if a is greater than b and *negative* if b is greater than a (regardless of the signs).
• $a - b$ is always the *opposite* of $b - a$.

Products, Quotients, and Powers of Negatives

❏ **Any product, quotient, or power is *negative* if it has an *odd* number of negatives and *positive* if it has an *even* number of negatives.**

e.g. $-12 \times 5 \times 7$ is negative: it has an odd number (1) of negatives.

$\dfrac{(-4x)(-3x)}{(-2x)(-6x^3)}$ is positive: it has an even number (4) of negatives.

$(-3)^{12}(5)^7(-2)^5$ is negative: it has an odd number (12 + 5 = 17) of negatives.

Inequalities and Negatives

❏ **Any inequality must be "flipped" whenever you multiply or divide both sides by a negative.**

e.g.   Solve $-3x > 6y - 3$ for x. Answer: we must divide both sides by –3 to get the x alone, but this means that the inequality "flips" because we changed the sign (just as 1 is less than 2 but –1 is greater than –2). So $x < -2y + 1$.

Concept Review 6: Negatives

Write the correct inequality (< or >) in each space.

1. $-\dfrac{3}{5}$ _____ $-\dfrac{2}{5}$ 2. -10 _____ -25 3. $-\dfrac{4}{7}$ _____ $-\dfrac{2}{5}$ 4. $\dfrac{3}{5}$ _____ $-\dfrac{2}{5}$

5. When does the expression $-x$ represent a *positive* number? _____

6. An inequality must be "flipped" whenever _____.

7. When is $x - y$ negative? _____

8. What is the simple way to tell quickly whether a product, quotient, or power is negative?

_____

_____

9. If $(x - y)(y - x) = -10$, then $(x - y)^2 =$ _____. (Think before doing any algebra!)

Simplify the following expressions **without** a calculator.

10. If $x \neq 2$, then $\dfrac{9x - 18}{18 - 9x} =$ _____.

13. $\dfrac{(-5)^3(-1)^{16}}{(2)^4(5)^3} =$ _____

11. $-13y^2 - (-4y^2) =$ _____

14. $-15 - (-9) =$ _____

12. $\dfrac{2}{-3} - \dfrac{-2}{-5}$ _____

15. $-5(-x)^6 \times -7x^{11} =$ _____

16. If $a(2 - x) > b(2 - x)$, then

$a > b$ only if _____

$a < b$ only if _____

Solve the following inequalities for x:

17. $-4x + 20 > 16$

18. $4x - 20 \geq 16$

19. $-20 - 4x < 16$

20. $-4x - 20 > -16$

17. _____

18. _____

19. _____

20. _____

SAT I Practice 6: Negatives

1   For all real numbers b, $-(-b - b - b - b) =$

(A) $-4b$ (B) $4b$ (C) b^4
(D) $-b^4$ (E) $4b^4$

2   If $k = (m - 1)(m - 2)(m - 3)$, then for which of the following values of m is k greater than 0?

(A) -2.47
(B) -1.47
(C) 0.47
(D) 1.47
(E) 2.47

3   For all real numbers w, $-w^2 - (-w)^2 =$

(A) $-w^4$
(B) $-2w^2$
(C) 0
(D) $2w^2$
(E) w^4

4   If $\dfrac{x}{y} > 1$, which of the following must be true?

    I. $m > n$

    II. $\dfrac{m}{n} > 0$

    III. $m > 1$

(A)   I only
(B)   II only
(C)   III only
(D)   I and II only
(E)   I and III only

5   If $x = -y$ and $x \neq 0$, then which of the following must be true?

    I. $x^2y^3 < 0$

    II. $(x + y)^2 = 0$

    III. $\dfrac{x}{y} < 0$

(A)   III only
(B)   I and II only
(C)   II and III only
(D)   I and III only
(E)   I, II, and III

6   If $mn^4p^5 > 0$ and $m < 0$, then which of the following expressions must be negative?

(A) mn
(B) m^2
(C) p^5
(D) mp
(E) np

7   If $0 < a < b < c < d < e < f$ and
$(a - b)(c - d)(e - f)(x) = (b - a)(d - c)(f - e)$
then $x =$

(A) -4
(B) -3
(C) -2
(D) -1
(E) 0

8   If the sum of the integers from 15 to 50, inclusive, is equal to the sum of the integers from n to 50, inclusive, and $n < 15$, then $n =$

(A) -50
(B) -49
(C) -35
(D) -15
(E) -14

9   If $-2x < -7$ and $y < 2.5$ then which of the following must be true?

    I. $xy > 0$
    II. $x - y > 0$
    III. $x > 3$

(A)   II only
(B)   I and II only
(C)   II and III only
(D)   I and III only
(E)   I, II, and III

10   A sequence of numbers begins with the numbers $-1, 1, 1, \ldots$, and each term afterward is the product of the preceding three terms. How many of the first 57 terms of this sequence are negative?

(A)   19   (B)   20   (C)   28
(D)   29   (E)   30

Answer Key 6: Negatives

Concept Review 6

1. $<$ 2. $>$ 3. $<$ 4. $>$

5. Whenever x is negative.

6. You multiply or divide by a negative on both sides.

7. Whenever y is greater than x (regardless of sign).

8. If the number of negatives in the term is odd, then the result is negative. If the number of negatives in the term is even, then the result is positive. Remember to add the exponents of all the negative numbers in the term.

9. 10. Notice that $y - x$ is the opposite of $x - y$. So $(x - y)(x - y)$ is the opposite of $(x - y)(y - x)$.

10. -1. Notice that $9x - 18$ and $18 - 9x$ must be opposites, and the quotient of nonzero opposites is always -1. ($-5/5 = -1$, $20/-20 = -1$, etc.)

11. $-9y^2$.

	$-13y^2 - (-4y^2)$
Change to addition:	$-13y^2 + 4y^2$
Commute:	$4y^2 + -13y^2$
Change to subtraction:	$4y^2 - 13y^2$
Swap and negate:	$-(13y^2 - 4y^2) = -9y^2$

12. $-16/15$.

	$\dfrac{2}{-3} - \dfrac{-2}{-5}$
Simplify fractions:	$-\dfrac{2}{3} - \dfrac{2}{5}$
Factor out -1:	$-\left(\dfrac{2}{3} + \dfrac{2}{5}\right)$
Zip-zap-zup:	$-\dfrac{10+6}{15} = -\dfrac{16}{15}$

13. $-1/16$.   Since there are an odd number (19) of negatives, the result is negative. Notice, too, that the powers of 5 cancel out.

14. -6 15. $35x^{17}$

16. $a > b$ only if $x < 2$ (and so $2 - x$ is positive). $a < b$ only if $x > 2$ (and so $2 - x$ is negative).

17. $x < 1$ 18. $x \geq 9$

19. $x > -9$ 20. $x < -1$

SAT I Practice 6

1. **B**

	$-(-b - b - b - b)$
Convert to addition:	$-(-b + -b + -b + -b)$
Distribute -1:	$(b + b + b + b)$
Simplify:	$4b$

2. **D**   Notice that $m - 1 > m - 2 > m - 3$. If the product is positive, then all three terms must be positive or one must be positive and the other two negative. They would all be positive only if $m > 3$, but no choice fits. If two terms are negative and one positive, then, by checking, $1 < m < 2$.

3. **B**   Don't forget the order of operations: powers before subtraction!

	$-w^2 - (-w)^2$
Simplify power:	$-w^2 - w^2$
Change to addition:	$-w^2 + -w^2$
Simplify:	$-2w^2$

4. **B**   If m/n is positive, then m and n must have the same sign. Using $m = -2$ and $n = -1$ disproves statements I and III. Statement II must be true because m and n must have the same sign.

5. **C**   The example $x = -1$ and $y = 1$ disproves statement I. Substituting $-y$ for x (because an expression can always be substituted for its equal) and simplifying in statements II and III proves that both are true.

6. **C**   Since m is negative, $n^4 p^5$ must be negative because the whole product is positive. n can be either positive or negative; n^4 will be positive in either case. Therefore, p^5 must be negative.

7. **D**   Since $x - y$ is always the opposite of $y - x$,

$(a - b)(c - d)(e - f)(x)$	$= (b - a)(d - c)(f - e)$
Substitute:	$= -(a - b) \times -(c - d) \times -(e - f)$
Simplify:	$= -(a - b)(c - d)(e - f)$

By comparing the two sides, x must equal -1.

8. **E**   If the two sums are equal, then the sum of the integers from n to 14, which are not included in the first sum, must "cancel out." That can only happen if n is -14.

9. **C**   Simplify the first inequality by dividing both sides by -2. (Don't forget to "flip" the inequality!) This gives $x > 3.5$. The example of $x = 4$ and $y = -1$ disproves statement I. Since x must be greater than y, statement II must be true. Since x is greater than 3.5, it must certainly be greater than 3, so statement III must be true.

10. **D**   The sequence follows the pattern $(-1, 1, 1, -1), (-1, 1, 1, -1), (-1, 1, 1, -1). \ldots$ Since the pattern is four terms long, it repeats $57 \div 4 = 14$ times, with a remainder of 1 (the remainder shows that it includes the first term of the 15th repetition), which means it includes $14(2) + 1 = 29$ negatives.

Lesson 7: Divisibility

Divisibility

❑ There are five different ways of saying that one integer, *a*, is a multiple of another integer *b*. Understand each phrasing.

- *a* **is divisible by** *b*.
- *a* **is a multiple of** *b*.
- *b* **is a factor of** *a*.
- **When** *a* **is divided by** *b*, **the remainder is 0.**
- *a/b* **is an integer.**

e.g.   42 is a multiple of 7, so

- 42 is divisible by 7.
- 42 is a multiple of 7.
- 7 is a factor of 42.
- When 42 is divided by 7, the remainder is 0.
- 42/7 is an integer (6).

❑ **To see if integer** *a* **is divisible by integer** *b*, **divide** *a* **by** *b* **on your calculator and see whether the result is an integer. Or use one of these "quick checks":**

- If an integer is a multiple of 3, its digits add up to a multiple of 3.

e.g.   345 is a multiple of 3 because
$3 + 4 + 5 = 12$, which is a multiple of 3.

- If an integer is a multiple of 5, it ends in 0 or 5.
- If an integer is a multiple of 6, it ends in an even digit and its digits add up to a multiple of 3.
- If an integer is a multiple of 9, its digits add up to a multiple of 9.

e.g.   882 is a multiple of 9 because
- $882 \div 9 = 98$ (which is an integer)
- Its digit sum is a multiple of 9: $8 + 8 + 2 = 18$ and $1 + 8 = 9$

- If an integer is a multiple of 10, it ends in 0.

Remainders

❑ **A remainder is a whole number "left over" when one whole number is divided by another whole number a whole number of times.** Think about giving balloons to kids: you can only have a whole number of balloons, a whole number of kids, and you can't give any kid a fraction of a balloon. If you try to divide 34 balloons among 4 kids, each kid can get 8 balloons, but then you will have 2 balloons "left over." This is your remainder.

❑ To find a remainder with a calculator, divide the two whole numbers on your calculator, then **multiply the "decimal part" of the result by the divisor.**

e.g.   What is the remainder when 34 is divided by 5?

$34 \div 5 = 6.8$ and $.8 \times 5 = 4!$

❑ Remainders can be very useful in solving SAT I "pattern" problems.

e.g.   What is the 50th term in this sequence?
7, 9, 3, 1, 7, 9, 3, 1 . . .

The pattern repeats every four terms. The remainder when 50 is divided by 4 is 2, so the 50th term is the same as the 2nd term, which is 9.

Primes, Evens, and Odds

❑ **A prime number** is any integer greater than 1 that is divisible only by 1 and itself (like 2, 3, 5, 7, 11, 13, 17 . . .).

❑ An **even number** is any multiple of 2. It can always be expressed as $2n$, where *n* is some integer. e.g. $28 = 2(14)$

❑ An **odd number** is any integer that is **not** a multiple of 2. Any odd number can be expressed as $2n + 1$, where *n* is some integer. e.g. $37 = 2(18) + 1$

❑ **Be careful not to confuse** *odd* **with** *negative* **(and** *even* **with** *positive*). Students commonly do this because *odd* and *negative* are "bad" words and *even* and *positive* are "good" words. **To avoid this mistake, pay special attention to the words** *odd*, *even*, *negative*, **and** *positive* **by underlining them when you see them in problems.**

Concept Review 7: Divisibility

1. What is a prime number? _____

2. What is a remainder? _____
   _____

3. An odd number is _____
   and can always be expressed as _____.

4. What can you do to avoid confusing *odd* with *negative* or *even* with *positive*? _____
   _____

5. How do you find a remainder with your calculator? _____
   _____

6. If an integer is divisible by k, 12, and 35, and k is a prime greater than 7, then the integer must also be divisible by which of the following? (Circle all that apply.)

   $3k$ $5k^2$ 10   24 $28k$ $k + 12$ 2 $35k$

7. When a whole number is divided by 7, what are the possible remainders? _____

8. What is the 100th term of this sequence? 3, 5, 7, 3, 5, 7 . . .   8. _____

9. What is the remainder when 357 is divided by 4?   9. _____

10. When x apples are divided equally among 7 baskets, one apple remains.   10. _____
    When those apples are divided equally among 9 baskets, one apple remains.
    If x is greater than 1 but less than 100, what is x?

    1, 2, 2, 1 . . .

11. In the sequence above, every term from the third onward is the quotient   11. _____
    of the previous term divided by the next previous term. For instance, the
    7th term is equal to the quotient of the 6th term divided by the 5th term.
    What is the 65th term of this sequence?

12. When an odd number is divided by 2, the remainder is always _____.

13. How many multiples of 6 between 1 and 100 are also multiples of 9?   13. _____

14. How many multiples of 6 between 1 and 100 are also prime?   14. _____

15. If z is an integer, which of the following must be odd? (Circle all that apply.)

    $5z$ $4z - 1$ $7z + 2$ z^2 $z^2 + 1$ z^3 $\dfrac{z}{2}$ $z^2 + z + 1$

16. If a divided by b leaves a remainder of r, then a must be _____ greater than a multiple of _____.

SAT I Practice 7: Divisibility

1 When an integer n is divided by 10, the remainder is 7. What is the remainder when n is divided by 5?

2 When 8 is divided by 12, the remainder is

(A) $\dfrac{1}{3}$ (B) $\dfrac{2}{3}$ (C) 4

(D) 8   (E) 12

3 If p is odd and q is even, then which of the following must be an odd number?

I. $p^2 + q^2$

II. $\dfrac{p^2}{q^2}$

III. $p^2 q^2$

(A) none   (B) I only
(C) I and II only   (D) I and III only
(E) I, II, and III

4   1, 3, 5, 7, 9, 1, 3, 5, 7, 9, 1 . . .

If the sequence above follows the pattern shown, what is the 103rd term of the sequence?

(A) 1   (B) 3   (C) 5
(D) 7   (E) 9

5
$$a\overline{)b}\ \ \text{remainder 3}$$
$$0$$

In the division problem shown above, if a and b are positive, which of the following must be true?

(A) $a = 3$ (B) $a = 3b$ (C) $b = 0$
(D) $b = 3$ (E) $b = 3a$

6 Which of the following is a counterexample to the statement: *All prime numbers are odd?*

(A) 2   (B) 3   (C) 9
(D) 11   (E) 12

7 If $\dfrac{k}{7}$ and $\dfrac{k}{12}$ are both positive integers, then which of the following must also be an integer?

(A) $\dfrac{k}{42}$ (B) $\dfrac{k}{24}$ (C) $\dfrac{k}{19}$

(D) $\dfrac{k}{15}$ (E) $\dfrac{k}{10}$

8 If a, b, c, d, and e are consecutive integers, then which of the following statements must be true?

I. This set contains 3 odd numbers.
II. This set contains a number divisible by 5.
III. $bc + 1$ is odd.

(A) I only   (B) II only
(C) I and II only   (D) II and III only
(E) I, II, and III

9 m and n are positive integers. If m is divided by n, the quotient is 7 with a remainder of 4. Which of the following expresses m in terms of n?

(A) $4n - 7$ (B) $7n - 4$ (C) $4n + 7$

(D) $\dfrac{n}{7} + 4$ (E) $7n + 4$

10 If a and b are positive integers and $\dfrac{a}{b} = 2.5$, then which of the following must be true?

I. $(a + b)$ is odd
II. $(a + b)$ is a multiple of 7

III. $\dfrac{5b}{a}$ is an integer

(A) II only   (B) I and III only
(C) I and II only   (D) II and III only
(E) I, II, and III

Answer Key 7: Divisibility

Concept Review 7

1. Any integer greater than one that is divisible only by 1 and itself.

2. The whole number "left over" when one whole number is divided by another whole number a whole number of times.

3. Any integer that is not divisible by 2. $2n + 1$.

4. Underline and think about those words when you see them in problems.

5. Divide the two integers, then multiply the decimal part of the result by the divisor (the number you divided by).

6. The least common multiple of k, 12, and 35 is $420k$, which is divisible by $3k$, 10, $28k$, 2, and $35k$.

7. 0, 1, 2, 3, 4, 5, and 6.

8. 3.   The pattern is 3 terms long, and 3 divided by 100 has a remainder of 1, so the 100th term is the same as the 1st.

9. 1

10. 64. The number must be 1 greater than both a multiple of 7 and a multiple of 9. The only multi-

ple of 7 and 9 that is between 1 and 100 is 63, and $63 + 1 = 64$.

11. 1/2. The sequence is
1, 2, 2, 1, 1/2, 1/2, 1, 2, 2, 1, 1/2, 1/2 . . . , so the pattern is 6 terms long. 65 divided by 6 leaves a remainder of 5, so the 65th term is the same as the 5th, which is 1/2.

12. 1

13. Five. The least common multiple of 6 and 9 is 18, and $100 \div 18 = 5.555 . . .$, which means that there are 5 multiples of 18 between 1 and 100.

14. None.   Prime numbers are divisible only by themselves and 1, but any multiple of 6 must also be divisible by 2 and 3.

15. $4z - 1$ and $z^2 + z + 1$ are the only expressions that must be odd. Since 4 is even, $4z$ is even, so $4z - 1$ must be odd. $z^2 + z + 1 = z(z + 1) + 1$, and since either z or $z + 1$ must be even, $z(z + 1)$ is even and $z(z + 1) + 1$ is odd.

16. If a divided by b leaves a remainder of r, then a must be r greater than a multiple of b.

SAT I Practice 7

1. **2.**   Since n leaves a remainder of 7 when divided by 10, it must be 7 more than a multiple of 10, like 7, 17, 27, etc. When any of these is divided by 5, the remainder is 2.

2. **D**   Don't confuse remainder with quotient. Remember to think of balloons and kids. If you had 8 balloons to divide among 12 kids, you'd have to keep all 8 balloons because there aren't enough to go around fairly. Also, you can use the calculator method, and divide 8 by 12, then multiply the result by 12.

3. **B**   Using $p = 1$ and $q = 2$ rules out II (1/4 is not an integer, let alone an odd number) and III (4 is even). $p^2 + q^2$ will always be odd, because the square of an odd is always odd and the square of an even is always even, and an odd plus an even is always odd.

4. **C**   The sequence that repeats is 5 terms long. 103 divided by 5 leaves a remainder of 3, so the 103rd term is the same as the 3rd term, which is 5.

5. **D**   For the statement to be correct, $b = a(0) + 3$, so $b = 3$.

6. **A**   A counterexample to the statement *All prime numbers are odd* would be a prime number that is not odd. The only even prime number is 2.

7. **A**   If $k/7$ and $k/12$ are both positive integers, then k must be a common multiple of 7 and 12. The least common multiple of 7 and 12 is 84. If we substitute 84 for k, (A) is the only choice that yields an integer.

8. **D**   Using the example of 2, 3, 4, 5, 6 disproves statement I. Since multiples of 5 occur every 5 consecutive integers, II must be true (remember that 0 is a multiple of every integer, including 5). Since bc will always be an even times an odd or an odd times an even, the result must always be even, so $bc + 1$ must be odd.

9. **E**   You might simplify this problem by picking values for m and n that work, like 46 and 6. (When 46 is divided by 6, the quotient is 7 with a remainder of 4.) If we substitute 6 for n, choice (E) is the only one that yields 46.

10. **D**   Using $a = 10$ and $b = 4$ disproves statement I. If a/b equals 5/2 and a and b are both integers, then $a = 5k$ and $b = 2k$, where k is an integer. Therefore $a + b = 7k$, so II is true. Also, since a/b equals 5/2, $b/a = 2/5$, so $5b/a = 10/5 = 2$, which is an integer, so III is true.

CHAPTER 11

ESSENTIAL ALGEBRA I SKILLS

1. Solving Equations

2. Systems

3. Working with Exponentials

4. Working with Roots

5. Factoring

6. Inequalities, Absolute Values, and Plugging In

7. Word Problems

Directions
1. [ ]   READ each Lesson slowly and carefully. Underline important points and take notes in the margins. Think about each example and what concept it illustrates.
2. [ ]   COMPLETE the Concept Review without referring back to the Lesson. Use the Concept Review to assess your understanding of the concepts.
3. [ ]   REVIEW the Lesson and make any necessary corrections to your Concept Review answers.
4. [ ]   CHECK your Concept Review answers with the Answer Key.
5. [ ]   ANSWER all of the questions in the SAT I Practice. Answer every question to the best of your ability.
6. [·]   CHECK your SAT I Practice answers with the Answer Key.
7. [ ]   REVIEW the questions you missed and try to find where your mistakes were.
8. [ ]   NOTE any questions that you may want to review with your tutor or teacher.

Lesson 1: Solving Equations

Equations as Balanced Scales

Algebra is really common sense once you start thinking of every equation as a balanced scale. The terms on either side of the equals sign must be "balanced," just like the weights on a scale.

❏ **All of the basic laws of algebra are the common-sense rules for keeping a scale balanced.** Imagine that you are the keeper of a scale, and you must keep it balanced. What would you do if someone took weights from one side of the scale? You'd remove an equal weight from the other side, of course. **This is a law of equality: anything you do to one side of the equation, you must do to the other to maintain the balance.**

e.g. If $12x - 8 = 28$, then what is the value of $3x - 2$?

Don't worry about solving for x, because that's not what the question is asking for. Notice that the expression you are given, $12x - 8$, is 4 times the expression you are looking for, $3x - 2$. So to turn the given expression into the one you want, divide by 4. Of course, you must do the same to the other side to keep the balance:

$$\frac{12x - 8}{4} = \frac{28}{4} \longrightarrow 3x - 2 = 7$$

Solving as Unwrapping

Solving simple algebraic equations is basically the same thing as unwrapping a present. (And it's just as fun, too, right?) Wrapping a present involves a sequence of steps: 1. Put the gift in the box. 2. Close the box. 3. Wrap the paper around the box. 4. Put the bow on. Here's the important part: unwrapping the present just means **inverting** those steps and **reversing** their order: 1. **Take off** the bow. 2. **Unwrap** the paper. 3. **Open** the box. 4. **Take out** the gift.

e.g. Solve for x: $5x^2 - 9 = 31$.

The problem is that x is not alone on the left side; it is "wrapped up" like a gift. How is it wrapped? Think of the order of operations for turning x into $5x^2 - 9$:

1. Square it (x^2)
2. Multiply by 5 $(5x^2)$
3. Subtract 9 $(5x^2 - 9)$

So to "unwrap" it, you **reverse** and **invert** the steps:

1. Add 9 $(5x^2 - 9) + 9 = 5x^2$
2. Divide by 5 $5x^2/5 = x^2$
3. Find the square roots (both of them!) $\pm\sqrt{x^2} = \pm|x|$

If you perform these steps to both sides, $5x^2 - 9 = 31$ transforms into $x = \pm\sqrt{8}$!

Watch Your Steps

To solve that last equation, we had to perform three operations. Many equations, as you probably know, require more steps to solve. It is very important that you keep track of your steps so that you can check your work if you need to. In other words, the equation we just solved should really look like this on your scratch paper:

$$5x^2 - 9 = 31$$

Step 1: $\underline{\qquad +9 \quad +9 \qquad}$

$$5x^2 \quad = 40$$

Step 2: $\underline{\dfrac{5}{} \qquad \dfrac{5}{}}$

$$x^2 \quad = 8$$

Step 3: $x \quad = \pm\sqrt{8}$

Check by Plugging Back In

❑ Always check your answer by plugging it back into the **original** equation to see if it works. Remember that solving an equation means simply finding the value of each unknown that makes the equation true.

e.g.   Are $\pm\sqrt{8}$ solutions to $5x^2 - 9 = 31$? Plug them in: $5\left(\pm\sqrt{8}\right)^2 - 9 = 5(8) - 9 = 40 - 9 = 31$ (Yes!)

Concept Review 1:
Solving Equations

1. Explain the Laws of Equality.

2. Are there any operations you can perform to both sides of an equation that will **not yield** a true equation? Explain.

Show your steps and check your work in solving the following equations.

3. $9x - 12 + 5x = 3x$

4. $(x - 4)^2 = 5$

5. $\dfrac{2x^2}{3} = x^2$

6. $\dfrac{x+2}{3} = \dfrac{x-5}{2}$

Solve the following equations for the given expression by performing **one operation** on both sides.

7. If $\dfrac{5x}{2} + 3 = 7$, then $10x + 12 =$ ___ Operation: _____ Solution: _____

8. If $18y + 12 = 7$, then $6y + 4 =$ ___ Operation: _____ Solution: _____

SAT I Practice 1:
Solving Equations

1 If $5d + 12 = 24$, then $5d - 12 =$

(A) −24   (B) −12   (C) 0
(D) 12   (E) 24

2 What number decreased by 7 equals 5 times the number?

(A) $-\dfrac{7}{4}$ (B) $-\dfrac{7}{5}$ (C) $-\dfrac{5}{7}$

(D) $-\dfrac{4}{7}$ (E) $\dfrac{4}{7}$

3 If $\dfrac{2y^2}{5} = y^2$, then $y + 5 =$

4 If $2x^2 - 5x = 9$, then $12x^2 - 30x =$

(A) −54   (B) −6   (C) 18
(D) 36   (E) 54

5 $$(p + 2)^2 = (p - 5)^2$$

The equation above is true for which of the following values of p?

(A) −2 and 5
(B) 2 and −5
(C) 0 and 1
(D) 1.5 only
(E) 3.5 only

6 If $\dfrac{5}{x} + \dfrac{7}{5} = 1$, what is the value of x?

(A) $-\dfrac{25}{2}$ (B) −7   (C) $-\dfrac{24}{7}$

(D) $-\dfrac{7}{5}$ (E) 7

7 The product of x and y is 36. If both x and y are integers, then what is the least possible value of $x - y$?

(A) −37   (B) −36   (C) −35
(D) −9   (E) −6

8 The graph of $y = f(x)$ contains the points $(-1, 7)$ and $(1, 3)$. Which of the following could be $f(x)$?

　I. $f(x) = |5x - 2|$
　II. $f(x) = x^2 - 2x + 4$
　III. $f(x) = -2x + 5$

(A) I only   (B) I and II only
(C) I and III only   (D) II and III only
(E) I, II, and III

9 If $20 - \sqrt{x} = 11$, which of the following gives all possible values of x?

(A) 9 only   (B) −9 and 9
(C) 81 only   (D) 81 and −81
(E) 961

10 For all positive values of m and n,
if $\dfrac{3x}{m - nx} = 2$, then $x =$

(A) $\dfrac{2m - 2n}{3}$ (B) $\dfrac{2m - 3}{2n}$

(C) $\dfrac{3 + 2n}{2m}$ (D) $\dfrac{2m}{3 + 2n}$

(E) $\dfrac{3}{2m - 2n}$

Answer Key 1: Solving Equations

Concept Review 1

1. The Laws of Equality say that whatever you do to one side of an equation you must do to the other side, to maintain the balance.

2. Yes. Dividing by 0 and taking the square root of a negative number are "undefined" operations in the real numbers. Be careful, then, when dividing both sides of an equation by an unknown, to check that the unknown could not possibly be 0.

3.

	$9x - 12 + 5x = 3x$
Commutative Law:	$14x - 12 = 3x$
Add 12, subtract $3x$:	$11x = 12$
Divide by 11:	$x = 12/11$

4.

	$(x - 4)^2 = 5$
Take square root:	$x - 4 = \pm\sqrt{5}$
Add 4:	$x = 4 \pm \sqrt{5}$

5.

	$\dfrac{2x^2}{3} = x^2$
Multiply by 3:	$2x^2 = 3x^2$
Subtract $2x^2$:	$0 = x^2$
Take square root:	$0 = x$

6.

	$\dfrac{x+2}{3} = \dfrac{x-5}{2}$
Cross-multiply:	$2x + 4 = 3x - 15$
Subtract $2x$:	$4 = x - 15$
Add 15:	$19 = x$

7. Operation: Multiply both sides by 4
   Solution: $10x + 12 = 28$

8. Operation: Divide both sides by 3
   Solution: $6y + 4 = 7/3$

SAT I Practice 1

1. **C**

	$5d + 12 = 24$
Subtract 24:	$5d - 12 = 0$

2. **A** Translate into an equation:

	$x - 7 = 5x$
Subtract x:	$-7 = 4x$
Divide by 4:	$-7/4 = x$

   You can also "test" the choices and see which one works, but that's probably more time-consuming.

3. **5** It's easiest to solve the equation for y, then add 5

	$\dfrac{2y^2}{5} = y^2$
Multiply by 5:	$2y^2 = 5y^2$
Subtract $2y^2$:	$0 = 3y^2$
Divide by 3:	$0 = y^2$
Take the square root:	$0 = y$
Add 5:	$5 = y + 5$

4. **E**

	$2x^2 - 5x = 9$
Multiply by 6:	$12x^2 - 30x = 54$

5. **D** Plugging in and checking is perhaps easiest here, but you could do the algebra too:

	$(p + 2)^2 = (p - 5)^2$
FOIL:	$p^2 + 4p + 4 = p^2 - 10p + 25$
Subtract p^2:	$4p + 4 = -10p + 25$
Subtract 4:	$4p = -10p + 21$
Add $10p$:	$14p = 21$
Divide by 14:	$p = 1.5$

6. **A**

	$\dfrac{5}{x} + \dfrac{7}{5} = 1$
Multiply by $5x$:	$25 + 7x = 5x$
Subtract $7x$:	$25 = -2x$
Divide by -2:	$-25/2 = x$

7. **C** Guess and check here. If $x = -36$ and $y = -1$, or $x = 1$ and $y = 36$, then $x - y = -35$.

8. **E** Just plug in the points $(-1, 7)$ and $(1, 3)$ to the equations, and confirm that the points "satisfy" all three equations.

9. **C**

	$20 - \sqrt{x} = 11$
Subtract 20:	$-\sqrt{x} = -9$
Multiply by -1:	$\sqrt{x} = 9$
Square both sides:	$x = 81$

10. **D**

	$\dfrac{3x}{m - nx} = 2$
Multiply by $m - nx$:	$3x = 2(m - nx)$
Distribute on right:	$3x = 2m - 2nx$
Add $2nx$:	$3x + 2nx = 2m$
Factor left side:	$x(3 + 2n) = 2m$
Divide by $(3 + 2n)$	$x = \dfrac{2m}{3 + 2n}$

Lesson 2: Systems

Systems

A system is simply a set of equations that are true at the same time, such as these:

$$3x - 2y = 12$$
$$x + 3y = 15$$

Although many values for x and y "satisfy" the first equation, like $(4, 0)$ and $(2, -3)$ (plug them in and check!), there is only one solution that works in **both** equations: $(6, 3)$. (Plug this into both equations and check!)

The Law of Substitution

❑ The **Law of Substitution** simply says that **if two things are equal, you can always substitute one for the other.**

e.g. $$\begin{cases} 3x - y^2 = 7 \\ y = x + 1 \end{cases}$$

The easiest way to solve this is to **substitute** the second equation (which is already "solved" for y) into the first, so that you **eliminate** one of the unknowns. Since $y = x + 1$, you can replace the y in the first equation with $x + 1$ and get

$$3x + (x + 1)^2 = 7$$

FOIL the squared binomial: $3x + x^2 + 2x + 1 = 7$
Combine like terms: $x^2 + 5x + 1 = 7$
Subtract 7: $x^2 + 5x - 6 = 0$
Factor the left side: $(x + 6)(x - 1) = 0$
Apply the Zero Product Property: $x = -6$ or $x = 1$
Plug values back into 2nd equation:

$$y = (-6) + 1 = -5$$
$$\text{or } y = (1) + 1 = 2$$

Solutions: $(-6, -5)$ and $(1, 2)$ (Check!)

Combining Equations

❑ If the two equations in the system are **alike** enough, you can sometimes solve them more easily by **combining equations**. The idea is simple: **if you add or subtract the corresponding sides of two true equations together, the result should also be a true equation, because you are adding equal things to both sides.** This strategy can be simpler than substitution:

e.g. $$\begin{cases} 2x - 5y = 7 \\ 3x + 5y = 23 \end{cases}$$ ⟵ Adding the corresponding sides will eliminate the y's from the system

Add equations: $5x = 30$
Divide by 5: $x = 6$

Plug this back in and solve for y:

$$2(6) - 5y = 7 \xrightarrow{\text{Simplify}} 12 - 5y = 7 \xrightarrow{-12}$$
$$-5y = -5 \xrightarrow{\div -5} y = 1$$

Special Kinds of "Solving"

❑ Sometimes a question gives you a system, but rather than asking you to solve for each unknown, it simply asks you to evaluate another expression. **Look carefully at what the question asks you to evaluate, and see whether there is a simple way of combining the equations (adding, subtracting, multiplying, dividing) to find the expression.**

e.g.   If $3x - 6y = 10$ and $4x + 2y = 2$, what is the value of $7x - 4y$?

Don't solve for x and y! Just notice that $7x - 4y$ equals $(3x - 6y) + (4x + 2y) = 10 + 2 = 12$.

"Letter-Heavy" Systems

❑ **An equation with more than one unknown, or a system with more unknowns than equations, is "letter-heavy." Simple equations and systems usually have just one solution, but these "letter-heavy" equations and systems usually have more than one solution, and you can often easily find solutions simply by "plugging in" values.**

e.g.   If $2m + 5n = 10$ and $m \neq 0$, then what is the value of $\dfrac{4m}{10 - 5n}$?

Answer: You can "guess and check" a solution to the equation pretty easily. Notice that $m = -5$, $n = 4$ works. If you plug these values into the expression you're evaluating, you'll see it simplifies to 2.

Concept Review 2: Systems

1. What is a system?

2. What are two algebraic methods for solving systems?

3. How do you check the solution of a system?

Solve the following systems by substitution, and check your solution.

4. $3x - 4y = 2$
   $x = y - 2$

5. $x^2 - 2y = 10$
   $y = 3x - 9$

6. $5m + 5 = 3n$
   $m = \dfrac{2}{5}n$

Solve the following systems by combination, and check your solution.

7. $a - b = 5$
   $a + b = 12$

8. $-3x - 5y = 20$
   $-3x - 4y = 14$

9. $\dfrac{x}{3} - \dfrac{y}{3} = -9$
   $\dfrac{x}{4} + \dfrac{y}{3} = 2$

Give three different solutions to each of the following "letter-heavy" systems.

10. $2x + 5y = 40$

    $x =$ _____ $y =$ _____

    $x =$ _____ $y =$ _____

    $x =$ _____ $y =$ _____

11. $-2a + 5b + c = 10$
    $a + b = 7$

    $a =$ _____ $b =$ _____ $c =$ _____

    $a =$ _____ $b =$ _____ $c =$ _____

    $a =$ _____ $b =$ _____ $c =$ _____

SAT I Practice 2: Systems

1 If $3x + 2y = 72$ and $y = 3x$, then $x =$

(A) 6
(B) 7
(C) 8
(D) 9
(E) 10

2 The difference of two numbers is 4 and their sum is −7. What is their product?

(A) −33.0
(B) −28.0
(C) −10.25
(D) 8.25
(E) 10.5

3 If $4m - 7n = 10$ and $2m + 2n = 4$, what is the value of $2m - 9n$?

4 If $9p = 3a + 1$ and $7p = 2a - 3$, then which of the following expresses p in terms of a?

(A) $\dfrac{3a+1}{7}$ (B) $\dfrac{2a-3}{9}$ (C) $\dfrac{2a}{63}$

(D) $\dfrac{7a}{9}$ (E) $\dfrac{a+4}{2}$

5 The cost of one hamburger and two large sodas is $5.40. The cost of three hamburgers and one large soda is $8.70. What is the cost of one hamburger?

(A) $1.50 (B) $1.95 (C) $2.40
(D) $2.50 (E) $2.75

6 If $m^6 = \dfrac{3}{y}$ and $m^5 = \dfrac{y^2}{6}$, then which of the following expresses m in terms of y?

(A) $\dfrac{18}{y^3}$

(B) $\dfrac{y^3}{18}$

(C) $\dfrac{y}{2}$

(D) $\dfrac{2}{y}$

(E) $\dfrac{18 - y^3}{6y}$

7 The sum of two numbers is 5 and their difference is 2. Which of the following could be the difference of their squares?

(A) −17
(B) −3
(C) 3
(D) 10
(E) 21

8 If $7x + 2y - 6z = 12$, and if x, y, and z are positive, then what is the value of $\dfrac{2+z}{7x+2y}$?

(A) 1/12
(B) 1/6
(C) 1/4
(D) 5/12
(E) 7/12

9 If $\dfrac{a}{2b} = \dfrac{3}{5}$ and $\dfrac{4b}{3c} = \dfrac{1}{7}$, then $\dfrac{a}{c} =$

(A) $\dfrac{2}{35}$ (B) $\dfrac{9}{70}$ (C) $\dfrac{8}{35}$

(D) $\dfrac{17}{70}$ (E) $\dfrac{9}{35}$

Answer Key 2: Systems

Concept Review 2

1. Any set of equations that are true at the same time.

2. Substitution and combination.

3. Plug the solutions back into the equations and check that both equations are true.

4. $(-10, -8)$
Substitute:	$3(y - 2) - 4y = 2$
Distribute:	$3y - 6 - 4y = 2$
Combine:	$-y - 6 = 2$
Add 6:	$-y = 8$
Multiply by -1:	$y = -8$

   Plug in and solve for x: $x = y - 2 = (-8) - 2 = -10$

5. $(4, 3)$ and $(2, -3)$
Substitute:	$x^2 - 2(3x - 9) = 10$
Distribute:	$x^2 - 6x + 18 = 10$
Subtract 10:	$x^2 - 6x + 8 = 0$
Factor:	$(x - 4)(x - 2) = 0$

   (Look over Lesson 5 if that step was tough!)
   Zero Product Property: $x = 4$ or $x = 2$

   Plug in and solve for y: $y = 3x - 9 = 3(4) - 9 = 3$
   or $= 3(2) - 9 = -3$

   So the solutions are $x = 4$ and $y = 3$ or
   $x = 2$ and $y = -3$.

6. $(2, 5)$
Substitute:	$5\left(\dfrac{2}{5}n\right) + 5 = 3n$
Simplify:	$2n + 5 = 3n$
Subtract $2n$:	$5 = n$

   Plug in to find m: $m = \dfrac{2}{5}(5) = 2$

7. $(8.5, 3.5)$
   $$\begin{array}{r} a - b = \ 5 \\ +a + b = 12 \\ \hline 2a = 17 \end{array}$$
Add the equations:	$2a = 17$
Divide by 2:	$a = 8.5$
Plug in to find b:	$(8.5) - b = 5$
Subtract 8.5:	$-b = -3.5$
Multiply by -1:	$b = 3.5$

8. $(10/3, -6)$
   $$\begin{array}{r} -3x - 5y = 20 \\ -(-3x - 4y = 14) \\ \hline -y = 6 \end{array}$$
Subtract the equations:	$-y = 6$
Multiply by -1:	$y = -6$
Plug in to find x:	$-3x - 5(-6) = 20$
Simplify:	$-3x + 30 = 20$
Subtract 30:	$-3x = -10$
Divide by -3:	$x = 10/3$

9. $(-12, 15)$ Add the equations to get $\dfrac{x}{3} + \dfrac{x}{4} = -7$
Combine fractions:	$\dfrac{7x}{12} = -7$
Multiply by 12:	$7x = -84$
Divide by 7:	$x = -12$
Plug in and solve for y:	$y = 15$

10. There are many solutions. Here are a few:
    $(0, 8)$; $(20, 0)$; $(10, 4)$; $(5, 6)$

11. There are many solutions. Here are a few:
    $(1, 6, 0)$; $(3, 4, -4)$; $(2, 5, 31)$; $(7, 0, 24)$

SAT I Practice 2

1. **C**
Substitute:	$3x + 2(3x) = 72$
Simplify:	$9x = 72$
Divide by 9:	$x = 8$

2. **D** Translate into equations:
   $$\begin{array}{r} x - y = \ 4 \\ x + y = -7 \\ \hline 2x = -3 \end{array}$$
Add the equations:	$2x = -3$
Divide by 2:	$x = -1.5$
Substitute:	$-1.5 + y = -7$
Add 1.5:	$y = -5.5$

   $(-1.5)(-5.5) = 8.25$

3. **6** Subtract them: $2m - 9n = (4m - 7n)$
   $- (2m + 2n)$
   $= 10 - 4 = 6$

4. **E** Subtracting gives $2p = a + 4$
   Divide by 2: $p = (a + 4)/2$

5. **C** Translate:
   $$\begin{array}{r} h + 2s = \ 5.40 \\ 3h + s = \ 8.70 \end{array}$$
Multiply 2nd eq. by 2:	$6h + 2s = 17.40$
	$-(h + 2s = \ 5.40)$
Subtract 1st equation:	$5h = 12.00$
Divide by 5:	$h = 2.40$

6. **A** Divide the first equation by the second:

   $$\frac{m^6}{m^5} = \frac{3}{y} \div \frac{y^2}{6}$$

   Simplify: $m = \dfrac{3}{y} \times \dfrac{6}{y^2} = \dfrac{18}{y^3}$

7. **D** Translate: $x + y = 5$ and $x - y = 2$

   Although you could solve this system by combining, it's easier to remember the "difference of squares" factoring formula:
   $x^2 - y^2 = (x + y)(x - y) = (5)(2) = 10$

8. **B** This is "letter-heavy," so you can guess and check a solution, like (2, 11, 4), and evaluate the expression: $\dfrac{2+(4)}{7(2)+2(11)} = \dfrac{6}{36} = \dfrac{1}{6}$. Or you can also just add $6z$ to both sides of the equation to get $7x + 2y = 12 + 6z$, then substitute:

$$\frac{2+z}{7x+2y} = \frac{2+z}{(12+6z)} = \frac{2+z}{6(2+z)} = \frac{1}{6}$$

9. **B** Multiply the equations:

$$\left(\frac{a}{2b}\right)\left(\frac{4b}{3c}\right) = \frac{2a}{3c} = \left(\frac{3}{5}\right)\left(\frac{1}{7}\right) = \frac{3}{35}$$

Multiply by $\dfrac{3}{2}$: $\quad \dfrac{a}{c} = \dfrac{3}{35}\left(\dfrac{3}{2}\right) = \dfrac{9}{70}$

Lesson 3:
Working with Exponentials

What Are Exponentials?

An **exponential** is simply any term with these three parts:

Coefficient — $4x^3$ — Exponent

Base

❏ **If a term seems not to have a coefficient or exponent, the coefficient or exponent is always assumed to be 1!**

e.g. $2x$ means $2x^1$ y^3 means $1y^3$

Expand to Understand

❏ Good students memorize the rules for working with exponentials, but **great students understand where the rules come from. They come from applying simple arithmetic to their "expanded" forms.**

e.g.   What is $(x^5)^2$ in simplest terms? Do you *add* exponents to get x^7? *Multiply* to get x^{10}? *Power* to get x^{25}?

The answer is clear when you expand the exponential. Just remember that *raising to the nth power* simply means *multiplying by itself* n times. So $(x^5)^2 = (x^5)(x^5) = (x·x·x·x·x)(x·x·x·x·x) = x^{10}$. Doing this helps you to **see and understand** the rule of "multiplying the powers."

Adding and Subtracting Exponentials

❏ **When adding or subtracting exponentials, you can combine only like terms, that is, terms with the same base and the same exponent.** When adding or subtracting like exponentials, remember to leave the bases and exponents alone.

e.g. $5x^3 + 6x^3 + 4x^2 = (5x^3 + 6x^3) + 4x^2 = x^3(5 + 6) + 4x^2 = 11x^3 + 4x^2$

Notice that combining like terms always involves the Law of Distribution (Chapter 10 Lesson 2).

Multiplying and Dividing Exponentials

You can simplify a **product** or **quotient** of exponentials when the bases are the same or the exponents are the same.

If the bases are the same, add the exponents (when multiplying) or subtract the exponents (when dividing) and leave the bases alone.

$$(5m^5)(12m^2) = (5)(m)(m)(m)(m)(m)(12)(m)(m)$$
$$= (5)(12)(m)(m)(m)(m)(m)(m)(m)$$
$$= 60m^7$$

$$\frac{6p^7}{3p^4} = \frac{6(p)(p)(p)(p)(p)(p)(p)}{3(p)(p)(p)(p)} = 2p^3$$

❏ **If the exponents are the same, multiply (or divide) the bases and leave the exponents alone.**

e.g. $$(3m^4)(7n^4) = (3)(m)(m)(m)(m)(7)(n)(n)(n)(n)$$
$$= (3)(7)(mn)(mn)(mn)(mn)$$
$$= 21(mn)^4$$

$$\frac{5(12)^5}{(3)^5} = \frac{5(12)(12)(12)(12)(12)}{(3)(3)(3)(3)(3)}$$

$$= 5\left(\frac{12}{3}\right)\left(\frac{12}{3}\right)\left(\frac{12}{3}\right)\left(\frac{12}{3}\right)\left(\frac{12}{3}\right)$$

$$= 5(4)^5$$

Raising Exponentials to Powers

❏ **When raising an exponential to a power, multiply the exponents, but don't forget to raise the coefficient to the power and leave the base alone.**

e.g. $$(3y^4)^3 = (3y^4)(3y^4)(3y^4)$$
$$= (3y·y·y·y)(3y·y·y·y)(3y·y·y·y)$$
$$= (3)(3)(3)(y·y·y·y)(y·y·y·y)(y·y·y·y)$$
$$= 27y^{12}$$

Concept Review 3: Working with Exponentials

1. The three parts of an exponential are the _____, _____, and _____.

2. When multiplying two exponentials *with the same base*, you should _____ the coefficients, _____ the bases, and _____ the exponents.

3. When dividing two exponentials *with the same exponent*, you should _____ the coefficients, _____ the bases, and _____ the exponents.

4. When multiplying two exponentials *with the same exponent*, you should _____ the coefficients, _____ the bases, and _____ the exponents.

5. When dividing two exponentials *with the same base*, you should _____ the coefficients, _____ the bases, and _____ the exponents.

6. To raise an exponential to a power, you should _____ the coefficient, _____ the base, and _____ the exponents.

Complete the tables:

	coefficient	base	exponent
7. -4^x			
9. xy^{-4}			

	coefficient	base	exponent
8. $(xy)^{-4}$			
10. $(3x)^9$			

Simplify, if possible.

11. $x^2y - 9x^2y =$ _____

12. $4x^3 + 2x^5 + 2x^3 =$ _____

13. $[(2)^{85} + (3)^{85}] + [(2)^{85} - (3)^{85}] =$ _____

14. $(3)^{2y}(5)^{2y} =$ _____

15. $6(29)^{32} \div 2(29)^{12} =$ _____

16. $18(6x)^m \div 9(2x)^m =$ _____

17. $(2x)^{m+1}(2x^2)^m =$ _____

18. $(3x^3(8)^2)^3 =$ _____

19. $(x^3 + y^5)^2 =$ _____

SAT I Practice 3: Working with Exponentials

1 If $g = -4.1$, then $\dfrac{-3g^2}{(-3g)^2} =$

(A) -1

(B) $-\dfrac{1}{3}$

(C) $-\dfrac{1}{9}$

(D) $\dfrac{1}{3}$

(E) 1

2 If $(200)(4{,}000) = 8 \times 10^m$, then $m =$

(A) 2
(B) 3
(C) 4
(D) 5
(E) 6

3 If $2a^2 + 3a - 5a^2 = 9$, then $a - a^2 =$

(A) 1
(B) 3
(C) 6
(D) 9
(E) 12

4 If $2^x = 10$, then $2^{2x} =$

(A) 20
(B) 40
(C) 80
(D) 100
(E) 200

5 If $5^x = y$ and x is positive, which of the following equals $5y^2$ in terms of x?

(A) 5^{2x}
(B) 5^{2x+1}
(C) 25^{2x}
(D) 125^{2x}
(E) 125^{2x+1}

6 If $9^x = 25$, then $3^{x-1} =$

7 If $p = \dfrac{3n}{m^3}$, then what is the effect on the value of p when n is multiplied by 4 and m is doubled?

(A) p is unchanged.
(B) p is halved.
(C) p is doubled.
(D) p is multiplied by 4.
(E) p is multiplied by 8.

8 For all real numbers n, $\dfrac{2^n \times 2^n}{2^n \times 2} =$

(A) 2

(B) 2^n

(C) 2^{n-1}

(D) $\dfrac{n^2}{n+1}$

(E) $\dfrac{2n}{n+1}$

9 If m is a positive integer, then which of the following is equivalent to $3^m + 3^m + 3^m$?

(A) 3^{m+1}
(B) 3^{3m}
(C) 3^{3m+1}
(D) 9^m
(E) 9^{3m}

Answer Key 3: Working with Exponentials

Concept Review 3

1. coefficient, base, and exponent

2. *multiply* the coefficients, *keep* the bases, and *add* the exponents.

3. *divide* the coefficients, *divide* the bases, and *keep* the exponents.

4. *multiply* the coefficients, *multiply* the bases, and *keep* the exponents.

5. *divide* the coefficients, *keep* the bases, and *subtract* the exponents.

6. *raise* the coefficient (to the power), *keep* the base, and *multiply* the exponents.

7. -4^x coefficient: -1; base: 4; exponent: x

8. $(xy)^{-4}$ coefficient: 1; base: xy; exponent: -4

9. xy^{-4} coefficient: x; base: y; exponent: -4

10. $(3x)^9$ coefficient: 1; base: $3x$; exponent: 9

11. $x^2y - 9x^2y = -8x^2y$

12. $4x^3 + 2x^5 + 2x^3 = (4x^3 + 2x^3) + 2x^5 = 6x^3 + 2x^5$

13. $[(2)^{85} + (3)^{85}] + [(2)^{85} - (3)^{85}] = 2(2)^{85} = (2)^{86}$

14. $(3)^{2y}(5)^{2y} = (15)^{2y}$

15. $6(29)^{32} \div 2(29)^{12} = (6/2)(29)^{32-12} = 3(29)^{20}$

16. $18(6x)^m \div 9(2x)^m = (18/9)(6x/2x)^m = 2(3)^m$

17. $(2x)^{m+1}(2x^2)^m = (2^{m+1})(x^{m+1})(2^m)(x^{2m}) = (2^{2m+1})(x^{3m+1})$

18. $(3x^3(8)^2)^3 = (3)^3(x^3)^3((8)^2)^3 = 27x^9(8)^6$

19. $(x^3 + y^5)^2 = (x^3 + y^5)(x^3 + y^5) = (x^3)^2 + 2x^3y^5 + (y^5)^2 = x^6 + 2x^3y^5 + y^{10}$

SAT I Practice 3

1. **B** You don't need to plug in $g = -4.1$. Just simplify:

   If $g \neq 0$, $\dfrac{-3g^2}{(-3g)^2} = \dfrac{-3g^2}{9g^2} = -\dfrac{1}{3}$

2. **D** $(200)(4,000) = 800,000 = 8 \times 10^5$

3. **B**

	$2a^2 + 3a - 5a^2 = 9$
Regroup:	$3a + (2a^2 - 5a^2) = 9$
Simplify:	$3a - 3a^2 = 9$
Factor:	$3(a - a^2) = 9$
Divide by 3:	$a - a^2 = 3$

4. **D**

	$2^x = 10$
Square both sides:	$(2^x)^2 = 10^2$
Simplify:	$2^{2x} = 100$

5. **B**

	$5^x = y$
Square both sides:	$(5^x)^2 = y^2$
Simplify:	$5^{2x} = y^2$
Multiply by 5:	$5(5^{2x}) = 5y^2$
"Missing" exponents = 1:	$5^1(5^{2x}) = 5y^2$
Simplify:	$5^{2x+1} = 5y^2$

6. 5/3 or 1.66 or 1.67

	$9^x = 25$
Take square root:	$\sqrt{9^x} = \sqrt{9}^x = \sqrt{25}$
Simplify:	$3^x = 5$
Divide by 3:	$3^x \div 3^1 = 5/3$
Simplify:	$3^{x-1} = 5/3 = 1.66$

7. **B** Begin by assuming $n = m = 1$.

   Then $p = \dfrac{3n}{m^3} = \dfrac{3(1)}{(1)^3} = 3$

   If n is multiplied by 4 and m is doubled, then

   $n = 4$ and $m = 2$, so $p = \dfrac{3n}{m^3} = \dfrac{3(4)}{(2)^3} = \dfrac{12}{8} = \dfrac{3}{2}$,

   which is half of the original value.

8. **C** (Remember that $2^n \times 2^n$ equals 2^{2n}, or 4^n, but **not** 4^{2n}!)

   $$\dfrac{2^n \times 2^n}{2^n \times 2}$$

   Cancel common factor 2^n: $\dfrac{2^n}{2}$

   Simplify: 2^{n-1}

9. **A** $3^m + 3^m + 3^m = 3(3^m) = 3^1(3^m) = 3^{m+1}$

Lesson 4: Working with Roots

What Are Roots?

The Latin word *radix* means *root* (remember that *radishes* grow underground), so the word *radical* means *the root of a number* (or *a person who seeks to change a system "from the roots up"*). What does the root of a plant have to do with the root of a number?

Think of a square with an area of 9 square units sitting on the ground:

The bottom of the square is "rooted" to the ground, and it has a length of 3. So we say that 3 is the *square root* of 9!

❑ **The square root of a number is what you must square to get the number.**

All positive numbers have two square roots. For instance, the square roots of 9 are 3 and –3.

The radical symbol, $\sqrt{}$, however, means only the **non-negative** square root. So although the square root of 9 equals either 3 or –3, $\sqrt{9}$ equals only 3.

The number inside a radical is called a **radicand**.

e.g.   If x^2 is equal to 9 or 16, then what is the least possible value of x^3?

x is the square root of 9 or 16, so it could be –3, 3, –4, or 4. Therefore, x^3 could be –27, 27, –64, or 64. The least of these, of course, is –64.

❑ Remember that $\sqrt{x^2}$ does not always equal x. It does, however, always equal $|x|$.

e.g.   Simplify $\sqrt{\left(\dfrac{3x+1}{y}\right)^2}$.

Don't worry about squaring first, just remember the rule above. It simplifies to $\left|\dfrac{3x+1}{y}\right|$.

Working with Roots

❑ Memorize the first nine **perfect squares:** 4, 9, 16, 25, 36, 49, 64, 81, 100. This will make working with roots easier.

❑ **To simplify a square root expression, factor any perfect squares from the radicand and simplify.**

e.g.   Simplify $3\sqrt{27}$.

$$3\sqrt{27} = 3\sqrt{9 \times 3} = 3\sqrt{9} \times \sqrt{3} = 3 \times 3 \times \sqrt{3} = 9\sqrt{3}$$

Simplify $\sqrt{m^2 + 10m + 25}$.

$$\sqrt{m^2 + 10m + 25} = \sqrt{(m+5)^2} = |m+5|$$

❑ **When adding or subtracting roots, treat them like exponentials: combine only like terms— those with the same radicand.**

e.g.   Simplify $3\sqrt{7} + 5\sqrt{2} + 13\sqrt{7}$.

$$3\sqrt{7} + 5\sqrt{2} + 13\sqrt{7} = \left(3\sqrt{7} + 13\sqrt{7}\right) + 5\sqrt{2} = 16\sqrt{7} + 5\sqrt{2}$$

❑ When multiplying or dividing roots, multiply or divide the **coefficients** and **radicands** separately.

e.g.   Simplify $\dfrac{8\sqrt{6}}{2\sqrt{2}}$.

$$\frac{8\sqrt{6}}{2\sqrt{2}} = \frac{8}{2}\sqrt{\frac{6}{2}} = 4\sqrt{3}$$

Simplify $5\sqrt{3x} \times 2\sqrt{5x^2}$.

$$5\sqrt{3x} \times 2\sqrt{5x^2} = (5 \times 2)\sqrt{3x \times 5x^2} = 10\sqrt{15x^3}$$

❑ You can also use the commutative and associative laws when simplifying expressions with radicals.

e.g.   Simplify $\left(2\sqrt{5}\right)^3$.

$$\left(2\sqrt{5}\right)^3 = 2\sqrt{5} \times 2\sqrt{5} \times 2\sqrt{5} = (2 \times 2 \times 2)\left(\sqrt{5} \times \sqrt{5}\right) \times \sqrt{5}$$

$$= 8 \times 5 \times \sqrt{5} = 40\sqrt{5}$$

Concept Review 4: Working with Roots

1. List the first ten perfect square integers greater than 1: _____

2. How can you tell whether two radicals are "like" terms?

3. An exponential is a perfect square only if its coefficient is _____ and its exponent is _____.

State whether each equation is true (T) or false (F). If it is false, rewrite the expression on the right side to correct it.

4. $2\left(3 \times \sqrt{x}\right) = 6\sqrt{2x}$ _____

5. $3\sqrt{2} + 5\sqrt{8} = 13\sqrt{2}$ _____

6. $\left(\sqrt{3x}\right)^5 = 9x^2\sqrt{3x}$ _____

7. $\sqrt{81x^2} = 9x$ _____

8. If $x^2 = 25$, then $x = $ _____ or _____.

9. If $x^2 = \sqrt{64^4}$ then $x = $ _____.

Simplify the following expressions, if possible.

10. $5\sqrt{7} - 8\sqrt{7} = $ _____

11. $\dfrac{6mn\sqrt{10m}}{3n\sqrt{5}} = $ _____

12. $\left(g\sqrt{5}\right)\left(g\sqrt{5}\right) = $ _____

13. $\left(2\sqrt{3}\right)^3 = $ _____

14. $5\sqrt{12} - 4\sqrt{27} = $ _____

15. $5\sqrt{52} = $ _____

16. $\sqrt{6} + \sqrt{3} = $ _____

17. $\left(3\sqrt{5}\right)\left(7\sqrt{2}\right) = $ _____

18. $\left(1 + \sqrt{2}\right)^2 = $ _____

19. $\dfrac{2\sqrt{2} + 4\sqrt{18}}{\sqrt{2}} = $ _____

SAT I Practice 4: Working with Roots

1

The square root of a certain positive number is twice the number itself. What is the number?

(A) $\dfrac{1}{8}$ (B) $\dfrac{1}{4}$ (C) $\dfrac{3}{8}$

(D) $\dfrac{1}{2}$ (E) 1

2

If $\dfrac{1}{2}x < \sqrt{x} < x$, what is one possible value of x?

3

If $a^2 + 1 = 10$ and $b^2 - 1 = 15$, what is the greatest possible value of $a - b$?

(A) −3   (B) −1   (C) 3
(D) 5   (E) 7

4

If $3y = \sqrt{\dfrac{2}{y}}$ then $y^3 =$

(A) $\dfrac{2}{9}$ (B) $\dfrac{4}{9}$ (C) $\dfrac{2}{3}$

(D) $\dfrac{4}{3}$ (E) 18

5

If $x^2 = 4$, $y^2 = 9$, and $(x - 2)(y + 3) \neq 0$, then $x^3 + y^3 =$

(A) −35   (B) −19   (C) 0
(D) 19   (E) 35

6

If m and n are both positive, then which of the following is equivalent to $\dfrac{2m\sqrt{18n}}{m\sqrt{2}}$?

(A) $3m\sqrt{n}$

(B) $6m\sqrt{n}$

(C) $4\sqrt{n}$

(D) $6\sqrt{n}$

(E) $8\sqrt{n}$

7

A rectangle has sides of length $\sqrt{a}$ cm and $\sqrt{b}$ cm. What is the length of a diagonal of the rectangle?

(A) $\sqrt{a} + \sqrt{b}$ cm

(B) $a + b$ cm

(C) $\sqrt{a + b}$ cm

(D) $\sqrt{a^2 + b^2}$ cm

(E) $\sqrt{ab}$ cm

8

The area of square A is ten times the area of square B. What is the ratio of the perimeter of square A to the perimeter of square B?

(A) $\sqrt{10}:4$ (B) $\sqrt{10}:2$

(C) $\sqrt{10}:1$ (D) $4\sqrt{10}:1$

(E) $40:1$

9

In the figure above, if n is a real number greater than 1, what is the value of x in terms of n?

(A) $\sqrt{n^2 - 1}$

(B) $\sqrt{n - 1}$

(C) $\sqrt{n + 1}$

(D) $n - 1$

(E) $n + 1$

Answer Key 4: Working with Roots

Concept Review 4

1. 4, 9, 16, 25, 36, 49, 64, 81, 100, 121

2. They are "like" if their radicands (what's inside the radical) are the same.

3. An exponential is a perfect square only if its co-efficient is *a perfect square* and its exponent is *even*.

4. False: $2\left(3 \times \sqrt{x}\right) = 2 \times 3 \times \sqrt{x} = 6\sqrt{x}$

5. True: $3\sqrt{2} + 5\sqrt{8} = 3\sqrt{2} + 10\sqrt{2} = 13\sqrt{2}$

6. True: $\left(\sqrt{3x}\right)^5 = \left(\sqrt{3x}\right)^4\left(\sqrt{3x}\right) = 9x^2\sqrt{3x}$

7. False if x is negative: $\sqrt{81x^2} = 9|x|$

8. 5 or –5

9. 64 or –64

10. $5\sqrt{7} - 8\sqrt{7} = -3\sqrt{7}$ (Law of Distribution)

11. $\dfrac{6mn\sqrt{10m}}{3n\sqrt{5}} = 2m\sqrt{2m}$

12. $\left(g\sqrt{5}\right)\left(g\sqrt{5}\right) = 5g^2$

13. $\left(2\sqrt{3}\right)^3 = 24\sqrt{3}$

14. $5\sqrt{12} - 4\sqrt{27} =$
$5\sqrt{4} \times \sqrt{3} - 4\sqrt{9} \times \sqrt{3} = 10\sqrt{3} - 12\sqrt{3} = -2\sqrt{3}$

15. $5\sqrt{52} = 5\sqrt{4} \times \sqrt{13} = 10\sqrt{13}$

16. $\sqrt{6} + \sqrt{3}$ can't be simplified (unlike terms).

17. $\left(3\sqrt{5}\right)\left(7\sqrt{2}\right) = 21\sqrt{10}$

18. $\left(1 + \sqrt{2}\right)^2 = \left(1 + \sqrt{2}\right)\left(1 + \sqrt{2}\right) = 1 + 2\sqrt{2} + 2 = 3 + 2\sqrt{2}$

19. $\dfrac{2\sqrt{2} + 4\sqrt{18}}{\sqrt{2}} = 2 + 4\sqrt{9} = 2 + 4 \times 3 = 2 + 12 = 14$

SAT I Practice 4

1. **B** The square root of ¼ is ½, because (½)² = ¼. Twice ¼ is also ½, because 2(¼) = ½. You can also set it up algebraically: $\sqrt{x} = 2x$

   Square both sides: $x = 4x^2$
   Divide by x (it's okay; x is positive): $1 = 4x$
   Divide by 4: $¼ = x$

2. Any number between 1 and 4 (but not 1 or 4). Guess and check is probably the most efficient method here. Notice that $\sqrt{x} < x$ only if $x > 1$, and $½x < \sqrt{x}$ only if $x < 4$.

3. **E** $a^2 = 9$, so $a = 3$ or –3. $b^2 = 16$, so $b = 4$ or –4. The greatest value of $a - b$, then, is 3 – (–4) = 7.

4. **A** $3y = \sqrt{\dfrac{2}{y}}$

   Square both sides: $9y^2 = \dfrac{2}{y}$
   Multiply by y: $9y^3 = 2$
   Divide by 9: $y^3 = 2/9$

5. **D** If $x^2 = 4$, then $x = 2$ or –2, and if $y^2 = 9$, then $y = 3$ or –3. But if $(x - 2)(y + 3) \neq 0$, then x cannot be 2 and y cannot be –3. Therefore, $x = -2$ and $y = 3$. $(-2)^3 + 3^3 = -8 + 27 = 19$

6. **D** $\dfrac{2m\sqrt{18n}}{m\sqrt{2}} = \left(\dfrac{2m}{m}\right)\sqrt{\dfrac{18n}{2}} = 2\sqrt{9n} = 6\sqrt{n}$

   Also, you can plug in easy positive values for m and n like 1 and 2, evaluate the expression on your calculator, and check it against the choices.

7. **C** The diagonal is the hypotenuse of a right triangle, so we can find its length with the Pythagorean Theorem: $\left(\sqrt{a}\right)^2 + \left(\sqrt{b}\right)^2 = d^2$

   Simplify: $a + b = d^2$
   Take the square root: $\sqrt{a + b} = d$

   Or you can plug in numbers for a and b, like 9 and 16, before you use the Pythagorean Theorem.

8. **C** Assume that the squares have areas of 10 and 1. The lengths of their sides, then, are $\sqrt{10}$ and 1, respectively, and the perimeters are $4\sqrt{10}$ and 4. $4\sqrt{10}:4 = \sqrt{10}:1$

9. **B** Use the Pythagorean Theorem:
   $1^2 + x^2 = \left(\sqrt{n}\right)^2$

   Simplify: $1 + x^2 = n$
   Subtract 1: $x^2 = n - 1$

   Take the square root: $x = \sqrt{n - 1}$ (Or plug in!)

Lesson 5: Factoring

Factoring

❑ **To factor means to write as a product.** All of the terms in a product are called **factors** of the product.

   e.g.   There are many ways to factor 12: 12×1, 6×2, 3×4, or $2 \times 2 \times 3$.

            Therefore, 1, 2, 3, 4, 6, and 12 are the **factors** of 12.

❑ Know how to factor a number into prime factors, and how to use those factors to find greatest common factors and least common multiples.

   e.g.   Two bells, A and B, ring simultaneously, then bell A rings once every 168 seconds and bell B rings every 360 seconds. What is the minimum number of seconds between simultaneous rings?

            This question is asking for the least common multiple of 168 and 360. The prime factorization of 168 is $2 \times 2 \times 2 \times 3 \times 7$ and the prime factorization of 360 is $2 \times 2 \times 2 \times 3 \times 3 \times 5$. A common multiple must have all of the factors that each of these numbers has, and the smallest of these is $2 \times 2 \times 2 \times 3 \times 3 \times 5 \times 7 = 2{,}520$. So they ring together every 2,520 seconds.

❑ **When factoring polynomials, think of "distribution in reverse."** This means that you can check your factoring by distributing, or FOILing the factors to make sure that the result is the original expression. For instance, to factor $3x^2 - 18x$, just think: what common factor must be "distributed" to what other factor to get this expression? Answer: $3x(x - 6)$ (Check by distributing.) To factor $z^2 + 5z - 6$, just think: what two binomials must be multiplied (by FOILing) to get this expression? Answer: $(z - 1)(z + 6)$ (Check by FOILing.)

The Law of FOIL:

$$(a + b)(c + d) = (a)(c + d) + (b)(c + d) \quad \text{(distribution)}$$
$$= ac + ad + bc + bd \quad \text{(distribution)}$$
$$\text{First + Outside + Inside + Last}$$

   e.g.   Factor $3x^2 - 18x$.

            Common factor is $3x$:
$3x^2 - 18x = 3x(x - 6)$ (check by distributing)

            Factor $z^2 + 5z - 6$.

            $z^2 + 5z - 6 = (z - 1)(z + 6)$ (check by FOILing)

Factoring Formulas

❑ **To factor polynomials, it often helps to know some common factoring formulas:**

Difference of Squares: $\quad x^2 - b^2 = (x + b)(x - b)$

Perfect Square Trinomials:
$$x^2 + 2xb + b^2 = (x + b)(x + b)$$
$$x^2 - 2xb + b^2 = (x - b)(x - b)$$

Simple Trinomials: $\quad x^2 + (a + b)x + ab = (x + a)(x + b)$

   e.g.   Factor $x^2 - 36$.

            This is a "difference of squares":
$x^2 - 36 = (x - 6)(x + 6)$.

            Factor $x^2 - 5x - 14$.

            This is a simple trinomial. Look for two numbers that have a sum of -5 and a product of -14. With a little guessing-and-checking, you'll see that -7 and 2 work. So $x^2 - 5x - 14 = (x - 7)(x + 2)$.

The Zero Product Property

❑ **Factoring is a great tool for solving equations if it's used with the Zero Product Property, which says that if the product of a set of numbers is 0, then at least one of the numbers in the set must be 0.**

   e.g.   Solve $x^2 - 5x - 14 = 0$.

            Factor: $(x - 7)(x + 2) = 0$

            Since their product is 0, either $x - 7 = 0$ or $x + 2 = 0$, so $x = 7$ or -2.

❑ **The only product property is the Zero Product Property.**

   e.g. $(x - 1)(x + 2) = 1$ **does not** imply that $x - 1 = 1$. This would mean that $x = 2$, which clearly doesn't work!

Concept Review 5: Factoring

1. What does it mean to factor a number or expression?

   _____

2. Write the four basic factoring formulas for quadratics.   _____

   _____

   _____

   _____

3. What is the Zero Product Property?

   _____

4. Write the prime factorization of 108.   4. _____

5. Find the least common multiple of $21mn$ and $75n^2$.   5. _____

6. Find the greatest common factor of $108x^6$ and $90x^4$.   6. _____

Factor and check by FOILing: FOIL

7. $1 - 49x^4$ _____   10. $\left(y + \sqrt{3}\right)\left(y - \sqrt{3}\right)$ _____

8. $m^2 + 7m + 12$ _____   11. $\left(\dfrac{x}{2} + \dfrac{1}{3}\right)\left(\dfrac{x}{5} + \dfrac{1}{2}\right)$ _____

9. $16x^2 - 40x + 25$ _____   12. $\left(3x - 2\sqrt{5}\right)^2$ _____

Solve by factoring and using the Zero Product Property. (Hint: each equation has two solutions.)

13. $4x^2 = 12x$ $x =$ _____ or _____   14. $x^2 - 8x = 33$ $x =$ _____ or _____

15. If $3xz - 3yz = 60$ and $z = 5$, then $x - y =$

SAT I Practice 5: Factoring

1 Chime A and chime B ring simultaneously at noon. Afterwards, chime A rings every 72 minutes and chime B rings every 54 minutes. What time is it when they next ring simultaneously?

(A)   3:18 pm   (B)   3:24 pm
(C)   3:36 pm   (D)   3:54 pm
(E)   4:16 pm

2 For all real numbers x and y, if $xy = 7$, then $(x - y)^2 - (x + y)^2 =$

(A) y^2 (B)   0   (C) -7
(D) -14 (E) -28

3 If for all real values of x,
$(x + a)(x + 1) = x^2 + 6x + a$, then $a =$

4

In the figure above, if $m \neq n$, what is the slope of the line segment?

(A) $m + n$ (B) $m - n$

(C) $\dfrac{m^2 - m}{n^2 - n}$ (D) $\dfrac{1}{m + n}$

(E) $\dfrac{1}{m - n}$

5 If $a^2 + b^2 = 8$ and $ab = -2$, then $(a + b)^2 =$

(A)   4   (B)   6   (C)   8
(D)   9   (E)   16

6 If $f^2 - g^2 = -10$ and $f + g = 2$, then what is the value of $f - g$?

(A) -20 (B) -12 (C) -8
(D) -5 (E)   0

7 If $x > 0$, then

$$\frac{x^2 - 1}{x + 1} + \frac{(x + 1)^2 - 1}{x + 2} + \frac{(x + 2)^2 - 1}{x + 3} =$$

(A) $(x + 1)^2$
(B) $(x - 1)^2$
(C) $3x - 1$
(D) $3x$
(E) $3(x + 1)^2$

8 If $y = 3p$ and $p \neq 2$, then $\dfrac{y^2 - 36}{(y - 6)^2} =$

(A)   1   (B) $\dfrac{p + 2}{p - 2}$ (C) $\dfrac{3p + 2}{3p - 2}$

(D) $\dfrac{3p + 2}{3p}$ (E) $\dfrac{9p^2 + 36}{9p^2 - 36}$

9 If $n - \dfrac{1}{n} = x$, then what is $n^2 + \dfrac{1}{n^2}$ in terms of x?

(A) $x^2 - 2$
(B) $x^2 - 1$
(C) x^2
(D) $x^2 + 1$
(E) $x^2 + 2$

Answer Key 5: Factoring

Concept Review 5

1. To write it as a product (result of multiplication).

2. $x^2 - b^2 = (x + b)(x - b)$
   $x^2 + 2xb + b^2 = (x + b)(x + b)$
   $x^2 - 2xb + b^2 = (x - b)(x - b)$
   $x^2 + (a + b)x + ab = (x + a)(x + b)$

3. If the product of a set of numbers is 0, then at least one of the numbers must be 0.

4. $108 = (2)(2)(3)(3)(3)$

5. $21mn = (3)(7)(m)(n)$ and $75n^2 = (3)(5)(5)(n)(n)$, so the least common multiple is $(3)(5)(5)(7)(m)(n)(n) = 525mn^2$.

6. $108x^6 = (2)(2)(3)(3)(3)(x)(x)(x)(x)(x)(x)$ and $90x^4 = (2)(3)(3)(5)(x)(x)(x)(x)$, so the greatest common factor is $(2)(3)(x)(x)(x)(x) = 6x^4$.

7. $1 - 49x^4 = (1 - 7x^2)(1 + 7x^2)$

8. $m^2 + 7m + 12 = (m + 4)(m + 3)$

9. $16x^2 - 40x + 25 = (4x - 5)(4x - 5) = (4x - 5)^2$

10. $\left(y + \sqrt{3}\right)\left(y - \sqrt{3}\right) = y^2 - y\sqrt{3} + y\sqrt{3} - \sqrt{3}^2 = y^2 - 3$

11. $\left(\dfrac{x}{2} + \dfrac{1}{3}\right)\left(\dfrac{x}{5} + \dfrac{1}{2}\right) = \left(\dfrac{x}{2}\right)\left(\dfrac{x}{5}\right) + \left(\dfrac{x}{2}\right)\left(\dfrac{1}{2}\right)$
    $\qquad + \left(\dfrac{1}{3}\right)\left(\dfrac{x}{5}\right) + \left(\dfrac{1}{3}\right)\left(\dfrac{1}{2}\right)$
    $= \dfrac{x^2}{10} + \dfrac{x}{4} + \dfrac{x}{15} + \dfrac{1}{6}$
    $= \dfrac{x^2}{10} + \dfrac{19x}{60} + \dfrac{1}{6}$

12. $\left(3x - 2\sqrt{5}\right)^2 =$
    $(3x)(3x) - (3x)\left(2\sqrt{5}\right) - (3x)\left(2\sqrt{5}\right) + \left(2\sqrt{5}\right)\left(2\sqrt{5}\right)$
    $= 9x^2 - 12x\sqrt{5} + 20$

13.
	$4x^2 = 12x$
Subtract 12x:	$4x^2 - 12x = 0$
Factor:	$4x(x - 3) = 0$
Use zero product property:	$x = 0$ or 12

14.
	$x^2 - 8x = 33$
Subtract 33:	$x^2 - 8x - 33 = 0$
Factor:	$(x - 11)(x + 3) = 0$
Use zero product property:	$x = 11$ or -3

15.
	$3xz - 3yz = 60$
Factor:	$3z(x - y) = 60$
Substitute $z = 5$:	$15(x - y) = 60$
Divide by 15:	$(x - y) = 4$

SAT I Practice 5

1. **C** $72 = (2)(2)(2)(3)(3)$ and $54 = (2)(3)(3)(3)$, so the least common multiple is $(2)(2)(2)(3)(3)(3) = 216$. 216 minutes is 3 hours 36 minutes.

2. **E** You can solve this one simply by plugging in $x = 7$ and $y = 1$ and evaluating $(7 - 1)^2 - (7 + 1)^2 = 36 - 64 = -28$. Or you could do the algebra: $(x - y)^2 - (x + y)^2$
FOIL:	$(x^2 - 2xy + y^2) - (x^2 + 2xy + y^2)$
Simplify:	$-4xy$
Substitute $xy = 7$:	$-4(7) = -28$

3. **5**
	$(x + a)(x + 1) = x^2 + 6x + a$
FOIL:	$x^2 + x + ax + a = x^2 + 6x + a$
Subtract x^2 and a:	$x + ax = 6x$
Factor:	$x(1 + a) = 6x$
Divide by x:	$1 + a = 6$
Subtract 1:	$a = 5$

4. **A** The slope is "the rise over the run," which is the difference of the y's divided by the difference of the x's:

$$\frac{m^2 - n^2}{m - n} = \frac{(m + n)(m - n)}{(m - n)} = m + n$$

Or you can just choose values for m and n, like 2 and 1, and evaluate the slope numerically. The slope between $(1, 1)$ and $(2, 4)$ is 3, and the expression in (A) is the only one that gives a value of 3.

5. **A** $(a + b)^2 = (a + b)(a + b) = a^2 + 2ab + b^2$
Commute:	$= a^2 + b^2 + 2ab$
Substitute $ab = -2$	
and $a^2 + b^2 = 8$:	$= (8) + 2(-2)$
	$= 4$

6. **D** Factor: $f^2 - g^2 = (f + g)(f - g)$
Substitute $f^2 - g^2 = -10$	
and $f + g = 2$:	$-10 = 2(f - g)$
Divide by 2:	$-5 = f - g$

7. **D** Plugging in $x = 1$ gives you $0 + 1 + 2 = 3$, and (D) is the only choice that yields 3. Or:

$$\frac{x^2 - 1}{x + 1} + \frac{(x+1)^2 - 1}{x + 2} + \frac{(x+2)^2 - 1}{x + 3}$$

$$= \frac{\cancel{(x+1)}(x-1)}{\cancel{x+1}} + \frac{(x+1+1)(x+1-1)}{\cancel{x+2}}$$

$$+ \frac{(x+2+1)(x+2-1)}{\cancel{x+3}}$$

$$= (x-1) + (x) + (x+1) = 3x$$

8. **B** $\dfrac{y^2 - 36}{(y-6)^2} = \dfrac{(y-6)(y+6)}{(y-6)(y-6)} = \dfrac{(y+6)}{(y-6)}$

Substitute $y = 3p$: $\dfrac{(3p+6)}{(3p-6)} = \dfrac{3(p+2)}{3(p-2)} = \dfrac{p+2}{p-2}$

9. **E** $\qquad n - \dfrac{1}{n} = x$

Square both sides:

$$\left(n - \frac{1}{n}\right)^2 = n^2 - 2 + \frac{1}{n^2} = (x)^2$$

Add 2: $\qquad n^2 + \dfrac{1}{n^2} = x^2 + 2$

Lesson 6:
Inequalities, Absolute Values,
and Plugging In

Inequalities as Unbalanced Scales

❑ Inequalities are just unbalanced scales. Nearly all of the laws of equality pertain to inequalities, with one exception. **When solving inequalities, keep the direction of the inequality (remember that "the alligator < always eats the bigger number") unless you divide or multiply by a negative, in which case you "switch" the inequality.**

e.g.   Solve $x^2 > 6x$ for x.

You might be tempted to divide both sides by x and get $x > 6$, but this incorrectly assumes that x is positive. **If x is positive, then $x > 6$, but if x is negative, then $x < 6$. (Switch the inequality when you divide by a negative!) But of course **any** negative number is less than 6, so the solution is either $x > 6$ or $x < 0$. (Plug in numbers to verify!)

Absolute Values as Distances

❑ The **absolute value of x,** written as $|x|$, means the **distance from x to 0 on the number line.** Since distances are never negative, neither are absolute values. For instance, since –4 is four units away from 0, we say $|-4| = 4$.

❑ The **distance** between numbers is found from their **difference.** For instance, the distance between 5 and –2 on the number line is $5 - (-2) = 7$. But differences can be negative, and distances can't! That's where absolute values come in. Mathematically, **the distance between a and b is $|a - b|$.**

e.g.   Graph the solution of $|x + 2| \geq 3$.

You can think about this in two ways. First think about distances. $|x + 2|$ is the same as $|x - (-2)|$, which is the distance between x and –2. So if this distance must be greater than or equal to 3, you can just visualize those numbers that are at least 3 units away from –2:

Or you can do it more "algebraically" if you prefer. The only numbers that have an absolute value greater than or equal to 3 are numbers greater than or equal to 3 or less than or equal to –3, right? Therefore, saying $|x + 2| \geq 3$ is the same as saying $x + 2 \geq 3$ or $x + 2 \leq -3$. Subtracting 2 from both sides of both inequalities gives $x \geq 1$ or $x \leq -5$, which confirms the answer by the other method.

Plugging In

After solving each of the examples above, you should, as with all equations and inequalities, **plug in** your solution to confirm that it works in the equation or inequality. But plugging in can also be a good way of solving multiple-choice problems that ask you to find an expression with variables rather than a numerical solution.

❑ **If a multiple-choice question has choices that contain unknowns, you can often simplify the problem by just plugging in values for the unknowns.** But **think** first: in some situations, plugging in is not the simplest method.

e.g.   If $y = r - 6$ and $z = r + 5$, which of the following expresses r in terms of y and z?

(A) $y + z - 1$

(B) $y + z$

(C) $y + z + 1$

(D) $\dfrac{y + z - 1}{2}$

(E) $\dfrac{y + z + 1}{2}$

If you pick r to be 6—it can be whatever you want, so pick an easy number!—then y is $6 - 6 = 0$ and z is $6 + 5 = 11$. The question is asking for an expression for r, so look for 6 among the choices. Plugging in your values gives (A) 10 (B) 11 (C) 12 (D) 5 (E) 6. Always evaluate **all** of the choices, because you must work by **process of elimination.** Only (E) gives 6, so it must be the right answer!

Concept Review 6: Inequalities, Absolute Values, and Plugging In

Express each of the following statements as equations or inequalities using absolute values:

1. The distance from y to 3 is less than 5.   _____

2. The distance from a to 2 is equal to the distance from b to -2.   _____

3. The distance from x to -1 is no greater than 10.   _____

4. The distance from a to b is no more than twice the distance from a to c.   _____

Graph the solution to each of the following inequalities on the given number line. Check your answer by testing points.

5. $|x - 3| < 2$

6. $y^2 \geq 4$

7. $6x > 2x^2$

8. $-3x \geq 12$

9. $5 - x^2 < 5$

10. $x + 3 < x - 1$

Solve the following problem by plugging in, then see if you can solve it "algebraically."

11. If $a = 2b - c$ and $5b = a + 1$, then which of the following expressions is equivalent to a?

   (A) $3b + c - 1$ (B) $3b - c + 1$ (C) $\dfrac{7b - c + 1}{2}$ (D) $\dfrac{7b - c - 1}{2}$ (E) $\dfrac{7b + c - 1}{2}$

SAT I Practice 6: Inequalities, Absolute Values, and Plugging In

1 If $2 - 4x < 20$, then which of the following could NOT be the value of x?

(A) -5 (B) -4 (C) -3
(D) -2 (E) -1

2 If $x < 0$, $xy > 0$, and $xyz > 0$, then which of the following expressions must be positive?

(A) x^2yz (B) xy^2z (C) xyz^2
(D) xy^2 (E) xz^2

3 Which of the following is equivalent to the statement $|x - 2| < 1$?

(A) $x < 3$ (B) $x < -1$
(C) $1 < x < 3$ (D) $-1 < x < 3$
(E) $-3 < x < -1$

4 If $|m| > -2$, then which of the following represents all possible values of m?

(A) $m > -2$ (B) $m > 2$
(C) $m > 2$ or $m < -2$ (D) $-2 < m < 2$
(E) all real numbers

5 If $r = 5w = 7a$ and $r \neq 0$, then what is the value of $r - w$ in terms of a?

(A) $28a$ (B) $\dfrac{28a}{5}$ (C) $3a$

(D) $\dfrac{7a}{5}$ (E) $\dfrac{a}{7}$

6 If x is the average (arithmetic mean) of k and 10 and y is the average (arithmetic mean) of k and 4, what is the average of x and y, in terms of k?

(A) $\dfrac{k+14}{4}$ (B) $\dfrac{k+14}{2}$

(C) $\dfrac{k+7}{2}$ (D) $7k$ (E) $14k$

7 If $m = 2x - 5$ and $n = x + 7$, which of the following expresses x in terms of m and n?

(A) $m - n + 2$ (B) $m - n + 12$

(C) $2(m - n + 12)$ (D) $\dfrac{m - n + 2}{2}$

(E) $\dfrac{m - n + 12}{2}$

8 What is the only integer n such that $20 - 2n > 5$ and $\dfrac{2n}{3} > 4$?

9 If $b = 2a - 4$ and $c = a + 2$, then which of the following expresses a in terms of b and c?

    I. $b - c + 6$

   II. $\dfrac{b + c + 2}{3}$

  III. $2c - b - 8$

(A) I only   (B) II only
(C) I and II only   (D) I and III only
(E) I, II, and III

10 Which of the following is equivalent to the statement "The distance from 1 to x is greater than the distance from 3 to x?"

    I. $|x - 1| > |x - 3|$
   II. $x > 3$ or $x < 1$
  III. $x > 2$

(A) I only   (B) I and II only
(C) II and III only   (D) I and III only
(E) I, II, and III

Answer Key 6: Inequalities, Absolute Values, and Plugging In

Concept Review 6

1. $|y - 3| < 5$

2. $|a - 2| = |b + 2|$

3. $|x + 1| \le 10$

4. $|a - b| \le 2|a - c|$

5. $|x - 3| < 2$

6.
$$y^2 \ge 4$$
Take the square root: $\quad |y| \ge 2$
Interpret without absolute value: $y \le -2$ or $y \ge 2$
Graph:

$$-4 \;\; -3 \;\; -2 \;\; -1 \;\;\; 0 \;\;\; 1 \;\;\; 2 \;\;\; 3 \;\;\; 4$$

7.
$$6x > 2x^2$$
Divide by x with conditions: if $x > 0$, then $6 > 2x$
  if $x < 0$, then $6 < 2x$
Simplify: if $x > 0$, then $3 > x$, so $0 < x < 3$
  if $x < 0$, then $3 < x$ (no solution)
Graph:
$$-4 \;\; -3 \;\; -2 \;\; -1 \;\;\; 0 \;\;\; 1 \;\;\; 2 \;\;\; 3 \;\;\; 4$$

8.
$$-3x \ge 12$$
Divide by -3: $\quad x \le -4$
Graph:
$$-8 \;\; -7 \;\; -6 \;\; -5 \;\; -4 \;\; -3 \;\; -2 \;\; -1 \;\;\; 0$$

9.
$$5 - x^2 < 5$$
Subtract 5: $\quad -x^2 < 0$
Multiply by -1 (and "switch"): $\quad x^2 > 0$
Take the square root: $\quad |x| > 0$
Interpret: $\quad x > 0$ or $x < 0$
Graph:
$$-4 \;\; -3 \;\; -2 \;\; -1 \;\;\; 0 \;\;\; 1 \;\;\; 2 \;\;\; 3 \;\;\; 4$$

10.
$$x + 3 < x - 1$$
Subtract x: $\quad 3 < -1$
But this is impossible, so there's no solution!

11. **(D)** If you plug in $a = 4$, then $b = 1$ and $c = -2$. Since you're looking for an expression that equals a, plug these in to the choices and see which one gives $a = 4$:

(A) $3(1) + (-2) - 1 = 0$ (B) $3(1) - (-2) + 1 = 6$

(C) $(7(1) - (-2) + 1)/2 = 5$ (D) $(7(1) - (-2) - 1)/2 = 4$

(E) $(7(1) + (-2) - 1)/2 = 2$

Since (D) is the only choice that gives 4, it is the right choice. To solve it algebraically, solve each equation for a:

$$a = 2b - c$$
$$\underline{a = 5b - 1}$$
Add the equations: $\quad 2a = 7b - c - 1$
Divide by 2: $\quad a = (7b - c - 1)/2$

SAT I Practice 6

1. **A** $2 - 4(-5) = 2 + 20 = 22$, which is not less than 20.

2. **C** To satisfy the inequalities, x must be negative, y must be negative, and z must be positive. You might choose $x = -1$, $y = -1$, and $z = 1$ to confirm that (C) is the only one that gives a positive value.

3. **C**
$$|x - 2| < 1$$
Translate without absolute value: $\quad -1 < x - 2 < 1$
Add 2: $\quad 1 < x < 3$

4. **E** All absolute values are greater than or equal to zero, so any value of m would satisfy $|m| > -2$.

5. **B** You can solve by plugging in for the unknowns, but be careful to choose values that work in the equation. The simplest values that work are $r = 35$, $w = 7$, and $a = 5$. In this case, $r - w = 35 - 7 = 28$. If you plug $a = 5$ into the choices, (B) is the only one that equals 28.

Or you can solve algebraically by expressing r and w in terms of a. $r = 7a$ and $w = \dfrac{7}{5}a$, so

$$r - w = 7a - \frac{7}{5}a = \frac{35}{5}a - \frac{7}{5}a = \frac{28a}{5}.$$

6. **C** You might plug in $k = 2$. Since x is the average of k and 10, $x = (2 + 10)/2 = 6$. Since y is the average of k and 4, $y = (2 + 4)/2 = 3$. The average of x and y, then, is $(6 + 3)/2 = 4.5$. If you then plug $k = 2$ into the choices, (C) is the only choice that equals 4.5.

7. **B**   Plug in $x = 3$. Then $m = 2(3) - 5 = 1$ and $n = (3) + 7 = 10$. The question asks for an expression that equals x, so look for 3 in the choices when you plug in $m = 1$ and $n = 10$. The only choice that gives you 3 is (B).

8. **7** $20 - 2n > 5$
   Subtract 20: $-2n > -15$
   Divide by -2: $n < 7.5$ (Don't forget the switch!)

The greatest integer n could be, then, is 7. Notice that 7 also satisfies the other inequality: $2(7)/3 = 4.666$, which of course is greater than 4.

9. **C**   Plugging in isn't good enough here, because more than one expression may be correct. The best method is substitution, using $b = 2a - 4$ and $c = a + 2$:

$$\text{I.} \quad b - c + 6 = (2a - 4) - (a + 2) + 6 = a \ (\text{Yes!})$$

$$\text{II.} \quad \frac{b + c + 2}{3} = \frac{(2a - 4) + (a + 2) + 2}{3} = \frac{3a}{3} = a$$
(Yes!)

$$\text{III.} \quad 2c - b - 8 = 2(a + 2) - (2a - 4) - 8 = 0$$
(No.)

10. **D**   The distance from 1 to x is $|x - 1|$ and the distance from 3 to x is $|x - 3|$, so I is clearly correct. To see why III is true, notice that 2 is the only number equidistant from 1 and 3, so all numbers that are farther from 1 than from 3 are greater than 2.

Lesson 7: Word Problems

A Word about Word Problems

Don't be afraid of word problems. The more words a problem has, the more information it provides to help you solve the problem. The key is simply to translate the words into mathematical expressions.

Algebraic Word Problems

Most word problems, are **algebraic word problems,** that is, problems that can be translated into an algebraic equation or system. As with all interesting problems, MAPS-CATCH helps you to solve them.

❑ **MAP** the problem: Read the entire problem carefully and think about the situation before you decide how to start. Try to "see" the whole problem situation in your mind. Understand what every quantity means. Note carefully what the question is asking you to find.

❑ **ANALYZE** the problem: Look at the parts of the problem, especially the unknowns. Give each unknown a convenient name, like x, n, or some other letter.

❑ Find the **PATTERNS** in the problem: Think carefully about the relationships among the quantities. Write an equation or inequality for each important statement in the problem. Remember: if you have one unknown, one equation will do, but if you have two unknowns, you need two equations. The following translation key can help you to set up the equation.

percent	means	$\div 100$		*is*	means	$=$		*decreased by*	means	$-$
of	means	*times*		*per*	means	$\div$		*is at least*	means	$\geq$
what	means	x		*x less than y*	means	$y - x$		*is no greater than*	means	$\leq$

❑ **SIMPLIFY** the problem: Don't introduce any more unknowns than are necessary.

❑ **CONNECT** to your algebra skills: Solve the equation or the inequality with the laws we discussed in earlier lessons.

❑ Consider **ALTERNATIVES:** Remember that you often have choices in solving equations or systems: consider your options and choose wisely.

❑ **THINK LOGICALLY:** Sometimes you can guess-and-check a solution without doing all the algebra!

❑ **CHECK** your answer: Read the problem again to check that your solution "works" in the problem. Remember that the solution to the equation is not necessarily the answer to the question! Read the problem carefully to make sure that you've found exactly what it's asking for.

e.g.　Ellen is twice as old as Julia. Five years ago, Ellen was three times as old as Julia. How old is Julia now? (Try this one before checking the explanation below.)

Let's say this is a grid-in question, so we can't just test the choices. Guessing and checking might work, but algebra might be more reliable. First think about the unknowns. The one we really care about is Julia's **current** age, so let's call that J. Ellen's current age is also unknown, so let's call that E. Now interpret the statements: *Ellen is twice as old as Julia* is easy to translate: $E = 2J$. But two unknowns require two equations, so interpret the next statement: *Five years ago, Ellen was three times as old as Julia.* Be careful: five years ago, Ellen was $E - 5$ years old and Julia was $J - 5$ years old. So the statement translates into $E - 5 = 3(J - 5)$. Now it's a system, and you know what to do:

$$E - 5 = 3(J - 5)$$

Distribute:	$E - 5 = 3J - 15$
Add 5:	$E = 3J - 10$
Substitute $E = 2J$:	$2J = 3J - 10$
Subtract $2J$:	$0 = J - 10$
Add 10:	$10 = J$

Now reread the problem and make sure the answer makes sense. If Julia is 10, Ellen must be 20, because she's twice as old. Five years ago, then, they were 5 and 15, and 15 is three times 5! It works!

Concept Review 7: Word Problems

For each of the following statements, specify and name the unknowns and translate the statement into an equation.

1. Mike is twice as old as Dave was 5 years ago.

2. The population of town A is 40% greater than the population of town B.

3. After 2/3 of the marbles are removed from a jar, 5 more than 1/6 of the marbles remain.

4. In a jar, there are 4 more than twice as many blue marbles as red marbles.

Solve the following word problems.

5. Three candy bars and two lollipops cost $2.20, and four candy bars and two lollipops cost $2.80. What is the cost of one lollipop?

6. At a football stadium, 2/3 of the seats were filled at the beginning of a game. At halftime, 1,000 people left the stadium, leaving 3/7 of the seats filled. What is the total number of seats in the stadium?

7. If the average of m and n is one-half of the average of s and t, then what is s in terms of m, n, and t?

8. A blue chip is worth 2 dollars more than a red chip, and a red chip is worth 2 dollars more than a green chip. If 5 green chips are worth m dollars, give an expression that represents the price, in dollars, of 10 blue chips and 5 red chips.

SAT I Practice 7: Word Problems

1 When x is subtracted from 24 and this difference is divided by x, the result is 3. What is x?

(A) 4
(B) 5
(C) 6
(D) 8
(E) 12

2 Three years ago, Nora was half as old as Mary is now. If Mary is four years older than Nora, how old is Mary now?

3 If the ratio of p to q is 9:7 and the ratio of q to r is 14:3, then what is the ratio of p to r?

(A) 1:6
(B) 27:98
(C) 2:5
(D) 5:2
(E) 6:1

4 Joan originally had twice as many books as Emily. After she gave Emily 5 books, Joan still had 10 more than Emily. How many books did Joan have originally?

5 The cost of living in a certain city rose 20% between 1960 and 1970, and rose 50% between 1960 and 1980. By what percent did the cost of living increase between 1970 and 1980?

(A) 15%
(B) 20%
(C) 25%
(D) 30%
(E) 35%

6 The Mavericks baseball team has a won-lost ratio of 7 to 5. If the team played a total of 48 games and no game ended in a tie, how many more games have the Mavericks won than they have lost?

7 When the Apex Pet Store first opened, the ratio of cats to dogs was 4 to 5. Since then, the number of cats has doubled, while the number of dogs has increased by 12. If the ratio of dogs to cats is now 1 to 1, how many cats did the store have when it opened?

8 Hillside High School has 504 students. One-quarter of the students are sophomores, and 3/7 of the sophomores are boys. If one-third of the sophomore girls take French, how many sophomore girls do *not* take French?

(A) 24
(B) 36
(C) 48
(D) 72
(E) 126

9 A jar contains only red, green, and blue marbles. If it is three times as likely that you randomly pick a red marble as a green marble, and five times as likely that you pick a green one as a blue one, which of the following could be the number of marbles in the jar?

(A) 38
(B) 39
(C) 40
(D) 41
(E) 42

Answer Key 7: Word Problems

Concept Review 7

1. m = Mike's current age, d = Dave's current age; $m = 2(d - 5)$

2. a = the population of town A, b = the population of town B; $a = 1.4b$

3. n = number of marbles in the jar; $n - (2/3)n = 5 + (1/6)n$

4. b = number of blue marbles, r = number of red marbles; $b = 4 + 2r$

5. c = cost of one candy bar, l = cost of one lollipop; $3c + 2l = 2.20$, and $4c + 2l = 2.80$.

   Subtract:
   $$4c + 2l = 2.80$$
   $$\underline{- (3c + 2l = 2.20)}$$
   $$c = .60$$

   Plug in to find l: $3(.60) + 2l = 2.20$
   Simplify: $1.80 + 2l = 2.20$
   Subtract 1.80: $2l = .40$
   Divide by 2: $l = .20$

6. n = number of seats in the stadium;
   $$(2/3)n - 1{,}000 = (3/7)n$$
   Subtract $(2/3)n$: $-1{,}000 = -(5/21)n$
   Multiply by $-(21/5)$: $4{,}200 = n$

7. $$\frac{m+n}{2} = \frac{1}{2}\left(\frac{s+t}{2}\right)$$
   Simplify: $\dfrac{m+n}{2} = \left(\dfrac{s+t}{4}\right)$
   Multiply by 4: $2m + 2n = s + t$
   Subtract t: $2m + 2n - t = s$

8. b = value of blue chip, r = value of red chip, g = value of green chip; $b = 2 + r$, $r = 2 + g$, and $5g = m$, so
   Cost of 10 blue and 5 red chips: $10b + 5r$
   Substitute $b = 2 + r$: $10(2 + r) + 5r$
   Simplify: $20 + 15r$
   Substitute $r = 2 + g$: $20 + 15(2 + g)$
   Simplify: $50 + 15g$
   Substitute $g = m/5$: $50 + 3m$

SAT I Practice 7

1. **C** You could test the choices here, or do the algebra:
   $$\frac{24 - x}{x} = 3$$
   Multiply by x: $24 - x = 3x$
   Add x: $24 = 4x$
   Divide by 4: $6 = x$

2. n = Nora's current age, m = Mary's current age.
   Interpret first sentence: $n - 3 = (1/2)m$
   Interpret second sentence: $m = n + 4$
   Subtract 4: $m - 4 = n$
   Substitute $n = m - 4$: $m - 4 - 3 = (1/2)m$
   Simplify: $m - 7 = (1/2)m$
   Subtract m: $-7 = -(1/2)m$
   Multiply by -2: $14 = m$

3. **E** $p/q = 9/7$, $q/r = 14/3$.
   Multiply: $\left(\dfrac{p}{q}\right)\left(\dfrac{q}{r}\right) = \dfrac{p}{r} = \left(\dfrac{9}{7}\right)\left(\dfrac{14}{3}\right) = \dfrac{6}{1}$

4. **40** J = number of books Joan had **originally**. E = number of books Emily had originally. $J = 2E$. After the exchange, Emily has $E + 5$ and Joan has $J - 5$ books, so $J - 5 = 10 + (E + 5)$.

   Simplify: $J - 5 = E + 15$
   Subtract 15: $J - 20 = E$
   Substitute into first equation: $J = 2(J - 20)$
   Solve for J: $J = 40$
   (Reread and check)

5. **C** Let x be the cost of living in 1960. In 1970, the cost of living was $1.2x$, and in 1980 it was $1.5x$. Use the percent change formula: $(1.5x - 1.2x)/1.2x = .25 = 25\%$.

6. **8** Let w = the number of games won and l = the number of games lost. $w/l = 7/5$ and $w + l = 48$.
   Multiply by l: $w = (7/5)l$
   Substitute into 2nd eq.: $(7/5)l + l = 48$
   Simplify: $(12/5)l = 48$
   Multiply by 5/12 $l = 20$
   Plug in to find w: $w + 20 = 48$
   Subtract 20: $w = 28$
   How many more games won than lost?
   $$w - l = 28 - 20 = 8$$

7. **16** Let c = number of cats originally, d = number of dogs originally. $c/d = 4/5$. Now the number of cats is $2c$ and the number of dogs is $d + 12$. If the ratio of dogs to cats is now 1 to 1, $2c = d + 12$.
   Cross-multiply: $5c = 4d$
   Divide by 4: $(5/4)c = d$
   Substitute: $2c = (5/4)c + 12$
   Subtract $(5/4)c$: $(3/4)c = 12$
   Multiply by 4/3: $c = 16$ (Reread and check)

8. **C** Number of sophomores = $(1/4)(504) = 126$. If 3/7 of the sophomores are boys, 4/7 are girls: $(4/7)(126) = 72$. If 1/3 of the sophomore girls take French, 2/3 do not: $(2/3)(72) = 48$.

9. **E** r, g, and b are the numbers of red, green, and blue marbles. $r = 3g$ and $g = 5b$. Total marbles = $r + g + b$.
   Substitute $r = 3g$ $3g + g + b = 4g + b$
   Substitute $g = 5b$ $4(5b) + b = 21b$
   So the total must be a multiple of 21, and $42 = 2(21)$.

CHAPTER 12

SPECIAL MATH PROBLEMS

1. New Symbol or Term Problems

2. Mean/Median/Mode Problems

3. Numerical Reasoning Problems

4. Rate Problems

5. Counting Problems

6. Probability Problems

Directions

1. [ ] READ each Lesson slowly and carefully. Underline important points and take notes in the margins. Think about each example and what concept it illustrates.
2. [ ] COMPLETE the Concept Review without referring back to the Lesson. Use the Concept Review to assess your understanding of the concepts.
3. [ ] REVIEW the Lesson and make any necessary corrections to your Concept Review answers.
4. [ ] CHECK your Concept Review answers with the Answer Key.
5. [ ] ANSWER all of the questions in the SAT I Practice. Answer every question to the best of your ability.
6. [ ] CHECK your SAT I Practice answers with the Answer Key.
7. [ ] REVIEW the questions you missed and try to find where your mistakes were.
8. [ ] NOTE any questions that you may want to review with your tutor or teacher.

Lesson 1:
New Symbol or Term Problems

New Symbol or Term Problems

❑ **Don't be intimidated by SAT I questions with strange symbols or new terms** that you haven't seen before. You're not **supposed** to have seen the symbol or term before. They just made it up for that problem! Just read the definition of the new symbol or term carefully, and use it to "translate" the expressions with the new symbol or term.

e.g.   Let the "kernel" of a number be defined as the square of its greatest prime factor. For instance, the kernel of 18 is 9, because the greatest prime factor of 18 is 3 (prime factorization: $18 = 2 \times 3 \times 3$), and 3^2 equals 9.

Question 1: What is the kernel of 39?

Answer: Don't worry about the fact that you haven't heard of a "kernel" before. Just read the definition carefully. By the definition, the kernel of 39 is the square of its greatest prime factor. So just find the greatest prime factor and square it. First, factor 39 into 3×13, so its greatest prime factor is 13, and $13^2 = 169$.

Question 2: What is the greatest integer less than 20 that has a kernel of 4?

Answer: This requires a bit more thinking. If a number has a kernel of 4, then 4 must be the square of its greatest prime factor, so its greatest prime factor must be 2. The only numbers that have a greatest prime factor of 2 are the powers of 2. The greatest power of 2 that is less than 20 is $2^4 = 16$.

e.g.   For all real numbers a and b, let the expression $a ¿ b$ be defined by the equation $a ¿ b = 10a + b$.

Question 3: What is $5 ¿ 10$?

Answer: Just substitute 5 for a and 10 for b in the given equation: $5 ¿ 10 = 10(5) + 10 = 60$.

Question 4: If $2.5 ¿ x = 50$, what is the value of x?

Answer: Just translate the left side of the equation: $2.5 ¿ x = 10(2.5) + x = 50$
Then solve for x: $25 + x = 50$
                          $x = 25$

Question 5: What is $1.5 ¿ (1.5 ¿ 1.5)$

Answer: According to the order of operations, evaluate what is in parentheses first:
$1.5 ¿ (1.5 ¿ 1.5)$
Substitute: $1.5 ¿ (10(1.5) + 1.5)$
Simplify: $1.5 ¿ (16.5)$
Substitute again: $10(1.5) + 16.5$
Simplify: $15 + 16.5 = 31.5$

Concept Review 1:
New Symbol or Term Problems

For questions 1–6, translate each expression into its simplest terms, using the definition of the new symbol.

The following definition pertains to questions 1–3:
 For any real number x, let $\S x$ be defined as the greatest integer less than or equal to x.

1. $\S-4.5$ $=$ _____

2. $\S-1.5 + \S 1.5$ $=$ _____

3. $\S\sqrt{15} + \S\sqrt{17}$ $=$ _____

The following definition pertains to questions 4–6:
 If q is any positive real number and n is an integer, let $q @ n$ be defined by the equation $q@n = \sqrt{q}^{\,n+1}$.

4. $8 @ 3$ $=$ _____

5. $9 @ (k-1)$ $=$ _____

6. $x^2 @ 0$ $=$ _____

7. If q is any positive real number and n is an integer, let $q @ n$ be defined by the equation $q@n = \sqrt{q}^{\,n+1}$. If $y @ 2 = 64$, what is the value of y?

8. For any integer n and real number x, let $x \wedge n$ be defined by the equation $x \wedge n = nx^{n-1}$. If $y \wedge 4 = -32$, what is the value of y?

9. For any integer n, let Ωn be defined as the sum of the distinct prime factors of n. For instance, $\Omega 36 = 5$, because 2 and 3 are the only prime factors of 36 and $2 + 3 = 5$. What is the smallest value of w for which $\Omega w = 12$?

SAT I Practice 1:
New Symbol or Term Problems

1 For all real numbers d, e, and f, let $d * e * f = de + ef + df$. If $2 * 3 * x = 12$, then $x =$

(A) $\dfrac{5}{6}$

(B) $\dfrac{6}{5}$

(C) $\dfrac{8}{5}$

(D) 2

(E) 6

2 If $b \neq 0$, let $a \# b = \dfrac{a^2}{b^2}$. If $x \# y = 1$, then which of the following statements must be true?

(A) $x = y$
(B) $x = |y|$
(C) $x = -y$
(D) $x^2 - y^2 = 0$
(E) x and y are both positive

3 On a digital clock, a time like 6:06 is called a "double" time because the number representing the hour is the same as the number representing the minute. Other such "doubles" are 8:08 and 9:09. What is the *smallest* time period between any two such doubles?

(A) 11 mins.   (B) 49 mins.
(C) 60 mins.   (D) 61 mins.
(E) 101 mins.

4 Two numbers are "complementary" if their reciprocals have a sum of 1. For instance, 5 and $\dfrac{5}{4}$ are complementary because $\dfrac{1}{5} + \dfrac{4}{5} = 1$.

If x and y are complementary, and if $x = \dfrac{2}{3}$, what is y?

(A) -2 (B) $-\dfrac{1}{2}$ (C) $-\dfrac{1}{3}$

(D) $\dfrac{1}{3}$ (E) 3

5 For $x \neq 0$, let $\$x = \dfrac{1}{x}$. What is the value of $\$\$5$?

6 For all non-negative real numbers x, let $\Diamond x$ be defined by the equation $\Diamond x = \dfrac{\sqrt{x}}{4}$. For what value of x does $\Diamond x = 1.5$?

(A) 0.3   (B) 6   (C) 12
(D) 14   (E) 36

7 For any integer n, let $[n]$ be defined as the sum of the digits of n. For instance, $[341] = 3+4+1 = 8$. If a is an integer greater than 0 but less than 1,000, which of the following must be true?

   I. $[10a] < [a]+1$
   II. $[[a]] < 20$
   III. If a is even, then $[a]$ is even

(A) none
(B) II only
(C) I and II only
(D) II and III only
(E) I, II, and III

8 For all integers, n, let $n\& = \begin{cases} 2n & \text{if } n \text{ is even} \\ n-3 & \text{if } n \text{ is odd} \end{cases}$
$13\&\& =$

(A) 10   (B) 13   (C) 20
(D) 23   (E) 26

Answer Key 1:
New Symbol or Term Problems

Concept Review 1

1. $\S-4.5 = -5$

2. $\S-1.5 + \S1.5 = -2 + 1 = -1$

3. $\S\sqrt{15} + \sqrt{17} = 3 + 4 = 7$

4. $8@3 = \left(\sqrt{8}\right)^4 = 64$

5. $9@(k-1) = \left(\sqrt{9}\right)^{k-1+1} = 3^k$

6. $x^2@0 = \left(\sqrt{x^2}\right)^{0+1} = |x|$

7.
$$y@2 = \left(\sqrt{y}\right)^{2+1} = 64$$

Simplify: $\left(\sqrt{y}\right)^3 = 64$

Take the cube root: $\sqrt{y} = 4$

Square: $y = 16$

8.
$$y^\wedge 4 = -32$$
Translate: $4y^{4-1} = -32$
Simplify and divide by 4: $y^3 = -8$
Take the cube root: $y = -2$

9. If $\Omega w = 12$, then w must be a number whose distinct prime factors add up to 12. The prime numbers less than 12 are 2, 3, 5, 7, and 11. Which of these have a sum of 12? (Remember you can't repeat any, because it says the numbers have to be *distinct*.) A little trial and error shows that the only possibilities are 5 and 7, or 2, 3, and 7. The smallest numbers with these factors are $5 \times 7 = 35$ and $2 \times 3 \times 7 = 42$. Since the question asks for the *least* such number, the answer is 35.

SAT I Practice 1

1. **B**
   Translate: $2 * 3 * x = 12$; $(2)(3) + (3)(x) + (2)(x) = 12$
   Simplify: $6 + 5x = 12$
   Subtract 6: $5x = 6$
   Divide by 5: $x = 6/5$

2. **D**   If $x \# y = 1$, then $(x^2/y^2) = 1$, which means $x^2 = y^2$. Notice that $x = -1$ and $y = 1$ is one possible solution, which means that
   (A) $x = y$
   (B) $x = |y|$
   (E) x and y are both positive
   are *not* necessarily true. Another simple solution is $x = 1$ and $y = 1$, which means that
   (C) $x = -y$
   is not necessarily true, leaving only
   (D) as an answer.

3. **B**   All of the consecutive "double times" are 1 hour and 1 minute apart except for 12:12 and 1:01, which are only 49 minutes apart.

4. **A**   If ⅔ and y are complementary, then the sum of their reciprocals is 1: $\frac{3}{2} + 1/y = 1$
   Subtract ½: $1/y = -1/2$
   Take the reciprocal of both sides: $y = -2$

5. **5**   The "double" symbol means you simply perform the operation twice. Start with 5, then $\$5 = 1/5$. Therefore, $\$\$5 = \$(1/5) = 1/(1/5) = 5$.

6. **E**
   $$\Diamond x = \frac{\sqrt{x}}{4} = 1.5$$
   Multiply by 4: $\sqrt{x} = 6$
   Square both sides: $x = 36$
   Plug in $x = 36$ to the original and see that it works.

7. **C**   If a is 12, which is even, then $[12] = 1 + 2 = 3$ is odd, which means that statement III is not necessarily true. (Notice that this eliminates choices (D) and (E).) Statement I is true because $[10a]$ will always equal $[a]$ because $10a$ has the same digits as a, but with an extra 0 at the end, which contributes nothing to the sum of digits. Therefore, $[10a] < [a] + 1$ is always true. Notice that this leaves only choice (C) as a possibility. To check statement II, though (just to be sure!), notice that the biggest sum of digits that you can get if a is less than 1,000 is from 999. $[999] = 9 + 9 + 9 = 27$; therefore, $[[999]] = [27] = 2 + 7 = 9$. It's possible to get a *slightly* bigger value for $[[a]]$ if a is, say, 991: $[[991]] = [19] = 10$, but you can see that $[[a]]$ will never approach 20.

8. **C**   Since 13 is odd, $13\& = 13 - 3 = 10$. Therefore, $13\&\& = 10\&$. Since 10 is even, $10\& = 2(10) = 20$.

Lesson 2: Mean/Median/Mode Problems

Average (Arithmetic Mean) Problems

Just about every SAT I will include at least one question about averages. These won't be simplistic questions like "What is the average of this set of numbers?" You will have to really understand the concept of averages beyond the basic formula.

You probably know the procedure for finding an average of a set of numbers: add them up and divide by how many numbers you have. For instance, the average of 3, 7, and 8 is $(3 + 7 + 8)/3 = 6$. You can describe this procedure with the "average formula":

$$\text{average} = \frac{\text{sum}}{\text{how many numbers}}$$

Since this is an algebraic equation, you can manipulate it just like any other equation, and get two more formulas:

$$\text{sum} = \text{average} \times \text{how many numbers}$$

$$\text{how many numbers} = \frac{\text{sum}}{\text{average}}$$

❏ **All three of these formulas can be summarized in one handy little "pyramid":**

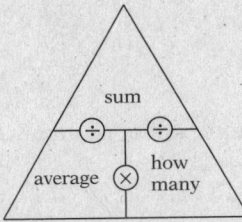

This is a great tool for setting up tough problems. To find any one of the three quantities, you simply need to find the other two, and then perform the operation between them. For instance, if the problem says, "The average (arithmetic mean) of five numbers is 30," just write 30 in the "average" place and 5 in the "how many" place. Notice that there is a multiplication sign between them, so multiply $30 \times 5 = 150$ to find the third quantity: their sum.

Medians

❏ A **median** is something that splits a set into two equal parts. Just think of the median of a highway: it splits the highway exactly in half. **The median of a set of numbers, then, is the middle number when they are listed in increasing order.** For instance, the median of $\{-3, 7, 65\}$ is 7, because the set has just as many numbers bigger than 7 as less than 7. **If you have an even number of numbers,** like $\{2, 4, 7, 9\}$, then the set doesn't have one "middle" number, so **the median is the average of the two middle numbers.** (So the median of $\{2, 4, 7, 9\}$ is $(4+7)/2 = 5.5$.)

When you take standardized tests like the SAT I, your score report often gives your score as a **percentile,** which shows the percentage of students whose scores were lower than yours. **If your percentile score is 50%, this means that you scored at the *median* of all the scores:** just as many (50%) of the students scored below your score as above your score.

❏ **The average (arithmetic mean) and the median are not always equal, but they are equal whenever the numbers are spaced symmetrically around a single number.**

e.g.   Consider any set of numbers that is evenly spaced, like 4, 9, 14, 19, and 24:

$$\xleftarrow{\qquad} \underset{4}{|} \quad \underset{9}{|} \quad \underset{14}{|} \quad \underset{19}{|} \quad \underset{24}{|} \xrightarrow{\qquad}$$

Notice that these numbers are spaced symmetrically about the number 14. This implies that the mean and the median both equal 14. This can be helpful to know, because finding the median of a set is often much easier than calculating the mean.

Modes

❏ Occasionally the SAT I may ask you about the **mode** of a set of numbers. **A mode is the number that appears the most frequently in a set.** (Just remember: MOde = MOst.) It's easy to see that not every set of numbers has a mode. For instance, the mode of $\{-3, 4, 4, 1, 12\}$ is 4, but $\{4, 9, 14, 19, 24\}$ doesn't have a mode.

Concept Review 2:
Mean/Median/Mode Problems

1. Draw the "average pyramid."

2. Explain how to use the average pyramid to solve a problem involving averages.

3. Define a median.

4. Define a mode.

5. In what situations is the mean of a set of numbers the same as its median?

6. The average (arithmetic mean) of four numbers is 15. If one of the numbers is 18, what is the average of the remaining three numbers?

7. The average (arithmetic mean) of 5 different positive integers is 25. If none of the numbers is less than 10, then what is the greatest possible value of one of these numbers?

8. Ms. Appel's class, which has 20 students, scored an average of 90% on a test. Mr. Bandera's class, which has 30 students, scored an average of 80% on the same test. What was the combined average score for the two classes?

SAT I Practice 2:
Mean/Median/Mode Problems

1 If $y = 2x + 1$, what is the average (arithmetic mean) of $2x$, $2x$, y, and $3y$, in terms of x?

(A) $2x$ (B) $2x + 1$ (C) $3x$
(D) $3x + 1$ (E) $3x + 2$

2 The average (arithmetic mean) of seven integers is 11. If each of these integers is less than 20, then what is the least possible value of any one of these integers?

(A) -113 (B) -77 (C) -37
(D) -22 (E) 0

3 The median of 8, 6, 1, and k is 5. What is k?

4 The average (arithmetic mean) of two numbers is z. If one of the two numbers is x, what is the value of the other number in terms of x and z?

(A) $z - x$ (B) $x - z$ (C) $2z - x$

(D) $x - 2z$ (E) $\dfrac{x + z}{2}$

5 A set of n numbers has an average (arithmetic mean) of $3k$ and a sum of $12m$, where k and m are positive. What is the value of n in terms of k and m?

(A) $\dfrac{4m}{k}$ (B) $\dfrac{4k}{m}$ (C) $\dfrac{k}{4m}$

(D) $\dfrac{m}{4k}$ (E) $36km$

6 The average (arithmetic mean) of 5, 8, 2, and k is 0. What is the median of this set?

(A) 0 (B) 3.5 (C) 3.75
(D) 5 (E) 5.5

7

Roll	Frequency
1	5
2	3
3	3
4	3
5	3
6	3

A die is rolled 20 times, and the outcomes are as tabulated above. If the average (arithmetic mean) of all of the rolls is a, the median of all the rolls is b, and the mode of all the rolls is c, then which of the following must be true?

I. $a = b$ II. $b > c$ III. $c = 5$

(A) I only   (B) II only
(C) I and II only   (D) II and III only
(E) I, II, and III

8 If a 30% salt solution is added to a 50% salt solution, which of the following could be the concentration of the resulting mixture?

I. 40%
II. 45%
III. 50%

(A) I only   (B) I and II only
(C) I and III only   (D) II and III only
(E) I, II, and III

9 Set A consists of five numbers with a median of m. If Set B consists of the five numbers that are two greater than each of the numbers in Set A, which of the following must be true?

I. The median of Set B is greater than m.
II. The average (arithmetic mean) of Set B is greater than m.
III. The greatest possible difference between two numbers in Set B is greater than the greatest possible difference between two numbers in Set A.

(A) I only   (B) I and II only
(C) I and III only   (D) II and III only
(E) I, II, and III

Answer Key 2:
Mean/Median/Mode Problems

Concept Review 2

1. It should look like this:

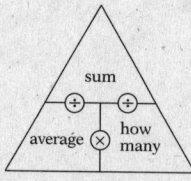

2. When two of the three values are given in a problem, write them in the pyramid and perform the operation between them. The result is the other value in the pyramid.

3. A median is the "middle" number when the numbers are listed in order. If there are an even number of numbers in the set, it is the average of the two middle numbers.

4. The number that appears the most frequently in a set.

5. When the numbers are evenly spaced, the mean is always equal to the median. This is true more generally if the numbers are distributed "symmetrically" about the mean, as in {–10, –7, 0, 7, 10}

6. If the average of four numbers is 15, then their sum must be (4)(15) = 60. If one of the numbers is 18, then the sum of the other three is 60 – 18 = 42. So the average of the other three is 42/3 = 14.

7. You need to read this problem super-carefully. If the average of the 5 numbers is 25, then their sum is (5)(25) = 125. If none of the numbers is less than 10, and since they are all *different integers*, the least that four of them can be is 10, 11, 12, and 13. Therefore, if x is the largest possible number in the set,

$$x + 10 + 11 + 12 + 13 = 125$$

Simplify: $x + 46 = 125$

Subtract 46: $x = 79$

8. If the 20 students in Ms. Appel's class averaged 90%, then they must have scored a total of (20)(90) = 1,800 points. Similarly, Mr. Bandera's class scored a total of (30)(80) = 2,400. The combined average is just the sum of all the scores divided by the number of scores: (1,800 + 2,400)/50 = 84.

Notice, too, that you can get a good estimate by just noticing that *if* there were an equal number of students in each class, the overall average would simply be the average of 80 and 90, which is 85. But since there are more students in Mr. Bandera's class, the average must be weighted more heavily toward 80.

SAT I Practice 2

1. **D** The average of 2x, 2x, y, and 3y is (2x + 2x + y + 3y)/4 = (4x + 4y)/4 = x + y. Substituting 2x + 1 for y gives x + (2x + 1) = 3x + 1.

2. **C** If the average of seven integers is 11, their sum is (7)(11) = 77. If each of these integers is less than 20, then the greatest any can be is 19. The question doesn't say that the integers must be different, so if x is the least possible of these integers, x + 19 + 19 + 19 + 19 + 19 + 19 = 77.

   Simplify: x + 114 = 77
   Subtract 114:   x = –37

3. **4** The median is the average of the two middle numbers. A little trial and error shows that 1, 4, 6, and 8 has a median of 5, so k must be 4.

4. **C** Call the number you are looking for y. The average of x and y is z, so set up the equation and solve:

   $$(x + y)/2 = z$$
   Multiply by 2: $x + y = 2z$
   Subtract x: $y = 2z - x$

5. **A** Just fill in the pyramid: n = 12m/3k = 4m/k.

6. **B** The average is 0, so (5 + 8 + 2 + k) = 0. Solving for k gives us k = –15. So we put the numbers in order: –15, 2, 5, 8. Since there are an even number of numbers, the median is the average of the two middle numbers: (2+5)/2 = 3.5.

7. **B** The most frequent number is 1, so c = 1. This means that statement III is untrue, and you can eliminate choices (D) and (E). To find the median, you need to find the average of the 10th and 11th numbers, when you arrange them in order. Since both of

these are 3, $b = 3$. Therefore, statement II is true, and you can eliminate choice (A). To find the average, just divide the sum by 20: $((1)(5) + (2)(3) + (3)(3) + (4)(3) + (5)(3) + (6)(3))/20 = 3.25$, so $a = 3.25$. Therefore, statement I is not true, so the answer is (B).

8. **B** When a 30% solution and a 50% solution are combined, the concentration must be anywhere between 30% and 50%, depending on how much of each you added. It can't be 50%, though, because the 30% solution dilutes it.

9. **A** If Set A were {0, 0, 10, 10, 10}, then its median, m, would be 10. Set B would be {2, 2, 12, 12, 12}. Inspection of Set B shows that it is a counterexample to statements II and III, leaving (**A**) as a possible answer.

Lesson 3:
Numerical Reasoning Problems

Arithmetic Reasoning

❏ Some of the most common problems on the SAT I are **numerical reasoning** problems, which ask you to think about what happens to numbers when you perform basic operations on them. You just need to know the common numerical and arithmetic rules and **think logically.**

e.g.   If $a + b$ is negative, which of the following CANNOT be negative?

(A) ab (B) ab^2 (C) a^2b
(D) a^2b^2 (E) $a - b$

Start by thinking about what **might** be true about a and b and what **must** be true about a and b. First think of possible values for a and b. –2 and 1 work, because $a + b = -2 + 1 = -1$. Notice that this proves that (A), (B), and (E) are incorrect, because they **can** be negative: (A) $ab = (-2)(1) = -2$, (B) $ab^2 = (-2)(1)^2 = -2$, and (E) $a - b = (-2) - (1) = -3$. But (C) $a^2b = (-2)^2(1) = 4$ is **positive,** so does that mean the answer is (C)? Not so fast! Your job is **not** to find which one **can be positive,** but rather which **cannot be negative.** Notice that (C) can be negative if a and b are, say, 1 and –2 (notice that $a + b$ is still negative, so those values work): (C) $a^2b = (1)^2(-2) = -2$. Therefore, by process of elimination, the answer is (D).

This question is much easier if you remember a simple fact: **if x is a real number, then x^2 is never negative.** If you don't know this already, play around with possible values of x until you see why this is true. Then look at choice (D) a^2b^2. a^2 can't be negative, and neither can b^2, so a^2b^2 can't be negative.

e.g.   If $m < n < p < r$, $mnpr = 0$, and $m + n + p + r = 0$, then which of the following must be true?

    I.   If m and n are negative, then $p = 0$.
    II. $np = 0$
    III. $m + r = 0$

(A) I only   (B) II only
(C) I and II only   (D) I and III only
(E) I, II, and III

The first statement, $m < n < p < r$, tells you that the alphabetical order is also the numerical order of the numbers. The second statement, $mnpr = 0$, tells you that one of the numbers must be 0. (This is the "Zero Product Property"!) The third statement, $m + n + p + r = 0$, tells you that you must have at least one positive and one negative, and all the numbers must "cancel out." This means that m can't be 0, because then none of the numbers would be negative, and r can't be 0, because then none of the numbers would be positive. Thus, either n or p is 0. This means that both I and II are necessarily true, so you can eliminate choices (A), (B), and (D). The example $m = -3, n = 0, p = 1, r = 2$ shows that statement III is not necessarily true, so the answer is (C).

Digit Problems

❏ You may see a question on the SAT I like the one below, where letters represent **digits.** Remember that **digits can only take the values 0, 1, 2, 3, 4, 5, 6, 7, 8, and 9.** Also remember that **you may have to consider "carried" digits when looking at a sum or product.** Lastly, **you may find it best to work from left to right rather than right to left.**

$$\begin{array}{r} 1BA \\ + 8B \\ \hline 211 \end{array}$$

e.g.   If A and B represent distinct digits in this addition problem, what is the value of $A - B$?

(A) –9   (B) –7   (C) 2
(D) 7   (E) 9

Look at the left (hundreds) column first. Since the sum has a 2 in the hundreds place, there must be a carry of 1 from the tens place. Therefore, $B + 8 +$ (carry from ones column, if any) = 11. This means $B = 2$ or 3. Trying each one shows that only $B = 2$ and $A = 9$ works, giving $129 + 82 = 211$. Therefore $A - B = 9 - 2 = 7$, so the answer is (D).

Concept Review 3: Numerical Reasoning Problems

1. If neither a nor b is 0: What is the relationship between $a \div b$ and $b \div a$?

$$\frac{a}{b} \quad \frac{b}{a} \qquad \text{reciprocals.}$$

2. What is the relationship between $a - b$ and $b - a$?

Complete the following "parity rules."

3. Odd × Even = _Even_

4. Even × Even = _Even_

5. Odd × Odd = ~~even~~ _odd_

6. Even + Even = _Even_

7. Odd + Even = _odd_

8. Odd + Odd = _even_

Complete the following "sign rules."

9. If n is odd, $(-1)^n =$ _____.

10. If n is even, $(-1)^n =$ _____.

11. If $x + y = 0$ and $x \neq 0$, then $x/y =$ _____.

12. Dividing by x is the same as multiplying by _____.

13. Subtracting $(x + 1)$ is the same as adding _____.

14. When a number is multiplied by its reciprocal, the result is _____.

15. When a number and its opposite are added, the result is _____.

16. When a number (other than 0) is divided by its opposite, the result is _____.

17. If a positive number is multiplied by a number greater than 1, what happens to it? _____

18. If a positive number is multiplied by a number between 0 and 1, what happens to it? _____

19. If a negative number is multiplied by a number greater than 1, what happens to it? _____

20. Is x always bigger than $-x$? Explain.

21. Is x^2 always bigger than x? Explain.

22. Is x^3 always bigger than x^2? Explain.

23. If x is between 0 and 1, then $1/x$ is _____.

24. If $a > b > 0$, then $\dfrac{a}{b}$ is _____.

25. If $b > a > 0$, then $\dfrac{a}{b}$ is _____.

6min

SAT I Practice 3:
Numerical Reasoning Problems

1

If m and n are both odd integers, which of the following must be true?

$M=3$
$n=5$

    I. $m^2 + n^2$ is even ✓
    II. $m^2 + n^2$ is divisible by 4
    III. $(m + n)^2$ is divisible by 4 ✓

  (A) none
  (B) I only
  (C) I and II only
  (D) I and III only ✓ ⓓ
  (E) I, II, and III

2

$$\begin{array}{r} 6AA \\ \times\ 8 \\ \hline 50B4 \end{array}$$

$8A = 4$
$A = \frac{4}{2}$

If A and B represent distinct digits in this correctly worked multiplication problem, what is the value of B?

  (A) 2   (B) 3   (C) 5
  (D) 6   (E) 8

Ⓑ

3

If j is the number of integers between 1 and 500 that are divisible by 9 and k is the number of integers between 1 and 500 that are divisible by 7, what is $j + k$?

  (A) 126   (B) 127   (C) 128
  (D) 129   (E) 130

Ⓐ

4

If 60 is written as the product of four integers, each greater than 1, then what is the sum of those integers?

a, b, c, d
$60 = abcd$

60

5 12

3 4 $+5$

$+3$

$2 + 2 = 4$

12

5

If n is an integer and 2^n is a factor of $1 \times 2 \times 3 \times 4 \times 5 \times 6 \times 7 \times 8 \times 9$, what is the *greatest* possible value of n?

$1 + 2 + 3 = 7$

  (A) 5   (B) 6   (C) 7
  (D) 8   (E) 9

 Ⓒ

6

If $p + pq$ is 4 times $p - pq$, and $pq \neq 0$, which of the following has exactly one possible value?

$p + pq = 4(p - pq)$

  (A) p
  (B) q $p + pq = 4p - 4pq$
  (C) pq $p(1 + q) = 4p(1 - pq)$
  (D) $p + pq$
  (E) $p - pq$ Ⓡ

7

If a, b, c, d, and e are whole numbers and $a(b(c + d) + e)$ is odd, then which of the following CANNOT be even?

whole = 0

  (A) a
  (B) b
  (C) c Ⓐ
  (D) d
  (E) e

8

$$a + b + c = 7$$
$$c + d + e = 9$$
$$ac + bd + ce = 16$$

If each letter in the sums above represents a different positive integer, then $c =$

  (A) 1   (B) 2   (C) 3
  (D) 4 ✓   (E) 5 Ⓓ

9

$$\begin{array}{r} ABB \\ +9B7 \\ \hline AA7C \end{array}$$

If A, B, and C are distinct digits in the correctly worked addition problem above, what is the value of $A + B + C$?

  (A) 4   (B) 9   (C) 14
  (D) 16   (E) 17

Ⓒ

Answer Key 3:
Numerical Reasoning Problems

Concept Review 3

1. They are reciprocals, so their product is 1.

2. They are opposites, so their sum is 0.

3. Odd × Even =   Even

4. Even × Even =   Even

5. Odd × Odd =   Odd

6. Even + Even =   Even

7. Odd + Even =   Odd

8. Odd + Odd =   Even

9. If n is odd, $(-1)^n = -1$.

10. If n is even, $(-1)^n = 1$.

11. If $x + y = 0$ and $x \neq 0$, then $x/y = -1$.

12. Dividing by x is the same as multiplying by $1/x$.

13. Subtracting $(x + 1)$ is the same as adding $-x - 1$.

14. When a number is multiplied by its reciprocal, the result is 1.

15. When a number and its opposite are added, the result is 0.

16. When a number (other than 0) is divided by its opposite, the result is −1.

17. It gets bigger.

18. It gets smaller.

19. It gets smaller (more negative).

20. No. If x is 0, then $-x$ is equal to x, and if x is negative, then $-x$ is greater than x.

21. No. If x is between 0 and 1, then x^2 is smaller than x. And if x is 0 or 1, then they are the same. If x is negative, then x^2 is positive, and therefore greater than x.

22. No. If x is between 0 and 1, then x^3 is smaller than x^2. And if x is 0 or 1, then they are the same. If x is negative, then x^2 is positive, and therefore greater than x^3.

23. greater than 1.   24. greater than 1.

25. between 0 and 1.

SAT I Practice 3

1. **D**   Start with the simplest odd values for m and n: $m = n = 1$. (There's no reason why m and n can't equal the same number!) Notice that $m^2 + n^2 = 1^2 + 1^2 = 2$, which isn't divisible by 4, so statement II is not necessarily true, and you can eliminate choices (C) and (E). Next, notice that m^2 and n^2 must both be odd, so $m^2 + n^2$ must be even, so statement I **is** necessarily true, and you can eliminate choice (A). $(m + n)^2$ must be a multiple of 4 because $m + n$ must be even (odd + odd = even), so it is a multiple of 2. When it is squared, it becomes a multiple of 4. So III is true, and the answer is (D).

2. **D**   Trial and error should show that A = 3. If A is less than 3, the product is too small. If greater than 3, the product is too large. Since $633 \times 8 = 5064$, B = 6.

3. **A** $500 \div 9 = 55.55$, so there are 55 multiples of 9 between 1 and 500. $500 \div 7 = 71.43$, so there are 71 multiples of 7 between 1 and 500. So $j + k = 55 + 71 = 126$.

4. **12**   Trial and error shows that the only way to write 60 as the product of four integers, each greater than 1, is $2 \times 2 \times 3 \times 5$. Their sum is $2 + 2 + 3 + 5 = 12$.

5. **C**   Do the prime factorization:

$1 \times 2 \times 3 \times 4 \times 5 \times 6 \times 7 \times 8 \times 9 = 1 \times 2 \times 3 \times (2 \times 2)$
$\times 5 \times (2 \times 3) \times 7 \times (2 \times 2 \times 2) \times (3 \times 3)$

Since there are 7 factors of 2, the greatest power of 2 that is a factor is 2^7.

6. **B**

	$p + pq = 4(p - pq)$
Distribute:	$p + pq = 4p - 4pq$
Divide by p:	$1 + q = 4 - 4q$

(This is OK as long as p is anything but 0.)

Add $4q$:	$1 + 5q = 4$
Subtract 1:	$5q = 3$
Divide by 5:	$q = 3/5$

Because p can have many possible values but q can only equal 3/5, **(B)** q is the only expression that has only one possible value.

7. **A** a cannot be even, because an even number times any other integer yields an even number, but $a(b(c + d) + e)$ is odd.

8. **A**   The only three different positive integers that have a sum of 7 are 1, 2 and 4. The only three different positive integers that have a sum of 9 are 1, 3 and 5 or 1, 2 and 6. But $1 + 2 + 6$ doesn't work, since that would have *two* numbers in common with the first set, but it may only have one, C. Since C is the only number they may have in common, it must be 1.

9. **C**   The only solution is $188 + 987 = 1{,}175$, so $A + B + C = 1 + 8 + 5 = 14$.

Lesson 4: Rate Problems

What Are Rates?

The word **rate** comes from the same Latin root as the word *ratio*. All rates are ratios. The most common type of rate is **speed,** which is a **ratio with respect to time,** as in *miles per hour* or *words per minute,* but some rates don't involve time at all, as in *miles per gallon.* Rate units always have *per* in their names: *miles **per** gallon, meters **per** second,* etc. *Per,* remember, means *divided by,* and is like the colon (:) or fraction bar in a ratio.

The Rate Pyramid

❑ **The name of any rate is equivalent to its formula.** For instance, *speed is miles per hour*

can be translated as $\quad \text{speed} = \dfrac{\text{number of miles}}{\text{number of hours}}$

or $\qquad\qquad\qquad \text{speed} = \dfrac{\text{distance}}{\text{time}}$

Since this formula is similar to the "average" formula, you can make a **rate pyramid.**

This can be a great tool for solving rate problems. If a problem gives you two of the quantities, just put them in their places in the pyramid, and do the operation between them to find the missing quantity.

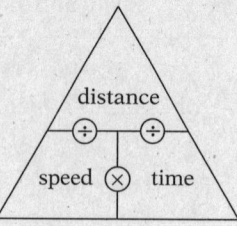

e.g.   How long will it take a car to travel 20 miles at 60 miles per hour?

Simply fill the quantities into the pyramid: 20 miles goes in the **distance** spot, and 60 miles an hour goes in the **speed** spot. Now what? Just do the division the way the diagram says: 20 miles ÷ 60 miles per hour = 1/3 hour.

Watch Your Units

❑ **Whenever you work with formulas, you can check your work by paying attention to units.** For instance, the problem above asks *how long,* so the calculation has to produce a **time** unit. Check the units in the calculation:

$$\frac{\text{miles}}{\dfrac{\text{miles}}{\text{hours}}} = \cancel{\text{miles}} \times \frac{\text{hours}}{\cancel{\text{miles}}} = \text{hours}$$

Two-Part Rate Problems

❑ Rate problems are tougher when they involve two parts. **When a problem involves, say, two people working together at different rates and times, or a two-part trip, you have to analyze the problem more carefully.**

e.g.   Toni bicycles to work at a rate of 20 miles per hour, then takes the bus home *along the same route* at a rate of 40 miles per hour. What is her average speed for the entire trip?

At first glance, it might seem that you can just average the two rates: (20 + 40)/2 = 30 miles per hour, since she is traveling the same distance at each of the two speeds. But this won't work, because she isn't spending the same **time** at each speed, and that is what's important. But if that's true, you might notice that she spends **twice** as much time going 20 miles per hour as 40 miles per hour (since it's half as fast), so instead of taking the average of 20 and 40, you can take the average of **two 20s** and a 40: (20 + 20 + 40)/3 = 26.67 miles per hour. Simple! But if that doesn't make sense to you, think of it this way: Imagine, for simplicity's sake, that her trip to work is 40 miles. (It doesn't matter what number you pick, and 40 is an easy number to work with here.) Now the average speed is simply the total distance divided by the total time (as the pyramid says). The total distance, there and back, is 80 miles. The total time is in two parts. Getting to work takes her 40 miles ÷ 20 miles per hour = 2 hours. Getting home takes her 40 miles ÷ 40 miles per hour = 1 hour. So the **total** time of the trip is 3 hours. The average speed, then, must be 80 miles ÷ 3 hours = 26.67 miles per hour!

Concept Review 4: Rate Problems

For each of the following rates, write the formula of the rate and the corresponding "rate pyramid."

1.   Speed is miles per hour.

2.   Efficiency is miles per gallon of fuel.

3.   Typing speed is pages per minute.

Find the missing quantity, including the units, in each of these rate situations.

4.   A train travels for 375 miles at 75 mph.

5.   A car that gets 28 miles per gallon uses 4.5 gallons of fuel.

6.   Harold can type 600 words in 5 minutes.

7.   A landscaper who cuts 1.6 acres of grass per hour cuts an 8-acre lot.

8.   A train leaves New York at 1:00 pm, going 50 mph, bound for Philadelphia, which is 90 miles away. If it makes no stops, at what time should it be expected to arrive?

9.   Anne can paint a room in 2 hours, and Barbara can paint a room in 3 hours. When they work together, their work rate is the sum of their rates working separately. How long should it take them to paint a room if they work together?

SAT I Practice 4: Rate Problems

1 Janice and Edward are editors at a newspaper. Janice can edit 700 words per minute and Edward can edit 500 words per minute. If each page of text contains 800 words, how many pages can they edit, working together, in 20 minutes?

2 Two cars leave the same point simultaneously, going in the same direction along a straight, flat road, one at 35 mph and one at 50 mph. After how many <u>minutes</u> will the cars be 5 miles apart?

3 What is the average speed, in miles per hour, of a sprinter who runs ¼ mile in 45 seconds? (1 hour = 60 minutes)

    (A) 11.25 mph   (B) 13.5 mph
    (C) 20 mph   (D) 22 mph
    (E) 25 mph

4 A car travels d miles in t hours and arrives at its destination 3 hours late. At what average speed, in miles per hour, should the car have gone in order to have arrived on time?

    (A) $t - 3$ (B) $\dfrac{t-3}{d}$ (C) $\dfrac{d}{t-3}$

    (D) $\dfrac{d}{t} - 3$ (E) $\dfrac{t}{d-3}$

5 If $x > 1$, how many hours does it take a train traveling at $x - 1$ miles per hour to travel $x^2 - 1$ miles?

    (A) $\dfrac{1}{x-1}$ (B) $\dfrac{1}{x+1}$ (C) x

    (D) $x - 1$ (E) $x + 1$

6 In 3 separate 1-mile races, Ellen finishes with times of x minutes, y minutes, and z minutes. What was her average speed, in miles per <i>hour</i>, for all three races? (1 hour = 60 minutes)

    (A) $\dfrac{x+y+z}{3}$ (B) $\dfrac{3}{x+y+z}$

    (C) $\dfrac{x+y+z}{180}$ (D) $\dfrac{180}{x+y+z}$

    (E) $\dfrac{x+y+z}{20}$

7 A hare runs at a constant rate of a mph, a tortoise runs at a constant rate of b mph, and $0 < b < a$. If they race each other for d miles, how many more hours, in terms of a, b, and d, will it take the tortoise to finish than the hare?

    (A) $\dfrac{a+b}{2d}$ (B) $\dfrac{d}{b} - \dfrac{d}{a}$

    (C) $\dfrac{b}{d} - \dfrac{a}{d}$ (D) $ad - bd$ (E) $a - b$

8 Sylvia drives 315 miles and arrives at her destination in 9 hours. If she had driven at an average rate that was 10 mph faster than her actual rate, how many hours sooner would she have arrived?

    (A) 1.75   (B) 2.00   (C) 2.25
    (D) 2.50   (E) 2.75

Answer Key 4: Rate Problems

Concept Review 4

1. Speed = #miles ÷ #hours

2. Efficiency = #miles ÷ #gallons

3. Typing speed = #pages ÷ #minutes

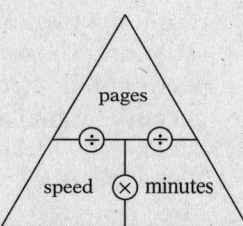

4. 375 miles ÷ 75 mph = 5 hours for the trip.

5. 28 miles per gallon × 4.5 gallons = 126 miles the car can go before it runs out of fuel.

6. 600 words ÷ 5 minutes = 120 words per minute is Harold's typing speed.

7. 8 acres ÷ 1.6 acres per hour = 5 hours for the job.

8. 90 miles ÷ 50 mph = 1.8 hours, or 1 hour 48 minutes for the entire trip. At 1 hour and 48 minutes after 1:00 pm, it is 2:48 pm.

9. Anne can paint 1 room in 2 hours, so her rate is ½ room per hour. Barbara can paint 1 room in 3 hours, so her rate is ⅓ room per hour. When they work together, their rate is ½ + ⅓ = ⅚ room per hour. So to paint 1 room would take 1 room ÷ ⅚ room per hour = ⅚ hours, or 1.2 hours, or 1 hour 12 minutes.

SAT I Practice 4

1. **30** Working together, they edit 700 + 500 = 1,200 words per minute. Since each page is 800 words, that's 1,200 words per minute ÷ 800 words per page = 1.5 pages per minute. In 20 minutes, then, they can edit 1.5 × 20 = 30 pages.

2. **20** Since the two cars are traveling in the same direction, their relative speed (that is, the speed at which they are moving away from each other) is 50 − 35 = 15 mph. In other words, they will be 15 miles farther apart each hour. Therefore, the time it takes them to get 5 miles apart is 5 miles ÷ 15 miles per hour = 1/3 hour, which is equivalent to 20 minutes.

3. **C** Since there are (60)(60) = 3,600 seconds in an hour, 45 seconds = 45/3,600 hour. Speed = distance ÷ time = 1/4 mile ÷ 45/3,600 hour = 3,600/180 = 20 miles per hour.

4. **C** To arrive on time, the car must take $t - 3$ hours for the whole trip. To travel d miles in $t - 3$ hours, the car must go $d/(t - 3)$ miles per hour.

5. **E** According to the rate pyramid, time = distance ÷ speed = $(x^2 - 1)$ miles ÷ $(x - 1)$ miles per hour =

$$\frac{x^2 - 1}{x - 1} = \frac{(x-1)(x+1)}{x-1} = x + 1 \text{ hours.}$$ Or you can pick a simple value for x, like 2, and solve numerically.

6. **D** Speed = miles ÷ hours. Her total time for the three races is $x + y + z$ minutes, which we must convert to hours by multiplying by the conversion factor (1 hour/60 minutes), which gives us $(x + y + z)/60$ hours. Since her total distance is 3 miles, her overall speed is 3 miles ÷ $(x + y + z)/60$ hours = $180/(x + y + z)$ miles per hour.

7. **B** If the hare's rate is a mph, then he covers d miles in d/a hours. Similarly, the tortoise covers d miles in d/b hours. The difference in their finishing times, then, is $d/b - d/a$.

8. **B** Sylvia's speed is 315 miles ÷ 9 hours = 35 mph. If she were to go 10 mph faster, then her speed would be 45 mph, so her time would be 315 miles ÷ 45 mph = 7 hours, which is 2 hours sooner.

Lesson 5: Counting Problems

The Fundamental Counting Principle

Some SAT I questions ask you to count things. Sometimes it's easy enough to just write out the things in a list and count them by hand. Other times, though, there will be too many, and it will help to use the Fundamental Counting Principle.

❑ To use the **Fundamental Counting Principle (FCP)**, you have to think of the things you're counting as coming from a **sequence of choices.** The Fundamental Counting Principle says that **the number of ways an event can happen is equal to the product of the choices that must be made to "build" the event.**

e.g.   How many ways can five people be arranged in a line?

You might consider calling the five people *A*, *B*, *C*, *D*, and *E*, and listing the number of arrangements. After a while, though, you'll see that this is going to take a lot of time, because there are a **lot** of possibilities. (Not to mention that it's really easy to miss some of them.) Instead, think of "building" the line with a sequence of choices: first pick the first person, then pick the second person, etc. There are five choices to make, so we'll have to multiply five numbers. Obviously, there are 5 people to choose from for the first person in line. Once you do this, though, there are only 4 people left for the second spot, then 3 for the third spot, etc. By the Fundamental Counting Principle, then, the number of possible arrangements is $5 \times 4 \times 3 \times 2 \times 1 = 120$.

e.g.   How many odd integers greater than 500 and less than 1,000 have an even digit in the tens place?

This seems a lot harder than it is. Again, think of "building" the numbers in question. All integers between 500 and 1,000 have three digits, so building the number involves choosing three digits and we must multiply three numbers together. If each number is between 500 and 1,000, then there are only five choices for the first digit: 5, 6, 7, 8, or 9. If the tens digit must be even, we have five choices again: 2, 4, 6, 8, or 0. If the entire number is odd, then we have five

choices for the last digit as well: 1, 3, 5, 7, or 9. Therefore, the total number of such integers is $5 \times 5 \times 5 = 125$.

Using Venn Diagrams to Keep Track of Sets

❑ Some counting problems involve "overlapping sets," that is, sets that contain elements that also belong in other sets. In these situations, Venn diagrams are very helpful for keeping track of things.

e.g.   A class of 29 students sponsored two field trips: one to a zoo and one to a museum. Every student attended at least one of the field trips, and 10 students attended both. If twice as many students went to the zoo as went to the museum, how many students went to the zoo?

Set up a Venn diagram of the situation. We represent the two sets—those who went to the museum and those who went to the zoo—as two overlapping circles, because some students went to both. Notice that there are three regions to consider. We know that 10 students are in the overlapping region, but we don't know how many are in the other two regions, so let's use algebra. Let's say that x students are in the first region, representing those who went to the museum but not to the zoo. This means that $x + 10$ students must have gone to the museum altogether. Since twice as many students went to the zoo, the total number in the zoo circle must be $2(x + 10) = 2x + 20$. Since 10 of these are already accounted for in the overlapping region, there must be $2x + 20 - 10 = 2x + 10$ in the third region. So now the diagram should look like this:

The total number of students is 29, so
$$(x) + (10) + (2x + 10) = 29$$
Simplify: $3x + 20 = 29$
Solve: $x = 3$
So the number of students who went to the zoo is $2(3) + 20 = 26$.

Concept Review 5: Counting Problems

1. What is the Fundamental Counting Principle?

2. How many different four-letter arrangements of the letters LMNO can be made if no letter can be repeated? Answer this first by listing all of the possible arrangements, then by using the Fundamental Counting Principle, and check that the two answers agree.

3. If the first digit of a 3-digit area code cannot be zero and the second digit is either 0 or 1, then how many different area codes are possible?

4. A baseball team has 6 players, each of whom can play in any of the three outfield positions: left field, center field, and right field. How many possible different arrangements of these players can the team place in the outfield? (This one is a bit harder to do by listing!)

5. Among a set of 40 sophomores, 20 students take French and 27 students take Spanish. If all of the students take either French or Spanish, how many students take both French *and* Spanish?

6. A box contains buttons, each of which is either blue or green and has either two or four holes. If there are four times as many blue buttons as green buttons and six times as many four-holed buttons as two-holed buttons, what is the *least* number of buttons that could be in the box?

SAT I Practice 5: Counting Problems

1 A pizzeria offers three different sizes of pizza, two different kinds of crust, and eight different choices for toppings. How many different one-topping pizzas are there to choose from?

(A) 13   (B) 16   (C) 24
(D) 48   (E) 60

(D)

2
                0, 2, 4, 6, 8

How many different integers between 30 and 70 contain only digits from the list above?

(A) 7   (B) 10   (C) 15
(D) 20   (E) 25

(B)

3 In how many ways can you arrange four different paintings in a line on a wall?

(A) 12   (B) 24   (C) 36
(D) 48   (E) 64

(B) $4 \times 3 \times 2 = $
        $4 \times 6 = 24$

4 At Lincoln County High School, 36 students are taking either calculus or physics or both, and 10 students are taking both calculus and physics. If there are 31 students in the calculus class, how many students are there in the physics class?

(A) 5   (B) 8   (C) 11
(D) 15   (E) 21

(D)

5 Dave's stickball team has six players. How many different six-player batting lineups can they make if Dave must bat second and either Zack or Paul must bat first?

(A) 48   (B) 96   (C) 192
(D) 256   (E) 720

$2 \times 1 \times 4 \times 3 \times 2 \times 1$ — (A)

5-1=4

6 Maria gave David x cards, gave Tina two more cards than she gave David, and gave Samuel five fewer cards than she gave Tina. In terms of x, how many cards did Maria give Tina, David, and Samuel all together?

(A) $3x + 9$ (B) $3x - 1$
(C) $3x - 3$ (D) $x - 3$
(E) $x - 1$

(B)

7 From a collection of six paintings, four are to be chosen to hang on a wall. How many different such arrangements are possible if every painting is different?

(A) 24   (B) 120   (C) 360
(D) 720   (E) 1,296

(C)

8 Every marble in a jar has either a dot, a stripe, or both. The ratio of striped marbles to non-striped marbles is 3:1, and the ratio of dotted marbles to non-dotted marbles is 2:3. If six marbles have both a dot and a stripe, how many marbles are there all together?

(A) 16   (B) 18   (C) 20
(D) 36   (E) 40

9 An ant must walk from one vertex of a cube to the "opposite" vertex (that is, the vertex that is farthest from the starting vertex) and back again to its starting position. It may only walk along the edges of the cube. For the entire trip, its path must traverse exactly six edges, and it *may* travel on the same edge twice. How many different six-edge paths can the ant choose from?

Answer Key 5: Counting Problems

Concept Review 5

1. The number of ways an event can happen is equal to the product of the choices that must be made to "build" the event.

2. Try listing all the "words" that start with L, then all that start with M, and so on:

LMNO	MLNO	NLMO	OLMN
LMON	MLON	NLOM	OLNM
LNMO	MNLO	NMLO	OMLN
LNOM	MNOL	NMOL	OMNL
LOMN	MOLN	NOLM	ONML
LONM	MONL	NOML	ONLM

   Whew! 24 in total. Annoying, but not impossible. Using the FCP makes it a **lot** easier: $4 \times 3 \times 2 \times 1 = 24$. That's it!

3. There are too many possibilities to list, but the FCP makes it easy: we have 9 choices for the first digit 2 choices for the second digit, and 10 choices for the last digit, and $9 \times 2 \times 10 = 180$.

4. "Build" the outfield from left to right. You have 6 players to choose from for left field, but then just 5 for center field and 4 for right field. $6 \times 5 \times 4 = 120$.

5. Since $20 + 27 - 40 = 7$, there must be 7 students who take both. This Venn diagram shows how it works out:

6. This one's tough. Say there are g green buttons. If there are four times as many blue buttons as green buttons, then there are $4g$ blue buttons, so $g + 4g = 5g$ buttons in total. So the total number of buttons must be a multiple of 5. Similarly, if there are n two-holed buttons, there must be $6n$ four-holed buttons, so the total number of buttons is $n + 6n = 7n$, so the total number of buttons is also a multiple of 7. The least common multiple of 5 and 7 is 35, so there are 35 marbles: 5 two-holed and 30 four-holed, and 7 green and 28 blue.

SAT I Practice 5

1. **D** Use the FCP: $3 \times 2 \times 8 = 48$.

2. **B** "Build" the number: If it's between 30 and 70, it must be a two-digit number that begins with 4 or 6. That's 2 choices. The second digit can be anything in the list, so that's 5 choices. $2 \times 5 = 10$

3. **B** Since there are four spaces, there are four decisions to make, so four numbers to multiply. You can choose from four paintings for the first spot, then three paintings for the second spot, etc. $4 \times 3 \times 2 \times 1 = 24$

4. **D** If there are 31 students in calculus but 10 of these are also taking physics, then $31 - 10 = 21$ students are taking only calculus. If there are 36 students taking either physics or calculus, but only 31 are taking calculus, then $36 - 31 = 5$ students are taking only physics. Therefore, the Venn diagram should look like this:

   As you can see, $5 + 10 = 15$ students are taking physics.

5. **A** "Build" the lineup. You have six spots to fill, and thus six decisions to make and six numbers to multiply. You only have two choices for the first spot (Zack or Paul) and one choice for the second spot (Dave), then you have four players left to fill the other slots, so you have four choices for the

third spot, then three for the fourth spot, etc. $2 \times 1 \times 4 \times 3 \times 2 \times 1 = 48$.

6. **B** David gets x cards. Tina gets two more cards than David, which is $x + 2$. Samuel gets five fewer cards than Tina, which is $x + 2 - 5 = x - 3$. So all together, $x + x + 2 + x - 3 = 3x - 1$.

7. **C** You have six choices for the first spot, then five for the second, then four for the third and three for the fourth. $6 \times 5 \times 4 \times 3 = 360$

8. **E** Set up the Venn diagram: Since the ratio of striped marbles to non-striped marbles is 3:1, $x + 6 = 3y$, and since the ratio of dotted marbles to non-dotted marbles is 2 to 3, $y + 6 = 2/3x$ and therefore $y = 2/3x - 6$. Substituting, we get $x + 6 = 3(2/3x - 6)$ or $x + 6 = 2x - 18$, so $x = 24$. Plug this back in to get $y = 2/3(24) - 6 = 10$. Total $= 24 + 6 + 10 = 40$.

9. **36** Draw the cube. To get from any vertex to its opposite vertex, the ant has $3 \times 2 \times 1$ possible paths. To see why, trace a path and notice it has three choices for the first edge, then two for the second, then only one option for the third. Since it must return to the opposite vertex, it has $3 \times 2 \times 1$ different paths it can take back. $3 \times 2 \times 1 \times 3 \times 2 \times 1 = 36$

Lesson 6: Probability Problems

Probability

❑ A probability is a number between 0 and 1 that represents the likelihood of an event. An event with a probability of 0 is impossible, and an event with a probability of 1 is certain. Most probabilities, of course, are somewhere in between 0 and 1. For instance, the probability of rolling a 5 on a fair die is ⅙. **It's best to think of a probability as a part-to-whole ratio.** There are six possible outcomes when you roll a die (the whole), but only one of them is 5 (the part). Thus, the probability of rolling a 5 is ⅙.

e.g.   What is the probability of rolling a sum of 5 on two dice?

Here is a table showing all the possible sums on a roll of two dice:

		Die 1					
		1	2	3	4	5	6
	1	2	3	4	5	6	7
	2	3	4	5	6	7	8
Die 2	3	4	5	6	7	8	9
	4	5	6	7	8	9	10
	5	6	7	8	9	10	11
	6	7	8	9	10	11	12

Clearly, there are four ways of getting a sum of 5 out of a possible 36, so the probability is ⁴⁄₃₆, or ⅑.

Geometrical Probability

❑ An SAT I question may ask you to find the probability that something hits a certain region, like a dart hitting a dartboard. In these situations, the probability is just **the ratio of the particular area to the entire area.**

e.g.   A landing target for skydivers consists of two concentric circles. The smaller circle has a radius of 3 meters, and the larger one has a radius of 6 meters. If a skydiver hits the target, what is the probability that she hits the smaller circle?

It might help to sketch the target:

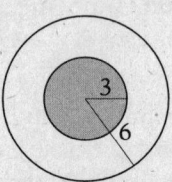

If she hits the target, then she hits an area that is $\pi(6)^2 = 36\pi$ square meters in area. The smaller circle, though, is only $\pi(3)^2 = 9\pi$ square meters in area, so the probability that she lands within the smaller region should be just $9\pi/36\pi = 1/4$.

Concept Review 6: Probability Problems

1. The probability of an impossible event is _____.

2. The probability of an event that is certain is _____.

3. If a jar contains 3 red marbles, 4 white marbles, and 5 blue marbles, then what is the probability of randomly choosing

   a red marble?   _____

   a white marble?   _____

   a blue marble?   _____

4. A jar contains five red marbles and ten white marbles.

   What is the probability of drawing a red marble? _____

   If three more red marbles are added, then what is the probability of drawing a red marble? _____

5. A jar contains 24 red and blue marbles. If the probability of selecting a red marble at random is $\frac{3}{8}$, then how many red marbles must be added so that the probability of randomly selecting a red marble becomes $\frac{1}{2}$?

6. A jar contains only black, white, and red marbles. The probability of choosing a white marble is $\frac{2}{3}$. If there are 4 times as many red marbles as black marbles, what is the least possible number of marbles in the jar?

SAT I Practice 6: Probability Problems

1

The figure above shows a spinner in the middle of a disc divided into six equal parts, each labeled with a number. What is the probability that the spinner will land on a number that is either even or greater than 5?

(A) $\frac{1}{6}$ (B) $\frac{1}{3}$ (C) $\frac{1}{2}$

(D) $\frac{2}{3}$ (E) $\frac{5}{6}$

2 A jar contains 10 blue marbles, 8 green marbles, and 14 red marbles. How many green marbles must be added so that the probability of choosing a green marble at random is $\frac{3}{4}$?

(A) 16   (B) 32   (C) 40
(D) 64   (E) 72

3 A fair six-sided die has faces bearing the numbers 1, 2, 3, 4, 5, and 6. When the die is thrown, the numbers on the five visible faces are added. What is the probability that this sum is greater than 18?

(A) $\frac{1}{6}$ (B) $\frac{1}{3}$ (C) $\frac{1}{2}$

(D) $\frac{2}{3}$ (E) $\frac{5}{6}$

4 A target consists of three concentric circles, with radii of 1 meter, 2 meters, and 3 meters. If an arrow that hits the target hits any point on the target with equal probability, what is the probability that an arrow that hits the target falls in the outermost region (between the second and third circles)?

(A) $\frac{1}{9}$ (B) $\frac{1}{3}$ (C) $\frac{\pi}{9}$

(D) $\frac{4}{9}$ (E) $\frac{5}{9}$

5 The probability of a meteor shower occurring in the skies above a particular island on any given night is $\frac{2}{25}$. Independently, the probability that any given night will be cloudless is $\frac{1}{4}$. What is the probability that, on any given night, there will be a meteor shower *and* it will be cloudless?

(A) $\frac{1}{50}$ (B) $\frac{3}{100}$ (C) $\frac{17}{200}$

(D) $\frac{4}{25}$ (E) $\frac{8}{25}$

6 A basket contains red, green, and yellow balls, all of equal size. The probability of choosing a green ball at random is $\frac{4}{7}$. If there are 3 times as many red balls as yellow balls, what is the probability of choosing a yellow ball at random?

7 A certain disease occurs in 1 person out of every 101 people. A test for the disease is 100% accurate for patients with the disease and 99% accurate for patients without it. That is, it gives a "false positive" 1% of the time even if the person tested doesn't have the disease. If you take this test and it returns a positive result, what is the probability that you have the disease?

(A) 1   (B) .99   (C) .95
(D) .50   (E) .01

Answer Key 6: Probability Problems

Concept Review 6

1. 0

2. 1

3. red marble: $\frac{3}{12}$, or $\frac{1}{4}$
   white marble: $\frac{4}{12}$, or $\frac{1}{3}$
   blue marble: $\frac{5}{12}$

4. What is the probability of drawing a red marble? $\frac{5}{15}$, or $\frac{1}{3}$
   If three more red marbles are added, what is the probability of drawing a red marble? $\frac{8}{18}$, or $\frac{4}{9}$

5. If the jar contains 24 red and blue marbles and the probability of selecting a red marble at random is 3/8, there must be $(\frac{3}{8})(24) = 9$ red marbles, and $24 - 9 = 15$ blue marbles. If the probability of drawing a red marble is to be ½, there must be as many red as blue marbles, so you must add $15 - 9 = 6$ marbles.

6. Let's say that the probability of drawing a black marble is x. Since there are 4 times as many red marbles as black marbles, the probability of drawing a red marble must be $4x$. The probability of choosing a white marble is $\frac{2}{3}$. Since we are certain to pick one of these colors, the sum of all of these probabilities must be 1: $x + 4x + \frac{2}{3} = 1$
   Simplify: $5x + \frac{2}{3} = 1$
   Subtract $\frac{2}{3}$: $5x = \frac{1}{3}$
   Divide by 5: $x = \frac{1}{15}$
   Therefore, $\frac{1}{15}$ of the marbles are black, $\frac{4}{15}$ of the marbles are red, and 2/3 of the marbles are white. The least common denominator of these fractions is 15, which means that 15 is the least possible number of marbles. In that case, there are 1 black marble, 4 red marbles, and 10 white marbles.

SAT I Practice 6

1. **D** Put an "x" through any number that is *either* even *or* greater than 5, or both. This gives us 8, 9, 2, and 6, which is 4 out of the 6 spaces, giving a probability of $\frac{4}{6}$, or $\frac{2}{3}$.

2. **D** If the probability of choosing a green marble is to be ¾, then ¾ of the marbles should be green and ¼ not green. There are 10 blue and 14 red, for a total of 24 "not green" marbles, and this will not change, since you are adding only green marbles. If this is ¼ of the total, then there must be $4(24) = 96$ marbles total after you add the extra green marbles. The jar now contains $10 + 8 + 14 = 32$ marbles, so you must add $96 - 32 = 64$ green marbles.

3. **B** The six sides of a die add up to $1 + 2 + 3 + 4 + 5 + 6 = 21$. The sum of any five faces can be greater than 18 only if the "down" face is 1 or 2 (so that the sum of the other faces is either $21 - 1 = 20$ or $21 - 2 = 19$. This is 2 possibilities out of 6 for a probability of $\frac{2}{6}$, or $\frac{1}{3}$.

4. **E** Sketch the target:
   You want to know the probability of the arrow hitting the outermost ring, which is the ratio of the area of the ring to the entire area of the target. The area of the whole target is $\pi(3)^2 = 9\pi$. The area of the outermost ring is $9\pi - \pi(2)^2$ (subtract the area of the middle circle from the area of the

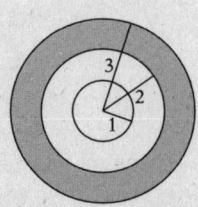

big circle) $= 9\pi - 4\pi = 5\pi$. So the probability is $5\pi/9\pi = 5/9$.

5. **A** Consider a stretch of 100 consecutive nights. If the probability of a meteor shower is $\frac{2}{25}$, then we should expect a meteor shower on $(\frac{2}{25})(100) = 8$ of those nights. If only 1/4 of the nights are cloudless, though, then $(\frac{1}{4})(8) = 2$ of the nights with a meteor shower, on average, should be cloudless. This gives a probability of $\frac{2}{100}$, or $\frac{1}{50}$. Mathematically, we can just multiply the two probabilities (as long as they are independent) to get the *joint* probability: $(\frac{2}{25})(\frac{1}{4}) = \frac{1}{50}$.

6. $\frac{3}{28}$ Call the probability of choosing a yellow ball x. If there are three times as many red balls as yellow balls, the probability of choosing a red ball must be $3x$. The probability of choosing a green ball is $\frac{5}{7}$. These probabilities must have a sum of 1:
   $$x + 3x + \frac{5}{7} = 1$$
   Simplify: $4x + \frac{5}{7} = 1$
   Subtract $\frac{5}{7}$: $4x = \frac{3}{7}$
   Divide by 4: $x = \frac{3}{28}$

7. **D** Most people would say that this probability is quite high, because the test is so reliable. But intuition is often wrong. Imagine that you test 101 people. Of these, on average, one will have the disease, and 100 will not. Since the test is 100% accurate for those who have the disease, that person will test positive. Of the 100 who do not have the disease, 99 will test negative, but one will test positive, because of the 1% "false positive" rate. So of those two who test positive, only one will have the disease; thus, the probability is ½.

CHAPTER 13

ESSENTIAL GEOMETRY SKILLS

Directions
1. [ ]   READ each Lesson slowly and carefully. Underline important points and take notes in the margins. Think about each example and what concept it illustrates.
2. [ ]   COMPLETE the Concept Review without referring back to the Lesson. Use the Concept Review to assess your understanding of the concepts.
3. [ ]   REVIEW the Lesson and make any necessary corrections to your Concept Review answers.
4. [ ]   CHECK your Concept Review answers with the Answer Key.
5. [ ]   ANSWER all of the questions in the SAT I Practice. Answer every question to the best of your ability.
6. [ ]   CHECK your SAT I Practice answers with the Answer Key.
7. [ ]   REVIEW the questions you missed and try to find where your mistakes were.
8. [ ]   NOTE any questions that you may want to review with your tutor or teacher.

Lesson 1: Lines and Angles

When Two Lines Cross

❏ When two lines cross, four angles are formed. **"Vertical" angles are equal, and look like this:**

Vertical angles

❏ Whenever two vertical angles are formed, another pair is also formed:

❏ Don't be fooled by diagrams that **look** like vertical angles, but aren't. **Vertical angles are formed by two and only two crossed lines.**

vertical   not vertical

❏ When two pairs of vertical angles are formed, four pairs of adjacent angles (side-by-side) are also formed. **Adjacent angles add up to 180°:**

adjacent angles

When a Line Crosses Parallel Lines

Imagine taking two crossed lines, making a "copy" of them, and sliding the copy down one of the lines so that together they look like this:

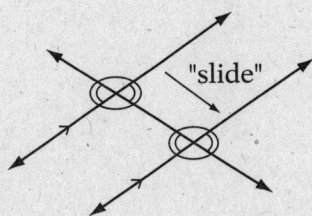

"slide"

❏ **This produces a pair of parallel lines crossed by a third line.**

❏ Since we've simply "copied" the four angles from the "top" intersection, you can figure out the relationship between any two angles in the diagram: **(1) all of the** *acute* **(less than 90°) angles are equal, (2) all of the "obtuse" (greater than 90°) angles are equal,** and **(3) any obtuse angle + any acute angle = 180°.**

❏ **To show that two lines are parallel,** use the **arrow marks** ">" like those in the figure above.

❏ **To show that two angles are equal,** use the **arc marks** ")" like those in the figure above.

❏ Don't be fooled by diagrams that only **look** as if they have two parallel lines crossed by another line. **Don't** *assume* **that two lines are parallel just because they look parallel.** You must be *given* that they are parallel.

To help yourself to see the relationships between angles in parallel line systems, you might try looking for these special "letters":

❑ **Angles that make Z's are equal:**

❑ **Angles that make C's or U's are supplementary (they have a sum of 180°):**

❑ **Angles that make F's are equal:**

Concept Review 1: Lines and Angles

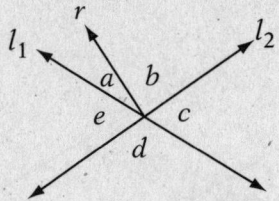

l_1 and l_2 are lines and r is a ray.

Questions 1 and 2 refer to the diagram above.

1. List all of the different pairs of angles that are congruent (equal).

2. List all of the different sets of angles that have a sum of 180°.

Mark the figure above to show the following information: **AD | HN, AI | BM** and **HD | JL.** Then list the angles in the figure that have each characteristic:

3. One angle equal to ∠10 _____

4. Two angles supplementary to ∠6 _____

5. Two angles supplementary to ∠9 _____

6. One angle equal to ∠15 _____

7. Three angles supplementary to ∠13 _____

State whether each of the following pairs is *supplementary* (have a sum of 180°), *equal,* or *neither.*

8. ∠13 and ∠7 _____

9. ∠13 and ∠6 _____

10. ∠2 and ∠9 _____

11. ∠14 and ∠9 _____

12. ∠7 and ∠3 _____

13. ∠1 and ∠2 _____

14. ∠6 and ∠7 _____

SAT I Practice 1:
Lines and Angles

1

Note: Figure not drawn to scale.

The figure above shows the intersection of three lines. $x =$

(A) 16
(B) 20
(C) 30
(D) 60
(E) 90

2

The figure above shows a parallelogram with one side extended. If $z = 40$, then $y =$

(A) 40°
(B) 60°
(C) 80°
(D) 110°
(E) 120°

3

Note: Figure not drawn to scale.

In the figure above, if $\ell_1 \parallel \ell_2$, then $a + b =$

(A) 130
(B) 270
(C) 280
(D) 290
(E) 310

4

In the figure above, if $l_1 \parallel l_2$, then what is the value of n in terms of m?

(A) $355 - 2m$
(B) $185 - 2m$
(C) $175 - 2m$
(D) $95 - 2m$
(E) $85 - 2m$

5

In the figure above if $l_1 \parallel l_2$, then $x =$

(A) 43°
(B) 69°
(C) 79°
(D) 101°
(E) 111°

6

In the figure above, if $\overleftrightarrow{FG} \parallel \overleftrightarrow{HJ}$ and $\overline{FJ}$ bisects $\angle HFG$, what is the measure of $\angle FJH$?

(A) 14°
(B) 38°
(C) 40°
(D) 56°
(E) 76°

7

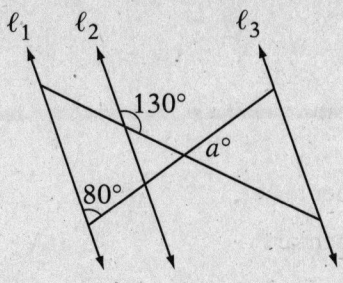

Note: Figure not drawn to scale.

In the figure above, if $\ell_1 \parallel \ell_2$ and $\ell_2 \parallel \ell_3$, then $a =$

(A) 50°
(B) 55°
(C) 60°
(D) 65°
(E) 70°

8

Note: Figure not drawn to scale.

In the diagram above, if $\ell_1 \parallel \ell_2$, then $x =$

(A) 65°
(B) 60°
(C) 50°
(D) 45°
(E) 40°

Answer Key 1:
Lines and Angles

Concept Review 1

1. Only c and e are congruent.

2. $a + b + c = 180°$, $c + d = 180°$, $d + e = 180°$, $e + a + b = 180°$

3. $\angle 5$

4. $\angle 7$ and $\angle 13$

5. $\angle 12$ and $\angle 14$

6. $\angle 4$

7. $\angle 11$, $\angle 8$, and $\angle 6$

8. equal

9. supplementary

10. neither

11. supplementary

12. neither

13. supplementary

14. supplementary

SAT I Practice 1

1. **C** Draw in the three angles that are "vertical," and therefore congruent, to the angles that are shown. Then choose any three adjacent angles, and notice that they form a straight angle. Therefore, $x + 2x + 3x = 180$. So $6x = 180$ and $x = 30$.

2. **B** The opposite angles in a parallelogram must be equal, and any two "consecutive angles" as you move around the figure must be supplementary. (Notice that consecutive angles form C's or U's. If you're not sure why this theorem is true, sketch a few sample parallelograms and work out the angles.) The angle opposite the $y°$ must also measure $y°$, and when this is added to the three $z°$ angles, they form a straight angle. Therefore, $y + 40 + 40 + 40 = 180$ and $y = 60$.

3. **E** In the triangle, the angles must have a sum of 180°. (See the next lesson for a simple proof.) Therefore, the other two angles in the triangle must have a sum of 50°. Pick values for these two angles that add up to 50°, and write them in. It doesn't matter how

you do it: 25° and 25°, 20° and 30°, 40° and 10°, as long as they add up to 50°. You can then find the values of a and b by noticing that they form straight angles with the interior angles. So if the interior angles are 25° and 25°, then a and b must both be 155.

4. **C** Notice that the $m°$ angle has a "corresponding" angle below that has the same measure. (Notice that they form an F.) Then $(m + 5) + n + m = 180$.

Simplify: $2m + 5 + n = 180$

Subtract $(5 + 2m)$: $n = 175 - 2m$

5. C Draw an extra line through the vertex of the angle that is parallel to the other two. Notice that this forms two "Z" pairs. Therefore, $x = 36 + 43 = 79$.

6. B There are many relationships here to take advantage of. Notice that $\angle HFG$ and the 76° angle form a "Z," so $\angle HFG = 76°$. Remember that "bisect" means to divide into two equal parts, so $\angle HFJ = \angle JFG = 38°$. Then notice that $\angle JFG$ and $\angle FJH$ form a "Z," so $\angle FJH = 38°$.

7. A Consider the triangle with the $a°$ angle. The other two angles in the triangle can be found from the given angles. Notice the "Z" that contains the two 80° angles and the "U" that contains the 130° and 50° angles. Therefore, $a + 80 + 50 = 180$, so $a = 50$.

8. E Draw two more parallel lines and work with the Z's. Your figure should look like the one above.

Lesson 2: Triangles

Angles in Polygons

Remembering what you learned about parallel lines in the last lesson, consider this diagram:

We drew line ℓ so that it is parallel to the opposite side of the triangle. Do you see the two Z's? The angles marked a are equal, and so are the angles marked c. We also know that angles that make up a straight line have a sum of 180°, so $a + b + c = 180$. The angles inside the triangle are also a, b, and c.

❑ Therefore, **the sum of angles in a triangle is always 180°.**

Every polygon with n sides can be divided into $n − 2$ triangles that share their vertices (corners) with the polygon:

5 sides,
3 triangles

7 sides,
5 triangles

❑ Therefore, **the sum of the angles in any polygon with n sides is $180(n − 2)°$.**

Angle-Side Relationships in Triangles

A triangle is like an alligator mouth with a stick in it: The wider the mouth, the bigger the stick, right?

❑ Therefore, **the largest angle of a triangle is always across from the longest side, and vice versa. Likewise, the smallest angle is always across from the shortest side.**

e.g.   In the figure below, 72 > 70, so $a > b$.

a / b
70° 72°

❑ **An isosceles triangle is a triangle with two equal sides. If two sides in a triangle are equal, then the angles across from those sides are equal, too, and vice versa.**

The Triangle Inequality

Look closely at the figure below. The shortest path from point A to point B is the line segment connecting them. Therefore, unless point C is "on the way" from A to B, that is, unless it's on $\overline{AB}$, **the distance from A to B through C must be longer than the direct route.** In other words:

❑ **The sum of any two sides of a triangle is always greater than the third side.**

❑ This means that **the length of any side of a triangle must be between the sum and the difference of the other two sides.**

$$12 − 10 < AB < 12 + 10$$
$$2 < AB < 22$$

The External Angle Theorem

❑ The extended side of a triangle forms an **external angle** with the adjacent side.

❑ **The external angle of a triangle is equal to the sum of the two "remote interior" angles.** Notice that this follows from our angle theorems:

$a + b + x = 180$ and $c + x = 180$;
therefore, $a + b = c$

Concept Review 2: Triangles

1. The sum of the measures of the angles in a quadrilateral is _____.

2. The sum of the measures in an octagon is _____.

3. In $\triangle ABC$, if the measure of $\angle A$ is 65° and the measure of $\angle B$ is 60°, then which side is longest? _____

4. The angles in an equilateral triangle must have a measure of _____.

5. Can an isosceles triangle include angles of 35° and 60°? Why or why not?

6. Draw a diagram to illustrate the External Angle Theorem.

7. If a triangle has sides of lengths 20 and 15, then the third side must be less than _____ but greater than _____.

8. Is it possible for a triangle to have sides of lengths 5, 8, and 14? Why or why not?

9. If an isosceles triangle includes an angle of 25°, the other two angles could have measures of _____ and _____ or _____ and _____.

10. In the figure above, $\overline{QS}$ and $\overline{RT}$ are diameters of the circle and P is *not* the center. Complete the statement below with >, <, or =.

$PQ + PR + PS + PT$ _____ $QS + RT$
(not shown)

SAT I Practice 2: Triangles

1

In the figure above, if $AB = BD$, then $x =$

(A) 25°
(B) 30°
(C) 35°
(D) 50°
(E) 65°

2

In the figure above, $a + b + c + d =$

3 The three sides of a triangle have lengths of 9, 16, and k. Which of the following could equal k?

    I.   6
    II. 16
    III. 25

(A) I only
(B) II only
(C) I and II only
(D) II and III only
(E) I, II, and III

4

Note: Figure not drawn to scale.

Which of the following statements about a and b in the figure above must be true?

    I. $a = b$
    II. $a + b = 90$
    III. $a < 60$

(A) I only
(B) II only
(C) I and II only
(D) II and III only
(E) I, II, and III

5

In the figure above, if $AD = DB = DC$, then $x + y =$

(A) 70
(B) 80
(C) 90
(D) 100
(E) 120

6

In the figure above, which of the following expresses a in terms of b and c?

(A) $180 - (b + c)$
(B) $180 - (b - c)$
(C) $90 - (b + c)$
(D) $90 - (b - c)$
(E) $b + c$

7

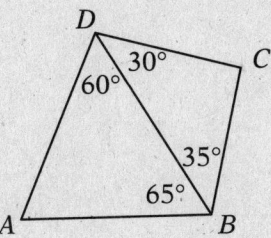

Note: Figure not drawn to scale.

Which of the following represents the correct ordering of the lengths of the five segments in the figure above?

(A) $AD > AB > DB > BC > DC$
(B) $AD > DB > AB > DC > BC$
(C) $AD > DB > AB > BC > DC$
(D) $AD > AB > DB > DC > BC$
(E) $AD > DB > DC > AB > BC$

8 A triangle has two sides of lengths 4 centimeters and 6 centimeters. Its area is n square centimeters, where n is a prime number. What is the greatest possible value of n?

(A) 11
(B) 12
(C) 19
(D) 23
(E) 24

Answer Key 2: Triangles

Concept Review 2

1. 360°

2. 1,080°

3. Draw a diagram. If the measure of ∠A is 65° and the measure of ∠B is 60°, then the measure of ∠C must be 55°, because the angles must have a sum of 180°. Since ∠A is the largest angle, the side opposite it, $\overline{BC}$, must be the longest side.

4. 60°. Since all the sides are equal, all the angles are, too.

5. No, because an isosceles triangle must have two equal angles, and the sum of all three must be 180°. Since $35 + 35 + 60 \neq 180$, and $35 + 60 + 60 \neq 180$, the triangle is impossible.

6. Your diagram should look something like this:

$a + b = c$

7. If a triangle has sides of lengths 20 and 15, then the third side must be less than 35 (their sum) but greater than 5 (their difference).

8. No. The sum of the two shorter sides of a triangle is always greater than the third side, but $5 + 8$ is not greater than 14. So the triangle is impossible.

9. 25° and 130° or 77.5° and 77.5°

10. Draw in the line segments PQ, PR, PS, and PT. Notice that this forms two triangles, ΔPQS and ΔPRT. Since any two sides of a triangle must have a sum greater than the third side, $PQ + PS > QS$, and $PR + PT > RT$. Therefore, $PQ + PR + PS + PT > QS + RT$.

SAT I Practice 2

1. **A**   If $AB = BD$, then, by the Isosceles Triangle Theorem, ∠BAD and ∠BDA must be equal. To find their measure, subtract 50° from 180° and divide by 2. This gives 65°. Mark up the diagram with this information. Since the angles in the big triangle have a sum of 180°, $65 + 90 + x = 180$, so $x = 25$.

2. **500** Drawing two diagonals shows that the figure can be divided into three triangles. (Remember that an n-sided figure can be divided into $n - 2$ triangles.) Therefore, the sum of all the angles is $3 \times 180° = 540°$. Subtracting 40° leaves 500°.

3. **B**   The third side of any triangle must have a length that is between the sum and the difference of the other two sides. Since $16 - 9 = 7$ and $16 + 9 = 25$, the third side must be between (but not including) 7 and 25.

4. **A**   Since the big triangle is a right triangle, $b + x$ must equal 90. The two small triangles are also right triangles, so $a + x$ is also 90. Therefore, $a = b$ and statement I is true. In one "solution" of this triangle, a and b are 65 and x is 25. (Put the values into the diagram and check that everything "fits.") This solution proves that statements II and III are not necessarily true.

5. **C**   If $AD = DB$, then, by the Isosceles Triangle Theorem, the angles opposite those sides must be equal. You should mark the other angle with an x also, as shown here. Similarly, if $DB = DC$, then the angles opposite those sides must be equal also, and they should both be marked y. Now consider the big triangle. Since its angles must have a sum of 180, $2x + 2y = 180$. Dividing both sides by 2 gives $x + y = 90$. (Notice that the fact that ∠ADB measures 100° doesn't make any difference!)

6. **E**   Label the two angles that are "vertical" to those marked b and c. Notice that the angle marked a is an "external" angle. By the External Angle Theorem, $a = b + c$.

8. **A**   Consider the side of length 4 to be the base, and "attach" the side of length 6. Notice that the triangle has the greatest possible height when the two sides form a right angle. Therefore, the greatest possible area of such a triangle is (1/2)(4)(6) = 12, and the minimum possible area is 0. The greatest prime number less than 12 is 11.

7. **D**   Write in the missing angle measures by using the fact that the sum of angles in a triangle is 180°. Then use the fact that the biggest side of a triangle is always across from the biggest angle to order the sides of each triangle.

Lesson 3:
The Pythagorean Theorem

The Pythagorean Theorem

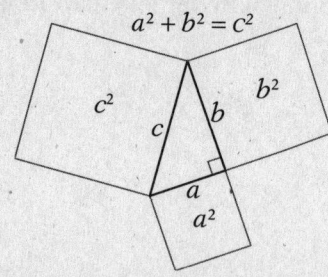

$$a^2 + b^2 = c^2$$

- ❏ The **Pythagorean Theorem** says that in any **right triangle, the sum of the squares of the two shorter sides is equal to the square of the longest side.**

- ❏ The Pythagorean Theorem does **not** apply to all triangles, **only to right triangles.**

- ❏ If you know two sides of any right triangle, **the Pythagorean Theorem can always be used to find the third side.**

  e.g.   What is x?

Pythagorean Theorem:	$9^2 + x^2 = 15^2$
Simplify:	$81 + x^2 = 225$
Subtract 81:	$x^2 = 144$
Take the square root:	$x = 12$

- ❏ You can also use the **Modified Pythagorean Theorem** to find whether a triangle is acute or obtuse:

  If $(side_1)^2 + (side_2)^2 < (\text{longest side})^2$, the triangle is **obtuse.** (If the stick gets bigger, the alligator's mouth gets wider!)

  If $(side_1)^2 + (side_2)^2 > (\text{longest side})^2$, the triangle is **acute.** (If the stick gets smaller, the alligator's mouth gets smaller!)

Special Right Triangles

Certain **special right triangles** show up frequently on the SAT I. **If you see that a triangle fits one of these patterns, it may save you the trouble of using the Pythagorean Theorem.** But be careful: **you must know two of three "parts" of the triangle in order to assume the third part.**

- ❏ **3-4-5 triangles:** More accurately, these can be called $3x$-$4x$-$5x$ triangles, because the **multiples** of 3-4-5 also make right triangles. Notice that the sides satisfy the Pythagorean Theorem.

  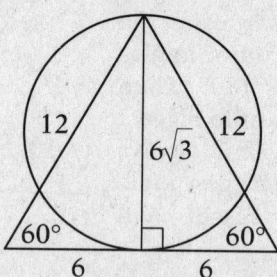

- ❏ **5-12-13 triangles** Likewise, these can be called $5x$-$12x$-$13x$ triangles, because the **multiples** of 5-12-13 also make right triangles. Notice that the sides satisfy the Pythagorean Theorem.

- ❏ **45°-45°-90° triangles** These triangles can be thought of as **squares cut on the diagonal.** This shows why the angles and sides are related the way they are. Notice that the sides satisfy the Pythagorean Theorem.

❑ **30°-60°-90° triangles**   These triangles can be thought of as **equilateral triangles cut in half.** This shows why the angles and sides are related the way they are. Notice that the sides satisfy the Pythagorean Theorem.

The Distance Formula

Say you want to find the distance between two points (x_1, y_1) and (x_2, y_2). Look carefully at this diagram and notice that you can find it with the Pythagorean Theorem. Just think of the distance between the points as the hypotenuse of a right triangle, and the Pythagorean Theorem becomes—lo and behold— the **distance formula!**

❑ According to the Pythagorean Theorem,

$$d^2 = (x_2 - x_1)^2 + (y_2 - y_1)^2$$

so

$$d = \sqrt{\left(x_2 - x_1\right)^2 + \left(y_2 - y_1\right)^2}$$

Concept Review 3:
The Pythagorean Theorem

1. Draw an example of each of the 4 "special" right triangles.

Use the **Modified Pythagorean Theorem** and the **Triangle Inequality** to find whether a triangle with the given side lengths is **acute, obtuse,** or **right,** or **impossible.**

2. 5, 6, 9

3. 2, 12, 12

4. 6, 8, 11

5. 2, 2, 12

6. 3, 4, 7

7. 1.5, 2, 2.5

8. The circle above has its center at P and an area of 16π. If $AP = AB$, what is the area of $\triangle ABC$? _____

9. The area of the triangle above is 30. What is the value of h? _____

10. What is the height of an equilateral triangle with sides of length $6\sqrt{3}$ cm? _____

11. Point P is at (0, 0), point M is at (4, 0), and point N is at (9, 12). What is the perimeter of $\triangle MNP$? _____

SAT I Practice 3: The Pythagorean Theorem

1 The length and width of a rectangle are in the ratio of 5:12. If the rectangle has an area of 240 square centimeters, what is the length, in centimeters, of its diagonal?

(A) 26
(B) 28
(C) 30
(D) 32
(E) 34

2 A spider on a flat horizontal surface walks 10 inches east, then 6 inches south, then 4 inches west, then 2 inches south. At this point, how many inches is the spider from its starting point?

(A) 8
(B) 10
(C) 12
(D) 16
(E) 18

3

In the figure above, *ABCF* is a square and Δ*EFD* and Δ*FCD* are equilateral. What is the measure of ∠*AEF*?

(A) 15°
(B) 20°
(C) 25°
(D) 30°
(E) 35°

4

In the figure above, an equilateral triangle is drawn with an altitude that is also the diameter of the circle. If the perimeter of the triangle is 36, what is the circumference of the circle?

(A) $6\sqrt{2}\pi$

(B) $6\sqrt{3}\pi$

(C) $12\sqrt{2}\pi$

(D) $12\sqrt{3}\pi$

(E) 36π

5

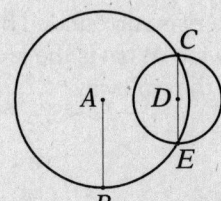

In the figure above, *A* and *D* are the centers of the two circles, which intersect at points *C* and *E*. $\overline{CE}$ is a diameter of circle *D*. If *AB = CE* = 10, what is *AD*?

(A) 5

(B) $5\sqrt{2}$

(C) $5\sqrt{3}$

(D) $10\sqrt{2}$

(E) $10\sqrt{3}$

6 Point H has coordinates $(2, 1)$, and point J has coordinates $(11, 13)$. If $\overline{HK}$ is parallel to the x-axis and $\overline{JK}$ is parallel to the y-axis, what is the perimeter of $\triangle HJK$?

7

A square garden with a diagonal of length $24\sqrt{2}$ meters is surrounded by a walkway 3 meters wide. What is the area, in square meters, of the walkway?

8

Note: Figure not drawn to scale.

In the figure above, what is the value of z?

(A)   15

(B) $15\sqrt{2}$

(C) $15\sqrt{3}$

(D) $30\sqrt{2}$

(E) $30\sqrt{3}$

Answer Key 3:
The Pythagorean Theorem

Concept Review 3

1. Your diagram should include one each of a $3x$ – $4x$ – $5x$, a $5x$ – $12x$ – $13x$, a $30° – 60° – 90°$, and a $45° – 45° – 90°$ triangle.

2. Obtuse: $5^2 + 6^2 = 61 < 9^2 = 81$

3. Acute: $2^2 + 12^2 = 148 > 12^2 = 144$

4. Obtuse: $6^2 + 8^2 = 100 < 11^2 = 121$

5. Impossible: $2 + 2$ isn't greater than 12

6. Impossible: $3 + 4$ isn't greater than 7

7. Right: $1.5^2 + 2^2 = 6.25 = 2.5^2$

8. Since the area of a circle is $\pi r^2 = 16\pi$, $r = 4$. Put the information into the diagram. Use the Pythagorean Theorem or notice that, since the hypotenuse is twice the shorter side, it is a $30° – 60° – 90°$ triangle. Either way, $CB = 4\sqrt{3}$, so the area of the triangle

   is $(bh)/2 = (4)(4\sqrt{3})/2 = 8\sqrt{3}$.

9. At first, consider the shorter leg as the base. In this case, the other leg is the height. Since the area is $(bh)/2 = 30$, the other leg must be 12. This is a 5-12-13 triangle, so the hypotenuse is 13. Now consider the hypotenuse as the base. Since $13h/2 = 30$, $h = 60/13 = 4.615$.

10. Your diagram should look like this: The height is

    $(3\sqrt{3})(\sqrt{3}) = 9$.

11. Sketch the diagram. Use the Pythagorean Theorem or distance formula to find the lengths. The perimeter is $4 + 13 + 15 = 32$.

SAT I Practice 3

1. **A**   Draw the rectangle. If the length and width are in the ratio of 5:12, then they can be expressed as $5x$ and $12x$. The area, then, is $(5x)(12x) = 60x^2 = 240$. So $x = 2$, and the length and width are 10 and 24. Find the diagonal with the Pythagorean Theorem:

   $10^2 + 24^2 = a^2$, so $100 + 576 = 676 = a^2$ and $d = 26$. (Notice that this is a 5-12-13 triangle times 2!)

2. **B**   Draw a diagram like this. The distance from the starting point to the finishing point is the hypotenuse of a right triangle with legs of 6 and 8. Therefore, the distance is found with Pythagoras:

   $6^2 + 8^2 = 36 + 64 = 100 = d^2$, so $d = 10$. (Notice that this is a 3-4-5 triangle times 2!)

3. **A**   Draw in the angle measures. All angles in a square are 90° and all angles in an equilateral triangle are 60°. Since all of the angles around point F add up to 360°, $\angle EFA = 360 – 60 – 60 – 90 = 150°$. Since $EF = AF$, ΔEFA is isosceles, so $\angle AEF = (180 – 150)/2 = 15°$.

4. **B**   If the perimeter of the triangle is 36, each side must have a length of 12. Since the altitude forms two $30° – 60° – 90°$ triangles, the altitude must have length $6\sqrt{3}$. This is also the diameter of the circle. The circumference of a circle is π times the diameter: $6\sqrt{3}\pi$.

5. **C**   Draw in AE and AC. Since all radii of a circle are equal, their measures are both 10 as well. Therefore ΔACE is equilateral, and AD divides it into two $30° – 60° – 90°$ triangles. You can use the Pythagorean Theorem, or just use the $30°$-$60°$-$90°$ relationships to see that $AD = 5\sqrt{3}$.

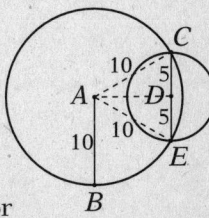

6. **36** Sketch a diagram. Point K has coordinates (11, 1). ΔHJK is a right triangle, so it satisfies the Pythagorean Theorem. Your diagram should look like this one. The perimeter is $9 + 12 + 15 = 36$.

7. **324** Since the garden is a square, the diagonal divides it into $45° – 45° – 90°$ triangles. Therefore the sides have a length of 24. The outer edge of the walkway is therefore $24 + 3 + 3 = 30$. The area of the walkway is the difference of the areas of the squares: $30^2 – 24^2 = 324$.

8. **B** The sum of the angles is 180°, so $x + x + 2x = 4x = 180$, and $x = 45$. Therefore the triangle is a $45° – 45° – 90°$ triangle. Since it is isosceles, $3y = 2y + 5$, and therefore $y = 5$. The three sides, then, have lengths of 15, 15, and $15\sqrt{2}$.

Lesson 4: Coordinate Geometry

Plotting Points

Some SAT I questions may ask you to work with points on the *x-y* plane (also known as the coordinate plane or the Cartesian plane, after the mathematician and philosopher René Descartes). **When plotting points, remember these four basic facts to avoid the common mistakes:**

❑ The coordinates of a point are always given **alphabetically:** the *x*-coordinate first, then the *y*-coordinate.

❑ The *x*-**axis** is always **horizontal** and the *y*-**axis** is always **vertical.**

❑ On the *x*-axis, the **positive** direction is to the **right** of the **origin** (where the *x* and *y* axes meet, point (0,0)).

❑ On the *y*-axis, the **positive** direction is **up** from the **origin** (where the *x* and *y* axes meet, point (0,0)).

Working with Slopes

❑ Every line has a **slope,** which is the **distance you move up or down as you move one unit to the right along the line.** Imagine walking between any two points on the line. As you move, you go a certain distance "up or down." This distance is called the rise. You also go a certain distance "left or right." This distance is called the **run.**

❑ **The slope is simply the rise divided by the run.**

$$\text{Slope} = \frac{rise}{run} = \frac{y_2 - y_1}{x_2 - x_1}$$

❑ You should be able to tell at a glance whether a slope has a *positive, negative,* or *zero* slope. **If the line goes up as it goes to the right, it has a positive slope. If it goes down as it goes to the right, it has a negative slope.** If it's horizontal, it has a zero slope.

❑ **If two lines are parallel,** they must have the same slope.

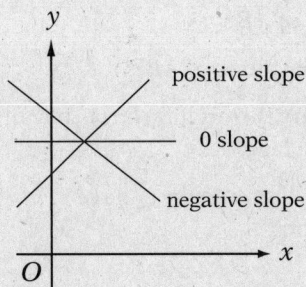

Finding Midpoints

The midpoint of a line segment is the point that divides the segment into two equal parts.

❑ Think of the **midpoint** as the **average of the two endpoints.**

$$\text{Midpoint} = \left(\frac{x_1 + x_2}{2}, \frac{y_1 + y_2}{2} \right)$$

Concept Review 4:
Coordinate Geometry

Questions 1–10 refer to the figure below.
Horizontal and vertical lines are spaced 1 unit apart.

1. What are the coordinates
   of point *A*?   _____

2. What are the coordinates of the
   midpoint of $\overline{AB}$?   _____

3. What is the slope of $\overline{AB}$?   _____

4. Draw a line through *B* that is parallel to the
   y-axis and label it ℓ_1.

5. What do all points on ℓ_1 have
   in common?   _____

6. Draw a line through *B* that is parallel to the *x*-axis
   and label it l_2.

7. Draw the line $y = -1$ and label it ℓ_3.

8. If point *A* is reflected over ℓ_2, what are the coordinates of its image?   _____

9. If line segment $\overline{AB}$ is rotated 90° clockwise about
   point *B*, what are the coordinates of the image of
   point *A*?   _____

10. If point *B* is the midpoint of line segment $\overline{AC}$,
    what are the coordinates of point *C*?   _____

Rectangle *ABCD* has an area of 108.
Note: Figure not drawn to scale.

Questions 11–15 pertain to the figure above.

11. $k =$ _____ $m =$ _____ $n =$ _____ $p =$ _____

12. What is the ratio of *AC* to
    the perimeter of *ABCD*?   _____

13. What is the slope of $\overline{DB}$?   _____

14. At what point do $\overline{AC}$ and
    $\overline{DB}$ intersect?   _____

15. If *B* is the midpoint of
    segment $\overline{DF}$, what are the
    coordinates of point *F*?   _____

Questions 16–18 pertain to the figure above.

16. What is the area of the triangle above?
                                         _____

17. If the triangle above were reflected over the line
    x = 3, what would be the least *x*-coordinate of any
    point on the triangle?   _____

18. If the triangle above were reflected over the line
    y = 1, what would the area of the new triangle be?

                                         _____

SAT I Practice 4: Coordinate Geometry

1 If point A has coordinates (3, 5), point B has coordinates (3, 2), and $ABCD$ is a square, which of the following could be the coordinates of point C?

(A) (4, 2)   (B) (6, 2)   (C) (6, 6)
(D) (4, 6)   (E) (8, 2)

2 If ℓ_1 is a horizontal line passing through (1, 8) and ℓ_2 is a vertical line passing through (–3, 4), then at what point do ℓ_1 and ℓ_2 intersect?

(A) (–3, 8)   (B) (1, 4)   (C) (–1, 6)
(D) (–2, 12)   (E) (0, 0)

3 The point (–3, 4) is on a circle with its center at the origin. Which of the following points must also be on the circle?

  I. (0, –5)
 II. (–4, –3)
III. (3, 4)

(A) I only   (B) II only
(C) I and II only   (D) II and III only
(E) I, II, and III

4 If the point (3, –7) is the center of a circle and the point (8, 5) is on the circle, what is the circumference of the circle?

(A) 13π (B) 15π (C) 18π
(D) 25π (E) 26π

5

In the figure above, point E is to be drawn so that $\triangle CDE$ has the same area as $\triangle ABC$. Which of the following could be the coordinates of E?

(A) (16, 5)   (B) (3, 8)   (C) (5, 12)
(D) (2, 16)   (E) (4, 24)

6

What is the area, in square units, of the shaded region in the figure above?

(A) 32
(B) 33
(C) 34
(D) 35
(E) 36

7

Note: Figure not drawn to scale

Points A and B lie on the line $y = 6$, as shown above. Lines ℓ_1 and ℓ_2 pass through the origin, and ℓ_1 has a slope of ½. If the distance from A to B is 4, what is the slope of line ℓ_2?

Answer Key 4: Coordinate Geometry

Concept Review 4

1. $(-2, 1)$

2. $(0.5, 2)$

3. ⅗

4. Your line should be vertical (straight up and down) and pass through B.

5. The x-coordinate of all the points is 3, so ℓ_1 can be described by the equation $x = 3$.

6. ℓ_2 should be horizontal (straight across) and pass through B.

7. ℓ_3 should be a horizontal (straight across) line one unit below the x-axis.

8. $(-2, 5)$

9. $(1, 8)$ (Notice that the new segment must be the same length as AB, but its slope is the negative reciprocal of AB's slope, that is, $-5/2$.)

10. $(8, 5)$

11. The area of the rectangle is 108, and its length DC is $14 - 2 = 12$. Therefore its height is $108/12 = 9$. Therefore $k - 1 = 9$, and $k = 10$.

   $m = 14$
   $n = 10$
   $p = 1$

12. AC is the hypotenuse of a right triangle with legs of 9 and 12. This is a 3-4-5 triangle times 3—a 9 – 12 – 15 triangle—so AC is 15. The perimeter of the rectangle is $9 + 12 + 9 + 12 = 42$. So the ratio of the diagonal to the perimeter is $15/42 = 5/14$.

13. The slope of DB is 3/4, or .75.

14. AC and DB intersect at the midpoint of each segment. The midpoint of AC is $((14 + 2)/2, (10 + 1)/2)$ $= (8, 5.5)$.

15. $(26, 19)$

16. Use the left side of the triangle as the base. This way, the base is vertical and the height is horizontal, so the lengths are easier to find. The base is 4 units and the height is 7 units, so the area is $(4 \times 7)/2 = 14$.

17. The reflection of the triangle over the line $x = 3$ is shown above. The "leftmost" point has an x-coordinate of 0.

18. No matter how the triangle is reflected, the area remains the same. The area is still 14.

SAT I Practice 4

1. **B** The vertices of a square must always be listed in consecutive order, so point C must follow consecutively after B and can be in either position shown in the figure at right. Therefore, C can be at $(0, 2)$ or $(6, 2)$.

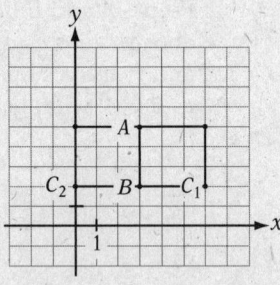

2. **A** The horizontal line passing through $(1, 8)$ is the line $y = 8$, and the vertical line passing through $(-3, 4)$ is the line $x = -3$. So they intersect at $(-3, 8)$.

3. **E** The distance from $(0, 0)$ to $(-3, 4)$ is 5, which is the radius of the circle. Therefore, any point that is 5 units from the origin is also on the circle. Each of the given points is also 5 units from the origin.

4. **(E)** The distance from $(3, -7)$ to $(8, 5)$ is $\sqrt{(8-3)^2 + (5-(-7))^2} = \sqrt{5^2 + 12^2} = 13$. The circumference is $2\pi r = 26\pi$.

5. **D** $\triangle ABC$ has a base of 4 and height of 8, so its area is $(4 \times 8)/2 = 16$. Since the base of $\triangle CDE$ is 2, its height must be 16 if it is to have the same area as $\triangle ABC$. The y-coordinate of E, then, must be 16 or -16.

6. **E** Draw a rectangle around the quadrilateral as in the figure at right. The rectangle has an area of $9 \times 8 = 72$. If we "remove" the areas of the four right triangles from the corners, the area of the shaded region will remain. $72 - 4 - 12 - 12.5 - 7.5 = 36$.

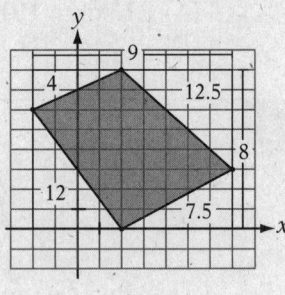

7. ⅜ The y-coordinate of point A is 6, which means the "rise" from O to A is 6. Since the slope of ℓ_1 is ½, the "run" must be 12. The "run" from O to B is $12 + 4 = 16$, and the "rise" is 6, so the slope of ℓ_2 is $6/16 = 3/8$.

Lesson 5:
Areas and Perimeters

The Formulas

The only area or perimeter formulas you will need for the SAT I will be given at the beginning of each section:

Reference Information

$A = \pi r^2$
$C = 2\pi r$

$A = \ell w$

$A = \frac{1}{2}bh$

$V = \ell wh$

$V = \pi r^2 h$

$c^2 = a^2 + b^2$

Special Right Triangles

The arc of a circle measures 360°.
Every straight angle measures 180°.
The sum of the measures of the angles in a triangle is 180°.

❑ **Make sure you can find the height of an obtuse triangle, when the height is "outside" the triangle:** The height always starts from the vertex opposite the base and must be perpendicular to the line containing the base.

❑ **Remember that any side of the triangle can be the base; rotate it if you need to.**

❑ **Don't confuse the area formula for a circle (πr^2) with the circumference formula ($2\pi r$).** Just remember that areas are measured in square units, so the area formula is the one with the radius squared.

Using Diagrams

❑ **If a geometry problem doesn't include a figure, draw one!** If it does include a diagram, **mark it up** with any information you find!

❑ You can use the diagram to estimate angle measures and lengths, **unless** it is labelled **"Note: Figure not drawn to scale,"** which means that the figure is drawn **inaccurately,** or **in only one of many different possible ways.** In this case, it often helps to **redraw the figure**—if it's drawn inaccurately, redraw it **accurately,** and see whether anything important changes. If it can be drawn in different ways, redraw it so that it is as **different**

as possible from the original, but **all of the given information is maintained.**

Strange Shapes

❑ Don't panic when you see a strange-looking shape on an SAT I. **Just notice how the shape relates to simple shapes.**

e.g.   In the figure below, the shaded region is constructed of only horizontal and vertical sides. That is, all angles are right angles. What is the perimeter of the shaded region?

Compare the shaded region to the rectangle, and **don't confuse perimeter with area!** Even though the **area** of the shaded region is clearly less than the area of the rectangle, their **perimeters** must be the same! How do we know? Consider the two different paths from A to B. Notice that all the horizontal segments of the "jagged" path add up in length to the horizontal part of the "simple" path along the rectangle. The same is true of the vertical parts. So the perimeter is 15 + 20 + 15 + 20 = 70.

e.g.   If the circle with center *C* has an area of 16π, what is the area of the shaded region?

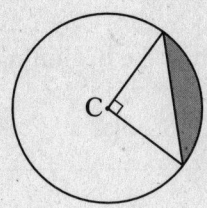

Piece together the strange shape from simple shapes. Notice that the shaded region is simply a quarter of the circle minus the triangle. If the area of the circle is 16π, then a quarter of the circle has an area of 4π. Since $\pi r^2 = 16\pi$, the radius must be 4. Therefore, the base and height of the triangle are both 4, and the area of the triangle is (4×4)/2 = 8. Therefore, the area of the shaded region is 4π − 8.

Concept Review 5:
Areas and Perimeters

Draw a diagram in the space below for the following situation:
The length and width of rectangle *ABCD* are integers. The area of *ABCD* is 32. Diagonal *AC* is extended to point *F* such that *C* is the midpoint of *AF*.

1.   If the area of *ABCD* is 32, what is the area of Δ*FDB*?

2.   What is the ratio of the area of Δ*FCB* to the area of Δ*FAD*?

Questions 3 and 4 pertain to the diagram below, in which *P* is the center of the semicircle.

3.   What is the area of the figure above?

4.   What is the perimeter of the figure above?

5.   The figure above consists of a rectangle and a curved path which is made up of 10 semicircles of equal diameter. If the total length of this curved path is 40π, then the area of the rectangle is
     (A)   40   (B)   80   (C)   96   (D)   192   (E)   384

SAT I Practice 5:
Areas and Perimeters

1

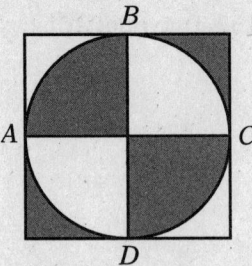

In the figure above, a circle is inscribed in a square and intersects the square at points *A*, *B*, *C*, and *D*. If *AC* = 12, what is the total area of the shaded regions?

(A) 18
(B) 36
(C) 18π
(D) 24π
(E) 72

2

In the figure above, *ABCD* is a rectangle and *P* and *R* are midpoints of their respective sides. What is the area of △*APR*?

(A) 54
(B) 68
(C) 72
(D) 78
(E) 96

3

A fence encloses three sides of a rectangular garden that is bordered on the other side by a barn, as shown in the figure above. If the total length of the fence is 44 meters and *p* is the length, in meters, of the fence parallel to the barn wall, then which of the following expresses the area of the garden?

(A) $22p - p^2$

(B) $\dfrac{44p - p^2}{2}$

(C) $22p$

(D) $\dfrac{22p - p^2}{2}$

(E) $44p - p^2$

4

What is the maximum number of pieces that can be cut from a paper circle with four straight cuts if none of the pieces are moved or folded between cuts?

(A) 7
(B) 8
(C) 9
(D) 10
(E) 11

5

In the figure above, all angles shown are right angles. What is the perimeter of the shaded region?

(A) 51
(B) 54
(C) 57
(D) 60
(E) 63

6

The figure above consists of a circle with radius 2 inscribed in an equilateral triangle in which all three interior angle bisectors are drawn. What is the total area of the shaded regions?

(A) $2\sqrt{3}$

(B) $\dfrac{2\pi + 2}{3}$

(C) $\dfrac{2\pi - 2}{3}$

(D) $2\pi + 2$

(E) $\pi + 2$

7

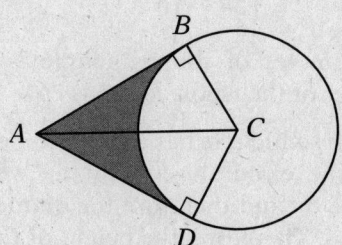

In the figure above, C is the center of the circle, $AC = 12$, and $\angle BAD = 60°$. What is the *perimeter* of the shaded region?

(A) $12 + 4\pi$

(B) $6\sqrt{3} + 4\pi$

(C) $6\sqrt{3} + 3\pi$

(D) $12\sqrt{3} + 3\pi$

(E) $12\sqrt{3} + 4\pi$

8

In the figure above, PR is the radius of the circle as well as a side of the rectangle. If the circle has an area of 4π and the rectangle has an area of 8, then what is the *perimeter* of the shaded region?

(A) $\pi + 8$

(B) $\pi + 10$

(C) $\pi + 12$

(D) $2\pi + 8$

(E) $2\pi + 12$

Answer Key 5:
Areas and Perimeters

Concept Review 5

Your diagram should look something like the one above, although the rectangle can also have dimensions of 1 and 32 or 2 and 16.

1. Think of the area of $\triangle FDB$ as the sum of the areas of $\triangle DCB$, $\triangle FDC$, and $\triangle FCB$. Each of these triangles has an area that is half of the rectangle, because each one has the same base and height as the rectangle. (If you have a tough time seeing this, think of BC as the base of $\triangle FCB$ and CD as the base of $\triangle FDC$. Since these triangles are obtuse, their heights are "outside" the triangles.) Therefore, the area of $\triangle FDB$ is $16 + 16 + 16 = 48$.

2. We just found that $\triangle FCB$ has an area of 16. The area of $\triangle FAD$ is the area of $\triangle FCD$ + the area of

$\triangle ADC$, which is $16 + 16 = 32$. Therefore, the ratio is 1:2.

3. Draw the extra segment as shown and determine its length from the Pythagorean Theorem. (It's a 3-4-5 right triangle times 2!) The area of the semicircle is $16\pi/2 = 8\pi$, the area of the rectangle is 40, and the area of the triangle is 24, for a total area of $64 + 8\pi$.

4. The perimeter of the semicircle is 4π, so the perimeter of the whole figure is $26 + 4\pi$.

5. (E) Each semicircle has a perimeter of 4π, which means the circumference of a "whole" circle would be 8π and therefore the diameter of each circle is 8. Therefore, the height of the rectangle is 16 and the length is 24. $24 \times 16 = 384$

SAT I Practice 5

1. **E** Move the shaded pieces around to see that they make up half of the square. The area of the square is $12 \times 12 = 144$, so the shaded region has area $144/2 = 72$.

2. **C** Find the area indirectly by subtracting the three right triangles from the rectangle. The rectangle has area $8 \times 24 = 192$, so the triangle has area $192 - 48 - 48 - 24 = 72$.

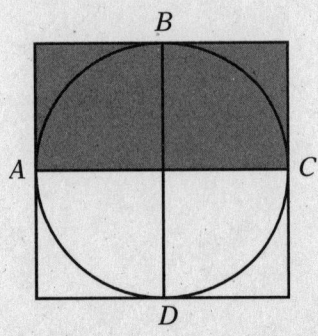

3. B The length of the garden is p. The width is half of $44 - p$. Therefore, the area is $p((44 - p)/2) = (44p - p^2)/2$.

4. E You get the maximum number of pieces (11) by making sure that each cut intersects every other previous cut in a new spot. Your diagram should look something like this, with six points of intersection in the circle.

5. B Draw the extra line shown here to see that the shaded region has a perimeter equal to a 10-by-17 rectangle. Therefore its perimeter is $10 + 17 + 10 + 17 = 54$.

6. A Move the pieces together to see that they form a right triangle. Since all of the interior angles of an equilateral triangle are 60° and the bisectors divide them in half, the triangle is a 30°-60°-90° triangle, so its base must be $2\sqrt{3}$, and the area is

$$\left((2\sqrt{3})(2)\right)/2 = 2\sqrt{3}.$$

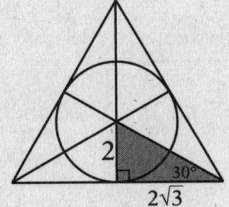

7. E The two right triangles have two pairs of equal sides (the two radii and the shared hypotenuse), so they must be congruent triangles. Arc BD is ⅓ of the circle, with circumference 12π. Therefore, you should be able to determine the measures shown in this diagram and see that the perimeter of the shaded region is $12\sqrt{3} + 4\pi$.

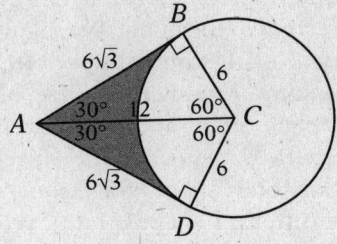

8. A If the circle has an area of 4π, its radius is 2. If the rectangle has an area of 8, its length must be 4. The arc portion of the shaded region is 1/4 of the circle with circumference 4π, so the perimeter is $2 + 2 + 4 + \pi = 8 + \pi$.

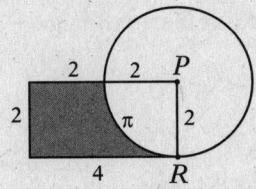

Lesson 6: Similar Figures

Similar Figures

❑ When you think of **similar** you probably think of **"almost the same, but not quite."** In mathematics, however, the word **similar** has a much more specific, technical meaning. Two figures are **similar if they are the same shape, but not necessarily the same size.** For instance, all circles are similar to each other, and all squares are similar to each other: there is only one "shape" for a circle, and only one "shape" for a square. But there are many different shapes that a rectangle may have, so two rectangles aren't necessarily similar.

❑ If two shapes are **similar,** then **all corresponding angles are equal** and **all corresponding lengths are proportional.**

❑ Use **proportions** to find the lengths of unknown sides in similar figures.

e.g.   What is x in the figure at left below?

Answer: The two triangles are similar because all of their corresponding angles are equal. (Even though only two pairs of angles are **given** as equal, we know that the other pair are equal also, because the angles in a triangle must add up to 180°.) So we can set up a proportion of corresponding sides:

$$\frac{10}{7} = \frac{x}{8}$$ Cross-multiply: $7x = 80$

Divide by 7: $x = 80/7 = 11.43$

❑ Two **triangles** are **similar** if any of the following is true:

• Two pairs of corresponding angles are equal. (If two pairs are equal, the third pair must be equal, too.)
• Two pairs of corresponding sides are proportional and the angles between them are equal.
• All three pairs of corresponding sides are proportional.

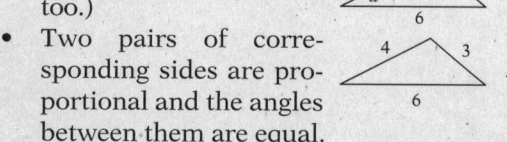

❑ Don't **assume** that two figures are similar just because they look similar. Make sure you can prove it!

Ratios of Areas

Consider two squares: one with a side length of 2 and the other with a side length of 3. Clearly, their sides are in the ratio of 2:3. What about their areas? That's easy: their areas are $2^2 = 4$ and $3^2 = 9$, so the areas are in a ratio of 4:9. This demonstrates a fact that is true of all similar figures:

❑ **If corresponding lengths of two similar figures have a ratio of $a:b$, then the areas of the two figures have a ratio of $a^2:b^2$.**

e.g.   A garden that is 30 feet long has an area of 600 square feet. A blueprint of the garden that is drawn to scale depicts the garden as being 3 inches long. What is the area of blueprint drawing of the garden?

Answer: It is tempting to want to say 60 square inches because 30:600 = 3:60. But **be careful:** the ratio of areas is the **square** of the ratio of lengths! You can draw a diagram, assuming the garden to be a rectangle. (The shape of the garden doesn't matter: it's convenient to draw the garden as a rectangle, but it doesn't have to be.) Or you can simply set up the proportion using the formula above:

$$\frac{x}{600} = \frac{3^2}{30^2} = \frac{9}{900}$$

Cross-multiply: $900x = 5,400$
Divide by 900: $x = 6$

Concept Review 6: Similar Figures

1. If two figures are similar, then their corresponding sides are _____ and their corresponding angles are _____.

2. What are the three sets of conditions of which any one is sufficient to show that two triangles are similar?

   a.

   b.

   c.

3. The hypotenuses of two similar right triangles are 4 centimeters and 6 centimeters long, respectively. If the area of the larger triangle is 27, what is the area of the smaller one?

Note: Figure not drawn to scale.

4. In the figure above, $\ell_1 \parallel \ell_2$, $AC = 4$, $BC = 5$, and $CE = 6$. What is the length of DE?

5. In a 5"-by-8" rectangular photograph, the image of a tree is 3" high. The photograph is then magnified until its area is 1,000 square inches. What is the height of the tree image in the larger photograph?

SAT I Practice 6:
Similar Figures

1 The ratio of the areas of two squares is 4:1. If the perimeter of the smaller square is 20, what is the perimeter of the larger square?

(A) 5
(B) 10
(C) 20
(D) 40
(E) 80

2 A scale drawing of a rectangular patio measures 5 centimeters by 7 centimeters. If the longer side of the actual patio is 21 feet, what is the area, in square feet, of the actual patio?

(A) 72
(B) 315
(C) 356
(D) 441
(E) 617

3

 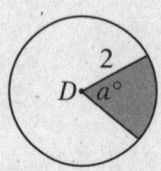

Note: Figure not drawn to scale.

In the figure above, C and D are the centers of the two circles with radii of 3 and 2, respectively. If the larger shaded region has an area of 9, what is the area of the smaller shaded region?

(A) 4
(B) 5
(C) 6
(D) 7
(E) 8

4

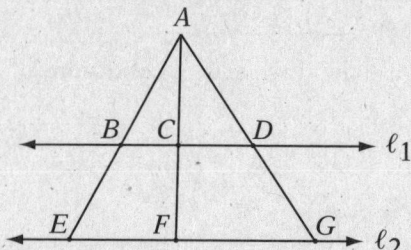

In the figure above, $\ell_1 \parallel \ell_2$. If $EF = x$, and $EG = y$, then which of the following represents the ratio of CD to BC?

(A) $1 - \dfrac{y}{x}$

(B) $1 + \dfrac{y}{x}$

(C) $\dfrac{y}{x} - 1$

(D) $1 - \dfrac{x}{y}$

(E) $1 + \dfrac{x}{y}$

5

A circular cone with a base of radius 5 has been cut as shown in the figure above. What is the height of the smaller cone?

(A) $\dfrac{8}{13}$

(B) $\dfrac{96}{13}$

(C) $\dfrac{96}{12}$

(D) $\dfrac{96}{5}$

(E) $\dfrac{104}{5}$

6

Note: Figure not drawn to scale.

In the figure above, what is the perimeter of the shaded trapezoid?

7

Note: Figure not drawn to scale.

In the figure above, $\overline{BD}$ is parallel to $\overline{EG}$, $AD = 6$, $DG = 4$, and $\triangle AEF$ has an area of 75. What is the area of $\triangle ABC$?

(A)   27
(B)   36
(C)   45
(D)   54
(E)   63

Answer Key 6: Similar Figures

Concept Review 6

1. If two figures are similar, then their corresponding sides are *proportional* and their corresponding angles are *equal* (or *congruent*).

2. a. two pairs of corresponding angles are equal
   b. two pairs of corresponding sides are proportional and the included angles are equal
   c. all three pairs of corresponding sides are proportional

3. The ratio of the sides is 4:6 or 2:3. The ratio of the areas is the square of the ratio of sides, which is 4:9. If x is the area of the smaller triangle, then $x/27 = 4/9$. Solving for x gives $x = 12$.

4. If $\ell_1 \mid \ell_2$, then the two triangles must be similar. Since corresponding sides are proportional, $AC/AE = BC/DE$.
   Substituting, this gives $\qquad$ $4/10 = 5/DE$.
   Cross-multiply: $\qquad\qquad$ $4DE = 50$
   Divide by 4: $\qquad\qquad\quad$ $DE = 12.5$

5. A 5"-by-8" rectangle has an area of 40 square inches. The ratio of areas, then, is 40:1,000, or 1:25. This is the square of the ratio of lengths, so the ratio of lengths must be 1:5. If x is the length of the larger tree image, then $3/x = 1/5$. Cross-multiplying gives $x = 15$, so the tree is 15 inches high in the larger photograph.

SAT I Practice 6

1. **D** If the ratio of the areas is 4:1, then the ratio of corresponding lengths is the square root: 2:1. If the perimeter of the smaller square is 20, then the perimeter of larger one is twice as big.

2. **B** Find the width of the patio with a proportion:

$$5/7 = x/21$$
Cross-multiply: $\qquad$ $7x = 105$
Divide by 7: $\qquad\quad$ $x = 15$

So the patio is a 15-foot-by-21-foot rectangle, which has an area of $15 \times 21 = 315$ square feet.

3. **A** The two regions are similar, because the central angles are the same. The ratio of their corresponding lengths is 3:2, so the ratio of their areas is 9:4. Since the larger area is 9, the smaller area must be 4.

4. **C** If EF has length x and EG has length y, then FG must have length $y - x$, as shown. Since the two lines are parallel, $\triangle ABC$ is similar to $\triangle AEF$ and $\triangle ACD$ is similar to $\triangle AFG$. Therefore $AC/CF = BC/x$ and $AC/CF = CD/(y - x)$. So $BC/x = CD/(y - x)$,

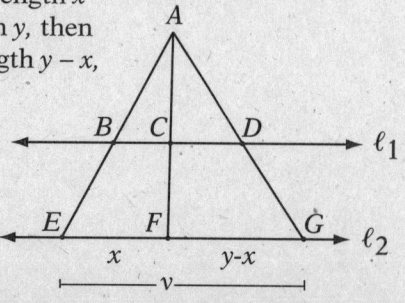

and therefore $CD/BC = (y - x)/x = y/x - 1$.

5. **B** The height of the larger cone can be found with the Pythagorean Theorem to be 12. (It's the old 5-12-13 right triangle!) Since the two triangles are similar, $x/12 = \tfrac{8}{3}$. Multiplying by 12 gives $x = 96/13$.

6. **28** The two triangles are similar because their corresponding angles are equal. Since they are right triangles, the missing sides can be found with the Pythagorean Theorem. Your diagram should look like the one above. The perimeter is $3 + 8 + 5 + 12 = 28$.

7. **A** Since the lines are parallel, $\triangle ABC$ is similar to $\triangle AEF$ and $\triangle ACD$ is similar to $\triangle AFG$. Therefore, $AD/AG = AC/AF = 6/10 = 3/5$. The ratio of areas between $\triangle ABC$ and $\triangle AEF$ is the square of the ratio of sides, which is $(3/5)^2 = 9/25$. Since $\triangle AEF$ has an area of 75, (the area of $\triangle ABC$)/75 = 9/25. So $\triangle ABC$ has an area of 27.

Lesson 7: Volumes and 3-D Geometry

Volume

The SAT I math section may include a question or two about volumes. Remember two things:

❑ **The volume of a container is nothing more than the number of "unit cubes" it can hold.**

❑ **The only volume formulas you will need are given to you in the "Reference Information" on every math section.**

e.g.　How many rectangular bricks measuring 2 inches by 3 inches by 4 inches must be stacked together (without mortar or any other material) to create a solid rectangular box that measures 15 inches by 30 inches by 60 inches?

Don't be too concerned with **how** the bricks could be stacked to make the box; there are many possible arrangements, but the arrangement doesn't affect the answer. All you need to know is that it can be done. If so, just looking at the volumes is enough: if you use n bricks, then the box must have a volume that is n times larger than the volume of one brick. Each brick has a volume of $2 \times 3 \times 4 = 24$ cubic inches. The box has a volume of $15 \times 30 \times 60 = 27{,}000$ square inches. The number of bricks, then, must be $27{,}000/24 = 1{,}125$.

3-D Distances

❑ **If you are trying to find the length of a line segment in three dimensions, look for a right triangle that has that segment as its hypotenuse.**

e.g.　The figure at right shows a cube with edges of length 4. If point C is the midpoint of edge BD, what is the length of $\overline{AC}$?

Draw segment $\overline{CE}$ to see that $\overline{AC}$ is the hypotenuse of right triangle $\triangle AEC$.

Leg $\overline{AE}$ has a length of 4, and leg $\overline{EC}$ is the hypotenuse of right triangle $\triangle EBC$, with legs of length 2 and 4. Therefore,

$$EC = \sqrt{2^2 + 4^2} = \sqrt{4 + 16} = \sqrt{20} \, ,$$

so　$AC = \sqrt{\left(\sqrt{20}\right)^2 + 4^2} = \sqrt{20 + 16} = \sqrt{36} = 6.$

❑ **One possible shortcut for finding lengths in three dimensions is the three-dimensional distance formula:**

$$d = \sqrt{\left(x_2 - x_1\right)^2 + \left(y_2 - y_1\right)^2 + \left(z_2 - z_1\right)^2}$$

e.g.　If you think of point A in the cube above as being the origin $(0, 0, 0)$, then point C can be considered to be $(4, 4, 2)$. The distance from A to C, then, is

$$\sqrt{\left(4 - 0\right)^2 + \left(4 - 0\right)^2 + \left(2 - 0\right)^2} = \sqrt{16 + 16 + 4} = \sqrt{36} = 6$$

Concept Review 7: Volumes and 3-D Geometry

1. What is the definition of volume?

2. Write the formula for the volume of a rectangular box.

3. Write the 3-D distance formula.

4. Graph the points $A(-2, 3, 1)$ and $B(2, 1, -2)$ on an x-y-z graph.

5. What is the distance from point A to point B in the figure above?

Container A   Container B

6. The two containers with rectangular sides in the figure above have the interior dimensions shown. Both containers rest on a flat, horizontal surface. Container A is filled completely with water, and then this water is poured, without spilling, into Container B. When all of the liquid is poured from Container A into Container B, what is the depth of the water in Container B?

SAT I Practice 7:
Volumes and 3-D Geometry

1 The length, width, and height of a rectangular box, in centimeters, are a, b, and c, where a, b, and c are all integers. The total surface area of the box, in square centimeters, is s, and the volume of the box, in cubic centimeters, is v. Which of the following must be true?

   I. v is an integer.
   II. s is an even integer.
   III.   The greatest distance between any two vertices of the box is $\sqrt{a^2+b^2+c^2}$.

   (A)   I only
   (B)   I and II only
   (C)   I and III only
   (D)   II and III only
   (E)   I, II, and III

2

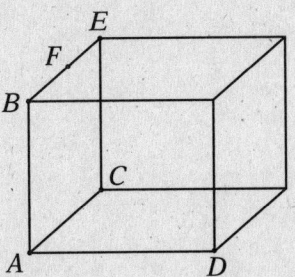

The figure above shows a rectangular box in which $AB = 6$, $AC = 5$, and $AD = 8$. What is the length of the shortest path from A to F that travels only on the edges of the box and does *not* pass through either point B or point C?

   (A)   27.5
   (B)   28.5
   (C)   29.5
   (D)   30
   (E)   30.5

3 A pool-filling service charges $2.00 per cubic meter of water for the first 300 cubic meters and $1.50 per cubic meter of water after that. At this rate, how much would it cost to have the service fill a rectangular pool of uniform depth that is 2 meters deep, 20 meters long, and 15 meters wide?

   (A) $450
   (B) $650
   (C) $800
   (D) $1,050
   (E) $1,200

4

In the figure above, a rectangular box has the dimensions shown. N is a vertex of the box, and M is the midpoint of an edge of the box. What is the length of $\overline{MN}$?

   (A) $\sqrt{63}$
   (B) $\sqrt{77}$
   (C) $\sqrt{98}$
   (D) $\sqrt{108}$
   (E) $\sqrt{125}$

5 A cereal company sells oatmeal in two sizes of cylindrical containers. The smaller container holds 10 ounces of oatmeal. If the larger container has twice the radius of the smaller container and 1.5 times the height, how many ounces of oatmeal does the larger container hold? (The volume of a cylinder is given by the formula $V = \pi r^2 h$.)

   (A)   30
   (B)   45
   (C)   60
   (D)   75
   (E)   90

6

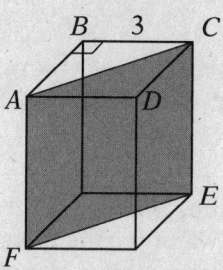

The figure above shows a rectangular solid with a volume of 72 cubic units. Base *ABCD* has an area of 12 square units. What is the area of rectangle *ACEF*?

7

The figure above shows a wedge-shaped holding tank that is partially filled with water. If the tank is 1/16 full, what is the depth of the water at the deepest part?

(A) 3
(B) 2
(C) 1.5
(D) 1
(E) 0.75

Answer Key 7: Volumes and 3-D Geometry

Concept Review 7

1. The volume of a solid is the number of "unit cubes" that fit inside of it.

2. $V = lwh$

3. $d = \sqrt{(x_2 - x_1)^2 + (y_2 - y_1)^2 + (z_2 - z_1)^2}$

4. Your graph should look like this one:

5. Using the 3-D distance formula,
$$d = \sqrt{(2-(-2))^2 + (1-3)^2 + (-2-1)^2}$$
$$= \sqrt{(4)^2 + (-2)^2 + (-3)^2}$$
$$= \sqrt{16+4+9} = \sqrt{29}$$

6. Since the water is poured without spilling, the volume of water must remain the same. Container A has a volume of $4 \times 6 \times 10 = 240$ cubic inches. Since Container B is larger, the water won't fill it completely, but will fill it only to a depth of h inches. The volume of the water can then be calculated as $8 \times 8 \times h = 64h$ cubic inches. Since the volume must remain the same, $64h = 240$, so $h = 3.75$ inches.

SAT I Practice 7

1. **E** $v = abc$, so if a, b, and c are integers, v must be an integer also and statement I is true. The total surface area of the box, s, is $2ab + 2bc + 2ac = 2(ab + bc + ac)$, which is a multiple of 2 and therefore even. So statement II is true. Statement III is true by the 3-D distance formula.

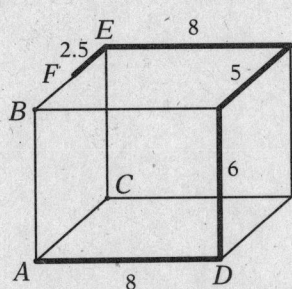

2. **C**   The path shown above is the shortest under the circumstances. The length of the path is

$8 + 6 + 5 + 8 + 2.5 = 29.5$.

3. **D**   The volume of the pool is $2 \times 20 \times 15 = 600$ cubic meters. The first 300 cubic meters cost $300 \times 2 = \$600$, and the other 300 cubic meters cost $300 \times 1.50 = \$450$, for a total of $\$1,050$.

4. **C**   Draw segment $\overline{NP}$ as shown. It is the hypotenuse of a right triangle, so you can find its length with the Pythagorean Theorem:

$$NP = \sqrt{8^2 + 5^2} = \sqrt{64+25} = \sqrt{89}$$

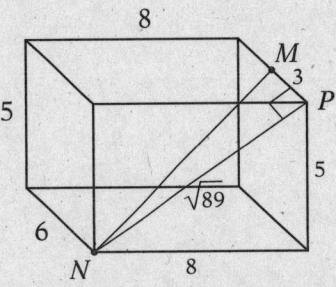

$\overline{NM}$ is the hypotenuse of right triangle $\triangle NPM$, so

$$NM = \sqrt{\left(\sqrt{89}\right)^2 + 3^2} = \sqrt{89+9} = \sqrt{98}$$

5. **C**   If the volume of the smaller container is $V = \pi r^2 h$, then the volume of the larger container is $\pi(2r)^2(1.5h) = 6\pi r^2 h = 6v$. So the larger container holds six times as much oatmeal as the smaller one. The smaller container holds 10 ounces of oatmeal, so the larger one holds $10 \times 6 = 60$ ounces.

6. **30** Mark up the diagram as shown. If the base has an area of 12, AB must be 4. If the volume of the box is 72, then the height must be $72/12 = 6$. AC must be 5, because it's the hypotenuse of a 3-4-5 triangle. So the rectangle has an area of $5 \times 6 = 30$.

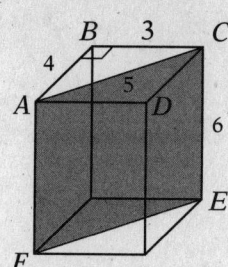

7. **A**   If the volume of the water is 1/16 the volume of the tank, the smaller triangle must have an area 1/16 that of the larger triangle. The two are similar, so the ratio of the lengths must be 1/4, because $1/16 = (1/4)^2$. Therefore, the depth of water is 1/4 the depth of the tank: $12/4 = 3$.

Lesson 8: Circles

Circle Basics

Okay, we all know a circle when we see one, but it often helps to know the **mathematical definition of a circle.**

❏ **A circle is all of the points in a plane that are a certain distance *r* from the center.**

❏ **The *radius* is the distance from the center to any point on the circle.**

 Radius means *ray* in Latin; a radius comes from the center of the circle like *a ray of light from the sun.*

❏ **The *diameter* is twice the radius: *d* = 2*r***

 Dia- means *through* in Latin, so the diameter is a segment that goes *all the way through* the circle.

The Circumference and Area of a Circle

It's easy to confuse the **circumference** formula with the **area** formula, because both formulas contain the same symbols arranged differently: *circumference* = 2π*r* and *area* = π*r*². There are two simple ways to avoid that mistake:

Reference Information

$A = \pi r^2$ $A = \ell w$ $A = \frac{1}{2} b$
$C = 2\pi r$

The arc of a circle measures 360°.

❏ Remember that the formulas for **circumference** and **area** are given in the **reference information** at the beginning of every math section:

❏ Remember that **area** is always measured in **square units,** so the **area** formula is the one with the "square:" *area* = π*r*².

Tangents

❏ **A tangent is a line that touches (or *intersects*) the circle at only one point.** Think of a plate balancing on its side on a table: the table is like a tangent line to the plate.

❏ **A tangent line is always perpendicular to the radius drawn to the point of tangency.** Just think of a bicycle tire (the circle) on the road (the

tangent): notice that the center of the wheel must be "directly above" where the tire touches the road, so the radius and tangent must be perpendicular.

e.g.   In the diagram above, point *M* is 7 units away from the center of circle *P*. If line *l* is tangent to the circle and *MR* = 5, what is the area of the circle?

 First, connect the dots. Draw *MP* and *PR* to make a triangle.

Since *PR* is a radius and *MR* is a tangent, they are perpendicular.

Since you know two sides of a right triangle, you can use the Pythagorean Theorem to find the third side: $5^2 + (PR)^2 = 7^2$
Simplify: $25 + (PR)^2 = 49$
Subtract 25: $(PR)^2 = 24$

$(PR)^2$ is the radius squared. Since the area of the circle is π*r*², it is 24π.

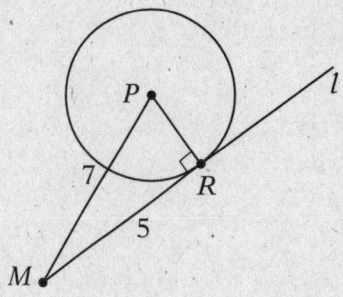

Concept Review 8: Circles

1. What is the formula for the circumference of a circle?

2. What is the formula for the area of a circle?

3. What is a tangent line?

4. What is the relationship between a tangent to a circle and the radius to the point of tangency?

5. In the figure above, $\overline{AB}$ is a tangent to circle C, $AB = 8$, and $AD = 6$. What is the circumference of circle C?

6. In the figure above, P and N are the centers of the circles and are 6 centimeters apart. What is the area of the shaded region?

SAT I Practice 8: Circles

1 Two circles, *A* and *B*, lie in the same plane. If the center of circle *B* lies on circle *A*, then in how many points could circle *A* and circle *B* intersect?

    I.   0
   II.   1
  III. 2

(A) I only
(B) III only
(C) I and III only
(D) II and III only
(E) I, II, and III

2 What is the area, in square centimeters, of a circle with a circumference of 16π centimeters?

(A) 8π
(B) 16π
(C) 32π
(D) 64π
(E) 256π

3 Point *B* lies 10 from point *A*, which is the center of the circle of radius 6. If a tangent line is drawn from *B* to the circle, what is the distance from *B* to the point of tangency?

4

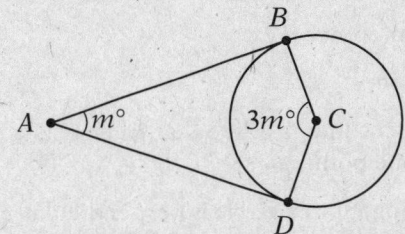

Note: Figure not drawn to scale.

In the figure above, $\overline{AB}$ and $\overline{AD}$ are tangents to circle *C*. What is the value of *m*?

5

Note: Figure not drawn to scale.

In the figure above, circle *A* intersects circle *B* in exactly one point, $\overleftrightarrow{CD}$ is tangent to both circles, circle *A* has a radius of 2, and circle *B* has a radius of 8. What is the length of $\overline{CD}$?

Answer Key 8: Circles

Concept Review 8

1. circumference = $2\pi r$

2. area = πr^2

3. A tangent line is a line that intersects a circle at only one point.

4. Any tangent to a circle is perpendicular to the radius drawn to the point of tangency.

5. Draw $\overline{BC}$ to make a right triangle, and call the length of the radius r. Then you can use the Pythagorean Theorem to find r:

$$8^2 + r^2 = (r+6)^2$$

FOIL: $\quad\quad\quad\quad 64 + r^2 = r^2 + 12r + 36$
Subtract r^2: $\quad\quad\quad 64 = 12r + 36$
Subtract 36: $\quad\quad\quad 28 = 12r$
Divide by 12: $\quad\quad\quad 7/3 = r$

The circumference is $2\pi r$, which is $2\pi(7/3) = 14\pi/3$.

6. Draw the segments shown here. Since PN is a radius of both circles, the radii of both circles have the same length. Notice that PN, PR, RN, PT, and NT are all radii, so they are all the same length; thus, $\triangle PNT$ and $\triangle PRN$ are equilateral triangles and their angles are all 60°. Now you can find the area of the left half of the shaded region. This is the area of the sector minus the area of $\triangle RNT$. Since $\angle RNT$ is 120°, the sector is 120/360, or ⅓, of the circle. The circle has area 36π, so the sector has area 12π. $\triangle RNT$ consists of two 30°-60°-90° triangles, with sides as marked, so its area is

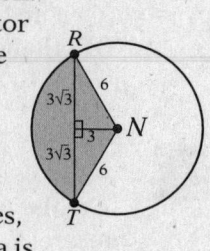

$(1/2)(6\sqrt{3})(3) = 9\sqrt{3}$. Therefore, half of the original shaded region is $12\pi - 9\sqrt{3}$, and the whole is $24\pi - 18\sqrt{3}$.

SAT I Practice 8

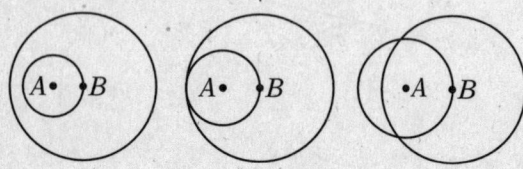

1. **E** The figure above demonstrates all three possibilities.

2. **D** The circumference = $2\pi r = 16\pi$. Dividing by 2π gives $r = 8$. Area = $\pi r^2 = \pi(8)^2 = 64\pi$.

3. **8** Draw a figure as shown, including the tangent segment and the radius extended to the point of tangency. You can find x with the Pythagorean Theorem:

Simplify: $\quad\quad\quad 6^2 + x^2 = 10^2$
$\quad\quad\quad\quad\quad\quad 36 + x^2 = 100$
Subtract 36: $\quad\quad\quad x^2 = 64$
Take the square root: $\quad\quad x = 8$

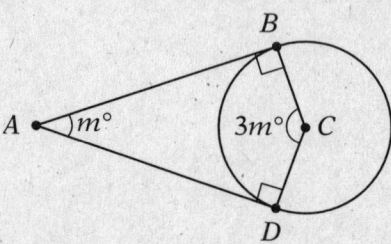

4. **45** Since $\overline{AB}$ and $\overline{AD}$ are tangents to the circle, they are perpendicular to their respective radii, as shown. The sum of the angles in a quadrilateral is 360°, so

$$m + 3m + 90 + 90 = 360$$

Simplify: $\quad\quad\quad 4m + 180 = 360$
Subtract 180: $\quad\quad\quad 4m = 180$
Divide by 4: $\quad\quad\quad m = 45$

5. **8** Draw the segments shown. Choose point E to make rectangle $ACDE$ and right triangle AEB. Notice that $CD = AE$, because opposite sides of a rectangle are equal. You can find AE with the Pythagorean Theorem:

$$(AE)^2 + 6^2 = 10^2$$

Simplify: $\qquad$ $(AE)^2 + 36 = 100$

Subtract 36: $\qquad$ $(AE)^2 = 64$

Take the square root: $\qquad$ $AE = 8$

Since $CD = AE$, $CD = 8$.

CHAPTER 14

ESSENTIAL ALGEBRA 2 SKILLS

1. Sequences

2. Functions

3. Transformations

4. Variation

5. Data Analysis

6. Negative and Fractional Exponents

Lesson 1: Sequences

Kinds of Sequences

A **sequence** is simply a list of numbers, each of which is called a **term.** The SAT I may ask you to identify and use a pattern in a sequence of numbers—for instance, "How many odd numbers are in the first 100 terms of the sequence 1, 2, 3, 1, 2, 3 . . . ?"

❑ An **arithmetic sequence** is a sequence in which each term is formed by **adding** a constant number to the previous term (e.g., 1, 5, 9, 13, 17, . . .). The **difference** between any two consecutive terms is always the same.

❑ A **geometric sequence** is a sequence in which each term is formed by **multiplying** the previous term by a constant (e.g., 2, 4, 8, 16, 32, 64, . . .). The **ratio** or **quotient** between any two consecutive terms is always the same.

What a Sequence Problem Will Ask For

Most sequence problems give the first few terms of the sequence, or the rule for generating them, and ask you to:

❑ **Find a specific term,** e.g., "What is the value of the 214th term of the sequence 1, 2, 3, 1, 2, 3, . . . ?"

❑ **Analyze a subset of the sequence,** e.g., "How many odd numbers are in the first 100 terms of the sequence 1, 2, 3, 1, 2, 3, . . . ?" or "What is the sum of the first 36 terms of the sequence 1, 2, 3, 1, 2, 3, . . . ?"

Three Steps to Solving a Sequence Problem

❑ Step 1: **Write out the first 6–8 terms** of the sequence following the rules they give you. Usually 5–8 terms is plenty.

❑ Step 2: **Identify the pattern and how often it repeats.** Perhaps "bracketing" the pattern will help it stand out.

❑ Step 3: **Use this pattern** and whole-number division (Chapter 10 Lesson 7) to solve the problem.

Some Sequence Practice

$$-1, 2, -2 \ldots$$

e.g.   The first three terms of a sequence are given above. Each subsequent term is found by dividing the preceding term by the term before that; for example, the third term is $2 \div -1 = -2$. What is the value of the 218th term in the sequence?

Begin by writing out the first 5–8 terms. The 3rd term of the sequence is $2 \div -1 = -2$. The 4th term is $-2 \div 2 = -1$. The 5th term is $-1 \div -2 = \frac{1}{2}$. The 6th term is $\frac{1}{2} \div -1 = -\frac{1}{2}$. The 7th term is $-\frac{1}{2} \div \frac{1}{2} = -1$. The 8th term is $-1 \div -1/2 = 2$.

$$[-1, 2, -2, -1, \tfrac{1}{2}, -\tfrac{1}{2},] -1, 2, \ldots$$

By now you should notice that the first two terms have repeated. The pattern is $-1, 2, -2, -1, \frac{1}{2}, -\frac{1}{2}$, and it repeats every 6 digits as shown with the bracket above.

The pattern repeats $218 \div 6 = 36\frac{2}{3}$ times, or 36 with a remainder of 2, which means that the 218th term is the same as the 2nd term of the sequence. Therefore, the 218th term is 2.

$$-1, 1, 0, -1, 1, 0, -1, 1, 0 \ldots$$

e.g.　　Given that the pattern above repeats indefinitely as shown, what is the sum of the first 43 terms?

They have written out the first 9 terms for you, so your first job is to identify the pattern.

$$[\underline{-1, 1, 0,}] -1, 1, 0, -1, \ldots$$

The pattern repeats every 3 digits, and the sum of each repetition is $-1 + 1 + 0 = 0$.

The pattern occurs $43 \div 3 = 14\text{-}\frac{1}{3}$ times, or 14 with a remainder of 1.

The 14 full repetitions have a sum of $14(0) = 0$. Since the 43rd term is -1, the sum is $0 + -1 = -1$.

Concept Review 1: Sequences

1. What is a geometric sequence?

2. If the pattern of a sequence repeats every 6 terms, how do you determine the 115th term of the sequence?

3. If the pattern of a sequence repeats every 4 terms, how do you find the sum of the first 32 terms of the sequence?

4. If a pattern repeats every 5 terms, how do you determine how many of the first 36 terms are negative?

5. What is the 30th term of the following geometric sequence?
    $$\frac{1}{9}, \frac{1}{3}, 1, 3, 9, \ldots$$

6. The first term in a sequence is 4, and each subsequent term is eight more than twice the preceding term. What is the value of the 6th term?

7. The word SCORE is written 200 times in a row on a piece of paper. How many of the first 143 letters are vowels?

8. The third term of a sequence is x. If each term in the sequence except the first is found by subtracting 3 from the previous term and dividing that difference by 2, what is the first term of the sequence in terms of x?

9. A 60-digit number is created by writing all the positive integers in succession beginning with 1. What is the 44th digit of the number?

SAT I Practice 1: Sequences

1 The first term in a sequence is x. Each subsequent term is three less than twice the preceding term. What is the 5th term in the sequence?

(A) $8x - 21$
(B) $8x - 15$
(C) $16x - 39$
(D) $16x - 45$
(E) $32x - 93$

2 $\frac{1}{8}, \frac{1}{4}, \frac{1}{2}, \ldots$

If the sequence above is geometric, what is the value of the 13th term?

(A) 2^7
(B) 2^8
(C) 2^9
(D) 2^{10}
(E) 2^{11}

3 The first term in a sequence is 400. Every subsequent term is 20 less than half of the immediately preceding term. What is the 4th term in the sequence?

4 In the number $0.\overline{148285}$, the digits 148285 repeat indefinitely. How many of the first 500 digits after the decimal point are odd?

(A) 83
(B) 166
(C) 167
(D) 168
(E) 332

5 5, 6, 5, 6, 6, 5, 6, 6, 6, 5, 6, 6, 6, 6, 5, . . .

In the sequence above, the first 5 is followed by one 6, the second 5 is followed by two 6s, and so on. If the sequence continues in this manner, how many 6s are there between the 44th and 47th appearances of the number 5?

(A) 91
(B) 135
(C) 138
(D) 182
(E) 230

6 The first term in a sequence is –5, and each subsequent term is 6 more than the immediately preceding term. What is the value of the 104th term?

(A) 607
(B) 613
(C) 618
(D) 619
(E) 625

7 What is the units digit of 3^{36}?

(A) 0
(B) 1
(C) 3
(D) 7
(E) 9

8   210, 70, . . .

After the first term in the sequence above, each odd-numbered term can be found by multiplying the preceding term by three and each even-numbered term can be found by multiplying the previous term by ⅓. What is the value of the 24th term?

9   If 640 and 160 are the first and second terms, respectively, of a geometric sequence, what is the value of the 6th term?

10   6, 4, . . .

After the first two terms in the sequence above, each odd-numbered term can be found by dividing the previous term by 2. For example, the 3rd term is equal to 4 ÷ 2 = 2. Each even-numbered term can be found by adding 8 to the previous term. For example, the 4th term is equal to 2 + 8 = 10. How many terms are there before the first non-integer term?

(A)   3
(B)   4
(C)   5
(D)   6
(E)   7

11   –2, 4, –8, . . .

The first three terms of a sequence are given above. If each subsequent term is the product of the preceding two terms, how many of the first 90 terms are negative?

(A)   16
(B)   30
(C)   45
(D)   60
(E)   66

Answer Key 1:
Sequences

Concept Review 1

1. In a geometric sequence, each term is equal to the previous term multiplied by a constant.

2. If the sequence repeats every six terms, you can find the 115th term by finding the remainder when 115 is divided by 6. Since $115 \div 6$ equals 19 with a remainder of 1, the 115th term will be the same as the first term.

3. Begin by finding the sum of the repeating pattern. Next, determine how many times the pattern occurs in the first 32 terms: $32 \div 4 = 8$ times. Then multiply the sum of the pattern by 8 to obtain the sum.

4. Count the number of negative terms in each repetition of the pattern, then find how many times the pattern repeats in the first 36 terms. Since $36 \div 5 = 7$ with a remainder of 1, the pattern repeats 7 times and is 1 term into the 8th repetition. Multiply the number of negative terms per repetition by 7 and if the 1st term of the sequence is negative, add 1 to the total.

5. This is a geometric sequence. Each term is the previous one times 3 ($1 \times 3 = 3$; $3 \times 3 = 9$, etc.). The first term of the sequence is 3^{-2}, and the 30th term is $3^{-2} \times 3^{29} = 3^{27}$.

6. The first term is 4. Second: $4(2) + 8 = 16$. Third: $16(2) + 8 = 40$. Fourth: $40(2) + 8 = 88$. Fifth: $88(2) + 8 = 184$. Sixth: $184(2) + 8 = 376$.

7. The pattern repeats every 5 terms, and each repetition contains 2 vowels. Since $143 \div 5 = 28$ with a remainder of 3, the first 143 letters contain $28 \times 2 = 56$ vowels plus the one vowel in the first 3 letters of the word SCORE, for a total of $56 + 1 = 57$.

8. Work backwards: x was found by subtracting 3 from the 2nd term and dividing by 2. Therefore, multiply x by 2 and add 3 to get the 2nd term: $2x + 3$. Repeat to find the first term: $2(2x + 3) + 3 = 4x + 9$.

9. The integers 1 through 9 represent the first 9 digits, and 10 through 19 represent the next 20 digits. Each integer thereafter contains 2 digits. 26 represents the 42nd and 43rd digits, so 2 is the 44th digit.

SAT I Practice 1

1. **D** The first term of the sequence is x. The second term is $2(x) - 3 = 2x - 3$. The third term is $2(2x - 3) - 3 = 4x - 6 - 3 = 4x - 9$. The fourth term is $2(4x - 9) - 3 = 8x - 18 - 3 = 8x - 21$. The fifth term is $2(8x - 21) - 3 = 16x - 42 - 3 = 16x - 45$.

2. **C** Each term in the sequence is the previous term times 2. The first term, $\frac{1}{8}$, is equal to 2^{-3}. To find the value of the 13th term, multiply the first term by 2 twelve times or by 2^{12} to get your answer.

$$2^{-3} \times 2^{12} = 2^{-3+12} = 2^{9}$$

3. **15** The first term is 400, after which each term is 20 less than $\frac{1}{2}$ the previous term. The second term is $\frac{1}{2}(400) - 20 = 180$. The third term is $\frac{1}{2}(180) - 20 = 70$. The fourth term is $\frac{1}{2}(70) - 20 = 15$.

4. **C** The sequence contains a repeating 6-term pattern: 148285. To find out how many times the pattern repeats in the first 500 terms, divide 500 by 6: $500 \div 6 = 83\text{-}\frac{1}{3}$. By the 500th term, the pattern has repeated 83 full times and is $\frac{1}{3}$ of the way through the 84th repetition. Each repetition of the pattern contains 2 odd digits, so in the 83 full repetitions there are $83 \times 2 = 166$ odd digits. In the first $\frac{1}{3}$ of the pattern there is one odd digit. Therefore there are $166 + 1 = 167$ odd digits.

5. **B** There will be $44 + 45 + 46 = 135$ 6s between the 44th and 47th appearances of 5.

6. **B** In this arithmetic sequence you must add 6 to each term. To get from the 1st to the 104th term you will add 103 terms, or 103 6s. The value of the 104th term is thus $-5 + (103)(6) = 613$.

7. **B** $3^{1} = 3$; $3^{2} = 9$; $3^{3} = 27$; $3^{4} = 81$; $3^{5} = 243$; $3^{6} = 729$ The units digits repeat in the pattern 3, 9, 7, 1, 3, 9, 7, 1. . . . $36 \div 4 =$ nine full repetitions. Since it goes in evenly, it must fall on the last term of the pattern, which is 1.

8. **70** The pattern alternates back and forth between 210 and 70. Each odd-numbered term is 210 and each even-numbered term is 70, so the 24th term is 70.

9. **5/8 or .625** The first term of the sequence is 640. Each term thereafter is $\frac{1}{4}$ of the immediately preceding term. The first six terms are 640, 160, 40, 10, 2.5, .625.
$.625 = 5/8$.

10. **D** The 3rd term of the sequence is $4 \div 2 = 2$. The 4th term is $2 + 8 = 10$. The 5th term is $10 \div 2 = 5$. The 6th term is $5 + 8 = 13$. The 7th term is $13 \div 2 = 6.5$, which is the first non-integer term.

11. **D** In this problem, only the signs of the terms matter. The first term is negative and the second is positive. The third term is $(-)(+) = -$. The 4th term is $(+)(-) = -$. The 5th term is $(-)(-) = +$. The 6th term is $(-)(+) = -$. The first 6 terms of the sequence are: $-$, $+$, $-$, $-$, $+$, $-$. The pattern $-$, $+$, $-$ repeats every 3 terms. In the first 90 terms, the pattern repeats $90 \div 3 = 30$ times. Each repetition contains 2 negative numbers, so in 30 full repetitions there are $30 \times 2 = 60$ negative numbers.

Lesson 2: Functions

The Definition of a Function

❑ A **function** is a formula used to calculate an **output** number (usually called y) from an **input** number (usually called x). In an equation like $f(x) = 3x + 2$, the term $f(x)$ represents the output of the function, which is the same as y,

❑ You can write a function like $f(x) = 3x + 2$ as $y = 3x + 2$ if it is clearer to you.

e.g. If $f(x) = 3x + 2$, what is the value of $f(3)$?

Answer: Plug in 3 for x and simplify:
$f(x) = 3x + 2$
$f(3) = 3(3) + 2 = 11$

e.g. If $f(x) = 3x + 2$, what is $f(3x)$?

Answer: Plug in $3x$ as the input and simplify:
$f(3x) = 3(3x) + 2 = 9x + 2$

Composition of Functions

You may be given two functions and asked to work with them together in "composition."

e.g. If $f(x) = 3x + 2$ and $g(x) = x^2$, what is $f(g(x))$?

Answer: Since $g(x) = x^2$, $f(g(x)) = f(x^2)$, by the law of substitution. Plug x^2 into $f(x)$ and simplify:
$f(x^2) = 3(x^2) + 2 = 3x^2 + 2$

❑ **When asked to find the value of $f(g(x))$ or $g(f(x))$, remember the rules of substitution. $f(g(x))$ means that x "goes into" the function g, then the result "goes into" the function f.**

Domain and Range

❑ The **domain** of a function is the set of all of the possible **inputs,** or "x values."

❑ When finding the domain of a function, remember that **you cannot divide by zero, and you can't take an even root (like $\sqrt{x}, \sqrt[4]{x}$ or $\sqrt[6]{x}$) of a negative number.** So if a function has a denominator, eliminate from the domain any values of x that make the denominator equal to zero. And if a function has an even root, eliminate from the domain any values of x that would make the radicand negative.

e.g. If $f(x) = \dfrac{3}{x-2}$, find the domain of $f(x)$.

Answer: We can't divide by zero, so $(x - 2) \neq 0$. Therefore, $x \neq 2$. Domain is all real numbers except $x = 2$, or simply $x \neq 2$.

e.g. If $f(x) = \sqrt{8x - 5}$, find the domain of $f(x)$.

Answer: We can't take the square root of a negative number, so $(8x - 5) \geq 0$. $8x \geq 5$, and therefore $x \geq 5/8$.

❑ The **range** of a function is the set of all of the possible **outputs,** or "y values."

e.g. If $f(x) = (x + 2)^2$, find the range over the domain $-3 \leq x \leq 0$.

Answer: Plug the integer values of the domain, $-3, -2, -1$, and 0, into the function to see that the range is $0 \leq y \leq 4$. Also, if you are skilled at graphing functions on your calculator, this may be the most efficient way to "see" the range.

Concept Review 2: Functions

1. What two rules should you remember when finding the domain of a function? How do you find the values of x that violate either rule?

2. How do you determine the range, or possible values of y, for a function over a given domain?

3. Define domain and range.

Find the domain of each of the following functions.

4. $f(x) = \dfrac{x+5}{x-4}$

5. $g(x) = \dfrac{\sqrt{x-5}}{x-6}$

6. $h(x) = 3x^2 - 4x + 5$

7. $k(x) = \sqrt{3x-6}$

8. If $f(x) = (x-2)^2 + 4$, what is the range of $f(x)$ over the domain $-1 \le x \le 3$?

Use the following definitions for questions 9–18:

$$f(x) = 3x + 4 \qquad g(x) = x^2 - 5 \qquad h(x) = 5x - 4 \qquad c(x) = \frac{2x}{x-6} \qquad p(x) = (x-4)^2$$

9. $f(5) =$

10. $g(x+2) =$

11. $h(f(x)) =$

12. $f(x)h(x) =$

13. What is the domain of $c(x)$?

14. $p(f(x)) =$

15. What is the domain of $\dfrac{f(x)}{h(x)}$?

16. $g(h(p(5))) =$

17. $g(3) - h(4) + p(6) =$

18. What is the range of $g(x)$?

SAT I Practice 2: Functions

1 If $f(x) = 3x^2 - 6$, then what is the value of $f(f(1))$?

(A) −33　(B) −17　(C) 21　(D) 27　(E) 75

2 Which of the following represents the domain

of the function $h(x) = \dfrac{\sqrt{2x-3}}{(x-5)}$?

(A) $x \neq -5$

(B) $x \neq 5$

(C) $x \geq \dfrac{3}{2}$

(D) $x \geq \dfrac{3}{2}, x \neq 5$

(E) All real numbers except $x = \dfrac{3}{2}$

3 If $f(x) = x^2 + 4$, then which of the following is equivalent to $f(x + 2)$?

(A) $x^2 + 8$　(B) $x^2 + 2x + 8$　(C) $x^2 + 4x + 8$

(D) $x^2 + 6$　(E) $x^2 - 4x + 8$

4 What is the range of the function $f(x) = x^2 + 1$ over the domain $-2 < x < 3$?

(A) $5 < y < 10$

(B) $5 < y < 9$

(C) $2 < y < 10$

(D) $1 < y < 9$

(E) $1 < y < 10$

5 **Questions 5 and 6 refer to the following definitions:**

$f(x) = 6x - 7$　　$g(x) = x^2 - 4$　　$h(x) = 3x$

What is the value of $h(g(4))$?

(A) 4　(B) 12　(C) 36　(D) 51　(E) 140

6 Which of the following represents $f(g(h(x)))$?

(A) $54x^2 - 31$

(B) $9x^2 - 4$

(C) $18x^2 - 31$

(D) $36x^2 - 14x + 5$

(E) $54x^2 - 17$

7 If $f(x) = \dfrac{3x-4}{2x}$ and $g(x) = 3 - x$, which of the following is NOT in the domain of $f(g(x))$?

(A) −3

(B) −1

(C) 0

(D) 1

(E) 3

8 If $f(x) = 2x + 5$ and $f(g(4)) = 21$, which of the following could be equivalent to $g(x)$?

I.　$3x - 4$

II.　$x + 7$

III.　$2x$

(A) I only

(B) II only

(C) I and II only

(D) I and III only

(E) I, II, and III

9 For which of the following functions does the range contain both positive and negative values over the domain $3 \leq x \leq 7$?

I.　$f(x) = 3x - 10$

II.　$g(x) = \dfrac{2x-7}{x-4}$

III.　$h(x) = \dfrac{5x+9}{x-6}$

(A) I only

(B) I and II only

(C) I and III only

(D) II and III only

(E) I, II, and III

10 Over the domain $-2 < x \leq 3$, which of the following functions contains the greatest value of y?

(A) $y = x^2 - 3$

(B) $y = \dfrac{x-5}{x+1}$

(C) $y = x$

(D) $y = 2x$

(E) $y = \dfrac{x+3}{x-2}$

Answer Key 2: Functions

Concept Review 2

1. Rule 1: You can't divide by zero. Rule 2: You can't take the even root of a negative number. If a function has a denominator, eliminate from the domain any values of x that make the denominator equal to zero. If a function has an even root, eliminate from the domain any values of x that would make the radicand negative.

2. If you are given a specific domain, plug in the integer values of x to see the range of values obtained.

3. The domain is the set of all of the possible inputs. The range represents the set of all of the possible outputs.

4. Don't divide by zero: $x - 4 \neq 0$, so $x \neq 4$.

5. Both rules apply: $x - 5 \geq 0$, so $x \geq 5$; and $x - 6 \neq 0$, so $x \neq 6$. Domain is $x \geq 5$; $x \neq 6$.

6. Neither rule applies: Domain = all real numbers.

7. Don't take square root of a negative: $3x - 6 \geq 0$, so $x \geq 2$.

8. To find the range, plug in the integer values within the domain. $f(-1) = (-3)^2 + 4 = 13$; $f(0) = (-2)^2 + 4 =$

8; $f(1) = (-1)^2 + 4 = 5$; $f(2) = (0)^2 + 4 = 4$; $f(3) = (1)^2 + 4 = 5$. Therefore, $4 \leq y \leq 13$.

9. $f(5) = 3(5) + 4 = 15 + 4 = 19$.

10. $g(x + 2) = (x + 2)^2 - 5 = (x^2 + 4x + 4) - 5 = x^2 + 4x - 1$

11. $h(f(x)) = h(3x + 4) = 5(3x + 4) - 4 = 15x + 20 - 4 = 15x + 16$

12. $f(x)h(x) = (3x + 4)(5x - 4) = 15x^2 - 12x + 20x - 16 = 15x^2 + 8x - 16$

13. Don't divide by zero! $x - 6 \neq 0$, so $x \neq 6$.

14. $p(f(x)) = p(3x + 4) = ((3x + 4) - 4)^2 = (3x)^2 = 9x^2$.

15. Don't divide by zero! $5x - 4 \neq 0$, so $5x \neq 4$; $x \neq 4/5$

16. $p(5) = (5 - 4)^2 = 1^2 = 1$; $h(p(5)) = h(1) = 5(1) - 4 = 1$; $g(h(p(5))) = g(1) = (1)^2 - 5 = -4$

17. $g(3) = (3)^2 - 5 = 4$; $h(4) = 5(4) - 4 = 16$; $p(6) = (6 - 4)^2 = 4$; $g(3) - h(4) + p(6) = 4 - 16 + 4 = -8$

18. The range of $g(x)$ is $y \geq -5$. Because x^2 is always greater than or equal to 0, $x^2 - 5$ must be greater than or equal to -5.

SAT I Practice 2

1. **C** First find the value of $f(1)$, which is $3(1)^2 - 6 = -3$. Now you can rewrite $f(f(1))$ as $f(-3)$ and solve. $f(-3) = 3(-3)^2 - 6 = 3(9) - 6 = 27 - 6 = 21$

2. **D** Both domain rules apply to this function. To avoid dividing by 0, $x - 5 \neq 0$, and therefore $x \neq 5$. To avoid taking the square root of a negative, set the radicand greater than 0 and solve for x: $(2x - 3) \geq 0$; $2x \geq 3$; $x \geq 3/2$. Therefore, D is the answer.

3. **C** Plug $(x + 2)$ into the function: $f(x + 2) = (x + 2)^2 + 4 = (x^2 + 2x + 2x + 4) + 4 = x^2 + 4x + 8$.

4. **E** Plug the integer values of the domain into the function to see what values you obtain: $f(-2) = (-2)^2 + 1 = 5$; $f(-1) = (-1)^2 + 1 = 2$; $f(0) = (0)^2 + 1 = 1$; $f(1) = (1)^2 + 1 = 2$; $f(2) = (2)^2 + 1 = 5$; $f(3) = (3)^2 + 1 = 10$. The value of y must be greater than 1 and less than 10.

5. **C** To find the value of $h(g(4))$, plug 4 into $g(x)$, then plug that solution into $h(x)$.
$g(4) = 4^2 - 4 = 16 - 4 = 12$, so $h(g(4)) = h(12)$
$h(12) = 3(12) = 36$

6. **A** $f(g(h(x))) = f(g(3x)) = f((3x)^2 - 4) = f(9x^2 - 4)$
$f(9x^2 - 4) = 6(9x^2 - 4) - 7 = 54x^2 - 24 - 7 = 54x^2 - 31$

7. **E** $f(g(x)) = \dfrac{3(3 - x) - 4}{2(3 - x)} = \dfrac{9 - 3x - 4}{6 - 2x} = \dfrac{5 - 3x}{6 - 2x}$

Since we can't divide by 0, $6 - 2x \neq 0$, so $x \neq 3$.

8. **D** $f(g(4)) = 2(g(4)) + 5$
Since this must equal 21: $2(g(4)) + 5 = 21$
Subtract 5: $2(g(4)) = 16$
Divide by 2: $g(4) = 8$

Now see which functions give an output of 8 when $x = 4$:

   I. If $g(x) = 3x - 4$, then $g(4) = 3(4) - 4 = 8$ (Check!)
   II. If $g(x) = x + 7$, then $g(4) = 4 + 7 = 11$ (Nope!)
   III. If $g(x) = 2x$, then $g(4) = 2(4) = 8$ (Check!)

9. **A** The function $f(x) = 3x - 10$ is negative when $x < 10/3 = 3.333\ldots$ and positive over the rest of the domain. The other functions are positive over the entire domain.

10. **B** The maximum value of any of the five functions occurs at $x = -2$, at which answer choice B = 7.
If $x = 3$, answer choices A, D, and E all equal 6.

Lesson 3: Transformations

Some SAT I math questions may ask you to "transform" functions of the form $y = f(x)$ graphically. You should understand how functions like $y = f(x + 2)$, $y = f(x) + 2$, $y = 2f(x)$, $y = \frac{1}{2} f(x)$, and $y = -f(x)$ relate to the basic function $y = f(x)$.

Horizontal Shift

❑ A **horizontal shift** moves the entire graph to the right or left but does not change its shape.

The graph of $y = f(x + k)$ is the graph of $y = f(x)$ **shifted k units to the left.**

The graph of $y = f(x - k)$ is the graph of $y = f(x)$ **shifted k units to the right.**

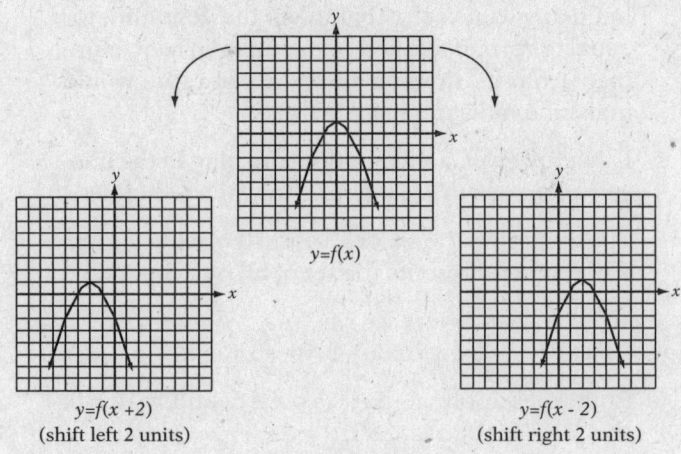

$y=f(x+2)$
(shift left 2 units)

$y=f(x-2)$
(shift right 2 units)

Vertical Shift

❑ A vertical shift moves the entire graph up or down but does not change its shape.

The graph of $y = f(x) + k$ is the graph of $y = f(x)$ **shifted up k units.**

The graph of $y = f(x) - k$ is the graph of $y = f(x)$ **shifted down k units.**

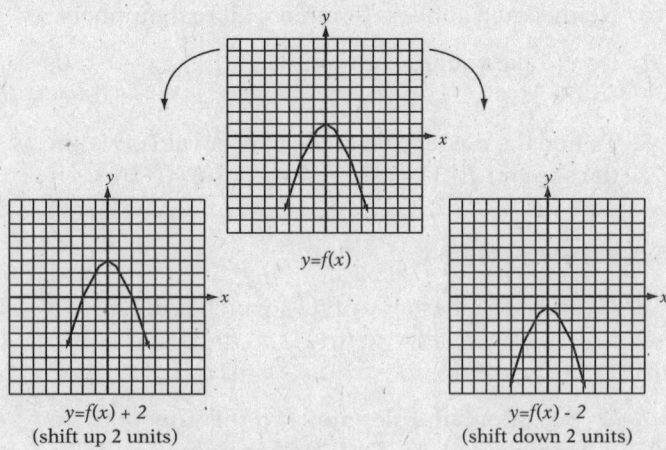

$y=f(x) + 2$
(shift up 2 units)

$y=f(x) - 2$
(shift down 2 units)

Reflected, Wide, and Narrow Functions

❑ The graph of $y = -f(x)$ is the **reflection of $y = f(x)$ over the x-axis.**

❑ The graph of $y = kf(x)$ is **wider than $y = f(x)$ if $0 < k < 1$ and narrower than $y = f(x)$ if $k > 1$.**

When a function is multiplied by a number greater than 1, its graph becomes "**narrower.**"

When a function is multiplied by a number between 0 and 1, it becomes "**wider.**"

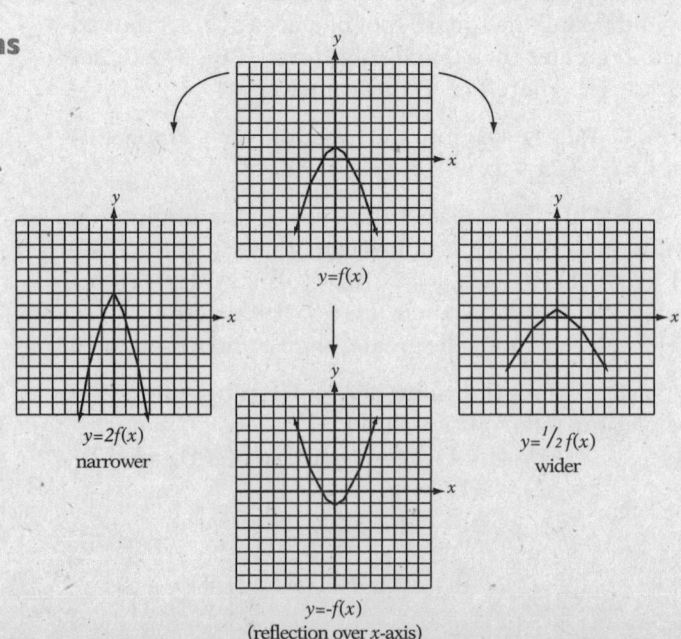

$y=2f(x)$
narrower

$y=\frac{1}{2}f(x)$
wider

$y=-f(x)$
(reflection over x-axis)

Concept Review 3: Transformations

1. What is a vertical shift?

2. What is a horizontal shift?

3. What transformation makes a graph look "narrower"?

4. What transformation makes a graph look "wider"?

5. What operation on a function reflects its graph over the x-axis?

Describe the effect the following transformations will have on the function $y = f(x)$:

6. $y = f(x) + 3$

7. $y = \frac{1}{2} f(x)$

8. $y = f(x) - 2$

9. $y = f(x + 2) - 3$

10. $y = f(2x)$

11. $y = f(x - 2) + 5$

12. $y = -f(x)$

13. $y = \frac{1}{2} f(x - 3) + 6$

Give the equation of the function that represents the given transformation of $y = f(x)$:

14. Shift left 3

15. Shift up 7 and right 2

16. Shift down 4

17. Shift down 2 and left 5

18. Shift right 6

19. Shift down 3 and right 4

20. Reflect over the x-axis

SAT I Practice 3: Transformations

1 Which of the following represents the equation of the graph formed when the graph of $y = (x + 1)^2$ is shifted 3 units up and 2 units to the left?

(A) $y = (x + 2)^2 + 3$ (B) $y = (x + 3)^2 + 3$
(C) $y = (x - 1)^2 + 2$ (D) $y = (x + 4)^2 + 2$
(E) $y = (x - 1)^2 + 3$

2 Which of the following transforms the graph of $y = x^3$ into the graph of $y - 4 = (x - 5)^3$?

(A) shift down 4, left 5
(B) shift down 4, right 5
(C) shift up 4, left 5
(D) shift up 4, right 5
(E) shift down 5, right 4

3

Given the graph of $y = f(x)$ above, which of the following represents the graph of $y = f(x - 5) + 3$?

(A)   (B)

(C)   (D)

(E)

4 Given the graph of $y = f(x)$ at right, which of the following represents the graph of $y = f(x) - 3$?

(A)   (B)

(C)   (D)

(E)

5 Which of the following functions best describes the transformed function on the right?

(A) $y = f(x + 3) + 4$
(B) $y = f(x - 3) + 3$
(C) $y = f(x - 4) + 4$
(D) $y = f(x - 3) + 4$
(E) $y = f(x + 4) + 3$

Answer Key 3: Transformations

Concept Review 3

1. A vertical shift moves the graph up or down but does not change its shape. For example, $y = f(x) + 4$ is $y = f(x)$ shifted *up* 4, and $f(x) - 3$ is $y = f(x)$ shifted *down* 3.

2. A horizontal shift moves the entire graph to the right or left but does not change its shape. For example, $f(x + 4)$ is $y = f(x)$ shifted *left* 4, and $f(x - 3)$ is $y = f(x)$ shifted *right* 3.

3. When a function is multiplied by a number greater than 1, its graph becomes "*narrower*."

4. When a function is multiplied by a number between 0 and 1, its graph becomes "*wider*."

5. Multiplying the function $y = f(x)$ by –1 (making $y = -f(x)$) causes the graph to be reflected over the x-axis. It effectively turns all the positive y-values negative and all the negative y-values positive.

6. $y = f(x) + 3$ will be shifted up 3.

7. $y = \frac{1}{2}f(x)$ will be twice as "wide."

8. $y = f(x) - 2$ will be shifted down 2.

9. $y = f(x + 2) - 3$ will be shifted down 3, left 2.

10. $y = f(2x)$ will be half as "wide."

11. $y = f(x - 2) + 5$ will be shifted up 5, right 2.

12. $y = -f(x)$ will be reflected across the x-axis.

13. $y = \frac{1}{2}f(x - 3) + 6$ will be twice as "wide," and shifted right 3 and up 6.

14. $y = f(x + 3)$

15. $y = f(x - 2) + 7$

16. $y = f(x) - 4$

17. $y = f(x + 5) - 2$

18. $y = f(x - 6)$

19. $y = f(x - 4) - 3$

20. $y = -f(x)$

SAT I Practice 3

1. **B**   When $y = (x + 1)^2$ is shifted 3 units up the equation becomes $y = (x + 1)^2 + 3$. When that is shifted 2 units to the left, the end result equation becomes:

$$y = ((x + 1) + 2))^2 + 3$$
$$y = (x + 3)^2 + 3.$$

2. **D**   When $y = x^3$ is shifted right 5, the equation becomes $y = (x - 5)^3$. When that is shifted up 4, the equation becomes $y = (x - 5)^3 + 4$. By subtracting 4 from each side, this equation can be rewritten as: $y - 4 = (x - 5)^3$.

3. **B**   When the equation $y = f(x)$ is transformed to $y = f(x - 5) + 3$, the resulting graph will be shifted up 3 and right 5. Answer choice A represents the graph of $y = f(x - 5) - 3$, because it is shifted right 5 and down 3. Choice B represents the graph of $y = f(x - 5) + 3$, because it is shifted right 5 and up 3. Choice C represents the graph of $y = f(x + 5) + 3$, because it is shifted left 5 and up 3. Choice D represents the graph of $y = f(x + 5) - 3$, because it is shifted left 5 and down 3. Choice E represents the graph of $y = f(x) + 3$, because it is just shifted up 3.

4. **C**   When the function $y = f(x)$ is transformed to $y = f(x) - 3$, the resulting graph will be shifted down 3. Choice A represents the graph of $y = f(x) - 2$ and is shifted down only 2. Choice B represents the graph of $y = f(x - 3)$ and is shifted right 3. Choice C represents the graph of $y = f(x) - 3$ and is shifted down 3. Choice D represents the graph of $y = f(x + 3)$ and is shifted left 3. Choice E represents the graph of $y = f(x) + 3$ and is shifted up 3.

5. **D**   In the second graph, the graph of the function $y = f(x)$ has been shifted up 4 and right 3. This would be properly represented by the equation $y = f(x - 3) + 4$.

Lesson 4: Variation

Direct Variation

❑ A relationship between two variables, x and y, is said to be **direct** if $y = kx$, where k is a nonzero constant.

❑ **In a direct variation, y increases whenever x increases and y decreases whenever x decreases.** More specifically, if x is multiplied by any number, y will be multiplied by that same number.

❑ The graph of a direct relationship is a line with a y-intercept of 0. (It passes through the origin.)

e.g.   If x varies directly with y and $x = 20$ when $y = 60$, then what is the value of x when $y = 150$?

Answer: First find the constant, k, by plugging in the values for x and y into the equation $y = kx$.
Plug in values of x and y: $60 = k(20)$
Divide by 20: $3 = k$
Rewrite equation with $k = 3$: $y = 3x$
Plug in new y value: $150 = 3x$
Divide by 3: $x = 50$

Inverse Variation

❑ A relationship between two variables, x and y, is said to be **inverse** if $y = \dfrac{k}{x}$, where k is a nonzero constant.

❑ **In an inverse variation, y decreases whenever x increases, and y increases whenever x decreases.** More specifically, the product of x and y is always the same: $xy = k$.

❑ The graph of an inverse relationship looks like this:

e.g.   If x varies indirectly with y, and $x = 40$ when $y = 10$, then what is the value of x when $y = 25$?

Answer: First find the constant, k, by plugging in the values for x and y into the equation $xy = k$.
Plug in values of x and y: $(40)(10) = k = 400$
Rewrite new equation: $xy = 400$
Plug in new y-value: $25x = 400$
Divide by 25: $x = 16$

Other Kinds of Variation

e.g.   If $y = x^2$, how is y affected when x is doubled?

Answer: Consider a simple value for x, like 1. If $x = 1$, then $y = (1)^2 = 1$. If x is doubled, then $x = 2$ and $y = (2)^2 = 4$. What was the change in y? It was quadrupled. Notice that this is true no matter what the starting value of x is.

e.g.   If $y = \dfrac{2x^2}{z}$, how is y affected when x and y are both doubled?

Answer: Consider simple values for x and z, like 1 and 2, respectively. (They don't have to be different, though; you can make them both 1 if you like.) If $x = 1$ and $z = 2$, then $y = \dfrac{2(1)^2}{2} = 1$. If you double x and z, y becomes $\dfrac{2(2)^2}{4} = 2$. What was the change in y? It was doubled.

Concept Review 4: Variation

1. What is direct variation?

2. What is inverse variation?

3. If m varies inversely with n and $m = 30$ when $n = 50$, what is the value of n when $m = 150$?

4. If w varies directly as v^3 and $w = 16$ when $v = 2$, what is the value of w when $v = 3$?

5. If m varies directly as n^2 and $m = 75$ when $n = 5$, what is the value of m when $n = 10$?

6. If b varies inversely as h and directly as p, and if $b = 20$ when $p = 40$ and $h = 10$, what is the value of p when $b = 40$ and $h = 3$?

For questions 7–9, write the function that best describes each of the following situations:

7. a varies directly as c and inversely as b.

8. c varies directly as the square of a and also directly as the cube of b.

9. b varies inversely as the square of c and directly as the square root of a.

10. z varies directly as the square of y and inversely as the cube of x. If $z = 16$ when $y = 8$ and $x = 2$, what is the value of z when $y = 4$ and $x = 4$?

11. m varies directly as n and inversely with the square of b. If $m = 4$ when $n = 4$ and $b = 3$, what is the value of m when $n = 9$ and $b = 9$?

12. If x varies directly as the cube root of y and directly as z and if $x = 18$ when $y = 27$ and $z = 2$, what is the value of z when $y = 125$ and $x = 60$?

SAT I Practice 4: Variation

1 The numbers of dollars m earned by a waiter varies directly as the number of hours he works h. If k is a constant, which of the following functions could represent this information?

(A) $m = kh$
(B) $m = h + k$
(C) $mh = k$
(D) $mk = h$
(E) $m = k - h$

2 If x varies inversely with y and if $x = 20$ when $y = 30$, then what is the value of x when $y = 100$?

(A) $\dfrac{3}{20}$
(B) 3
(C) 6
(D) $\dfrac{20}{3}$
(E) 10

3 If $f(x,y) = x^2y^3$ and $f(a,b) = 10$, what is the value of $f(2a, 2b)$?

(A) 50 (B) 100 (C) 160
(D) 320 (E) 640

4 The time it takes to paint a room varies inversely as the number of people who help paint. If four people paint the room in ten hours, how long will it take five people to paint the room?

5 If $f(x,y,z) = \dfrac{2x}{y^2z}$, and $f(a,b,c) = 20$, which of the following is equal to 40?

(A) $f(.5a, 2b, 4c)$
(B) $f(.5a, .5b, .5c)$
(C) $f(2a, .5b, 4c)$
(D) $f(2a, 2b, .5c)$
(E) $f(4a, .5b, c)$

6 The force needed to stretch a spring is proportional to the distance the spring is stretched. If a 40-pound weight is attached to the spring, it stretches 8 inches. How many inches would it stretch if a 100-pound weight were attached?

7 If r varies directly with s and t, and $r = 20$ when $s = 2$ and $t = 5$, what is the value of t when $r = 40$ and $s = 5$?

(A) 4
(B) 8
(C) 10
(D) 12
(E) 20

8 The number of minutes m it takes c children to eat b brownies varies directly as the number of brownies and inversely as the number of children. If it takes 5 children 20 minutes to eat 25 brownies, how many minutes should it take 15 children to eat 60 brownies?

(A) 12
(B) 14
(C) 16
(D) 25
(E) 240

9 If a varies directly as b and inversely as c, and if $a = 10x + 5$ when $c = 2$, and $b = 10$, what is the value of a when $b = 4$ and $c = 2x + 1$?

Answer Key 4: Variation

Concept Review 4

1. Two variables, y and x, vary directly if $y = kx$, where k is a constant.

2. Two variables, y and x, vary directly if $y = \dfrac{k}{x}$, where k is a constant, or $xy = k$.

3. Set up the equation: $mn = k$; then plug in and solve for k: $(30)(50) = 1{,}500 = k$. Now plug the new value of m into the equation $mn = 1{,}500$ and solve for n: $(150)(n) = 1{,}500$, so $n = 10$.

4. Set up the equation: $w = kv^3$, then plug in and solve for k: $16 = k(2)^3 = 8k$, so $k = 2$. Now plug in the new value of v; $w = 2(3)^3 = 2(27) = 54$.

5. Set up the equation: $m = kn^2$, then plug in and solve for k: $75 = k(5)^2 = 25k$, so $k = 3$. Now plug in the new value of n: $m = 3(10)^2 = 3(100) = 300$.

6. $b = \dfrac{kp}{h}$; $20 = \dfrac{k(40)}{10}$; $200 = 40k$; $k=5$. $b = \dfrac{5p}{h}$; $bh = 5p$; $(40)(3) = 5p$; $120 = 5p$; $p = 24$

7. $a = \dfrac{kc}{b}$ \qquad 8. $c = ka^2b^3$ \qquad 9. $b = \dfrac{k\sqrt{a}}{c^2}$

10. First set up the equation: $z = \dfrac{ky^2}{x^3}$ or $zx^3 = ky^2$.

    Rearrange and solve for k: $k = \dfrac{zx^3}{y^2} = \dfrac{16(2)^3}{(8)^2} = 2$.

    $z = \dfrac{2x^3}{y^2} = \dfrac{2(4)^3}{(4)^2} = 8$

11. Set up the equation: $m = \dfrac{kn}{b^2}$. Plug in and solve

    for k: $4 = \dfrac{k(4)}{(3)^2}$, so $36 = 4k$ and $k = 9$. Therefore,

    $m = \dfrac{9n}{b^2}$. If $b = 9$ and $n = 9$, then $m = \dfrac{9(9)}{(9)^2}$ and

    $m = 1$.

12. Plug in to $x = kz\sqrt[3]{y}$: \qquad $18 = 2kz\sqrt[3]{27}$

    Simplify: \qquad\qquad\qquad $18 = 2k(3) = 6k$

    Divide by 6: \qquad\qquad\qquad $3 = k$

    Plug in values to $x = 3z\sqrt[3]{y}$: \quad $60 = 3z\sqrt[3]{125} = 15z$

    Divide by 15: \qquad\qquad\qquad\quad $z = 4$

SAT I Practice 4

1. **A** If m and h vary directly, then $m = kh$.

2. **C** First write the relationship: $x = \dfrac{k}{y}$ and solve for k.

   You can rewrite the equation as $xy = k$, plug in your values, and solve: $(20)(30) = k = 600$. $xy = 600$. Plug in the new values and solve: $(x)(100) = 600$, so $x = 6$.

3. **D** The notation $f(x,y)$ means that the function has two inputs, x and y. Since x is squared by the function, doubling x (from a to $2a$) *quadruples* the value of the function because $2^2 = 4$. Since y is cubed by the function, doubling y (from b to $2b$) *multiplies the function by eight*, because $2^3 = 8$. Doing both will have the effect of multiplying the function by $(2^2)(2^3) = 2^5 = 32$. So if the original function value is 10, the new one is $10 \times 32 = 320$.

4. **8** Since p and h are inversely related, their relationship can be expressed as $k = ph$. Solve for k by plugging in the given values: $k = (4)(10) = 40$. The relationship is $(p)(h) = 40$. Now plug in the new value of p and solve for h: $(5)(h) = 40$, so $h = 8$.

5. **C** The function $f(x)$ is directly proportional to x, inversely proportional to the square of y, and inversely proportional to z. Doubling x (from a to $2a$) has the effect of doubling the value of the function. Since the function is inversely proportional to the *square* of y, halving y (from b to $.5b$) would multiply the function by 4. Finally, quadrupling z (from c to $4c$) divides the function by 4. So the result of all three changes in choice (C) is to multiply the function by $2 \times 4 \div 4 = 2$. Therefore, the function value is $(2)(20) = 40$.

6. **20** The equation for the relationship is $f = kx$. Plug in the given values: $40 = 8k$, so $k = 5$. The function is $f = 5x$. Plug in $f = 100$ and solve for x: $100 = 5x$; $x = 20$.

7. **A** The equation is $r = kst$. First find the value of k by plugging in the values: $20 = k(2)(5)$, so $k = 2$. Therefore, the equation is $r = 2st$. Plug in the new values and solve: $40 = (2)(5)(t)$, so $t = 4$.

8. **C** $m = \dfrac{kb}{c}$. Plug in to solve for k: $20 = \dfrac{k(25)}{(5)}$;

   $20 = 5k$, so $k = 4$. Now solve for the new value of m:

   $m = \dfrac{4(60)}{(15)} = 16$.

9. **4** $a = \dfrac{kb}{c}$. Plug in to solve for k: $(10x + 5) = \dfrac{k(10)}{(2)}$.

   Simplify: \qquad $10x + 5 = 5k$

   Divide by 5: \quad $2x + 1 = k$

   The original formula becomes:

   $$a = (2x + 1)(b)/c$$

   Plug in $c = 2x + 1$: \quad $a = \dfrac{(2x+1)(4)}{(2x+1)} = 4$

Lesson 5: Data Analysis

Scatterplots and Lines of Best Fit

A **scatterplot** is a collection of data points plotted on a graph that can be used to visualize the relationship between two variables.

A **line of best fit** is a straight line that best represents the data of a scatterplot. It can sometimes be estimated by connecting the "outermost" points of the plot or by drawing a line that "hugs" the points closely and divides the points roughly in half. This line is not an exact representation of the relationship between the two variables, but it can often be used to make predictions.

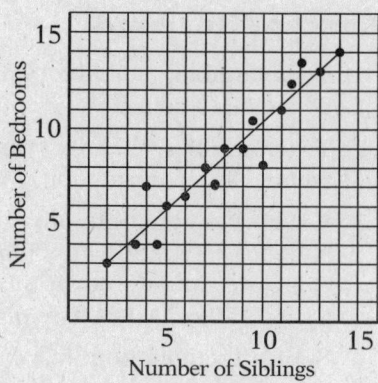

To **interpolate** is to estimate a value that lies between data points on the graph.

To **extrapolate** is to use the line of best fit to estimate a value that lies beyond the points on the graph.
An **outlier** is a data point, such as (1, 11) or (15.5, 10) in the graph above, that does not "fit with" the rest of the data.

❑ **The SAT I will not ask you to find the exact equation of a line of best fit.**
❑ **You may be asked whether the slope of the line of best fit is positive or negative and perhaps whether it is greater than or less than 1.**

e.g.   What is the approximate slope of the line of best fit in the scatterplot above?

Answer: To estimate the slope of a line of best fit, pick two points on your line of best fit and use the slope equation to solve for m. It appears that the line of best fit connects the points (2, 3) and (13, 14),

so $m = \dfrac{14-3}{13-2} = 1$.

Tables, Charts, and Graphs

❑ A **table** is a set of data arranged in rows and columns.
❑ **When given a table, first read the labels carefully to understand what the table values represent.**
❑ Some SAT I questions may ask you to complete the data in a table, or to solve for variables in a table. You might be asked to **cross-reference** information in two or more tables. **Be sure you know how the two tables are related.**

e.g.   If the Thompsons own as many pieces of electronic equipment as the Shields, how many black and white televisions does the Thompson family own?

Household Electronic Equipment

	Thompson Family	Shields Family
Computers	2	3
Televisions	x	4
Stereos	2	2

Televisions

	Black & White	Color
Thompson	y	4
Shields	1	3

Answer: The Shields own $2 + 3 + 4 = 9$ pieces of equipment.

Using the "television" table, use the fact that the Thompsons have 5 TVs:

Therefore: $9 = 2 + 2 + x$
Subtract 4: $x = 5$
$y + 4 = 5$
Subtract 4: $y = 1$ black and white TV

❑ As with tables, **first read the labels of pie charts carefully to understand what the data represent.**
❑ **In a pie chart, a sector that contains $x\%$ of the total data has a central angle of $(x/100)(360°)$.**

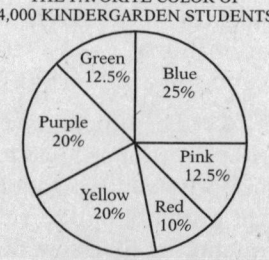

THE FAVORITE COLOR OF 4,000 KINDERGARDEN STUDENTS

e.g.   In the pie chart at right, what is the angle measure of the sector represented by the students who prefer the color purple?

Answer: Purple accounts for 20% of the circle, or 20% of 360°. $(0.2)(360°) = 72°$

Concept Review 5: Data Analysis

1. What is a line of best fit?

2. How is a line of best fit created?

3. How do you estimate the slope of a best fit line?

4. When given percentages in a pie chart, how do you determine how many degrees each sector represents?

Questions 5 and 6 refer to the bar graph at right:

5. The largest percent increase in number of accidents occurred between which two days of the week?

6. Approximately what percentage of the accidents occurred on Friday, Saturday, or Sunday?

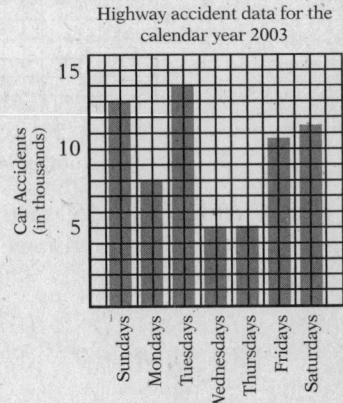

Questions 7–9 refer to the pie chart at right:

7. The pie chart shows the results of a survey that asked 4,000 kindergarten students their favorite color. How many more students said blue was their favorite color than said yellow was their favorite color?

8. What is the degree measure of the sector of the circle that represents red?

9. Using the data in the pie chart, how many students would have to change their answer to blue in order for blue to account for 50% of the data?

Questions 10–11 refer to the tables at right:

10. According to the tables, which school ordered the most amusement park tickets?

11. If all the students who went to Coaster Heaven from New Haven Public and Hamden High bought 5-day passes, how much more money did Hamden High spend than New Haven Public did at Coaster Heaven?

Number of Amusement Park Tickets Ordered			
	Adventure City	Galaxy Island	Coaster Heaven
Hamden High	36	28	81
New Haven Public	64	23	64
Waterbury High	53	31	51

Price of Admission			
	1-day pass	2-day pass	5-day pass
Adventure City	$40.00	$75.00	$150.00
Galaxy Island	$45.00	$85.00	$175.00
Coaster Heaven	$50.00	$94.00	$200.00

SAT I Practice 5: Data Analysis

1

Questions 1 and 2 refer to the following information:

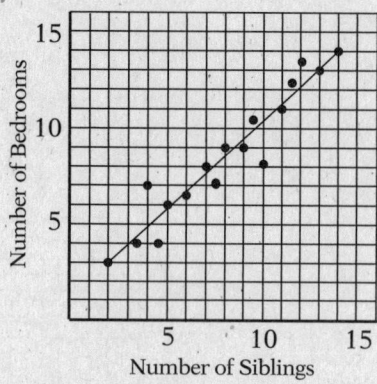

Which of the following best approximates the slope (in pounds/week) of the line of best fit for this data?

(A) $m > 1$ (B) $0 < m < 1$ (C) $m = 1$
(D) $-1 < m < 0$ (E) $m < -1$

2

If the line of best fit for the data presented above passed through the points $(32, 6.5)$ and $(39.5, 8.0)$, it can be estimated that a baby born at 28 weeks would most nearly weigh how many pounds?

(A) 5.3   (B) 5.5   (C) 5.7   (D) 5.9   (E) 6.1

3

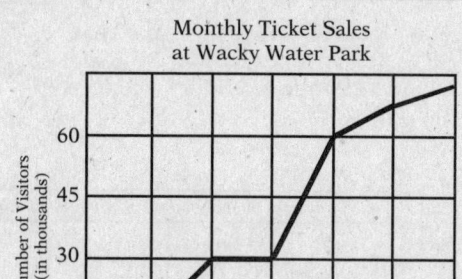

Monthly Ticket Sales at Wacky Water Park

According to the graph above, Wacky Water Park experienced its largest increase in park attendance between which two consecutive months?

(A) March and April   (B) April and May
(C) May and June   (D) June and July
(E) July and August

4

Cost/Revenue Analysis for the Trinket Factory

	Revenue per unit	Cost per unit
Widgets	$w	$4
Gadgets	$x	$3
Tinkers	$6	$y

The table above shows the per unit revenue and cost of 3 products at the Trinket Factory. If profit equals revenue minus cost, how much profit do they make if they produce and sell 2 of each item?

(A) $2w + 2x - 2y - 2$ (B) $2y - 2x - 2w - 2$
(C) $w + x - y - 1$ (D) $x + 2w + y - 7$
(E) $2x + 2y - 2w + 2$

5

Questions 5 and 6 refer to the following diagrams:

Cost of Food		
	Sandwich	Sandwich and Fries
Turkey	$ 4.50	$ 5.50
Ham	$ 5.00	$ 6.00
Veggie	$ 3.75	$ 4.75

Number of sandwiches ordered at a local deli			
	Turkey	Ham	Veggie
Boys	75	80	22
Girls	40	35	64

Based on the tables above, if every boy bought a sandwich without fries and every girl bought a sandwich with fries, how much more money did the boys spend at the deli than the girls?

6

If the girls who bought turkey sandwiches have $206 in total to spend on their lunches, what is the greatest number of turkey sandwiches with fries they could buy without exceeding their budget?

(A) 23
(B) 24
(C) 25
(D) 26
(E) 27

Answer Key 5: Data Analysis

Concept Review 5

1. A best fit line is a straight line that "hugs" the data most closely on a scatterplot.

2. It can be created by connecting the "outermost" points on the plot or by drawing a line that best "hugs" the points and divides them in half. Try to ignore any outliers that don't fit with the rest of the data.

3. For the SAT I, you just need to be able to tell if a slope is positive or negative, or perhaps greater or less than 1. Positive slopes go up to the right, and negative slopes go down to the right. If the slope is positive and the "rise" is greater than the "run," the slope is greater than 1; if the rise is less than the run, the slope is less than 1.

4. If you know what percent of the data are in a sector of the pie chart, multiply the percentage by 360° to obtain the degree measure of that sector (e.g., a sector that represents 40% of the circle would be $(.40)(360°) = 144°$).

5. The biggest percent change occurs between Thursday and Fridays.
Percent change = $(100\%)(10.5 - 5)/(5) = 110\%$.

6. There were a total of $13 + 7 + 14 + 5 + 5 + 10.5 + 11.5 = 66$ thousand accidents; 35 of them occurred on Friday, Saturday or Sunday. $35/66 = 53\%$

7. 25% of the kids said blue was their favorite color. 25% of 4,000 = $0.25 \times 4,000 = 1,000$. 20% of the kids said yellow was their favorite color. 20% of $4,000 = 0.20 \times 4,000 = 800$. $1,000 - 800 = 200$ kids.

8. The color red represents 10% of the circle, which is 10% of 360°. $\dfrac{10(360)}{100} = 36°$.

9. There are currently $(.25)(4,000) = 1,000$ votes for blue. In order for blue to be 50% of the circle, it would need $(.50)(4,000) = 2,000$ votes. Therefore, 1,000 votes must change.

10. Hamden High ordered $36 + 28 + 81 = 145$ tickets. New Haven Public ordered $64 + 23 + 64 = 151$. Waterbury High ordered $53 + 31 + 51 = 135$.

11. 81 Hamden High students bought 5-day passes at $200.00/pass, spending $(81)(200) = \$16,200$. 64 students at New Haven Public bought 5-day passes at $200/pass, spending $(64)(200) = \$12,800$. The difference is $\$16,200 - \$12,800 = \$3,400$.

SAT I Practice 5

1. **B** A line connecting (32, 6.5) and (39.5, 8.0) is a good line of fit, and has a slope of $1.5/7.5 = 0.2$, which is between 0 and 1.

2. **C** If the slope is about 0.2, you can use the slope equation to solve: $\dfrac{(y_2 - y_1)}{(x_2 - x_1)} = 0.2$

   Plug in values: $\dfrac{(6.5 - y_1)}{(32 - 28)} = 0.2$

   Simplify: $\dfrac{(6.5 - y_1)}{(4)} = 0.2$

   Multiply by 4: $(6.5 - y_1) = 0.8$
   Subtract 6.5: $-y_1 = -5.7$
   Divide by -1: $y_1 = 5.7$

3. **C** From March to April: $30 - 15 = 15,000$
   From April to May: $30 - 30 = 0$
   From May to June: $60 - 30 = 30,000$
   From June to July: $65 - 60 = 5,000$
   From July to August: $69 - 65 = 4,000$

4. **A** The revenue generated from 2 widgets, 2 gadgets, and 2 tinkers is $2w$, $2x$, and $2(6)$, respectively. The cost of producing 2 widgets, 2 gadgets, and 2 tinkers is $8, $6, and $2y$, respectively. Therefore, the total profit can be found by subtracting the cost from the revenue: $(2w + 2x + 12) - (8 + 6 + 2y) = 2w + 2x - 2y - 2$.

5. **86** The boys bought only sandwiches and spent $(\$4.50)(75) + (\$5.00)(80) + \$3.75(22) = \$820.00$. If the girls bought only sandwiches with fries, then they spent $(\$5.50)(40) + (\$6.00)(35) + \$4.75(64) = \$734.00$. $\$820.00 - \$734.00 = \$86.00$

6. **D** If x = sandwiches: $x(4.5) + (40 - x)(5.5) = 206$
   Distribute: $4.5x + 220 - 5.5x = 206$
   Combine like terms: $-1.0x = -14$
   Divide by -1: $x = 14$

   There were $(40 - x) = 40 - 14 = 26$ meals with fries.

Lesson 6: Negative and Fractional Exponents

Exponents Review

In Chapter 11, Lesson 3, we discussed the practical definition of exponentials:

❑ **The expression x^n means x multiplied by itself n times.**

This is a useful definition when you need to evaluate something like 4^3: you simply multiply $4 \times 4 \times 4$ and get 64. But what about expressions like 4^0 or 4^{-3} or $4^{1/2}$? How do you multiply 4 by itself 0 times, or −3 times, or half of a time? It doesn't make much sense to think of it that way. So to understand such expressions, you must expand your understanding of exponents.

Zero and Negative Exponents

Using what you have learned in Lesson 1 of this chapter, what are the next three terms of this sequence?

81, 27, 9, 3, _____, _____, _____

The rule seems to be "divide by 3," so the next three terms are 1, $\frac{1}{3}$, and $\frac{1}{9}$.

Now, what are the next three terms of this sequence?

3^4, 3^3, 3^2, 3^1, _____, _____, _____

Here, the rule seems to be "reduce the power by 1," so that the next three terms are 3^0, 3^{-1}, and 3^{-2}.

Notice that **the two sequences are exactly the same,** that is, $3^4 = 81$, $3^3 = 27$, $3^2 = 9$, and $3^1 = 3$. This means that the pattern can help us to understand zero and negative exponents: $3^0 = 1$, $3^{-1} = \frac{1}{3}$, and $3^{-2} = \frac{1}{9}$. Now, here's the million-dollar question:

Without a calculator, how do you write 3^{-7} without a negative exponent?

If you follow the pattern you should see that $3^{-7} = \frac{1}{3^7}$ and, in general:

❑ $x^0 = 1$ and $x^{-n} = \frac{1}{x^n}$.

❑ **Notice that raising a positive number to a negative power *does not* produce a negative result.** For instance 3^{-2} does **not** equal −9; it equals $\frac{1}{9}$.

Fractional Exponents

What if a number is raised to a **fractional** exponent? For instance, what does $8^{1/3}$ mean? To understand expressions like this, you have to use the basic rules of exponents from Chapter 11, Lesson 3. Specifically, you need to remember that $x^n \times x^m = x^{m+n}$.

$(8^{1/3})^3 = 8^{1/3} \times 8^{1/3} \times 8^{1/3}$. Using the rule above, $8^{1/3} \times 8^{1/3} \times 8^{1/3} = 8^{1/3 + 1/3 + 1/3} = 8^1 = 8$. In other words, when you raise $8^{1/3}$ to the 3rd power, the result is 8. This means that $8^{1/3}$ is the same as the cube root of 8, and, in general:

❑ **The expression $x^{1/n}$ means $\sqrt[n]{x}$, or the nth root of x.** For example, $\sqrt{a}$ can be written as $a^{1/2}$.

e.g.   What is the value of $16^{3/4}$?

Answer: The first step is to see that $16^{3/4}$ is the same as $(16^{1/4})^3$ (because $(16^{1/4})^3 = 16^{1/4} \times 16^{1/4} \times 16^{1/4} = 16^{3/4}$). Using the definition above, $16^{1/4}$ is the 4th root of 16, which is 2 (because $2^4 = 16$). So $(16^{1/4})^3 = 2^3 = 8$.

❑ **The expression $x^{m/n}$ means the nth root of x raised to the mth power.** For instance, $4^{3/2}$ means the square root of 4 raised to the third power, or $2^3 = 8$.

Concept Review 6: Negative and Fractional Exponents

Evaluate the following expressions without a calculator.

1. 5^{-2}

2. $9^{1/2}$

3. 2^{-5}

4. $25^{-1/2}$

5. $4^{3/2}$

6. $\left(\dfrac{16}{25}\right)^{-3/2}$

Simplify the following expressions, eliminating any negative or fractional exponents.

7. $x^{1/3}$

8. $(4g)^{1/2}$

9. $4x^{-2}$

10. $(4y)^{-2}$

11. $(9m)^{3/2}$

12. $(27b)^{1/3}/(9b)^{-1/2}$

13. If $x^{3/4} = 27$, what is the value of x?

14. If $b^{-1/2} = 4$, what is the value of b?

15. If $(2^m)^{-6} = 16$, what is the value of 2^{3m}?

SAT I Practice 6: Negative and Fractional Exponents

1 If $4^n = 20$, then what is the value of 4^{-n}?

2 If $5^4 \times m = 5^2$, then $m =$

(A) -5^2
(B) 5^{-2}
(C) $\frac{1}{5}$
(D) $5^{1/2}$
(E) $\frac{1}{2}$

3 If $2^m \times 2^m \times 2^m \times 2^m = 2$, then $m =$

4 For all values of n, $\dfrac{3 \times 3^{2n}}{9^n} =$

(A) 3
(B) $\left(\dfrac{2}{3}\right)^n$
(C) 3^n
(D) 9^2
(E) 9^n

5 If x is a positive number, then $\dfrac{x^{3/2} \times x^{1/2}}{x^{-4/2}} =$

(A) $x^{\frac{3}{4}}$

(B) $x^{-\frac{1}{4}}$

(C) $x^{\frac{3}{4}}$

(D) $\sqrt{x}^{3}$

(E) $\sqrt{x}^{5}$

6 If $x = a^5 = b^3$ and x is positive, then $ab =$

(A) $x^{1/15}$
(B) $x^{1/8}$
(C) $x^{8/15}$
(D) x^8
(E) x^{15}

Answer Key 6: Negative and Fractional Exponents

Concept Review 6

1. $5^{-2} = 1/(5^2) = 1/25$

2. $9^{1/2} = \sqrt{9} = 3$

3. $2^{-5} = 1/(2^5) = 1/32$

4. $25^{-1/2} = 1/\left(25^{1/2}\right) = 1/\sqrt{25} = 1/5$

5. $4^{3/2} = \left(4^{1/2}\right)^3 = \left(\sqrt{4}\right)^3 = 2^3 = 8$

6. $(16/25)^{-3/2} = 1/(16/25)^{3/2} = (25/16)^{3/2} = ((25/16)^{1/2})^3$
   $= \left(\sqrt{\dfrac{25}{16}}\right)^3 = \left(\dfrac{5}{4}\right)^3 = \dfrac{125}{64}$

7. $x^{1/3} = \sqrt[3]{x}$

8. $\left(4g\right)^{1/2} = \sqrt{4g} = 2\sqrt{g}$

9. $4x^{-2} = 4/x^2$

10. $(4y)^{-2} = 1/(4y)^2 = 1/(16y^2)$

11. $\left(9m\right)^{3/2} = \left(\left(9m\right)^{1/2}\right)^3 = \left(3\sqrt{m}\right)^3 = 27m\sqrt{m}$

12. $\left(27b\right)^{1/3}\big/\left(9b\right)^{-1/2} = \left(27b\right)^{1/3} \times \left(9b\right)^{1/2} = 3b^{1/3} \times 3b^{1/2}$
    $= 9b^{1/6} = 9\sqrt[6]{b}$

13. $x^{3/4} = 27$

    Raise both sides to the
       4/3 power: $(x^{3/4})^{4/3} = 27^{4/3}$
    Simplify: $x^1 = (27^{1/3})^4$
    Simplify: $x = 3^4$
    Simplify: $x = 81$

14. $b^{-1/2} = 4$

    Raise both sides to the
       −2 power: $(b^{-1/2})^{-2} = 4^{-2}$
    Simplify: $b^1 = 1/(4^2)$
    Simplify: $b = 1/16$

15. $(2^m)^{-6} = 16$
    Simplify: $2^{-6m} = 16$
    Raise to the −1/2 power: $2^{3m} = 16^{-1/2}$
    Simplify: $2^{3m} = 1/\sqrt{16}$
    Simplify: $2^{3m} = 1/4$

SAT I Practice 6

1. **1/20 or 0.05** $4^{-n} = 1/4^n = 1/20$

2. **B** $5^4 \times m = 5^2$
   Divide by 5^4: $m = 5^2/5^4$
   Simplify (subtract exponents): $m = 5^{-2}$

3. **1/4, or 0.25** $2^m \times 2^m \times 2^m \times 2^m = 2$
   Simplify (add exponents): $2^{4m} = 2$
   Exponents must be equal: $4m = 1$
   Divide by 4: $m = 1/4$

4. **A** $\dfrac{3 \times 3^{2n}}{9^n}$

   Write as powers of 3: $\dfrac{3^1 \times 3^{2n}}{\left(3^2\right)^n}$

   Simplify denominator: $\dfrac{3^1 \times 3^{2n}}{3^{2n}}$

   Divide numerator and
       denominator by 3^{2n}: $3^1/1 = 3$

   Perhaps a simpler method is to simply pick n to
   be 0 (because n can be any number). This gives
   $(3 \times 3^0)/9^0 = (3 \times 1)/1 = 3$. The only choice that
   equals 3 when $n = 0$ is (A).

5. **E** $\dfrac{x^{3/2} \times x^{1/2}}{x^{-4/2}} =$

   Simplify numerator (add exponents): $\dfrac{x^{4/2}}{x^{-1/2}}$

   Simplify quotient
   (subtract exponents): $x^{4/2-(-1/2)}$

   Simplify exponent: $x^{5/2}$

   Rewrite as a root: $\left(\sqrt{x}\right)^5$

6. **C** $x = a^5 = b^3$
   Solve for a (raise to the 1/5): $x^{1/5} = a$
   Solve for b (raise to the 1/3): $x^{1/3} = b$
   Multiply a and b: $ab = x^{1/5} \times x^{1/3}$
   Simplify (add exponents): $ab = x^{1/5 + 1/3}$
   Simplify: $ab = x^{8/15}$

   (Remember the quick way to add fractions:
   "zip-zap-zup" from Chapter 10 Lesson 3.)

CHAPTER 15

WRITING A GREAT ESSAY

1. Know What They're Looking For

2. Examine the Assignment Closely

3. Brainstorm Creatively

4. Prepare with "Source Summaries"

5. Write a Strong and Creative Thesis

6. Organize Your Thoughts

7. Write Logically

8. Write Clearly

9. Write Concisely

10. Write Forcefully

11. Write Masterfully

12. Finish with a Bang

Lesson 1: Know What They're Looking For

Why an Essay?

The first section of your SAT I is a 25-minute writing assignment **designed to assess how well you can express your ideas in writing—that is, make a point using clear and specific examples and reasoning. It is not simply an assessment of "what you know," and it isn't a spelling or grammar test.** Many colleges regard this as one of the most important elements of the SAT I, because essays are often a big part of college evaluation.

They'll Grade Its SOCS Off!

❑ **Two people will read your essay and grade its SOCS off! That is, they will grade it on the basis of:**

- **Substance.** Did you answer the question thoughtfully? Did you take a forceful and interesting position? Did you develop your response logically? Did you give strong, specific examples or provide meaningful explanations?
- **Organization.** Did you organize the essay around a clear thesis? Did you relate each paragraph to that thesis? Did you use paragraphs effectively? Did you provide transitions between paragraphs when necessary? Did you provide a thoughtful introduction? Did you conclude the essay appropriately?
- **Clarity.** Did you use precise language? Did you explain all terms or ideas that you needed to? Did you use strong verbs and nouns? Did you avoid overuse of the verb "to be"? Did you avoid the passive voice? Did you avoid cliché? Did you avoid redundancy?
- **Style.** Did you vary sentence length, structure, and syntax for impact? Did you avoid needless repetition of terms? Were you creative? Did you use humor? Did you use effective vocabulary?

The Assignment

❑ The essay assignment will most likely ask you to do one of the following:

- **Agree or Disagree.** Read a statement, then write an essay explaining why you agree or disagree with it.
- **Compare Statements.** Read two statements, then write an essay explaining why you agree with one of the statements more than with the other.
- **Complete the Statement.** Read an incomplete statement, then write an essay in which you explain how you would complete the statement.

❑ There is never a "right" or "wrong" response to any of the assignments, and the assignments will never ask **specifically** about your knowledge in any academic subject. You should, however, use your knowledge of **history, science,** or **literature and the arts** to find appropriate examples to illustrate your points whenever it is appropriate.

How Long Should It Be?

❑ Quality is much more important than quantity. Nevertheless, it's hard to get a great score with fewer than three paragraphs. **You should plan to write four paragraphs, and add a fifth if you have enough time and substance.**

❑ Many of us have been taught the "standard" five-paragraph essay format. However, you should know that **many "perfect" (12-point) essays on the SAT I are only four paragraphs long.** It is hard, however, to get a perfect score with fewer than four paragraphs. This is because the graders must evaluate your **organization,** and this includes productive use of paragraphs.

Practice 1: Know What They're Looking For

SAT I Essay Grading Review

1. What does it mean for an essay to have good substance?

2. What does it mean for an essay to have strong organization?

3. What does it mean for an essay to be clear?

4. What does it mean for an essay to have an effective and interesting style?

5. How long should your SAT I essay be?

Check your answers with the Answer Key at the end of the chapter.

Lesson 2: Examine the Assignment Closely

Read the Assignment Carefully

☐ **Always take a couple of minutes to read the assignment very carefully (two or three times), and underline any important phrases.** Do you have to **agree or disagree with a statement? Choose between two statements? Complete a statement?** Also, notice whether the assignment expects you to use just **one example** and explain it carefully, or if it allows you to use **several examples.**

Do Precisely What the Assignment Says

☐ **The first thing a reader will assess is whether you've done what the assignment says.** If the assignment tells you to take a stance, **don't** talk about how silly or difficult taking a stance is. If it asks you to comment on a quote, comment on the **statement** the quote makes, **not just the general topic** that it addresses. For instance, if the assignment asks you to agree or disagree with the statement *Every cloud has a silver lining,* **don't** write an essay arguing that "there are too many 'clouds' in our lives."

☐ **One of the biggest mistakes writers make is starting to write without first carefully considering the assignment.** Below are some examples of different approaches to writing assignments. Note how the first approach "misses the mark," that is, discusses the right topic but does **not** answer the right question. The "bad approaches" sometimes discuss more interesting issues than the "good approaches," but that doesn't mean they will get better scores. **You are not permitted to change to a different topic even if that topic is more interesting.**

Assignment	OFF the mark	ON the mark
Who is your hero and why?	Discuss your belief that pro athletes shouldn't be heroes and that we don't value true heroism anymore.	Pick a person you admire; define what a hero is to you and show how he or she exemplifies heroic qualities.
Has technology mostly benefited humankind or harmed it?	Discuss how internet companies have made so much money on IPOs, and explain why technology stocks are a good investment.	Discuss the cost vs. benefits of technology through many eras with three examples.
Vince Lombardi said, "Winning isn't everything; it's the only thing." Do you agree or disagree?	Describe how important the arts and music are to a good education, and argue that they are more important than sports.	Describe an experience with an out-of-control father at a soccer match to show how focusing on winning alone harms kids.
"Every cloud has a silver lining." Agree or disagree?	Explain how "clouds" represent difficult times. Show how some people, for instance the poor, have more "clouds" than do other people, and this isn't fair.	Describe a difficult situation in your life that made you stronger for having endured it.

Define Your Terms

☐ Your assignment will probably ask you to discuss an abstract concept or value. **Don't discuss complicated, abstract concepts without *defining* them first.** Defining your terms is the first step in communication, and communication is the essence of writing. **If your readers disagree with how you are using a term, you will not be able to convince them of your point.**

Practice 2: Examine the Assignment Closely

Defining Terms Practice

Below are some examples of common terms that may show up on an SAT I writing assignment and that you should define if you use them in an essay. Avoid a simplistic "dictionary" definition. Think carefully about each one, then write a simple but useful definition of each term in your own words. Include a well-chosen example, if it helps to illustrate your definition.

1. Democracy

2. Courage

3. Adventure

4. Liberty

5. Political power

6. Discipline

Lesson 3: Brainstorm Creatively

Take Six to Eight Minutes

To write a great essay, you must brainstorm creatively and organize your thoughts **before you write.** If you do these well, the rest of the essay will flow smoothly and (relatively) easily. If you don't take the time to brainstorm and organize, your essay will probably flounder.

❑ **Plan to spend six to eight minutes at the beginning of each essay assignment reading the assignment carefully, brainstorming about what example(s) you will use, thinking about what position you will take, and writing a quick outline.** Don't worry about running out of time: these tasks are critical to writing a good essay, and will save you time in the long run.

Do all of your brainstorming on paper, not just in your head. The SAT I will give you room to scribble notes. Use it. Write down thoughts; connect them; cross them out; underline them; do whatever your creative brain tells you to do. **But remember: when brainstorming, turn off your internal "critic." Don't dismiss ideas right away. Think about them for a bit, and you may find that the ideas you were going to throw away are the best ones after all!**

Think of Good Examples *Before* Taking Your Position

Most students think that the first thing to do after reading the assignment is to take a position. **In fact, analyzing the problem should always come before making a thesis.** Since your position is going to rest on your example(s) and your explanation, you should think about the examples and explanations first.

❑ After you have read the assignment carefully and have defined your terms, ask yourself: **"What is the most interesting example I can think of to clearly support a position on this issue?"** The SAT I essay is an excellent opportunity to show off what you know and how creative a thinker you are. Try to think of an example that other students aren't likely to think of, but that you can discuss with authority.

Find your example(s) *before* you decide about your position on the issue. If the assignment asks you to *agree* or *disagree* with a statement, **try to think of good examples to support each side of the issue.** Then think about which example(s) would produce the more substantial and interesting essay.

Go Off the Beaten Path

❑ **Try your best to avoid a "run-of-the-mill" response.** Although there is no such thing as a "wrong" response to these assignments, there certainly is such a thing as a "boring" response. Nothing will put a reader to sleep faster than writing about how Michael Jordan is your hero because he is the greatest basketball player ever and he does things for charity. Thousands of other students are probably going to say the exact same thing, or something close to it. If you can go off the beaten path, and describe why Maya Angelou is your hero because she sculpts the written word as no one else does, or Noam Chomsky because of his commitment to justice and peace and because of his contributions to linguistics, you will make a reader sit up and think that you are a very special writer and thinker.

Another reason to go off the beaten path is that it will keep you on your toes, and this almost always leads to better writing. When you take the "easy" position, you are likely to fall into lazy writing habits (which we will discuss later) like cliché, redundancy, and vagueness.

Practice 3: Brainstorm Creatively

Brainstorming Practice

Give yourself six minutes for each exercise below. Use the space below each question to practice brainstorming. Write down all the words, ideas, associations, people, events, books, etc., that pertain to the issue implied by the question. **Don't censor or criticize any idea; just get it down on the paper.** Then, in the last few minutes, try to organize your thoughts into ideas for individual paragraphs. Try to find one idea for each of four paragraphs. (Don't write the paragraphs, though.)

1.   Should safety always be first?

2.   Is the pen always mightier than the sword?

Show this work to your teacher or tutor. Discuss ways of efficiently releasing your creativity and connecting to your academic knowledge.

Lesson 4: Prepare with "Source Summaries"

What Is a College Hill Coaching "Source Summary"?

❑ **Good writers must be prepared to give good examples to support their claims.** A well-chosen and well-explained example often means the difference between a mediocre essay and a great essay. The College Hill Coaching "Source Summary" helps you to prepare to write good essays by helping you to summarize what you know about important "source material" for essays: novels, historical events, people, cultural movements, etc., so that you can use them well.

A Source Summary is simply a summary of the key ideas about a topic: **themes, theses,** and **examples** that you can use in a persuasive essay. Two examples are given below. Notice that each summary focuses only on the information that you would use in an essay on the given theme. It includes the important details you need to mention in order to sound as if you know what you're talking about.

Sample Source Summaries

Book, Person, or Event   *Jane Eyre* by Charlotte Bronte

Themes	Theses	Examples
Feminism	Women are more constrained by society than men are.	Jane complains about what society expects of her, and that men aren't held to such high moral standards.
Social status	In 19th-century England, one's status in society had to do with breeding rather than ability.	Jane is disgusted by how she is treated by Rochester's houseguests.
Love	Love is blind and often irrational.	Rochester marries Jane while literally blind. Jane overlooks Rochester's previous marriage.
Independence	Independence can open one to new experiences, but can also lead to tragic isolation and inability to connect emotionally with others.	Orphaned as a child, Jane learns that she must fend for herself, and that others don't necessarily have her best interests in mind. She doubts Rochester's love for her at first, and takes an assumed name to avoid revealing herself to Reverend St. John Rivers.

Book, Person, or Event   *D-Day* or *Operation Overlord* June 6, 1944, Normandy, France

Themes	Theses	Examples
Strategic planning	Intelligent planning pays off.	Operation Overlord was a monumental achievement. Thousands of soldiers had to keep it secret. Not since 1688 had an invading army crossed the English Channel. Over 800 planes brought paratroopers, and another 300 dropped 13,000 bombs. Within weeks, 20,000 tons of supplies per day were being brought ashore.
Loss	Great achievements require great losses.	By nightfall, 100,000 soldiers had landed, but over 9,000 were dead or wounded.
Bravery	To accomplish great things, we must conquer our fears.	Many went ashore knowing that they would die. From D-Day until Christmas 1944, Allied soldiers captured German prisoners at the rate of 1,000 per day.

Practice 4: Prepare with "Source Summaries"

Source Summaries Make copies of this sheet and summarize the major books, people, and events you have recently studied. Try to make a Source Summary for at least 10 different topics of study.

Book, Person, or Event _____

Themes   Theses   Examples

Book, Person, or Event _____

Themes   Theses   Examples

Book, Person, or Event _____

Themes   Theses   Examples

Discuss these examples with your teacher or tutor to see if your analyses are "on the mark."

Lesson 5: Write a Strong and Creative Thesis

The Importance of a Good Thesis

Good short essays revolve around a good thesis. If your thesis is weak or dull, your essay will be weak or dull. Once you have brainstormed about the topic and examples, focus on a strong, creative thesis.

❏ **After a few minutes of brainstorming, write "THESIS:" on your scratch paper, then write the strongest, most creative one-sentence thesis that you can support.** The thesis should capture the essence of the essay in one well-crafted sentence. This sentence should be **concise, interesting, specific,** and **informative.**

Below are some examples of weak theses and strong theses. The weak theses may be true, but they show little insight into the topic, and are run-of-the-mill observations. The strong theses are more thoughtful and creative, and have a wider scope.

Assignment	Weak Thesis	Strong Thesis
Has technology been good for humankind or bad?	• Good, because it has given us computers, video games, and DVDs. • Bad, because kids spend too much time online and playing video games.	• Good, because it has given us tools for exploring the universe and uncovering its secrets. • Bad, because it impedes genuine social interaction, and separates us from nature.
Vince Lombardi said, "Winning isn't everything; it's the only thing." Do you agree or disagree?	• Disagree: we focus too much on winning and not enough on sportsmanship. • Agree: we should always strive to win, because that's what sports are all about.	• Agree: we love sports because our genes, which we inherit from our hunter ancestors, compel us to. • Disagree: winning is only a very small part of a successful and happy life, and here are some things that make us happier than winning.
"Every cloud has a silver lining." Agree or disagree?	• Agree, because I once had a bad experience that had a good side. • Disagree, because there are some experiences that are just tragic.	• Agree, because every trial can strengthen a person for having endured it, as these examples from literature show. • Disagree, because interpreting every tragedy in a Panglossian way prevents us from solving important problems like the following.

"Play Devil's Advocate"

Don't worry—**"playing devil's advocate"** doesn't mean selling your soul to the devil for a good essay grade. It simply means **addressing objections to your argument to strengthen it.** If you want to persuade a good reader, you must address common objections to your thesis. For instance, if your thesis is "Competition for grades creates a bad learning environment," a reader might object: "But competition motivates students to do their best, much as it motivates athletes." Your argument will not be complete until you address this objection. So you might address it this way in your essay:

> *Although many will say that competition motivates students to do their best, much as it motivates athletes, such objections misrepresent real learning. A decent artist is not motivated to create great art by the mere thought of "defeating" other artists, but to express a capacity that makes her more in tune with nature and with her own humanity. Similarly, some children do not learn merely to get better grades than other kids (if they did, then how would they learn to speak, to walk, to tell jokes, and the myriad other things they learn outside of school?) but to make themselves more competent and happier human beings.*

❏ Every good thesis must argue **against** something as well as argue **for** something. A good thesis should acknowledge the common objections to it, and address them thoughtfully. As you compose your thesis, **"play devil's advocate."**

Practice 5: Write a Strong and Creative Thesis

Strong and Creative Thesis Practice

Look again at the questions from Practice 3. Now that you have brainstormed about these questions, and understand the difference between a weak thesis and a strong thesis, write a **strong thesis,** in one sentence, to answer the two questions.

1. Should safety always be first?

2. Is the pen always mightier than the sword?

Devil's Advocate Practice

To play devil's advocate and write a strong thesis, you must be able to look at opposing sides of an issue. After each of the following questions, write two thesis statements, one for the "pro" position and one for the "con" position.

3. Should criminal trials be televised?

     Yes, because:

     No, because:

4. Is jealousy ever a good thing?

     Yes, because:

     No, because:

5. Does wealth make people happier?

     Yes, because:

     No, because:

Discuss your answers with your teacher or tutor, focusing on whether your responses are creative and forceful.

Lesson 6: Organize Your Thoughts

Write a Quick Four- or Five-Point Outline

❑ Once you have written a strong and creative thesis and brainstormed a good example or two, you are **almost** ready to write. Your last step should be to quickly organize the other three or four paragraphs. **This outline should be very brief: simply write one short sentence that captures the gist of each paragraph.**

Writing a quick outline helps you to avoid one of the most common writing problems: redundancy. Students who do not plan their paragraphs usually end up repeating themselves too much; their essays don't "go anywhere." Good organization helps you to **develop** your thoughts. Once you've stated your thesis and example, what then? You have many options: you can explain your example in more detail, you can give another example, you can address an objection, and so on.

Understand the Function of Paragraphs

Think of paragraphs as "mini-chapters" of your essay. Each one must be complete in itself, but must also be part of a whole. When you start a new paragraph, you signal that you are doing something new: giving a new example, analyzing a new idea, presenting a counter-argument, or the like. Your paragraphs give your essay **structure.** (For more on structure, see Chapter 7, Lesson 3.) You might like a standard "top-down" (thesis at the beginning) structure:

Paragraph 1: State thesis and summarize reasons or examples.

Paragraph 2: Explain first reason or example.

Paragraph 3: Explain second reason or example.

Paragraph 4: Conclude with an extension or clarification of your thesis.

This is a simplification of the standard "five-paragraph" essay structure. We have simplified it to four paragraphs, because five paragraphs may be too much to write in 25 minutes, and because **most essays that get perfect scores have only four paragraphs. Writing more than four paragraphs is usually too hard, and writing fewer than four paragraphs indicates weak development.**

You might also want to use a "bottom-up" (thesis near the end) structure like this:

Paragraph 1: Begin with a quick story that introduces the topic.

Paragraph 2: Analyze the significance of the story.

Paragraph 3: State and explain your thesis that follows from the story.

Paragraph 4: Generalize from this thesis and connect it to a broader scope of ideas.

❑ **There is no one "right" structure; choose the structure that works best with your ideas, your examples, and your style.**

Practice 6: Organize Your Thoughts

Organization Review

1. What is the difference between a "top-down" essay structure and a "bottom-up" essay structure?

2. What should a good outline consist of?

Check your answers with the Answer Key at the end of the chapter.

Organization Practice

Spend a few minutes reading and brainstorming about each of the questions below. Then write a brief four-point outline with thesis, development, and conclusion. Capture just the essence of your argument, and **be brief.**

3. Is honesty always the best policy?

    1. THESIS:

    2.

    3.

    4. CONCLUSION:

4. What is an example of true courage?

    1. THESIS:

    2.

    3.

    4. CONCLUSION:

Discuss your outlines with your teacher or tutor, focusing on whether your outlines show good development.

Lesson 7: Write Logically

Be Specific

❑ Your argument is much more effective when you discuss **real and specific examples rather than hypothetical and general ones.** You can generalize in your thesis and conclusion, but be specific everywhere else.

Consider this paragraph:

Although our Constitution provides us with the right to bear arms, this right should not be a universal one. That's not what the Second Amendment was intended for. A lot of times it's not appropriate and just plain dangerous or foolish. This is obvious to anyone who reads newspapers or watches the TV news and knows about what is going on in the world.

The argument isn't effective because it gives no specifics. Consider this improvement:

Although our Constitution provides us with the right to bear arms, this right was intended only to protect citizens from the tyranny of government, and not to arm citizens against one another. In many places, for instance in schools and other public places, the right to bear arms does not enhance public safety. Even the popular argument that it makes our homes safer is absurd. Rather, it merely increases the likelihood that a problematic situation like an argument will turn deadly, as it did last month when an eight-year-old boy shot his six-year-old sister to death in New Jersey.

This revision is more forceful because it turns the generalizations into specifics, and gives concrete examples.

Help Your Reader with Logical Transitions

❑ **Provide your readers with "guideposts" to help them to understand the logical relationships between your ideas.** These guideposts, which usually come at the beginning of a paragraph or a sentence, are called **transitions.** They include words like *however* (to indicate a contrast), *therefore* (to indicate a result), *furthermore* (to indicate an extension of an argument), *first, second,* or *third* (to indicate a sequence of examples or reasons), *nevertheless* (to indicate irony), and so on.

Consider the following paragraphs:

Every first-year chemistry or physics student learns that opposite charges attract and like charges repel. If we try to force two positive charges together, they will fly apart as soon as we release them. Similarly, if we try to hold a positive charge apart from a negative charge, they will fly together as soon as we release them.

The nucleus of an atom consists of a collection of positively charged protons and uncharged neutrons squashed together in a very small space. Negatively charged electrons remain in "shells" that never touch the nucleus.

You should notice that the facts in these paragraphs don't "fit" logically. If like charges fly apart, then how on earth could they remain together in a nucleus? Also, if unlike charges fall toward each other, why don't the negative electrons fall into the positive nucleus? However, the second paragraph provides no logical "guideposts" to indicate this surprising relationship between these ideas. A good writer should acknowledge the contrasts between the ideas of the first paragraph and the ideas of the second paragraph with **logical transitions.** Notice how this revision provides the necessary transitions:

Every first-year chemistry or physics student learns that opposite charges attract and like charges repel. If we try to force two positive charges together, they will fly apart as soon as we release them. Similarly, if we try to hold a positive charge apart from a negative charge, they will fly together as soon as we release them.

***However,** science students are also told that the nucleus of an atom consists of a collection of positively charged protons and uncharged neutrons squashed together in a very small space. They are also told that negatively charged electrons remain in "shells" that never touch the nucleus. How can this be?*

You need to think carefully about the logic of individual sentences, as well.

Not logical: *The bill was in committee, and the opposition of several senators killed it because of the unpopular amendments that they attached to it.*

Better: *Several senators who opposed the bill killed it in committee by attaching unpopular amendments to it.*

Practice 7: Write Logically

Logical Transition Practice

Rewrite the second sentence of each of the following pairs so that it includes a logical transition from the previous one.

1. *We knew that the game would be hard fought. We never thought it would last 8 hours and 20 innings.*

   _____

   _____

2. *There were thousands of visitors in town for the game. It was almost impossible to find a hotel room.*

   _____

   _____

3. *The theory of evolution has had a profound effect on scientific thought. It has influenced many artists and writers.*

   _____

   _____

4. *We knew that punishing the culprits would do no good. We took no action against them.*

   _____

   _____

5. *Perfect games are rare. In the last two years, only one was bowled in the entire state.*

   _____

   _____

6. *There were several reasons for the delay. The bus driver had the wrong directions.*

   _____

   _____

Check your answers with the Answer Key at the end of the chapter.

Lesson 8: Write Clearly

Use Natural Language

❑ Good writing follows more rules than conversational speech does, but this doesn't mean that good writing is stiff and unnatural. Convoluted and abstract language doesn't make "better" writing. **Although you should avoid wordiness and egregious grammatical errors, natural language is always better than overly formal language.**

This sentence is far too stiff and unnatural:

An individual person's lack of tolerance and inability to appreciate and even enjoy different aspects in other individuals is a concept that negatively affects the ability of a community to avoid hatred and establish the environment in which we would like to bring our children up.

It is much more effective when phrased more naturally and concisely:

We create a much more peaceful society when we learn to appreciate the differences in others.

Use Personal and Concrete Nouns

Is the following sentence easy to understand?

My concerns in general center on numerous omissions of relevant facts and quotes, which had the effect of diminishing the extent of the apparent support of free expression, and the force of the moral arguments for free expression, and of enhancing the support of those who are vigilant against dangerous speech, and obscuring the more extreme arguments made on their behalf.

No. Why not? Just look at the nouns:

My <u>concerns</u> in general center on numerous <u>omissions</u> of relevant <u>facts</u> and <u>quotes</u>, which had the <u>effect</u> of <u>diminishing</u> the <u>extent</u> of the apparent <u>support</u> of free <u>expression</u>, and the <u>force</u> of the moral <u>arguments</u> for free <u>expression</u>, and of <u>enhancing</u> the <u>support</u> of those who are vigilant

against dangerous <u>speech</u>, and <u>obscuring</u> the more extreme <u>arguments</u> made on their <u>behalf</u>.

These nouns are all **impersonal** and **abstract,** so they are hard to relate to. **Personal nouns** refer to the things in your readers' common experience, things that they personally understand. **Concrete** nouns refer to things that can be **seen, heard, smelled, tasted,** or **touched.** Of course, if you are talking about ideas, you will need to use abstract nouns, but don't use any more than are necessary. Not many people can keep track of 18 abstract and impersonal nouns in a single sentence. Here's a good revision:

Some <u>people</u> have left out relevant <u>facts</u> in this <u>discussion</u>, and have therefore minimized how much <u>people</u> support free <u>expression</u> and maximized how much <u>people</u> want to eliminate offensive <u>speech</u>. <u>They</u> have also ignored or obscured the crazy and illogical <u>arguments</u> against offensive <u>speech</u>. In fact, the majority of <u>Americans</u> support free <u>expression</u>, and regard it as a moral <u>necessity</u>.

Without question, this conveys the author's ideas much more clearly and effectively.

❑ **Minimize abstract and impersonal nouns.** When they pile up, your thoughts become hard to follow.

Eliminate Jargon

❑ **Jargon** like *win-win scenario, thinking outside the box, bulletizing the issues, targeting a goal, bottom line, downside, facilitate, prioritize, optimize, time frame, mutually beneficial, parameter, utilize,* etc., **annoys good readers,** particularly when simpler, more common words suffice.

Jargony: *If we think outside the box and prioritize our concerns, I'm sure we can facilitate a win-win scenario for all parties.*

Better: *If we think creatively and set our priorities, I'm sure we can find a solution that everyone will like.*

Practice 8: Write Clearly

Clarification Practice

Rewrite the following sentences to eliminate stiffness, vagueness, and jargon.

1. *The concept of competition is an essential element with regard to the ability of society to encourage people to achieve excellence.*

   _____

   _____

   _____

2. *The consideration of all ideas of our employees is done by our management with the thinking that only the most quality concepts will elevate to the forefront.*

   _____

   _____

   _____

3. *A concern in the general population with regard to the ability of the government to optimize the positive use of federal funds has accelerated in recent times.*

   _____

   _____

   _____

4. *When one is placing the emphasis on the deterioration of the individual concern for others and personal moral responsibility, the role of social institutions is ignored.*

   _____

   _____

   _____

Check your answers with the Answer Key at the end of the chapter.

Lesson 9: Write Concisely

Eliminate Wordiness

❑ **The fewer words you can use to convey an idea, the better.** You won't impress readers by making them work hard or by confusing them. When you use wordy or unnatural language, a good reader will think that you don't have command over your words, or that you're stalling because you don't have anything interesting to say.

Wordy: *Courage is a value that is very difficult to be found in and among individuals in the world today, even though it is clearly something that nearly everyone of every persuasion and creed finds to be an extremely important and valuable element of human morality.*

Better: *Courage today is rare, and so all the more precious.*

❑ **Avoid wordy phrases like those below. Use the concise versions.**

Wordy	Concise	Wordy	Concise
has a reaction	*reacts*	*in the event that*	*if*
has a dependence on	*depends*	*regardless of the fact that*	*although*
provides enforcement	*enforces*	*in our world today*	*today*
is in violation of	*violates*	*in this day and age*	*today*
has knowledge of	*knows*	*being that*	*because*
achieves the maximization of	*maximizes*	*due to the fact that*	*because*
provides opposition to	*opposes*	*at this point in time*	*now*
is reflective of	*reflects*	*at the present moment*	*now*
give consideration to	*consider*	*are aware of the fact*	*know*
lend assistance to	*assist*	*make contact with*	*contact*

Watch Your Prepositional Phrases

❑ **Sometimes even good writers can get ambushed by prepositional phrases. Like most things, prepositional phrases are fine in moderation. But too many—particularly when they are strung together—make a sentence wordy and unclear.**

Wordy: *Few people in the media recognize their responsibility to the public for writing fair and unbiased pieces for the sake of expanding their readers' trust in their representations of the world around them.* (7 prepositional phrases)

Better: *Few journalists understand that they must sustain scrupulous impartiality in order to maintain the trust of their readers.* (1 prepositional phrase)

Avoid Redundancy

❑ Eliminate any word or phrase that conveys an idea already stated or implied in the sentence.

Redundant: *We are now serving breakfast **at this time.***
Better: *We are now serving breakfast.*

Redundant: *The best elements of her previous works were combined **together** in this symphony.*
Right: *The best elements of her previous works were combined in this symphony.*

Redundant: *They could always rely on him to tell the **honest** truth.*
Right: *They could always rely on him to tell the truth.*

Practice 9: Write Concisely

Redundancy Sweeping Practice

Eliminate any redundancies in the following sentences.

1. *An effective and good manager must need to rely on sound, solid management principles as well as past experience.*

2. *Both parents as well as students should have input into the new testing plan.*

3. *Many cleaning substances should not be combined together, because violent reactions could result.*

4. *Even if each and every citizen contributed to the effort, it would still take several years to complete.*

5. *The food and blankets dropped for the suffering refugees were far from sufficient enough to ward off the hunger and cold.*

6. *We watched the jet until it disappeared from view.*

Tightening-Up Practice

Rewrite the following sentences to eliminate wordiness.

7. *In this day and age, all too many people have a dependence on television as their exclusive source of information.*

   _____

   _____

8. *Few people are aware of the fact that such gambling is in violation of federal law.*

   _____

   _____

9. *Due to the fact that corporations endeavor to achieve the maximization of profit, they rarely put their focus on environmental needs.*

   _____

   _____

10. *In the event that your boss expresses opposition to your proposal at the meeting, consider having a head-to-head conversation with her about it personally.*

    _____

    _____

11. *It is certainly clear that too few people give consideration to the fact that economic strength is often reflective of the hopes of consumers.*

    _____

    _____

Check your answers with the Answer Key at the end of the chapter.

Lesson 10: Write Forcefully

Eliminate Weak Verbs—Uncover the "Lurking Verbs"

❑ Take an essay you've written recently and circle all of the verbs. How many are forms of the verb *to be*, like *is, are, was,* and *were*? Probably too many. *To be* is the most overused verb in the English language, and it is also the **weakest.** Other weak verbs are *to exist* and *to have*. Too many of these verbs in your writing make it weak and lifeless. **If your writing contains too many weak verbs, find the stronger lurking verbs in the sentence, and rewrite it. Lurking verbs are words in the sentence that aren't verbs but should be, because they convey the idea or action of the sentence more effectively.**

Weak: *The mice **have** a tendency to overeat when they are in the absence of this hormone.*

Stronger: *The mice **tend** to overeat when they **lack** this hormone.*

The original verbs, *have* and *are*, are weak. More effective verbs are "lurking" as nouns in the first sentence: *tendency* and *absence* seem to carry the main ideas, but they are nouns. Notice how much more forceful the revision is because these ideas were transformed into verbs.

Weak: *We **will not be** tolerant of anyone who **is** disrespectful of the opposing players.*

Stronger: *We won't **tolerate** anyone who **disrespects** the opposing players.*

Use Clear and Active Verbs

Consider this example of a weak and unclear sentence:

The most aggressive of the new companies, whose priorities are characterized by their capital commitment to market share and name recognition, will be seen as the "players" in their niche, and may see an extension of share overvaluation, despite weak product development or business models.

Why is this sentence so weak and vague? It's filled with jargon, abstract nouns, and weak and passive verbs. Here's a much more effective revision:

Investors like aggressive companies that are committed to making themselves well-known and to building their share of the market. As a result, investors put a lot of money into these companies, thereby overvaluing them, even though the companies often have weak products or business models.

We've cut out the jargon, used more concrete nouns, included more logical connections, and found stronger verbs. We also replaced the **passive verb** with an **active verb.** A passive verb places the noun performing the action **after** the verb, as in *The ball **was hit** by the boy,* or eliminates the noun performing the action altogether, as in *The ball **was hit.*** In the original sentence above, the verb is in the passive voice and doesn't convey a clear thought: *The companies will be seen as "players."* Seen by whom? It doesn't say, so the sentence is unclear. Notice that the revision makes this clear: *Investors like companies.* This tells us what's happening, and who's doing it.

❑ **Use the passive voice sparingly: don't say *The ball was hit by the boy* when you can say *The boy hit the ball.* The passive voice often makes a sentence needlessly wordy and vague.**

Eliminate Clichés

❑ Phrases like *give it 110%, go for the gold, rip it to shreds, in the lap of luxury, keep at arm's length, pick up the pieces, cross that bridge when we come to it, go to town,* and so on are **clichés. A cliché** is an overused phrase. **Whenever you use a cliché in your writing, a good reader will think you are being lazy, or that you cannot think of an original way to convey your idea. Instead, use your own, original words to convey your thoughts.**

Clichéd: *Believe me, I felt like a fish out of water giving that speech, but I sucked it up and gave it a go.*

Better: *Although the prospect of speaking in front of the class intimidated me, I tried to focus on my words rather than my fear.*

Practice 10: Write Forcefully

Cliché Sweeping Practice

Rewrite each sentence to eliminate any clichés.

1. *Many people these days are fond of saying that the youth of this day and age are lazy as dogs.*

   _____

   _____

2. *They say that kids are nothing but couch potatoes who sit like bumps on a log playing video games or watching MTV.*

   _____

   _____

3. *For all intents and purposes, this assumption is dead wrong.*

   _____

   _____

4. *As a matter of fact, many of my friends are thinking more about careers that will change the world as we know it rather than careers that will just chase the almighty dollar.*

   _____

   _____

Verb Strengthening Practice

Rewrite the following sentences to strengthen the verbs. Uncover any good "lurking" verbs.

5. *This action is in violation of the company's own contract.*

   _____

6. *The village was affected to a devastating degree by the earthquake.*

   _____

7. *My failure on the test was reflective of the fact that I didn't study.*

   _____

8. *The movie was considered by the critics to be dull and hackneyed.*

   _____

9. *The bold maneuver was made by the army under the cover of night.*

   _____

10. *Outside the office were a dozen chairs filling the hallway.*

   _____

Check your answers with the Answer Key at the end of the chapter.

Lesson 11: Write Masterfully

Vary Your Sentence Length Wisely

Consider the following paragraph:

Many people buy into the cliché "guns don't kill people; people kill people." On its surface, this statement seems obviously true. However, some deep thought and analysis about this statement, its assumptions and implications, shows clearly that it is mistaken.

Not bad, but consider the following revision:

Many people buy into the cliché "guns don't kill people; people kill people." On its surface, this statement seems obviously true. It's not.

Why is the last sentence of the revision more effective than the last sentence of the first paragraph? Because it's short. When it follows a series of lengthy, informative sentences, a short sentence hits the reader like a slap in the face and drives home an important point.

❑ Good writers always think about the length of their sentences. **Long sentences may be necessary for explaining complex ideas, but very short sentences are often best for emphasizing important points.**

Eliminate Sentences to Nowhere

❑ **Eliminate sentences that state the obvious, are hopelessly vague, or don't move your thesis forward.** Sometimes a sentence that seemed profound when you first wrote it may turn out to be nonsensical or unintelligible. Every sentence should convey a fresh and interesting idea that moves your argument forward. Any sentence that fails to do that should be eliminated.

If you must eliminate a sentence from your essay, cross it out neatly. Don't worry about erasing it completely, and don't be concerned about the essay's looking "perfect." The readers understand that you would have been more neat if you had had the time, and won't penalize you for eliminating an unnecessary sentence.

e.g. *Life is characterized by the ups and downs one experiences while living from day to day.*

The writer probably thought that this sentence was profound when she wrote it. But it really doesn't say anything at all. Saying that *life has ups and downs* is just stating the obvious. No rational person would disagree with that. The writer should eliminate this sentence.

e.g. *Every country seeks a constant prosperity in its growth.*

This sentence is so vague and uninteresting that it's hardly worth saving. How can a country *seek* anything? Maybe the people can, but not the country. Saying that people seek prosperity is a pretty uninteresting observation. Do they really seek *constant prosperity*? What does that even mean? And what the heck is *prosperity in their growth*? Clearly, this is a sentence to nowhere.

Choose Your Words Carefully

❑ Good writers have good vocabularies. They know that one well-chosen "bargain" word is often worth six modifiers.

Weak diction: *I walked through the finish line as if my legs were ridiculously heavy, and sat down exhausted.*

Strong diction: *I lumbered through the finish line and collapsed.*

❑ Don't use overblown vocabulary unnecessarily. Fancy words are often distracting.

Overblown diction: *An astute scribe shall always eschew superfluous grandiloquence.*

Effective diction: *Good writers use big words only when necessary.*

Practice 11: Write Masterfully

Sentence Variation Practice

Cross out the sentence in each paragraph that is too long. Then rewrite the sentence to increase its impact.

1. *Many neoconservatives love to claim that lowering taxes actually raises government revenue. Any rational examination of this claim shows clearly that it is wrong, or at least not as simple as they are claiming. In fact, the government's tax revenue depends on many things other than the tax rate.*

    _____

    _____

2. *My mother sat me down and explained to me how important it is to spend money wisely. After listening to her carefully, I understood the point she was trying to make. I began keeping better track of my accounts and became a wiser consumer.*

    _____

    _____

Bargain Word Practice

Find a single word or shorter phrase to capture the idea in bold.

3. *David **looked very closely at** his test results.*

    _____

4. *The girls in the car **talked on and on about meaningless things** for hours.*

    _____

5. *The coach **gave us a long, harsh, and critical speech** about our lack of effort in the first half.*

    _____

Toning Down Practice

Tone down the fancy vocabulary in the sentences below.

6. *When a practitioner of medicine suggests an appropriate remedy for a malady, it is best that the person to whom it was offered utilizes it strictly according to the instructions.*

    _____

7. *Plebeians execrate prevaricators, while aristocrats lionize them.*

    _____

Check your answers with the Answer Key at the end of the chapter.

Lesson 12: Finish with a Bang

What a Good Conclusion Does

❏ Your conclusion should do one of the following:

- **Make a broader connection to your thesis:** Discuss an implication of your thesis by connecting it to your own life, society at large, a particular problem, the future, etc.
- **Offer a solution:** If your essay describes a problem, offer some ideas of how to fix it.
- **Refine or clarify your thesis:** Address objections to your point of view, or clarify important points.

Don't Just Summarize

❏ **A conclusion provides closure to the essay and should leave the reader with something to think about. A conclusion should not be just a "recap" of your essay.** Don't merely restate your thesis in different words. **A good conclusion must present a *new* idea.** Read good essays in magazines like the *New Yorker* and the *Atlantic Monthly,* and in the *New York Times* Op-Ed page, and you will see that good writers **never** say "In conclusion, . . ." or "As I have proven in this essay, . . ." So you shouldn't say that, either.

Don't Tell Us What You're Doing— Just Do It

❏ **Many writers are distractingly self-conscious.** They say things like *It is my opinion that drugs are dangerous* instead of *Drugs are dangerous.* All competent readers know that your essay presents your opinion. **You don't need to tell them that you're giving your opinion; just give it.**

Weak and self-conscious:

> *I believe that bullies are often people who don't like themselves. It's just my opinion, of course, but those who have to pick on the weak can't really feel good about themselves, as I can demonstrate with a few examples.*

Stronger:

> *Bullies are often people who don't like themselves. Those who have to pick on the weak can't really feel good about themselves.*

❏ **Similarly, don't tell your readers that you are concluding your essay. Just conclude.** Don't say *In conclusion, . . .* or *As my examples clearly prove, . . .*

> e.g. *As I said in the beginning, every cloud has a silver lining, and this has been shown in this essay with the examples of some wars and individual diseases. Both of these are bad things overall which sometimes can have good things come out of them. This shows that. . . .*

This conclusion seems to be saying: "Well, I guess it's time for the conclusion. In case you weren't paying attention, here's what I just finished saying." This is not what a conclusion should do; it should present new and interesting thoughts connected to the thesis. This conclusion merely repeats the thesis and doesn't give the readers anything new to think about. In fact, it insults the readers by assuming that they can't remember what they just read. Compare it to this revision:

> *Of course, wars are among the most tragic of all human events. If wars can have beneficial outcomes, then surely we can see the good in lesser tragedies. Perhaps if we could take such a positive perspective on our everyday problems, we would live happier lives.*

This conclusion is more effective because it **extends the thesis** to a wider sphere, **offers a suggestion,** and **leaves the readers thinking** without insulting them.

Practice 12: Finish with a Bang

Conclusion Review

1. What are the three things that a good conclusion can do?

2. What does it mean for your writing to be self-conscious?

Self-Consciousness Sweeping Practice

Rewrite the following sentences to make them less self-conscious.

3. *I think that classes should not start until 9:00 am, because I believe students need more rest than they are getting.*

   _____

   _____

4. *As I have shown with these examples, there are many factors to consider when choosing a college.*

   _____

   _____

5. *It is my opinion that more money should be spent, in my school and schools like it, on music programs.*

   _____

   _____

6. *These examples abundantly demonstrate that goals are important in life, as I said earlier.*

   _____

   _____

Check your answers with the Answer Key at the end of the chapter.

Chapter 15 Answer Key

Practice 1

1. It means that you respond with a thoughtful and interesting thesis and provide relevant, specific examples and clear, logical explanations.

2. It means that you use paragraphs to develop, support, and explain your thesis, and that you conclude effectively.

3. It means that you avoid needless jargon, wordiness, cliché, or abstraction, and define terms as necessary.

4. It means that you vary your sentence structure appropriately, are concise, and choose your words wisely.

5. Four or five paragraphs.

Practice 6

1. A "top-down" essay states the thesis at the beginning, and a "bottom-up" essay states it near the end of the essay.

2. Four brief sentences: the thesis, the topic sentence of paragraph 2, the topic sentence of paragraph 3, and the concluding idea.

Practice 7

1. *We knew that the game would be hard fought.* **However,** *we never thought it would last 8 hours and 20 innings.*

2. *There were thousands of visitors in town for the game.* **Therefore,** *it was almost impossible to find a hotel room.*

3. *The theory of evolution has had a profound effect on scientific thought.* **Furthermore,** *it has influenced many artists and writers.*

4. *We knew that punishing the culprits would do no good.* **Therefore,** *we took no action against them.*

5. *Perfect games are rare.* **In fact,** *in the last two years, only one was bowled in the entire state.*

6. *There were several reasons for the delay.* **First,** *the bus driver had the wrong directions.*

Practice 8

1. *Competition encourages excellence.*

2. *Our managers consider all ideas from our employees, and use the best ones.*

3. *People are increasingly concerned that the government is wasting money.*

4. *When we focus exclusively on personal moral responsibility, we ignore the importance of social institutions.*

Practice 9

1. *An effective and good manager must need to rely on sound, solid management principles as well as past experience.*

2. *Both parents as well as students should have input into the new testing plan.*

3. *Many cleaning substances should not be combined together, because violent reactions could result.*

4. *Even if each and every citizen contributed to the effort, it would still take several years to complete.*

5. *The food and blankets dropped for the suffering refugees was far from sufficient enough to ward off the hunger and cold.*

6. *We watched the jet until it disappeared from view.*

7. *Today, too many people depend on television as their exclusive source of information.*

8. *Few people know that such gambling violates federal law.*

9. *Because corporations try to maximize profit, they rarely focus on environmental needs.*

10. *If your boss opposes your proposal at the meeting, consider talking to her about it.*

11. *Too few people realize that economic strength often reflects the hopes of consumers.*

Chapter 15 Answer Key

Practice 10

1. *Many people today think that young people are lazy.*

2. *They say that they spend too much time playing video games or watching MTV.*

3. *They are wrong.*

4. *In fact, many of my friends are choosing careers that help others rather than make themselves rich.*

5. *This action violates the company's own contract.*

6. *The earthquake devastated the village.*

7. *I failed the test because I hadn't studied.*

8. *The critics complained that the movie was dull and hackneyed.*

9. *The army maneuvered boldly under the cover of night.*

10. *A dozen chairs filled the hallway outside the office.*

Practice 11

1. *Many neoconservatives love to claim that lowering taxes actually raises government revenue.* **They are wrong. It's not that simple.** *In fact, the government's tax revenue depends on many things other than the tax rate.*

2. *My mother sat me down and explained to me how important it is to spend money wisely.* **I got the message.** *I began keeping better track of my accounts and became a wiser consumer.*

3. *David* **scrutinized** *his test results.*

4. *The girls in the car* **babbled** *for hours.*

5. *The coach* **harangued us** *about our lack of effort in the first half.*

6. *When a doctor prescribes something for you, follow the directions carefully.*

7. *Ordinary people hate liars, but noblemen love them.*

Practice 12

1. Make a broader connection to the thesis; offer a solution; refine or clarify the thesis.

2. It means that you are telling your reader that you are doing something rather than simply doing it.

3. *Classes should not start until 9:00 am, because students need more rest than they are getting.*

4. *There are many factors to consider when choosing a college.*

5. *More money should be spent on school music programs.*

6. *Goals are important in life.*

## CHAPTER 16

ESSAY WRITING PRACTICE

20 Practice SAT I Essay Assignments

Practice Essay 1

Time—25 minutes

Directions for Writing the Essay

Plan and write an essay that answers the question below. Do NOT write on another topic. An essay on another topic will receive a score of 0.

Two readers will grade your essay based on how well you develop your point of view, organize and explain your ideas, use specific and relevant examples to support your thesis, and use clear and effective language. How well you write is much more important than how much you write, but to cover the topic adequately you should plan to write several paragraphs.

Your essay must be written only on the lines provided on your answer sheet. You will have enough space if you write on every line, avoid wide margins, and keep your handwriting to a reasonable size. Your essay will be read by people who are not familiar with your handwriting, so write legibly.

You may use this sheet for notes and outlining, but these will not be graded as part of your essay.

Consider carefully the issue discussed in the following passage, then write an essay that answers the question posed in the assignment.

> Without a clear goal to focus our energy and drive us to grow, we cease to be truly alive. We become inert particles floating on the sea of life. This is true of not only ourselves, but our institutions—our families, our corporations, and our societies. The moment we cease to grow, we begin to die.

Assignment: **Is growth necessary to a happy and productive life?** Write an essay in which you answer this question and discuss your point of view on this issue. You may discuss personal or institutional growth. Support your position logically with examples from literature, the arts, history, politics, science and technology, current events, or your experience or observation.

Write your essay on your answer sheet.

PRACTICE ESSAY 1

PRACTICE ESSAY I

Practice Essay 2

Time—25 minutes

Directions for Writing the Essay

Plan and write an essay that answers the question below. Do NOT write on another topic. An essay on another topic will receive a score of 0.

Two readers will grade your essay based on how well you develop your point of view, organize and explain your ideas, use specific and relevant examples to support your thesis, and use clear and effective language. How well you write is much more important than how much you write, but to cover the topic adequately you should plan to write several paragraphs.

Your essay must be written only on the lines provided on your answer sheet. You will have enough space if you write on every line, avoid wide margins, and keep your handwriting to a reasonable size. Your essay will be read by people who are not familiar with your handwriting, so write legibly.

You may use this sheet for notes and outlining, but these will not be graded as part of your essay.

Consider carefully the issue discussed in the following passage, then write an essay that answers the question posed in the assignment.

> Our leaders love to tell us that only victory will do, as if they are imparting great wisdom. They seek only to defeat the enemy, to achieve the goal. Yet many times a loss, particularly one that is hard fought, is more valuable than victory. We cannot live a life full of only victories, nor should we. The quality of our lives depends as much on how we manage our losses as on how we achieve our victories.

Assignment: **Can a loss ever be more valuable than a victory?** Write an essay in which you answer this question and discuss your point of view on this issue. Support your position logically with examples from literature, the arts, history, politics, science and technology, current events, or your experience or observation.

Write your essay on your answer sheet.

PRACTICE ESSAY 2

PRACTICE ESSAY 2

Practice Essay 3

Time—25 minutes

Directions for Writing the Essay

Plan and write an essay that answers the question below. Do NOT write on another topic. An essay on another topic will receive a score of 0.

Two readers will grade your essay based on how well you develop your point of view, organize and explain your ideas, use specific and relevant examples to support your thesis, and use clear and effective language. How well you write is much more important than how much you write, but to cover the topic adequately you should plan to write several paragraphs.

Your essay must be written only on the lines provided on your answer sheet. You will have enough space if you write on every line, avoid wide margins, and keep your handwriting to a reasonable size. Your essay will be read by people who are not familiar with your handwriting, so write legibly.

You may use this sheet for notes and outlining, but these will not be graded as part of your essay.

Consider carefully the issue discussed in the following passage, then write an essay that answers the question posed in the assignment.

> Adventure seekers who merely crave the rush of adrenaline that accompanies risky feats do not demonstrate true courage. Courage is not fearlessness but the willingness to face our unmitigated fears and vulnerabilities, particularly those fears that make us think less of ourselves.

Assignment: **What is one example of true courage?** Write an essay in which you answer this question and explain the reasons for your choice. You may choose an example from literature, the arts, history, politics, science and technology, current events, or your experience or observation.

Write your essay on your answer sheet.

PRACTICE ESSAY 3

PRACTICE ESSAY 3

Practice Essay 4

Time—25 minutes

Directions for Writing the Essay

Plan and write an essay that answers the question below. Do NOT write on another topic. An essay on another topic will receive a score of 0.

Two readers will grade your essay based on how well you develop your point of view, organize and explain your ideas, use specific and relevant examples to support your thesis, and use clear and effective language. How well you write is much more important than how much you write, but to cover the topic adequately you should plan to write several paragraphs.

Your essay must be written only on the lines provided on your answer sheet. You will have enough space if you write on every line, avoid wide margins, and keep your handwriting to a reasonable size. Your essay will be read by people who are not familiar with your handwriting, so write legibly.

You may use this sheet for notes and outlining, but these will not be graded as part of your essay.

Consider carefully the issue discussed in the following passage, then write an essay that answers the question posed in the assignment.

> Communicating technology was supposed to turn the world into a "global village," enhancing our relationships with others and our understanding of other cultures. Yet I fear it has rendered us more polarized and less articulate. Instant communication allows us to proclaim what is on our minds before we've analyzed it, substantiated it, or rendered it coherent, let alone eloquent.

Assignment: **Do modern means of communication make our society better or worse?** Write an essay in which you answer this question and explain your point of view on this issue. Support your position logically with examples from your reading, current events, or your experience or observation.

Write your essay on your answer sheet.

PRACTICE ESSAY 4

PRACTICE ESSAY 4

Practice Essay 5

Time—25 minutes

Directions for Writing the Essay

Plan and write an essay that answers the question below. Do NOT write on another topic. An essay on another topic will receive a score of 0.

Two readers will grade your essay based on how well you develop your point of view, organize and explain your ideas, use specific and relevant examples to support your thesis, and use clear and effective language. How well you write is much more important than how much you write, but to cover the topic adequately you should plan to write several paragraphs.

Your essay must be written only on the lines provided on your answer sheet. You will have enough space if you write on every line, avoid wide margins, and keep your handwriting to a reasonable size. Your essay will be read by people who are not familiar with your handwriting, so write legibly.

You may use this sheet for notes and outlining, but these will not be graded as part of your essay.

Consider carefully the issue discussed in the following passage, then write an essay that answers the question posed in the assignment.

> Being truly human as a member of a society means seeing injustice and working to fix it. The human mind is endowed with not only the ability to perceive the world and act instinctively, but to visualize a better future and endeavor to realize it.

Assignment: **What is one great injustice in the world, and how should it be addressed?** Write an essay in which you answer this question and explain the reasons for your choice. You may draw inspiration and support from literature, the arts, history, politics, science and technology, current events, or your experience or observation.

Write your essay on your answer sheet.

PRACTICE ESSAY 5

PRACTICE ESSAY 5

Practice Essay 6

Time—25 minutes

Directions for Writing the Essay

Plan and write an essay that answers the question below. Do NOT write on another topic. An essay on another topic will receive a score of 0.

Two readers will grade your essay based on how well you develop your point of view, organize and explain your ideas, use specific and relevant examples to support your thesis, and use clear and effective language. How well you write is much more important than how much you write, but to cover the topic adequately you should plan to write several paragraphs.

Your essay must be written only on the lines provided on your answer sheet. You will have enough space if you write on every line, avoid wide margins, and keep your handwriting to a reasonable size. Your essay will be read by people who are not familiar with your handwriting, so write legibly.

You may use this sheet for notes and outlining, but these will not be graded as part of your essay.

Consider carefully the issue discussed in the following passage, then write an essay that answers the question posed in the assignment.

> Acquiring knowledge is like scaling a mountain. The proper attitude in reaching a summit, however, is to marvel not so much at one's achievement as at the glorious view of the unknown beyond. A well-educated person is known not so much for the questions he or she can answer as for the questions he or she can ask.

Assignment: **What is one great question that every educated person should ask?** Write an essay in which you indicate what this question should be and explain the reasons for your choice. You may draw inspiration and support from literature, the arts, history, politics, science and technology, current events, or your experience or observation.

Write your essay on your answer sheet.

PRACTICE ESSAY 6

PRACTICE ESSAY 6

Practice Essay 7

Time—25 minutes

Directions for Writing the Essay

Plan and write an essay that answers the question below. Do NOT write on another topic. An essay on another topic will receive a score of 0.

Two readers will grade your essay based on how well you develop your point of view, organize and explain your ideas, use specific and relevant examples to support your thesis, and use clear and effective language. How well you write is much more important than how much you write, but to cover the topic adequately you should plan to write several paragraphs.

Your essay must be written only on the lines provided on your answer sheet. You will have enough space if you write on every line, avoid wide margins, and keep your handwriting to a reasonable size. Your essay will be read by people who are not familiar with your handwriting, so write legibly.

You may use this sheet for notes and outlining, but these will not be graded as part of your essay.

Consider carefully the issue discussed in the following passage, then write an essay that answers the question posed in the assignment.

> Some people spend their lives waiting for the one great challenge that will define them. Every society needs such people, who forge into the unknown and lay new foundations. But society also depends very much on those who meet the small challenges, like feeding mouths and minds and hearts.

Assignment: **Are we defined more by great challenges in our lives or small, everyday challenges?** Write an essay in which you answer this question and discuss your point of view on this issue. Support your position logically with examples from literature, the arts, history, politics, science and technology, current events, or your experience or observation.

Write your essay on your answer sheet.

PRACTICE ESSAY 7

PRACTICE ESSAY 7

Practice Essay 8

Time—25 minutes

Directions for Writing the Essay

Plan and write an essay that answers the question below. Do NOT write on another topic. An essay on another topic will receive a score of 0.

Two readers will grade your essay based on how well you develop your point of view, organize and explain your ideas, use specific and relevant examples to support your thesis, and use clear and effective language. How well you write is much more important than how much you write, but to cover the topic adequately you should plan to write several paragraphs.

Your essay must be written only on the lines provided on your answer sheet. You will have enough space if you write on every line, avoid wide margins, and keep your handwriting to a reasonable size. Your essay will be read by people who are not familiar with your handwriting, so write legibly.

You may use this sheet for notes and outlining, but these will not be graded as part of your essay.

Consider carefully the issue discussed in the following passage, then write an essay that answers the question posed in the assignment.

> Freedom requires the eradication of repression from tyrants and from want, but eliminating these is not enough. We must also eliminate the means by which we oppress ourselves, through our peeves, our addictions, and in our insecurities. This may involve strengthening the restraints within ourselves.

Assignment: **Does freedom require eliminating all restraints, or does it require creating or strengthening certain restraints?** Write an essay in which you answer this question and discuss your point of view on this issue. Support your position logically with examples from literature, the arts, history, politics, science and technology, current events, or your experience or observation.

Write your essay on your answer sheet.

PRACTICE ESSAY 8

PRACTICE ESSAY 8

Practice Essay 9

Time—25 minutes

Directions for Writing the Essay

Plan and write an essay that answers the question below. Do NOT write on another topic. An essay on another topic will receive a score of 0.

Two readers will grade your essay based on how well you develop your point of view, organize and explain your ideas, use specific and relevant examples to support your thesis, and use clear and effective language. How well you write is much more important than how much you write, but to cover the topic adequately you should plan to write several paragraphs.

Your essay must be written only on the lines provided on your answer sheet. You will have enough space if you write on every line, avoid wide margins, and keep your handwriting to a reasonable size. Your essay will be read by people who are not familiar with your handwriting, so write legibly.

You may use this sheet for notes and outlining, but these will not be graded as part of your essay.

Consider carefully the issue discussed in the following passage, then write an essay that answers the question posed in the assignment.

> We employ many devices to maintain or create peace among countries—trade agreements, cultural exchanges, treaties. But nothing unites humanity as well as a common foe. Mutual fear of nature or of foreign ideologies is perhaps the greatest diplomacy we know.

Assignment: **What is the most significant means of bringing people together in peace?** Write an essay in which you answer this question and discuss your point of view on this issue. Support your position logically with examples from literature, the arts, history, politics, science and technology, current events, or your experience or observation.

Write your essay on your answer sheet.

PRACTICE ESSAY 9

PRACTICE ESSAY 9

Practice Essay 10

Time—25 minutes

Directions for Writing the Essay

Plan and write an essay that answers the question below. Do NOT write on another topic. An essay on another topic will receive a score of 0.

Two readers will grade your essay based on how well you develop your point of view, organize and explain your ideas, use specific and relevant examples to support your thesis, and use clear and effective language. How well you write is much more important than how much you write, but to cover the topic adequately you should plan to write several paragraphs.

Your essay must be written only on the lines provided on your answer sheet. You will have enough space if you write on every line, avoid wide margins, and keep your handwriting to a reasonable size. Your essay will be read by people who are not familiar with your handwriting, so write legibly.

You may use this sheet for notes and outlining, but these will not be graded as part of your essay.

Consider carefully the issue discussed in the following passage, then write an essay that answers the question posed in the assignment.

> We love best not what gives the greatest pleasure, but what comes through the greatest effort, because this effort provides meaning. A plastic medallion received after completing a marathon is not just a $2.00 trinket, but the representation of months of effort and sacrifice. The best things in life are not free, but come at the expense of hard work.

Assignment: **Do we love things most that come at a great cost, or are the best things in life truly free?** Write an essay in which you answer this question and discuss your point of view on this issue. Support your position logically with examples from literature, the arts, history, politics, science and technology, current events, or your experience or observation.

Write your essay on your answer sheet.

PRACTICE ESSAY 10

PRACTICE ESSAY 10

Practice Essay 11

Time—25 minutes

Directions for Writing the Essay

Plan and write an essay that answers the question below. Do NOT write on another topic. An essay on another topic will receive a score of 0.

Two readers will grade your essay based on how well you develop your point of view, organize and explain your ideas, use specific and relevant examples to support your thesis, and use clear and effective language. How well you write is much more important than how much you write, but to cover the topic adequately you should plan to write several paragraphs.

Your essay must be written only on the lines provided on your answer sheet. You will have enough space if you write on every line, avoid wide margins, and keep your handwriting to a reasonable size. Your essay will be read by people who are not familiar with your handwriting, so write legibly.

You may use this sheet for notes and outlining, but these will not be graded as part of your essay.

Consider carefully the issue discussed in the following passage, then write an essay that answers the question posed in the assignment.

> Defeating an enemy by force always has profound, and usually unforeseen, consequences. Destroying another requires destroying a part of one's own humanity, and strengthening resentment in others. It is better to understand one's enemy, to learn the subtler but more enobling art of persuasion and coexistence.

Assignment: **Is it more important to defeat your enemy or to understand your enemy?** Write an essay in which you answer this question and discuss your point of view on this issue. Support your position logically with examples from literature, the arts, history, politics, science and technology, current events, or your experience or observation.

Write your essay on your answer sheet.

PRACTICE ESSAY 11

PRACTICE ESSAY 11

Practice Essay 12

Time—25 minutes

Directions for Writing the Essay

Plan and write an essay that answers the question below. Do NOT write on another topic. An essay on another topic will receive a score of 0.

Two readers will grade your essay based on how well you develop your point of view, organize and explain your ideas, use specific and relevant examples to support your thesis, and use clear and effective language. How well you write is much more important than how much you write, but to cover the topic adequately you should plan to write several paragraphs.

Your essay must be written only on the lines provided on your answer sheet. You will have enough space if you write on every line, avoid wide margins, and keep your handwriting to a reasonable size. Your essay will be read by people who are not familiar with your handwriting, so write legibly.

You may use this sheet for notes and outlining, but these will not be graded as part of your essay.

Consider carefully the issue discussed in the following passage, then write an essay that answers the question posed in the assignment.

> A person's greatness derives from the many small moral choices one makes moment by moment. To be born into great wealth, power, or ability is not to be great at all. Rather, greatness only comes from the continual choice to use that endowment wisely, to struggle with the needs of humanity as a member of its family.

Assignment: **Are human beings more the products of their endowments, or of their choices?** Write an essay in which you answer this question and discuss your point of view on this issue. Support your position logically with examples from literature, the arts, history, politics, science and technology, current events, or your experience or observation.

Write your essay on your answer sheet.

PRACTICE ESSAY 12

PRACTICE ESSAY 12

Practice Essay 13

Time—25 minutes

Directions for Writing the Essay

Plan and write an essay that answers the question below. Do NOT write on another topic. An essay on another topic will receive a score of 0.

Two readers will grade your essay based on how well you develop your point of view, organize and explain your ideas, use specific and relevant examples to support your thesis, and use clear and effective language. How well you write is much more important than how much you write, but to cover the topic adequately you should plan to write several paragraphs.

Your essay must be written only on the lines provided on your answer sheet. You will have enough space if you write on every line, avoid wide margins, and keep your handwriting to a reasonable size. Your essay will be read by people who are not familiar with your handwriting, so write legibly.

You may use this sheet for notes and outlining, but these will not be graded as part of your essay.

Consider carefully the issue discussed in the following passage, then write an essay that answers the question posed in the assignment.

> We tend to think that rewarding people for doing good things is always better than punishing them for doing bad things. We often fail, however, to realize that rewards can be oppressive, too. Giving someone a prize for doing something he or she would do anyway often makes that person feel manipulated. What's worse, competition for prizes, which invariably occurs when rewards are doled out systematically, often breeds resentment and division rather than cooperation.

Assignment: **Are reward systems, like grades, prizes and work bonuses, effective means of controlling human behavior?** Write an essay in which you answer this question and discuss your point of view on this issue. Support your position logically with examples from literature, the arts, history, politics, science and technology, current events, or your experience or observation.

Write your essay on your answer sheet.

PRACTICE ESSAY 13

PRACTICE ESSAY 13

Practice Essay 14

Time—25 minutes

Directions for Writing the Essay

Plan and write an essay that answers the question below. Do NOT write on another topic. An essay on another topic will receive a score of 0.

Two readers will grade your essay based on how well you develop your point of view, organize and explain your ideas, use specific and relevant examples to support your thesis, and use clear and effective language. How well you write is much more important than how much you write, but to cover the topic adequately you should plan to write several paragraphs.

Your essay must be written only on the lines provided on your answer sheet. You will have enough space if you write on every line, avoid wide margins, and keep your handwriting to a reasonable size. Your essay will be read by people who are not familiar with your handwriting, so write legibly.

You may use this sheet for notes and outlining, but these will not be graded as part of your essay.

Consider carefully the issue discussed in the following passage, then write an essay that answers the question posed in the assignment.

> History books record the deeds of the great inventors, warriors, explorers, and artists, but the real fabric of society is determined by consumers and ordinary workers—not those who make, but those who use; not those who find, but those who settle; not those who fight, but those who repair the damage.

Assignment: **Which is more important to a society: the demands of consumers or the dreams of artists, discoverers, and inventors?** Write an essay in which you answer this question and discuss your point of view on this issue. Support your position logically with examples from literature, the arts, history, politics, science and technology, current events, or your experience or observation.

Write your essay on your answer sheet.

PRACTICE ESSAY 14

PRACTICE ESSAY 14

Practice Essay 15

Time—25 minutes

Directions for Writing the Essay

Plan and write an essay that answers the question below. Do NOT write on another topic. An essay on another topic will receive a score of 0.

Two readers will grade your essay based on how well you develop your point of view, organize and explain your ideas, use specific and relevant examples to support your thesis, and use clear and effective language. How well you write is much more important than how much you write, but to cover the topic adequately you should plan to write several paragraphs.

Your essay must be written only on the lines provided on your answer sheet. You will have enough space if you write on every line, avoid wide margins, and keep your handwriting to a reasonable size. Your essay will be read by people who are not familiar with your handwriting, so write legibly.

You may use this sheet for notes and outlining, but these will not be graded as part of your essay.

Consider carefully the issue discussed in the following passage, then write an essay that answers the question posed in the assignment.

> Paradise is not to be found in a life of plenty and ease, free from all suffering. Without challenges to meet, pain to which we can compare delight, and barriers to surmount, paradise would be tedium. Give me the pain and inspiration of struggle over the perfection of your heaven.

Assignment: **Is it better to seek difficult challenges, or to seek relief from difficult challenges?** Write an essay in which you answer this question and discuss your point of view on this issue. Support your position logically with examples from literature, the arts, history, politics, science and technology, current events, or your experience or observation.

Write your essay on your answer sheet.

PRACTICE ESSAY 15

PRACTICE ESSAY 15

Practice Essay 16

Time—25 minutes

Directions for Writing the Essay

Plan and write an essay that answers the question below. Do NOT write on another topic. An essay on another topic will receive a score of 0.

Two readers will grade your essay based on how well you develop your point of view, organize and explain your ideas, use specific and relevant examples to support your thesis, and use clear and effective language. How well you write is much more important than how much you write, but to cover the topic adequately you should plan to write several paragraphs.

Your essay must be written only on the lines provided on your answer sheet. You will have enough space if you write on every line, avoid wide margins, and keep your handwriting to a reasonable size. Your essay will be read by people who are not familiar with your handwriting, so write legibly.

You may use this sheet for notes and outlining, but these will not be graded as part of your essay.

Consider carefully the issue discussed in the following passage, then write an essay that answers the question posed in the assignment.

> Oscar Wilde once said that the only thing worse than being talked about was *not* being talked about. Today it seems we have taken this witticism to its logical extreme. Some people make their lives as "personalities" whose only job is to get their names in the media. They lack any discernible talents except self-promotion.

Assignment: **Is fame a good thing or a bad thing?** Write an essay in which you answer this question and discuss your point of view on this issue. Support your position logically with examples from literature, the arts, history, politics, science and technology, current events, or your experience or observation.

Write your essay on your answer sheet.

PRACTICE ESSAY 16

PRACTICE ESSAY 16

Practice Essay 17

Time—25 minutes

Directions for Writing the Essay

Plan and write an essay that answers the question below. Do NOT write on another topic. An essay on another topic will receive a score of 0.

Two readers will grade your essay based on how well you develop your point of view, organize and explain your ideas, use specific and relevant examples to support your thesis, and use clear and effective language. How well you write is much more important than how much you write, but to cover the topic adequately you should plan to write several paragraphs.

Your essay must be written only on the lines provided on your answer sheet. You will have enough space if you write on every line, avoid wide margins, and keep your handwriting to a reasonable size. Your essay will be read by people who are not familiar with your handwriting, so write legibly.

You may use this sheet for notes and outlining, but these will not be graded as part of your essay.

Consider carefully the issue discussed in the following passage, then write an essay that answers the question posed in the assignment.

> History books are inclined to focus on power gained through military or political conquest, but power is maintained most efficiently by ideology—control over the symbols of a society and over the framework of debate. This way, popular opinion is controlled without raising popular anger or resentment.

Assignment: **How do people gain power over others?** Write an essay in which you answer this question and discuss your point of view on this issue. Support your position logically with examples from literature, the arts, history, politics, science and technology, current events, or your experience or observation.

Write your essay on your answer sheet.

PRACTICE ESSAY 17

PRACTICE ESSAY 17

Practice Essay 18

Time—25 minutes

Directions for Writing the Essay

Plan and write an essay that answers the question below. Do NOT write on another topic. An essay on another topic will receive a score of 0.

Two readers will grade your essay based on how well you develop your point of view, organize and explain your ideas, use specific and relevant examples to support your thesis, and use clear and effective language. How well you write is much more important than how much you write, but to cover the topic adequately you should plan to write several paragraphs.

Your essay must be written only on the lines provided on your answer sheet. You will have enough space if you write on every line, avoid wide margins, and keep your handwriting to a reasonable size. Your essay will be read by people who are not familiar with your handwriting, so write legibly.

You may use this sheet for notes and outlining, but these will not be graded as part of your essay.

Consider carefully the issue discussed in the following passage, then write an essay that answers the question posed in the assignment.

> We can hardly become complete human beings without identifying with at least one social group—family, social clique, political party, ethnic group, nation or religion. Yet, by distinguishing "us" from "them," these group identities are also the source of great injustices like prejudice and war.

Assignment: **Is group identity a good thing or a bad thing?** Write an essay in which you answer this question and discuss your point of view on this issue. Support your position logically with examples from literature, the arts, history, politics, science and technology, current events, or your experience or observation.

Write your essay on your answer sheet.

PRACTICE ESSAY 18

PRACTICE ESSAY 18

Practice Essay 19

Time—25 minutes

Directions for Writing the Essay

Plan and write an essay that answers the question below. Do NOT write on another topic. An essay on another topic will receive a score of 0.

Two readers will grade your essay based on how well you develop your point of view, organize and explain your ideas, use specific and relevant examples to support your thesis, and use clear and effective language. How well you write is much more important than how much you write, but to cover the topic adequately you should plan to write several paragraphs.

Your essay must be written only on the lines provided on your answer sheet. You will have enough space if you write on every line, avoid wide margins, and keep your handwriting to a reasonable size. Your essay will be read by people who are not familiar with your handwriting, so write legibly.

You may use this sheet for notes and outlining, but these will not be graded as part of your essay.

Consider carefully the issue discussed in the following passage, then write an essay that answers the question posed in the assignment.

> I have been gravely disappointed with the . . . moderate who is more devoted to "order" than to justice; who prefers a negative peace which is the absence of tension to a positive peace which is the presence of justice . . . Shallow understanding from people of good will is more frustrating than absolute misunderstanding from people of ill will. Lukewarm acceptance is much more bewildering than outright rejection.
>
> Excerpted from Martin Luther King, Jr., *Letter from a Birmingham Jail*

Assignment: **Are there certain kinds of peace that are unacceptable?** Write an essay in which you answer this question and discuss your point of view on this issue. Support your position logically with examples from literature, the arts, history, politics, science and technology, current events, or your experience or observation.

Write your essay on your answer sheet.

PRACTICE ESSAY 19

PRACTICE ESSAY 19

Practice Essay 20

Time—25 minutes

Directions for Writing the Essay

Plan and write an essay that answers the question below. Do NOT write on another topic. An essay on another topic will receive a score of 0.

Two readers will grade your essay based on how well you develop your point of view, organize and explain your ideas, use specific and relevant examples to support your thesis, and use clear and effective language. How well you write is much more important than how much you write, but to cover the topic adequately you should plan to write several paragraphs.

Your essay must be written only on the lines provided on your answer sheet. You will have enough space if you write on every line, avoid wide margins, and keep your handwriting to a reasonable size. Your essay will be read by people who are not familiar with your handwriting, so write legibly.

You may use this sheet for notes and outlining, but these will not be graded as part of your essay.

Consider carefully the issue discussed in the following passage, then write an essay that answers the question posed in the assignment.

> Human beings can attain a worthy and harmonious life if only they are able to rid themselves, within the limits of human nature, of the striving for the wish fulfillment of material kinds. The goal is to raise the spiritual values of society.
>
> Albert Einstein

Assignment: **Is the desire for "wish fulfillment of material kinds" a good or a bad thing?** Write an essay in which you answer this question and discuss your point of view on this issue. Support your position logically with examples from literature, the arts, history, politics, science and technology, current events, or your experience or observation.

Write your essay on your answer sheet.

PRACTICE ESSAY 20

PRACTICE ESSAY 20

Sample Essays: Practice Essay 1

Consider carefully the issue discussed in the following passage, then write an essay that answers the question posed in the assignment.

> Without a clear goal to focus our energy and drive us to grow, we cease to be truly alive. We are inert particles floating on the sea of life. This is true of not only ourselves, but our institutions—our families, our corporations, and our societies. The moment we cease to grow, we begin to die.

Assignment: **Is growth necessary to a happy and productive life?** Write an essay in which you answer this question and discuss your point of view on this issue. You may discuss personal or institutional growth. Support your position logically with examples from literature, the arts, history, politics, science and technology, current events, or your experience or observation.

Sample 1: 12 points out of 12

Ever since the Enlightenment, Western thought has been dominated by the idea that humans are endowed with "natural rights," which include not only the right to free speech and the pursuit of happiness, but the right to dominate the natural world and even other "less civilized" societies. The growth of an individual or a society, we believe, is limited only by one's imagination. But not only is eternal growth an illusion, to pursue it is a danger.

Today, our media trumpet the benefits of "growth." A company cannot be satisfied with providing a consistent product or service over time; it must keep growing and expanding, preferably swallowing up competitors to produce more and more value for investors. A school cannot be satisfied with consistently meeting the diverse needs of its students; it must graduate a higher and higher percentage of its students, who must get higher and higher test scores, and get into better and better colleges. But such "growth" only serves the psychological needs of deluded consumers; it provides no real value. CEOs feel compelled to "cook the books" and educators likewise feel compelled to "manipulate" test scores or cheat outright so that the illusion of "growth" can be maintained.

As a society, we must learn to see that the only worthwhile growth in society is that which enhances personal growth. Better profits mean nothing unless they are from a company that helps people to experience life more fully, and not merely give them tasty snack foods or mindless entertainment to consume. Higher test scores mean nothing unless they reflect students who are better problem solvers and more empathetic and happier human beings.

Growth is not a universal good. Just because a statistic is going up doesn't mean the world is getting better. Our statistics-obsessed society has to learn to appreciate the quality of life around us more than the quantities that summarize and, sometimes, eviscerate it.

Evaluation: *Insightful and informed response; expert use of vocabulary and sentence structure; good organization.*

Sample 2: 12 points out of 12

My keyboard felt like a world unto itself. The ghosts of Muddy Waters and Stevie Ray Vaughan and Dave Brubeck and Gustav Mahler and, I admit it, even Raffi, were an ether that engulfed the keyboard and infused my fingers, arms and body, so that I had no choice but to play, to give a sound dimension to this world. Sometimes the music that came out was just an etude that I had practiced for Mrs. Parker years before, but sometimes, magically, it was a completely new form that seemed conjured from that ether like a genie from a bottle.

Sometimes my buddy Paul would pick up on the vibe and we'd jam for hours. Our band, the Badunks, was my whole world. But two years later, that all changed. The spark wasn't there any more between Paul and me, and as soon as we stopped growing musically, Badunk began to die.

I think about those years a lot now, and I guess it was inevitable. Paul is a smart guy and, unlike me, he was inspired by history and physics and started to groove on DBQs and equations instead of NRBQ and The Persuasions. We both got girlfriends, and you know how love isn't nearly as inspirational when it's no longer just out of reach. We just weren't able to find the time to jam together, to write together, to just talk music together. Even though Paul and I are still best friends, I feel like I've lost my real best friend—music.

I guess music is a person. You have to nurture it if you want it to stick around. If you don't give it what it needs, which is your whole commitment, your whole soul, then it begins to wither into those dried-up jingles you hear on shampoo or dog food commercials.

Evaluation: *Personal and colloquial approach very consistent and effective; great use of imagery and metaphor.*

Sample Essays: Practice Essay 2

Consider carefully the issue discussed in the following passage, then write an essay that answers the question posed in the assignment.

> Our leaders love to tell us that only victory will do, as if they are imparting great wisdom. They seek only to defeat the enemy, to achieve the goal. Yet many times a loss, particularly one that is hard fought, is more valuable than victory. We cannot live a life full of only victories, nor should we. The quality of our lives depends as much on how we manage our losses as on how we achieve our victories.

Assignment: **Can a loss ever be more valuable than a victory?** Write an essay in which you answer this question and discuss your point of view on this issue. Support your position logically with examples from literature, the arts, history, politics, science and technology, current events, or your experience or observation.

Sample 1: 12 points out of 12

My father always says, "It's not whether you win or lose, it's how you play the game." I can understand his point; playing hard and fair is its own reward. We become stronger by learning how to lose gracefully. But sometimes it *is* whether you win or lose. Sometimes, nothing but victory will do.

There are hundreds, maybe thousands, of stories of people who tried to invent flying machines. Nearly all of them are relegated to oblivion or, at best, quaint mentions in arcane history books or old film clips accompanied by a silly trombone. But we all know the Wright Brothers. They're emblazoned on every license plate in North Carolina. We know them for one reason only: they succeeded. They got a big hunk of wood and metal to fly. If their struggles led only to another hapless nose-dive off a cliff, their workshop would long ago have been forgotten and replaced by a Piggly Wiggly.

Without question, World War II was hard fought by America, as much as we tried to avoid getting involved. In the end, we lost well over a quarter of a million American lives to the struggle. Would it have been worth it had we not defeated Hitler, Mussolini and Hirohito? We could hardly claim any benefit if we had lost, and allowed hundreds of thousands of more "undesirables" to be incinerated by Hitler and his henchmen.

Sometimes, a loss, hard fought, is more valuable than an easy victory. But whether this is true depends on the worthiness of the goal. If we are true explorers, true noble warriors, true visionaries, then it is our responsibility to envision goals that are worth every sacrifice to achieve.

Evaluation: *Clearly articulated and insightful thesis; solid examples; effective use of language; great organization.*

Sample 2: 12 points out of 12

I studied my hindquarters off for that test. I had two Starbucks mocha javas (don't tell my mom) to help me stay up until 2:00 am studying for the darn physics test (circular motion and gravitation—yuk) and I still got a C–! For months afterward, I swore that physics was the most ridiculous subject ever. But something about that C– really got to me. I started to wonder why some people would spend their lives studying this subject that seemed so difficult to understand.

I took it as a personal challenge. I guess I felt a lot like an athlete feels when he loses a playoff game, but knows that, if he had just worked harder, he could have won the whole championship. So I started to look into physics. I picked up a book called "Surely You're Joking, Mr. Feynman" about a Noble Prize–winning physicist and how he saw the world. I was hooked. Richard Feynman convinced me that trying to solve the great riddles of physics could be profoundly rewarding, and even fun.

It helped a great deal, too, I think, that I was now confronting physics on my own terms. I wasn't reading this book because it was assigned, but because I wanted to read it (and because my dad said it was hilarious).

And I wasn't thinking about physics because I had a test to study for, but because the problems were interesting to think about.

If I had gotten an A on that physics test, instead of a C–, I probably would not have gotten mad enough to venture into the world of physics on my own. I would not have immersed myself in the relativistic twin paradox, or the question of how black holes are formed. I could have done the opposite, as my friends have done, and just shunned science for the rest of my life. I'm glad I didn't. Sometimes a loss, hard fought, is more valuable than an easy victory.

Evaluation: *Although very colloquial, the style is used to good effect; well organized; solid support and details.*

Sample Essays: Practice Essay 3

Consider carefully the issue discussed in the following passage, then write an essay that answers the question posed in the assignment.

> Adventure seekers who merely crave the mitigating rush of adrenaline that accompanies risky feats do not demonstrate true courage. Courage is not fearlessness but the willingness to face our unmitigated fears and vulnerabilities, particularly those fears that make us think less of ourselves.

Assignment: **What is one example of true courage?** Write an essay in which you answer this question and explain the reasons for your choice. You may choose an example from literature, the arts, history, politics, science and technology, current events, or your experience or observation.

Sample: 12 points out of 12

Courage is not fearlessness but the willingness to face fear. One example of true courage is Pip, the hero of *Great Expectations*. In the early chapters, in which he meets the escaped criminal from the prison ship on the moors and later at Mrs. Haversham's where he meets the lovely girl who tempts him and treats him with adolescent cruelty, he shows great courage.

Why Pip? Let us examine true "courage." If fear is an element, historical examples are hard to assess, for we must see inside the historical figure, read his emotions. This is hard to do. The soldier in battle. The leader of the soldier in battle. He may be brave or craven, foolish or calculating. He may declare himself without fear and be sick with it, or being modest and self-deprecating, declare himself in fear of his life, when in fact, in his heart, he is without fear.

You look inside yourself. You look back at the moments when true courage was needed. Was it there? You confronted the class bully, knowing you would be beaten up. You were scared. You know you were, because you wet your pants. You faced him. You know because you got beat up. Was this true courage? There were so many other emotions, so many other feelings, so many motives.

There was a certain girl who would soothe your wounds, comfort you. There was anger. There was foolishness. You were on the playground with a crowd around and you were playing to the crowd. Maybe he wasn't such a bad kid after all.

So we turn to Dickens. Pip's fear is palpable. We are inside his head and we know the fear is there. We watch as he summons his courage to face it. We feel ourselves in the same situation, so carefully contrived to test the mettle of an adolescent, and we know that he was braver than we would have been.

So, that is why Pip emerges as one of the great characters of literature, and one the courageous heroes. An ordinary human, in a situation that might happen to any reader, or at least one the reader can imagine happening to him.

Evaluation: *Although it would be great if the author had remembered some of the characters' names, the analysis is deep yet engaging. The examination of courage is insightful and clear. The use of informal language and the second person (you) and first person plural (we) are very effective and draw the reader into the reasoning.*

Notice the author's effective use of informal language and the second person. Sometimes, teachers forbid such language in essays because "that's not the way a good essay is supposed to be written." This is simply untrue. Great writers use these devices often. The important thing is to do them well, in the service of solid and persuasive reasoning.

Sample Essays: Practice Essay 4

Consider carefully the issue discussed in the following passage, then write an essay that answers the question posed in the assignment.

> Communicating technology was supposed to turn the world into a "global village," enhancing our relationships with others and our understanding of other cultures. Yet I fear it has rendered us more polarized and less articulate. Instant communication allows us to proclaim what is on our minds before we've analyzed it, substantiated it, or rendered it coherent, let alone eloquent.

Assignment: **Do modern means of communication make our society better or worse?** Write an essay in which you answer this question and explain your point of view on this issue. Support your position logically with examples from your reading, current events, or your experience or observation.

Sample: 12 points out of 12

Communication technology has made the world a "global village," enhancing our understanding of other cultures as never before. Technology has made this possible by granting instant access to a variety of international popular cultures. The internet has allowed people worldwide to sample music, read literature and peruse news items from other cultures, exposing them to artistic ideas and perspectives previously too obscure to find by chance. Before such advances in technology, cross-cultural understanding was more difficult to achieve.

As recently as the early 1990s, a college student might need to spend days in the library, or take an expensive trip, to begin to understand another culture. Not everyone had access to these resources and, as such, the gap was often too vast to bridge. Although technology has not made multi-national enlightenment universal, it has allowed millions to take a more active role in the world around them. MP3s have played a pivotal part in this transition from ignorance to semi-enlightenment. By exposing listeners to artists such as Ireland's Damien Rice, the Internet took control out of the hands of record companies, allowing consumers to decide what should be in demand. People were given insight into a world beyond their own.

We are a global village in more than just music and pop culture. The internet has greatly enhanced our understanding of people in foreign lands—their concerns, their religious views, their political status—and we have become more aware of how similar we are even though we may be thousands of miles apart. Without communication technology, many people have no access to the world outside of their own towns and, as such, have no opportunity to explore other cultures by themselves.

Because of communication technology, the world is now, literally, at our fingertips. With the proper amount of initiative and curiosity, anyone can now delve into the volumes of information available on topics previously locked away in library towers and distant cities. While the internet does not offer the personal feel of a firsthand encounter, it still manages to bring the world together and provide limitless amounts of information. Communication technology has enhanced the average understanding of the world as a whole, creating a less ignorant and provincial lifestyle for millions of people worldwide.

Evaluation: *Clearly organized, with relevant, specific examples.*

Sample Essays: Practice Essay 5

Consider carefully the issue discussed in the following passage, then write an essay that answers the question posed in the assignment.

> Being truly human as a member of a society means seeing injustice and working to fix it. The human mind is endowed with not only the ability to perceive the world and act instinctively, but to visualize a better future and endeavor to realize it.

Assignment: **What is one great injustice in the world, and how should it be addressed?** Write an essay in which you answer this question and explain the reasons for your choice. You may draw inspiration and support from literature, the arts, history, politics, science and technology, current events, or your experience or observation.

Sample: 12 points out of 12

One great injustice that has not been adequately addressed is the perception that depression is a sign of weakness. The human mind is a complex puzzle. Psychological theories, diagnoses and treatments are constantly changing and may never be fully understood. Unfortunately, people tend to dismiss theories that don't provide simple answers.

At best, psychologists can create a rough map of tendencies and patterns, connecting them as often as possible to findings in neurology and thus lending them a sense of scientific validity. Diagnosing a complex disease like depression involves examining a wide constellation of symptoms over a long period of time. This doesn't satisfy skeptics. Someone with the flu will show clear symptoms like fever, nausea, and congestion. A depressed person will have less measurable symptoms like lethargy, emotional polarity or apathy. Skeptics tend to view these as simply a lack of will. They do not understand that depression is an illness just like influenza or cancer. Someone with a tumor can't just think happy thoughts and pretend it is not there. The same can be said about clinical depression.

People suffering from depression are unfairly stigmatized. They resist seeking help and so lead lives filled with unnecessary pain. Those lucky enough to find help are often ashamed to tell their peers. Friends often misconstrue symptoms of depression as personal slights: Why didn't she call me? Why is he not fun anymore? Bonds are thus broken due to miscommunication.

Depression alters one's life at least as dramatically as more "accepted" illnesses do. People suffering from depression need others to understand the limitations depression imposes. They need to be allowed to heal. Advances in anti-depressants and mood stabilizers can help ease these adjustments, but social pressure makes it nearly impossible for the victims of depression to live in a suitable environment.

Emotional disorders are a remarkably sad facet of life. To lose control over one's emotions is to lose track of hope. A world that denies one's suffering makes this situation even worse. The key to resolving this problem is education. People of all ages need to understand how prevalent depression is and that it is not a cause for embarrassment. Hopefully, we will one day live in a world where emotional disorders will be treated with the same tolerance and compassion as "traditional" illnesses.

Evaluation: *Very thoughtful thesis, well reasoned and articulated.*

Sample Essays: Practice Essay 6

Consider carefully the issue discussed in the following passage, then write an essay that answers the question posed in the assignment.

> Acquiring knowledge is like scaling a mountain. The proper attitude in reaching a summit, however, is to marvel not so much at one's achievement as at the glorious view of the unknown beyond. A well-educated person is known not so much for the questions he or she can answer as for the questions he or she can ask.

Assignment: **What is one great question that every educated person should ask?** Write an essay in which you indicate what this question should be and explain the reasons for your choice. You may draw inspiration and support from literature, the arts, history, politics, science and technology, current events, or your experience or observation.

Sample: 12 points out of 12

A well-educated person is known more for the questions he or she asks than for the questions he or she can answer. One great question that I think every educated person should ask is whether the news they read and hear is based on objective facts or subjective views. Within moments, any important news story will be studied, filmed, and disseminated for an entire world to see. Televisions broadcast this information for global audiences and, instantaneously, a world opinion is formed. But does this presentation resemble more closely an objective analysis or a "spun" interpretation of an image-conscious presenter?

Most people think of "news" as the factual story of what is going on in the world. Few would say that the news is a script produced by businessmen seeking ratings and profits, although this is an uncontroversial fact that's hard to deny. Most people either accept what they see in the media as facts or cynically dismiss everything they hear as propaganda. Hiding somewhere in between these two extremes is perspective, the ability to independently judge what is factual and, from that, to create a unique and personal view.

We are continually bombarded with flashy images, scandalous revelations, and sound bites devoid of context. Journalists interpret and explain the news for us, encouraging us to sit quietly rather than think. An educated person must view this programming with a skeptical eye. Every story is tainted by subjectivity, no matter how distant the producer. The educated viewer, however, must be disciplined enough to recognize how the corporate media "spins" the news. By analyzing the differences among storytellers, the viewer can better understand what is real and what is merely opinion.

Information can be potent. Truthful information, in particular, has the power to unite or fracture, to enlighten or confirm previously held beliefs. Unfortunately, truth is slippery, easily lost in the swirling winds of global communication. Educated people must pursue the truth by asking questions and resisting the urge to accept every image flashed before them. Education teaches us to analyze situations from multiple angles whenever possible. Those who have embraced the moral value of critical thinking will apply that ideal to the world around them, treating every bit of news only as a piece of information open to debate and intense analysis.

Evaluation: *Very fluent use of language. Well-organized and well analyzed.*

Sample Essays: Practice Essay 7

Consider carefully the issue discussed in the following passage, then write an essay that answers the question posed in the assignment.

> Some people spend their lives waiting for the one great challenge that will define them. Every society needs such people, who forge into the unknown and lay new foundations. But society also depends very much on those who meet the small challenges, like feeding mouths and minds and hearts.

Assignment: **Are we defined more by great challenges in our lives or small, everyday challenges?** Write an essay in which you answer this question and discuss your point of view on this issue. Support your position logically with examples from literature, the arts, history, politics, science and technology, current events, or your experience or observation.

Sample: 12 points out of 12

My geometry teacher was Mrs. Leuty. Everyone hated her. But she showed me the meaning of little things.

Outside of the classroom she was never referred to as Mrs. Leuty, but as "Leuty," or "old Lady Leuty," and she wasn't even old. She dressed plainly, with minimal makeup, like a teacher. She had short-heeled black leather shoes that tied. Usually she wore a cardigan. She never smiled or joked.

Geometry was a regents exam, one exam prepared and supervised by the state regents. Every geometry student in the State of New York took the same exam on the same day in June. Mrs. Leuty focused our entire class on that one day. That one test. It was to be our entire mark. The first half of the year she taught geometry. The second half she taught taking the test.

One day she gave a sample test. I finished early and was looking around the room when she came down the aisle, ripped the test from my desk and tore it into pieces in front of the class. When I protested she said that the appearance of cheating was just as bad as cheating. The penalty was the same.

As June approached and spring began to turn to summer, she made us stay in every lunch period for an extra half hour, and work on axioms and corollaries.

The worst student in the class was Doug Lane. He was a lazy red-haired kid. He loved lunch hour on the school playground. He had a dog named Bo, who would sit outside the school waiting for him. Sometimes we could hear Bo whining. Doug would look vacantly out the window as we struggled.

Doug was the only one of us that Leuty was nice to. She let him bring Bo into the lunch sessions, and the dog sat by Doug's feet as he studied. One day she said, "People (she called us "people"), we should all hope that someday someone loves us the way that dog loves Douglas."

She was the only teacher I ever hated and the best teacher I ever had.

Evaluation: *The passage makes its point strongly without ever being didactic. The narrative is clear and effective precisely because the author does not overexplain anything. Very approachable style.*

Sample Essays: Practice Essay 8

Consider carefully the issue discussed in the following passage, then write an essay that answers the question posed in the assignment.

> Freedom requires the eradication of repression from tyrants and from want, but eliminating these is not enough. We must also eliminate the means by which we oppress ourselves, through our peeves, our addictions, and in our insecurities. This may involve strengthening the restraints within ourselves.

Assignment: **Does freedom require eliminating all restraints, or does it require creating or strengthening certain restraints?** Write an essay in which you answer this question and discuss your point of view on this issue. Support your position logically with examples from literature, the arts, history, politics, science and technology, current events, or your experience or observation.

Sample: 12 points out of 12

In "Bread and Wine," Ignazio Silone states that freedom is not something you get as a present. You must fight for it. George Orwell said, "Never trade freedom for security. It is always a bad bargain." Silone tells us to fight the external bonds, Orwell speaks of an internal bond. The idea of liberty is a strong one, both an external and an internal one. As Silone points out, it is not a gift. It must be seized and defended.

By American standards, much of the world is not free, and even in America today, people are trading freedom for security. There are many tests which weaken the internal bonds. One is hunger. How hungry must you be before you will trade your freedom for a loaf of bread? In parts of the world where starvation is a way of life, the quest for freedom must wait.

This leads to one of the arguments for the cause of the success of terrorism and religious extremism. A recent economic study highlighted in THE ECONOMIST points to the success of the Taliban extremists in Afghanistan. The Taliban were tolerated because they provided bread and a kind of security. The lesson perhaps is that the internal bonds demanding liberty cannot form until the stomach is satisfied.

In a recent article on the India/Pakistan eternal war in the mountains of Kashmir, by journalist Kevin Fedarko, Fedarko describes a visit to a ski resort operating in the war zone. The young man who owns and operates the resort had an interesting view on terrorism. He said that he had for some time a fear of terror and a desire to sacrifice his freedom to travel the world to be safe, but then he convinced himself that there was nowhere to hide. Terrorism was everywhere and would always exist. So, he says, when I realized I could be killed anywhere, I became free again. I travel wherever I want and do what I want to do.

Evaluation: *Well analyzed and argued. Somewhat exploratory rather than focused, but effective nonetheless.*

Sample Essays: Practice Essay 9

Consider carefully the issue discussed in the following passage, then write an essay that answers the question posed in the assignment.

> We employ many devices to maintain or create peace among countries—trade agreements, cultural exchanges, treaties. But nothing unites humanity as well as a common foe. Mutual fear of nature or of foreign ideologies is perhaps the greatest diplomacy we know.

Assignment: **What is the most significant means of bringing people together in peace?** Write an essay in which you answer this question and discuss your point of view on this issue. Support your position logically with examples from literature, the arts, history, politics, science and technology, current events, or your experience or observation.

Sample: 12 points out of 12

Nothing unifies humanity as well as a common foe. This thought can be said to explain the triumph of the Allied forces in WW II, the French and American Revolution, and other great triumphs in western history. However, this uplifting thought has a dark corollary, because the common foe is usually another segment of humanity.

The great modern historian, T. Ruiz, at UCLA writes and lectures extensively on the middle ages. He explains western history not as a progression from barbarism to high civilization, but as a continuing series of clashes of man against man, advancing only in the increasing number of victims resulting from more powerful weaponry. In all these clashes the victors (who after all write the history of the event) see and explain their success as due to unified humanity against the common foe.

To take a sweeping view of western history after the fall of the Roman Empire, we see a European Society for hundreds of years without borders, without governments, without kings, without commerce, without land ownership, somewhat of an empty slate by modern political and economic terms. As the world changed from a medieval world to a modern world, we can observe some changes which came about by the unification against a common foe. The rise of the nation state was made possible by the emergence of the "king" who united his subjects by invention of a common foe (e.g. "France"). Witchcraft, antisemitism and other concepts of "otherness," can be argued to be offshoots of the movement toward nation states. And these evils are caused by the invention of a common foe.

The nation state, antisemitism, witchcraft all came about as inventions of the modern era. The Crusades, to expel the Arabs from Europe, the fallout from which we are still experiencing, is perhaps nothing but a political example of the successful search for a common enemy. Political, of course, because they occurred in the era when the king realized that religion was too important to be left to the Pope.

As history marches on, we have the modern success of genocide as the ultimate success possible from the unification against the common enemy. The lesson perhaps is that when humanity unifies against a common enemy, make sure you're not the enemy.

Evaluation: *Excellent specific examples. Well analyzed and organized.*

Sample Essays: Practice Essay 19

Consider carefully the issue discussed in the following passage, then write an essay that answers the question posed in the assignment.

> We love best not what gives the greatest pleasure, but what comes through the greatest effort, because this effort provides meaning. A plastic medallion received after completing a marathon is not just a $2.00 trinket, but the representation of months of effort and sacrifice. The best things in life are not free, but come at the expense of hard work.

Assignment: **Do we love things most that come at a great cost, or are the best things in life truly free?** Write an essay in which you answer this question and discuss your point of view on this issue. Support your position logically with examples from literature, the arts, history, politics, science and technology, current events, or your experience or observation.

Sample: 12 points out of 12

We love best not that which gives great pleasure, but what comes through great effort. What do we mean by "love"? For one may love one's mother, chocolate and fine art, all in different ways and all of which usually come with little effort. But perhaps love means "value," as in one loves freedom and one loves life. It is often observed that those who have had to fight for freedom love it more, and those who have recovered from near death accidents or disease have a greater love of freedom and life.

It is an American phenomenon that freedoms are valued so highly because so many Americans have suffered religious or political persecution and suffered great hardship to escape to this country. However, there are many things one loves which are not achieved through great effort, and there are many things achieved through great effort that one comes to hate. The Rubaiyat of Omar Khayyam expresses a way to achieve love, contentment and happiness without effort. It suggests the less effort the better. John Ruskin said, "Life without work is guilt, life without art is brutality," suggesting that effort and love are two separate things.

The Calvinists, and the Protestant ethic, suggest that the only thing worth achieving is achieved through hard work. Or perhaps, they suggest that hard work in itself gives satisfaction. Although something achieved through effort is valued (loved) more highly than the same thing received as a gift, many things are loved intensely without regard to the effort expended.

Although some have discarded the Cartesian duality of mind and body, perhaps it is a real separation. Great effort satisfies the body primarily. The body loves to work. Love, on the other hand, satisfies the mind or the soul.

As Ruskin suggests, if I work hard to achieve a pot of gold, I may find love of riches does not satisfy, but if I work hard to create a work of art, and craft a beautiful shaped and molded chair, I may find that I love this chair more than any other in the world.

Evaluation: *Although the thesis is somewhat diffuse, it is very insightful and well analyzed. The essay makes good use of specific and relevant examples.*

CHAPTER 17

ATTACKING THE GRAMMAR QUESTIONS

Lesson 1: Don't Sweat the Small Stuff

Know what "mistakes" don't matter

Many English teachers have their own grammatical "pet peeves." They may take points off your essays because you split an infinitive or started a sentence with a conjunction. Some of these "rules" are based on sound rules of good writing, but many are debatable quibbles that aren't tested on the SAT I. **To do well on the Writing portion of the SAT I, you should know what grammatical issues to ignore as well as what to focus on.**

❑ **The SAT I will expect you to notice and fix only "uncontroversial" grammatical errors,** that is, those errors that every good writing teacher would agree are violations of sound rules of good writing. The following are some of the grammatical "problems" that your teacher may not like, but which the SAT I will probably avoid entirely.

Don't worry about *who* vs. *whom*

The Bad Advice: Never use *who* as the object of a verb or preposition; use *whom* for that purpose. For instance, never say: *Who are you voting for?* but rather *For whom are you voting?*

The Textbook Approach: All textbooks agree that *who* is preferred as the **subject of a verb** or as a **predicate nominative.** (If these terms sound a bit unfamiliar, see Chapter 18 Lesson 6.) They also generally agree that *whom* is usually preferred as the **object of a verb or preposition.** For instance, *The stage was crowded by dozens of fans, all of whom wanted Sting's autograph* sounds much better than *The stage was crowded by dozens of fans, all of who wanted Sting's autograph.*

However, there are many situations in which using *whom* is technically correct, but makes a sentence sound too formal. For instance, *For whom are you voting?* is excessively formal, even for most published prose. So it is often acceptable to write *Who are you voting for?* Linguists know that pronouns in English have been evolving away from "case markers" for many centuries. For instance, where English used to have the subjective *thou* and the objective

thee, it now has just one word: *you.* Quite likely, English is evolving away from *whom* in the same way.

❑ **How the SAT I Views It:** Because the use of *whom* is not cut and dried, you probably won't see any *who/whom* questions on the SAT I. If, however, one does show up, just remember that using *who* vs. *whom* is just like using *he* vs. *him.* For instance, just as we'd say *We gave the book to him,* we should likewise say *We gave the book to whom?*

Don't worry about splitting infinitives

The Bad Advice: Never split an infinitive. For instance, don't say **to boldly go** *where no man has gone before* . . . but rather **to go boldly** *where no man has gone before.* . . .

The Textbook Approach: An **infinitive** is a *to* phrase, like *to drop,* that represents the basic form of a verb. (See Chapter 18, Lesson 3.) We say that the infinitive is "split" when we stick an adverb between the 2 words; as in *The news caused the stock price* **to suddenly drop.** In this case, it would sound better just to keep the infinitive together: *The news caused the stock price* **to drop suddenly.**

However, some ideas can't be expressed clearly and concisely without splitting infinitives. For instance:

The company plans **to more than double** *its revenue next year.*

The new policy is expected **to thoroughly discourage** *unfair discrimination in those departments where it remains.*

"Unsplitting" the infinitives in either of these sentences will either make the sentence awkward or change the meaning of the sentence. Try it and see!

❑ **How the SAT I Views It:** Split infinitives **won't show up on the SAT I grammar section. In your essay, though, avoid splitting infinitives if you can. (In most situations, you can do it without a problem.)**

Don't worry about ending a sentence with a preposition

The Bad Advice: Never end a sentence with a preposition. For instance, don't say *What are you looking for?* but rather ***For** what are you looking?*

The Textbook Approach: Winston Churchill once said, after someone had chastised him about this rule, *"That is the type of arrant pedantry up with which I will not put!"* That beautifully awkward statement shows very nicely that some sentences sound much better with a preposition at the end! Most textbooks agree.

Certainly, many sentences that end in a preposition sound awkward or weak and should be reworded. For instance:

> *One remarkable aspect of Rivera's delivery is the seeming effortlessness he releases his fastball with.*

This sentence is much more effective when rephrased without the preposition at the end:

> *One remarkable aspect of Rivera's delivery is the seeming effortlessness with which he releases his fastball.*

❑ **How the SAT I Views It:** Don't worry too much about ending sentences with prepositions. The grammar questions won't ask you to correct such errors. In your essay, however, try to avoid ending a sentence in a preposition unless the alternative is too awkward or formal. For instance, for most purposes, saying *What are you looking for?* is better than saying *For what are you looking?*

Don't worry about starting a sentence with *And, But,* or *Because*

The Bad Advice: Never start a sentence with ***And, But,*** or ***Because.***

The Textbook Approach: This seems to be more of a problem to some teachers than to textbooks.

> *Next to the groundless notion that it is incorrect to end an English sentence with a preposition, perhaps the most widespread of many false beliefs about the use of our language is the equally groundless notion that it is incorrect to begin one with "but" or "and." As in the case of the super-*stition about the prepositional ending, no textbook supports it, but apparently about half of our teachers of English go out of their way to handicap their pupils by inculcating it. One cannot help wondering whether those who teach such monstrous doctrine ever read any English themselves.*

> —Charles Allen Lloyd,
> *We Who Speak English, and*
> *Our Ignorance of Our Mother Tongue* (1938)

This rule most likely evolved as a rule against sentence fragments, as in *He ate the cookies. Because he was hungry.* This clearly should be rephrased to remove the fragment: *He ate the cookies because he was hungry.*

But we can find myriad examples of perfectly good sentences (by perfectly good writers) starting with *And, But,* or *Because,* but notice that in each case the sentence conveys a **complete thought:**

> *Because of the war the situation in hospitals is, of course, serious.*

> —E. B. White, "A Weekend with the Angels,"
> in *The Second Tree from the Corner* (1954)

> *If we view the paragraph as a discursive development of a proposition, we can predict that the topic sentence of the paragraph in question will generate a development based on objectives. And this is exactly what we do find.*

> —W. Ross Winterowd,
> *Rhetoric: A Synthesis* (1968)

> *But it must not be assumed that intelligent thinking can play no part in the formation of the goal and of ethical judgments.*

> —Albert Einstein, "Science and Religion,"
> (1939) in *Ideas and Opinions* (1954)

❑ **How the SAT I Views It:** Avoid starting a sentence with *And, But,* or *Because* only if it produces a sentence fragment or makes an illogical transition. Otherwise, if it's done properly, starting a sentence with *And, But,* or *Because* can make a sentence stronger. **Never, however, follow a semicolon (;) or colon (:) with *and* or *but*, because what follows a semicolon or colon must always be an *independent clause*.** (See Chapter 18, Lesson 15.)

Don't worry about starting sentences with words like *Hopefully* or *Clearly*

The Bad Advice: Never start a sentence with an adverb like *Hopefully, Clearly,* or *Fortunately,* **because such words do not properly modify the verb of the sentence.** For instance, those who abide by this rule regard a sentence like *Clearly, the fog obscured her vision dramatically* to be utterly illogical because the verb, *obscured,* cannot logically be modified by the adverb *clearly.* If something is *obscured,* it must by definition be *unclear!*

The Textbook Approach: All good textbooks agree that this is a nonsensical rule. The word *Clearly* in the sentence above does not modify the verb at all, and almost every listener knows that. The word *Clearly* is called a **sentence modifier: it conveys the speaker's attitude toward the *statement* the sentence makes as a whole.** In effect, the word *Clearly* in the sentence above means *I consider the following fact to be obvious:* but in a much more elegant way.

Here is a partial list of some common sentence modifiers:

accordingly	admittedly	arguably	hopefully
clearly	curiously	fortunately	sadly
ironically	paradoxically	regrettably	
strangely	theoretically	consequently	

❑ **How the SAT I Views It:** Don't even think about this as a problem. **Some adverbs can describe the speaker's attitude toward a statement rather than modify a verb.** It's ok to say things like *Sadly, the party was cancelled.*

Don't worry about possessive antecedents

The Bad Advice: Never use a pronoun that refers to a possessive noun. For instance, don't say ***Nathanael West's** novel portrays the nihilistic culture that he encountered in early 20th-century Hollywood,* because the pronoun *he* must refer to a noun, but *Nathanael West's* is a possessive **adjective.**

The Textbook Approach: Very few good grammar textbooks consider this a problem. In reading the sentence above, for instance, no one would be confused about who *he* refers to; no harm, no foul. Interestingly, though, the 2002 PSAT writing section contained the following sentence:

Toni Morrison's genius enables <u>her to create</u>
                                      A

novels <u>that arise from</u> <u>and express</u> the injustice
        B   C

African Americans <u>have endured.</u>   <u>No error</u>
               D   E

The ETS's original answer was E. But some teachers complained, because *her* refers to a possessive: *Toni Morrison's.* They argued that A could be considered the proper response. As a result, the ETS threw out the question.

❑ **How the SAT I Views It:** You can be sure that the test writers at ETS are going to be extra careful about writing sentences like that one again! So don't worry about possessive antecedents. All you need to know about using definite pronouns is given in Chapter 18 Lesson 5. **In short, simply make sure that every definite pronoun has a clear antecedent.**

Don't worry about *that* vs. *which*

The Bad Advice: Be very careful about using *that* and *which.*

The Textbook Approach: Good grammar textbooks suggest that *which* is best used in "nonrestrictive" clauses and *that* is best used in "restrictive" clauses. What the heck does that mean? A restrictive clause is one that gives **essential** information about the noun that precedes it, as in *All of the books **that are on that table** are for sale.* A nonrestrictive clause, as you have probably guessed, is one that gives **incidental, or nonessential,** information about the noun that precedes it, as in *All of the books, which amount to only about ten, are nonfiction.* Still too complicated?

Here's a simple rule: ***which* almost always follows a comma; if there's no comma, *that* will probably work better.**

Second simple rule: ***what* usually works better than *that which.***

Not good: *Second Federal was the only bank in town **which** did not practice redlining.*

Better: *Second Federal was the only bank in town **that** did not practice redlining.*

Not good: *The corporation approved spending $12 million on the commercial **which** lasted all of 20 seconds.*

Better: *The corporation approved spending $12 million on the commercial, **which** lasted all of 20 seconds.*

Not good: *We pursue most fervently **that which** we cannot have.*

Better: *We pursue most fervently **what** we cannot have.*

❑ **How the SAT I Views It:** Don't worry about *that* vs. *which* on the multiple-choice grammar section. On your essay, though, use the simple rules above to decide about using *that* and *which*, but don't make a big deal of it.

Don't worry too much about *bad/badly* and *good/well*

The Bad Advice: Don't say *I feel good*, say *I feel well* instead. Likewise, don't say *I feel bad* or *This tastes bad*, but rather *I feel badly* or *This tastes badly* because *badly* is an adverb modifying the verb *feel* or *taste*.

The Textbook Approach: Both *I feel good* and *I feel well* are okay. In both cases, *feel* is a **linking verb** that joins *I* to an adjective. Although some people will say that *well* is an adverb meaning *in a competent manner*, in this sentence it is instead an adjective meaning *healthy*, as in *The gerbils were sick, but now they are well*. The *bad/badly* rule, however, is just plain wrong. *I feel badly* and *This tastes badly* are illogical, because in both cases the verb is a **linking verb, and should be followed by an adjective, not an adverb.** The correct wording is *I feel bad* or *This tastes bad*.

❑ **How the SAT I Views It:** The sentences *I feel good*, *I feel well*, and *I feel bad* are all okay. The sentence *I feel badly*, however, is a "hypercorrection" suggested by those who think they know better, but are mistaken.

Don't worry about disappearing *that*s

The Bad Advice: Never say *I like the sweater you gave me*, say *I like the sweater **that** you gave me* instead.

The Textbook Approach: Either sentence is fine. The sentence *I like the sweater you gave me* uses what textbooks call **acceptable ellipsis. Ellipsis** is leaving out one or more words from a sentence because they are unnecessary to the meaning of the sentence. Since no one would ever be confused about what *I like the sweater you gave me* means, there's no need for the *that*.

❑ **How the SAT I Views It:** Don't worry about disappearing *that*s.

Concept Review 1: Don't Sweat the Small Stuff

Read the "corrections" to the following sentences. If it is a "good" correction, that is, a correction of a widely accepted rule of grammar, write "valid" in the space next to the sentence. If it is instead an arbitrary "hyper-correction," write "don't worry."

1. *The lunch box I had when I was a kid had a picture of the Backstreet Boys on it.*

   Correction: *The lunch box **that** I had when I was a kid. . . .*   _____

2. *Neither of us are going on the field trip.*

   Correction: *Neither of us **is** going on the field trip.*   _____

3. *Because the first flight was delayed so long, we missed the connection in Denver.*

   Correction: ***We missed the connection in Denver because** the first flight. . . .*   _____

4. *Hopefully the rain will let up soon.*

   Correction: ***I hope that** the rain will let up soon.*   _____

5. *We were concerned about the affect the storm would have on the beachside community.*

   Correction: *We were concerned about the **effect** the storm would have. . . .*   _____

6. *But we all knew that his claim was untrue.*

   Correction: ***Nevertheless,** we all knew that his claim was untrue.*   _____

7. *I wish she was more optimistic about the trip.*

   Correction: *I wish she **were** more optimistic about the trip.*   _____

8. *Helen was always arguing against her friends.*

   Correction: *Helen was always arguing **with** her friends.*   _____

9. *David was always the son she was proudest of.*

   Correction: *David was always the son **of whom** she was proudest.*   _____

10. *We discovered that someone had stole the entire tea set from the closet.*

    Correction: *We discovered that someone **had stolen** the entire tea set from the closet.*   _____

Answer Key 1: Don't Sweat the Small Stuff

1. Don't worry.

   It's fine to leave out the word *that* in a sentence like *The lunch box that I had when I was a kid had a picture of the Backstreet Boys on it,* because the sentence is clear either way.

2. Valid.

   Because *neither* is a singular pronoun, it must take a singular verb (see Chapter 18 Lesson 1).

3. Don't worry.

   It's okay to start a sentence with *Because.*

4. Don't worry.

   It's okay to start a sentence with a sentence modifier like *Hopefully.*

5. Valid.

   This is a **diction error** (see Chapter 18 Lesson 11). *Affect* is a verb meaning *to influence,* but *effect* is a noun meaning *result.*

6. Don't worry *too* much, but be careful.

   It can be okay to start a sentence with a conjunction like *But,* particularly when the sentence addresses a previous remark by another speaker, but make sure that such a sentence isn't better just incorporated into the previous one.

7. Valid.

   The phrase *I wish* indicates that the verb to follow is in the **subjunctive mood** (see Chapter 18 Lesson 14). The subjunctive form is *were,* not *was.*

8. Valid.

   This is an **idiom error** (see Chapter 18 Lesson 10). Pay attention to prepositions, and make sure they conform to standard English idiom.

9. Don't worry *too* much, but be careful.

   Ending a sentence with a preposition isn't necessarily "wrong." What matters more is the precision, flow, and tone of the sentence as a whole. Try rephrasing the sentence to avoid ending in a preposition, but if this alters the tone or flow inappropriately, then leave it alone.

10. Valid.

    This is the incorrect form of the **past participle** (see Chapter 18 Lesson 13).

Lesson 2: Attacking "Identifying Sentence Errors" Questions

What are "Identifying Sentence Errors" questions?

The first questions on the grammar portion of the SAT I are "Identifying Sentence Errors" questions. These questions give you a sentence with four underlined parts and ask you whether the sentence contains an error in grammar or diction. If it does, you simply choose the underlined portion that contains the error. If it does not, choose E, for "no error."

❑ **Any error in these sentences must be correctable by replacing *only* the underlined portion of the sentence. Every other part of the sentence must be assumed to be correct, and no parts of the sentence may be moved to correct the problem.**

e.g.   The team <u>diligently</u> practiced and
                          A

prepared a clever game plan, but they
<u>B</u>   <u>C</u>

never got the opportunity to use the

<u>most ingenious plays</u> in the game.
                    D

<u>No error</u>
E

Answer: Some might prefer to say the team *practiced diligently* rather than the team *diligently practiced*. But choosing A would be incorrect, because this "correction" would involve **moving** a word rather than merely **replacing** it. Remember, **every other part of the sentence must remain unchanged.** In fact, either phrasing is fine: the adverb can come before or after the verb. There is a grammatical mistake here, however—do you see it? The definite pronoun *they* is plural, but its antecedent is *team*, which is singular. So choice C is the correct response, and should be replaced by *it*.

Listen for the clunker

❑ The best way to begin an "Identifying Sentence Errors" question is to take the most commonsense approach: first **read the entire sentence normally, and listen for any part of the sentence that sounds bad.** If something sounds wrong, chances are pretty good that a rule of grammar or usage is being violated.

If you are a native speaker of English, you can probably "trust your ear" on the easier questions (that is, those near the beginning of the section). If it sounds wrong, it probably is. But on more difficult questions, your instinct may be less reliable.

Make sure it's a real mistake

❑ Of course, just "trusting your ear" can only get you so far. Therefore, you should **do your best to identify the error and be sure that it's a real grammatical mistake, and not just a word or phrase that you would "say differently."**

e.g.   <u>Had the speeches been</u> any longer,
                    A

the assembly <u>would have needed to be</u>
                              B

extended <u>into</u> the next <u>class period</u>.
              C   D

<u>No error</u>
E

Answer: The first phrase, *Had the speeches been,* may sound strange to your ear. You may prefer to say *If the speeches had been. . . .* But both phrases are acceptable; the original doesn't violate any rule of grammar. Similarly, instead of *would have needed to be,* you might have said *would have had to be.* But this is merely a matter of preference; the original does not violate any grammatical rule. **Every grammatical rule that you need to know for the SAT I is discussed in great detail in Chapter 18.** For this question, the correct response is E.

The Tougher Questions: Process of Elimination

❑ **What if your ear doesn't catch a mistake? The sentence could be correct, or perhaps it contains a subtle error. In these cases, begin by eliminating the parts that are clearly okay. If you can get it down to just two choices, it's better to guess than to leave it blank.**

The Tougher Questions: The Systematic Approach

❑ If you're not sure whether a section contains an error, take a **systematic approach. This requires, however, that you be familiar with the 15 grammatical issues discussed in Chapter 18.**

To attack an "Identifying Sentence Errors" question systematically, look at each underlined portion in turn, and check the common errors as needed:

If it contains a verb

- Does the verb agree with its subject in person and number? (Subject-verb disagreement, Chapter 18 Lesson 1)
- Is it the right tense? (Tricky tenses, Chapter 18 Lesson 9)
- Does it require the subjunctive mood? If so, is it the correct form? (The subjunctive mood, Chapter 18 Lesson 14)
- If it's a past participle, is it the correct form? (Irregular verbs, Chapter 18 Lesson 13)

If it contains a pronoun

- Does it have a clear antecedent? (Pronoun agreement, Chapter 18 Lesson 5)
- Does it agree in number and person with its antecedent? (Pronoun agreement, Chapter 18 Lesson 5)
- Is it the proper case, that is, subjective (*I, he, she, we, they*), objective (*me, him, her, us, them*) or possessive (*my, your, his, her, our, their*)? (Pronoun case, Chapter 18 Lesson 6)

If it contains a preposition

- Is it the proper preposition for the "attached" word, or is it an idiom error? (Idiom errors, Chapter 18 Lesson 10)

If it contains an adjective or adverb

- Is it near the item it is modifying, or is it misplaced or dangling? (Dangling and misplaced participles, other misplaced modifiers, Chapter 18 Lessons 7 and 8)
- Is it in the correct form? (Other modifier problems, Chapter 18 Lesson 12)
- Is it logical? (Other modifier problems, Chapter 18 Lesson 12)

If it is part of a comparison

- Are the things being compared the same kind of thing? (Comparison problems, Chapter 18 Lesson 4)
- Are any of the "two" vs. "many" errors being made? (Comparison problems, Chapter 18 Lesson 4)
- Are any of the "countable" vs. "uncountable" errors being made? (Comparison problems, Chapter 18 Lesson 4)
- Are the things being compared in parallel grammatical form? (Parallelism, Chapter 18 Lesson 3)

If it is part of a list

- Does it have parallel structure with the other items in the list? (Parallelism, Chapter 18 Lesson 3)

If a word seems misspelled or unusual

- Is the wrong word being used? (Diction errors, Chapter 18 Lesson 11)

Don't fear perfection

❑ A good multiple-choice test should distribute answers evenly, so in a set of 5-choice questions, each choice should be right about 20% (1/5) of the time. Of course, this is true of choice E (No error). Your test should include about 13 "Identifying Sentence Errors" questions, so you should expect between 1 and 3 to have an answer of E (No error).

SAT I Practice 2: Attacking "Identifying Sentence Errors" Questions

The following sentences may contain errors in grammar, usage, diction (choice of words), or idiom. Some of the sentences are correct. No sentence contains more than 1 error.

If the sentence contains an error, it is underlined and lettered. The parts that are not underlined are correct.

If there is an error, select the part that must be changed to correct the sentence.

If there is no error, choose (E).

EXAMPLE:

By the time <u>they reached</u> the halfway point
          A

<u>in the race</u>, most <u>of the runners</u> <u>hadn't hardly</u>
  B   C   D

begun to hit their stride.   <u>No error</u>
                         E

EXAMPLE ANSWER:

(D)

1 The abundance <u>of</u> recent <u>business failures</u>
          A   B

<u>have intimidated</u> many <u>prospective</u>
    C   D

entrepreneurs.   <u>No error</u>
                E

2 When scientists <u>theorize</u> about the traits that
             A

all humans have come to share, they must be

keenly aware <u>of the fact</u> that these traits
           B

<u>are evolving</u> over <u>thousands of generations</u>.
   C   D

<u>No error</u>
 E

3 The entire industry has steadfastly maintained

<u>their</u> position <u>that</u> tobacco <u>is not addictive</u>
 A   B   C

and that smoking <u>is an inalienable right</u>
               D

of consumers.   <u>No error</u>
            E

4 <u>In bestowing</u> the award, the critics' guild
   A

praised the head writer, <u>saying that</u> her writing
                B

for the television series continued to be

consistently more <u>intelligent and provocative</u>
                  C

than <u>anything on the air</u>.   <u>No error</u>
     D   E

5 The <u>challenge</u> of Everest, its conquerors claim,
     A

is far more the <u>lack of oxygen</u> at its rarefied
          B

heights <u>than even</u> the <u>precarious</u> ice falls or
       C   D

precipitous ascents.   <u>No error</u>
               E

6 Those who talk more <u>respectful</u>
              A

<u>to their employers</u> are <u>more likely</u> to have their
    B   C

<u>grievances</u> addressed.   <u>No error</u>
   D   E

Answer Key 2: Attacking "Identifying Sentence Errors" Questions

1. **C**   The subject is *abundance,* which is singular, so the verb should be *has intimidated.* (Chapter 18, Lesson 1.)

2. **C**   The phrase *over thousands of generations* indicates that the evolution occurred over an extended time in the past. This means that the verb should be in the **present perfect** form: *have evolved.* (Chapter 18, Lesson 9.)

3. **A**   *Their* is a plural pronoun, but it refers to *industry,* which is singular, so the pronoun should be *its.* (Chapter 18, Lesson 5.)

4. **D**   Since the sentence indicates that the show *continued to be,* it must have been still on the air. Since it could not be better written than itself, choice D should be replaced by *anything else on the air.* (Chapter 18, Lesson 9.)

5. **E**   The sentence is correct.

6. **A**   This word is modifying the verb *talk,* so it should be in the form of an **adverb:** *respectfully.* (Chapter 18, Lesson 12.)

Lesson 3: Attacking "Improving Sentences" Questions

What are "Improving Sentences" questions?

The second set of questions on the grammar section of the SAT I are "Improving Sentences" questions. Here, you are given a sentence with only one underlined portion. This underlined portion may or may not contain one or more errors in grammar or examples of wordiness or awkwardness. If the portion contains an error, you are to choose the best correction among the choices. If it is correct, choose (A), which leaves the sentence as it is.

Identify the mistake

❑ "Improving Sentences" questions, unlike the "Identifying Sentence Errors" questions, require you to **fix mistakes** rather than merely to **find** them. Therefore, it is more important that you try to **identify the error (if there is one) as well as how to correct it, before looking at the choices.**

Having a "correction" in mind often makes it easier to pick out the best answer. The correct choice won't always be exactly the same as your correction, but chances are pretty good that it will be close.

❑ **The sentence may have more than one mistake, so don't just stop at identifying one; see whether there is another!**

Eliminate the clunkers, but be careful!

❑ As with the other questions, **read the sentence naturally,** and let your ear tell you if anything sounds wrong. **If the underlined portion contains an obvious error discussed in Chapter 18, eliminate (A) immediately. Also, immediately eliminate any choices that repeat the same error that (A) has.**

❑ **BE CAREFUL! Make sure the error in each choice is really an error, and remember that often there is more than one way to fix a mistake.**

Consider the following question:

e.g. The coaches weren't as interested in winning games during *spring training, they considered it* as an opportunity to experiment with different permutations of players.

(A) spring training, they considered it
(B) spring training; but they considered it
(C) spring training, but
(D) spring training as they were in using it
(E) spring training they were in using it

Answer: You might read the sentence and say: "It's a run-on sentence. We can't splice two sentences together like that without a semicolon, a colon, or a conjunction." (If you don't know about this rule, read Chapter 18, Lesson 15.) So you might go through the choices and cross out those that also don't contain a semicolon or conjunction, leaving you with (B) and (C). But these don't work. (D) is the correct answer because it is the only one that logically completes the *as* comparison.

Check

❑ **Always reread the sentence with your correction (if any) as the last step to check your answer. Make sure the "corrected" sentence sounds good to your ear.**

The shorter the better

❑ **If the sentence sounds okay to your ear on the first reading, it probably is.** But it may contain a subtle error. So, just to be safe, **read any choices that are shorter than the original. If you can find a choice that says the same thing more concisely, and without error, then it's probably the better choice.** Wordiness violates a rhetorical rule: **all else being equal, the shorter the better.**

e.g. Several reviewers suggested that the article was not only frequently inaccurate, *but additionally it was needlessly obtuse and, ultimately, it was insubstantial.*

(A) but additionally it was needlessly obtuse and, ultimately, it was insubstantial

(B) but it was also needlessly obtuse and it was ultimately also insubstantial

(C) but they also commented on the needless obtuseness and also the ultimate insubstantiality

(D) although it was also needlessly obtuse and ultimately insubstantial

(E) but also needlessly obtuse and ultimately insubstantial

Answer: The sentence here doesn't have any blatant grammatical gaffe, but it is wordy and awkward. Don't pick (A) immediately just because you don't spot a problem. Notice that choices (B), (D), and (E) are substantially shorter. The most elegant and concise is choice (E).

Check for danglers

❑ Improving Sentences questions are good for testing for **dangling modifiers** (see Chapter 18, Lessons 7 and 8). **Most Improving Sentences sections contain at least one sentence with a dangling modifier that needs to be fixed, so watch for it.** If a sentence begins with a modifying phrase, the noun it modifies must follow the comma.

e.g. *Chosen from the best players from around the country,* the coaches found the recruits to be extraordinarily easy to work with.

(A) Chosen from the best players from around the country

(B) Being chosen from the best players from throughout the county

(C) Having chosen the best players from around the county

(D) Being the best players from throughout the entire county

(E) The best players having been chosen by them from throughout the county

Answer: Who was *chosen from the best players from around the county*? The sentence implies that it is *the recruits* who were chosen. Certainly *the coaches* were not the ones chosen, so the underlined modifying phrase is **dangling** (see Chapter 18, Lessons 7 and 8). The modifying phrase that begins the sentence must modify the *coaches*, since that is what follows, so (C) is the best choice.

Watch out for "extra" problems

❑ Although your choice may correct one mistake, it might contain another. **Always reread the sentence with your choice to make sure there are no "extra" problems.**

e.g. The entire editorial staff worked *diligent for completing* the article in time for the midnight deadline.

(A) diligent for completing

(B) diligent in order to complete

(C) diligently for completing

(D) diligent to complete

(E) diligently to complete

Answer: The most obvious problem is that *diligent* should be *diligently*, because it modifies a verb (*wrote*), not a noun. But don't jump right to choice (C) just because it makes that correction. The sentence also contains an idiom error: to show purpose, *to complete* should be used instead of *for completing*. The best answer is (E).

SAT I Practice 3: Attacking "Improving Sentences" Questions

Each of the sentences below contains one underlined portion. The portion may contain one or more errors in grammar, usage, construction, precision, diction (choice of words), or idiom. Some of the sentences are correct.

Consider the meaning of the original sentence, and choose the answer that best expresses that meaning. If the original sentence is best, choose (A), because it repeats the original phrasing. Choose the phrasing that creates the clearest, most precise, and most effective sentence.

EXAMPLE:

The children *couldn't hardly believe their eyes.*

(A) couldn't hardly believe their eyes
(B) would not hardly believe their eyes
(C) could hardly believe their eyes
(D) couldn't nearly believe their eyes
(E) could hardly believe his or her eyes

EXAMPLE ANSWER:

(C)

1 *Being highly efficient and with plentiful fuel, physicists consider nuclear fusion to represent* a profoundly promising source of energy.

(A) Being highly efficient and with plentiful fuel, physicists consider nuclear fusion to represent
(B) Being so efficient and its sources so plentiful, physicists consider nuclear fusion to be
(C) Because nuclear fusion is so efficient and its fuel so plentiful, physicists consider it to be
(D) Being an efficient and plentiful energy source, nuclear fusion is what physicists considered as being
(E) For an energy source that physicists consider efficient and plentiful, nuclear fusion is

2 Committed to improving student achievement, *the use of standardized tests in the elementary grades by the administration has increased dramatically.*

(A) the use of standardized tests in the elementary grades by the administration has increased dramatically
(B) standardized tests have been used by the administration increasingly in the elementary grades
(C) the administration has used standardized tests increasingly in the elementary grades
(D) the use of standardized tests by the administration has increased dramatically in the elementary grades
(E) the administration have used more standardized tests in the elementary grades

3 More and more athletes are turning to yoga as a means of *increasing flexibility, refining balance, to control their energy, and they can use it to enhance their awareness of their bodies.*

(A) increasing flexibility, refining balance, to control their energy, and they can use it to enhance their awareness of their bodies.
(B) increasing their flexibility, refining their balance, controlling their energy, and enhancing their body awareness.
(C) increasing one's flexibility, balance, energy, and body awareness.
(D) to increase flexibility, to refine balance, to control energy and the enhancement of the awareness of one's body.
(E) increasing the flexibility and the balance and controlling the energy and the awareness of the body.

4 Many of the rights granted by the Constitution were not regarded by the founding fathers *as self-evident at all, but rather* the subject of often vicious debate.

(A) as self-evident at all, but rather
(B) so much as self-evident at all as they were more
(C) so self-evidently as they were
(D) as self-evident as
(E) as being self-evident, but nevertheless were

Answer Key 3: Attacking "Improving Sentences" Questions

1. **C** The original sentence is awkward and contains a dangling participle (Chapter 18, Lesson 7). *Being* is the participle, but the noun that it modifies does not follow the participial phrase. Furthermore, the logic of the sentence is unclear. Choice C shows the essential cause-and-effect relationship.

2. **C** The original sentence contains a **dangling participle** (Chapter 18, Lesson 7). *Committed* is the participle, and the participial phrase must be followed by the noun it modifies. *Who* is *committed?* Certainly not *the use of standardized tests,* but rather *the administration.* Notice that choice E is incorrect because it contains subject-verb disagreement (Chapter 18, Lesson 1).

3. **B** The original sentence violates the Law of Parallelism (Chapter 18, Lesson 3). In a list, all items should, as far as possible, have the same grammatical form. Choice C is parallel and concise, but it changes the meaning of the sentence from the original, and uses the pronoun *one's* inappropriately.

4. **A** The original sentence is best.

Lesson 4: Attacking "Improving Paragraphs" Questions

What Are "Improving Paragraphs" Questions?

The last section on the SAT I Grammar section is the "Improving Paragraphs" section. In this section, you are given a draft of a short essay that needs revision. You are then asked questions regarding how to improve the passage.

❑ Although all "Improving Paragraphs" questions refer to the passage, these questions are not like Critical Reading questions, except in one regard: **some of the questions may require you to think about the overall purpose of the essay.**

Most "Improving Paragraphs" questions are of one of common types:

"Isolated Sentences" Questions

These questions require only that you consider a single sentence and consider ways to improve it. These are very much like the "Improving Sentences" questions, except that often choice (A) does not repeat the selected portion of the sentence. In other words, there may not be a "No error" choice.

e.g.   Which of the following is the best way to revise sentence 7 (reproduced below)?

If the students would of known in advance about the shortage, they could have prevented the crisis.

(A) If the students would have known in advance
(B) It being that the students might have known in advance
(C) If the students had known in advance
(D) Being known in advance
(E) If it had been that the students knew in advance   (Answer: C)

"Sentences in Context" Questions

These questions may appear similar to the "Isolated Sentences" questions, but they will contain key phrases like

In context . . .	Considering the passage as a whole . . .
Taking the third paragraph into account . . .	Which of the following provides the best transition . . .

These phrases indicate that **you must think about the previous sentences, or the passage as a whole, to understand how best to improve the sentence.** Therefore, don't treat these questions like "Isolated Sentence" questions, but read the sentences immediately preceding the given sentence and **think about how to relate them logically.**

❑ "Sentences in Context" questions often focus on **transitions,** those words or phrases that serve as logical guideposts for a reader. They include words like **therefore, yet, nonetheless, although, furthermore,** and so on. When answering a "Sentences in Context" question, **pay special attention to these transition words, and think about whether they make sense.**

e.g.   In context, which of the following is the best version of sentence 12 (reproduced below)?

The racers were shivering as the race began.

(A) (As it is now.)
(B) Nevertheless, the racers were shivering
(C) Furthermore, the racers were shivering
(D) Therefore, the racers were shivering
(E) All the while, the racers were shivering

Answer: Of course, the correct answer depends on what immediately precedes sentence 12. For instance, if the previous sentence were *The race organizers had arranged for large, powerful heaters to be placed all around the starting line,* then (B) would provide the most logical transition, because it indicates something unexpected. If, however, the previous sentence were *The temperature had plummeted 20 degrees in the hours before the race was to start,* then (D) would make more sense because it shows a cause and effect.

"Inserting, Moving, and Removing Sentences" Questions

Some "Improving Paragraphs" questions will ask you how inserting, moving, or removing sentences in paragraphs might improve the unity or logic of the paragraph.

> e.g. Which of the following sentence contributes the least to the cohesiveness of the third paragraph?
>
> Which of the following is the most logical order for the sentences in the second paragraph?
>
> Which of the following would be most the suitable sentence to insert after sentence 5?

❏ These questions require you to consider how the sentences fit together in a paragraph. A paragraph may require an extra sentence or phrase to clarify an idea. Also, any sentence that doesn't pertain to the main idea of the paragraph should be removed. A paragraph may also be more logical if the sentences are rearranged.

Attacking the "Improving Paragraphs" Questions

❏ There are two basic approaches to attacking the "Improving Paragraphs" questions. You may want to **skim the questions and answer the "Isolated Sentences" questions first,** because these do not require you to understand the passage as a whole. For many students, this helps to give them a sense of control over the questions, and helps them to get through the questions more efficiently.

❏ Or, if you prefer, you may want to **skim the passage first** to get an idea of what the passage is about before looking at the questions. Many students prefer to get a "feel" for the passage as a whole, because this gives them more confidence as they answer the questions. **Don't worry about reading the passage as carefully as you would read a Critical Reading passage, however. Just get a general sense of what the author is trying to do.** Although some of the questions may require an understanding of the passage as a whole, most will not.

SAT I Practice 4: Attacking "Improving Paragraphs" Questions

Below is a draft of an essay that needs improvement. Some sentences may contain grammatical errors, and the paragraphs may need to be altered to improve their logic, clarity, and cohesiveness. Read the passage and answer the questions that follow.

(1) *John D. Rockefeller, Jr., was born in 1854 as the only son of America's richest man and first billionaire.* (2) *Intensely shy as a child and young man, he came out of his shell at Brown University, where he was elected president of the junior class and senior manager of the football team.* (3) *After graduating from Brown, John had the opportunity to follow his father into the oil business and add to the family fortune.* (4) *He soon discovered that wealth, rather than being something to hoard, was "an instrumentality of constructive social living."* (5) *Because of the hard-nosed business practices of John's father, John D. Rockefeller, Sr., the name Rockefeller had become synonymous with greed and trade-busting.* (6) *The younger John decided that he could make this better.*

(7) *Perhaps no American has ever done more in the area of philanthropy than John D. Rockefeller, Jr.* (8) *He created charitable foundations like the Rockefeller Foundation, the Rockefeller Institute, and the General Education Board.* (9) *He sponsored the construction of Rockefeller Center in New York City, financed the reconstruction of Colonial Williamsburg, which stands to this day as an invaluable historical treasure, and donated the land in New York City for the United Nations complex.*

(10) *The scope of Rockefeller's conservation efforts, also, was profound.* (11) *He donated thousands of acres of land to national parks like Acadia, Shenandoah, the Great Smoky Mountains, and the Grand Tetons.* (12) *He also financed the construction of museums in Yellowstone, the Grand Canyon, and Mesa Verde.*

(13) *John D. Rockefeller, Jr., is considered the father of philanthropy in the United States never before or since has any one person made such an impact on public institutions.* (14) *Although always willing to support a good cause, Rockefeller never sought accolades for himself.* (15) *He was offered dozens of honorary degrees from prestigious universities, and declined all but one, from his alma mater.*

1 In context, which of the following is the best revision of the underlined portion of sentence 4 (reproduced below)?

<u>He soon discovered</u> that wealth, rather than being something to hoard, was "an instrumentality of constructive social living."

(A) However, he soon discovered
(B) Furthermore, he soon discovered
(C) He would only have soon discovered
(D) Therefore, he soon discovered
(E) When he soon discovered

2 Where is the most logical place to insert the following sentence?

John's discovery of philanthropy could hardly have come at a better time for the Rockefellers.

(A) After sentence 1
(B) After sentence 3
(C) After sentence 4
(D) Before sentence 7, to begin the second paragraph
(E) After sentence 8

3 Which of the following revisions of sentence 6 (reproduced below) best improves its clarity in the context of the first paragraph?

The younger John decided that he could make this better.

(A) The younger John, the son of John D. Rockefeller, Sr., decided that he could make this better.
(B) The younger John decided that he could restore the prestige of his family name.
(C) The younger John, who was affectionately called "Johnny D," decided that he could make this better.
(D) This was something that the younger John himself thought he could improve greatly.
(E) But this was something that young John knew he could do something about the problem of his family honor.

Answer Key 4: Attacking "Improving Paragraphs" Questions

1. **A** Sentence 3 indicates that John could have added to the family fortune. Sentence 4 indicates that he did not, but rather used the money for philanthropic purposes. This contrast of ideas should be accompanied by a contrasting transition, as provided by the word *however*.

2. **C** Because sentence 4 introduces John's "discovery of philanthropy," and because sentence 5 explains why it "could hardly have come at a better time," the sentence belongs most logically between sentence 4 and sentence 5.

3. **B** The original sentence is unclear because the word *this* does not have a clear antecedent; that is, it is unclear what *this* refers to. A reader could probably figure out that it refers to the problem with the Rockefeller reputation, discussed in the previous sentence, but sentence 5 does not actually contain the words *the problem with the Rockefeller reputation,* so the reference is unclear. Choice B is the only sentence that clarifies that reference.

CHAPTER 18

ESSENTIAL GRAMMAR SKILLS

1. Subject-Verb Disagreement

2. Trimming Sentences

3. Parallelism

4. Comparison Problems

5. Pronoun-Antecedent Disagreement

6. Pronoun Case

7. Dangling and Misplaced Participles

8. Other Misplaced Modifiers

9. Tricky Tenses

10. Idiom Errors

11. Diction Errors

12. Other Modifier Problems

13. Irregular Verbs

14. The Subjunctive Mood

15. Coordinating Ideas

Lesson 1: Subject-Verb Disagreement

Finding Verbs

The verb is the most important part of a sentence, but verbs aren't always easy to spot. Consider the word *swim* in the sentences *The ducks swim in the pond* and *The ducks love to swim.* In the first sentence, *swim* is the verb. In the second sentence, *swim* is part of a noun phrase. (*To swim* is the **thing** that the ducks *love.*) So how do we spot verbs?

❑ **A verb is what conveys the essential meaning of a clause** (a string of words that convey an idea). Every idea requires a verb. The sentence *The ducks swim in the pond* says that *Something swims somewhere,* so the verb is *swim.* The sentence *The ducks love to swim* says that *Something loves something,* so the verb is *love.* Every verb requires a **subject,** that is, what *does* the verb. In both sentences, the subject is *ducks.* A verb may also require an *object,* that is, what *receives* the verb. In *The ducks love to swim,* the object is *to swim,* because that is the *thing* that is *loved.*

> e.g. *When David approached third base, the coach waved him home.*

> This sentence contains two related ideas, so it contains two **clauses,** and therefore two **verbs:**

> Clause 1: *When David **approached** third base*
> Verb: *approached*   Subject: *David*
> Object: *third base*
> Clause 2: *the coach **waved** him home*
> Verb: *waved*   Subject: *the coach*
> Object: *him*

Subject-Verb Disagreement (SVD)

❑ **Every verb must agree in number** (singular or plural) **with its subject. Subject-verb disagreement** is one of the most common errors tested for on the SAT I. If you are a native speaker of English, the best way to check for subject-verb disagreement is to find the subject and verb (ignoring all the intervening words) and **say them together.**

> e.g. *The people, who are easily persuaded by corporate sponsored media, spends very little time analyzing issues.* (The verb is *spends*

and its subject is *people.* But *people spends* sounds wrong, because *spends* is the "third person singular" form—as in *he spends*—but *people* is plural, so the phrase should be *people spend.*)

Tricky Plurals and Singulars

These rules will help you to check whether a verb agrees in "number" with its subject:

❑ Phrases like *Sam and Bob* are **plural,** but phrases like *Sam, in addition to Bob,* are **singular.** Phrases that start *as well as . . . , together with . . . , along with . . . ,* or *in addition to . . .* are **interrupters,** which are not part of the main subject.

❑ These words are **singular:** *each, anyone, anybody, anything, another, neither, either, every, everyone, someone, no one, somebody, everything, little,* and *much.* To check for SVD, you can replace any of them with ***it.***

❑ These words are **plural:** *phenomena* (singular: *phenomenon*), *media* (singular: *medium*), *data* (singular: *datum*), and *criteria* (singular: *criterion*). To check for SVD, you can replace any of them with ***they.***

❑ All of the following can be either **singular or plural,** according to the noun that follows the *of: none (of), any (of), some (of), most (of), more (of),* and *all (of).*

❑ Verbs that follow subjects of the form *either A or B* and *neither A nor B* must **agree with B,** the noun closer to the verb.

Inverted Sentences

❑ Usually the subject comes **before** the verb, but **inverted** clauses have the subject **after** the verb. For instance, sentences that start *There is . . .* or *There are . . .* are inverted. To check subject-verb agreement in these sentences, first "uninvert" them.

> e.g. *There <u>are</u> many <u>flies</u> in the barn.* (inverted) =
>   V   S
> *Many <u>flies</u> <u>are</u> in the barn.* (uninverted)
>   S   V

Concept Review 1:
Subject-Verb Disagreement

Next to each noun or noun phrase, write "S" if it is singular or "P" if it is plural.

1. *Neither rain nor snow* _____
2. *Crowd of rowdy fans* _____
3. *Media* _____
4. *Criterion* _____
5. *One or two* _____
6. *Everything* _____
7. *Either of the candidates* _____
8. *Phenomena* _____

Circle the subject in each sentence, and choose the correct verb.

9. *Neither of the cars (is/are) equipped with anti-lock brakes.*
10. *The flock of geese (was/were) startled by the shotgun blast.*
11. *The data on my computer (was/were) completely erased when the power failed.*
12. *Mathematics and history (is/are) my favorite subjects.*
13. *None of the roast (was/were) eaten.*
14. *All of the games (was/were) played on real grass fields.*
15. *Pride and Prejudice (is/are) my favorite Jane Austen novel.*
16. *Neither of the twins (is/are) allergic to penicillin.*
17. *Much of what I hear in those lectures (goes/go) in one ear and out the other.*
18. *Amy, along with Jamie and Jen, (is/are) applying to Mount Holyoke.*
19. *None of the books (was/were) considered fit for public consumption.*
20. *All of the eggplant (was/were) used to make the sauce.*
21. *Amid the lilies and wildflowers (was/were) one solitary rose.*
22. *Either Ben or his brothers (is/are) in charge of bringing the drinks.*
23. *There (is/are) hardly even a speck of dirt left on the carpet.*
24. *"Stop right there!" (shouts/shout) the Bailey brothers, who are standing in front of me.*
25. *Either the Donovans or Dave (is/are) going to bring the plates.*
26. *There (is/are) at least a hundred people here.*

"Uninvert" the following sentences so that the verb follows the subject, then choose the correct verb form.

27. *There (is/are), in my opinion, far too many smokers in this restaurant.*

   _____

28. *Over that hill (is/are) thousands of bison.*

   _____

29. *Riding on the bus among the children (was/were) over a dozen commuters.*

   _____

30. *Never before (has/have) there been such voices heard here.*

   _____

31. *Absent from the article (was/were) any mention of the director's previous Broadway failures.*

   _____

Worksheet 1:
Subject-Verb Disagreement

Label each verb in the following sentences with a "V" and each subject with an "S." If any verbs are incorrect, cross them out and write the correct form in the blank.

1. We were horrified to discover that there was more than 3 mice living in the attic.   _____

2. Either the president or one of her aides are going to coordinate the project.   _____

3. There is nearly always 2 or 3 guards posted at each entrance.   _____

4. Every player on both the Falcons and the Rockets were at the party after the game.   _____

5. There has been a theater and a toy store in the mall ever since it opened.   _____

6. Either Eric or his brother is hosting the party this year.   _____

7. There is no fewer than 6 crayons in this box.   _____

8. The therapy can resume as planned because neither of the twins are allergic to penicillin.   _____

9. The proceeds from the sale of every auctioned item goes to charity.   _____

10. Economics, particularly with its dependence on the behavior of consumers and producers, has always struck me as more of a human science than a mathematical one.   _____

11. There is more than 3 years remaining on her contract.   _____

12. Neither of the girls were frightened by the wild animals that scurried incessantly past their tent.   _____

13. The technology behind high-definition television, DVDs, and CDs have transformed nearly every aspect of the home entertainment industry.   _____

14. Every player on both teams were concerned about the goalie's injury.   _____

15. The company's sponsorship of charitable foundations and mentorship programs have garnered many commendations from philanthropic organizations.   _____

16. Neither the children nor their parents utters a word when Mrs. Denny tells her stories.   _____

17. How important is your strength training and your diet to your daily regimen?   _____

Answer Key 1: Subject-Verb Disagreement

Concept Review 1

1. *S*
2. *S*
3. *P*
4. *S*
5. *P*
6. *S*
7. *S*
8. *P*
9. s: *neither*, v: *is*
10. s: *flock*, v: *was*
11. s: *data*, v: *were* (*data* is plural)
12. s: *Mathematics and history*, v: *are*
13. s: *none (roast)*, v: *was*
14. s: *all (games)*, v: *were*
15. s: *Pride and Prejudice*, v: *is*
16. s: *neither*, v: *is*
17. s: *much*, v: *goes*
18. s: *Amy*, v: *is*
19. s: *none (books)*, v: *were*
20. s: *all (eggplant)*, v: *was*
21. s: *rose*, v: *was*
22. s: *brothers*, v: *are*
23. s: *speck*, v: *is*
24. s: *Bailey brothers*, v: *shout*
25. s: *Dave*, v: *is*
26. s: *people*, v: *are*
27. *Far too many smokers, in my opinion, are in this restaurant.*
28. *Thousands of bison are over that hill.*
29. *Among the children, over a dozen commuters were riding on the bus.*
30. *Such voices have never before been heard here.*
31. *Any mention of the director's previous Broadway failures was absent from the article.*

Worksheet 1

1. s: *we*, v: *were* (correct); s: *mice*, v: *was* (change to *were*)
2. s: *one*, v: *are* (change to *is*)
3. s: *guards*, v: *is* (change to *are*)
4. s: *every player*, v: *were* (change to *was*)
5. s: *a theater and a toy store*, v: *has been* (change to *have been*)
6. s: *his brother*, v: *is* (correct)
7. s: *crayons*, v: *is* (change to *are*)
8. s: *therapy*, v: *can resume* (correct); s: *neither*, v: *are* (change to *is*)
9. s: *proceeds*, v: *goes* (change to *go*)
10. s: *economics*, v: *has struck* (correct)
11. s: *years*, v: *is* (change to *are*)
12. s: *neither*, v: *were* (change to *was*)
13. s: *technology*, v: *have transformed* (change to *has transformed*)
14. s: *every player*, v: *were* (change to *was*)
15. s: *sponsorship*, v: *have garnered* (change to *has garnered*)
16. s: *their parents*, v: *utters* (change to *utter*); s: *Mrs. Denny*, v: *tells*
17. s: *your strength training and your diet*, v: *is* (change to *are*)

Lesson 2: Trimming Sentences

Why Trim?

❑ Spotting SVD errors is often easier when you "trim" the sentence, that is, eliminate nonessential modifiers to leave the "core" of the sentence. What remains after you "trim" a sentence should still be a grammatically correct and complete sentence.

How to "Trim" a Sentence

❑ **Step 1: Cross out all nonessential prepositional phrases.**
e.g. *The bird ~~in the cage~~ began singing.*

A **preposition** is a word that shows relative position or direction. It can complete one of the following sentences:

The squirrel ran _____ the tree.
Democracy is government _____ the people.

Examples include *to, from, of, for, by, in, before, with, beyond,* and *up.*

A **prepositional phrase** is the preposition and the noun phrase that follows, including its modifiers.

e.g. *from sea to shining sea   in the beginning with hat in hand*

❑ **Step 2: Cross out all interrupting phrases.**
e.g. *The committee, ~~ignoring tradition~~, will approve the measure.*

An **interrupting phrase** is a modifying phrase that interrupts the flow of the sentence. Interrupters are generally separated from the main sentence by commas or dashes.

❑ **Step 3: Cross out all other nonessential modifiers and modifying phrases.**
e.g. *~~Having traveled so far,~~ the ~~baseball~~ team hardly wanted to forfeit the ~~championship~~ game.*

Modifiers are **adjectives** and **adverbs,** as well as modifying phrases like **participial phrases** (see Lesson 7). Most modifiers are not essential to a sentence, but some are. Use your best judgment. One kind of essential adjective is a **predicate adjective,** that is, an adjective that is linked to the subject by a linking verb, as in *Martha is <u>smart</u>.*

Trimming a sentence helps you to spot SVD more easily.

Original: *My chief concern with this budget and the other proposals on the table are the cuts in school funds.*

Trimmed: *My concern are the cuts.*

Revised: *My concern <u>is</u> the cuts.*

Who Kicked Whom?

When you write, trim your sentences to play the "Who kicked whom?" exercise. Look at the subject-verb-object ("Who kicked whom?") core, and see if it clearly and forcefully conveys the thought you want to convey.

Original: *The lack of economic programs and no big country's being ready to join it symbolized the problems the League of Nations had in getting established.*

Trimmed: *The lack and no country's being ready symbolized the problems.* (Yikes! That doesn't make a shred of sense; rewrite it.)

Revised: *Two problems plagued the establishment of the League of Nations: its lack of viable economic programs and its lack of support from the larger countries.*

Concept Review 2:
Trimming Sentences

1. What are the three types of words or phrases that can be eliminated when "trimming" a sentence?

   _____

2. Why is it sometimes helpful to "trim" a sentence?

   _____

   _____

3. Circle all of the prepositions in the list below.

   of   beyond   for   and   with   the   an   without   some   along   below

4. What is a prepositional phrase?

   _____

5. Write four examples of prepositional phrases.

   _____

   _____

Write the trimmed version of each sentence on the line below it, correcting any verb problems.

6. *The team of advisors, arriving ahead of schedule, were met at the airport by the Assistant Prime Minister.*

   _____

7. *The flock of birds that darted over the lake were suddenly an opalescent silver.*

   _____

8. *Carmen, along with her 3 sisters, are unlikely to be swayed by arguments supporting David's position.*

   _____

Write the trimmed version of each sentence on the line below it, then rewrite the sentence to make it clearer and more forceful, changing the subject and verb entirely, if necessary.

9. *Nearly inevitably, advancements, or those being popularly regarded as such, have to do with modifications, not overhaul.*

   Trimmed: _____

   Revised: _____

10. *The development of the new country's governmental system was affected in a negative regard by the rebels' lack of cohesiveness.*

   Trimmed: _____

   Revised: _____

Worksheet 2:
Trimming Sentences

Write the "trimmed" version of each sentence, circling the verbs and subjects and correcting any agreement errors.

1. Juggling the demands of both school and my social agenda often seem too much to bear.
   _____

2. Others on the committee, like the chairwoman Amanda Sanders, is concerned about the lack of attention given to school safety.
   _____

3. The waiters' professional demeanor—particularly their keen knowledge, their attention to detail, and their cordiality—are what makes dining there such a sublime culinary experience.
   _____
   _____

4. The system by which candidates for local political offices are selected is archaic and, many contend, unfair.
   _____

5. The abundance of companies that fail in their first year of business contribute to an intimidating economic climate.
   _____

6. When scientists theorize about the traits that all humans have come to share, they must be keenly aware of the fact that these traits have evolved over millions of generations.
   _____
   _____

7. The entire industry of tobacco companies and distributors has steadfastly maintained their position that tobacco is not addictive and that smoking is an inalienable right of consumers.
   _____
   _____

8. The challenge of Mount Everest, its conquerors claim, is far more the lack of oxygen at its rarefied heights than even the precarious ice falls or precipitous ascents.
   _____

9. One in every 3 Americans agree strongly with the statement: "Anyone who would run for political office is not worth voting for."
   _____

10. The fact that humans have committed so many atrocities have forced some historians to adopt a cynical perspective on human nature.
   _____
   _____

Answer Key 2: Trimming Sentences

Concept Review 2

1. Prepositional phrases, interrupting phrases, and nonessential modifiers

2. Trimming reveals subject-verb disagreement errors and reveals how clear and forceful the sentence is.

3. Prepositions: *of, beyond, for, with, without, along, below*

4. A prepositional phrase is a preposition and the noun or noun phrase that follows it.

5. Examples might include *in the tree, without hesitation, beyond gimmicks,* and *over two million hungry customers.*

6. *The team were* (change to *was*) *met.*

7. *The flock were* (change to *was*) *silver.*

8. *Carmen are* (change to *is*) *unlikely to be swayed.*

9. Trimmed: *Advancements have to do with modifications.*

The verb *(have to do with)* is weak, vague, and inactive, and the subject *(advancements)* and object *(modification)* are abstract and vague. To improve the sentence, think about the *intended* meaning of the sentence, and use stronger and less abstract terms. Here's a good revision:

Typically, societies progress by making small modifications to their institutions, not by overhauling them completely.

10. Trimmed: *The development was affected.*

The verb *(was affected)* is weak, passive, and vague. Here's a good revision:

The incohesiveness of the rebels hindered the development of the new government.

Worksheet 2

1. *Juggling the demands seem* (change to *seems*) *too much to bear.*

2. *Others is* (change to *are*) *concerned.*

3. *The demeanor are* (change to *is*) *what makes dining there a sublime experience.*

4. *The system is archaic and unfair.* (correct)

5. *The abundance contribute* (change to *contributes*) *to an intimidating climate.*

6. *They must be keenly aware that these traits have evolved over millions of generations.* (correct)

7. *The industry has maintained their* (change to *its*) *position that tobacco is not addictive and that smoking is an inalienable right.*

8. *The challenge is far more the lack of oxygen than the precarious ice falls or precipitous ascents.* (correct)

9. *One agree* (change to *agrees*) *with the statement: "Anyone who would run for political office is not worth voting for."*

10. *The fact have forced* (change to *has forced*) *some*

Lesson 3: Parallelism

The Law of Parallelism

❑ When you **compare** or list items in a sentence, the items should have the **same grammatical form.** That is, if the first item is an infinitive (or a gerund, or an adjective, etc.) the other item(s) should be, too.

Wrong: *She hated **to take** charge, **draw** attention to herself, and **she hated seeming** like a know-it-all.*
(The three items have different forms. The sentence sounds best if they are all **gerunds.**)

Right: *She hated **taking** charge, **drawing** attention to herself, and **seeming** like a know-it-all.*

Wrong: *Believe it or not, I like **to read** more than I like **going** to parties.*
(The first item is an **infinitive,** but the second is a **gerund.** Make them the same form.)

Right: *Believe it or not, I like **to read** more than I like **to go** to parties.*

Also right: *Believe it or not, I like **reading** more than I like **going** to parties.*

Parallel Constructions

❑ In all constructions like the following, the words or phrases that replace *A* and *B* must be parallel:

A is like B	*A more than B*	*prefer A to B*
neither A nor B	*either A or B*	*both A and B*
the more A,	*the better A,*	*not only A*
* the less B*	* the better B*	* but also B*
not A but B	*less A than B*	*more A than B*

Infinitives vs. Gerunds

Infinitives are verblike phrases like *to run, to see,* and *to think,* which usually act as **nouns.**

Gerunds are also verblike words, like *running, seeing,* and *thinking,* and they also often act as **nouns.**

I like pizza.   I like to swim.   I like swimming.

What kind of word is *pizza*? Obviously a noun. But notice that in the sentences above, *to swim* (infinitive) and *swimming* (gerund) are playing the same role as *pizza* did in the first sentence. So they must be nouns here, too!

❑ Usually, gerunds and infinitives are interchangeable. But in some situations, one is preferable to the other:

- The gerund often indicates a **general class** of activity, while the infinitive indicates a **specific** activity.

  Good: ***Kayaking** (not to kayak) is a healthful sport, but can sometimes be dangerous.*

  Good: *Curtis and Dan want **to kayak** (not kayaking) this afternoon.*

- The infinitive indicates a stronger **connection between subject and action** than does the gerund.

  Unclear: *Cara has always loved **dancing**.*

  (Does Cara simply like to watch dancing, or does she herself do the dancing?)

  Clearer: *Cara has always loved **to dance**.*

  (This sentence clearly indicates that Cara herself dances.)

- The infinitive often indicates **purpose or intention** better than does the gerund.

  Awkward: *We have supplied cars **for transporting** the guests back to their hotel rooms.*

  Better: *We have supplied cars **to transport** the guests back to their hotel rooms.*

Concept Review 3: Parallelism

1. In what situations do you have to obey the Law of Parallelism?

In each of the sentences below, circle the words or phrases that are parallel, then write the *form* of those words or phrases (adjectives, prepositional phrases, gerunds, infinitives, nouns, etc.) in the blank.

2. You can register for the test by mail, by phone, or on the Web. _____

3. Having good study practices is even more important than working hard. _____

4. The more you get to know her, the more you will like her. _____

5. The produce is not only exceptionally fresh but also reasonably priced. _____

6. The show is less a concert than it is a 3-hour nightmare. _____

Complete each of the sentences below with the appropriate word or phrase—infinitive or gerund—using the given verb.

7. (exercise) _____ is essential, but so is (eat) _____ intelligently.

8. The purpose of this trip is (show) _____ you what life was like in the 18th century.

9. I have always loved (dance) _____, although my condition has always prevented me from doing it myself.

10. Is it better (study) _____ a little each night, or a lot the night before?

11. The director called a meeting (discuss) _____ the coordination of the marketing phase.

Correct any infinitive/gerund problems in the sentences below.

12. The defendant was unwilling to give up his right of having his lawyer present at all questioning.

13. I would not dream to try out for the team until I have learned to throw a football.

14. Even the reinforced concrete breakwater could not prevent the water to inundate the village.

15. Within the next 3 weeks, we plan having all of the work on the roof completed.

Fix the parallelism errors in the following sentences.

16. I like working with Miss Bennett because she is very supportive and has a lot of knowledge.

_____

17. I can't decide whether I should give Maria the tickets or Caitlyn.

_____

18. The movie was both beautifully directed and the acting was a joy to watch.

_____

Worksheet 3: Parallelism

In the following sentences, circle all parts that should be parallel, and correct any problems.

1. Personal digital assistants can be not only practical, but also entertain for hours on end.

   _____

2. Filling out applications for summer jobs is about as much fun as when you take the SAT.

   _____

3. My lab partners were more concerned about getting the lab done quickly than about what grade they might get.

   _____

4. To say she is excitable is like saying Bill Gates is well off.

   _____

5. The sheer magnitude of the structure was awesome, but I thought the aesthetics were less than appealing.

   _____

6. The elegance of a proof lies more in its conciseness and clarity than in how clever it is.

   _____

7. I bought my tickets, reserved the hotel room, and I planned the itinerary myself.

   _____

8. We had to build our own shelters, orient ourselves without instruments, and we even had to hunt and gather our own food.

   _____

9. The rebels were neither disciplined nor did they have any overall strategy.

   _____

10. She was concerned not only with getting good grades, but also wanted to understand the material.

    _____

11. Patients with chronic fatigue syndrome tend to exhibit lethargy, a reduced affect and they often feel depressed.

    _____

12. Taxpayers often prefer to pay high property taxes to the paying of high sales taxes.

    _____

13. Riding that roller coaster was like a trip over a waterfall in a barrel.

    _____

14. As a teacher, she loved to inspire creativity in her students, even more than she loved receiving accolades.

    _____

Answer Key 3: Parallelism

Concept Review 3

1. When comparing or listing things in a sentence.

2. *by mail; by phone; on the web*   prepositional phrases

3. *having; working*   gerunds

4. *you get to know her; you will like her*   clauses

5. *exceptionally fresh; reasonably priced*   adverb-adjectives

6. *concert; 3-hour nightmare*   nouns

7. *<u>Exercising</u> is essential, but so is <u>eating</u> intelligently.*

8. *The purpose of this trip is <u>to show</u> you what life was like in the 18th century.* The infinitive shows purpose more effectively than the gerund does.

9. *I have always loved <u>dancing</u>, although my condition has always prevented me from doing it myself.* Since the speaker cannot dance, the infinitive is inappropriate.

10. *Is it better <u>to study</u> a little each night, or a lot the night before?* The infinitive shows a clearer link between the action and a particular subject.

11. *The director called a meeting <u>to discuss</u> the coordination of the marketing phase.* The infinitive shows purpose more effectively than the gerund does.

12. *The defendant was unwilling to give up his right <u>to have</u> his lawyer present at all questioning.*

13. *I would not dream <u>of trying</u> out for the team until I have learned to throw a football.*

14. *Even the reinforced concrete breakwater could not prevent the water <u>from inundating</u> the village.*

15. *Within the next 3 weeks, we plan <u>to have</u> all of the work on the roof completed.*

16. *I like working with Miss Bennett because she is very supportive and <u>knowledgeable</u>.*

17. *I can't decide whether I should give <u>the tickets to Maria or Caitlyn</u>.*

18. *The movie's <u>directing was beautiful</u> and the <u>acting was a joy to watch</u>.*

Worksheet 3

1. *Personal digital assistants can be not only practical, but also <u>entertaining</u> for hours on end.*

2. *Filling out applications for summer jobs is about as much fun as <u>taking</u> the SAT.*

3. *My lab partners were more concerned about getting the lab done quickly than about <u>getting a good grade</u>.*

4. *<u>Saying</u> she is excitable is like saying Bill Gates is well off.*

5. *The sheer magnitude of the structure was awesome, but (omit I thought) the aesthetics were less than appealing.*

6. *The elegance of a proof lies more in its conciseness and clarity than in <u>its cleverness</u>.*

7. *I bought my tickets, reserved the hotel room, and (omit I) planned the itinerary myself.*

8. *We had to build our own shelters, orient ourselves without instruments, and <u>even hunt</u> and gather our own food.*

9. *The rebels <u>lacked both discipline and</u> overall strategy.*

10. *She was concerned not only with getting good grades, but <u>also with understanding</u> the material.*

11. *Patients with CFS tend to exhibit lethargy, a reduced affect, and often <u>depression</u>.*

12. *Taxpayers often prefer <u>paying</u> high property taxes to <u>paying</u> high sales taxes.*

13. *Riding that roller coaster was like <u>taking</u> a trip over a waterfall in a barrel.*

14. *As a teacher, she loved <u>inspiring</u> creativity in her students, even more than (omit she loved) receiving accolades.*

Lesson 4: Comparison Problems

Illogical Comparisons

❑ Any items being compared in a sentence must be logically comparable, that is, in the same general category. Always compare *apples* to *apples*, not *apples* to *car batteries*! Also, comparisons must obey the Law of Parallelism.

Wrong: *Her chances of getting an A aren't much better than the lottery.*
(*Chances* and *the lottery* aren't comparable things! We must compare *chances* to *chances*.)

Right: *Her chances of getting an A aren't much better than **her chances of winning** the lottery.*

❑ It is always illogical to say that something is different from itself. Watch out for sneaky contrasts like this:

Wrong: *She has played in more concerts than any cellist in her school.*
(Of course, she hasn't played in more concerts than herself!)

Right: *She has played in more concerts than any other cellist in her school.*

Fewer/Less, Number/Amount, and Many/Much

❑ Use the words *fewer, number,* or *many* only in reference to **countable** things (like *cars, dollars,* and *popsicles*) and *less, amount,* or *much* only in reference to **uncountable** things (like *traffic, money,* and *food*). It is a common mistake to use *less* when you should use *fewer*.

Wrong: *There have been a lot less fans at the games ever since the owners raised ticket prices.*
(Since fans can be counted, *less* doesn't work. Use *fewer* instead.)

Right: *There have been a lot **fewer** fans at the games ever since the owners raised ticket prices.*

Wrong: *The team owners showed concern about the increasing **amount** of dangerously rowdy fans.*

Right: *The team owners showed concern about the increasing **number** of dangerously rowdy fans.*

Between/Among, More/Most, and -er/-est

❑ Use *between, more,* and any *-er* adjectives only when comparing **exactly 2 things.** Use *among, most,* and *-est* adjectives when comparing **more than 2 things.**

Wrong: *The two superpowers seemed to be in a constant battle to see who was **strongest.***

Right: *The two superpowers seemed to be in a constant battle to see who was **stronger.***

Wrong: *Of the dozens of students in the club, Deborah was the **more** popular.*

Right: *Of the dozens of students in the club, Deborah was the **most** popular.*

Number Shift

❑ Things that you compare should, if possible, agree in number. Be sure they are **both plural** or **both singular.**

Wrong: *They were both hoping to be **a winner.***

Right: *They were both hoping to be **winners.***

Wrong: *The sailors' main **point of reference was** the two lighthouse beacons.*

Right: *The sailors' main **points of reference were** the two lighthouse beacons.*

Concept Review 4: Comparison Problems

1. How do you know whether to use *fewer* or *less* in a comparison?

2. How do you know whether to use *more* or *most* in a comparison?

In each sentence, underline any items that are being compared or equated. Below the sentence, state whether the comparison is *logical* or *illogical*. If it is illogical or contains another error in comparison, correct the sentence.

3. *The critics' guild praised the show, saying that it was consistently more intelligent and provocative than anything on the air.*

   _____

4. *Team unity and commitment to practice were regarded by the players as the key to their success.*

   _____

5. *Mathematics lessons in Japanese classrooms, unlike American classrooms, are often focused on solving a single complex problem rather than many simplistic problems.*

   _____

6. *Increasingly, modern singers, like Gregorian chanters, are becoming adept at melisma, the singing of many notes on a single syllable.*

   _____

7. *The electric-combustion engines of the new hybrid cars burn much more cleanly and efficiently than conventional cars.*

   _____

8. *To the critics of the time, the surrealists were as inscrutable, if not more so, than the dadaists.*

   _____

9. *In modern warfare, unlike the past, combatants rarely meet face to face, and are detected as often by video as by sight.*

   _____

10. *Most people vastly prefer turning the pages of a real book to scrolling through the screens of an electronic novel.*

    _____

Worksheet 4:
Comparison Problems

Correct any errors in the comparisons in the following sentences.

1. *I prefer a lot of modern poetry to Shakespeare.*

   _____

2. *Her suitcase would not close because she had packed too much of her towels into it.*

   _____

3. *The year-end bonus was equally divided between Parker, Herriot, and me.*

   _____

4. *Many students wanted to be a lifeguard at the club.*

   _____

5. *The toughest thing about her class is you have to do tons of homework every night.*

   _____

6. *Mr. Forstadt's comments, like so many coaches, didn't spare the players' feelings in the least.*

   _____

7. *After several days in the woods, we became concerned that we had packed a lot less meals than we would need.*

   _____

8. *Even in the 21st century, women throughout the globe are treated like a slave, or, worse yet, like a non-person.*

   _____

9. *I've always preferred observational humor to those quirky prop comedians.*

   _____

10. *It was remarkable that the children had donated so much toys to others who were barely needier than they.*

    _____

11. *The formal structure of the sonnet imposes far more discipline on the mind of the poet than formless free verse.*

    _____

12. *The theories of true anarchists, unlike modern antistatists, do not promote social chaos, but rather organization without authority.*

    _____

13. *Those passengers with a disability will be permitted to board the plane first.*

    _____

14. *The reason we lost the game is because our captain had torn his ACL.*

    _____

15. *Voter apathy and cold weather were a reason that turnout was so poor at this year's election.*

    _____

16. *Having studied Faulkner and Hemingway, I've come to believe that Hemingway is the best writer, although Faulkner tells the best stories.*

    _____

Answer Key 4: Comparison Problems

Concept Review 4

1. *Fewer* is used to compare <u>countable</u> things, while *less* is used to compare <u>uncountable</u> things.

2. *More* is used only when comparing <u>exactly 2</u> things, while *most* is used when comparing <u>more than 2</u>.

3. *The show* is compared to *anything on the air.* Illogical: *the show* can only be better than *anything <u>else</u> on the air.*

4. *Team unity and commitment* are equated with *the key.* Illogical: they are *the <u>keys</u> to their success.*

5. *Mathematics lessons* are compared to *American classrooms.* Illogical: they should be compared to <u>*the lessons in*</u> *American classrooms.*

6. *Modern singers* are compared to *Gregorian chanters.* Logical and correct.

7. *The engines* are compared to *conventional cars.* Illogical: they should be compared to <u>*those in conventional cars.*</u>

8. *The surrealists* are compared to *the dadaists.* Logical, but grammatically incorrect: *the surrealists were regarded as being as inscrutable <u>as the dadaists, if not more so.</u>*

9. *In modern warfare* is compared to *the past.* Illogical: *In modern warfare, unlike <u>warfare in</u> the past . . .*

10. *Turning* is compared to *scrolling.* Logical and correct.

Worksheet 4

1. *I prefer a lot of modern poetry to <u>the poetry of Shakespeare.</u>*

2. *Her suitcase would not close because she had packed too <u>many</u> of her towels into it.*

3. *The year-end bonus was equally divided <u>among</u> Parker, Harriot, and me.*

4. *Many students wanted to be <u>lifeguards</u> at the club.*

5. *The toughest thing about her class is <u>having</u> to do tons of homework every night.*

6. *Mr. Forstadt's comments, like <u>those of</u> so many coaches, didn't spare the players' feelings in the least.*

7. *After several days in the woods, we became concerned that we had packed a lot <u>fewer</u> meals than we would need.*

8. *Even in the 21st century, women throughout the globe are treated like <u>slaves,</u> or, worse yet, like <u>nonpersons.</u>*

9. *I've always preferred observational humor to <u>quirky prop comedy.</u>*

10. *It was remarkable that the children had donated so <u>many</u> toys to others who were barely needier than they.*

11. *The formal structure of the sonnet imposes far more discipline on the mind of the poet than <u>does the formlessness of</u> free verse.*

12. *The theories of the original anarchists, unlike <u>those of</u> modern antistatists, do not promote social chaos, but rather organization without authority.*

13. *Those passengers with <u>disabilities</u> will be permitted to board the plane first* or *<u>Any passenger</u> with a disability will be permitted to board the plane first.*

14. *The reason we lost the game is <u>that</u> our captain had torn his ACL.*

15. *Voter apathy and cold weather were <u>the reasons</u> that turnout was so poor at this year's election.*

16. *Having studied Faulkner and Hemingway, I've come to believe that Hemingway is the <u>better</u> writer, although Faulkner tells the <u>better</u> stories.*

Lesson 5: Pronoun-Antecedent Disagreement

Pronouns

A **pronoun** is a word (such as *it, he, she, what,* or *that*) that substitutes for a noun. A pronoun is either **definite** (like *it, you, she,* and *I*) and refers to a specified thing (or person or place or idea) or **indefinite** (like *anyone, neither,* and *those*), and does **not** refer to a specific thing (or person or place or idea).

Definite Pronouns and Antecedents

❑ Every definite pronoun refers to a noun called an **antecedent.** The pronoun **must agree in number** (singular or plural) **and kind** (personal or impersonal) with the pronoun.

Wrong: *Everyone should brush **their** teeth 3 times a day.*
           (Because *everyone* is singular, *their* is the wrong pronoun.)

Right: *Everyone should brush **his** or **her** teeth 3 times a day.*

Wrong: *David was the one **that** first spotted the error.*
           (The pronoun *that* is impersonal, but of course, *David* is a person.)

Right: *David was the one **who** first spotted the error.*

❑ The antecedent of a definite pronoun should be clear, not ambiguous.

Wrong: *Roger told Mike that **he** was going to start the next game.*
           (Who was going to start? Roger or Mike?)

Right: *Mike learned that he was going to start the next game when Roger told him so.*

Interrogative Pronouns

An interrogative pronoun (like *what, where, why,* and *when*) usually asks a question or refers to an un-

known, as in ***Where** are my keys?* But sometimes it can be used as a definite pronoun. When it is, remember two points:

❑ Use ***what*** only to refer to a **thing, *where*** to refer to a **place, *when*** to refer to a **time, *why*** to refer to a **reason, *who*** to refer to a **person,** and ***how*** to refer to an **explanation.**

Wrong: *An anachronism is **when** something doesn't fit in with its time period.*
           (An anachronism isn't a time, is it? It's a thing.)

Right: *An anachronism is something **that** doesn't fit in with its time period.*

❑ When following a comma, an interrogative pronoun usually takes the **immediately preceding** noun as its antecedent.

Wrong: *The actors will design their own sets, **who** are participating in the workshop.*
           (This is awkward because the *sets* are not what the pronoun *who* is logically referring to.)

Right: *The actors **who** are participating in the workshop will design their own sets.*

Pronoun Consistency

❑ **Be consistent** with any pronouns you use to refer to the same thing more than once in a sentence.

Wrong: *Even when **one** is dieting, **you** should always try to get enough vitamins.*
           (It sounds like we can't make up our minds about whom we're talking to!)

Right: *Even when **one** is dieting, **one** should always try to get enough vitamins.*

Concept Review 5: Pronoun-Antecedent Disagreement

1. Name three definite pronouns: _____

2. Name three indefinite pronouns: _____

3. Every _____ pronoun requires a specific antecedent.

4. What is an antecedent?

    _____

    _____

After each interrogative pronoun, write what kind of noun it must represent.

5. *what*   _____

6. *where*   _____

7. *how*   _____

8. *when*   _____

9. *why*   _____

10. *who*   _____

Circle all pronouns in the following sentences, and make any corrections that may be necessary.

11. *There are too many legal situations where misrepresentation seems to be standard practice.*

    _____

12. *If a student wants to memorize the meaning of a word, you should begin by understanding the concept it represents.*

    _____

13. *Caroline passed the phone to Julia, but she couldn't bring herself to speak.*

    _____

14. *Neither of the dogs wanted to give up their territory to the other.*

    _____

15. *David volunteered to be a ticket taker, not wanting to be the one that cleaned the aisles after the show.*

    _____

16. *They lost the game, which is why they didn't celebrate afterwards.*

    _____

Worksheet 5: Pronoun-Antecedent Disagreement

Correct any pronoun errors in each of the following sentences.

1. *Although the British parliament conducts debate under very formal and decorous rules, they can often produce very animated arguments.*

2. *Brown has always been committed to assisting their students by providing him or her with any necessary financial aid.*

3. *The media ignored the reports, probably because it believed they were not what the public were ready to hear.*

4. *The agency decided that they would give control of the project exclusively to Fiona and me.*

5. *Each of the girls wanted their idea for the logo design to be considered.*

6. *No one who has been through the first week of boot camp ever believes that they will make it through the entire 6 weeks.*

7. *Although you shouldn't read carelessly, one doesn't need to read slowly, either.*

8. *Neither gentleman thought that their team could win the championship.*

9. *Students sometimes aren't ready to handle the extra work when his or her courses become more demanding.*

10. *Many modern novels are concerned with situations where love goes unrequited.*

11. *Everybody is expected to do their share.*

12. *The entire team turned out to be robots who had been programmed to play lacrosse.*

13. *The radio station's board of directors drafted a proposal modifying their advertising policies.*

14. *The museum received so many donations that they actually had to return over a million dollars to the benefactors.*

15. *They usually give the most points to the skater that makes the fewest mistakes.*

16. *I like movies where the guy gets the girl.*

17. *Each swimmer will have a lane to themselves.*

18. *Who was the one that made the error in the third inning?*

Answer Key 5: Pronoun-Antecedent Disagreement

Concept Review 5

1. *I, you, she, he, it, they, we, us, them,* etc.

2. *anyone, everybody, each, either, one*

3. definite

4. An antecedent is the noun that a definite pronoun refers to.

5. a thing

6. a place

7. an explanation

8. a time

9. a reason

10. a person

11. pronouns: *there, where. There are too many legal situations in which misrepresentation seems to be standard practice. (Situations* aren't places, they're things.)

12. pronouns: *you, it. If a student wants to memorize the meaning of a word, he or she should begin by understanding the concept it represents.* (Agreement)

13. pronouns: *she, herself. Caroline passed the phone to Julia, but Julia couldn't bring herself to speak.* (Ambiguous antecedent)

14. pronouns: *neither, their. Neither of the dogs wanted to give up its territory to the other. (Neither* is singular.)

15. pronouns: *one, that. David volunteered to be a ticket taker, not wanting to be the one who cleaned the aisles after the show.* (David's a *who.*)

16. pronouns: *they, which, why, they.* (The sentence is correct because *which* refers to the clause *they lost the game*.)

Worksheet 5

1. *Although the British parliament conducts debate under very formal and decorous rules, it can often produce very animated arguments.*

2. *Brown has always been committed to assisting its students by providing them with any necessary financial aid.*

3. *The media ignored the reports, probably because they believed that those reports were not what the public was ready to hear.*

4. *The agency decided that it would give control of the project exclusively to Fiona and me.*

5. *Each of the girls wanted her idea for the logo design to be considered.*

6. *No one who has been through the first week of boot camp ever believes that he or she will make it through the entire 6 weeks.*

7. *Although you shouldn't read carelessly, you don't need to read slowly, either.*

8. *Neither gentleman thought that his team could win the championship.*

9. *Students sometimes aren't ready to handle the extra work when their courses become more demanding.*

10. *Many modern novels are concerned with situations in which love goes unrequited.*

11. *Everybody is expected to do his or her share.*

12. *The entire team turned out to be robots that had been programmed to play lacrosse.*

13. *The radio station's board of directors drafted a proposal modifying its advertising policies.*

14. *The museum received so many donations that it actually had to return over a million dollars to the benefactors.*

15. *They usually give the most points to the skater who makes the fewest mistakes.*

16. *I like movies in which the guy gets the girl.*

17. *Each swimmer will have a lane to herself (or himself).*

18. *Who was the one who made the error in the third inning?*

Lesson 6: Pronoun Case

Pronoun Cases

Every pronoun has a **case,** which indicates its relationship to a verb or noun. There are four common cases.

> **Subjective** (or *nominative*) pronouns (*I, you, he, she, we, they, who,* etc.) are used primarily as subjects of verbs.

> **Objective** pronouns (*me, you, him, her, them, whom,* etc.) are used primarily as **objects of verbs.**

> **Possessive** pronouns (*my/mine, her/hers, their/ theirs, whose* etc.) show **attribution or ownership.**

> **Reflexive** pronouns (*myself, yourself, himself, herself, themselves,* etc.) show an **object equated with the subject** or show **emphasis.**

Subjective Pronouns

Subjective pronouns are used only as **subjects** of verbs or **as predicate nominatives.**

Subject of real verb:	*Jenna and I were the only two at the meeting.*
Subject of implied verb:	*My brother is taller than I (am).* (Although the verb isn't written, its meaning is implied.)
Predicate nominative:	*The winner of the prize was she.*

❑ **A predicate nominative** is a pronoun or noun "linked" to the subject by a linking verb. It takes the **subjective case.**

> e.g. <u>Matthew</u>   <u>is</u>   <u>the new captain of the team</u>.
>   subject   l. verb   predicate nominative
>
> <u>The mountain</u> <u>became</u>   <u>a violent volcano</u>.
>   subject   l. verb   predicate nominative

Objective Pronouns

Objective pronouns are used as **objects of verbs** or as **objects of prepositions.**

Object of verb:	*My father struggled to raise my brother and* **me.**
Object of preposition:	*This should be a great opportunity for you and* **her.**

❑ When you have a compound phrase like *Tom and me* and *the coach and them,* deciding the case of the pronoun is easier if you leave out the other part of the phrase:

Sheila and (her or she?) took the cab uptown. ——— **She** *took the cab uptown* not **Her** *took the cab uptown.*

It was made for you and (me or I?) ——— *It was made for* **me** *not It was made for* **I.**

Possessive Pronouns

❑ **Don't** use the **objective case** when you should use the **possessive case** before a gerund:

Wrong:	*I resent* **you** *taking the car without asking.*
Right:	*I resent* **your** *taking the car without asking.* (The object of the verb *resent* is *taking:* the *taking* is what *I resent,* so using the objective pronoun *you* only confuses things. Since it's not *you whom I resent,* the possessive case *your* makes sense.)

Reflexive Pronouns

❑ Reflexive pronouns are used in only two ways: to show that a subject and object are the same, as in "I pinched **myself** to make sure I wasn't dreaming," or to emphasize a noun or pronoun, as in "I **myself** would never say such a thing." Never use a reflexive pronoun where an objective pronoun is required. Wrong: The crowd applauded Carl and **myself.** Right: The crowd applauded Carl and **me.**

Concept Review 6: Pronoun Case

1. Name four subjective pronouns: _____

2. Subjective pronouns are used as _____

   or _____

3. Name 4 objective pronouns: _____

4. Objective pronouns are used as _____

   or _____

5. Name 4 possessive pronouns: _____

6. Name 4 reflexive pronouns: _____

7. Reflexive pronouns are used to _____

   or _____

Choose the correct pronoun in each sentence below.

8. *The climb was much easier for them than it was for Jeff and (I/me/myself).*

9. *The other contestants did not seem as confident as (he/him).*

10. *Within a week, George and (me/I) will have completed the project.*

11. *(Us/We) detectives are always careful to follow every lead.*

12. *Every student should make (his or her/their) own study plan.*

13. *They never seem to listen to the opinions of (us/we) students as they should.*

Worksheet 6: Pronoun Case

Choose the correct pronoun in each sentence below.

1. *The university presented the honor to David and (he/him).*

2. *After the game, we all agreed that no one had played harder than (he/him).*

3. *Justine and (me/I) have always been closest friends.*

4. *There is no point in (our/us) delaying the tests any longer.*

5. *I shall grant immortality to (he/him) who can pull the sword from the stone.*

6. *It seems quite clear that you and (I/me) will have to work together to solve this problem.*

7. *It might be hard for (him and me/he and I) to agree.*

8. *The other cheerleaders and (her/she) needed to practice on the weekend.*

9. *The tabloid media were thrilled about (him/his) making such a fool of himself in public.*

10. *(We/Us) and the other members debated the issue for over 2 hours.*

11. *The owners of the club offered my wife and (me/I) a free bottle of wine with dinner.*

12. *No other runner on the team could outrun (myself/me).*

13. *The teachers were getting tired of (him/his) constantly falling asleep in class.*

14. *The ballpark always held a special attraction for Dave and (I/me).*

15. *Our friends gave a party for Ingrid and (I/me/myself).*

16. *In anticipation of the trip, I bought (me/myself) a nice new suitcase.*

Answer Key 6: Pronoun Case

Concept Review 6

1. *I, he, she, you, we, they, who*

2. *subjects of verbs* or *predicate nominatives*

3. *me, him, her, you, us, them, whom*

4. *objects of verbs* or *objects of prepositions*

5. *my, mine, her, hers, his, your, yours, their, theirs, our, ours*

6. *myself, yourself, himself, herself, ourselves, themselves*

7. *show that the object of the verb is the same as the subject* or *emphasize an adjacent noun or pronoun*

8. *The climb was much easier for them than it was for Jeff and me*. (object of a preposition)

9. *The other contestants did not seem as confident as he (did).* (subject of an implied verb)

10. *Within a week, George and I will have completed the project.* (subject of a verb)

11. *We detectives are always careful to follow every lead.* (subject of a verb)

12. *Every student should make his or her own study plan.* (possessive modifier of noun; must agree with singular antecedent)

13. *They never seem to listen to the opinions of us students as they should.* (object of a preposition)

Worksheet 6

1. *The university presented the honor to David and him.* (object of a preposition)

2. *After the game, we agreed that no one had played harder than he.* (*than he did*: subject of an implied verb)

3. *Justine and I have always been closest friends.* (subject)

4. *There is no point in our delaying the tests any longer.* (*Delaying* is the object of the preposition, so the pronoun should not be objective.)

5. *I shall grant immortality to him who can pull the sword from the stone.* (object of a preposition)

6. *It seems quite clear that you and I will have to work together to solve this problem.* (subject)

7. *It might be hard for him and me to agree.* (object of a preposition)

8. *The other cheerleaders and she needed to practice on the weekend.* (subject)

9. *The tabloid media were thrilled about his making such a fool of himself in public.* (*Making* is the object of the preposition)

10. *We and the other members debated the issue for over 2 hours.* (subject)

11. *The owners of the club offered my wife and me a free bottle of wine with dinner.* (object of a verb)

12. *No other runner on the team could outrun me.* (object of a verb)

13. *The teachers were getting tired of his constantly falling asleep in class.* (*Falling* is the object, so the pronoun should not be in the objective case.)

14. *The ballpark always held a special attraction for Dave and me.* (object of a preposition)

15. *Our friends gave a party for Ingrid and me.* (object of a preposition)

16. *In anticipation of the trip, I bought myself a nice new suitcase.* (The object and subject represent the same person, so the object should be in the reflexive case.)

Lesson 7: Dangling and Misplaced Participles

What Is a Participle?

❏ There are two kinds of **participles:**

Present participles always end in -ing, e.g., colliding, writing, swimming, eating, fighting.

Past participles often end in -ed or -en, but not always, e.g., collided, written, swum, eaten, fought.

A participle is a verb form used when the verb is **a phrase with a helping verb,** as in the following sentences:

e.g. *I was <u>walking</u> through the lobby.*
We had been <u>talking</u> for over an hour.

I have not yet <u>begun</u> to fight.
The chairs were <u>pushed</u> against the wall.

Participles as Verbs or Adjectives

A participle can be used as a **verb part** (with a helping verb), as in *He is **writing** his term paper* or *They have **taken** the car.* It can also be used as an **adjective,** as in *Don't trust a **smiling** salesman* or *I like **frozen** treats.*

❏ Don't confuse **present participles** with **gerunds.** They look the same, but they play very different roles. Present participles act as **verb parts** or **adjectives** (as above), but gerunds act as **nouns,** as in ***Writing** is harder than it looks.* (*Writing* is the subject of the verb *is,* so it is a noun and a gerund.)

Dangling and Misplaced Participial Phrases

❏ A **participial phrase** is a modifying phrase that includes a participle. Such a phrase always describes something, so it acts like an adjective or adverb. It is usually separated from the main part of the sentence by one or more commas.

e.g. ***Eating ravenously,** the vultures remained on the carcass until it was picked clean.*

*The runners, **exhausted from the final sprint,** stumbled over the finish line.*

❏ If a participial phrase starts a sentence, the word it modifies **must follow immediately after the comma.**

Wrong: *After **having studied** all night, the professor postponed the test until Friday.*

(The participial phrase modifies a noun. Who had studied all night? Certainly not *the professor,* so the modifying phrase **dangles.**)

One way to correct a dangling participle is simply to place the correct noun next to the participial phrase:

Better: *After **having studied** all night, **I** was frustrated to learn that the professor had postponed the test until Friday.* (*I* answers the question: *who had studied?*)

Another way is to incorporate a subject into the participial phrase, turning it into a dependent clause:

Better: *After **I had studied** all night, the professor postponed the test until Friday.*

❏ Every participial phrase **should be as close as possible to the word it modifies.** If a modifier sounds as if it modifies the wrong thing, it is "misplaced" and must be moved.

Wrong: *Bob found his watch **walking to the bathroom.***
(Was the watch *walking?* Of course not, so the participial phrase is misplaced.)

Better: ***Walking to the bathroom,** Bob found his watch.*

Also good: *Bob found his watch as he was **walking to the bathroom.***

Wrong: *It was difficult for William to hear the announcements **waiting for the train.***
(Were the *announcements* waiting for the train? Of course not.)

Better: ***While waiting for the train,** William found it difficult to hear the announcements.*

Concept Review 7: Dangling and Misplaced Participles

1. If a participial phrase followed by a comma begins a sentence, it must be followed by

_____

Give the past and present participle forms of each of the following verbs.

2. *push*   past participle _____   present participle _____

3. *run*   past participle _____   present participle _____

4. *take*   past participle _____   present participle _____

Identify the underlined word as a *gerund* or a *present participle*.

5. *I've loved <u>singing</u> ever since I was a little girl.*   5. _____

6. *I doubt that they would be <u>working</u> this late at night.*   6. _____

7. *<u>Calling</u> me a bum was a very mean thing to do.*   7. _____

Circle the participle in each sentence, then write whether it is an *adjective* or *verb participle.*

8. *We saw the meteorite as it was falling from the sky.*   8. _____

9. *We saw the falling meteorite.*   9. _____

10. *The urn was tarnished and chipped.*   10. _____

11. *The urn was chipped at the auction.*   11. _____

12. *The evidence was damaging to the defense.*   12. _____

13. *I could never have run so fast without those shoes.*   13. _____

Circle the participle in each sentence, then rewrite the sentence so that the participle does not "dangle."

14. *Looking at your essay, it seems to me that you need to be more specific.*

_____

15. *Turning the corner, the stadium came into our view.*

_____

16. *Although exhausted after the night's work, Martha's creative instincts compelled her to keep writing.*

_____

17. *Without waiting for an answer, David's eagerness got the better of him, and he left in a flash.*

_____

18. *Thinking her friends were right behind her, it was frightening for Alison to discover that they were gone.*

_____

Worksheet 7: Dangling and Misplaced Participles

Circle the participles in the following sentences, then rewrite the sentence, if necessary, to correct any "dangling" participles.

1. *Although angered by the irrationality of his opponent, Senator Sanchez's plan was to address each point calmly.*

   _____

2. *Watching from the bridge, the fireworks bloomed spectacularly over the water.*

   _____

3. *Without admitting her transgression, the club found it hard to forgive Megan.*

   _____

4. *Although mildly discolored by the harsh sunlight, the sofa has retained much of its original beauty.*

   _____

5. *Exhausted from the day's climbing, the looming storm forced the hikers to pitch an early camp.*

   _____

6. *Having studied for hours, it was very disappointing that I did so poorly on the exam.*

   _____

7. *Without being aware of it, termites can infest your home if you don't take the proper precautions.*

   _____

8. *Before working at the bank, no one thought I could hold such a responsible position.*

   _____

9. *Lacking any real sailing skills, David's concern was mainly with keeping the ship afloat.*

   _____

10. *Not wanting to be fooled again, she had her husband followed by a private investigator.*

   _____

Answer Key 7: Dangling and Misplaced Participles

Concept Review 7

1. the noun phrase that it modifies

2. past participle *pushed*, present participle *pushing*

3. past participle *run* (not *ran*), present participle *running*

4. past participle *taken* (not *took*), present participle *taking*

5. gerund (It's the object of the verb *loved*.)

6. present participle (The verb is *would be working*.)

7. gerund (It's the subject of the verb *was*.)

8. participle: *falling*, verb participle

9. participle: *falling*, adjective

10. participles: *tarnished* and *chipped*, adjectives

11. participle: *chipped*, verb participle

12. participle: *damaging*, adjective

13. participle: *run*, verb participle

Each revised sentence below represents only one possible revision to correct the dangling participle. We have chosen what seems to be the clearest and most concise of the possibilities.

14. participle: *looking. It seems to me, <u>as I look at your essay,</u> that you need to be more specific.*

15. participle: *turning. <u>As we turned</u> the corner, the stadium came into view.*

16. participle: *exhausted. Although <u>Martha was</u> exhausted after the night's work, <u>her</u> creative instincts compelled her to keep writing.*

17. *David's eagerness got the better of him, <u>and without waiting for an answer,</u> he left in a flash.*

18. *Thinking her friends were right behind her, <u>Alison was frightened</u> to discover that they were gone.*

Worksheet 7

Each revised sentence below represents only one possible revision to correct the dangling participle. We have chosen what seems to be the clearest and most concise of the possibilities.

1. participle: *angered. Although angered by the irrationality of his opponent, <u>Senator Sanchez planned</u> to address each point calmly.*

2. participle: *watching. <u>As we watched</u> from the bridge, the fireworks bloomed spectacularly over the water.*

3. participle: *admitting. <u>Because Megan would not admit</u> her transgression, the club found it hard to forgive <u>her</u>.*

4. participle: *discolored. Although mildly discolored by the harsh sunlight, the sofa has retained much of its original beauty. (Correct)*

5. participle: *exhausted. <u>The looming storm forced the hikers, exhausted from the day's climbing, to pitch an early camp.</u>*

6. participle: *having. Having studied for hours, <u>I was very</u> disappointed to do so poorly on the exam.*

7. participle: *being. Without <u>your</u> being aware of it, termites can infest your home if you don't take the proper precautions.*

8. participle: *working. Before <u>I started</u> working at the bank, no one thought I could hold such a responsible position.*

9. participle: *lacking. Lacking any real sailing skills, <u>David was mainly concerned</u> with keeping the ship afloat.*

10. participle: *wanting. Not wanting to be fooled again, she had her husband followed by a private investigator. (Correct)*

Lesson 8:
Other Misplaced Modifiers

The Law of Proximity

❑ Any modifier **should be as close as possible to the word it modifies.**

Of course, there are many other kinds of modifying phrases besides participial phrases, and you should familiarize yourself with them.

Misplaced Prepositional Phrases

Prepositional phrases are modifying phrases. They are sometimes **adjectives,** which means they modify nouns:

> e.g. *The dog **in the car** was barking.* (The prepositional phrase answers the question *which **dog?***)

They may also be **adverbs,** which means they modify verbs, adjectives, or other adverbs:

> e.g. *David walked **into the pole.*** (The prepositional phrase answers the question *where did David walk?*)

❑ Like any modifying phrase, a prepositional phrase can be misplaced:

> Wrong: **As a physician,** *it was difficult for me to see such suffering.*

The prepositional phrase *as a physician* answers the question *what is my role?* So it modifies *I,* not *it:*

> Right: **As a physician,** *I found it difficult to see such suffering.*

Misplaced Appositives

An **appositive** is a noun phrase that accompanies and expands another noun, as in

> *Franklin, **the only one of us who owned a car,** agreed to drive us all to the game.*

❑ An appositive must always be adjacent to the noun it modifies.

> Wrong: **A splendid example of late synthetic cubism,** *Picasso painted* Three Musicians *in the summer of 1924.*
> (Of course, Picasso is not an example of synthetic cubism, so the appositive is dangling.)

> Better: **A splendid example of late synthetic cubism,** Three Musicians *was painted by Picasso in the summer of 1924.*

> Better: *Picasso painted* Three Musicians, **a splendid example of late synthetic cubism,** *in the summer of 1924.*

Misplaced Infinitives

Recall, from Lesson 3, that an **infinitive** is the basic *to* _____ form of a verb that usually serves as a **noun,** as in *I love **to shop.*** Infinitives can also serve as **adjectives.**

> e.g. *We have a lot more math problems **to do.***
> (It answers the question *what kind of **problems** are they?*)

They can also serve as **adverbs.**

> e.g. *We are working **to earn** money for the trip.* (It answers the question *why are we **working?***)

❑ Because infinitives are often modifiers, they can be misplaced.

> Wrong: **To get** *our attention, we saw Mr. Genovese take out a giant boa constrictor.*
> (*To get* answers the question *why did he **take** it out?* So *take* should be the closest verb to the phrase.
> We can rearrange the sentence in a couple of ways to fix this.)

> Right: **To get** *our attention, Mr. Genovese took out a giant boa constrictor.*

> Right: *We saw Mr. Genovese take out a giant boa constrictor **to get** our attention.*

Concept Review 8: Other Misplaced Modifiers

Label each underlined phrase as a participial phrase (PART), a prepositional phrase (PREP), an appositive (APP), or an infinitive phrase (INF). Although the SAT I will NOT ask you to use these terms to label phrases, this exercise will help you to spot modifier errors more easily.

1. My friend _the lawyer_ told me that I should never sign any contract _without first reading it carefully_.

2. We should go _to the meeting_ _to see whether they need our help_ _with the planning_.

3. _Despite spraining her ankle_, our first mate was able to navigate our schooner _into port_.

4. Four score and seven years ago our fathers brought forth _on this continent_, a new nation, _conceived in liberty_, and _dedicated to the proposition that all men are created equal_.

5. Now we are engaged _in a great civil war_, _testing whether that nation or any nation so conceived and so dedicated, can long endure_.

6. We have come _to dedicate a portion_ _of that field_ as a final resting place _for those who here gave their lives_ that that nation might live.

7. It is for us _the living_, rather, _to be dedicated here_ _to the unfinished work_ which they who fought here have thus far so nobly advanced.

8. It is rather _for us_ _to be here_ _dedicated to the great task_ _remaining before us_—that _from these honored dead_ we take increased devotion _to that cause_ _for which_ they gave the last full measure of devotion—that we here highly resolve that these dead shall not have died in vain—that this nation, _under God_, shall have a new birth of freedom—and that government _of the people_, _by the people_, _for the people_, shall not perish from the earth.

9. We _the people_, in order _to form a more perfect union_, establish justice, ensure domestic tranquility, provide _for the common defense_, promote the general welfare and secure the blessings of liberty to ourselves and our posterity, do ordain and establish this Constitution _for the United States of America_.

Worksheet 8:
Other Misplaced Modifiers

In each of the following sentences, underline and label all participial phrases (PART), prepositional phrases (PREP), appositives (APP), and infinitive phrases (INF), and rewrite any sentence to fix any misplaced modifiers.

1. *Without so much as a blink, the gleaming sword was unsheathed by the warrior.*
   _____

2. *To maintain good health, physicians suggest that both vigorous exercise and good eating habits are required.*
   _____

3. *We found my lost earring walking through the parking lot.*
   _____

4. *Having run for over 4 hours, the finish line was still 10 miles ahead of her.*
   _____

5. *Even with a sprained ankle, the coach forced Adam back into the game.*
   _____

6. *To find a good restaurant, there are many good online guides to help you.*
   _____

7. *In search of a good calculator, not a single store in the mall could help me.*
   _____

8. *A dutiful wife and mother, we were surprised to hear Carol complaining about domestic life.*
   _____

9. *To get a good jump out of the starting blocks, most sprinters say that good body positioning is essential.*
   _____

10. *Among the most sought-after collectibles on the market, we found the antique toys at a garage sale.*
    _____

Answer Key 8:
Other Misplaced Modifiers

Concept Review 8

1. *the lawyer* (APP)
   without first reading it carefully (PREP)
2. *to the meeting* (PREP)
   to see whether they need our help (INF)
   with the planning (PREP)
3. *Despite spraining her ankle* (PREP containing a PART)
   into port (PREP)
4. *on this continent* (PREP)
   conceived in liberty (PART containing a PREP)
   dedicated to the proposition that all men are created equal (PART containing a PREP)
5. *in a great civil war* (PREP)
   testing whether that nation . . . (PART)
6. *to dedicate a portion* (INF)
   of that field (PREP)
   for those who here gave their lives (PREP)

7. *the living* (APP)
   to be dedicated here (INF containing a PART)
   to the unfinished work (PREP)
8. *for us* (PREP)
   to be here (INF)
   dedicated to the great task (PART containing a PREP)
   remaining before us (PART containing a PREP)
   from these honored dead (PREP)
   to that cause (PREP)
   for which (PREP)
   under God (PREP)
   of the people (PREP)
   by the people (PREP)
   for the people (PREP)
9. *the people* (APP)
   to form a more perfect union (INF)
   for the common defense (PREP)
   of the United States of America (PREP)

Worksheet 8

Each of these answers provides only one possible correction. On some sentences, other corrections are possible.

1. *Without so much as a blink* (PREP), the gleaming sword was unsheathed *by the warrior* (PREP).
   Correction: *Without so much as a blink, the warrior unsheathed the gleaming sword.*
2. *To maintain good health* (INF), physicians suggest that both vigorous exercise and good eating habits are required.
   Correction: *Physicians suggest that both vigorous exercise and good eating habits are required to maintain good health.*
3. We found my lost earring *walking through the parking lot* (PART containing a PREP).
   Correction: *Walking through the parking lot, we found my lost earring.*
4. *Having run for over 4 hours* (PART containing a PREP), the finish line was still 10 miles ahead *of her* (PREP).
   Correction: *Although she had run for over 4 hours, the finish line was still 10 miles ahead of her.*
5. Even *with a sprained ankle* (PREP), the coach forced Adam back *into the game* (PREP).
   Correction: *Even through Adam had a sprained ankle, the coach forced him back into the game.*

6. *To find a good restaurant* (INF), there are many good online guides *to help you* (INF).
   Correction: *There are many good online guides to help you find a good restaurant.*
7. *In search of a good calculator* (PREP), not a single store *in the mall* (PREP) could help me.
   Correction: *Not a single store in the mall could help me find a good calculator.*
8. *A dutiful wife and mother* (APP), we were surprised to hear Carol complaining *about domestic life* (PREP).
   Correction: *We were surprised to hear Carol, a dutiful wife and mother, complaining about domestic life.*
9. *To get a good jump* (INF) *out of the starting blocks* (PREP), most sprinters say that good body positioning is essential.
   Correction: *Most sprinters say that good body positioning is essential for getting a good jump out of the starting blocks.*
10. *Among the most sought-after collectibles* (PREP) *on the market* (PREP), we found the antique toys *at a garage sale* (PREP).
    Correction: *We found the antique toys, which are among the most sought-after collectibles on the market, at a garage sale.*

Lesson 9: Tricky Tenses

Verb Tenses

The **tense** of a verb is what indicates its place and extent in time. There are two common situations in which tenses can be tricky: those with "perfect" verbs and those with "timeless" verbs.

"Perfect" Verbs

You use the **perfect tenses** whenever you need to indicate that some event is **completed** before some other point in time. (Here, the word *perfect* means *complete*, not *flawless*.) They are usually **relative** tenses, that is, they show a particular relationship to another verb or reference to time within the sentence. All perfect tenses use the helping verb *to have*, as in we **had walked,** we **have walked,** and *we* **will have walked.**

❑ The **past perfect tense** shows that an event had been completed before another point in the past. You can think of it as the "past past" tense.

  e.g. *By the time we* **arrived** *at the reception, Glen* **had** *already* **given** *the toast.*

  past perfect   past   now
  ───────┼────────────┼────────────┼──────▶ time
      had given   arrived

❑ When a sentence contains two past tense verbs, check whether one event was completed before the other. If so, the earlier event should be given the past perfect tense.

❑ The **present perfect tense,** unlike the other perfect tenses, usually does not show completion, but that an event either **extends from the past to the present** or **occurs at an extended or unspecified time in the past.** You can think of it as the "past plus present" tense or the "unspecific past."

  e.g. *She* **has been** *so nice to me.*
  (This means *she was nice to me* and also *she still is nice to me.* It combines past and present.)

  e.g. *We* **have taken** *only two tests this semester.*
  (The taking of the tests did not happen at one specific time, but over an extended time in the past.)

❑ The **future perfect tense** shows that something will have been completed before some time in the future.

  e.g. *By* **Friday,** *we* **will have completed** *the entire project.*

         now   future perfect   future
  ◀───────┼────────────┼────────────┼──────▶ time
              will have completed   Friday

❑ Participles must be "perfect," too, when they indicate an action completed before another action.

  e.g. ***Having walked*** *all night, we were desperate to find rest at dawn.*
  (The *walking* was **completed** by dawn, so the participle is "past perfect.")

"Timeless" Verbs

❑ When you need to discuss a theory, an artistic work, or a general nonhistorical fact, the verb that describes it is "timeless" and should take the **present tense** by default.

Wrong: *The ancient Greek philosopher Zeno believed that all motion was an illusion.*

Right: *The ancient Greek philosopher Zeno believed that all motion is an illusion.*
  (The *believing* is in the past, since Zeno's long gone, but the theory is timeless.)

Concept Review 9: Tricky Tenses

1. When are the perfect tenses used?

2. What kinds of ideas are conveyed by "timeless" present-tense verbs?

Circle the correct verb in each of the following sentences:

3. Glen (came/has come) to work exhausted this morning because he (stayed/had stayed) up all last night.

4. Already, and without (spending/having spent) so much as an hour on research, Dale (wrote/has written) the first draft of her essay.

5. (Developing/Having developed) the first compressed-air automobile, he (hoped/had hoped) to reveal it to the world at the exposition.

6. Shakespeare's tragedies (were/are) concerned with the deepest aspects of the human condition.

The meaning of the following sentence is ambiguous.

His legs ached because he ran farther than he ever had [run] before.

Rewrite it using the correct tenses to indicate that

7. The aching started before he finished running: _____

8. The aching started after he finished running: _____

Fix any tense problems in the following sentences.

9. Right after school, we had gone to Mario's for a pizza and a few Cokes.

_____

10. Finding no evidence against the accused, the detective had to release him.

_____

11. Being captured by the rebels, David soon began to fear he would never escape.

_____

12. When I got home, I wrote an essay on the baseball game that I saw that afternoon.

_____

Worksheet 9: Tricky Tenses

Correct any tense errors in the following sentences.

1. *By the time the committee had adjourned, it voted on all 4 key proposals.*

   _____

2. *In the evening, we had a nice meal with the same group of people we skied with that afternoon.*

   _____

3. *By the time I am done with finals, I will write 4 major papers.*

   _____

4. *Being nominated for office, Ellen felt that she had to run an honest campaign.*

   _____

5. *It surprised us to learn that Venus was almost the same size as Earth.*

   _____

6. *Reading* The Sun Also Rises, *I feel as if I've learned a great deal about bullfighting.*

   _____

7. *Most Oscar nominees claimed that they were happy simply to be nominated.*

   _____

8. *When the epidemic struck Rwanda, the entire population had suffered.*

   _____

9. *I have never felt so free as when I am running.*

   _____

10. *Centuries ago, physicians had believed that illnesses were caused by imbalances in bodily fluids.*

    _____

11. *David has been the president of the club ever since it was founded.*

    _____

12. *Over the last several years, real estate values increased by over 20%.*

    _____

13. *Students often worry excessively about grades and will forget about actually understanding the concepts.*

    _____

14. *We need not bother to patch the hull now that the entire boat had been inundated.*

    _____

15. *By the time we arrived at the tent where the reception would be held, the caterers set up all the chairs.*

    _____

16. *We will have been in this house for 3 years in February.*

    _____

Answer Key 9: Tricky Tenses

Concept Review 9

1. when showing that an event was completed before another event, or, in the case of the present perfect tense, when showing that an event occurs over an extended time in the past or extends from the past to the present

2. theories, general nonhistorical facts, and works of art

3. Glen _came_ to work exhausted this morning because he _had stayed_ up all last night. (The _staying up_ was completed before he _came to work_.)

4. Already, and without _having spent_ so much as an hour on research, Dale _has written_ the first draft of her essay. (The word _already_ establishes the current time as a reference point. Since the verbs indicate actions completed prior to now, they take the present perfect tense.)

5. _Having developed_ the first compressed-air automobile, he _hoped_ to reveal it to the world at the exposition. (He must have _developed_ it before he could _hope to reveal it_.)

6. Shakespeare's tragedies _are_ concerned with the deepest aspects of the human condition. (His works are still available to us, so they get the present tense.)

7. His legs ached because he _was running_ farther than he ever had before.

8. His legs ached because he _had run_ farther than he ever had before.

9. Right after school, we _went_ to Mario's for a pizza and a few Cokes. (No need for past perfect.)

10. _Having found_ no evidence against the accused, the detective had to release him. (The search for evidence was completed before the release.)

11. _Having been_ captured by the rebels, David soon began to fear he would never escape. (The capture occurred before his fear set in.)

12. When I got home, I wrote an essay on the baseball game that I _had seen_ that afternoon. (The _writing_ happened after the _seeing_.)

Worksheet 9

1. By the time the committee _adjourned_, it _had voted_ on all 4 key proposals. (The voting was completed before the adjournment, so it should take the perfect tense.)

2. In the evening, we had a nice meal with the same group of people we _had skied_ with that afternoon. (The skiing was completed before the meal, so it should take the perfect tense.)

3. By the time I am done with finals, I _will have written_ 4 major papers. (The writing will be completed before the finals.)

4. _Having been nominated_ for office, Ellen felt that she had to run an honest campaign. (The _nomination_ must be completed before the _running_ can start.)

5. It surprised us to learn that Venus _is_ almost the same size as Earth. (Facts take the present tense.)

6. _Having read_ The Sun Also Rises, I feel as if I've learned a great deal about bullfighting. (Since the learning occurred over an extended time in the past, the present perfect tense is appropriate; since the _reading_ was prior to or simultaneous with the _learning_, it must also be in the perfect form.)

7. Most Oscar nominees claimed that they were happy simply to _have been nominated_. (The _nominating_ must have been completed if they are happy about the outcome.)

8. When the epidemic struck Rwanda, the entire population _suffered_. (Since the _suffering_ occurred when the epidemic _struck_, the two verbs should have the same tense.)

9. I _never feel_ so free as when I am running. (This expresses a general fact, so it is "timeless.")

10. Centuries ago, physicians _believed_ that illnesses were caused by imbalances in bodily fluids. (Since this expresses a theory that has been disproven, it is not "timeless," but relegated to the past.)

11. David has been the president of the club ever since it was founded. (Correct)

12. Over the last several years, real estate values _have increased_ by over 20%. (The increase occurred over an extended time in the past.)

13. Students often worry excessively about grades and _forget_ about actually understanding the concepts. (Tense consistency requires the present tense.)

14. We need not bother to patch the hull now that the entire boat _has been_ inundated. (The present perfect is needed to show the connection to the present, which is implied by the present-tense verb _bother_.)

15. By the time we arrived at the tent where the reception would be held, the caterers _had set up_, all the chairs. (The _setting up_ was completed before we _arrived_.)

16. We will have been in this house for 3 years in February. (Correct)

Lesson 19: Idiom Errors

What Is an Idiom?

Idioms are common phrases with quirky, nonliteral meanings. Most idioms, like *carry through, across the board, come on strong, get your feet wet, bang for the buck, all ears, pull your leg, eat crow,* etc., are so ingrained in our language that we hardly notice that their meanings are so nonliteral. We appreciate our idioms when we hear someone speak who has just learned English, since the idioms take the longest to learn.

Watch Your Prepositions

The SAT I won't expect you to memorize the thousands of idioms in the English language, but it does expect you to recognize **preposition errors.** Remember from Lesson 2 that prepositions are words like *to, from, of, for, by, in, before, with, beyond,* and *up* that show relative position or direction. Certain idiomatic phrases, like *arguing with,* require a particular preposition. (That is, saying something like *She was arguing **against** her brother* is not a proper idiom.) The choice of preposition is not usually a matter of logic, as in the sentence.

> *The house was on fire, so the firefighters put it out.*

This sentence contains two prepositions, *on* and *out,* but neither is used literally or logically: the house wasn't really "on" a fire, and the firemen didn't put the fire "out." But if you tried to make the sentence literal and logical, it would sound ridiculous or overly stilted:

> *The house was aflame, so the firefighters extinguished the blaze.*

So idioms are an important part of clear and effective language.

❑ When you notice a preposition in a sentence, always ask: "Is that preposition necessary, and if so, is it the correct preposition for that particular phrase?"

Wrong: *We were no longer satisfied **at the level of** service we were receiving.*
(The prepositions are *at* and *of.* The idiom *level of service* is correct, but the idiom *satisfied at* is not. The correct idiom is *satisfied with.*)

Right: *We were no longer satisfied **with** the level of service we were receiving.*

ESP: Eliminate Superfluous Prepositions

❑ Casual speech often uses extra prepositions. When you write, however, try to eliminate unnecessary prepositions. Notice that in phrases like the following, the preposition is unnecessary and thus "nonstandard."

e.g. *The pole did not extend ~~out~~ far enough.*

> *Since my injury, it hurts to climb ~~up~~ the stairs.*

> *Although clearly angry, the students were not yet ready to fight ~~against~~ the ruling.*

> *We were unsuccessful in our attempt to extract ~~out~~ the chemical from the venom.*

> *The illness can make one dizzy and prone to falling ~~down~~.*

> *If you don't hurry, you'll miss ~~out on~~ all the fun!*

> *There were plenty of volunteers to help ~~out~~ with the race.*

> *Before we prepare the steaks, we should fry ~~up~~ some peppers.*

> *Her speed and strength helped her to dominate ~~over~~ her opponents.*

Concept Review 10:
Idiom Errors

Choose the correct preposition or phrase (if any) to complete each of the following sentences. If no word or phrase is required, circle—.

1. *I prefer spaghetti (to/over/more than/—) linguine.*

2. *The students were protesting (against/over/—) the decision to cut financial aid.*

3. *We are all concerned (about/with/—) your decision to drop out of school.*

4. *It took nearly an hour to open (up/—) the trunk.*

5. *Eleanor has always been concerned (with/about/—) feminist issues.*

6. *We all agreed (on/with/about/—) the decision to go skiing rather than hiking.*

7. *She would not agree (to/on/with/about) the plea bargain.*

8. *We found dozens of old photographs hidden (in/—) between the pages.*

9. *Good study habits are necessary (to/for/in) academic success.*

10. *The new house color is not very different (from/than/to/—) the old one.*

11. *His girlfriend was angry (with/at/—) him for not calling sooner.*

12. *It will be many years before we fill (up/—) all the pages in this photo album.*

13. *They were both angry (about/at/with) the boys' behavior.*

14. *You should plan (to come/on coming) before 6:00 p.m.*

15. *Matt was kicked off (of/—) the team for drinking at a party.*

16. *We will make sure that your contract complies (with/to/—) the laws of your state.*

17. *After the operation, Denise was no longer capable (of playing/to play) the violin.*

Worksheet 10: Idiom Errors

Consider the idiom in each sentence and fill in the correct preposition, if one is required.

1. *The interview provided insight _____ what great directors think about.*

2. *We were very angry _____ him for ignoring our phone calls.*

3. *Her tests include questions that seem very different _____ those that we see in the homework.*

4. *My mother preferred my singing _____ my practicing guitar.*

5. *Detective Simone ran in pursuit _____ the perpetrators.*

6. *We had to shoo the cat off _____ the car.*

7. *When she arrived on campus, she felt truly independent _____ her parents for the first time.*

8. *They scoured the bedroom in search _____ the missing bracelet.*

9. *We were very angry _____ the exorbitant price of gasoline at the corner gas station.*

10. *Although they were friends, they always seemed to be arguing _____ each other.*

11. *I am concerned _____ your failure to pass the last few quizzes.*

12. *We all agreed _____ the color scheme for the wedding.*

13. *Tony had to climb _____ the ladder to get to the top bunk.*

14. *As a public defender, he was very concerned _____ the legal issue of search and seizure.*

15. *It was hard not to agree _____ her offer of a free movie ticket.*

16. *The vaccine was intended to protect everyone working on the project _____ disease.*

17. *I could hardly pay attention in class because I was daydreaming _____ the prom.*

18. *Allison and her sister both excel _____ dance and music.*

19. *I could never dream _____ confronting the coach with such a trivial concern.*

20. *I arrived at the meeting too late to raise my objection _____ the proposal.*

21. *The third edition of this book really doesn't differ very much at all _____ the first two.*

22. *I beg to differ _____ you, but your story does not fit my recollection at all.*

23. *If we don't act soon, we may miss _____ the opportunity to lock in the lowest rates.*

Answer Key 10: Idiom Errors

Concept Review 10

1. I prefer spaghetti <u>to</u> linguine.

2. The students were protesting (none needed) *the* decision to cut financial aid.

3. We are all concerned <u>about</u> your decision to drop out of school. (*Concerned about* means *worried about.*)

4. It took nearly an hour to open (none needed) *the* trunk.

5. Eleanor has always been concerned <u>with</u> feminist issues. (*Concerned with* means *occupied with* or *involved in.*)

6. We all agreed <u>on</u> the decision to go skiing rather than hiking. (You *agree on* mutual decisions or plans.)

7. She would not agree <u>to</u> the plea bargain. (You *agree to* offers.)

8. We found dozens of old photographs hidden (none needed) *between* the pages.

9. Good study habits are necessary <u>to</u> (or sometimes <u>for</u>) academic success.

10. The new house color is not very different <u>from</u> the old one. (Use *than* only with **comparatives** like *bigger; different* is not a comparative.)

11. His girlfriend was angry <u>with</u> him for not calling sooner. (You get *angry with* people.)

12. It will be many years before we fill (none needed) all the pages in this photo album.

13. They were both angry <u>about</u> the boys' behavior. (You get *angry about* situations.)

14. You should plan <u>to come</u> before 6:00 p.m. (*Plan to* means *make a plan to,* but *plan on* means *rely on.*)

15. Matt was kicked off (none needed) the team for drinking at a party.

16. We will make sure that your contract complies <u>with</u> the laws of your state.

17. After the operation, Denise was no longer capable <u>of playing</u> the violin.

Worksheet 10

1. The interview provided insight <u>into</u> what great directors think about.

2. We were very angry <u>with</u> him for ignoring our phone calls.

3. Her tests include questions that seem very different <u>from</u> those that we see in the homework.

4. My mother preferred my singing <u>to</u> my practicing guitar.

5. Detective Simone ran in pursuit <u>of</u> the perpetrators.

6. We had to shoo the cat off (none needed) the car.

7. When she arrived on campus, she felt truly independent <u>of</u> her parents for the first time.

8. They scoured the bedroom in search <u>of</u> the missing bracelet.

9. We were very angry <u>about</u> the exorbitant price of gasoline at the corner gas station.

10. Although they were friends, they always seemed to be arguing <u>with</u> each other.

11. I am concerned <u>about</u> your failure to pass the last few quizzes.

12. We all agreed <u>on</u> the color scheme for the wedding.

13. Tony had to climb (none needed) *the* ladder to get to the top bunk.

14. As a public defender, he was very concerned <u>with</u> the legal issue of search and seizure.

15. It was hard not to agree <u>to</u> her offer of a free movie ticket.

16. The vaccine was intended to protect everyone working on the project <u>from</u> disease.

17. I could hardly pay attention in class because I was daydreaming <u>about</u> the prom.

18. Allison and her sister both excel <u>in</u> dance and music.

19. I could never dream <u>of</u> confronting the coach with such a trivial concern.

20. I arrived at the meeting too late to raise my objection <u>to</u> the proposal.

21. The third edition of this book really doesn't differ very much at all <u>from</u> the first two.

22. I beg to differ <u>with</u> you, but your story does not fit my recollection at all.

23. If we don't act soon, we may miss (none needed) the opportunity to lock in the lowest rates.

Lesson 11: Diction Errors

What Are Diction Errors?

❑ Diction errors are "wrong word" errors. If an SAT I sentence contains a word that sounds *almost* right but not quite, it may well be a diction error. Study this list of words so that you can spot common diction errors:

Commonly Confused Words

accept/except: To *accept* something means to *agree to take it.* <***accept** an offer*> To *except* something is to *exclude* it.

adapt/adopt/adept: To *adapt* something means to *make it suitable for a particular purpose* (from *apt,* which means *appropriate* or *suitable*). To *adopt* means to *choose as one's own.* Someone *adept* is *highly skilled.* <*an **adept** player*>

affect/effect: To *affect* means to *influence.* <*It **affected** me deeply.*> An *effect* is a *result or consequence.* <*It had a good **effect.***> They are easily confused because to *affect* means to *have an effect* on something.

allude/elude/allusion/illusion: To *allude to* something means to *make a subtle or indirect reference* to it. To *elude* something means to *escape from it.* An *allusion* is a *subtle reference,* but an *illusion* is a *deception* or *misconception.*

ambivalent/ambiguous: When you're *ambivalent* you *have conflicting feelings* about something. <*I feel **ambivalent** about the party.*> Something *ambiguous* is *unclear* or *having more than one interpretation.* <*an **ambiguous** signal*>

compliment/complement: A *compliment* is a *praising personal comment.* A *complement* is something that *completes or makes a whole.* (Notice the **ple** in complement and complete.)

cite/site/sight: To *cite* means to *mention as a source of information* or to *commend for meritorious action.* <***cite** an article in her essay*> A *site* is a *place where a planned activity occurs.* To *sight* means to *see at a specific location.*

council/counsel: A *council* is a *committee.* <*the executive **council***> To *counsel* is to *give advice.* <*He **counseled** me.*>

discrete/discreet: *Discrete* means *distinct.* <*A watch contains dozens of discrete parts.*> Someone *discreet* is *prudently modest.* <*Act **discreetly.***>

elicit/illicit: To *elicit* means to *bring out or to call forth.* <*The joke **elicited** laughter.*> *Illicit* means *unlawful.*

eminent/imminent: Someone *eminent* is *prominently distinguished.* <*an **eminent** historian*> Something *imminent* is *about to occur.* <***imminent** doom*>

phase/faze: A *phase* is a *stage in a process.* <*third **phase** of the project*> The idiom to *phase out* means to *eliminate in stages.* To *faze* someone means to *disturb his or her composure.* <*I was a bit **fazed** by the interruption.*>

flaunt/flout: To *flaunt* something means to *show it off.* <***flaunt** your talents*> To *flout* something means to *show contempt for it.* <***flout** the rules*>

gambit/gamut: A *gambit* is a *careful strategy* or an *opening move.* The *gamut* is the *complete range.* <*run the **gamut***>

imply/infer: To *imply* means to *suggest* or *hint at,* but to *infer* means to *draw a conclusion from evidence.*

its/it's, their/they're, whose/who's, your/you're: Apostrophes can show possession (as in *David's bike*) or indicate missing letters in a contraction (as in *can't* as a contraction of *cannot*). In each of the confusing word pairs above, apostrophes indicate **contraction,** not possession: *it's = it is* or *it has, they're = they are, you're = you are,* and *who's = who is* or *who has.* The possessives are the ones without apostrophes.

morale/moral: *Morale* (n: mor-AL) is *shared enthusiasm for and dedication to a goal.* <*The team's **morale** was very high after the win.*> A *moral* (n: MOR-al) is a *lesson* or *principle about good behavior.* <*The story had a nice **moral.***>

precede/proceed/proceeds: To *precede* something means to *come before it* (*pre-* before). To *proceed* means to *go on, usually after a pause* (*pro-* forward). *Proceeds* are *funds received from a venture.* <***proceeds** from the raffle*>

principal/principle: A *principal* is your *pal—the head of a school.* It's also the *initial investment in an interest-bearing account.* (Money in the bank can be a pretty good *pal,* too, eh?) A *principle* is a *guiding rule.*

reticent/reluctant: Someone *reticent* is *reserved* or *reluctant to talk freely.* Don't use it to mean *reluctant.*

Concept Review 11: Diction Errors

Circle any diction errors in each of the following sentences, and write the correct word(s) in the blank.

1. Although most of the manuscripts were signed by their authors, some were written unanimously. _____

2. It was hard for the comic to illicit even the slightest laugh from the crowd. _____

3. She seems to have a hard time excepting compliments. _____

4. We needed to adopt the old engine to fit the new go-cart. _____

5. I like all flavors of ice cream accept mocha. _____

6. The imminent congresswoman was reelected easily. _____

7. While his activities were clearly immoral, they were not elicit. _____

8. The committee decided to adapt the new rules regarding membership. _____

9. She thought it wise to be discrete about her previous relationship with the defendant. _____

10. The counsel will decide how to finance the new city park. _____

11. Rather than cooperating with the rest of the team, Richard is always trying to flaunt the rules. _____

12. His knowledge of sports runs the gambit from table tennis to arena football. _____

13. The jury should not imply guilt from the defendant's refusal to answer these questions. _____

14. We were amazed at how adapt a juggler Carl was. _____

15. Rather than eliminate the department all at once, they decided to faze it out gradually. _____

16. Dogs barking can often signal eminent danger. _____

17. Training a dog is easy, once you've got it's attention. _____

18. She was sending mixed signals, so it was ambivalent whether she really wanted to go. _____

19. After our vacation, we decided to precede with the plan. _____

20. They don't seem to tolerate anyone who does not abide by their principals. _____

21. I was trying to infer that I should be considered for the new position. _____

22. I always felt reticent to talk in class. _____

23. Deanne was not even phased by the fire alarm. _____

24. The vitamins didn't have as great an affect as I thought they would. _____

25. She was the principle benefactor of the new hospital ward. _____

26. The police officer was sighted for her efforts in the hostage rescue. _____

27. She made an illusion to the fact that she was once a beauty queen. _____

28. Even the most trivial news seems to effect the stock price immediately. _____

29. David felt ambiguous about testifying against his partner. _____

30. The moral of the troops was at an all-time low during the Christmas season. _____

31. That scarf really compliments your outfit. _____

32. The meaning of that poem alludes me. _____

33. Her study of gorillas has been sited in several major books. _____

Worksheet 11: Diction Errors

Circle any diction errors in each of the following sentences, and write the correct word(s) in the blank.

1. *The reason we canceled the trip is because Wynona couldn't come on that weekend.*   _____

2. *Most of the meeting was spent honing in on the final plans for building the float.*   _____

3. *Matt was finally kicked off the starting squad for flaunting the team rules.*   _____

4. *I tried to stay awake for the lecture, but I was so disinterested that I dozed off before the professor was half finished.*   _____

5. *Ms. Davis said that we should always try and speak as if we were trying to hold a conversation with a person in the very back of the auditorium.*   _____

6. *Jennifer was very reticent to speak about the incident, even many years after it occurred.*   _____

7. *The article mentioned the low voter turnout in order to infer that the senator may not have been elected by a true majority.*   _____

8. *Even the 10-run deficit didn't seem to phase the manager; he refused to waver in his optimism.*   _____

9. *We decided that it was prudent to wait until the debris was cleared before we preceded.*   _____

10. *Although the police initially had many solid leads, the suspect alluded them for several months.*   _____

11. *It may be years before we understand how pollution from the new power plant might effect the regional environment.*   _____

12. *The new online store's musical offerings run the gambit from arias to zydeco.*   _____

13. *Heather was the principle author of the study that was recently published in a prominent scientific magazine.*   _____

14. *We were thrilled to get such an imminent expert on world affairs to speak at our colloquium on such short notice.*   _____

15. *All of the invited guests accept Anthony arrived promptly.*   _____

16. *Mrs. Sullivan went on all period about the illusions to Victorian society in Alice in Wonderland.*   _____

17. *For nearly the entire semester, I felt so inhabited that I never so much as razed my hand in class.*   _____

18. *Since they did not have a plan for the project, they decided to refer their approval until later.*   _____

19. *Try as they might, the hikers could not find the anecdote to the snake venom.*   _____

20. *The acid solution was so potent that we had to delude it with water before we could use it safely.*   _____

21. *The symbols on the cave walls are ambivalent; scientists have been debating their meaning for decades.*   _____

22. *Despite the setbacks with the caterers, the Breedens managed to give a splendidly eloquent party.*   _____

23. *As someone committed to fairness in education, she could not accept the iniquity of the admissions policy.*   _____

Answer Key 11: Diction Errors

Concept Review 11

1. Although most of the manuscripts were signed by their authors, some were written _anonymously_.
2. It was hard for the comic to _elicit_ even the slightest laugh from the crowd.
3. She seems to have a hard time _accepting_ compliments.
4. We needed to _adapt_ the old engine to fit the new go-cart.
5. I like all flavors of ice cream _except_ mocha.
6. The _eminent_ congresswoman was re-elected easily.
7. While his activities were clearly immoral, they were not _illicit_.
8. The committee decided to _adopt_ the new rules regarding membership.
9. She thought it wise to be _discreet_ about her previous relationship with the defendant.
10. The _council_ will decide how to finance the new city park.
11. Rather than cooperating with the rest of the team, Richard is always trying to _flout_ the rules.
12. His knowledge of sports runs the _gamut_ from table tennis to arena football.
13. The jury should not _infer_ guilt from the defendant's refusal to answer these questions.
14. We were amazed at how _adept_ a juggler Carl was.
15. Rather than eliminate the department all at once, they decided to _phase_ it out gradually.
16. Dogs barking can often signal _imminent_ danger.
17. Training a dog is easy, once you've got _its_ attention.
18. She was sending mixed signals, so it was _ambiguous_ whether she really wanted to go.
19. After our vacation, we decided to _proceed_ with the plan.
20. They don't seem to tolerate anyone who does not abide by their _principles_.
21. I was trying to _imply_ that I should be considered for the new position.
22. I always felt _reluctant_ to talk in class.
23. Deanne was not even _fazed_ by the fire alarm.
24. The vitamins didn't have as great an _effect_ as I thought they would.
25. She was the _principal_ benefactor of the new hospital ward.
26. The police officer was _cited_ for her efforts in the hostage rescue.
27. She made an _allusion_ to the fact that she was once a beauty queen.
28. Even the most trivial news seems to _affect_ the stock price immediately.
29. David felt _ambivalent_ about testifying against his partner.
30. The _morale_ of the troops was at an all-time low during the Christmas season.
31. That scarf really _complements_ your outfit.
32. The meaning of that poem _eludes_ me.
33. Her study of gorillas has been _cited_ in several major books.

Worksheet 11

1. The reason we canceled the trip is _that_. . . . (The reason is a thing.)
2. Most of the meeting was spent _homing in on_. . . .
3. Matt was finally kicked off the starting squad for _flouting_. . . .
4. I tried to stay awake for the lecture, but I was so _uninterested_. . . . (Disinterested means impartial.)
5. Ms. Davis said that we should always _try to_. . . .
6. Jennifer was very _reluctant_ to speak. . . .
7. The article mentioned the low voter turnout in order to _imply_. . . .
8. Even the 10-run deficit didn't seem to _faze_ the manager. . . .
9. We decided that it was prudent to wait until the debris was cleared before we _proceeded_.
10. Although the police initially had many solid leads, the suspect _eluded_ them for several months.
11. It may be years before we understand how pollution from the new power plant might _affect_ the regional environment.
12. The new online store's musical offerings run the _gamut_ from arias to zydeco.
13. Heather was the _principal_ author of the study. . . .
14. We were thrilled to get such an _eminent_ expert. . . .
15. All of the invited guests _except_ Anthony arrived promptly.
16. Mrs. Sullivan went on all period about the _allusions_. . . .
17. For nearly the entire semester, I felt so _inhibited_ that I never so much as _raised_ my hand in class.
18. Since they did not have a plan for the project, they decided to _defer_ their approval until later.
19. Try as they might, the hikers could not find the _antidote_. . . .
20. The acid solution was so potent that we had to _dilute_ it with water before we could use it safely.
21. The symbols on the cave walls are _ambiguous_; scientists have been debating their meaning for decades.
22. Despite the setbacks with the caterers, the Breedens managed to give a splendidly _elegant_ party. (Eloquent means well-spoken.)
23. As someone committed to fairness in education, she could not accept the _inequity_. . . . (Iniquity is sin.)

Lesson 12:
Other Modifier Problems

Adjectives vs. Adverbs

❑ Don't use an **adjective** to do an the job of an **adverb. Adjectives** (like *green, generous,* and *gargantuan*) are words that modify **nouns. Adverbs** (like *gently, globally,* and *grossly*) are words that modify **verbs, adjectives,** or **other adverbs.**

Wrong: *I was impressed by how **cogent** his argument was presented.*
(Although the *argument* was *cogent,* the modifier in this sentence is intended to answer the question *how was it **presented?*** Since it modifies a verb, it is an **adverb** and should take the *-ly* form.)

Right: *I was impressed by how **cogently** his argument was presented.*

❑ An **adverb** may also be used to modify the statement that a **whole sentence** makes.

Okay: *Clearly, the dust storm obscured the rider's vision.*
(Some people claim that the adverb *clearly* must modify the verb *obscured,* and say that it's illogical for something to be *obscured clearly,* because *obscured* is the opposite of *clear.* However, **adverbs can be used to modify the statement as a whole** rather than the verb it contains. In this case, *Clearly* means *What follows is a clear and obvious statement,* but it's much more concise, wouldn't you agree?)

❑ Two common modifiers, *fast* and *well,* can be used as either adjectives or adverbs. *Fast* is an adjective in *The car is fast,* but it is an adverb in *He talks too fast,* describing how he *talks. Well* is an adjective meaning *healthy* in *I haven't been well lately,* but it is an adverb in *She sings very well,* describing how she *sings.*

Comparative Adjectives and Adverbs

❑ Use the proper form when using comparative modifiers. **Comparative adjectives** take one of two forms: *fast* becomes comparative by adding *-er* to make *faster,* but *adorable* becomes compara-

tive by adding *more* to make *more adorable.* (*Adorabler* just doesn't sound right, does it?) **Comparative adverbs** almost always start with *more* as in *more rapidly,* but some irregular (that is, non "*-ly*") adverbs can take *-er,* as in *She runs **faster** than anyone else in the class.*

Wrong: *The briefcase feels **more light** than it did this morning.* (This is not the proper idiom.)

Right: *The briefcase feels **lighter** than it did this morning.*

Wrong: *Please try to hold the baby **gentler** next time.* (*Gentler* is a comparative adjective, not an adverb.)

Right: *Please try to hold the baby **more gently** next time.*

❑ Some modifiers should not take the comparative form because they are **absolutes.** For instance, it is illogical for one thing to be *more unique* than another thing, because *unique* means *one of a kind,* and this shows an absolute quality.

Wrong: *The loss was made **more inevitable** by the injury to our starting pitcher.* (It's either *inevitable* or it's not!)

Right: *The loss was made **inevitable** by the injury to our starting pitcher.*

Eliminate Redundancy

❑ A **redundancy** is an unnecessary repetition of an idea. **Eliminate all redundancies from your writing.** To check whether a word or phrase is redundant, reread the sentence without that word or phrase. If the meaning of the sentence remains unchanged, then the word or phrase is redundant.

Wrong: *With only seconds **remaining to go** in the game, Michael **sped quickly** down the court.*
(Since *remaining* means roughly the same as *to go,* we don't need both. Also, to *speed* means to *move quickly,* so *sped quickly* is redundant.)

Right: *With only seconds **remaining** in the game, Michael **sped** down the court.*

Concept Review 12: Other Modifier Problems

Give the comparative form of each adjective or adverb.

1. *gentle* _____

2. *precious* _____

3. *gently* _____

4. *lovely* _____

5. *quiet* _____

6. *sporty* _____

7. Circle the absolute modifiers in the list below.

wild	*impossible*	*sufficient*	*final*	*fatal*
complete	*inevitable*	*responsive*	*tolerable*	*willing*
entire	*effective*	*ideal*	*universal*	*unique*

8. What is the correct comparative form of an absolute modifier?

In each of the following sentences, circle the modifying words or phrases and label them *adjectives* (ADJ), *adverbs* (ADV), or *sentence modifiers* (SMOD).

9. *The music was overwhelmingly beautiful.*

10. *The other store is far less convenient than the one on the corner.*

11. *David unknowingly picked up the wrong bag.*

12. *Unfortunately, we could hardly see the band from our awful seats.*

13. *The best thing to do is to wait patiently.*

14. *Personally, I vastly prefer bison meat to beef.*

15. *Most likely, the lacrosse team left on the first bus.*

16. *I almost never watch television anymore.*

17. Cross out any redundant words or phrases in the paragraph below. (Hint: there are at least 10 redundancies.)

When we refer back to past history, we can see that whenever a new innovation is introduced for the first time, people rarely accept the whole entire concept, at least not right away. If and when something threatens the ways of the past, people don't part easily with their old ways. Although not everyone necessarily needs to maintain the status quo, consistency and predictability make people feel comfortable. Even when technology comes up with a way to do things better, people often continue on with their older, less efficient ways. For instance, it's not uncommon for people to use e-mail while at the same time continuing to correspond via "snail mail." If they would quickly pause for a moment, they would see that they can communicate more effectively through the Internet—and save some trees!

Worksheet 12:
Other Modifier Problems

Correct any modifier problems in the sentences below.

1. *The latest political commercials make their points stronger than previous ones.*

2. *My shirt smelled quite foully after rugby practice.*

3. *Recent technological advances have made it easier to extract minuscule chemical traces from geological samples.*

4. *We never usually get to go to such elegant restaurants.*

5. *Although both of my parents have pretty level heads, my father is the most patient.*

6. *The third graders weren't hardly interested in going to the museum after school.*

7. *I could always sing in front of a crowd easier than I could give a speech.*

8. *In many areas of the country, wind energy can be converted to electricity even more efficient than fossil energy.*

9. *I felt surprisingly well after Saturday's 10-mile run.*

10. *The microscopic size of the fracture made it more impossible to detect, even with special instruments.*

11. *The committee had never been so unanimous as they were on the most recent vote.*

12. *These measures won't barely address the state's deficit.*

13. *The teacher never told us about the test until the day before.*

14. *We weren't real sure that the plan would work.*

15. *Students never usually bother to examine the veracity of the "facts" they are supposed to memorize in history class.*

16. *Gena's guess was the most correct of anyone's in the class.*

Answer Key 12: Other Modifier Problems

Concept Review 12

1. *gentler*
2. *more precious*
3. *more gently*
4. *more lovely*
5. *quieter*
6. *sportier*
7. absolutes: *impossible, inevitable, ideal, complete, final, universal, entire, sufficient, fatal, unique*
8. Trick question! Of course, absolute modifiers are absolute *because* they have no comparative forms.
9. *overwhelmingly* (ADV modifying the ADJ *beautiful*); *beautiful* (ADJ)
10. *other* (ADJ); *far* (ADV modifying the ADJ *less convenient*); *less* (ADV modifying the ADJ *convenient*); *convenient* (ADJ); *on the corner* (ADJ prep phrase)
11. *unknowingly* (ADV); *wrong* (ADJ)
12. *unfortunately* (SMOD); *hardly* (ADV modifying the V *see*); *from our awful seats* (ADV prep phrase modifying V *see*); *awful* (ADJ)
13. *best* (ADJ); *to do* (ADJ infinitive); *patiently* (ADV)
14. *personally* (SMOD); *vastly* (ADV modifying V *prefer*); *to beef* (ADV prep phrase modifying V *prefer*)
15. *most* (ADV modifying ADJ *likely*); *likely* (ADJ); *lacrosse* (ADJ); *on the first bus* (ADV prep phrase modifying V *left*); *first* (ADJ)
16. *almost* (ADV modifying ADV *never*); *never* (ADV modifying V *watch*); *anymore* (ADV modifying V *watch*)
17. When we refer to history, we can see that whenever <u>an</u> innovation is introduced, people rarely accept the entire concept, at least not right away. When something threatens the ways of the past, people don't part easily with their old ways. Although not everyone needs to maintain the status quo, consistency and predictability make people feel comfortable. Even when technology comes up with a way to do things better, people often continue with their older, less efficient ways. For instance, it's not uncommon for people to use e-mail while continuing to correspond via "snail mail." If they would pause for a moment, they would see that they can communicate more effectively through the Internet—and save some trees!

Worksheet 12

1. *The latest political commercials make their points <u>more strongly</u> than previous ones.* (Use adverb, not adjective.)
2. *My shirt smelled quite <u>foul</u> after rugby practice.* (Here, the modifier is an adjective describing the shirt. The verb *smelled* is acting as a linking verb.)
3. *Recent technological advances have made it easier to extract minuscule chemical traces from geological samples.* (Correct)
4. *We <u>rarely</u> get to go to such elegant restaurants.* (The use of *never* is illogical.)
5. *Although both of my parents have pretty level heads, my father is the <u>more</u> patient.* (Use *more* when comparing two things.)
6. *The third graders <u>were hardly</u> interested in going to the museum after school.* (Double negative)
7. *I could always sing in front of a crowd <u>more easily</u> than I could give a speech.* (Use adverb, not adjective.)
8. *In many areas of the country, wind energy can be converted to electricity even <u>more efficiently</u> than fossil energy.*
9. *I felt surprisingly well after Saturday's 10-mile run.* (This is okay, but only if you mean that you are in a state of generally good health. If, however, you mean to say that you don't feel fatigued or achy, it is better to use *good* rather than *well*.)
10. *The microscopic size of the fracture made it <u>impossible</u> to detect, even with special instruments.* (*Impossible* is an absolute adjective.)
11. *The committee had never been so <u>unified</u> as they were on the most recent vote.* (*Unanimous* is an absolute, but *unified* is not.)
12. *These measures <u>won't</u> address the state's deficit.* (Double negative)
13. *The teacher <u>didn't tell</u> us about the test until the day before.* (The use of *never* is illogical.)
14. *We weren't <u>really</u> sure that the plan would work.* (The modifier is an adverb modifying the adjective *sure*.)
15. *Students <u>rarely</u> bother to examine the veracity of the "facts" they are supposed to memorize in history class.* (*Never usually* is illogical.)
16. *Gena's guess was the most <u>nearly</u> correct of anyone's in the class.* (*Correct* is an absolute modifier, but guesses can *approach* correctness in varying degrees.)

Lesson 13: Irregular Verbs

Know Your Irregulars

❑ When using the perfect tenses or using participial phrases, you must use the **past participle** of the verb rather than the **past tense** form of the verb. Don't mix them up!

❑ For many verbs, the two forms are the same, as in *we **walked*** (past) and *we had **walked*** (past perfect), but for many "irregular" verbs, they are different, as in *we **ate*** (past) and *we had **eaten*** (past perfect). You should know the irregular forms of common verbs.

Infinitive	Past tense	Past participle
to arise	*arose*	*arisen*
to awake	*awoke*	*awoken*
to beat	*beat*	*beaten*
to begin	*began*	*begun*
to blow	*blew*	*blown*
to break	*broke*	*broken*
to burst	*burst*	*burst*
to cast	*cast*	*cast*
to come	*came*	*come*
to creep	*crept*	*crept*
to do	*did*	*done*
to draw	*drew*	*drawn*
to drink	*drank*	*drunk*
to drive	*drove*	*driven*
to forsake	*forsook*	*forsaken*
to get	*got*	*got, gotten*
to go	*went*	*gone*
to hurt	*hurt*	*hurt*
to kneel	*kneeled, knelt*	*knelt*
to know	*knew*	*known*
to lay (to put or place)	*laid*	*laid*
to lie (to recline)	*lay*	*lain*
to ride	*rode*	*ridden*
to run	*ran*	*run*
to speak	*spoke*	*spoken*
to shrink	*shrank*	*shrunk, shrunken*
to sink	*sank*	*sunk*
to speak	*spoke*	*spoken*
to spring	*sprang*	*sprung*
to take	*took*	*taken*
to tear	*tore*	*torn*
to write	*wrote*	*written*

Concept Review 13:
Irregular Verbs

Complete the following sentences with the correct form of the verb:

1. We would have _____ (to ride) even further if we had had the time.

2. Until now, that issue hasn't _____ (to arise).

3. Before we won last week's game, we hadn't _____ (to beat) the Cougars in 10 years.

4. I would not have _____ (to drink) the punch if I had known that it had liquor in it.

5. We searched everywhere, but our friends had _____ (to go) out for the evening.

6. Had I never _____ (to know) about video games, I would have _____ (to get) perfect grades last semester.

7. At last night's concert, the band _____ (to sing) all of its greatest hits.

8. The Donnellys have _____ (to run) their corner store for over 20 years.

9. They had hardly _____ (to speak) about the incident until that night.

10. I can't believe you put my wool sweater in the dryer and _____ (to shrink) it.

11. His batting average has really _____ (to sink) ever since his injury.

12. She had _____ (to speak) for so long that the other speakers didn't have time to finish their presentations.

13. It seems as if the tulips _____ (to spring) out of the ground overnight.

14. We should have _____ (to take) that shortcut to work.

15. If we had jumped over that fence, the polar bear would have _____ (to tear) us to shreds.

16. I promise you that by next month I will have _____ (to write) the first 4 chapters of the book.

Worksheet 13: Irregular Verbs

Circle the past participle(s) or past tense verbs in each sentence, and make any necessary corrections.

1. Elisha could never have went to the state finals if I had not convinced her to join the team in the first place.

2. In retrospect, it seems I might have took too much time on the essay portion of the test.

3. While we played video games, Danny lay on the couch all afternoon.

4. Most people find it amazing that, millions of years ago, life sprung from a primordial swamp.

5. After we had placed our bets, we lay our cards on the table.

6. Carl would have tore his uniform if he had not stopped his slide at the last second.

7. The generals forsook their own troops to surrender and save their own lives.

8. When the temperature sunk below zero, the pipes bursted like water balloons.

9. The assets of the company were froze as soon as it declared bankruptcy.

10. Promptly at 6 o'clock, the assistant cook rung the bell for dinner, and the whole camp raced up the hill.

11. I was concerned about buying a cotton warm-up suit, and sure enough, it shrunk two sizes after the first wash.

12. By the time they pitched camp for the night, they had ridden over 30 miles.

13. George needed his friends more than ever, but they had forsook him.

14. We sung just about every song we knew, then we went to bed.

15. The senator could have spoke a lot longer, but she yielded the floor to her colleague.

Answer Key 13: Irregular Verbs

Concept Review 13

1. We would have <u>ridden</u> even further if we had had the time.

2. Until now, that issue hasn't <u>arisen</u>.

3. Before we won last week's game, we hadn't <u>beaten</u> the Cougars in 10 years.

4. I would not have <u>drunk</u> the punch if I had known that it had liquor in it.

5. We searched everywhere, but our friends had <u>gone</u> out for the evening.

6. Had I never <u>known</u> about video games, I would have <u>gotten</u> perfect grades last semester.

7. At last night's concert, the band <u>sang</u> all of its greatest hits.

8. The Donnellys have <u>run</u> their corner store for over 20 years.

9. They had hardly <u>spoken</u> about the incident until that night.

10. I can't believe you put my wool sweater in the dryer and <u>shrank</u> it.

11. His batting average has really <u>sunk</u> ever since his injury.

12. She had <u>spoken</u> for so long that the other speakers didn't have time to finish their presentations.

13. It seems as if the tulips <u>sprang</u> out of the ground overnight.

14. We should have <u>taken</u> that shortcut to work.

15. If we had jumped over that fence, the polar bear would have <u>torn</u> us to shreds.

16. I promise you that by next month I will have <u>written</u> the first 4 chapters of the book.

Worksheet 13

1. Elisha could never have <u>gone</u> to the state finals if I had not convinced her to join the team in the first place.

2. In retrospect, it seems I might have <u>taken</u> too much time on the essay portion of the test.

3. While we played video games, Danny lay on the couch all afternoon. (Correct)

4. Most people find it amazing that, millions of years ago, life <u>sprang</u> from a primordial swamp.

5. After we had placed our bets, we <u>laid</u> our cards on the table.

6. Carl would have <u>torn</u> his uniform if he had not stopped his slide at the last second.

7. The generals forsook their own troops to surrender and save their own lives. (Correct)

8. When the temperature <u>sank</u> below zero, the pipes <u>burst</u> like water balloons.

9. The assets of the company were <u>frozen</u> as soon as it declared bankruptcy.

10. Promptly at 6 o'clock, the assistant cook <u>rang</u> the bell for dinner, and the whole camp raced up the hill.

11. I was concerned about buying a cotton warm-up suit, and sure enough, it <u>shrank</u> two sizes after the first wash.

12. By the time they pitched camp for the night, they had ridden over 30 miles. (Correct)

13. George needed his friends more than ever, but they had <u>forsaken</u> him.

14. We <u>sang</u> just about every song we knew, then we went to bed.

15. The senator could have <u>spoken</u> a lot longer, but she yielded the floor to her colleague.

Lesson 14:
The Subjunctive Mood

What is the "Mood" of a Verb?

The **mood** of a verb is its *factuality* or *urgency*. There are three moods of verbs in English.

Indicative mood: Most verbs are in the **indicative mood,** meaning they indicate something **real or factual,** as in *I am going to the park.*

Subjunctive mood: Verbs in the **subjunctive mood** indicate something **hypothetical, conditional, wishful, suggestive,** or **counter to fact,** as in *I wish **I were going** to the park.*

Imperative mood: Verbs in the **imperative mood** indicate a **direct command,** as in ***Go** to the park!*

❑ The only "tricky" mood in English is the **subjunctive mood.** Questions about the subjunctive mood are possible on the SAT I, but they are not very common. You should recognize the common situations in which the subjunctive mood must be used, and know how to change the form of the verb accordingly.

❑ The subjunctive mood is usually indicated by **auxiliaries** like *would, should, might,* and *may,* or if the verb is *to be,* by the forms *were* and *be.*

e.g. *He **would feel** better if only he would eat.*	(Hypothetical)
*If **I were** faster, I could play wide receiver.*	(Hypothetical)
*We thought that she **might win** the election, but she lost by a lot.*	(Counter to fact)
*He plays as though he **were** not even injured.*	(Counter to fact)
*I wish that he **would not act** so superior.*	(Wishful)
*I wish **I were** 2 inches taller.*	(Wishful)
*I truly doubt that she **would ever say** such a thing.*	(Doubtful)
*I think she **might be** in over her head.*	(Doubtful)
*She said that we **should practice** harder.*	(Suggestion)
*He asks that we **be** there at 6 o'clock sharp.*	(Indirect command)

Don't Overdo It

❑ The subjunctive mood is slowly disappearing from the English language. Many subjunctive forms from the past now sound old-fashioned and are no longer "standard" English.

*Archaic: We must all respect the office of the presidency, no matter who **be** the current officeholder.*

*Better: We must all respect the office of the presidency, no matter who **is** the current officeholder.*

*Archaic: If that **be** so, we may see dramatic changes in the market.*

*Better: If that **is** so, we may see dramatic changes in the market.*

Watch Your Ifs

❑ One very common mistake is using the construction *if . . . would have . . .* as a past subjunctive form. The correct form is *if . . . had. . . .*

Wrong: If he would have arrived a minute sooner, he would not have missed her.

Right: If he had arrived a minute sooner, he would not have missed her.

Concept Review 14:
The Subjunctive Mood

1. Name 5 auxiliaries that indicate the subjunctive mood.

2. What does the subjunctive mood indicate?

Circle the correct subjunctive verb form in each of the following sentences.

3. *If I (was/were) a little faster, I'd be able to anchor the relay team.*

4. *In fact, I (was/were) only 5 years old at the time.*

5. *He would feel better if only he (ate/would eat).*

6. *He asks that we (are/be) there at 6 o'clock sharp.*

7. *I wish that he (were/was) not so presumptuous about my motives.*

8. *If he (would have/had) caught the ball, the inning would be over now.*

9. *If I (was/were) a rock star, I'd tour all over Europe.*

10. *He plays as though he (was/were) not even injured.*

11. *I wish I (was/were) 6 inches taller.*

12. *I think she (might be/is) in over her head.*

13. *If she (would have/had) campaigned harder, she might have won the election.*

14. *I cannot tell whether he (is/be) friend or foe.*

Worksheet 14:
The Subjunctive Mood

Circle the verb(s) in each sentence. If the verb mood is incorrect, cross it out and write in the correction.

1. We doubted that she will get enough votes to force a runoff, let alone win outright. _____

2. If I was going to take the SAT tomorrow, I'd be sure to get plenty of sleep tonight. _____

3. If I would have known that it would take this long, I'd have gone out for a snack. _____

4. I would have liked to have been there just to see the panicked look on his face. _____

5. The camp counselors asked that we were in our beds with lights out promptly at 10 o'clock. _____

6. David ran as if he was carrying a refrigerator on his back. _____

7. I wish that we would have paid the extra $50 a night to get a better room. _____

8. Miss Hannigan demanded that we be silent unless spoken to and should always do what we're told. _____

9. He spoke as if he was an expert in the field of international relations. _____

10. I would have remembered to have left a generous tip, but I left my wallet at home. _____

11. Had I known beforehand, I would not have mentioned her ex-boyfriend. _____

12. If the rest of the class would have voted the way I did, we wouldn't be taking the test today. _____

Answer Key 14: The Subjunctive Mood

Concept Review 14

1. *might, may, would, could, should*

2. That the verb indicates something hypothetical, conditional, suggestive, wishful, or counter to fact.

3. *If I <u>were</u> a little faster, I'd be able to anchor the relay team.*

4. *In fact, I <u>was</u> only five years old at the time.*

5. *He would feel better if only he <u>would eat</u>.*

6. *He asks that we <u>be</u> there at 6 o'clock sharp.*

7. *I wish that he <u>were</u> not so presumptuous about my motives.*

8. *If he <u>had</u> caught the ball, the inning would be over now.*

9. *If I <u>were</u> a rock star, I'd tour all over Europe.*

10. *He plays as though he <u>were</u> not even injured.*

11. *I wish I <u>were</u> 6 inches taller.*

12. *I think she <u>might be</u> in over her head.*

13. *If she <u>had</u> campaigned harder, she might have won the election. (Don't say If she would have. . . .)*

14. *I cannot tell whether he <u>is</u> friend or foe. (The form be is formally correct also, but such usage is now considered archaic.)*

Worksheet 14

1. *We doubted that she <u>would</u> get enough votes to force a runoff, let alone win outright.*

2. *If I <u>were</u> going to take the SAT tomorrow, I'd be sure to get plenty of sleep tonight.*

3. *If I <u>had</u> known that it would take this long, I'd have gone out for a snack.*

4. *I would have liked to <u>be</u> there just to see the panicked look on his face.*

5. *The camp counselors asked that we <u>be</u> in our beds with lights out promptly at 10 o'clock.*

6. *David ran as if he <u>were</u> carrying a refrigerator on his back.*

7. *I wish that we <u>had</u> paid the extra $50 a night to get a better room.*

8. *Miss Hannigan demanded that we be silent unless spoken to and (omit should) always do what we're told.*

9. *He spoke as if he <u>were</u> an expert in the field of international relations.*

10. *I would have remembered to <u>leave</u> a generous tip, but I left my wallet at home.*

11. *Had I known beforehand, I would not have mentioned her ex-boyfriend. (Correct)*

12. *If the rest of the class <u>had</u> voted the way I did, we wouldn't be taking the test today.*

Lesson 15: Coordinating Ideas

Complex and Compound Sentences

Many sentences contain more than one complete idea, or **clause.** These are called **compound sentences** (if the individual clauses can stand alone as sentences) or **complex sentences** (if one or more of the individual clauses **cannot** stand alone as sentences). **The ideas in sentences must coordinate logically with each other.**

> e.g. *As we walked in the door, Bernie jumped all over us.*
> (This is a **complex sentence** because the first clause, *As we walked in the door,* cannot stand alone as a sentence. This is called a **dependent clause.** The second clause, however, *Bernie jumped all over us,* is an **independent clause,** and can stand alone as a sentence.)
>
> *He was very excited to see us: we had been away for nearly a full hour!*
> (This is a **compound sentence** because the two clauses are **independent.**)

Run-On Sentences

❑ If **two independent clauses** are joined only by a comma, this is an error called a **run-on** sentence or a **comma splice.** (A run-on sentence isn't just a sentence that's too long!) To join two independent clauses in one sentence, you must use a **colon** (:), **a semicolon** (;), or a **conjunction like *but, or, yet, for, and, nor,* or *so.*** (Mnemonic: BOYFANS)

Wrong: *I have taken several science courses this year, my favorite was neuroscience.*
          (Two independent clauses are joined only by a comma, so the sentence is a run-on.)

Right: *I have taken several science courses this year; my favorite was neuroscience.*
          (Because the two clauses are closely related, they can be joined with a semicolon.)

Right: *I have taken several science courses this year, but my favorite was neuroscience.*

(Here the two clauses are joined with the conjunction *but.* This changes the meaning slightly from the previous version; it emphasizes the contrast between the **group** of courses in the first clause and the **single** course in the second clause.)

Wrong: *The ride was more harrowing than they expected, several times the car nearly skidded off the mountain.*

Right: *The ride was more harrowing than they expected: several times the car nearly skidded off the mountain.*
          (The colon is more appropriate than a semicolon here, because the second clause **explains** the first.)

The Colon and Semicolon

❑ The **semicolon** (;) is used primarily to join two closely related independent clauses in a single sentence. When using a semicolon to join clauses, make sure they are **independent;** that is, they can stand alone as sentences.

Wrong: *The test was unbelievably difficult; and hardly anyone finished it on time.*
          (A semicolon or a conjunction should be used to join the clauses, but not both.)

Right: *The test was unbelievably difficult; hardly anyone finished it on time.*

❑ The **colon** (:) is used in much the same way as a semicolon is used, but it also implies that an **explanation** will follow.

Unclear: *The meeting went well and everyone was impressed by my presentation.*
          (This sentence is a bit ambiguous: did the meeting go well **because** of the successful presentation, or for another reason?)

Better: *The meeting went well: everyone was impressed by my presentation.*
          (This makes the relationship between the clauses clearer: the second explains the first.)

Concept Review 15:
Coordinating Ideas

1. When should a semicolon be used to join clauses?

2. When should a colon be used to join clauses?

3. What is a run-on sentence?

4. Name the seven conjunctions that can join independent clauses.

Write a sentence that logically and concisely incorporates the given clauses, with the first clause as the main clause.

5. Confederates in the Attic *has received widespread critical acclaim. It was written by Tony Horwitz. It portrays the legacy of the Civil War in the modern South. It is poignant and funny.*

   _____

   _____

   _____

6. *Many of the rights given by the Constitution were bitterly contested by the Founding Fathers. Many people believe that the Founding Fathers agreed unanimously to safeguard those rights for us. The Constitution is much more a political compromise than a steadfast commitment to a set of ideals.*

   _____

   _____

   _____

7. *The Sapir-Whorf hypothesis has been largely disproven. It claims that our thoughts are guided and limited by constraints on our language. Scientists now understand that having thoughts and expressing them are very different things.*

   _____

   _____

   _____

8. *Corporations can effectively control the opinions of the people through the media. They can do this to a large degree because the people don't believe they are being manipulated. This happens in free and democratic societies. Unlike totalitarian societies, free and democratic societies do not use force to ensure popular compliance.*

   _____

   _____

   _____

Worksheet 15: Coordinating Ideas

Make any necessary corrections to the following sentences to coordinate the clauses logically and concisely.

1. *Standardized test results can help measure the progress of individual students, and they are far less able to measure the effectiveness of entire school systems.*

   _____

   _____

2. *A consistent program of vigorous aerobic exercise maintains cardiovascular health, it also helps your brain to work more effectively.*

   _____

   _____

3. *If the Mets could just get some consistent relief pitching; they might be able to put a winning streak together.*

   _____

   _____

4. *We never should have bought the plane tickets, and it would have been much easier to drive.*

   _____

   _____

5. *The convention was not the success they had hoped it would be, their lead presenter came down with the flu; the salesman who had to fill in had never given a presentation in front of an audience.*

   _____

   _____

6. *Since 1998, the civil war in the Democratic Republic of Congo has been the deadliest since World War II, it has claimed over 3.3 million lives.*

   _____

   _____

7. *Mrs. Donovan seems to inspire every one of her students to achieve; she inspires them despite having to manage classes that sometimes number over 35 students.*

   _____

   _____

8. *The lab took us twice as long to complete as any of our other labs; but it was also the most worthwhile.*

   _____

   _____

Answer Key 15: Coordinating Ideas

Concept Review 15

1. When the two clauses are independent and are very closely related.

2. When the two clauses are independent and the second clause explains the first.

3. A sentence that joins two independent clauses without a colon, a semicolon, or a conjunction.

4. BOYFANS: *but, or, yet, for, and, nor, so*

5. Tony Horwitz's book Confederates in the Attic, *a poignant and funny portrayal of the legacy of the Civil War in the modern South, has received widespread critical acclaim.*

6. *Although many people believe that the Founding Fathers agreed unanimously to safeguard our rights* in the Constitution, many of those rights were bitterly contested by the Founding Fathers; in fact, the Constitution is much more a political compromise than a steadfast commitment to a set of ideals.

7. *The Sapir-Whorf hypothesis, which claims that our thoughts are guided and limited by constraints on our language, has been largely disproven, and scientists now understand that having thoughts and expressing them are very different things.*

8. *Even in free and democratic societies, corporations can effectively control the opinions of the people not through force, as totalitarian societies do, but through the media, largely because the people don't believe they are being manipulated.*

Worksheet 15

1. *Standardized test results can help measure the progress of individual students, <u>but</u> they are far less able to measure the effectiveness of entire school systems.*

2. *A consistent program of vigorous aerobic exercise maintains cardiovascular health <u>and</u> helps your brain to work more effectively.*

3. *If the Mets could just get some consistent relief pitching, they might be able to put a winning streak together.*

4. *We never should have bought the plane tickets; it would have been much easier to drive.*

5. *The convention was not the success they had hoped it would be; their lead presenter came down with the flu, <u>and</u> the salesman who had to fill in had never given a presentation in front of an audience.*

6. *Since 1998, the civil war in the Democratic Republic of Congo has been the deadliest since World War II, <u>claiming</u> over 3.3 million lives.*

7. *<u>Despite having to manage classes that sometimes number</u> over 35 students, Mrs. Donovan seems to inspire every one of her students to achieve.*

8. *The lab took us twice as long to complete as any of our other labs, but it was also the most worthwhile.*

CHAPTER 19

FOUR PRACTICE SAT I TESTS WITH DETAILED ANSWER KEYS

PRACTICE TEST 1

ANSWER SHEET

SECTION 1

Write your essay for Section 1 in the space below and on the next page.

_____

_____

_____

_____

_____

_____

_____

_____

_____

_____

_____

_____

_____

_____

_____

_____

_____

_____

_____

_____

_____

_____

_____

_____

_____

_____

_____

_____

_____

Section I

Time—25 minutes

Directions for Writing the Essay

Plan and write an essay that answers the question below. Do NOT write on another topic. An essay on another topic will receive a score of 0.

Two readers will grade your essay based on how well you develop your point of view, organize and explain your ideas, use specific and relevant examples support your thesis, and use clear and effective language. How well you write is much more important than how much you write, but to cover the topic adequately you should plan to write several paragraphs.

Your essay must be written only on the lines provided on your answer sheet. You will have enough space if you write on every line, avoid wide margins, and keep your handwriting to a reasonable size. Your essay will be read by people who are not familiar with your handwriting, so write legibly.

You may use this sheet for notes and outlining, but it will not be graded as part of your essay.

Consider carefully the issue discussed in the following passage, then write an essay that answers the question posed in the assignment.

> An entertainment-driven culture runs the risk of encouraging passivity among its citizens. If they can experience something vicariously through a movie, television show, or video game, why should they get involved with the activity itself? It's safer, after all, to watch someone scale a mountain than to do it yourself. The effect of this passivity, of course, is an apathetic frame of mind. We cease to care very about so many things because they are experienced, at best, second-hand.

Assignment: **Is apathy a problem in today's** Write an essay in which you answer this question and discuss your point of this issue. Support your position logically with examples from literature, the history, politics, science and technology, current events, or your experience or observation.

Write your essay on your answer sheet.

Section 2

Time—25 minutes
20 Questions

2

Directions for Multiple-Choice Questions

In this section, solve each problem, using any available space on the page for scratchwork. Then decide which is the best of the choices given and fill in the corresponding oval on the answer sheet.

- You may use a calculator on any problem. All numbers used are real numbers.
- Figures are drawn as accurately as possible EXCEPT when it is stated that the figure is not drawn to scale.
- All figures lie in a plane unless otherwise indicated.

Reference Information

$A = \pi r^2$
$C = 2\pi r$
$A = \ell w$
$A = \frac{1}{2} bh$
$V = \ell wh$
$V = \pi r^2 h$
$c^2 = a^2 + b^2$
Special Right Triangles

The arc of a circle measures 360°.
Every straight angle measures 180°.
The sum of the measures of the angles in a triangle is 180°.

---

1 If $x = 3$ and $5x = 3x + y$, then $y =$

(A) 1.5
(B) 2
(C) 3
(D) 4
(E) 6

$5(3) = 3(3) + y$

$15 - 9 = y$

6

---

2 A store sells a package of 6 batteries for $4 and a package of 24 of the same batteries for $12. If you need to buy 48 of these batteries, how much money will you save by buying them in packages of 24 rather than packages of 6?

(A) $4
(B) $8
(C) $12
(D) $16
(E) $20

3

Which of the following points does NOT lie in the shaded region above?

(A) (1, 1)
(B) (1, 4)
(C) (3, 3)
(D) (4, 1)
(E) (5, 5)

GO ON TO THE NEXT PAGE ▶▶▶

4 If $\frac{1}{3}$ of $2x$ is 5, what is $\frac{2}{3}$ of $4x$?

(A)   5
(B)   10
(C)   15
(D)   20
(E)   25

$\frac{1}{3}(2x) = 5$

(D)

5 If n is a positive integer that is divisible by 12 and 16, then n must also be divisible by

(A)   28
(B)   32
(C)   48
(D)   96
(E)   192

$12 = 4 \cdot 3$
$16 = 4 \cdot 4$

(C)

6

Note: Figure not drawn to scale

$90 - 60$
In the figure above, if $a - b = 10$, then $a =$
75 65

(A)   60
(B)   65
(C)   70
(D)   75
(E)   80

$a = b$

$180 - 40 = 140$

(D)

7 If n is an integer, which of the following must be even?

(A) $\frac{n}{2}$
(B) $n + 2$
(C) $2n + 1$
(D) n^2
(E) $n^2 + n$

(E)

8 Mike sold a total of 48 sodas at a snack stand. The stand sells only cola and root beer. If he sold twice as many colas as root beers, how many root beers did he sell?

(A)   32
(B)   24
(C)   18
(D)   16
(E)   8

$x = r$
$2x = c$
$3x = 48$

(D)

9 If m and n are both squares of integers, which of the following is NOT necessarily the square of an integer?

(A) $9m$ ✓
(B) mn ✓
(C) m^2
(D) $9mn$
(E) $9m - 9n$

(E)

2

10 If $a + b = 9$, $a - c = 14$, and $a = 10$, then $c - b =$

(A) −5
(B) −3
(C) 3
(D) 5
(E) 23

$10 + b = 9$
-10
$b = -1$

$10 - c = 14$
-10
$-c = 4$
$c = -4$

$-4 - 1 = -3$

11 If set $M = \left\{ \dfrac{1}{6}, \dfrac{1}{4}, \dfrac{2}{3}, \dfrac{5}{6} \right\}$ and if x and y are both elements of set M, then what is the maximum possible value of $5x - 5y$?

(A) $\dfrac{10}{3}$

(B) 4

(C) $\dfrac{25}{6}$

(D) $\dfrac{14}{3}$

(E) 5

$5\left(\dfrac{5}{6}\right) - 5\left(\dfrac{1}{6}\right)$

$\dfrac{25}{6} - \dfrac{5}{6}$

$\dfrac{20}{6}$

12

0	1	2	3	4	5
1	2	4	7		
2	4	8	15		
3	7	15	x		
4					
5					

With the exception of the shaded squares, every square in the figure above contains the sum of the number in the square directly above it and the number in the square directly to its left. For example, the number 4 in the unshaded square above is the sum of the 2 in the square above it and the 2 in the square directly to its left. What is the value of x?

(A) 6
(B) 7
(C) 8
(D) 15
(E) 30

13 If a, b, and c are positive even integers such that $a < b < c$ and $a + b + c = 60$, then the greatest possible value of c is

(A) 36
(B) 40
(C) 42
(D) 54
(E) 57

14 The population of Bumpton increased by 10% from 1980 to 1990 and decreased by 10% from 1990 to 2000. What is the net percent change in the population of Bumpton from 1980 to 2000?

(A) −9%
(B) −1%
(C) +0%
(D) +1%
(E) +9%

$100 - 110$
$110 - 99$

15 Each female of a certain species of fish lays 100 eggs each fall and then dies. If only 30% of these eggs mature to become egg-producing females the next year, then how many egg-producing females will descend from a single egg-producing female 2 years after she first lays eggs?

(A) 900
(B) 9,000
(C) 18,000
(D) 27,000
(E) 810,000

16   If $x > 0$ and $x = 5y$, then $\sqrt{x^2 - 2xy + y^2} =$

(A) $2y$

(B) $y\sqrt{6}$

(C) $4y$

(D) $16y$

(E) $24y$

$\sqrt{(5y)^2 - 2(5y)(y) + y^2}$

$\sqrt{25y^2 - 10y^2 + y^2}$

$\sqrt{16y^2}$

$4y$

17   If $x > x^2$, which of the following must be true?

    I. $x < 1$ ✓

    II. $x > 0$ ✓

    III. $x^2 > 1$

(A)   I only

(B)   II only

(C)   I and II only

(D)   I and III only

(E)   I, II, and III

18

$$A \qquad\qquad B \qquad C$$

$$\overleftarrow{\quad}\underset{-x-4}{|}\quad\underset{0}{|}\;\underset{x}{|}\quad\underset{3x+2}{|}\overrightarrow{\quad}$$

Which of the following represents the distance from the midpoint of $\overline{AB}$ to the midpoint of $\overline{BC}$ on the number line above?

(A) $\dfrac{3x+2}{2}$

(B) $2x - 1$

(C) $2x + 3$

(D) $3x + 1$

(E) $4x$ ✓

$\dfrac{-x-4+x}{2} = -2$

$x + 3x + 2 = 4x + 2 = 2(2x+1)$

$-2, 2x+2$

$\sqrt{(2x+2-2)^2} = \sqrt{4x^2} = 2x$

19

P is the center of the circle above and $PQ = QR$. If $\triangle PQR$ has an area of $9\sqrt{3}$, what is the area of the shaded region?

(A) $36\pi - 9\sqrt{3}$

(B) $24\pi - 9\sqrt{3}$

(C) $18\pi - 9\sqrt{3}$

(D) $9\pi - 9\sqrt{3}$

(E) $6\pi - 9\sqrt{3}$

20   In a class of 160 seniors, the ratio of boys to girls is 3 to 5. In the junior class, the ratio of boys to girls is 3 to 2. When the two classes are combined, the ratio of boys to girls is 1 to 1. How many students are in the junior class?

(A)   400

(B)   360

(C)   200

(D)   180

(E)   160

$3x + 5x = 160$

$8x = 160$

$x = 20$

$60 \qquad 100$

$3x + 2x = 160$

$100 \qquad\qquad 60$

32

STOP   *You may check your work, on this section only, until time is called.*

Section 3

Time—25 minutes
24 Questions

Each of the sentences below is missing 1 or 2 portions. Read each sentence, then select the word or words that most logically complete the sentence, taking into account the meaning of the sentence as a whole.

Example:

Rather than accepting the theory unquestioningly, Deborah regarded it with -------.

   (A) mirth
   (B) sadness
   (C) responsibility
   (D) ignorance
   (E) skepticism

Correct response: (E)

---

1 Julia feared that her 6-month hiatus from playing the piano would cause her musical skills to -------.

   (A) atrophy
   (B) align
   (C) develop
   (D) reconcile
   (E) disseminate

2 Senator Harris is widely viewed as a ------- orator; his speeches are full of ------- commentary and domineering opinions.

   (A) vindictive . . . pedantic
   (B) conciliatory . . . treacherous
   (C) didactic . . . moralizing
   (D) dogmatic . . . meek
   (E) simplistic . . . prosaic

3 Walter's ------- was beginning to annoy his co-workers; although they appreciated the thought he gave to his decisions, his inability to make up his mind was growing tiresome.

   (A) vacillation
   (B) solicitation
   (C) rejuvenation
   (D) admonishment
   (E) professionalism

4 To succeed as a writer, one needs a great deal of -------; successful writers are ------- even in the face of countless rejections.

   (A) affluence . . . haughty
   (B) pertinacity . . . apologetic
   (C) intimidation . . . resilient
   (D) tenacity . . . relentless
   (E) stoutness . . . craven

5 Although direct, forceful stances usually appeal to voters on the campaign trail, candidates usually resort to ------- during debates to avoid alienating any potential supporters.

   (A) pontification
   (B) circumlocution
   (C) logic
   (D) exaggeration
   (E) brevity

6 Counselors in the prison rehabilitation program must have faith in the ------- of those who have committed felonies, yet be wary of -------; they must believe that criminals can change, but know that they can often return to their old habits.

   (A) mutability . . . astuteness
   (B) variability . . . consistency
   (C) coarseness . . . responsibility
   (D) persuasion . . . transcendence
   (E) malleability . . . relapse

GO ON TO THE NEXT PAGE ▶▶▶

7 Marullus' reference to "chimney-tops" during his monologue in *Julius Caesar* is considered by some historians ------ since such things are unlikely to have existed in Rome in the 1st century B.C.

(A) a miscalculation
(B) an anachronism
(C) an idiom
(D) an interlocutor
(E) a mirage

8 The letter "h" at the end of Pittsburgh is ------ of American sentiments soon after World War I; it was added as part of a movement during that time to make the names of American cities sound less German.

(A) an inference
(B) an analogy
(C) a vestige
(D) an anomaly
(E) a quandary

Each passage below is followed by one or two questions based on its content. Answer each question based on what is stated or implied in the preceding passage.

Questions 9–10 are based on the following passage.

Although countries can construct redoubtable
stone barriers to separate "us" from "others,"
Line no barrier is stronger than language. We infer
volumes from the language of another,
5 whether he is erudite or philistine, whether
she is noble or mean. Our labels, too, can be
impenetrable walls: we are "freedom fighters,"
they are "terrorists"; we are the "faithful," they
are the "infidels." Those people who use such
10 wall-language are the Manichaeans,[1] those
who refuse to see, or cannot see, shades of
gray, the subtle truths of humanity. Their
"truths" are the most dangerous weapons,
wielded by the blind and the ignorant.

[1] those who believe in absolute good and evil

9 In this paragraph, language is characterized primarily as

(A) biased
(B) enlightening
(C) difficult to understand
(D) unifying
(E) changeable

10 In line 4, the word "volumes" most nearly means

(A) spaces
(B) editions
(C) measurements
(D) an abundance
(E) capacities

Questions 11–12 are based on the following passage.

It may be difficult for adults to learn not to interfere but rather to support the child's desire
Line for freedom and autonomy. For example, if
you watch a boy of three trying to tie his
5 shoes, you may see him work with extraordinary motivation even though the loops aren't
matched; and well over half the time as he
tries for the final knot, he ends up with two
separate laces, one in each hand. Then watch
10 his parents as they watch their children attempt a task like this. Too often the parent
will step in and take over, tie the shoes the
"right way" and defeat the child's growing attempt at self-mastery. The same goes for
15 putting on boots, coats, and even playing with
toys. It is exceedingly easy to fall into the trap
of almost always responding negatively to a
child at this age. Commonly, a parent might
say no up to 200 times a day at this stage.
20 Such nagging not only is aversive in the extreme, but also a constant reminder to the
child of his or her lack of self-control.

Second paragraph: *Educational Psychology: A Developmental Approach*, Norman A. Sprinthall et al., McGraw-Hill 1994, p. 149

GO ON TO THE NEXT PAGE ▶▶▶

11 The passage suggests that helping a boy to tie his shoes the "right way" (line 13) can be

(A) necessary to his self-esteem
(B) important to his personal hygiene
(C) appropriate only if the boy has the necessary fine motor skills
(D) essential to teaching him patience
(E) harmful to his autonomous development

12 The passage indicates that negative responses to a child can lead to the child's

(A) rebellion
(B) feeling of helplessness
(C) persistence in the task
(D) mimicking of the negative behavior
(E) anger

The questions below are based on the content of the preceding passage. The questions are to be answered on the basis of what is stated or implied in the passage itself or the introductory material that precedes the passage.

Questions 13–18 are based on the following passage.

The following is an essay about T. S. Eliot, an American poet of the early 20th century, and the Modernist movement, of which he was a part.

Modernism is the most peculiar of all artistic movements of the twentieth century and the
Line most difficult to pin down since people started coming up with "movements" in the first
5 place. Modernism is the only thing that strikes more fear into the heart of an English under-graduate than the idea of going to a lecture. Critics and academics, not unwisely, prefer their artistic movements to be readily compre-
10 hensible and clearly enough defined to make some logical sense. Modernism, however, will not be tamed. It is straggly, begins nowhere and with no one in particular, and ends only when its writers have started to baffle even
15 themselves. One treads carefully through its key texts: James Joyce's *Ulysses*, T. S. Eliot's *The Waste Land* (both 1922), and Virginia Woolf's *Mrs. Dalloway* (1925). The authors of these aberrations, these posturing, egotistical,
20 lunatic, kaleidoscopic works of blatant and self-conscious genius, have laid literary land-mines throughout their works. Joyce said of

Ulysses that "I've put in so many enigmas and puzzles that it will keep the professors busy
25 for centuries arguing over what I meant, and that's the only way of insuring one's immortal-ity." This statement sums up the enigma of modernism (if one can be said to sum up an enigma) in that it contains arrogance min-
30 gling with modesty, cleverness tied up in self-effacing humour, and above all absurdity with a purpose. Plots, such as they exist at all in modernist writing, are submerged beneath wave upon wave of classical allusions, ar-
35 chaisms, neologisms, foreign languages, quo-tations, swear words and other hyper-literary and meta-literary indulgences. If I haven't made it clear already, it is hard not to love modernism. It is hard to work out what ex-
40 actly it is.

Recently, while browsing in an Oxford bookshop, a friend of mine picked up a copy of *Finnegans Wake*—James Joyce's final book—and read the first page. Between tears
45 of laughter, he managed to indicate to me that he couldn't understand a word of it. It is hard not to sympathise with the outsider's at-titude so amply demonstrated by my friend's outburst of shock and wonder. To find one of
50 our most famous authors writing gibberish is rather heartening. Yet we remain outsiders to the work. *Finnegans Wake*, you see, is em-blematic of all that is right and wrong with modernism. It took a spectacularly long time
55 to write and was finally published in 1939, seventeen years after its predecessor, *Ulysses*. That probably had something to do with the fact that over 40 different languages crept into its catalogue of portmanteau words
60 (ersatz words consisting of two or more real words or word elements, like those of Lewis Carroll in his poem "Jabberwocky"). The re-sulting book is uniquely inventive and at the same time uniquely confusing. In that sense,
65 it is the perfect example of a modernist text. It alienates its readers just as it tries to mimic how they think. The English mod-ernist novel is a sociopath and a cad: danger-ous and reprehensible but somehow roguishly
79 likeable.

Excerpted from *T. S. Eliot and the Elitism of Modernism*, by David Pinching, on Bibliomania.com

GO ON TO THE NEXT PAGE ▶▶▶

13 In the first paragraph, the author characterizes Modernism as which of the following?

      I. self-centered
     II. ill-defined
   III. politically oriented

(A) I only
(B) II only
(C) I and II only
(D) II and III only
(E) I, II, and III

14 The passage suggests that critics and academics dislike artistic movements that are

(A) enigmatic
(B) comprehensible
(C) wide-ranging
(D) inventive
(E) socially conscious

15 The "landmines" in lines 21–22 are

(A) episodes in novels that refer to violence
(B) criticisms of the works of other novelists
(C) new methods of analyzing literature
(D) literary devices intended to baffle academics
(E) limitations that publishers place on an author's work

16 The reference to "wave upon wave" (line 34) suggests that, in Modernist fiction, plot is

(A) a powerfully moving element
(B) secondary to other considerations
(C) dominant over diction
(D) characterized by redundancy
(E) dangerous

17 The author's overall attitude toward Modernism can best be described as

(A) ambivalent
(B) reverential
(C) cynical
(D) indignant
(E) jocular

18 The final sentence of the passage employs each of the following EXCEPT

(A) simile
(B) juxtaposition
(C) personification
(D) contrast
(E) metaphor

The questions below are based on the content of the preceding passage. The questions are to be answered on the basis of what is stated or implied in the passage itself or the introductory material that precedes the passage.

Questions 19–24 are based on the following passage.

The following is an excerpt from a book on genomics, the new science of gathering and using the information encoded in the genes of an organism.

Biology is being reborn as an information science, a progeny of the Information Age. As in-
Line formation scientists, biologists concern themselves with the messages that sustain life,
5 such as the intricate series of signals that tell a fertilized egg to develop into a full-grown organism, or the orchestrated response the immune system makes to an invading pathogen. Molecules convey information, and it is their
10 messages that are of paramount importance. Each molecule interacts with a set of other molecules and each set communicates with another set, such that all are interconnected. Networks of molecules give rise to cells; networks
15 of cells produce multicellular organisms; networks of people bring about cultures and societies; and networks of species encompass ecosystems. Life is a web and the web is life.
    Ironically, it was the euphoria for molecules
20 that touched off this scientific revolution. In the 1980s only a tiny percentage of the millions of different molecular components of living beings was known. In order to gain access to these molecules, a new science and even a
25 new industry had to be created. Genomics is the development and application of research tools that uncover and analyze thousands of different molecules at a time. This new approach to biology has been so successful that
30 universities have created entire departments devoted to it, and all major pharmaceutical companies now have large genomics divisions. Genomics has granted biologists unprecedented access to the molecules of life,
35 but this is more than just a technological revolution. Through genomics massive amounts of biological information can be converted into an electronic format. This directly links the

GO ON TO THE NEXT PAGE ▶▶▶

life sciences to the information sciences,
40 thereby facilitating a dramatically new framework for understanding life.

Information is a message, a bit of news. It
may be encoded or decoded. It may be conveyed by smoke signals, pictures, sound
45 waves, electromagnetic waves, or innumer-
ous other media, but the information itself is
not made of anything. It has no mass. Furthermore, information always has a sender
and an intended receiver. This implies an un-
50 derlying intent, meaning, or purpose. Information theory thus may seem unfit for the
cold objectivism of science. The focus of the
information sciences, however, is not so
much on information content, but rather on
55 how messages are conveyed, processed, and
stored.

Advances in this area have been great and
have helped to propel the remarkable development of the computer and telecommunication
60 industries. Could these forces be harnessed to
better understand the human body and to improve human health?

19 The primary purpose of this passage is to

(A) refute a theory
(B) describe the origins of a mis-
conception
(C) analyze different perspectives on a
phenomenon
(D) describe a new trend in a field of study
(E) suggest a new method of teaching

20 The passage mentions each of the following
as an example of elements interrelating to
form a larger whole EXCEPT

(A) molecules forming a cell
(B) organisms forming an ecosystem
(C) pathogens forming the immune system
(D) individuals forming a society
(E) cells forming an organism

Transducing the Genome, Gary Zweiger, McGraw-Hill, pp. xi–xii

21 The passage mentions the "orchestrated response" (line 7) primarily as an example of

(A) the coordinated efforts of scientists
(B) molecules conveying information
(C) the work being done to promote
genomics
(D) the similarity between cells and
computers
(E) an unrealized potential

22 According to the passage, the "dramatically
new framework" (lines 40–41) is one in which

(A) new university buildings are being built
(B) the immune system attacks a pathogen
(C) networks of molecules give rise to cells
(D) genomics research receives more
federal funding
(E) biological data is translated into a new
form

23 According to the passage, information theory
"may seem unfit for the cold objectivism of
science" (line 51–52) because

(A) it is better suited to commercial indus-
try than to academic study
(B) it can be conveyed by sound waves
(C) it suggests that messages may have
meaning or purpose
(D) it is not rigorously studied
(E) it analyzes biological information

24 Which of the following best describes the
function of the final paragraph in relation to
the rest of the passage?

(A) It modifies a theory presented earlier.
(B) It provides a solution to a problem
mentioned earlier.
(C) It raises doubts about the value of
genomics.
(D) It indicates actual and potential consequences of genomics.
(E) It mentions a viable alternative to
genomics.

STOP *You may check your work, on this
section only, until time is called.*

Section 4

Time—25 minutes
35 Questions

Directions for "Improving Sentences" Questions

Each of the sentences below contains one underlined portion. The portion may contain one or more errors in grammar, usage, construction, precision, diction (choice of words), or idiom. Some of the sentences are correct.

Consider the meaning of the original sentence, and choose the answer that best expresses that meaning. If the original sentence is best, choose (A), because it repeats the original phrasing. Choose the phrasing that creates the clearest, most precise, and most effective sentence.

EXAMPLE:	EXAMPLE ANSWER

The children <u>couldn't hardly believe their eyes.</u>   (C)
  (A)   couldn't hardly believe their eyes
  (B)   would not hardly believe their eyes
  (C)   could hardly believe their eyes
  (D)   couldn't nearly believe their eyes
  (E)   could hardly believe his or her eyes

1 The controversial themes, which resonate with recent political events, <u>explain why the book is selling at such a feverish pace.</u>

(A)   explain why the book is selling at such a feverish pace
(B)   explains the feverish pace of the book
(C)   explain the reason for the pace of the book's feverish sales
(D)   explains why the book's selling pace is so feverish
(E)   is why the book is selling well.

2 One of the best features of the journalist's lifestyle is <u>you never know what's next.</u>

(A)   you never know what's next
(B)   it's so unpredictable
(C)   that you never know what's next
(D)   one can never predict what's next
(E)   its unpredictability

3 Despite having an engaging personality and an outstanding education, <u>Greg's search for a satisfying job was fruitless.</u>

(A)   Greg's search for a satisfying job was fruitless
(B)   Greg searched fruitlessly for a satisfying job
(C)   Greg's job search was fruitless because he insisted on a satisfying job
(D)   the satisfying job that Greg sought was nowhere to be found
(E)   Greg searched for a satisfying job, but it was fruitless

4 The plot of the movie was neither plausible <u>and it was not even faithful to the novel.</u>

(A)   and it was not even faithful to the novel
(B)   nor was it faithful to the novel
(C)   nor faithful to the novel
(D)   and certainly not faithful to the novel
(E)   yet hardly faithful to the novel

GO ON TO THE NEXT PAGE ▶▶▶

5 We were astonished that the package <u>had took so long to get to its destination.</u>

(A) had took so long to get
(B) had took so long getting
(C) had taken so long in its getting
(D) had taken so long to get
(E) had been so long getting

4 ▶ **6** The committee agreed that the new principal should be able to inspire teachers, uphold tradition, and, above all, <u>he or she must maintain a scholarly atmosphere.</u>

(A) he or she must maintain a scholarly atmosphere
(B) they should maintain a scholarly atmosphere
(C) maintain a scholarly atmosphere
(D) keep things scholarly
(E) he or she should keep things scholarly

7 Although critics say that many have portrayed Othello with more passion than <u>he, they can't help but admire his acting.</u>

(A) he, they can't help but admire his acting
(B) him, they can't help but admire his acting
(C) he, they can't help but admire him acting
(D) him, they can't help but admire him acting
(E) him, they must only admire his acting

8 <u>Neither of the battling rams seemed to feel the pain of their wounds.</u>

(A) Neither of the battling rams were slowed by the pain of their wounds.
(B) Neither of the battling rams was slowed by the pain of its wounds.
(C) Neither ram, that was battling, was slowed by the pain of their wounds.
(D) Neither ram, who were battling, were slowed by the pain of its wounds.
(E) Neither of the battling rams was slowed by the pain of their wounds.

9 Walking into her house after a hard day's work, <u>Liz's family surprised her with a warm, delicious meal and a clean house.</u>

(A) Liz's family surprised her with a warm, delicious meal and a clean house
(B) Liz was surprised to find a warm, delicious meal and a clean house, courtesy of her family
(C) Liz's family made her a warm, delicious meal and cleaned the house, surprising her
(D) Liz found a warm, delicious meal and a clean house surprising her from her family
(E) a warm, delicious meal and a clean house surprised Liz, courtesy of her family

10 An increasing number of students are coming to realize that an education at a public university can be <u>as good, if not better, than an elite private college.</u>

(A) as good, if not better, than an elite private college
(B) as good, if not better, as one at an elite private college
(C) as good as, if not better, than an elite private college education
(D) as good an education as, if not better, than one at an elite private college
(E) as good as, if not better than, one at an elite private college

11 <u>S. J. Perelman, whose hallmark of a grandiloquent writing style is</u> widely regarded as one of the finest American wits of all time.

(A) S. J. Perelman, whose hallmark of a grandiloquent writing style is
(B) Being that his hallmark is a grandiloquent writing style, S. J. Perelman is
(C) S. J. Perelman's grandiloquent writing style is his hallmark and is
(D) S. J. Perelman and his hallmark of a grandiloquent writing style are
(E) S. J. Perelman, whose hallmark is a grandiloquent writing style, is

---

Directions for Identifying Sentence Error Questions

The following sentences may contain errors in grammar, usage, diction (choice of words), or idiom. Some of the sentences are correct. No sentence contains more than 1 error.

If the sentence contains an error, it is underlined and lettered. The parts that are not underlined are correct.

If there is an error, select the part that must be changed to correct the sentence.

If there is no error, choose (E).

EXAMPLE:
By the time they reached the halfway point
                A
in the race, most of the runners hadn't hardly
         B   C   D
begun to hit their stride.   No error
                                        E

SAMPLE ANSWER:

(D)

---

12 The lack of progress

in international relations reveals that
      A   B
governments must study the art of
                  C
diplomacy much closer.   No error
              D   E

13 Because Deborah has been a representative
                          A
for over 20 years and also her popularity
                          B
among her constituents, few are willing
        C
to challenge her in an election.   No error
  D   E

14 Caravaggio demonstrated the great range
                    A
of his artistic talent in such paintings as
        B   C
"Bacchus" and "Basket of Fruit," painted in

1593 and 1596, respectfully.   No error
                      D   E

15 Grizzly bears rarely show aggression toward
                  A
humans, but they will protect their territory
  B
from anyone whom they
  C
would have considered to be a threat.
          D
No error
  E

16 The choir's rendition of "America the

Beautiful" was stirring, particularly after
              A
the children had finished their presentation
                  B   C
on the meaning of freedom.   No error
      D   E

17 Andre suggested to the board that both the
                  A
fund deficit and the disillusionment of the
                        B
investors were a problem that
                  C
had to be addressed immediately.
          D
No error
  E

GO ON TO THE NEXT PAGE ▶▶▶

4 ➤

18 Because Phillips reasoned that either

accepting or rejecting the proposal were
A   B
going to upset some political faction,
                          C
he decided to delay the vote until

after his reelection.   No error
D   E

19 The Attorney General spoke at length about
                          A
the detrimental effects of having less
                    B   C
defense attorneys to serve indigent
                      D
defendants.   No error
                E

20 The service at Centro is much better than
                  A
the other restaurants we frequent, so
        B
we prefer to go there when
    C
we are entertaining guests.   No error
        D   E

21 Before the curtain rose, Anthony wished
                          A
that he were back in bed, only dreaming
        B   C
about performing in front of

hundreds of strangers rather than actually
        D
doing it.   No error
            E

22 James, like many parents, believes that if a
                              A
child can read at a very young age, they will
                  B   C
grow to have exceptional literary
                  D
talent.   No error
            E

23 The decline of the Enlightenment
        A
was hastened not only by tyrants but also
    B
because of intellectual opposition.   No error
    C   D   E

24 Although he pitched professionally for 3
                          A
decades, Nolan Ryan never lost any velocity
                          B
on his fastball, and few maintained such
                              C
control over so many pitches as he.
    D
No error
    E

25 The Senator and his opponent, Thomas
                      A
Cowher, were running a very tight race until

he made a racially insensitive comment that
B   C
offended many voters.   No error
    D   E

26 Just when those who were observing
                  A
the heart transplant procedure assumed

the worst, the surgeons themselves are most
    B   C   D
confident.   No error
            E

27 Although testing for unsafe levels of
        A   B
asbestos particles is widely advocated for
                              C
houses built before 1950, many home
        D
owners ignore this suggestion.   No error
                                    E

GO ON TO THE NEXT PAGE ▶▶▶

28 Between my brother <u>and I</u> <u>existed</u> a strong
　　　　　　　　　 A　　 B
bond that did not weaken even <u>when</u> he
　　　　　　　　　　　　　　　　 C
chose to live <u>thousands of miles</u> away on a
　　　　　　　 D
different continent.　<u>No error</u>
　　　　　　　　　　　　 E

29 <u>Writing about</u> the folk duo, *The Indigo Girls,*
　　　 A
one critic <u>has suggested</u> that <u>their</u> longevity
　　　　　　 B　　　　　　　　 C
is <u>due to</u> its ability to remain faithful to an
　　 D
honest musical style while stretching the

boundaries of convention.　<u>No error</u>
　　　　　　　　　　　　　　　　 E

Directions for "Improving Paragraphs" Questions

Below is an early draft of an essay. It requires revision in many areas.

The questions that follow ask you to make improvements in sentence structure, diction, organization, and development. Answering the questions may require you to understand the context of the passage as well as the rules of standard written English.

4

Questions 30–35 pertain to the following passage.

(1) For thousands of years, philosophers have debated whether humans discover mathematics or it is something that has been invented. (2) Plato believed that perceived mathematical objects like lines were only vague shadows of abstract "ideals" that exist outside of human experience. (3) Circular objects or circles drawn on paper aren't "really" circles. (4) Rather, they are just a flawed approximation of the perfect circular form. (5) So, in this sense, Plato believed that mathematics was something revealed imperfectly to humans, not invented by them. (6) Many students surely wish that mathematics had not been invented at all. (7) A position that opposes Plato's idealism is called mathematical intuitionism, which is the belief that all mathematics is the product of human minds.

(8) There is one good way to understand the difference between idealism and intuitionism. (9) Look at big numbers. (10) An idealist would say that all numbers, no matter how large, truly exist, even if no one has ever actually calculated them. (11) An intuitionist, on the other hand, might say that some numbers may be so big that they are physically impossible to calculate or express in a meaningful way, and so do not truly "exist."

(12) Another point of view that is different from these ones is one that says that it is a pointless thing to ask the question as to whether mathematical objects "really exist" or not. (13) This view simply regards mathematics as a tool for interpreting information from the world around us. (14) This view is essentially a compromise between idealism and intuitionism. (15) Although it acknowledges that mathematics reaches beyond the mind of a mathematician, it also denies that it has any meaning outside of the mind. (16) The concept of a circle is not a reflection of an abstract "ideal," and also it is not completely a human invention. (17) Instead it is a concept that we form in our minds after perceiving and thinking about many circular objects in the world around us.

30 Which of the following is the best revision of the underlined portion of sentence 1 (reproduced below)?

For thousands of years, philosophers have debated whether <u>humans discover mathematics or it is something that has been invented.</u>

(A) humans discover mathematics or invent it
(B) humans so much discover mathematics as they do invent it
(C) the discovery of mathematics is what humans do or the invention
(D) humans discover mathematics or if it is invented
(E) mathematics is something discovered or if humans invent it

31 In context, which of the following is the most logical revision of the underlined portion of sentence 3 (reproduced below)?

<u>Circular objects</u> or circles drawn on paper aren't "really" circles.

(A) Nevertheless, circular objects
(B) According to his reasoning, circular objects
(C) Furthermore, circular objects
(D) Secondly, circular objects
(E) All the while, circular objects

32 Which of the following is the best revision of sentence 4 (reproduced below)?

Rather, they are just a flawed approximation of the perfect circular form.

(A) But instead they are only a flawed approximation of the perfect circular form.
(B) Rather, they are only flawed approximations of the perfect circular form.
(C) Rather, their forms are merely an approximation of circular perfection alone.
(D) Instead, their approximation of the perfect circular form mentioned above is imperfect.
(E) Rather, their perfection as circular forms is only an approximation of it.

33 Which of the following sentences contributes least to the unity of the first paragraph?

(A) Sentence 3
(B) Sentence 4
(C) Sentence 5
(D) Sentence 6
(E) Sentence 7

34 Which of the following is the best way to combine sentences 8 and 9 (reproduced below)?

There is one good way to understand the difference between idealism and intuitionism. Look at big numbers.

(A) One good way to understand the difference between idealism and intuitionism is the following: look at large numbers.
(B) It is a good way to understand the difference between idealism and intuitionism in considering large numbers.
(C) The consideration of large numbers provides one good way toward the understanding of the difference between idealism and intuitionism.
(D) To consider large numbers is to have one good way of understanding the difference between idealism and intuitionism.
(E) One good way to understand the difference between idealism and intuitionism is to consider large numbers.

35 In context, which of the following is the best revision of sentence 12 (reproduced below)?

Another point of view that is different from these ones is one that says that it is a pointless thing to ask the question as to whether mathematical objects "really exist" or not.

(A) A third point of view regards it as pointless to ask whether mathematical objects "really exist."
(B) Another, completely different, point of view is the one that regards asking whether or not mathematical objects "really exist" as pointless.
(C) Asking whether mathematical objects "really exist" is pointless, according to another, third, different point of view.
(D) The asking of whether mathematical objects "really exist" is a pointless thing, says a third point of view.
(E) Another different point of view says it is pointless to ask about whether mathematical objects "really exist" or not.

STOP

You may check your work, on this section only, until time is called.

Section 5

Time — 25 minutes
18 Questions

5

Directions for Multiple-Choice Questions

In this section, solve each problem, using any available space on the page for scratchwork. Then decide which is the best of the choices given and fill in the corresponding oval on your answer sheet.

- You may use a calculator on any problem. All numbers used are real numbers.
- Figures are drawn as accurately as possible EXCEPT when it is stated that the figure is not drawn to scale.
- All figures lie in a plane unless otherwise indicated.

Reference Information

$A = \pi r^2$
$C = 2\pi r$
$A = \ell w$
$A = \frac{1}{2} bh$
$V = \ell wh$
$V = \pi r^2 h$
$c^2 = a^2 + b^2$
Special Right Triangles

The arc of a circle measures 360°.
Every straight angle measures 180°.
The sum of the measures of the angles of a triangle is 180°.

---

1 If $2x = 10$ and $3y = 12$, then $4x + 6y =$

(A) 10
(B) 12
(C) 22
(D) 32
(E) 44

2 The average (arithmetic mean) of three numbers is 5. If one of the numbers is 4, what is the sum of the other two numbers?

(A) 8
(B) 9
(C) 10
(D) 11
(E) 12

3

The figure above shows a rectangle intersected by a line. If $b = 2a$, then $d + e + g + h =$

(A) 120
(B) 240
(C) 300
(D) 320
(E) 360

GO ON TO THE NEXT PAGE ▶▶▶

4 For all real numbers x where $x \geq 1$, let
$f(x) = \sqrt{\sqrt{x} - 1}$. What is the value of $f(100)$?

(A)   3
(B)   9
(C)   10
(D)   27
(E)   100

5 If $3^{k+m} = 243$ and $2^m = 8$, then what is the value of 2^k?

(A)   2
(B)   4
(C)   6
(D)   8
(E)   10

6 The average (arithmetic mean) of four different even integers is 50. If none of the numbers is greater than 60, what is the least possible value of any one of the numbers?

(A)   26
(B)   27
(C)   28
(D)   29
(E)   30

7 In a certain soccer league, each of the five teams plays every other team in the league exactly three times each season. How many games are played in total in one season?

(A)   15
(B)   24
(C)   30
(D)   60
(E)   120

8 Pump A, working alone, can fill a tank in 3 hours, and pump B can fill the same tank in 2 hours. If the tank is empty to start and pump A is switched on for one hour, after which pump B is also switched on and the two work together, how many *minutes* will pump B have been working by the time the pool is filled?

(A)   48
(B)   50
(C)   54
(D)   60
(E)   64

Directions for Student-Produced Response Questions

Each of the questions in this section requires you to solve the problem and enter your answer in a grid, as shown below.

- If your answer is ⅔ or .666 . . . , you must enter **the most accurate value the grid can accommodate,** but you may do this in one of four ways:

Start in first column

Grid result here

Start in second column

Grid as a truncated decimal

Grid as a rounded decimal

- In the example above, gridding a response of 0.67 or 0.66 is **incorrect** because it is less accurate than those above.
- The scoring machine cannot read what is written in the top row of boxes. You **MUST** fill in the numerical grid accurately to get credit for answering any question correctly. You should write your answer in the top row of boxes only to aid your gridding.
- Do **not** grid in a mixed fraction like $3\frac{1}{2}$ as $\boxed{3\ |\ 1\ |\ /\ |\ 2}$, because it will be interpreted as $\frac{31}{2}$. Instead, convert it to an improper fraction like $\frac{7}{2}$ or a decimal like 3.5 before gridding.
- None of the answers will be negative, because there is no negative sign in the grid.
- Some of the questions may have more than one correct answer. You must grid only one of the correct answers.
- You may use a calculator on any of these problems.
- All numbers in these problems are real numbers.
- Figures are drawn as accurately as possible EXCEPT when it is stated that the figure is not drawn to scale.
- All figures lie in a plane unless otherwise indicated.

---

9   If four times a certain number is decreased by 5, the result is 25. What is the number?

10   For every integer m greater than 1, let «m» be defined as the sum of the integers from 1 to m, inclusive. For instance,
«4» = 1 + 2 + 3 + 4 = 10.
What is the value of «7» − «5»?

11

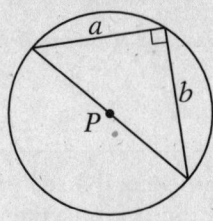

If the circumference of the circle above is 10π, then what is the value of $a^2 + b^2$?

12 A, B, C, D

How many different three-letter arrangements of the letters above are possible if no letter may be repeated? (An arrangement like ABC is distinct from an arrangement like BCA.)

13   If $96{,}878 \times x^2 = 10{,}200$, then $\dfrac{10{,}200}{5x^2 \times 96{,}878} =$

14   Every term in a certain sequence is one less than three times the previous term. If the fourth term of this sequence is 95, what is the 1st term of the sequence?

15   If $4 + \sqrt{b} = 7.2$, what is the value of $4 - \sqrt{b}$?

16   Admission to a museum is $10 for each adult and $5 for each child. If a group of 30 people pays a total of $175 in admission, how many adults are in the group?

17

The perimeter of the isosceles triangle above is 24. If the ratio of a to b is 2 to 3, what is the value of b?

18

Note: Figure not drawn to scale

In the figure above, $AB = 6$, $BC = 6$, and $CD = 2$. What is AD?

STOP   *You may check your work, on this section only, until time is called.*

5

Section 6

Time — 25 minutes
24 Questions

Each of the sentences below is missing one or two portions. Read each sentence, then select the word or words that most logically complete the sentence, taking into account the meaning of the sentence as a whole.

Example:

Rather than accepting the theory unquestioningly, Deborah regarded it with -------.

    (A)   mirth
    (B)   sadness
    (C)   responsibility
    (D)   ignorance
    (E)   skepticism

Correct response: (E)

1 The strange signal detected by the radio telescope, rather than being taken as evidence of a new cosmological phenomenon, was instead treated as merely ------- of the equipment itself.

    (A)   a malfunction
    (B)   a bulwark
    (C)   an anthology
    (D)   a mutation
    (E)   a transfer

2 The long-standing divisions among the indigenous ethnic groups in the region have created an ------- problem that may never be solved without international intervention.

    (A)   impotent
    (B)   intractable
    (C)   evanescent
    (D)   irate
    (E)   insipid

3 The ease with which the army's defenses were breached surprised the opposing general, who expected resistance to be far more ------- than it was.

    (A)   ephemeral
    (B)   compatible
    (C)   egregious
    (D)   tolerable
    (E)   imposing

4 Although dependence on electronic devices has ------- in recent years, the increased efficiency of common appliances has ------- the demand on the power grid.

    (A)   abated . . . decreased
    (B)   surged . . . attenuated
    (C)   increased . . . compromised
    (D)   diminished . . . reduced
    (E)   flourished . . . elevated

5 Although persecution at the hands of ------- landowners vanquished the will of many, it ------- the dreams of revolution among the hardier insurgents.

    (A)   despotic . . . squandered
    (B)   cruel . . . destroyed
    (C)   amenable . . . bore
    (D)   celebrated . . . initiated
    (E)   ruthless . . . forged

GO ON TO THE NEXT PAGE ▶▶▶

Each passage below is followed by questions based on its content. Answer each question based on what is stated or implied in the passage or the introductory material that precedes it.

Questions 6–9 are based on the following passage.

Passage 1

The following is from a recent commentary on Jean-Jacques Rousseau (1712–1778), a French philosopher during the Enlightenment.

Taken as a whole, Rousseau's writings attacked the Age of Reason, gave impetus to the
Line Romantic movement by emphasizing feeling (leading Goethe to say that "feeling is all"), re-
5 vived religion even though he had doubts about some traditional teachings, provided a new direction for education (his book *Émile* was considered by some the best work on education since Plato's *Republic*), inspired the
10 French Revolution, made a unique impact on political philosophy, and, more than the writing of any of his contemporaries, influenced several subsequent philosophers, especially Immanuel Kant. On one occasion, Kant was
15 so absorbed in reading Rousseau's *Émile* that he forgot to take his celebrated daily walk. While Kant admitted that it was David Hume who awakened him from his dogmatic slumbers regarding the theory of knowledge, it was
20 Rousseau who showed him the way to a new theory of morality. So impressed was Kant by the insights of Rousseau that he hung a picture of him on the wall of his study, convinced that Rousseau was the Newton of the moral world.

Passage 2

25 The roses we lay at Rousseau's feet for this theory of Natural Rights tend to overwhelm the less fragrant of his ideas. He persisted in believing in the nobility of the primitive state of nature, and that women's nature was to serve
30 men. His assertions about Natural Rights of Man laid the philosophical foundation of American independence, but his worship of emotion over reason and of "negative education" gave generations of parents permission to ignore the
35 need to discipline and teach their children.

First paragraph: from "Rousseau: A Romantic in the Age of Reason," from *Socrates to Sartre*, McGraw-Hill, 1999, p. 278
Second paragraph: Copyright 2005 Christopher Black. All rights reserved.

6 Passage 1 suggests that Goethe

(A) was at the forefront of the Age of Reason
(B) was a traditionalist
(C) was influenced by Rousseau
(D) opposed the Romantic movement
(E) inspired much of Rousseau's work

7 Passage 1 mentions Kant's "daily walk" (line 16) in order to emphasize

(A) Kant's forgetfulness
(B) Kant's commitment to healthful practices
(C) the dogmatic nature of Rousseau's writings
(D) the effect of Rousseau's philosophy on Kant
(E) Kant's close friendship with Rousseau

8 Unlike Passage 1, Passage 2 characterizes Rousseau's emphasis on emotion as

(A) insincere
(B) innovative
(C) harmful
(D) temporary
(E) necessary

9 Both passages credit Rousseau with

(A) attacking the Age of Reason
(B) inspiring revolutionary thought
(C) encouraging discipline
(D) praising the primitive state of nature
(E) establishing the Romantic movement

GO ON TO THE NEXT PAGE ▶▶▶

The questions below are based on the content of the preceding passage. The questions are to be answered on the basis of what is stated or implied in the passage itself or the introductory material that precedes the passage.

Questions 10–16 pertain to the following passage.

The following passage was written by an American essayist in 2003 about the status of capitalism.

In response to a journalist's question, "What do you think about Western civilization?"
Line Mahatma Gandhi is said to have replied, "It would be a good idea." Any honest person
5   who values the concept of the free market, who believes in the promise of open economic competition, would say the same thing about capitalism. We hear our politicians, and of course the corporate news and entertainment
10 media, speaking as if the United States were a model of free-market capitalism, as if anyone could start a business to create and sell a product or service without the obstruction of the government. The truth is quite different.
15 Those we hear saying such things are quite often voices that are bankrolled by large corporations, which themselves are often protected from competition by mutual agreement with the federal government.
20   The concept of free trade is simple: if Company A can produce and distribute a product more efficiently and at a higher quality than Company B, it should be allowed to do so, and to charge any price for it that free consumers
25 are willing to pay. Although Company B would likely suffer as a result, humanity would benefit from freer and cheaper access to high-quality goods. Sometimes free trade works nicely, as when Company A is in the
30 United States and Company B is in India. Then, agreements are signed to "open up" India to the cheaper goods made by Company A, even if doing so crushes Company B because, we say, consumers have a right to
35 cheap, high-quality goods. But if Company A were in India and Company B were in the United States, the story would likely be very different.
        This isn't an idle example. India developed
40 a pharmaceutical industry many years ago that could produce drugs very cheaply that

would save tens of thousands of lives each year. In a free-market economy, the Indian pharmaceutical industry would have been
45 allowed to make drugs and get them to the people who needed them. But that would mean that western pharmaceutical companies would make less profit. Of course, it's not that the American pharmaceutical companies
50 don't care about Indian children dying because they can't get drugs; it's just that their responsibility is to their stockholders. They must maximize profits. But the "free market" was getting in the way. So they simply
55 changed the rules.
        Thus, in 1994 India "agreed" (that is, gave in to Western pressure) to "liberalize" its pharmaceutical industry by allowing its largest drug companies to be sold to Western
60 interests, thereby reducing competition. Drug prices predictably shot up, putting them out of reach of people who needed them, but the Western corporations made more money. It was a big triumph for the
65 "liberalization" of markets, but a great blow to free markets.
        In a free economy, businesses are also expected to wager their own capital on success in the marketplace. The adventurous entre-
70 preneur is a moral icon in the United States. The American pharmaceutical industry, however, receives over half a billion dollars annually in federal tax dollars in the form of research grants to develop medications and
75 vaccines that they can then patent and sell back to consumers at monopolistic prices. The legislators who sponsor these grants know that their campaigns will likely receive reciprocal monetary benefit as a result. What
80 is worse, most American voters accept this system happily because they believe that they are simply helping to find cures for diseases. The reality, however, is very different: by discouraging the competition that leads to real
85 progress, this system of protectionism is actually a huge impediment to the elimination of disease.

10 The quotation from Mahatma Gandhi (lines 3–4) suggests that Gandhi believed that Western civilization was

(A) on the decline
(B) the beneficiary of unfair economic practices
(C) antithetical to progress in Asia
(D) a great triumph
(E) an unrealized concept

11 The "voices" mentioned in line 16 can be inferred to include all of the following EXCEPT

(A) American politicians
(B) leaders like Mahatma Gandhi
(C) television journalists
(D) some leaders of large corporations
(E) those who believe that the United States is faithful to the capitalist ideal

12 The primary function of the second paragraph (lines 20–38) is to

(A) illustrate a debate
(B) provide a statistical analysis
(C) explain a concept
(D) give historical background
(E) describe a popular viewpoint

13 By saying that "the story would likely be very different" (lines 37–38), the passage suggests that

(A) the rules of a free market are selectively applied
(B) trade laws favor smaller countries
(C) American companies produce the best products
(D) Asian countries are moving away from the free market
(E) American companies share the same interests as Indian companies

14 The quotation marks around particular words in the fourth paragraph (lines 56–66) serve primarily to indicate that those words are

(A) being used ironically
(B) technical economic terms
(C) adaptations of foreign words
(D) recently coined
(E) direct quotations from a document described earlier

15 The "triumph" described in line 64 is characterized as

(A) a rare success for free markets
(B) a legislative victory
(C) a breakthrough in the development of inexpensive drugs
(D) a tragic violation of the principle of free trade
(E) a success that was based on luck

16 The passage suggests that the "entrepreneur" (lines 69–70) differs from executives in the pharmaceutical industry in that the entrepreneur

(A) does not abide by free-market ideals
(B) risks his or her own money
(C) does not hire employees from overseas
(D) works more closely with representatives in Washington
(E) needs less money to start a typical business

The questions below are based on the content of the preceding passage. The questions are to be answered on the basis of what is stated or implied in the passage itself or the introductory material that precedes the passage.

Questions 17–24 pertain to the following passage.

The following passage is an excerpt from Mary Shelley's Frankenstein, *written in 1831.*

Natural philosophy, and particularly chemistry, became nearly my sole occupation.
Line I read with ardor those works, so full of genius and discrimination, that modern inquir-
5 ers have written on these subjects. I attended the lectures and cultivated the acquaintance of the men of science of the university. In M. Waldman I found a true friend. His gentleness was never tinged by dogmatism, and his
10 instructions were given with an air of frankness and good nature that banished every idea of pedantry. In a thousand ways he smoothed for me the path of knowledge and made the most abstruse inquiries clear and facile to my
15 apprehension.

As I applied so closely, it may be easily conceived that my progress was rapid. My

GO ON TO THE NEXT PAGE ▶▶▶

ardor was indeed the astonishment of the students, and my proficiency that of the mas-
20   ters. None but those who have experienced them can conceive of the enticements of science. A mind of moderate capacity which closely pursues one study must infallibly arrive at great proficiency in that study; and I,
25   who continually sought the attainment of one object of pursuit and was solely wrapped up in this, improved so rapidly that at the end of two years I made some discoveries in the improvement of some chemical instru-
30   ments, which procured me great esteem and admiration at the university. When I had arrived at this point and had become as well acquainted with the theory and practice of natural philosophy as depended on the
35   lessons of any of the professors at Ingolstadt, my residence there being no longer conducive to my improvements, I thought of returning to my friends and my native town, when an incident happened that protracted
40   my stay.
      Whence, I often asked myself, did the principle of life proceed? It was a bold question, and one which has ever been considered as a mystery; yet with how many things are we
45   upon the brink of becoming acquainted, if cowardice or carelessness did not restrain our inquiries. I revolved these circumstances in my mind and determined thenceforth to apply myself more particularly to those branches of
50   natural philosophy which relate to physiology. Unless I had been animated by an almost supernatural enthusiasm, my application to this study would have been irksome and almost intolerable. To examine the causes of life, we
55   must first have recourse to death. I became acquainted with the science of anatomy, but this was not sufficient; I must also observe the natural decay and corruption of the human body. In my education my father had taken
60   the greatest precautions that my mind should be impressed with no supernatural horrors. I do not ever remember to have trembled at a tale of superstition or to have feared the apparition of a spirit. Darkness had no effect
65   upon my fancy, and a churchyard was to me merely the receptacle of bodies deprived of life, which, from being the seat of beauty and strength, had become food for the worm. I saw how the fine form of man was degraded
70   and wasted; I beheld the corruption of death succeed to the blooming cheek of life; I saw how the worm inherited the wonders of the eye and brain. I paused, examining and ana-

lyzing all the minutiae of causation, as exem-
75   plified in the change from life to death, and death to life, until from the midst of this darkness a sudden light broke in upon me—a light so brilliant and wondrous, yet so simple, that while I became dizzy with the immensity of
80   the prospect which it illustrated, I was surprised that among so many men of genius who had directed their inquiries towards the same science, that I alone should be reserved to discover so astonishing a secret.

17 In the first paragraph, the narrator indicates that the instruction given to him by M. Waldman was

(A)   haughty
(B)   challenging
(C)   easily understood
(D)   obscure
(E)   expensive

18 In line 15, the word "apprehension" most nearly means

(A)   fear
(B)   reservation
(C)   imprisonment
(D)   understanding
(E)   arrest

19 The narrator indicates that proficiency in an academic study requires which of the following?

        I.   genius
        II. diligence
        III. financial resources

(A)   I only
(B)   II only
(C)   I and II only
(D)   II and III only
(E)   I, II, and III

Excerpted from *Frankenstein* by Mary Shelley, public domain, edited for length

GO ON TO THE NEXT PAGE ▶▶▶

20 The narrator indicates that he considered leaving Ingolstadt because he

(A) had learned all he could from its instructors
(B) was acutely homesick
(C) was offered another job
(D) had a negative experience with a professor there
(E) had become ill

21 In saying that he was "animated by an almost supernatural enthusiasm" (lines 51–52) the narrator suggests that he

(A) was easily influenced by superstition
(B) loved lecturing at Ingolstadt
(C) was passionate about studying the physiology of life and death
(D) was excited about the prospect of returning home
(E) wanted to learn more about the origin of certain superstitions

22 The "seat of beauty and strength" (lines 67–68) is a reference to

(A) the churchyard
(B) the human body
(C) the worm
(D) the university at Ingolstadt
(E) the narrator's studies

23 In line 71, the phrase "succeed to" most nearly means

(A) inspire
(B) thrive
(C) replace
(D) proceed to
(E) promote

24 The final sentence of the passage suggests that the narrator feels

(A) intimidated by the enormous task before him
(B) grateful to those who instructed him
(C) anxious about the moral dilemma posed by his work
(D) baffled by particular scientific principles
(E) privileged to be on the verge of a momentous discovery

6

STOP

You may check your work, on this section only, until time is called.

Section 7

Time—20 Minutes
16 Questions

Directions for Multiple-Choice Questions

In this section, solve each problem, using any available space on the page for scratchwork. Then decide which is the best of the choices given and fill in the corresponding oval on your answer sheet.

- You may use a calculator on any problem. All numbers used are real numbers.
- Figures are drawn as accurately as possible EXCEPT when it is stated that the figure is not drawn to scale.
- All figures lie in a plane unless otherwise indicated.

Reference Information

$A = \pi r^2$
$C = 2\pi r$
$A = \ell w$
$A = \frac{1}{2} bh$
$V = \ell wh$
$V = \pi r^2 h$
$c^2 = a^2 + b^2$
Special Right Triangles

The arc of a circle measures 360°.
Every straight angle measures 180°.
The sum of the measures of the angles of a triangle is 180°.

---

1 Which of the following integers is 2 greater than a multiple of 7?

(A)   14
(B)   15
(C)   16
(D)   17
(E)   18

2 A store sells oranges for 20 cents each, but for every 4 oranges you buy, you may buy a fifth for only 5 cents. How many oranges can you buy from this store for $3.40?

(A)   14
(B)   17
(C)   18
(D)   19
(E)   20

3 If r is a positive number and s is a negative number, all of the following must represent positive numbers EXCEPT:

(A) $-r + s$

(B) $r - s$

(C) $\dfrac{r}{s^2}$

(D) rs^2

(E) $(rs)^2$

GO ON TO THE NEXT PAGE ▶▶▶

4 Which of the following expresses the number that is 12 less than the product of 3 and $x + 1$?

(A) $x - 8$
(B) $x + 37$
(C) $3x - 11$
(D) $3x - 9$
(E) $3x + 15$

5 One bag of grass seed covers 5,000 square feet. If each bag costs $25, how much will it cost to buy enough grass seed to cover a square area that is 200 feet by 200 feet?

(A) $25
(B) $100
(C) $200
(D) $1,000
(E) $2,000

6

Note: Figure not drawn to scale

In the right triangle above, what is the value of w?

(A) 30
(B) 60
(C) 90
(D) 120
(E) 150

7 Three integers have a sum of 7 and a product of 0. If the difference of the greatest number and the least numbers is 11, then the least of these numbers is

(A) −18
(B) −11
(C) −9
(D) −2
(E) 0

8 Four points lie on a circle. How many different triangles can be drawn with 3 of these points as vertices?

(A) 4
(B) 5
(C) 6
(D) 7
(E) 8

9 If a, b, and c are consecutive positive integers such that $a < b < c$ and abc is NOT a multiple of 4, then which of the following must be true?

(A) a is even
(B) b is even
(C) c is even
(D) $a + b + c$ is odd
(E) abc is odd

Questions 10–12 refer to the following graph.

PARTICIPATION IN FUND RAISER
FOR 5 CLASSES

Percent participation in 2002

10 For which class was the change in percent participation the greatest from 2002 to 2003?

(A) A
(B) B
(C) C
(D) D
(E) E

11 If class *B* and class *E* each had 100 students in 2002 and 2003, then, in total, how many more students participated in the fund raiser from class *E* than from class *B* over the 2 years?

(A) 10
(B) 20
(C) 30
(D) 40
(E) 60

12 In 2002, the same number of students participated in the fund raiser from class *C* as from class *D*. If class *D* contained 120 students in 2002, how many students were there in class *C* in 2002?

(A) 90
(B) 100
(C) 120
(D) 140
(E) 160

13 If $x = -1$ is a solution of the equation $x^2 = 4x + c$ where c is a constant, what is another value of x that satisfies the equation?

(A) −5
(B) −2
(C) 1
(D) 2
(E) 5

14   1, 2, 6, 7, 9

A three-digit integer is to be formed from the digits listed above. If the first digit must be odd, either the second or the third digit must be 2, and no digit may be repeated, how many such integers are possible?

(A) 6
(B) 9
(C) 18
(D) 24
(E) 30

15 If 1 pound of grain can feed 5 chickens or 2 pigs, then 10 pounds of grain can feed 20 chickens and how many pigs?

(A) 8
(B) 10
(C) 12
(D) 24
(E) 40

16

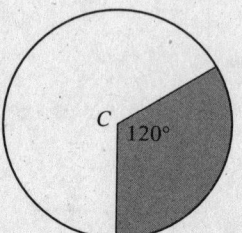

Point *C* is the center of the circle on the figure above. The shaded region has an area of 3π square centimeters. What is the *perimeter* of the shaded region in centimeters?

(A) $2\pi + 6$
(B) $2\pi + 9$
(C) $2\pi + 12$
(D) $3\pi + 6$
(E) $3\pi + 12$

STOP

You may check your work, on this section only, until time is called.

Section 8

Time — 20 minutes
19 Questions

Each of the sentences below is missing one or two portions. Read each sentence, then select the word or words that most logically complete the sentence, taking into account the meaning of the sentence as a whole.

Example:

Rather than accepting the theory unquestioningly, Deborah regarded it with -------.

    (A) mirth
    (B) sadness
    (C) responsibility
    (D) ignorance
    (E) skepticism

Correct response: (E)

8

1 The studio's most recent movies reflect a ------- of many different artistic visions rather than the ------- of a single director.

    (A) conglomeration . . . insubordination
    (B) prudence . . . unity
    (C) bastion . . . despair
    (D) synthesis . . . dominance
    (E) conspiracy . . . retreat

2 Rather than endeavoring to write timeless fiction with lasting value, many novelists cater to the ------- tastes of those modern readers who read a book once and then discard it.

    (A) immoral
    (B) fleeting
    (C) valuable
    (D) solid
    (E) intellectual

3 Although many investors may tolerate short-term declines in the value of their securities, few will accept a ------- downturn in the stock market.

    (A) protracted
    (B) contemporaneous
    (C) transient
    (D) surreptitious
    (E) fickle

4 In most societies, athletes are ------- in the same way that successful warriors were celebrated by civilizations in years past.

    (A) invoked
    (B) repudiated
    (C) lionized
    (D) vilified
    (E) beguiled

5 Dobson's overconfident and arrogant manner during press conferences was beginning to irritate his associates; there was no need to be ------- about the success of an endeavor that had yet to be launched.

    (A) superficial
    (B) capricious
    (C) pious
    (D) deferential
    (E) supercilious

6 Although few literary critics approved of her criticism of the ------- society in which she lived, Virginia Woolf remained a ------- opponent of the male hegemony that hindered women's pursuit of professional and artistic success.

    (A) matriarchal . . . pugnacious
    (B) patriarchal . . . vociferous
    (C) avuncular . . . belligerent
    (D) prejudiced . . . rudimentary
    (E) liberal . . . negligent

The passages below are followed by questions based on their content and the relationship between the passages. The questions are to be answered on the basis of what is stated or implied in the passages themselves or the introductory material that precedes them.

Questions 7–19 pertain to the following passage.

The following are 2 essays on the American English spelling reform movement. Passage 1 was written in 1906 by the humorist Ellis Parker Butler. Passage 2 was written by a modern American writer in 2003.

Passage 1

My own opinion of the spelling profession is that it has nothing to do with genius, except to kill it. I know that Shakespeare was a promis-
Line cuous sort of speller, even as to his own name, and no one can deny that he was a greater ge-
5 nius than Noah Webster. The reason America so long lagged behind Europe in the produc-tion of genius is that America, for many decades, was the slave of the spelling-book. No man who devotes the fiery days of his youth to
10 learning to spell has time to be a genius.

Serena says, and I agree with her, that it is the jealousy of a few college professors who are trying to undermine the younger writers. They know that it is excusable to spell incor-
15 rectly now, but they want this new phonetic spelling brought into use so that there shall be no excuse for bad spelling, and that then, Ser-ena says, self-made authors like me, who never can spell but who simply blaze with ge-
20 nius, will be hooted out of the magazines to make room for a stupid sort of literature that is spelled correctly. Serena looks upon the whole thing as a direct, personal stab at me. I look at it more philosophically.

25 To me it seems that the spelling reformers are entirely on the wrong track. Their pro-posed changes are almost a revolution, and we Americans do not like sudden changes. We like our revolutions to come about gradually.
30 Think how gradually automobiles have come to pass. If, in our horse age, the streets had suddenly been covered with sixty horsepower snorters going thirty miles an hour and smelling like an eighteenth-century literary
35 debate, and killing people right and left, we Americans would have arisen and destroyed

every vestige of the automobile. But the auto-mobile came gradually—first the bicycle, then the motorcycle, and so, by stages, to the pre-
40 sent monsters. So slowly and progressively did the automobile increase in size and num-ber that it seemed a matter of course. We take to being killed by the automobile quite natu-rally now.

45 Of course, the silent letters in our words are objectionable. They are lazy letters. We want no idle class in America, whether tramp, aristocrat, or silent letter, but we do not kill the tramp and the aristocrat. We set them to
50 work, or we would like to. My theory of spelling reform is to set the idle letters to work.

Take that prime offender, *although*. *Altho* does all the work, and *ugh* sits on the fence
55 and whittles. I would put *ugh* to work. *Ugh* is a syllable in itself. I would have the *ugh* follow the pronounced *altho* as a third syllable. Doubtless the asthmatic islanders who con-cocted our English language actually pro-
60 nounced it so.

I propose to have some millionaire endow my plan, and Serena and I will then form a so-ciety for the reforming of English pronuncia-tion. I will not punch out the *i* of any chief,
65 nor shall any one drag *me* from any pro-gramme, however dull. I will pronounce *programme* as it should be pronounced— *pro-grammy*—and, as for *chief*, he shall be pronounced *chy-ef*.

70 The advantage of this plan is manifest. It is so manifest that I am afraid it will never be adopted.

Serena's plan is, perhaps, less intellectual, but more American. Serena's plan is to ignore
75 all words that contain superfluous letters. She would simply boycott them. Serena would have people get along with such words as are already phonetically spelled. Why should peo-ple write *although*, when they can write
80 *notwithstanding that*, and not have a silent let-ter in it? I have myself often written a phrase twelve words long to stand instead of a single word I did not know how to spell. In fact, I abandoned my Platonic friendship for Serena,
85 and replaced it with ardent love, because I did know how to spell *sweetheart*, but could not remember whether she was my *friend* or *freind*.

Passage 2

For centuries, thinkers as notable as Ben-
90   jamin Franklin have registered the same complaint about English spelling: it is needlessly
complicated and inconsistent in pronunciation. Silent letters abound, and *ough* is pronounced six different ways in the words
95   *tough, bough, through, bought, although,* and
cough. Franklin wanted to change the alphabet and institute new spelling rules to make
English more sensible, more usable, and easier to learn. Such good ideas have been
100   around a long time, and we should put them
to rest for three good reasons.

      First, English, like most languages, has di-
alects. In Boston, *Korea* and *career* are homo-
phones. In San Francisco, they are not. To
105   spell them the same way would be to impose a
"preferred" dialect on all Americans, forcing
us all to talk like South Enders and violating
our precious value of democracy over elitism.
Failure to do so would result in chaos. Would
110   a novelist from Alabama who was educated at
Brown write in her native drawl, her adopted
New England dialect, or the homogenized
English of the educated elite? In a democratic
society, isn't one of the great benefits of a lan-
115   guage-wide spelling system that it obscures
those spoken dialects that are so often used to
stratify and separate us?

      Second, languages evolve, adopting words
from other languages, coining new ones, and
120   changing pronunciations over time. The silent
letters in the word *eight,* a bane of the "rational" speller, are the echoes of the German
acht, the Latin *octo,* the Greek *okto* and even
(faintly) the Sanskrit *asta.* The spelling may be
125   vexing to some, but it is a historical treasure
trove to others. Furthermore, this example
shows the folly of trying to standardize
spelling by linking it with pronunciation. The
words won't stand still.
130   Third, languages are not influenced very
much by plan or reason; they develop by
evolving conventions of usage. They are cultural artifacts, not legislated standards.
Spelling is like football: there may be lots of
135   silly and illogical things in it, but that doesn't
mean you have a snowball's chance in hell of
replacing the rules.

7 In the first paragraph of Passage 1, Noah
Webster is mentioned as an example of

(A)   a genius who was a poor speller
(B)   one of the first spelling reformers
(C)   a man devoted to proper spelling
(D)   a famous playwright
(E)   one who shares the author's opinion

8 Serena regards phonetic spelling as a "personal stab" (line 24) at the author of Passage
1 because its proponents

(A)   have a history of vindictiveness
(B)   do not like hard work
(C)   are well educated
(D)   are wealthy
(E)   want to eliminate the author's excuse
for poor spelling

9 The success of "Serena's plan" (line 74) depends on the ability of people to

(A)   change their habits of pronunciation
(B)   spell correctly
(C)   perfect their handwriting skills
(D)   learn an entirely new alphabet
(E)   change their writing habits

10 By saying that Serena's plan is "more American" (line 75), the author of Passage 1 implies
that Americans

(A)   are good spellers
(B)   regard writers with disdain
(C)   are inclined to protest
(D)   do not read enough
(E)   can't take a joke

11 In Passage 1, the author's theory of spelling
reform differs from that of Serena in that the
author

(A)   wants to alter the pronunciation of
words that Serena wants to ignore
(B)   regards Shakespeare as a genius but
Serena does not
(C)   wants to change the alphabet but
Serena does not
(D)   seeks to simplify spelling, while
Serena does not
(E)   understands how to alter American
habits but Serena does not

GO ON TO THE NEXT PAGE ▶▶▶

12 The author of Passage 1 claims to have fallen in love with Serena because

(A) his spelling skills were weak
(B) they agreed on a plan for phonetic spelling
(C) she helped him to understand philosophy
(D) they shared a distaste for automobiles
(E) they were both writers

13 The "chaos" mentioned in line 110 refers to

(A) the difficulty of spelling words with silent letters
(B) the challenge of getting scholars to agree
(C) the many ways of pronouncing *ough*
(D) the possibility of many sets of spelling rules for different dialects
(E) the disagreement among linguists regarding spelling reform

14 According to Passage 2, "one of the great benefits of a language-wide spelling system" (lines 115–116) is that it

(A) simplifies commonly misspelled words
(B) discourages social distinctions implied by pronunciation
(C) eliminates silent letters
(D) makes it easier to translate words from English to other languages
(E) imposes a preferred dialect

15 Passage 2 mentions the word "eight" as an example of

(A) a word with a spelling that is edifying to some
(B) a commonly mispronounced word
(C) a word with a spelling that the author believes should be simplified
(D) a recently coined term
(E) a word that has remained unchanged for centuries

16 The tone of the two passages differs in that Passage 1 is

(A) jocular, whereas Passage 2 is logical
(B) cynical, whereas Passage 2 is whimsical
(C) analytical, whereas Passage 2 is lighthearted
(D) scientific, whereas Passage 2 is satirical
(E) strident, whereas Passage 2 is reflective

17 With which of the following statements would the authors of both passages most likely agree?

(A) The rules of English spelling need to be changed.
(B) Modern conventions of grammar are illogical.
(C) Americans are lazy.
(D) Conventions of language are not easily changed.
(E) Writers should read widely to perfect their craft.

18 If the author of Passage 1 were serious about his plan for reforming English pronunciation, the author of Passage 2 would likely regard that plan as

(A) a necessary addition to phonetic spelling
(B) a logical alternative to the current system
(C) inferior to the plan for phonetic spelling
(D) unworkable because it disregards the way that conventions of language develop
(E) a more plausible plan than Serena's

19 In both passages, the word "although" is regarded as

(A) a word that is commonly mispronounced
(B) a word that is difficult to spell
(C) an example of an idiosyncracy of English that some consider problematic
(D) a word that reveals much about the development of the English language
(E) a word that can easily be eliminated from the English language

 STOP

You may check your work, on this section only, until time is called.

Section 9

Time — 10 minutes
14 Questions

Directions for "Improving Sentences" Questions

Each of the sentences below contains one underlined portion. The portion may contain one or more errors in grammar, usage, construction, precision, diction (choice of words), or idiom. Some of the sentences are correct.

Consider the meaning of the original sentence, and choose the answer that best expresses that meaning. If the original sentence is best, choose (A), because it repeats the original phrasing. Choose the phrasing that creates the clearest, most precise, and most effective sentence.

EXAMPLE: EXAMPLE ANSWER

The children couldn't hardly believe their eyes.   (C)
   (A)   couldn't hardly believe their eyes
   (B)   would not hardly believe their eyes
   (C)   could hardly believe their eyes
   (D)   couldn't nearly believe their eyes
   (E)   could hardly believe his or her eyes

---

1 The chef's assistant cut the vegetables and laid them on the table, he then started to prepare the meat.

(A)   The chef's assistant cut the vegetables and laid them on the table, he
(B)   The vegetables were cut and laid on the table by the chef's assistant when he
(C)   After cutting the vegetables and laying them on the table, the chef's assistant
(D)   The chef's assistant, having cut the vegetables and laying them on the table,
(E)   Laying on the table, the chef's assistant who cut the vegetables

2 Practicing their rebuttals ahead of time helps the forensics team members to become a better debater.

(A)   helps the forensics team member to become a better debater
(B)   helps forensic team members to become better debaters
(C)   helping the forensics team members to become better debaters
(D)   is helpful to the forensics team members who become better debaters
(E)   the forensics team member becomes a better debater

3 *Billy the Bobcat,* like other children's stories, have elements that can only be fully appreciated by adults.

(A)   like other children's stories have
(B)   like other children's stories, has
(C)   a children's story, like others, has
(D)   is like other stories for children in that they have
(E)   like that of other children's stories, has also

4 Ernest Rutherford, a New Zealand scientist when measuring the charge and mass of alpha particles, discovered that they are virtually identical to the nuclei of helium atoms.

(A)   a New Zealand scientist when measuring the charge and mass of alpha particles,
(B)   a New Zealand scientist who measured the charge and mass of alpha particles
(C)   a New Zealand scientist which measured the charge and mass of alpha particles,
(D)   measuring the charge and mass of alpha particles, was a scientist when he
(E)   being the one who measured the mass and charge of alpha particles as a scientist,

GO ON TO THE NEXT PAGE ▶▶▶

5 Oxytocin is the hormone that triggers uterine contractions during <u>labor, as well as</u> the preliminary contractions known as Braxton Hicks.

(A) labor, as well as
(B) labor, as well as being the hormone that triggers
(C) labor, causing as well
(D) labor; and also causes
(E) labor; also causing

6 During the Clinton presidency, <u>the U.S. enjoyed more than any time in its history peace and economic well being</u>.

(A) the U.S. enjoyed more than any time in its history peace and economic well being
(B) the U.S. enjoying more than any other time in its history peace and economic well being
(C) more peace and economic well being was enjoyed by the U.S. than any other time
(D) economic peace and well being was enjoyed by the U.S. more so than any other time in the country's history
(E) the U.S. enjoyed more peace and economic well being than at any other time in its history

7 The final three months of the year tend to be profitable for technology companies <u>because of increased consumer demand being around the holidays</u>.

(A) because of increased consumer demand being around the holidays
(B) because of increasing consumer demand occurs around the holidays
(C) an increased consumer demand around the holidays makes it so
(D) because consumer demand increases around the holidays
(E) because the increased consumer demand is what occurs around the holidays

8 As his moviemaking career began to wane, Jerry Lewis remained in the public eye by hosting a variety show and <u>on an annual telethon with benefits for the Muscular Dystrophy Association</u>.

(A) on an annual telethon with benefits for the Muscular Dystrophy Association
(B) an annual telethon with benefits to the Muscular Dystrophy Association
(C) benefiting the Muscular Dystrophy Association with his annual telethon
(D) an annual telethon benefiting the Muscular Dystrophy Association
(E) the Muscular Dystrophy Association with an annual telethon

9 The development of bebop is attributed in large part to Dizzy Gillespie and also saxophonist Charlie Parker; <u>and their unique styles helped to contribute to and typified the bebop sound</u>.

(A) and their unique styles helped to contribute to and typified the bebop sound
(B) their unique styles contributed to and typified the bebop sound
(C) it was their unique styles that contributed to and were typifying the bebop sound
(D) but their unique styles helped contribute to the typical bebop sound
(E) the bebop sound was helped by the contributions of their unique styles and typified it

10 Many critics believe that video games <u>are harmful to children that contain violent imagery</u>.

(A) are harmful to children that contain violent imagery
(B) containing violent imagery are harmful to children
(C) that contain violent imagery that harms children
(D) containing violent imagery that are harmful to children
(E) harmful to children containing violent imagery

11 Walking hand-in-hand along the boardwalk, <u>a vendor stopped the couple to try to sell them lemonade</u>.

(A) a vendor stopped the couple to try to sell them lemonade
(B) the couple was stopped by a vendor who tried to sell them lemonade
(C) trying to sell them lemonade, a vendor stopped the couple
(D) a vendor stopped the couple to try and sell them lemonade
(E) the couple having been stopped by the vendor who tried to sell them lemonade

12 Professor Peterson had just stepped into the classroom <u>and that was when he discovered</u> that several lab manuals were missing.

(A) and that was when he found out
(B) and then he discovered
(C) when he discovered
(D) after which he discovered
(E) discovering soon thereafter

13 Parents today spend more time working <u>than</u> 30 years ago.

(A) than
(B) than have
(C) than of the parents of
(D) than did parents
(E) than of the parents

14 The anthropologists would have considered their research a success <u>if they would have found a language that shares lexical elements with the Borneans they were studying</u>.

(A) if they would have found a language that shares lexical elements with the Borneans they were studying
(B) had they found a language that shares lexical elements with that of the Borneans they were studying
(C) if they found a language that shares lexical elements with the Borneans they were studying
(D) if they had found a language that shares lexical elements with the Borneans they were studying
(E) if they would have found a language that shares lexical elements with that of the Borneans they were studying

9

STOP

You may check your work, on this section only, until time is called.

ANSWER KEY

Section 2 Math	Section 5 Math	Section 7 Math	Section 3 Critical Reading	Section 6 Critical Reading	Section 8 Critical Reading	Section 4 Writing	Section 9 Writing
1. E	1. E	1. C	1. A	1. A	1. D	1. A	1. C
2. B	2. D	2. E	2. C	2. B	2. B	2. E	2. B
3. E	3. C	3. A	3. A	3. E	3. A	3. B	3. B
4. D	4. A	4. D	4. D	4. B	4. C	4. C	4. B
5. C	5. B	5. C	5. B	5. E	5. E	5. D	5. A
6. D	6. A	6. C	6. E	6. C	6. B	6. C	6. E
7. E	7. C	7. D	7. B	7. D	7. C	7. A	7. D
8. D	8. A	8. A	8. C	8. C	8. E	8. B	8. D
9. E	9. 7.5	9. B	9. A	9. D	9. E	9. B	9. B
10. B	10. 13	10. A	10. D	10. E	10. C	10. E	10. B
11. A	11. 100	11. E	11. E	11. B	11. A	11. E	11. B
12. E	12. 24	12. E	12. B	12. C	12. A	12. D	12. C
13. D	13. 0.2 or 1/5	13. E	13. C	13. A	13. D	13. B	13. D
14. B	14. 4	14. C	14. A	14. A	14. B	14. D	14. B
15. A	15. 0.8	15. C	15. D	15. D	15. A	15. D	
16. C	16. 5	16. A	16. B	16. B	16. A	16. E	
17. C	17. 9		17. A	17. C	17. D	17. C	
18. C	18. 10		18. A	18. D	18. D	18. B	
19. E			19. D	19. B	19. C	19. C	
20. C			20. C	20. A		20. B	
			21. B	21. C		21. E	
			22. E	22. B		22. C	
			23. C	23. C		23. C	
			24. D	24. E		24. E	
						25. B	
						26. C	
						27. E	
						28. A	
						29. C	
						30. A	
						31. B	
						32. B	
						33. D	
						34. E	
						35. A	

# Right (A):	Questions 1–8 # Right (A):	# Right (A):	# Right (A):	# Right (A):	# Right (A):	# Right (A):	# Right (A):
# Wrong (B):		# Wrong (B):	# Wrong (B):	# Wrong (B):	# Wrong (B):	# Wrong (B):	# Wrong (B):
# (A)–¼ (B):	# Wrong (B):	# (A)–¼ (B):	# (A)–¼ (B):	# (A)–¼ (B):	# (A)–¼ (B):	# (A)–¼ (B):	# (A)–¼ (B):
	# (A)–¼ (B):						
	Questions 9–18 # Right (A):						

SCORE CONVERSION TABLE

How to score your test

Use the answer key on the previous page to determine your raw score on each section. **Your raw score on each section except Section 5 is simply the number of correct answers minus ¼ of the number of wrong answers. On Section 5, your raw score is the sum of the number of correct answers for questions 1–18 minus ¼ of the number of wrong answers for questions 1–8.** Next, add the raw scores from Sections 3, 4, and 7 to get your Math raw score, and add the raw scores from Sections 6 and 9 to get your Writing raw score. Write the three raw scores here:

Raw Critical Reading score: _____ Raw Math score: _____ Raw Writing score: _____

Use the table below to convert these to scaled scores.

Scaled scores: Critical Reading: _____ Math: _____ Writing: _____

Raw Score	Critical Reading Scaled Score	Math Scaled Score	Writing Scaled Score	Raw Score	Critical Reading Scaled Score	Math Scaled Score	Writing Scaled Score
67	800			32	520	550	610
66	800			31	510	550	600
65	790			30	510	540	580
64	780			29	500	530	570
63	760			28	490	530	560
62	750			27	490	520	550
61	730			26	480	510	540
60	720			25	480	500	530
59	700			24	470	490	520
58	700			23	460	480	510
57	690			22	460	480	500
56	680			21	450	470	490
55	670			20	440	460	480
54	660	800		19	440	450	470
53	650	790		18	430	450	460
52	650	760		17	420	440	450
51	640	740		16	420	430	440
50	630	720		15	410	420	440
49	620	710	800	14	400	410	430
48	620	700	800	13	400	410	420
47	610	680	800	12	390	400	410
46	600	670	790	11	380	390	400
45	600	660	780	10	370	380	390
44	590	650	760	9	360	370	380
43	590	640	740	8	350	360	380
42	580	630	730	7	340	350	370
41	570	630	710	6	330	340	360
40	570	620	700	5	320	330	350
39	560	610	690	4	310	320	340
38	550	600	670	3	300	310	320
37	550	590	660	2	280	290	310
36	540	580	650	1	270	280	300
35	540	580	640	0	250	260	280
34	530	570	630	−1	230	240	270
33	520	560	620	−2 or less	210	220	250

SCORE CONVERSION TABLE FOR WRITING COMPOSITE
[ESSAY + MULTIPLE CHOICE]

Calculate your writing raw score as you did on the previous page and grade your essay from a 1 to a 6 according to the standards that follow in the detailed answer key.

Essay score: _____ Raw Writing score: _____

Use the table below to convert these to scaled scores.

Scaled score: Writing: _____

Raw Score	Essay Score 0	Essay Score 1	Essay Score 2	Essay Score 3	Essay Score 4	Essay Score 5	Essay Score 6
-2 or less	200	230	250	280	310	340	370
-1	210	240	260	290	320	360	380
0	230	260	280	300	340	370	400
1	240	270	290	320	350	380	410
2	250	280	300	330	360	390	420
3	260	290	310	340	370	400	430
4	270	300	320	350	380	410	440
5	280	310	330	360	390	420	450
6	290	320	340	360	400	430	460
7	290	330	340	370	410	440	470
8	300	330	350	380	410	450	470
9	310	340	360	390	420	450	480
10	320	350	370	390	430	460	490
11	320	360	370	400	440	470	500
12	330	360	380	410	440	470	500
13	340	370	390	420	450	480	510
14	350	380	390	420	460	490	520
15	350	380	400	430	460	500	530
16	360	390	410	440	470	500	530
17	370	400	420	440	480	510	540
18	380	410	420	450	490	520	550
19	380	410	430	460	490	530	560
20	390	420	440	470	500	530	560
21	400	430	450	480	510	540	570
22	410	440	460	480	520	550	580
23	420	450	470	490	530	560	590
24	420	460	470	500	540	570	600
25	430	460	480	510	540	580	610
26	440	470	490	520	550	590	610
27	450	480	500	530	560	590	620
28	460	490	510	540	570	600	630
29	470	500	520	550	580	610	640
30	480	510	530	560	590	620	650
31	490	520	540	560	600	630	660
32	500	530	550	570	610	640	670
33	510	540	550	580	620	650	680
34	510	550	560	590	630	660	690
35	520	560	570	600	640	670	700
36	530	560	580	610	650	680	710
37	540	570	590	620	660	690	720
38	550	580	600	630	670	700	730
39	560	600	610	640	680	710	740
40	580	610	620	650	690	720	750
41	590	620	640	660	700	730	760
42	600	630	650	680	710	740	770
43	610	640	660	690	720	750	780
44	620	660	670	700	740	770	800
45	640	670	690	720	750	780	800
46	650	690	700	730	770	800	800
47	670	700	720	750	780	800	800
48	680	720	730	760	800	800	800
49	680	720	730	760	800	800	800

Detailed Answer Key

Section I

The following essay received 12 points out of a possible 12, meaning that it demonstrates *clear and consistent competence* in that it

- develops an insightful point of view on the topic
- demonstrates exemplary critical thinking
- uses effective examples, reasons, and other evidence to support its thesis
- is consistently focused, coherent, and well-organized
- demonstrates skillful and effective use of language and sentence structure
- is largely (but not necessarily completely) free of grammatical and usage errors

Consider carefully the issue discussed in the following passage, then write an essay that answers the question posed in the assignment.

> An entertainment-driven culture runs the risk of encouraging passivity among its citizens. If they can experience something vicariously through a movie, television show or video game, why should they get involved with the activity itself? It's safer, after all, to watch someone scale a mountain than to do it yourself. The effect of this passivity, of course, is an apathetic frame of mind. We cease to care deeply about so many things because they are experienced, at best, second-hand.

Assignment: **Is apathy a problem in today's society?** Write an essay in which you answer this question and discuss your point of view on this issue. Support your position logically with examples from literature, the arts, history, politics, science and technology, current events, or your experience or observation.

Every society seems to have platitudes about laziness, like "idle hands are the devil's workshop." This is because, to a society, the value of an individual is little more than his or her productivity. For many people, the worst kind of laziness is apathy, being too lazy to even care. But the fact is that we couldn't survive if we cared about everything that was worth caring about. We would go insane. Furthermore, those who complain about apathy are usually the great manipulators of the world, trying to blame others for their own failures.

Holden Caulfield seemed to be apathetic to his teachers at Pencey Prep. But he was far from apathetic; indeed, he probably cared too much. His brother's death and the suicide of a classmate affected him deeply, although he had trouble articulating his grief. He saw what the adults in his world seemed unable to see: the hypocrisy and meanness in the world. If he didn't get away from the things that the teachers and other adults wanted him to care about, he probably would have gone crazy. Indeed, those adults thought he was crazy, but to Holden, it was the hypocritical world that was mad. His desperation to protect him-

self from the unbearable "phoniness" in the world led him, ironically, to often be phony himself. He hated his own hypocrisy, but he had to experience it to understand it. What others saw as apathy and cynicism was just his way of making it in the world.

Holden was quick to see that those who complained about his laziness and apathy were just the ones who wanted to control him because they couldn't control their own lives. Teachers too often assume that, if their students aren't "performing," they must be lazy and apathetic. "You're so smart. You would do well if you would just apply yourself." Teachers see this kind of comment as supporting, but it is supremely degrading, and it covers up the teachers' inability to inspire or even understand their students.

Some people even go so far as to assume that entire societies are lazy or apathetic, simply because they do not share their same sensibilities or "productivity," failing to see that productivity is often the product, not just of hard work, but of material and logistical advantage. I don't have to work as hard, for instance, to be "productive" as a teenager in rural China, because I have free access to a computer, the internet, a local library, and helpful adult professionals. The Chinese teenager might be far more intelligent, diligent and resourceful than I, but far less "productive."

Perhaps a sign of maturity and virtue in a society is the degree to which it values its citizens independently of their "productivity." Every human being desires to build a better world in his or her own way. Sometimes that way does not involve making more money, getting better grades, or doing what society has established as "productive."

The following essay received 8 points out of a possible 12, meaning that it demonstrates *adequate competence* in that it

- develops a point of view on the topic
- demonstrates some critical thinking, but perhaps not consistently
- uses some examples, reasons, and other evidence to support its thesis, but perhaps not adequately
- shows a general organization and focus, but shows occasional lapses in this regard
- demonstrates adequate but occasionally inconsistent facility with language
- contains occasional errors in grammar, usage and mechanics

The greatest danger to the modern world is not terrorists who have been indoctrinated into a twisted world view, but the masses of people who are indifferent to them, or even sympathize with them. "Live and let live," so many people say. "They have a right to their point of view that women are animals and that someone who speaks against their religion should have his tongue cut out. That is just their way of thinking." This apathy to the dangers of the world is even more dangerous than the terrorists themselves.

In Madrid, a band of Al Qaeda terrorists decided that it was a good idea, in March of 2004, to blow up 200 innocent commuters on a train so that they could influence the upcoming elections in Spain. They proclaimed that they love death more than westerners love life. They were hoping that the Spanish people would then be so frightened that they would elect a leader who would take Spain's troops out of Iraq, as Al Qaeda wished. And that is exactly what happened.

The people of Spain didn't care enough to realize that they were doing exactly what the terrorists were hoping they would do. The voters of Spain probably believed that they were making it less likely that the terrorists would strike again, but it was probably the exact opposite. The terrorists love to know that their violence scares people, and the Spanish people gave them what they wanted. Contrast this with the American response to terrorism: zero tolerance.

The worst evil occurs when good people do nothing. Millions of supposedly "good" German people sat on their hands as millions of "unwanted" Jews, gays and foreigners were slaughtered. Now, millions of people sit on their hands as religious fanatics look at the slaughter of innocent people as their ticket to paradise. It is unreasonable to believe that those with warped hatred of western cultures will stop their hatred and their evil deeds merely because they are appeased by weak governments.

The following essay received 4 points out of a possible 12, meaning that it demonstrates *some incompetence* in that it

- has a seriously limited point of view
- demonstrates weak critical thinking
- uses inappropriate or insufficient examples, reasons, and other evidence to support its thesis
- is poorly focused and organized, and has seriously problems with coherence
- demonstrates frequent problems with language and sentence structure
- contains errors in grammar and usage that obscure the author's meaning seriously

When people don't care about something, it's hard to get anything done. If a team has players that don't really want to play, for instance, it's almost impossible to get them to win a game, even if you're a master motivator. That's why it's so important to care about things and not have apathy.

If you don't care about something, also, it's just really difficult to be happy. You don't have anything to look forward to in life. Some people don't really care about school, and they just listen to their iPods and can't wait to hang out with their friends or play their XBoxes when they get home. College doesn't mean anything to them, and you can tell that they are miserable people. It's one thing to question your teachers and wonder whether the things you learn in school are relevant for your life, but it's entirely different to not even care about what you do in school even a little bit.

Research has shown that you can't really get anywhere without an education, so if you don't care about school you might as well not care about having any kind of successful life. If they would just find something important that they could care about, like a sport or a musical instrument or a job or something like that, then they might have something they could focus there life for, and have some positive purpose in life. Criminals probably come about because early on they didn't really learn to care about anything important, and that is the real tragedy. and foreigners were slaughtered. Now, millions of people sit on their hands as religious fanatics look at the slaughter of innocent people as their ticket to paradise. It is unreasonable to believe that those with warped hatred of western cultures will stop their hatred and their evil deeds merely because they are appeased by weak governments.

Detailed Answer Key

Section 2

1. **E** Just substitute 3 for x: $5x = 3x + y$
   Substitute: $5(3) = 3(3) + y$
   Simplify: $15 = 9 + y$
   Subtract 9: $6 = y$
   (Chapter 11 Lesson 1: Solving Equations)

2. **B** To buy 48 batteries in packages of 24, you will need two packages, which will cost 2($12) = $24. To buy them in packages of 6, you will need 8 packages, which will cost 8($4) = $32. Buying in packages of 24 will save $ 32 – $24 = $8.
   (Chapter 12 Lesson 4: Rate Problems)

3. **E** You can probably solve this one best by quickly graphing each point and just inspecting. Clearly, (5, 5) lies outside the region.
   (Chapter 13 Lesson 4: Coordinate Geometry)

4. **D** Interpret the statement as an equation:
   $(\frac{1}{3})(2x) = 5$
   Multiply by 2: $(\frac{2}{3})(2x) = 10$
   Multiply by 2: $(\frac{2}{3})(4x) = 20$
   (Chapter 11 Lesson 7: Word Problems)

5. **C** The smallest positive integer that is divisible by 12 and 16 is 48. If n is 48, the only factor among the choices is (C) 48.
   (Chapter 10 Lesson 7: Divisibility)
   (Chapter 11 Lesson 5: Factoring)

6. **D** The sum of the angles in a triangle is 180°, so
   $a + b + 40 = 180$
   Subtract 40: $a + b = 140$
   Add the given equation: $\underline{+ (a - b) = 10}$
   $2a = 150$
   Divide by 2: $a = 75$
   (Chapter 13 Lesson 2: Triangles)
   (Chapter 11 Lesson 2: Systems)

7. **E** Choose n = 1 as an example. Plugging this in to the choices gives answers of (A) ½ (B) 3 (C) 3 (D) 1 (E) 2. The only even number here is (E) 2.
   (Chapter 12 Lesson 3: Numerical Reasoning Problems)

8. **D** Let c be the number of colas that Mike sold and r be the number of root beers. Since the total sold is 48, $c + r = 48$. Since he sold twice as many colas as root beers, $c = 2r$. Substituting this into the first equation gives

Simplify: $2r + r = 48$
$3r = 48$
Divide by 3: $r = 16$
(Chapter 11 Lesson 7: Word Problems)

9. **E** Pick two perfect squares for m and n, like 4 and 9. Plugging these in to the examples gives (A) 36 (B) 36 (C) 16 (D) 324 (E) -45. The only choice that is not a perfect square is (E) -45.
   (Chapter 11 Lesson 4: Working with Roots)

10. **B** One option is to solve each equation by plugging in 10 for a: $a + b = 10 + b = 9$
    Subtract 10: $b = -1$
    Second equation: $10 - c = 14$
    Subtract 10: $-c = 4$
    Divide by -1: $c = -4$
    So $c - b = -4 - (-1) = -4 + 1 = -3$
    (Chapter 10 Lesson 6: Negatives)

11. **A** To maximize $5x - 5y$, maximize the value of x and minimize the value of y. The greatest x can be is $\frac{5}{3}$, and the least y can be is $\frac{1}{3}$. So $5x - 5y = 5(\frac{5}{3}) - 5(\frac{1}{3}) = \frac{25}{3} - \frac{5}{3} = \frac{20}{3} = 6\frac{2}{3}$.
    (Chapter 10 Lesson 3: Fractions)
    (Chapter 12 Lesson 3: Numerical Reasoning Problems)

12. **E** Fill in the table above and to the left of the x by following the rule, like this:

0	1	2	3	4	5
1	2	4	7		
2	4	8	15		
3	7	15	x		
4					
5					

This shows that $x = 15 + 15 = 30$.
(Chapter 14 Lesson 5: Data Analysis)

13. **D** To maximize c you must minimize the value of $a + b$. Since the numbers must be positive and even, the least values that a and b can have are 2 and 4:
    $a + b + c = 60$
    Plug in: $2 + 4 + c = 60$
    Simplify: $6 + c = 60$
    Subtract 6: $c = 54$
    (Chapter 12 Lesson 3: Numerical Reasoning Problems)

14. B It is easier to pick a simple value for the "starting" population in 1980, like 100. Since the population increased by 10% from 1980 to 1990, the 1990 population must have been (100)(1.10) = 110. Since it decreased by 10% from 1990 to 2000, the 2000 population must have been (110)(0.90) = 99. From 1980 to 2000, then, the percent change was (99 − 100)/100 = −1/100 = −1%.
(Chapter 10 Lesson 5: Percents)

15. A An egg-producing female lays 100 eggs. Only 30% of these eggs become egg-producing females, which is (.30)(100) = 30 egg-producing females the next year. These 30 lay 100 eggs each, or 3,000 eggs. If 30% of these eggs become egg-producing females the next year, this yields (0.30)(3,000) = 900 in 2 years.

16. C Although you may substitute $5y$ for x as a first step, it's probably easier to simplify the expression first:

$$\sqrt{\left(x^2 - 2xy + y^2\right)}$$

Factor: $\sqrt{(x-y)^2}$

Simplify: $|x - y|$

Substitute: $|5y - y|$

Simplify: $|4y| = 4y$
(Chapter 11 Lesson 4: Working with Roots)
(Chapter 11 Lesson 5: Factoring)
(Chapter 11 Lesson 6: Inequalities, Absolute Values, and Plugging In)

17. C Think of numbers that are larger than their squares. This excludes negatives, because the squares of negatives are always positive. It also excludes numbers greater than 1, because the squares of these are bigger than the original numbers. Therefore, $0 < x < 1$. This means I and II are true, but not III.
(Chapter 12 Lesson 3: Numerical Reasoning Problems)

18. C Believe it or not, you don't need to find the 2 midpoints in order to answer this question. You need to know only that the distance between the 2 midpoints is half of the distance between the 2 endpoints. The distance between the endpoints is $(3x + 2) − (−x − 4) = 3x + 2 + x + 4 = 4x + 6$. Half of this is $2x + 3$.
(Chapter 13 Lesson 4: Coordinate Geometry)

19. E Since all radii of a triangle are equal, $PQ = PR$. Since $PQ = QR$ too, the triangle must be equilateral. Since its area is $9\sqrt{3}$, the lengths have the measures shown in the diagram. The circle has a radius of 6. The shaded region is equal to the area of the sector minus the area of the triangle. Since the central angle is 60°, the sector has an area that is ⅙ of the whole circle, or $(\frac{1}{6})(\pi(6)^2) = 6\pi$. Subtracting the area of the triangle gives $6\pi − 9\sqrt{3}$.

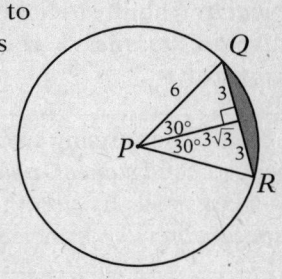

(Chapter 13 Lesson 3: The Pythagorean Theorem)
(Chapter 13 Lesson 5: Areas and Perimeters)
(Chapter 13 Lesson 8: Circles)

20. C If the ratio of boys to girls in a class is 3 to 5, then 3/(3 + 5) = ⅜ of the class is boys and 5/(3 + 5) = 5/8 of the class is girls. This means there are (⅜)(160) = 60 boys and (⅝)(160) = 100 girls in the senior class. Similarly, the fraction of boys in the junior class is ⅜ and the fraction of girls is ⅝. If there are x students in the junior class, then there are (⅜)x boys and (⅝)x girls in the junior class. If the ratio of boys to girls is 1:1 when the classes are combined, then

$$60 + (\tfrac{3}{8})x = 100 + (\tfrac{5}{8})x$$

Subtract 60 and (⅜)x: $(\frac{1}{5})x = 40$
Multiply by 5: $x = 200$
(Chapter 11 Lesson 7: Word Problems)
(Chapter 10 Lesson 4: Ratios and Proportions)

Section 3

1. A A *six-month hiatus* (break) would cause her skills to *weaken*, something she might fear. *atrophy* = weaken from disuse; *align* = line up; *disseminate* = spread like seed

2. C *Domineering* opinions are overbearing and preachy. *vindictive* = inspired by revenge; *pedantic* = acting like a know-it-all; *conciliatory* = acting to bring people together; *treacherous* = betraying someone's confidence; *didactic* = preachy; *dogmatic* = condescendingly preachy; *prosaic* = ordinary

3. A The missing word must refer to Walter's *inability to make up his mind*. *vacillation* = inability to make up one's mind; *solicitation* = request for help; *rejuvenation* = restoration of one's youth; *admonishment* = mild reproof

4. **D** If a writer is *successful . . . even in the face of . . . rejections,* he or she must be very *persistent. affluence* = wealth; *haughty* = arrogant; *pertinacity* = strong persistence; *resilient* = able to endure hardship; *tenacity* = ability to hold fast; *relentless* = unwilling to give up; *stoutness* = courage or sturdiness; *craven* = cowardly

5. **B** The missing word must be in contrast to *direct, forceful stances. pontification* = haughty, self-important speech; *circumlocution* = indirect, evasive speech; *brevity* = conciseness

6. **E** The parallelism of the two clauses helps you to complete the sentence. If counselors *believe that criminals can change,* then they must *have faith in their changeability.* If they realize *that they can often return to their old habits,* they must by wary of *recidivism* (tendency to fall into old habits). *mutability* = changeability; *astuteness* = keen ability; *transcendence* = the quality of exceeding; *malleability* = ability to be bent; *relapse* = falling back into old ways

7. **B** If something is out of place in time, it is an *anachronism. anachronism* = something out of place in time; *idiom* = phrase with a meaning that is different from its literal meaning; *interlocutor* = someone who takes part in a conversation

8. **C** The sentence indicates that the "h" was evidence of an earlier time. *inference* = conclusion based on evidence; *analogy* = useful comparison; *vestige* = remaining trace; *anomaly* = unusual event; *quandary* = perplexing situation

9. **A** The passage states that language is used as *impenetrable walls* (line 7) between people, having biased connotations favoring one group over another.

10. **D** By saying that *we infer volumes* (lines 3–4), the author means that *we draw a lot of conclusions.*

11. **E** The passage states that instructing a child to tie shoes *the right way will defeat the child's growing attempt at self-mastery* (lines 12–14).

12. **B** The last sentence states that *nagging* is a *constant reminder of his or her lack of self-control* (lines 21–22).

13. **C** The author states that Modernism is *egotistical* (line 19) and *self-conscious* (line 21) and also that it *begins nowhere and with no one in particular* (lines 12–13), suggesting that it is both *self-centered* and *ill-defined,* but the paragraph does not mention Modernism being *politically oriented.*

14. **A** The passage states that *Critics and academics . . . prefer their artistic movements to be readily comprehensible* (lines 8–10), so they do *not* like those that are hard to understand.

15. **D** The quotation from James Joyce in the next sentence describes these *landmines as enigmas and puzzles that . . . will keep the professors busy for centuries arguing over what I meant* (lines 21–25). In other words, they are literary devices placed in his novels to baffle professors.

16. **B** The passage states that *plots . . . are submerged beneath wave after wave of . . . hyper-literary and meta-literary indulgences* (lines 32–37), so it suggests that plot is not as important as other things.

17. **A** The author states that it is *hard not to love modernism* (lines 38–39) but also uses critical terms like *posturing* (line 19) *aberrations* (line 19) to describe it. In the last two lines, he refers to modernism as *reprehensible but somehow roguishly likeable.* This is a very *ambivalent* characterization of modernism.

18. **A** The comparison is a *metaphor* but not a *simile* because it states that the *modernist novel* is *a sociopath. Juxtaposition* is the placement of two images one on top of the another, as in *a sociopath and a cad. Personification* is giving human qualities to something that is not human.

19. **D** The purpose of the passage is to introduce the reader to the new science of genomics.

20. **C** A *pathogen* (line 8) is not part of the *immune system* (lines 7–8) but rather what the immune system responds to.

21. **B** The *orchestrated response* of *the immune system* (lines 7–8) is mentioned as an example of how *molecules convey information* (line 9).

22. **E** The fact that *through genomics massive amounts of information can be converted into an electronic format* (lines 36–38) is what *facilitates a dramatically new framework for understanding life* (lines 40–41).

23. **C** The passage suggests that *information theory . . . may seem unfit for . . . science* (lines 50–52) because *information . . . implies an underlying intent* (lines 49–50).

24. **D** The final paragraph indicates that genomic advances *have helped to propel the remarkable development of the computer and telecommunication industries* (lines 58–60) and suggests that they may help to *improve human health* (lines 61–62). This discusses *actual and potential consequences.*

Section 4

1. A The sentence is correct.

2. E The underlined phrase should be a noun phrase that represents *one of the best features of the journalist's lifestyle.* Only (C) and (E) are noun phrases, and (E) is much clearer.
(Chapter 18 Lesson 4: Comparison Problems)

3. B The opening participial phrase modifies *Greg* and not *Greg's search.*
(Chapter 18 Lesson 7: Dangling and Misplaced Participles)

4. C Idiom requires *neither* to be followed by *nor*, and parallelism requires the *nor* to be followed by an adjective.
(Chapter 18 Lesson 10: Idiom Errors)

5. D The past participle of *to take* is *taken*, not *took.*
(Chapter 18 Lesson 13: Irregular Verbs)

6. C Although choice (D) is parallel in structure, its phrasing is nonstandard. The phrasing in (C) is both parallel and clear.
(Chapter 18 Lesson 3: Parallelism)

7. A The pronoun *he* is the subject of an implied verb: *he (did)*, so it is correctly in the subjective form. Also, the phrase *admire his acting* is correct, because the object of the verb is *acting*, not *him.*
(Chapter 18 Lesson 6: Pronoun Case)

8. B *Neither* is the subject of the verb, as well as the antecedent of the pronoun. Since it is singular, the verb should be *was* and the pronoun should be *its.*
(Chapter 18 Lesson 1: Subject-Verb Disagreement)
(Chapter 18 Lesson 5: Pronoun-Antecedent Disagreement)

9. B The participle *walking* modifies *Liz*, not *Liz's family.* Choice (D) makes this correction, but the modifiers are awkward and unclear.
(Chapter 18 Lesson 7: Dangling and Misplaced Participles)
(Chapter 18 Lesson 12: Other Modifier Problems)

10. E The phrase *if not better* is an interrupter, so the sentence should read well even if it is omitted. The only phrasing that meets this criterion is (E).
(Chapter 18 Lesson 2: Trimming Sentences)

11. E The original is not a sentence but a fragment.
(Chapter 18 Lesson 15: Coordinating Ideas)

12. D The phrase *much closer* modifies the verb *study* and so should be in adverbial form: *much more closely.*
(Chapter 18 Lesson 12: Other Modifier Problems)

13. B The two clauses must be parallel: *has been so popular* would make this clause parallel to the first.
(Chapter 18 Lesson 3: Parallelism)

14. D This is a diction error. *Respectfully* means full of respect, which makes no sense here. The word should be *respectively.*
(Chapter 18 Lesson 11: Diction Errors)

15. D The verb *would have considered* is in the wrong tense and mood. It should be *consider.*
(Chapter 18 Lesson 9: Tricky Tenses)
(Chapter 18 Lesson 14: The Subjunctive Mood)

16. E The sentence is correct.

17. C The *fund deficit and the disillusionment* are not a single problem, but two *problems.*
(Chapter 18 Lesson 4: Comparison Problems)

18. B The subject of the verb is *either accepting or rejecting.* If the subject of a verb is an *either . . . or* construction, the verb must agree with the noun after the *or*, which in this case is *rejecting.* Since this is a singular noun, the verb should be *was.*
(Chapter 18 Lesson 1: Subject-Verb Disagreement)

19. C Since *defense attorneys* can be counted, the correct comparative word is *fewer*, not *less.*
(Chapter 18 Lesson 4: Comparison Problems)

20. B It is illogical to compare *service* to *other restaurants.* The phrase should be *the service at the other restaurants.*
(Chapter 18 Lesson 3: Parallelism)

21. E The sentence is correct.

22. C This pronoun refers to *a child*, so it must be the singular *his or her.*
(Chapter 18 Lesson 5: Pronoun-Antecedent Disagreement)

23. C The phrase *not only A but also B* indicates a parallel structure. To make the structure parallel, the phrase should be replaced with *by.*
(Chapter 18 Lesson 3: Parallelism)

24. E The sentence is correct.

25. **B** The pronoun *he* is ambiguous. We are not certain which individual it is referring to. To correct the error, *he* should be changed to either Thomas Cowher or the Senator.
(Chapter 18 Lesson 5: Pronoun-Antecedent Disagreement)

26. **C** The sentence indicates that this occurred in the past by saying those who *were observing*. Therefore *are* should instead be *were*.
(Chapter 18 Lesson 1: Subject-Verb Disagreement)

27. **E** The sentence is correct

28. **A** Between my brother and *I* should instead be between my brother and *me*. Subjective pronouns, such as *I*, should only be used as subjects. Objective pronouns, including *me*, can be used as objects of verbs or as objects of prepositions.
(Chapter 18 Lesson 6: Pronoun Case)

29. **C** The critic is writing about a *duo*, which is a singular subject. The *their* should therefore be replaced by *its*.
(Chapter 18 Lesson 5: Pronoun-Antecedent Disagreement)

30. **A** Choice (A) is the most concise and clear, and the phrasing is parallel.
(Chapter 18 Lesson 3: Parallelism)
(Chapter 18 Lesson 15: Coordinating Ideas)

31. **B** Sentence 3 presents an example of Plato's reasoning as described in sentence 2. Choice (C) may be tempting, but since the sentence does not extend the idea from sentence 2 but only provides an example, the word *furthermore* is inappropriate.
(Chapter 18 Lesson 15: Coordinating Ideas)

32. **B** The pronoun *they* and the noun *approximations* should agree in number. Choice (B) provides the most straightforward phrasing.
(Chapter 18 Lesson 5: Pronoun-Antecedent Disagreement)
(Chapter 18 Lesson 15: Coordinating Ideas)

33. **D** Sentence 6 does not fit because it shifts the discussion to what students dislike, rather than the nature of mathematical objects.

34. **E** Choice (E) provides the most logical, concise, and clear phrasing.

35. **A** Choice (A) provides the most logical, concise, and clear phrasing.

Section 5

1. **E** If $2x = 10$, then $4x = 20$, and if $3y = 12$, then $6y = 24$, so $4x + 6y = 20 + 24 = 44$.
(Chapter 9 Lesson 4: Simplifying Problems)

2. **D** Set up the equation: $(a + b + 4)/3 = 5$
Multiply by 3: $a + b + 4 = 15$
Subtract 4: $a + b = 11$
(Chapter 12 Lesson 2: Mean/Median/Mode Problems)

3. **C** If $b = 2a$, then $a + 2a = 180$, because the 2 angles form a linear pair. So $3a = 180$ and $a = 60$. Your diagram should now look like this:

So $d + e + g + h = 60 + 60 + 120 + 60 = 300$.
(Chapter 13 Lesson 1: Lines and Angles)

4. **A** Substitute $x = 100$ into the function:
$\sqrt{\sqrt{100} - 1} = \sqrt{10 - 1} = \sqrt{9} = 3$
(Chapter 14 Lesson 2: Functions)

5. **B** If $2^m = 8$, then $m = 3$. So $3^{k+3} = 243$. Checking the powers of 3 shows that $k + 3 = 5$. Therefore, $k = 2$, so $2^k = 2^2 = 4$.
(Chapter 11 Lesson 3: Working with Exponentials)

6. **A** If four numbers have an average of 50, they have a sum of $4 \times 50 = 200$. The numbers are all *different* and all *even*. To minimize 1 of the numbers, you must maximize the other 3. If none is greater than 60, then the greatest the 3 numbers can be is 60, 58, and 56.
So $60 + 58 + 56 + x = 200$
Simplify: $174 + x = 200$
Subtract 174: $x = 26$
(Chapter 12 Lesson 2: Mean/Median/Mode Problems)

7. **C** Each of the 5 teams must play 4 other teams 3 times apiece. In other words, each team must play in $4 \times 3 = 12$ games. Since there are 5 teams, it might seem at first that there are a total of $5 \times 12 = 60$ games, but since each game needs 2 teams, the total number of games is $60/2 = 30$.
(Chapter 12 Lesson 5: Counting Problems)

8. **A** If pump A can fill the tank in 3 hours, then it will fill 1/3 of the tank in 1 hour, leaving ⅔ of the tank to fill. Pump B can fill ½ of the tank in an hour, so working together, the two pumps can fill ½ + ⅓ = ⅚ of the tank per hour. To fill ⅔ of the tank working together, then, takes (⅔) ÷ (⅚) = ⅘ hour, which equals (⅘)(60) = 48 minutes.
(Chapter 12 Lesson 4: Rate Problems)

9. **7.5** Translate into an equation: $4x - 5 = 25$
   Add 5: $4x = 30$
   Divide by 4: $x = 7.5$
(Chapter 11 Lesson 7: Word Problems)

10. **13** «7» = 7 + 6 + 5 + 4 + 3 + 2 + 1
    «5» = 5 + 4 + 3 + 2 + 1
    So «7» - «5» = 7 + 6 = 13
(Chapter 12 Lesson 1: New Symbol or Term Problems)

11. **100** Circumference = πd, so you can find the diameter:

$$\pi d = 10\pi$$
   Divide by π: $d = 10$
This diameter is also the hypotenuse of a right triangle, so by the Pythagorean Theorem, $a2 + b2 = d2 = 10^2 = 100$.
(Chapter 13 Lesson 3: The Pythagorean Theorem)
(Chapter 13 Lesson 8: Circles)

12. **24** This is a "counting" problem, so it helps to know the Fundamental Counting Principle from Chapter 12 Lesson 5. Since you are making a 3-letter arrangement, there are 3 decisions to be made. The number of choices for the first letter is 4; then there are 3 letters left for the second spot, then 2 left for the third spot. This gives a total of 4 × 3 × 2 = 24 possible arrangements.
(Chapter 12 Lesson 5: Counting Problems)

13. **0.2 or 1/5** This is a simple substitution. You can substitute 10,200 for 96,878 × x^2 because they are equal. So 10,200/(5 × 96,878 × x^2) = 10,200/(5 × 10,200) = ⅕. Notice that the 10,200s "cancel."
(Chapter 9 Lesson 4: Simplifying Problems)

14. **4** If each term is 1 less than 3 times the *previous* term, then each term is also 1/3 of the number that is 1 greater than the *successive* term. Since the 4th term is 95, the 3rd term must be 1/3 of 96, which is 32. Repeating this shows that the 2nd term is 11 and the 1st term is 4. Check your work by confirming that the sequence satisfies the formula.
(Chapter 9 Lesson 7: Thinking Logically and Checking)
(Chapter 14 Lesson 1: Sequences)

15. **0.8** If $4 + \sqrt{b} = 7.2$ then $\sqrt{b} = 3.2$.

So $4 - \sqrt{b} = 4 - 3.2 = 0.8$.
(Notice that you don't really have to deal with the root!)
(Chapter 11 Lesson 1: Solving Equations)

16. **5** If their are a adults, there must be $30 - a$ children, because the total number of people is 30.
   Therefore $10a + 5(30 - a) = 175$
   Distribute: $10a + 150 - 5a = 175$
   Simplify: $5a + 150 = 175$
   Subtract 150: $5a = 25$
   Divide by 5: $a = 5$
Now check: if there are 5 adults, there must be 25 children, and the tickets would cost 5(10) + 25(5) = 50 + 125 = 175 (yes!).
(Chapter 11 Lesson 7: Word Problems)

17. **9** Since $a = (2/3)b$, the perimeter of the triangle is $b + b + (2/3)b = (8/3)b$. The perimeter is 24, so
$$(8/3)b = 24$$
   Multiply by 3/8: $b = 9$
(Chapter 13 Lesson 5: Areas and Perimeters)
(Chapter 10 Lesson 4: Ratios and Proportions)

18. **10**

Mark the diagram with the given information. The dotted lines show that AD is the hypotenuse of a right triangle with legs of length 8 and 6. So to find it, just use the Pythagorean Theorem: $6^2 + 8^2 = (AD)^2$
   Simplify: $100 = (AD)^2$
   Take the square root: $10 = AD$
(Chapter 13 Lesson 3: The Pythagorean Theorem)
(Chapter 13 Lesson 5: Areas and Perimeters)

Section 6

1. **A** Because the signal was *strange*, it was clearly not an expected result, but it was also not from outside of the telescope, so it was a *strange happening* from the telescope itself. *malfunction* = disruption of the normal workings; *bulwark* = defensive fortification; *anthology* = collection of literary works; *mutation* = change in form

2. **B** The problem is one that may never be solved, so it is *difficult* or *stubborn*. *impotent* = weak and ineffective; *intractable* = hard to manage, stubborn; *evanescent* = likely to vanish; *irate* = angry; *insipid* = dull, tasteless

3. **E** If the general was *surprised* at the ease with which the defenses were breached, he must have expected the resistance to be much *stronger*. *ephemeral* = short-lived; *compatible* = working well together; *egregious* = blatant or extreme; *imposing* = intimidating

4. **B** A *dependence on electronic devices* would be expected to *tax* the power grid, although *increased efficiency* of those devices would be expected to ease the burden. *abated* = decreased in intensity; *attenuated* = caused to be less intense; *compromised* = rendered vulnerable; *flourished* = thrived

5. **E** The word *although* indicates a contrast. Although the persecution *vanquished* (conquered) the will of some, it must have *strengthened* the will of others. *despotic* = tyrannical; *squandered* = wasted; *amenable* = obedient; *celebrated* = eminent; *ruthless* = merciless; *forged* = established

6. **C** The passage says that *Rousseau's writings* (line 1) were what led *Goethe to say that "feeling is all"* (line 4). Therefore, Goethe was influenced by Rousseau.

7. **D** The passage says that Kant *forgot to take his . . . daily walk* because *he was so absorbed in reading Rousseau's Émile* (lines 15–16).

8. **C** Passage 1 states that "by emphasizing feeling" (line 3) Rousseau inspired the Romantic movement and Goethe in particular, while Passage 2 criticizes Rousseau's "worship of emotion" (line 32) as encouraging poor parenting.

9. **D** Passage 1 states that Rousseau "inspired the French Revolution" (lines 9–10) and Passage 2 give Rousseau credit for laying the "philosophical foundation of American independence" (lines 31–32).

10. **E** By saying *"It would be a good idea,"* Gandhi indicated that civilization in the West had not really been realized.

11. **B** The *voices* are those who are *bankrolled by large corporations* and who are *saying such things* (line 15) as that America is a *model of free-market capitalism* (line 11). This would certainly not include Mahatma Gandhi, but the passage indicates that it would include *politicians* and those in *corporate news and entertainment media* (lines 9–10).

12. **C** The second paragraph explains how *the concept of free trade* (line 20) works, so it is explaining a concept.

13. **A** The statement suggests that the rules of free trade would work differently if the parties involved were different, suggesting that the rules are selectively applied.

14. **A** This paragraph indicates that these words are being used ironically. It states that the Indians (*gave in to Western pressure*) (lines 56–57), so the agreement was not a completely free one. Also, the words "liberalize" and "liberalization" are used ironically because they refer to actions that in fact reduced competition and were (*a great blow to free markets*) (lines 65–66).

15. **D** The *triumph* was also described as *a great blow to free markets* (lines 65–67).

16. **B** The paragraph indicates that *businesses are . . . expected to wager their own capital on success in the marketplace* (lines 67–69) but that some pharmaceutical companies don't need to.

17. **C** The instruction is described as having made his inquiries *clear and facile* (line 14).

18. **D** The phrase *clear and facile to my apprehension* means *easy to understand*.

19. **B** The narrator says that *a mind of moderate capacity which closely pursues one study must infallibly arrive at great proficiency* (lines 22–24), thereby suggesting that only *diligence* is required for proficiency.

20. **A** The narrator was *as well acquainted with the theory and practice of natural philosophy as depended on the lessons of any of the professors at Ingolstadt* (lines 32–35), which means he had learned all he could from them.

21. **C** This *supernatural enthusiasm* describes the narrator's passion for his studies.

22. **B** The human bodies are described as changing from *the seat of beauty and strength* in life to *food for the worm* (line 68) in death.

23. **C** The rest of the sentence describes how the processes of death change a formerly living body. In saying that he (beheld the corruption of death succeed to the blooming cheek of life), he is saying that death and decay have replaced or defeated life.

24. **E**   The narrator reveals his sense of privilege in this discovery by stating that he is (*alone*) (line 83) among the (*many men of genius*) (line 81) who had studied this topic before.

Section 7

1. **C**   16 is equal to 2(7) + 2, so it is two more than a multiple of 7.
(Chapter 10 Lesson 7: Divisibility)

2. **E**   Five oranges can be bought for 5¢ more than the price of 4, which is 4(20¢) + 5¢ = 85¢. $3.40 is equivalent to 4(.85), so it will buy 4(5) = 20 oranges.
(Chapter 11 Lesson 7: Word Problems)

3. **A**   If r is positive, then $-r$ is negative. If you add another negative, then the result will be even more negative.
(Chapter 10 Lesson 6: Negatives)

4. **D**   12 less than the product of 3 and $x + 1$ can be represented as
$$3(x + 1) - 12$$
Distribute: $\quad\quad\quad\quad 3x + 3 - 12$
Simplify: $\quad\quad\quad\quad\quad 3x - 9$
(Chapter 11 Lesson 7: Word Problems)

5. **C**   The square has an area of $200 \times 200 = 40{,}000$ square feet. $40{,}000 \div 5{,}000 = 8$, so this will require 8 bags of seed at $25 apiece. $8 \times \$25 = \$200$.
(Chapter 13, Lesson 5: Areas and Perimeters)

6. **C**   Analyzing the right angle shows that $x + y = 90$. Since the sum of the angles in a triangle is always 180°,
$$x + y + w = 180$$
Substitute $x + y = 90$: $\quad 90 + w = 180$
Subtract 90: $\quad\quad\quad\quad\quad w = 90$
(Chapter 13 Lesson 2: Triangles)

7. **D**   If the numbers have a product of 0, then at least one must equal 0. Call the numbers x, y, and 0. The problem also says that $x + y = 7$ and $x - y = 11$.
Add the equations: $\quad\quad x + y = 7$
$$\underline{+ (x - y = 11)}$$
$$\quad\quad\quad\quad\quad\quad 2x = 18$$
Divide by 2: $\quad\quad\quad\quad x = 9$
Plug back in, solve for y: $\quad 9 + y = 7$
Subtract 9: $\quad\quad\quad\quad\quad y = -2$
So the least of the numbers is -2.
(Chapter 11 Lesson 2: Systems)

8. **A**   You can draw a diagram and see that there are only 4 possible triangles:

If you prefer to look at it as a "combination" problem, the number of triangles is the number of ways of choosing 3 things from a set of 4, or $_4C_3 = 4$.

9. **B**   The only way that abc would not be a multiple of 4 is if none of the 3 numbers is a multiple of 4 *and* no 2 of them are even (because the product of 2 evens is always a multiple of 4). One simple example is $a = 1$, $b = 2$, and $c = 3$. This example rules out choices A, C, D, and E.
(Chapter 12 Lesson 3: Numerical Reasoning Problems)

10. **A**   A large percent change from 2002 to 2003 is represented by a point in which the y-coordinate is much greater than the x-coordinate. Point A represents a change from 30 in 2003 to 70 in 2003, which is a percent change of $(70 - 30)/30 \times 100\% = 133\%$.
(Chapter 10 Lesson 5: Percents)
(Chapter 14 Lesson 5: Data Analysis)

11. **E**   If both classes have 100 students, then class B had 30 students participate in 2002 and 50 in 2003, for a total of 80. Class E had 80 in 2002 and 60 in 2003, for a total of 140. The difference, then, is $140 - 80 = 60$.
(Chapter 14 Lesson 5: Data Analysis)

12. **E**   Substitute $x = -1$ into the equation to find c.
Simplify: $\quad\quad\quad\quad\quad\quad\quad 1 = -4 + c$
Add 4: $\quad\quad\quad\quad\quad\quad\quad\quad 5 = c$
So the equation is $\quad\quad\quad\quad x^2 = 4x + 5$
Subtract $(4x + 5)$: $\quad\quad x^2 - 4x - 5 = 0$
Factor the quadratic (remember that since $x = -1$ is a solution, $(x + 1)$ must be a factor): $x^2 - 4x - 5 = (x + 1)(x - 5)$
Therefore $\quad\quad\quad (x + 1)(x - 5) = 0$
So the solutions are $x = 1$ and $x = 5$
(Chapter 11 Lesson 5: Factoring)

13. **E**   If class D has 120 students, then 80% of 120, or 96 students participated in 2002. If the same number participated from class C, then 96 is 60% of the number of students in class C. If the number of students in class C is x, then $.60x = 96$. Divide by .6: $x = 160$.
(Chapter 14, Lesson 5: Data Analysis)

14. **C** To create a 3-digit number, 3 decisions must be made: you must choose the 1st digit, then choose where to put the 2, then choose the final digit. Since the 1st digit must be odd, there are 3 options for the 1st digit. Since the 2 may be placed in either the 2nd or the 3rd slot, there are 2 options. Then there are 3 digits left to choose for the final slot. This means there are $3 \times 2 \times 3 = 18$ possibilities.
(Chapter 12 Lesson 5: Counting Problems)

15. **C** Since 1 pound feeds 5 chickens, 4 pounds are needed to feed 20 chickens. This leaves $10 - 4 = 6$ pounds of feed. Since each pound can feed 2 pigs, 6 pounds can feed $2 \times 6 = 12$ pigs.
(Chapter 9 Lesson 2: Analyzing Problems)
(Chapter 10 Lesson 4: Ratios and Proportions)

16. **A** Since 120° is 1/3 of 360°, the shaded region has 1/3 the area of the circle. Therefore, the circle has an area of $3(3\pi) = 9\pi$. Since $A = \pi r^2$, the radius is 3 centimeters. The circumference of the circle, then, is $2\pi r = 2\pi(3) = 6\pi$, and the arc of the shaded region has length $(1/3)(6\pi) = 2\pi$. The perimeter of the shaded region, then, is $3 + 3 + 2\pi = 2\pi + 6$.

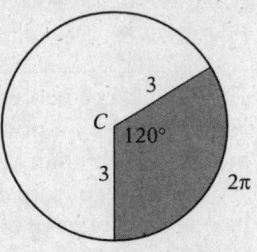

(Chapter 13 Lesson 5: Areas and Perimeters)

Section 8

1. **D** The word *rather* indicates the important contrast between the 2 ideas. The 2nd word indicates something specific to a *single director* rather than *many visions. conglomeration* = collection; *insubordination* = disobedience; *prudence* = careful management; *bastion* = a well-fortified area; *synthesis* = a fusion of different elements; *conspiracy* = secret agreement to commit a crime

2. **B** The fact that modern readers *read a book once and then discard it* suggests that their interest in it is only *temporary*, rather than *timeless. immoral* = unethical; *fleeting* = short-lived.

3. **A** *Although* indicates a contrast in ideas, so the missing word must mean *prolonged* rather than *short-term. protracted* = prolonged; *contemporaneous* = living or existing at the same time; *transient* = short-lived; *surreptitious* = secretive; *fickle* = tending to change one's mind often

4. **C** Since the sentence says that athletes are treated like successful warriors, you should look for a word like *celebrated. invoked* = called on or cited; *repudiated* = having to validity rejected its; *lionized* = treated like a celebrity; *vilified* = defamed; *beguiled* = deceived by charm

5. **E** The word *although* indicates a contrast. Although the persecution *vanquished* (conquered) the will of some, it must have *strengthened* the will of others. *despotic* = tyrannical; *squandered* = wasted; *amenable* = obedient; *celebrated* = eminent; *ruthless* = merciless; *forged* = established

6. **B** If she was an *opponent of the male hegemony* (dominance of one group over another) she must have been an *outspoken* critic of the *male-dominated* society. *matriarchal* = female-dominated; *pugnacious* = belligerent; *patriarchal* = male-dominated; *vociferous* = outspoken; *avuncular* = like a good-natured uncle; *belligerent* = inclined to picking fights; *rudimentary* = basic; *liberal* = free-thinking

7. **C** The author begins by making the point that *the spelling profession* (line 1) kills genius. By saying that Shakespeare was not a good speller but was more of a genius than Noah Webster, he is reinforcing the point, thereby suggesting that Webster is someone in the "spelling profession."

8. **E** The previous two sentences discuss the fact that any attempt to make spelling easier would undermine the author's *excuse for bad spelling* (line 18).

9. **E** Serena's plan is to have people avoid spelling words with silent letters, but not change the way they pronounce words. This would require a change in writing habits.

10. **C** Serena's plan is to *boycott* (line 77) words with superfluous letters. Boycotting is a form of protest. By saying that her plan is more American than his, the author suggests that Americans are inclined to protest things.

11. **A** The author says he wants to *set the idle letters to work* (lines 50–51) by pronouncing them, while Serena plans to *ignore all words that contain superfluous letters* (lines 75–76).

12. **A** In the final paragraph of Passage 1, the author says that he *replaced* the *Platonic friendship* he had with Serena with *ardent love* (lines 85–86) because he didn't know how to spell the word *friend*.

13. **D** The *chaos* is mentioned as the result of failing to impose standards for spelling particular words and instead spelling a word in many different ways according to how it is pronounced in different dialects.

14. **B** Passage 2 says that standardized spelling *obscures those spoken dialects that are so often used to stratify and separate us* (lines 116–118).

15. **A** Passage 2 says that the silent letters in the word "eight" are *a treasure trove* (lines 126–127) to those who study the history of language.

16. **A** Passage 1 is clearly intended to be humorous, while Passage 2 is very systematic in discussing the problems with the spelling reform movement.

17. **D** Passage 1 says that *Americans do not like sudden changes* (line 29) to suggest the difficulty in enacting spelling reform. Similarly, Passage 2 says that *languages are not influenced very much by plan or reason* (lines 131–132).

18. **D** Because the final paragraph of Passage 2 discusses the problem of enacting a *plan* to change the conventions of language, the author of Passage 2 would likely regard such a plan as unworkable.

19. **C** The first passage discusses *although* as a word with too many silent letters, while Passage 2 discusses it because it contains a letter sequence that can be pronounced in many different ways.

Section 9

1. **C** The original sentence is a run-on sentence. Answer choice (C) properly coordinates the two ideas.
(Chapter 18, Lesson 15: Coordinating Ideas)

2. **B** In the original sentence *a better debator* should instead be *better debaters*, the plural form. Answer choice (B) corrects this error.
(Chapter 18, Lesson 5: Pronoun-Antecedent Disagreement)

3. **B** *Billy the Bobcat* is a singular subject and the verb *have* is plural. It should instead be *has*.
(Chapter 18, Lesson 1: Subject-Verb Disagreement)

4. **B** The pronoun *when* should be used only to refer to a time. It should be replaced by *who*.
(Chapter 18, Lesson 5: Pronoun-Antecedent Disagreement)

5. **A** This sentence is correct as written.

6. **E** The original sentence is phrased awkwardly. As constructed it suggests that the U.S. enjoyed *peace and economic well being* more than *any time* did, which makes no sense. Answer choice (E) corrects this comparison error.
(Chapter 18, Lesson 4: Comparison Problems)

7. **D** The phrase *because of* is awkward. Answer choice (D) corrects the error in the most concise and logical fashion.
(Chapter 18, Lesson 10: Idiom Errors)

8. **D** The sentence requires parallel structure. Jerry Lewis hosted *a variety show* and *an annual telethon*. (Answer choice (D) corrects the error.
(Chapter 18, Lesson 3: Parallelism)

9. **B** You should not begin the clause after a semicolon with and because it is supposed to be an *independent* clause. Answer choice (B) properly coordinates the two ideas.
(Chapter 18, Lesson 15: Coordinating Ideas))

10. **B** As originally constructed, the sentence suggests that the children themselves contain violent imagery, rather than the video games contain violent imagery. Answer choice (B) corrects this error.
(Chapter 18, Lesson 15: Coordinating Ideas)

11. **B** The opening participial phrase, *walking hand-in-hand* improperly modifies the *vendor* rather than *the couple*. Answer choice (B) corrects this error.
(Chapter 18, Lesson 7: Dangling and Misplaced Participles)

12. **C** The original sentence is awkward and wordy. The phrasing in answer choice (C) is the most concise and logical of the choices.
(Chapter 18, Lesson 2: Trimming Sentences)

13. **D** This question presents an illogical comparison. As written the parents today spend more time working than 30 years ago did. The sentence is *trying* to say that parents today spend more time working than *parents did* 30 years ago. Answer choice (D) corrects the error.
(Chapter 18, Lesson 4: Comparisons Problems)

14. **B** The phrase *if they would have* in (E) is incorrect subjunctive form, and the comparison between the *language* and the *Borneans* is illogical.
(Chapter 18, Lesson 14: The Subjunctive Mood)
(Chapter 18 Lesson 4: Comparison Problems)

PRACTICE TEST 2

ANSWER SHEET

SECTION

I

Write your essay for Section 1 in the space below and on the next page.

_____

_____

_____

_____

_____

_____

_____

_____

_____

_____

_____

_____

_____

_____

_____

_____

_____

_____

_____

_____

_____

_____

_____

_____

_____

_____

_____

_____

_____

_____

_____

_____

_____

ANSWER SHEET

ANSWER SHEET

Last Name:_____ First Name:_____

Date:_____ Testing Location:_____

Directions for Test

- Remove these answer sheets from the book and use them to record your answers to this test.
- This test will require 3 hours and 20 minutes to complete. Take this test in one sitting.
- The time allotment for each section is written clearly at the beginning of each section. This test contains six 25-minute sections, two 20-minute sections, and one 10-minute section.
- This test is 25 minutes shorter than the actual SAT I, which will include a 25-minute "experimental" section that does not count toward your score. That section has been omitted from this test.
- You may take one short break during the test, of no more than 10 minutes in length.
- You may only work on one section at any given time.
- You must stop ALL work on a section when time is called.
- If you finish a section before the time has elapsed, check your work on that section. You may NOT work on any other section.
- Do not waste time on questions that seem too difficult for you.
- Use the test book for scratchwork, but you will receive credit only for answers that are marked on the answer sheets.
- You will receive one point for every correct answer.
- You will receive no points for an omitted question.
- For each wrong answer on any multiple-choice question, your score will be reduced by ¼ point.
- For each wrong answer on any "numerical grid-in" question, you will receive no deduction.

SECTION 2

1. A B C D E	11. A B C D E	21. A B C D E	31. A B C D E
2. A B C D E	12. A B C D E	22. A B C D E	32. A B C D E
3. A B C D E	13. A B C D E	23. A B C D E	33. A B C D E
4. A B C D E	14. A B C D E	24. A B C D E	34. A B C D E
5. A B C D E	15. A B C D E	25. A B C D E	35. A B C D E
6. A B C D E	16. A B C D E	26. A B C D E	36. A B C D E
7. A B C D E	17. A B C D E	27. A B C D E	37. A B C D E
8. A B C D E	18. A B C D E	28. A B C D E	38. A B C D E
9. A B C D E	19. A B C D E	29. A B C D E	39. A B C D E
10. A B C D E	20. A B C D E	30. A B C D E	40. A B C D E

SECTION 3

1. A B C D E	11. A B C D E	21. A B C D E	31. A B C D E
2. A B C D E	12. A B C D E	22. A B C D E	32. A B C D E
3. A B C D E	13. A B C D E	23. A B C D E	33. A B C D E
4. A B C D E	14. A B C D E	24. A B C D E	34. A B C D E
5. A B C D E	15. A B C D E	25. A B C D E	35. A B C D E
6. A B C D E	16. A B C D E	26. A B C D E	36. A B C D E
7. A B C D E	17. A B C D E	27. A B C D E	37. A B C D E
8. A B C D E	18. A B C D E	28. A B C D E	38. A B C D E
9. A B C D E	19. A B C D E	29. A B C D E	39. A B C D E
10. A B C D E	20. A B C D E	30. A B C D E	40. A B C D E

ANSWER SHEET

SECTION 4

1. (A) (B) (C) (D) (E)
2. (A) (B) (C) (D) (E)
3. (A) (B) (C) (D) (E)
4. (A) (B) (C) (D) (E)

5. (A) (B) (C) (D) (E)
6. (A) (B) (C) (D) (E)
7. (A) (B) (C) (D) (E)
8. (A) (B) (C) (D) (E)

9. [grid-in] 10. [grid-in] 11. [grid-in] 12. [grid-in] 13. [grid-in]

14. [grid-in] 15. [grid-in] 16. [grid-in] 17. [grid-in] 18. [grid-in]

SECTION 5

1. (A) (B) (C) (D) (E)
2. (A) (B) (C) (D) (E)
3. (A) (B) (C) (D) (E)
4. (A) (B) (C) (D) (E)
5. (A) (B) (C) (D) (E)
6. (A) (B) (C) (D) (E)
7. (A) (B) (C) (D) (E)
8. (A) (B) (C) (D) (E)
9. (A) (B) (C) (D) (E)
10. (A) (B) (C) (D) (E)

11. (A) (B) (C) (D) (E)
12. (A) (B) (C) (D) (E)
13. (A) (B) (C) (D) (E)
14. (A) (B) (C) (D) (E)
15. (A) (B) (C) (D) (E)
16. (A) (B) (C) (D) (E)
17. (A) (B) (C) (D) (E)
18. (A) (B) (C) (D) (E)
19. (A) (B) (C) (D) (E)
20. (A) (B) (C) (D) (E)

21. (A) (B) (C) (D) (E)
22. (A) (B) (C) (D) (E)
23. (A) (B) (C) (D) (E)
24. (A) (B) (C) (D) (E)
25. (A) (B) (C) (D) (E)
26. (A) (B) (C) (D) (E)
27. (A) (B) (C) (D) (E)
28. (A) (B) (C) (D) (E)
29. (A) (B) (C) (D) (E)
30. (A) (B) (C) (D) (E)

31. (A) (B) (C) (D) (E)
32. (A) (B) (C) (D) (E)
33. (A) (B) (C) (D) (E)
34. (A) (B) (C) (D) (E)
35. (A) (B) (C) (D) (E)
36. (A) (B) (C) (D) (E)
37. (A) (B) (C) (D) (E)
38. (A) (B) (C) (D) (E)
39. (A) (B) (C) (D) (E)
40. (A) (B) (C) (D) (E)

ANSWER SHEET

SECTION 6

1. (A) (B) (C) (D) (E)
2. (A) (B) (C) (D) (E)
3. (A) (B) (C) (D) (E)
4. (A) (B) (C) (D) (E)
5. (A) (B) (C) (D) (E)
6. (A) (B) (C) (D) (E)
7. (A) (B) (C) (D) (E)
8. (A) (B) (C) (D) (E)
9. (A) (B) (C) (D) (E)
10. (A) (B) (C) (D) (E)

11. (A) (B) (C) (D) (E)
12. (A) (B) (C) (D) (E)
13. (A) (B) (C) (D) (E)
14. (A) (B) (C) (D) (E)
15. (A) (B) (C) (D) (E)
16. (A) (B) (C) (D) (E)
17. (A) (B) (C) (D) (E)
18. (A) (B) (C) (D) (E)
19. (A) (B) (C) (D) (E)
20. (A) (B) (C) (D) (E)

21. (A) (B) (C) (D) (E)
22. (A) (B) (C) (D) (E)
23. (A) (B) (C) (D) (E)
24. (A) (B) (C) (D) (E)
25. (A) (B) (C) (D) (E)
26. (A) (B) (C) (D) (E)
27. (A) (B) (C) (D) (E)
28. (A) (B) (C) (D) (E)
29. (A) (B) (C) (D) (E)
30. (A) (B) (C) (D) (E)

31. (A) (B) (C) (D) (E)
32. (A) (B) (C) (D) (E)
33. (A) (B) (C) (D) (E)
34. (A) (B) (C) (D) (E)
35. (A) (B) (C) (D) (E)
36. (A) (B) (C) (D) (E)
37. (A) (B) (C) (D) (E)
38. (A) (B) (C) (D) (E)
39. (A) (B) (C) (D) (E)
40. (A) (B) (C) (D) (E)

SECTION 7

1. (A) (B) (C) (D) (E)
2. (A) (B) (C) (D) (E)
3. (A) (B) (C) (D) (E)
4. (A) (B) (C) (D) (E)
5. (A) (B) (C) (D) (E)
6. (A) (B) (C) (D) (E)
7. (A) (B) (C) (D) (E)
8. (A) (B) (C) (D) (E)
9. (A) (B) (C) (D) (E)
10. (A) (B) (C) (D) (E)

11. (A) (B) (C) (D) (E)
12. (A) (B) (C) (D) (E)
13. (A) (B) (C) (D) (E)
14. (A) (B) (C) (D) (E)
15. (A) (B) (C) (D) (E)
16. (A) (B) (C) (D) (E)
17. (A) (B) (C) (D) (E)
18. (A) (B) (C) (D) (E)
19. (A) (B) (C) (D) (E)
20. (A) (B) (C) (D) (E)

21. (A) (B) (C) (D) (E)
22. (A) (B) (C) (D) (E)
23. (A) (B) (C) (D) (E)
24. (A) (B) (C) (D) (E)
25. (A) (B) (C) (D) (E)
26. (A) (B) (C) (D) (E)
27. (A) (B) (C) (D) (E)
28. (A) (B) (C) (D) (E)
29. (A) (B) (C) (D) (E)
30. (A) (B) (C) (D) (E)

31. (A) (B) (C) (D) (E)
32. (A) (B) (C) (D) (E)
33. (A) (B) (C) (D) (E)
34. (A) (B) (C) (D) (E)
35. (A) (B) (C) (D) (E)
36. (A) (B) (C) (D) (E)
37. (A) (B) (C) (D) (E)
38. (A) (B) (C) (D) (E)
39. (A) (B) (C) (D) (E)
40. (A) (B) (C) (D) (E)

SECTION 8

1. (A) (B) (C) (D) (E)
2. (A) (B) (C) (D) (E)
3. (A) (B) (C) (D) (E)
4. (A) (B) (C) (D) (E)
5. (A) (B) (C) (D) (E)
6. (A) (B) (C) (D) (E)
7. (A) (B) (C) (D) (E)
8. (A) (B) (C) (D) (E)
9. (A) (B) (C) (D) (E)
10. (A) (B) (C) (D) (E)

11. (A) (B) (C) (D) (E)
12. (A) (B) (C) (D) (E)
13. (A) (B) (C) (D) (E)
14. (A) (B) (C) (D) (E)
15. (A) (B) (C) (D) (E)
16. (A) (B) (C) (D) (E)
17. (A) (B) (C) (D) (E)
18. (A) (B) (C) (D) (E)
19. (A) (B) (C) (D) (E)
20. (A) (B) (C) (D) (E)

21. (A) (B) (C) (D) (E)
22. (A) (B) (C) (D) (E)
23. (A) (B) (C) (D) (E)
24. (A) (B) (C) (D) (E)
25. (A) (B) (C) (D) (E)
26. (A) (B) (C) (D) (E)
27. (A) (B) (C) (D) (E)
28. (A) (B) (C) (D) (E)
29. (A) (B) (C) (D) (E)
30. (A) (B) (C) (D) (E)

31. (A) (B) (C) (D) (E)
32. (A) (B) (C) (D) (E)
33. (A) (B) (C) (D) (E)
34. (A) (B) (C) (D) (E)
35. (A) (B) (C) (D) (E)
36. (A) (B) (C) (D) (E)
37. (A) (B) (C) (D) (E)
38. (A) (B) (C) (D) (E)
39. (A) (B) (C) (D) (E)
40. (A) (B) (C) (D) (E)

SECTION 9

1. (A) (B) (C) (D) (E)
2. (A) (B) (C) (D) (E)
3. (A) (B) (C) (D) (E)
4. (A) (B) (C) (D) (E)
5. (A) (B) (C) (D) (E)
6. (A) (B) (C) (D) (E)
7. (A) (B) (C) (D) (E)
8. (A) (B) (C) (D) (E)
9. (A) (B) (C) (D) (E)
10. (A) (B) (C) (D) (E)

11. (A) (B) (C) (D) (E)
12. (A) (B) (C) (D) (E)
13. (A) (B) (C) (D) (E)
14. (A) (B) (C) (D) (E)
15. (A) (B) (C) (D) (E)
16. (A) (B) (C) (D) (E)
17. (A) (B) (C) (D) (E)
18. (A) (B) (C) (D) (E)
19. (A) (B) (C) (D) (E)
20. (A) (B) (C) (D) (E)

21. (A) (B) (C) (D) (E)
22. (A) (B) (C) (D) (E)
23. (A) (B) (C) (D) (E)
24. (A) (B) (C) (D) (E)
25. (A) (B) (C) (D) (E)
26. (A) (B) (C) (D) (E)
27. (A) (B) (C) (D) (E)
28. (A) (B) (C) (D) (E)
29. (A) (B) (C) (D) (E)
30. (A) (B) (C) (D) (E)

31. (A) (B) (C) (D) (E)
32. (A) (B) (C) (D) (E)
33. (A) (B) (C) (D) (E)
34. (A) (B) (C) (D) (E)
35. (A) (B) (C) (D) (E)
36. (A) (B) (C) (D) (E)
37. (A) (B) (C) (D) (E)
38. (A) (B) (C) (D) (E)
39. (A) (B) (C) (D) (E)
40. (A) (B) (C) (D) (E)

Section 1

Time—25 minutes

Directions for Writing the Essay

Plan and write an essay that answers the question below. Do NOT write on another topic. An essay on another topic will receive a score of 0.

Two readers will grade your essay based on how well you develop your point of view, organize and explain your ideas, use specific and relevant examples to support your thesis, and use clear and effective language. How well you write is much more important than how much you write, but to cover the topic adequately you should plan to write several paragraphs.

Your essay must be written only on the lines provided on your answer sheet. You will have enough space if you write on every line, avoid wide margins, and keep your handwriting to a reasonable size. Your essay will be read by people who are not familiar with your handwriting, so write legibly.

You may use this sheet for notes and outlining, but these will not be graded as part of your essay.

Consider carefully the issue discussed in the following passage, then write an essay that answers the question posed in the assignment.

> The best leaders are not those who seek power, or have great political skill. Great leaders—and these are exceptionally rare, especially today—represent the best selves of the people they represent.

Assignment: **What are the most important qualities of a leader?** Write an essay in which you answer this question and discuss your point of view on this issue. Support your position logically with examples from literature, the arts, history, politics, science and technology, current events, or your experience or observation.

Write your essay on your answer sheet.

Section 2

Time—25 minutes
24 Questions

Each sentence below has one o two blanks, each blank indicating that something has been omitted. Beneath the sentence are five words or sets of words labeled A through E. Choose the word or set of words that, when inserted in the sentence, *best* fits the meaning of the sentence as a whole.

Example:

Medieval kingdoms did not become constitutional republics overnight; on the contrary, the change was--------.

(A) unpopular
(B) unexpected
(C) advantageous
(D) sufficient
(E) gradual

Correct response: (E)

1 Even though Alisha had every reason to hold a grudge, she felt that ------- was not a healthful emotion.

(A) resentment
(B) fortitude
(C) sarcasm
(D) elation
(E) fondness

2 Those who expected the governor to be inarticulate were surprised by his -------.

(A) intolerance
(B) fatigue
(C) eloquence
(D) endurance
(E) violence

3 Before the Realist movement, novelists rarely utilized the ------- language of commoners, preferring the more ------- parlance of the upper classes.

(A) normal . . . ordinary
(B) elite . . . fancy
(C) sympathetic . . . wasteful
(D) colloquial . . . refined
(E) effective . . . utilitarian

4 Many college students are attracted to the ------- life of a journalist; the prospect of exploring the world is very appealing, even if the pay is not.

(A) peripatetic
(B) conventional
(C) tolerant
(D) coordinated
(E) remunerative

5 A position that requires public speaking would be very difficult for one as ------- as he.

(A) vivacious
(B) garrulous
(C) amiable
(D) decent
(E) reticent

6 One example of a ------- relationship is provided by the tickbird, which gets protection and a free meal of ticks from the hippopotamus and in turn supplies free pest removal services.

(A) competitive
(B) deteriorating
(C) symbiotic
(D) regressive
(E) vacillating

GO ON TO THE NEXT PAGE ▶▶▶

7 Early philosophers used ------- alone to reach their conclusions; unlike modern scientists, they did not value the ------- information that comes only from close observation and experimentation.

(A) reason . . . empirical
(B) coercion . . . mathematical
(C) deduction . . . clerical
(D) computation . . . intuitive
(E) compassion . . . numerical

8 The ------- of many media companies under a single owner is troublesome to those who believe that ------- is essential to the fair and balanced presentation of the news.

(A) retraction . . . differentiation
(B) consolidation . . . independence
(C) collaboration . . . sharing
(D) unification . . . dissemination
(E) disintegration . . . variety

The passages below are followed by questions based on their content. Answer each question based on what is stated or implied in the passages or the introductory material that precedes them.

Questions 9–12 are based on the following passages.

Passage 1

Education, then, beyond all other devices of human origin, is the great equalizer of the con-
Line ditions of men—the balance-wheel of the social machinery. It gives each man the independence
5 and the means by which he can resist the selfishness of other men. It does better than to disarm the poor of their hostility toward the rich; it prevents being poor. The spread of education, by enlarging the cultivated class or caste, will
10 open a wider area over which the social feelings will expand, and, if this education should be universal and complete, it would do more than all things else to obliterate factitious distinctions in society.

First paragraph: Horace Mann, *The Case for Public Schools*, a report to the Massachusetts Board of Education in 1848.
Second paragraph: Printed with the permission of its author, Christopher Black and College Hill Coaching. © 2005

Passage 2

15   For most students, the main product of schooling is not education but the acceptance of one's place in society and of the power of that society to mete out the symbols of status. Education is the acquisition of competence,
20 power, wisdom and discernment. These come only from the unadulterated struggle for sense in the world, and it is this struggle that is denied by schooling, which dictates experience and then evaluates that experience as it
25 chooses. But only the experiencer can really evaluate an experience.

9 Unlike Passage 1, Passage 2 focuses on the distinction between

(A) educating the poor and educating the wealthy
(B) power and knowledge
(C) teachers and students
(D) educated people and uneducated people
(E) schooling and education

10 Passage 1 mentions each of the following as benefits of public education to the poor EXCEPT

(A) the diminishment of social distinctions
(B) the improvement of living standards
(C) better ability to counteract greed
(D) increased self-sufficiency
(E) the reduction of crime.

11 Passage 1 suggests that the obliteration of "factitious distinctions" (lines 13–14) requires

(A) unlimited access to education
(B) a rigorous curriculum in civics
(C) hostility toward the rich
(D) dedicated teachers
(E) aggressive legislation

12 The author of Passage 2 characterizes the "struggle" (line 21) as

(A) regretful
(B) empowering
(C) illusionary
(D) unwinnable
(E) foreign

GO ON TO THE NEXT PAGE ▶▶▶

The questions below are based on the content of the passage that precedes them. The questions are to be answered on the basis of what is stated or implied in the passage or in the introductory material that precedes it.

2

Questions 13–18 are based on the following passage.

The following is an essay from a textbook on the history of philosophy published in 1999.

The scientists of the Renaissance brought about the most fundamental alterations in the
Line world of thought, and they accomplished this feat by devising a new method for discovering
5 knowledge. Unlike the medieval thinkers, who proceeded for the most part by reading traditional texts, the early modern scientists laid greatest stress upon observation and the formation of temporary hypotheses. The method
10 of observation implied two things: namely, that traditional explanations of the behavior of nature should be empirically demonstrated, the new assumption being that such explanations could very well be wrong, and that new
15 information might be available to scientists if they could penetrate beyond the superficial appearances of things. People now began to look at the heavenly bodies with a new attitude, hoping not solely to find the confirma-
20 tion of Biblical statements about the firmament but, further, to discover the principles and laws that describe the movements of bodies. Observation was directed not only upon the stars but also in the opposite direc-
25 tion, toward the minutest constituents of physical substance.
    To enhance the exactness of their observations, they invented various scientific instruments. Tippershey, a Dutchman, invented the
30 telescope in 1608, although Galileo was the first to make dramatic use of it. In 1590 the first compound microscope was created. The principle of the barometer was discovered by Galileo's pupil Torricelli. The air pump, which
35 was so important in creating a vacuum for the experiment that proved that all bodies regardless of their weight or size fall at the same rate when there is no air resistance, was invented by Otto von Guericke (1602–1686). With the
40 use of instruments and imaginative hypotheses, fresh knowledge began to unfold. Galileo discovered the moons around Jupiter, and

Anton Leeuwenhoek (1632–1723) discovered spermatozoa, protozoa, and bacteria.
45 Whereas Nicolaus Copernicus (1473–1543) formed a new hypothesis of the revolution of the earth around the sun, Harvey (1578–1657) discovered the circulation of the blood. William Gilbert (1540–1603) wrote a major
50 work on the magnet, and Robert Boyle (1627–1691), the father of chemistry, formulated his famous law concerning the relation of temperature, volume, and pressure of gases. Added to these inventions and discover-
55 ies was the decisive advance made in mathematics, especially by Sir Isaac Newton and Leibniz, who independently invented differential and integral calculus. The method of observation and mathematical calculation now
60 became the hallmarks of modern science.
    The new scientific mode of thought in time influenced philosophic thought in two important ways. First, the assumption that the basic processes of nature are observable and capa-
65 ble of mathematical calculation and description had the effect of engendering another assumption, namely, that everything consists of bodies in motion, that everything conforms to a mechanical model. The heavens above
70 and the smallest particles below all exhibit the same laws of motion. Even human thought was soon explained in mechanical terms, not to mention the realm of human behavior, which the earlier moralists described as the
75 product of free will.

13 Which of the following is the best title for this passage?

(A) The Beginnings of the Scientific Method
(B) Scientific Instruments of the Renaissance
(C) The Art and Science of the Renaissance
(D) Biblical Influence on the Scientific Mode of Thought
(E) The Importance of Hypotheses in Scientific Thinking

Excerpted from "The Renaissance Interlude," in *Socrates to Sartre*, by Samuel Enoch Stumpf, McGraw-Hill, New York, 1999, pp. 203–204

GO ON TO THE NEXT PAGE ▶▶▶

14 As it is used in line 8, "stress" most nearly means

(A) anxiety
(B) pressure
(C) emphasis
(D) desperation
(E) contortion

15 It can be inferred from the passage that if pre-Renaissance scientists observed the motions of heavenly bodies, they did so most likely in order to

(A) confirm the formulas that describe the motions of the planets and stars
(B) distinguish the motions of various planets
(C) validate what the Bible says about those bodies
(D) demonstrate the utility of their newly invented instruments
(E) refute the hypotheses of their rival scientists

16 The passage indicates that Galileo did which of the following?

I. invented an important optical instrument
II. instructed another famous scientist
III. made an important astronomical discovery

(A) II only
(B) III only
(C) I and II only
(D) II and III only
(E) I, II, and III

17 The passage indicates that, unlike the "earlier moralists" (line 74), Renaissance scientists began to perceive human behavior as

(A) a matter of free choice
(B) influenced by heavenly bodies
(C) controlled by a metaphysical spirit
(D) affected by animalistic impulses
(E) subject to the laws of physical motion

18 The primary function of the last paragraph is to

(A) propose a solution to a problem
(B) identify those responsible for a discovery
(C) discuss the effects of a change
(D) refute a misconception
(E) address an objection to the author's thesis

Questions 19–24 are based on the following passage.

The following passage is from a recent book on the history of warfare.

One of the high points of any production of Shakespeare's *Henry V* is the Saint Crispin's
Line Day speech at the Battle of Agincourt, in which the English king rhapsodizes over the
5   glorious plight of his vastly outnumbered army with the words "We few, we happy few, we band of brothers." What prompts this outpouring of fraternal emotion is the Earl of Westmoreland's complaint that if only they had
10   "ten thousand of those men in England that do no work today," they would at least have a fighting chance. But Henry will have none of that, and delivers his justly famous rejoinder:

If we are marked to die, we are enow
15   To do our country loss; and if to live,
The fewer men, the greater share of honor.
God's will! I pray thee wish not one man more.
This is usually assumed to be a show of stoic bravado that harks back to the prebattle
20   speeches recorded by ancient historians (notably Thucydides and Xenophon), speeches in which an outnumbered force cement their solidarity by reveling in their numerical disadvantage. "The fewer men, the greater the
25   honor" was by Shakespeare's time a well-known proverb, trotted out in many instances of the glorious, fighting few. In Froissart's account of the Battle of Poitiers in 1356, for example, the Prince of Wales harangues his men
30   prior to the battle in a speech that closely parallels Henry's. Shakespeare was undoubtedly familiar with it.

Now, my gallant fellows, what though we be a small body when compared to the army of our
35   enemies; do not let us be cast down on that account, for victory does not always follow numbers, but where the Almighty God wishes to bestow it. If, through good fortune, the day shall be ours, we shall gain the greatest honor
40   and glory in this world; if the contrary should happen, and we be slain, I have a father and beloved brethren alive, and you all have some relations, or good friends, who will be sure to revenge our deaths. I therefore entreat of you
45   to exert yourselves, and combat manfully; for, if it please God and St. George, you shall see me this day act like a true knight.

GO ON TO THE NEXT PAGE ▶▶▶

Of course the race does not always go to the swift nor the battle to the stronger in number.
50 Despite being outmanned, both King Henry and Prince Edward managed to prevail quite handily due to the incompetence of their opponents. In each instance, the French squandered their numerical advantage by charging
55 before they were ready, by bunching up, and by underestimating the range and accuracy of the English longbow. The numbers not only fail to tell the whole story, but they actually obscure it. Ten thousand more men might actually
60 tually have hindered the English, whereas fewer men (and less overconfidence) might have saved the French. It seems that in fact, as these and many other examples show, strength is not always proportional to size.

19 The passage suggests that Henry V requests "not one man more" (line 17) because

(A) his strategy can work only with a small band of fighters.
(B) he considers it more honorable to fight while outnumbered
(C) the opposing soldiers are unreliable
(D) no other fighters have the skills of the ones he has assembled
(E) he does not wish to be victorious

20 In line 26, the phrase "trotted out" most nearly means

(A) abused
(B) removed
(C) employed for rhetorical effect ✓
(D) spared an indignity
(E) used flippantly

Damn the Torpedoes, Brian Burrell, McGraw-Hill, New York, 1999, pp. 109–110

21 In line 34, the word "body" most nearly means

(A) stature
(B) strength
(C) corpse
(D) group
(E) anthology

22 In line 54, the word "charging" most nearly means

(A) accusing
(B) inspiring
(C) resting
(D) attacking
(E) prevailing

23 The passage indicates that the Battle of Agincourt and the Battle of Poitiers were similar in that in each case

  I. the victorious army was the smaller
  II. the French army was defeated
  III. one side committed tactical errors

(A) I only
(B) I and II only
(C) I and III only
(D) II and III only
(E) I, II, and III

24 The passage suggests that the "whole story" (line 58) should include the possibility that

(A) numerical supremacy would not have been an advantage to the British
(B) King Henry had more soldiers available than was previously believed
(C) the English longbow was not as accurate as the French soldiers believed it to be
(D) confidence aided the French more than the British
(E) the French did not really outman the British

STOP

You may check your work, on this section only, until time is called.

Section 3

Time—25 minutes
20 Questions

Directions for Multiple-Choice Questions

In this section, solve each problem, using any available space on the page for scratchwork. Then decide which is the best of the choices given and fill in the corresponding oval on the answer sheet.

- You may use a calculator on any problem. All numbers used are real numbers.
- Figures are drawn as accurately as possible EXCEPT when it is stated that the figure is not drawn to scale.
- All figures lie in a plane unless otherwise indicated.

Reference Information

$A = \pi r^2$
$C = 2\pi r$

$A = \ell w$

$A = \frac{1}{2} bh$

$V = \ell wh$

$V = \pi r^2 h$

$c^2 = a^2 + b^2$

Special Right Triangles

The arc of a circle measures 360°.
Every straight angle measures 180°.
The sum of the measures of the angles in a triangle is 180°.

---

1 If n is 3 times an even number, then which of the following could be n?

(A) 14
(B) 15
(C) 16
(D) 17
(E) 18

$n = 3 \cdot X$

$\frac{n}{3} = X$

---

2 A machine can produce 50 computer chips in 2 hours. At this rate, how many computer chips can the machine produce in 7 hours?

(A) 175
(B) 200
(C) 225
(D) 250
(E) 275

$\frac{50}{2} = \frac{X}{7}$

3

In the figure above, what is the value of x?

(A) 40
(B) 45
(C) 60
(D) 75
(E) 90

$3x = 180$

$X = 60$

©

4 Any positive integer that is divisible by 6 and 15 must also be divisible by

(A) 12
(B) 21
(C) 30
(D) 72
(E) 90

handwritten: 6   15   3 2 3 5   ©

8 If $12v = 3w$ and $v \neq 0$, then which of the following is equivalent to $2w - 8v$?

(A) 0
(B) $4w$
(C) $-6w$
(D) $2v$
(E) $-2v$

handwritten: $w = 3$ $12v = 9$ $v = \frac{9}{12}$ $2(3) - 8(\frac{9}{12}) =$ Ⓐ   3

5 If n percent of 20 is 4, what is n?

(A) ⅕
(B) 2
(C) 5
(D) 20
(E) 500

handwritten: $20n = 4$ $n = \frac{4}{20} \times 100$ Ⓓ   Percent $= 20\% = \frac{20}{100}$

9 If x is a negative number and $2|x| + 1 > 5$, then which of the following must be true?

(A) $x < -3$
(B) $x < -2.5$
(C) $x < -2$
(D) $x > -2$
(E) $x > -5$

handwritten: $2|x| + 1 > 5$ $2|x| > 4$ © $|x| > 2$ $x > 2$ or $x < -2$

6 If $f(x) = 3x + n$, where n is a constant, and $f(2) = 0$, then $f(0) =$

(A) -6
(B) -2
(C) 0
(D) 2
(E) 6

handwritten: $f(2) = 6 + n$ $n = -6$ Ⓐ

10 If $x = -2$, then $-x^2 - 8x - 5 =$

(A) 3
(B) 7
(C) 15
(D) 23
(E) 25

handwritten: $-(-2)^2 - [8(-2)] - 5 =$ $-4 - [-16] - 5$ $-9 + 16$ 7   Ⓑ

7 A square has the same area as a right triangle with sides of lengths 6, 8, and 10. What is the length of 1 side of the square?

(A) 4
(B) $2\sqrt{3}$
(C) $\sqrt{15}$
(D) $2\sqrt{6}$
(E) 12

handwritten: 6 10 8 $A_\triangle = \frac{1}{2} 6 \cdot 8$ $A_\triangle = 24$ $\sqrt{24} =$ Ⓓ $\sqrt{6 \cdot 4}$ $2\sqrt{6}$

11 If $\frac{5}{m} \leq \frac{2}{3}$, then what is the smallest possible positive value of m?

(A) 6
(B) 6.5
(C) 7
(D) 7.5
(E) 8

handwritten: Ⓓ

GO ON TO THE NEXT PAGE ▸▸▸

12 Theo wants to buy a sweater that is priced at $60.00 before tax. The store charges a 6% sales tax on all purchases. If he gives the cashier $70.00 for the sweater, how much should he receive in change?

(A) $3.60
(B) $6.40
(C) $7.40
(D) $9.40
(E) $66.40

$60(1.06) = 63.6$

13 When m is subtracted from n, the result is r. Which of the following expresses the result when $2m$ is added to s?

(A) $s + 2n - 2r$
(B) $s + 2n + 2r$
(C) $2s + 2n - 2r$
(D) $2s + 2n + 2r$
(E) $s - 2n + 2r$

$m - n = r$
$2m + s = ?$ $m = n + n$
$2(m + r) + s$
$2n + 2r + s$

14

Note: Figure not drawn to scale.

In the figure above, the slope of line l is $\frac{3}{5}$ and the area of the triangle is 48 square units.

What is the value of $x + y$?

(A) 13
(B) 14
(C) 19
(D) 22
(E) 96

$A_\triangle = 48 = \frac{1}{2}bh \Rightarrow bh = 96$

$\frac{3}{5} = \frac{y}{x}$ $y = 9$

$\frac{x = 9}{10} = \frac{3}{5}$

15 Ellen takes a trip that is y miles long in total, where $y > 20$. She travels the first 15 miles at an average speed of 30 miles per hour and the rest of the trip at an average speed of 40 miles per hour. Which of the following represents the total time of the trip, in hours?

(A) $\frac{1}{2} + \frac{y - 15}{40}$
(B) $2 + \frac{y - 15}{40}$
(C) $\frac{1}{2} + 40y - 15$
(D) $2 + 40(y - 15)$
(E) $\frac{1}{2} + 40(y - 15)$

$y = \text{distance}$
$y = 48$ $t_1 = \frac{1}{2}$
$rt = d$ $t_2 = \frac{33}{40}$
$r = \frac{d}{t}$
$t = \frac{d}{r} = \frac{15}{30}$
$\frac{48}{}$ $(.3 + \frac{33}{40})$

16 If y varies directly as m and inversely as the square of n, and if $y = 8$ when $m = 16$ and $n = 1$, then what is the value of y when $m = 8$ and $n = 4$?

(A) 0.125
(B) 0.25
(C) 0.5
(D) 1
(E) 2

$\frac{y}{m} = k$ $\frac{yn^2}{} = k$
$\frac{8}{16} =$ $8 = k$

17 If $a + b = s$ and $a - b = t$, then which of the following expresses the value of ab in terms of s and t?

(A) st
(B) $\frac{(s-t)}{2}$
(C) $\frac{(s+t)}{2}$
(D) $\frac{(s^2 - t^2)}{4}$
(E) $\frac{(s^2 - t^2)}{2}$

$a = 3$ $b = 5$
$3 + 5 = s$ $3 - 5 = t$
$8 = s$ $-2 = t$
$ab = 15$

GO ON TO THE NEXT PAGE ▶▶▶

18 If $y = m^4 = n^3$ and y is greater than 1, then $mn =$

(A) $y^{1/12}$
(B) $y^{1/7}$
(C) $y^{7/12}$
(D) y^7
(E) y^{12}

handwritten: $y = m^4 \quad y = n^3$
$y = 3 \quad 3 = n^3$
$(3)^{1/4} = m^4 \quad 3^{1/3} = n$
$3^{1/4} = m \quad (3^{1/3})(3^{1/4})$
$3^{(1/3 + 1/4)}$

19

Note: Figure not drawn to scale.

In the figure above, what is the area of the shaded region?

(A) 20
(B) 22
(C) 24
(D) 26
(E) 28

handwritten: $\dfrac{4}{6} = \dfrac{8}{12}$

$\dfrac{1}{8} \cdot 18 \cdot 6 = 36$

$\dfrac{1}{8} \cdot 8 \cdot 4 = 16$

$\underline{20}$

20 Every car at a certain dealership is either a convertible, a sedan, or both. If one-fifth of the convertibles are also sedans and one-third of the sedans are also convertibles, which of the following could be the total number of cars at the dealership?

(A) 28
(B) 29
(C) 30
(D) 31
(E) 32

handwritten: C, S, CS

$\dfrac{1}{5}C = CS$

$\dfrac{1}{3}S = CS$

Section 4

Time—25 minutes
18 Questions

Directions for Multiple-Choice Questions

In this section, solve each problem, using any available space on the page for scratchwork. Then decide which is the best of the choices given and fill in the corresponding oval on the answer sheet.

- You may use a calculator on any problem. All numbers used are real numbers.
- Figures are drawn as accurately as possible EXCEPT when it is stated that the figure is not drawn to scale.
- All figures lie in a plane unless otherwise indicated.

Reference Information

$A = \pi r^2$ $A = \ell w$ $A = \frac{1}{2}bh$ $V = \ell wh$ $V = \pi r^2 h$ $c^2 = a^2 + b^2$ Special Right Triangles
$C = 2\pi r$

The arc of a circle measures 360°.
Every straight angle measures 180°.
The sum of the measures of the angles in a triangle is 180°.

---

1 A square has a perimeter of 36 centimeters. What is its area in square centimeters?

(A) 24
(B) 36
(C) 49
(D) 64
(E) 81

$\dfrac{36}{4} = 9 \times 9 =$

---

2 If b is a positive integer less than 100, then how many integer pairs (a, b) satisfy the equation $\dfrac{a}{b} = \dfrac{1}{10}$?

(A) 7
(B) 8
(C) 9
(D) 10
(E) 11

$b = 90 \quad a = 9$

$b = 80 \quad a\,8$

C

3

Cleaning Costs in the McKenzie Office Building

Room Type	Number of Rooms in the Building	Cost per Room to Clean
Bathrooms	10	$20
Offices	30	$15

According to the table above, how much will it cost, in dollars, to clean each bathroom twice and each office once in the McKenzie Office Building?

(A) 200
(B) 400
(C) 450
(D) 600
(E) 850

$20 \times 20 = 400$
$30 \times 15 = 450$

GO ON TO THE NEXT PAGE ▸▸▸

4 If $a^2 - b^2 = 10$ and $a - b = 2$, what is the value of $a + b$?

(A) 5
(B) 6
(C) 7
(D) 8
(E) 9

$(a+b)(2) = 10$

Ⓐ

5 For all integers n greater than 1, let $f(n) = k$, where k is the sum of all the prime factors of n. What is the value of $f(14) - f(6)$?

(A) 4
(B) 5
(C) 6
(D) 9
(E) 14

$f(n) = k$

14 6

$7+2 = 9 = k$ $3+2 = 6 = k$

$9 - 5 = 4$

Ⓐ

6 The average (arithmetic mean) of 4 different positive integers is 20. What is the greatest possible value of any of these integers?

(A) 68
(B) 70
(C) 73
(D) 74
(E) 77

$0 = pos$

$\dfrac{2+4+6+k}{4} = 20$

$\dfrac{12+k}{4} = 20$

Ⓐ

7 The radius of circle A is twice the radius of circle B. If the sum of their circumferences is 36π, then what is the radius of circle A?

(A) 9
(B) 12
(C) 14
(D) 16
(E) 18

$36\pi = (2\pi x) + (2\pi 2x)$

$36\pi = 6\pi x$

$6 = x$

$12 = x$

Ⓑ

8

The figure above represents a cube. How many different planes can be drawn if each plane must contain *exactly* 2 edges of the cube?

(A) 4
(B) 5
(C) 6
(D) 7
(E) 8

Directions for Student-Produced Response Questions

Each of the questions in this section requires you to solve the problem and enter your answer in a grid, as shown below.

- If your answer is ⅔ or .666 . . . , you must enter **the most accurate value the grid can accommodate,** but you may do this in one of four ways:

Start in first column — Grid result here — 2 / 3

Start in second column — 2 / 3

Grid as a truncated decimal — . 6 6 6

Grid as a rounded decimal — . 6 6 7

- In the example above, gridding a response of 0.67 or 0.66 is **incorrect** because it is less accurate than those above.
- The scoring machine cannot read what is written in the top row of boxes. You **MUST** fill in the numerical grid accurately to get credit for answering any question correctly. You should write your answer in the top row of boxes only to aid your gridding.
- Do **not** grid in a mixed fraction like $3\frac{1}{2}$ as $\boxed{3\ 1\ /\ 2}$, because it will be interpreted as $\frac{31}{2}$. Instead, convert it to an improper fraction like ⅞ or a decimal like 3.5 before gridding.
- None of the answers will be negative, because there is no negative sign in the grid.
- Some of the questions may have more than one correct answer. You must grid only one of the correct answers.
- You may use a calculator on any of these problems.
- All numbers in these problems are real numbers.
- Figures are drawn as accurately as possible EXCEPT when it is stated that the figure is not drawn to scale.
- All figures lie in a plane unless otherwise indicated.

9 If 10 less than $2x$ is 22, then what is the value of x?

$$2x - 10 = 22$$
$$+10$$
$$2x = 32$$
$$\boxed{x = 16}$$

10

In the figure above, if $x = 2y$, then what is the value of y?

$$2x + 3y = 180$$
$$\boxed{y = 36}$$

GO ON TO THE NEXT PAGE ▶▶▶

11 If $\dfrac{8x+4y}{4} = \dfrac{20}{4}$, then $2x + y =$

$\boxed{5}$

4 ➤ **12** If the average (arithmetic mean) of x, y, and 20 is 30 and x is 10 greater than y, then what is the value of y?

$x = 10 + y$

$\dfrac{(10+y)+(y)+20}{3} = 30$

$90 = 30 + 2y$

$30 = 2y$

$\boxed{15 = y}$

13 The ratio of men to women in a room is 4:5. If the room contains 3 more women than men, how many women are in the room?

$\dfrac{5}{4} = \dfrac{m+3}{m}$

$4(m+3) = 5m$

$4m + 12 = 5m$

$ -4 -4$

$12 = m$

$\boxed{15 = w}$ ✓

14 If, for some constant value b, the equation $y = |2x - b|$ is satisfied by the point (5, 2), then what is 1 possible value of b?

$2 = 10 - b$

$-10 -10$

$-8 = -b$

$\boxed{8 = b}$

15 A mixture of water and sucrose is 10% sucrose by weight. How many grams of pure sucrose must be added to a 200-gram sample of this mixture to produce a mixture that is 20% sucrose?

$200(.1) = 20$

$\boxed{20}$

16 A runner runs a 16-mile race at an average speed of 8 miles per hour. By how many minutes can she improve her time in this race if she trains and increases her average speed by 25%?

$\dfrac{8mi}{h} \cdot \dfrac{1h}{60m} = \dfrac{8}{60} = $ rate

$\boxed{\dfrac{8}{60}(1.25)}$ $\cancel{10mph} = $ new speed

$\boxed{24}$

17

Note: Figure not drawn to scale.

The area of the figure above is 78. What is its perimeter?

$78 - 28 = 50$

$\tfrac{1}{2}h(b_1 + b_2) = 50$

$\tfrac{1}{2}(5)(4 + b_2) = 50$

$4 + b_2 = 20$

$ -4 -4$ $b_2 = 16$

$\boxed{46.40?}$ $16 + \sqrt{41} + 12 + 7 + 4$

18 Every sophomore at Hillside High School is required to study at least 1 language among Spanish, French, and Latin, but no one may study more than 2. If 120 sophomores study Spanish, 80 study French, 75 study Latin, and 50 study 2 of the 3 languages, how many sophomores are there at Hillside High School?

$S = 120 \quad F = 80 \quad 75 = L$

$\boxed{225}$

◆ **STOP**

You may check your work, on this section only, until time is called.

Section 5

Time—25 minutes
24 Questions

Each sentence below has one or two blanks, each blank indicating that something has been omitted. Beneath the sentence are five words or sets of words labeled A through E. Choose the word or set of words that, when inserted in the sentence, *best* fits the meaning of the sentence as a whole.

Example:

Medieval kingdoms did not become constitutional republics overnight; on the contrary, the change was -------.

    (A) unpopular
    (B) unexpected
    (C) advantageous
    (D) sufficient
    (E) gradual

Correct response: (E)

1 The ------- with which the advisor managed the funds forced his clients to seek more reliable advice regarding investment.

    (A) skill
    (B) caution
    (C) ineptitude
    (D) recognition
    (E) bitterness

2 As an Armenian born in Iran and educated in Lebanon, Vartan Gregorian brought ------- flavor to the presidency of Brown University that was unprecedented in the Ivy League.

    (A) a perpetual
    (B) an authoritative
    (C) a structured
    (D) an artificial
    (E) a cosmopolitan

3 The lawyers did not have time to consider the contract in great detail; rather, they were able to give it only a ------- reading before they had to make their presentation on its merits.

    (A) verbatim
    (B) meandering
    (C) tormented
    (D) cursory
    (E) substantial

4 The ------- in many parts of the city has made the ------- of infectious diseases more rapid, because pathogens spread quickly in close quarters.

    (A) overcrowding . . . propagation
    (B) squalor . . . circulation
    (C) poverty . . . deterioration
    (D) congestion . . . elimination
    (E) proximity . . . resilience

5 Much research in neuroscience today endeavors to ------- the mechanisms by which our brains turn the ------- data from our sense organs into coherent and understandable information.

    (A) enhance . . . quality of
    (B) restore . . . absence of
    (C) enlighten . . . source of
    (D) attenuate . . . dearth of
    (E) elucidate . . . deluge of

GO ON TO THE NEXT PAGE ▸▸▸

The passages below are followed by questions based on their content. Answer each question based on what is stated or implied in the passages.

Questions 6–7 are based on the following passage.

Line
5

10

15

Towards the middle and the end of the sixteenth century there were many students and scholars possessing a great deal of erudition, but very little means of subsistence. Nor were their prospects very encouraging. They first went through that bitter experience, which, since then, so many have made after them—that whoever seeks a home in the realm of intellect runs the risk of losing the solid ground on which the fruits for maintaining human life grow. The eye directed towards the Parnassus is not the most apt to spy out the small tortuous paths of daily gain. To get quick returns of interest, even though it be small, from the capital of knowledge and learning has always been, and still is, a question of difficult solution.

6 The "fruits" mentioned in line 10 represent

(A) spiritual growth
(B) artistic skill
(C) technological progress
(D) the means of acquiring food and shelter
(E) scientific knowledge

7 The "question" in line 16 is whether

(A) money can buy happiness
(B) intellectuals can earn a good living
(C) society can construct effective schools
(D) old ideas are relevant to modern society
(E) scholars are happier than merchants

Questions 8–9 are based on the following passage.

Line
5

10

15

When there exists an inherited or instinctive tendency to the performance of an action, or an inherited taste for certain kinds of food, some degree of habit in the individual is often or generally requisite. We find this in the paces of the horse, and to a certain extent in the pointing of dogs; although some young dogs point excellently the first time they are taken out, yet they often associate the proper inherited attitude with a wrong odour, and even with eyesight. I have heard it asserted that if a calf be allowed to suck its mother only once, it is much more difficult afterwards to rear it by hand. Caterpillars which have been fed on the leaves of one kind of tree, have been known to perish from hunger rather than to eat the leaves of another tree, although this afforded them their proper food, under a state of nature.

8 The "pointing of dogs" (line 7) is mentioned primarily as an example of

(A) an innate habit
(B) a behavior that humans find useful
(C) a skill that is hard to learn
(D) an ability that many other animals also have
(E) a skill that helps animals to find food

9 Which of the following best summarizes the main point of the paragraph?

(A) People will eat only what they are genetically determined to eat.
(B) All animal behavior is instinctive.
(C) Cows and other animals should not be fed by humans.
(D) Habits in animals are impossible to break.
(E) Inherited tendencies manifest themselves in behavioral habits.

First paragraph: Jacob Feis. *Shakspere and Montaigne*, c. 1890. Public domain
Second paragraph: Charles Darwin. *The Expression of the Emotions in Man and Animals*. 1872. Public domain

GO ON TO THE NEXT PAGE ▶▶▶

The passages below are followed by questions based on their content. The questions are to be answered on the basis of what is stated or implied in the passage itself or in the introductory material that precedes them.

Questions 10–16 are based on the following passage.

The following is an excerpt from an essay entitled Political Ideals, *written in 1917 by Bertrand Russell.*

It is not one ideal for all men, but a separate ideal for each separate man, that has to be real-
Line ized if possible. Every man has it in his being to develop into something good or bad: there is
5 a best possible for him, and a worst possible. His circumstances will determine whether his capacities for good are developed or crushed, and whether his bad impulses are strengthened or gradually diverted into better channels.
10 But although we cannot set up in any detail an ideal of character which is to be univer-sally applicable—although we cannot say, for instance, that all men ought to be industrious, or self-sacrificing, or fond of music—there are
15 some broad principles which can be used to guide our estimates as to what is possible or desirable.
      We may distinguish two sorts of goods, and two corresponding sorts of impulses.
20 There are goods in regard to which individual possession is possible, and there are goods in which all can share alike. The food and cloth-ing of one man is not the food and clothing of another; if the supply is insufficient, what one
25 man has is obtained at the expense of some other man. This applies to material goods gen-erally, and therefore to the greater part of the present economic life of the world. On the other hand, mental and spiritual goods do not
30 belong to one man to the exclusion of an-other. If one man knows a science, that does not prevent others from knowing it; on the contrary, it helps them to acquire the knowl-edge. If one man is a great artist or poet, that
35 does not prevent others from painting pic-tures or writing poems, but helps to create the atmosphere in which such things are possible. If one man is full of good-will toward others, that does not mean that there is less goodwill
40 to be shared among the rest; the more good-will one man has, the more he is likely to cre-ate among others.

In such matters there is no possession, be-cause there is not a definite amount to be
45 shared; any increase anywhere tends to pro-duce an increase everywhere.
      There are two kinds of impulses, corre-sponding to the two kinds of goods. There are possessive impulses, which aim at acquiring or
50 retaining private goods that cannot be shared; these center in the impulse of property. And there are creative or constructive impulses, which aim at bringing into the world or mak-ing available for use the kind of goods in which
55 there is no privacy and no possession.
      The best life is the one in which the cre-ative impulses play the largest part and the possessive impulses the smallest. This is no new discovery. The Gospel says: "Take no
60 thought, saying, What shall we eat? or What shall we drink? Or Wherewithal shall we be clothed?" The thought we give to these things is taken away from matters of more impor-tance. And what is worse, the habit of mind
65 engendered by thinking of these things is a bad one; it leads to competition, envy, domi-nation, cruelty, and almost all the moral evils that infest the world. In particular, it leads to the predatory use of force. Material posses-
70 sions can be taken by force and enjoyed by the robber. Spiritual possessions cannot be taken in this way. You may kill an artist or a thinker, but you cannot acquire his art or his thought. You may put a man to death because
75 he loves his fellow-men, but you will not by so doing acquire the love which made his happi-ness. Force is impotent in such matters; it is only as regards material goods that it is effec-tive. For this reason the men who believe in
80 force are the men whose thoughts and desires are preoccupied with material goods.

10 Which of the following best summarizes the main point of the passage?

(A) People should strive harder to appreci-ate the arts.
(B) Nothing can be possessed exclusively by one person.
(C) Societies need strong laws against stealing.
(D) Creativity is of higher value than possessiveness.
(E) Scarce resources should be shared equally in a society.

GO ON TO THE NEXT PAGE ▸▸▸

11 The passage mentions "food and clothing" (lines 22–23) primarily as examples of things that

(A) everyone needs to survive
(B) create a positive atmosphere of sharing
(C) many underdeveloped countries lack
(D) cannot be shared as freely as other things
(E) are hard to find

12 As it is used in line 43, "such matters" can be inferred to refer to situations in which

(A) people must compete for ownership of goods
(B) artists struggle to sell their works
(C) people strive to be industrious
(D) philosophers endeavor to define human ideals
(E) possessing a good does not deny it to someone else

13 In line 51, the phrase "impulse of" most nearly means

(A) reaction against
(B) restriction of
(C) sharing of
(D) fear of
(E) desire for

14 According to the author, "force is impotent in such matters" (line 77) because

(A) violence cannot influence another person's thoughts
(B) moral people do not engage in violence
(C) spiritual things cannot be acquired coercively
(D) a good person will always be protected by friends
(E) reason is more powerful than physical force

15 In the last paragraph, the author indicates that his thesis is not

(A) ancient
(B) a matter of logic
(C) relevant to those who are already happy
(D) original
(E) universal

16 Which of the following examples, if it existed, would most directly refute the main point of the author?

(A) a person who finds a large sum of money and gives it to charity
(B) an invention that benefits all of humankind even though it was created only to make money for its inventor
(C) a tyrant who murders intellectuals in order to maintain his authority
(D) a thief who steals in order to feed his starving family
(E) an army that invades another country and plunders its wealth

Questions 17–24 are based on the following passage.

The following passage was written for The Atlantic Monthly *in 1902 by Native American writer Zitkala-Sa, also known as Gertrude Simmons Bonnin.*

The racial lines, which once were bitterly real, now serve nothing more than marking
Line out a living mosaic of human beings. And even here men of the same color are like the ivory
5 keys of one instrument where each represents all the rest, yet varies from them in pitch and quality of voice. Thus with a compassion for all echoes in human guise, I greet the solemn-faced "native preacher" whom I find awaiting
10 me. I listen with respect for God's creature, though he mouth most strangely the jangling phrases of a bigoted creed.
    As our tribe is one large family, where every person is related to all the others, he ad-
15 dressed me:
    "Cousin, I came from the morning church service to talk with you."
    "Yes," I said interrogatively, as he paused for some word from me.
20   Shifting uneasily about in the straight-backed chair he sat upon, he began: "Every holy day (Sunday) I look about our little God's house, and not seeing you there, I am disappointed. This is why I come today. Cousin, as
25 I watch you from afar, I see no unbecoming behavior and hear only good reports of you, which all the more burns me with the wish that you were a church member. Cousin, I was taught long years ago by kind missionar-

30   ies to read the holy book. These godly men
taught me also the folly of our old beliefs.

     "There is one God who gives reward or pun-
ishment to the race of dead men. In the upper
region the Christian dead are gathered in un-
35   ceasing song and prayer. In the deep pit below,
the sinful ones dance in torturing flames.

     "Think upon these things, my cousin, and
choose now to avoid the after-doom of hell
fire!" Then followed a long silence in which he
40   clasped tighter and unclasped again his inter-
locked fingers.

     Like instantaneous lightning flashes came
pictures of my own mother's making, for she,
too, is now a follower of the new superstition.
45   "Knocking out the chinking of our log
cabin, some evil hand thrust in a burning
taper of braided dry grass, but failed of his intent, for the fire died out and the half burned
brand fell inward to the floor. Directly above
50   it, on a shelf, lay the holy book. This is what
we found after our return from a several days'
visit. Surely some great power is hid in the sacred book!"

     Brushing away from my eyes many like pic-
55   tures, I offered midday meal to the converted
Indian sitting wordless and with downcast
face. No sooner had he risen from the table
with "Cousin, I have relished it," than the
church bell rang.

60   Thither he hurried forth with his afternoon
sermon. I watched him as he hastened along,
his eyes bent fast upon the dusty road till he
disappeared at the end of a quarter of a mile.

     The little incident recalled to mind the copy
65   of a missionary paper brought to my notice a
few days ago, in which a "Christian" pugilist[1]
commented upon a recent article of mine,
grossly perverting the spirit of my pen. Still I
would not forget that the pale-faced mission-
70   ary and the aborigine are both God's creatures,
though small indeed their own conceptions of
Infinite Love. A wee child toddling in a wonder
world, I prefer to their dogma my excursions
into the natural gardens where the voice of the
75   Great Spirit is heard in the twittering of birds,
the rippling of mighty waters, and the sweet
breathing of flowers. If this is Paganism, then
at present, at least, I am a Pagan.

---

17 The main purpose of the passage as a whole is to

(A)   describe one person's perspective on an attempt at religious conversion
(B)   compare Native American religious tra-dition to European religious tradition
(C)   analyze the rise of Christianity in Na-tive American tribes
(D)   refute a misconception about the nature of Paganism
(E)   describe a conflict between the author and her mother

18 The reference to "pitch and quality of voice" (lines 6–7) serves to emphasize

(A)   the variety in vocal quality of religious singers
(B)   the harshness with which many preachers rebuke their congregations
(C)   the sounds that the author hears in nature
(D)   the author's inability to understand what the native preacher is saying
(E)   the differences among members of the same race

19 In the first paragraph, the author character-izes the preacher primarily as

(A)   respectful
(B)   articulate
(C)   uneducated
(D)   intolerant ✓
(E)   compassionate

20 According to the passage, the preacher ad-dressed the author as "cousin" because

(A)   it is customary for preachers to refer to church members with that term
(B)   the tribe members are all related
(C)   the preacher's mother and the author's mother are sisters
(D)   the preacher had forgotten the au-thor's name
(E)   the author refused to answer to her given name

---

[1]One who fights for a cause; also, a prize fighter

GO ON TO THE NEXT PAGE ▶▶▶

21 According to the passage, the native preacher and the author's mother are alike in that they both

(A) have experienced attempted arson
(B) must travel a great deal
(C) have similar religious beliefs
(D) relish the midday meal
(E) enjoy excursions into the natural gardens

22 In line 68, the word "spirit" most nearly means

(A) apparition
(B) lively nature
(C) intent
(D) fear
(E) presence

23 In the final paragraph, the author characterizes herself primarily as

(A) mature
(B) creative
(C) vengeful
(D) repressed
(E) awed

24 The author mentions "conceptions of Infinite Love" (lines 71–72) in order to emphasize which of the following characteristics of the "pale-faced missionary" (lines 69–70)?

(A) small-mindedness
(B) reluctance to persist in the attempt to convert the author to Christianity
(C) generosity toward aborigines
(D) sympathy for animals
(E) high intelligence

STOP   *You may check your work, on this section only, until time is called.*

Section 6

Time—25 minutes
35 Questions

Directions for "Improving Sentences" Questions

Each of the sentences below contains one underlined portion. The portion may contain one or more errors in grammar, usage, construction, precision, diction (choice of words), or idiom. Some of the sentences are correct.

Consider the meaning of the original sentence, and choose the answer that best expresses that meaning. If the original sentence is best, choose (A), because it repeats the original phrasing. Choose the phrasing that creates the clearest, most precise, and most effective sentence.

EXAMPLE:

The children <u>couldn't hardly believe their eyes.</u>
  (A)   couldn't hardly believe their eyes
  (B)   would not hardly believe their eyes
  (C)   could hardly believe their eyes
  (D)   couldn't nearly believe their eyes
  (E)   could hardly believe his or her eyes

EXAMPLE ANSWER

(C)

---

1 Claims about harmful effects of the genetic alteration of vegetables <u>is more speculation than documented fact</u>.

  (A)   is more speculation than documented fact
  (B)   are more with speculation than of a documented fact
  (C)   is more of a speculation than a documented fact
  (D)   are more speculation than documented fact
  (E)   are a matter of more speculation than documented fact

2 <u>Having passed</u> the test for certification, Mackenzie was looking forward to finding a challenging teaching position in her home town.

  (A)   Having passed
  (B)   Passing
  (C)   Being that she passed
  (D)   If she had passed
  (E)   For her passing

3 Having once been a provincial schoolmaster, <u>Jean-Paul Sartre's writing was always oriented more towards clear instruction than pontification</u>.

  (A)   Jean-Paul Sartre's writing was always oriented more towards clear instruction than pontification
  (B)   Jean-Paul Sartre always wrote to instruct more than to pontificate
  (C)   the writings of Jean-Paul Sartre were always oriented more toward instruction than pontification
  (D)   Jean-Paul Sartre was oriented in his writing more toward instruction than pontification
  (E)   Jean-Paul Sartre's writing was more to instruct than to pontificate

GO ON TO THE NEXT PAGE ▶▶▶

4 Adam Smith was a professor of philosophy, <u>a commissioner of customs, and founded the field of modern economics</u>.

(A) a commissioner of customs, and founded the field of modern economics
(B) worked as commissioner of customs, and founded the field of modern economics
(C) a commissioner of customs, and the founder of the field of modern economics
(D) commissioned customs, and was the founder of the field of modern economics
(E) a commissioner of customs, and was the founder of the field of modern economics

5 John Locke was one of the first philosophers to attack the principle of <u>primogeniture, the practice of handing the monarchy down</u> to the king's first-born son.

(A) primogeniture, the practice of handing the monarchy down
(B) primogeniture; the practice of handing the monarchy down
(C) primogeniture being the practice of handing the monarchy down
(D) primogeniture that which handed down the monarchy
(E) primogeniture this was the practice of handing the monarchy down

6 The nation's fledgling economy struggled <u>because the investment from other countries into its major industries was lacking from most of them</u>.

(A) because the investment from other countries into its major industries was lacking from most of them
(B) because few other countries were willing to invest in its major industries
(C) due to the fact that few other countries would have invested in its major industries
(D) because of the lack of investment from few other countries in its major industries
(E) for the lack of investment in its major industries from other countries

7 The corporation began construction on the new building in January, but <u>there is still no completion</u>.

(A) there is still no completion
(B) they have yet to complete it
(C) it has yet to complete the project
(D) they have not still completed it yet
(E) it isn't hardly done yet

8 Having spread more quickly than antibiotics could be distributed, <u>doctors were prevented from effectively treating the virulent disease</u>.

(A) doctors were prevented from effectively treating the virulent disease
(B) doctors could not effectively treat the virulent disease because it thwarted them
(C) the doctors who were trying to treat it effectively were prevented by the virulent disease
(D) the virulent disease prevented itself from its being treated effectively by the doctors
(E) the virulent disease prevented the doctors from treating it effectively

9 Although psychologist B. F. <u>Skinner, who is best known as the man who popularized behaviorism, he</u> also wrote a utopian novel entitled *Walden Two*.

(A) Skinner, who is best known as the man who popularized behaviorism, he
(B) Skinner, who is best known as the man who popularized behaviorism,
(C) Skinner is best known as the man who popularized behaviorism, he
(D) Skinner popularized behaviorism, for which he is well known, nevertheless he
(E) Skinner, who is best known as the man who popularized behaviorism, is the one who

10 Singing for over 2 hours, Anita's hoarseness prevented her hitting the high notes.

(A) Singing for over 2 hours, Anita's hoarseness prevented her hitting the high notes.
(B) Singing for over 2 hours, Anita was unable to hit the high notes because of her hoarseness.
(C) Having sung for over 2 hours, Anita's hoarseness prevented her from hitting the high notes.
(D) Having sung for over 2 hours, Anita was no longer able to hit the high notes because of her hoarseness.
(E) Having sung for over 2 hours, Anita's ability to hit the high notes was prevented by her hoarseness.

11 Some philosophers maintain that language is essential to formulating certain thoughts; others, that even the most complex thoughts are independent of words.

(A) thoughts; others, that
(B) thoughts, however, that others maintain that
(C) thoughts others suggest that
(D) thoughts and that others believe
(E) thoughts but others, however, that

Directions for "Identifying Sentence Error" Questions

The following sentences may contain errors in grammar, usage, diction (choice of words), or idiom. Some of the sentences are correct. No sentence contains more than 1 error.
If the sentence contains an error, it is underlined and lettered. The parts that are not underlined are correct.
If there is an error, select the part that must be changed to correct the sentence.
If there is no error, choose (E).

EXAMPLE:

By the time <u>they reached</u> the halfway point
                        A

<u>in the race,</u> <u>most of the runners</u> <u>hadn't hardly</u>
        B   C   D
begun to hit their stride. <u>No error</u>
                                     E

SAMPLE ANSWER:

(D)

6

---

12 Ellen turned around <u>quick</u> and noticed
                                 A

<u>that the dog</u> that <u>had been following</u> her was
        B   C

now <u>gone</u>.   <u>No error</u>
         D   E

13 Marlena was honored not only for her

<u>initiative</u> in establishing the fund for war
     A

refugees but also <u>in devoting</u> so much
                            B

<u>of her own time</u> and money
         C

<u>to its success</u>.   <u>No error</u>
         D   E

14 The Medieval era in music <u>is considered</u>
                                             A

<u>by most</u> scholars <u>to begin</u> during the reign
     B   C
of Pope Gregory and to have ended

<u>around the middle of</u> the 15th century.
                D
<u>No error</u>
     E

15 Neither the artists <u>who were</u> at the vanguard
                                   A

of the Expressionist movement <u>or even</u> the
                                            B

critics <u>of the era</u> could have foreseen
             C

<u>the impact</u> of this new mode on the general
        D
public.   <u>No error</u>
                 E

16 Several members <u>of the safety commission</u>
                                 A

<u>suggested</u> that lowering the speed limit
     B

<u>on the road</u> would not necessarily result in
         C

<u>less</u> accidents.   <u>No error</u>
     D   E

17 By the time the operation <u>was completed</u>,
                                             A

5 surgeons <u>spent</u> over 20 hours <u>performing</u>
                 B   C
more than a dozen <u>procedures</u>.   <u>No error</u>
                            D   E

GO ON TO THE NEXT PAGE ▶▶▶

18 Not until the recent scandal <u>has</u> the
　　　　　　　　　　　　　　A
newspapers published <u>anything</u> even
　　　　　　　　　　　　B
vaguely <u>negative</u> about the company or
　　　　　C
<u>its executives</u>.　<u>No error</u>
　　D　　　　　　E

19 <u>After falling asleep</u> on a horse-drawn bus in
　　　　A
Belgium in 1865, Friedrick Kekule had a

<u>dream, it led</u> to <u>his discovery</u> of the structure
　　B　　　　　　C
of the benzene molecule.　<u>No error</u>
　　　D　　　　　　　　　　　E

20 The movement <u>to establish</u> women's issues
　　　　　　　　A
as important <u>subjects of study</u> <u>have had</u>
　　　　　　　B　　　　　　C
a profound impact on the curricula

<u>offered in colleges</u> today.　<u>No error</u>
　　D　　　　　　　　　　E

21 Legends and folk stories inevitably become

transformed and <u>exaggerated</u> as they are
　　　　　　　　A
<u>passed down</u> through the generations, often
　　B
in order <u>to conform</u> to changing political
　　　　　C
and <u>social standards</u>.　<u>No error</u>
　　　D　　　　　　　　　E

22 Although the remarks <u>were made</u> to the
　　　　　　　　　　　A
entire group, <u>everyone</u> at the meeting could
　　　　　　　B
tell <u>that they were</u> particularly intended
　　　C
<u>for Maria and I</u>.　<u>No error</u>
　　D　　　　　　　E

23 By all accounts, the restructuring of the

federal department was <u>successive</u>,
　　　　　　　　　　A
<u>eliminating</u> unnecessary layers
　B
<u>of bureaucracy</u> and dozens of
　C
<u>wasteful procedures</u>.　<u>No error</u>
　　D　　　　　　　　　E

24 The professor <u>suggested</u> that
　　　　　　　A
<u>those who wished</u> to attend the lecture next
　　B
week <u>be in the classroom</u> 10 minutes
　　　　C
<u>earlier than usual</u>.　<u>No error</u>
　　D　　　　　　　　E

25 While in office a President <u>can usually</u>
　　　　　　　　　　　　A
pass more legislation, <u>and with fewer</u>
　　　　　　　　　　　B
procedural obstacles, when the Congress

and the administration are <u>underneath</u> the
　　　　　　　　　　　　　C
<u>control of</u> the same political party.
　D
<u>No error</u>
　E

26 A quick <u>inspection</u> of Kurt's art collection
　　　　　A
<u>would show clearly</u> that <u>he has</u> a discerning
　　B　　　　　　　　C
eye for <u>exemplary works</u> of art.　<u>No error</u>
　　　　D　　　　　　　　　　E

27 <u>Surprisingly</u> absent from the debate <u>were</u>
　　　　A　　　　　　　　　　　　　　　B
the vice president's arrogance <u>that</u> he
　　　　　　　　　　　　　　　　　　C
typically displays <u>in such</u> forums.　<u>No error</u>
　　　　　　　　　　D　　　　　　　　E

28 Of the numerous strains of *Streptococcus*

bacteria <u>that are known</u> to cause
　　　　　　　A
infections, type B is the <u>more</u> dangerous
　　　　　　　　　　　　　　B
<u>for pregnant women</u> about <u>to give</u>
　　　　C　　　　　　　　　　　D
birth.　<u>No error</u>
　　　　　E

29 Since 2001, the company <u>has spent</u>
　　　　　　　　　　　　　　　A
<u>more time on</u> employee training than
　　　B
<u>they did</u> in the previous 10 years <u>combined</u>.
　　C　　　　　　　　　　　　　　　D
<u>No error</u>
　E

Directions for "Improving Paragraphs" Questions

Below is an early draft of an essay. It requires revision in many areas.

The questions that follow ask you to make improvements in sentence structure, diction, organization, and development. Answering the questions may require you to understand the context of the passage as well as the rules of standard written English.

Questions 30–35 are based on the following passage.

(1) Most great scientists and artists are familiar with the so-called "eureka phenomenon." (2) This is the experience that a thinker has when, after they thought about a problem long and hard, they suddenly come upon a solution in a flash when they are no longer thinking about it. (3) The name of the phenomenon comes from the legend of Archimedes. (4) He had been thinking for days about a hard problem that had come from the king, King Hieron II. (5) The problem was how to determine whether the king's crown was pure gold without destroying it. (6) As he was bathing, the solution to the problem came to Archimedes in a flash and he ran naked through the streets of Syracuse shouting "Eureka!" meaning "I have found it!"

(7) Students should understand this also. (8) You have probably had the experience of thinking about a paper or a math problem for so long that it's like one's brain gets frozen. (9) When this happens, it is best to get away from the problem for a while rather than obsess about it. (10) Isaac Asimov, one of the most prolific writers of all time, used to go to the movies every time he got writer's block. (11) He claimed that he always came out of the movie knowing exactly how to get his story back on track.

(12) Unfortunately, many students today don't have time for that. (13) They feel so much pressure to get everything done—their homework, their jobs, their sports, their extracurricular activities—that they think that taking "time out" to relax their brains is just a costly waste of time. (14) This is really too bad because very often relaxation is more valuable to a student than just more hard work.

30 Which of the following is the best revision of the underlined portion of sentence 2 (reproduced below)?

This is the experience that a thinker has when, after they thought about a problem long and hard, they suddenly come upon a solution in a flash when they are no longer thinking about it.

(A) that a thinker has when, after they thought long and hard about a problem, their solution suddenly arises like a flash

(B) that thinkers have when a solution suddenly had arisen like a flash after they were thinking long and hard about a problem

(C) that a thinker has when, after having thought long and hard about a problem, they suddenly come upon a solution

(D) that thinkers have when, after having thought long and hard about a problem, they suddenly come upon a solution

(E) that thinkers have when, thinking long and hard about a problem, they suddenly come upon a solution in a flash

6

31 Which of the following is the best way to combine sentences 3, 4, and 5?

(A) The name of the phenomenon comes from the legend of Archimedes, who had been thinking for days about how to determine whether King Hieron II's crown was pure gold without destroying it.

(B) Archimedes had been thinking for days about how to determine whether King Hieron II's crown was pure gold without destroying it, and this is where the name of the phenomenon comes from.

(C) The legend of Archimedes thinking about how to determine whether King Hieron II's crown was pure gold without destroying it is the origin of the name of the phenomenon.

(D) The phenomenon is named for Archimedes and his thinking for days about how to determine whether King Hieron II's crown was pure gold without destroying it.

(E) The name of the phenomenon was from Archimedes, and his thinking for days about how to determine without destroying it whether King Hieron II's crown was pure gold.

32 Which of the following revisions of sentence 7 most clearly and logically introduces the second paragraph?

(A) This historical episode is something that all students should learn about in school.

(B) Understanding this phenomenon may help students to improve their studies.

(C) Nevertheless, this episode is something that all students should know.

(D) Understanding this episode requires a more thorough understanding of its historical setting.

(E) Many have tried to understand this phenomenon, but few have succeeded.

33 Which of the following is the best revision of the underlined portion of sentence 8 (reproduced below)?

You have probably had the experience of thinking about a paper or a math problem for so long that it's like one's brain gets frozen.

(A) it seems that your brain gets frozen
(B) one's brain gets frozen
(C) your brain seems to freeze
(D) your brains seem to freeze
(E) one's brain seems to freeze

34 Where is the best place to insert the following sentence?

Perhaps if students could work such little excursions into their busy study schedules, they would have similar "eureka" experiences.

(A) after sentence 7
(B) after sentence 8
(C) after sentence 9
(D) after sentence 10
(E) after sentence 11 (as the last sentence of the second paragraph)

35 In context, which of the following revisions of the underlined portion of sentence 12 (reproduced below) is most effective at making it clearer and more specific?

Unfortunately, many students today don't have time for that.

(A) today have hardly even 1 hour for such things
(B) today, unlike those in Archimedes' time, don't have time to go to the movies
(C) today don't have time for such excursions
(D) of modern times lack sufficient time for the kinds of things explained above
(E) today lack sufficient time for things like this

STOP

You may check your work, on this section only, until time is called.

Section 7

Time—20 minutes
16 Questions

Directions for Multiple-Choice Questions

In this section, solve each problem, using any available space on the page for scratchwork. Then decide which is the best of the choices given and fill in the corresponding oval on your answer sheet.

- You may use a calculator on any problem. All numbers used are real numbers.
- Figures are drawn as accurately as possible EXCEPT when it is stated that the figure is not drawn to scale.
- All figures lie in a plane unless otherwise indicated.

Reference Information

$A = \pi r^2$ $A = \ell w$ $A = \frac{1}{2} bh$ $V = \ell wh$ $V = \pi r^2 h$ $c^2 = a^2 + b^2$ Special Right Triangles
$C = 2\pi r$

The number of degrees of arc in a circle is 360°.
The measure in degrees of a straight angle is 180°.
The sum of the measures in degrees of the angles of a triangle is 180°.

---

1 If four apples cost 20 cents, then, at this rate, how much would 10 apples cost?

(A) $.40
(B) $.50
(C) $.60
(D) $.70
(E) $.80

1 = 5c
50
(B)

---

2 If $2^b = 8$, then $3^b =$

(A) 6
(B) 9
(C) 27
(D) 64
(E) 81

b = 3
$3^3 = 27$
(C)

---

3 How much greater is the average (arithmetic mean) of a, b, and 18 than the average of a, b, and 12?

(A) 2
(B) 3
(C) 4
(D) 5
(E) 6

$\frac{a+b+18}{3}$, *$\frac{a+b+12}{3}$*

$\frac{18}{3} = 6$ *$\frac{12}{3} = 4$*

(A)

GO ON TO THE NEXT PAGE ▶▶▶

4 The first day of a particular month is a Tuesday. What day of the week will it be on the 31st day of the month?

(A) Wednesday
(B) Thursday
(C) Friday
(D) Saturday
(E) Sunday

$d_1 = T$
$d_8 = T$
$d_{15} = T$
$d_{22} = T$
$d_{29} = T$

(B)

5 How many integer pairs (m, n) satisfy the statements $0 < m + n < 50$ and $\frac{m}{n} = 8$?

(A) 5
(B) 6
(C) 7
(D) 8
(E) more than 8

int = + or −
m+n < 60
$\frac{m}{n} = 8$

$\frac{8n}{1n}$

$\left(\frac{8}{1} \quad \frac{8}{31} \right)$ (D)

6 If $y\%$ of 50 is 32, then what is 200% of y?

(A) 16
(B) 32
(C) 64
(D) 128
(E) 256

$\frac{Y(50)}{100} = 32$
$\frac{50}{100} = \frac{1}{2}$
$y = 64$
$2y =$

(D)

7 For $x > 0$, the function $g(x)$ is defined by the equation $g(x) = x + x^{1/2}$. What is the value of $g(16)$?

non neg

(A) 16
(B) 20
(C) 24
(D) 64
(E) 272

$g(16) = 16 + \sqrt{16}$
$16 + 4$
$= 20$

(B)

8

Note: Figure not drawn to scale.

In the figure above, if the slope of $\overline{AB}$ is $-\frac{3}{4}$, what is the area of $\triangle ABO$?

(A) 54
(B) 72
(C) 96
(D) 108
(E) 192

$A = (0, 12)$ $B = (X, 0)$
$\frac{-3}{4} = \frac{X - 0}{0 - 12}$
$\frac{-3}{4} = \frac{X}{-12}$ (A)
$9 = X$

9 $-1, 1, 2, -1, 1, 2, -1, 1, 2, \ldots$

The sequence above continues according to the pattern shown. What is the sum of the first 25 terms of this sequence?

(A) 15
(B) 16
(C) 18
(D) 19
(E) 21

$3 \times 8 = 24$
$(2)8 = 16 - 1 = 15$

(A)

10 A jar contains only white and blue marbles of identical size and weight. The ratio of the number of white marbles to the number of blue marbles is 4 to b. If the probability of choosing a white marble from the jar at random is $\frac{1}{4}$, then what is the value of b?

(A) 1
(B) 2
(C) 6
(D) 12
(E) 16

$\frac{\#w}{\#b} = \frac{4}{b} = \frac{1}{3}$
$\frac{3}{4} \quad \frac{1}{4} \quad \sqrt{b = 12}$

(D)

GO ON TO THE NEXT PAGE ▶▶▶

11 The area of a right triangle is 10 square centimeters. If the length of each leg, in centimeters, is a positive integer, then what is the *least* possible length, in centimeters, of the hypotenuse?

(A) $\sqrt{29}$
(B) $\sqrt{41}$
(C) $\sqrt{101}$
(D) $\sqrt{104}$
(E) $\sqrt{401}$

≥ 1 $A = 10 cm^2$

$\sqrt{1^2+1^2} = \sqrt{2}$

12 If y is a number less than 0 but greater than -1, which of the following expressions has the greatest value?

(A) $100y$
(B) y^2
(C) y^3
(D) y^4
(E) y^5

$y = neg \#$

$-1 < y < 0$

$-.5$

13 If at least one wuzzle is grumpy, then some fuzzles are lumpy.

If the statement above is true, then which of the following must also be true?
(A) If all wuzzles are grumpy, then all fuzzles are lumpy.
(B) If no wuzzle is grumpy, then all fuzzles are lumpy.
(C) If all fuzzles are lumpy, then all wuzzles are grumpy.
(D) If no wuzzle is grumpy, then no fuzzle is lumpy.
(E) If no fuzzle is lumpy, then no wuzzle is grumpy.

if, this, then that

if not that, then not this

14 Six buses are to carry 200 students on a field trip. If each bus must have no more than 40 students and no fewer than 30 students, then what is the greatest number of buses that can have 40 students?

(A) 6
(B) 5
(C) 4
(D) 3
(E) 2

$40x$ $30 = 1$
200 $30 = 2$
$3\cancel{0}$ 3
170 $= 4$
          $\cancel{10} = 5$
          $40 = 6$

15 The volume of right cylinder A is twice the volume of right cylinder B. If the height of cylinder B is twice the height of cylinder A, then what is the ratio of the radius of cylinder A to the radius of cylinder B?

(A) 1 to 2
(B) 1 to 1
(C) $\sqrt{2}$ to 1
(D) 2 to 1
(E) 4 to 1

$V_a = 2V_b$ $h_b = 6$
$h_b = 2h_a$ $h_a = 3$

$V = \pi r^2 h$

$V_a = \pi(3)r^2 = 3\pi r^2$
$V_b = 6\pi r^2 = 6\pi r^2$
$3\pi r_a^2 = 2(6\pi r_b^2)$

16 In a set of 30 different positive integers, every number is even and/or a multiple of 3. If 22 of these numbers are even and 15 are multiples of 3, then how many of these numbers are multiples of 6?

(A) 23
(B) 22
(C) 15
(D) 11
(E) 7

$\dfrac{3\pi r_a^2}{3\pi} = \dfrac{12\pi r_b^2}{3\pi}$ $\dfrac{r_a^2}{r_b^2}$

$\sqrt{\dfrac{r_a^2}{r_b^2}} = \sqrt{\dfrac{4}{1}} = \dfrac{2}{\sqrt{1}}$

$\dfrac{2}{1}$

STOP   *You may check your work, on this section only, until time is called.*

Section 8

Start:
753
803

Time—20 minutes
19 Questions

Each of the sentences below is missing one or two portions. Read each sentence, then select the word or words that most logically complete the sentence, taking into account the meaning of the sentence as a whole.

Example:

Rather than accepting the theory unquestioningly, Deborah regarded it with -------.

(A) mirth
(B) sadness
(C) responsibility
(D) ignorance
(E) skepticism

Correct response: (E)

1 The evidence for ESP is ------- at best, so very few reputable scientists are willing to even ------- that the phenomenon exists.

(A) meager . . . regret
(B) unconvincing . . . suggest
(C) plentiful . . . admit
(D) paltry . . . deny
(E) strong . . . assume

2 The concept that the Earth is round was once ------- theory, but is now accepted as an inarguable truth.

(A) an incontrovertible
(B) a mellifluous
(C) an admirable
(D) a dubious
(E) an accurate

3 The controversy within the party produced a ------- that broke it into several factions even before the matter could be fully discussed among the members.

(A) unanimity
(B) schism
(C) caucus
(D) commemoration
(E) prognostication

4 Horace Mann, widely acknowledged as the father of American public schooling, ------- the Massachusetts legislature to institute a system for ------- universal access to education.

(A) petitioned . . . restricting
(B) established . . . denying
(C) persuaded . . . ensuring
(D) tolerated . . . requiring
(E) discouraged . . . vouchsafing

5 The light from most stars takes millions of years to reach us, so not only is the present existence of these stars -------, but so are the very concepts of "the present" and "existence."

(A) debatable
(B) methodical
(C) indecorous
(D) imperious
(E) profuse

6 Although many parents prefer to be ------- when their children broach sensitive personal subjects, others resort instead to ------- so as to make any potentially offensive matters seem less objectionable.

(A) honest . . . anachronism
(B) intolerant . . . laudation
(C) clandestine . . . obligation
(D) candid . . . euphemism
(E) forthright . . . coercion

GO ON TO THE NEXT PAGE ▶▶▶

The passages below are followed by questions based on their content and the relationship between the passages. The questions are to be answered on the basis of what is stated or implied in the passages or the introductory material that precedes them.

Questions 7–19 are based on the following passages.

The following 2 passages concern the use of "reinforcers," which are rewards or punishments used to encourage desired behaviors, and "contingencies," which are the arrangements of those reinforcers to shape behavior.

Passage 1

"Avoid compulsion," said Plato in *The Republic*, "and let your children's lessons take the form of play." Horace, among others, recom-
Line mended rewarding a child with cakes. Eras-
5   mus tells of an English gentleman who tried to teach his son Greek and Latin without punishment. He taught the boy to use a bow and arrow and set up targets in the shape of Greek and Latin letters, rewarding each hit with a cherry. He also fed the boy letters cut from de-
10 licious biscuits. Privileges and favors are often suggested, and the teacher may be personally reinforcing as friend or entertainer. In indus-
trial education students are paid for learning. Certain explicit contrived reinforcers, such as
15 marks, grades, and diplomas, are characteris-
tic of education as an institution. (These sug-
gest progress, but like progress they must be made reinforcing for other reasons.) Prizes are intrinsically reinforcing. Honors and
20 medals derive their power from prestige or esteem. This varies between cultures and epochs. In 1876 Oscar Wilde, then 22 years old and halfway toward his B.A. at Oxford, got a "first in Mods." He wrote to a friend: ". . . I
25 did not know what I had got till the next morning at 12 o'clock, breakfasting at the Mitre, I read it in the *Times*. Altogether I swaggered horribly but am really pleased with myself. My poor mother is in great delight,
30 and I was overwhelmed with telegrams on Thursday from everyone I knew." The con-
temporary student graduating *summa cum laude* is less widely acclaimed.
Although free of some of the by-products of
35 aversive control, positive reinforcers of this sort are not without their problems. Many are effective only in certain states of deprivation which are not always easily arranged. Making

a student hungry in order to reinforce him
40 with food would raise personal issues which are not entirely avoided with other kinds of reinforcers. We cannot all get prizes, and if some students get high grades, others must get low.
45 But the main problem again is the contin-
gencies. Much of what the child is to do in school does not have the form of play, with its naturally reinforcing consequences, nor is there any natural connection with food or a
50 passing grade or a medal. Such contingencies must be arranged by the teacher, and the arrangement is often defective. The boy men-
tioned by Erasmus may have salivated slightly upon seeing a Greek or Latin text, and he was
55 probably a better archer, but his knowledge of Greek and Latin could not have been appre-
ciably improved. Grades are almost always given long after the student has stopped behaving as a student. We must know that such
60 contingencies are weak because we would never use them to shape skilled behavior. In industrial education pay is usually by the hour—in other words, contingent mainly on being present. Scholarships are contingent on
65 a general level of performance. All these con-
tingencies could no doubt be improved, but there is probably good reason why they remain defective.

Passage 2

Even if they don't study it as a philosophi-
70 cal matter, all teachers must at some point confront the issue of whether, when, and how to punish or reward student behavior. Unless a teacher is blessed with a class full of highly motivated adult-pleasers, it is nearly impossi-
75 ble to avoid the need to nudge students in one direction or another. Simple suggestion works occasionally, but not frequently enough. Rea-
soning sometimes works, too, but explaining the logical nuances of behavioral standards is
80 often time-consuming and too often falls on deaf ears. So the practical question becomes: the carrot or the stick?
Most educators and psychologists agree that reward is always better than punishment,
85 but a small yet vocal group of psychologists

First passage: B. F. Skinner, *The Technology of Teaching*, © 1968 Prentice-Hall, pp. 149–150.
Second passage: © 2004 Christopher Black. All rights reserved. Reprinted by permission of the author.

GO ON TO THE NEXT PAGE ▸▸▸

have maintained since the 1960s that reward is often just as harmful as punishment, if not more so. Their arguments are subtle but very persuasive. Educators like Alfie Kohn and psy-
90　chologists like Edward Deci claim that careful study has shown that the introduction of a reward system, like gold stars on an attendance sheet or extra recess time for good behavior, changes the nature of the desired behavior
95　completely, and not for the better. For instance, Deci conducted a study in which people were given a puzzle to solve. Some were given money as a "reward" for solving the puzzle and others were simply asked to solve
100　the puzzle. Afterwards, both groups were left alone but watched carefully. Those who had been paid stopped playing, but those who had not been paid continued. Deci concluded that the subjects who were paid probably con-
105　strued the task as being manipulative: the experimenter was trying to get them to do something through bribery. The unpaid subjects, however, were more likely to see the task as fun and worth doing for its own sake.
110　This study and many like it have profound implications for the classroom. Several experiments have demonstrated that "pay-to-read" programs, where students are given money or certificates to read books, have surprisingly
115　negative effects on literacy. Such programs usually get kids to "read" a lot more books, but their reading skills and, far more importantly, their love of reading decline. Such programs, research suggests, turn reading into a
120　performance rather than a fulfilling personal experience. They encourage students to read books only superficially and only to get the reward. What is worse, like Deci's puzzle-solvers, the students don't want to continue
125　reading after the payments stop. Books have become only enrichment for the pocket, not enrichment for the mind.

Of course, the human mind is an enormously complex machine, and it would be a
130　mistake to use these few experiments to generalize that all rewards are bad. Certainly, honest and mindful praise from a respected teacher can do a great deal to encourage not only good behavior but rigorous intellectual
135　curiosity. Parents and teachers, however, need to be very aware of children's need to feel in control of themselves.

7 It can be inferred that the "English gentleman" (line 5) believed that good teaching utilized

(A) punishment
(B) well-written books
(C) reward
(D) humor
(E) careful grading

8 The parenthetical remark in lines 17–19 is intended to caution educators against

(A) failing to make grades and diplomas meaningful to students
(B) punishing students unnecessarily
(C) employing dull lessons
(D) emphasizing entertainment over rigor
(E) using rewards as reinforcers

9 Passage 1 indicates that "cultures and epochs" (lines 22–23) vary in the ways that

(A) universities choose from among their applicants
(B) academic awards are effective as motivators
(C) universities teach literature
(D) students are paid money for learning
(E) the media portray educational crises

10 The Wilde story in lines 23–32, "In 1876 . . . everyone I knew,'" is intended to illustrate

(A) how the modern cultural perception of academic honors differs from that of a previous era
(B) a particularly effective teaching strategy
(C) how a famous author used rewards to teach his students
(D) the dangerous effects of using academic rewards
(E) the point that Plato makes in the first sentence

GO ON TO THE NEXT PAGE ▶▶▶

11 Passage 1 mentions which of the following as "problems" (line 37) inherent in the use of positive reinforcers in education?

    I. difficulties in scheduling the reinforcers
   II. limitations in the supply of reinforcers
  III. the fact that rewards encourage only superficial learning

(A) I only
(B) II only
(C) I and II only
(D) I and III only
(E) I, II, and III

12 In the final paragraph of Passage 1, the author suggests that grades are problematic as reinforcers because they

(A) cannot be given to every student
(B) do not provide sensual gratification, as food does
(C) are not publicized enough
(D) are not given immediately after the desired behavior is exhibited
(E) are not as useful to the student as money

13 The sentence that begins on line 78, "Reasoning sometimes works . . . on deaf ears" is intended to describe the interaction between

(A) those who promote the use of punishments and those who oppose it
(B) educators and philosophers
(C) parents and teachers
(D) teachers and administrators
(E) teachers and students

14 In Passage 2, Alfie Kohn and Edward Deci (lines 90–91) are mentioned as examples of

(A) teachers who use rewards as reinforcers
(B) experts who question the effectiveness of rewards as reinforcers
(C) scientists on opposite sides of a debate
(D) educators who prefer negative reinforcers to positive reinforcers
(E) educators who advocate a careful schedule of contingencies for students

15 In saying that "the introduction of a reward system . . . changes the nature of the desired behavior" (lines 92–94), the author of Passage 2 indicates that

(A) many people object to the use of punishments in school
(B) teachers find it difficult to find the right kinds of rewards for student performance
(C) experts disagree about the effects of rewards on human behavior
(D) such systems tend to decrease student interest in the activity for its own sake
(E) not enough study has been done on the effectiveness of rewards in education

16 Deci's conclusion about the experiment described in Passage 2 (lines 96–110) assumes that the subjects in the study

(A) are well educated
(B) are highly proficient at solving puzzles
(C) have not participated in reward systems before
(D) can make inferences about the motives of the experimenter
(E) have some teaching experience

17 The author of Passage 2 mentions that "the human mind is an enormously complex machine" (lines 129–130) in order to suggest that

(A) a simplistic theory about the effectiveness of rewards is unwise
(B) people cannot be easily fooled
(C) many learning disabilities require special attention
(D) teachers often find it hard to teach certain subjects
(E) Deci's experiment was poorly constructed

GO ON TO THE NEXT PAGE ▶▶▶

18 The description of the "problems" (line 37) with positive reinforcers in Passage 1 would most likely be regarded by Edward Deci as

(A) thorough and fair
(B) presumptuous and incomplete
(C) unfair to educators
(D) erroneous in concluding that the methods of the "gentleman" were ineffective
(E) likely correct, but worthy of further study

19 Which of the following assumptions is shared by the authors of both passages?

(A) Rewards are ineffective as reinforcers of behavior.
(B) Honors and grades are necessary elements of institutional education.
(C) Good teaching is always focused on play.
(D) Negative feedback is not an effective teaching tool.
(E) If prizes are to be used in a classroom, there must be enough for all students.

8

STOP   *You may check your work, on this section only, until time is called.*

Section 9

Time—10 minutes
14 Questions

Directions for "Improving Sentences" Questions

Each of the sentences below contains 1 underlined portion. The portion may contain one or more errors in grammar, usage, construction, precision, diction (choice of words), or idiom. Some of the sentences are correct.

Consider the meaning of the original sentence, and choose the answer that best expresses that meaning. If the original sentence is best, choose (A), because it repeats the original phrasing. Choose the phrasing that creates the clearest, most precise, and most effective sentence.

EXAMPLE:	EXAMPLE ANSWER:
The children <u>couldn't hardly believe their eyes</u>.	(C)

(A)   couldn't hardly believe their eyes
(B)   would not hardly believe their eyes
(C)   could hardly believe their eyes
(D)   couldn't nearly believe their eyes
(E)   could hardly believe his or her eyes

---

1 <u>Choreographer Alvin Ailey's works, whose style is rooted in the techniques of modern dance, jazz dance and ballet, draw upon African American themes.</u>

(A)   Choreographer Alvin Ailey's works, whose style is rooted in the techniques of modern dance, jazz dance and ballet, draw upon African American themes.
(B)   Alvin Ailey has a style of a choreographer that is rooted in the techniques of modern dance, jazz dance and ballet of which also draws upon African American themes.
(C)   The works of choreographer Alvin Ailey, which draw upon African American themes, have a style that is rooted in the techniques of modern dance, jazz dance, and ballet.
(D)   Choreographer Alvin Ailey's works, which have a style that is rooted in the techniques of modern dance, jazz dance, and ballet, drawing upon African American themes.
(E)   Alvin Ailey's style, a choreographer, is rooted in the techniques of modern dance and jazz dance and ballet which also draws upon African American themes.

2 <u>The mountain climbers getting this far, they</u> did not want to return without having reached the peak.

(A)   The mountain climbers getting this far, they
(B)   Having gotten this far, the mountain climbers
(C)   To have gotten this far, the mountain climbers
(D)   The mountain climbers having gotten so far that they
(E)   Mountain climbers getting this far

3 Although usually even-tempered, <u>Rachel's irritation with her supervisor caused her to become</u> uncharacteristically cantankerous.

(A)   Rachel's irritation with her supervisor caused her to become
(B)   Rachel being irritated by her supervisor caused her to become
(C)   Rachel was irritated by her supervisor, and so became
(D)   her supervisor caused Rachel through irritation to become
(E)   Rachel, due to her supervisor's irritation, caused her to become

GO ON TO THE NEXT PAGE ▶▶▶

4 Because Alberta worked harder than her associates, she assumed that her salary would be higher than the other workers in the firm.

(A) would be higher than the
(B) was higher than that of the
(C) had been higher than the
(D) being higher than the salary of
(E) was highest of the

5 The police chief was hoping that by assigning an extra officer to the patrol he would decrease the amount of elicit behavior in the neighborhood.

(A) would decrease the amount of elicit
(B) would be able to decrease the elicit
(C) would decrease the amount of illicit
(D) might be able to lessen that of the illicit
(E) decreases the amount of illicit

6 Watching from the balcony, the paraders marched triumphantly through the streets below us.

(A) Watching from the balcony
(B) While watching from the balcony
(C) As we had been watching from the balcony
(D) As we watched from the balcony
(E) From the balcony, while watching,

7 By the time we arrived at the campsite where the troop would be staying, the counselors set up all the tents.

(A) the counselors set up all the tents
(B) setting up all the tents were the counselors
(C) set up by the counselors are the tents
(D) the tents are set up by the counselors
(E) the counselors had set up all the tents

8 By the time the movie had finished, neither Eric nor his daughters was able to stay awake because of the boredom caused by the film's inferior plot.

(A) neither Eric nor his daughters was able to stay awake because of the boredom caused by the film's inferior plot
(B) staying awake was an impossibility for Eric and his daughters because of the boredom caused by the inferiority of the plot
(C) neither Eric nor his daughters were able to stay awake because of the boredom caused by the film's inferior plot
(D) Eric and his daughters was unable to stay awake because of the boredom caused by the film's inferior plot
(E) the film's inferior plot had made it impossible for neither Eric nor his daughters to stay awake

9 An outstanding tennis player, Erica was concerned not only with working her way to the top of the national rankings, but also wanted to compete with class and dignity.

(A) also wanted to compete with class and dignity
(B) also with competing with class and dignity
(C) also with wanting to have competed with class and dignity
(D) she also wanted to compete with class and dignity
(E) she was also wanting to compete with class and dignity

10 Roberto volunteered to be an usher, not wanting to be the one that had to clean up the petals after the ceremony.

(A) that had to clean up the petals after the ceremony
(B) which had to clean up the petals after the ceremony
(C) who had to clean up the petals after the ceremony
(D) cleaning the petals up after the ceremony
(E) who was to be cleaning the petals after the ceremony

11 Rebecca liked to read <u>books, of which she found autobiographies to be the most interesting</u>.

(A) books, of which she found autobiographies to be the most interesting
(B) books, the most fascinating of which to her she found the autobiographies
(C) books, autobiographies being the most interesting she found
(D) books; she found autobiographies to be the most interesting
(E) books, to which autobiographies were the most interesting

12 Forced to live apart from his family and to move from place to place to avoid detection by the government's ubiquitous informers, <u>St. Pierre adopting a number of disguises</u>.

(A) St. Pierre adopting a number of disguises
(B) St. Pierre having adopted a number of disguises
(C) had adopted for St. Pierre a number of disguises
(D) a number of disguises by St. Pierre had adopted
(E) St. Pierre had to adopt a number of disguises

13 The Santa Catalina <u>Mountains, forming 12 million years ago during a period when the Western North American Continent was stretching</u>, cracking into blocks, bordered by steep faults.

(A) Mountains, forming 12 million years ago during a period when the Western North American Continent was stretching
(B) Mountains were formed 12 million years ago during a period when the Western North American Continent was being stretched
(C) Mountains, having been formed 12 million years ago during a period when the Western North American Continent was stretching
(D) Mountains was formed 12 million years ago during a period when the Western North American Continent was being stretched.
(E) Mountains had been formed during a period 12 million years ago when the Western North American Continent was stretching.

14 The most challenging aspect of the project is <u>we have to coordinate our work carefully</u>.

(A) we have to coordinate our work carefully
(B) we must coordinate our work carefully
(C) our coordination of our work carefully
(D) coordinating our work carefully
(E) in careful coordination of our work

9

STOP

You may check your work, on this section only, until time is called.

ANSWER KEY

Section 3 Math	Section 4 Math	Section 7 Math	Section 2 Critical Reading	Section 5 Critical Reading	Section 8 Critical Reading	Section 6 Writing	Section 9 Writing
1. E	1. E	1. B	1. A	1. C	1. B	1. D	1. C
2. A	2. C	2. C	2. C	2. E	2. D	2. A	2. B
3. C	3. E	3. A	3. D	3. D	3. B	3. B	3. C
4. C	4. A	4. B	4. A	4. A	4. C	4. B	4. B
5. D	5. A	5. A	5. E	5. E	5. A	5. A	5. C
6. A	6. D	6. D	6. C	6. D	6. D	6. B	6. D
7. D	7. B	7. B	7. A	7. B	7. C	7. C	7. E
8. A	8. C	8. C	8. C	8. B	8. A	8. E	8. C
9. C	9. 16	9. A	9. E	9. E	9. B	9. C	9. B
10. B	10. 36	10. D	10. B	10. D	10. A	10. D	10. C
11. D	11. 5	11. B	11. A	11. D	11. C	11. A	11. D
12. B	12. 30	12. B	12. B	12. E	12. D	12. A	12. E
13. A	13. 15	13. E	13. A	13. E	13. E	13. B	13. B
14. D	14. 8 or 12	14. E	14. C	14. C	14. B	14. C	14. D
15. A	15. 25	15. D	15. C	15. D	15. D	15. B	
16. B	16. 24	16. E	16. D	16. B	16. D	16. D	
17. D	17. 52	17. E	17. E	17. A	17. A	17. B	
18. C	18. 225		18. C	18. E	18. B	18. A	
19. A			19. B	19. D	19. D	19. B	
20. A			20. C	20. B		20. C	
			21. D	21. C		21. E	
			22. D	22. C		22. D	
			23. E	23. E		23. A	
			24. A	24. A		24. E	
						25. C	
						26. E	
						27. B	
						28. B	
						29. C	
						30. D	
						31. A	
						32. B	
						33. C	
						34. E	
						35. C	

Right (A): ___

Wrong (B): ___

(A)−1/4 (B): ___

Questions 1–8
Right (A): ___
Wrong (B): ___
(A)−1/4 (B): ___

Questions 9–18
Right (A): ___

SCORE CONVERSION TABLE

How to score your test

Use the answer key on the previous page to determine your raw score on each section. **Your raw score on each section except Section 4 is simply the number of correct answers minus ¼ of the number of wrong answers. On Section 4, your raw score is the sum of the number of correct answers for questions 1–18 minus ¼ of the number of wrong answers for questions 1–8.** Next, add the raw scores from Sections 3, 4, and 7 to get your Math raw score, and add the raw scores from sections 6 and 9 to get your Writing raw score. Write the three raw scores here:

Raw Critical Reading score: _____   Raw Math score: _____   Raw Writing score: _____

Use the table below to convert these to scaled scores.

Scaled scores: Critical Reading: _____   Math: _**40.75**___   Writing: _____

41=630= all due to time
= careless errors.

goal

Raw Score	Critical Reading Scaled Score	Math Scaled Score	Writing Scaled Score	Raw Score	Critical Reading Scaled Score	Math Scaled Score	Writing Scaled Score
67	800			32	520	550	610
66	800			31	510	550	600
65	790			30	510	540	580
64	780			29	500	530	570
63	760			28	490	530	560
62	750			27	490	520	550
61	730			26	480	510	540
60	720			25	480	500	530
59	700			24	470	490	520
58	700			23	460	480	510
57	690			22	460	480	500
56	680			21	450	470	490
55	670			20	440	460	480
54	660	800		19	440	450	470
53	650	790		18	430	450	460
52	650	760		17	420	440	450
51	640	740		16	420	430	440
50	630	720		15	410	420	440
49	620	710	800	14	400	410	430
48	620	700	800	13	400	410	420
47	610	680	800	12	390	400	410
46	600	670	790	11	380	390	400
45	600	660	780	10	370	380	390
44	590	650	760	9	360	370	380
43	590	640	740	8	350	360	380
42	580	630	730	7	340	350	370
41	570	630	710	6	330	340	360
40	570	620	700	5	320	330	350
39	560	610	690	4	310	320	340
38	550	600	670	3	300	310	320
37	550	590	660	2	280	290	310
36	540	580	650	1	270	280	300
35	540	580	640	0	250	260	280
34	530	570	630	−1	230	240	270
33	520	560	620	−2 or less	210	220	250

Handwritten annotations: "miss 1 on each" (boxed, near Math Scaled Score 740–800 area); "700 Goal" (boxed, at Math raw 48); "630" (boxed, at Math raw 41); "C 48" (at raw 48).

SCORE CONVERSION TABLE FOR WRITING COMPOSITE
[ESSAY + MULTIPLE CHOICE]

Calculate your writing raw score as you did on the previous page and grade your essay from a 1 to a 6 according to the standards that follow in the detailed answer key.

Essay score: _____   Raw Writing score: _____

Use the table below to convert these to scaled scores.

Scaled score: Writing: _____

Raw Score	Essay Score 0	Essay Score 1	Essay Score 2	Essay Score 3	Essay Score 4	Essay Score 5	Essay Score 6
-2 or less	200	230	250	280	310	340	370
-1	210	240	260	290	320	360	380
0	230	260	280	300	340	370	400
1	240	270	290	320	350	380	410
2	250	280	300	330	360	390	420
3	260	290	310	340	370	400	430
4	270	300	320	350	380	410	440
5	280	310	330	360	390	420	450
6	290	320	340	360	400	430	460
7	290	330	340	370	410	440	470
8	300	330	350	380	410	450	470
9	310	340	360	390	420	450	480
10	320	350	370	390	430	460	490
11	320	360	370	400	440	470	500
12	330	360	380	410	440	470	500
13	340	370	390	420	450	480	510
14	350	380	390	420	460	490	520
15	350	380	400	430	460	500	530
16	360	390	410	440	470	500	530
17	370	400	420	440	480	510	540
18	380	410	420	450	490	520	550
19	380	410	430	460	490	530	560
20	390	420	440	470	500	530	560
21	400	430	450	480	510	540	570
22	410	440	460	480	520	550	580
23	420	450	470	490	530	560	590
24	420	460	470	500	540	570	600
25	430	460	480	510	540	580	610
26	440	470	490	520	550	590	610
27	450	480	500	530	560	590	620
28	460	490	510	540	570	600	630
29	470	500	520	550	580	610	640
30	480	510	530	560	590	620	650
31	490	520	540	560	600	630	660
32	500	530	550	570	610	640	670
33	510	540	550	580	620	650	680
34	510	550	560	590	630	660	690
35	520	560	570	600	640	670	700
36	530	560	580	610	650	680	710
37	540	570	590	620	660	690	720
38	550	580	600	630	670	700	730
39	560	600	610	640	680	710	740
40	580	610	620	650	690	720	750
41	590	620	640	660	700	730	760
42	600	630	650	680	710	740	770
43	610	640	660	690	720	750	780
44	620	660	670	700	740	770	800
45	640	670	690	720	750	780	800
46	650	690	700	730	770	800	800
47	670	700	720	750	780	800	800
48	680	720	730	760	800	800	800
49	680	720	730	760	800	800	800

Detailed Answer Key

Section 1

The following essay received 12 points out of a possible 12. This means that, according to the graders, it

- develops an insightful point of view on the topic
- demonstrates exemplary critical thinking
- uses effective examples, reasons, and other evidence to support its thesis
- is consistently focused, coherent and well-organized
- demonstrates skillful and effective use of language and sentence structure
- is largely (but not necessarily completely) free of grammatical and usage errors

Consider carefully the issue discussed in the following passage, then write an essay that answers the question posed in the assignment.

> The best leaders are not those who seek power, or have great political skill. Great leaders—and these are exceptionally rare, especially today—represent the best selves of the people they represent.

Assignment: **What are the most important qualities of a leader?** Write an essay in which you answer this question and discuss your point of view on this issue. Support your position logically with examples from literature, the arts, history, politics, science and technology, current events, or your experience or observation.

There is no more important decision that a citizen can make than one's choice of a leader. I am inclined to agree with Thomas Hobbes, who believed that humans are hardly better than other mammals without a social contract that binds us to work together as a society. Artists could not survive in a society that does not provide a means of trading art for food. Great teachers cannot survive in a society without a means of trading wisdom for shelter. This requires a social order, a division of labor, and a group we call leaders. Yet we know that power corrupts, and absolute power corrupts absolutely. So how do we maintain a just society when we must bestow corrupting powers upon members of that society?

Those who seek power are too often not our best leaders, but rather our best politicians. George Bush, John F. Kennedy and Ronald Reagan came to power not so much because of their visionary leadership but because of their appeal to a television-viewing audience. The problems with democracy are well known. In order to become elected, most politicians must appeal to a broad range of citizens. To gain this appeal, they must pander to their constituents, and often take conflicting or equivocal stances on issues. Of course, the politicians claim that they are taking "forceful stances" to "bring the people together." But it is far more likely that they are simply doing their best to make everyone happy without putting their feet in their mouths.

So why is democracy the best way of electing a leader? Because the alternatives are much worse. To gain power, one must either use force or pander to those who do. Which is a better alternative? A country is weak if its people do not support it, and, at the very least, a democracy can claim a good degree of public support. Even more importantly, only a democracy allows for the possibility of finding a reluctant leader with genuine leadership skills. It doesn't happen often enough, but when it does, it is breathtaking. Witness the phenomenon of Howard Dean's campaign for the 2004 Democratic nomination for president, or Ross Perot's run in 1992. Neither was ultimately successful, but both demonstrated the potential of motivated citizens to change their country.

Without democracy, there is no hope for an ordinary citizen to change his or her country. What makes America great is not that its policies are always correct. Indeed, they are often deeply flawed. What makes America great is that it is run by those who are not even seeking power: the citizens.

The following essay received 8 points out of a possible 12, meaning that it demonstrates *adequate competence* in that it

- develops a point of view on the topic
- demonstrates some critical thinking, but perhaps not consistently
- uses some examples, reasons, and other evidence to support its thesis, but perhaps not adequately
- shows a general organization and focus, but shows occasional lapses in this regard
- demonstrates adequate but occasionally inconsistent facility with language
- contains occasional errors in grammar, usage and mechanics

Someone once said that great men don't seek greatness but have it thrust upon them. I think this is true, because those who have really changed the world were not slick politicians but rather people who had such great leadership skill and charisma that others forced them into leadership roles. Good examples of this are Jesus, Mahatma Gandhi, Mother Theresa and George Washington.

After his great victories in the American Revolutionary War against Great Britain, George Washington wanted to retire to his farm in Virginia and live out the rest of his days as a humble farmer. He did not want to become the political leader of a brand new country. But the Continental Congress looked to him for leadership, and sought him out to be the first President of the United States. Washington saw that his country needed him and answered the call.

Similarly, Mahatma Gandhi did not seek personal power, but only justice for his people. His humility and selflessness are what made him one of the great leaders of the twentieth century, and a model for the cause of nonviolent activism.

It is unfortunate that today only millionaires with big political connections seem to have any chance at being elected to national office. Maybe they have a shot at a local race, but the congress and the presidency seem to be off limits. The answer is to get more involved in politics yourself, as a voter, and avoid voting for candidates just because they are popular but instead because they have good souls.

The following essay received 4 points out of a possible 12, meaning that it demonstrates *some incompetence* in that it

- has a seriously limited point of view
- demonstrates weak critical thinking
- uses inappropriate or insufficient examples, reasons, and other evidence to support its thesis
- is poorly focused and organized, and has seriously problems with coherence
- demonstrates frequent problems with language and sentence structure
- contains errors in grammar and usage that obscure the author's meaning seriously

I'm not sure how it can be that you can be the best person to be in power if you don't want to be. In this country, at least, running for president or something like that takes a lot of effort, and I think you have to be a really hard worker in order to become president or senator.

An example of somebody who is a hard worker who got into office is former president Bill Clinton. Although many people think he had indiscretions in office, he came from a very poor family where he was only raised by his mother because his father left the family when he was young. He worked really hard and became a Rhodes scholar and was elected as governor at a very young age. He knew even when he was a very young kid that he wanted to become a great leader like John F. Kennedy.

Clinton was a good leader because he understood where a lot of people were coming from. He wasn't just a rich guy who got into office because he had rich relatives who got him there. I don't think you can say that the best leaders are the ones who don't want to be in office. If you didn't want to be in office, then you shouldn't run.

Section 2

1. A   Alisha was holding a *grudge*, which is a feeling of resentment.
resentment = ill will; *fortitude* = strength of mind to endure; *sarcasm* = wit used to ridicule; *elation* = extreme joy

2. C   There were people who expected the governor to be *inarticulate* (unable to speak clearly), so they would be surprised if he were *articulate*. *intolerance* = inability to put up with something; *fatigue* = tiredness; *eloquence* = persuasiveness in speech; *endurance* = ability to last, often through hard times

3. D   The *language of commoners* would be logically described as *common*. But the novelists preferred another kind of *parlance* (speech): that of the *upper* classes. A word such as *elegant* would work nicely. *elite* = superior; *sympathetic* = compassionate; *colloquial* = characteristic of everyday language; *refined* = precise, elegant; *utilitarian* = practical, stressing utility

4. A   The second half of this sentence presents a definition. The word in the blank should mean "*exploring the world*." *peripatetic* = walking from place to place; *conventional* = customary; *tolerant* = willing to put up with something; *coordinated* = well-matched; *remunerative* = profitable

5. E   A position that requires public speaking would be *difficult* for a person who does not like to speak or is afraid of crowds. *vivacious* = full of life; *garrulous* = talkative; *amiable* = friendly; *reticent* = hesitant to share one's feelings or opinions with others

6. C   The tickbird gets something from the hippopotamus, and the hippopotamus gets something from the tickbird; it's a *give-and-receive* relationship. *deteriorating* = diminishing in quality; *symbiotic* = of mutual benefit; *regressive* = going backwards; *vacillating* = going back and forth

7. A   This sentence establishes a contrast between how *modern scientists* think and how *early philosophers* thought. The contrast shows that the early philosophers were not using experiments as much as their own minds to draw conclusions and that the modern scientists rely more on experimental data to draw their conclusions. *empirical* = relying on the observations made from experiments; *coercion* = pressure on someone to act; *deduction* = reaching a conclusion through the use of logic; *clerical* = relating to office work; *intuitive* = known innately

8. B   The first blank should be a word like *merging* or *unification*, because many companies are under a *single owner*. This would be *troublesome* to those who value *independence*. *retraction* = taking something back; *differentiation* = finding a difference between 2 things; *consolidation* = combining of multiple things into 1 common entity; *collaboration* = working together on something; *dissemination* = the spread of something

9. E   Passage 2 distinguishes between education and schooling. It states that the *main product of schooling is not education* (lines 15–16) and that the struggle that defines education *is denied by schooling* (lines 22–23). Passage 1 makes no such distinction, and speaks of education as if it is inseparable from the idea of schooling.

10. B   Farmers raise most food by *a rotation of plants belonging to the most different orders: nature follows what may be called a simultaneous rotation*. They both are using a similar system.

11. A   The passage suggests that education *is the great equalizer* and that *the spread of education will open a wider area over which the social feelings will expand*. It concludes by commenting that *if this education should be universal and complete* it would *obliterate factitious distinctions in society*.

12. B   Passage 2 states that education, which is *the acquisition of competence, power, wisdom and discernment* (lines 19–20), is achieved only through the *struggle for sense in the world* (lines 21–22). Therefore, this struggle is empowering.

13. A   "The Beginnings of the Scientific Method" is the best title, because this passage begins by discussing the scientists of the Renaissance and how they *brought about the most fundamental alterations in the world of thought . . . by devising a new method for discovering knowledge* (lines 1–5). This new method was the scientific method.

14. C   Saying that *the early modern scientists laid greatest stress upon observation and the formation of temporary hypotheses* (lines 7–9) is like saying they *emphasized* observation and hypotheses.

15. C   In lines 19–21 the passage suggests that earlier scientists were simply trying *to find the confirmation of Biblical statements about the firmament*.

16. D Choice II is confirmed in lines 31–33: *The principle of the barometer was discovered by Galileo's **pupil*** (student) *Torricelli.* Choice III is confirmed in lines 41–42: *Galileo discovered the moons around Jupiter.*

17. E The final paragraph states that Renaissance scientists believed *that everything consists of bodies in motion, that everything conforms to a mechanical model. The heavens above and the smallest particles below all exhibit the same laws of motion*—even, as it says in the next sentence, *human thought* (lines 69–72).

18. C The final paragraph discusses how the scientific method changed the way science was done.

19. B The passage mentions in lines 22–24 that many military leaders *cement their solidarity by reveling* (taking delight) *in their numerical disadvantage.* They considered it more honorable to fight with fewer men and beat a larger opponent.

20. C Stating that *a well-known proverb* was ***trotted out** in many instances of the glorious, fighting few* (lines 25–27), in this context, is like saying that the proverb was *used for rhetorical effect* because it was used to persuade and inspire the troops.

21. D When the prince says that *we be a small **body** when compared to the army of our enemies,* he is saying that they are a small army or group of men.

22. D This sentence is discussing the tactical errors of the French in two different battles. The phrase *charging before they were ready* simply means *attacking before they were ready.*

23. E All 3 of these facts are true and are mentioned in the passage.

24. A The passage states in the final paragraph that *ten thousand more men might actually have hindered the English* (lines 59–60) and that *it seems that in fact . . . strength is not always proportional to size* (lines 62–64).

Section 3

1. E Since *n* is equal to 3 times an even number, you can eliminate any answer choice that is not a multiple of 3 (A, C, and D). Answer choice B: $15 = 3 \times 5$; 5 is an odd number, so this answer choice is out. Answer choice E: $18 = 3 \times 6$; 6 is an even number.
(Chapter 12 Lesson 3: Numerical Reasoning Problems)

2. A Set up a ratio: $\dfrac{50 \text{ chips}}{2 \text{ hours}} = \dfrac{x \text{ chips}}{7 \text{ hours}}$
Cross-multiply: $350 = 2x$
Divide by 2: $175 = x$
(Chapter 10 Lesson 4: Ratios and Proportions)

3. C Angles that form a straight angle have a sum of 180°:
$$x + 2x = 180°$$
Combine like terms: $3x = 180°$
Divide by 3: $x = 60°$
(Chapter 13 Lesson 1: Lines and Angles)

4. C Find the smallest number that is divisible by both 15 and 6 and see which answer choice works.
Multiples of 15: 15, **30**, 45, . . .
Multiples of 6:   6, 12, 18, 24, **30**, . . .
(Chapter 10 Lesson 7: Divisibility)

5. D $n\%$ of 20 is 4
$$\frac{n}{100} \times 20 = 4$$
Simplify: $.20n = 4$
Divide by .20: $n = 20$
(Chapter 10 Lesson 5: Percents)

6. A $f(x) = 3x + n$
Plug in 2 for *x*: $f(2) = 3(2) + n = 0$
Simplify: $6 + n = 0$
Subtract 6: $n = -6$
Substitute for *n*: $f(x) = 3x - 6$
Plug in 0 for *x*: $f(0) = 3(0) - 6 = -6$
(Chapter 14 Lesson 2: Functions)

7. D First find the area of the right triangle:

Area = ½(base)(height)
Area = ½(8)(6) = 24

Next, set up an equation for the area of a square.
Area = (side)²
Substitute 24 for area: $24 = (\text{side})^2$
Take the square root: $\sqrt{24} = \text{side}$
Simplify the radical: $2\sqrt{6} = \text{side}$

(Chapter 13 Lesson 5: Areas and Perimeters)

8. **A**   You are told that: $12v = 3w$
Divide by 3: $4v = w$
Multiply by 2: $8v = 2w$
The question asks for the value of: $2w - 8v$
Substitute for $2w$: $8v - 8v = 0$
Alternatively, you can try finding values for v and w that work, like 1 and 4, and plug them in to $2w - 8v$ and into the choices and find the match.
(Chapter 11 Lesson 1: Solving Equations)

9. **C** $2|x| + 1 > 5$
Subtract 1: $2|x| > 4$
Divide by 2: $|x| > 2$
Interpret the absolute value: $x > 2$ OR $x < -2$
You are told that x is negative, so $x < -2$ is the answer.
(Chapter 11 Lesson 6: Inequalities, Absolute Values, and Plugging In)

10. **B** $-x^2 - 8x - 5$
Substitute -2 for x: $-(-2)^2 - 8(-2) - 5$
Square -2: $-(4) - 8(-2) - 5$
Simplify: $-4 + 16 - 5 = 7$
When evaluating $-x^2$, don't forget to square the value *before* taking its opposite!
(Chapter 11 Lesson 1: Solving Equations)

11. **D** $\dfrac{5}{m} \le \dfrac{2}{3}$
Cross-multiply: $15 \le 2m$
Divide by 2: $7.5 \le m$
Since m is greater than *or equal to* 7.5, D is the answer.
(Chapter 11 Lesson 6: Inequalities, Absolute Values, and Plugging In)

12. **B**   First find the price after the 6% sales tax:
$60.00 \times .06 = \$3.60$ tax
$60.00 + \$3.60 = \$63.60$ price with tax
(A simpler way is just to multiply 60 by 1.06.)
Now find how much change Theo received:
$70.00 - \$63.60 = \$6.40$ change
(Chapter 10 Lesson 5: Percents)

13. **A**   Write an equation for the first sentence.
$n - m = r$
Because none of the answer choices contain m, solve for m in terms of r and n: $n - m = r$
Add m: $n = r + m$
Subtract r: $n - r = m$
Now write an expression for what the question asks for:
$s + 2m$
Substitute for m: $s + 2(n - r)$
Distribute: $s + 2n - 2r$
Alternatively, you can substitute numbers for n, m, and r, making sure they "work," and get a numerical answer to the question.
(Chapter 11 Lesson 1: Solving Equations)

14. **D**   Two points on line l are $(0, 0)$ and $(10, y)$. Find the slope of the line:
$$m = \frac{y_2 - y_1}{x_2 - x_1} = \frac{y - 0}{10 - 0} = \frac{y}{10} = \frac{3}{5}$$
Cross-multiply: $5y = 30$
Divide by 5: $y = 6$
Since $y = 6$, the height of the triangle is 6. Find the area:
$A = \frac{1}{2}$(base)(height)
Substitute 48 for A: $48 = \frac{1}{2}$(base)(6)
Simplify: $48 = 3$(base)
Divide by 3: $16 = $ base $= x$
Now find $x + y = 16 + 6 = 22$.
(Chapter 13 Lesson 4: Coordinate Geometry)

15. **A**   Ellen travels the first 15 miles at 30 miles per hour. Find out how much time that takes:
$d = (rate)(time)$
Plug in known values: $15 = 30t$
Divide by 30: $\frac{1}{2}$ hour $= t$
The rest of the trip, which is $(y - 15)$ miles long, she travels at an average speed of 40 miles per hour:
$d = (rate)(time)$
Plug in known values: $(y - 15) = 40t$
Divide by 40: $\dfrac{y - 15}{40} = t$
Add the 2 times together to find the total time:
$$\frac{1}{2} + \frac{y - 15}{40}$$
(Chapter 12 Lesson 4: Rate Problems)

16. **B**   Set up the relationship in equation form:
$$y = \frac{km}{n^2}$$
Plug in what you're given: $8 = \dfrac{k(16)}{(1)^2}$
Simplify: $8 = 16k$
Divide by 16: $\frac{1}{2} = k$
Write the new equation: $y = \dfrac{\frac{1}{2}(m)}{(n)^2}$
Plug in new values: $y = \dfrac{\frac{1}{2}(8)}{(4)^2} = \dfrac{4}{16} = \dfrac{1}{4}$
(Chapter 14 Lesson 4: Variation)

17. D

$$a + b = s$$
$$\underline{a - b = t}$$

Add straight down: $2a \quad = s + t$

Divide by 2: $a = \dfrac{s + t}{2}$

$$a + b = s$$
$$\underline{a - b = t}$$

Subtract straight down: $2b = s - t$

Divide by 2: $b = \dfrac{s - t}{2}$

Find the product: $(a)(b) = \left(\dfrac{s+t}{2}\right)\left(\dfrac{s-t}{2}\right) = \left(\dfrac{s^2 - t^2}{4}\right)$

(Chapter 11 Lesson 2: Systems)

18. C $y = m^4 = n^3$

The answer is in terms of y alone, so find m and n in terms of y: $y = m^4$

Take the 4th root: $y^{1/4} = m$

     $y = n^3$

Take the cube root: $y^{1/3} = n$

Find the product mn: $mn = (y^{1/4})(y^{1/3}) = y^{1/3 + 1/4}$

Add exponents: $mn = y^{7/12}$

(Chapter 14 Lesson 6: Negative and Fractional Exponents)

19. A   This question deals with similar triangles:

Set up ratio: $\dfrac{6}{12} = \dfrac{4}{x}$

Cross-multiply: $6x = 48$
Divide by 6: $x = 8$

Area of big triangle = ½(base)(height) = ½(12)(6) = 36
Area of small triangle = ½(base)(height) = ½(8)(4) = 16
Shaded area = area of big triangle – area of small triangle = 36 – 16 = 20
(Chapter 13 Lesson 6: Similar Figures)
(Chapter 13 Lesson 5: Areas and Perimeters)

20. A   Set up a Venn diagram to visualize the information.

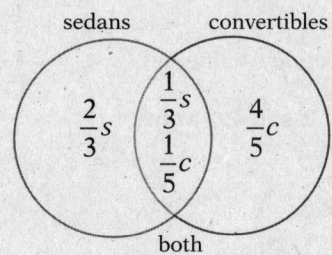

Notice that ⅓ the number of sedans must equal ⅕ the number of convertibles. Say the number of convertible sedans is x. If this is ⅓ the number of sedans, then there must be $3x$ sedans in total, and $3x - x = 2x$ of these are *not* convertibles. Similarly, if x is ⅕ the number of convertibles, then there must be $5x$ convertibles altogether, and $5x - x = 4x$ of these are *not* sedans. So now your diagram can look like this:

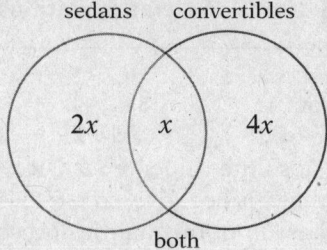

So there must be a total of $2x + x + 4x = 7x$ cars at the dealership. The only choice that is a multiple of 7 is A: 28.
(Chapter 12 Lesson 5: Counting Problems)

Section 4

1. E

Perimeter of a square = $4s$
     $36 = 4s$

Divide by 4: $9 = s$

Area of a square $= (s)^2$

Area $= (9)^2 = 81$

(Chapter 13 Lesson 4: Areas and Perimeters)

2. C

     $\dfrac{a}{b} = \dfrac{1}{10}$

Cross-multiply: $b = 10a$

Try positive integer values of a to see how many work:

a	1	2	3	4	5	6	7	8	9
b	10	20	30	40	50	60	70	80	90

There are 9 integer pairs that satisfy the equation.

(Chapter 12 Lesson 3: Numerical Reasoning Problems)

3. E   The 10 bathrooms cost $20 each to clean:
     Total cost = $20 × 10 = $200

To clean each bathroom twice would cost:
     $200 × 2 = $400

There are 30 offices, and they cost $15 each to clean:
     Total cost = $15 × 30 = $450

To clean each office once and each bathroom twice will cost: $400 + $450 = $850

(Chapter 14 Lesson 5: Data Analysis)

4. **A**   Remember the "difference of squares" factoring formula: $a^2 - b^2 = (a - b)(a + b)$

    Substitute: $10 = (2)(a + b)$

    Divide by 2: $5 = a + b$

(Chapter 11 Lesson 5: Factoring)

---

5. **A**

To find the value of $f(14)$, find all the factors of 14:

        1, <u>2</u>, <u>7</u>, 14

There are two prime factors, 2 and 7.

        $2 + 7 = 9$

        $f(14) = 9$

To find the value of $f(6)$, find all the factors of 6:

        1, <u>2</u>, <u>3</u>, 6

There are two prime factors, 2 and 3.

        $2 + 3 = 5$

        $f(6) = 5$

     $f(14) - f(6) = 9 - 5 = 4$

(Chapter 14 Lesson 2: Functions)

---

6. **D**   First write an equation to find the average.

$$\frac{a + b + c + d}{4} = 20$$

Multiply by 4: $a + b + c + d = 80$

If you want a to be as large as possible, make b, c, and d as small as possible. You are told that they are all *different* positive integers: $a + b + c + d = 80$

    Let $b = 1, c = 2, d = 3$: $a + 1 + 2 + 3 = 80$

    Combine like terms: $a + 6 = 80$

    Subtract 6: $a = 74$

(Chapter 12 Lesson 2: Mean/Median/Mode Problems)

---

7. **B**   Let the radius of circle A $= a$ and the radius of circle B $= b$. It is given that $a = 2b$. The circumference of a circle can be found with the equation $C = 2\pi r$. The sum of their circumferences is 36π.

        $36\pi = 2\pi a + 2\pi b$

    Divide by π: $36 = 2a + 2b$

    Substitute for a: $36 = 2(2b) + 2b$

    Simplify: $36 = 4b + 2b$

    Combine like terms: $36 = 6b$

    Divide by 6: $6 = b$

    Solve for a: $a = 2(b) = 2(6) = 12$

(Chapter 13 Lesson 5: Areas and Perimeters)

8. **C**   This is a visualization problem. The 6 possible planes are illustrated below. Notice that the 6 faces of the cube "don't count," because each of those contains *4* edges of the cube.

(Chapter 13 Lesson 7: Volumes and 3-D Geometry)

---

9. **16**   Set up an equation: $2x - 10 = 22$

    Add 10: $2x = 32$

    Divide by 2: $x = 16$

(Chapter 11 Lesson 1: Solving Equations)

---

10. **36**

There are 180° on 1 side of a line:

      $2y + y + y + y = 180°$

  Combine like terms: $5y = 180°$

  Divide by 5: $y = 36°$

(Chapter 13 Lesson 1: Lines and Angles)

11. **5**   Think simple: What's the simplest way to turn $8x + 4y$ into $2x + y$? Just divide by 4!

$$8x + 4y = 20$$
Divide by 4: $$2x + y = 5$$

(Chapter 11 Lesson 1: Solving Equations)

(Chapter 9 Lesson 4: Simplifying Problems)

12. **30**   Set up equations: $$\frac{x + y + 20}{3} = 30$$

$$x = y + 10$$
Substitute for x: $$\frac{y + 10 + y + 20}{3} = 30$$

Combine like terms: $$\frac{2y + 30}{3} = 30$$

Multiply by 3: $$2y + 30 = 90$$
Subtract 30 $$2y = 60$$
Divide by 2: $$y = 30$$

Check by noticing that the 3 numbers are 20, 30, and 40. You should easily see that their average is 30.

(Chapter 12 Lesson 2: Mean/Median/Mode Problems)

(Chapter 9 Lesson 7: Thinking Logically and Checking)

13. **15**   Ratios such as 4:5 can also be written as $4x:5x$. So the number of men m is $4x$ and the number of women w is $5x$.

Plug those values into the equation $w = m + 3$

$$5x = 4x + 3$$
Subtract $4x$: $$x = 3$$
Plug 3 in to $5x$: $$w = 5x = 5(3) = 15$$

(Chapter 10 Lesson 4: Ratios and Proportions)

14. **8 or 12** $$y = |2x - b|$$
Plug in (5, 2): $$2 = |2(5) - b|$$
Simplify: $$2 = |10 - b|$$
$$(10 - b) = 2 \text{ or } (10 - b) = -2$$
Subtract 10: $$-b = -8 \text{ or } -b = -12$$
Multiply by -1: $$b = 8 \text{ or } b = 12$$

(Chapter 11 Lesson 6: Inequalities, Absolute Values, and Plugging In)

15. **25**   First calculate how many grams of sucrose there are in 200 grams of a 10% mixture.

$$(200 \text{ grams})(.10) = 20 \text{ grams of sucrose}$$

Since you will be adding x grams of sucrose, the total weight of sucrose will be $20 + x$ grams, and the total weight of the mixture will be $200 + x$ grams. Since the fraction that will be sucrose is 20%,

$$\frac{20 + x}{200 + x} = \frac{20}{100}$$

Cross-multiply: $$(20 + x)(100) = 20(200 + x)$$
Distribute: $$2{,}000 + 100x = 4{,}000 + 20x$$
Subtract 2,000: $$100x = 2{,}000 + 20x$$
Subtract $20x$: $$80x = 2{,}000$$
Divide by 80: $$x = 25$$

(Chapter 10 Lesson 5: Percents)

(Chapter 10 Lesson 4: Ratios and Proportions)

16. **24**   First calculate how long the race took.
$$distance = rate \times time$$
$$16 = (8)(time)$$
Divide by 8: $$2 \text{ hours} = time = 120 \text{ minutes}$$

Next, find the new rate that is 25% faster:
$$new\ rate = (8)(1.25) = 10 \text{ mph}$$

Calculate how long the new race would take:
$$distance = rate \times time$$
$$16 = (10)(time)$$
Divide by 10: $$1.6 \text{ hours} = time = 96 \text{ minutes}$$

So she can improve her time by $(120 - 96) = 24$ minutes.

(Chapter 12 Lesson 4: Rate Problems)

17. **52**

Break a shape like this into recognizable 4-sided figures and triangles that are easier to deal with.

The area of the rectangle on the left is $7 \times 4 = 28$. The area of the rectangle on the right is $5 \times 4 = 20$. The sum of those two areas is $28 + 20 = 48$. The area remaining for the triangle is the difference $78 - 48 = 30$. Set up an equation for the area of a triangle to solve for x:

$$\text{Area} = \tfrac{1}{2}(\text{base})(\text{height})$$
$$30 = \tfrac{1}{2}(5)(\text{height})$$

Divide by $\tfrac{1}{2}$: $\quad 60 = 5(\text{height})$

Divide by 5: $\quad 12 = \text{height}$

To find the hypotenuse of the right triangle, set up the Pythagorean Theorem and solve:

$$5^2 + 12^2 = c^2$$
$$25 + 144 = c^2$$
$$169 = c^2$$
$$c = 13$$

(Or just notice that it's a 5-12-13 triangle!)

To find the perimeter of the figure, add up all of the sides:

$$13 + 12 + 4 + 5 + 7 + 4 + 7 = 52$$

(Chapter 13 Lesson 5: Areas and Perimeters)
(Chapter 13 Lesson 3: The Pythagorean Theorem)

18. **225** Set up a 3-circle Venn diagram to visualize this information.

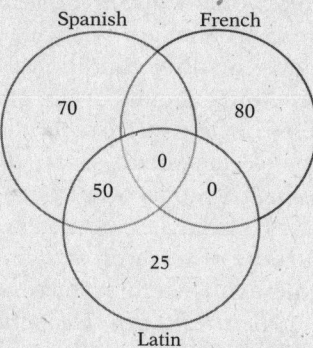

Fifty students study 2 of the 3 languages, so let's say that 50 students study both Spanish and Latin. (It doesn't matter *which* 2 languages those 50 students take; the result turns out the same.) This means that 0 students study both Spanish and French both French and Latin and 0 students study all three languages.

There are 120 Spanish students in all. There are therefore $120 - 50 = 70$ students who study Spanish alone. There are 80 French students in all, all of whom study just French, and there are 75 total Latin students including $75 - 50 = 25$ students who study only Latin.

This means that there are $70 + 50 + 80 + 25 = 225$ sophomores at Hillside High School.

(Chapter 12 Lesson 5: Counting Problems)

Section 5

1. **C** The clients were forced to seek more *reliable* investment advice, so the manager must have managed their funds badly. *ineptitude* = lack of skill

2. **E** Vartan is Armenian; he was born in Iran and educated in Lebanon and is now president of the American Brown University. He has a lot of *worldly* experience. *perpetual* = lasting forever; *authoritative* = showing authority; *cosmopolitan* = worldly

3. **D** They didn't consider it in great detail, so the reading must have been *without great care*. *verbatim* = word for word; *meandering* = wandering; *tormented* = feeling anguish or pain; *cursory* = quick and without care; *substantial* = of substance, quite large

4. **A** If the *pathogens* (infectious agents) spread more quickly in close quarters, the *crowding* would be a problem. This would cause the disease to *spread*. *propagation* = reproduction, increase in number; *squalor* = horrible or dirty conditions; *circulation* = moving of something around from place to place; *poverty* = state of being poor; *deterioration* = wearing down; *congestion* = crowdedness; *proximity* = closeness; *resilience* = ability to recover from a challenge

5. **E** The purpose of research is to find answers to questions of interest. Therefore, the research *endeavors* (attempts) to *determine* or *understand* the mechanisms by which our brains do things. If the data must be turned into *coherent and understandable information*, it must not have been coherent to begin with, but rather just a big rush of information. *enhance* = make better; *attenuate* = reduce in amount; *dearth* = scarcity, lack; *elucidate* = make clear; *deluge* = huge flood

6. **D** The *fruits* mentioned in line 10 refer to the means of acquiring food and shelter, because they are described as the *fruits for maintaining human life.*

7. **B** The question is whether one can *get quick returns of interest* (make money) *from the capital of knowledge and learning* (from one's education) (lines 13–15).

8. **A** The pointing of dogs is mentioned as an *instinctive tendency to the performance of an action* (lines 1–2).

9. **E** Inherited tendencies tend to show themselves in the behavior of an organism. The paragraph mentions the calf and the caterpillar as examples of organisms with instincts that show themselves in later behavior.

10. **D** The final paragraph begins with *The best life is the one in which the creative impulses play the largest part and the possessive impulses the smallest* (lines 56–58).

11. **D** Lines 22–26 say that *the food and clothing of one man is not the food and clothing of another; if the supply is insufficient, what one man has is obtained at the expense of some other man.* Therefore, food and clothing exist in finite amounts and can be used up.

12. **E** This section of the passage discusses matters such as *good will* (line 38), *science* (line 31), and *painting pictures or writing poems* (lines 35–36) as things that are not denied to someone else when 1 person possesses them.

13. **E** This sentence discusses the *possessive impulses* (line 49) as distinct from the *creative impulses* discussed in the next sentence. The *impulse of property* in lines 51–52 is the *desire to possess property.*

14. **C** This statement echoes the point made in lines 55–56 that *spiritual possessions cannot be taken in this way,* that is, by force.

15. **D** Lines 58–59 say *This is no new discovery* and goes on to cite the Gospel as a prior source expressing the same opinions as Russell's.

16. **B** The author's main point is that creativity is of higher value than possessiveness. The invention mentioned in answer choice B was created to make money for its inventor (a possessive and materialistic motive) but has the side effect of benefitting all of humankind.

17. **A** The passage discusses the perspective one Native American has on the appearance of the *new superstition* (line 44). It discusses how some villagers have taken to the new religion and also mentions one fellow tribe member's attempting to convert the main character.

18. **E** In saying that *men of the same color are like the ivory keys of one instrument where each represents all the rest, yet varies from them in pitch and quality of voice* (lines 4–7), the author is saying that people of the same race possess important differences.

19. **D** The author describes the preacher as *mouth[ing] most strangely the jangling phrases of a bigoted creed* (lines 11–12), indicating that she considers him to be an intolerant person. She describes herself as having *compassion* (line 7) and *respect* (line 10), but does not attribute these qualities to the preacher.

20. **B** Lines 13–14 say that *our tribe is one large family, where every person is related to all the others.*

21. **C** Both the preacher and the author's mother have become followers of *the new superstition* (line 44).

22. **C** In saying that a *pugilist commented upon a recent article of mine, grossly perverting the spirit of my pen* (lines 66–68) the author is saying that the pugilist distorted the author's words in a grotesque way.

23. E The author characterizes herself as *a wee child toddling in a wonder world* (lines 72–73), indicating that she is in awe of the world around her. Although one might expect her to be vengeful in response to the *pugilist* (line 66) who *grossly pervert[ed] the spirit of [her] pen* (line 68), there is no indication in the paragraph that she is vengeful.

24. A The author says in lines 68–72 that *still I would not forget that the pale-faced missionary and the aborigine are both God's creatures, though **small indeed in their own conceptions of Infinite Love***. In other words, the author respects the missionary but believes he is small-minded.

Section 6

1. D The verb must agree with the plural subject *claims*. Choice D is most concise and correct.
(Chapter 18 Lesson 1: Subject-Verb Disagreement)

2. A The original sentence is best.

3. B The participial phrase opening the sentence modifies Sartre himself, not his *writing*. This being the case, the phrase dangles.
(Chapter 18 Lesson 7: Dangling and Misplaced Participles)

4. C Choice C best follows the law of parallelism.
(Chapter 18 Lesson 3: Parallelism)

5. A The original sentence is best.

6. B Choice B is the most concise, logical, and complete.
(Chapter 15 Lesson 9: Write Concisely)

7. C The original phrasing contains an incomplete thought. Choice C is by far the most concise and direct.
(Chapter 18 Lesson 15: Coordinating Ideas)

8. E The participle *having spread* modifies the *disease*, not the *doctors*.
(Chapter 18 Lesson 7: Dangling and Misplaced Participles)

9. C The original phrasing contains an incomplete thought. Choice C is by far the most concise and direct.
(Chapter 18 Lesson 15: Coordinating Ideas)

10. D The participle *singing* modifies *Anita*, not her hoarseness. Furthermore, the participle is in the wrong form; it should be in the perfect form *having sung*, because only the *previous* singing could have contributed to her hoarseness.
(Chapter 18 Lesson 7: Dangling and Misplaced Participles)
(Chapter 18 Lesson 9: Tricky Tenses)

11. A The original sentence is best.

12. A The word *quick* is an adjective and can thus modify only a noun. But since it modifies the verb *turned*, the adverb *quickly* is needed here.
(Chapter 18 Lesson 12: Other Modifier Problems)

13. B This sentence violates the law of parallelism. If she is known *for her initiative*, she should also be known *for devoting her own time*.
(Chapter 18 Lesson 3: Parallelism)

14. C Since the Medieval era is long past, its *beginning* is "completed" or, in grammar terms, "perfect." So this phrase should be the "perfect" form of the infinitive: *to have begun*.
(Chapter 18 Lesson 9: Tricky Tenses)

15. B The word *neither* is almost always part of the phrase *neither of . . .* or *neither A nor B*. So choice B should read *nor even*.
(Chapter 18 Lesson 10: Idiom Errors)

16. D The word *less* is used to compare only quantities that can't be counted. If the quantities are countable, as accidents are, the word should be *fewer*.
(Chapter 18 Lesson 4: Comparison Problems)

17. B To convey the proper sequence of events, the perfect tense is required: *had spent*.
(Chapter 18 Lesson 9: Tricky Tenses)

18. A The subject of the verb *has* is the plural noun *newspapers*. (The sentence is "inverted," because the subject follows the verb.) The proper form of the verb, then, is *have*.
(Chapter 18 Lesson 1: Subject-Verb Disagreement)
(Chapter 18 Lesson 2: Trimming Sentences)

19. B The original sentence has a "comma splice" that incorrectly joins 2 sentences with only a comma. A better phrasing is *dream that led*.
(Chapter 18 Lesson 15: Coordinating Ideas)

20. C The subject of the verb is the singular noun *movement,* so the proper verb form is *has led.*
(Chapter 18 Lesson 1: Subject-Verb Disagreement)
(Chapter 18 Lesson 2: Trimming Sentences)

21. E The sentence is correct as written.

22. D This is a prepositional phrase, so the pronoun is the object of the preposition and should be in the objective case. The correct phrasing is *for Maria and me.*
(Chapter 18 Lesson 6: Pronoun Case)

23. A The word *successive* means *consecutive,* so it does not make sense in this context. The right word is *successful.*
(Chapter 18 Lesson 11: Diction Errors)

24. E The sentence is correct as written.

25. C The word *underneath* means that it is physically *below* something else. It should be changed to *under.*
(Chapter 18 Lesson 10: Idiom Errors)

26. E The sentence is correct as written.

27. B The subject of the verb *were* is *arrogance,* which is singular. It should instead be *was.*
(Chapter 18 Lesson 11: Subject-Verb Disagreement)

28. B The sentence mentions there are *numerous* strains of the bacteria, which means that *more* should instead be *most.*
(Chapter 18 Lesson 4: Comparison Problems)

29. C The subject *company* is singular. Therefore, *they* should instead be *it.*
(Chapter 18 Lesson 5: Pronoun-Antecedent Disagreement)

30. D Choice D is most consistent, logical, and concise.

31. A Choice A is most logical.
Chapter 15 Lesson 7: Write Logically)

32. B The first paragraph ends with the description of an idea. The second paragraph begins with an illustration of how students experience this idea in their daily lives and then goes on to explain how it can help them get through their *brain freezes.* Choice B is the best introduction to the paragraph, because it explains that a student using the phenomenon can improve his or her studies.
(Chapter 15 Lesson 7: Write Logically)

33. C The sentence begins using the pronoun *you,* so that usage should be maintained throughout the sentence. Option D is incorrect because a person has only 1 brain.
(Chapter 18 Lesson 5: Pronoun Agreement)

34. E Sentence 11 concludes a discussion of Isaac Asimov's "eureka" experience. The additional sentence expands upon that idea, relating it back to the lives of students.
(Chapter 15 Lesson 7: Write Logically)

35. C Choice C is the most concise and logical revision.
(Chapter 15 Lesson 7: Write Logically)
(Chapter 15 Lesson 9: Write Concisely)

Section 7

1. B Set up a ratio to solve this problem:

$$\frac{4 \text{ apples}}{20 \text{ cents}} = \frac{10 \text{ apples}}{x \text{ cents}}$$

Cross-multiply: $\qquad 4x = 200$
Divide by 4: $\qquad x = 50 \text{ cents}$
(Chapter 10 Lesson 4: Ratios and Proportions)

2. C Solve for *b:* $\qquad 2^b = 8$
$\qquad\qquad\qquad\qquad b = 3$
Plug in 3: $\qquad\qquad 3^b = 3^3 = 27$
(Chapter 11 Lesson 3: Working with Exponentials)

3. A The sum of *a, b,* and 18 is 6 greater than the sum of *a, b,* and 12. Since there are 3 terms in the group, it follows that the average of *a, b,* and 18 would be $6 \div 3 = 2$ greater than the average of *a, b,* and 12.
(Chapter 12 Lesson 2: Mean/Median/Mode Problems)

4. B If you have the patience, you can write out a quick calendar for yourself to track the days:

Su	M	T	W	**Th**	F	Sa
		1	2	3	4	5
6	7	8	9	10	11	12
13	14	15	16	17	18	19
20	21	22	23	24	25	26
27	28	29	30	**31**		

Or you can use the simple fact that successive Tuesdays (like any other days) are always 7 days apart. Therefore, if the 1st of the month is a Tuesday, so are the 8th, the 15th, the 22nd, and the 29th. Therefore, the 30th is a Wednesday and the 31st is a Thursday.

(Chapter 12 Lesson 3: Numerical Reasoning Problems)

5. A From the given information: $m = 8n$

$$0 < m + n < 50$$

Substitute for m: $0 < 8n + n < 50$

Combine like terms: $0 < 9n < 50$

Divide by 9: $0 < n < 5\frac{5}{9}$

Since n must be an integer, n can be 1, 2, 3, 4, or 5.

(Chapter 11 Lesson 6: Inequalities, Absolute Values, and Plugging In)

6. D First find the value of y: $y\%$ of 50 is 32.

Simplify: $\dfrac{y}{100} \times 50 = 32$

Cross-multiply: $50y = 3{,}200$

Divide by 50: $y = 64$

What is 200% of 64?

Interpret: $2.00 \times 64 = 128$

(Chapter 10 Lesson 5: Percents)

7. B $g(x) = x + x^{1/2}$

Plug in 16 for x: $g(16) = 16 + 16^{1/2}$

Take square root of 16: $g(16) = 16 + 4$

Combine like terms: $g(16) = 20$

(Chapter 14 Lesson 2: Functions)

8. C The slope of the line is $-\frac{3}{4}$, so use the slope equation and the coordinates of point A (0, 12) to find the coordinates of point B $(x, 0)$:

$$m = \frac{y_2 - y_1}{x_2 - x_1} = \frac{0 - 12}{x - 0} = \frac{-12}{x} = -\frac{3}{4}$$

Cross-multiply: $4(-12) = -3(x)$

Simplify: $-48 = -3x$

Divide by -3: $16 = x$

The base of the triangle is 16, and its height is 12.

Area = ½(base)(height)

Substitute: Area = ½(16)(12)

Simplify: Area = 96

(Chapter 13 Lesson 4: Coordinate Geometry)

9. A Find the sum of each repetition of the pattern: $-1 + 1 + 2 = 2$

Next, determine how many times the pattern repeats in the first 25 terms: $25 \div 3 = 8$ with a remainder of 1.

Multiply the sum of the pattern by 8 to obtain the sum of the first 24 terms: $2 \times 8 = 16$

The 25th term is -1, which makes the sum $16 + -1 = 15$. (Chapter 14 Lesson 1: Sequences)

10. D The ratio of white marbles to blue marbles is 4 to b. The probability of randomly selecting a white marble from the jar is ¼. This means that 1 out of every 4 marbles in the jar is white and 3 out of every 4 marbles are blue. If there are 4 white marbles, then there are $4 \times 3 = 12$ blue marbles.

(Chapter 10 Lesson 4: Ratios and Proportions)

11. B Area = ½(base)(height)

Substitute: 10 = ½(base)(height)

Divide by ½: 20 = (base)(height)

The base and the height are both integers. Find all the "factor pairs" of 20: 1, 20; 2, 10; and 4, 5

Plug each pair into the Pythagorean Theorem to find the least possible length of the hypotenuse:

$$a^2 + b^2 = c^2$$
$$4^2 + 5^2 = c^2$$

Combine like terms: $41 = c^2$

Take square root: $\sqrt{41} = c$

$$a^2 + b^2 = c^2$$
$$2^2 + 10^2 = c^2$$

Combine like terms: $104 = c^2$

Take square root: $\sqrt{104} = c$

$$a^2 + b^2 = c^2$$
$$1^2 + 20^2 = c^2$$

Combine like terms: $401 = c^2$

Take square root: $\sqrt{401} = c$

$\sqrt{41}$ is the shortest possible hypotenuse.

(Chapter 13 Lesson 5: Areas and Perimeters)
(Chapter 13 Lesson 3: The Pythagorean Theorem)

12. B $-1 < y < 0$

This means that y is a negative decimal fraction. Answer choices A, C, and E will all be negative numbers. Answer choices B and D are positive numbers. When you raise a simple fraction to a positive number larger than 1, it gets smaller. $y^4 < y^2$, which makes B the greatest value. Pick a value like $y = -\frac{1}{2}$ and see.

(Chapter 12 Lesson 3: Numerical Reasoning Problems)

13. E Any statement of the form *"If A is true, then B is true"* is logically equivalent to *"If B is not true, then A is not true."* Try this with some common-sense examples of such statements. For instance, saying *"If I am under 16 years old, then I am not allowed to drive"* is the same as saying *"If I am allowed to drive, then I must not be under 16 years old."* The statement in E is logically equivalent to the original.

(Chapter 9 Lesson 7: Thinking Logically and Checking)

14. E If each bus contained only the minimum number of students, the buses would accommodate $6 \times 30 = 180$ students. But since you have 200 students to accommodate, you have 20 more students to place. To maximize the number of 40-student buses, place 10 more students in 2 of the buses. Therefore, a maximum of 2 buses can have 40 students.

(Chapter 12 Lesson 3: Numerical Reasoning Problems)

15. D The volume of a cylinder is equal to $\pi r^2 h$. Let's say that the radius of cylinder A is a and the radius of cylinder B is b. Since the height of cylinder B is twice the height of cylinder A, if the height of cylinder A is h, then the height of cylinder B is $2h$. The volume of A is twice that of B: $\pi a^2 h = 2\pi b^2 (2h)$

Simplify: $\pi a^2 h = 4\pi b^2 h$
Divide by π: $a^2 h = 4b^2 h$
Divide by h: $a^2 = 4b^2$
Take the square root of both sides: $a = 2b$
Divide by b: $\dfrac{a}{b} = \dfrac{2}{1}$

(Chapter 13 Lesson 7: Volumes and 3-D Geometry)

16. E First notice that any multiple of 6 is an even number that is divisible by 3, since $2 \times 3 = 6$. Set up a Venn diagram to help visualize the information, letting x represent how many of the numbers are multiples of 6.

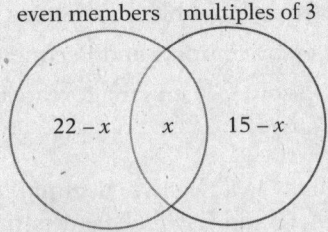

even members   multiples of 3

There are 30 numbers in the set, so set up an equation using the values in the Venn diagram and solve for x:
$$(22 - x) + (x) + (15 - x) = 30$$

Combine like terms: $37 - x = 30$
Add x: $37 = 30 + x$
Subtract 30: $7 = x$

So there are 7 multiples of 6 in this set.

(Chapter 12 Lesson 5: Counting Problems)

Section 8

1. B A *reputable* scientist is well-known and well-respected. Saying *the evidence is ------- at best* indicates that there is not much evidence at all. It must be *flimsy*. Reputable scientists would not likely *admit* that a phenomenon exists if the evidence is weak. *meager* = scanty, deficient; *regret* = feel bad about an action, wish it hadn't happened; *paltry* = lacking worth

2. D The concept that the Earth is round is *now accepted an an inarguable truth*. It can be inferred that it was at some point a fact that was thought to be wrong. *incontrovertible* = cannot be questioned; *mellifluous* = smooth flowing; *dubious* = doubtful

3. B A profound break of a political party or religion into factions is a *schism*. (The Latin word *schisma* = split.) *unanimity* = full agreement; *schism* = division into factions; *caucus* = meeting of party members; *commemoration* = event that honors something or someone; *prognostication* = prediction

4. C As the father of the American public school system, Horace Mann would *pressure* or *push* the Massachusetts legislature to institute a system for *ensuring* or *guaranteeing* universal access to eduction. *petitioned* = requested, lobbied for; *vouchsafing* = conceding, granting

5. A Since the light from most stars takes millions of years to reach us, it is plausible to imagine that by the time we see the light the star might actually no longer be there. This would make the present existence of these stars *questionable*. *debatable* = disputable; *methodical* = systematic; *indecorous* = not proper; *imperious* = acting as if one is superior to another; *profuse* = abundant

6. D The *although* establishes a contrast. Something that makes *any potentially offensive matters seem less objectionable* is, by definition, a *euphemism*. The 1st blank should therefore be a word that contrasts with euphemism, like *straightforward*. *anachronism* = something out of place in time; *intolerant* = unable to put up with something; *laudation* = extreme praise; *clandestine* = secret, hidden; *candid* = honest, straightforward; *euphemism* = the substitution of an inoffensive term for an offensive one; *forthright* = honest; *coercion* = pressure on someone to act

7. C The English gentleman *tried to teach his son Greek and Latin without punishment, . . . rewarding his son with cherries and biscuits* (lines 5–11).

8. **A**   In saying that *marks, grades, and diplomas . . . must be made reinforcing for other reasons* (lines 16–19), the author is saying that such things will not reinforce behavior by themselves but must be made to represent something more meaningful.

9. **B**   The passage says that how *honors and medals derive their power from prestige or esteem* is what *varies between cultures and epochs* (lines 20–23). When Oscar Wilde got a *"first in Mods"* in 1876, he was the talk of the town. But the contemporary student graduating *summa cum laude* is *less widely acclaimed* (lines 33–34).

10. **A**   The story follows the statement that how *honors and medals derive their power from prestige or esteem* is what *varies between cultures and epochs*. Therefore, the story is intended to illustrate that fact.

11. **C**   Statement I is supported by lines 37–39, which say that certain kinds of reinforcements (like food) *are not always easily arranged*. Statement II is supported by line 43: *We cannot all get prizes*. The selection does not mention anything about rewards' encouraging only superficial learning.

12. **D**   In lines 58–60, the passage says that *grades are almost always given long after the student has stopped behaving as a student*. It then goes on to discuss how *such contingencies are weak* (lines 60–61).

13. **E**   The paragraph as whole discusses the need for teachers to address the issues of whether, when, and how to punish or reward student behavior, so it is about teacher-student interactions.

14. **B**   Kohn and Deci are mentioned as examples of experts who believe *that reward is often just as harmful as punishment, if not more so* (lines 87–89).

15. **D**   The second paragraph of Passage 2 goes on to argue that those who are doing a task without a reward continue to perform the task because they see it as being "fun," whereas those who do it for a reward stop playing because they are no longer being paid to continue. The activity's sole value comes from the payment they get for it, not from the enjoyment they get from participating.

16. **D**   We are told that Deci concluded that the *subjects who were paid probably construed* (interpreted) *the task as being manipulative* (lines 105–106). In order to draw such conclusions, the subjects would have to make inferences about the motivations of the experimenter.

17. **A**   The author follows that statement with *it would be a mistake to use these few experiments to generalize that all rewards are bad* (lines 130–132). These statements caution against an overly simplistic theory about the effectiveness of rewards.

18. **B**   Deci's opinion is that the introduction of a reward system changes things for the worse. He would see the description of the *problems* mentioned in line 37 as presumptuous because they presume that the rewards actually have a positive effect and incomplete because they do not mention all of the problems that he sees in reward systems.

19. **D**   Both authors agree that positive feedback is a more effective teaching mechanism than negative feedback. Passage 1 mentions the need of good educators to *teach . . . without punishment* (lines 6–7) and mentions the negative *by-products of aversive control* (control by punishment) (lines 35–36). Passage 2 mentions that *most educators and psychologists agree that reward is always better than punishment* (lines 84–85), and since the writer goes on to criticize even reward systems, he implies that punishment is most certainly a bad teaching technique.

Section 9

1.   **C**   The word *whose* should refer to Alvin Ailey, but the way the sentence is constructed, it is referring to Alvin Ailey's *works*. Answer choice (C) corrects this error in the most concise and logical fashion.

(Chapter 18 Lesson 2: Trimming Sentences)

2.   **B**   When a participle is used to indicate an action that is completed before another action, it should be *perfect. Getting* this far should instead be *Having gotten.*

(Chapter 18 Lesson 9: Tricky Tenses)

3.   **C**   The sentence is improperly describing Rachel's irritation as being even-tempered. In reality, it should be *Rachel* who is even-tempered. Answer choice (C) corrects this error.

(Chapter 18 Lesson 7: Dangling and Misplaced Participles)

4.   **B**   This is a comparisons error. The literal translation of the sentence as written suggests that Alberta's salary is higher in the air than her co-workers are. It needs to be changed so that the sentence is comparing Alberta's salary to the *salary of her coworkers.*

(Chapter 18 Lesson 4: Comparison Problems)

5. **C** The word *elicit* means to call forth or draw out. The word should be *illicit,* which means unlawful.

(Chapter 18 Lesson 11: Diction Errors)

6. **D** The paraders were not watching from the balcony. The sentence needs to be changed so that the subjects represented by the final pronoun *us* are the ones watching from the balcony.

(Chapter 18 Lesson 7: Dangling and Misplaced Participles))

7. **E** The sentence contains two past tense verbs and one event was completed before the other. The tents were set up before they arrived. So *set up* needs to be in the past perfect tense—*had set up.*

(Chapter 18 Lesson 9: Tricky Tenses)

8. **C** When using neither . . . nor . . . phrasing, the verb should match in number the subject that follows the *nor.* Because daughters is plural, *was* should instead be *were.*

(Chapter 18 Lesson 1: Subject-Verb Disagreement)

9. **B** When using not only A but also B, the words or phrases that replace A and B must be parallel. It should be replaced by not only *with working* but also *with wanting.*

(Chapter 18 Lesson 3: Parallelism)

10. **C** To correct this sentence, the word *that* should be replaced with *who,* sine Roberto is a *person.*

(Chapter 18 Lesson 5: Pronoun-Antecedent Disagreement)

11. **D** Answer choice (D) connects the two clauses most effectively.

(Chapter 18 Lesson 15: Coordinating Ideas)

12. **E** When reading this sentence you should ask yourself: "who was forced to live apart from his family?" The answer to that question, St. Pierre, is what should immediately follow the comma after *informers.*

(Chapter 18 Lesson 7: Dangling and Misplaced Participles)

13. **B** The gerund form, *forming,* is not correct and needs to be changed to past tense *formed.* Choice (B) works best.

(Chapter 18 Lesson 9: Tricky Tenses)

14. **D** What follows the linking verb is must be a noun phrase representing *the most challenging aspect,* not an independent clause, as in the original. Choice (D) works best.

(Chapter 18 Lesson 15 Coordinating Ideas)

PRACTICE TEST 3

ANSWER SHEET

SECTION

1

Write your essay for Section 1 in the space below and on the next page.

ANSWER SHEET

ANSWER SHEET

Last Name:_____ First Name:_____

Date:_____ Testing Location:_____

Directions for Test

- Remove these answer sheets from the book and use them to record your answers to this test.
- This test will require 3 hours and 20 minutes to complete. Take this test in one sitting.
- The time allotment for each section is written clearly at the beginning of each section. This test contains six 25-minute sections, two 20-minute sections, and one 10-minute section.
- This test is 25 minutes shorter than the actual SAT I, which will include a 25-minute "experimental" section that does not count toward your score. That section has been omitted from this test.
- You may take one short break during the test, of no more than 10 minutes in length.
- You may only work on one section at any given time.
- You must stop ALL work on a section when time is called.
- If you finish a section before the time has elapsed, check your work on that section. You may NOT work on any other section.
- Do not waste time on questions that seem too difficult for you.
- Use the test book for scratchwork, but you will receive credit only for answers that are marked on the answer sheets.
- You will receive one point for every correct answer.
- You will receive no points for an omitted question.
- For each wrong answer on any multiple-choice question, your score will be reduced by ¼ point.
- For each wrong answer on any "numerical grid-in" question, you will receive no deduction.

SECTION 2

1. Ⓐ Ⓑ Ⓒ Ⓓ Ⓔ   11. Ⓐ Ⓑ Ⓒ Ⓓ Ⓔ   21. Ⓐ Ⓑ Ⓒ Ⓓ Ⓔ   31. Ⓐ Ⓑ Ⓒ Ⓓ Ⓔ
2. Ⓐ Ⓑ Ⓒ Ⓓ Ⓔ   12. Ⓐ Ⓑ Ⓒ Ⓓ Ⓔ   22. Ⓐ Ⓑ Ⓒ Ⓓ Ⓔ   32. Ⓐ Ⓑ Ⓒ Ⓓ Ⓔ
3. Ⓐ Ⓑ Ⓒ Ⓓ Ⓔ   13. Ⓐ Ⓑ Ⓒ Ⓓ Ⓔ   23. Ⓐ Ⓑ Ⓒ Ⓓ Ⓔ   33. Ⓐ Ⓑ Ⓒ Ⓓ Ⓔ
4. Ⓐ Ⓑ Ⓒ Ⓓ Ⓔ   14. Ⓐ Ⓑ Ⓒ Ⓓ Ⓔ   24. Ⓐ Ⓑ Ⓒ Ⓓ Ⓔ   34. Ⓐ Ⓑ Ⓒ Ⓓ Ⓔ
5. Ⓐ Ⓑ Ⓒ Ⓓ Ⓔ   15. Ⓐ Ⓑ Ⓒ Ⓓ Ⓔ   25. Ⓐ Ⓑ Ⓒ Ⓓ Ⓔ   35. Ⓐ Ⓑ Ⓒ Ⓓ Ⓔ
6. Ⓐ Ⓑ Ⓒ Ⓓ Ⓔ   16. Ⓐ Ⓑ Ⓒ Ⓓ Ⓔ   26. Ⓐ Ⓑ Ⓒ Ⓓ Ⓔ   36. Ⓐ Ⓑ Ⓒ Ⓓ Ⓔ
7. Ⓐ Ⓑ Ⓒ Ⓓ Ⓔ   17. Ⓐ Ⓑ Ⓒ Ⓓ Ⓔ   27. Ⓐ Ⓑ Ⓒ Ⓓ Ⓔ   37. Ⓐ Ⓑ Ⓒ Ⓓ Ⓔ
8. Ⓐ Ⓑ Ⓒ Ⓓ Ⓔ   18. Ⓐ Ⓑ Ⓒ Ⓓ Ⓔ   28. Ⓐ Ⓑ Ⓒ Ⓓ Ⓔ   38. Ⓐ Ⓑ Ⓒ Ⓓ Ⓔ
9. Ⓐ Ⓑ Ⓒ Ⓓ Ⓔ   19. Ⓐ Ⓑ Ⓒ Ⓓ Ⓔ   29. Ⓐ Ⓑ Ⓒ Ⓓ Ⓔ   39. Ⓐ Ⓑ Ⓒ Ⓓ Ⓔ
10. Ⓐ Ⓑ Ⓒ Ⓓ Ⓔ   20. Ⓐ Ⓑ Ⓒ Ⓓ Ⓔ   30. Ⓐ Ⓑ Ⓒ Ⓓ Ⓔ   40. Ⓐ Ⓑ Ⓒ Ⓓ Ⓔ

SECTION 3

1. Ⓐ Ⓑ Ⓒ Ⓓ Ⓔ   11. Ⓐ Ⓑ Ⓒ Ⓓ Ⓔ   21. Ⓐ Ⓑ Ⓒ Ⓓ Ⓔ   31. Ⓐ Ⓑ Ⓒ Ⓓ Ⓔ
2. Ⓐ Ⓑ Ⓒ Ⓓ Ⓔ   12. Ⓐ Ⓑ Ⓒ Ⓓ Ⓔ   22. Ⓐ Ⓑ Ⓒ Ⓓ Ⓔ   32. Ⓐ Ⓑ Ⓒ Ⓓ Ⓔ
3. Ⓐ Ⓑ Ⓒ Ⓓ Ⓔ   13. Ⓐ Ⓑ Ⓒ Ⓓ Ⓔ   23. Ⓐ Ⓑ Ⓒ Ⓓ Ⓔ   33. Ⓐ Ⓑ Ⓒ Ⓓ Ⓔ
4. Ⓐ Ⓑ Ⓒ Ⓓ Ⓔ   14. Ⓐ Ⓑ Ⓒ Ⓓ Ⓔ   24. Ⓐ Ⓑ Ⓒ Ⓓ Ⓔ   34. Ⓐ Ⓑ Ⓒ Ⓓ Ⓔ
5. Ⓐ Ⓑ Ⓒ Ⓓ Ⓔ   15. Ⓐ Ⓑ Ⓒ Ⓓ Ⓔ   25. Ⓐ Ⓑ Ⓒ Ⓓ Ⓔ   35. Ⓐ Ⓑ Ⓒ Ⓓ Ⓔ
6. Ⓐ Ⓑ Ⓒ Ⓓ Ⓔ   16. Ⓐ Ⓑ Ⓒ Ⓓ Ⓔ   26. Ⓐ Ⓑ Ⓒ Ⓓ Ⓔ   36. Ⓐ Ⓑ Ⓒ Ⓓ Ⓔ
7. Ⓐ Ⓑ Ⓒ Ⓓ Ⓔ   17. Ⓐ Ⓑ Ⓒ Ⓓ Ⓔ   27. Ⓐ Ⓑ Ⓒ Ⓓ Ⓔ   37. Ⓐ Ⓑ Ⓒ Ⓓ Ⓔ
8. Ⓐ Ⓑ Ⓒ Ⓓ Ⓔ   18. Ⓐ Ⓑ Ⓒ Ⓓ Ⓔ   28. Ⓐ Ⓑ Ⓒ Ⓓ Ⓔ   38. Ⓐ Ⓑ Ⓒ Ⓓ Ⓔ
9. Ⓐ Ⓑ Ⓒ Ⓓ Ⓔ   19. Ⓐ Ⓑ Ⓒ Ⓓ Ⓔ   29. Ⓐ Ⓑ Ⓒ Ⓓ Ⓔ   39. Ⓐ Ⓑ Ⓒ Ⓓ Ⓔ
10. Ⓐ Ⓑ Ⓒ Ⓓ Ⓔ   20. Ⓐ Ⓑ Ⓒ Ⓓ Ⓔ   30. Ⓐ Ⓑ Ⓒ Ⓓ Ⓔ   40. Ⓐ Ⓑ Ⓒ Ⓓ Ⓔ

ANSWER SHEET

SECTION 4

1. Ⓐ Ⓑ Ⓒ Ⓓ Ⓔ   11. Ⓐ Ⓑ Ⓒ Ⓓ Ⓔ   21. Ⓐ Ⓑ Ⓒ Ⓓ Ⓔ   31. Ⓐ Ⓑ Ⓒ Ⓓ Ⓔ
2. Ⓐ Ⓑ Ⓒ Ⓓ Ⓔ   12. Ⓐ Ⓑ Ⓒ Ⓓ Ⓔ   22. Ⓐ Ⓑ Ⓒ Ⓓ Ⓔ   32. Ⓐ Ⓑ Ⓒ Ⓓ Ⓔ
3. Ⓐ Ⓑ Ⓒ Ⓓ Ⓔ   13. Ⓐ Ⓑ Ⓒ Ⓓ Ⓔ   23. Ⓐ Ⓑ Ⓒ Ⓓ Ⓔ   33. Ⓐ Ⓑ Ⓒ Ⓓ Ⓔ
4. Ⓐ Ⓑ Ⓒ Ⓓ Ⓔ   14. Ⓐ Ⓑ Ⓒ Ⓓ Ⓔ   24. Ⓐ Ⓑ Ⓒ Ⓓ Ⓔ   34. Ⓐ Ⓑ Ⓒ Ⓓ Ⓔ
5. Ⓐ Ⓑ Ⓒ Ⓓ Ⓔ   15. Ⓐ Ⓑ Ⓒ Ⓓ Ⓔ   25. Ⓐ Ⓑ Ⓒ Ⓓ Ⓔ   35. Ⓐ Ⓑ Ⓒ Ⓓ Ⓔ
6. Ⓐ Ⓑ Ⓒ Ⓓ Ⓔ   16. Ⓐ Ⓑ Ⓒ Ⓓ Ⓔ   26. Ⓐ Ⓑ Ⓒ Ⓓ Ⓔ   36. Ⓐ Ⓑ Ⓒ Ⓓ Ⓔ
7. Ⓐ Ⓑ Ⓒ Ⓓ Ⓔ   17. Ⓐ Ⓑ Ⓒ Ⓓ Ⓔ   27. Ⓐ Ⓑ Ⓒ Ⓓ Ⓔ   37. Ⓐ Ⓑ Ⓒ Ⓓ Ⓔ
8. Ⓐ Ⓑ Ⓒ Ⓓ Ⓔ   18. Ⓐ Ⓑ Ⓒ Ⓓ Ⓔ   28. Ⓐ Ⓑ Ⓒ Ⓓ Ⓔ   38. Ⓐ Ⓑ Ⓒ Ⓓ Ⓔ
9. Ⓐ Ⓑ Ⓒ Ⓓ Ⓔ   19. Ⓐ Ⓑ Ⓒ Ⓓ Ⓔ   29. Ⓐ Ⓑ Ⓒ Ⓓ Ⓔ   39. Ⓐ Ⓑ Ⓒ Ⓓ Ⓔ
10. Ⓐ Ⓑ Ⓒ Ⓓ Ⓔ   20. Ⓐ Ⓑ Ⓒ Ⓓ Ⓔ   30. Ⓐ Ⓑ Ⓒ Ⓓ Ⓔ   40. Ⓐ Ⓑ Ⓒ Ⓓ Ⓔ

SECTION 5

1. Ⓐ Ⓑ Ⓒ Ⓓ Ⓔ   5. Ⓐ Ⓑ Ⓒ Ⓓ Ⓔ
2. Ⓐ Ⓑ Ⓒ Ⓓ Ⓔ   6. Ⓐ Ⓑ Ⓒ Ⓓ Ⓔ
3. Ⓐ Ⓑ Ⓒ Ⓓ Ⓔ   7. Ⓐ Ⓑ Ⓒ Ⓓ Ⓔ
4. Ⓐ Ⓑ Ⓒ Ⓓ Ⓔ   8. Ⓐ Ⓑ Ⓒ Ⓓ Ⓔ

9.   10.   11.   12.   13.

14.   15.   16.   17.   18.

ANSWER SHEET

SECTION 6

1. Ⓐ Ⓑ Ⓒ Ⓓ Ⓔ	11. Ⓐ Ⓑ Ⓒ Ⓓ Ⓔ	21. Ⓐ Ⓑ Ⓒ Ⓓ Ⓔ	31. Ⓐ Ⓑ Ⓒ Ⓓ Ⓔ
2. Ⓐ Ⓑ Ⓒ Ⓓ Ⓔ	12. Ⓐ Ⓑ Ⓒ Ⓓ Ⓔ	22. Ⓐ Ⓑ Ⓒ Ⓓ Ⓔ	32. Ⓐ Ⓑ Ⓒ Ⓓ Ⓔ
3. Ⓐ Ⓑ Ⓒ Ⓓ Ⓔ	13. Ⓐ Ⓑ Ⓒ Ⓓ Ⓔ	23. Ⓐ Ⓑ Ⓒ Ⓓ Ⓔ	33. Ⓐ Ⓑ Ⓒ Ⓓ Ⓔ
4. Ⓐ Ⓑ Ⓒ Ⓓ Ⓔ	14. Ⓐ Ⓑ Ⓒ Ⓓ Ⓔ	24. Ⓐ Ⓑ Ⓒ Ⓓ Ⓔ	34. Ⓐ Ⓑ Ⓒ Ⓓ Ⓔ
5. Ⓐ Ⓑ Ⓒ Ⓓ Ⓔ	15. Ⓐ Ⓑ Ⓒ Ⓓ Ⓔ	25. Ⓐ Ⓑ Ⓒ Ⓓ Ⓔ	35. Ⓐ Ⓑ Ⓒ Ⓓ Ⓔ
6. Ⓐ Ⓑ Ⓒ Ⓓ Ⓔ	16. Ⓐ Ⓑ Ⓒ Ⓓ Ⓔ	26. Ⓐ Ⓑ Ⓒ Ⓓ Ⓔ	36. Ⓐ Ⓑ Ⓒ Ⓓ Ⓔ
7. Ⓐ Ⓑ Ⓒ Ⓓ Ⓔ	17. Ⓐ Ⓑ Ⓒ Ⓓ Ⓔ	27. Ⓐ Ⓑ Ⓒ Ⓓ Ⓔ	37. Ⓐ Ⓑ Ⓒ Ⓓ Ⓔ
8. Ⓐ Ⓑ Ⓒ Ⓓ Ⓔ	18. Ⓐ Ⓑ Ⓒ Ⓓ Ⓔ	28. Ⓐ Ⓑ Ⓒ Ⓓ Ⓔ	38. Ⓐ Ⓑ Ⓒ Ⓓ Ⓔ
9. Ⓐ Ⓑ Ⓒ Ⓓ Ⓔ	19. Ⓐ Ⓑ Ⓒ Ⓓ Ⓔ	29. Ⓐ Ⓑ Ⓒ Ⓓ Ⓔ	39. Ⓐ Ⓑ Ⓒ Ⓓ Ⓔ
10. Ⓐ Ⓑ Ⓒ Ⓓ Ⓔ	20. Ⓐ Ⓑ Ⓒ Ⓓ Ⓔ	30. Ⓐ Ⓑ Ⓒ Ⓓ Ⓔ	40. Ⓐ Ⓑ Ⓒ Ⓓ Ⓔ

SECTION 7

1. Ⓐ Ⓑ Ⓒ Ⓓ Ⓔ	11. Ⓐ Ⓑ Ⓒ Ⓓ Ⓔ	21. Ⓐ Ⓑ Ⓒ Ⓓ Ⓔ	31. Ⓐ Ⓑ Ⓒ Ⓓ Ⓔ
2. Ⓐ Ⓑ Ⓒ Ⓓ Ⓔ	12. Ⓐ Ⓑ Ⓒ Ⓓ Ⓔ	22. Ⓐ Ⓑ Ⓒ Ⓓ Ⓔ	32. Ⓐ Ⓑ Ⓒ Ⓓ Ⓔ
3. Ⓐ Ⓑ Ⓒ Ⓓ Ⓔ	13. Ⓐ Ⓑ Ⓒ Ⓓ Ⓔ	23. Ⓐ Ⓑ Ⓒ Ⓓ Ⓔ	33. Ⓐ Ⓑ Ⓒ Ⓓ Ⓔ
4. Ⓐ Ⓑ Ⓒ Ⓓ Ⓔ	14. Ⓐ Ⓑ Ⓒ Ⓓ Ⓔ	24. Ⓐ Ⓑ Ⓒ Ⓓ Ⓔ	34. Ⓐ Ⓑ Ⓒ Ⓓ Ⓔ
5. Ⓐ Ⓑ Ⓒ Ⓓ Ⓔ	15. Ⓐ Ⓑ Ⓒ Ⓓ Ⓔ	25. Ⓐ Ⓑ Ⓒ Ⓓ Ⓔ	35. Ⓐ Ⓑ Ⓒ Ⓓ Ⓔ
6. Ⓐ Ⓑ Ⓒ Ⓓ Ⓔ	16. Ⓐ Ⓑ Ⓒ Ⓓ Ⓔ	26. Ⓐ Ⓑ Ⓒ Ⓓ Ⓔ	36. Ⓐ Ⓑ Ⓒ Ⓓ Ⓔ
7. Ⓐ Ⓑ Ⓒ Ⓓ Ⓔ	17. Ⓐ Ⓑ Ⓒ Ⓓ Ⓔ	27. Ⓐ Ⓑ Ⓒ Ⓓ Ⓔ	37. Ⓐ Ⓑ Ⓒ Ⓓ Ⓔ
8. Ⓐ Ⓑ Ⓒ Ⓓ Ⓔ	18. Ⓐ Ⓑ Ⓒ Ⓓ Ⓔ	28. Ⓐ Ⓑ Ⓒ Ⓓ Ⓔ	38. Ⓐ Ⓑ Ⓒ Ⓓ Ⓔ
9. Ⓐ Ⓑ Ⓒ Ⓓ Ⓔ	19. Ⓐ Ⓑ Ⓒ Ⓓ Ⓔ	29. Ⓐ Ⓑ Ⓒ Ⓓ Ⓔ	39. Ⓐ Ⓑ Ⓒ Ⓓ Ⓔ
10. Ⓐ Ⓑ Ⓒ Ⓓ Ⓔ	20. Ⓐ Ⓑ Ⓒ Ⓓ Ⓔ	30. Ⓐ Ⓑ Ⓒ Ⓓ Ⓔ	40. Ⓐ Ⓑ Ⓒ Ⓓ Ⓔ

SECTION 8

1. Ⓐ Ⓑ Ⓒ Ⓓ Ⓔ	11. Ⓐ Ⓑ Ⓒ Ⓓ Ⓔ	21. Ⓐ Ⓑ Ⓒ Ⓓ Ⓔ	31. Ⓐ Ⓑ Ⓒ Ⓓ Ⓔ
2. Ⓐ Ⓑ Ⓒ Ⓓ Ⓔ	12. Ⓐ Ⓑ Ⓒ Ⓓ Ⓔ	22. Ⓐ Ⓑ Ⓒ Ⓓ Ⓔ	32. Ⓐ Ⓑ Ⓒ Ⓓ Ⓔ
3. Ⓐ Ⓑ Ⓒ Ⓓ Ⓔ	13. Ⓐ Ⓑ Ⓒ Ⓓ Ⓔ	23. Ⓐ Ⓑ Ⓒ Ⓓ Ⓔ	33. Ⓐ Ⓑ Ⓒ Ⓓ Ⓔ
4. Ⓐ Ⓑ Ⓒ Ⓓ Ⓔ	14. Ⓐ Ⓑ Ⓒ Ⓓ Ⓔ	24. Ⓐ Ⓑ Ⓒ Ⓓ Ⓔ	34. Ⓐ Ⓑ Ⓒ Ⓓ Ⓔ
5. Ⓐ Ⓑ Ⓒ Ⓓ Ⓔ	15. Ⓐ Ⓑ Ⓒ Ⓓ Ⓔ	25. Ⓐ Ⓑ Ⓒ Ⓓ Ⓔ	35. Ⓐ Ⓑ Ⓒ Ⓓ Ⓔ
6. Ⓐ Ⓑ Ⓒ Ⓓ Ⓔ	16. Ⓐ Ⓑ Ⓒ Ⓓ Ⓔ	26. Ⓐ Ⓑ Ⓒ Ⓓ Ⓔ	36. Ⓐ Ⓑ Ⓒ Ⓓ Ⓔ
7. Ⓐ Ⓑ Ⓒ Ⓓ Ⓔ	17. Ⓐ Ⓑ Ⓒ Ⓓ Ⓔ	27. Ⓐ Ⓑ Ⓒ Ⓓ Ⓔ	37. Ⓐ Ⓑ Ⓒ Ⓓ Ⓔ
8. Ⓐ Ⓑ Ⓒ Ⓓ Ⓔ	18. Ⓐ Ⓑ Ⓒ Ⓓ Ⓔ	28. Ⓐ Ⓑ Ⓒ Ⓓ Ⓔ	38. Ⓐ Ⓑ Ⓒ Ⓓ Ⓔ
9. Ⓐ Ⓑ Ⓒ Ⓓ Ⓔ	19. Ⓐ Ⓑ Ⓒ Ⓓ Ⓔ	29. Ⓐ Ⓑ Ⓒ Ⓓ Ⓔ	39. Ⓐ Ⓑ Ⓒ Ⓓ Ⓔ
10. Ⓐ Ⓑ Ⓒ Ⓓ Ⓔ	20. Ⓐ Ⓑ Ⓒ Ⓓ Ⓔ	30. Ⓐ Ⓑ Ⓒ Ⓓ Ⓔ	40. Ⓐ Ⓑ Ⓒ Ⓓ Ⓔ

SECTION 9

1. Ⓐ Ⓑ Ⓒ Ⓓ Ⓔ	11. Ⓐ Ⓑ Ⓒ Ⓓ Ⓔ	21. Ⓐ Ⓑ Ⓒ Ⓓ Ⓔ	31. Ⓐ Ⓑ Ⓒ Ⓓ Ⓔ
2. Ⓐ Ⓑ Ⓒ Ⓓ Ⓔ	12. Ⓐ Ⓑ Ⓒ Ⓓ Ⓔ	22. Ⓐ Ⓑ Ⓒ Ⓓ Ⓔ	32. Ⓐ Ⓑ Ⓒ Ⓓ Ⓔ
3. Ⓐ Ⓑ Ⓒ Ⓓ Ⓔ	13. Ⓐ Ⓑ Ⓒ Ⓓ Ⓔ	23. Ⓐ Ⓑ Ⓒ Ⓓ Ⓔ	33. Ⓐ Ⓑ Ⓒ Ⓓ Ⓔ
4. Ⓐ Ⓑ Ⓒ Ⓓ Ⓔ	14. Ⓐ Ⓑ Ⓒ Ⓓ Ⓔ	24. Ⓐ Ⓑ Ⓒ Ⓓ Ⓔ	34. Ⓐ Ⓑ Ⓒ Ⓓ Ⓔ
5. Ⓐ Ⓑ Ⓒ Ⓓ Ⓔ	15. Ⓐ Ⓑ Ⓒ Ⓓ Ⓔ	25. Ⓐ Ⓑ Ⓒ Ⓓ Ⓔ	35. Ⓐ Ⓑ Ⓒ Ⓓ Ⓔ
6. Ⓐ Ⓑ Ⓒ Ⓓ Ⓔ	16. Ⓐ Ⓑ Ⓒ Ⓓ Ⓔ	26. Ⓐ Ⓑ Ⓒ Ⓓ Ⓔ	36. Ⓐ Ⓑ Ⓒ Ⓓ Ⓔ
7. Ⓐ Ⓑ Ⓒ Ⓓ Ⓔ	17. Ⓐ Ⓑ Ⓒ Ⓓ Ⓔ	27. Ⓐ Ⓑ Ⓒ Ⓓ Ⓔ	37. Ⓐ Ⓑ Ⓒ Ⓓ Ⓔ
8. Ⓐ Ⓑ Ⓒ Ⓓ Ⓔ	18. Ⓐ Ⓑ Ⓒ Ⓓ Ⓔ	28. Ⓐ Ⓑ Ⓒ Ⓓ Ⓔ	38. Ⓐ Ⓑ Ⓒ Ⓓ Ⓔ
9. Ⓐ Ⓑ Ⓒ Ⓓ Ⓔ	19. Ⓐ Ⓑ Ⓒ Ⓓ Ⓔ	29. Ⓐ Ⓑ Ⓒ Ⓓ Ⓔ	39. Ⓐ Ⓑ Ⓒ Ⓓ Ⓔ
10. Ⓐ Ⓑ Ⓒ Ⓓ Ⓔ	20. Ⓐ Ⓑ Ⓒ Ⓓ Ⓔ	30. Ⓐ Ⓑ Ⓒ Ⓓ Ⓔ	40. Ⓐ Ⓑ Ⓒ Ⓓ Ⓔ

Section 1

Time—25 minutes

Directions for Writing the Essay

Plan and write an essay that answers the question below. Do NOT write on another topic. An essay on another topic will receive a score of 0.

Two readers will grade your essay based on how well you develop your point of view, organize and explain your ideas, use specific and relevant examples to support your thesis, and use clear and effective language. How well you write is much more important than how much you write, but to cover the topic adequately you should plan to write several paragraphs.

Your essay must be written only on the lines provided on your answer sheet. You will have enough space if you write on every line, avoid wide margins, and keep your handwriting to a reasonable size. Your essay will be read by people who are not familiar with your handwriting, so write legibly.

You may use this sheet for notes and outlining, but these will not be graded as part of your essay.

Consider carefully the issue discussed in the following passage, then write an essay that answers the question posed in the assignment.

> Many among us like to blame violence and immorality in the media for a "decline in morals" in society. Yet these people seem to have lost touch with logic. Any objective examination shows that our society is far less violent or exploitative than virtually any society in the past. Early humans murdered and enslaved each other with astonishing regularity, without the help of gangsta rap or Jerry Bruckheimer films.

Assignment: **Does violence and immorality in the media make our society more dangerous and immoral?** Write an essay in which you answer this question and discuss your point of view on this issue. Support your position logically with examples from literature, the arts, history, politics, science and technology, current events, or your experience or observation.

Write your essay on your answer sheet.

Section 2

Time—25 minutes
20 Questions

Directions for Multiple-Choice Questions

In this section, solve each problem, using any available space on the page for scratchwork. Then decide which is the best of the choices given and fill in the corresponding oval on the answer sheet.

- You may use a calculator on any problem. All numbers used are real numbers.
- Figures are drawn as accurately as possible EXCEPT when it is stated that the figure is not drawn to scale.
- All figures lie in a plane unless otherwise indicated.

Reference Information

$A = \pi r^2$
$C = 2\pi r$

$A = \ell w$

$A = \frac{1}{2} bh$

$V = \ell wh$

$V = \pi r^2 h$

$c^2 = a^2 + b^2$

Special Right Triangles

The arc of a circle measures 360°.
Every straight angle measures 180°.
The sum of the measures of the angles in a triangle is 180°.

---

1 If $(x + 4) + 7 = 14$, what is the value of x?

(A) 3
(B) 7
(C) 11
(D) 17
(E) 25

$X + 11 = 14$

Ⓐ

---

2 Erica spends $.95 each day for her newspaper subscriptions. She would like to determine the approximate amount she spends during the month of July, which has 31 days. Which of the following would provide her with the best estimate?

(A) $.50 × 30
(B) $1.00 × 30
(C) $1.50 × 30
(D) $.50 × 35
(E) $1.00 × 35

$.95 × 31 = 29.45$

≈ 29
or
≈ 30

3

Note: Figure not drawn to scale.

In the figure above, lines l, m, and n intersect in a single point. What is the value of $w + x$?

(A) 40
(B) 70
(C) 90
(D) 130
(E) 140

GO ON TO THE NEXT PAGE ▶▶▶

4 Let the function g be defined by the equation $g(x) = 3x + 4$. What is the value of $g(5)$?

(A) 8
(B) 11
(C) 15
(D) 19
(E) 23

$g(5) = 15 + 4$

(D)

7 Chris buys a chocolate bar and a pack of gum for $1.75. If the chocolate bar costs $.25 more than the pack of gum, how much does the pack of gum cost?

(A) $.25
(B) $.50
(C) $.75
(D) $1.00
(E) $1.50

$b + g = 1.75$

$b = g + .25$

$\therefore 2g + .25 = 1.75$

$2g = 15$

$g =$

(L)

5 If $x > y$, which of the following equations expresses the fact that when the difference between x and y is multiplied by their sum, the product is 18?

(A) $(x - y)^2 = 18$
(B) $(x + y)^2 = 18$
(C) $(x - y) \div (x + y) = 18$
(D) $x^2 - y^2 = 18$
(E) $x^2 + y^2 = 18$

(D)

$(x - y)(x + y) = 18$

8 40% of 80 is what percent of 96?

(A) 20%
(B) 30%
(C) 33⅓%
(D) 50%
(E) 66⅔%

$.4(80) = x \cdot 96$

(C)

6 If $3\sqrt{x} - 7 = 20$, what is the value of x?

(A) 3
(B) 9
(C) 27
(D) 36
(E) 81

$3\sqrt{x} = 27$

$\dfrac{}{3} \quad \dfrac{}{3}$

$\sqrt{x}^2 = 9^2$

$x = 81$

(E)

9 If l, m, and n are positive integers greater than 1; $lm = 21$; and $mn = 39$, then which of the following must be true?

(A) $n > l > m$
(B) $m > n > l$
(C) $m > l > n$
(D) $l > n > m$
(E) $n > m > l$

$lm = 21$

$nm = 39$

$n > l$

$39 \quad 21 \quad \dfrac{1}{n} =$

$\diagdown \quad \diagdown$

$13 \ \circled{3} \quad 7 \ \circled{3}$

(A)

GO ON TO THE NEXT PAGE ▶▶▶

10

Annual Profits for ABC Company
(in thousands of dollars)

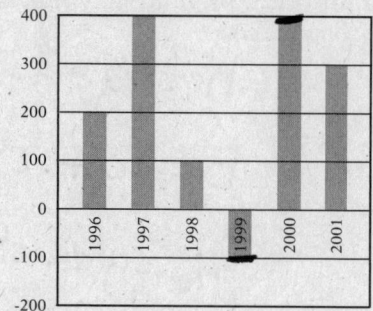

According to the graph above, ABC Company showed the greatest change in profits between which 2 years?

(A) 1996 and 1997
(B) 1997 and 1998
(C) 1998 and 1999
(D) 1999 and 2000 ✓ (D)
(E) 2000 and 2001

11

In a 9th-grade class, 12 students play soccer, 7 students play tennis, and 9 students play lacrosse. If 4 students play exactly 2 of the 3 sports and all other students play only 1, how many students are in the class?

(A) 28
(B) 24 ✓ $(12+7+9)-4$
(C) 20
(D) 18
(E) 16   (B)

12

The point (14, 14) is the center of a circle, and (2, 9) is a point on the circle. What is the length of a diameter of the circle?

(A) 24
(B) 26   (B)
(C) 50   •14,14
(D) 144π
(E) 169π

$r = \sqrt{(14-2)^2 + (14-9)^2}$

$d = 26$ $r = \sqrt{(12)^2 + (5)^2}$

$\sqrt{144 + 25}$

$\boxed{r = 13}$

13

The population of Boomtown doubles every 18 months. In January of 2000, its population was exactly 12,000. At this rate, approximately when should the population reach 96,000?

(A) January 2003
(B) July 2004 $P(t) = 12,000 (2)$
(C) January 2006
(D) July 2007
(E) January 2012   96000

$\frac{18}{12} = 1.5$ (A)

$pop = 8 \times 18 =$ $\frac{96000}{1200}$ (E)

14

In how many different ways can 5 students of different heights be arranged in a line if the tallest student cannot be on either end?

(A) 24
(B) 25 $4 \cdot 2 \cdot 1 \cdot 1 \cdot 3$
(C) 72
(D) 96 $8 \cdot 3 =$
(E) 120

(A) $\underline{3}\ \underline{2}\ \underline{1}\ \underline{4}$
4 3 2   3

15

Note: Figure not drawn to scale.

In the figure above, $a > 90$ and $b = c + 3$. If a, b, and c are all integers, what is the greatest possible value of b?

(A) 43
(B) 46 ✓ $90 = c + 3 + c$
(C) 60
(D) 86 $90 = 2c + 3$
(E) 89

87

43.5 = c

(B)

GO ON TO THE NEXT PAGE ▸▸▸

Anste-A_BDC

16

In the figure above, $\triangle ACF$ is equilateral, with sides of length 4. If B, D, and E are the midpoints of their respective sides, what is the sum of the areas of the shaded regions?

(A) $3\sqrt{2}$ (B) $3\sqrt{3}$ (C) $4\sqrt{2}$

(D) $4\sqrt{3}$ (E) $6\sqrt{3}$

$h = \sqrt{4^2 - 2^2}$
$h = \sqrt{16-4}$
$h = \sqrt{12}$

$A_{ACF} = \frac{1}{2}\sqrt{12} \cdot 2$
$A_{ACF} = 2\sqrt{2}$

17

Given the graph of $y = f(x)$ above, which of the following sets represents all values of x for which $f(x) \geq 1$?

(A) all real numbers
(B) $x \geq 1$
(C) $-5 \leq x \leq -1$; $1 \leq x \leq 5$
(D) $-4 \leq x \leq -2$; $2 \leq x \leq 4$ ✓
(E) $x \leq -4$; $x \geq 4$

18

X: {2, 4, 6, 8, 10} 5
Y: {1, 3, 5, 7, 9} 5

If a is a number chosen randomly from set X and b is a number chosen randomly from set Y, what is the probability that ab is greater than 20 but less than 50?

(A) 1/5   (B) 6/5   (C) 7/25
(D) 3/5   (E) 18/25

STOP

You may check your work, on this section only, until time is called.

19 If $w^a \times w^5 = w^{15}$ and $(w^4)^b = w^{12}$, what is the value of $a + b$?

(A) 6
(B) 7
(C) 11
(D) 12
(E) 13

$w^{(a+5)} = w^{15}$ $w^{4b} = w^{12}$
$a + 5 = 15$ $b = 3$
$a = 10$

2

20

Given the graph of $y = f(x)$ above, which of the following represents the graph of $y = f(x - 2)$?

(A)

(B)

(C)

(D)

(E)

Section 3

Time—25 minutes
24 Questions

Each of the sentences below is missing one or two portions. Read each sentence, then select the word or words that most logically complete the sentence, taking into account the meaning of the sentence as a whole.

Example:

Rather than accepting the theory unquestioningly, Deborah regarded it with -------.

(A) mirth
(B) sadness
(C) responsibility
(D) ignorance
(E) skepticism

Correct response: (E)

1 Although he purchased his computer only 10 months ago, rapid improvements in technology have left Raúl with ------- machine.

(A) an obsolete (B) an adjunct
(C) a novel (D) an automated
(E) an elusive

2 Only if the number of applicants continues to -------- can the admissions committee justify offering more scholarships in order to increase the number of applications.

(A) mushroom (B) expand (C) plummet
(D) satiate (E) burgeon

3 My father is so ------- that he will never even consider another person's viewpoint to be valid if it is different from his own.

(A) pragmatic (B) dogmatic (C) phlegmatic
(D) cordial (E) curt

4 J. K. Rowling's *Harry Potter* series is a collection of works that are ------- for children but are still ------- to adults.

(A) penned . . . prosaic
(B) employed . . . morose
(C) censored . . . incongruous
(D) designed . . . tedious
(E) authored . . . engaging

5 Julia approaches her homework assignments in such ------- way that it is very difficult to believe that she is at the top of her class.

(A) an adept (B) a diligent (C) a fanatical
(D) an extroverted (E) a laggardly

6 The President was such a ------- orator that his opponents were always supremely cautious about agreeing to debate him.

(A) redoubtable (B) staid (C) magnanimous
(D) weak (E) stoic

7 The newest clothing line revealed at the show was an eclectic mix that ranged from the modest and unadorned to the ------- and garish.

(A) austere (B) prophetic (C) cordial
(D) ostentatious (E) solitary

8 Neil Campbell's textbook *Biology* is ------- and yet -------; it includes all of the essential information without ever being verbose.

(A) compendious . . . circumlocutory
(B) reprehensible . . . terse
(C) comprehensive . . . concise
(D) praiseworthy . . . grandiloquent
(E) painstaking . . . redundant

GO ON TO THE NEXT PAGE ▶▶▶

The passages below are followed by questions based on their content. Answer each question based on what is stated or implied in the passages or the introductory material preceding them.

Questions 9–12 are based on the following passages.

Passage 1

The following is from President Bill Clinton's first inaugural address.

Today, a generation raised in the shadows of the Cold War assumes new responsibilities in a
Line world warmed by the sunshine of freedom, but threatened still by ancient hatreds and new
5 plagues. Raised in unrivaled prosperity, we inherit an economy that is still the world's strongest, but is weakened by business failures, stagnant wages, increasing inequality, and deep divisions among our own people. When
10 George Washington first took the oath I have just sworn to uphold, news traveled slowly across the land by horseback, and across the ocean by boat. Now the sights and sounds of this ceremony are broadcast instantaneously to
15 billions around the world. Communications and commerce are global. Investment is mobile. Technology is almost magical, and ambition for a better life is now universal.

Passage 2

The following is a commentary on America written in 2005 by an American writer.

The people of the world, save the majority
20 of our own citizens, are growing to appreciate the difference between America and the United States. America is the heart and mind of the world. It is an ideal to which all free-thinking men and women aspire. It is the
25 spirit of hope, freedom, vision and creativity. But the United States, at least since the turn of the century, has become something different. It constantly grasps at the cloak of America, but this cloak fits our current leaders
30 quite poorly. Our leaders have become dominated by fear and its value as a political tool. They speak incessantly of freedom but revel in repression. They speak of a "culture of life" but revel in the culture of siege and war. The

35 hope, freedom, vision and creativity of America have slipped through their fingers, and they have little hope of recapturing it. In America, that task is left to the people.

9 The word "unrivaled" in line 5 most nearly means

(A) without enemies
(B) supremely abundant
(C) militarily superior
(D) unimaginable
(E) highly intelligent

10 Which of the following best describes the contrast between the "people" (line 9) as characterized in Passage 1 and the "citizens" (line 20) as characterized in Passage 2?

(A) the "people" are ignorant, while the "citizens" are well-educated
(B) the "people" lack fortitude, while the "citizens" are courageous
(C) the "people" are worldly, while the "citizens" are parochial
(D) the "people" are proud of their leaders, while the "citizens" are not
(E) the "people" lack unity, while the "citizens" lack awareness

11 Passage 1 makes all of the following claims about the state of society EXCEPT that

(A) an increasing number of people are happy with their lives
(B) information is disseminated more rapidly than in the past
(C) the current economy is strong
(D) social inequities are deepening
(E) workers' incomes are not increasing

12 Unlike the author of Passage 1, the author of Passage 2 does which of the following?

(A) contrasts an ideal with a reality
(B) explains a study
(C) compares the past with the present
(D) describes an injustice
(E) acknowledges a responsibility

GO ON TO THE NEXT PAGE ▶▶▶

The passages below are followed by questions based on their content. The questions are to be answered on the basis of what is stated or implied in the passage itself or in the introductory material that precedes them.

3

Questions 13-19 are based on the following passage.

The following passage is adapted from a short story published by a Russian author in the late 1970s.

What is all this? he thought, terrified. And yet . . . do I love her, or don't I? That is the
Line question!

5   But she, now that the most important and difficult thing had at last been said, breathed lightly and freely. She, too, stood up and, looking straight into Ognev Alexeyich's face, began to talk quickly, irrepressibly and ardently.

10   Just as a man who is suddenly overwhelmed by terror cannot afterwards remember the exact order of sounds accompanying the catastrophe which stuns him, Ognev could not remember Vera's words and phrases. His memory retained only the substance of her speech
15   itself and the sensation her speech produced in him. He remembered her voice, as though it were choked and slightly hoarse from excitement, and the extraordinary music and passion of her intonation. Crying, laughing, the tears
20   glittering on her eyelashes, she was telling him that even from the first days of their acquaintance she had been struck by his originality, his intellect, his kind intelligent eyes, with the aims and objects of his life; that she had fallen pas-
25   sionately, madly and deeply in love with him; that whenever she had happened to come into the house from the garden that summer and had seen his coat in the vestibule or heard his voice in the distance, her heart had felt a cold
30   thrill of delight, a foretaste of happiness; that even the silliest jokes made her laugh helplessly, and in each figure of his copybook she could see something extraordinarily clever and grandiose; that his knotted walking stick
35   seemed to her more beautiful than the trees.
       The forest and the wisps of fog and the black ditches alongside the road seemed to fall silent, listening to her, but something bad and strange was taking place in Ognev's
40   heart. . . . Vera was enchantingly beautiful as she told him of her love, she spoke with eloquence and passion, but much as he wanted to, he could feel no joy, no fundamental hap-

piness, but only compassion for Vera, and
45   pain and regret that a good human being should be suffering because of him. The Lord only knows whether it was his bookish mind that now began to speak, or whether he was affected by that irresistible habit of objectivity
50   which so often prevents people from living, but Vera's raptures and suffering seemed to him only cloying and trivial. At the same time he was outraged with himself and something whispered to him that what he was now see-
55   ing and hearing was, from the point of view of human nature and his personal happiness, more important than any statistics, books or philosophical truths . . . And he was annoyed and blamed himself even though he himself
60   did not understand why he was to blame.

13 Which of the following best describes the characterization of the man and the woman in the first two paragraphs?

(A) He is confused, while she is passionate.
(B) He is angry, while she is jocular.
(C) He is stoic, while she is serene.
(D) He is ambivalent, while she is anxious.
(E) He is disdainful, while she is whimsical.

14 The author suggests that one "who is suddenly overwhelmed by terror" (line 10) is temporarily

(A) vindictive
(B) defensive
(C) cautious
(D) disoriented
(E) resentful

15 The description of "the catastrophe" (lines 11-12) serves primarily to suggest that

(A) the couple has endured a terrible accident
(B) Ognev is devastated by Vera's harsh words
(C) Ognev is deeply troubled by Vera's passionate expression of love
(D) Ognev holds Vera responsible for a crime
(E) Vera has told Ognev a horrible secret

GO ON TO THE NEXT PAGE ▸▸▸

16 In line 24, "objects" most nearly means

(A) possessions
(B) facts
(C) decorations
(D) goals
(E) complaints

17 The passage suggests that the "bad and strange" (line 39) thing that was taking place in Ognev's heart was his

(A) eagerness
(B) sadism
(C) jealousy
(D) hatred
(E) disaffection

18 In lines 57–58, "statistics, books or philosophical truths" are mentioned as examples of things that

(A) Vera does not understand
(B) Ognev and Vera share reluctantly
(C) Ognev abandoned long ago
(D) Vera loves passionately
(E) Ognev inexplicably values more highly than passion

19 The primary function of the final paragraph is to show Ognev's

(A) struggle to understand his own feelings
(B) anger about Vera's misrepresentation of her feelings
(C) frustration with the voices in his head
(D) outrage with his inability to understand a philosophical concept
(E) appreciation of Vera's beauty

Questions 20–24 are based on the following passage.

The following is part of an introduction to the publication of a speech delivered by President Lyndon B. Johnson in the 1960s.

"Somehow you never forget what poverty and hatred can do when you see its scars on
Line the hopeful face of a young child." So spoke President Lyndon B. Johnson in the course of
5 one of the most deeply felt, and deeply moving, addresses ever delivered by an American president. The date was March 15th, 1965; the occasion was an extraordinary joint session at night of the Senate and the House of Repre-
10 sentatives, televised across the nation. It was the "time of Selma"—only a few days after the historic mass demonstration in support of voter registration in Alabama, in which many of the peaceful marchers were physically at-
15 tacked and one of them, a white clergyman from the north, was killed. The nation itself was a shocked witness, via television, of much of that unforgettable scene: the long rows of marchers, a cross section of African Americans
20 and whites, Californians and New Yorkers, resolutely striding, smiling, singing to hide their exhaustion, trying not to see the hate-twisted faces and shouting menace of the sidewalk crowd, trying not to fear the armored
25 troopers and police with their notorious supporting artillery of dogs, clubs, and cattle prods.

This was the moment chosen by the President, himself a Southerner with a reputation
30 for compromise, to bear witness before the nation, and to call upon his former associates of Congress to stand up and be counted with him—more specifically, to take action on a bill which would correct the conspicuous
35 weakness of the 1964 Civil Rights Bill, its failure to protect the right of African Americans to vote "when local officials are determined to deny it." In forthright terms, President Johnson spelled out the full cruelty and ingenuity
40 of that discrimination, and crisply defined the central issue involved: "There is no Constitutional issue here. The command of the Constitution is plain. There is no moral issue. It is wrong—deadly wrong—to deny any of your
45 fellow Americans the right to vote in this

GO ON TO THE NEXT PAGE ▶▶▶

country. There is no issue of state's rights or national rights. There is only the struggle for human rights."

50 The President spoke slowly, solemnly, with unmistakable determination. His words and his manner were perfectly synchronized; indeed he made the nationwide audience aware of how deeply personal the issue of African American rights was to him. He recalled his

55 own southern origins, and his shattering encounter with Mexican-American children as a young schoolteacher ("They never seemed to know why people disliked them, but they knew it was so because I saw it in their eyes.")

60 He spoke more directly, more explicitly, and more warmly of the human experience of prejudice than any president before him. But he also placed the problem of African American rights in a broader frame of reference—

65 that of poverty and ignorance, bigotry and fear. "Their cause must be our cause too. Because it is not just African Americans, but really it's all of us, who must overcome the crippling legacy of bigotry and injustice. And

70 we shall overcome."

20 In the first paragraph, the marchers are characterized as

(A) ruthless
(B) gleeful
(C) intellectual
(D) stoic
(E) shocked

21 The passage indicates that the 1964 Civil Rights Act was deficient in that it did not

(A) sufficiently pressure local officials to extend voting privileges to all citizens
(B) provide enough funds to promote voter registration drives
(C) punish felons who committed hate crimes
(D) provide military protection for the Selma marchers
(E) invest in minority-owned businesses

22 In line 55, *shattering* most nearly means

(A) exploding
(B) disturbing
(C) fragmenting
(D) violent
(E) loud

23 The quotation in lines 57–59 ("They never seemed ... in their eyes") indicates that Johnson

(A) understood the political process at a young age
(B) was unfamiliar with Mexican-American customs
(C) empathized strongly with his students
(D) was a victim of bigotry
(E) was unaware of the difficulties his students faced

24 The passage indicates that Johnson, unlike previous presidents, handled the issue of civil rights by

(A) successfully integrating the issue into his reelection campaign
(B) approaching the cause with objectivity and impartiality
(C) speaking clearly to reporters using terms they wanted to hear
(D) focusing primarily on the Mexican American population
(E) directly addressing the public on the issue and describing it in personal terms

STOP

You may check your work, on this section only, until time is called.

Section 4

Time—25 minutes
35 Questions

Directions for "Improving Sentences" Questions

Each of the sentences below contains 1 underlined portion. The portion may contain 1 or more errors in grammar, usage, construction, precision, diction (choice of words), or idiom. Some of the sentences are correct.

Consider the meaning of the original sentence, and choose the answer that best expresses that meaning. If the original sentence is best, choose (A), because it repeats the original phrasing. Choose the phrasing that creates the clearest, most precise, and most effective sentence.

EXAMPLE:
The children <u>couldn't hardly believe their eyes</u>.
(A) couldn't hardly believe their eyes
(B) would not hardly believe their eyes
(C) could hardly believe their eyes
(D) couldn't nearly believe their eyes
(E) could hardly believe his or her eyes

EXAMPLE ANSWER
(C)

1 Exhausted from a day of hiking across steep, rain-soaked paths, the <u>group of campers were relieved upon the final reaching of the car</u>.

(A) group of campers were relieved upon the final reaching of the car
(B) camping group became relieved after they got to the car
(C) group of campers was relieved to finally reach the car
(D) campers were relieved after the car was finally reached
(E) group was relieved after the campers finally reached the car

2 Theodore Roosevelt's first term as President <u>was marked by a ferocious battle between labor and management</u> in Pennsylvania's anthracite coal mines.

(A) was marked by a ferocious battle between labor and management
(B) marked a ferocious battle between labor and management
(C) battled ferociously with labor and management
(D) was marked ferociously by labor and management's battle
(E) was marking a ferocious battle between labor and management

3 Timid and self-conscious, <u>Timothy never managed to give full expression towards his feelings for Jessica.</u>

(A) Timothy never managed to give full expression towards his feelings for Jessica.
(B) Timothy never managed full expression of his feelings towards Jessica.
(C) Jessica never heard Timothy's full expression of his feelings.
(D) Timothy never managed to fully express his feelings for Jessica.
(E) Timothy's full expression of his feelings never reached Jessica.

4 Knowing that this was his last chance, Sherman stayed up all night <u>studying in preparation for the exam.</u>

(A) studying in preparation for the exam.
(B) studying for the exam.
(C) studying for preparation for the exam.
(D) to study in order to get ready for the exam.
(E) for studying for the exam.

GO ON TO THE NEXT PAGE ▶▶▶

5 Disgruntled with the United States and disillusioned by battle, Hemingway <u>led an exodus of expatriate authors on an overseas journey</u> across the Atlantic Ocean following World War I.

(A) led an exodus of expatriate authors on an overseas journey
(B) leads an exodus of expatriate authors on an overseas journey
(C) led an exodus of expatriate authors
(D) led expatriate authors on an overseas exodus
(E) during an expatriate author exodus, journeyed

6 Renowned for his straightforward, honest presentation of the news, <u>Walter Cronkite, which became a fixture in the homes</u> of an entire American generation.

(A) Walter Cronkite, which became a fixture in the homes
(B) Walter Cronkite, who became a fixture in the homes
(C) Walter Cronkite became a home fixture
(D) Walter Cronkite, who was a fixture, became home
(E) Walter Cronkite became a fixture in the homes

7 <u>Known for his patience, understanding, and how easily he can be approached</u>, Professor Wilson has developed close relationships with many of his colleagues and students.

(A) Known for his patience, understanding, and how easily he can be approached
(B) Known for his patience, understanding, and the ability to be approached
(C) Known for his patience, understanding, and approachability
(D) Knowing his patience, understanding, and ability to be approached
(E) Known for his patience, for his understanding, and his approachability

8 Auto racing, often thought of as a regional phenomenon, <u>therefore is quite popular</u> throughout the nation.

(A) therefore is quite popular
(B) henceforth is quite popular
(C) is thus quite popular
(D) is actually quite popular
(E) in retrospect, is quite popular

9 Unable to wait until her birthday, <u>Julia sneaked downstairs in an effort to open</u> several of her presents.

(A) Julia sneaked downstairs in an effort to open
(B) Julia, sneaking downstairs and opening
(C) Julia sneaked downstairs and opened
(D) Julia sneaked downstairs in opening
(E) Julia, as a result of sneaking downstairs, opened

10 Many parents detest music featuring explicit lyrics, <u>believing that which encourages inappropriate behavior</u>.

(A) believing that which encourages inappropriate behavior
(B) that which they believe encourages inappropriate behavior
(C) believing that it encourages inappropriate behavior
(D) of the belief that it encourages inappropriate behavior
(E) that which encourages inappropriate behavior, they believe

11 Perhaps best known for his untiring defense of the downtrodden, <u>Clarence Darrow's stunning oratory often devastated his opponents</u>.

(A) Clarence Darrow's stunning oratory often devastated his opponents
(B) Clarence Darrow often devastated his opponents with his stunning oratory
(C) the stunning oratory of Clarence Darrow often devastated his opponents
(D) Clarence Darrow devastated his opponents often with the stunning nature of his oratory
(E) Clarence Darrow's devastated opponents were stunned by his oratory

GO ON TO THE NEXT PAGE ▸▸▸

Directions for "Identifying Sentence Error" Questions

The following sentences may contain errors in grammar, usage, diction (choice of words), or idiom. Some of the sentences are correct. No sentence contains more than 1 error.

If the sentence contains an error, it is underlined and lettered. The parts that are not underlined are correct.

If there is an error, select the part that must be changed to correct the sentence.

If there is no error, choose (E).

EXAMPLE: SAMPLE ANSWER:

By the time <u>they reached</u> the halfway point
A

in the race, <u>most of the runners</u> <u>hadn't hardly</u>
B   C   D

begun to hit their stride.   <u>No error</u>
                      E

(D)

---

12 The local dairy company is <u>one of the most</u>
A

<u>efficient</u> in the state, <u>so</u> it is surprising that
B   C

the delivery of our milk products over the last

few days <u>have been</u> late.   <u>No error</u>
       D   E

13 <u>Last summer</u> <u>we stayed in</u> a charming cottage
A   B

<u>whose rooms are</u> spacious and <u>well decorated</u>.
   C   D

<u>No error</u>
  E

14 <u>This holiday season</u>, several members of the
A

committee <u>are</u> sponsoring a dinner to raise
       B

money for their <u>efforts</u> to encourage
            C

<u>responsible</u> driving.   <u>No error</u>
  D   E

15 The lavish photographs and fascinating

diagrams <u>in the biology textbook</u> <u>was</u> so
          A   B

engaging that I seriously <u>considered</u>
               C

becoming <u>a zoologist</u>.   <u>No error</u>
      D   E

16 Behavioral scientists <u>believe</u> that the way
A

chimpanzees <u>form friendships</u> and alliances
          B

is <u>very similar</u> <u>to humans</u>.   <u>No error</u>
   C   D   E

17 When the window <u>was opened</u>, the <u>affects</u> of
              A   B

the cool spring breeze were <u>felt immediately</u>
                       C

by the <u>uncomfortable workers</u>.   <u>No error</u>
      D   E

18 The probability <u>of getting hit</u> by lightning
A

<u>are fewer than</u> the probability <u>of winning</u>
   B   C

the lottery, <u>although both are</u> minuscule.
           D

<u>No error</u>
  E

19 My mother <u>has always believed</u> that everyone
A

<u>should clean</u> <u>their</u> room <u>thoroughly</u> each
  B   C   D

morning or risk bad luck all day.   <u>No error</u>
                            E

20 Eric <u>was so grateful</u> to us for <u>allowing him</u> to
           A   B
spend a weekend <u>on the island</u> that he <u>bought</u>
                   C   D
us back a lovely fruit basket.   <u>No error</u>
                                      E

21 <u>Although</u> we had expected poor service at
    A
the resort, <u>we were</u> more than <u>satisfied at</u> the
              B   C
attention <u>we received</u> throughout our stay.
          D
<u>No error</u>
  E

22 After we <u>had ate</u> a leisurely meal, we walked
         A
<u>down the street</u> and <u>discovered</u> a jazz club
    B   C
where a talented young trio <u>was playing</u>.
                          D
<u>No error</u>
  E

23 <u>Jules and I</u> have been at the same school
    A
<u>since</u> we <u>were</u> 5 years old and <u>will even go</u>
  B   C   D
to college together next fall. <u>No error</u>
                                E

24 <u>Despite</u> the fact that <u>they had</u> lived in France
    A   B
<u>until</u> they were 8 years old, neither of the
    C
boys <u>are</u> able to speak French any more.
       D
<u>No error</u>
  E

25 Some doctors <u>believe that</u> taking vitamins
               A
<u>on a daily basis</u> <u>help</u> decrease a patient's
    B   C
susceptibility <u>to infection</u>. <u>No error</u>
               D   E

26 When my parents <u>went</u> out to dinner, they
               A
left me <u>underneath</u> the <u>control of</u> our
        B   C
babysitter, <u>who lived</u> next door to us.
            D
<u>No error</u>
  E

27 Since 2001, the company <u>has spent</u> <u>more on</u>
                      A   B
employee training than <u>they did</u> in the
                  C
previous 10 years <u>combined</u>. <u>No error</u>
              D   E

28 <u>When teaching</u> high-school students, <u>one</u>
    A   B
must not only command respect but

<u>one should</u> develop rapport <u>as well</u>.
  C   D
<u>No error</u>
  E

29 Since the experiments began, the scientists

<u>have discovered</u> that <u>they</u> can separate the
    A   B
reagents more effectively <u>by using</u> a
                 C
centrifuge machine <u>and not</u> by shaking
             D
the tubes. <u>No error</u>
        E

Directions for "Improving Paragraphs" Questions

Below is an early draft of an essay. It requires revision in many areas.

The questions that follow ask you to make improvements in sentence structure, diction, organization, and development. Answering the questions may require you to understand the context of the passage as well as the rules of standard written English.

Questions 30–35 pertain to the following passage.

(1) While known when he was the President for his abundant energy and muscular build as an adult, Theodore Roosevelt's build as a child was actually quite puny. (2) Stricken with asthma, he was taught early that strenuous physical activity might be dangerous to his health and that, in fact, it might even be fatal. (3) Determined to overcome this obstacle, Roosevelt trained his body relentlessly and built his impressive girth through sheer grit and determination. (4) That these childhood passions stayed with him throughout his adult life should not be surprising. (5) Physical activities, though, were not the only childhood fascination to play a prominent role later in his life.

(6) A skilled hunter, Roosevelt spent much of his leisure time hunting various forms of game. (7) Beginning during his undergraduate days at Harvard, he spent significant time in snow-covered Maine forests as well as the arid deserts of the Dakota territory. (8) As a child, Theodore was so enraptured by birds, he would spend hours observing and writing about them, even phonetically spelling out their various calls and songs. (9) Upon reaching government office, Roosevelt became the first true conservationist, pushing for laws to protect wildlife and resources. (10) He cherished nature in all its forms, seeking to understand its variety through research and experience.

(11) By openly maintaining these passions while in political office, Roosevelt redefined the role of the American politician. (12) While his predecessors had often been aloof with regard to their own personal feelings, Roosevelt advertised his sense of morality by talking openly about it repeatedly with citizens and reporters in speeches and newspapers. (13) In the dawning of a new, industrialized age, Roosevelt chose to take on controversial issues, battling through the spoils system, disputes between management and labor, and the question of imperialism.

30 In context, which of the following is the best revision of sentence 1 (reproduced below)?

While known when he was the President for his abundant energy and muscular build as an adult, Theodore Roosevelt's build as a child was actually quite puny.

(A) While Theodore Roosevelt was known for his energy and muscular build, but the President was actually a quite puny child.

(B) Although known for his abundant energy and muscular build as an adult, President Theodore Roosevelt was actually quite puny as a child.

(C) While puny as a child, Theodore Roosevelt was known for his abundant energy and muscular build while being President.

(D) As President, Theodore Roosevelt was known for his abundant energy and muscular build, not for being puny as a child.

(E) Theodore Roosevelt was puny as a child and was known for his abundant energy and muscular build as President.

31 In context, which of the following is the best revision of the underlined portion of sentence 3 (reproduced below)?

Determined to overcome this obstacle, Roosevelt trained his body relentlessly and built his impressive girth through sheer grit and determination.

(A) (no revision needed)
(B) that this obstacle should be overcome
(C) to overcome such ideas that became obstacles
(D) not to allow this to become an obstacle standing in his way
(E) to take obstacles out of his way

32 Where is the most appropriate place to move sentence 4?

(A) Before sentence 1
(B) Before sentence 2
(C) Before sentence 6, to start the 2nd paragraph
(D) After sentence 10, to end the 2nd paragraph
(E) After sentence 13

33 Which of the following provides the most logical ordering of the sentences in paragraph 2?

(A) 7, 9, 10, 6, 8
(B) 8, 10, 7, 6, 9
(C) 8, 10, 9, 6, 7
(D) 9, 7, 8, 10, 6
(E) 7, 10, 8, 6, 9

34 If the author wanted to make sentence 7 more specific, which of the following details would fit best in the context of the 2nd paragraph?

(A) Roosevelt's age
(B) information about Roosevelt's course of study
(C) details of Roosevelt's activities in the deserts and forests
(D) an explanation of why the climate of Maine is so different from the climate of the Dakota territory
(E) information about Roosevelt's political affiliation prior to these excursions

35 Where is the best place to insert the following sentence?

His brazen moves were often criticized, but Theodore Roosevelt will go down in the annals of history as a man who was always true to himself, whether as a private citizen or as President of the United States.

(A) Before sentence 1
(B) After sentence 1
(C) After sentence 5
(D) Before sentence 11
(E) After sentence 13

STOP

You may check your work, on this section only, until time is called.

Section 5

Time—25 minutes
18 Questions

start: 10:37
end: 11:02

5

Directions for Multiple-Choice Questions

In this section, solve each problem, using any available space on the page for scratchwork. Then decide which is the best of the choices given and fill in the corresponding oval on the answer sheet.

- You may use a calculator on any problem. All numbers used are real numbers.
- Figures are drawn as accurately as possible EXCEPT when it is stated that the figure is not drawn to scale.
- All figures lie in a plane unless otherwise indicated.

Reference Information

$A = \pi r^2$
$C = 2\pi r$

$A = \ell w$

$A = \frac{1}{2}bh$

$V = \ell w h$

$V = \pi r^2 h$

$c^2 = a^2 + b^2$

Special Right Triangles

The arc of a circle measures 360°.
Every straight angle measures 180°.
The sum of the measures of the angles in a triangle is 180°.

1

$2x°$ $3x°$

Note: Figure not drawn to scale.

In the figure above, what is the value of $2x$?

(A) 36
(B) 72
(C) 90
(D) 108
(E) 132

$5x = 180$

$x = 36$

2

While at the laundromat, Erica wrote down the phone number for a nearby pizzeria. Unfortunately, the paper got wet and she could no longer read the last 2 digits. If she dials what she knows of the number and guesses on the missing digits, how many phone numbers does she have to choose from, if she knows only that neither of the last 2 digits is odd?

(A) 5
(B) 25
(C) 36
(D) 50
(E) 100

$10 \times 5 = 50$

5

(D)

GO ON TO THE NEXT PAGE ▶▶▶

3

In the figure above, what is the value of
$a + b + c + d$?

(A)   56
(B)   128
(C)   256
(D)   264
(E)   322

4   If $f(x) = x^2 - 4$, for what positive value of x
does $f(x) = 32$?

(A)   5
(B)   6
(C)   7
(D)   8
(E)   9

5   If the average (arithmetic mean) of x, $x + 1$,
$x + 4$, $2x$, and $5x$ is 11, what is the median of
these numbers?

(A)   5
(B)   9
(C)   10
(D)   11
(E)   25

6   Twenty students in a chemistry class took a
test on which the overall average score was
75. If the average score for 12 of those students was 83, what was the average score for
the remaining members of the class?

(A)   60
(B)   61
(C)   62
(D)   63
(E)   64

7

In the figure above, the vertices of square
$EFGH$ are on the diagonals of square $ABCD$. If
$EF = 8\sqrt{2}$ and $AB = 14\sqrt{2}$, what is the sum of
the lengths $AE + BF + CG + DH$ (heavier lines)?

(A)   24
(B)   28
(C)   32
(D)   36
(E)   38

8

$$\begin{array}{r} RS \\ + \underline{SR} \\ TR4 \end{array}$$

In the correctly worked addition problem
above, each letter represents a different nonzero digit. What is the value of $2R + T$?

(A)   4
(B)   5
(C)   10
(D)   11
(E)   13

GO ON TO THE NEXT PAGE ▶▶▶

Directions for Student-Produced Response Questions

Each of the questions in this section requires you to solve the problem and enter your answer in a grid, as shown below.

- If your answer is 2/3 or .666 . . . , you must enter **the most accurate value the grid can accommodate,** but you may do this in one of four ways:

Start in first column

Start in second column

Grid as a truncated decimal

Grid as a rounded decimal

Grid result here

5

- In the example above, gridding a response of 0.67 or 0.66 is **incorrect** because it is less accurate than those above.
- The scoring machine cannot read what is written in the top row of boxes. You **MUST** fill in the numerical grid accurately to get credit for answering any question correctly. You should write your answer in the top row of boxes only to aid your gridding.
- Do **not** grid in a mixed fraction like $3\frac{1}{2}$ as $\boxed{3}\ \boxed{1}\ \boxed{/}\ \boxed{2}$, because it will be interpreted as $\frac{31}{2}$.
  Instead, convert it to an improper fraction like 7/2 or a decimal like 3.5 before gridding.
- None of the answers will be negative, because there is no negative sign in the grid.
- Some of the questions may have more than 1 correct answer. You must grid only 1 of the correct answers.
- You may use a calculator on any of these problems.
- All numbers in these problems are real numbers.
- Figures are drawn as accurately as possible EXCEPT when it is stated that the figure is not drawn to scale.
- All figures lie in a plane unless otherwise indicated.

9 For all real numbers n, let $\boxed{n}$ be defined by $\boxed{n} = \dfrac{n^2}{16}$. What is the value of $\boxed{4}^2$?

10 If b and d are integers such that $15 < b < 25$ and $5 < d < 10$, what is the greatest possible value of $\dfrac{b}{d}$?

$b = 24$

$d = 6$

$\dfrac{24}{6} = \boxed{4}$

11 If the sum of two numbers is 4 and their difference is 2, what is their product?

$x+y=4$
$x-y=2$
$2x=6$
$x=3$ $y=1$
$\boxed{3}$

12

L 8   16 P 8 M
8   8
$\sqrt{6^2+8^2}$
O 16 N

Note: Figure not to scale.

In rectangle $LMNO$ above, P is the midpoint of side $\overline{LM}$. If the perimeter of the rectangle is 48 and side $\overline{LM}$ is twice the length of side $\overline{LO}$, what is the area of the shaded region?

$P=48$ $LM=2LO$
$48=2LO+2LO+LO+LO$
$48=6LO$
$8=LO$
$\boxed{B6}$

13 If $64^3 = 4^x$, what is the value of x?

$(4^3)^3 = 4^x$
$\boxed{x=9}$

14 Points P, Q, R, and S lie on a line in that order. If $\overline{PS}$ is twice as long as $\overline{PR}$ and 4 times as long as $\overline{PQ}$, what is the value of $\dfrac{QS}{PQ}$?

$\boxed{3}$

15 If $f(x) = \dfrac{(x-1)(2x-1)}{(x-2)(3x-1)}$, what is one possible value of x for which $f(x)$ is not a real number?

$\boxed{2}$

16 If the sum of five consecutive even integers is 110, what is the value of the least of these integers?

$\boxed{20}$

17

NUMBER OF APPLICANTS TO COLLINS COLLEGE	
YEAR	APPLICANTS
1980	15,000
1985	18,000
1990	20,000
1995	24,000
2000	25,000

According to the data in the table above, by what percent did the number of applicants to Collins College increase from 1990 to 1995? (Disregard the % symbol when entering your answer into the grid. For instance, grid 50% as 50.)

18 A jar contains only black, white, and red marbles. If randomly choosing a black marble is 4 times as likely as randomly choosing a white marble and randomly choosing a red marble is 5 times as likely as randomly choosing a black marble, then what is the smallest possible number of marbles in the jar?

$\dfrac{1}{4} = \dfrac{w}{b}$

$4w=b$ $5b=b$

$\boxed{20}$

STOP

You may check your work, on this section only, until time is called.

Section 6

Time—25 minutes
24 Questions

Each of the sentences below is missing one or two portions. Read each sentence, then select the word or words that most logically complete the sentence, taking into account the meaning of the sentence as a whole.

Example:

Rather than accepting the theory unquestioningly, Deborah regarded it with -------.

(A) mirth
(B) sadness
(C) responsibility
(D) ignorance
(E) skepticism

Correct response: (E)

1 If John had not been there to ------- when tensions began to rise at the meeting, a fight would surely have ensued.

(A) intervene
(B) coalesce
(C) harass
(D) intermingle
(E) exacerbate

2 The defendant hoped that the testimony of the surprise witness would corroborate his alibi and ------- him of the crime of which he had been accused.

(A) convoke
(B) synthesize
(C) impeach
(D) absolve
(E) magnify

3 Rachel's ------- driving is not surprising, given that she spends ------- hours each day ensnarled in traffic delays.

(A) antipathy for . . . delightful
(B) penchant for . . . uncountable
(C) predilection for . . . dreary
(D) proclivity for . . . desperate
(E) aversion to . . . insufferable

4 Many medical practices once considered "state of the art" are now thought to be ------- by physicians who are often incredulous that such barbaric acts were once -------.

(A) primitive . . . sanctioned
(B) ingenious . . . approved
(C) boorish . . . censured
(D) innovative . . . endorsed
(E) foolhardy . . . condemned

5 The Prime Minister had vetoed the proposal several times in the past; thus, it came as a great surprise to the public when he ------- the same law in his most recent speech.

(A) articulated
(B) sanctioned
(C) denounced
(D) initiated
(E) abbreviated

GO ON TO THE NEXT PAGE ▶▶▶

The passages below are followed by questions based on their content. Answer each question based on what is stated or implied in the passages or the introductory material preceding them.

Questions 6–7 are based on the following passage.

Line

The reverence for their goddess of protection accounts for the respect Navajos show to the women of their tribe. The tradition is that a man never lifts his hand against a woman,
5 although it is not an unusual thing for a squaw to administer a sound thrashing to a warrior husband who has offended her. All of the sheep, which constitute the great wealth of the tribe, are owned by the women, and in
10 the various families the line of descent is always on the side of the women. The Navajos have little or no idea of a future existence but are firm believers in the transmigration of souls. For this reason they have great rever-
15 ence for different animals and birds, which are supposed to be the re-embodiment of departed spirits of Navajos.

6 Based on the information in the passage, with which of the following statements would the author most likely agree?

(A) Navajo warriors obey their wives obsequiously.
(B) Birds are a particularly vital food source for the Navajo.
(C) A Navajo man who disrespects a woman would likely face censure.
(D) The Navajo do not believe in reincarnation.
(E) In the winter, the Navajo migrate to warmer climates.

7 The word "administer" in line 6 most nearly means

(A) manage
(B) maintain
(C) govern
(D) rehearse
(E) dispense

Questions 8–9 are based on the following passage.

Line

"Dying with dignity" is a topic that has inspired deep debate among the members of the medical community. Should an individual be allowed to determine when he or she wants to
5 die? Should a person who is merely receiving palliative care that provides no hope of a cure be allowed to tell a doctor to stop all treatment so she can die in peace? How can a doctor know if a patient has the mental capacity
10 to decide for herself that the time has come to stop fighting the disease? It is a challenging and persistent debate.

8 As used in line 6, "palliative" most nearly means

(A) punitive
(B) remedial
(C) analgesic
(D) curative
(E) altruistic

9 The passage suggests that in cases of extreme illness, doctors may have difficulty in determining their patients'

(A) state of mind
(B) prognosis
(C) quality of life
(D) tolerance of pain
(E) ability to remember facts

First paragraph: *The Navajo Indians*, William M. Edwardy; *Harper's Weekly*, July 1890
Second paragraph: *Copyright 2004 Mark Anestis. All rights reserved.*

GO ON TO THE NEXT PAGE ▶▶

The passages below are followed by questions based on their contents. Answer each question based on what is stated or implied in the passages or the introductory material preceding them.

Questions 10–16 pertain to the following passage.

The following passage is excerpted from a recent book about seismology, the study of earthquakes.

In the 1970s, there was great optimism about earthquake prediction. A few so-called earth-
Line quake precursors had come to light, and there
was even a theory (known as dilatancy) put
5 forth to explain many of the phenomena that
come before a large earthquake. A series of
foreshocks is an example of a precursor. However, since foreshocks look just like any other
earthquakes, they are not in themselves very
10 useful in prediction. From all points around
the globe, there are numerous anecdotal reports about other precursors, earthquake folk-
lore, if you will.

Many widely reported earthquake precur-
15 sors are related to groundwater. A few hours
before a large earthquake, marked changes
have been reported in the level or flow of wells
and springs. Groundwater has also reportedly
changed temperature, become cloudy, or ac-
20 quired a bad taste. Occasionally, electrostatic
phenomena such as earthquake lights (similar
to St. Elmo's fire that appears on ships during
electrical storms) and changes in the local
magnetic field have been reported. Anecdotal
25 reports also persistently include the strange
behavior of animals, which might be linked to
electrostatic phenomena or foreshocks.
Changes in strain and creep (silent tectonic
motion, without accompanying earthquake)
30 along a fault normally locked by friction could
also be considered precursors.
In China in the 1970s, it became popular
for people to predict earthquakes using "backyard" measurements such as the monitoring
35 of well levels and observation of farm animals.
At least one earthquake, the Haicheng quake
in 1975, was successfully predicted and a
town evacuated, proving that, at least in some
cases, earthquake prediction is possible. The
40 Haicheng earthquake had hundreds of foreshocks, making it an easier-than-average
earthquake to predict. Groundwater changes

and anomalous animal behavior were also reported (for example, hibernating snakes sup-
45 posedly awoke and froze to death). In China,
"evacuation" meant that compulsory outdoor
movies were shown, so that when the quake
did happen and the town was severely dam-
aged, no one was killed. But Chinese seismol-
50 ogists missed predicting the catastrophic
Tangshan earthquake, in which at least
250,000 reportedly perished.

10 Which of the following is the best title for this passage?

(A) The Effects of Earthquakes on Groundwater
(B) The Search for Earthquake Precursors
(C) A Novel Theory of the Origin of Earthquakes
(D) A History of Chinese Earthquakes
(E) How Animals Anticipate Earthquakes

11 The passage indicates that foreshocks are *not . . . very useful* (lines 9–10) in predicting earthquakes because they

(A) are exceptionally difficult to detect
(B) occur simultaneously with changes in groundwater
(C) are not part of the theory of dilatancy
(D) interfere with electrostatic phenomena
(E) are impossible to distinguish from earthquakes themselves

12 According to the passage, which of the following features of groundwater have been reported to change immediately prior to an earthquake (lines 16–20)?

   I. density
  II. clarity
 III. flow

(A) II only
(B) III only
(C) I and II only
(D) II and III only
(E) I, II, and III

Excerpted from *Furious Earth* by Ellen J. Prager, McGraw-Hill, New York, 2000, pp. 80–81

GO ON TO THE NEXT PAGE ▸▸▸

13 Which of the following could be considered a logical inconsistency in the passage?

(A) The passage states that foreshocks are not useful predictors of earthquakes but then cites foreshocks as instrumental to predicting an earthquake.

(B) The passage says that the Chinese are interested in predicting earthquakes but then says that they were devastated by the Tangshan earthquake.

(C) The passage reports that animals behaved strangely before an earthquake but then attributes this behavior to electrostatic phenomena.

(D) The passage states that the town of Haicheng was safely evacuated but then says that its citizens were forced to watch outdoor movies.

(E) The passage suggests that both strain and creep could be considered earthquake precursors.

14 Which of the following best describes the function of the third paragraph?

(A) to describe an application of a theory
(B) to provide an alternative perspective
(C) to recount a scientific experiment
(D) to summarize the ancient origins of a theory
(E) to demonstrate the difficulties of employing a technique

15 The passage suggests that the Tangshan earthquake

(A) was caused by strain and creep
(B) was preceded by changes in the groundwater
(C) caused more damage than the Haicheng earthquake did
(D) was preceded by several foreshocks
(E) was anticipated by the theory of dilatancy

16 In line 46, the word "evacuation" is placed in quotations in order to

(A) imply that an action was ineffective
(B) indicate that it is an archaic term
(C) emphasize the primitiveness of Chinese scientific methods
(D) suggest that a certain practice was unconventional
(E) underscore that an action was intended, but not implemented

Questions 17–24 pertain to the following passage.

The following passage contains an excerpt taken from an anthology of autobiographies of American women.

On landing in America, a grievous disappointment awaited us; my father did not
Line meet us. He was in New Bedford, Massachusetts, nursing his grief and preparing to return
5   to England, for he had been told that the *John Jacob Westervelt* had been lost at sea with every soul on board. One of the missionaries who met the ship took us under his wing and conducted us to a little hotel, where we remained until
10   father had received his incredible news and rushed to New York. He could hardly believe that we were really restored to him; and even now, through the mists of more than half a century, I can still see the expression in his wet eyes
15   as he picked me up and tossed me into the air.

I can see, too, the toys he brought me— a little saw and a hatchet, which became the dearest treasures of my childish days. They were fatidical[1] gifts, that saw and hatchet; in
20   the years ahead of me I was to use tools as well as my brothers did, as I proved when I helped to build our frontier home.

We went to New Bedford with father, who had found work there at his old trade; and
25   here I laid the foundations of my first childhood friendship, not with another child, but with my next-door neighbor, a ship-builder. Morning after morning, this man swung me on his big shoulder and took me to his ship-
30   yard, where my hatchet and saw had violent exercise as I imitated the workers around me. Discovering that my tiny petticoats were in

[1]prophetic

GO ON TO THE NEXT PAGE ▶▶▶

my way, my new friends had a little boy's suit
made for me; and thus emancipated, at this
35 tender age, I worked unwearyingly at his side
all day long and day after day.
    The move to Michigan meant a complete
upheaval in our lives. In Lawrence we had
around us the fine flower of New England
40 civilization. We children went to school; our
parents, though they were in very humble circumstances, were associated with the leading
spirits and the big movements of the day.
When we went to Michigan, we went to the
45 wilderness, to the wild pioneer life of those
times, and we were all old enough to keenly
feel the change.
    Every detail of our journey through the
wilderness is clear in my mind. My brother
50 James met us at Grand Rapids with what, in
those days, was called a lumber-wagon, but
which had a horrible resemblance to a vehicle
from the health department. My sisters and I
gave it one cold look and turned from it; we
55 were so pained by its appearance that we refused to ride in it through the town. Instead,
we started off on foot, trying to look as if we
had no association with it, and we climbed
into the unwieldy vehicle only when the city
60 streets were far behind us.

17 Immediately upon arriving in America, the
author was cared for by

(A) John Jacob Westervelt
(B) her father
(C) a missionary
(D) a childhood friend
(E) a shipbuilder neighbor

18 In line 12, the word "restored" most nearly
means

(A) updated
(B) refurbished
(C) put into storage
(D) deposited
(E) returned

19 Which of the following best describes the relationship between the narrator and the men
in her life?

(A) She gladly provides for their needs.
(B) She considers herself their equal.
(C) She feels overly dependent on them.
(D) She wishes to avoid them.
(E) She believes that they suppress her
     wishes.

20 The author was "emancipated" (line 34) so
that she might more easily

(A) spend time with her father
(B) play with her young friends
(C) travel throughout New Bedford
(D) work with tools
(E) move to Michigan

21 In line 43, the word "movements" most nearly
means

(A) travels
(B) cosmetic alterations
(C) cultural changes
(D) physical actions
(E) mechanical workings

22 The author indicates that she regarded New
England as superior to Michigan in that New
England

  I. had humbler citizens
 II. was more culturally developed
III. had finer gardens

(A) II only
(B) III only
(C) I and II only
(D) II and III only
(E) I, II, and III

6

Excerpted from "The Story of a Pioneer" by Anna Howard Shaw,
   in *Autobiographies of American Women: An Anthology*
   © 1992 by Jill Ker Conway, ed., pp. 475–477

GO ON TO THE NEXT PAGE ▶▶▶

23 The author's attitude toward her move to Michigan is best described as

(A) eager
(B) awed
(C) fearful
(D) resentful
(E) bewildered

24 The sisters refused to ride in the lumber wagon mainly because

(A) they were embarrassed by its appearance
(B) they felt it was unsafe
(C) they had bad memories of it
(D) it was cold
(E) it lacked sufficient room for both of them

6 ➤

STOP

You may check your work, on this section only, until time is called.

Section 7

Time—20 minutes
16 Questions

Directions for Multiple-Choice Questions

In this section, solve each problem, using any available space on the page for scratchwork. Then decide which is the best of the choices given and fill in the corresponding oval on your answer sheet.

- You may use a calculator on any problem. All numbers used are real numbers.
- Figures are drawn as accurately as possible EXCEPT when it is stated that the figure is not drawn to scale.
- All figures lie in a plane unless otherwise indicated.

Reference Information

$A = \pi r^2$ $A = \ell w$ $A = \frac{1}{2} bh$ $V = \ell wh$ $V = \pi r^2 h$ $c^2 = a^2 + b^2$ Special Right Triangles
$C = 2\pi r$

The number of degrees of arc in a circle measures 360.
The measure in degrees of a straight angle is 180.
The sum of the measures in degrees of the angles of a triangle is 180.

---

1 If $4x + 5 = 20$, what is the value of $4x + 8$?

(A) 3
(B) 7
(C) 16
(D) 23
(E) 30

2 If one serving of cereal is $\frac{1}{3}$ cup, how many servings are in 3 pints of cereal? (1 pint = 2 cups)

(A) 3
(B) 9
(C) 18
(D) 27
(E) 36

3

If the radius of the circle with center O above is 4, what is the length of arc RST?

(A) 2π
(B) 4π
(C) 8π
(D) 12π
(E) 16π

4

30°

x

14

$2x$

$x\sqrt{3}$

$7\sqrt{3}$

$x = 7$

Note: Figure not drawn to scale.

In the triangle above, what is the value of x?

(A) 7

(B) $7\sqrt{2}$

(C) $7\sqrt{3}$

(D) $14\sqrt{3}$

(E) $28\sqrt{3}$

5

For $x > 0$, let ∇x be defined by the equation $\nabla x = 3x - 3$. Which of the following is equivalent to $\dfrac{\nabla 7}{\nabla 3}$?

$\nabla = 3x - 3 = 3(x - 1)$

(A) $\nabla 2$

(B) $\nabla 3$

(C) $\nabla 6$

(D) $\nabla 8$

(E) $\nabla 9$

$\dfrac{3(7-1)}{3(3-1)} = \dfrac{6}{2} = 3$

Ⓐ

6

Stephanie can clean a pool in 1 hour, and Mark can clean the same pool in 1.5 hours. If the rate at which they work together is the sum of their rates working separately, how many minutes should they need to clean the pool if they work together? (1 hour = 60 minutes)

(A) 24 minutes

(B) 36 minutes

(C) 60 minutes

(D) 72 minutes

(E) 100 minutes

$r \times t = w$

$S = 60 \quad M = 90$

$90 \times \dfrac{x \cdot 60}{(90)60}$

$90(60)$

7

Which of the following has the greatest value?

(A) $(100^3)^4$

(B) $(100^5)(100^6)$

(C) $(10,000)^4$

(D) $(100^2 \times 100^2)^2$

(E) $(1,000,000)^3$

$100^{12} = 10$

$100^{30} = 10^{2 \cdot 30} = 10^{60}$

100^{12}

10^{24}

Ⓑ

$(10^2)^3$

$(10^{10})(10^{12})$

$\dfrac{100^{11}}{10^{22}}$

8

$\dfrac{2}{3}$

Line m (not shown) is the reflection of line l over the x-axis. What is the slope of line m?

(A) 3/2

(B) 2/3

(C) 0

(D) −2/3

(E) −3/2

9

If $a^2 + b^2 = 4$ and $ab = 5$, what is the value of $(a + b)^2$?

$a^2 + 2ab + b^2 =$

(A) 10

(B) 12

(C) 14

(D) 16

(E) 18

$4 + 2(5) =$

14

Ⓒ

10

The figure above shows the dimensions, in feet, of a stone slab. How many of these slabs are required to construct a rectangular patio 24 feet long and 12 feet wide?

(A) 18

(B) 20

(C) 24

(D) 36

(E) 48

GO ON TO THE NEXT PAGE ▶▶▶

7

11 $12,000 in winnings for a golf tournament were distributed in the ratio of 7:2:1 to the 1st-, 2nd-, and 3rd-place finishers, respectively. How much money did the 1st-place finisher receive?

(A) $1,200
(B) $1,700
(C) $2,400
(D) $8,400
(E) $10,000

$\frac{7}{7+3} = \frac{7}{10}$

$\frac{7}{10}(12000)$

(D)

12 If $2x + 3y = 7$ and $4x - 5y = 12$, what is the value of $6x - 2y$?

(A) 5
(B) 8
(C) 15
(D) 17
(E) 19

$7 + 12 = 19$

(E)

13 If r and s are positive integers and $s + 1 = 2r$, which of the following must be true?

I. s is odd
II. r is even
III. $\dfrac{s}{r} + \dfrac{1}{r}$ is an integer

(A) I only
(B) III only
(C) I and II only
(D) I and III only
(E) I, II, and III

$\frac{s+1}{3+1} =$

$\frac{s+1}{r} = 2$

(D)

14 A bag contains 6 chips, numbered 1 through 6. If 2 chips are chosen at random without replacement and the values on those 2 chips are multiplied, what is the probability that this product will be greater than 20?

(A) 1/30
(B) 1/15
(C) 2/15
(D) 1/5
(E) 13/15

$1, 2, 3, 4, 5, 6$

$(4 \cdot 6) (5 \cdot 6)$

$\frac{3}{36} = \frac{4}{36} = \frac{1}{9}$

(B)

15

$2, -4, -8, 32, -, -, +$

In the sequence above, each term after the 2nd is equal to the product of the 2 preceding terms. For example, the 3rd term, −8, is the product of 2 and −4. How many of the first 100 terms of this sequence are negative?

(A) 33
(B) 34
(C) 50
(D) 66
(E) 67

(D)

16

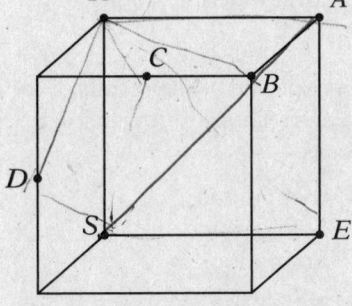

In the figure above, points C and D are midpoints of edges of a cube. A triangle is to be drawn with R and S as 2 of the vertices. Which of the following points should be the 3rd vertex of the triangle if it is to have the largest possible perimeter?

(A) A
(B) B
(C) C
(D) D
(E) E

(B)

STOP

You may check your work, on this section only, until time is called.

7

Section 8

Time—20 minutes
19 Questions

Each of the sentences below is missing one or two portions. Read each sentence, then select the word or words that most logically complete the sentence, taking into account the meaning of the sentence as a whole.

Example:

Rather than accepting the theory unquestioningly, Deborah regarded it with -------.

(A) mirth
(B) sadness
(C) responsibility
(D) ignorance
(E) skepticism

Correct response: (E)

8

1 The latest review for the restaurant was -------, suggesting that the ------- cuisine came close to compensating for the insipid decor.

(A) glowing . . . indefatigable
(B) banal . . . mediocre
(C) ambivalent . . . sublime
(D) severe . . . piquant
(E) antiquated . . . tepid

2 As unexpected as the results of the experiment were, Dr. Thompson refused to characterize them as -------.

(A) meticulous
(B) belligerent
(C) anomalous
(D) convergent
(E) warranted

3 The executives could only hope that the company's poor 1st-quarter performance was not ------- of the year to come.

(A) an amalgam
(B) a harbinger
(C) an arbiter
(D) a deception
(E) a talisman

4 Around 1850, abolitionist and author Frederick Douglass sought to ------- those oppressed by slavery by facilitating the underground railroad, a widespread network of individuals and organizations that worked to transport former slaves out of bondage.

(A) evaluate   (B) encumber   (C) unfetter
(D) disorient   (E) forgo

5 Known for her ------- and decorative poetry, the author demonstrated her ------- by scribing a keenly analytical mystery novel.

(A) flamboyant . . . immutability
(B) austere . . . elegance
(C) unadorned . . . flexibility
(D) florid . . . versatility
(E) grandiloquent . . . insurgence

6 Because the mechanisms by which cancers attack the body are so -------, scientists have been ------- in their efforts to find a universal cure.

(A) efficacious . . . bilked
(B) multifarious . . . stymied
(C) conspicuous . . . thwarted
(D) consistent . . . hampered
(E) lucid . . . proscribed

GO ON TO THE NEXT PAGE ▶▶▶

The questions below are based on the content of the two passages that precede them and the relationship between the passages. The questions are to be answered on the basis of what is stated or implied in the passage itself or the introductory material that precedes the passage.

Questions 7–19 pertain to the following passages.

The following passages are excerpts from a recent debate between two well-known astronomers. The author of passage 1 is a professor of geological sciences and the author of passage 2 is a principal scientist in the Department of Space Studies in Boulder, Colorado.

Passage 1

There is a cultural assumption that there are many alien civilizations. This stems in no
Line small way from the famous estimate by Frank Drake—known as the "Drake Equation"—that
5   was later amended by Drake and Carl Sagan. They arrived at an estimate that there are perhaps a million intelligent civilizations in the Milky Way Galaxy alone.

The Drake and Sagan estimate was based
10   on their best guess about the number of planets in the galaxy, the percentage of those that might harbor life, and the percentage of planets on which life not only could exist but could have advanced to culture. Since our
15   galaxy is but one of hundreds of billions of galaxies in the universe, the number of intelligent alien species would be numbered in the billions. Surely, if there are so many intelligent aliens out there, then the number of
20   planets with life must be truly astronomical. But what if the Drake and Sagan estimates are way off? If, as could be the reality, our civilization is unique in the galaxy, does that mean that there might be much less life in
25   general as well?

In my view, life in the form of microbes or their equivalents is very common in the universe, perhaps more common than even Drake and Sagan envisioned. However, complex life
30   is likely to be far more rare than commonly assumed. Life on earth evolved from single celled organisms to multi-cellular creatures

with tissues and organs, climaxing in animals and higher plants. But is Earth's particular
35   history of life—one of increasing complexity to an animal grade of evolution—an inevitable result of evolution, or even a common one? Perhaps life is common, but complex life— anything that is multicellular—is not.

40   On Earth, evolution has undergone a progressive development of ever more complex and sophisticated forms leading ultimately to human intelligence. Complex life—and even intelligence—could conceivably arise faster
45   than it did on Earth. A planet could go from an abiotic state to a civilization in 100 million years, as compared to the nearly 4 billion years it took on Earth. Evolution on Earth has been affected by chance events, such as the
50   configuration of the continents produced by continental drift. Furthermore, I believe that the way the solar system was produced, with its characteristic number and planetary positions, may have had a great impact on the
55   history of life here.

It has always been assumed that attaining the evolutionary grade we call animals would be the final and decisive step. Once we are at this level of evolution, a long and continuous
60   progression toward intelligence should occur. However, recent research shows that while attaining the stage of animal life is one thing, maintaining that level is quite another. The geologic record has shown that once evolved,
65   complex life is subject to an unending succession of planetary disasters, creating what are known as "mass extinction" events. These rare but devastating events can reset the evolutionary timetable and destroy complex life while
70   sparing simpler life forms. Such discoveries suggest that the conditions allowing the rise and existence of complex life are far more rigorous that are those for life's formation. On some planets, then, life might arise and ani-
75   mals eventually evolve—only to be soon destroyed by a global catastrophe.

Passage 2

It is always shaky when we generalize from experiments with a sample size of one. So we have to be a bit cautious when we fill the cos-
80   mos with creatures based on the time scales of Earth history (it happened so fast here, therefore it must be easy) and the resourcefulness of Earth life (they are everywhere where

First passage: Peter Ward, *Great Debates Part I*, Astrobiology Magazine, 2003
Second passage: David Grinspoon, *Great Debates Part III*, Astrobiology Magazine, 2003

there is water). This is one history, and one
85 example of life.

I am not convinced that the Earth's
carbon-in-water example is the only way for
the universe to solve the life riddle. I am not
talking about silicon, which is a bad idea, but
90 systems of chemical complexity that we have
not thought of, which may not manifest themselves at room temperature in our oxygen atmosphere. The universe is constantly more
clever than we are, and we learn about com-
95 plex phenomena, like life, more through exploration than by theorizing and modeling.
I think there are probably forms of life out
there which use different chemical bases than
we, and which we will know about only when
100 we find them, or when they find us.

An obvious rejoinder to this is, "But no one
has invented another system that works as
well as carbon-in-water." That is true. But to
this I would answer, "We did not invent
105 carbon-in-water!" We discovered it. I don't
believe that we are clever enough to have
thought of life based on nucleic acids and pro-
teins if we hadn't had this example handed to
us. This makes me wonder what else the uni-
110 verse might be using for its refined, evolving
complexity elsewhere, in other conditions that
seem hostile to life as we know it.

I think it is a mistake to look at the many
specific peculiarities of Earth's biosphere and
115 how unlikely such a combination of characteristics seems, and to then conclude that
complex life is rare. This argument can only
be used to justify the conclusion that planets
exactly like Earth, with life exactly like Earth-
120 life, are rare.

My cat, "Wookie" survived life as a near
starving alley cat and wound up as a beloved
house cat through an unlikely series of bio-
graphical accidents, which I won't take up
125 space describing but, trust me, given all of the
incredible things that had to happen in just
the right way, it is much more likely that there
would be no Wookie than Wookie. From this I
do not conclude that there are no other cats
130 (The Rare Cat Hypothesis), only that there are
no other cats exactly like Wookie.

Life has evolved together with the Earth. Life
is opportunistic. The biosphere has taken advantage of the myriad of strange idiosyncrasies
135 that our planet has to offer. So it is easy to look
at our biosphere and conclude that this is the
best of all possible worlds; that only on such a
world could complex life evolve. My bet is that
many other worlds, with their own peculiar

140 characteristics and histories, co-evolve their
own biospheres. The complex creatures on
those worlds, upon first developing intelligence
and science, would observe how incredibly well
adapted life is to the many unique features of
145 their home world. They might naively assume
that these qualities, very different from Earth's,
are the only ones that can breed complexity.

7 The discussion of the Drake equation in the
first paragraph indicates that the author
holds which of the following assumptions?

(A) The Drake equations are too compli-
      cated for most people to understand.
(B) Mathematical formulas can influence
      public opinion.
(C) Sagan did not substantially alter the
      Drake equation.
(D) Mathematics tend to obscure scientific
      exploration.
(E) Drake was not as reputable a scientist
      as Sagan was.

8 Which of the following best describes the
function of the third paragraph?

(A) It asks more questions similar to those
      posed in the second paragraph.
(B) It provides more background informa-
      tion on the debate discussed in the
      passage.
(C) It explains a comment made in the
      second paragraph.
(D) It defines an important term men-
      tioned in the second paragraph.
(E) It presents an opinion contrary to one
      presented in the second paragraph.

9 In line 46, the word "abiotic" most nearly
means

(A) resistant to bacteria
(B) devoid of life
(C) highly populated
(D) extremely advanced
(E) quick growing

10 Which of the following best summarizes the main idea of Passage 1?

(A) The conditions that support complex life may be much more difficult to maintain than is widely assumed.
(B) The Drake equation is not a valid predictor of life in the universe.
(C) Evolution on Earth has made it very unlikely that there would be complex life on other planets.
(D) The number of planets in the universe with complex life is astronomical.
(E) Conditions allowing for the existence of microbes are rare.

11 In line 57, "grade" most nearly means

(A) level
(B) slope
(C) evaluation
(D) life
(E) quantity

12 The author of Passage 1 makes all of the following claims in support of his argument EXCEPT

(A) Complex life on Earth was due in part to haphazard events.
(B) Higher life forms sometimes face the likelihood of extinction due to catastrophic events.
(C) The Earth's carbon-in-water example is probably not the only way for life to come into existence.
(D) Simple forms of life are far more common than highly evolved life forms.
(E) The evolution of life can be affected by the positions of planets around a star.

13 The "sample size of one" (line 78) refers to

(A) the Milky Way galaxy
(B) Drake and Sagan's data
(C) the planet Earth
(D) the Sun of our solar system
(E) mass extinction events

14 The quotations in lines 101–105 serve to

(A) show how the author would respond to someone who disagrees with him
(B) illustrate an argument for why there is no life on neighboring planets
(C) explain a theory the author has disagreed with his entire career
(D) describe a conversation the author had with a colleague
(E) illustrate the author's confusion about the origin of alternate life forms

15 The author includes the anecdote in lines 121–131 in order to

(A) compare his cat to the complex life forms in nearby galaxies
(B) give supporting evidence to the claim that life in the universe is unique to the Earth
(C) caution scientists about drawing premature conclusions from one specific occurrence
(D) mock scientists who believe that animals such as cats can live on other planets
(E) show the result of an evolutionary process

16 In saying that "Life is opportunistic" (lines 132–133), the author of Passage 2 suggests that

(A) only the most cunning animals survive
(B) evolution takes advantage of the unique features of many different environments
(C) humans will likely always be the dominant species on Earth
(D) the theory of evolution is probably wrong
(E) all life forms seek to dominate others

17 The author of Passage 2 suggests that the "complex creatures" discussed in lines 141–147 are likely to believe that

(A) technological advancements are critical to their survival
(B) life is unique to planet Earth
(C) there is no life on other planets
(D) life on all planets originates in the same manner
(E) carbon is essential to the creation of life

GO ON TO THE NEXT PAGE ▶▶▶

18 The author of Passage 1 would most likely respond to the statement in Passage 2 that "The biosphere . . . offer" (lines 133–135) by saying that

(A) our planet also offers many dangers to the biosphere
(B) the biosphere is filled with far more complex life forms
(C) life on Earth has not evolved to such a high level
(D) our planet does not offer so many idiosyncrasies
(E) carbon is one of the most complex elements in the universe

19 The authors of both passages would most likely agree with which of the following statements?

(A) The estimates made by the Drake Equation are surprisingly accurate.
(B) Mass extinction events are not a factor in predicting the existence of extraterrestrial life.
(C) Mathematical models are the most helpful means of learning about the development of life in the universe.
(D) There is likely an abundance of life in the universe that has yet to be discovered.
(E) Complex life is very common in the universe.

STOP *You may check your work, on this section only, until time is called.*

Section 9

Time—10 minutes
14 Questions

Directions for "Improving Sentences" Questions

Each of the sentences below contains one underlined portion. The portion may contain one or more errors in grammar, usage, construction, precision, diction (choice of words), or idiom. Some of the sentences are correct.

Consider the meaning of the original sentence, and choose the answer that best expresses that meaning. If the original sentence is best, choose (A), because it repeats the original phrasing. Choose the phrasing that creates the clearest, most precise, and most effective sentence.

<table>
<tr><td>EXAMPLE:
The children <u>couldn't hardly believe their eyes</u>.
(A) couldn't hardly believe their eyes
(B) would not hardly believe their eyes
(C) could hardly believe their eyes
(D) couldn't nearly believe their eyes
(E) could hardly believe his or her eyes</td><td>EXAMPLE ANSWER
(C)</td></tr>
</table>

9

1 His morning routine included eating an English muffin with grape jelly, <u>then to drink coffee from a styrofoam cup</u>, and sitting down to draw his daily comic strip.

(A) then to drink coffee from a styrofoam cup
(B) drinking coffee from a styrofoam cup
(C) then drink coffee from a styrofoam cup
(D) from a styrofoam cup he would drink coffee
(E) he would drink coffee from a styrofoam cup

2 Pretending to be hurt to avoid running sprints at the end of practice, <u>Mark's attempt failed to convince</u> his coach.

(A) Mark's attempt failed to convince
(B) Mark's attempted to fail to convince
(C) Mark attempt to convince failed
(D) Mark failed to convince
(E) Mark failed but attempt to convince

3 The flier describing the details of the blood drive requested that we <u>are in the hospital lobby</u> promptly at 10 A.M.

(A) are in the hospital lobby
(B) should get at the hospital lobby
(C) be in the hospital lobby
(D) would be to the hospital lobby
(E) should have been at the lobby of the hospital

4 <u>Known for his temper, impatience, and how easily he can be irritated</u>, Dr. McGee was not well-liked by his patients.

(A) Known for his temper, impatience, and how easily he can be irritated
(B) Knowing his temper, impatience and irritability
(C) Known for his temper, impatience and irritability
(D) Known for his temper, impatience and irritation
(E) Known for his temper, for his impatience and his irritability

GO ON TO THE NEXT PAGE ▶▶▶

5 <u>Winning</u> the final match, Courtney gave a gracious speech thanking her competitor, the sponsors, and the spectators.

(A) Winning
(B) Having won
(C) Being that she won
(D) If she had won
(E) For her winning

6 Generally regarded as the most influential social science treatise of the 20th century, <u>John Maynard Keynes wrote a book, *The General Theory of Employment Interest and Money* that</u> forever changed the way scientists looked at the economy.

(A) John Maynard Keynes wrote a book, *The General Theory of Employment Interest and Money* that
(B) a book by John Maynard Keynes, *The General Theory of Employment Interest and Money,* that
(C) John Maynard Keynes' book *The General Theory of Employment Interest and Money* had already
(D) John Maynard Keynes wrote a book *The General Theory of Employment Interest and Money* having
(E) John Maynard Keynes' book *The General Theory of Employment Interest and Money*

7 <u>Neither of the warriors were aware of the massive wounds they had suffered</u> because each was so intently focused on vanquishing the other.

(A) Neither of the warriors were aware of the massive wounds they had suffered
(B) Neither of the warriors was aware of the massive wounds they had suffered
(C) The wounds suffered by the warriors who were not aware
(D) Having suffered massive wounds, neither of the warriors was aware
(E) Despite the wounds suffered, neither of the warriors was aware

8 The Chief of Staff stayed up the entire night to <u>prepare</u> the President's speech for the following night.

(A) to prepare
(B) in preparing
(C) for the preparation of
(D) in order for preparation of
(E) for preparing

9 Twenty-foot high waves crashed into the shore, covering the stores along the <u>boardwalk and many cars in the parking lots were swept away</u>.

(A) boardwalk and many cars in the parking lots were swept away
(B) boardwalk with many cars in the parking lot having been swept away
(C) boardwalk and sweeping away many cars in the parking lot
(D) boardwalk, and the sweeping away of many cars in the parking lot
(E) boardwalk; sweeping away many cars having been in the parking lot

10 <u>The life of the ShinZanu tribesman of the Australian Outback, which are realistically depicted in the books written by Ronald Skinner</u>.

(A) The life of the ShinZanu tribesman of the Australian Outback, which are realistically depicted in the books written by Ronald Skinner.
(B) The books written by Ronald Skinner realistically depict the life of the ShinZanu tribesman of the Australian Outback.
(C) The life of the ShinZanu tribesmen of the Australian Outback being realistically depicted in the books written by Ronald Skinner.
(D) Ronald Skinner realistically depicting in his books the life of the ShinZanu tribesmen of the Australian Outback.
(E) Ronald Skinner, whose books realistically depicting the life of the ShinZanu tribesmen of the Australian Outback.

11   <u>At the age of seven, my father took me to a</u>
<u>baseball game for the very first time.</u>

(A)   At the age of seven, my father took me
to a baseball game for the very first
time.

(B)   At the age of seven, my father took me
to my first baseball game.

(C)   My father took me at seven years old
to a baseball game for the first time.

(D)   When I was seven years old, my father
took me to my first baseball game.

(E)   At the age of seven, I was being taken
by my father to my first baseball game.

12   Dealing skillfully with Congress, President
Ronald Reagan <u>obtained legislation to stim-</u>
<u>ulate economic growth, curb inflation, in-</u>
<u>crease employment, and strengthen national</u>
<u>defense</u>.

(A)   obtained legislation to stimulate economic growth, curb inflation, increase
employment, and strengthen national
defense

(B)   obtained legislation to stimulate economic growth, curb inflation, increase
employment, and strengthening
national defense

(C)   obtaining legislation to stimulate economic growth, curbing inflation,
increasing employment, and strengthening national defense

(D)   obtained legislation to stimulate economic growth, to curb inflation,
increasing employment, and
strengthen national defense

(E)   had obtained legislation to stimulate
economic growth, to curb inflation, to
increase employment, and to
strengthen national defense

13   <u>If anyone asks for a doctor, send them</u> directly to the nurses' station for immediate
assistance.

(A)   If anyone asks for a doctor, send them

(B)   Having asked for a doctor, send them

(C)   When anyone asks for a doctor, they
should be sent

(D)   Had anyone asked for a doctor, send
them

(E)   Send anyone who asks for a doctor

14   <u>Even if they have been declawed as kittens</u>,
adult cats often run their paws along tall objects as if to sharpen their claws.

(A)   Even if they have been declawed as
kittens

(B)   Even though they should have been
declawed when being kittens

(C)   Even when being declawed as kittens

(D)   Declawed when kittens nevertheless

(E)   Declawed as kittens

9

STOP   *You may check your work, on this*
section only, until time is called.

ANSWER KEY

Section 2 Math	Section 5 Math	Section 7 Math	Section 3 Critical Reading	Section 6 Critical Reading	Section 8 Critical Reading	Section 4 Writing	Section 9 Writing
☐ 1. A	☐ 1. B	☐ 1. D	☐ 1. A	☐ 1. A	☐ 1. C	☐ 1. C	☐ 1. B
☐ 2. B	☐ 2. B	☐ 2. C	☐ 2. C	☐ 2. D	☐ 2. C	☐ 2. A	☐ 2. D
☐ 3. D	☐ 3. C	☐ 3. A	☐ 3. B	☐ 3. E	☐ 3. B	☐ 3. D	☐ 3. C
☐ 4. D	☐ 4. B	☐ 4. C	☐ 4. E	☐ 4. A	☐ 4. C	☐ 4. B	☐ 4. C
☐ 5. D	☐ 5. B	☐ 5. A	☐ 5. E	☐ 5. B	☐ 5. D	☐ 5. C	☐ 5. B
☐ 6. E	☐ 6. D	☐ 6. B	☐ 6. A	☐ 6. C	☐ 6. B	☐ 6. E	☐ 6. C
☐ 7. C	☐ 7. A	☐ 7. A	☐ 7. D	☐ 7. E	☐ 7. B	☐ 7. C	☐ 7. B
☐ 8. C	☐ 8. D	☐ 8. B	☐ 8. C	☐ 8. E	☐ 8. E	☐ 8. D	☐ 8. A
☐ 9. A	☐ 9. 1	☐ 9. C	☐ 9. B	☐ 9. A	☐ 9. B	☐ 9. C	☐ 9. C
☐ 10. D	☐ 10. 4	☐ 10. D	☐ 10. E	☐ 10. B	☐ 10. A	☐ 10. C	☐ 10. B
☐ 11. B	☐ 11. 3	☐ 11. D	☐ 11. A	☐ 11. E	☐ 11. A	☐ 11. B	☐ 11. D
☐ 12. B	☐ 12. 32	☐ 12. E	☐ 12. A	☐ 12. D	☐ 12. C	☐ 12. D	☐ 12. A
☐ 13. B	☐ 13. 9	☐ 13. D	☐ 13. A	☐ 13. A	☐ 13. C	☐ 13. C	☐ 13. E
☐ 14. C	☐ 14. 3	☐ 14. C	☐ 14. D	☐ 14. A	☐ 14. A	☐ 14. E	☐ 14. A
☐ 15. B	☐ 15. 2 or 1/3 or .333	☐ 15. D	☐ 15. C	☐ 15. C	☐ 15. C	☐ 15. B	
☐ 16. B	☐ 16. 18	☐ 16. B	☐ 16. D	☐ 16. D	☐ 16. B	☐ 16. D	
☐ 17. D	☐ 17. 20		☐ 17. E	☐ 17. C	☐ 17. D	☐ 17. B	
☐ 18. C	☐ 18. 25		☐ 18. E	☐ 18. E	☐ 18. A	☐ 18. B	
☐ 19. E			☐ 19. A	☐ 19. B	☐ 19. D	☐ 19. C	
☐ 20. D			☐ 20. D	☐ 20. D		☐ 20. D	
			☐ 21. A	☐ 21. C		☐ 21. C	
			☐ 22. B	☐ 22. A		☐ 22. A	
			☐ 23. C	☐ 23. D		☐ 23. E	
			☐ 24. E	☐ 24. A		☐ 24. D	
						☐ 25. C	
						☐ 26. B	
						☐ 27. C	
						☐ 28. E	
						☐ 29. B	
						☐ 30. B	
						☐ 31. A	
						☐ 32. D	
						☐ 33. B	
						☐ 34. C	
						☐ 35. E	

# Right (A):	Questions 1–8	# Right (A):	# Right (A):	# Right (A):	# Right (A):	# Right (A):	# Right (A):
	# Right (A):						
# Wrong (B):	# Wrong (B):	# Wrong (B):	# Wrong (B):	# Wrong (B):	# Wrong (B):	# Wrong (B):	# Wrong (B):
# (A)–¼(B):	# (A)–¼(B):	# (A)–¼(B):	# (A)–¼(B):	# (A)–¼(B):	# (A)–¼(B):	# (A)–¼(B):	# (A)–¼(B):
	Questions 9–18						
	# Right (A):						

SCORE CONVERSION TABLE

How to score your test

Use the answer key on the previous page to determine your raw score on each section. **Your raw score on each section except Section 5 is simply the number of correct answers minus ¼ of the number of wrong answers. On Section 5, your raw score is the sum of the number of correct answers for questions 1–18 minus ¼ of the number of wrong answers in questions 1–8.** Next, add the raw scores from Sections 3, 4, and 7 to get your Math raw score, and add the raw scores from sections 6 and 9 to get your Writing raw score. Write the three raw scores here:

Raw Critical Reading score: _____   Raw Math score: _____   Raw Writing score: _____

Use the table below to convert these to scaled scores.

Scaled scores: Critical Reading: _____   Math: _____   Writing: _____

Raw Score	Critical Reading Scaled Score	Math Scaled Score	Writing Scaled Score	Raw Score	Critical Reading Scaled Score	Math Scaled Score	Writing Scaled Score
67	800			32	520	550	610
66	800			31	510	550	600
65	790			30	510	540	580
64	780			29	500	530	570
63	760			28	490	530	560
62	750			27	490	520	550
61	730			26	480	510	540
60	720			25	480	500	530
59	700			24	470	490	520
58	700			23	460	480	510
57	690			22	460	480	500
56	680			21	450	470	490
55	670			20	440	460	480
54	660	800		19	440	450	470
53	650	790		18	430	450	460
52	650	760		17	420	440	450
51	640	740		16	420	430	440
50	630	720		15	410	420	440
49	620	710	800	14	400	410	430
48	620	700	800	13	400	410	420
47	610	680	800	12	390	400	410
46	600	670	790	11	380	390	400
45	600	660	780	10	370	380	390
44	590	650	760	9	360	370	380
43	590	640	740	8	350	360	380
42	580	630	730	7	340	350	370
41	570	630	710	6	330	340	360
40	570	620	700	5	320	330	350
39	560	610	690	4	310	320	340
38	550	600	670	3	300	310	320
37	550	590	660	2	280	290	310
36	540	580	650	1	270	280	300
35	540	580	640	0	250	260	280
34	530	570	630	−1	230	240	270
33	520	560	620	−2 or less	210	220	250

SCORE CONVERSION TABLE FOR WRITING COMPOSITE
[ESSAY + MULTIPLE CHOICE]

Calculate your writing raw score as you did on the previous page and grade your essay from a 1 to a 6 according to the standards that follow in the detailed answer key.

Essay score: _____   Raw Writing score: _____

Use the table below to convert these to scaled scores.

Scaled score: Writing: _____

Raw Score	Essay Score 0	Essay Score 1	Essay Score 2	Essay Score 3	Essay Score 4	Essay Score 5	Essay Score 6
-2 or less	200	230	250	280	310	340	370
-1	210	240	260	290	320	360	380
0	230	260	280	300	340	370	400
1	240	270	290	320	350	380	410
2	250	280	300	330	360	390	420
3	260	290	310	340	370	400	430
4	270	300	320	350	380	410	440
5	280	310	330	360	390	420	450
6	290	320	340	360	400	430	460
7	290	330	340	370	410	440	470
8	300	330	350	380	410	450	470
9	310	340	360	390	420	450	480
10	320	350	370	390	430	460	490
11	320	360	370	400	440	470	500
12	330	360	380	410	440	470	500
13	340	370	390	420	450	480	510
14	350	380	390	420	460	490	520
15	350	380	400	430	460	500	530
16	360	390	410	440	470	500	530
17	370	400	420	440	480	510	540
18	380	410	420	450	490	520	550
19	380	410	430	460	490	530	560
20	390	420	440	470	500	530	560
21	400	430	450	480	510	540	570
22	410	440	460	480	520	550	580
23	420	450	470	490	530	560	590
24	420	460	470	500	540	570	600
25	430	460	480	510	540	580	610
26	440	470	490	520	550	590	610
27	450	480	500	530	560	590	620
28	460	490	510	540	570	600	630
29	470	500	520	550	580	610	640
30	480	510	530	560	590	620	650
31	490	520	540	560	600	630	660
32	500	530	550	570	610	640	670
33	510	540	550	580	620	650	680
34	510	550	560	590	630	660	690
35	520	560	570	600	640	670	700
36	530	560	580	610	650	680	710
37	540	570	590	620	660	690	720
38	550	580	600	630	670	700	730
39	560	600	610	640	680	710	740
40	580	610	620	650	690	720	750
41	590	620	640	660	700	730	760
42	600	630	650	680	710	740	770
43	610	640	660	690	720	750	780
44	620	660	670	700	740	770	800
45	640	670	690	720	750	780	800
46	650	690	700	730	770	800	800
47	670	700	720	750	780	800	800
48	680	720	730	760	800	800	800
49	680	720	730	760	800	800	800

Detailed Answer Key

Section 1

The following essay received 12 points out of a possible 12. This means that, according to the graders, it

- develops an insightful point of view on the topic
- demonstrates exemplary critical thinking
- uses effective examples, reasons, and other evidence to support its thesis
- is consistently focused, coherent and well-organized
- demonstrates skillful and effective use of language and sentence structure
- is largely (but not necessarily completely) free of grammatical and usage errors

Consider carefully the issue discussed in the following passage, then write an essay that answers the question posed in the assignment.

> Many among us like to blame violence and immorality in the media for a "decline in morals" in society. Yet these people seem to have lost touch with logic. Any objective examination shows that our society is far less violent or exploitative than virtually any society in the past. Early humans murdered and enslaved each other with astonishing regularity, without the help of gangsta rap or Jerry Bruckheimer films.

Assignment: **Does violence and immorality in the media make our society more dangerous and immoral?** Write an essay in which you answer this question and discuss your point of view on this issue. Support your position logically with examples from literature, the arts, history, politics, science and technology, current events, or your experience or observation.

One of the most misguided notions of conventional wisdom is that depicting violence in the media makes our society more violent. A close examination shows that this claim is baseless. Societies with severe restrictions on violence in the media tend to be more, not less, violent than those with no such restrictions. Indeed, despite the popular myth of a more peaceful past, societies were far more violent before the advent of movies, television, and video games. Societies that restrict access to "immoral" western movies are the same ones that call their citizens to violent and irrational holy war.

As Michael Moore pointed out poignantly in the movie "Bowling for Columbine," Americans kill each other with firearms at a far greater rate than almost any other first-world nation. But he is quick to point out that our media is not more violent than those in Japan or Germany or even Canada, which have rates of violence that are a full order of magnitude lower than ours. Indeed, the killers among us are not likely to spend a lot of time listening to Marilyn Manson or playing Mortal Kombat on their Playstations, despite what our more nearsighted and sanctimonious politicians and preachers would like us to believe. Ted Kaczynski, the Unabomber, lived in a one-room shack without electricity or running water, let alone cable. But even if murderers like Kaczynski were video game addicts, attributing their motives to media violence would be missing the point entirely.

People who are habitually violent have adopted a "war mentality." They tend to see the world in black-and-white, us-against-them terms. Tragically, our leaders tend to have this very same mentality, but they couch it in "patriotism." Lobbing cruise missiles and landing marines in another country is not considered a horrible last resort, but a patriotic duty. If we wish to understand why Americans are more violent than the Japanese, violence in the media will hold no answers; Japanese kids watch just as much violence. Foreign policy is far more telling: which country has leaders who engage in violence against other countries at every opportunity, and constantly try to convince us that it's right?

If our pundits and politicians were truly concerned about making a safer world—and there are many reasons to believe they are not, since they profit the most from a fearful citizenry—they would begin by acknowledging that violence is almost a desperate grab for control from a person or people who believe they are being repressed. If we want a more peaceful and noble society, then we will stop coercing other countries with violence and economic oppression. As Franklin Roosevelt said, "We have nothing to fear but fear itself." We are the most fearful nation on the planet, and we are paying for it.

People say that society today is much more violent due to all of the media portrayal of violence we see on a daily basis. The nightly news is often made up entirely of stories about murders, muggings, arson, and other gruesome crimes. The most successful shows on television are the investigative crime shows in which they solve disturbing murder mysteries. Movies like the Lord of the Rings contain gory fight scenes that show the death of hundreds of characters. It's hard even to find a video game anymore that doesn't somehow relate back to fighting.

Those who don't believe that violence breeds violence would argue that the United States murder rate had declined to its lowest level in 30 years and that this is proof that the violence in the media has not in fact made for a more violent society. But what they conveniently leave out is the fact that at the same time, youth gun killings were on the rise. This is who is being affected by the increased exposure to violence—the children. It is perhaps the video game violence and television/movie violence that can be held responsible.

Kids today are growing up in a society where violence is everywhere. It is difficult for a child to go through the day without witnessing some violent act on TV or hearing about a gruesome murder on the radio. A recent study we learned about in class concluded that because of what they see on television, children become immune to violence, accept it as something that is part of a "normal" life, and they often times will attempt to imitate what they see on television because it "looks fun."

Something needs to be done to reverse this trend of growing violence in our country and tighter regulation of the amount of violence on television, in music, and in the movies would be a great place to start. The youth of this country need to be reminded that violence is not an acceptable part of daily existence and that it should be avoided at all costs.

The following essay received 4 points out of a possible 12, meaning that it demonstrates *some incompetence* in that it

- has a seriously limited point of view
- demonstrates weak critical thinking
- uses inappropriate or insufficient examples, reasons, and other evidence to support its thesis
- is poorly focused and organized and has serious problems with coherence
- demonstrates frequent problems with language and sentence structure
- contains errors in grammar and usage that obscure the author's meaning seriously

Believing that the violence in the media has made the members of our society like violent murderers is an absurd notion. Sure, there are lots video games on the market that involve fighting ninjas and battling army troops. Yes, nightly television shows on the public television networks show many a violent episode. Sure, the nightly news is covered with violent crimes and such. For instance, the popular music of this era is full of violent references and foul language. But, no experiment or statistics that I have seen proves the above statement to be true. Just because a teenager kills over 500 fake people on his ninja fighting videogame, it does not mean that after he turns off the game console that he will run outside in his ninja costume and start attacking the people in his neighborhood. It is absurd to say that violence is because of all the violence on video games television. Actually I think that video games make you better at eye-hand coordination which is a valuable skill. Hundreds of years before video games and movies and television, there were murder and violence. Human beings are violent people and the exposure to violence does not make us more violent than we already were. If we did not have all of these impressive technological advances such as radio, television and film, we would still be committing acts of violence. There will always be violent humans that are ready to hurt others to get what they want and eliminating violent references from our music and television shows might even make people madder.

Section 2

1. A
$$(x+4)+7=14$$
Subtract 7: $\quad x+4=7$
Subtract 4: $\quad x=3$
(Chapter 11 Lesson 1: Solving Equations)

2. B Write out a mathematical equation for how you would actually find the cost for the month: $\$.95 \times 31$. Answer choice B, $\$1.00 \times 30$, is closest to that amount.
(Chapter 10 Lesson 1: Numbers and Operations)

3. D A linear angle measures 180°. Write an equation:
$$w+x+50=180°$$
Subtract 50°: $\quad w+x=130°$
(Chapter 13 Lesson 1: Lines and Angles)

4. D
$$g(x)=3x+4$$
Substitute 5 for x: $\quad g(5)=3(5)+4$
Simplify: $\quad g(5)=15+4=19$
(Chapter 14 Lesson 2: Functions)

5. D The difference between x and y is $(x-y)$.
The sum of x and y is $(x+y)$.
The product of those two is equal to 18:
$$(x-y)(x+y)=18$$
FOIL: $\quad x^2-xy+xy-y^2=18$
Combine like terms: $\quad x^2-y^2=18$
(Chapter 11 Lesson 5: Factoring)

6. E
$$3\sqrt{x}-7=20$$
Add 7: $\quad 3\sqrt{x}=27$
Divide by 3: $\quad \sqrt{x}=9$
Square both sides: $\quad x=81$
(Chapter 11 Lesson 4: Working with Roots)

7. C Let b = cost of chocolate bar and g = cost of gum.
$$b+g=\$1.75$$
Chocolate bar is $\$.25$ more: $\quad b=\$.25+g$
Substitute for b: $\quad \$.25+g+g=\$1.75$
Combine like terms: $\quad \$.25+2g=\$1.75$
Subtract $\$.25$: $\quad 2g=\$1.50$
Divide by 2: $\quad g=\$.75$
(Chapter 11 Lesson 1: Solving Equations)

8. C First find 40% of 80: $.40 \times 80 = 32$

Now find what percent of 96 is 32.

Translate: $\quad \dfrac{x}{100}\times 96=32$

Multiply by 100: $\quad 96x=3,200$
Divide by 96: $\quad x=33\frac{1}{3}$
(Chapter 10 Lesson 5: Percents)

9. A If $lm=21$ and both l and m are integers, then m must either 1, 3, 7, or 21. If $mn=39$, however, then m must also be a factor of 39, so it must be 3. Therefore, $l=21/3=7$ and $n=39/3=13$, so $n>l>m$.
(Chapter 11 Lesson 6: Inequalities, Absolute Values, and Plugging In)

10. D There's no need to do a lot of calculation here. Look for the 2 adjacent bars with the greatest positive difference between them. Since 1999 shows the least profits of all the years on the graph and 2000 shows the greatest profits of any year on the graph, 1999–2000 must have the greatest change in profit.
(Chapter 14 Lesson 5: Data Analysis)

11. B A Venn diagram can help you with this problem: Imagine that the 4 students who play 2 sports play soccer and tennis. (It doesn't matter which specific pair of sports they play.) This means that $12-4=8$ students play just soccer, $7-4=3$ students play just tennis, and 9 students play just lacrosse. This shows that there is a total of $9+8+4+3=24$ students.
(Chapter 12 Lesson 5: Counting Problems)

12. B To solve this problem, you need to find the distance between the center of the circle (14, 14) and the point on the circle (2, 9). To do this, you can use the distance formula.

You can also draw a right triangle connecting the two points. It gives you a triangle with one leg of 5 and one leg of 12. Set up the Pythagorean Theorem and solve for r.

$$5^2+12^2=r^2$$
Simplify: $\quad 25+144=r^2$
Combine like terms: $\quad 169=r^2$
Take square root: $\quad 13=r$
The diameter is twice the radius $=2(r)=2(13)=26$.
(Chapter 13 Lesson 3: The Pythagorean Theorem)

13. B The population doubles every 18 months. Start with January of 2000 and start doubling.

	January 2000	12,000
18 months later:	July 2001	24,000
18 months later:	January 2003	48,000
18 months later:	July 2004	96,000

(Chapter 12 Lesson 3: Numerical Reasoning Problems)

14. C Use the Fundamental Counting Principle from Chapter 12 Lesson 5. To arrange these students, 5 choices must be made. First select the students for each end. Since one of the 5 (the tallest) cannot go on either end, you have 4 students to choose from for 1 end and then, once that choice has been made, 3 students to choose from for the other end:

$$\underset{*}{4} \; \_\_ \; \_\_ \; \_\_ \; \underset{*}{3}$$

Now fill the remaining spots. There are 3 students left to choose from for the 2nd spot:

$$\underset{*}{4} \; 3 \; \_\_ \; \_\_ \; \underset{*}{3}$$

Then, once that selection has been made, there are 2 for the next spot, then 1 for the remaining spot:

$$4 \; 3 \; 2 \; 1 \; 3$$

To find the total number of possible arrangements, simply multiply: $4 \times 3 \times 2 \times 1 \times 3 = 72$.
(Chapter 12 Lesson 5: Counting Problems)

15. B From the diagram, we know that $a + b + c = 180$, and we know that $b = c + 3$.

If you want b to be as large as possible, then you need to make the sum of a and c as small as possible. The smallest integer value of a possible is 91. So let's say that $a = 91$.

Substitute 91 for a:	$91 + b + c = 180$
Substitute $c + 3$ for b:	$91 + c + 3 + c = 180$
Combine like terms:	$94 + 2c = 180$
Subtract 94:	$2c = 86$
Divide by 2:	$c = 43$

So 43 is the largest possible value of c; this means that $43 + 3 = 46$ is the largest possible value of b.
(Chapter 13 Lesson 2: Triangles)

16. B Begin by finding the area of the big equilateral triangle. An equilateral triangle with sides of length 4 has a height of $2\sqrt{3}$, because the height divides the triangle into 2 30°–60°–90° triangles.

Area = ½(base)(height) = ½(4)($2\sqrt{3}$) = $4\sqrt{3}$

The big triangle is divided into 4 equal parts, 3 of which are shaded, so the shaded area is ¾ of the total area.

Shaded area = ¾($4\sqrt{3}$) = $3\sqrt{3}$
(Chapter 13 Lesson 5: Areas and Perimeters)

17. D Just look at the graph and draw a line at $y = 1$.

The y-values of the graph are at or above that line from $x = -4$ to $x = -2$ and from $x = 2$ to $x = 4$.
(Chapter 14 Lesson 2: Functions)

18. C This table shows all of the $5 \times 5 = 25$ possible values of ab:

x	2	4	6	8	10
1	2	4	6	8	10
3	6	12	18	24	30
5	10	20	30	40	50
7	14	28	42	56	70
9	18	36	54	72	90

Of those, only the 7 shaded values are greater than 20 and less than 50, so the probability is 7/25.
(Chapter 12 Lesson 6: Probability Problems)

19. E

$$(w^a)(w^5) = w^{15}$$

Simplify:	$w^{5+a} = w^{15}$
Equate the exponents:	$5 + a = 15$
Subtract 5:	$a = 10$

$$(w^4)^b = w^{12}$$

Simplify:	$w^{4b} = w^{12}$
Equate the exponents:	$4b = 12$
Divide by 4:	$b = 3$

So $a + b = 10 + 3 = 13$.
(Chapter 11 Lesson 3: Working with Exponentials)

20. D The graph of $y = f(x - 2)$ is the graph of $y = f(x)$ shifted to the right 2 units without changing its shape. Therefore, the "peak" at point (6, 4) should shift to (8, 4).
(Chapter 14 Lesson 3: Transformation)

Section 3

1. **A**   The word *although* indicates a contrast. Raúl purchased his computer only 10 months ago, but technology has been improving so fast that it is already *outdated*. *obsolete* = outdated; *adjunct* = auxiliary, or additional; *novel* = new, innovative; *elusive* = hard to catch

2. **C**   The admissions committee is looking to justify offering more scholarships to increase the number of applications, so the number of applicants must be *decreasing*. *mushroom* = expand rapidly; *plummet* = decrease rapidly; *satiate* = satisfy; *burgeon* = grow

3. **B**   If the father will not consider another person's viewpoint to be valid if it differs from his own, he must be pretty *stubborn* or *arrogant*. *pragmatic* = practical; *dogmatic* = arrogantly authoritative; *phlegmatic* = sluggish; *cordial* = polite; *curt* = abrupt and rude

4. **E**   The books are written for children but are still *enjoyable* to adults. *penned* = written; *prosaic* = dull; *morose* = gloomy; *censored* = cleansed of profanity; *incongruous* = not compatible; *tedious* = boring, dull; *authored* = written; *engaging* = captivating, interesting

5. **E**   Julia is at the top of her class, but if this is hard to believe, she must approach her work in a *lazy* or *irresponsible* way. *adept* = skilled; *diligent* = hardworking; *fanatical* = obsessive and crazy; *extroverted* = outgoing; *laggardly* = slow-moving, lagging behind

6. **A**   The President's opponents were always cautious about debating him, so the President must be *highly skilled* or *intimidating* or *mean*. *redoubtable* = formidable, imposing; *staid* = calm, not outwardly emotional; *magnanimous* = generous; *stoic* = indifferent to pain or pleasure

7. **D**   The new clothing line was described as being *eclectic* (containing much variety). It ranged from *modest* (not showy) and *unadorned* (undecorated) to -------- and *garish* (flashy). By parallelism, the missing word should be in opposition to the word *modest*. *austere* = severe, stern; *prophetic* = able to tell the future; *cordial* = polite; *ostentatious* = showy; *solitary* = alone

8. **C**   The textbook *includes all of the essential information* but it is not *verbose* (wordy); the 2 missing words should be parallel to *containing lots of information* and *not verbose*. *compendious* = succinct; *circumlocutory* = talking around the subject, indirect; *reprehensible* = blameworthy; *terse* = concise; *comprehensive* = including a large amount of information; *concise* = brief and to the point; *grandiloquent* = speaking in a pompous manner; *painstaking* = done with great care; *redundant* = repetitive

9. **B**   Saying that we were *raised in unrivaled prosperity* is like saying that the economy has been very strong and *abundant*.

10. **E**   The "people" are plagued by *deep divisions* (line 9), and the *citizens* are the only ones who are not *growing to appreciate the difference between America and the United States* (lines 21–23). Therefore, the *people* lack unity, while the *citizens* lack awareness.

11. **A**   Don't miss the word *EXCEPT* in the question. Choice B is supported in line 14, choice C in line 7, choice D in line 8, and choice E in line 8. The last lines say that *ambition for a better life is universal*, implying that *not* everyone is happy with the status of their lives.

12. **A**   Unlike Passage 1, Passage 2 discusses the difference between the ideal of America and the reality of the United States

13. **A**   The questions in the opening lines show the man's *confusion*, and the woman is said to talk *ardently* (passionately).

14. **D**   The author says that one *who is suddenly overwhelmed by terror cannot afterwards remember the exact order of sounds accompanying the catastrophe which stuns him*—that is, he becomes disoriented.

15. **C**   Line 11 suggests that Ognev is stunned by a *catastrophe*. The context of the passage makes it clear that this catastrophe is the expression of love from Vera, which Ognev has difficulty understanding.

16. **D**   In saying that *she had been struck by . . . the aims and objects of his life* (lines 23–25) the author is saying that she was impressed with Ognev's *life goals*.

17. **E**   In lines 42–44, the passage states that *much as he wanted to, he could feel no joy; no fundamental happiness*. In other words, the *bad and strange* thing was *disaffection*.

18. **E**   In lines 51–52, the passage states that *Vera's raptures and suffering seemed to him* (Ognev) *to be only cloying* (excessively sweet) *and trivial* (of little significance). He felt her passion to be unimportant and was *outraged at himself* for feeling this way. To him, his *statistics, books or philosophical truths* were more important than this passion.

19. **A**   The final sentence of the passage states that *he was annoyed and blamed himself even though he himself did not understand why he was to blame*. Ognev is confused and uncertain about how he *should* feel about Vera's passion. He feels indifference but thinks he should feel something different.

20. D In lines 21–22 the marchers are described as *singing to hide their exhaustion* and then as *trying not to fear. . . .* This commitment to hiding emotion is *stoicism.*

21. A Lines 35–38 criticize the bill's *failure to protect the right of African Americans to vote "when local officials are determined to deny it."* In other words, it did not sufficiently pressure local officials to extend voting rights to all citizens.

22. B In context, saying that *his . . . encounter with Mexican-American children* was *shattering* is like saying that the encounter bothered the President and had a major impact on the way he approached civil rights issues later in his career.

23. C Johnson indicates that he inferred, by looking into his students' eyes, that they knew that others disliked them. This indicates a strong empathy with his students, because he inferred it not from their words but from their expressions.

24. E Lines 52–54 say that Johnson *made the nationwide audience aware of how deeply personal the issue of African American rights was to him* and lines 60–62 that *he spoke more directly, more explicitly, and more warmly of the human experience of prejudice than any president before him.* In other words, he addressed it directly and in personal terms.

Section 4

1. C The word *group* is the singular subject, so the verb should be *was.*
(Chapter 18 Lesson 1: Subject-Verb Disagreement)

2. A The original phrasing is best.

3. D *Timothy* must follow the opening modifiers, because he is the one who is *timid and self-conscious.* The original phrasing is wrong, however, because *give full expression towards* is awkward and unidiomatic. Choice B is wrong because *managed full expression of* is awkward and unidiomatic.
(Chapter 18 Lesson 10: Idiom Errors)
(Chapter 18 Lesson 8: Other Misplaced Modifiers)

4. B The phrase *studying in preparation for* is awkward, redundant, and unidiomatic.
(Chapter 18 Lesson 12: Other Modifier Problems)
(Chapter 18 Lesson 10: Idiom Errors)

5. C The phrase *on an overseas journey* is redundant because the next phrase is *across the Atlantic Ocean.*
(Chapter 18 Lesson 12: Other Modifier Problems)

6. E The original phrasing is a sentence fragment. Choice E is better than choice C because, idiomatically, being a *home fixture* means being an *appliance,* while being a *fixture in the homes* means being a *welcome figure in the homes.*
(Chapter 18 Lesson 15: Coordinating Ideas)

7. C This phrasing is most parallel and concise.
(Chapter 18 Lesson 3: Parallelism)

8. D The use of *therefore* in the original phrasing is illogical, because the ideas in the sentence are related not as a cause and effect but rather as a contrast. The use of *actually* in choice D conveys the appropriate irony.
(Chapter 18 Lesson 15: Coordinating Ideas)
(Chapter 15 Lesson 7: Write Logically)

9. C Because the sneaking is not a part of the *effort to open several of her presents* but rather an action that preceded it, the original phrasing is awkward and illogical.
(Chapter 15 Lesson 7: Write Logically)

10. C The definite pronoun *it* is required to relate it to its antecedent *music.*
(Chapter 18 Lesson 5: Pronoun Antecedent Disagreement)

11. B The opening participial phrase modifies *Clarence Darrow,* not his oratory, so the original phrasing leaves a dangling participle. Choice B is less awkward than D.
(Chapter 18 Lesson 7: Dangling and Misplaced Participles)

12. D The subject of this verb is *delivery,* which is singular, so the verb should be *has been.*
(Chapter 18 Lesson 1: Subject-Verb Disagreement)

13. C The pronoun *whose* is personal and so should not refer to an inanimate object like a *charming cottage.* A better phrase here is *with rooms that are.*
(Chapter 18 Lesson 5: Pronoun-antecedent Disagreement)

14. E The sentence is correct.

15. B The subject of this verb is *photographs . . . and diagrams,* which is plural, so the verb should be *were.*
(Chapter 18 Lesson 1: Subject-Verb Disagreement)

16. **D**   This is a comparison error. The *way in which chimpanzees form friendships* cannot logically be compared to *humans*. Instead, the phrase should be *to the way humans form friendships*.
(Chapter 18 Lesson 4: Comparison Problems)

17. **B**   As a noun, *affects* means *feelings or emotions*, so its use here is a diction error. The proper word is *effects*.
(Chapter 18 Lesson 11: Diction Errors)

18. **B**   There are 2 errors in this phrase. First, the subject *probability* is singular, so the verb should be *is*. Second, a probability can be *lower* than another, but not *fewer* than another.
(Chapter 18 Lesson 1: Subject-Verb Disagreement)
(Chapter 18 Lesson 4: Comparison Problems)

19. **C**   *Everyone* is singular, so the pronoun should be changed to the singular *his or her*.
(Chapter 18 Lesson 5: Pronoun-Antecedent Disagreement)

20. **D**   The word *bought* is the past tense of the verb *to buy*. But Eric clearly did not *buy back* the basket. The correct word here is *brought*.
(Chapter 18 Lesson 11: Diction Errors)

21. **C**   People are satisfied *with* things, not *at* them.
(Chapter 18 Lesson 10: Idiom Errors)

22. **A**   The phrase *had ate* is an incorrect past perfect form. The correct form is *had eaten*. In this case, however, the word *after* conveys the time sequence, so the past perfect form isn't strictly necessary: *ate* (but not *had ate*) is an acceptable alternative.
(Chapter 18 Lesson 9: Tricky Tenses)

23. **E**   The sentence is correct.

24. **D**   The word *neither* is a singular subject of the verb, so the correct form is *is*.
(Chapter 18 Lesson 1: Subject-Verb Disagreement)

25. **C**   The subject of the verb *help* is *taking*, which is singular. Think of the subject as *it*. The word *help* should instead be *helps*.
(Chapter 18 Lesson 1: Subject-Verb Disagreement)

26. **B**   The word *underneath* means physically below something. The word should instead be *under*.
(Chapter 18 Lesson 10: Idiom Error)

27. **C**   The subject *they* is referring to *the company*, which is singular. *They* should instead be *it*.
(Chapter 18 Lesson 1: Subject-Verb Disagreement)

28. **E**   The sentence is correct.

29. **B**   The subject *they* is ambiguous. It is not easy to tell if the *they* is referring to the *experiments* or the *scientists*.
(Chapter 18 Lesson 5: Pronoun-Antecedent Disagreement)

30. **B**   This phrasing is the most concise and logical of the choices.
(Chapter 15 Lesson 7: Write Logically)

31. **A**   The original phrasing is best.

32. **D**   Because the sentence refers to *these passions*, it is most logically placed after those passions are described. It also provides a logical transition to the third paragraph.
(Chapter 15 Lesson 7: Write Logically)

33. **B**   This order places the sentences in proper logical and chronological order: (8) identifies his childhood passion, (10) identifies his goals for this passion, (7) proceeds to his college years, (6) mentions where he pursued his passions, and (9) describes the connection between these passions and his later career.
(Chapter 15 Lesson 7: Write Logically)

34. **C**   The paragraph as a whole discusses Roosevelt's passion for nature, so details about his activities in these natural settings would be relevant.
(Chapter 15 Lesson 7: Write Logically)

35. **E**   This sentence would be a good conclusion to the passage because it gives historical perspective to the specific ideas in the passage.
(Chapter 15 Lesson 12: Finish with a Bang)

Section 5

1. **B**   There are 180° on the side of a line.

$$2x + 3x = 180°$$

Combine like terms: $5x = 180°$
Divide by 5: $x = 36°$
Multiply by 2: $2x = 72°$
(Chapter 13 Lesson 1: Lines and Angles)

2. **B**   Erica knows that *neither* of the last two digits is odd, so each is 0, 2, 4, 6, or 8. Since there are 5 possibilities for each digit, there are $5 \times 5 = 25$ possible arrangements.
(Chapter 12 Lesson 5: Counting Problems)

3. **C** There are 180° in a triangle. Set up equations for the two triangles in the figure.

$$a + b + 52 = 180$$
Subtract 52: $$a + b = 128$$
$$c + d + 52 = 180$$
Subtract 52: $$c + d = 128$$
$$a + b + c + d =$$
Substitute: $$128 + 128 = 256$$

(Chapter 13 Lesson 2: Triangles)

4. **B** $$f(x) = x^2 - 4$$
Set $f(x)$ equal to 32: $$x^2 - 4 = 32$$
Add 4: $$x^2 = 36$$
Take positive square root: $$x = 6$$

(Chapter 14 Lesson 2: Functions)

5. **B** Set up an equation to find the average.

$$\frac{x + (x+1) + (x+4) + 2x + 5x}{5} = 11$$

Multiply by 5: $$x + (x + 1) + (x + 4) + 2x + 5x = 55$$
Combine like terms: $$10x + 5 = 55$$
Subtract 5: $$10x = 50$$
Divide by 10: $$x = 5$$
Plug in 5 for x to find the values:

$$x, (x + 1), (x + 4), 2x, 5x$$
$$5, 6, 9, 10, 25$$

The median is the middle number, which is 9.
(Chapter 12 Lesson 2: Mean/Median/Mode Problems)

6. **D** If 20 students scored an average of 75 points, then the sum of their scores is $20 \times 75 = 1{,}500$ total points.

If 12 of those students scored an average of 83 points, then the sum of their scores is $12 \times 83 = 996$ points.

Therefore, the remaining 8 students scored $1{,}500 - 996 = 504$ points altogether, so their average score is $504 \div 8 = 63$ points.

(Chapter 12 Lesson 2: Mean/Median/Mode Problems)

7. **A** The sides of square *EFGH* all have length $8\sqrt{2}$. A diagonal of this square can be found with the Pythagorean Theorem: $(8\sqrt{2})^2 + (8\sqrt{2})^2 = \overline{EG}^2$.

Simplify: $$128 + 128 = \overline{EG}^2$$
$$256 = \overline{EG}^2$$
Take square root: $$16 = \overline{EG}$$

(Or, more simply, you can remember that the length of the diagonal of a 45°-45°-90° triangle is the length of the side times $\sqrt{2}$. So the diagonal is $8\sqrt{2} \times \sqrt{2} = 16$.) By the same reasoning, since the sides of square *ABCD* all have length $14\sqrt{2}$: $\overline{AD} = 14\sqrt{2} \times \sqrt{2} = 28$.

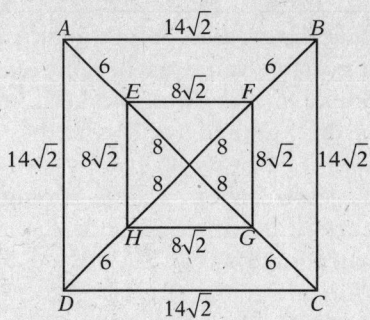

Notice that $\overline{AC} = \overline{AE} + \overline{EG} + \overline{CG}$; therefore, $28 = \overline{AE} + 16 + \overline{CG}$, so $\overline{AE} + \overline{CG} = 12$. By the same reasoning, $\overline{BF} + \overline{DH} = 12$, so $\overline{AE} + \overline{BF} + \overline{CG} + \overline{DH} = 24$.
(Chapter 13 Lesson 3: The Pythagorean Theorem)

8. **D** Although you were probably taught to add the "rightmost" digits first, here the "leftmost" digits provide more information about the number, so it's best to start there.

$$\begin{array}{r} RS \\ +SR \\ \hline TR4 \end{array}$$

The largest possible 3-digit number that can be formed by adding two 2-digit numbers is $99 + 99 = 198$. Therefore, T must be 1.

$$\begin{array}{r} RS \\ +SR \\ \hline 1R4 \end{array}$$

Therefore, there must be a "carry" of 1 from the addition of $R + S$ in the 10s column. Looking at the units column tells us that $S + R$ yields a units digit of 4, so $S + R = 14$. The addition in the 10s column tells us that $R + S + 1 = R + 10$. (The "+10" is needed for the carry into the 100s column.)

$$R + S + 1 = R + 10$$
Substitute $R + S = 14$: $$14 + 1 = R + 10$$
Subtract 10: $$5 = R$$
So $2R + T = 2(5) + 1 = 11$.
(Chapter 12 Lesson 3: Numerical Reasoning Problems)

9. **I** $$\boxed{n} = \frac{n^2}{16}$$

If it helps, you can think of this as $f(n) = \dfrac{n^2}{16}$
Find the value of $(f(4))^2$

Plug in 4 for n: $$f(4) = \frac{4^2}{16} = \frac{16}{16} = 1$$

Plug in 1 for $f(4)$: $$((f(4))^2 = (1)^2 = 1$$

(Chapter 12 Lesson 1: New Symbol or Term Problems)

10. 4   To find the greatest possible value of b/d, find the greatest possible value of b and the least possible positive value of d. Since they are both integers, the greatest possible value of b is 24 and the least possible value of d is 6. $24 \div 6 = 4$.
(Chapter 12 Lesson 3: Numerical Reasoning Problems)

11. 3   Set up equations:

$$x + y = 4$$
$$\underline{x - y = 2}$$

Add straight down: $2x = 6$
Divide by 2: $x = 3$
Plug in 3 for x: $3 + y = 4$
Subtract 3: $y = 1$
Final product: $(x)(y) = (3)(1) = 3$
(Chapter 11 Lesson 2: Systems)

12. 32   Let $LM = x$, and let $LO = y$. Since x is twice the length of y, $x = 2y$.

$$x + x + y + y = P$$

Substitute for x: $2y + 2y + y + y = P$
Combine terms: $6y = P$
Plug in 48 for P: $6y = 48$
Divide by 6: $y = 8$
Solve for x: $x = 2y = 2(8) = 16$

To find the area of the shaded region, you might notice that if PM is the base of the shaded triangle, then LO is the height, so area = ½(base)(height) = ½(8)(8) = 32.

If you don't notice this, you can find the shaded area by finding the area of the rectangle and subtracting the areas of the two unshaded triangles.

Area of rectangle = (length)(width)
Area of rectangle = $(x)(y) = (16)(8) = 128$

Area of triangle PLO = ½(base)(height)
Area of triangle PLO = ½(8)(8) = 32

Area of triangle MNO = ½(base)(height)
Area of triangle MNO = ½(16)(8) = 64

Area of triangle OPM = 128 − 64 − 32 = 32
(Chapter 13 Lesson 5: Areas and Perimeters)

13. 9 $64^3 = 4^x$

Substitute 4^3 for 64: $(4^3)^3 = 4^x$
Simplify: $4^9 = 4^x$
Equate the exponents: $x = 9$
(Chapter 11 Lesson 3: Working with Exponentials)

14. 3   Draw a line with points P, Q, R, and S on the line in that order. You are given that $\overline{PS} = 2\overline{PR}$ and that $\overline{PS} = 4\overline{PQ}$, so choose values for those lengths, like $\overline{PS} = 12$, $\overline{PR} = 6$, and $\overline{PQ} = 3$.

This means that $\overline{QS} = 9$, so $\overline{QS}/\overline{PQ} = 9/3 = 3$.
(Chapter 9 Lesson 2: Analyzing Problems)

15. 2 or ⅓ or .333
If $f(x)$ is not a real number, it must have a denominator of 0. Therefore, either $(x - 2)$ or $(3x - 1)$ is 0.
Set $(x - 2) = 0$ and solve for x: $(x - 2) = 0$
Add 2: $x = 2$
Set $(3x - 1) = 0$ and solve for x: $(3x - 1) = 0$
Add 1: $3x = 1$
Divide by 3: $x = ⅓$
(Chapter 14 Lesson 2: Functions)

16. 18   Since these numbers are "evenly spaced," their mean (average) is equal to their median (middle number). The average is easy to calculate: 110/5 = 22. Therefore, the middle number is 22, so the numbers are 18, 20, 22, 24, and 26.

Alternatively, you can set up an equation to find the sum of 5 consecutive unknown even integers, where x is the least of these:

$$x + (x + 2) + (x + 4) + (x + 6) + (x + 8) = 110$$
Combine like terms: $5x + 20 = 110$
Subtract 20: $5x = 90$
Divide by 5: $x = 18$

So the 5 integers are 18, 20, 22, 24, and 26.
(Chapter 12 Lesson 2: Mean/Median/Mode Problems)

17. 20   Use the percent change formula:

$$\frac{\text{Final} - \text{Original}}{\text{Original}} \times (100\%)$$

$$\frac{24{,}000 - 20{,}000}{20{,}000} \times (100\%) = 20\%$$

(Chapter 10 Lesson 5: Percents)

18. 25   Let b = the number of black marbles, w = the number of white marbles, and r = the number of red marbles in the jar. If you are 4 times as likely to choose a black marble as a white one, then $b = 4w$. If you are 5 times as likely to choose a red marble as a black one, then $r = 5b$. To find the least possible number of marbles in the jar, imagine you have only 1 white marble. This would mean you have 4(1) = 4 black marbles and 5(4) = 20 red marbles, for a total of $1 + 4 + 20 = 25$ marbles.

In general, you can represent the total number of marbles as

$$\text{total} = b + w + r$$

Since $r = 5b$: $\text{total} = b + w + 5b$

Since $b = 4w$: $\text{total} = 4w + w + 5(4w)$

Simplify: $\text{total} = 4w + w + 20w$

Simplify: $\text{total} = 25w$

In other words, the number of marbles in the jar must be a multiple of 25. The smallest positive multiple of 25 is, of course, 25.

(Chapter 12 Lesson 6: Probability Problems)

Section 6

1. **A**   If the fight did not ensue, John must have *intervened* to stop it. *intervene* = get in the way of something; *coalesce* = fuse together; *intermingle* = mix together; *exacerbate* = make worse

2. **D**   The defendant hoped the testimony would *corroborate* (support) his alibi, which would *clear him of blame*. *convoke* = call together; *synthesize* = generate; *absolve* = free of blame; *impeach* = accuse

3. **E**   Being *ensnarled* (tied up) in traffic is an unpleasant experience that Rachel would have an *aversion to* or *dislike for*. *antipathy* = feeling against; *penchant* = liking; *predilection* = liking; *proclivity* = tendency to do something; *aversion* = feeling of dislike; *insufferable* = intolerable

4. **A**   If the practices are no longer considered *state of the art*, they must now be considered *outdated* or *unsophisticated*. The physicians are *incredulous* (not able to believe) that such barbaric acts were once *supported* or *condoned*. *primitive* = old, unsophisticated; *sanctioned* = approved; *ingenious* = incredible, brilliant; *boorish* = rude, *censured* = publicly condemned; *innovative* = new; *endorsed* = supported; *foolhardy* = recklessly bold; *condemned* = criticized

5. **B**   The Prime Minister had vetoed the law in the past many times, so he didn't want it to pass. What would come *as a great surprise?* The Prime Minister's suddenly *supporting* the law. *articulated* = expressed clearly; *championed* = defended; *denounced* = spoke out against; *initiated* = began; *abbreviated* = shortened

6. **C**   Lines 3–4 state that the *tradition is that a man never lifts his hand against a woman*. Furthermore, if a man offends a woman, she is entitled to give him *a sound thrashing* (line 6). Therefore, a man who disrespected a woman would face *censure*.

7. **E**   Saying that *it is not an unusual thing for a squaw to administer a sound thrashing to a warrior husband* (lines 5–7) is like saying that it is not unusual for her to *give* him a beating, or *dispense* it.

8. **C**   Lines 5–6 say that *merely receiving palliative care . . . provides no hope of a cure*. Therefore, palliative care only reduces the discomfort of the symptoms, without curing the disease, as something *analgesic* does.

9. **A**   Lines 8–11 ask, *How can a doctor know if a patient has the mental capacity to decide for herself that the time has come to stop fighting the disease?* This question indicates that there may be some difficulty in determining a patient's *state of mind*.

10. **B**   The first sentence of the passage says *there was great optimism about earthquake prediction*. Each paragraph discusses potential *precursors*, or predictors, of earthquakes.

11. **E**   Lines 8–10 say that because *foreshocks look just like any other earthquake, they are not in themselves very useful in prediction*.

12. **D**   Support for choice II can be found in line 19, which says that groundwater has *become cloudy* prior to an earthquake. Choice III is supported in lines 16–18, which say that *before a large earthquake, marked changes have been reported in the level or flow of wells and springs*. Nothing is said about density changes in the groundwater.

13. **A**   The passage says (lines 8–10) that *since foreshocks look just like any other earthquakes, they are not in themselves very useful in prediction* but later (lines 40–42) mentions that because *the Haicheng earthquake had hundreds of foreshocks*, it was *easier than average . . . to predict*, thereby suggesting that foreshocks are, in fact, useful in predicting earthquakes.

14. **A**   This paragraph describes a particular application of the theory of earthquake prediction, described in the previous paragraphs, which led to scientists' predicting a large earthquake and saving many lives. Although this is said to have *prov[ed] that . . . earthquake prediction is possible* (lines 38–39), it was not a scientific experiment, as there was no control group.

15. **C**   Lines 49–50 mention that *seismologists missed predicting* the Tangshan earthquake and that over 250,000 people died. This was far worse than the Haicheng earthquake, which was *successfully predicted*, so that many lives were saved.

16. D The word "evacuation" in line 46 is placed in quotations to indicate that it is not being used in the traditional sense. The task of evacuating a population from a natural disaster does not typically involve showing movies, so doing so is unconventional.

17. C Lines 7–8 say that *one of the missionaries who met the ship took us under his wing.*

18. E Saying that *he could hardly believe that we were really restored to him* is like saying he couldn't believe that we were returned to him.

19. B The narrator states that she could *use tools as well as [her] brothers did* (lines 20–21), that her first childhood friendship was with a male ship-builder next door, and that she was eager and able to work with the ship-builders around her. Thus, she conveys a clear sense that she considers herself the equal of the males in her life.

20. D The author was emancipated from her confining clothing so that she could work with tools, such as her hatchet, in the shipyard.

21. C The *big movements of the day* refer to the changes in culture and *civilization* (line 43).

22. A Choice II is supported by lines 38–40, which say that *we had around us the fine flower of New England civilization,* as opposed to Michigan, which the author characterizes as *the wilderness* (line 45). The passage does not suggest that New England had finer gardens or humbler citizens than Michigan had.

23. D The author describes the move to Michigan as a complete upheaval (lines 37–38), and an unwelcome move from the fine flower of New England civilization (lines 39–40), thereby suggesting that she resents the move. She conveys no sign of bewilderment, fear or awe in this passage, since she describes the move with insight and equanimity.

24. A The passage says that the sisters *were so pained by* (the lumber wagon's) *appearance that we refused to ride in it* (lines 55–56) and that they wanted to *look as if we had no association with it* (lines 57–58).

Section 7

1. D

$$4x + 5 = 20$$

Add 3:
$$4x + 8 = 23$$

(Chapter 11 Lesson 1: Solving Equations)

2. C First find out how many cups are in 3 pints.

Set up a ratio: $\dfrac{1\text{ pint}}{2\text{ cups}} = \dfrac{3\text{ pints}}{x\text{ cups}}$

Cross-multiply: $x = 6$ cups

Set up ratio to solve for servings:

$$\dfrac{1\text{ serving}}{\dfrac{1}{3}\text{ cups}} = \dfrac{x\text{ servings}}{6\text{ cups}}$$

Cross-multiply: $\quad\quad\quad\quad \frac{1}{3}x = 6$

Divide by $\frac{1}{3}$: $\quad\quad\quad\quad x = 18$

(Chapter 10 Lesson 4: Ratios and Proportions)

3. A Since the angle shown is a right angle, the arc represents $\frac{1}{4}$ of the circumference.

length of arc = $\frac{1}{4}(2\pi r)$

Substitute 4 for r: length of arc = $\frac{1}{4}(2\pi(4))$

Simplify: length of arc = 2π

(Chapter 13 Lesson 8: Circles)

4. C This question tests your understanding of 30°-60°-90° triangles. The hypotenuse, which corresponds to $2x$, is 14. This means that the base is $x = 7$. The height is therefore $x\sqrt{3} = 7\sqrt{3}$.

(Chapter 13 Lesson 5: Areas and Perimeters)
(Chapter 13 Lesson 3: The Pythagorean Theorem)

5. A Given that $\nabla x = 3x - 3$, find $\nabla 7$.

$$\nabla 7 = 3x - 3$$

Plug in 7 for x: $\quad\quad 3(7) - 3 = 18$

Find $\nabla 3$: $\quad\quad\quad\quad \nabla 3 = 3x - 3$

Plug in 3 for x: $\quad\quad 3(3) - 3 = 6$

$$\dfrac{\nabla 7}{\nabla 3} = \dfrac{18}{6} = 3$$

Be careful not to pick answer choice (B) $\nabla 3$, because $\nabla 3 = 3(3) - 3 = 6$, not 3. Answer choice (A) $\nabla 2$ is correct, because $\nabla 2 = 3(2) - 3 = 3$.

(Chapter 12 Lesson 1: New Symbol or Term Problems)

6. B A little common sense should tell you that they will not need a full hour to clean the pool, because Stephanie can clean it in an hour all by herself, but Mark is helping. Therefore, you should eliminate choices (C), (D), and (E) right away. You might also notice that it can't take less than 30 minutes, because that is how long it would take if they both cleaned 1 pool per hour (so that the 2 working together could clean it in half the time), but Mark is slower, so they can't clean it quite that fast. This eliminates choice (A) and leaves (B) as the only possibility.

But you should know how to solve this problem if it were not a multiple-choice question, as well:

Stephanie's rate for cleaning the pool is 1 pool per hour. Mark's rate for cleaning the pool is 1 pool ÷ 1.5 hours = $\frac{2}{3}$ pools per hour. Combined, they can clean $1 + \frac{2}{3} = \frac{5}{3}$ pools per hour. Set up a rate equation using this rate to determine how much time it would take to clean 1 pool:

$$1 \text{ pool} = (\tfrac{5}{3} \text{ pools per hour})(\text{time})$$

Divide by $\frac{5}{3}$: $\frac{3}{5}$ hours to clean the pool
Multiply by 60: $\frac{3}{5}(60) = 36$ minutes
(Chapter 12 Lesson 4: Rate Problems)

7. A Change each expression to a base-10 exponential: *Silly*

(A) $= ((10^2)^3)^4 = 10^{24}$
(B) $= ((10^2)^5)((10^2)^6) = (10^{10})(10^{12}) = 10^{22}$
(C) $= ((10^4)^4) = 10^{16}$
(D) $= (((10^2)^2)((10^2)^2))^2 = ((10^4)(10^4))^2 = (10^8)^2 = 10^{16}$
(E) $= (10^6)^3 = 10^{18}$
(Chapter 11 Lesson 3: Working with Exponentials)

8. B Consider the points $(0, 2)$ and $(3, 0)$ on line l. When these points are reflected over the x-axis, $(0, 2)$ transforms to $(0, -2)$ and $(3, 0)$ stays at $(3, 0)$ because it is on the x-axis. You can then use the slope formula to find the slope of line m:

$$\frac{y_2 - y_1}{x_2 - x_1} = \frac{0 - (-2)}{3 - 0} = \frac{2}{3}$$

It's helpful to notice that whenever a line is reflected over the x-axis (or the y-axis, for that matter—try it), its slope becomes the opposite of the original slope.
(Chapter 13 Lesson 4: Coordinate Geometry)

9. C
	$(a+b)^2 = (a+b)(a+b)$
FOIL:	$a^2 + ab + ab + b^2$
Combine like terms:	$a^2 + 2ab + b^2$
Plug in 5 for ab:	$a^2 + 2(5) + b^2$
Simplify:	$a^2 + b^2 + 10$
Plug in 4 for $a^2 + b^2$:	$4 + 10 = 14$

(Chapter 11 Lesson 5: Factoring)

10. D The total area of the patio to be constructed is $24 \times 12 = 288$ ft^2. The slab shown in the figure has an area of 8 ft^2. Therefore, to fill the patio you will need $288 \div 8 = 36$ slabs.
(Chapter 13 Lesson 5: Areas and Perimeters)

11. D The prize money ratio can also be written as $7x:2x:1x$. Because the total prize money is \$12,000,
$$7x + 2x + 1x = 12,000$$
Combine like terms: $10x = 12,000$
Divide by 10: $x = 1,200$
The first place prize is $7x = 7(1,200) = \$8,400$.
(Chapter 10 Lesson 4: Ratios and Proportions)

12. E Always read the problem carefully and notice what it's asking for. Don't assume that you must solve for x and y here. Finding the value of $6x - 2y$ is much simpler than solving the entire system:
$$2x + 3y = 7$$
$$\underline{4x - 5y = 12}$$
Add straight down: $6x - 2y = 19$
(Chapter 11 Lesson 2: Systems)

13. D Think carefully about the given information and what it implies, then try to find counterexamples to disprove the given statements. For instance, try to disprove statement I by showing that s can be even. Imagine $s = 2$:
$$s + 1 = 2r$$
Substitute 6 for s: $6 + 1 = 2r$
Combine like terms: $7 = 2r$
Divide by 2: $3.5 = r$ (nope)
This doesn't work because r must be an integer. Why didn't it work? Because $2r$ must be even, but if s is even, then $s + 1$ must be odd and cannot equal an even number, so s must always be odd and statement I is true. (Eliminate choice (B).)

Statement II can be disproven with $r = 1$:
$$s + 1 = 2r$$
Substitute 1 for r: $s + 1 = 2(1)$
Subtract 1: $s = 1$ (okay)
Since 1 is an integer, we've proven that r is not necessarily even, so II is false. (Eliminate choices (C) and (E).)

Since we still have 2 choices remaining, we have to check ugly old statement III. Try the values we used before. If $r = 1$ and $s = 1$, then $\frac{s}{r} + \frac{1}{r} = \frac{1}{1} + \frac{1}{1} = 2$, which is an integer. But is it always an integer? Plugging in more examples can't prove that it will ALWAYS be an integer, because we can never test all possible solutions. We can prove it easily with algebra, though. Since $s + 1 = 2r$:

Divide by r: $\dfrac{s+1}{r} = 2$

Distribute: $\dfrac{s}{r} + \dfrac{1}{r} = 2$

Since 2 is an integer, statement III is necessarily true.
(Chapter 12 Lesson 3: Numerical Reasoning Problems)
(Chapter 9 Lesson 7: Thinking Logically and Checking)

14. C Find all the possible products of the values on two chips: (1)(2) = 2; (1)(3) = 3; (1)(4) = 4; (1)(5) = 5; (1)(6) = 6; (2)(3) = 6; (2)(4) = 8; (2)(5) = 10; (2)(6) = 12; (3)(4) = 12; (3)(5) = 15; (3)(6) = 18; (4)(5) = 20; (4)(6) = 24; (5)(6) = 30. There are 15 different combinations of chips. Of these, only the last 2 yield products that are greater than 20. So the probability is 2/15.
(Chapter 12 Lesson 6: Probability Problems)

15. D In this problem, only the signs of the terms matter. By following the rule of the sequence, you should see that the first 6 terms of the sequence are: +, −, −, +, −. −, . . . The pattern {+, −, −} repeats forever. In the first 100 terms, the pattern repeats 100 ÷ 3 = 33⅓ times. Because each repetition contains 2 negative numbers, in 33 full repetitions there are 33 × 2 = 66 negative numbers. The 100th term is the 1st term of the next pattern, which is positive, so the total number of negative terms is 66.
(Chapter 14 Lesson 1: Sequences)

16. B Draw the 5 triangles. The simplest way to solve this problem is to compare the choices 1 pair at a time. For instance, it should be clear just by inspection that $RB > RA$ and $SB > SA$, so we can eliminate A. Similarly, it should be clear that $RB > RC$ and $SB > SC$, so we can eliminate C. Likewise, since $RB > RD$ and $SB > SD$, we can eliminate D. Finally, we compare B with E. Since RB and RE are each a diagonal of one of the square faces, they must be equal. But SB is clearly longer than SE, because SB is the hypotenuse of triangle SEB, while SE is one of the legs.
(Chapter 13 Lesson 7: Volumes and 3-D Geometry)
(Chapter 9 Lesson 7: Thinking Logically and Checking)

Section 8

1. C If the review suggested that the décor of the restaurant was insipid (tasteless), but that the cuisine came close to *compensating* for it, the review must have been part positive and part negative, that is, *ambivalent*. *indefatigable* = untiring; *banal* = lacking originality; *ambivalent* = characterized by conflicting feelings; *sublime* = supreme, impressive; *piquant* = spicy; *tepid* = lukewarm

2. C The sentence suggests that Dr. Thompson should have characterized the results as unusual, but didn't. *meticulous* = concerned with detail; *belligerent* = prone to fighting; *anomalous* = deviating from the norm; *convergent* = coming together; *warranted* = appropriate to the situation

3. B They would hope that bad news did not predict further bad news. *amalgam* = a combination of diverse elements; *harbinge* = omen; *arbiter* = judge; *talisman* = an object with magical power

4. C To bring slaves *out of bondage* is to *free* or *unfetter* them. *encumber* = burden; *forgo* = relinquish

5. D A writer who can produce both *decorative poetry* and a *keenly analytical mystery novel* is a *versatile* writer, that is, she is able to write in divergent styles. *flamboyant* = ornate; *immutability* = permanence, unchangeability; *austere* = plain; *florid* = ornate; *grandiloquent* = characterized by pompous language

6. B The word *because* indicates that the sentence shows a cause-and-effect relationship. There are several ways to complete this sentence logically, but the only one among the choices is (B), because *multifarious* (widely varied) mechanisms would logically "stymie" (impede) scientists who are trying to investigate them. *efficacious* = capable of producing a desired effect; *bilked* = cheated; *conspicuous* = obvious; *thwarted* = prevented; *hampered* = hindered; *lucid* = clear; *proscribed* = forbidden

7. B If the *cultural assumption that there are many alien civilizations . . . stems in no small way from . . . the "Drake Equation,"* then this equation has had quite an influence on public opinion.

8. E The first two paragraphs discuss how the Drake Equation has led to the belief that there are many alien civilizations in the universe. The third paragraph discusses the author's contrasting view that there is indeed probably much simple life in the universe but very little if any other complex life.

9. B The sentence states that *a planet could go from an abiotic state to a civilization in 100 million years* thereby implying that a *civilization* must, by definition, not be *abiotic*. B is the only choice that necessarily cannot apply to a civilization.

10. A The author states his thesis in lines 38–39: *perhaps life is common, but complex life is not,* and goes on to explain this thesis, stating in lines 61–67 that *research shows that while attaining the stage of animal life is one thing, maintaining that level is quite another. . . . Complex life is subject to an unending succession of planetary disasters, creating what are known as mass-extinction events.*

11. A The phrase *the evolutionary grade we call animals* refers to the *level* of life form produced by evolution.

12. C Statement (A) is supported in lines 48–50, statement (B) is supported in lines 74–76, statement (D) is supported in lines 38–39, and statement (E) is supported in lines 51–55.

13. C The *sample size of one* refers to the uniqueness of *Earth history* (line 78).

14. A The first quotation in lines 101–103 is described as a *rejoinder,* or an opposing response, to the author's thoughts. The author then responds with his own quotation.

15. C The author says that he does not *conclude that there are no other cats (Rare Cat Hypothesis), only that there are no other cats exactly like Wookie* in order to convey the idea that one should not draw conclusions based on 1 occurrence.

16. B The author says that *life is opportunistic* to summarize the next statement that *the biosphere has taken advantage of the myriad of strange idiosyncrasies that our planet has to offer.*

17. D The passage says that these creatures *might naively assume that these qualities, very different from Earth's, are the only ones that can breed complexity,* that is, that all life evolved the same way.

18. A The author of Passage 1 believes that complex life, once evolved, faces numerous dangers that push it toward extinction. The author would point this fact out in response to the statement in lines 134–135 of Passage 2.

19. D The author of Passage 1 says in line 26, *In my view, life in the form of microbes or their equivalents is very common in the universe, perhaps more common than even Drake and Sagan envisioned.* The author of Passage 2 says in line 138, *My bet is that many other worlds, with their own peculiar characteristics and histories, co-evolve their own biospheres.* Both authors seem to agree that there is a lot of undiscovered life out there in the universe.

Section 9

1. B When you list items in a sentence, the items should have the same grammatical form. If the first item is in the gerund, they should all be in the gerund. Because the sentence says *Eating* an english muffin and *sitting* down, *drink coffee* should instead be *drinking coffee.*
(Chapter 18 Lesson 3: Parallelism)

2. D As written the sentence suggests that Mark's *attempt* was pretending to be hurt rather than Mark himself. Answer choice (D) corrects this error.
(Chapter 18 Lesson 7: Dangling and Misplaced Participles)

3. C The verb *are* is the improper tense. It should be *be* as in answer choice (C).
(Chapter 18 Lesson 9: Tricky Tenses)

4. C When you list items in a sentence, the items should have the same grammatical form. If the first term is in the noun form, then they all should be in the noun form. Because the sentence says *his temper, impatience, how easily he can be irritated* should instead be *irritability.*
(Chapter 18 Lesson 3: Parallelism)

5. B Before she gave the *gracious speech,* she won the match. The verb *winning* should instead be in the *past perfect form, having won.*
(Chapter 18 Lesson 9: Tricky Tenses)

6. C The sentence begins by describing something that was the most influential science treatise of the 20th century. The pronoun to follow the comma should describe this treatise. Choice (C) corrects the error in the most logical and concise fashion.
(Chapter 18 Lesson 7: Dangling and Misplaced Participles)

7. B The subject *neither* is singular and therefore *were* should instead be *was.*
(Chapter 18 Lesson 1: Subject-Verb Disagreement)

8. A This sentence is correct as written.

9. C Because the waves were described to have been *covering* the stores (gerund form), the verb *swept* should also be in the gerund form—*sweeping.*
(Chapter 18 Lesson 3: Parallelism)

10. B The problem with this question is that it is not a complete sentence as written. Answer choice (B) corrects that flaw in the most logical fashion.
(Chapter 18 Lesson 15: Coordinating Ideas)

11. **D**   The problem with this sentence is that it suggests that the father was 7 years old when he took his son to the game. That is not likely. Answer choice (D) best corrects the problem.
(Chapter 18 Lesson 7: Dangling and Misplaced Participles)

12. **A**   This sentence is correct as written

13. **E**   The pronoun them refers to a plural subject. However, anyone is singular. Answer choice (E) clears up this pronoun-antecedent disagreement in the most concise and logical way
(Chapter 18 Lesson 5: Pronoun-Antecedent Disagreement)

14. **A**   Although the original phrasing is not the most concise option, it is the only one that logically coordinates the ideas in the sentence.

PRACTICE TEST 4

ANSWER SHEET

SECTION

1

Write your essay for Section 1 in the space below and on the next page.

_____
_____
_____
_____
_____
_____
_____
_____
_____
_____
_____
_____
_____
_____
_____
_____
_____
_____
_____
_____
_____
_____
_____
_____
_____
_____
_____
_____
_____
_____
_____

ANSWER SHEET

SECTION 4

1. (A) (B) (C) (D) (E)   11. (A) (B) (C) (D) (E)   21. (A) (B) (C) (D) (E)   31. (A) (B) (C) (D) (E)
2. (A) (B) (C) (D) (E)   12. (A) (B) (C) (D) (E)   22. (A) (B) (C) (D) (E)   32. (A) (B) (C) (D) (E)
3. (A) (B) (C) (D) (E)   13. (A) (B) (C) (D) (E)   23. (A) (B) (C) (D) (E)   33. (A) (B) (C) (D) (E)
4. (A) (B) (C) (D) (E)   14. (A) (B) (C) (D) (E)   24. (A) (B) (C) (D) (E)   34. (A) (B) (C) (D) (E)
5. (A) (B) (C) (D) (E)   15. (A) (B) (C) (D) (E)   25. (A) (B) (C) (D) (E)   35. (A) (B) (C) (D) (E)
6. (A) (B) (C) (D) (E)   16. (A) (B) (C) (D) (E)   26. (A) (B) (C) (D) (E)   36. (A) (B) (C) (D) (E)
7. (A) (B) (C) (D) (E)   17. (A) (B) (C) (D) (E)   27. (A) (B) (C) (D) (E)   37. (A) (B) (C) (D) (E)
8. (A) (B) (C) (D) (E)   18. (A) (B) (C) (D) (E)   28. (A) (B) (C) (D) (E)   38. (A) (B) (C) (D) (E)
9. (A) (B) (C) (D) (E)   19. (A) (B) (C) (D) (E)   29. (A) (B) (C) (D) (E)   39. (A) (B) (C) (D) (E)
10. (A) (B) (C) (D) (E)   20. (A) (B) (C) (D) (E)   30. (A) (B) (C) (D) (E)   40. (A) (B) (C) (D) (E)

SECTION 5

1. (A) (B) (C) (D) (E)   5. (A) (B) (C) (D) (E)
2. (A) (B) (C) (D) (E)   6. (A) (B) (C) (D) (E)
3. (A) (B) (C) (D) (E)   7. (A) (B) (C) (D) (E)
4. (A) (B) (C) (D) (E)   8. (A) (B) (C) (D) (E)

9.   10.   11.   12.   13.

14.   15.   16.   17.   18.

ANSWER SHEET

SECTION 6

1. (A) (B) (C) (D) (E)   11. (A) (B) (C) (D) (E)   21. (A) (B) (C) (D) (E)   31. (A) (B) (C) (D) (E)
2. (A) (B) (C) (D) (E)   12. (A) (B) (C) (D) (E)   22. (A) (B) (C) (D) (E)   32. (A) (B) (C) (D) (E)
3. (A) (B) (C) (D) (E)   13. (A) (B) (C) (D) (E)   23. (A) (B) (C) (D) (E)   33. (A) (B) (C) (D) (E)
4. (A) (B) (C) (D) (E)   14. (A) (B) (C) (D) (E)   24. (A) (B) (C) (D) (E)   34. (A) (B) (C) (D) (E)
5. (A) (B) (C) (D) (E)   15. (A) (B) (C) (D) (E)   25. (A) (B) (C) (D) (E)   35. (A) (B) (C) (D) (E)
6. (A) (B) (C) (D) (E)   16. (A) (B) (C) (D) (E)   26. (A) (B) (C) (D) (E)   36. (A) (B) (C) (D) (E)
7. (A) (B) (C) (D) (E)   17. (A) (B) (C) (D) (E)   27. (A) (B) (C) (D) (E)   37. (A) (B) (C) (D) (E)
8. (A) (B) (C) (D) (E)   18. (A) (B) (C) (D) (E)   28. (A) (B) (C) (D) (E)   38. (A) (B) (C) (D) (E)
9. (A) (B) (C) (D) (E)   19. (A) (B) (C) (D) (E)   29. (A) (B) (C) (D) (E)   39. (A) (B) (C) (D) (E)
10. (A) (B) (C) (D) (E)   20. (A) (B) (C) (D) (E)   30. (A) (B) (C) (D) (E)   40. (A) (B) (C) (D) (E)

SECTION 7

1. (A) (B) (C) (D) (E)   11. (A) (B) (C) (D) (E)   21. (A) (B) (C) (D) (E)   31. (A) (B) (C) (D) (E)
2. (A) (B) (C) (D) (E)   12. (A) (B) (C) (D) (E)   22. (A) (B) (C) (D) (E)   32. (A) (B) (G) (D) (E)
3. (A) (B) (C) (D) (E)   13. (A) (B) (C) (D) (E)   23. (A) (B) (C) (D) (E)   33. (A) (B) (C) (D) (E)
4. (A) (B) (C) (D) (E)   14. (A) (B) (C) (D) (E)   24. (A) (B) (C) (D) (E)   34. (A) (B) (C) (D) (E)
5. (A) (B) (C) (D) (E)   15. (A) (B) (C) (D) (E)   25. (A) (B) (C) (D) (E)   35. (A) (B) (C) (D) (E)
6. (A) (B) (C) (D) (E)   16. (A) (B) (C) (D) (E)   26. (A) (B) (C) (D) (E)   36. (A) (B) (C) (D) (E)
7. (A) (B) (C) (D) (E)   17. (A) (B) (C) (D) (E)   27. (A) (B) (C) (D) (E)   37. (A) (B) (C) (D) (E)
8. (A) (B) (C) (D) (E)   18. (A) (B) (C) (D) (E)   28. (A) (B) (C) (D) (E)   38. (A) (B) (C) (D) (E)
9. (A) (B) (C) (D) (E)   19. (A) (B) (C) (D) (E)   29. (A) (B) (C) (D) (E)   39. (A) (B) (C) (D) (E)
10. (A) (B) (C) (D) (E)   20. (A) (B) (C) (D) (E)   30. (A) (B) (C) (D) (E)   40. (A) (B) (C) (D) (E)

SECTION 8

1. (A) (B) (C) (D) (E)   11. (A) (B) (C) (D) (E)   21. (A) (B) (C) (D) (E)   31. (A) (B) (C) (D) (E)
2. (A) (B) (C) (D) (E)   12. (A) (B) (C) (D) (E)   22. (A) (B) (C) (D) (E)   32. (A) (B) (C) (D) (E)
3. (A) (B) (C) (D) (E)   13. (A) (B) (C) (D) (E)   23. (A) (B) (C) (D) (E)   33. (A) (B) (C) (D) (E)
4. (A) (B) (C) (D) (E)   14. (A) (B) (C) (D) (E)   24. (A) (B) (C) (D) (E)   34. (A) (B) (C) (D) (E)
5. (A) (B) (C) (D) (E)   15. (A) (B) (C) (D) (E)   25. (A) (B) (C) (D) (E)   35. (A) (B) (C) (D) (E)
6. (A) (B) (C) (D) (E)   16. (A) (B) (C) (D) (E)   26. (A) (B) (C) (D) (E)   36. (A) (B) (C) (D) (E)
7. (A) (B) (C) (D) (E)   17. (A) (B) (C) (D) (E)   27. (A) (B) (C) (D) (E)   37. (A) (B) (C) (D) (E)
8. (A) (B) (C) (D) (E)   18. (A) (B) (C) (D) (E)   28. (A) (B) (C) (D) (E)   38. (A) (B) (C) (D) (E)
9. (A) (B) (C) (D) (E)   19. (A) (B) (C) (D) (E)   29. (A) (B) (C) (D) (E)   39. (A) (B) (C) (D) (E)
10. (A) (B) (C) (D) (E)   20. (A) (B) (C) (D) (E)   30. (A) (B) (C) (D) (E)   40. (A) (B) (C) (D) (E)

SECTION 9

1. (A) (B) (C) (D) (E)   11. (A) (B) (C) (D) (E)   21. (A) (B) (C) (D) (E)   31. (A) (B) (C) (D) (E)
2. (A) (B) (C) (D) (E)   12. (A) (B) (C) (D) (E)   22. (A) (B) (C) (D) (E)   32. (A) (B) (C) (D) (E)
3. (A) (B) (C) (D) (E)   13. (A) (B) (C) (D) (E)   23. (A) (B) (C) (D) (E)   33. (A) (B) (C) (D) (E)
4. (A) (B) (C) (D) (E)   14. (A) (B) (C) (D) (E)   24. (A) (B) (C) (D) (E)   34. (A) (B) (C) (D) (E)
5. (A) (B) (C) (D) (E)   15. (A) (B) (C) (D) (E)   25. (A) (B) (C) (D) (E)   35. (A) (B) (C) (D) (E)
6. (A) (B) (C) (D) (E)   16. (A) (B) (C) (D) (E)   26. (A) (B) (C) (D) (E)   36. (A) (B) (C) (D) (E)
7. (A) (B) (C) (D) (E)   17. (A) (B) (C) (D) (E)   27. (A) (B) (C) (D) (E)   37. (A) (B) (C) (D) (E)
8. (A) (B) (C) (D) (E)   18. (A) (B) (C) (D) (E)   28. (A) (B) (C) (D) (E)   38. (A) (B) (C) (D) (E)
9. (A) (B) (C) (D) (E)   19. (A) (B) (C) (D) (E)   29. (A) (B) (C) (D) (E)   39. (A) (B) (C) (D) (E)
10. (A) (B) (C) (D) (E)   20. (A) (B) (C) (D) (E)   30. (A) (B) (C) (D) (E)   40. (A) (B) (C) (D) (E)

Section 1

Time—25 minutes

Directions for Writing the Essay

Plan and write an essay that answers the question below. Do NOT write on another topic. An essay on another topic will receive a score of 0.

Two readers will grade your essay based on how well you develop your point of view, organize and explain your ideas, use specific and relevant examples to support your thesis, and use clear and effective language. How well you write is much more important than how much you write, but to cover the topic adequately you should plan to write several paragraphs.

Your essay must be written only on the lines provided on your answer sheet. You will have enough space if you write on every line, avoid wide margins, and keep your handwriting to a reasonable size. Your essay will be read by people who are not familiar with your handwriting, so write legibly.

You may use this sheet for notes and outlining, but these will not be graded as part of your essay.

Consider carefully the issue discussed in the following passage, then write an essay that answers the question posed in the assignment.

> We like to believe that physical phenomena, animals, people and societies obey predictable rules, but such rules, even when carefully ascertained, have their limits. Every rule has its exceptions.

Assignment: **What is one particularly interesting "exception" to a rule?** Write an essay in which you answer this question and discuss your point of view on this issue. Support your position logically with examples from literature, the arts, history, politics, science and technology, current events, or your experience or observation.

Write your essay on your answer sheet.

Section 2

Time—25 minutes
20 Questions

Directions for Multiple-Choice Questions

In this section, solve each problem, using any available space on the page for scratchwork. Then decide which is the best of the choices given and fill in the corresponding oval on the answer sheet.

- You may use a calculator on any problem. All numbers used are real numbers.
- Figures are drawn as accurately as possible EXCEPT when it is stated that the figure is not drawn to scale.
- All figures lie in a plane unless otherwise indicated.

Reference Information

$A = \pi r^2$
$C = 2\pi r$

$A = \ell w$

$A = \frac{1}{2}bh$

$V = \ell wh$

$V = \pi r^2 h$

$c^2 = a^2 + b^2$

Special Right Triangles

The arc of a circle measures 360°.
Every straight angle measures 180°.
The sum of the measures of the angles in a triangle is 180°.

---

1 A playground with an area of 3,600 square feet is to be divided into 6 different play stations. What is the average (arithmetic mean) area, in square feet, of the 6 stations?

(A) 400
(B) 500
(C) 600
(D) 700
(E) 800

2 If $3a = 15$ and $4b = 10$, what is the value of $\dfrac{a}{b}$?

(A) $\dfrac{1}{2}$

(B) $\dfrac{2}{3}$

(C) $\dfrac{3}{2}$

(D) 2

(E) $\dfrac{5}{2}$

3

SALARIES AT ULTRA CORP

Salary (in thousands of dollars)

Employee 1
Employee 2
Employee 3
Employee 4
Employee 5

1992 1994 1996 1998 2000

The graph above shows the salaries of 5 employees at UltraCorp over an 8-year period. Which employee's salary has risen at the fastest rate over this period?

(A) Employee 1
(B) Employee 2
(C) Employee 3
(D) Employee 4
(E) Employee 5

GO ON TO THE NEXT PAGE ▶▶▶

616

4 One bucket of fried chicken serves either 3 adults or 5 children. If the Memorial Day fair committee wants to have enough chicken to serve 100 children and 60 adults, how many buckets of chicken are needed?

(A) 29
(B) 32
(C) 35
(D) 40
(E) 45

100 / 5 → 70   60/3 = 20

5 $(5x - 3x + 4)(3x + 6x - 2) =$

(A) $9x^2 + 16x - 4$
(B) $18x^2 + 32x - 8$
(C) $18x^2 - 40x + 8$
(D) $72x^2 + 20x - 8$
(E) $72x^2 - 20x + 8$

$(2x+4)(9x-2) = 18x^2 - 4x + 36x$

6

Note: Figure not drawn to scale.

In the figure above, $l \parallel m$ and $z = 55$. What is the value of $a + b + c$?

(A) 235
(B) 265
(C) 275
(D) 305
(E) 315

7 If $7\sqrt{x} + 16 = 79$, what is the value of x?

(A) 3
(B) 6
(C) 9
(D) 27
(E) 81

$7\sqrt{x} = 63$ $\sqrt{x}^2 = 9^2$ x

8 Each term in a sequence of numbers, except for the 1st term, is 2 less than the square root of the previous term. If the 3rd term of this sequence is 1, what is the 1st term?

(A) 1
(B) 9
(C) 11
(D) 121
(E) 123

$n_3 = 1$ $\sqrt{121} = 11 - 2$ $\sqrt{9} = 3 - 2 = 1$

9

In the figure above, rectangle $ABCD$ has an area of 90 and is divided into 15 smaller squares. What is the sum of the areas of the shaded regions?

(A) 39
(B) 42
(C) 45
(D) 48
(E) 51

$\dfrac{90}{2} =$

10 For all x greater than 2, let ☆x☆ be defined as the sum of the positive integers less than x.

What is the value of ☆16☆ − ☆13☆?

(A) 27
(B) 29
(C) 42
(D) 45
(E) 54

$15 + 14 + 13$

GO ON TO THE NEXT PAGE ▶▶▶

11

$$X3\text{0}$$
$$+ 5\text{0}X$$
$$\overline{1,33X \, \text{=8}}$$

In the correctly worked addition problem above, X and Y represent 2 different digits. What digit does X represent?

(A) 0
(B) 1
(C) 4
(D) 8 ∪   (D)
(E) 9

12

$$x, y, 3y$$

If the average (arithmetic mean) of the 3 numbers above is $3x$ and $x \neq 0$, what is y in terms of x?

(A) $\dfrac{x}{2}$

(B) $2x$

(C) $3x$

(D) $x + 7$

(E) $3x - 3$

$$\frac{x + y + 3y}{3} = 3x$$

$$x + 4y = 9x$$
$$-x \qquad -x$$
$$4y = 8x$$
$$y = \frac{8x}{4} = \frac{8x}{8}$$

(B)

13

Note: Figure not drawn to scale.

In the figure above, what is the value of x in terms of w?

(A) $w - 2$
(B) $w - 1$
(C) w ∪ (C)
(D) $w + 1$
(E) $w + 2$

14

When r is divided by 10, the remainder is 9. What is the remainder when $r + 2$ is divided by 5?

(A) 0
(B) 1
(C) 3
(D) 4
(E) 14

15

If five distinct lines lie in a plane, then at most how many distinct points can lie on two or more of these lines?

(A) 6 ∪
(B) 7
(C) 8   (A)
(D) 9
(E) 10

16

A pile of playing cards consists of only kings, jacks, and queens. If the probability of randomly choosing a king is $\dfrac{1}{4}$ and the probability of randomly choosing a queen is $\dfrac{2}{7}$, what is the probability of randomly choosing a jack?

(A) $\dfrac{3}{7}$

(B) $\dfrac{13}{28}$

(C) $\dfrac{15}{28}$

(D) $\dfrac{4}{7}$

(E) $\dfrac{9}{14}$

17

Note: Figure not drawn to scale.

In the figure above, $\triangle VXT$ is equilateral and $WU = WY$. If the measure of $\angle VWU$ is twice the measure of $\angle VUW$, what is the measure of $\angle TUY$?

(A) 55°
(B) 60°
(C) 65°
(D) 70°
(E) 75°

$X + 2X = 120$
$3X = 120$
$X = 40$
$2X = 80$

$180 - (65 + 40) =$

18 If m and n are positive numbers, what percent of $m - 4$ is $n + 2$?

(A) $\dfrac{100(n+2)}{(m-4)}\%$

(B) $\dfrac{m-4}{n+2}(100)\%$

(C) $\dfrac{100n+2}{(m-4)}\%$

(D) $\dfrac{m-4}{100n}\%$

(E) $\dfrac{n+2}{m-4}\%$

$m - 4 = 100$
$n - 2 = 4$

$\left(\dfrac{100}{4}\right)100$ 100 is 25

$\dfrac{n+2(100)}{m-4}$ 25 is 25%

$\dfrac{25(100}{100}$

19 The Greenwich Cinema charges the same price for every ticket it sells. At a matinee showing, the theater sold tickets for all but 6 seats. At the evening showing, the theater sold tickets for every seat, as well as 5 additional standing-room-only tickets at full price. If the theater collected \$912 in ticket revenue for the matinee and \$1,000 for the evening showing, what is the seating capacity of the theater?

(A) 116
(B) 120
(C) 124
(D) 130
(E) 135

$X = $ mat.
$X + 6 = $ tot.
$X + 6 + 5 = X + 11 = $ evening

$\begin{array}{c} 11 \\ \underline{6} \\ 13 \end{array}$ $\begin{array}{c} 1000 \\ -\ 912 \\ \hline 88 \end{array}$

$17.6 = $ price per ticket

20 The price of a certain stock was d dollars on January 1, 2003. The price decreased by 20% in January, increased by 40% in February, decreased by 25% in March, and increased by 25% in April. In terms of d, what was the price of the stock at the end of April?

(A) 0.80d
(B) 0.84d
(C) 1.05d
(D) 1.12d
(E) 1.20d

$17.6(X+6) = 912$

$X + 6$

$100 = d$
$100 - 20 = 80$
$80(1.4) = 112$
$112(1 - .25) = 84$
$84(1.25) = 105$

You may check your work, on this section only, until time is called.

Section 3

Time—25 minutes
24 Questions

Each of the sentences below is missing one or two portions. Read each sentence, then select the word or words that most logically complete the sentence, taking into account the meaning of the sentence as a whole.

Example:

Rather than accepting the theory unquestioningly, Deborah regarded it with -------.

    (A) mirth
    (B) sadness
    (C) responsibility
    (D) ignorance
    (E) skepticism

Correct response: (E)

1 Jacques Lugard's world-renowned 34th-Street bistro is known best for its ------- main courses, but many go there simply to enjoy the restaurant's ------- desserts.

    (A) delectable . . . scrumptious
    (B) unpalatable . . . tantalizing
    (C) divine . . . bland
    (D) debilitating . . . uninspired
    (E) savory . . . mediocre

2 Decades of political ------- have left the region on the brink of war; the slightest ------- could cause it to explode into destructive conflict.

    (A) dissension . . . construct
    (B) tension . . . communication
    (C) harmony . . . instigation
    (D) strife . . . provocation
    (E) unanimity . . . agitation

3 For over 500 years, the *Mona Lisa*'s smile has been the source of much ------- among art historians, who continue to interpret her enigmatic smile in many different ways.

    (A) assent
    (B) deliberation
    (C) concurrence
    (D) remuneration
    (E) reconciliation

4 Even after his death, Elvis Presley continues to be one of the most ------- singers of all time; every year hundreds of thousands of fans travel to his hometown to pay tribute to his memory.

    (A) satirized
    (B) unexalted
    (C) revered
    (D) despised
    (E) shunned

5 Professional poker player Howard Lederer is known as "the professor" because of the ------- tactics he uses to outthink his opponents.

    (A) entertaining
    (B) obscure
    (C) cerebral
    (D) transparent
    (E) outlandish

6 Detractors of the new building say that it is ------- aesthetically and furthermore that, far from being the financial ------- that its developers claimed it would be, the project has cost the city dearly in lost revenue.

    (A) an eyesore . . . adversary
    (B) an enhancement . . . gratuity
    (C) an embellishment . . . windfall
    (D) a defacement . . . calamity
    (E) an atrocity . . . boon

GO ON TO THE NEXT PAGE ▶▶▶

7 Nineteenth-century author Edgar Allen Poe was acclaimed for his ------- inventiveness; he had an unmatched ability to write ------ tales of cruelty and torture that mesmerized his readers.

(A) tenuous . . . spellbinding
(B) grotesque . . . enthralling
(C) interminable . . . sacrilegious
(D) eclectic . . . sadistic
(E) chimerical . . . mundane

8 DNA evidence taken from the scene of the crime was used to ------- the defendant; the genomic "fingerprint" taken from the blood sample was not a match for the accused, thus proving his innocence.

(A) perambulate
(B) expedite
(C) incriminate
(D) exculpate
(E) equivocate

The passages below are followed by questions based on their content. Answer each question based on what is stated or implied in the passages or the introductory material preceding them.

Questions 9–10 are based on the following passage.

Debussy, though less radical harmonically than Schoenberg, preceded him in starting
Line the breakdown of the old system. Debussy, one of the most instinctive musicians who
5 ever lived, was the first composer of our time who dared to make his ear the sole judge of what was good harmonically. With Debussy, analysts found chords that could no longer be explained according to the old harmony. If
10 one had asked Debussy why he used such chords, I am sure he would have given the only possible answer: "I like it that way!" It was as if one composer finally had confidence in his ear. I exaggerate a little, for, after all,
15 composers have never had to wait for theoreticians to tell them what or what not to do. On the contrary, it has always been the other way about—theoreticians have explained the logic of the composer's thought after he has
20 instinctively put it down.

9 It can be inferred from the passage that the "old system" (lines 2–3) most likely involved

(A) a way of developing musical intuition
(B) a rigid method for writing musical harmonies
(C) a means by which musicians could incorporate the ideas of theoreticians into their music
(D) a method of transcribing music that arose spontaneously from a musician's imagination
(E) methods that theoreticians used for distinguishing the harmonies of different composers

10 The passage characterizes Debussy primarily as being

(A) less self-assured than other composers of his time
(B) reverential of traditional musical forms
(C) preoccupied more with musical theory than with practice
(D) harmonically inventive
(E) derisive of musical theoreticians

Questions 11–12 are based on the following passage.

Imagine flying in a hot-air balloon over the lush, green canopy of a rainforest. Through
Line the clouds and mist you can barely make out the treetops and a few of the birds flying
5 among them. What lies hidden in the undergrowth? How many organisms are there, what do they look like, and how do they behave? Using a rope and bucket you blindly drag the rainforest from above hoping to ensnare some
10 of its inhabitants or the materials that make up its infrastructure. But alas, with such feeble and limited means you can learn little about the environment and life below. For years this is essentially how we have studied
15 the ocean—blindly sampling the sea with limited and relatively ineffective methods. Even

First paragraph: *What to Listen for in Music*, Aaron Copland, McGraw-Hill, 1957, pp. 73–74
Second paragraph: *The Oceans*, Ellen J. Prager; McGraw-Hill, 2000, p. xii–xiii

GO ON TO THE NEXT PAGE ▶▶▶

today, with technology as advanced as it is, study of the ocean remains a difficult and expensive task. Whether through large-scale
20 satellite imagery, small-scale chemical and biological measures, or even the collecting of fossil impressions of ancient sea creatures, all aspects of oceanographic study require some type of observation or sample collection, and
25 herein lies the problem.

11 The passage describes a trip in a hot-air balloon primarily in order to

    (A) describe the variety of life forms in the rainforest

    (B) make an analogy to ocean exploration

    (C) exemplify the advanced equipment that land-based biologists have at their disposal

    (D) show the difficulties that most biologists encounter in extracting samples from the rainforest

    (E) demonstrate how methods of biological exploration have evolved over time

12 The "small-scale chemical and biological measures" (lines 20–21) are mentioned primarily as examples of

    (A) methods that are not as cost-effective or simple as the author would like

    (B) challenges for the explorer of the rainforest

    (C) technologies that hold great promise for revealing the nature of oceanic life

    (D) techniques that require little or no training to employ

    (E) inexpensive means of exploring the deepest parts of the ocean

The passages below are followed by questions based on their content. Answer each question based on what is stated or implied in the passages or the introductory material preceding them.

Questions 13–17 are based on the following passage.

The following is an excerpt from a book about the history of primitive art.

Pictures from the earliest artistic periods are the traces of a primal concept of the
Line world. In spite of the thematic treatment of real creatures we can still recognize, paintings
5 of animals or men from the early Stone Age are charged with magical strength, exaggerated and concentrated as they are into forms of existential experience. They fulfilled still other functions beyond the mere representa-
10 tion of the visible.

The degree of naïveté in archaic primitive art varies. A certain naïveté is always present when observation of nature is not overlaid with rational thought. Art first had to discover
15 the world and to invent ways of making it perceivable. Along with visible things, invisible forces too were given form and substance and began to make their appearance. And as they achieved form they took on permanence.
20 The early hunters attempted to influence the chance fortunes of the hunt through magical practices. The power of magic was as real to them as the power of the stone ax they had invented. Art ensnared the form of the animal.
25 Whenever the figure of woman appears it is a sign of fertility; representations of men are rarer, and when they occur they show him in his role as hunter. Man does not yet look beyond the borders of existence that mark his
30 practical life. Magic precedes the fall of man into knowledge.

It must have meant a considerable revolution in prehistoric times when man discovered that he did not have to live solely from
35 hunting, that not only the animals but indeed all of nature round about him was full of life. Stars and seasons take their rhythms from unknown forces; a mysterious power functioning beyond human understanding, propitious or

40 forbidding, helpful or threatening; forces of
ancestors, spirits, and demons, and forces of
the departed and the coming gods.
With the transition from the early to the
late Stone Age there appears the first stylistic
45 change in art. The original naturalism based
on observation and experience gives way to a
geometrically stylized world of forms discoverable only through thought and speculation.
Prehistoric man, leaving behind him the
50 life of the hunter and gatherer, invents abbre-
viations and pictographic signs which are no
longer pictures proper but rather thought
models, reflections of his more settled existence as a beginning herdsman and farmer.
55 Following the late Stone Age, the art of the
Bronze Age—which in Asia dates from the middle of the third millennium B.C. and which
began in Europe around 2100 B.C.—contains,
as does the art of the Iron Age as well, elements
60 of naïveté and inventive immediacy side by side
with highly developed, formalized compositions. The bronze sculptures of the Celts and
the Illyrians are ample witnesses to them.
With the substitution of conceptual ratio-
65 nalization for more primitive, mythical explanations of the world, a kind of art arises in
which objective criteria of reality and the natural laws of optics come into play. The simplicity and vividness of the naïve become
70 more rare.
The art of the period of the catacombs was
informed with the naturalistic naïveté of late
antiquity. In medieval Christian art, which
was averse to any spatial illusions, a "moral"
75 perspective dominated; all action was pressed
onto the holy, two-dimensional surface.
While the primitive and instinctual accompanies the course of art until the Renaissance, it
recedes in the face of the humanistic concept of
80 the world and the discovery of linear and aerial
perspective. High art forsakes the realm of instinct in exchange for the province of reason.
But parallel with it, in folk art and among
so-called primitive peoples, naïve representa-
85 tion lives on.

13 The first paragraph suggests that the "primal concept of the world" (lines 2–3) involved

(A) a belief that art was more important even than hunting
(B) a need to preserve a record of events for the future
(C) a focus on the realistic depiction of animals
(D) a sense that paintings can have powers beyond what can be seen
(E) a desire to communicate with animals

14 In line 6, the word "charged" most nearly means

(A) exchanged
(B) approached violently
(C) accused
(D) trampled
(E) filled

15 The "stylistic change" (lines 44–45) is a transition from

(A) representations of real things to representations of ideas
(B) magical applications of art to representations of hunting scenes
(C) depictions of gods to depictions of herdsmen
(D) art used to depict the natural environment to art used for magical rituals
(E) a focus on the theme of hunting to a focus on the theme of fertility

16 The "bronze sculptures of the Celts and the Illyrians" (line 62) are mentioned primarily as examples of

(A) a new appreciation of three-dimensional art
(B) art with both primitive and formal characteristics
(C) a revival of the art of the Stone Age
(D) illustrations of the herding life
(E) art with moralistic themes

GO ON TO THE NEXT PAGE ▶▶▶

17 The passage indicates that, unlike the "art of the period of the catacombs" (line 71), Renaissance art is characterized by

(A) an appreciation of three-dimensional forms
(B) an emphasis on religious themes
(C) representations of magical creatures
(D) a primitive view of the world
(E) a focus on the realm of instinct

Questions 18–24 are based on the following passage.

The following passage, from a modern textbook on anthropology, discusses a debate among biologists and anthropologists about how humans evolved.

Does evolution occur gradually or in "punctuated equilibria"? Charles Darwin, a gradualist, maintained that life forms arise from others in a gradual and orderly fashion.
5 Small modifications that accumulate over the generations add up to major changes after millions of years. Gradualists cite intermediate fossils as evidence for their position, contending that there would be even more
10 transitional forms if it weren't for gaps in the fossil record.

The advocates of the punctuated equilibrium model believe that long periods of equilibrium, during which species change little,
15 are interrupted (punctuated) by sudden changes—evolutionary leaps. One reason for such jumps in the fossil record may be extinction followed by invasion by a closely related species. For example, a sea species may die
20 out when a shallow body of water dries up, while a closely related species will survive in deeper waters. Then, later, when the sea reinvades the first locale, the protected species will extend its range to the first area. Another
25 possibility is that when barriers are removed, a group may replace, rather than succeed, a related one because it has a trait that makes it adaptively superior in the environment they now share.
30 When a major environmental change occurs suddenly, one possibility is for the pace of evolution to increase. Another possibility is extinction. The earth has witnessed several mass extinctions—worldwide ecosystem ca-
tastrophes that affect multiple species. The
35 biggest one divided the era of "ancient life" (the Paleozoic) from the era of "middle life" (the Mesozoic). This mass extinction occurred 245 million years ago, when 4.5 million of the earth's estimated 5 million species
40 (mostly invertebrates) were wiped out. The second biggest extinction, which occurred 65 million years ago, destroyed the dinosaurs and many other Mesozoic species. One explanation for the extinction of the dinosaurs is
45 that a massive, long-lasting cloud of gas and dust arose from the impact of a huge meteorite. The cloud blocked solar radiation and therefore photosynthesis, ultimately destroying most plants and the chain of animals that
50 fed on them.

The hominid fossil record exemplifies both gradual and rapid change, confirming that evolution can be faster or slower depending on the rate of environmental change, the
55 speed with which geographic barriers rise or fall, and the value of the group's adaptive response. Australopithecine teeth and skulls show some gradual transitions. For example, some of the fossils that are intermediate be-
60 tween *Australopithecus* and early *Homo* combine a larger brain (characteristic of *Homo*) with huge back teeth and supportive structures (characteristic of the australopithecines). However, there is no doubt that the
65 pace of hominid evolution sped up around 18 million years ago. This spurt resulted in the emergence (in just 200,000 years) of *Homo erectus*. This was followed by a long period of relative stability. The probable key to the
70 rapid emergence of *Homo erectus* was a dramatic change in adaptive strategy: greater reliance on hunting through improved tools and other cultural means of adaptation. The new economy, tools, and phenotype arose and
75 spread rapidly, then remained fairly stable for about 1 million years.

Anthropology: The Exploration of Human Diversity, Conrad Phillip Kottak, McGraw-Hill, 1997, p. 161

GO ON TO THE NEXT PAGE ▶▶▶

18 The passage suggests that the existence of "transitional forms" (line 10) would demonstrate

(A) how some species have come to dominate others
(B) how life first arose on earth
(C) the gradual nature of evolution
(D) the divisions in the scientific community over the manner in which evolution occurs
(E) how barriers arise between species

19 The example of the two "sea species" (line 19) described in the second paragraph is intended to demonstrate

(A) the differences between the demands of an aquatic environment and the demands of a terrestrial environment
(B) how the fossil record can misrepresent the history of a species
(C) the manner in which one species gradually evolves into a more advanced one
(D) a current theory of how mass extinctions occur
(E) how punctuated evolution can occur

20 According to the passage, the dinosaurs most likely became extinct because

(A) they were struck by a large meteorite
(B) their food supply was eliminated
(C) a more dominant species invaded their environment and destroyed them
(D) the earth's temperature increased dramatically after the impact of a meteorite
(E) a sudden ice age destroyed their environment

21 In line 63, the word "supportive" most nearly means

(A) providing evidence
(B) secondary
(C) emotionally sustaining
(D) weight-bearing
(E) scientific

22 According to the passage, the early Mesozoic era differed from the late Paleozoic era chiefly in that the early Mesozoic era

(A) was no longer dominated by the dinosaurs
(B) was characterized by the rise of *Homo erectus*
(C) was characterized by a greater diversity of life than that in the late Paleozoic era
(D) was far colder than the late Paleozoic era
(E) contained far fewer species than the late Paleozoic era did

23 According to the passage, "the pace of hominid evolution sped up around 18 million years ago" (lines 65–67) most likely because

(A) *Australopithecus* developed a larger brain
(B) *Homo erectus* developed better means of hunting and social interaction
(C) *Homo erectus* invaded and took over the environment of *Australopithecus*
(D) *Australopithecus* developed large teeth, which enabled it to eat a wider variety of foods
(E) a natural catastrophe, perhaps a meteor, destroyed many species that were competing with the hominids

24 Given the information in the passage as a whole, how would the author most likely answer the opening question of the passage?

(A) The gaps in the fossil record indicate clearly that all organisms evolve in punctuated equilibrium.
(B) The example of *Homo erectus* demonstrates that no species can remain stable for very long.
(C) The rapidity with which species evolve depends on many factors, so evolution can occur gradually or in a punctuated manner.
(D) Only occasional mass extinctions interrupt the gradual evolution of species.
(E) The father of evolution, Charles Darwin, was correct in believing that all species evolve gradually over long periods of time.

STOP You may check your work, on this section only, until time is called.

Section 4

Time—25 minutes
35 Questions

Directions for "Improving Sentences" Questions

Each of the sentences below contains one underlined portion. The portion may contain one or more errors in grammar, usage, construction, precision, diction (choice of words), or idiom. Some of the sentences are correct.

Consider the meaning of the original sentence, and choose the answer that best expresses that meaning. If the original sentence is best, choose (A), because it repeats the original phrasing. Choose the phrasing that creates the clearest, most precise, and most effective sentence.

<table>
<tr><td>EXAMPLE:</td><td>EXAMPLE ANSWER:</td></tr>
</table>

The children <u>couldn't hardly believe their eyes.</u>
- (A) couldn't hardly believe their eyes
- (B) would not hardly believe their eyes
- (C) could hardly believe their eyes
- (D) couldn't nearly believe their eyes
- (E) could hardly believe his or her eyes

EXAMPLE ANSWER:
(C)

---

1 Renowned for his skills on the trumpet, Louis Armstrong also <u>thrilling listeners with his remarkable and unique singing voice</u>.

- (A) thrilling listeners with his remarkable and unique singing voice
- (B) thrilled listeners with his remarkable and unique singing voice
- (C) with his remarkable and unique singing voice thrilled listeners
- (D) thrilled listeners remarkably with his singing voice that was unique
- (E) thrilling listeners, his remarkable and unique singing voice

2 Like children, cats often develop a love for certain <u>toys, creating games and diversions</u> that can occupy them for hours.

- (A) toys, creating games and diversions
- (B) toys and creating games and diverting
- (C) toys and in creating games and diversions
- (D) toys; and these create games and diversions
- (E) toys, the creation of games and diversions

3 Marcus Garvey argued that assimilation into mainstream culture, far from being a panacea for African Americans, <u>would be a distracting factor from their ultimate goals</u>.

- (A) would be a distracting factor from their ultimate goals
- (B) would factor to distract them from their ultimate goals
- (C) would, for their ultimate goals, be a distraction
- (D) distracting them from their ultimate goals
- (E) would distract them from their ultimate goals

4 Pretending to be sick to avoid taking her chemistry test, <u>Chandra's attempt failed to convince</u> her parents.

- (A) Chandra's attempt failed to convince
- (B) Chandra's attempt to convince failed
- (C) Chandra attempted to fail to convince
- (D) Chandra failed to convince
- (E) Chandra failed but attempted to convince

5 <u>Believing his speech to be superior to the other candidates</u>, Walter walked confidently into the assembly hall.

(A) Believing his speech to be superior to the other candidates
(B) Believing his speech superior to the other candidates
(C) Of the belief that his speech was superior to the other candidates
(D) Believing his speech to be superior to those of the other candidates
(E) Of the belief that his speech was superior over the other candidates

6 <u>Undeterred by her parents' opposition</u>, Rachel changed majors during her junior year, convinced that she had found her calling in the study of romantic poetry.

(A) Undeterred by her parents' opposition
(B) Undeterred and opposed by her parents
(C) Undeterred by her parents whose opposition
(D) Her parents' opposition undeterring her
(E) Undeterred to her parents opposition

7 The field commanders quickly realized that they had lost command of their troops, who had become scattered, <u>undisciplined, and most were becoming demoralized</u>.

(A) undisciplined, and most were becoming demoralized
(B) were losing discipline and morale
(C) undisciplined, and demoralized
(D) were undisciplined, and they were demoralized
(E) and had become undisciplined and demoralized

8 Standardized tests, some argue, do not indicate a student's academic skill but <u>rather their ability to memorize and use a set of test-taking tricks</u>.

(A) rather their ability to memorize and use a set of test-taking tricks
(B) instead it tests your ability to memorize and use test-taking tricks
(C) also the ability to memorize and use a set of test-taking tricks
(D) rather the ability to memorize and use a set of test-taking tricks
(E) instead the ability of memorizing and using a set of test-taking tricks

9 Muhammad Ali, known almost as much for his controversies outside the ring as for his glory within <u>it, becoming a great American icon</u>.

(A) it, becoming a great American icon
(B) it, has become a great American icon
(C) it; has thereby become a great American icon
(D) it; he has become a great American icon
(E) it, and so has become a great American icon

10 The brochure describing the camp requested that we <u>are at the registration center</u> promptly at noon.

(A) are at the registration center
(B) should be getting to the registration center
(C) should get at the registration center
(D) would be to the registration center
(E) be at the registration center

11 Without such detailed information about the disaster, the agency could not <u>have allocated the proper resources to distribute</u> the necessary food, medicine, and clothing.

(A) have allocated the proper resources to distribute
(B) allocate the proper resources in order for the distribution of
(C) be allocating the proper resources to distribute
(D) have been allocating the proper resources for the distribution of
(E) allocated the proper resources to distribute

GO ON TO THE NEXT PAGE ▸▸▸

Directions for "Identifying Sentence Error" Questions

The following sentences may contain errors in grammar, usage, diction (choice of words), or idiom. Some of the sentences are correct. No sentence contains more than 1 error.

If the sentence contains an error, it is underlined and lettered. The parts that are not underlined are correct.

If there is an error, select the part that must be changed to correct the sentence.

If there is no error, choose (E).

4 →

EXAMPLE:
By the time <u>they reached</u> the halfway point
            A

<u>in the race</u>, <u>most of the runners</u> <u>hadn't hardly</u>
  B   C   D
begun to hit their stride. <u>No error</u>
                 E

SAMPLE ANSWER:

(D)

---

12 After all the <u>children's</u> names were <u>wrote</u>
           A   B
down, they were <u>allowed</u> to proceed to
               C
recess, <u>joining the rest</u> of their classmates
         D
outside. <u>No error</u>
         E

13 Because each of the candidates had a very

<u>different position on</u> <u>on the matter</u>, the
     A   B
voters were <u>able to select</u> from a very diverse
         C
set of options <u>from which to choose</u>.
                D
<u>No error</u>
  E

14 The film was <u>a watershed</u> in art <u>history: its</u>
            A   B
stylistic innovations <u>catalyzed</u> a revolution
            C
<u>in American movies</u>. <u>No error</u>
    D   E

15 An <u>astute tactician</u>, an experienced player,
     A
and <u>charismatic as a leader</u>, Terrence was
     B
<u>an obvious choice</u> to be the next captain
     C
<u>of the soccer team</u>. <u>No error</u>
    D   E

16 His chronic back pain and <u>strong dislike</u> for
                    A
manual labor were <u>a reason</u> why Thomas
           B
<u>refused</u> to help the others <u>shovel snow</u> from
  C   D
the driveway. <u>No error</u>
         E

17 Tabitha had a <u>maddening</u> habit of extending
          A
trips <u>unnecessarily</u>, <u>leading friends</u> on
     B   C
<u>roundabout, circuitous</u> routes. <u>No error</u>
    D   E

GO ON TO THE NEXT PAGE ▶▶▶

18 The <u>subtle oration</u> left Perry <u>confused; he</u>
          A   B

was not confident that he <u>truly understood</u>
                                      C

the message <u>eluded</u> to by the speaker.
             D

<u>No error</u>
  E

19 Still nervous <u>hours after watching</u> the
                       A

horror movie, Annie <u>clutching</u> her sheets
                        B

<u>tighter every time</u> a noise from the street
      C

<u>reached</u> her ear.   <u>No error</u>
  D   E

20 Throwing her shoe, <u>stomping on the floor,</u>
                     A

and screaming at the top of her lungs, the

<u>demonstrative girl</u> persisted <u>in arguing</u> her
       B   C

point, <u>leaving her parents</u> at a loss as to how
          D

to subdue her.   <u>No error</u>
                E

21 Ariel was <u>dumbfounded</u> when she did not
           A

get into <u>her favorite college</u>, because her
          B

grade point average was higher than

<u>the rest of her classmates</u> and her
        C

after-school activities were <u>so impressive.</u>
                      D

<u>No error</u>
  E

22 The <u>emissary for</u> the committee stated that
       A

<u>their</u> position <u>on the matter</u> remained
  B   C

neutral and that no amount of <u>cajolery</u>
                    D

would cause a shift in either direction.

<u>No error</u>
  E

23 Brian hopes that his training program

<u>will help</u> him <u>to become faster</u> and stronger
  A   B

than <u>both</u> of his chief rivals for the position
      C

of quarterback, each of whom <u>receive</u> more
                    D

practice time with the varsity team.

<u>No error</u>
  E

24 The magician's skill <u>left</u> the children
               A

both <u>awestruck and inspired</u>; they all
        B

left the party <u>convinced that</u>, if they
           C

<u>tried hard enough</u>, they could pull a rabbit
       D

out of any hat.   <u>No error</u>
                E

25 The genre of romance literature, now

<u>primarily associated</u> with love stories,
      A

actually <u>encompass</u> a much broader range
        B

of themes <u>including</u> chivalry, heroism
        C

<u>and travel</u> to foreign lands.   <u>No error</u>
  D   E

26 The settlers <u>experimented</u> for months
　　　　　　　　A
<u>to find</u> the best method <u>to channel</u> water
　B　　　　　　　　　　C
from the river to <u>their</u> fields and homes.
　　　　　　　　D

<u>No error</u>
　E

4

27 Ms. Parker <u>read</u> the account with <u>so much</u>
　　　　　　A　　　　　　　　　　B
emotion and urgency <u>as</u> we could clearly
　　　　　　　　　　C
envision ourselves <u>embroiled</u> in the battle
　　　　　　　　　　D
ourselves.　<u>No error</u>
　　　　　　　E

28 Several college coaches came to the

tournament hoping to find <u>perspective</u>
　　　　　　　　　　　　　　A
players <u>who</u> demonstrated <u>not only</u>
　　　B　　　　　　　　C
strong basketball skills but also the ability

<u>to work</u> as members of a team.　<u>No error</u>
　D　　　　　　　　　　　　　　　E

29 In the school's new camp <u>for the performing</u>
　　　　　　　　　　　　　　　A
<u>arts</u> students choreograph <u>their own</u> dances,
　A　　　　　　　　　　　　B
develop <u>their acting skills</u>, and <u>will write</u>
　　　　　C　　　　　　　　　D
and perform their own plays.　<u>No error</u>
　　　　　　　　　　　　　　E

GO ON TO THE NEXT PAGE ▶▶▶

Questions 30–35 refer to the following passage.

(1) Few people have had as strong an impact on an industry as the impact that Charlie Chaplin had on the world of film. (2) Born into an impoverished London family, Chaplin crossed the Atlantic and became a pioneer in silent comedic movies. (3) Charlie's mother suffered from severe mental illness, which forced her to spend time institutionalized. (4) Early in his film career, Chaplin developed his signature character, the "Little Tramp," who amused audiences repeatedly with his clever physical comedy and endearing sensitivity. (5) Modest yet clearly intelligent, shy yet always at the center of action, the Tramp's embodiment was of the genius of Chaplin's artistry.

(6) Being writer, director, and editing his own work, Chaplin faced a daunting challenge with the rise of "talkie" films, which dried up the market for the Tramp. (7) His response was to take on the additional role of composer, writing beautiful scores to accompany his work and thus allowing the Tramp to remain speechless. (8) Whether it was the mastery of his work or the audience's tendency, during the Great Depression, to identify with his character, Chaplin managed to defy the odds and maintain a tremendous level of popularity and success in the face of technological advancement.

(9) A vocal liberal in a time of conservative rule, he became a target for men like Senator Joseph McCarthy and his House Un-American Activities Committee. (10) While he managed to avoid being named to McCarthy's Hollywood Ten, a list of blacklisted entertainment industry figures suspected of Communist connections, he drew the ire of J. Edgar Hoover with the messages imbedded within his films. (11) The fascination with Chaplin went beyond his artistic genius, however.

(12) Chaplin saw the dangers in Hitler's rise to power before most of the world had heard of the dictator. (13) He saw industry becoming mechanized and impersonal and believed in a connection between the atomic bomb and murder. (14) Outraged at what they viewed as subversive propaganda created by an immoral man, the United States government revoked Chaplin's re-entry visa during a trip to London in 1952. (15) Sixty-three years old and tired of fighting against a force unwilling to hear his message, Chaplin agreed to exile rather than to going back to America and facing interrogation and lived the rest of his years in Europe. (16) He returned twenty years later to receive an Academy Award for lifetime achievement.

30 Which of the following is the best revision of the underlined portion of sentence 1 (reproduced below)?

Few people have had as strong an impact on an industry as the impact that Charlie Chaplin had on the world of film.

(A) the impact that Charlie Chaplin had on the world of film
(B) Charlie Chaplin had on the world of film
(C) the impact upon the world of film by Charlie Chaplin
(D) Charlie Chaplin's impact on the world of film
(E) Charlie Chaplin and his impact on the world of film

31 Which sentence contributes least to the unity of the first paragraph?

(A) sentence 1
(B) sentence 2
(C) sentence 3
(D) sentence 4
(E) sentence 5

GO ON TO THE NEXT PAGE ▶▶▶

32 Which of the following is the best version of the underlined portion of sentence 5 (reproduced below)?

Modest yet clearly intelligent, shy yet always at the center of action, the <u>Tramp's embodiment was of the genius of Chaplin's artistry</u>.

(A) (no revision needed)
(B) Tramp was embodied for the genius of Chaplin's artistry
(C) Tramp and his embodiment of the genius of Chaplin's artistry
(D) Tramp embodied the genius of Chaplin's artistry
(E) Tramp's embodiment and the genius of Chaplin's artistry

33 Which of the following is the best version of the underlined portion of sentence 6 (reproduced below)?

<u>Being writer, director, and editing his own work</u>, Chaplin faced a daunting challenge with the rise of "talkie" films, which dried up the market for the Tramp.

(A) (no revision needed)
(B) Writing, directing, and being editor of his own work
(C) Being writer of his own work, directing and editing too
(D) Writing his own work, directing, and editing also
(E) As the writer, director, and editor of his own work

34 What is the most logical way to rearrange the sentences in paragraph 3?

(A) 11, 9, 10
(B) 10, 11, 9
(C) 11, 10, 9
(D) 9, 11, 10
(E) 10, 9, 11

35 In context, which of the following sentences best precedes sentence 12 as an introduction to the 4th paragraph?

(A) But Chaplin did not let his politics overwhelm his art.
(B) Chaplin's films allowed audiences to escape from hard political and economic times.
(C) Chaplin's fame and power came to dominate Hollywood.
(D) These messages addressed political and moral issues both inside and outside of the United States.
(E) Chaplin would never again be the same actor he once was.

STOP *You may check your work, on this section only, until time is called.*

Section 5

Time—~~20~~ 25 minutes
18 Questions

Directions for Multiple-Choice Questions

In this section, solve each problem, using any available space on the page for scratchwork. Then decide which is the best of the choices given and fill in the corresponding oval on your answer sheet.

- You may use a calculator on any problem. All numbers used are real numbers.
- Figures are drawn as accurately as possible EXCEPT when it is stated that the figure is not drawn to scale.
- All figures lie in a plane unless otherwise indicated.

Reference Information

$A = \pi r^2$ $A = \ell w$ $A = \frac{1}{2} bh$ $V = \ell wh$ $V = \pi r^2 h$ $c^2 = a^2 + b^2$ Special Right Triangles
$C = 2\pi r$

The arc of a circle measures 360°.
Every straight angle measures 180°.
The sum of the measures of the angles in a triangle is 180°.

---

1 Eric earns a 5% commission on each $200 stereo that he sells. How many stereos must he sells to earn $100?

(A)   5
(B)   10
(C)   15
(D)   20
(E)   25

$[200(x)].05 = 100$

(B)

2

Jane's Discount Music Superstore
Holiday Sales

	CDs	DVDs	Total
New		4,500	7,500
Used			
Total	7,000	7,000	14,000

Jane's Discount Music Superstore sells both new and used CDs and DVDs. On the basis of the information listed above, how many used DVDs were sold during the holiday season?

(A)   2500
(B)   3000
(C)   4000
(D)   6500
(E)   7000

GO ON TO THE NEXT PAGE ▶▶▶

3 One bag of potatoes of a certain brand weighs 40 ounces. Five pounds of these potatoes cost $4.00. If Larry has exactly $20.00 to spend on potatoes, what is the maximum number of bags he can buy? (1 pound = 16 ounces)

(A)   7
(B)   8
(C)   9
(D) 10
(E) 11

handwritten: 5×16 = 80, 2b = $4, b = $2, (D)

4

handwritten: h=3

What is the area of the shaded region in the figure above?

(A) 15
(B) 20
(C) 25
(D) 30
(E) 35

handwritten: 5×5=25, b×h = 2•5 = 10, 35, (e)

5

The rectangular solid above is constructed of 12 cubes that each have a volume of 8 cubic inches. What is the surface area of the solid?

(A)   32
(B)   48
(C)   96
(D) 128
(E) 144

handwritten: 12•8 = 96, 96 = V of whole, V = L×W×H, (e)

6 Set M consists of the consecutive integers from −15 to y, inclusive. If the sum of all of the integers in set M is 70, how many numbers are in the set?

(A) 33
(B) 34
(C) 35
(D) 36
(E) 37

7 In a round robin tennis tournament involving 7 players, each player will play every other player twice. How many total matches will be played in the tournament?

(A) 21
(B) 28
(C) 42
(D) 48
(E) 56

8

The figure above shows a right prism, the base of which is a quarter of a circle with center C. If the area of each base of the prism is 12.5π and the volume of the solid is 300π, what is the distance from point A to point B?

(A) 24
(B) 26
(C) 28
(D) 30
(E) 32

GO ON TO THE NEXT PAGE ▶▶▶

Directions for Student-Produced Response Questions

Each of the questions in this section requires you to solve the problem and enter your answer in a grid, as shown below.

- If your answer is 2/3 or .666 . . . , you must enter **the most accurate value the grid can accommodate,** but you may do this in one of four ways:

Start in first column

Start in second column

Grid as a truncated decimal

Grid as a rounded decimal

Grid result here

- In the example above, gridding a response of 0.67 or 0.66 is **incorrect** because it is less accurate than those above.
- The scoring machine cannot read what is written in the top row of boxes. You **MUST** fill in the numerical grid accurately to get credit for answering any question correctly. You should write your answer in the top row of boxes only to aid your gridding.
- Do **not** grid in a mixed fraction like $3\frac{1}{2}$ as $\boxed{3}\ \boxed{1}\ \boxed{/}\ \boxed{2}$, because it will be interpreted as $\frac{31}{2}$.
  Instead, convert it to an improper fraction like 7/2 or a decimal like 3.5 before gridding.
- None of the answers will be negative, because there is no negative sign in the grid.
- Some of the questions may have more than 1 correct answer. You must grid only 1 of the correct answers.
- You may use a calculator on any of these problems.
- All numbers in these problems are real numbers.
- Figures are drawn as accurately as possible EXCEPT when it is stated that the figure is not drawn to scale.
- All figures lie in a plane unless otherwise indicated.

9

In the figure above, if $x = y + 1$, what is the value of $3y + 3$?

10

Note: Figure not drawn to scale.

In the figure above, $AB = BC = CD = AD$ and quadrilateral $ABCD$ has an area of 480 square inches. What is the perimeter, in inches, of quadrilateral $ABCD$?

GO ON TO THE NEXT PAGE ▶▶▶

11

$$f(x) = 7x + 2$$
$$g(x) = x^2 - 5$$

Given the functions above, what is the value of $f(g(3))$?

12

How much less than x is $\dfrac{6x-9}{5} - \dfrac{x+6}{5}$?

5

13

If a and b are positive integers, $a + b < 20$, and the product ab is an even number, what is the largest possible value of a?

14

U	V
W	X
Y	Z

Note: Figure not drawn to scale.

In the figure above, a large rectangle is divided into 6 smaller rectangles that each have integer lengths and widths. The areas of rectangles *U*, *V*, and *W* are 18, 21, and 12, respectively. If the area of the entire figure is 117, what is the area of rectangle *Z*?

15

An elementary school class of 55 students is planning a field trip to a nearby aquarium. The price of admission is $15 per person. However, for groups of 60 or more people, the price is reduced to $13 per person. How much money would the class save by buying 60 tickets at the discounted price and using only 55 of them, instead of buying 55 individual tickets?

16

Points *W*, *X*, *Y*, and *Z* lie on a line in that order. If $WY = 15$, *X* is the midpoint of $\overline{WY}$, and $YZ = 2WX$, what is the length of $\overline{XZ}$?

17

For all numbers r and s, let $r \,\square\, s$ be defined by $r \,\square\, s = \dfrac{rs^2}{r-s}$. If $3 \,\square\, 2 = x$, what is the value of $x \,\square\, 3$?

18

Note: Figure not drawn to scale.

In $\triangle ABC$ above, $\overline{DC}$ is perpendicular to $\overline{AB}$, $BC = 5\sqrt{2}$, and $AD = 2DB$. What is the area of $\triangle ABC$?

STOP

You may check your work, on this section only, until time is called.

Section 6

Time—25 minutes
24 Questions

Each of the sentences below is missing one or two portions. Read each sentence, then select the word or words that most logically complete the sentence, taking into account the meaning of the sentence as a whole.

Example:

Rather than accepting the theory unquestioningly, Deborah regarded it with -------.

(A) mirth
(B) sadness
(C) responsibility
(D) ignorance
(E) skepticism

Correct response: (E)

1 The knee-jerk reflex is nearly ------- because it produces an immediate muscular response without sending information to the brain.

(A) transient
(B) instantaneous
(C) stagnant
(D) revitalized
(E) consecutive

2 Although starved and emaciated, the 2 stray cats nevertheless summoned the energy to fight ------- for the scraps of food.

(A) humanely
(B) vigilantly
(C) fluently
(D) ferociously
(E) dispassionately

3 Jennifer's ------- demeanor irritated her peers, who hated listening to her supercilious and pretentious remarks.

(A) reticent
(B) belligerent
(C) lofty
(D) self-effacing
(E) discomfited

4 The art of the sushi master takes years to grasp; only after years of ------- will a chef in training have the ------- to create his or her own work.

(A) apprenticeship . . . autonomy
(B) tutelage . . . ineptitude
(C) dormancy . . . sovereignty
(D) cultivation . . . boorishness
(E) quiescence . . . authority

5 The journalist had been called ------- by her editors because of her ability to get news stories before anyone else, but she later admitted that she had received early information from privileged sources, rather than through -------, as many thought.

(A) prophetic . . . prescience
(B) premeditated . . . predilection
(C) dismissive . . . omniscience
(D) preeminent . . . reluctance
(E) insolvent . . . foresight

GO ON TO THE NEXT PAGE ▸▸▸

The passages below are followed by questions based on their content. Answer each question based on what is stated or implied in the passages or the introductory material preceding them.

Questions 6–9 are based on the following passages.

Passage 1

The very differentness of the medieval universe from our own invites our study of it, for
Line we cannot fully appreciate the world we live in until we contrast it with a different *weltan-*
5 *schauung*, or "world picture," and the older cosmology is indeed very unlike our own. For example, C. S. Lewis has pointed out that where our universe is thought to be dark, the other one was presumed to be illuminated;
10 and while Pascal could be disturbed by the silence of the vast spaces between the stars, the universe was formerly thought to produce the "music of the spheres" that only the wise man could hear. Furthermore, the often-heard
15 charge that the earth-centered universe of former times was the product of man's sense of self-importance is questionable, for we may observe in a medieval poet and philosopher like Dante that although the spheres are first
20 described as surrounding the earth, they are then more properly seen in an inverted order surrounding God, so that God, not man, is at the center.

Passage 2

The mystical works of Hildegard of Bingen,
25 a 12th century German nun and daughter of a knight, reveal a great deal about the medieval mind. One of the earliest known composers of hymns, she also wrote plays and other works based on her migraine-inspired visions. She
30 also composed treatises, like Physica, that analyzed the physical world from a religious perspective. Hildegard's science was based on the Aristotelian categories of earth, water, air and fire, and on the then-common view of the rela-
35 tionship between mankind and nature: "All the elements served mankind and, sensing that man was alive, they busied themselves in aiding his life in every way."

6 Both passages are primarily concerned with

(A) describing the discoveries of great medieval scientists
(B) providing examples of how medieval thinkers perceived the world
(C) disproving modern assumptions about medieval history
(D) questioning medieval scientific theories
(E) showing the influence of religion on everyday life in medieval Europe

7 In Passage 1, the "other one" (line 9) refers to

(A) the far side of the galaxy
(B) the earth in contrast with outer space
(C) the sun
(D) the medieval universe
(E) an alternative cosmological theory

8 Pascal is mentioned in the passage primarily as an example of someone

(A) who could hear the "music of the spheres"
(B) who was among the first scientists to explore the medieval universe
(C) whose "world picture" was different from that of medieval times
(D) whose cosmology is very similar to that of poets like Dante
(E) who assumed that the universe was illuminated

9 Hildegard's view of the world as described in Passage 2 differs from Dante's view of the world as described in Passage 1 primarily in terms of its

(A) focus on religion
(B) assumption that the universe is ordered
(C) application of scientific methods
(D) public acceptance
(E) anthropocentrism

The passages below are followed by questions based on their content. Answer each question based on what is stated or implied in the passages or the introductory material preceding them.

Questions 10-16 pertain to the following passage.

The following passage was written by a naturalist about his studies of the wildlife in the African plains, particularly Serengeti National Park in Tanzania.

How can so many wild animals manage to survive in the Serengeti? Their migrations of Line course tell part of the story. By moving from place to place with the changing seasons, they
5 do not overuse and damage the grass in any one area. But other, less obvious factors also are involved.

Here on the eastern plains in January, it is clear that most of the animals are eating the
10 abundant grass that springs up like a well-mown lawn between low clumps of Sodom apple and indigo plants. Nearly all of them, from 1,500-pound eland bulls to tiny 10-pound Thomson's gazelle calves, are grazers, rather
15 than browsers, which feed on shrubs or the leaves of trees. Singly or in pairs, long lines, or little groups, they move over the green pastures, never remaining long in one place. Where the grass is all short, as it will be when
20 it has been heavily grazed, all the animals apparently eat much the same sort of grass. But where the grass is of varied lengths and toughness, we can see that each animal copes differently with the available fodder.
25 The herds of zebras tend to roam in areas separate from the rest of the grazing multitude. Unlike all the other grazers on the plain, they have teeth in both jaws. This enables them to deal with taller, coarser grass than can
30 the other herbivores. All the rest are various species of antelope, which nip off the grass between their lower incisors and toothless upper palates. Thus, the zebras eat down the longer grasses to a certain level and then move on.
35 Following the zebras come the wildebeests and, in better-wooded areas, hartebeests. These animals eat the grass down a stage further, until it is really short. (They also eat new growth before it has had a chance to grow
40 tall.) Then the Thomson's gazelles take over.

With their tails flicking constantly, they nibble at the individual leaves of the tussocks and on the tiny plants that grow between them. By the time all of them have finished, the plain resem-
45 bles a closely but rather unevenly mown lawn.

Thus, one species or another of animal often predominates over a great expanse of the plain, depending on the height to which the grass has grown or has been grazed. Finally,
50 when all has been eaten down rather short, most of the grazers leave the area altogether.

Two or three weeks later, when more rain has brought on fresh growth, the herds may return to feed over the area again. Perhaps
55 they move about in response to the intensity of local showers, which can vary a good deal over a distance of only a mile or two. In any case, the result of their returning again and again to the same areas is to keep the grass
60 green and short, just as the repeated mowing of a lawn in summer does.

If, as a result of badly drawn park boundaries or some other cause, the migrant herds of Serengeti were confined to either the west-
65 ern woodlands or the eastern short-grass plains, they would be forced to return to the same areas too often and would eventually so weaken the grass that it would die out. But as they eat it down, they move away and the
70 grass recovers.

10 As a whole, this passage is primarily concerned with

(A) criticizing human intervention in a natural habitat
(B) describing the life cycle of particular plants
(C) suggesting a way to avert a natural disaster
(D) showing how to distinguish grazers from browsers
(E) describing how a particular ecosystem works

Excerpted from *The Life of the African Plains*, Leslie Brown, McGraw-Hill, 1972, pp. 69–71

GO ON TO THE NEXT PAGE ▸▸▸

11 Lines 22–24 ("Where the grass . . . the available fodder") discuss the relationship between

(A) what they eat
(B) the seasons and relative animal populations
(C) plant size and dietary variety
(D) zebras and antelopes
(E) climate and plant health

12 According to the passage, browsers differ from grazers primarily in terms of

(A) what they eat
(B) how quickly they eat
(C) their weight
(D) how they digest their food
(E) the season in which they migrate

13 The passage indicates that the various species of antelope that graze on the Serengeti

(A) feed on shrubs and leaves of trees
(B) lack upper teeth
(C) can easily eat tall and coarse grass
(D) usually graze with zebras
(E) tend to consume all of the vegetation in an area before moving on

14 The passage suggests that the sequence of grazers described in the 3rd and 4th paragraphs—zebras followed by wildebeests followed by Thomson's gazelles—is generally maintained UNLESS

(A) the grazers arrive at a new pasture
(B) the grass is of various lengths and textures
(C) there are browsers among them
(D) fresh rains have fallen
(E) all of the available grass is short

15 According to the passage, rain affects the feeding habits of Serengeti grazers primarily by

(A) flooding and destroying some of the pastures
(B) forcing the browsers to take shelter under trees
(C) rendering the plants edible again
(D) weakening the grass
(E) confining the herds to high plateaus

16 The final paragraph suggests that maintaining the grasslands of the Serengeti requires

(A) freedom of the grazers to move as they wish
(B) frequent rainless periods
(C) frequent removal of dead plants
(D) the restriction of grazers to the woodlands
(E) a separation of grazers and browsers

Questions 17–24 are based on the following passage.

The following is an excerpt from an essay by George Bernard Shaw, written in 1889, on the economic basis of socialism.

All economic analyses begin with the cultivation of the earth. To the mind's eye of the
Line astronomer the earth is a ball spinning in space without ulterior motives. To the bodily
5 eye of the primitive cultivator it is a vast green plain, from which, by sticking a spade into it, wheat and other edible matters can be made to spring. To the eye of the sophisticated city man this vast green plain appears rather as a
10 great gaming table, your chances in the game depending chiefly on the place where you deposit your stakes. To the economist, again, the green plain is a sort of burial place of hidden treasure, where all the forethought and indus-
15 try of man are set at naught by the caprice of the power which hid the treasure. The wise and patient workman strikes his spade in here, and with heavy toil can discover nothing but a poor quality of barley, some potatoes,
20 and plentiful nettles, with a few dock leaves to cure his stings. The foolish spendthrift on the other side of the hedge, gazing idly at the sand glittering in the sun, suddenly realizes that the earth is offering him gold—is dancing it be-
25 fore his listless eyes lest it should escape him. Another man, searching for some more of this tempting gold, comes upon a great hoard of coal, or taps a jet of petroleum. Thus is Man mocked by Earth his stepmother, and never
30 knows as he tugs at her closed hand whether it contains diamonds or flints, good red wheat or a few clayey and blighted cabbages. Thus too he becomes a gambler, and scoffs at the theorists who prate of industry and honesty

35 and equality. Yet against this fate he eternally
    rebels. For since in gambling the many must
    lose in order that the few may win; since dis-
    honesty is mere shadow-grasping where
    everyone is dishonest; and since inequality is
40 bitter to all except the highest, and miserably
    lonely for him, men come greatly to desire
    that these capricious gifts of Nature might be
    intercepted by some agency having the power
    and the goodwill to distribute them justly
45 according to the labor done by each in the
    collective search for them. This desire is
    Socialism; and, as a means to its fulfillment,
    Socialists have devised communes, kingdoms,
    principalities, churches, manors, and finally,
50 when all these had succumbed to the old
    gambling spirit, the Social Democratic State,
    which yet remains to be tried. As against
    Socialism, the gambling spirit urges man to
    allow no rival to come between his private in-
55 dividual powers and Stepmother Earth, but
    rather to secure some acres of her and take
    his chance of getting diamonds instead of cab-
    bages. This is private property or Unsocialism.
    Our own choice is shown by our continual
60 aspiration to possess property, our common
    hailing of it as sacred, our setting apart of the
    word Respectable for those who have attained
    it, our ascription of pre-eminent religiousness
    to commandments forbidding its violation,
65 and our identification of law and order among
    men with its protection. Therefore is it vital to
    a living knowledge of our society that Private
    Property should be known in every step of its
    progress from its source in cupidity to its end
70 in confusion.

Shaw, George Bernard and H. G. Wilshire. Various authors. See
    Contents. *Fabian Essays in Socialism.* New York: Humboldt
    Publishing Co., ed. George Bernard Shaw, H. G. Wilshire,
    and W. D. P. Bliss, 1891. [Online] available from http://www.
    econlib.org/library/

17 Which of the following best summarizes the
        main idea of this passage?

(A) Socialism provides the best means for
     humanity to manage the capricious-
     ness of nature.

(B) Astronomers, farmers, and economists
     have much to learn from each other.

(C) Patient and diligent farmers will
     always be rewarded.

(D) Foolish people are often just as lucky
     as industrious workers.

(E) All people properly aspire to own
     property and earn respectability.

18 The "primitive cultivator" (line 5) is

(A) a supernatural creator
(B) an astronomer
(C) a farmer
(D) a machine
(E) a philosopher

19 According to the passage, the perspective of
the "astronomer" (line 3) differs primarily
from the perspective of the "foolish spendthrift" (line 21) in that the astronomer views
the earth as

(A) generous, while the spendthrift views
     the earth as stingy

(B) a beautiful gem, while the spendthrift
     views the earth as a dull, sandy
     expanse

(C) dangerously capricious, while the
     spendthrift views the earth as a source
     of unlimited riches

(D) lacking regard for humankind, while
     the spendthrift views the earth as
     generous

(E) moving in an orderly fashion, while
     the spendthrift views the earth's move-
     ments as dangerously random

20 The "closed hand" in line 30 refers to

(A) the strength of the farmer
(B) the tendency of the earth to hide its
     treasures
(C) the abundance of resources that
     spring from the earth
(D) the laziness of the foolish spendthrift
(E) the fact that the earth is inanimate and
     lacking will

GO ON TO THE NEXT PAGE ▸▸▸

21 The author mentions "industry and honesty and equality" (lines 34–35) in order to make the point that

(A) some moral habits are not as valuable as many claim
(B) fate tends to favor those who are virtuous
(C) too many people disdain ethical behavior
(D) the natural order reflects a moral order
(E) hard work and morality are their own reward

6 →

22 The "fate" mentioned in line 35 is the fate of

(A) the hard-working farmer
(B) the theorist who preaches honesty and equality
(C) the gambler
(D) the owner of private property
(E) the socialist

23 The author qualifies his view of the "Social Democratic State" by indicating that it

(A) appeals to the gambling instinct
(B) will discourage workers from being industrious
(C) places a high value on selfishness
(D) encourages people to be wasteful
(E) has not yet been attempted

24 The sentence "Our own choice . . . its protection" (lines 59–66) suggests that most people of the author's era

(A) are deeply religious
(B) are becoming skeptical of the concept of respectability
(C) place a high value on the concept of private property
(D) desire a socialist democratic state
(E) are not as industrious as they believe themselves to be

STOP   *You may check your work, on this section only, until time is called.*

Section 7

Time—20 minutes
16 Questions

Directions for Multiple-Choice Questions

In this section, solve each problem, using any available space on the page for scratchwork. Then decide which is the best of the choices given and fill in the corresponding oval on your answer sheet.

- You may use a calculator on any problem. All numbers used are real numbers.
- Figures are drawn as accurately as possible EXCEPT when it is stated that the figure is not drawn to scale.
- All figures lie in a plane unless otherwise indicated.

Reference Information

$A = \pi r^2$
$C = 2\pi r$ $\quad A = \ell w \quad\quad A = \frac{1}{2}bh \quad V = \ell wh \quad\quad V = \pi r^2 h \quad\quad c^2 = a^2 + b^2 \quad$ Special Right Triangles

The number of degrees of arc in a circle is 360.
The measure in degrees of a straight angle is 180.
The sum of the measures in degrees of the angles of a triangle is 180.

---

1 If $3x + 5x + 8x = 32$, what is the value of x?

(A) 1
(B) 2
(C) 3
(D) 4
(E) 5

2 If $\left(\frac{1}{x}\right)\left(\frac{x}{3}\right)(6x) = 8$, then $x =$

(A) 1
(B) 2
(C) 3
(D) 4
(E) 5

3 If $5b - 10 \geq 15$, which of the following expresses all of the possible values of b?

(A) $b \geq 5$
(B) $b \geq 1$
(C) $b \geq 9$
(D) $b \leq 1$
(E) $b \leq 5$

4 If $t\%$ of 60 is 30% of 50, what is the value of t?

(A) 12
(B) 15
(C) 25
(D) 30
(E) 35

Handwritten work:
$\frac{60t}{100} = \frac{30}{100} \cdot 50$

$60t = 150\emptyset$

$\frac{60t}{100} = 15$

$t =$

Ⓒ $\frac{t}{100} \cdot 60 = \frac{30 \cdot 50}{100}$
$\qquad\qquad 2$
$\qquad\qquad 15$

5 If it takes 40 minutes to write h holiday cards, then in terms of h, how many holiday cards can be written at that rate in 8 hours?

Handwritten work:
$\frac{h}{40} = \frac{x}{8 \cdot 60}$
$\quad\quad\quad 480$
$12h = x$

(A) $\frac{5}{h}$

$\frac{h}{40m} \cdot \frac{60m}{1} =$

(B) $8h$

(C) $12h$

(D) $\frac{5}{h}$

$4 \, 8 \, \frac{3h}{2} = \frac{h}{8}$

(E) $\frac{12}{h}$

$12h$ Ⓒ

6

$$\begin{array}{cccccccc} A & B & C & & D & & E \\ \bullet & \bullet & \bullet & & \bullet & & \bullet \end{array}$$
$$-2 \qquad -1 \qquad 0 \qquad 1 \qquad 2$$

Which of the labeled points on the number line above could represent the product -1.5×1.25?

(A) A ✓ Ⓐ
(B) B
(C) C
(D) D
(E) E

7 If 4 people share 100 baseball cards and each person must receive a different positive whole number of cards, what is the greatest possible number of cards any one person may have?

Handwritten work: $1, 2, 3 + x = 100$
$\qquad\qquad 6 + x = 100$

(A) 28
(B) 29
(C) 94 ✓
(D) 95 $1, 2, 3, 94$
(E) 97

Ⓒ

8

Fuel Efficiency over Time

Age of car (in years)	1	2	3	4	5
Miles per gallon	36	35	31	26	20

Which of the following graphs best represents the data presented in the table above?

9 If the sum of 7 integers is even, at most how many of these integers could be odd?

(A) 3
(B) 4
(C) 5
(D) 6 ✓ Ⓓ
(E) 7

10 In a particular year, if January 22 is the 4th Wednesday of the month, what is the date of the 4th Monday in January?

(A) January 20
(B) January 21
(C) January 26
(D) January 27 ✓
(E) January 28

1
8
15
22

Ⓓ

Th, F, S, Su, M

11

The graph above shows the number of teachers in Hamden who live in a house, the number of teachers who live in an apartment and the number of each who use gas or oil heat. Of the teachers who use gas heat, what fraction live in a house?

(A) $\dfrac{60}{100}$

(B) $\dfrac{73}{100}$ $\dfrac{60}{60+13} = \dfrac{60}{73}$

(C) $\dfrac{60}{80}$

(D) $\dfrac{60}{73}$ ✓ Ⓓ

(E) $\dfrac{73}{80}$

Average Speed

12 If $5x + 7y = 18$ and $2x - 4y = 6$, what is the value of $7x + 3y$?

(A) 7
(B) 12
(C) 19
(D) 24 ✓ Ⓓ
(E) 31

㉔

$\dfrac{T}{N} = A$

rate
$r \times t = d$
$r = \dfrac{d}{t}$

$24 + 24$

13

$180 - Y$ $z°$ $180 - ((180-y)-z)$ 861
$y°$ $x°$ $180 - +y+z$
$x°$ $x°$ 1360
m

$y = z + x$
$y - z = x$

In the figure above, if $l \parallel m$, what is the value of x in terms of y and z?

(A) $y - z$ ✓
(B) $z - y$ Ⓐ
(C) $z + y$
(D) $180 - y - z$
(E) $90 - z - y$

14 Julie Ann commutes to work one morning at an average speed of 40 mph. She returns home along the same route at an average speed of 24 mph. If she spends a total of 2 hours traveling to and from work that day, how many miles is her commute to work?

(A) 24   Ⓑ
(B) 30
(C) 32
(D) 34
(E) 40

$R \times T = D$

40	X	40X
24	2-X	24(2-X)
		48-24X

$40X = 48 - 24X$
$+24X \qquad +24X$

$64X = 48$
$X = .75$

15

$y = f(x)$

Given the graph of $y = f(x)$ above, which of the following represents the graph of $y = f(x - 2) + 4$?

(A)

(B)

(C)

(D)

(E)

16

Note: Figure not drawn to scale.

Line segment $\overline{BD}$ is tangent to the circle with center O at point A. If $\overline{DO} = \overline{BO} = 12$, what is the area of the _unshaded region_ of $\triangle BOD$?

(A) $36\sqrt{3} - 12\pi$

(B) $36\sqrt{2} - 12\pi$

(C) $36 - 12\pi$

(D) $72\sqrt{2} - 36\pi$

(E) $72\sqrt{3} - 36\pi$

7

STOP   You may check your work, on this section only, until time is called.

Section 8

Time—20 minutes
19 Questions

Each of the sentences below is missing one or two portions. Read each sentence, then select the word or words that most logically complete the sentence, taking into account the meaning of the sentence as a whole.

Example:

Rather than accepting the theory unquestioningly, Deborah regarded it with -------.

    (A) mirth
    (B) sadness
    (C) responsibility
    (D) ignorance
    (E) skepticism

Correct response: (E)

8

1 The ------- with which technology is advancing makes it difficult for businesses to stay current, and as a result, they often find themselves using ------- equipment.

    (A) urgency . . . progressive
    (B) swiftness . . . conventional
    (C) torpidity . . . antiquated
    (D) lassitude . . . innovative
    (E) rapidity . . . outdated

2 The ------- of James Joyce's early works, which used clear prose to reveal the inner dimensions of his characters, gave way to ------- and arcane style of writing in such books as Ulysses and Finnegans Wake, which explored character through neologisms and obscure literary tricks.

    (A) inspiration . . . an emotional
    (B) lucidity . . . an opaque
    (C) vagueness . . . a simple
    (D) popularity . . . a concise
    (E) anachronism . . . a derivative

3 Critics of former British Prime Minister Winston Churchill complained that he too often acted -------, choosing his strategies arbitrarily without much explanation.

    (A) diligently
    (B) impulsively
    (C) viciously
    (D) malevolently
    (E) savagely

4 Sixteenth-century British monarch Henry VIII was a king who demanded ------- from his courtiers; he did not hesitate to execute anyone who acted irreverently.

    (A) insolence
    (B) impudence
    (C) truculence
    (D) deference
    (E) ignominy

GO ON TO THE NEXT PAGE ▶▶▶

5 In the 1600s, Italian scientist Galileo Galilei was ------- and sentenced to life in prison for being a ------- when, contrary to church teachings, he proposed that the sun, rather than the earth, was the center of the universe.

(A) ostracized . . . hermit
(B) venerated . . . demagogue
(C) hallowed . . . revisionist
(D) denounced . . . heretic
(E) reviled . . . luminary

6 Known for her ------- and iconoclastic stance on most political matters, the Senator had a hard time securing the votes of the more ------- party members during her presidential campaign.

(A) contentious . . . orthodox
(B) controversial . . . litigious
(C) disingenuous . . . vituperative
(D) dissident . . . idolatrous
(E) heretical . . . polemical

8

The passages below are followed by questions based on their content and the relationship between them. Answer the questions on the basis of what is stated or implied in the passages or the introductory material that precedes them.

Questions 7–19 are based on the following passages.

The following passages present 2 viewpoints on the assimilation of ex-slaves into American culture in the late 19th century. Passage 1 is from a speech given by Booker T. Washington, an African American ex-slave and prominent educator, at the Atlanta Exposition in 1895. Passage 2 is an excerpt from a paper entitled The Conservation of Races *written by W. E. B. Du Bois in 1897.*

Passage 1

A ship lost at sea for many days suddenly sighted a friendly vessel. From the mast of the
Line unfortunate vessel was seen a signal, "Water, water; we die of thirst!" The answer from the
5 friendly vessel at once came back, "Cast down your bucket where you are." And a second, third and fourth signal for water were answered, "Cast down your bucket where you

are." The captain of the distressed vessel, at
10 last heeding the injunction, cast down his bucket, and it came up full of fresh, sparkling water from the mouth of the Amazon River. To those of my race who depend upon bettering their condition in a foreign land or who
15 underestimate the importance of cultivating friendly relations with the Southern white man, who is their next-door neighbor, I would say: "Cast down your bucket where you are"— cast it down in making friends in every manly
20 way of the people of all races by whom we are surrounded.

Cast it down in agriculture, in mechanics, in commerce, in domestic service, and in the professions. And in this connection it is well
25 to bear, when it comes to business, pure and simple, it is in the South that the Negro[1] is given a man's chance in the commercial world, and in nothing is this Exposition more eloquent than in emphasizing this chance.
30 Our greatest danger is that in the great leap from slavery to freedom we may overlook the fact that the masses of us are to live by the production of our hands, and fail to keep in mind that we shall prosper in proportion as
35 we learn to dignify and glorify common labor and put brains and skill into the common occupations of life; shall prosper in proportion as we learn to draw the line between the superficial and the substantial, the ornamental
40 gew-gaws of life and the useful. No race can prosper till it learns that there is as much dignity in tilling a field as in writing a poem. It is at the bottom of life we must begin, and not at the top. Nor should we permit our grievances
45 to overshadow our opportunities.

To those of the white race who look to the incoming of those of foreign birth and strange tongue and habits for the prosperity of the South, were I permitted I would repeat what I
50 say to my own race, "Cast down your bucket where you are." Cast it down among the eight millions of Negroes whose habits you know, whose fidelity and love you have tested in days when to have proved treacherous meant the ruin of your firesides. Cast down your bucket
56 among these people who have, without strikes and labor wars, tilled your fields, cleared your forests, built your railroads and cities, and brought forth treasures from the bowels of the

[1]African American

60 earth, and helped make possible this magnifi-
cent representation of the progress of the
South. Casting down your bucket among my
people, helping and encouraging them as you
are doing on these grounds, and to education
65 of head, hand and heart, you will find that
they will buy your surplus land, make blos-
som the waste places in your fields, and run
your factories.

Passage 2

Here, then, is the dilemma, and it is a puz-
70 zling one, I admit. No Negro who has given
earnest thought to the situation of his people
in America has failed, at some time in life, to
find himself at these cross-roads; has failed to
ask himself at some time: What, after all, am
75 I? Am I an American or am I a Negro? Can I
be both? Or is it my duty to cease to be a
Negro as soon as possible and be an American? If I strive as a Negro, am I not perpetuat-
ing the very cleft that threatens and separates
80 Black and White America? Is not my only possible practical aim the subduction of all that is
Negro in me to the American? Does my black
blood place upon me any more obligation to
assert my nationality than German, or Irish or
85 Italian blood would?

It is such incessant self-questioning and the
hesitation that arises from it, that is making
the present period a time of vacillation and
contradiction for the American Negro; com-
90 bined race action is stifled, race responsibility
is shirked, race enterprises languish, and the
best blood, the best talent, the best energy of
the Negro people cannot be marshalled to do
the bidding of the race. They stand back to
95 make room for every rascal and demagogue
who chooses to cloak his selfish deviltry under
the veil of race pride.

Is this right? Is it rational? Is it good policy?
Have we in America a distinct mission as a
100 race—a distinct sphere of action and an opportunity for race development, or is self-
obliteration the highest end to which Negro
blood dare aspire?

If we carefully consider what race prejudice
105 really is, we find it, historically, to be nothing
but the friction between different groups of
people; it is the difference in aim, in feeling, in
ideals of two different races; if, now, this difference exists touching territory, laws, lan-
110 guage, or even religion, it is manifest that
these people cannot live in the same territory
without fatal collision; but if, on the other

hand, there is substantial agreement in laws,
language and religion; if there is a satisfactory
115 adjustment of economic life, then there is no
reason why, in the same country and on the
same street, two or three great national ideals
might not thrive and develop, that men of different races might not strive together for their
120 race ideals as well, perhaps even better, than
in isolation. Here, it seems to me, is the reading of the riddle that puzzles so many of us.
We are Americans, not only by birth and by
citizenship, but by our political ideals, our
125 language, our religion. Farther than that, our
Americanism does not go. At that point, we
are Negroes, members of a vast historic race
that from the very dawn of creation has slept,
but half awakening in the dark forests of its
130 African fatherland. We are the first fruits of
this new nation, the harbinger of that black
tomorrow which is yet destined to soften the
whiteness of the Teutonic today. We are that
people whose subtle sense of song has given
135 America its only American music, its only
American fairy tales, its only touch of pathos
and humor amid its mad money-getting plu-
tocracy. As such, it is our duty to conserve our
physical powers, our intellectual endowments,
140 our spiritual ideals; as a race we must strive
by race organization, by race solidarity, by
race unity to the realization of that broader
humanity which freely recognizes differences
in men, but sternly deprecates inequality in
145 their opportunities of development.

7 Passage 1 is primarily concerned with

(A) educating former slave owners about
the social plight of African Americans
(B) describing the many cultural contributions of African Americans
(C) presenting an argument for creating
schools to educate former slaves
(D) convincing African Americans and
white Americans to work together to
build a vibrant Southern economy
(E) preventing future labor strikes

GO ON TO THE NEXT PAGE ▶▶▶

8 The author of Passage 1 specifically addresses each of the following audiences EXCEPT

(A) Southern whites who were active in the movement to end slavery
(B) Southern whites who are considering hiring foreign laborers
(C) African Americans who seek to improve their social conditions
(D) Southern whites who have employed African Americans in the past
(E) African Americans who do not consider it necessary to build friendly relationships with Southern whites

9 Passage 1 suggests that, upon hearing the first response from the friendly vessel, the captain of the distressed vessel was

(A) elated
(B) arrogant
(C) incredulous
(D) indifferent
(E) angry

10 In the sentence beginning on line 24, "And in this connection . . . emphasizing this chance," the author of Passage 1 suggests that the Exposition at which he is speaking

(A) is overly concerned with superficial things
(B) does not represent the full spectrum of the American population
(C) provides excellent economic opportunities for African Americans
(D) is in distress, much like the ship in his story
(E) will encourage African Americans to seek employment in the North

11 The author of Passage 1 mentions "writing a poem" in line 42 in order to suggest that

(A) manual labor is a worthy activity
(B) poetry can convey emotions more effectively than prose
(C) expanding literacy should be a major focus of the Exposition
(D) African Americans should consider careers in writing
(E) political leaders should be more articulate

12 The questions in lines 74–85 are intended to represent the thoughts of

(A) a former slave owner
(B) one who is doubtful about the morality of slavery
(C) an African American who is seeking a new life in a foreign country
(D) an African American who is concerned with the issue of race identity
(E) any political leader who represents a substantial population of African Americans

13 In line 93, the word "marshalled" most nearly means

(A) arrested
(B) discovered
(C) organized for a purpose
(D) interrogated
(E) determined

14 The sentence that begins on line 94, "They stand back . . . the veil of race pride," suggests that those who incessantly question themselves run the risk of

(A) violating the law
(B) alienating friends
(C) losing gainful employment
(D) falling under the influence of disreputable people
(E) squandering their education

15 The phrase "that point" in line 126 refers to the boundary between

(A) the needs of the dominant class of society and the needs of the minority classes
(B) the past and the future
(C) white Americans and African Americans
(D) the qualities that bind all Americans and the qualities that make one race unique
(E) those who support racial discrimination and those who oppose it

GO ON TO THE NEXT PAGE ▶▶▶

16 The term "broader humanity" (lines 142–143) refers to people who

(A) hinder the progress of African Americans

(B) acknowledge the substantial cultural contributions African Americans have made to American culture

(C) believe that all races deserve equal opportunity in society

(D) seek a better life outside of their home countries

(E) have little understanding of cultures beyond their own

17 The 2 passages differ in their characterizations of the contributions of African Americans to American culture in that the 1st passage emphasizes

(A) agricultural contributions, while the 2nd emphasizes scientific innovations

(B) religious heritage, while the 2nd emphasizes political contributions

(C) musical innovations, while the 2nd emphasizes social contributions

(D) contributions of the past, while the 2nd focuses only on potential contributions in the future

(E) economic contributions, while the 2nd emphasizes artistic contributions

18 Unlike the "black tomorrow" (lines 131–132) described in Passage 2, the vision of the future of African Americans described in Passage 1 involves

(A) the incorporation of African Americans into the dominant system rather than a change in dominant American cultural values

(B) the restructuring of political institutions rather than maintenance of the status quo

(C) the reeducation of all Americans rather than the submission of one race to another

(D) a strong reliance on the lessons of the past rather than a complete rejection of the past

(E) travel to foreign lands rather than the commitment to stay in America

8

19 Which of the following best characterizes the tone each author takes toward the dominant American culture of his time?

(A) The author of Passage 1 is sarcastic, while the author of Passage 2 is respectful.

(B) The author of Passage 1 is tongue-in-cheek, while the author of Passage 2 is didactic.

(C) The author of Passage 1 is aggressive, while the author of Passage 2 is nonchalant.

(D) The author of Passage 1 is pontifical, while the author of Passage 2 is colloquial.

(E) The author of Passage 1 is deferential, while the author of Passage 2 is assertive.

STOP

You may check your work, on this section only, until time is called.

Section 9

Time—10 minutes
14 Questions

Directions for "Improving Sentences" Questions

Each of the sentences below contains 1 underlined portion. The portion may contain 1 or more errors in grammar, usage, construction, precision, diction (choice of words), or idiom. Some of the sentences are correct.

Consider the meaning of the original sentence, and choose the answer that best expresses that meaning. If the original sentence is best, choose (A), because it repeats the original phrasing. Choose the phrasing that creates the clearest, most precise, and most effective sentence.

EXAMPLE:
The children couldn't hardly believe their eyes.
(A) couldn't hardly believe their eyes
(B) would not hardly believe their eyes
(C) could hardly believe their eyes
(D) couldn't nearly believe their eyes
(E) could hardly believe his or her eyes

EXAMPLE ANSWER:
(C)

1 Neither the strength of the army nor how agile they were was able to compensate for the superior strategy of its enemy.

(A) nor how agile they were
(B) nor their agility
(C) nor its agility
(D) or how agile it was
(E) or its agility

2 Although Georgia preferred to perform with her fellow band members, they were not used by her when she sang at the opening ceremony.

(A) they were not used by her
(B) they were not used by she
(C) it was her who did not use them
(D) she had not used them
(E) she did not use them

3 Without rehearsing at all the previous week, the troupe performed the first act of the play in full costume.

(A) Without rehearsing
(B) Being that they didn't rehearse
(C) They didn't rehearse
(D) Without having rehearsed
(E) They hadn't even rehearsed

4 Not since the beginning of the resistance movement has the major media outlets acknowledged the scope of the opposition.

(A) has the major media outlets acknowledged the scope of the opposition
(B) have the major media outlets acknowledged the scope of the opposition
(C) have the scope of the opposition been acknowledged by the major media outlets
(D) has it been acknowledged by the major media outlets what the scope is of the opposition
(E) have the major media outlets been acknowledging the scope of the opposition

5 We would be healthier today if we have had to hunt and scavenge for our food as our ancestors did.

(A) if we have had to hunt and scavenge
(B) having hunted and scavenged
(C) if we would have hunted and scavenged
(D) for hunting and scavenging
(E) if we had to hunt and scavenge

GO ON TO THE NEXT PAGE ▶▶▶

6

<u>Against popular opinion</u>, college students with strong reasoning skills are more successful than students with strong memorization skills.

(A) Against popular opinion
(B) Not what popular opinion says
(C) Contrary to popular opinion
(D) Opposite to what popular opinion says
(E) Contrary to what popular opinion says

7

The school renovations should be planned <u>so as to minimize disruption and inconvenience to teachers and students</u>.

(A) so as to minimize disruption and inconvenience to teachers and students
(B) for the minimizing of disruptions and inconvenience to teachers and students
(C) so that teachers and students have minimum disruptions and inconvenience
(D) to minimize disruption and inconvenience on the part of teachers and students
(E) in order for the minimization of disruption and inconvenience to teachers and students

8

Dina, having struggled for months <u>to find a job as a writer</u>; she finally took a position at a local advertising agency.

(A) to find a job as a writer; she finally
(B) to find a job as a writer, finally
(C) for finding a job as a writer, finally
(D) finding a job as a writer, finally
(E) to find a job as a writer, so she finally

9

The fall of the Roman Empire was precipitated not so much by foreign invaders as <u>by the delusions and indulgences of its ruling class</u>.

(A) by the delusions and indulgences of its ruling class
(B) because of the delusions and indulgences of their ruling class
(C) the delusions and indulgences of its ruling class did
(D) it was by the delusions and indulgences of its ruling class
(E) the delusions and indulgences of its ruling class

10

If the preliminary sales numbers are reliable, then Hannigan's first book appears <u>like it is a success</u>.

(A) like it is a success
(B) like a success
(C) a success
(D) to be a success
(E) as a success

11

The response to the revised proposal has been much more favorable than <u>the original one</u>.

(A) the original one
(B) the original one was
(C) the response to the original one
(D) to the one that was originally given
(E) to the original one

12

The discovery was made by a team of <u>scientists trying to locate a gene responsible for producing a particular enzyme, but they found instead</u> a set of genetic triggers for a predisposition to heart disease.

(A) scientists trying to locate a gene responsible for producing a particular enzyme, but they found instead
(B) scientists; trying to locate a gene responsible for producing a particular enzyme, but they found instead
(C) scientists who, trying to locate a gene responsible for producing a particular enzyme, instead found
(D) scientists that tried to locate a gene responsible for producing a particular enzyme, instead finding
(E) scientists who instead, in trying to find a gene responsible for producing a particular enzyme, found

GO ON TO THE NEXT PAGE ▶▶▶

13 The strongest opposition to the sale of alcohol in the United States came in the late nineteenth century, <u>and this is the time when religious movements</u> preaching temperance were sweeping the nation.

(A) and this is the time when religious movements
(B) when religious movements were
(C) and this is when religious movements
(D) at the time in which religious movements were
(E) when religious movements

14 Professor Angleton valued conciseness highly, telling his students to edit their papers thoroughly <u>for eliminating any extra superfluous</u> information in the text.

(A) for eliminating any extra superfluous
(B) to eliminate any extra superfluous
(C) and eliminate any superfluous
(D) having eliminated any superfluous
(E) in eliminating any superfluous

9 →

STOP

You may check your work, on this section only, until time is called.

ANSWER KEY

Section 2 Math	Section 5 Math	Section 7 Math	Section 3 Critical Reading	Section 6 Critical Reading	Section 8 Critical Reading	Section 4 Writing	Section 9 Writing
1. C	1. B	1. B	1. A	1. B	1. E	1. B	1. C
2. D	2. A	2. D	2. D	2. D	2. B	2. A	2. E
3. A	3. D	3. A	3. B	3. C	3. B	3. E	3. D
4. D	4. E	4. C	4. C	4. A	4. D	4. D	4. B
5. B	5. D	5. C	5. C	5. A	5. D	5. D	5. E
6. D	6. C	6. A	6. E	6. B	6. A	6. A	6. C
7. E	7. C	7. C	7. B	7. D	7. D	7. C	7. A
8. D	8. B	8. C	8. D	8. A	8. A	8. D	8. B
9. C	9. 135	9. D	9. B	9. E	9. C	9. B	9. A
10. C	10. 104	10. D	10. D	10. E	10. C	10. E	10. D
11. D	11. 30	11. D	11. B	11. C	11. A	11. A	11. C
12. B	12. 3	12. D	12. A	12. A	12. D	12. B	12. C
13. C	13. 18	13. A	13. D	13. B	13. C	13. C	13. E
14. B	14. 28	14. B	14. E	14. E	14. D	14. E	14. C
15. E	15. 45	15. B	15. A	15. C	15. D	15. B	
16. B	16. 22.5	16. A	16. B	16. A	16. C	16. B	
17. E	17. 12		17. A	17. A	17. E	17. D	
18. A	18. 37.5		18. C	18. C	18. A	18. D	
19. B			19. E	19. D	19. E	19. B	
20. C			20. B	20. B		20. E	
			21. D	21. A		21. C	
			22. E	22. C		22. B	
			23. B	23. E		23. D	
			24. C	24. C		24. E	
						25. B	
						26. C	
						27. C	
						28. A	
						29. D	
						30. B	
						31. C	
						32. D	
						33. E	
						34. A	
						35. D	

15 = understanding
the question.
They means
now inverse/ons
can form

Ever

# Right (A): 19	Questions 1–8 # Right (A):	# Right (A): 16	# Right (A):	# Right (A):	# Right (A):	# Right (A):	# Right (A):
# Wrong (B): 1	# Wrong (B):	# Wrong (B): 0	# Wrong (B):	# Wrong (B):	# Wrong (B):	# Wrong (B):	# Wrong (B):
# (A)–¼ (B): 18.75	# (A)–¼ (B):	# (A)–¼ (B):	# (A)–¼ (B):	# (A)–¼ (B):	# (A)–¼ (B):	# (A)–¼ (B):	# (A)–¼ (B):
	Questions 9–18 # Right (A):						

SCORE CONVERSION TABLE

How to score your test

Use the answer key on the previous page to determine your raw score on each section. **Your raw score on each section except Section 4 is simply the number of correct answers minus ¼ of the number of wrong answers. On Section 4, your raw score is the sum of the number of correct answers for questions 1–8 minus ¼ of the number of wrong answers for questions 1–8 plus the total number of correct answers for questions 9–18.** Next, add the raw scores from Sections 3, 4, and 7 to get your Math raw score, and add the raw scores from sections 6 and 9 to get your Writing raw score. Write the three raw scores here:

Raw Critical Reading score: _____ Raw Math score: _____ Raw Writing score: _____

Use the table below to convert these to scaled scores.

Scaled scores: Critical Reading: _____ Math: _____ Writing: _____

Raw Score	Critical Reading Scaled Score	Math Scaled Score	Writing Scaled Score	Raw Score	Critical Reading Scaled Score	Math Scaled Score	Writing Scaled Score
67	800			32	520	550	610
66	800			31	510	550	600
65	790			30	510	540	580
64	780			29	500	530	570
63	760			28	490	530	560
62	750			27	490	520	550
61	730			26	480	510	540
60	720			25	480	500	530
59	700			24	470	490	520
58	700			23	460	480	510
57	690			22	460	480	500
56	680			21	450	470	490
55	670			20	440	460	480
54	660	800		19	440	450	470
53	650	790		18	430	450	460
52	650	760		17	420	440	450
51	640	740		16	420	430	440
50	630	720		15	410	420	440
49	620	710	800	14	400	410	430
48	620	700	800	13	400	410	420
47	610	680	800	12	390	400	410
46	600	670	790	11	380	390	400
45	600	660	780	10	370	380	390
44	590	650	760	9	360	370	380
43	590	640	740	8	350	360	380
42	580	630	730	7	340	350	370
41	570	630	710	6	330	340	360
40	570	620	700	5	320	330	350
39	560	610	690	4	310	320	340
38	550	600	670	3	300	310	320
37	550	590	660	2	280	290	310
36	540	580	650	1	270	280	300
35	540	580	640	0	250	260	280
34	530	570	630	−1	230	240	270
33	520	560	620	−2 or less	210	220	250

SCORE CONVERSION TABLE FOR WRITING COMPOSITE
[ESSAY + MULTIPLE CHOICE]

Calculate your writing raw score as you did on the previous page and grade your essay from a 1 to a 6 according to the standards that follow in the detailed answer key.

Essay score: _____   Raw Writing score: _____

Use the table below to convert these to scaled scores.

Scaled score: Writing: _____

Raw Score	Essay Score 0	Essay Score 1	Essay Score 2	Essay Score 3	Essay Score 4	Essay Score 5	Essay Score 6
-2 or less	200	230	250	280	310	340	370
-1	210	240	260	290	320	360	380
0	230	260	280	300	340	370	400
1	240	270	290	320	350	380	410
2	250	280	300	330	360	390	420
3	260	290	310	340	370	400	430
4	270	300	320	350	380	410	440
5	280	310	330	360	390	420	450
6	290	320	340	360	400	430	460
7	290	330	340	370	410	440	470
8	300	330	350	380	410	450	470
9	310	340	360	390	420	450	480
10	320	350	370	390	430	460	490
11	320	360	370	400	440	470	500
12	330	360	380	410	440	470	500
13	340	370	390	420	450	480	510
14	350	380	390	420	460	490	520
15	350	380	400	430	460	500	530
16	360	390	410	440	470	500	530
17	370	400	420	440	480	510	540
18	380	410	420	450	490	520	550
19	380	410	430	460	490	530	560
20	390	420	440	470	500	530	560
21	400	430	450	480	510	540	570
22	410	440	460	480	520	550	580
23	420	450	470	490	530	560	590
24	420	460	470	500	540	570	600
25	430	460	480	510	540	580	610
26	440	470	490	520	550	590	610
27	450	480	500	530	560	590	620
28	460	490	510	540	570	600	630
29	470	500	520	550	580	610	640
30	480	510	530	560	590	620	650
31	490	520	540	560	600	630	660
32	500	530	550	570	610	640	670
33	510	540	550	580	620	650	680
34	510	550	560	590	630	660	690
35	520	560	570	600	640	670	700
36	530	560	580	610	650	680	710
37	540	570	590	620	660	690	720
38	550	580	600	630	670	700	730
39	560	600	610	640	680	710	740
40	580	610	620	650	690	720	750
41	590	620	640	660	700	730	760
42	600	630	650	680	710	740	770
43	610	640	660	690	720	750	780
44	620	660	670	700	740	770	800
45	640	670	690	720	750	780	800
46	650	690	700	730	770	800	800
47	670	700	720	750	780	800	800
48	680	720	730	760	800	800	800
49	680	720	730	760	800	800	800

Detailed Answer Key

Section I

The following essay received 12 points out of a possible 12. This means that it demonstrates clear and consistent competence in that it

- develops an insightful point of view on the topic
- demonstrates exemplary critical thinking
- uses effective examples, reasons, and other evidence to support its thesis
- is consistently focused, coherent and well-organized
- demonstrates skillful and effective use of language and sentence structure
- is largely (but not necessarily completely) free of grammatical and usage errors

Consider carefully the issue discussed in the following passage, then write an essay that answers the question posed in the assignment.

> We like to believe that physical phenomena, animals, people and societies obey predictable rules, but such rules, even when carefully ascertained, have their limits. Every rule has its exceptions.

Assignment: **What is one particularly interesting "exception" to a rule?** Write an essay in which you answer this question and discuss your point of view on this issue. Support your position logically with examples from literature, the arts, history, politics, science and technology, current events, or your experience or observation.

One particularly interesting exception to a rule is the orbit of Mercury. For hundreds of years, Sir Isaac Newton's laws of motion and gravity stood as a testament to the power of mathematics to describe the universe. Newton's equations showed that the moon did not revolve around the earth because the gods willed it to, or because of the abstract perfection of a circular orbit. Rather, it circled the earth because doing so obeyed a simple mathematical formula: Newton's Universal Law of Gravitation. It was a singular achievement in the history of science.

The equation was not only elegant, but enormously powerful. It was used to predict the existence of two new planets before they were even seen: Neptune and Pluto. Astronomers actually began to doubt the power of the Universal Law of Gravitation when they noticed that Uranus was not behaving the way the equation said it should. Its orbit was wobblier than Newton's law predicted. Could the law be incorrect? A few careful scientists noticed that the law could still be correct if another planet, further from the sun, were tugging at Uranus. Indeed, astronomers looked carefully and found a planet they called Neptune. As even further confirmation of Newton's law, irregularities in Neptune's orbit led astronomers to find Pluto exerting yet another tiny gravitational tug at the edge of the solar system. It seemed that Newton's equation could do no wrong.

But it was wrong. When astronomers began to notice irregularities in Mercury's orbit, they surmised, naturally, that another planet must be near the sun tugging at Mercury. They even went so far as to call the undiscovered planet Vulcan. But even the most careful observations revealed no such planet. How could this equation, so powerful and elegant, be wrong? It turned out that Newton's equation broke down a bit as gravitational force became great, as it did near the sun. It wasn't until the 20th century that Einstein's theory of General Relativity tweaked Newton's equation to make it explain the precession of Mercury's orbit.

The value of Mercury's orbit, in fact, lies not so much in its ability to "prove" Einstein's theory as in its ability to disprove Newton's. It was the exception to a very powerful rule. It seems to suggest that, in science, nothing is truly sacred; everything must be examined. If one of the most powerful and elegant equations in all of science—one that had been "proven" time and again by rigorous experiment—could turn out to be wrong (albeit only by a tiny bit, in most ordinary circumstances), how much can we trust our own beloved "truths" about our universe? So many of us believe we know at least a few things that are "absolutely true." But can we say that we are more insightful, intelligent, or rigorous than Isaac Newton? Perhaps we should be more like the scientists, and look for the holes in our theories.

The following essay received 8 points out of a possible 12, meaning that it demonstrates *adequate competence* in that it

- develops a point of view on the topic
- demonstrates some critical thinking, but perhaps not consistently
- uses some examples, reasons, and other evidence to support its thesis, but perhaps not adequately
- shows a general organization and focus, but shows occasional lapses in this regard
- demonstrates adequate but occasionally inconsistent facility with language
- contains occasional errors in grammar, usage, and mechanics

When we are children, everyone—parents, teachers and friends—tells us that we should never lie. It's even one of the ten commandments in the Bible. This is a rule that many believe should have no exceptions. It is just something you should not do. Lying is bad, and being truthful is good. End of story.

But I believe that this rule has its exceptions, as many rules do. Sometimes lying can even be considered the right thing to do. It's obviously not good to lie just because you don't feel like telling the truth or just because you might look better if you lie. There has to be a good reason to deceive someone in order for it to be a valid action.

For instance, sometimes telling the truth can really hurt a situation more than it helps. For example, my friend is in a dance company, and I went to see her in the Nutcracker dance performance this past weekend. Even though she was pretty good, the whole thing was long, boring, and a lot of the dancers were not very good. I know that she would not want to hear that. So instead of telling her the truth, I lied and told her how great it was. This is what is called a 'white lie.' Yes, I was deceiving her, but there was really very little to come from telling her the truth that the show was a disaster. What is the point of telling the truth there if it is only going to hurt everyone involved?

Recently, I watched a documentary about the Vietnam War. The documentary focused on a troop of 25 soldiers and their experience in the war and how they grew closer together as a group as the time went by. One of the soldiers, a 16 year old boy who had lied about his age so that he could fight, died because he made a bad decision and chased after a Vietnamese soldier into the woods without anyone else to back him up. Part of the reasoning behind this action, they explained, was because he spent his entire life trying to prove to his parents that he was not a failure at everything and that he could be a hero. A fellow troopmate knew what he had done, knew the struggle for respect he was going through at home, and wrote the formal letter home to the family telling them how their son had died in an honorable fashion saving several members of the troop with his heroism. Some might argue that it was bad to lie about his death, but I would argue that this was a valiant thing done by the soldier who wrote the letter because it allowed the family to feel better about the death of their young son in a war so many miles away.

To summarize, in general, it is best not to lie. But there are in fact situations where it is better to tell partial truths than the whole truth. It is important to avoid lying whenever possible, but it is also important to know when it is OK to tell a slight variation to the truth.

> The following essay received 4 points out of a possible 12, meaning that it demonstrates *some incompetence* in that it
>
> - has a seriously limited point of view
> - demonstrates weak critical thinking
> - uses inappropriate or insufficient examples, reasons, and other evidence to support its thesis
> - is poorly focused and organized, and has serious problems with coherence
> - demonstrates frequent problems with language and sentence structure
> - contains errors in grammar and usage that obscure the author's meaning seriously

A lot of rules have exceptions because there are different circumstances for everybody and also people grow up and the old rules don't apply anymore. One afternoon back in elementary school, I got in trouble when I took my friend's Capri-Sun drink out of his lunchbox and took a sip without asking his permission. My teacher caught me in the act and yelled at me reciting the "Golden Rule." She said: How would you feel if he took your drink and had some without asking you? I guess I would have been pretty annoyed. I hate it when people drink from the same glass as me. It seemed like a pretty fair rule that I should only do things to other people that I would be OK with them doing to me.

This interaction with my 3rd grade teacher stuck with me throughout my education experience and I heard her voice in my head many times as I was about to perform questionable acts upon others around me. It kept me from doing a lot of pranks like I used to do like tie Eric's shoelaces together and putting hot pepper flakes in Steve's sandwich one afternoon while he went off to get himself another cup of water.

But this rule seemed to get a bit more difficult to follow as I got older and found myself in more complex relationships. Sometimes I wanted to be treated in ways that my friends did not want to be treated. I wanted my friends to call me each night so that we could talk and catch up on the day's events so I would call each of them every night to chat. This annoyed my friends though who did not like talking on the phone. Or, I would always point out to my friends when something they were wearing did not look good because I wanted to be told such things so that I did not embarrass myself. This made a LOT of my friends very angry at me and cost me a few good friendships.

"Do unto others" is a rule that requires a bit of thought and a lot of good judgment. Doing unto others things that I was hoping they would do to me sometimes cost myself friendships. I think it is better to reserve that rule for things that I might consider negative rather than positive.

Detailed Answer Key

Section 2

1. **C** It does not matter how big each station is. All that matters is the total area and *how many* stations there are.

$$\text{average} = \frac{\text{total}}{\text{pieces}} = \frac{3{,}600 \text{ ft}^2}{6 \text{ stations}} = 600 \text{ ft}^2$$

(Chapter 13 Lesson 5: Areas and Perimeters)
(Chapter 12 Lesson 2: Mean/Median/Mode Problems)

2. **D** Solve for a and b: $\quad 3a = 15$
    Divide by 3: $\qquad\qquad\qquad a = 5$
    $\qquad\qquad\qquad\qquad\qquad\quad 4b = 10$
    Divide by 4: $\qquad\qquad\qquad b = 2.5$
    Plug in a and b: $\qquad \dfrac{a}{b} = \dfrac{5}{2.5} = 2$

(Chapter 11 Lesson 1: Solving Equations)

3. **A** Pick the employee whose line has the largest positive slope. This is Employee 1. Her line has the largest "rise over run." Her salary increases approximately $20,000 in 8 years, or roughly $2,500 per year.
(Chapter 14 Lesson 5: Data Analysis)

4. **D** Use unit analysis and solve:

$$100 \text{ children} \times \frac{1 \text{ bucket}}{5 \text{ children}} = 20 \text{ buckets}$$

$$60 \text{ adults} \times \frac{1 \text{ bucket}}{3 \text{ adults}} = 20 \text{ buckets}$$

Total number of buckets = 20 + 20 = 40
(Chapter 10 Lesson 4: Ratios and Proportions)

5. **B** $\qquad\qquad (5x - 3x + 4)(3x + 6x - 2)$
    Combine like terms: $\quad (2x + 4)(9x - 2)$
    FOIL: $\qquad\qquad (18x^2 - 4x + 36x - 8)$
    Combine like terms: $\quad 18x^2 + 32x - 8$
(Chapter 11 Lesson 5: Factoring)

6. **D**

Linear pair: $\qquad\qquad\qquad z + x = 180$
Substitute: $\qquad\qquad\qquad 55 + x = 180$
Subtract 55: $\qquad\qquad\qquad x = 125$
Since lines l and m are parallel:
$\quad$ Corresponding: $\qquad\qquad z = d = 55$
$\qquad\qquad\qquad\qquad\qquad\qquad x = c = 125$
$\quad$ Alternate interior: $\qquad\quad z = a = 55$
$\qquad\qquad\qquad\qquad\qquad\qquad x = c = 125$
$\qquad a + b + c = 55 + 125 + 125 = 305$
(Chapter 13 Lesson 1: Lines and Angles)

7. **E** $\qquad\qquad\qquad\qquad 7\sqrt{x} + 16 = 79$

Subtract 16: $\qquad\qquad\qquad 7\sqrt{x} = 63$
Divide by 7: $\qquad\qquad\qquad \sqrt{x} = 9$
Square both sides: $\qquad\qquad x = 81$
(Chapter 11 Lesson 4: Working with Roots)

8. **D** Work backwards with this problem. Each term, starting with the second, is 2 less than the square root of the previous term. So to work backwards and find the previous term, add 2 and then square the sum: $\qquad$ 2nd term $= (1 + 2)^2 = 3^2 = 9$
$\qquad\qquad\qquad\qquad$ 1st term $= (9 + 2)^2 = 11^2 = 121$
(Chapter 14 Lesson 1: Sequences)

9. **C** Before trying to solve this with geometrical formulas, analyze the figure. The rectangle is divided into 15 squares. Each of the 15 squares is split into 2 identical triangles, which means there are 30 triangles total. Of those 30 triangles, 15 of them are shaded in, or *half* of the figure. This means that half of the area, or 45, is shaded.
(Chapter 13 Lesson 5: Areas and Perimeters)
(Chapter 9 Lesson 2: Analyzing Problems)
(Chapter 9 Lesson 4: Simplifying Problems)

10. **C** The long way:

$\bigstar16 = 15 + 14 + 13 + 12 + 11 + 10 + 9 + 8 + 7 + 6 + 5 + 4 + 3 + 2 + 1 = 120$

$\bigstar13 = 12 + 11 + 10 + 9 + 8 + 7 + 6 + 5 + 4 + 3 + 2 + 1 = 78$

$\bigstar16 - \bigstar13 = 120 - 78 = 42$

More simply, this can be solved without actually calculating the sums. Just focus on the terms in the sum of $\bigstar16$ that are not "cancelled" by the terms in $\bigstar13$:

$\bigstar16 - \bigstar13 = 15 + 14 + 13 = 42$

(Chapter 12 Lesson 1: New Symbol or Term Problems)

11. D Look at the right (units) column first.

$$Y + X = X$$

Subtract X: $Y = 0$
Look at the 10s column: $3 + Y = 3$
Because $Y = 0$, we know there is no carried digit.
Look at the left (1,000s) column:

$$X + 5 = 13$$

Subtract 5: $X = 8$
(Chapter 12 Lesson 3: Numerical Reasoning Problems)

---

12. B Write out an equation given the average:

$$\frac{x + y + 3y}{3} = 3x$$

Multiply by 3: $x + y + 3y = 9x$
Combine like terms: $x + 4y = 9x$
Subtract x: $4y = 8x$
Divide by 4: $y = 2x$
(Chapter 12 Lesson 2: Mean/Median/Mode Problems)

---

13. C

The simplest method is to use the Triangle External Angle Theorem, which says that the measure of an "exterior angle" of a triangle equals the sum of the measures of the two "remote interior angles," so $x = y + z$ and $w = (z - 1) + (y + 1) = y + z$. Therefore, $w = x$.

Another, more involved method is to write an equation for each triangle:
Triangle on left: $y + z + (180 - x) = 180$
Subtract 180: $y + z - x = 0$
Add x: $y + z = x$
Triangle on right: $(y + 1) + (z - 1) + (180 - w) = 180$
Subtract 180 and simplify: $y + z - w = 0$
Add w: $y + z = w$
Substitute w for $y + z$: $w = x$
(Chapter 13 Lesson 2: Triangles)

---

14. B Pick a value for r, like 19, that makes this statement true. (r must be 9 more than some multiple of 10.) If r is 19, then $r + 2$ is 21. When 21 is divided by 5, it leaves a remainder of 1.
(Chapter 10 Lesson 7: Divisibility)

---

15. E

The best way to solve this problem is to draw the lines. With each line you draw, attempt to create as many intersection points as possible. The maximum number of intersection points possible with 5 lines is 10, as shown above.
(Chapter 9 Lesson 2: Analyzing Problems)

---

16. B The probability of selecting a king is 1/4, and the probability of selecting a queen is 2/7. To find the probability of randomly choosing a jack, add up the probabilities of choosing a king and a queen and subtract that sum from 1. $\frac{1}{4} + \frac{2}{7}$
Find a common denominator: $\frac{7}{28} + \frac{8}{28} = \frac{15}{28}$
Subtract from 1: $1 - \frac{15}{28} = \frac{13}{28}$
(Chapter 12 Lesson 6: Probability Problems)

---

17. E

Since $\triangle VXT$ is equilateral, its angles all measure 60°. Mark the diagram as shown.
If $WU = WY$, then $\angle WUY = \angle WYU = 65°$.
$\angle VWU$ ($2x°$) is twice as large as $\angle VUW$ ($x°$).

There are 180 degrees in a triangle: $x + 2x + 60° = 180°$
Combine like terms: $3x + 60° = 180°$
Subtract 60°: $3x = 120°$
Divide by 3: $x = 40°$
The angles on one side of a line add up to 180°:
$$40° + 65° + \angle TUY = 180°$$
Combine like terms: $105° + \angle TUY = 180°$
Subtract 105°: $\angle TUY = 75°$
(Chapter 13 Lesson 2: Triangles)

18. **A** The question asks: what percent of $m - 4$ is $n + 2$?

Translate the question: $\dfrac{x}{100} \times (m - 4) = n + 2$

Multiply by 100: $x(m - 4) = 100(n + 2)$

Divide by $(m - 4)$: $x = \dfrac{100(n + 2)}{m - 4}$

(Chapter 10 Lesson 5: Percents)

19. **B** At the matinee, all but 6 seats were filled and the theater collected $912. At the evening showing, all the seats were sold plus 5 extra tickets and they collected $1,000. Let x = the number of seats in the theater. Let y = the price per ticket in the theater. Set up equations to represent the amount of money collected:

Matinee showing: $(x - 6)y = \$912$

Divide by $(x - 6)$: $y = \dfrac{912}{(x - 6)}$

Evening showing: $(x + 5)y = \$1,000$

Divide by $(x + 5)$: $y = \dfrac{1000}{(x + 5)}$

Set up equation: $\dfrac{912}{(x - 6)} = \dfrac{1000}{(x + 5)}$

Cross-multiply: $(912)(x + 5) = (1,000)(x - 6)$
Distribute: $912x + 4,560 = 1,000x - 6,000$
Add 6,000: $912x + 10,560 = 1,000x$
Subtract 912x: $10,560 = 88x$
Divide by 88: $120 = x$

(Chapter 11 Lesson 7: Word Problems)

20. **C** Work month by month with the price:
Start of Jan: d
After Jan: $d - .2d = .8d$
After Feb: $.8d + (.4)(.8d) = 1.12d$
After Mar: $1.12d - (.25)(1.12d) = .84d$
After Apr: $.84d + (.25)(.84d) = 1.05d$

(Chapter 11 Lesson 7: Word Problems)
(Chapter 10 Lesson 5: Percents)

Or, more simply, remember that each percent change is a simple multiplication: $d(.8)(1.4)(.75)(1.25) = 1.05d$.

(Chapter 9 Lesson 6: Finding Alternatives)

Section 3

1. **A** The bistro is world-renowned, so it is famous and successful. Both words should be positive. *delectable* = pleasing to the taste; *scrumptious* = delicious; *unpalatable* = bad tasting; *tantalizing* = exciting because kept out of reach; *debilitating* = sapping energy; *savory* = pleasing to the taste

2. **D** The 1st word represents something that could put a country on the *brink of war*. The 2nd word represents something that could cause it to *explode into destructive conflict*. *dissension* = disagreement; *harmony* = concord; *instigation* = provocation; *strife* = violent disagreement; *provocation* = rousing of anger; *unanimity* = complete agreement; *agitation* = disturbance

3. **B** For over 500 years, art historians have argued about the emotion behind the *Mona Lisa*'s *enigmatic* (mysterious) smile. This would make the painting the source of much *debate* or *discussion*. *assent* = agreement; *deliberation* = discussion of all sides of an issue; *concurrence* = agreement; *remuneration* = payment for goods or services; *reconciliation* = the act of resolving an issue

4. **C** Every year, crowds of people travel to Elvis's hometown to pay *tribute* (respect). Therefore, he was a very *well-respected* or *admired* musician. *satirized* = made fun of, mocked; *unexalted* = not praised; *revered* = respected, worshipped; *despised* = hated; *shunned* = avoided

5. **C** The poker player uses *tactics* (strategies) to *outthink* his opponents, so his tactics must be intellectual. This is why he is called "the professor." *obscure* = not well understood; *cerebral* = using intellect; *transparent* = easily understood; *outlandish* = bizarre, unusual

6. **E** Detractors are critics who would likely say something negative about the aesthetics of the building, whereas its developers would likely claim that the project would be a *great success*. *adversary* = opponent; *enhancement* = something that improves the appearance or function of something else; *gratuity* = tip; *embellishment* = decoration or exaggeration; *windfall* = unexpected benefit; *defacement* = act of vandalism; *calamity* = disaster; *atrocity* = horrific crime; *boon* = benefit

7. **B** Poe wrote tales of cruelty and torture, so they must have been *horrific*. His tales mesmerized his readers, so they must have been *hypnotizing*. *tenuous* = flimsy; *spellbinding* = mesmerizing; *grotesque* = distorted, horrifying, outlandish; *enthralling* = captivating; *interminable* = never-ending; *sacrilegious* = grossly disrespectful; *eclectic* = deriving from a variety of sources; *sadistic* = taking pleasure in others' pain; *chimerical* = unrealistically fanciful, illusory; *mundane* = everyday, common

8. **D** The DNA evidence was vital to proving the defendant's innocence. The missing word should mean to *prove innocent* or *free from blame*. *perambulate* = walk through; *expedite* = speed up; *incriminate* = accuse of a crime; *exculpate* = free from blame; *equivocate* = avoid telling the whole truth

9. **B** Debussy is said to have started the *breakdown of the old system* (line 3) and then to have been the *first . . . who dared to make his ear the sole judge of what was good harmonically* (lines 6–7). Therefore, the old system did not allow this and was a rigid method for writing harmonies.

10. **D** The passage as a whole describes Debussy's inventiveness as a composer of musical harmony.

11. **B** The hot-air balloon trip is an analogy for the difficulties involved in exploring the ocean.

12. **A** These are examples of the *limited and relatively ineffective methods* (lines 15–16) that make ocean exploration *a difficult and expensive task* (lines 18–19).

13. **D** This *primal concept* is revealed by the fact that the paintings of Stone Age artists are charged with *magical strength* and *fulfilled . . . other functions beyond the mere representation of the visible* (lines 9–10).

14. **E** To be *charged with magical strength* is to be *filled with magical strength*.

15. **A** The *stylistic change* was from the *naturalism based on observation and experience* to a *geometrically stylized world of forms discoverable . . . through thought and speculation* (lines 45–48). In other words, artists were depicting ideas rather than just objects and animals.

16. **B** The sculptures are said to be *ample witnesses* (line 63) to the fact that art of this period contained *elements of naïveté . . . side by side with . . . formalized compositions* (lines 59–62).

17. **A** The passage states that Renaissance art is characterized by the *discovery of linear and aerial perspective* (lines 80–81), that is, the ability to imply depth in painting, while the earlier *art of the period of the catacombs* (line 71) *was averse to any spatial illusions* and contained action *pressed onto the holy, two-dimensional surface* (lines 75–76).

18. **C** *Transitional forms* (line 10) are described as fossils that gradualists would cite as *evidence for their position* (line 8), which is that evolution proceeds gradually.

19. **E** This case is mentioned as an illustration of the theory of *punctuated equilibrium* (lines 12–13).

20. **B** The passage says that *one explanation for the extinction of the dinosaurs* is that a meteorite created a *cloud of gas and dust* that destroyed *most plants and the chain of animals that fed on them* (lines 44–51).

21. **D** This sentence is discussing fossil evidence., The supportive structures are those bones that support the weight of the body.

22. **E** The passage states in lines 35–38 that the biggest mass extinction in history happened between the Paleozoic era and the Mesozoic era, thereby implying that there were far fewer species in the early Mesozoic era than there were in the late Paleozoic era.

23. **B** In lines 70–74, the passage states that *the probable key to the rapid emergence of* Homo erectus *was a dramatic change in adaptive strategy: greater reliance on hunting through improved tools and other cultural means of adaptation.*

24. **C** The author presents several examples of mass extinctions and environmental changes that would likely lead to punctuated evolution but also describes species like *Homo erectus*, which *remained fairly stable for about 1 million years* (lines 76–77).

Section 4

1. **B** The original phrasing is a fragment. Choice B completes the thought clearly and concisely.
(Chapter 15 Lesson 8: Write Clearly)

2. **A** The original phrasing is best.

3. **E** This phrasing is concise, complete, and in the active voice.
(Chapter 15 Lesson 9: Write Concisely)

4. **D** The participle *pretending* modifies *Chandra* and not *Chandra's attempt,* so the participle dangles. Choice D corrects the problem most concisely.
(Chapter 18 Lesson 7: Dangling and Misplaced Participles)

5. **D** The original phrasing contains a comparison error, comparing *his speech* to the *candidates.* Choice D best corrects the mistake.
(Chapter 18 Lesson 4: Comparison Problems)

6. **A** The original phrasing is best.

7. **C** The original phrasing is not parallel. Choice C maintains parallelism by listing 3 consecutive adjectives.
(Chapter 18 Lesson 3: Parallelism)

8. **D** The pronoun *their* does not agree with its antecedent, *student.* Choice (C) is close, but including the word *also* implies that the tests do indicate academic skill.
(Chapter 18 Lesson 5: Pronoun-antecedent Disagreement)

9. **B** The original phrasing is a sentence fragment. Choices (C) and (D) are incorrect because semicolons must separate independent clauses.
(Chapter 18 Lesson 15: Coordinating Ideas)

10. **E** The phrase *requested that* indicates that the idea to follow is **subjunctive.** The correct subjunctive form here is *be.*
(Chapter 18 Lesson 14: The Subjunctive Mood)

11. **A** The original phrasing is best.

12. **B** The past participle form of *to write* is *written.*
(Chapter 18 Lesson 13: Irregular Verbs)

13. **D** This phrase is redundant and should be omitted.
(Chapter 18 Lesson 12: Other Modifier Problems)

14. **E** The sentence is correct.

15. **B** This phrase lacks parallel structure. A good revision is *a charismatic leader.*
(Chapter 18 Lesson 3: Parallelism)

16. **B** The sentence indicates two reasons, not one.
(Chapter 18 Lesson 4: Comparison Problems)

17. **D** This phrase is redundant. *Circuitous* means *roundabout.*
(Chapter 18 Lesson 12: Other Modifier Problems)

18. **D** *Eluded* means *evaded,* so this is a diction error. The correct word here is *alluded,* meaning *hinted at.*
(Chapter 18 Lesson 11: Diction Errors)

19. **B** As it is written, the sentence is a fragment. Change *clutching* to *clutched* to complete the thought.
(Chapter 18 Lesson 15: Coordinating Ideas)

20. **E** The sentence is correct.

21. **C** This is a comparison error. A *grade point average* cannot be higher than *her classmates,* but rather higher than *those of the rest of her classmates.*
(Chapter 18 Lesson 4: Comparison Problems)

22. **B** Both the *emissary* and the *committee* are singular, so the pronoun *their* should be changed to *its* (if it refers to the committee) or *his* or *her* (if it refers to the emissary).
(Chapter 18 Lesson 5: Pronoun-Antecedent Disagreement)

23. **D** The verb *receive* does not agree with the singular subject *each* and so should be changed to *receives.*
(Chapter 18 Lesson 1: Subject-Verb Disagreement)

24. **E** The sentence is correct.

25. **B** The subject of this sentence is *genre,* so the correct conjugation of the verb is *encompasses.*
(Chapter 18 Lesson 1: Subject-Verb Disagreement)

26. **C** The proper idiom is *method of channeling* or *method for channeling.*
(Chapter 18 Lesson 10: Idiom Error)

27. **C** The sentence does not make a comparison, but rather indicates a result, so the word *as* should be replaced with *that.*
(Chapter 18 Lesson 10: Idiom Error)

28. **A** The word *perspective* is a noun meaning point of view. In this context, the proper word is *prospective,* which is an adjective meaning *having the potential to be.*
(Chapter 18 Lesson 11: Diction Error)

29. **D** The list of camp activities should be parallel. The verbs should consistently be in the present tense, so *will write* should be changed to *write.*
(Chapter 18 Lesson 3: Idiom Error)

30. **B** This phrasing is concise and parallel and makes a logical comparison.
(Chapter 18 Lesson 3: Parallelism)

31. **C** Chaplin's mother's mental illness is not pertinent to the main ideas of paragraph 1.
(Chapter 15 Lesson 7: Write Logically)

32. D In the original phrasing, the opening modifiers are left dangling. Choice D corrects this problem most concisely.
(Chapter 18 Lesson 8: Other Misplaced Modifiers)

33. E This choice is most parallel.
(Chapter 18 Lesson 3: Parallelism)

34. A Sentence 11 introduces the idea that some were interested in more than Chaplin's art. Sentence 9 expands on this fact with the specific example of Senator McCarthy's interest in Chaplin's political beliefs. Sentence 10 extends the ideas in sentence 9.
(Chapter 18 Lesson 15: Coordinating Ideas)

35. D This sentence provides the best transition from the idea that Chaplin's films contained political messages to a discussion of their specific messages about domestic and international issues.
(Chapter 15 Lesson 7: Write Logically)

Section 5

1. B Eric earns a 5% commission on each $200 stereo, so he makes $(\$200)(.05) = \$10$ per stereo. So if he makes $100 on x stereos, $\quad 10x = 100$
Divide by 10: $\qquad x = 10$
(Chapter 11 Lesson 1: Solving Equations)
(Chapter 10 Lesson 5: Percents)

2. A Fill in the table:

Jane's Discount Music Superstore
Holiday Sales

	CDs	DVDs	Total
New	3,000	4,500	7,500
Used	4,000	2,500	6,500
Total	7,000	7,000	14,000

Since 7,000 out of the total of 14,000 items sold were CDs, $14,000 - 7,000 = 7,000$ were DVDs. Since 4,500 of these DVDs were new, $7,000 - 4,500 = 2,500$ were used.
(Chapter 14 Lesson 5: Data Analysis)

3. D Set up a ratio: $\qquad \dfrac{5 \text{ pounds}}{\$4.00} = \dfrac{x \text{ pounds}}{\$20.00}$

Cross-multiply: $\qquad 4x = 100$
Divide by 4: $\qquad x = 25$

$$25 \text{ pounds} \times \dfrac{16 \text{ ounces}}{1 \text{ pound}} = 400 \text{ ounces}$$

Set up a proportion: $\dfrac{1 \text{ bag}}{40 \text{ ounces}} = \dfrac{x \text{ bags}}{400 \text{ ounces}}$

Cross-multiply: $\qquad 40x = 400$
Divide by 40: $\qquad x = 10 \text{ bags}$
(Chapter 10 Lesson 4: Ratios and Proportions)

4. E
Divide this complex-looking shape into a square and 2 right triangles.

$\text{Area}_{\text{square}} = (5)(5) = 25$
$\text{Area}_{\text{triangle}} = \frac{1}{2}(2)(5) = 5$

Total shaded area $= \text{Area}_{\text{square}} + \text{Area}_{\text{triangle}} + \text{Area}_{\text{triangle}} = 25 + 5 + 5 = 35$
(Chapter 13 Lesson 5: Areas and Perimeters)

5. D If each of the small cubes has a volume of 8 cubic inches, then each side of the smaller cubes must be 2 inches long. So the dimensions of the box are 6, 4, and 4. To find the surface area, use the formula:

$\qquad SA = 2lw + 2lh + 2wh$
Plug in values: $\qquad SA = 2(6)(4) + 2(6)(4) + 2(4)(4)$
Simplify: $\qquad SA = 48 + 48 + 32 = 128$
(Chapter 13 Lesson 7: Volumes and 3-D Geometry)

6. **C** Don't waste time doing the calculation: $-15 + -14 + -13 + -12 + -11 + -10 + -9 + -8 + -7 + -6 + -5 + -4 + -3 + -2 + -1 + 0 + 1 + 2 + 3 + 4 + 5 + 6 + 7 + 8 + 9 + 10 + 11 + 12 + 13 + 14 + 15 + 16 + 17 + 18 + 19$. Instead, think logically. The sum of the numbers from -15 to $+15$ is 0. They cancel out completely: $-15 + 15 = 0$, $-14 + 14 = 0$, $-13 + 13 = 0$, etc. Therefore, y must be greater than 15. With a little checking, it's easy to see that $16 + 17 + 18 + 19 = 70$, so $y = 19$. The total number of integers from -15 to 19, inclusive, is $19 - (-15) + 1 = 35$.
(Chapter 12 Lesson 3: Numerical Reasoning Problems)

7. **C** The general strategy is to find out how many matches there are if each plays every other player once and multiply that by 2.

Opponents:
Player 1: 2, 3, 4, 5, 6, 7   6
Player 2: 3, 4, 5, 6, 7   5
Player 3: 4, 5, 6, 7   4
Player 4: 5, 6, 7   3
Player 5: 6, 7   2
Player 6: 7   1
Total head to-head-matchups: 21
Since they play each opponent twice, there is a total of $21 \times 2 = 42$ matches.
(Chapter 12 Lesson 5: Counting Problems)

8. **B**
The area of the base of the prism is 12.5π. Since this is one-quarter of a circle, the entire circle has an area of $4(12.5\pi) = 50\pi$.

$$\pi r^2 = \text{area}$$
Substitute: $\pi r^2 = 50\pi$
Divide by π: $r^2 = 50$

Take square root: $r = \sqrt{50}$
You are told that the volume of the prism is 300π. Since this is ¼ of a cylinder, the entire cylinder would have a volume of $4(300\pi) = 1,200\pi$.

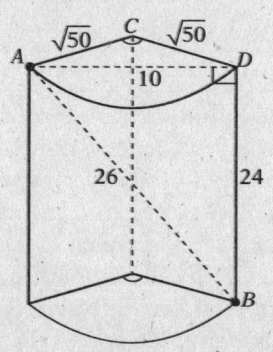

$\pi r^2 h = \text{volume of a cylinder}$
Substitute: $\pi r^2 h = 1,200\pi$
Divide by π: $r^2 h = 1,200$
Substitute $r = \sqrt{50}$: $\left(\sqrt{50}\right)^2 h = 1,200$
Simplify: $50h = 1,200$
Divide by 50: $h = 24$

Finally, to find the distance from point A to point B, notice that AB is the hypotenuse of a right triangle with legs AD and DB. First you must find the value of AD:

$$\left(\sqrt{50}\right)^2 + \left(\sqrt{50}\right)^2 = (AD)^2$$
Simplify: $50 + 50 = 100 = (AD)^2$
Take square root: $10 = AD$
Solve for AB: $(AD)^2 + (DB)^2 = (AB)^2$
Substitute: $(10)^2 + (24)^2 = (AB)^2$
Simplify: $100 + 576 = (AB)^2$
Combine like terms: $676 = (AB)^2$
Take square root: $26 = AB$
(Chapter 13 Lesson 3: The Pythagorean Theorem)
(Chapter 13 Lesson 7: Volumes and 3-D Geometry)

9. **135** Set up an equation: $x + (3y + 3) = 180°$
Substitute $y + 1$ for x: $y + 1 + 3y + 3 = 180°$
Combine like terms: $4y + 4 = 180°$
Subtract 4: $4y = 176°$
Divide by 4: $y = 44°$
Solve for $3y + 3$: $3(44) + 3 = 135°$
(Chapter 13 Lesson 1: Lines and Angles)

10. **104**
Quadrilateral $ABCD$ is composed of 2 identical triangles, each with an area of 240 square inches.

Area of $\triangle ABC = \frac{1}{2}bh$
$240 = \frac{1}{2}(20)(h)$
$h = 24$ inches

To solve for side BC, set up the Pythagorean Theorem:

$$10^2 + 24^2 = (BC)^2$$
Simplify: $100 + 576 = (BC)^2$
Combine like terms: $676 = (BC)^2$
Take the square root: $26 = BC$
(Or simply notice that each right triangle is a classic 5-12-13 triangle times 2: 10-24-26.)

The perimeter of quadrilateral $ABCD =$
$$26 + 26 + 26 + 26 = 104$$
(Chapter 13 Lesson 5: Areas and Perimeters)

11. 30 If 2 things are equal, you can substitute either one for the other. Since $g(x) = x^2 - 5$,

$$f(g(x)) = f(x^2 - 5)$$

Plug $x^2 - 5$ into $f(x)$ and simplify:

$$f(x) = 7(x^2 - 5) + 2$$

Distribute: $\quad\quad\quad 7x^2 - 35 + 2$

Plug in 3 for x: $\quad\quad 7(3)^2 - 35 + 2$

Simplify: $\quad\quad\quad 63 - 35 + 2 = 30$

(Chapter 14 Lesson 2: Functions)

---

12. 3 Start by simplifying the expression:

$$\frac{6x - 9}{5} - \frac{x + 6}{5} = \frac{6x - 9 - x - 6}{5}$$

Combine like terms: $\quad \dfrac{5x - 15}{5}$

Simplify: $\quad\quad\quad\quad x - 3$

This expression is 3 less than x.

(Chapter 11 Lesson 1: Solving Equations)

---

13. 18 Approach this problem logically, but keep the restrictions in mind. If we want the *largest* possible value of a and $a + b < 20$, try $a = 19$. But that is not a possibility, because b is a positive integer and so can be no less than 1, and $19 + 1$ is equal to, not less than 20. Therefore, the largest value of a that fits the restriction is 18. If $a = 18$ and $b = 1$, then $ab = (18)(1) = 18$, an even number.

(Chapter 12 Lesson 3: Numerical Reasoning Problems)

---

14. 28 Since rectangle U and rectangle V share a side with integer length, this length must be a common factor of 18 and 21.

Similarly, the side that rectangle U and rectangle W share must be a common factor of 18 and 12. Therefore, the common side between U and V is 3, and the common side between U and W is 6. So U is a

	6		7
U	3	V	
W 6	2	X 7	
Y 6	x	Z 7	

6-by-3 rectangle, V is a 7-by-3 rectangle, and W is a 6-by-2 rectangle, which means rectangle X must have an area of 14. The sum of the areas of those 4 rectangles is $18 + 21 + 12 + 14 = 65$. The area of the entire rectangle is given as 117. Thus, the area of rectangles Y and Z together must be $117 - 65 = 52$. Set up an equation:

$$6x + 7x = 52$$

Combine like terms: $\quad 13x = 52$

Divide by 13: $\quad\quad\quad x = 4$

If $x = 4$, then the area of rectangle Z is $4 \times 7 = 28$.

(Chapter 13 Lesson 5: Areas and Perimeters)

---

15. 45 Begin by finding the amount the class would spend on 55 regular-price tickets: $55 \times \$15 = \$825$. Then calculate how much 60 discounted tickets cost: $60 \times \$13 = \$780$. Then subtract to find the amount saved: $\$825 - \$780 = \$45$.

(Chapter 12 Lesson 3: Numerical Reasoning Problems)

---

16. 22.5

W ————15———— Y

The length of $\overline{WY}$, as shown above, is 15.

W —7.5— X —7.5— Y ——15—— Z

Point X is the midpoint of $\overline{WY}$, so $WX = XY = 7.5$. $YZ = 2WX = 2(7.5) = 15$. So $XZ = 22.5$.

(Chapter 9 Lesson 2: Analyzing Problems)

---

17. 12

$$r \square s = \frac{rs^2}{r - s}$$

Solve for x:

$$3 \square 2 = \frac{(3)(2^2)}{3 - 2} = \frac{12}{1} = 12 = x$$

$$x \square 3 = 12 \square 3 = \frac{(12)(3^2)}{12 - 3} = \frac{108}{9} = 12$$

(Chapter 12 Lesson 1: New Symbol or Term Problems)

---

18. 37.5

Since $\overline{DC} \perp \overline{AB}$, angle CDB is a right angle, so $\triangle CDB$ is a 45°-45°-90° right triangle. Therefore, $DB = DC = 5$. Since $AD = 2DB$, $AD = (5)(2) = 10$.

The area of $\triangle ABC = \frac{1}{2}(b)(h) = \frac{1}{2}(15)(5) = 37.5$.

(Chapter 13 Lesson 5: Areas and Perimeters)

Section 6

1. B The reflex produces an *immediate* (or *instantaneous*) response. *transient* = short-lived; *stagnant* = not moving; *revitalized* = filled with new life and energy

---

2. D Although the cats are *emaciated* (excessively thin) and *starved for food*, summoning energy would help them to fight *hard* or *aggressively* for the scraps. *humanely* = with mercy; *vigilantly* = in a watchful way; *fluently* = smoothly; *ferociously* = fiercely

3.   **C** Jennifer *irritated* her peers with her *supercilious* (overly proud) and *pretentious* (haughty) remarks. These are characteristic of an arrogant or showy demeanor. *reticent* = reserved, unwilling to speak; *belligerent* = warlike; *lofty* = pompous; *self-effacing* = modest; *discomfited* = uneasy, uncomfortable

4.   **A** The first part of the sentence indicates that a sushi master's work is not easily learned. Therefore, much *training* and *studying* are required to become a master chef. *Apprenticeship*, *tutelage*, and *cultivation* are all good choices for the 1st word. This training will give someone the *autonomy* to create his or her own work. *apprenticeship* = working as a beginner under the assistance of an instructor; *autonomy* = independence; *tutelage* = instruction; *ineptitude* = lack of skill; *dormancy* = lack of activity; *sovereignty* = supreme authority; *cultivation* = the act of improving; *boorish* = rude, lacking manners; *quiescent* = not active

5.   **A** The journalist had a reputation for breaking news early, almost as if she were *able to see the future*. Later she admitted that she had privileged sources and did not use *prophecy* at all. *prophetic* = able to tell the future; *prescience* = knowledge of future events; *premeditated* = planned ahead of time; *predilection* = preference; *dismissive* = indifferent; *omniscience* = total knowledge; *preeminent* = superior; *reluctance* = resistance; *insolvent* = bankrupt; *foresight* = thinking ahead

6.   **B** Neither passage describes a discovery, but rather the world picture (line 5) of the medieval mind (lines 26–27), that is, medieval theories about the nature of the universe. Although Passage 1 provides a counterexample to an often-heard charge (lines 14–15), Passage 2 does not attempt to disprove any assumptions. Neither passage questions the medieval theories presented. Instead, the passages merely describe those theories. Lastly, neither passage discusses the everyday life in medieval Europe.

7.   **D** The passage states that where our universe is thought to be dark, the other one was presumed to be illuminated, which means that the medieval universe was perceived to be full of light, unlike our modern universe.

8.   **C** Pascal is said to be *disturbed by the silence of the vast spaces between the stars* (lines 10–11), in contrast to the medieval thinkers who *formerly thought* that the universe produced *the "music of the spheres"* (lines 12–13).

9.   **E** Dante's theory is described in Passage 1 to counter the charge that medieval thinkers were focused on man's sense of self-importance (lines 16–17), but Hildegard's theory presented in the final sentence of Passage 2 is clearly anthropocentric, or human-centered. The world views of both Dante and Hildegard are focused on religion and an ordered hierarchy, but neither addresses scientific methods. Lastly, Passage 1 does not discuss the public acceptance of Dante's theory.

10.   **E** This passage is concerned primarily with describing the relationships among the plants, animals and climate of the Serengeti. Therefore, it is describing how a particular ecosystem works. Although the passage mentions human intervention tangentially in the last paragraph, where it refers to badly drawn park boundaries, it is not a central focus of the passage. Although it does mention individual plants, the passage as a whole does not focus on them, but instead shows how they play a role in a larger ecosystem. It does not mention natural disasters, and only mentions the distinction between grazers and browsers as a minor point.

11.   **C** These sentences suggest that the variety in the diet of grazers increases with the length of the grass. When the grass is short, all the animals apparently eat much the same sort of grass, but when it is long, they diversify their diets.

12.   **A** Browsers are said to *feed on shrubs or the leaves of trees* (lines 15–16), as opposed to the grazers, which eat *the abundant grass that springs up like a well-mown lawn* (lines 10–11).

13.   **B** The passage states that *unlike all the other grazers on the plain,* (zebras) *have teeth in both jaws* (lines 27–28). *All the rest* (besides the zebras) *are various species of antelope* (lines 30–31), which have *toothless upper palates* (lines 32–33).

14.   **E** The second paragraph states that *where the grass is all short . . . all the animals apparently eat the same sort of grass . . . but where the grass is of varied lengths . . . each animal copes differently with the available fodder* (lines 19–24). This difference is then described in the third paragraph, where the grazing sequence is specified.

15.   **C** The rains are said to bring on *fresh growth* (lines 52–53), encouraging the grazers to return to old grazing lands.

16. **A** This paragraph states that if the *migrant herds . . . were confined* (lines 63–64), they would *so weaken the grass that it would die out* (lines 67–68). So maintaining the grasslands requires that the animals not be confined.

17. **A** The thesis of the passage is that *men come greatly to desire that these capricious gifts of Nature* (that is, the natural resources that are hard for some and easy for others to find , by luck alone) *might be intercepted by some agency having the power and the goodwill to distribute them justly. . . . This desire is Socialism* (lines 41–47).

18. **C** This primitive cultivator is a person who tries to stick a spade into the earth and make wheat and other edible matters spring from it. This is a farmer. Although the author uses figurative and metaphorical language throughout the passage, this particular phrase is being used literally.

19. **D** The *astronomer* is said to regard the earth as simply *a ball . . . without ulterior motives* (lines 3–4), while the *foolish spendthrift . . . suddenly realizes that the earth is offering him gold* (lines 21–24). Therefore, the astronomer regards the earth as impersonal, while the spendthrift regards it as generous.

20. **B** The *closed hand* represents the tendency of the *Earth* to hide its *diamonds* and *good red wheat* (lines 31–32).

21. **A** The author is discussing how capricious nature is in revealing its resources, and suggests that anyone trying to harvest the earth's resources must become a gambler (line 33), and scoff at theorists who prate (speak inconsequentially) of moral virtues such as industry and honesty and equality. Therefore, the author is suggesting that these virtues are not as valuable as many people claim they are.

22. **C** This fate is the fate of the *gambler* (line 33), who is at the whim of mother earth.

23. **E** The author states that the *Social Democratic State . . . remains to be tried* (lines 51–52).

24. **C** The author states that *our own choice* (that is, the choice of his society) *is shown by our continual aspiration to possess property* (lines 59–60).

Section 7

1. **B** $3x + 5x + 8x = 32$
   Combine like terms: $16x = 32$
   Divide by 16: $x = 2$
   (Chapter 11 Lesson 1: Solving Equations)

2. **D** $\left(\dfrac{1}{x}\right)\left(\dfrac{x}{3}\right)(6x) = 8$
   Simplify: $2x = 8$
   Divide by 2: $x = 4$
   (Chapter 11 Lesson 1: Solving Equations)

3. **A** $5b - 10 \geq 15$
   Add 10: $5b \geq 25$
   Divide by 5: $b \geq 5$
   (Chapter 11 Lesson 6: Inequalities, Absolute Values, and Plugging In)

4. **C** First find 30% of 50: $(.3)(50) = 15$
   t% of 60 is 15

   Set up equation: $\dfrac{t}{100} = \dfrac{15}{60}$

   Cross-multiply: $60t = 1{,}500$
   Divide by 60: $t = 25$
   (Chapter 10 Lesson 5: Percents)

5. **C** First convert 8 hours into minutes:

   $$\dfrac{8 \text{ hours}}{x \text{ minutes}} = \dfrac{1 \text{ hour}}{60 \text{ minutes}}$$

   Cross-multiply: $x = 480$ minutes
   Then set up a ratio to answer the question:

   $$\dfrac{480 \text{ minutes}}{y \text{ cards}} = \dfrac{40 \text{ minutes}}{h \text{ cards}}$$

   Cross-multiply: $40y = 480h$
   Divide by 40: $y = 12h$
   (Chapter 11 Lesson 7: Word Problems)
   (Chapter 10 Lesson 4: Ratios and Proportions)

6. **A** First find the product of $-1.5 \times 1.25 : -1.875$. Point A is closest to -1.875 on the number line presented.
   (Chapter 10 Lesson 1: Numbers and Operations)

7. **C** If the 4 people must each have a different positive number of cards, then the least that 3 may have is 1, 2, and 3 cards. This leaves a maximum of $100 - 6 = 94$ for the remaining person.
   (Chapter 12 Lesson 3: Numerical Reasoning Problems)

8.   **C**   A quick plot of the data listed in the table will point you to answer choice C.

Since the miles per gallon are decreasing as the age increases, you can eliminate choice A. There is no point where the data levels out, which eliminates answer choice D. Finally, because it is not decreasing at a constant rate, you can eliminate choices B and E.
(Chapter 14 Lesson 5: Data Analysis)

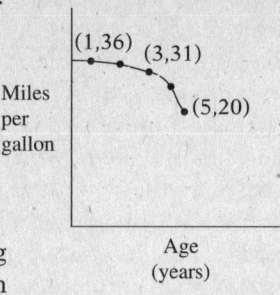

9.   **D**   If the question is *at most* how many of these integers *could* be odd, begin by imagining that ALL of them are odd. The integers may be the same, so imagine that they are all 1: $1 + 1 + 1 + 1 + 1 + 1 + 1 = 7$. But 7 is odd, so try 6 odds and 1 even: $1 + 1 + 1 + 1 + 1 + 1 + 2 = 8$. Therefore, the most that could be odd is 6.
(Chapter 12 Lesson 3: Numerical Reasoning Problems)

10.   **D**   You can write out a quick calendar for yourself to track the days:

Su	M	T	W	**Th**	F	Sa
	1	2	3	4	5	
6	7	8	9	10	11	12
13	14	15	16	17	18	19
20	21	22	23	24	25	26
27	28	29	30	**31**		

If you do this problem too quickly, you might assume that since the 4th Wednesday is the 22nd, the 4th Monday would be the 20th. But the 1st Monday comes after the 1st Wednesday, which makes the 4th Monday the 27th.
(Chapter 12 Lesson 3: Numerical Reasoning Problems)

11.   **D**   Be careful with this question. Make sure you understand the chart before choosing an answer. The question asks about teachers who use gas heat. There are $60 + 13 = 73$ teachers who use gas heat, and 60 of these live in a house.
(Chapter 14 Lesson 5: Data Analysis)
(Chapter 10 Lesson 3: Fractions)

12.   **D**   "Stack" the equations:
$$5x + 7y = 18$$
$$\underline{2x - 4y = 6}$$
Add straight down: $7x + 3y = 24$
(Chapter 11 Lesson 2: Systems)

13.   **A**

Starting with the angle marked $x°$ in the original figure, you can mark its vertical angle $x°$ as well. Since line l is parallel to line m, the corresponding angle in the top triangle is also $x°$. Set up an equation for the triangle:
$$x + z + (180 - y) = 180$$
Subtract 180: $x + z - y = 0$
Add y: $x + z = y$

(You might also simply notice that the angle marked $y°$ is an "exterior" angle to the triangle, so its measure is equal to the sum of the 2 "remote interior" angles: $y = x + z$.)
Subtract z: $x = y - z$
(Chapter 13 Lesson 1: Lines and Angles)
(Chapter 13 Lesson 2: Triangles)

14.   **B**   This problem involves rates, so it helps to recall the rate equation: $d = rt$.

Because she travels home *along the same route,* you can use d for the distance both to and from work. Because she spends a total of 2 hours in the car, if she spends t hours on the way to work, she will spend $2 - t$ hours on the way home from work.
Set up rate equations for both legs of the trip:
To work: $d = 40(t)$
From work: $d = 24(2 - t)$
Set the expressions equal: $40t = 24(2 - t)$
Distribute: $40t = 48 - 24t$
Add $24t$: $64t = 48$
Divide by 64: $t = .75$
Plug 0.75 in for t and solve for d: $d = 40(.75) = 30$
Check by confirming that plugging $t = .75$ into the other rate equation gives the same distance from home to work.
(Chapter 12 Lesson 4: Rate Problems)

15.   **B**   The graph of the original function will be shifted up 4 and right 2. Answer choice B shows the proper representation of the new graph.
(Chapter 14 Lesson 3: Transformation)

16. **A**

Line segment $\overline{BD}$ is tangent to the circle at point A, so angles BAO and DAO are right angles. This means that both $\triangle DAO$ and $\triangle BAO$ are 30°-60°-90° triangles.

Using the 30°-60°-90° reference information at the beginning of this section, you can find the values of the remaining sides of the triangles.

Find the area of $\triangle BOD$:   Area $= \dfrac{1}{2}$(base)(height)

Plug in values: Area $= \dfrac{1}{2}\left(12\sqrt{3}\right)(6) = 36\sqrt{3}$

The radius of the circle is 6, so the area of the entire circle can be found using the equation Area $= \pi r^2 = \pi(6)^2 = 36\pi$.

The shaded region of the circle makes up 120°, or ⅓ of the circle. Therefore, the area of the shaded region is equal to ⅓$(\pi r^2) = $ ⅓$(36\pi) = 12\pi$.

The area of the unshaded region of the triangle can be found by subtracting the area of the shaded region from the total area of the triangle: $36\sqrt{3} - 12\pi$.
(Chapter 13 Lesson 2: Triangles)
(Chapter 13 Lesson 8: Circles)

Section 8

1. **E** If businesses are having a hard time staying current, their equipment must be *old* or *outdated* because technology is advancing at a *fast rate. urgency* = pressing importance; *progressive* = advancing forward; *conventional* = standard; *torpidity* = lethargy; *antiquated* = outdated; *lassitude* = lack of energy; *innovative* = inventive, novel

2. **B** The sentence states that one feature of Joyce's work *gave way* to another, suggesting that first missing word is a noun that directly contrasts the adjective in the second blank. The second word is paired with *arcane*, which means *secret* or *little-understood*. This word must also describe works that feature *neologisms* (invented words) and *obscure literary tricks*. Therefore the first word should mean something like *clarity* and the second phrase should include an adjective like *hard to understand. lucidity* = clarity; *opaque* = very difficult to understand or translate; *concise* = brief and to the point; *anachronism* = quality of being out of place in time; *derivative* = copied from others

3. **B** Churchill was known to *choose his strategies arbitrarily* (without logical reason), so he was *whimsical* or *impulsive. diligent* = working with great effort; *impulsive* = acting without thought; *vicious* = evil, harsh; *malevolent* = wishing harm, malicious

4. **D** If the king executed those who acted irreverently (without respect), he must have demanded *utmost respect. insolence* = brazen rudeness; *impudence* = disrespect; *truculence* = inclination to pick fights; *deference* = respect; *ignominy* = humiliation

5. **D** Since Galileo contradicted church teachings, he was a *heretic. ostracized* = cut off from society; *hermit* = one who seeks solitude; *venerated* = worshipped; *demagogue* = powerful leader; *hallowed* = respected as holy; *revisionist* = one who rethinks or reshapes a commonly accepted view; *denounced* = accused or condemned for being a villain; *heretic* = one who holds controversial opinions; *reviled* = attacked with harsh language; *luminary* = one who inspires others

6. **A** The Senator is known for her *iconoclastic* views, which means that she goes against the party line. Because of this, she would have a tough time getting *traditional* party members to support her. *contentious* = quarrelsome; *orthodox* = traditional; *litigious* = prone to bringing lawsuits; *disingenuous* = insincere; *vituperative* = using harsh censure or condemnation; *dissident* = disagreeing; *heretical* = going against standard beliefs; *polemical* = pertaining to a highly controversial political or intellectual position

7. **D** This is an address to the Atlanta Exposition (as the introduction indicates), and the author is clearly addressing those in *the commercial world* (lines 27–28) and entreating ex-slaves and Southern whites to work together for their mutual benefit.

8. **A** The author does not directly address those in the antislavery movement but does address (B) *those of the white race who look to the incoming of those of foreign birth . . . for the prosperity of the South* (lines 46–49), (C) *those of my race who depend upon bettering their condition* (lines 13–14), (D) those for whom African Americans have *tilled your fields, cleared your forests . . .* (lines 57–58), and (E) those African Americans who *underestimate the importance of cultivating friendly relations with the Southern white man* (lines 15–17).

9. **C** The captain did not heed the 1st, 2nd, or 3rd call but heeded the 4th call *at last* (lines 9–10), suggesting that he did not believe the responses were helpful at first.

10. **C** The phrase *this chance* refers to the *man's chance* (that African Americans can have) *in the commercial world* (lines 27–28).

11. **A** In saying that *there is as much dignity in tilling a field as in writing a poem* (lines 41–42), the author is saying that such manual labor is valuable work.

12. **D** These indicate the thoughts of a *Negro who has given earnest thought to the situation of his people in America* (lines 70–72).

13. **C** In saying that because of *incessant self-questioning* (line 86) *. . . the best energy of the Negro people cannot be marshalled to do the bidding of the race* (lines 92–94), the author means that introspection keeps African Americans from organizing themselves to meet the needs of their race.

14. **D** Such people are said to *make room for every rascal and demagogue who chooses to cloak his selfish deviltry under the veil of race pride* (lines 95–97); that is, they allow themselves to be influenced by selfish and evil people.

15. **D** *That point* refers to the point *farther than* (which) *our Americanism does not go* (lines 125–126). In other words, this is the point up to which African Americans share much in common with all Americans but beyond which they are a unique people.

16. **C** This *broader humanity* is that which *freely recognizes differences in men, but sternly deprecates* (disapproves of) *inequality in their opportunities of development* (lines 142–145). In other words, its members value equal opportunity for all races.

17. **E** Passage 1 focuses on the manual labor that African Americans have performed in tilling fields, clearing forests, building railroads and cities, etc., while the author of Passage 2 emphasizes contributions like *the subtle sense of song that has given America its only American music, its only American fairy tales, its only touch of pathos and humor. . . .* (lines 134–137).

18. **A** The *black tomorrow* in Passage 2 is the influence of African Americans in softening *the whiteness of the Teutonic today* (line 133), which suggests a change in the dominant culture. Passage 1, on the other hand, envisions a future in which African Americans make *friends in every manly way of the people of all races by whom we are surrounded* (lines 19–21) and incorporate themselves into the existing dominant industries of *agriculture, mechanics, . . . commerce, . . .* (and) *domestic service* (lines 22–23).

19. **E** Passage 1 indicates that the dominant culture can give the African American *a man's chance in the commercial world* (lines 27–28) and contains many *opportunities* (line 45). Passage 2 is more assertive in suggesting that African Americans have changed and will continue to change the dominant culture: *We are the first fruits of this new nation, the harbinger of that black tomorrow which is yet destined to soften the whiteness of the Teutonic today* (lines 130–133).

Section 9

1. **C** The parallel idiom *neither . . . nor* requires that the phrase following *neither* and the phrase following *nor* have the same grammatical form. The only choice that maintains proper idiom and parallelism is C.
(Chapter 18 Lesson 3: Parallelism)

2. **E** This sentence contains three clauses, each of which has the same subject, *Georgia*. The underlined clause, however, is in the passive voice, unlike the other two. It should be changed to the active voice like the others.
(Chapter 18 Lesson 3: Parallelism)

3. **D** Since any rehearsal would have been completed before the performance, the participle in the underlined phrase should be in the perfect form *having rehearsed*. Choice B also uses the nonstandard phrase *being that,* and choices C and E create run-on sentences.
(Chapter 18 Lesson 9: Tricky Tenses)

4.   **B** In the original sentence, the subject *outlets* does not agree with the verb *has acknowledged*. In choice C, the subject *scope* disagrees with the verb *have been acknowledged*. Choice D is awkward and choice E uses an illogical verb tense. Choice B conveys the idea clearly and grammatically.
(Chapter 18 Lesson 1: Subject Verb Disagreement)

5.   **E** The original verb *have had* is in the imperative mood, but should be in the subjunctive mood because it conveys a hypothetical condition. Choice E conveys the mood correctly.
(Chapter 18 Lesson 14: The Subjunctive Mood)

6.   **C** The statement made in the main clause is not *against* popular opinion, but rather is *contrary* to it. Although choice E uses the proper modifier, it illogically suggests that an opinion can *say* something.
(Chapter 18 Lesson 15: Coordinating Ideas)

7.   **A** The original sentence is the most logical and effective option.

8.   **B** The original phrase misuses the semicolon, because the phrase preceding it is not an independent clause. Similarly, choice E uses the conjunction *so* to join two clauses, but the first is not independent, so the sentence is ungrammatical. Choices C and D use the unidiomatic phrases *struggled for finding* and *struggled finding*. Choice B avoids these problems, and is clear and effective.
(Chapter 18 Lesson 15: Coordinating Ideas)

9.   **A** The original phrasing is best. It provides the parallel form required by the comparative idiom *not so much by . . . as by . . .*, whereas the others violate parallel form.

10. **D** The original phrasing is unidiomatic. The correct idiom is *A appears to be B*.
(Chapter 18 Lesson 10: Idiom Errors)

11. **C** The comparison is logically between the *response* to the revised proposal and the *response* to the original proposal. Choice C is the only one that makes the correct logical and parallel comparison.
(Chapter 18 Lesson 4: Comparison Errors)

12. **C** The original phrasing breaks the idea into two independent clauses. But since it conveys one central idea, it is more effectively phrased with a single independent clause and a modifying phrase. Choice C does this effectively, idiomatically and concisely.
(Chapter 18 Lesson 15: Coordinating Ideas))

13. **E** The original phrasing is unnecessarily wordy and does not effectively coordinate the ideas in the sentence. Choice C has the same problem. Choices B and D create clauses with uncoordinated verbs. Only choice E conveys the idea concisely and effectively.
(Chapter 18 Lesson 15: Coordinating Ideas)

14. **C** The phrase *extra superfluous* is redundant, and the phrase *to edit for eliminating* is unidiomatic. Choice C is clear and concise.
(Chapter 18 Lesson 12: Other Modifier Problems)

A right triangle has a leg of length 3 and a hypotenuse of length 4. What is the length of the other side?

If n is a positive real number, what is the simplest way to express $n^2 \times n^3$?

The average of 3 consecutive even integers is 80. What is the least of these integers?

Stephanie bought a sweater for $42.40, including a 6% sales tax. What was the price before tax?

If $5 - 2(x - 3) = 9$, then what is the value of x?

Note: *Figure not drawn to scale*
In the figure above, what is the value of $a + b$?

Formula/Concept:
When you multiply exponentials with the same base, you **add** the exponents.

Correct answer: n^5 $(n^2)(n^3) =$
   Add the exponents: $(n^{2+3}) = n^5$

Common mistake: n^6
This is the result if you mistakenly multiply the exponents.

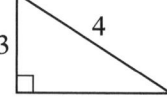

Formula/Concept:
The Pythagorean Theorem

Correct answer: $\sqrt{7}$ $3^2 + x^2 = 4^2$
   Subtract 9: $x^2 = 7$
   Take square root: $x = \sqrt{7}$

Common mistake: 5
Don't assume it is a 3-4-5 triangle. In such a triangle, the 3-4 sides must both be **legs.**

Formula/Concept:
To find the price before a 6% tax, **divide** the final price by 1.06.

Correct answer: $40
        $42.40 = (1.06)(x)$
Divide by 1.06: $40.00 = x$

Common mistake: $39.86
This is the result if you mistakenly deduct 6% of $42.40 (which is $2.54), from $42.40.

Formula/Concept:
If a set of numbers is "evenly" spaced, the average is the same as the middle number.

Correct answer: 78
If the average of consecutive even numbers is 80, then 80 must be the "middle" number in the set, so the numbers are 78, 80, 82.

Common mistake: 79
Don't overlook the fact that the numbers are **even.**

Formula/Concept:
$(n - 2)180°$ = the sum of the angles in an n-sided figure.

Correct answer: 250
The sum of the angles is $(5 - 2)(180°) = 540°$, so $105° + 93° + 92° + a + b = 540°$. Therefore, $a + b = 250°$.

Common mistake: 70
This is the result if you mistakenly think the sum is 360° instead of 540°.

Formula/Concept:
Distributing with negative numbers

Correct answer: 1 $5 - 2(x - 3) = 9$
Distribute: $5 - 2x + 6 = 9$
Combine like terms: $11 - 2x = 9$
Subtract 11: $-2x = -2$

Common mistake: -5
This results from improperly distributing the -2.

At the beginning of 1999, stock in ABC company cost $100 per share. It increased by 25% in 1999, decreased by 20% in 2000, decreased by 20% in 2001, and increased by 15% in 2002. What was the price at the end of 2002?

Shaquille O'Neal made 4 of his first 12 free throws. How many consecutive shots x must he hit for his free-throw percentage to reach 60%?

If the average of x, $x + 2$, and $2x + 8$ is 6, what is the value of x?

If a triangle has two sides of length 8 and 12, then what is the largest possible integer length of the third side?

A set consists of the integers from −12 to n. If the sum of the members of that set is 42, how many integers are in the set?

If 10 students in a class of 16 have an average score of 82 on a physics test and the remaining students have an average score of 90, what is the average score of the entire class?

Formula/Concept: Ratios and Proportions

Correct answer: 8 $\dfrac{4+x}{12+x} = .6$

Cross-multiply: $(4 + x) = (12 + x)(.6)$
Distribute: $4 + x = 7.2 + .6x$
Subtract .6x: $4 + .4x = 7.2$
Subtract 4: $.4x = 3.2$
Divide by .4: $x = 8$

Common mistake: 4
This is the result if you forget to add the quantity x to the denominator as well as the numerator.

Formula/Concept: Percent change

e.g.   To *increase* a value by 20%, multiply by 1.20
       To *decrease* a value by 10%, multiply by 0.90

Correct answer: 92   1999 = $100
$(100)(1.25) = 125$ 2000 = $125
$(125)(.8) = 100$ 2001 = $100
$(100)(.8) = 80$ 2002 = $80
$(80)(1.15) = 92$ 2003 = $92

Common mistake: 100   This is result if you simply add up the percent changes instead of calculating the changes as above: 25 - 20 - 20 + 15 = 0.

Formula/Concept:
The Triangle Inequality:
$|B - A| < C < |B + A|$

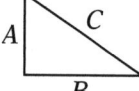

Correct answer: 19
$(B - A) < C < (B + A)$
Substitute for A and B: $(12 - 8) < C < (12 + 8)$
Simplify: $4 < C < 20$

Common mistake: 20
This is the common error that can be made if you mistakenly set $4 \leq C \leq 20$.

Formula/Concept: $\dfrac{sum}{\#} = average$
Average formula:

Correct answer: 2

$\dfrac{x + (x + 2) + (2x + 8)}{3} = 6$

Multiply by 3: $x + (x + 2) + (2x + 8) = 18$
Combine like terms: $4x + 10 = 18$
Subtract 10 $4x = 8$
Divide by 4: $x = 2$

Common mistake: 5
This is the result if you mistakenly think that there are 5 numbers instead of 3.

Formula/Concept: Weighted Averages
If two numbers being averaged have different "weights," you must remember to account for that when finding the average.

Correct answer: 85

$\dfrac{10(82) + 6(90)}{16} = \dfrac{820 + 540}{16} = 85$

Common mistake: 86
This is the result if you mistakenly take the "simple" average of the two scores, 82 and 90, rather than taking their *weighted* average.

Formula/Concept: Integer arithmetic

Correct answer: 28
Remember that the sum of the numbers from -12 to 12 is 0, because the negative integers "cancel" the positives. 13 + 14 + 15 = 42, so n must be 15. To find the number of integers in the set, just subtract the first from the last and add 1.

Common mistake: 27
This is the result if you forget that 0 is an integer or simply subtract the least from the greatest to count the integers in the set.

If the area of square ABCD in the figure above is 100 ft², then what is the circumference of inscribed circle O?

In 1984, a share of stock in Black's Oil Trust cost $3. By 2000, it had increased to $15 per share. What is the percent increase in the price of the stock from 1984 to 2000?

If $(x + 4)(x - 4) = 65$, then what is the value of x^2?

If the third Friday in January occurs on the 15th, what is the date of the fourth Wednesday in January?

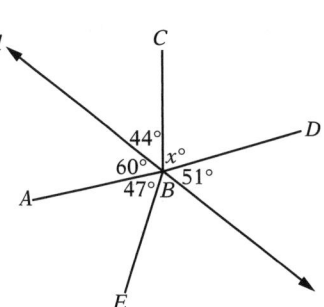

Note: Figure not drawn to scale.

In the figure above, line segments $\overline{AB}$, $\overline{EB}$ $\overline{CB}$, and $\overline{DB}$ intersect line l at point B. What is the value of x?

At a department store, all shirts are priced at s dollars, but if you buy one shirt at full price, you can buy any number of additional shirts at a $2 discount per shirt. What is the cost of buying x shirts at this sale?

Formula/Concept: Using Patterns
Correct answer: 27th
Make a calendar:

M	T	W	Th	F	Sa	Su
				1	2	3
4	5	**6**	7	8	9	10
11	12	**13**	**14**	**15**	16	17
18	19	**20**	21	22	23	24
25	26	**27**	28	29	30	31

Common mistake: **20th**
This is the result if you mistakenly assume, without drawing a calendar to confirm, that the third Wednesday occurs before the third Friday. In this particular month, the first Wednesday is after the first Friday.

Formula/Concept: Circumference $= 2\pi r = \pi d$

Correct answer: **10π**
Area of square $= (\text{side})^2$
Substitute 100 for area: $100 = (\text{side})^2$
Take square root: $10 = \text{side of square}$
diameter $d = \text{side of square}$
Use circumference $C = \pi d = \pi(10) = 10\pi$
formula

Common mistake: 25π
This is the result if you confuse the area formula with the circumference formula.

Formula/Concept: A linear angle measures 180°.

Correct answer: **85°**
$44° + x° + 51° = 180°$
Combine like terms: $95° + x° = 180°$
Subtract 95°: $x° = 85°$

Common mistake: **47°**
This is the result if you mistakenly think that angles CBD and ABE are vertical angles. But vertical angles must involve intersecting lines, not line segments. There are no vertical angles in this figure.

Formula/Concept:

$$\text{Percent change} = \frac{final - original}{original} \times 100\%$$

Correct answer: **400%**

$$\text{Percent change} = \frac{15 - 3}{3} \times 100\% = 400\%$$

Common mistake: **500%**
This is the result if you mistakenly find what percent 15 is of 3 instead of finding the percent **change** from 3 to 15.

Formula/Concept: Translating words into expressions

Correct answer: $s + (x - 1)(s - 2)$
The first shirt costs s dollars, and each additional shirt costs $(s - 2)$ dollars. Don't multiply the $(s - 2)$ by x, because this would account for the first shirt twice. Only $(x - 1)$ shirts are priced at $(s - 2)$ dollars.

Common mistake: $s + (x)(s - 2)$
This is the result if you forget that only $x - 1$ shirts are discounted, rather than all (x) shirts.

Formula/Concept: FOILing
$$(a + b)(a - b) = a^2 - ab + ab + b^2$$

Correct answer: **81**
$(x + 4)(x - 4) = 65$
FOIL: $x^2 - 4x + 4x - 16 = 65$
Combine like terms: $x^2 - 16 = 65$
Add 16: $x^2 = 81$

Common mistake: 9
This is result if you mistakenly solve for x instead of x^2.

If *w* divided by ¼ is equal to 32, then what is the value of *w*?

Point *W* is on line segment *XY* such that $\frac{XW}{WY} = \frac{3}{4}$. If *WY* = 12 then what is *XY*?

At Holston Hospital, a "team" consists of 1 resident and 2 medical students. If there are 4 residents and 5 medical students in the emergency department, how many different teams could be formed?

For all values of *x*, let $x = \frac{x-2}{4}$.

Which of the following is equal to $\boxed{34} - \boxed{10}$?

(A) $\boxed{6}$
(B) $\boxed{8}$
(C) $\boxed{14}$
(D) $\boxed{24}$
(E) $\boxed{26}$

If the average of 5, 6, 8, *x*, and 8 is 6, then what is the median of the set?

When 34 is divided by 6, the remainder is *n*. What is the remainder when *n* is divided by 2?

Formula/Concept: Ratios and Proportions

Correct answer: 21 $\dfrac{XW}{WY} = \dfrac{3}{4}$

Plug in 12 for WY: $\dfrac{XW}{12} = \dfrac{3}{4}$

Cross-multiply: $4XW = 36$
Divide by 4: $XW = 9$
Solve for XY: $XY = 9 + 12 = 21$

Common mistake: 9
This is the result if you solve for XW instead of XY.

Formula/Concept: To divide by a fraction, multiply by its reciprocal.

Correct answer: **8**
Write an equation: $w \div \tfrac{1}{4} = 32$
Multiply by the reciprocal: $w \times 4 = 32$
Divide by 4: $w = 8$

Common mistake: **128**
This is the result if you divide 32 by $\tfrac{1}{4}$ instead of multiplying it by $\tfrac{1}{4}$.

Formula/Concept: New Symbols/Functions
Correct answer: **E**

$\boxed{34} = \dfrac{34 - 2}{4} = \dfrac{32}{4} = 8$ $\boxed{10} = \dfrac{10 - 2}{4} = \dfrac{8}{4} = 2$

$\boxed{34} - 10 = 8 - 2 = 6$ $\boxed{26} = \dfrac{26 - 2}{4} = \dfrac{24}{4} = 6$

Common mistake: **A**
This is the result if you do not notice that the answer choices are also in boxes.

Formula/Concept: The Fundamental Counting Principle

Correct answer: $4 \times 5 \times 4 \div 2 = \mathbf{40}$
The number of options for choosing a resident is 4, since there are 4 residents. The number of different pairs of interns is 10, because there are 5 options for intern A and then 4 options for intern B, but since choosing AB is the same as choosing BA, we must divide this set by 2.

Common mistake: **100 or 80**
This is the result of $4 \times 5 \times 5$ or $4 \times 5 \times 4$.

Formula/Concept: Remainders
Correct answer: **0**

$$6\overline{)34}\;\;{}^{5\,R4} \quad -30 \quad \underline{} \quad 4$$

$$2\overline{)4}\;\;{}^{2\,R0} \quad -4 \quad \underline{} \quad 0$$

Common mistake: **2**
This is the result if you find the **quotient** rather than the remainder.

Formula/Concept: Median = middle number
Mean = average

Correct answer: 6 $\dfrac{5 + 6 + 8 + x + 8}{5} = 6$

Multiply by 5: $5 + 6 + 8 + x + 8 = 30$
Combine like terms: $27 + x = 30$
Subtract 27: $x = 3$
Find the median: $\cancel{3}, \cancel{5}, 6, \cancel{8}, \cancel{8}$
Common mistake: **8**
This is the result if you confuse **mode** with **median.**

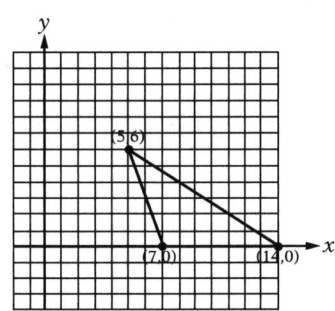

What is the area of the triangle in the figure above?

A printer can produce 50 pages in 3 minutes. At this rate, how many pages can it print in 300 minutes?

The slope of line l is $-\frac{1}{2}$. If two points on line l are $(2, 4)$ and $(x, -2)$, what is the value of x?

If $f(x) = (x - 2)^2$, what is the range of this function over the domain $-2 \le x \le 3$?

There are 25 students in Ms. Jamison's 4th-grade homeroom class. If 12 of her students have a cat, 19 have a dog, and every student has at least 1 pet, how many students have both a cat and a dog?

If b varies inversely as the square of c and directly as a, and $b = 4$ when $c = 4$ and $a = 8$, then what is the value of b when $a = 18$ and $c = 6$?

Formula/Concept: Ratios and Proportions

Correct answer: **5,000**

Set up a ratio: $\dfrac{50 \text{ pages}}{3 \text{ minutes}} = \dfrac{x \text{ pages}}{300 \text{ minutes}}$

Cross multiply: $15{,}000 = 3x$

Divide by 3: $5{,}000 = x$

Common mistake: **18**

This is the result if you set up the ratio improperly.

$$\dfrac{50 \text{ pages}}{3 \text{ minutes}} = \dfrac{300 \text{ minutes}}{x \text{ pages}}$$

Formula/Concept: Area = ½(base)(height)

Correct answer: **21**

The base of the triangle is the distance from (7, 0) to (14, 0), which is $14 - 7 = 7$. The height is the distance from the x-axis to (5, 6), which is $6 - 0 = 6$.

$$\text{Area} = \tfrac{1}{2}(7)(6) = 21$$

Common mistake: **17.5**

This is the common error that can be made if you use 5 as the height instead of 6.

Formula/Concept:
The range of a function is the set of all of the possible outputs, or "y-values."

Correct answer: $0 \le y \le 16$

Plug in the integer values of the domain and find the range:
$f(-2) = 16$; $f(-1) = 9$; $f(0) = 4$; $f(1) = 1$; $f(2) = 0$; $f(3) = 1$. This yields a range of $0 \le y \le 16$. Or you could graph it:

Common mistake: $1 \le y \le 16$

This results if you try to find the range by plugging in only the two domain endpoints, ignoring the points in between.

Formula/Concept: $\text{slope} = \dfrac{\text{rise}}{\text{run}} = \dfrac{y_2 - y_1}{x_2 - x_1}$

Correct answer: 14 $\quad \text{slope} = \dfrac{y_2 - y_1}{x_2 - x_1} = \dfrac{-2 - 4}{x - 2} = \dfrac{-1}{2}$

Cross-multiply: $2(-6) = -1(x - 2)$

Simplify: $-12 = -x + 2$

Subtract 2: $-14 = -x$

Divide by -1: $14 = x$

Common mistake: **−1**

This is the result if you mistakenly calculate "run over rise" for the slope: $\dfrac{x_2 - x_1}{y_2 - y_1}$

Formula/Concept: Direct and Inverse Variation

Correct answer: **4**

$b = \dfrac{ka}{c^2} \qquad 4 = \dfrac{k(8)}{(4)^2}$

Cross-multiply: $64 = 8k$

Divide by 8: $k = 8$

Set up new equation: $b = \dfrac{8a}{c^2} \qquad b = \dfrac{8(18)}{(6)^2} = \dfrac{144}{36} = 4$

Common mistake: ½

This is the result if you inversely relate b to the square **root** of c instead of relating it to the square of c.

Formula/Concept: Venn Diagrams

Correct answer: **6**

Let x represent the number of students with both cats and dogs:

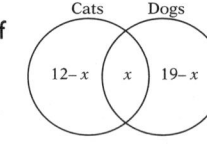

$$(12 - x) + (19 - x) + x = 25$$

Combine like terms: $31 - x = 25$

Subtract 31: $-x = -6$

Divide by -1: $x = 6$

Common mistake: **25 or 31**

This is the result if you confuse "a cat **and** a dog" with "a cat **or** a dog."

If $5 - 2|x| > -9$, find the range of possible values for x.

If $-1 < w < 0$, then which of the following statements is true?

    (A) $w < w^2 < w^3$
    (B) $w^2 < w < w^3$
    (C) $w < w^3 < w^2$
    (D) $w^3 < w^2 < w$
    (E) $w^3 < w < w^2$

$-2, 0, 2, -2, 0, 2, -2, 0, 2, \ldots$

The sequence above continues according to the pattern shown. What is the sum of the first 31 terms of this sequence?

A jar contains only red and white marbles. If the probability of randomly selecting a white marble from the jar is ¼ and there are 15 red marbles in the jar, how many white marbles are there?

The sum of a set of 7 integers is 67. If each of these numbers must be less than 14, what is the smallest possible value of any one number in the set?

Jim takes the same train to and from work each day. One winter day, during the morning commute, the train averaged 80 miles per hour. During the evening commute, due to ice on the track, the train averaged only 48 miles per hour. If Jim spent 2 hours in the train that day, how many miles is the train ride to work?

Formula/Concept: Powers of Fractions

Correct answer: **C**

Plug in a number for w:

Plug in $-\frac{1}{2}$ for w:

$$w = -\tfrac{1}{2}$$
$$w^2 = (-\tfrac{1}{2})^2 = \tfrac{1}{4}$$
$$w^3 = (-\tfrac{1}{2})^3 = -\tfrac{1}{8}$$

Rank the values of w, w^2, w^3: $-\tfrac{1}{2} < -\tfrac{1}{8} < \tfrac{1}{4}$

Common mistake: **A or E**

You might choose E if you forget that $-\tfrac{1}{8} > -\tfrac{1}{2}$. You might choose A if you forget that squaring any negative number will result in a positive number.

Formula/Concept:
Solving absolute value inequalities

Correct answer: $-7 < x < 7$

$$5 - 2\,|\,x\,| > -9$$

Subtract 5: $-2\,|\,x\,| > -14$

Divide by -2: (swap the inequality) $|\,x\,| < 7$

Take away absolute value: $-7 < x < 7$

Common mistake: $x > 7$ or $x < -7$

This is the common error that can be made if you forget to swap the inequality when dividing or multiplying by a negative number.

Formula/Concept: Ratios and Probability

Correct answer: **5**

If the probability of selecting a white marble is $\tfrac{1}{4}$, then the probability of selecting a red marble is $1 - \tfrac{1}{4} = \tfrac{3}{4}$.

Set up a ratio: $\dfrac{red}{total} = \dfrac{3}{4}$ $\dfrac{15}{total} = \dfrac{3}{4}$

Cross-multiply: $60 = 3(total)$

Divide by 3: $20 = total = $ white + red

Solve for white: $20 = $ white + 15

Subtract 15:   white = 5 marbles

Common mistake: **20**

This is the result if you answer for the **total** number of marbles instead of the number of **white** marbles.

Formula/Concept:
Sequence problems: finding the sum of a random number of terms

Correct answer: **−2**

The pattern repeats every 3 digits, and the sum of each repetition is $-2 + 0 + 2 = 0$. The pattern occurs $31 \div 3 = 10\tfrac{1}{3}$ times, or 10 with remainder 1. The 10 full repetitions have a sum of $10(0) = 0$. Since the 31st term is -2, the sum is $0 + -2 = -2$.

Common mistake: **0**

This is the common error that can be made if you forget to add the 31st term after finding out that the pattern occurs $10\tfrac{1}{3}$ times.

Formula/Concept: Distance = Rate × Time

Correct answer: **60**   (because he takes the same train, the distance is the same going in both directions.)

To work: $d = (80)(t)$

From work: $d = (48)(2 - t)$

Set them equal: $80t = 48(2 - t)$

Distribute: $80t = 96 - 48t$

Add 48t: $128t = 96$

Divide by 128: $t = .75$ hours

Plug in .75 for t: $d = 80(.75) = 60$ miles

Common mistake: **64**

This is the result if you average the two speeds, 80 and 48, and then using that speed of 64 to calculate a distance of 64 miles to work.

Formula/Concept: Numerical Reasoning

Correct answer: **−11**

$$a + b + c + d + e + f + g = 67$$

If you want g to be as **small** as possible, then make the sum of the other numbers as **large** as possible: Substitute 13 for a through f:

$$13 + 13 + 13 + 13 + 13 + 13 + g = 67$$

Combine like terms: $78 + g = 67$

Common mistake: **4**

This is the result if you assume the integers must be **different**: 13, 12, 11, 10, 9, and 8.

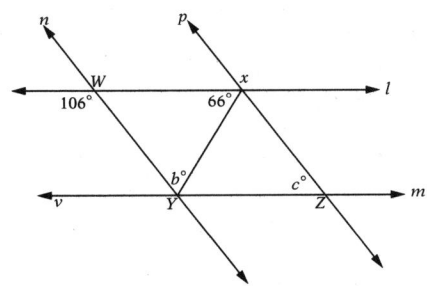

Note: Figure not drawn to scale.

In the figure above, if $l \parallel m$ and $n \parallel p$, what is the value of $b + c$?

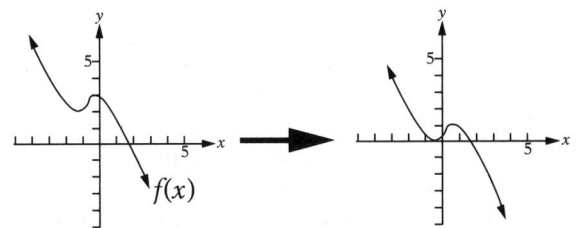

Given the graph of $y = f(x)$ shown above and the transformed graph on the right, what is the equation of the new function?

If the rectangular solid above has a volume of 162 cubic inches, what is the surface area of the solid?

Instructions for studying with Root Smart Cards

1st **point:**   Define the word on the front of the card

2nd **point:**   Give the meaning of the root in bold.

3rd **point:**   List at least **three** words that contain the root.

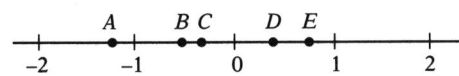

Which point corresponds to the result when the numbers corresponding to points E and B are multiplied?

magn**anim**ous

Formula/Concept: Transformations of Functions

Correct answer: $y = f(x - 1) - 2$
The graph is shifted **down** two units, which turns $y = f(x)$ into $y = f(x) - 2$.
The graph is then shifted to the **right** one unit, which turns $y = f(x) - 2$ into $y = f(x - 1) - 2$.

Common mistake: $y = f(x - 2) - 1$
This is the result if you mistakenly reverse the vertical and horizontal shifts.

Formula/Concept:
Parallel lines and alternate interior, corresponding, and alternate exterior angles.

Correct answer: 114
Angle $ZYX = 66°$ and angle $ZYW = 106°$ because they form a "Z".
$b = 40°$ because $106°$ $- 66° = 40°$. Angle $VYW = 74°$ because $180 - 106 = 74°$. $c = 74°$ because of corresponding angles. $b + c = 40° + 74° = 114°$.

Mistake:
$80°$. If you think b and c are 40.

definition of the word

definition of the root

examples of words

Formula/Concept: Volume = lwh
Surface area (SA) = $2lw + 2lh + 2wh$
Correct answer: **198** volume = lwh
$162 = (9)(6)(h)$
Divide by 54: $3 = h$
SA = $2lw + 2lh + 2wh$
Plug in and solve: SA = $2(9)(6) + 2(9)(3) + 2(6)(3)$
Simplify: SA = $108 + 54 + 36 = 198$
Common mistake: 99
This is the result if you forget to count the 3 unshown faces when calculating the surface area.

magn**anim**ous = generous

anima = life, spirit

animal, **anim**ate, pusill**anim**ous, un**anim**ous, in**anim**ate

Formula/Concept: Numerical Reasoning

Correct answer: **C**
Assign approximate values to the points:
$A = -1.25$; $B = -0.50$; $C = -0.35$; $D = .35$; $E = .70$
$(E)(B) =$
Plug in values: $(0.70)(-0.50) = -0.35$

Common mistake: D
This is the result if you forget that $(.7)(-.5)$ is negative.

eloquent

peripatetic

immoral

propensity

sacro**sanct**

anthropology

peripatetic = wandering from place to place

peri = around

pericardium, **peri**stalsis, **per**ambulate,
periscope, **peri**pheral, **peri**od

eloquent = fluent in speech

loqu = to talk

loquacious, ventri**loqu**ist, e**locu**tion,
circum**locu**tion, inter**locu**tion

propensity = a tendency

pro = forward, forth

procrastinate, **pro**pagate, **pro**found,
provocative, **pro**lific, **pro**voke,
prophesy, **pro**phetic, **pro**ject, **pro**mote

immoral = lacking morals

im, in, ir = not

immodest, **im**material, **im**mature,
immeasurable, **im**perceptible,
irresponsible, **in**tractable, **im**pregnable

Caution: **in**flammable = easily ignited
invaluable = priceless
infamous = famous for bad deeds

anthropology = the study of humankind

anthropos = humankind

mis**anthrop**e, phil**anthrop**ist,
anthropocentric, **anthrop**omorphic

sacro**sanct** = regarded as sacred

sanctus = holy

sanctimonious, **sanct**ion, **sanct**ify, **sanct**uary

abject

subconscious

anarchy

placid

tractable

theocracy

subconscious = occuring in the mind but beyond conscious awareness

sub = under, secretly

subtle, **sub**cutaneous, **sub**liminal, **sub**lime, **sub**terfuge, **sub**sequent, **sub**servient, **sub**marine

abject = miserable

ab = away

abdicate, **ab**scond, **ab**duct, **ab**erration, **ab**solve, **ab**scess, **ab**omination

placid = calm

plac = to please

placate, **plac**ebo, com**plai**sant, com**plac**ent, dis**please**, **plea**

anarchy = absence of government

an = without

anecdote, **an**aerobic, **an**algesic, **an**emia, **an**esthetic, **an**onymous

theocracy = a government ruled by religious authority

theo = god

a**the**ist, **theo**logy, en**thu**siasm, pan**the**ist, mono**the**ism

tractable = easily managed

tract = together

sub**tract**, abs**tract**, at**tract**, **tract**or, in**tract**able, dis**tract**, con**tract**, **tract**ion

convoca**tion**

epitaph

tenacity

soliloquy

in**cite**

com**ple**ment

epitaph = an inscription on a tombstone

epi = upon

epicenter, **epi**demic, **ep**hemeral,
epilepsy, **epi**dermis, **epi**tome, **epi**logue

con**voca**tion = an assembly or meeting

vocare = to call

vocabulary, pro**voke**, con**voke**,
in**voke**, re**voke**, **voca**tion,
ad**voca**te, equi**voca**te

soliloquy = a speech to oneself

solus = alone

sole, solo, solitaire,
solitary, **soli**tude, **soli**psism

tenacity = persistence

tenere = to hold

sus**tain**, abs**tain**, con**tain**, de**tain**,
ob**tain**, enter**tain**, **ten**able, per**tain**,
per**tina**city, re**tain**

com**ple**ment = to complete the whole

plere = to fill

accom**pli**sh, re**ple**te,
de**ple**te, supp**le**ment

in**cite** = to provoke

citare = to summon, to call

citation, ex**cite**, re**cite**, resus**cita**te, soli**cit**

pro**pon**ent

biology

eulogy

apocryphal

circum**scribe**

etymo**logy**

biology = the study of life

bio = life

biogenesis, **bio**graphy, **bio**nics, **bio**psy, **bio**sphere

pro**pon**ent = a supporter; an advocate

ponere = to place

im**pose**, inter**pose**, op**pon**ent, op**po**site, ex**pon**ent, ex**po**sition, ex**po**und, post**pone**, ap**po**sitive

apocryphal = of doubtful authenticity

apo = away from

apocalypse, **apho**rism, **apo**state, **apo**plexy, **apo**stle, **apo**thecary, **apo**logy

eulogy = praise; a praise-filled speech given at someone's funeral

eu = good

euphemism, **eu**calyptus, **eu**charist, **eu**genics, **eu**karyote, **eu**phoria, **eu**rhythmic

etymo**logy** = the study of the origin of words

logos = study of

astro**logy**, archaeo**logy**, geo**logy**, onco**logy**, bio**logy**, paleonto**logy**, psycho**logy**, etymo**logy**, theo**logy**, patho**logy**, anthropo**logy**

circum**scribe** = to determine the limits of; to draw a line around

scribe = to write

in**scribe**, con**scrip**tion, de**scrip**tion, sub**scrip**tion, in**scrip**tion

paramount

levity

orthodox

in**cis**ive

equanimity

irre**ver**ent

levity = the state of being light, frivolity

levis = light in weight

e**lev**ator, re**liev**e, **lev**itate,
al**lev**iate, e**lev**ate, ob**liv**ion

paramount = of extreme importance

para = beside, next to, beyond

paraphrase, **para**site, **para**medic,
paranoia, **para**llel, **para**digm, **para**gon

in**cis**ive = clear in expression, penetrating

cis = cut

s**cis**sors, con**cis**e, s**cis**m,
pre**cis**e, pre**cis**ion, de**cis**ive

orthodox = traditional

orthos = correct, straight

orthography, **ortho**dontics, un**ortho**dox,
orthopedic, **ortho**doxy

irre**ver**ent = disrespectful

vereri = respect
verus = truth

re**ver**e, re**ver**ent, re**ver**end, **ver**acity,
verify, **ver**isimilitude, **ver**itable

equanimity = calm, even-temperedness

equi = equal

equinox, **equi**valent, **equa**lize,
equality, **equi**potential, in**equa**lity,
equitable, **equa**tor, **equa**lize

denigrate

misanthrope

ob**sequi**ous

ex**culp**ate

im**pul**sive

antipathy

misanthrope = one who hates humankind

mis = bad, wretched, hatred

miser, **mis**ery, **mis**erly, **mis**erable, **mis**carriage, **mis**chief, **mis**creant, **mis**direct, **mis**cue, **mis**demeanor, **mis**feasance, **mis**conduct

denigrate = to speak poorly of; to belittle

de = down, off

delineate, **de**scend, **de**mote, **de**cline, **de**moralize, **de**ride, **de**bate, **de**brief, **de**bunk, **de**capitate, **de**ciduous, **de**crepit, **de**cry, **de**ficient, **de**pict

ex**culp**ate = free from blame

culp = blame

dis**culp**ate, **culp**rit, **culp**able, in**culp**ate, mea **culp**a

ob**sequi**ous = overly submissive

sequi = to follow

sequience, pro**secu**te, **segue**, sub**sequ**ent, pur**sue**, non **sequi**tur

antipathy = strong feeling against

anti = against

antisocial, **anti**biotic, **ant**onym, **anti**septic, **ant**agonist

im**pul**sive = acting on impulse without much forethought

pel, pul = to push

com**pel**, im**pel**, ex**pel**, pro**pul**sion, pro**pel**, re**pul**sive, pro**pel**ler

a**pathy**

audible

"A stitch in time saves nine."

The statement above suggests that taking your time to do something well rather than rushing to get it done quickly will save time in the long run.

For 1 point each, generate a "furthermore," a "however," and a "for example" statement to this thesis.

"A bird in the hand is worth two in the bush."

The statement above suggests that it is better to opt for something certain than it is to try and achieve the impossible.

For 1 point each, generate a "furthermore," a "however," and a "for example" statement to this thesis.

"What's past is prologue."

The statement above suggests that it is important to remember the past because of the lessons it has for us all, but also that there is much to come in the future.

For 1 point each, generate a "furthermore," a "however," and a "for example" statement to this thesis.

"All that matters is that you try your best."

For 1 point each, generate an "I agree, because" and an "I disagree, because" thesis statement and a "for example" or a "nevertheless" statement for each point of view.

audible = able to be heard

aud = to hear

auditorium, **aud**ition, **aud**io,
audit, **aud**itory, in**aud**ible, **aud**ience

apathy = lack of feeling

pathos = emotion

sym**pathy**, em**pathy**, anti**pathy**,
osteo**pathy**, **path**ogen, **path**etic, psycho**path**

Because there are so many possible answers to this question, we have not given specific examples for the point allocation. Ask a teacher, friend, parent, or tutor to score this card for you:

Give 1 point for each statement made by the student that is interesting, well thought out, and relevant to the given thesis.

Because there are so many possible answers to this question, we have not given specific examples for the point allocation. Ask a teacher, friend, parent, or tutor to score this card for you:

Give 1 point for each statement made by the student that is interesting, well thought out, and relevant to the given thesis.

Because there are so many possible answers to this question, we have not given specific examples for the point allocation. Ask a teacher, friend, parent, or tutor to score this card for you:

Give 1 point for each statement made by the student that is interesting, well thought out, and relevant to the given thesis.

Because there are so many possible answers to this question, we have not given specific examples for the point allocation. Ask a teacher, friend, parent, or tutor to score this card for you:

Give 1 point for each statement made by the student that is interesting, well thought out, and relevant to the given thesis.

"Everything you can imagine can become reality."

For 1 point each, generate a "furthermore," a "however," and a "for example" statement to this statement made by Pablo Picasso.

"All that glitters is not gold."

For 1 point each, generate a "furthermore," a "however," and a "for example" statement to this thesis.

"It is better to be safe than sorry."

For 1 point each, generate a "furthermore," a "however," and a "for example" statement to this thesis.

Is money the root of all evil?

For 1 point each, generate a "yes, because" and a "no, because" thesis statement and a "for example" or a "nevertheless" statement for each point of view.

"Too many cooks spoil the broth."

For 1 point each, generate a "furthermore," a "however," and a "for example" statement to this thesis.

Is ignorance bliss?

For 1 point each, generate a "yes, because" and a "no, because" thesis statement and a "for example" or a "nevertheless" statement for each point of view.

Because there are so many possible answers to this question, we have not given specific examples for the point allocation. Ask a teacher, friend, parent, or tutor to score this card for you:

Give 1 point for each statement made by the student that is interesting, well thought out, and relevant to the given thesis.

Because there are so many possible answers to this question, we have not given specific examples for the point allocation. Ask a teacher, friend, parent, or tutor to score this card for you:

Give 1 point for each statement made by the student that is interesting, well thought out, and relevant to the given thesis.

Because there are so many possible answers to this question, we have not given specific examples for the point allocation. Ask a teacher, friend, parent, or tutor to score this card for you:

Give 1 point for each statement made by the student that is interesting, well thought out, and relevant to the given thesis.

Because there are so many possible answers to this question, we have not given specific examples for the point allocation. Ask a teacher, friend, parent, or tutor to score this card for you:

Give 1 point for each statement made by the student that is interesting, well thought out, and relevant to the given thesis.

Because there are so many possible answers to this question, we have not given specific examples for the point allocation. Ask a teacher, friend, parent, or tutor to score this card for you:

Give 1 point for each statement made by the student that is interesting, well thought out, and relevant to the given thesis.

Because there are so many possible answers to this question, we have not given specific examples for the point allocation. Ask a teacher, friend, parent, or tutor to score this card for you:

Give 1 point for each statement made by the student that is interesting, well thought out, and relevant to the given thesis.

Is honesty the best policy?

For I point each, generate a "yes, because" and a "no, because" thesis statement and a "for example" or a "nevertheless" statement for each point of view.

Are women more constrained by society than men are?

For I point each, generate a "yes, because" and a "no, because" thesis statement and a "for example" or a "nevertheless" statement for each point of view.

Is the rapid advance of technology good or bad for humankind?

For I point each, generate a "yes, because" and a "no, because" thesis statement and a "for example" or a "nevertheless" statement for each point of view.

The most important thing for a leader to understand is history.

For I point each, generate an "I agree, because" and an "I disagree, because" thesis statement and a "for example" or a "nevertheless" statement for each point of view.

"There is a time and a place for censorship."

For I point each, generate a "yes, because" and a "no, because" thesis statement and a "for example" or a "nevertheless" statement for each point of view

For I point each, rewrite the sentences below to eliminate any wordiness, redundancy, clichés, or grammatical errors.

1. Veteran pitchers rely on past experience to know how to pitch to the best hitters.
2. It was clear that my son planned on asking me the question until I said yes.
3. In this day and age, too much emphasis is placed on how much annual income a person makes when trying to measure success.

Because there are so many possible answers to this question, we have not given specific examples for the point allocation. Ask a teacher, friend, parent, or tutor to score this card for you:

Give 1 point for each statement made by the student that is interesting, well thought out, and relevant to the given thesis.

Because there are so many possible answers to this question, we have not given specific examples for the point allocation. Ask a teacher, friend, parent, or tutor to score this card for you:

Give 1 point for each statement made by the student that is interesting, well thought out, and relevant to the given thesis.

Because there are so many possible answers to this question, we have not given specific examples for the point allocation. Ask a teacher, friend, parent, or tutor to score this card for you:

Give 1 point for each statement made by the student that is interesting, well thought out, and relevant to the given thesis.

Because there are so many possible answers to this question, we have not given specific examples for the point allocation. Ask a teacher, friend, parent, or tutor to score this card for you:

Give 1 point for each statement made by the student that is interesting, well thought out, and relevant to the given thesis.

1. **Redundancy:** Veteran pitchers rely on ~~past~~ experience to know how to pitch to the best hitters.

2. **Infinitive versus gerund:** It was clear that my son planned ~~on asking~~ **to ask** me the question until I said yes.

3. **Wordiness:** ~~In this day and age~~ **Today**, too much emphasis is placed on ~~how much~~ annual income ~~a person makes~~ when ~~trying to measure~~ **measuring** success.

Because there are so many possible answers to this question, we have not given specific examples for the point allocation. Ask a teacher, friend, parent, or tutor to score this card for you:

Give 1 point for each statement made by the student that is interesting, well thought out, and relevant to the given thesis.

"It is always good to follow authority."

For 1 point each, generate a "yes, because" and a "no, because" thesis statement and a "for example" or a "nevertheless" statement for each point of view.

For 1 point each, rewrite the sentences below to eliminate any wordiness, redundancy, clichés, or grammatical errors.

1. There are many reasons making it irresponsible to allow your children to do whatever they want every day after school simply because you are too busy at work to keep them in line.
2. When a bear is chasing you, one should not make loud noises and avoid sudden movements.
3. Put your pencils down; we are now at this time going to collect your test booklets.

For 1 point each, rewrite the sentences below to eliminate any wordiness, redundancy, clichés, or grammatical errors.

1. The company is looking to hire individuals who can think outside the box.
2. In the event that I am unable to make the wedding due to the fact that I am away on business, I hope that you are aware of the fact that I will be there in spirit.
3. We always give it 110% when we are on the field, and if we fail this year, we'll pick up the pieces and try again next year.

"Misfortune reveals your true friends."

For 1 point each, give 3 examples from literature, history, current events, or your own experiences that support this statement made by Aristotle.

For 1 point each, rewrite the sentences below to eliminate any wordiness, redundancy, clichés, or grammatical errors.

1. Ever since she was a young child, Ella has loved singing.
2. A diamond of perfect clarity is an object that is very difficult to find in the marketplace today.
3. Regardless of the fact that the best parts of the Star Wars trilogy have been combined together into one action-packed DVD, I still found it to be boring and uninteresting.

"Real integrity is doing the right thing, knowing that nobody's going to know whether you did it or not."

For 1 point each, give 3 examples from literature, history, current events, or your own experiences that support this statement made by Oprah Winfrey.

1. **Wordiness:** It is irresponsible to allow your children to do whatever they want after school simply because you are busy.

2. **Parallelism:** When a bear is chasing you, ~~one~~ **you** should ~~not~~ make **neither** loud noises ~~and avoid~~ **nor** sudden movements.

3. **Redundancy:** Put your pencils down; we are now ~~at this time~~ going to collect your test booklets.

Because there are so many possible answers to this question, we have not given specific examples for the point allocation. Ask a teacher, friend, parent, or tutor to score this card for you:

Give 1 point for each statement made by the student that is interesting, well thought out, and relevant to the given thesis.

Because there are so many possible answers to this question, we have not given specific examples for the point allocation. Ask a teacher, friend, parent, or tutor to score this card for you:

Give 1 point for each statement made by the student that is interesting, well thought out, and relevant to the given thesis.

1. **Jargony:** The company is looking to hire individuals who can think ~~outside the box~~ **creatively**.

2. **Wordiness:** ~~In the event that~~ **If** I am unable to make the wedding ~~due to the fact that~~ **because** I am away on business, I hope that you ~~are aware of the fact~~ **know** that I will be there in spirit.

3. **Clichés:** We always ~~give it 100%~~ **try our hardest** ~~we are~~ on the field, and if we fail this year, we'll ~~pick up the pieces~~ **regroup** and try again next year.

Because there are so many possible answers to this question, we have not given specific examples for the point allocation. Ask a teacher, friend, parent, or tutor to score this card for you:

Give 1 point for each statement made by the student that is interesting, well thought out, and relevant to the given thesis.

1. **Unclear:** Ever since she was a young child, Ella has loved ~~singing~~ **to sing**. OR Ever since she was a young child, Ella has loved **listening to others sing.**

2. **Wordiness:** A diamond of perfect clarity is **rare.** ~~an object that is very difficult to find in the marketplace today~~.

3. **Wordiness:** ~~Regardless of the fact that~~ **Although** the best parts of the Star Wars trilogy have been combined ~~together~~ into one action-packed DVD, **it was still dull.** ~~I still found it to be boring and uninteresting~~.

For 1 point each, rewrite the sentences below to eliminate any wordiness, redundancy, clichés, or grammatical errors.

1. Although the movie was different than its predecessor, it is nevertheless filled with similar themes and ideas.
2. Frustrated and tired, the struggling poet threw his notebook which hit the floor and let out a scream.
3. When Madonna's music was first introduced to the public, they had criticized it for being inappropriate and controversial.

"Knowledge is power."

For 1 point each, give 3 examples from literature, history, current events, or your own experiences that support this statement made by Sir Francis Bacon.

Who is your hero and why?

You will receive points for an answer that is thought-provoking, clear, and original. You will also receive a point for writing a strong concluding thought on heroism in general.

Give 3 examples from literature, history, current events, or your own experiences that demonstrate something meaningful about <u>courage</u>.

Does government-mandated testing affect education in a positive or a negative way?

For 1 point each, generate a "yes, because" and a "no, because" thesis statement and a "for example" or a "nevertheless" statement for each point of view.

Give 3 examples from literature, history, current events, or your own experiences that describe <u>an individual's overcoming adversity</u>.

Because there are so many possible answers to this question, we have not given specific examples for the point allocation. Ask a teacher, friend, parent, or tutor to score this card for you:

Give 1 point for each statement made by the student that is interesting, well thought out, and relevant to the given thesis.

1. **Idiom error, tense error:** Although the movie was different ~~than~~ **from** its predecessor, it ~~is~~ **was** nevertheless ~~filled~~ **concerned** with similar themes and ideas.

2. **Coordination error:** Frustrated and tired, the struggling poet **let out a scream and** threw his notebook, which hit the floor. ~~and let out a scream.~~

3. **Redundancy/Tense error:** When Madonna's music was ~~first~~ introduced, ~~to~~ the public~~, they had~~ criticized it for being inappropriate and controversial.

Because there are so many possible answers to this question, we have not given specific examples for the point allocation. Ask a teacher, friend, parent, or tutor to score this card for you:

Give 1 point for each reference made by the student that is interesting, well thought out, and relevant to the given thesis.

Because there are so many possible answers to this question, we have not given specific examples for the point allocation. Ask a teacher, friend, parent, or tutor to score this card for you:

1st **point: for a response that is unique and thought-provoking.**
2nd **point: for a good "because" statement**
3rd **point: for a good concluding thought on heroism in general**

Because there are so many possible answers to this question, we have not given specific examples for the point allocation. Ask a teacher, friend, parent, or tutor to score this card for you:

Give 1 point for each reference made by the student that is interesting, well thought out, and relevant to the given thesis.

Because there are so many possible answers to this question, we have not given specific examples for the point allocation. Ask a teacher, friend, parent, or tutor to score this card for you:

Give 1 point for each statement made by the student that is interesting, well thought out, and relevant to the given thesis.

Should criminal trials be televised?

For 1 point each, generate a "yes, because" and a "no, because" thesis statement and a "for example" or a "nevertheless" statement for each point of view.

Give 3 examples from literature, history, current events, or your own experiences that demonstrate something meaningful about treachery.

Give 3 examples from literature, history, current events, or your own experiences that say something meaningful about devotion.

One thing undervalued in today's society is. . . .

You will receive points for answers that are thought-provoking, clear, and original. Write 3 thesis statements that complete the phrase above.

Give 3 examples from literature, history, current events, or your own experiences that say something meaningful about the power of knowledge.

I have done many memorable things in my life, but the one moment I will never forget is. . .

You will receive points for an answer that is thought-provoking, clear, and original. You will also receive a point for writing a strong concluding thought on what makes a moment unforgettable.

Because there are so many possible answers to this question, we have not given specific examples for the point allocation. Ask a teacher, friend, parent, or tutor to score this card for you:

Give 1 point for each reference made by the student that is interesting, well thought out, and relevant to the given thesis.

Because there are so many possible answers to this question, we have not given specific examples for the point allocation. Ask a teacher, friend, parent, or tutor to score this card for you:

Give 1 point for each statement made by the student that is interesting, well thought out, and relevant to the given thesis.

Because there are so many possible answers to this question, we have not given specific examples for the point allocation. Ask a teacher, friend, parent, or tutor to score this card for you:

Give 1 point for each thesis written by the student that is interesting, well thought out, and relevant to the given phrase.

Because there are so many possible answers to this question, we have not given specific examples for the point allocation. Ask a teacher, friend, parent, or tutor to score this card for you:

Give 1 point for each reference made by the student that is interesting, well thought out, and relevant to the given thesis.

Because there are so many possible answers to this question, we have not given specific examples for the point allocation. Ask a teacher, friend, parent, or tutor to score this card for you:

1st point: for a response that is unique and thought-provoking.
2nd point: for a good "because" statement.
3rd point: for a good concluding thought on unforgettable moments.

Because there are so many possible answers to this question, we have not given specific examples for the point allocation. Ask a teacher, friend, parent, or tutor to score this card for you:

Give 1 point for each reference made by the student that is interesting, well thought out, and relevant to the given thesis.